Ministry
to Word and
Sacraments

Ministry to Word and Sacraments

History and Theology

Bernard Cooke

FORTRESS PRESS

Philadelphia

COPYRIGHT © 1976 BY FORTRESS PRESS

Library of Congress Catalog Card Number 75–36459

ISBN 0–8006–0440–7

Second printing 1977

6485E77   Printed in the United States of America   1–440

Contents

Preface

Acquiring more accurate understanding of Christian ministry is not an incidental item on the agenda of the church today; it is basic to everything Christianity claims to be and attempts to do. In a world of staggering problems and "mind-blowing" potential, it would be foolish to waste time and energy on what is not the genuine ministerial role of the church, and in the process leave undone the very things Christians are meant to achieve.

At the time I began work on this book, more than a decade ago, there was an almost total lack of serious theological writing about Christian ministry and priesthood. In these last few years, however, a considerable volume of literature on the topic has appeared, as the review of recent publications contained in this book's Introduction will indicate. Yet, as that review also indicates, there is still very little of a synthetic historical and theological nature. This book is an attempt to fill part of that gap.

Very probably the absence of such synthetic presentations suggests the questionable wisdom of attempting such an enterprise. It is obvious that an accurate account of the historical evolution of Christian ministry and of the accompanying understanding of that ministry is close to impossible; not only is the evidence massive and diverse, but the interpretation of that evidence as indicating certain patterns of historical relationship rather than others involves constant judgment—philosophical, religious, historical, literary. In the last analysis such judgment cannot avoid being personal.

To then go on and reflect theologically about this historical evolution is to face still further dangers: the threat that the very basis of one's theologizing is conjecture about what happened, rather than solid evidence about the historical process; the threat of limiting one's theological perspective to the problematic and presuppositions of the past, and not remaining open to the new and creative possibilities which the present and the future require; the threat that one's supposed search for the *logos* of God's action in and through the historical existence of the Christian ministry may be a process of seeking justification for one's a priori views about that divine action or about the function of Christian ministry.

But this moment in the life of the Christian church and of mankind seems to demand that we run the risk of such scholarly inadequacy. We are faced with inescapable practical questions: What should we do to further human history, to alleviate the oppression and suffering of most of the human race, to foster the movement towards freedom and dignity? In other words, how should we minister effectively to one another? And in this present—and in many ways new—need for ministry, is there anything specifically "Christian" that members of the church can undertake? Certainly, much of the classic performance of Christian ministry by clerical "professionals" is outdated; and the widespread role-identity crisis among ordained clergy (in all the churches) indicates that the precise function of Christian ministry is today unclear.

Certain features of this present book should be mentioned, so that its contents and conclusions can be better appraised. First of all, the ideal of being comprehensive in the historical portions had to be severely limited: most adequate treatment is given to the historical development of the Roman Catholic tradition (for the obvious reason that I am best acquainted with this), and serious effort has been made to take account of the major strains of Protestant thought and practice. This latter was done in order to indicate a basic common development and a common problematic; it was done also because we can no longer honestly do theology within the limited traditions of our own Christian denomination. Ideally, I would have done the same with Orthodox theologians and the historical experience of the Eastern Christian churches, but my understanding of the roots and background of Orthodox thinking and practice is so limited that I distrusted my ability to avoid a distorted presentation. This lack in the book is a serious one; I hope that it will be compensated for by the work done within Orthodox theological circles. And as for the kinds of comparative study (anthropological, sociological, psychological) relating Christianity to other instances of ministerial service: this was beyond the scope of the present book, but it certainly is part of the more comprehensive understanding of the phenomenon of Christian ministry.

Something should be said about the function footnotes play in this present book. Even within the modest perimeters of study to which the book is limited, a great mass of material had to be arranged carefully and coherently. Work with primary source material had, of course, to form the heart of the research for the book's historical sections, but it would have been presumptuous (even if it had been possible) to redo all the scholarship of first-rate historians and theologians on various topics. Consequently, much of the research behind this book consisted in examining the way these scholars had dealt with the historical evidence, then complementing it by elements that they had not researched, and at times differing with their procedures or with their conclusions. It is this critical dependence upon secondary

sources that is reflected in the footnotes: these notes serve the indispensable function of referring the reader to writings that can provide an amplification or corrective for my own treatment of a given point.

Simply to make the material manageable and to allow the patterns of historical evolution to become visible, it has often been necessary to give conclusions without all the detailed supporting evidence; but I have hoped that the footnote references will lead readers to the lengthier presentations of a given matter—and so to agreement or disagreement with my analysis. In many cases, too, the secondary studies to which reference is made provide in more accessible form the relevant historical texts; many of these books can be found in libraries that do not have on hand the Greek or Latin *Patrologia* or Mansi or the *Corpus Reformatorum* or the *Monumenta Germaniae Historica*.

Since the footnotes are such an intrinsic part of the historical sections of this book, it may seem strange that no notes at all are provided for the theological reflections that conclude each of the book's five parts. Though these theological reflections are heavily dependent upon the thought of others, I was neither able in many instances to determine exactly my indebtedness nor willing to claim that my opinion was supported by a given theologian (or theologians). More than that, I think it is important that the ideas contained in those sections be evaluated in themselves and not on the basis of their having come from this or that prominent theologian, much as I value the ideas of these theologians. Instead of providing this kind of footnote reference to what is being done by theologians today, I tried to indicate this more globally in the lengthy review of current literature that is provided in the introduction. Anyone who is familiar with this current writing will recognize quite readily my own heavy indebtedness to men like Congar, Rahner, Audet, and Thurian.

Finally, a word about the arrangement of the book. Early research for the book was tentatively arranged according to the classic topics of ministry of word, ministry of sacrament, and ministry of forming Christian community. Very early, however, the historical evidence indicated the inadequacy of this triple division: a great deal of material began to cluster around the ill-defined "ministry of helping others," and even more around the notion of "passing judgment." The book, then, evolved into five main parts: the *first* describes the basic role of the ministry in the historical development of the Christian community; the *second* concentrates on the ministry of word; the *third* deals with the broad area of "service" to those in need; the *fourth* studies the areas of judgment, authority, and jurisdiction as attached to the church's ministry; the *fifth* investigates the ministry of sacramental leadership, the sacramental character of all ministry, and the relation in Christianity between ministry and priesthood. Prior to these five principal divisions of the book there is a lengthy introduction whose purpose is to present the questions about Christian ministry and priesthood that confront the present-day church and to indicate the main currents of thought on this topic within the past quarter-century or so.

Within each of the five main parts, there is a description of the historical evolution of thought and practice and a concluding theological reflection. Though inspired by and grounded in history, the theological discussion is not just the drawing of conclusions from the historical precedents; rightly or wrongly, it is an attempt to get at the "essence" of Christian ministry and priesthood, so that this insight may be a guide to evaluating historical developments and to planning practical Christian activity in the present and future. For this reason, the theological portions are presented as relatively freestanding. Yet, I feel that they are inextricably bound up with the historical study that precedes them; it was the study of the historical process of Christian ministry that

led me to the theological positions I present.

The advance of theology is a pattern of alternating analysis and synthesis, each preparing for and making possible the other. Hopefully, this present book in its attempt to provide a historical and theological synthesis of understandings about Christian ministry will do two things: bring together much of the analytic work that has been done, so that an overall view of ministry can be obtained; and make clearer the real questions and possibilities that face us today, so that further analysis will be directed to those areas of understanding which will allow the Christian community to exercise more fruitfully the ministries that are properly its in today's world.

After more than a decade of working on this book, it is literally impossible to list all those to whom I am indebted, particularly all those students and confreres, both ministerial and academic, whose shared ideas and experiences and reactions provided stimulus and nurture for my own reflection. Some special gratitude should be expressed to Yale Divinity School for the year of research fellowship that made possible the core research for this book, a year that would have been much less fruitful without the kindness and help of the divinity school's chief librarian, Mr. Raymond Morris, and of his staff. To two other libraries also I am particularly indebted, those at Marquette University and at the University of Windsor. In the process of preparing the manuscript and arranging indices I had the valuable assistance of Michael Loveland, Marcia Stroko, and Peter Wickerson, and most importantly of Lucy Turner. Roland Tapp and Norman Hjelm of Fortress Press deserve my gratitude for their editorial efficiency and friendly professionalism. Most specially I am indebted to Pauline, who has done so much to broaden my understanding of what Christian ministry can and should be, and whose years-long encouragement helped bring this book into being.

Introduction

Important issues often tend to be side-tracked or taken for granted; perhaps they seem so obvious by their constant presence, perhaps humans instinctively avoid them because of the major risk they often entail or because the difficulty of facing them is too great. Whatever reasons one may assign, the fact is that the major issue of the nature and exercise of Christian ministry has until quite recently been neglected in the theology of every Christian denomination.

Yet, one would have expected just the opposite. There can be no doubt about the central and focal position of Christian priesthood and ministry in the interlocked complex of Christian faith and life. Whatever view one takes of Christian ministry is inseparably tied to one's view of the church, of Christ, of the church's role in the transformation of human life. No important aspect of faith or theology can be reassessed—and today every aspect is being radically reassessed—without impact on one's view of Christian ministry.

Ecumenically, the centrality of the matter is quite apparent and has been repeatedly acknowledged as such by those most closely connected with ecumenical discussion and activity. Were there to be essential agreement on the nature of Christian ministry, there would inevitably be that kind of common understanding of worship and church membership and ecclesiastical structure which would in effect indicate the basic reunion of Christians into one community. The fact that such reunion does not yet exist, despite increasing bonds of understanding and charity among separated churches, testifies to the present divergence of teaching about Christian ministry; and there is increasing awareness that this question must be confronted, theologically and pastorally, if the movement towards Christian union is to reach fulfillment.

A basic difficulty arises, of course, from the very centrality of ministry in the reality that is Christianity, and therefore the centrality of one's understanding about ministry in the understanding one has of the church. One really cannot hope to give an adequate explanation of this one element of Christianity without taking into consideration every other important element. On the other hand, forthright confrontation of this issue could well be a safeguard against superficial ecumenical agreement on allied questions of ecclesiology or Christology.

From a practical and pastoral point of view, it is unfortunate that more attention was not given to the theology of ministry. It would have helped prepare for the widespread and often agonizing problems of clerical self-identity, problems that are felt today in every religious group. Those who have devoted their lives to ministry in the church are less certain of their precise role, and many have found their clerical self-understanding deeply challenged, if not repudiated, by the developments and crises of contemporary life. When one remembers that theological study has been until very recently confined to ordained ministers, it is indeed puzzling that there should have been so little done to clarify the role of those engaged in specialized ministry in the church.

It would not be honest, however, to intimate that there is at present a total vacuum regarding theological study of Christian priesthood and ministry. The past half-century has seen some small beginnings, the past decade an accelerated activity; but there has been little in the way of major historical or theological studies that would have equipped us to face the rapid, one might justifiably say explosive, changes of thought and life-style that have occurred in practically every Christian group. For the most part, the study that has been made of Christian ministry falls more into the categories of sociological, psychological, or legal research; such study makes it possible to undertake now a more careful theological analysis.

One of the clearest indices of the pattern of theological study of ministry during the past few decades is the sequence of discussion on the topic undertaken by the World Council of Churches, especially by its Commission on Faith and Order. In the years before it was brought under the aegis of the WCC as a commission of that body, the Faith and Order movement had indicated interest in probing further the question of ministry, and some writing on the topic did appear in Faith and Order publications. Yet, explicit attention to the question lapsed, and interest in it was overshadowed by other matters which, however, had long-range implications for the understanding of Christian ministry. In its fourth world conference (in Montreal in 1963), the Faith and Order Commission could report:

> The question of the ministry has not been prominent in Faith and Order discussion for some twenty-five years. In those years there has, of course, been a continuing spate of books about ministry, many of them of the kind which attempts the constructive re-statement of the doctrine of a particular church or confessional tradition in the light of criticism from other traditions. This type of work can be a valuable, indeed essential, element in the whole ecumenical conversation.
>
> But it is probably true to say that two other things have exercised a far greater and fresher influence on thinking about the ministry in those

twenty-five years. One of these is the recovery of a doctrine of the whole Church as the people of God, and of a positive and indeed creative understanding of the laity in consequence. The other is the accompanying recovery of the sense that the Church, the ministry, and the congregation are all alike in basic principle missionary, though much of the structure we have inherited from the past makes it difficult to practise this principle and to act upon it.[1]

Even at Montreal there was no theological commission assigned the specific task of studying Christian ministry, though the topic of ministry and order was on the agenda of a worldwide conference for the first time since Edinburgh in 1937.

That twenty-five year period, during which formal discussion of Christian ministry had to a large extent lapsed in Faith and Order studies, saw the convening of the first three world meetings of the World Council of Churches. None of these worldwide gatherings dealt with the question, except briefly in relation to some other programmed area of study. The picture is not, however, quite as negative as it might seem: many of the emergent questions and issues that engaged the attention of these three meetings, especially issues of international order and justice, were reflections of the new situation and new view that are today demanding a radical reexamination of Christian ministry.

At the initial meeting, in Amsterdam in 1948, the general theme "Man's Disorder and God's Design" directed attention most basically to the activity of Christians in the world —and therefore to ministry in the broad sense. But there was no explicit examination of specialized ministry, even in the report of Study Section II which dealt with evangelism.[2] Instead, there was a concentration of attention on the contribution of Christians, positive and negative, to the world of post–World War II 1948; and an attempt to see how cooperative Christian involvement in the needs of mankind could bear witness to the gospel and be a force for the reunification of Christians.

Again, at Evanston in 1954, the problem of

ordained ministry was practically ignored. An exception was the Orthodox insistence on the apostolic succession as an essential to true union; but while this intervention was respectfully received, it had little practical bearing on the progress of the meeting's discussions.[3] One can see some reflection of the attitude of the Evanston conference in the listing of key topics that were suggested to Faith and Order for follow-up study. Ministry is not mentioned, though two of the suggested topics—worship, and the nature of the church—necessarily involve ministry. However, from a long-range viewpoint the report of Section 6 on the laity and its ministry is important, for it reflects the growing emphasis on the laity and its involvement in the "secular" world.[4] In tone much like Vatican II's Constitution on the Church, which it preceded by a decade, Section 6's report lays stress on the notion of the church as "the people of God" and points to the ministry that is common to all members of the church. One of the interesting features of this report is the stress it lays on work as central to the ministry of the laity. The report does advert to a special ministry possessed by the clergy, but only very succinctly and in passing: "The clergy have their appointed function in the Church, the ministry of Word and Sacrament."[5]

At least if one can use the official documentation as a guide, the 1961 World Council meeting in New Delhi indicated little change in the relative lack of attention paid to the ordained ministry. Actually, there was an even clearer concentration on the ministry of the entire church and a broadening of the scope of Christian ministry to include practically all acts of service:

> There is an urgent need for all church members to recover the true meaning of certain words; to learn that the laity is really the *Laos*, that is, the whole People of God in the world, including, of course, those who have been ordained; to learn that ministry means any kind of service by which a Christian, exercising his particular skill and gift, however humble, helps his fellow Christians or his fellow men in the name of Christ. A far richer fellowship and team-spirit is bound to ap-

pear as soon as the whole Church comes to realize its function as the People of God, which God himself has provided with many kinds of ministry, in which one special kind of ministry, that of the ordained clergy, is set apart to strengthen and teach, to encourage and unite all the several witnesses in their various callings whose ministry is set in the heart of the secular world's manifold activity.[6]

But if New Delhi did not produce any clarification of the manner in which its member churches viewed the specialized ministry of the ordained, and did not even add the topic of ministry to the areas suggested for special study by the Faith and Order Commission, the report from its Section on Unity did point to divergent understandings of ministry as one of the greatest barriers to union:

> All agree that the whole Body is a royal priesthood. Yet one of the most serious barriers to unity is our diverse understanding of the nature of the ministry within the corporate priesthood. All who have engaged in church union negotiations testify to this fact. . . . Here, biblical, theological and historical studies must be continued to seek to lay before the churches that which is necessary to have a true ministry according to God's Word.[7]

In reading this statement, one gets the definite impression that its awareness of divergent views on ministry being a barrier to unity is the result of concrete experience in ecumenical endeavor. To this extent it differs from the recognition at Lund nine years earlier, at the third world conference of Faith and Order, of the problem of ministry, a recognition that seems to have rested more on the intrinsic relationship of theological issues. Under "unsolved problems regarding unity" the Lund conference had said:

> Worship is always the worship of the whole people of God, the whole Church. The leadership of this worship can on some occasions be entrusted to any member. Yet most of our Churches believe that our Lord has called forth in his Church a stated ministry. To this ministry alone the leadership of certain acts of wor-

ship is restricted. For some of us this restriction rests on the belief that the Church by the guidance of the Holy Spirit calls some of its members to this or that function. For others it is based on the belief that the Holy Spirit gives to some members of the Church the appropriate grace of holy orders. Again, some Churches emphasize the ministerial priesthood as definitely distinct from the priesthood of all believers.

We recognize that questions regarding the character of the ministry, priestly and prophetic, continue to be grave obstacles to unity. Behind them lie fundamental problems concerning the nature of grace and the person and work of Christ. These questions must be faced fully and frankly. Fruitful discussion here may well render less intractable the differences in defining the meaning of apostolic ministry and validity.[8]

Situated just about midway in the twenty-five-year inattention to the theology of ministry to which we have already alluded, this statement from Lund did little to arouse practical interest in careful investigation of the matter. It would seem that the actual encounter with divergent views on ministry, as churches engage in serious attempts at union, will alone provide the incentive for thorough research into the question. This kind of serious study did not yet have impact on the agenda or proceedings of the Uppsala meeting of the World Council of Churches; but it was called for a year earlier at the Bristol meeting of Faith and Order, when the report of Section 3 (On Ministry, Church Union Negotiations, etc.) outlined in detail a study on ordination and proposed a timetable for its implementation. And in proposing a course of action to be taken by the World Council with regard to the Consultation on Church Union negotiations, this same report urged that: "The present study on the Ministry be prosecuted with great urgency, with particular reference to the theological understanding of ordination and the place of episcopacy."[9]

One reflection of the slowly increasing attention given to ministry by the World Council and particularly by Faith and Order is the "Report of the Study Commission on Institutionalism" which was presented in 1963. In-

cluded in this penetrating and balanced investigation of the institutional elements of Christianity are two fairly lengthy discussions of priesthood and ministry which we will examine later.[10] Though these two passages are succinct presentations of theological understanding, conclusions from historical and systematic evidence which itself could not be presented because of restrictions of space, they reflect the growing awakening among theologians of various churches to the need for radical examination of Christian priesthood and ministry.

Finally, at the Faith and Order meeting of 1971 (in Louvain) a more detailed examination of Christian ministerial priesthood was given in the study report on the ordained ministry.[11] The report is quite theological in its outlook and interests, but it is largely reportorial in style and content—indicating the general trend of present-day discussion, the new atmosphere caused by such influences as Vatican II, and the questions that have come to explicit theological formulation. This is quite understandable, since its purpose is to clarify the extent of common understanding about ministry that exists among the Christian churches; in general, the report points to an encouraging growth of agreement, and it is hopeful about the future mutual acceptance of ministries. However, the report is not meant to be a scholarly analysis of the relevant theological issues, and it is not that; perhaps its greatest value lies in the way it mirrors the basic trends of theological discussion and sets the various questions about Christian ministry into a unified context.[12]

However, important though they be, the World Council and its Faith and Order Commission are but reflections of the much broader life and activity of the member churches. And when one turns to the theological activity in these constituent churches —and in other important Christian churches that do not belong to the World Council— one gets the definite impression that momentum has been slowly building up in scholarly circles, a momentum that may soon result in the production of a synthetic study of Christian ministry and priesthood. In many ways, Anglican scholars provided much of the thrust during the 1930s and 1940s,[13] and the fruit of their work was still evident in the 1968 Lambeth Conference, specifically in its report on renewal in ministry,[14] and in the discussions on union between Anglicans and other Christians. One can point also to important studies undertaken by officially appointed groups or by individual theologians within many of the other Christian churches. One thinks immediately of the Lutheran studies of the episcopal office, studies that have drawn from both biblical and Lutheran confessional sources. Or of the United Presbyterian Church's "Contemporary Statement of Faith," with the commentary statements that prepared for and accompanied its appearance. Or of the statements produced by various official joint commissions (Anglican-Orthodox, Lutheran–Roman Catholic, etc.). Certainly, one of the most tantalizing and creative developments has been the discussion connected with the Consultation on Church Union.[15] Tentative and uncertain though the status and future of this consultation is, the extent to which various confessional traditions flowed into its statements on ministry and received a measure of common acceptance gives hope that somewhere in the future of serious theological reflection we may arrive at insights and convictions that pave the way for genuine and lasting reunion of Christians.[16]

In Roman Catholic theological developments, one inevitably thinks of the documents produced by Vatican II, even though this council has been criticized for neglecting the question of priesthood in its deliberations.[17] While it is true that comparatively little was done to clarify the role of priests within the Catholic church, the central position of discussion about episcopacy indicates the importance of the council's statements for one who wishes to study the present state of Roman Catholic thought on priesthood and ministry. Moreover, the reorientation of Catholic thought about the identity and function of the laity, which was not initiated by the council but did find there a most important official

support, has far-reaching implications for Roman Catholic thought about the ordained ministry.

Few aspects of the documents from Vatican II received more attention—and rightly so—than the emphasis on the dignity and role of lay people in the church. Going explicitly beyond the early twentieth-century position that lay activity in the church was essentially one of aiding the bishops in their apostolic task, the council's key document, the Constitution on the Church ("Lumen gentium"), speaks about the initiative and responsibility that lay men and women should exercise by virtue of their baptism.[18] This same document, moving away from the political state as a model for understanding the church, describes the entire church as "the people of God"—not a new notion, but one that had long been overlaid with legalistic and organizational patterns of thought. It is this entire people that possesses a share in the prophetic, royal, and priestly ministry that Christ continues to exercise in and through his church.[19]

It would be naive to suppose that the statements of Vatican II represent a full and effective break with the centuries of appropriating to the clergy the "active" side of the church's life. Yet, groundwork has been laid for developments which—as far as one can foresee—will revolutionize the pattern of church life. Understandably, despite its openness to the need for reexamination of the structures and activity of the church, the council still clung to much of the "traditional" view of the church: as composed of clergy and laity; as made up of two groups, *ecclesia docens* and *ecclesia discens*; as deriving its life and power and order "from on high" through the channel of the papacy and the hierarchy. Expressing not the front-line speculation of theologians but the broad consensus of the episcopacy that was charged with the institutional responsibilities of church life, Vatican II felt compelled to retain and repeat the older formulations at the same time that it was enunciating newer insights that challenged the old.[20]

Perhaps no place is this apparent inconsistency more observable than in the description of the nature and role of the hierarchy. Commentators on Vatican II are agreed that one of the key contributions of the council to the advance of understanding about the church was its examination of episcopacy, particularly its position on the collegiality of the episcopacy.[21] Its statement on this latter point, a definite step away from the overemphasis on the papal role that has marked Roman Catholic thought for many decades, especially since Vatican I, is brief but filled with implications. Yet, without being negatively critical, one must say that the conciliar fathers did not thoroughly face these implications; for side by side with the newer views one finds a repetition of Vatican I's formulations. It is impossible to avoid some ultimate conflict between the two sets of statements.[22] The tensions that have developed in Roman Catholic circles in the years since the council are to some extent rooted in this ambiguity of the conciliar documents, since divergent views can each justify their positions by statements taken from the decrees of Vatican II.

Despite these limitations, the decrees of Vatican II do represent a new stage in the development of Roman Catholic thought about the nature of Christian ministry, and as such these decrees deserve careful analysis by theologians, particularly by those working within that tradition. In a context of doctrine that considers ministerial priesthood to be sacramental in the strict sense, and considers it to be grounded in some form of divine institution, the origin and nature and function of the episcopal college are at the very heart of theological study of Christian ministry. Whether it is true or not, one often hears it stated as obvious, that all ordained ministry in the church is an extension of the episcopacy, it does seem true that careful investigation of the episcopal office is a basic element in any thorough study of Christian ministry.[23]

Vatican II did produce specific decrees on the episcopal office and on the ministry of ordained priests; but its more advanced thinking on ministry is found (and in somewhat fragmentary fashion) in other documents. The Constitution on the Church is of particular interest. With its stress on the basic unity of all Christians as the people of God, its clear statements on the equality and responsibility of the laity within the community, and its teaching on the collegiality of the pastoral office, this decree provides the principles for a basic reconsideration of ministerial priesthood. If laypeople in the church are really to exercise the share in Christ's priesthood about which this decree speaks, it is clear that they will become involved in many forms of activity that were previously thought to be proper to the clergy. This has raised the question— by no means a purely speculative one in the post–Vatican II situation of the Roman Catholic church—as to what functions are intrinsically reserved to those possessing priestly ordination.

Vatican II's pastoral constitution on the church in the modern world (*"Gaudium et spes"*) does not go beyond *"Lumen gentium"* in the principles it enunciates; but it does spell out in greater detail the areas of apostolic involvement to which the laity are directed.[24] Even more important, the whole tone of this unprecedented conciliar document is one of openness to the contemporary world situation and of concern for the needs of all men and women today. Implicitly this calls for a thoroughgoing appraisal of the worth and effectiveness of present apostolic activity within the church. More specifically, the relative importance of "secular" involvement as against strictly "religious" activities has come to the fore. Vatican II was certainly not raising this issue for the first time, for movements such as the worker-priests in France had been wrestling with it for many years and with mixed success, but the council directed the attention of the entire church to this matter. An easy solution to the question is to assign the secular activities to the laity and the sacred functions to the ordained, but the deeper implications of the conciliar decrees forbid such a resolution of the issue: the laity have a real share in the most sacred actions of the church—preaching of the gospel and the Eucharistic worship of God; on the other hand, the ordained do not lose the rights or responsibility to act in the secular order which belongs to them because of their baptism.

The Decree on the Life and Ministry of Priests does not probe into the deeper questions raised by *"Lumen gentium"* and by the existential situation of twentieth-century Christianity. On the other hand, it does provide a fairly comprehensive exposition of the standard Roman Catholic explanation of ordained ministry.[25] It sees the ordained as directed in pastoral concern to all men, but bearing a special responsibility for those who are members of the Christian community. They are to minister to these latter by word and sacrament, not just for their own sake but so that they in turn can work for the betterment of human life.

While it does reflect quite faithfully the common Catholic theology of the priestly ministry, the decree is not basically a theological explanation but rather a piece of pastoral guidance for ordained priests. As such, it does not even advert to the important issues it avoids, for example, whether the proper role of the ordained consists in fulfilling an office or in providing leadership through an exceptionally faithful Christian life. Moreover, it gives no theological grounding for its description of the function and desirable life-style of priests. The decree is not a pioneering document; it is a summation of the more common opinion within the Roman Catholic church at the time of Vatican II, and as such it provides little guidance for theological exploration into the nature of ministry or for creative expressions of ministry in response to contemporary needs. At the same time, by the very generality of its position it leaves an open opportunity for scholars to probe into the questions of ministry through biblical, historical, and systematic studies.

In the decade since Vatican II there has been a rapidly increasing interest in ministry and priesthood and some efforts to push beyond the positions enunciated at the council. For the moment, however, the theological

studies are quite fragmentary and uneven in quality. Catholic theologians are realizing that the questions about ministry are central and critical; and this is already leading to more searching and thorough study. Just one indication of this new awareness: The 1969 convention of the Catholic Theological Society of America was devoted to papers and discussion on Christian ministry, and a number of valuable orientations towards further study emerged.

In both Catholic and Protestant churches, the past decade has seen a new impetus in the study of priesthood and ministry. One of the more important ingredients in this effort has been the activity of theologians and churchmen working for reunion of the Christian churches. And as we already mentioned, one of the most creative and theologically important developments has been the Consultation on Church Union (COCU). Embracing churches that espoused episcopal and presbyterian views of church polity (and therefore of ministry), views that seemed radically incompatible, COCU managed to formulate a position that was at least tentatively acceptable to sincere and theologically trained people in both camps. Themselves the result of considerable study and debate, the sections of COCU's "Plan for Union" and of its earlier "Principles of Church Union" that deal with ministry laid down a position that can well serve as a hypothesis to be tested by biblical, historical, and systematic research. As now formulated (and despite the very uncertain future of the Consultation), COCU's statements point to the discovery of a genuine commonality in theological understanding, a commonality that will still honor a pluralism of insight and safeguard the legitimate traditions of the various churches. Whether such a pluralistic community of understanding is achievable remains to be seen; but the hope of reaching such a goal is a stimulus to careful and imaginative study of Christian ministry.[26]

For Roman Catholic theologians interested in the question of ministry and more specifically interested in finding some understanding and some pastoral implementation of ministry that will make Christian reunion possible, the COCU formulation is particularly interesting. Though its language is admittedly hypothetical and quite general, it appears to contain no element that is clearly irreconcilable with the essentials of Catholic thinking. What would result if the generalities were reduced to the concrete details of practice we cannot say; but as they stand, the COCU statements seem to open a positive avenue for reflection, discussion, and interaction between Roman Catholicism and other Christian communities.[27]

Even more encouraging have been the serious and progressively advancing theological discussions between Roman Catholics and several other churches in the United States. Joint commissions of Anglicans and Roman Catholics, Lutherans and Roman Catholics, etc., have in a relatively short time produced an important body of statements, expressing basic agreement on a number of key issues including ministry. While it is true that these statements are not official confessional documents and that they have not received approbation by the participant churches as "official doctrine," they are nevertheless the product of careful joint study by prominent theologians and high-level churchmen who are acting by official appointment. Actually, the extent of agreement that has been reached is somewhat surprising; and there are some indications that it is proving to be a bit of an embarrassment to top-level administrators in the churches.

Reluctance to move on the part of highly placed ecclesiastics may slow down the process of structural reunion, but it will probably have little influence on the theological study of ministry. One of the effects of the work that has been done by the various joint commissions is an increased possibility for genuinely ecumenical growth of theological understanding. Into these interchurch discussions (as also into the COCU negotiations) have flowed the credal and theological traditions of the various churches; these have become increasingly the common heritage of all

the theologians involved in this common study. What may be emerging is a community of understanding that is not one of completely uniform insight possessed by all but an awareness on the part of each theological tradition that the other views are complementary to its own and, though different, still within the limits of acceptability as explanation of orthodox Christian faith.

Besides ecumenical dialogue, a number of other factors brought the question of Christian ministry and priesthood to theologians' attention during the post–World War II period, though relatively little publication on the question as such appeared prior to 1965. There were indications, however, in the writing on related matters (or in nontheological discussions of ministry) that the war was a watershed in religious thought in general and particularly in thought about the institutionalized aspects of Christianity. And this shift in Christian attitudes indicated the extent to which the experience of the war had crystallized many of the religious trends of previous decades and inaugurated a new period in the practice of Christianity.

Not for the first time, but with new awareness, the Christian churches began to worry about the shortage of ordained ministers.[28] There was, of course, the loss of ministerial manpower due to the war years themselves; but the more serious problem was the obvious drop-off in vocations to the ministry. For the moment, the problem was a European one— and a chronic difficulty in Latin America. North America would experience the vocational crisis just a bit later.

More deeply, there was anxious questioning about the effectiveness of the classic methods of pastoral activity. Religious sociology, beginning to acquire form as a developed discipline, provided evidence to support the fears about decline in formal Christian practice.[29] Experiments in more relevant pastoral activity, such as the worker-priest effort in France, excited interest and received considerable attention, raising incidentally many issues regarding the nature of Christian apostolate and the particular function of the ordained.

Basic structures of ministerial activity, such as the parish, came under scrutiny; and serious suggestions were made that many such structures were no longer viable.[30]   All this had its effect in a growing distrust of seminary training, in a suspicion that the methods that were appropriate to another time were outdated in the second half of the twentieth century.[31]

One of the aspects of pastoral activity that was most severely challenged during these postwar years was that of religious instruction; and the 1950s and 60s saw an important catechetical renewal.[32]   Very rapidly the questions raised in religious education triggered broader questions about the entire apostolic effort of the church—homiletic, liturgical, etc.   Moreover, the increased utilization of laity for such catechetical work made it rather clear that such ministry was not confined to, though still for the moment controlled by, the clergy.   Even technical theological study was deeply affected, as people began to doubt the value of ivory-tower theological reflection and to ask if all theology should not be "kerygmatic."

Of all the developments during those decades, none had a greater effect on the theology of Christian ministry than the renewed emphasis on the laity.   We have already seen the influence this had on discussion within the World Council of Churches, which reflected the situation in the member churches. In Roman Catholicism, the pre–World War II movements such as Catholic Action and the Jocists matured into more autonomous activity that was now called "the apostolate of the laity."   Theologically, a number of important studies appeared, such as those by Congar, Philips, and Rahner, who were destined to have a determining influence on Vatican II.[33] The increasing study of the laity and of its relationship to ministry and priesthood began to affect the theology of baptism and confirmation, the theology of the sacramental character, and ecclesiology as a whole.   For one thing, it revived Catholic interest in the common priesthood of the community.[34]

Another major influence was the liturgical revival within the Christian churches, most prominently in the Roman Catholic community, and the historical and theological research that triggered and accompanied it. The postwar appearance of Jungmann's *Missarum Solemnia* (in 1948), of Chavasse's work on the *Gelasian Sacramentary* (in 1958), and of M. Andrieu's studies on the Roman ordinals were milestones in the historical clarification of sacramental practice in the Latin church; but they were only part of the massive scholarly effort that laid the groundwork for more accurate theological analysis of sacramental ministry.[35]   Some of these studies touched directly on ministry, as did Nussbaum's investigation of the monastic practice of private masses.[36]

When we turn to the explicit treatment of Christian ministry and priesthood during the 1950s and early 60s, it is immediately apparent that the bulk of the literature dealt with what we might call the "spirituality" of the minister.   There was widespread discussion of the need to develop the prayer life (and the life of faith in general) of the ordained, to nurture their Christian understanding with the fruit of modern Scripture scholarship, to deepen their commitment to the needs of their fellow men.   But there was also a somewhat new stress on what might be (and often were) called the "natural virtues," i.e., those human qualities of sympathy and competence and social graciousness which equipped the ordained minister to deal on a genuinely personal (though professional) level with those he wished to assist.[37]   This, of course, was closely linked to the changing "job description" of the ministry, with the rapidly developing shift to activities like counseling and social work, and with the consequent need for various kinds of technical training.

In Roman Catholic circles, a large percentage of the influential writing along these lines was constituted by papal documents, which were already numerous under Pius XII but came out with even greater frequency during the years of John XXIII and Paul VI.[38]   Granted the serious and solid content of these documents and of the commentaries upon them, they contributed little to the advance of theological understanding, since they embraced unquestioningly the theology of ministerial priesthood that was then standard in seminary courses. Much the same can be said about discussion relating to the seminary formation of candidates for ordination.[39]

In this Catholic literature about the spirituality of priests, there was already observable a mounting pressure to reconsider the discipline of clerical celibacy. Official statements frequently adverted to the "traditional" foundations for the law, and some theological effort was made to scrutinize the nature of priestly celibacy.[40] The awareness of the serious need to appraise imposed celibacy was great enough to make it a "behind doors" topic at Vatican II, but Vatican pressure kept the topic off the formal conciliar agenda. Most of this theological writing was noticeably repetitive of the standard explanations;[41] but there was a ground swell of opinion that questioned this classic justification and that sought a more adequate approach to clerical celibacy.[42]

Along a more strictly theological line, there was a considerable body of scholarly writing during this time that reexamined the "sources." Some of this concerned the scriptural, particularly the New Testament, foundations for a theology of ministry and priesthood, some of it dealt with the historical evolution of ministerial life and activity, and some of it studied critically the classic confessional or theological formulations within the different Christian churches.[43] For the most part, this material was only loosely integrated in *Festschriften* or in the published proceedings of such conferences as that at Paris' Centre de pastorale liturgique in 1954/55 (which produced *Etudes sur le sacrement de l'ordre*, published in 1957 and translated into English as *The Sacrament of Holy Orders* in 1962).

However, the badly needed synthetic work was beginning to emerge as part of a revitalized ecclesiology. Since this was the outgrowth of a theological evolution that goes back at least as far as J. A. Mohler (in the early nineteenth century), many influences

fed it; but much of the credit for organizing systematic theology and historical evidence into a new and coherent construct must go to Yves Congar.

At the heart of the creative developments in ecclesiology was the "rediscovery" of the mystery dimension of the church, which was already heralded by such nineteenth-century theologians as Scheeben and Passaglia, formulated in important (though somewhat divergent) studies of Mersch and Tromp in the 1930s and early 40s, and brought to popular attention by Pius XII's encyclical *"Mystici corporis"* in 1943. Implicit in the notion of the church being the body of Christ is the idea of the church's sacramentality; and the publication in 1953 of Semmelroth's *Die Kirche als Ursakrament* indicated that theology was now dealing formally with this aspect of the Christian community. Finally, when the appearance of Durrwell's book on the resurrection of Christ and Rahner's and Schillebeeckx's writings on the relation between Christ and the church and the sacraments drew attention to the redemptive presence of the risen Christ to the church, the soteriological underpinnings for a deepened view of the church were provided.[44]

Any serious attempt to deal theologically with the structures of the church is confronted with the episcopacy; and most of the historical polemic concerning the nature of the church has focused on this one institution. Obviously, the Reformation and post-Reformation theologies about the church had not resolved the disputed issues that dealt with episcopacy; and both Trent and Vatican I had bequeathed as unfinished business the doctrinal clarification of the bishop's office and function. The matter lay dormant for several decades after Vatican I, but surfaced in mid-twentieth century and received widespread attention with Pope John's announcement of Vatican II. Actually, the Arbesle symposium in 1960 on the episcopacy (edited by H. Bouesse and A. Mandouze under the title *L'évêque dans l'Eglise du Christ*, Paris, 1963) indicated the scholarly concentration on the topic even prior to preparation for the council.

Before the agenda of Vatican II was formulated, books and articles and conferences of various kinds began discussing the episcopate, particularly the relationship of the bishops to the papacy. In 1961 came Torrell's *La théologie de l'épiscopat au premier concile du Vatican*, K. Rahner and J. Ratzinger's *Episkopat und primat*, and G. Thil's *Primaute pontificale et prérogatives épiscopales*. The next year saw the important collection of essays edited by Y. Congar and R.-D. Dupuy, *L'épiscopat et l'Eglise universelle*; some of the essays dealt with the early historical context of the episcopate, others (such as Congar's important article on "La Hierarchie comme service selon le N.T. et la tradition") opened up new directions for theological reflection and stressed the collegiality of the bishops. Also in 1962 came T. Urresti's *El binomio "primado-episcopado,"* and from the 22nd Semana Española de Teologia the volume *Teologia del episcopado*, both of them more "traditional" in outlook than the Congar-Dupuy book.

As the council itself began to draw attention to episcopal collegiality, more theological writing dealt with this topic. Some of it, such as W. Bertrams' *De relatione inter episcopatum et primatum* (Rome, 1963) and J. Alonso's *De corpore seu "collegio episcopali"* (Rome, 1964), was noticeably reactionary and defensive of Vatican prerogatives. Other writing, such as the articles of G. Dejaifve and D. Stanley, suggested the historical and theological bases for moving in the direction of episcopal collegiality.[45] One of the articles to which attention should be drawn because of its theological depth was that of P. Anciaux, "L'épiscopat (ordo episcoporum) comme réalité sacramentelle."[46] Anciaux places stress on the transmission and exercise of apostolic *jurisdiction*; the article is one of the most cogent *theological* arguments for the intrinsic appropriateness of jurisdiction to Christian ministry, a conclusion that the present book will contest.

Despite the concentration on episcopacy, some of the theological discussion of Orders during these years did deal with the presbyterate—for example, the pioneering work of J. Lecuyer (crystallized in *Le sacerdoce dans le mystère du Christ*, Paris, 1957, and in his article on the episcopacy in the *Dictionnaire de spiritualité*). However, much of this, including Lecuyer's own work, was dominated by the question of episcopal-presbyteral relation.[47] For the most part, the theological writing about Christian ministry and priesthood was still cast in the classic post-Tridentine mold; though some of the best of it, for example, C. Dillenschneider's *Le Christ, l'unique Prêtre et nous ses prêtres* (Paris, 1960) and H. Bouesse's *Le sacerdoce chrétien* (Paris, 1957), incorporated a great deal of the newer theological insights, particularly in discussion of the priesthood of Christ himself. An excellent popular reflection of up-to-date Catholic theology of priesthood and ministry on the eve of Vatican II was furnished by the Lenten series (in Notre Dame Cathedral, Paris) of A.-M. Carre in 1959 (*Le vrai visage du prêtre*), 1960 (*Le sacerdoce des laïcs*), and 1961 (*Prêtres et laïcs apôtres de Jésus-Christ*), with the very sequence of topics moving from ordained ministry towards the ministry of the whole community, suggesting that the reconsideration of ordained ministry was intrinsically linked with the reemphasis on the function of the laity. Some indication of the direction in which more creative theology might proceed was provided by *La tradition sacerdotale*, a series of studies emanating from the Catholic faculty of Lyon.[48] But, for the most part, there was little theological study done on priesthood and ministry, even less that could be considered progressive, and most of this latter occurred in writings that dealt more formally with pastoral practice.[49]

Before the formal closing of Vatican II on December 8, 1965, the council's final session had issued three decrees that would provide the basis for much of the Roman Catholic discussion of priesthood in the consequent decade: *"Christus Dominus"* (on the office and ministry of the bishops), *"Presbyterorum ordinis"* (on the ministry and life of priests), and *"Optatam totius"* (on priestly formation). Almost immediately a number of commentaries appeared (as they did on other conciliar documents), ranging from the short explanation accompanying the published text[50] to lengthier analysis of the text.[51] While it would be impossible to summarize the content of these commentaries or of those that continued to come out during the next few years,[52] there was somewhat general agreement that emphasis had shifted from the cultic to the diakonal in Vatican II's treatment of Christian priesthood, and that the basic question of the relation between the priesthood of the people and that of the ordained had been advanced by the council but not satisfactorily resolved. Incidentally, it is interesting to note how a scholarly study such as J. Colson's *Ministre de Jésus-Christ ou le sacerdoce de l'Evangile* (Paris, 1966) draws attention to early Christian stress on the priesthood of the community.

These documents (along with other relevant documents of Vatican II, particularly the Constitution on the Church) provided the stimulus for a broad range of articles and books about ministry and priesthood, from the cautious and conservative view of J. Galot in "Le Sacerdoce dans la doctrine du concile,"[53] to the more optimistically open attitude of E. Fairweather and G. Baum in *The Ecumenist*.[54] One of the more exploratory articles (and one that mirrored the way in which theology about ministry and priesthood was, for the moment, between the "old" and the "new") was that of A. de Bovis, which moved quite clearly to an emphasis on the priest's role as sacrament of Christ, but then placed this in a juridical context. The priesthood of the ordained is distinctive because they exercise the *authority* of Christ in the sacraments.[55] An interesting feature of this immediate post–Vatican II period is that the large international gatherings of theologians, e.g., at St. Xavier College (Chicago) and Notre Dame University in 1966, and in Toronto in 1967, to reflect on the council paid scant attention to the documents on the priesthood.

Apart from such commentary on Vatican II and some continuing work on the scriptural and historical sources, there was still very little *theological* writing on ministry and priesthood.[56] An exception was H. Küng's *Die Kirche* (Freiburg, 1967), a considerable portion of which dealt with the ministerial institutions of the church. A lengthy study that had manifest ecumenical objectives, Küng's book stressed the New Testament (especially the Pauline) writings as normative evidence and emphasized the charismatic aspect of Christian ministry.[57] Another exception was the speculative essay of W. Dodd in the December 1967 issue of *Theological Studies*.[58] Recognizing both the community-forming finality of priesthood and the essentially sacramental role of the ordained minister, Dodd saw the ordained minister as the sacrament of Christ the Head in the formation of community. This article carries a step beyond that of de Bovis, and it opens up a number of promising leads for further theological work. One should also mention G. Tavard's "The Function of the Minister in the Eucharistic Celebration: An Ecumenical Approach," a stimulating analysis of the celebrant's role in Eucharist.[59]

Generally speaking, the writing that dealt with practical pastoral applications of Vatican II's documents was more progressive and imaginative. For one thing, it was often linked with enthusiastic writing about the new role of the laity. In the afterglow of Vatican II, it seemed that the incorporation of laypeople into the active life of the church would proceed more rapidly than has actually happened. Suggested changes in patterns of ministerial activity were linked to suggested changes in the life-style of the ordained—and the most radical of such suggestions was the abolition of imposed clerical celibacy.[60] J.-P. Audet's study of the primitive Christian ministry presented cogent reasons for a positive approach to married ministry and brought into question the link between the discipline of celibacy and early Christian spirituality.[61] And R. Bunnik's two articles in *Cross Currents* subjected the classic arguments for imposed celibacy to radical but careful scrutiny, and concluded with a proposal for optional celibacy.[62] E. Schillebeeckx made a balanced and open contribution to the discussion with his *Autour du célibat du prêtre* (Paris, 1967). But any expectation that such theological reflection might have an impact on official policy was deflated by the appearance in June 1967 of Paul VI's encyclical *"Sacerdotalis caelibatus,"* which simply repeated the standard explanation, dismissed the arguments raised against imposed celibacy, and was clearly intended to shut off further debate on the topic. However, debate intensified.

As one reflects on theological activity in the two years following the council, it appears that the most creative contributions to the theology of priesthood and ministry came from adjoining questions. In the wake of the Constitution on the Sacred Liturgy and as the fruition of the liturgical movement that had made that document possible, there was an important development of thought about the Eucharist. For one thing, Vatican II's recognition of the laity's function in the life of the church implied a much more positive and intrinsic role for them in the Eucharistic action —the liturgical monopoly of the ordained minister could no longer prevail. Besides, the stress in Vatican II on the "word" aspect of the Eucharist, supported by important theological reflection on "word and sacrament,"[63] drew attention to the evangelical character of Eucharist and to the prophetic aspect of the celebrant's function.

Another question that had far-reaching implications for ministry and priesthood was that of sacramental validity. Some historical and theological study had already thrown doubt on the accepted Roman Catholic understanding of "valid" as applied to sacramental efficacy; but Vatican II's *Decree on Ecumenism*, which recognized an intrinsic effectiveness in Protestant sacramental activity, made some shift in understanding inevitable. These implications were delineated in F. van Beeck's important essay "Towards an Ecumenical Understanding of the Sacraments,"[64] which challenged the notion of validity and the claim of the Roman Catholic

community to a monopoly on genuine sacramental ministry.

But beyond the issues we have mentioned so far lay yet deeper problems, problems that carried theological reflection (and Christian life) beyond the horizons of Vatican II. For one thing, there was the so-called secularization of human existence, which brought into question the entire ministerial enterprise of the Christian churches. Was any of the traditional ministry of word and sacrament meaningful in a "world come of age," in a world where God was proclaimed to be dead? One can see the fundamental character of this challenge by perusing the printed report of the Third International Conference for Inter-European Sacerdotal Exchange, held at Luzern, September 18–22, 1967. Composed of some ninety experts in profane as well as sacred sciences, the conference brought some of the most advanced biblical-pastoral-theological reflection into confrontation with the data about ministry provided by the behavioral and social sciences, and made it quite clear that the present moment in the church's life calls for a reappraisal of ministerial priesthood that reaches far beyond the perspective of Vatican II. The crisis in which the church finds itself today is a fundamental crisis of faith; and the difficulty of maintaining authentic Christian faith in the present-day world faces ordained ministers as well as (or perhaps more than) the laity.[65]

The end of the 1960s witnessed an increase in writing about ministerial priesthood, but progressive theological contribution was still quite rare. A collection of essays such as J. Frisque and Y. Congar's *Les prêtres: Formation, ministère, et vie* (Paris, 1968) contained much of value; and the *Concilium* series dealt with a number of issues that touched on priesthood and ministry—apostolic succession, the Eucharist, sacramental theology, liturgy. But with one exception, to which we will allude in a moment, the volumes of *Concilium*, though they constituted the most consistent source of creative theology in the postconciliar years, did not grapple with the deeper theological questions of ministry and priesthood.[66] The exception was *The Identity of the Priest* (*Concilium*, vol. 43), which appeared in 1969 and contained an excellent group of articles. Two of these are especially significant for their theological orientation: W. Kasper's "A New Dogmatic Outlook on the Priestly Ministry" (pp. 20–33) concentrates on the function of community leadership and on promoting unity; and K. Rahner's "What Is the Theological Starting Point for a Definition of the Priestly Ministry?" (pp. 80–84) suggests as an answer that "the priest is he who . . . preaches the Word of God by mandate of the Church as a whole and therefore officially, and in such a way that he is entrusted with the highest levels of sacramental intensity of this Word" (p. 85).

Conferences of various kinds on the crisis of the priesthood became quite common; but most of these concerned themselves with more practical pastoral issues and did little probing into basic theological questions. An exception was the 1969 meeting of the Catholic Theological Society of America. The ministerial priesthood was taken as the general theme, and a number of worthwhile papers set the stage for the participants' discussion. R. Dillon's "Ministry as Stewardship of the Tradition in the New Testament" was a careful contribution to the already extensive literature on primitive Christianity's church order; J. Powers raised several key questions about ministerial powers and office in "The Concept of Validity in Ministry"; A. Cunningham's paper on "Ministry of Women in the Church" was a thoughtful but progressive view of a question that was becoming more and more discussed (and unavoidable!); and J. O'Brien raised both practical and theological questions in his "Theology of the Presbyterium."[67]

One of the more significant contributions during these two years was made by J. Blenkinsopp, *Celibacy, Ministry, Church* (New York, 1968). Leaving aside, for the moment, the early portion of the book which deals critically with the discipline of clerical celibacy and specifically with the encyclical "*Sacerdotalis caelibatus*" (which had come out the previous year), the major portion of the book is a careful examination of the biblical evidence for the origins of Christian ministry, a short appraisal of the historical process by which emphasis shifted to cultic minister, and some imaginative suggestions of the forms that Christian ministry could take at the present time. The historical portion of Blenkinsopp's thesis was complemented and deepened by the article of J. Moingt, "Caractère et ministère sacerdotal."[68] Moingt traces the evolution of stress on the cultic in Christian ministry, argues persuasively that a critical element in this evolution was the development of a theology of sacramental character in terms of the "power to sacrifice," and concludes by urging that the "character of Orders" be thought through in terms of word as well as cult.

The fact, however, that Blenkinsopp began his book with the matter of celibacy, and sees this as the root issue, reflected the atmosphere of those years. The focus of discussion was on the practical issues of celibacy and ecclesiastical authority rather than on the nature of priesthood and ministry. Controversy about the discipline of imposed clerical celibacy became increasingly heated at the turn of the decade, and the topic was discussed from every imaginable angle.[69] Paul VI's "*Sacerdotalis caelibatus*" failed to stop the debate, and growing pressure finally forced the question onto the agenda of the world synod of bishops in 1971. Negative reaction to the encyclical was voiced bluntly in articles such as A. Antweiler's in *Orientierung*;[70] and equally strong affirmative voices were heard, like that of the United States bishops in their annual statement. Almost everyone writing on the topic mentioned that celibacy was not *the* basic problem; but the widespread unrest in this matter was symptomatic of the uncertainty and ferment in the Roman Catholic community, and particularly in its clergy. From a theological point of view, the massive quantity of writing was not particularly fruitful: the papal encyclical had said nothing about celibacy that had not been often repeated before, and the same was true of most of the encyclical's defenders. The bulk of their effort was directed to answering the objections raised against imposed celibacy; with rare exceptions (such as Blenkinsopp's book) there was little that the critics of the discipline of clerical celibacy added to what one could find, for example, in Bunnik's earlier (1966) articles.

Another encyclical of Paul VI, "*Humanae vitae*" (in July 1968), contributed both to the turbulent internal situation of the Roman Catholic clergy and to the theological clarification of issues related to Christian ministry. The issue of contraception was one that deeply concerned ordained ministers within the Roman Catholic community, for their church's official stand on this issue had caused no little anguish and perplexity to both confessors and their penitents. And (without essaying any judgment on the encyclical's content) it seems safe to say that the pope's action removed neither anguish nor perplexity. It quickly became apparent, however, that the fundamental questions raised by the encyclical were not those concerning the morality of contraception but those related to authority within the church, more specifically to teaching authority. So, for example, in the well-respected "Notes on Moral Theology," published each year in *Theological Studies*, R. McCormick in 1969 spent ten pages describing the diverse reactions to the encyclical and twenty-five pages on the authority of the *magisterium*.[71]

Radical questioning of ecclesiastical authority was not new with "*Humanae vitae*," but the encyclical brought discussion to a head. Aspects of the problem were, of course, latent in many of the discussions and documents of Vatican II. More than one of the studies that dealt with the crisis in the ordained clergy emphasized the issues of authority—whether the intrinsic nature of that authority or (more frequently) the manner in which it was exercised. Probably no book had drawn sharper attention to the question, delineated its elements more clearly, and studied in more scholarly fashion the scriptural sources from which careful reflection must proceed, than J.

McKenzie's *Authority in the Church* (New York, 1966). But now at the end of the 1960s there was an intensive concentration on the matter of teaching authority, and (quite logically) on what was the ultimate instance of such authority: papal infallibility.[72]

The theological link of ecclesiastical authority with ordained ministry comes in the study of "office." Quite a number of books and articles on this topic already existed (actually, it is the center of all the literature concerning church order in early Christianity —and thereafter), most of them historical in character, a few (such as H. von Balthasar's *Church and World*) of them analytic, and a few appraising the contemporary situation (like A. Hayen's "L'obéissance dans l'Eglise").[73] Attention should be drawn to E. Schillebeeckx's article "The Catholic Understanding of Office in the Church," certainly one of the most important reconsiderations of "office" and of "sacramental character" in current theology.[74]

Roman Catholics were far from being the only ones in the 1960s concerned about the "*crise du ministère*" or engaged in trying to understand more adequately the nature of Christian ministry and priesthood, though Vatican II and the disputes about celibacy gave added drama to the Catholic situation. To give only a few instances—for we can make no attempt to describe the entire picture: One can glimpse the extensive Lutheran research in this area by reading the volume *Episcopacy in the Lutheran Church* (edited by I. Asheim and V. Gold, Philadelphia, 1970); or examining the essays by Lutheran theologians in *Eucharist and Ministry* (vol. 4 of *Lutherans and Catholics in Dialogue*)—one can notice an increasing ecumenical openness in Lutheran scholarship, coupled with a characteristic fidelity to confessional traditions. This same combination is strikingly illustrated in G. Lindbeck's "The Lutheran Doctrine of Ministry: Catholic and Reformed,"[75] an article that is particularly good in clarifying the traditional Lutheran emphasis on the primacy of the ministry of word.[76] In Anglican circles, a key reflection of theological attitudes in the 1960s is contained in the *Lambeth Essays on Ministry*, a series of studies prepared for (and approved by) the Lambeth Conference of 1968.[77] From a theological point of view the most probing contribution was that of L. Houlden (pp. 39–50); he works to develop the understanding of traditional priestly notions such as "sacrifice" and "mediation" by insisting on the fact that God works through the ordained in *sacramental* fashion. And in continental Reformed theology, the writings of J.-J. von Allmen and M. Thurian's very important *Sacerdoce et ministère* (Taizé, 1970) gave evidence of the theological depth of their tradition and of that tradition's radical compatibility with other traditions, more specifically with the Roman Catholic, on the matter of priesthood. Thurian's conclusions, in particular, are strikingly congruent with acceptable Catholic views; yet, there is no question of compromise or infidelity to his own tradition, but rather a depth of insight that transcends many of the misunderstandings and false oppositions.

Overall, there were clear indications by the beginning of the 1970s of a convergence of views among theologians of the various churches regarding the nature of ministry and priesthood—the convergence was far from total, but it was quite evident that all the churches faced the same problems and questions, theological and practical. Moreover, as the decade began, it was evident that one could no longer talk about a dearth of research and writing about ministry and priesthood; there was a flood of publication, and a fair amount of this contributed to a more accurate theological understanding.[78]

For the most part, the theological work on ministry continued to be published as shorter pieces, and then was gathered together in collections of essays. The papers from the 1969 meeting of the Downside Symposium appeared in 1970: they covered a wide range of approaches—historical, sociological, theological—and represented the viewpoints of a number of churches.[79] Perhaps the most important insight one gets from reading these papers is the emergence of the question about

priestly character as central: what really is meant when one speaks about a person or function as "priestly"? Dom Leclercq's remarks on this (pp. 53–75) are particularly intriguing, as he shows the way in which the medieval developments constitute a secularization of Christian ministry rather than a clerico-sacralization of the Christian community. Another worthwhile collection was *Existenzprobleme des Priesters* (edited by F. Henrich), particularly the essay of K. Lehmann; and *Il sacerdozio ministeriale*, the papers from a meeting of Italian theologians in 1969; and *Teologia del sacerdocio*, issuing from a similar meeting of Spanish theologians in the same year. These indicate the spreading concern in theological circles for a clarification of the basic issues—the nature of priesthood, the specific role of the ordained in the church, the meaning of priestly character.

One of the collections that drew most attention—since it was prepared as a working paper for the 1971 synod of bishops in Rome—was *Le ministère sacerdotal*.[80] The purpose of this study, which was the corporate product of a committee of prominent theologians, dictated its orientation: it remains within the confines of the formulations of Vatican II, and explicates some of the latent implications of the council. Actually, one can find much more depth in the first two volumes of Herder's projected five-volume series, *Der priesterliche Dienst*: in the first of these, *Ursprung und Frühgeschichte*, by A. Diessler, H. Schlier, and J.-P. Audet, the origins of Christian priesthood are studied—the insights of Schlier and Audet into the context and "atmosphere" of early Christian ministry are of considerable value; in the second volume, *Wesen und Vollmacht des Priestertums nach dem Lehramt*, K. Becker reviews the official teaching of the Catholic church on priesthood, and indicates some of the historical factors that conditioned this teaching at different stages of its evolution.[81]

The most complete, and one of the most coherently planned, collection was *Sacerdoce et célibat*, edited by J. Coppens as a volume in the *Bibliotheca Ephemeridum Theolog-*

icarum Lovaniensium.[82] From both a theological and an exegetico-historical point of view, the volume is filled with carefully researched insights and marked by balanced scholarly judgment—the section on celibacy provides more that is "new," particularly in its historical portions, than does the section on priesthood. To some extent, the outlook of the volume is projected in Coppen's essay "Le sacerdoce chrétien" (pp. 49–99), which uses the 1969 letter on priesthood of the German hierarchy as a framework for his own reflections on the historical origin and evolution of priesthood. As his own conclusion (and that of the German bishops), Coppens draws attention to the ordained priesthood as sacrament—certainly an important and genuine conclusion; however, one cannot but ask whether a certain clericalism still lurks in Coppens' view, for the ordained ministry as sacrament (as Coppens explains that) seems to monopolize the sacramentality of the community.

In the historical portion of its study of clerical celibacy, *Sacerdoce et célibat* performs a real service. H. Crouzel's article, "Le célibat et la continence dans l'Eglise primitive," not only complements R. Gryson's *Les origines du célibat ecclésiastique*, which appeared in 1970, but does so by studying the viewpoint and motivation underlying those early Christian developments—which makes Crouzel's essay one of the few attempts to deal with the *theological* understanding of celibacy. In three consequent essays, A. Stickler, J. Coppens, and J.-P. Massaut trace the evolution of celibacy up to the time of Trent. The volume does little to study the post-Tridentine developments.

Because of its breadth of coverage, the *Concilium* series deserves somewhat separate treatment. With 1970, a new *Concilium* collection was launched, and an overview of the issues that touched upon ministry or upon allied topics indicates three tendencies in the early 70s: a growing convergence of discussion (among Roman Catholic theologians, and among theologians from the different churches); a growing awareness of the need to give some *theological* explanation of priesthood and ministry; and increased attention to the broader problems of "secularity," religious faith, and world development, into which any realistic understanding of Christian ministry must fit. Three of the 1972 volumes are particularly relevant; and though their content is too varied and rich to summarize, their titles indicate the range of discussion they contain: *The Plurality of Ministries* (edited by H. Küng and W. Kasper), *The Unifying Role of the Bishop* (edited by E. Schillebeeckx), *Office and Ministry in the Church* (edited by R. Murphy and B. van Iserl).

Separate mention should also be made of the volumes issuing from the large-scale study of priestly life and ministry undertaken by the United States Catholic bishops. Initiated in 1967 as a project to study in depth all the important aspects of ministerial priesthood (especially in the form it had taken in the United States), the multifaceted study was completed in 1971 and presented in summary fashion to the bishops at their national meeting that year.[83] Quite symptomatically, the only major portion of the study that was not subsequently published by the bishops was that dealing with the *theology* of priesthood and ministry.[84]

Throughout the late 1960s and the early 70s, longer scholarly studies of specialized aspects of the question continued to appear: A. Lemaire's thorough and balanced study *Les ministères aux origines de l'Eglise* (Paris, 1971); R. Gryson's study on the early history of celibacy (already referred to above); J.-P. Massaut's two volumes, *Josse Clichtove, l'humanisme et le réforme du clergé* (Paris, 1968); R. Brown, *Priest and Bishop* (New York, 1970); R. Corriveau, *The Liturgy of Life* (Montreal, 1970). And some few more substantive articles, such as J. Moingt's "Nature du sacerdoce ministériel,"[85] worked towards a systematizing of current theological reflection. But what was still missing was a more complete synthesis by a Roman Catholic theologian that would compare with Thurian's *Sacerdoce et ministère.*[86]

Discussion of ecclesiastical authority, more

specifically papal teaching authority, continued, and in the early 1970s it revolved around H. Küng's *Unfehlbar? Eine Anfrage.*[87] Debate on the book's methodology and conclusions, and more broadly on the issues the book raised, was widespread and quite heated. The most publicized aspect of the debate was the exchange between Küng and K. Rahner, carried on in the pages of *Stimmen der Zeit.*[88]

However, time may show that the most penetrating and significant contribution to the discussion was made by B. Tierney in his article in a special issue of *Journal of Ecumenical Studies* and in his recently published *Origins of Papal Infallibility, 1150–1350.*[89]

Not directly involved in the infallibility debate, but having considerable importance for its ultimate resolution, was the joint study by Lutheran and Roman Catholic scholars, *Peter in the New Testament* (edited by R. Brown, K. Donfried, J. Reumann), which appeared in 1973.[90] Its careful analysis of the various New Testament traditions regarding Peter and its clear but nuanced conclusions about Peter's historical activity and about early Christianity's evolving view of Peter throw considerable light on primitive Christianity's understanding of ministry.

Another question came into prominence in the 1960s and early 70s, one whose practical implications may be sweeping for the church of the future: this was the question of ordaining women to the ministry. While the discussion was not limited to Catholic circles, and while a portion of the controversy dealt with the role of women in the various ministries (teaching, healing, etc.) whose distinctiveness and autonomy were beginning to be recognized, the focus of attention was clearly on ordination to priesthood, i.e., to full liturgical ministry as understood in the Catholic tradition.[91]

Considering the very recent emergence of theological reflection on this question, it is quite remarkable how rapidly thought about this topic has evolved. Instead of the common assumption (which prevailed until after World War II) that "priestly ordination" was by the very nature of things limited to males,

there is a growing *theological* consensus that no intrinsic barriers stand in the way of admitting women to full ministry as liturgical celebrants.[92] No doubt, there are still strong objections to ordaining women—on what are claimed to be practical or cultural grounds, and the answer to such objections will be part of the broader movement towards recognizing the full equality of women.[93]

However, it is important that exclusion of women from certain areas of the church's ministry can no longer be facilely supported by theological reasons.[94] No doubt, the resolution of the question will be deeply affected by the entire evolution of thought and practice regarding ministry today—the recognized pluralism of ministries, the separation of ministry (even "ordained" ministry) from "clerical," the distinction between ministry as function and as profession, etc. While the acceleration of "women's liberation" in human society has unquestionably been a major psychological impulse in the discussion about ordination of women, the major theological impulse may very well be the post–World War II rediscovery of the laity.[95]

Although the brief review we have just given of post–World War II writing about ministry and priesthood purposely focused on more strictly theological publications, this is not meant to suggest that the existential situation of Christian ministry during those years provided no insights for theology. Just the contrary; the ferment in the church as a whole and particularly in clerical circles made theological confrontation of many issues unavoidable, and challenged any number of presuppositions and conclusions that theologians and churchmen had rather complacently accepted up to that point. For that reason, a brief look at the crisis within the Roman Catholic clergy and some suggestions of the way in which this is linked to theological understandings may be appropriate to this introduction—though there will be nothing new in these comments. Concentration on the problem within the Roman Catholic community in no way implies that it is unique to that church; but the Catholic situation is more striking and in many ways paradigmatic for the church as a whole. Moreover, since the following description may seem to imply some critical judgment, it is better for the author to confine himself to his own tradition, with which he is experientally familiar.

That some kind of crisis exists in the Catholic priesthood—decline in vocations, decision by many ordained priests to leave the institutional structures of their ministry, uncertainty among many clergy as to their Christian and professional identity and function—is apparent. Objective evaluation of the situation demands that one neither ignore the problem nor overdramatize it. Such vocational uncertainty is not peculiar to the Roman Catholic ministry—in various ways, all the Christian churches are faced with the same questions about the professional identity of the ordained minister—nor is it confined to the ministry, since most of the classic professions are faced with the question of their function in a world whose social structure is rapidly changing. For most Catholics, however, there is a special difficulty in applying such evolutionary views to the priesthood: its unchanging character was itself a clear reflection of the unchanging sameness of the church; but today everything points to a future pattern of priestly life and activity that would in many respects be hard for yesterday's Catholics to recognize.

Priests in the Roman Catholic church are situated between bishop and people, bearing responsibilities in both directions; and both of these relationships are being questioned by today's priests. What precisely is the position of the priest vis-à-vis his bishop, or the bishops as a group, or the bishop of Rome? Can it be one of simple and unquestioning compliance with any directive that comes to him from the episcopal level? Is his priestly task one of carrying out the orders given him by higher authority, or is it one of exerting initiative and creativity in forming his people as Christians, even if this conflicts with the wishes, perhaps even the orders, of the bishop?

True, many of the problems between priests and bishops are situated on the practical level of human relationships. All too many bishops are humanly out of touch with their priests, and the administrative burdens of their present episcopal role make it difficult, if not almost impossible, to remedy this situation. In some instances, the bishops have misconstrued the notion of "monarchical" as applied to the episcopal office, and so deal with priests (and others as well) in authoritarian fashion. Nor can the blame—if there is blame—be placed on one side alone: most priests are reluctant to form too close a personal relationship with their bishop; they tend to treat him as a "boss" rather than as a brother apostle; and bishops often find themselves socially isolated from their priests. Yet, deeper than these human elements of the problem lie the theological issues. The operative attitudes of both priests and bishops towards one another are to a large extent the result of the point of view on episcopal authority that they were taught during their years of seminary training, a point of view that has been fortified by ecclesiastical structures and procedures that are grounded in that same point of view. The question we must ask ourselves is whether the theology of episcopacy and priesthood that found expression in seminary classrooms and diocesan chanceries is correct.

While it may not be as sharply controversial, the priest's relation to the Christian people with whom he works is also undergoing basic change. Sociologically, Catholics in a country like the United States have become more established socially, financially more secure, better educated—and probably more "secularized" in their attitudes. Besides, the most dedicated and best informed (i.e., informed about their faith) among them are now aware of the new dimensions in Christian life and activity that have been promised by Vatican II. With the new insistence on initiative and responsibility for forming one's own conscience, lay men and women who previously would have been content to allow their pastor to be their conscience are now making their own adult decisions quite independently of direct priestly guidance. Probably nothing has done more to accelerate this whole process than the controversy about contraception, the impossible situation in which it placed so many priests with regard to advising people in the confessional, and the dawning awareness on the part of large numbers of Catholic laity that the Christian decision in the matter was ultimately theirs to face.

But what, then, is the role of the pastor towards his people? Is he merely to service their strictly "spiritual" needs, providing the Eucharist and baptism and opportunity for confession? Is he to concentrate on religious education, forming the laity to carry out the tasks that he himself previously fulfilled? Or is he, in the last analysis, just another member of the Christian community who should now join in apostolic equality with other members of the community to work for the betterment of human life? And if it seems that this betterment will be best fostered by the activity of nonreligious institutions, such as governmental agencies, should he not devote himself to such social activism rather than continue a pastoral ministry that seems somewhat sterile and out of touch with contemporary man's deepest needs?

Inevitably, such questioning raises doubts about the life-style of the ordained clergy. On principle and by design the ordained priest has had a somewhat isolated and detached existence. He was "taken from among men" and was not meant to be as other men; his clerical celibacy was the sign of this superior level of life he had espoused. Priesthood had become, and is still considered to be, not just a function but a state in life; it remains to be seen whether this view that has prevailed for many centuries corresponds with the intrinsic nature of Christian ministry. What happens to the clergy as a distinct caste within the church if one takes seriously the current emphasis on the unity of that church as one "people of God"? or if one discovers that Christian ministry (even sacramental ministry) need not be a full-time profession? or if theological reflection indicates that "dedication" in a true Christian sense may mean not detachment from people but identification with them? One could go on with ques-

tions, but the basic point seems incontrovertible: finding a life-style (or life-styles) appropriate to the ordained ministry will be dependent upon the theological answers about the nature and function of ministry in the church.

However, the down-to-earth, vital adjustment of ministry to our developing world situation will not wait upon full theological clarification—life must go on, even in the midst of doubt and obscurity. And it is good that such tentative probings for new forms take place, painful and misunderstood as they often may be. Without them, theology itself would be working too much in the abstract, out of touch with what is one of its principal sources: the dynamic action of the Spirit in Christians as they try to express their faith through the patterns of their daily lives. At the same time, there is a critical need for the kind of relevant and creative theological insight that could provide some guidance for these searchings towards new forms.

Whatever else one might wish to say about studies into the nature of Christian ministry today, they are not purely academic exercises, a playful reconsideration of something that is really quite well understood already. The basic inadequacy of our present understanding of Christian priesthood and ministry is only too painfully apparent. Taking only the Roman Catholic theology of priesthood as an example (and obviously it is not an isolated example), it might be good to seek some of the roots of this inadequacy—so that in turn this can help guide our search for further understanding.

First, the notion of "priesthood" that prevailed in Roman Catholic circles for many centuries was formed in a period of history when legal categories were the dominant way of thinking about human society, whether ecclesiastical or civil. Already by the time of Cyprian, Christian ministry was thought of as "office"; and since by that time the model of the civil state is already shaping Christian thought about the church as institution, understanding of ecclesiastical office is influenced by the notion of civil office. This tendency becomes increasingly pronounced in later centuries when there was an actual confusion of ecclesiastical and civil office. But long before this practical aspect of the problem arose, the late patristic and medieval church tried to clarify the reality of priesthood and ministry by issuing laws to regulate the existence of the ordained. Like all positive legislation, these laws dealt with the external social relationships of those in the clerical state (to one another and to other members of the church); and such laws almost necessarily treated the clergy as a class in society, rather than dealing with ministry as an essentially charismatic function. Despite the profound challenge to this pattern of thinking that came with the reform movements of the fourteenth to sixteenth centuries, the legal expression of the church's being continued to exert a normative influence in Catholic understanding of the ministerial priesthood. The present-day fascination of most bishops with the prescriptions of canon law and their appeal to it as the primary guide for interpreting their own role and that of the priests working with them indicate that the legal way of envisaging the ministerial function is still very influential.

Secondly, the Roman Catholic view of ministry has been strongly influenced by papal theology, which is the final intensification of the dichotomy of the church into clergy and laity. With Vatican II a period of reaction has set in which may lead to a more balanced view of the church; but it will not be easy to remove from Catholic thought the image of the pyramid—with the pope at the top, immediately over the bishops, who are over the priests, who in turn are over the laity, with all power and authority and sanctification coming down from the top. In such a view, those ordained to the ministry, even the bishops, are thought of as carrying out the apostolate that originates with the pope; the directives for valid and profitable ministry issue from Rome; and the authenticity of one's ministerial activity is judged by the criterion of conformity to Roman norms. The ordained priest is looked upon as the lowest level of the

"active" portion of the church, which is distinguished from and directed to the laity. This is the point of departure in thinking about the priest's function, rather than his basic Christian identity and coresponsibility with the laity. One realizes this when he reflects that fidelity to the priestly role has been gauged essentially by the priest's conformity to authority directives rather than by his identification with the needs and concerns of the mass of people.

Thirdly, the backdrop for Catholic thought about the ordained ministry has been the division of the Christian community into the parish structure. Obviously, the organization of Christians into parishes has a long and fruitful history and a great deal to recommend it. It is altogether possible that such parish organization will continue to be the most desirable form of Christian community in many situations. But it is *one* form of organizing a Christian community; it is not identical with Christian community. And in the present-day world of increasing urbanization it is questionable how effective parish structures are in many instances. To think of the ordained minister as essentially related to a parish is, then, to tie oneself to something less than essential. It limits one's understanding of what may well be the most basic finality of the ministry, its purpose of creating Christian community, for it tends to see the parish as the community par excellence, and any other grouping of Christians is thought of as accidental and only improperly a true Christian community. Even priests themselves, engaged in some context other than a parish—e.g., in university education—have allowed themselves to be classified as part-time or "hyphenated" priests, as if they were exercising their ministerial function only when they were engaged partially in what parish priests do full-time.

Clearly, if explanations of priestly ministry and existence have been controlled by the notion of the parish, and this latter has found its definition essentially in canonical terms, this has reinforced the view of the ordained ministry as a caste within the church and as a state in life. Priests, living in the parish rectory, govern and care for all the details of the parish; they are in charge, for they have been given their authority by the bishop within the framework of canon law. They are responsible for the parish buildings and other possessions; they provide Mass and confessions, baptize, marry, and bury; in many cases they are ultimately in charge of a school attached to the parish, though most of the routine academic management has been entrusted to others. What role they play or should play in applying the gospel to local economic, social, or political conditions is somewhat vague; and most of the influential members of their congregations prefer that it remain vague—priests should remain apart from all this.

Fourthly, it is generally assumed that all the clearly Christian things an ordained priest has done he has done by virtue of his priestly ordination—an apparently logical but really misleading assumption. During the centuries when the intrinsic role of the laity was overlooked or even explicitly denied, much of the basic Christian responsibility for witness and service was appropriated by the ordained clergy (and by religious communities which were at least sociologically, if not canonically, identified with the clergy). To say that the clergy arrogated to themselves the activity and responsibility that is actually common to the entire people is not to criticize them; for in many cases they performed heroically and filled what otherwise would have been a vacuum. But what is important, if one is to understand the nature and limits of the ministry as such, is that one distinguish between the functions a man performs by virtue of his baptism and basic membership in the Christian community and the functions he performs by virtue of his ordination to ministry. Though we need to examine the matter more carefully, there are good grounds for suspecting that much of the present activity of the ordained belongs properly to any Christian—though not all Christians have the dedication or freedom to undertake it.

Fifthly, Roman Catholic thinking about priestly ministry has been controlled by a view of sacramental causality that employed the phrase *"ex opere operato"* without at times understanding it too accurately. It would be unjust and naive to accuse responsible Catholic thought of seeing the action of sacraments as magic; yet Catholic theologians must also admit that such terms as "sacramental grace," "sacramental character," and "grace of office" aroused only the vaguest of understandings, even among graduates of seminary. One can, of course, take refuge in saying that the realities denominated by such terms are in the realm of mystery; but this is to give way to fideism and to make all ministerial activity a blind striving towards an unknown goal.

What is more commonly taught and believed by ordained ministers in the Catholic church is that they received some special spiritual endowment and power with their ordination; this permits them to effect spiritual transformation in others through the administration of the sacraments. Above all, the power given by priestly ordination enables them to function as consecrators in the celebration of the Eucharist. Possession of this special power, the character of Orders, is lifelong and irremovable; it is what differentiates the action of an ordained minister from that of an unordained person who would perform exactly the same external action, e.g., celebrating the Eucharist. In the latter case, the action would not be valid; it would not be the action of the Eucharist, but an empty gesture. It is clear, then, that the question of "validity" that is so central and abrasive in ecumenical discussions is closely tied to this "intrinsic quality" understanding of priestly being and activity.

Sixthly, Catholic thought about the ordained minister and his function is closely linked to the understanding of terms like "sacrifice," "dedication," "sanctification"; and as current theological reflection reexamines the meaning of these, there is a concomitant questioning of "priesthood." To take just one aspect as illustration: "Dedication" has traditionally carried the implication of "set apart from the ordinary." This meaning is certainly basic to the idea of dedication, but reflection on Christ's own act of dedication in his death and resurrection apparently leads to the conclusion that the characteristic Christian sense of dedication is that of self-giving to others in love and service. Thus, it involves not removal from other men and their daily concerns but instead a profound identification with them. We will have to examine in much greater depth such theological study, but for the moment we can point to the implications that this study can have for our understanding of the activity and life-style that is appropriate to ordained priesthood.

Relatively unexplored though the question was until very recently, the main lines of investigation into priesthood and ministry now seem basically clear. Further work may dispel this impression, but there seems to be a consistent listing of needed research and analysis that has been provided by the various scholars and study groups that have dealt with the matter in the past decade. It seems beyond question that the reality of Christian ministry will have to be investigated in the context of a total ecclesiology, for ministry exists within the church and for the sake of the church, and its nature and finality are therefore determined by the life and activity of the whole church. This would seem immediately to discourage any thorough study of priesthood until lengthier analyses of allied areas of ecclesiology have been completed; but such need not be the conclusion. What it does indicate is that one cannot expect any definitive conclusions to result from the present wave of writing about ministry. Hopefully the work done will be accurate and imaginative enough to lay out the groundwork for further study and to define the questions that demand scholarly examination. After all, if the Christian church is a vital and historically evolving reality, the task of ecclesiology (and within that the task of a theology of ministry) will be unending.

Because ministry is part of a changing community, serious theological study will have to draw from the resources of contemporary social and behavioral sciences. Thus far, exploitation of the work done in these scientific fields has been very limited on the part of theologians. Most of the studies on priesthood and ministry have been governed by categories of thought that came out of a past that was dominated by philosophical and legal ways of thinking; and while these ways of thinking are to be respected, they can no longer be considered all-sufficient. Whether social scientific investigation of Christian ministry, or for that matter of Christianity as a social phenomenon, is advanced enough to provide the desired data is questionable; however, it may well be that the attempt of theologians to draw from what has been done can serve as a guide and incentive for further study.

Recent "rediscovery" of the priesthood and ministry possessed by the Christian people as a whole makes it quite obvious that the specialized ministry exercised by the ordained cannot be studied in isolation. Rather, theologians of every Christian church are faced with the task of distinguishing—if that is possible—the functions of ordained ministers from those of the entire community. A number of facile answers to that question have been given—e.g., that the ordained individual ministers to the Christian community itself, while the entire community ministers to the needs of mankind. However, none of these proposed answers comes to grips with the full spectrum of biblical and historical evidence, nor with the presently developing situation within the churches. Even if it is possible to describe accurately this community-minister relationship as it existed in the past, one is still faced with a value judgment that must flow from correct theological principles: Should the pattern of the past continue to exist within Christianity as it works to make itself a source of transformation in the emerging world of today?

One element that recurs consistently in credal statements and theological analyses is the relationship of specialized ministry to word and sacrament; through these two agencies the ordained are to minister to the faith of the community. Though the agreement of the various churches on this point is rather striking, the uniformity of view is not as real as it appears. "Word" and "sacrament" are terms that are understood quite differently in different confessional groups; and the understanding of a ministry of word and sacrament is therefore quite diverse. The very frequency of the phrase, however, demands that it be carefully studied. Yet, the prospect of doing so is a bit frightening: one can immediately see lurking on the horizon all the contemporary debates about hermeneutics, about Christianity as basically event or *kerygma*, about the function of symbol and sacrament, etc.

One specific aspect of this question that cannot be neglected is the long-standing contention of several Christian churches that the specialized ministry itself is a sacramental reality in the strict usage of that term. We noticed earlier that scholarly reflection during the past decade is drawing attention to this topic. It may well be that the attempt to find some element in ordained ministry that will discriminate between it and the function of the church as a whole will come to focus on the question: is there really a sacrament of orders? No doubt this evokes some of the classic theological tensions that have separated Christian thought: the function of mediation in Christian life, the "supernaturality" of divine action in and through the church, the dependence (or independence) of faith vis-à-vis ecclesiastical institutions; but honest theological investigation cannot dodge the issue.

Along a somewhat different line, there is common agreement that whatever the specialized ministry may be, it exists for the sake of the community as a whole. At least in the theoretical order, this is almost a truism. Understanding of this principle, however, immediately fragments when one sees what different Christian churches mean by the

word "community" when applied to Christianity. In reality we are faced with what has already been mentioned, that a theology of ministry can only exist as part of an integral ecclesiology. There may be, though, an avenue of research: perhaps in deepening the notion of "community," studying the particular way in which Christianity is meant to be community, and examining the nonstructural elements of Christian community, we can discover the ways in which certain persons (or groups of persons) can function in ordered fashion to foster that community. This approach may permit us to think more creatively about the forms of specialized ministry that our present religious situation demands.

Finally, a theology of ministry and priesthood cannot avoid one of the most persistent and aggravating of religious questions: the necessity and effectiveness (validity) of institutionalized religious forms. Today this question is being proposed in its most radical expression: not only is there a question about the appropriateness of present institutional structures and the proposal to replace them with something more relevant but the question is being asked whether in the life and activity of the Christian people there is place for any kind of settled institutions. Obviously, such a broad question contains a number of subquestions: What is meant by "office" in the church? What kind of power and authority can legitimately be exercised in the church? Does authentic Christian mission, now that we see that it entails involvement with the "outside world," demand a structure of specialized Christian institutions, or should Christians act through the institutions of secular society? And if Christianity does demand some institutions of its own, are there some of these that must be common to the entire church, or can there be a considerable pluralism of forms without impairing the essential unity of Christians?

NOTES

1. *The Fourth World Conference on Faith and Order. Montreal, 1963* (London, 1964), p. 26.
2. See D. Gaines, *The World Council of Churches* (Petersborough, N.H., 1966), pp. 275–306.
3. See *The Evanston Report* (London, 1955), pp. 92–95.
4. *Ibid.*, pp. 160–73.
5. *Ibid.*, p. 169.
6. *The New Delhi Report* (New York, 1962), p. 88.
7. *Ibid.*, p. 121.
8. *The Third World Conference on Faith and Order. Lund, 1952* (London, 1953), pp. 41–42.
9. *New Directions in Faith and Order. Bristol, 1967* (London, 1968), p. 148.
10. See *Faith and Order Findings* (London, 1963), pp. 3–29; see also *Institutionalism and Church Unity* (London, 1963).
11. *Faith and Order, Louvain, 1971. Study Reports and Documents* (Geneva, 1971), pp. 78–101.
12. In its reaction to the study report, the Faith and Order Commission noted the trend towards convergence, but listed a number of theological issues that require deeper study; see pp. 223–24.
13. The best known and probably most influential study was *The Apostolic Ministry*, ed. K. Kirk (London, 1946).
14. See *Lambeth Essays on Ministry*, the working papers prepared for the 1968 conference; for a description of the conference and its achievements, see the report of C. Ryan in *Theological Studies* 29 (1968), pp. 597–636.
15. On the origin and growth of COCU, see P. Crow, "The Church—A New Beginning," *Church Union at Midpoint*, ed. P. Crow and W. Boney (New York, 1972), pp. 20–37.
16. This is expressed by several of the contributors to *Church Union at Midpoint*.
17. Fear of such neglect was already voiced during the council by some of its participants; see, e.g., the remarks of Cardinal Meyer and Cardinal de Barros Camara, *Commentary on the Documents of Vatican II*, ed. H. Vorgrimler (New York, 1969), vol. 4, pp. 192–94.
18. *Lumen gentium (Constitution on the Church)*, 30–38 (*The Documents of Vatican II*, ed. W. Abbott [New York, 1966], pp. 56–65).
19. *Lumen gentium*, 34–36 (*Documents of Vatican II*, pp. 60–62).
20. This is but one expression of one of the underlying problems that influenced the entire proceedings of Vatican II, the question of the irreformability of previous dogmatic statements of the church, or, for that matter, of previous doctrinal statements of the papacy.
21. See C. Moeller, *Vatican II: An Interfaith Appraisal* (Notre Dame, 1966), pp. 143–46.
22. See K. Rahner, *Commentary on the Documents of Vatican II*, vol. 1 (1967), pp. 186–218, for a commentary on chap. 3 of *Lumen gentium*.
23. Historically, the bulk of discussion about the official ministry of the church has involved debate about the nature and necessity of episcopacy. This continues to be the case in today's reflection on Christian priesthood and ministry; the COCU discussions are a case in point.
24. See *Documents of Vatican II* (Abbott ed.), pp. 199–316; and *Vatican II: An Interfaith Appraisal*, pp. 397–517.
25. See *Documents of Vatican II* (Abbott ed.), pp. 532–79. See also J. Lecuyer's commentary on the decree in *Commentary on the Documents of Vatican II*, vol. 5, pp. 183–297.
26. See M. Marty, "The New Generation and COCU," *Church Union at Midpoint*, pp. 178–89.

27. See the essays by J. Ford (pp. 99–112) and J. Hotchkin (pp. 215–21) in *Church Union at Midpoint*; both these Roman Catholic theologians manifest the positive resonance with COCU that is possible for theologians in that church. However, the deepest analysis of COCU's openness to the Catholic tradition is given by the Episcopalian scholar W. Wolf on pp. 80–98 of the same volume. For related developments in the U.S. and Europe, see A. Dulles, "Ministry and Intercommunion," *Theological Studies* 34 (1973), pp. 643–78.

28. See, e.g., R. Mols, "Le problème sacerdotale en Europe," *Nouvelle revue théologique* 82 (1960), pp. 513–16.

29. During the two decades after World War II, France and the Low Countries were almost alone in serious application of sociological methods to the study of Christian practice. More recently, there has been important growth of religious sociology in both South and North America—the latter reflected in the publications of the Society for the Scientific Study of Religion.

30. See F. Houtart, "Faut-il abandonner la paroisse dans la ville moderne?" *Nouvelle revue théologique* 77 (1955), pp. 602–13.

31. A short review of some of the many Roman Catholic meetings and books devoted to revision of seminary training is given by J. Walsh in *Theological Studies* 26 (1965), pp. 482–90. For the parallel discussion in Protestant circles, see *Theological Education*, the publication of the American Association of Theological Schools. Begun in 1964, the periodical is a rich mine of current American views on the nature and purpose and prospects of Christian ministry.

32. A flood of writing—some of it critical of existent practice, some of it studying the principles that should govern appropriate religious education, some of it a creative attempt to provide instruments for better teaching—accompanied this movement. By following two journals, *Religious Education* (published in New York by the Religious Education Association) and *Lumen vitae* (published in Brussels by the religious education center of the same name), one can obtain a complete overview of the developments during the past quarter century.

33. Y. Congar, *Jalons pour une théologie du laïcat* (Paris, 1953), perhaps the most influential book in shaping Catholic thought about the laity in the 1950s; G. Philips, *Le rôle du laïcat dans l'Eglise* (Paris, 1954); K. Rahner, "Ueber das Laienapostolat," *Schriften*, vol. 2 (1955), pp. 339–73. This had appeared the previous year as three articles in *Der grosse Entschluss*.

34. A catalyst in Catholic discussion was provided by Pius XII's two encyclicals "*Mystici corporis*" (1943) and "*Mediator Dei*" (1947), which unavoidably but not too clearly dealt with the relation between the priesthood of the ordained and the priesthood of the laity. See P. Palmer, "Lay Priesthood: Towards a Terminology," *Theological Studies* 10 (1949), pp. 235–50.

35. Though this scholarship concentrated on the Eucharistic liturgy and comparatively little attention was devoted to the ordinational liturgy (apart from a flurry of writing that accompanied Pius XII's constitution on the form of presbyteral ordination, "*Sacramentum ordinis*," in 1947), all study of the sacramental liturgies ultimately helps clarify the church's ordained ministry of sacrament.

36. O. Nussbaum, *Kloster, Priestermonch, und Privatmesse* (Bonn, 1961).

37. See U. Holmes, *The Future Shape of Ministry* (New York, 1971), pp. 114–200; his description of the shift in ministerial activity is concerned primarily wth the Episcopalian community in the United States, but indicates the more general developments.

38. The 1959 centennial of the death of the Curé d'Ars occasioned a rash of writing about the pastoral function, including Pope John's "*Sacerdotii nostri*"; but very little of it was theological in nature. For a summary of papal teaching on the topic from Pius X to Pius XII, see *Notre sacerdoce*, ed. Msgr. Veuillot (Paris, 1954). In the light of later developments it is interesting to read the two short but excellent introductions to this collection: the one by Veuillot, who later became cardinal archbishop of Paris, and the other by Msgr. Montini, the future Paul VI.

39. See, e.g., E. Bergh, "La formation sacerdotale dans les états de perfection," *Nouvelle revue théologique* 79 (1957), pp. 941–56. This article reflects also the continuing de-

bate about the "spiritualities" proper to clerical religious and to diocesan clergy: see also R. Carpentier, "Vocation sacerdotale, vocation religieuse," *ibid.*, 84 (1962), pp. 142–63.

40. One of the more detailed studies was that of H. Doms, *Vom Sinn des Zölibats* (Regensberg, 1954); he tries to ground clerical celibacy in the sacramentalism of Christ as mediator and to apply the universalism, etc., of Christ's mediation to the ordained clergy. For a balanced criticism of Dom's views, see R. Carpentier's review in *Nouvelle revue théologique* 78 (1956), p. 538.

41. E.g., G. Bertrams, *Le célibat du prêtre* (Paris, 1961).

42. See the references to the literature of this post–World War II period contained in R. Bunnik, "The Question of Married Priests," *Cross Currents* 15 (1965), pp. 407–31; and *ibid.*, 16 (1966), pp. 81–112.

43. In general, the scriptural study was much more complete, with such careful studies as E. Schweizer's *Gemeinde und Gemeindeordnung* (1959); H. von Campenhausen's *Kirchliches Amt und geistliche Vollmacht* (1953), whose treatment extends up to the end of the third century; K. Schelkle's *Jüngerschaft und Apostelamt* (1961); or J. Colson's *L'évêque dans les communautés primitives* (1951). Two extensive bibliographies provided by A. Lemaire cover quite thoroughly and analytically the biblical studies on ministry: pp. 219–35 in his *Les ministères aux origines de l'Eglise* (Paris, 1971) give extensive reference to works published up to that point; and his excellent review article in *Biblical Theology Bulletin* 3 (1973), pp. 133–66, deals with the most recent publication in the biblical field. Historical study was much more uneven, with only the first few Christian centuries receiving much attention. Research into confessional literature, though usually of much higher quality than earlier post-Reformation polemic, was very limited. One can point to only a few works like H. Lieberg's *Amt und Ordination bei Luther und Melanchthon* (Göttingen, 1962), or L. Schummer's *Le ministère pastoral dans l' "Institution Chrétienne" de Calvin* (Wiesbaden, 1965), or the study of Trent and its background by Jedin and Lortz.

44. F. Durrwell, *La resurrection du Christ* (Paris, 1950); E. Schillebeeckx, *De Christusontmoeting als sacrament* (Antwerp, 1957); K. Rahner, *Die Kirche und Sakramente* (Freiburg, 1960). In many ways, Durrwell's study was anticipated by the valuable work of W. Kunneth whose *Theologie der Auferstehung* (1st ed., 1933) was influential in Protestant circles but little known by Catholic scholars until quite recently.

45. See G. Dejaifve, "Episcopat et collège apostolique," *Nouvelle revue théologique* 85 (1963), pp. 805–18; D. Stanley, "The New Testament Basis for the Concept of Collegiality," *Theological Studies* 25 (1964), pp. 197–216.

46. This article appeared in *Nouvelle revue théologique* 85 (1963), pp. 139–359.

47. In Protestant circles, especially in Great Britain (because of the interest of some in finding a basis for better understanding between the Presbyterian and Anglican communions), there were parallel studies into episcopacy and presbyterate: the studies of two Scottish theologians published in 1955, J. Reid, *The Biblical Doctrine of the Ministry* (Edinburgh, 1955), and T. Torrance, *Royal Priesthood* (London, 1955), provide an interesting difference in tone and purpose.

48. Published at Le Puy in 1959, this volume contains a good selective bibliography of works on priesthood and ministry up to 1958.

49. One of the finest of these theological approaches to the pastorate was J.-J. von Allmen's *La vie pastorale* (Neuchâtel, 1968).

50. E.g., F. Norris's commentary in the Paulist Press edition of the two documents on the priesthood (New York, 1966).

51. Probably the most detailed and reflective commentary was that contained in pt. 3, pp. 9–239, of the German commentary edited by H. Vorgrimler and published by Herder (Freiburg) from 1966–68.

52. E.g., S. Ryan's article, "The Hierarchical Structure of the Church," *Vatican II: The Constitution on the Church*, ed. K. McNamara (London, 1968), pp. 163–234.

53. *Nouvelle revue théologique* 88 (1966), pp. 1044–61.

54. E. Fairweather, "Renewal of the Episcopate: An Anglican Evaluation," *Ecumenist* 4 (1965–66), pp. 1–4; and G. Baum, "The Ministerial Priesthood," *ibid.*, pp. 4–7.

55. A. de Bovis, "Le presbyterat selon Vatican II," *Nouvelle revue théologique* 89 (1967), pp. 1009–42.

56. For a rather complete bibliography of work during these years, see *Ephemerides theologicae lovanienses* 43 (1967), pp. 205–7; 44 (1968), pp. 212–15, 487–91; 45 (1969), pp. 215–20, 429–33; 46 (1970), pp. 217–20; 47 (1971), pp. 230–35.

57. In scholarly circles the reaction to Küng's book was quite mixed; for one of the more critical reviews (and one that gives reference to other judgments on the book), see J. Coppens, *ibid.*, 46 (1970), pp. 121–30, and 47 (1971), pp. 484–88.

58. W. Dodd, "Toward a Theology of Priesthood," *Theological Studies* 28 (1967), pp. 683–705.

59. *Journal of Ecumenical Studies* 4 (1967), pp. 629–49.

60. For a select bibliography of writings on celibacy between 1963 and 1967, see *Concilium*, vol. 43, pp. 172–74.

61. J.-P. Audet, *Mariage et célibat dans le service pastoral de l'Eglise* (Paris, 1967).

62. R. Bunnik, "The Question of Married Priests," *Cross Currents* 15 (1965), pp. 407–31; 16 (1966), pp. 81–112.

63. See esp. K. Rahner's "Wort und Eucharistie," *Schriften*, vol. 4 (1967), pp. 313–35; and T. Stanks, "The Eucharist: Christ's Self-communication in a Revelatory Event," *Theological Studies* 28 (1967), pp. 27–50.

64. *Journal of Ecumenical Studies* 3 (1966), pp. 57–112.

65. For two frank and urgent presentations of this problem, see M. Bellet, *Ceux qui perdent la foi* (Paris, 1965); and M. Thurian, *La foi en crise* (Taizé, 1968).

66. Some mention, however, should be made of B. Dupuy's "Is There a Dogmatic Distinction Between the Function of Priests and the Function of Bishops?" *Apostolic Succession*, vol. 34 of *Concilium* (New York, 1968), pp. 74–86. Dupuy comes up with this important conclusion: ". . . It seems impossible to establish theologically a radical difference between the functions of the bishop and those of the priest" (p. 85).

67. See *Catholic Theological Society of America Proceedings* 24 (1969). Dillon's article is on pp. 10–62, Powers' on pp. 109–20, Cunningham's on pp. 124–41, and O'Brien's on pp. 151–60. An article that can be profitably read in conjunction with O'Brien's is that of T. O'Meara, "Toward a Roman Catholic Theology of the Presbytery," *Heythrop Journal* 10 (1969), pp. 390–404.

68. *Recherches de science religieuse* 56 (1968), pp. 563–89.

69. For a description of the celibacy controversy in Europe, see *Herder Correspondence* 6 (1969), pp. 270–84; a reflection of North American discussion on the topic is contained in *Celibacy: The Necessary Option*, ed. G. Frein (New York, 1968). See also the report contained in the latter portion of *The Identity of the Priest*, vol. 43 of *Concilium*.

70. In the April 1968 issue, pp. 96–99.

71. *Theological Studies* 30 (1969), pp. 635–68; also his remarks on "The Magisterium and Theology" in *Catholic Theological Society of America Proceedings* 24 (1969), pp. 239–54.

72. See, e.g., the clear (and standard) presentation of G. Thils, *L'infaillibilité pontificale* (Gembloux, 1969); or *L'infaillibilité*, ed. E. Castelli (Paris, 1970), the essays presented at the meeting in Rome at the Centre international des études humanistes.

73. H. Urs von Balthasar, *Church and World* (New York, 1967), pp. 44–111; A. Hayen, *L'obéissance dans l'Eglise* (Brussels, 1969). Though its approach is sociological and juridical rather than theological, mention should be made of J. Dauvillier's lengthy study of primitive church structures, *Les temps apostoliques: 1er siècle* (Paris, 1970); its value is diminished by its neglect of contemporary New Testament exegesis.

74. *Theological Studies* 30 (1969), pp. 567–87.

75. *Ibid.*, pp. 589–612.

76. In the conclusion to his article Lindbeck poses two questions to Roman Catholic theologians. In the first question he adverts to some of the discussion now going on in Catholic circles about "validity," the importance of the local community, reevaluat-

ing episcopal office in terms of "service," etc., and he asks, "How seriously can these theological speculations be taken? Can they be successfully harmonized with the description of the hierarchical office in, e.g., chapter 3 of *Lumen gentium*?" Anticipating the conclusions of our own historical study, which will consider such basic issues, we can say that present Catholic theological speculation should be taken quite seriously. It seems that one can find a concurrence of such responsible speculation with one facet of *Lumen gentium*'s description of the episcopal office, for (as we indicate elsewhere) that description is itself somewhat ambiguous and not totally consistent with principles enunciated in other conciliar (i.e., Vatican II) statements. In his second question Lindbeck asks whether Roman Catholics are "irrevocably committed to the view that the legitimacy of the office ultimately guarantees the authenticity of proclamation, while the sons of the Reformation are equally committed to the converse, that the authenticity of proclamation is the only guarantee for the legitimacy of the office." This present study will grapple with this question, particularly in treating the question of authoritative teaching; but it does seem that if Catholic scholars must regain an insight into the fact that any ecclesial proclamation of the gospel finds its validation in the truth of the gospel itself and in the presence of the Spirit of truth (the Spirit of prophecy) in the act of proclamation, the sons of the Reformation must help us ascertain the means of determining the authentic normative word of God and the means of discerning the presence or absence of Christ's Spirit in any situation of proclamation. The issue is unquestionably fundamental, but it seems that one is faced not with an insurmountable opposition but with a dialectic that is intrinsic to Christianity because it is grounded in the Incarnation of God's own Word.

77. They were circulated privately in 1968, and then published the following year. For a broader view of developments in Anglican circles, see Holmes, *Future Shape of Ministry*.

78. The most complete bibliography (going back to 1966) is that being published by the Office National du Clergé in Montreal. In *Theological Studies* 32 (1971), pp. 489–99, J. Crehan has a review of work done since Vatican II, but it is quite selective and omits much of basic importance. Limited to publication in the biblical field, but providing a most helpful review of work by New Testament scholars, is A. Lemaire's article (see n. 43 above) in *Biblical Theology Bulletin* 3 (1973), pp. 133–66.

79. *The Christian Priesthood*, ed. N. Lash and J. Rhymer (London, 1970).

80. *Le ministère sacerdotal: Rapport de la Commission international de théologie* (Paris, 1971).

81. *Der priestliche Dienst* (Freiburg, 1970).

82. Published Gembloux/Louvain, 1971. It is interesting and instructive to compare the positions espoused in this volume, positions grounded in the document produced by the German hierarchy, with the conclusions of the Dutch Pastoral Council in 1970; for an analytic report on this latter, see R. Rousseau, "A New Kind of Priesthood? Some Reflections on the Dutch Pastoral Council," *American Ecclesiastical Review* 164 (1971), pp. 232–41.

83. See J. Ellis, ed., *The Catholic Priest in the United States: Historical Investigations* (Collegeville, Minn., 1971); E. Kennedy and V. Heckler, *The Catholic Priest in the United States: Psychological Investigations* (Washington, D.C., 1972); A. Greeley, *The Catholic Priest in the United States: Sociological Investigations* (Washington, D.C., 1972). In conjunction with the last of these, see A. Greeley, *Priests in the United States: Reflections on a Survey* (Garden City, N.Y., 1972).

84. For an account of the difficulties encountered by the report of the theological subcommittee (and an account of the bishops' reception of the rest of the reports), see the articles (*passim*) during 1971 in the *National Catholic Reporter*.

85. *Recherches de science religieuse* 58 (1970), pp. 237–72.

86. H. Holstein's *Hiérarchie et peuple de Dieu* (Paris, 1970) is an interesting and theologically solid reflection on Vatican II's *Lumen gentium*, and though open in spirit to newer developments in the church, it does not move progressively into post–Vatican II theology. Y. Congar's *Ministères et communion écclésiale* (Paris, 1971) comes much nearer to what is needed; for one thing it is illuminating to have Congar trace the

evolution of his own views since the writing of *Jalons pour une théologie du laïcat.* However, the book is a collection of articles Congar has written on different occasions, and though it reflects the coherence of his own personal thought, it is not an attempt to give a synthetic view of Christian ministry. One of the more intriguing studies was A. Feuillet's *Le sacerdoce du Christ et de ses ministres* (Paris, 1972), a biblico-theological study of John 17. It opens up a number of interesting views (such as the relation between John and Hebrews on the matter of Christian priesthood), but the discussion seems controlled throughout by the presupposition that ministerial priesthood is seen as somehow basic to Christianity from the time of the New Testament.

87. Published in 1970, it was translated into English the following year: *Infallible? An Inquiry* (Garden City, N.Y., 1971).

88. K. Rahner, "Kritik an Hans Küng," *Stimmen der Zeit* 186 (1970), pp. 361–77; H. Küng, "Im Interesse der Sache: Antwort an Karl Rahner," *ibid.*, 187 (1971), pp. 43–64, 105–22; K. Rahner, "Replik, Bemerkungen zu: Hans Küng, Im Interesse der Sache," *ibid.*, pp. 145–60. As an example of American response, see the symposium in the April 24, 1971, issue of *America.*

89. See *Journal of Ecumenical Studies* 8 (1971), pp. 841–64; *Origins of Papal Infallibility, 1150–1350* (Leiden, 1973).

90. See *Peter in the New Testament*, ed. R. Brown, K. Donfried, J. Reumann (Minneapolis, 1973).

91. For reviews of the considerable literature on the topic, see J. Brothers, "Women in Ecclesial Office," vol. 80 of *Concilium* (1973), pp. 109–22; M. Rowe, "Women in the Church," *Herder Correspondence* 6 (1969), pp. 291–98. See also the two survey articles in the December 1975 issue of *Theological Studies* by M. O'Neill ("Toward a Renewed Anthropology," pp. 725–36) and A. Patrick ("Women and Religion," pp. 737–65). This issue of *Theological Studies*, devoted entirely to the question of women's role in the church, contains several worthwhile articles which reflect key aspects of present discussion.

92. See R. van Eyden, "The Place of Women in Liturgical Functions," vol. 72 of *Concilium* (1972), p. 78. Thus, the question as to *whether* women should be ordained to the ministry of liturgical celebration ("priestly ordination") would seem to be a theological nonquestion, i.e., a matter of removing supposed theological arguments against such ordination. This is not to say that the *nature* of such ministerial functioning by women is not a relevant and important theological issue, e.g., the effect such a development would have on the symbolisms attached to the church, liturgical actions, etc. Exercise of full ministerial function by women (and also by married couples as such) would apparently lead to some intriguing and basic theological reflection. For brief suggestions as to lines such reflection on women's ministerial role might take, see A. Cunningham, "The Ministry of Women in the Church," *Catholic Theological Society of America Proceedings* 24 (1969), pp. 124–41.

93. For the relation of the ordination question to the broader problem of sexual discrimination within the church, see M. Daly, *The Church and the Second Sex* (New York, 1968); on the background of such devaluation of women's role, see R. Reuther, ed., *Images of Women in the Judaeo-Christian Tradition* (New York, 1973).

94. Granted that it was a somewhat isolated voice, the intervention of Cardinal G. Flahiff in the 1971 synod of bishops, insisting that traditional views about women's role in the church's ministry must be seriously challenged, is an indication that the theological discussion has begun to affect even the official attitudes towards the ministry of women. See *International Documentation on the Contemporary Church* (*IODC*) 38 (1971), pp. 52–55.

95. It is significant that leading proponents of ordaining women to full ministerial function do not advocate admitting women to clerical circles, i.e., they do not favor retaining clerical division from the remainder of the Christian community. See Brothers, pp. 116–17. This is the position taken by H. van der Meer in his *Women Priests in the Catholic Church* (Philadelphia, 1973) and by the translators of the volume, Arlene and Leonard Swidler, in their "Afterword" to the book. Van der Meer's volume is, incidentally, the most thorough study of the topic that has appeared to date.

PART ONE

Ministry as Formation
of Community

The New Testament Evidence

Methodological Presuppositions

When one attempts to study the phenomenon of a religious community, or of any particular aspect of its structure and activity, he must apply ordinary epistemological principles in a unique way.[1] The reason is quite apparent: he is dealing with faith in the transcendent, and no ordinary tools of human discovery and appraisal can determine whether this faith is unfounded opinion or whether it actually reflects the real state of affairs. So it must be with our study of the phenomenon of Christian ministry and/or priesthood. Only partially can one follow the normal paths of investigation in which one depends on the fact that the nature of a given reality is reflected in its activity, and that it can be known therefore in terms of that activity. The problem is that the activity itself can only be known in terms of that goal to which the activity is directed and which it achieves; but in the case of Christian ministry and priesthood the goal (according to explicit traditional teaching) lies beyond human comprehension, beyond adequate description, beyond immediate perception. Quite simply, the goal's very existence is a matter of faith.

Despite this built-in limitation, our study will attempt, in the light of available evidence, to look at the historical reality of Christian ministry in action.[2] What have those designated as "official ministers" actually done in different historical and geographical situations, and what has the Christian community as a whole done in those aspects of the church's life that more directly touch on

ministry and priesthood? Moreover, in this activity what goal has been achieved, or at least intended?

As the theologian undertakes such a discovery and analysis of historical data (and then later proceeds to reflect on its meaning) his task is complicated because he must take seriously the two levels of reality in Christianity.[3] There is the observable element in the life of the Christian community: its structure and overt activity, its size and influence, its formulated doctrine and liturgical practice, its interaction with other historical forces such as civil governments or cultural movements. All this the theologian must investigate as carefully as he can; at this level he shares his task with the historian,[4] the social scientist, the literary critic—i.e., with all the various disciplines that can look at the historical reality of Christianity as a purely human phenomenon that can be studied in the same manner as any other human institution.

There is also the mystery level of Christianity,[5] accepted as real by those who profess Christian faith but escaping the ambit of "secular" research. At this level the church is viewed as the historical externalizing (the Body) of the risen Christ as he continues his redemptive function among men,[6] and viewed as the expression of the power of Christ's Spirit working to transform human life by the love of God.[7] In this perspective the external elements of the church's existence —its organizational structures, its formulation of liturgy and doctrine, its involvement in the social life of mankind—are seen as the result of the divine activity that finds an outlet through the being and action of the Christian community.[8] The history of the church then appears as the organic evolution of that divine-human community which grows out of the resurrection of Christ.[9]

What complicates the theologian's task still further is the fact that it does not suffice to study both the levels we have just described; for theology itself indicates that it is inaccurate to speak of these as "two levels." Rather, it is precisely *in* the phenomenal aspects of Christian life, social and individual, that the divine action is occurring; the very history of the church's thought and institutions *is* the history of the Spirit's redeeming action; it is *in* the life of mankind, and more particularly in the life of the Christian community, that the believer is meant to discover the God who reveals himself through his saving action.[10] For this reason, the theologian's involvement in and dependence upon those "secular" studies that clarify the observable reality of Christian history are absolutely essential; but, without prejudicing the accuracy of his historical research, he must *as a theologian* take account of the "mystery depth" which Christian faith sees as present in the historical data.

From this latter point of view, the dynamism governing the activity and development of Christianity is seen to be eschatological, i.e., the finality of the church's being and life is directed to a fulfillment that transcends history, the power working within the church is the "new life" of the Spirit which will culminate in man's full sharing in the human fulfillment of the risen Christ.[11] Exactly what this future realization of mankind's potential will be remains an object of hope rather than of clear knowledge ("Now I see, as in a mirror, darkly . . ."); but the death and resurrection of Jesus himself is meant to be a revelation of the essence of this *eschaton*.[12]

Whatever the exact nature of this final fulfillment, the Christian gospel proclaims that it will be a situation of true community, a community embracing all men who truly wish such personal sharing with one another and with God.[13] Christian faith (which the theologian attempts to probe and to clarify) holds that the achievement of this teleology is what should (and in some enigmatic fashion does) guide the historical evolution of the church and of the ministries within the church.

Because its existence is basically eschatological, because from one point of view "it is not of this world,"[14] because it quite obviously has not achieved the goal towards which the Spirit is moving it, it would seem that the church cannot be adequately known. This could imply that any understanding we have of Christianity is therefore partially erroneous. However, there are several saving features in the situation, at least, if one views the matter from the perspective of Christian faith.

First, the essential reality of the goal towards which the church is progressing is known, known through the revelation that comes with the death and resurrection of Jesus and that is preached as the gospel in every age of history. Second, in the view of Christian faith the *eschaton*, while obviously pertaining to the future, is not entirely non-existent in the present. The risen Christ, who is in himself the essential core of the eschatological fulfillment, is already in the context of "the next life"; moreover, with the power of his Spirit he is present and operative in the midst of the Christian community as he leads it to its goal. Third, if one views the church as a living reality, the Body of Christ animated by his Spirit, the final and fully mature state of its existence will be the outgrowth of its historically emerging life. The church is meant to become what it already is, only more so, which means that this life at any given moment in history points to the past out of which it grew and gives some (even though often indefinite) promise about the future.

It is precisely this pointing to the future that Christians try to assess at those critical spots in history when a basic reevaluation and possible realignment of the church's life is demanded, as it is today. If true prophets arise at such moments, blessed is that generation of Christians; for it is the prophet's function to provide guidance for this moment. But in the absence of the prophet, or as a helpful complement to him, the theologians of the church are meant to discover from the sources of Christian revelation some of those elements that are intrinsic to the church's nature and that can indicate the path the future must take in order to fulfill that nature.

This, then, is the manner in which theological study of Christian ministry and priesthood must read the historical evidences of the church's life. The observable realities of ministerial and priestly activity must be the prime source of theological analysis. Formulations of this activity (and of the functions it expresses), whether they be doctrinal or legal or institutional, must be scrutinized with care. Such formulations express the Christian community's understanding of its ministry and priesthood, and they also express the inner nature of the church as a ministering community. However, an integral theological analysis must push yet further: the external expressions of ministry and priesthood must be studied as the embodiment of the community's faith and (still more profoundly) as the "incarnation" of the Spirit's activity.

What emerges, then, methodologically is a three-faceted object for our study: (1) the external institutions of ministry/priesthood, which can be studied quite competently by "secular" scholarship; (2) the Christian faith and understanding that underlie these external institutions, faith and understanding that can be studied only partially by "secular" scholars, because true "inner" knowledge demands faith that can experientially identify with the Christian community's faith; and (3) the divine action that takes place in and through Christian ministry/priesthood, an action that can be known only in faith.

Community as Christianity's Goal

Because of its radical importance for the entire study of ministry and priesthood, the community dimension of Christianity can appropriately be given some special initial emphasis. It is unlikely that any careful stu-

dent of Christian tradition would contest the fact that the formation of community among men through their community with Christ is *a* goal of Christianity's existence and activity. Rather, it is a question of emphasis: does one see this as lying at the very heart of "salvation," of "worship," of "giving glory to God," of "forgiveness of sin"; or is the establishment of community viewed as a somewhat peripheral result of the cumulative salvation of individual humans? Clear insight into this seemingly esoteric distinction and into the position that one takes of the question is of considerable practical importance. We are just emerging from a period of religious history when the drawbacks of excessive individualism became painfully apparent. Yet, there is no need for us to swing to the opposite end of the pendulum, giving community a priority over the individual. We should be able to draw from contemporary studies in social sciences and psychology, as well as from history and Christian revelation, and realize that community and individual are inseparably interdependent; to stress either to the neglect of the other would be to dilute or misdirect our civic and social activity and our religious zeal.

When one turns to the biblical sources of theology, the emphasis on community is quite evident:[15] God's special revealing action begins with the formation of a people, Israel; and the historical evolution of that people under divine influence constitutes the very essence of what we call "Old Testament revelation."[16] Christianity itself starts as a community of believers, united by their faith in the resurrection of Christ and living in shared expectation of that eschatological fulfillment which is described as "the heavenly Jerusalem." It is not difficult to assemble New Testament texts that point to the fostering of Christian community as the goal towards which are directed the behavior of Christians, the efforts of the specialized ministry, and the redeeming action of Christ himself in his Spirit. Having done this (as we will have to do in the following pages) there still remains a basic question: what kind of community are we discussing? In terms of our larger objective, i.e., to discover the essential elements of Christian ministry and priesthood, this question is critical. Upon its answer depends our understanding of the ministry, for there seems to be little doubt but that the specialized ministry, if it has any special objective, is directed to nurturing the life and activity of the community as a whole. Hence, the question our study will have to address to the documents of Christian history, beginning with the New Testament, will not be "Is Christian ministry directed to formation of community?" but "To what kind of community is Christian ministry directed?"

Christ's Ministry

Though they may neglect it in the course of their practical Christian activity, all Christian churches in all periods of history admit in some form the principle that Christ alone is the ultimate possessor of priesthood and ministry and authority in the church.[17] This means that the understanding of Christ's own ministry is determinative of any insight into Christian ministry, whether it be the ministry of the community as a whole or that of the ordained minister. Actually, the basic question, "What did Christ do, and what, if anything, is he still doing?" is at the very heart of the view one takes of Christianity. Differences of position on this fundamental issue lie at the root of the credal and institutional oppositions of the various Christian churches. Neither theological honesty nor ecumenical effectiveness permits us today to avoid this issue, thorny though it be. Hence, it seems logical to begin our study of the New Testament texts by seeking in them some insight into primitive Christianity's faith about the risen Lord's activity in their midst.

Needless to say, we are here confronted with the entire matter of early Christian faith in the resurrection of Jesus and with the extremely divergent interpretations of that faith that are given by present-day scholars.[18] Since the whole of soteriology is involved in this issue (and it is not our purpose to treat more than the role of ministry in salvation),

we will not enter into the complications of the question regarding the continuity between the historical Jesus and the risen one whom the Christians acclaimed as Messiah and Lord. For our purposes it will suffice to note that the Christians who produced the New Testament writings believed in some such continuity, and they believed also in some continuing influence of the Risen One in their lives and destiny.[19] At the very least, the meaning of his death and subsequent glorification transformed the meaning and purpose of their own existence.[20] More than that, his own Spirit moved in their midst to animate and direct their communal and individual life, transforming them into sons of God.[21]

The precise question is whether the risen Christ is seen only as an object of faith commitment, by whose teachings and example Christians are constantly transformed[22] and who thereby find historical fulfillment in such continuing "imitation"; or whether he is seen also as an ever present and governing agent in the life of the Christian community, not an idea or an ideal but a living person.[23] In the second of these perspectives he continues to witness to his Father's saving love, he continues to offer sacrifice for the remission of sin, he continues to give himself in love to men who accept him in faith. If one can take Paul's writings as an indication of early Christian faith, it would seem that there is much to indicate that the primitive church thought of its risen Lord as thus dynamically and personally present in its midst.[24] Paul's own initial experience of the Risen One, so paradigmatic for all his future experience and understanding, seems unmistakable: the Christ of the Pauline "vision" was a conscious person present in familiar dialogue with Saul. He was neither a voice from the past, nor the personification of an ethical ideal, nor the projection of Saul's own frustrated religious expectations.

It is true, of course, that Paul's teaching about the salvific effect of Jesus' death is expressed in the past tense, in terms of what Jesus *did*; it could not be otherwise about the historical fact of Jesus' dying. However, in the saving mystery Jesus' death and resurrection are inseparable: without the second the first is meaningless. Begun in the past, a past to which Paul himself is not direct witness, the redeeming act of Christ continues into the present and future. Of this, Paul claims to be the witness. Paul sees his own role as co-worker with and ambassador of Christ (1 Cor. 4:1; 2 Cor. 5:20); he speaks of himself as introducing others into the life of Christ (1 Cor. 4:16), and as exercising the authority of Christ himself (1 Thess. 4:2). This would be strange language if Paul did not see the risen Christ as a contemporary reality with which he was in contact.

This Pauline perspective is not singular in the New Testament writings. The tenth chapter of Matthew reflects the manner in which Christian evangelization was looked upon as being sent by Christ himself;[25] the Lucan viewpoint is dominated by the risen Lord whose presence to the Christian people is the replacement of the *kebod* attached to the Jerusalem Temple;[26] and the Johannine literature is unintelligible apart from the living Lord who imparts eternal life to those who accept him in faith (John 6), the Lord who invites his disciples to abide in him as he abides in them (John 15).

But if the risen Christ is alive and active in his church, what is the nature of the "ministry" that he continues to carry on among his brethren? There are many ways in which one can view this activity of the risen Christ; it is a role of witness (Rev. 1:5), of reconciliation (Col. 1:22), of granting the Spirit of sonship (Gal. 4:4), of giving life (John 6), of redemption from wickedness (Gal. 1:4). But basic to all these categories is the notion of formation of community: the risen Christ has unified men to himself in his death and resurrection; but it is this death and resurrection that also reunited men to God (2 Cor. 5:19; Gal. 4:4), reconciling men who had alienated themselves from the divine (Col. 1:22). The reconciliation has also a horizontal dimension: through his death and resurrection Christ has broken down the walls of division that had separated men from one another

(Eph. 2:11–16). Sin which consists so basically in alienation,[27] man from God, men from one another, man from his very self, has been overcome through the love of Christ expressed in his supreme act of self-giving. Thus his self-gift in death and resurrection links him to his disciples as a bridegroom to his bride (Eph. 5). With his full power and authority as risen Lord, Christ sends his own Spirit of love as the ultimate unifying principle of mankind and principally of the community of believers.

Probably no place does the community-forming function of the risen Christ find more profound expression in the New Testament literature than in the Pauline usage of the notion of "body" (1 Cor. 12:12–27; Eph. 4:4–16) and the corresponding Johannine figure of the vine (John 15). The risen Christ acts as the source of life and unity; while he is distinct from his disciples, he forms with them a vital unity which is the very link that binds them to one another in an unparalleled instance of human community. True, it is a community of believers, but the faith that links them is not that of a shared assent to some religious truth, but rather the common bond with the person of the risen Lord who abides with them and gives them his very Spirit.

Later we will have occasion to probe more deeply into the fact that the risen Christ gives of himself in vivifying fashion precisely as the Word; but for the moment it is important to point out the social teleology of his action in the church. It is not just that his activity has to it a social aspect; the very heart of the action is one of establishing community. While Christ gives himself in profound intimacy to each believer, he does so in order to bring that believer into deep communion with the heavenly Father and with all others who acknowledge Christ and the Father in faith.

Aware of the absolutely unique character of "community" as it is verified in the social unity achieved by the risen Christ among his disciples, we can then look at another key biblical category of thought without danger of reading it legalistically. That is the notion of "covenant." It is hard to find a manner of thinking that is more pervasive in Old Testament writing as a description of Israel's relation to God.[28] And in the New Testament, the work of Christ is unquestionably seen as the establishment of the "new covenant"; more than that, in the mystery of his death and resurrection he is himself the very reality of that new covenant.[29] Once we reflect on the basic position of this manner of New Testament thinking about the function of the risen Christ, it becomes apparent how central in that function is the formation of the believing community—which is the very idea of covenant.[30]

However, if the New Testament writers (and the primitive church whose faith they reflect) looked on the death and resurrection of Jesus as the establishment of the new covenant, they viewed the public ministry as the preparation for that action. Jesus' preaching and deeds of compassionate healing not only announce but even make present in inchoative fashion that definitive step in the establishment of God's kingdom in a new covenant which comes with Jesus' death and resurrection.[31] In the outlook of early Christianity the entire public ministry of Jesus was within the context of forming a new "covenant people," and it was governed by that goal. Without having to probe into the ticklish but important question of Jesus' own consciousness of the exact purpose of his ministry,[32] one can draw from the evidence of New Testament texts a strong argument for the fact that early Christianity, in all the various traditions represented in the New Testament, saw the activity of the risen Christ as fulfilling and standing in continuity with what Jesus had done historically.[33] For this reason scenes such as that related in Matthew 10 could provide catechetical guidance for the church's cooperation with the risen Lord.[34]

Everything, then, in Jesus' earthly activity was meant to lead to that community of faith that actually emerged as early Christianity. The ministry that Jesus exercised finds its full and triumphant expression only with his death and resurrection. It is then that he be-

comes fully the Christ, gives the supreme prophetic witness, is enabled as Servant-Lord to give himself fully in love for the forgiveness of sin, functions as head of the community which is his body.[35] And it is then that the true meaning and value of his earthly life and ministry can be seen. As a matter of fact, it cannot be seen fully even then; the community that emerges is itself an incomplete and eschatological reality, it is a goal only partially achieved, and the full scope of Jesus' earthly and risen ministry will be understood with the final achievement of human history when the bride, freed from all wrinkles and blemishes, will finally be ready for the bridegroom to present to his Father (Eph. 5:27).

In the midst of the widespread diversity of opinion as to how the New Testament texts are to be interpreted, and the extent to which they really reflect the activity and mentality of Jesus, it does seem that we can find two areas of general agreement which are particularly important for our study: (1) The presentation of Jesus' work, in both its earthly and "heavenly" stages, is provided as guidance for the early Christians in their own living and action. (2) The "work" of Christ, accomplished essentially in death and resurrection, is somehow carried on in the church through the power of the Spirit. Though our study will eventually have to take account of the full gamut of discussion regarding the meaning of Christ's resurrection and its implications for the understanding of Christian ministry, suffice it for now to establish the fact that the early Christians saw themselves as charged with the task of building up the community that Jesus had initiated.

That the early Christians saw themselves entrusted with some "God-given" role is part and parcel of their understanding of themselves as an eschatological reality, as a pilgrim community. Without dramatizing the "deception" of early Christianity with regard to the early advent of the Parousia, it does seem that the first generation of Christians only gradually realized the fact that they themselves were to be part of the ongoing mystery of salvation and not only the heralds of its final achievement in the resurrection of Christ.[36] Paradoxically, the death and resurrection of Jesus was without question the culmination of the *magnalia Dei*; it was the action of salvation, the "day of the Lord," the "last days"; yet, there remained for Christians to "fill up what was lacking in the sufferings of Christ." The paradox becomes acceptable only in the situation where the very ministry of the Christian people is the continuing ministry of the risen Lord himself, the externalization of the saving Spirit he has sent upon his disciples.

At first sight, the texts of the New Testament seem to indicate that the ministry of the Christian community as a whole is for the most part "inward-directed" to the building up of the *ekklesia* itself. Not that this is to be understood in a pejorative sense, for we will see shortly that this does involve a resultant movement *ad extra*; but we may be faced with the conclusion that the early decades of Christianity had not yet refined an understanding of the church's role in the world.[37] Certainly, most of the ministrations to which Christians are urged in the writings of the New Testament have to do with building up the life of the community itself. Christians are to do good to all men in love, "but especially to fellow believers" (Gal. 6:10). The Johannine insistence on mutual love as "the great commandment," while not confined to the relation among Christians, seems quite clearly to find its primary expression in that context: "By this shall all men know that you are my disciples, that you have love for one another" (John 13:35). The objective of praising God, which functions in Christ's own ministry, will be achieved through Christians' service to one another in the sharing of their goods. The priestly overtones of such ministry is quite interesting: the phrase used is *diakonia tes leitourgias tautes* (2 Cor. 9:12).

The whole church shares in the ministry of preaching the gospel, of witnessing to the death and resurrection of Christ (Phil. 1:7, 14). This seems to be accomplished in great part by the very intrinsic growth in loving community of the people themselves. Their daily life is their sacrifice (Rom. 12:1); they have their diverse functions (*diakoniai*), but these are for the sake of the whole body; they are all to teach and exhort, but to do this for one another (Col. 3:16). Living out its faith constitutes for the community its sacrifice, its offering (Phil. 2:17); and this seems quite clearly linked to Jesus' own servant ministry (which is described in the immediately preceding verses in Phil. 2). Again, it seems that Paul places considerable stress on the suffering of the early Christians—probably in the context of prophetic witness (Phil. 1:27–30).

Certainly, there is not a limitation of ministry to the needs of Christians alone; the parable of the Samaritan, the scene at Jacob's well, the cure of the daughter of the Syro-Phoenician woman, all state explicitly that no narrow chauvinism is to characterize Christian ministry. Such limitation to intramural interests would be a denial of the mission character that is essential to the Christian community.[38] Nor is evangelization of nonbelievers or service of non-Christians a ministry limited to designated individuals; definite tasks are on occasion assigned to individuals or groups, as to Paul or the Twelve; but the basic function of witnessing to the gospel in word and deed pertains to all in the community.[39] Yet, one cannot avoid the impression that the principal ministry of the community is exercised by *being*, precisely by being a community of faith and love, and as such bearing witness to the presence of God's saving action in Christ and the Spirit.[40]

Having seen that the nurture of community among themselves is basic to the ministry that is common to all Christians (it is also a fundamental objective of the specialized charismata given to individuals), can one on the basis of New Testament evidence conclude that this common ministry extends outward to the establishment of community among all men? It is tempting to so conclude, and there seems to be little difficulty (as we will see later) in proceeding theologically to draw such conclusions from principles contained in the New Testament literature. However, merely on the basis of explicit New Testament statements, the evidence is fragmentary at best that the Christians of the first decades looked upon themselves as commissioned to form mankind into unity.[41] Indeed, they are to be peacemakers (Matt. 5:9). Also, they realize that Christ destroyed the barriers that traditionally separated men (Eph. 2:11–22), but do they see such removal of barriers as happening outside the Christian community itself? More basic, does early Christianity envisage any providential unity into which the events of non-Christian living fit as a positive manifestation of the redeeming mystery of Christ? To some extent the language of Ephesians 3–5 when it talks about "the mystery" would seem to point in this direction. Yet the "theology of history" we find in Revelation seems to limit the realization of history to "the kingdom of the saints" and to those who have formally come into its compass through baptism in Christ.[42] The "other kingdoms" are apparently cast in the role of that which must be overcome and destroyed.[43] Throughout the Pauline corpus, the Synoptic traditions, and the Johannine writings, world history seems to be merely the given framework in the midst of which the destiny of the people of God is to be achieved. Little hint, if any, is given that the ministry of the gospel is to touch and transform that history.[44] Instead, the preaching of the gospel is meant to draw men from that world and to convert them to the kingdom of God.[45] What must give one pause, however, in forming too facile a conclusion in this regard is the cosmic vision of the captivity Epistles, where God is described as having reconciled all creation to himself in Christ, and where the church's role is one of working to achieve this end (Eph. 1:4–14; Col. 1:9–23).

Specialized Ministries Within the Community

When we turn to the New Testament treatment of the specialized ministries within the community, we are provided much fuller textual evidence. It is here, too, that we encounter all the semantic and historical problems (about the exact historical referent of terms such as *episkopos, presbyteros, apostolos, diakonos*) that have been discussed at length, to the point where one asks whether it is possible to gain further understanding by more study.[46] Probably we will have to settle for less than certainty about the exact historical situation of ministry in the first few decades of the church, but it may be that certain guidelines can be extracted from the evidence that is at our disposal.[47]

One of these principles deals directly with this present chapter's emphasis on community: whatever special charisms or functions do exist, they are meant to increase the vitality and unity of the Christian people. Paul's writings are perhaps most explicit in this matter. His own preaching of the gospel is aimed at bringing into existence a community of believers, and his continuing exhortation of his converts is directed to avoiding dissensions in their midst. He reminds the churches that whatever charisms are given, these are for the one body (1 Cor. 12:12). He sees prophecy as superior to tongues, precisely because prophecy is directly related to building up the community of faith (1 Cor. 14:22). Superior to all other gifts of the Spirit is charity which is itself the very bond of unity (1 Cor. 13). If Paul himself has authority (and this would seem to apply to others also), it is given to him from the Lord for the building up of the community (2 Cor. 10:8); he is the co-worker with God, but "the work" in question is the community itself (1 Cor. 3:9).

Ephesians reiterates the teaching of the early Pauline letters: the various gifts that come from the Spirit are all for the sake of the one body; they are diverse because the needs of the body are diverse; and no particular function can claim precedence over others (Eph. 4:7–13). While the Pastorals deal explicitly with the role of the *presbyteros/ episkopos*,[48] it is clear that this function and the suitability of a given individual to occupy this position are measured against the welfare of the community (1 Tim. 3:1–7; Tit. 1:5–9).

In the Gospels, the pastoral office, whether spoken of generally or applied to the Twelve or to Peter, is quite clearly one of fostering the communal life of the believing followers of Jesus.[49] Jesus' own work is described as one of molding his groups of followers into a unity. His exhortations to fraternal communion are perhaps more explicitly stated in the Johannine texts, but the Synoptics share with John the basically community-oriented view of Jesus' work as one of bringing into being the new people of God in the *koine diatheke*.[50] Those who are commissioned to special responsibility within the apostolic community are meant to carry on essentially the same task as Jesus: to shepherd the flock.[51] Acts presents basically the same evidence: the early Christians grouped together in closely knit communities, bound together by their faith and concern for one another, and expressing this deeper unity in their worship and, at least in some instances, by their sharing of earthly goods; and in their midst certain more prominent members were charged in differing fashion with preserving and developing this community of Christian life.[52]

In speaking as we have, however, about the orientation of ministry, whether that common to all the faithful or that possessed by certain designated individuals, we may well be accused of approaching the texts with a priori assumptions: is it legitimate to assume a common pattern of primitive Christian life, one that would justify use of the term "community" for the common objective of early Christianity? This very objection, which is unquestionably valid if one is thinking of "community" in institutional or structural terms, brings us face to face with a most important issue.[53] The community envisaged by the New Testament writers as a goal of Christian ministry (including the ministry of Christ himself) is not basically a matter of social arrangement. Rather, it is the deeper reality involved in people sharing a common insight into the meaning of life. In this case it is the insight of faith grounded in the death and resurrection of Christ, the reality of a mature and concerned love of people for one another, the reality of truly common objectives and hopes.[54] Such deeper unity may express itself in different patterns of community life, ac-

cording to the backgrounds or specific historical situation of people, as apparently it did to some extent in the early decades of Christianity. But beneath the diverse social patterns of the early *ekklesiai* lay the unifying reality of Christ to whom all the churches gave the tribute of their faith, the unifying influence of Christ's Spirit, the unifying influence of the common gospel they all accepted and to which they all witnessed.[55]

In facing our present-day question about the intrinsic nature of Christian ministry, it is critically important to keep in mind that it is this more profound level of Christian community which must be seen as a governing objective for ministry. This is not to accept the notion of an institutionless Christianity; later we will indicate that this is an impossible idea. Nor is it to assert that one must, through some form of historical archaism, return to the exact multiplicity of forms that marked the first emergence of church life. But it is to assert the primacy of the "spiritual" dimension of Christian community; it is to recognize that all external forms brought into being or sustained in being by the church are for the sake of this communion in faith and love and worship, and all questions about the retention or reshaping or evolution of these forms are to be answered in the light of this finality.[56]

So far, there is general agreement (at least theoretically) among the various Christian churches today. Controversy begins when one raises the question: Were not some external structures (e.g., the episcopacy) God-given to achieve the goal we have been describing; and are they not therefore indispensable to any genuine Christian community, and by their existence the cause and guarantee of the deeper level of community? In all probability this same question can be applied to Scripture, to sacraments, to ecclesiastical office, but our purpose is to examine only the question of ecclesiastical office. Even if one so limits the question to the institution of a specially designated ministry, it is highly doubtful whether the question can be settled on the basis of New Testament evidence. For one thing, the very differences of view about Christian life and activity for which the several churches find support as they read the New Testament texts are the differences that distinguish their opposing hermeneutical presuppositions.[57]

Relation to Jewish Ministry

Of the many influences that impinged upon Christianity as it came into existence, that of the religion of Old Testament Israel was certainly of unique importance. Not only were very many of the earliest Christians drawn from the Jewish community, but Jesus himself was Jewish and thoroughly steeped in the traditions of his people. The New Testament portrayal of Jesus depicts him as understanding his own identity and mission against the background of Israel's religious history; and while it is difficult to determine the exact extent to which the New Testament texts bring us into contact with the historical reality of Jesus of Nazareth, his "Jewishness" is probably one of the most trustworthy elements in the New Testament picture.

On the other hand, the New Testament communities very soon saw that there was also a radical distinctiveness of Christianity vis-à-vis Judaism.[58] Determining the nature and extent of this "newness" is critically important for our study, since there are some indications that later periods in the church's history involved a loss of insight about the uniqueness of Christianity and a tendency to revert to the thought and institutional patterns of the Old Testament.[59] If such historical regression did occur, Christians today are faced with the task of evaluating this fact critically against the faith of the infant church, and perhaps recovering some of the vision of the distinctiveness of Christ and of his redemptive work in the church. This is a many-faceted question, but the precise purposes of our study demand that we examine only two elements with care: the manner in which early Christianity's view of itself as a community with a priestly mission corresponded to Israel's notion of itself as a community, and the respective views of the two communities

regarding the role of ministerial groups in fostering the community's life.[60]

New Testament evidence, as far back as we can trace it, points to a tension in early Christianity's view of its relation to Judaism.[61] Increasingly, though not without decades of conflict within the church itself, the Christians broke with Judaism and emphasized the differences that separated them.[62] Yet, throughout, the fundamental thread of continuity joined them with the Old Testament traditions and with the evolution of Israel as a religious entity. The church was the "new Israel," the new people of God, which entered into the inheritance promised to Abraham.[63] Its community existence was grounded in the new covenant effected in Jesus' death and resurrection; but this new covenant stood as the fulfillment of the covenant dispensation that Old Testament thought traced back to Sinai.[64] Actually, the total event of Christianity was viewed as realization of the promises, explicit or implicit, contained in Old Testament revelation and history—"that the Scriptures might be fulfilled."[65] Christianity's emergence on the historical scene in the resurrection of Jesus and in the sending of the Spirit is that "day of the Lord" which polarized the eschatological view of Israel's great prophets.[66] The church is the awaited "kingdom of the saints," dedicated as was Old Testament Israel to the worship of God but seeing its worship as already perfected in the sacrifice of its high priest Jesus, who is both Son of man and Messiah.[67]

Yet, while a deep current of continuity bound together Judaism and early Christianity, it flowed at the level of faith in the God of revelation rather than at the surface level of religious institutions.[68] In contrast to Old Testament Israel, where religious life not only depended upon the external structures of social and political life but was practically indistinguishable from them, the early Christian communities were based almost exclusively on faith in Jesus as Lord and Messiah. It would be too much to say that no social, political, or cultural factors contributed to the unification of the men and women who formed the infant church.[69] Indeed, the patterns of Jewish life and worship made a significant contribution to the way of life that characterized the early Christian groups.[70] Yet, neither common culture, nor common social customs, nor common political affiliation formed the true unification in the early decades of Christianity. Jewish religious cult with its detailed observances, Jewish law, the authoritative guidance of the Jewish priesthood (which historically had absorbed a good deal of the governing role of the vanished kingship)[71]—with these Christianity broke after a short period of hesitation.[72]

Perhaps even more important, there seems to have been no particular inclination on the part of early Christians to substitute for these Jewish institutions a parallel structure of their own. The New Testament literature gives evidence, on the contrary, of an early insight into the universality of the gospel, which militated against its restriction to any limiting context of culture, law, or national identity.[73] Old Testament religion, certainly in the form it took in late Judaism, was marked by a high degree of institutionalization and by a somewhat narrow nationalism that stood in contrast to the broader viewpoint of some of the prophets.[74] Christianity accepted neither of these, in large part because of the strong stand taken by Paul in defense of his apostolate among the Gentiles.[75]

Of particular interest for us is the fact that apparently there was little felt need to provide for the early Christians any of the priestly mediation so insisted upon in Judaism.[76] This is the more striking if, as Acts seems to indicate, a fair number of Jewish priests were converted to the gospel of Christ.[77] Moreover, this stands in distinction to the situation of the Qumran community, where the official Jerusalem priesthood was rejected as illegitimate but where the assumption was that the continuity of true Israelitic priesthood belonged to the Qumran priests themselves, and that in the day of God's salvation this authentic priesthood would be restored as the privileged mediators of God's actions.[78] Of the three key "offices" of medi-

ation that emerged in Old Testament Israel—king, priest, and prophet—only that of prophet (significantly in its charismatic and noninstitutionalized form) is found operative in the early decades of Christianity.[79]

However, it might well be a mistake to confine our study of the ministries of early Christianity and their relationship to the ministerial office of Old Testament Israel to the classic categories of priest, prophet, and king. Two important functions of later Judaism seem to have had some influence on the emerging social structure of the infant Christian community, and therefore deserve some special attention: the role of the elders in Jewish communities, and the role of the teachers of Israel's traditions. While it would not be accurate to confine the role of the Jewish elders to the final centuries before Christ, for the influence of elders within the local community had been important long before that, it seems that this role acquired increased importance in the postexilic period, particularly in those communities which could not easily remain in close contact with Jerusalem.[80] Even in Jerusalem, the Sanhedrin, which functioned as a supreme tribunal, was an assembly of key elders of that community whose influence extended even to Jews in the Diaspora.[81] And though they did not admit the authority of the established high priesthood which functioned within the Jerusalem Sanhedrin, dissident sects such as that at Qumran still retained the pattern of a ruling group of elders for their own community.[82] All indications are that the early Christian communities that grew out of a basically Palestinian background found it natural to give a body of elders (presbyteroi) some power of guidance over local communities.[83]

What seems quite interesting, and in the last analysis may be of basic importance, is that one finds in neither Old Testament texts nor in the New Testament writings any claim that this "office" of elder was of special divine institution—in opposition to the claims made for kingship, priesthood, and even prophecy. Rather, the role of the elders in Old Testament Israel seems to have resulted quite naturally from the intrinsic needs of the group, to have been the outgrowth of family and clan authority structures, and to have been essentially judicial in nature.[84] In the early Christian churches neither the origin nor the exact function of the elders is clear, but the existence of such groups of guiding *presbyteroi* was apparently a common (if not universal) pattern. The presbyterate does not seem to have derived from the special corporate role of the Twelve at the beginnings of the church, nor from the kind of special charism given the prophet or apostle.[85] In Jerusalem it does seem that the presbyterate emerged only after the Twelve had gone on to other places; but even here there is no evidence that the *presbyteroi* were looked upon as successors of the Twelve in their pastoral role.

Instead, the quick emergence of established groups of presbyters seems to have resulted from the possession of natural leadership plus some form of community designation, though this latter did not have to take formal shape. In some cases the designation might have resulted from the actions of someone like Paul who as a "founding father" of a community would leave some members in charge.[86] In any event, it seems quite clear that the concrete needs of the Christian community dictated the existence of these Christian elders, and their precise function as contrasted with that of the Jewish elders of the time was specified by the nature of Christianity as a new people grounded in faith in the risen Christ and entrusted with the prophetic preaching of the gospel.[87]

Just as the role of the elders seems to have arisen from the practical needs of the community, so, too, did the role of the teacher. Later we will examine in depth the function of teaching within the ministry of the word of revelation; for now we only indicate that both in Judaism and in early Christianity there existed a group of recognized teachers distinct from either prophet or institutionalized priesthood, and that in both instances the activity of such teachers was directed to unifying the

people in faith.[88] One of the clearest indications of the social dimension of their activity is the fact that these teachers, even though their "appointment" was based on their own understanding and/or training rather than on any official designation, were clearly intended to teach within an established tradition of belief.[89] The understanding that they were privileged to possess was not for their own sake but was a heritage to be passed on for the sake of the people.

One of the interesting features of these two "nonoffice" roles of elder and teacher is that the continuity between Israel and Christianity is here much stronger than with the classic priest-prophet-king roles. This may well have strong implications for contemporary Jewish-Christian dialogue, for the cleavage between the teacher-led reality which is rabbinic Judaism and the teacher-led reality which is Christianity may not be as great as that between Judaism and a Christianity that is thought of as based on episcopal monarchs. Moreover, the historical fact that the Judaism contemporary with the origin of Christianity was largely fashioned by teachers may help explain why the early Christians did not feel keenly the need to set up a formally institutionalized priesthood.

In comparing the notion of ministry in early Christianity with that found in Judaism prior to it, one must take notice of the manner in which the ministry of the community as a whole was envisaged. Here, it seems that a basic difference existed. Apart from a "breakthrough" at the time of the great prophets, particularly in Deutero-Isaiah and in the book of Jonas, Old Testament writings as well as the later nonbiblical literature of Judaism reflect a certain narrow self-containment. Israel is not seen as standing totally apart from the destiny of other peoples; rather, it stands as a center of focus, a source of salvation to which others must come;[90] it does not reach outward to the world either in evangelization or in service. Christianity, on the contrary, was marked almost immediately by a thrust outward.[91] The Christian communities possessed a gospel that was meant for all men; theirs was a mission to preach that good news to the "ends of the earth."[92]

It would be excessive to claim that the early Christians saw clearly the extent of the service that they were to extend to all men. Even after centuries of slow development in this direction, today's Christianity is not totally adjusted to this notion.[93] Yet, the Pauline teaching states that Christian charity is to be extended to all men, though primarily to those of the faith (Gal. 6:10). Gospel parables like that of the good Samaritan manifest a universality of view that breaks with Judaism's tendency to nationalism (Luke 10:30–37). More importantly, the explicit Christian teaching that Jesus of Nazareth had died and risen for all men (2 Cor. 5:14–15), that this constituted the very heart of his "service" (Phil. 2:8), and that the ministry of Christians consisted in extending this very service to all men (Mark 16:15–16) makes it clear that a universal horizon governed the mentality of the early Christians,[94] even if they did not see the full implications of this for the transformation of mankind's social existence.

In such a context, the role of "ministers" within the community inevitably takes on a different orientation. While they function for the well-being of the religious community itself, they also act as guides and stimulants for the community as it directs itself outward in witness and service.[95] Much of the leadership and instruction in this case consists in the example of apostolic dedication provided by the leaders.[96] In this light it is significant how often Paul in his exhortations to the early churches urges them to be as he is (1 Cor. 11:1), and how the theme of Jesus' call to discipleship is so prominent in the mentality of the Gospel writers.[97]

Moreover, the difference between early Christianity and Judaism relative to leadership within the community is closely bound up with the viewpoint reflected in the description of Pentecost in Acts 2. Here, in the speech of Peter, the claim is made that charism as a basis for special ministry is not con-

fined to an elite within the Christian community. Instead, since this is now "the day of the Lord," the promised Spirit of God is poured out on the entire people, all share in diverse ways in the special guidance of this Spirit, the entire people is prophetic. The Spirit is a radically democratic principle in the communal life of the disciples of Jesus; no one because of his particular gift is permitted to ignore the manifestation of the Spirit in each of his brethren.[98]

At the same time, the New Testament literature testifies to the early Christian belief that the key ministerial roles of Israel found an idealized fulfillment in the "new Israel." Basic to this view is the manner in which Jesus himself is seen to recapitulate these roles in his own ministry of service.[99] Though he occupies no political office nor seeks such, he is the Messiah who realizes the ideal unattained by the historical kingship of Israel. Enjoying no part in the function or structure of Israelitic priesthood, his own worship of the Father definitively replaces the sacrificial ritual of the Old Testament law. Without formalized rabbinic training, he is the supreme teacher who reveals the new law. He is the great prophet, he is the one who fulfills the Old Testament prophetic movement by his own prophetic activity and by being in his death and resurrection the act of divine salvation anticipated by the prophets of old.

Called to a discipleship which is not one of *succeeding* the Christ in his historical role, continuing what he began and then handed over to them when he passed beyond history, but rather one in which the risen Lord remains present to them and works through them, the Christian communities see themselves as sharing in this fuller ministry.[100] Like *the* Servant, who by his loving obedience and gift of self even unto death brought salvation to his brethren and established the kingdom of God and his own Lordship,[101] they are to rule as the kingdom of the saints by their service. Doing this, they will bear prophetic witness to the word spoken through them, for in living out the new law they will be recognized as disciples of the Risen

One.[102] Their mediation will not be through office but through life itself, their life of faith that will lead to eternal life.[103]

Christian Ministry and Comparative Religious Studies

While the relation of early Christianity to Judaism was immediate and involved some dependence, and for that reason the comparison between them is of special importance, it is also instructive to view the origins of the church in the light of elements common to religions in general. Like everything else in Christianity, there is (if one accepts Christian faith) a radical transformation of these elements by the death and resurrection of Christ; but seeing *what* it is that he transforms gives added insight into the nature of "redemption" as well as into the characteristic genius of Christianity as a religion.[104]

First, like most religious groups throughout history, the early Christians were convinced that their identity as a people of faith was grounded in an "event." In essence, this event had constituted a divine "election" by which they were singled out as the chosen ones of the god, picked to fulfill a particular destiny in the course of following the will of this divinity. We are here in the presence of a cast of mind that one finds as a recurring element in religious groups. Whether it be the insight granted to Gautama beneath the Bo-tree, or the mystic communications given to Mohammed, or the freeing of Israel from Egypt in the exodus, or the mythic kind of "happenings" that one finds at the roots of such religions as those of ancient Egypt or Mesopotamia, of the American Indians, or of Polynesia, practically all religious groups connect their belief and practice to "something that the divinity did." And in most cases this divine action was performed through the "founder" of the religion, whether he be historical or legendary.[105]

What is intriguing about Christianity is that it apparently manages to combine two seemingly contradictory positions that divide such religions one from another: either the "event" in question is really rooted in historical happenings, in real time, or it is mythic

projection into the discovery of recurring happenings in nature or human society—it occurs not in real time but in sacral time.[106] In the first case, the religious community looks back to the historical event and sees itself as continuing the implications of that divine act; in the second case, the community sees the event as transcending ordinary time and therefore as contemporary with itself. It seems that only in Christianity does one find the claim that the originating event, in this case the death and resurrection of Jesus (the *event* and not just its implications and impact), is both historical happening and continuously contemporary with the believing community during its historical experience.[107] If this is truly unique to Christianity, it follows that its view of ministry, whether that of the community as a whole or that of specialized ministers within the community, will of necessity be quite distinctive when compared with other religions.[108]

Second, in many of the world's great religions, the influence of the founder is of major and lasting importance, though this pertains only to those cases where we can identify this founder as an historical personage, such as Mohammed or Confucius or Christ. One of the factors that enters the picture at this point (and sociologists of religion have drawn attention to its importance in formation of community) is the somewhat nebulous reality of personal charism.[109] Beyond unusual intellectual endowments or gifts of expression or unique sensitivity, there seems to be involved a very special power of attracting men and women to a new way of life. Because of this unique magnetism, the religious founder is able to gather about him a nucleus of dedicated followers who form the bridge between him and the historical continuity of the religion.[110] These men (and those who succeed them) minister to the message and memory of the founder, thus perpetuating his impact as a constituting force in the religious community's existence.[111] This generic role of "ministry" is distinguished in each case by the particular manner in which each "founder" brought the religious community into existence.

What is interesting, and may prove to be of capital importance in our study of Christian ministry, is the prominence in such religious founders of the task of teaching. Granted all the special charismatic power just mentioned, the major task of most of the founders of the world's great religions seems to have been one of teaching. Possessed of a new vision of human life and destiny, they felt compelled to communicate this to others; and the faith of their followers was fashioned into communal unity by this teaching. This would seem to say that teaching is one of the most basic forms of religious ministration. It would therefore dictate a careful study of this role in the life of the Christian church.

Third, closely allied with this element of teaching is the influence in various religious groups of tradition.[112] Retention and diffusion of the original insights, even though they may have to be adapted and expanded over the course of the historical existence of the religious community, is vital to the essential identity of the group. Moreover, because the original teaching is always viewed as a special truth communicated by "god" to men, it is seen as a precious treasure to be safeguarded and transmitted to each new generation as its heritage. Within his body of "revealed truth" a key role has always been given to the code of behavior which the believers are meant to follow; this law of life indicates to the community the path that will lead to fulfilling its destiny, and indicates to the individual believer the secure way of following "the will of God" and so obtaining his blessing.[113]

Clearly, Christianity has emphasized the element of tradition ever since the apostolic church.[114] Yet, because of its belief that the original manifestation of the divine in Jesus of Nazareth continues as contemporary event as a result of his resurrection, the notion of tradition, and therefore the ministry of transmitting this tradition, takes on unique form.[115] What is meant to be handed on in the church is not just traditional teaching nor codified religious law, but contact with the risen Lord. This applies with special importance to the ethical traditions of Christianity, for the law of Christ consisted essentially in his "follow me" and the early disciples saw that their own following of Christ handed on the tradition of Christian behavior to the communities with whom they worked.[116]

Fourth, the element most immediately identified with religion in most people's thinking is cultic worship. But, such identification of religion with cult runs into difficulties when one is dealing with the more intellectualized forms of Buddhism or Hinduism or even Islam. However, cult in some form or other does seem quite basic to a faith community's celebration of its religious identity;[117] and historically nearly all religions have had a designated group of men and women who minister in special fashion to the cult and to the shrine.[118] Without attempting now to describe the "new" approach to cult that characterizes Christianity, we can simply note that the early Christians unquestionably thought of themselves as a worshiping community, gathered together for the praise of "the Father of our Lord, Jesus Christ." Moreover, in the actual social formation of the early church no action so consistently brought Christians together and forged their specific social identity as did "the breaking of the bread."[119]

What is less clear is the manner in which a designated group of cultic functionaries came into existence in the early church. That some such group, charged not only with liturgical but with overall direction of the community, is identifiably existent by the end of the second century seems clear from the evidence we possess. But what constituted the grounds on which these men based their claim to special cultic role? Given the early Christian insistence on the "spirituality" of their worship, how did the function of the "hierarch" in Christianity differ from that of cultic personages in other religions? These are large questions that demand close analysis. They are unavoidable, since it is clear that Christianity is, though perhaps in exceptional fashion, basically a community existing in history for the purpose of worship.

Fifth, like practically every other historical instance with which we are familiar, the Christian community quickly developed within it a "ruling class." To this group was entrusted the preservation and nurture of the founder's original impact and heritage, the traditions stemming from him and from the community's own religious experience, the formation of people's understanding of the way of life that is proper to the community, and the patterns of ritual by which the community enunciates to itself and to its divinity the relation it bears to that divinity. And, as in other historical instances, this ruling group quickly devises institutional forms through which it seeks to guarantee the original insight and spirit of the community. Such an attempt can be only partially successful, for it is the very nature of religious experience to resist reduction to external formalization. So, with all the specific differentiation deriving from the Christian belief that the community is animated by the Spirit of Christ, the earliest decades of the church are already marked by a tension between the institutional and charismatic factors in the community.

It would be a mistake to judge Christianity on the basic assumption that the ideal situation is that of least institutionalization. While the founder's immediate impact is still felt during his lifetime and shortly thereafter, this may suffice to inspire and unite his disciples; but as this becomes weakened by historical distance, some structures of social unification must come into being if the community's continuance is to be safeguarded. According to the Christian belief reflected in the New Testament writings, this should not be the case for Christianity, since the risen Christ is always with them. Still, the historical fact is that traditional forms of life and teaching and worship played a growing role in unifying the church. The emerging ministry was intended to serve these forms and thereby the community.

Conclusions: Ministry in Relation to Community

In later chapters we will examine the New Testament texts for clarification about the early church's view on the three key aspects of

Christian ministry—of the word, of sacrament, and of service. At this point in our study, recognizing the extent to which detailed study of these three (along with the activity of judgment which assumed major historical importance) will modify our present statements, it might still be good to draw some conclusion about the New Testament's view of ministry in relation to community. More specifically, we might try to isolate some of the viewpoints that are distinctive of the early church.

(1) Central to the entire discussion is the distinctive position of Christianity's founder to the community he establishes. As the head of his body, which is the church, he is throughout history the preeminent member of the community, abiding with it and acting through and with it for the redemption of mankind.[120] This alters the outlook on authoritative office within the Christian community, for it is Christ and he alone who holds authority in his own name. While there is "delegation" of this authority, this is not true in the sense that others exercise this authority in his stead. Rather, they minister to his continuing function of preeminent charismatic leadership. They bear witness to his guiding presence. They allow his Spirit to work through them for the direction and nurture of the community. Their own being and activity translate sacramentally his abiding and transforming presence.[121]

(2) To an extent that is hard to parallel in the history of religious communities, early Christianity exists apart from civic involvements. Aware that its members must also function in the secular structures of human life, it still remains uninvolved in these, living out the principle "Render to Caesar the things that are Caesar's. . . ." It neither depends upon non-Christian social institutions for its own internal cohesion and vitality, nor does it see itself as contributing to the well-being of these institutions except insofar as its members are faithful to their civic duties. The kingdom it works to establish "is not of this world" and so in its own internal dynamics it remains quite impartial to the function-

ing of secular society. With a naive simplicity (which history and its own internal missionary thrust will inevitably alter) the early Christian community views itself as a thoroughly "otherworldly" movement. It is in the world but not "of the world."[122] Unavoidably this conditions the manner of discovering or devising ministries that will suitably foster its vitality; and at least in theory it excludes the model of the political structure as an apt parallel for thinking about Christian community and ministry. "The lords of the gentiles dominate their subjects; but it is not so in my kingdom. . . ."

(3) As they see it in faith, the early Christian communities not only owe their origin to the event of Christ's death and resurrection, they continued to live that event. They were constantly formed by it as the center of their experience, and they gathered to celebrate it in their Eucharistic assemblies.[123] Their worship for this reason took on a distinctive character: it was historical commemoration in a new sense, and it was tied to the communal life of the people rather than to any designated "shrines" or to detailed liturgical ritual.[124] In such a context, there was no need for a priestly group entrusted with care of shrine and ceremonial; rather, the care of the people provided for the care of their worship. In some ways, one is almost back to that primitive sociological situation in which the family or clan structure of life and social order provides for cult without any special group of cultic ministers.[125]

(4) Of the three prominent mediatorial functions that early Christians would have known from their Old Testament heritage (priest, prophet, and king), it is that of prophet which gains the ascendancy in the life and thought of early Christianity. Significantly, the "office" of prophet is the least structured and institutionalized of the three. And even within the reality of prophecy, it is not with the organized prophetic groups of Old Testament times that Christians see themselves linked, but with the charismatic prophets whose "vocation" was independent of officially recognized prophetic groups and

derived directly from divine choice. Moreover, the "office" of prophet was not only seen as the most basic; it absorbed into itself the idealized functions of both king and priest. One can see this in the description given of Jesus' own ministry and mission; his activity is essentially prophetic, and the texts indicate that this was his own manner of envisaging his role.[126] The same was true of his disciples, who were sent forth to spread his prophetic message.[127] Even worship was subsumed under this prophetic function, for there are clear indications that the early celebration of the Eucharist was seen as proclamation of the word (e.g., John 6).[128]

(5) Prophetic ministry would, then, seem to be the essential pattern of pastoral service within the infant church. Those who with special designation provided for the faith and unity of the churches were to do so most basically through their witness, the witness of their words and the witness of their lives.[129] Yet, to some extent, this prophetic role was not confined to a special group; all those who belonged to the community possessed the prophetic charism and task. This seems to be the clear meaning of Acts 2, where in the explanation of Pentecost given by Peter, the gift of the prophetic Spirit is communicated to the entire assembly. The Spirit animating and unifying the Christian people was the Spirit of prophecy, hence each Christian is meant to bear prophetic witness to his fellow Christians as well as to nonbelievers.[130] This may well mean that our explanation of distinctive functions within early Christianity must distinguish aspects of prophecy rather than distinguish other roles from prophecy.

(6) Attention should be drawn to an element connected with Christian prophecy, the notion of "discipleship."[131] We have already adverted to the general phenomenon of a religious founder's immediate followers enjoying a special role, but it seems that we are in the presence of something quite distinctive when dealing with early Christianity. Here it is a question of the disciples spreading the teaching of their master, but more than that they are the very embodiment of his continu-

ing teaching and witness.[132] They are themselves the living instance of the mystery they proclaim; who and what they are, as well as what they do and say, form a central and necessary part of their ministry.[133] Old Testament charismatic prophecy already exemplified this to a considerable extent,[134] and we find the ideal of such "personification of the message" in the figure of the Servant in Deutero-Isaiah.[135] Yet, Christian discipleship goes an important step further: the very presence of the risen Christ is somehow "located" in the Christian believers; Christ is still continuing to live out his redeeming destiny in his followers. They are a sign, a sacrament, of his redeeming activity.

NOTES

1. Some indication of the complexity of this question is provided by the extensive bibliography of works by sociologists, anthropologists, etc., that treat of the method in which religious phenomena should be studied, works which testify to great divergence of opinion. One can see this reflected in such works as the anthology of readings *Religion in Philosophical and Cultural Perspective*, ed. J. Feaver and W. Horosz (Princeton, 1967), or in the comparative study by H. Duncan, *Symbols and Social Theory* (New York, 1969). Dealing more specifically with the Christian scholar's methodological problems are: J. Robinson's "A Critical Inquiry into the Scriptural Bases of Confessional Hermeneutics," *Journal of Ecumenical Studies* 3 (Winter, 1966), pp. 36–56; K. Rahner's "The Hermeneutics of Eschatological Assertions," *Theological Investigations* (Baltimore, 1966), vol. 4, pp. 323–46; and E. Schillebeeckx', *God the Future of Man* (New York, 1968), pp. 3–49.

2. At present, historical studies of Christian ministry are quite fragmentary. One can, of course, obtain a considerable body of information from the better histories of the church, e.g., the Fliche-Martin *Histoire de l'Eglise depuis les origines jusqu'à nos jours* (Paris, 1935—), and the new Herder *Handbook of Church History* (New York, 1965—). More detailed studies of specific elements are to be found in volumes such as *The Apostolic Ministry*, ed. K. Kirk (London, 1946) or the more recent *The Sacrament of Holy Orders* (Collegeville, Minn., 1962), which resulted from a conference sponsored (in 1955) by the Centre de Pastorale Liturgique in Paris. But there is lacking anything like a serious synthetic historical presentation.

3. This point is strongly emphasized by Y. Congar in his *L'ecclésiologie du Haut Moyen Age* (Paris, 1968) where he criticizes the inadequacy of a historical study of medieval ecclesiology that would confine itself to examining theological understanding of church institutions.

4. For a review of ecclesiastical history, its history and function, see H. Jedin's introduction in *Handbook of Church History*, vol. 1, pp. 1–56.

5. See K. Rahner, "The Concept of Mystery in Catholic Theology," *Theological Investigations*, vol. 4, pp. 36–73.

6. See F. Durrwell, *The Resurrection* (New York, 1960), pp. 250–348; also, E. Mersch, *Theology of the Mystical Body* (St. Louis, 1951), pp. 520–93.

7. See Durrwell, pp. 234–35; Vatican II, *Constitution on the Church*, 48.

8. See *Constitution on the Church*, 35–38.

9. Since the risen Christ, head of the Body, is the preeminent member of this community which he animates by his Spirit, any authentic ministry (whether of the community as a whole or of a specialized group within the community) can be considered *de iure divino* independent of when it emerges in the history of the church. Actually, the demarcation between *de iure divino* and *de iure humano* tends to vanish if one views the church as Body of Christ, as a sacramental reality. These two terms seem rather to be distinguishing what is absolutely necessary to the intrinsic nature of the church, as opposed to what is historically incidental. Or from another point of view this distinction may have been an attempt to find some criterion for evaluating certain external elements of the church's life that emerge in the course of history.

To ask the question "What is *de iure divino?*" in the sense of "What did God himself will the church to be?" seems to be based on the notion of a conceptualized divine decree. What seems more acceptable theologically than this divine "prevision" and predetermination of the church's history is a view that sees God working through the secondary causality of human history, with the incarnate Word working *ab intra* in this history as the risen Christ, and the Christian community responding in freedom to the transforming presence of God in the risen Christ and his Spirit. In other words, the view one has of "Providence" seems quite clearly to control the view one has of notions such as "divine institution," *"de iure divino."*

10. This would seem to be what is implied in calling the church the sacrament of Christ, or in the approach to prayer enunciated by Ignatius Loyola (among others), "seeing God in all things." On the former see H. de Lubac, *The Splendour of the Church* (New York, 1956), pp. 120–42. On the latter see J. de Guibert, *The Jesuits: Their Spiritual Doctrine and Practice* (Chicago, 1964), pp. 44–73; M. Giuliani, "Trouver Dieu en toutes choses," *Christus* 6 (1955), pp. 172–94; and E. Coreth, "In actione contemplativus," *Zeitschrift für katholische Theologie* 76 (1954), pp. 55–82.

11. See *Constitution on the Church*, 48.

12. See Durrwell, pp. 250–87.

13. This seems quite clearly to be the mentality of Revelation as it speaks of the "heavenly Jerusalem." Such imagery of a heavenly city is obviously linked with the prominent New Testament (esp. Johannine) theme of "abiding," which itself stands in continuity with the Old Testament notion of "promised land." On the relation of Revelation's view of the heavenly temple and the heavenly Jerusalem to the presence of God, see Y. Congar, *The Mystery of the Temple* (London, 1962), pp. 204–48.

14. For a discussion of the knotty question of reconciling the various New Testament texts about "the world" (more specifically such Johannine texts as 3:16, 6:51, 14:17, 16:8, 18:36), see R. Brown, *The Gospel According to John* (New York, 1966), vol. 29, pp. 508–10; vol. 29A (New York, 1970), pp. 705, 711–14, 852; also A. Richardson, *Introduction to the Theology of the New Testament* (New York, 1958), pp. 206–14; J. Macquarrie, *Principles of Christian Theology* (New York, 1966), pp. 240–41; J. Bonsirven, *Theology of the New Testament* (Westminster, Md., 1963), pp. 39–40.

15. As indications of the common insistence on this point, see G. von Rad, *Old Testament Theology* (New York, 1965), vol. 1, pp. 392–98 (in discussing the increasing emergence of individualism in Israel's spirituality, von Rad takes the basic tendency towards corporate identity as a presupposition); W. Eichrodt, *Theology of the Old Testament* (Philadelphia, 1961), vol. 1, pp. 36–69; R. Schnackenburg, *Christian Existence in the New Testament* (Notre Dame, 1968), pp. 12–16; and idem, *The Church in the New Testament* (New York, 1965), pp. 11–35.

16. See B. Cooke, *The God of Space and Time* (New York, 1970), pp. 28–34.

17. As contemporary examples: "It is our common belief that, in the New Covenant of the Lord Jesus Christ, he alone is priest in his own right" (*Towards Reconciliation: The Interim Statement of the Anglican-Methodist Unity Commission* [London, 1967], p. 12); "In the bishops, therefore, for whom the priests are assistants, Our Lord Jesus Christ, the supreme High Priest, is present in the midst of those who believe. For sitting at the right hand of God the Father, He is not absent from the gatherings of his high priests, but above all through their excellent service he is preaching the Word of God to all nations, and constantly administering the sacraments of faith to those who believe." (*Constitution on the Church*, 21.) "All ministry in the Church is rooted in the ministry of Christ himself, who glorifies the Father in the power of the Holy Spirit. Christ stirs up, calls, strengthens and sends those whom he has chosen for the whole ministry of his Church or for the special ministry, making them the instruments of his message and of his work." (*The Fourth World Conference on Faith and Order. Montreal, 1963*, ed. Rodger and Vischer [London, 1964], p. 64.)

18. For one of the most recent theological studies, see W. Pannenberg, *Jesus—God and Man* (Philadelphia, 1968), pp. 53–114.

19. This seems clearly indicated in a passage like Romans 8. For a discussion of the

relation between the historical Jesus and the risen Christ, see X. Leon-Dufour, *The Gospels and the Jesus of History* (New York, 1968), pp. 204–76.

20. Rom. 8; 1 Cor. 15.

21. Gal. 4:6–7; see Durrwell, pp. 103–7.

22. Such exemplarism as an explanation of salvation is often attributed to Abelard and before him to Pelagius. The attribution is certainly dubious in the case of Abelard (see J. Sikes, *Peter Abailard* [Cambridge, 1932], pp. 204–11) and not perfectly clear in that of Pelagius (see R. Hedde and E. Amann, "Pelagianisme," *Dictionnaire de théologie catholique*, vol. 12 [1933], col. 684). It is in more recent times that it has become a common, if not-too-theologically formulated, view of many who call themselves Christians but see Jesus only as a great human being.

23. See B. Cooke, "Sacraments as Continuing Acts of Christ," *Catholic Theological Society of America Proceedings* 16 (1961), pp. 43–68.

24. See A. Wikenhauser, *Pauline Mysticism* (New York, 1960), pp. 65–91; T. Manson, *The Servant Messiah* (Cambridge, 1961), pp. 98–99.

25. See Bornkamm-Barth-Held, *Tradition and Interpretation in Matthew* (London, 1963), pp. 17–19.

26. See H. Conzelmann, *The Theology of St. Luke* (New York, 1961), pp. 80–83, 120–25; R. Laurentin, *Structure et théologie de Luc I–II* (Paris, 1957), pp. 123–31.

27. On basic categories of sin, see E. Beaucamp and S. Lyonnet, "Péché," in *Dictionnaire de la Bible, Supplement* (Paris, 1962), vol. 7.

28. See esp. Eichrodt, *Theology of the Old Testament*; he takes covenant as the basic category for his development of the Old Testament theology.

29. See B. Cooke, "Synoptic Presentation of the Eucharist as Covenant Sacrifice," *Theological Studies* 21 (1960), pp. 1–44.

30. See Schnackenburg, *Church in the N.T.*, pp. 149–64.

31. It is still valuable to reflect upon the view of Thomas Aquinas regarding the redemptive causality exercised by the actions of Jesus' public ministry. See *Summa Theol.* 3, qq. 39–40.

32. On Christ's consciousness of himself and his mission, see R. Brown, *Jesus—God and Man* (Milwaukee, 1967), pp. 39–102.

33. As already indicated above (nn. 18, 19), there is considerable recent study of this continuity; good examples are G. Bornkamm, *Jesus of Nazareth* (New York, 1960), and E. Kaesemann, *New Testament Questions Today* (London, 1969), pp. 23–65.

34. See D. Stanley, "The New Testament Basis for the Concept of Collegiality," *Theological Studies* 25 (1964), pp. 197–216.

35. See Durrwell, pp. 108–50, for a discussion of the effect of the resurrection on Jesus himself.

36. See H. Küng, *The Church* (New York, 1967), pp. 54–87.

37. See Schnackenburg, *Church in the N.T.*, pp. 176–87.

38. On the missionary character of Christianity, see *ibid.*, pp. 135–40; also *Mission and Witness*, ed. P. Burns (Westminster, Md., 1964).

39. *Constitution on the Church*, 12.

40. *Ibid.*, 10, 12. See also K. Rahner, *The Church and the Sacraments* (New York, 1963), which develops this theme of the community's faith and love making present the redeeming presence of God. Rahner's essay points to the immense implications of this viewpoint for theological reflection about salvation or the church or Christology. Basically it would mean that the principle from which such reflection would proceed is the insight that the heart of Jesus' own ministry is his act of sacrifice, which is his very manner of being as the risen one.

41. On the ambiguity of early Christian thought on this question, see Schnackenburg, *Church in the N.T.*, pp. 135–49.

42. *Ibid.*, pp. 113–17.

43. Rev. 11:7–15, 17–18.

44. Obviously, the world-view (esp. in its eschatological elements) of early Christianity has wide-reaching implications. For a review and analysis of recent writing (by such men as Cullmann, Balthasar, Dawson, and Marrou) on this matter of Christian thought and history, see J. Connolly, *Human History and the Word of God* (New York, 1965).

45. Such withdrawal from the world is, obviously, half of a dialectical attitude that has always characterized Christian behavior, the other half being an involvement with the problems of mankind. Different periods of history and different currents of thought have stressed now one, now the other, of these poles. See H. de Lubac's perceptive discussion in *Splendour of the Church* (New York, 1956), pp. 92–119, and in *Catholicism* (New York, 1950), pp. 181–95.

46. The scholarly writings of the past two decades (to take an arbitrary date that excludes important writings by Battifol, Bultmann, Harnack, Lebreton, and others) appear to have thoroughly sifted, analyzed, and commented upon whatever data is available to us. Congar, von Campenhausen, Schweizer, Daniélou, Colson, Küng, and Schnackenburg, to name only some of the more prominent authors, have dealt with the matter in detail and from various perspectives. To quite an extent a consensus emerges concerning the general picture, but disagreement on details (some of them fairly important) seems unresolvable, unless some new data is discovered (which seems unlikely) or some fresh approach to understanding the historical evidence appears.

47. It seems better to postpone until later the analysis of church structure in the New Testament until we have studied further the nature of ministry; this may help us avoid certain preconceptions in reading the New Testament evidence.

48. Implicitly the Pastorals may also give us (in the role attributed to Timothy and Titus themselves) some evidence for the traveling ministry; see J. Daniélou, *The Theology of Jewish Christianity* (London, 1964), pp. 346–56. See also, J. Meier, "*Presbyteros* in the Pastoral Epistles," *Catholic Biblical Quarterly* 35 (1973), pp. 323–45.

49. See K. Schelkle, *Discipleship and Priesthood* (New York, 1965), pp. 33–58.

50. See Cooke, "Synoptic Presentation," pp. 28–32.

51. See Schelkle, pp. 39–42.

52. See Schnackenburg, *Church in the N.T.*, pp. 17–34.

53. For examples of the manner in which social scientists utilize the notion of community in studying religious phenomena, see J. Wach, *Sociology of Religion* (Chicago, 1944), pp. 27–33; or T. O'Dea, *The Sociology of Religion* (Englewood Cliffs, N.J., 1966), pp. 47–60.

54. See F. Hauck, "*Koinos*," *Theological Dictionary of the New Testament* (hereafter referred to as *TDNT*) vol. 3, pp. 796–809.

55. See E. Schweizer, *Church Order in the New Testament* (London, 1961), pp. 163–70.

56. This emphasis on the inner reality of the church is, of course, a constant refrain throughout Christian history, with such diverse personalities as Luther, Gregory VII, Thomas More, Gerson, Bernard of Clairvaux, and Joachim of Flora insisting on it.

57. See J. Robinson, "A Critical Inquiry into the Scriptural Bases of Confessional Hermeneutics," *Journal of Ecumenical Studies* 3 (1966), pp. 35–56.

58. See Schnackenburg, *Church in the N.T.*, pp. 118–23.

59. This topic will be discussed at length in later portions of the book, see pp. 541–42, 577–78.

60. On Old Testament thinking about the manner in which ministry (to impose our later categories upon Old Testament thought and life) functioned as service to the community, see R. de Vaux, *Ancient Israel* (New York, 1961), pp. 345–57.

61. See Schnackenburg, *Church in the N.T.*, pp. 77–84, 149–57; also Küng, pp. 107–25.

62. See Bonsirven, pp. 371–76.

63. On New Testament usage of these terms, see the carefully qualified remarks of Küng, pp. 114–25.

64. See Cooke, "Synoptic Presentation."

65. See W. G. Kummel, *Promise and Fulfillment* (London, 1961).

66. For a discussion of the diversity of views among the Old Testament prophets on the nature of this "day of the Lord," see J. Lindblom, *Prophecy in Ancient Israel* (Oxford, Basil Blackwell, 1962; Philadelphia: Fortress Press, 1976), pp. 360–422.

67. Heb. 4:14—5:10.

68. The question of the relationship between the two testaments which has intrigued thinkers since the time of the New Testament literature itself remains today a hotly debated issue. See the divergent views of von Rad, vol. 2, pp. 319–409; J. Bonsirven, *Le règne de Dieu* (Paris, 1957), pp. 201–8; W. Eichrodt, "Les rapports du Nouveau et de l'Ancien Testament," *Le problème biblique dans le protestantisme* (Neuchâtel, 1955), pp. 105–30. Küng, pp. 107–50, studies the relations of Christianity in its inception to Judaism, but extends this into the critically important matter of present-day relationships between Judaism and Christianity.

69. Though the evidence for his thesis is not too apparent, S. Brandon in his recent *Jesus and the Zealots* (Manchester, 1967) draws attention to the need to look carefully at the political factors that may have influenced the origins of Christianity. A more moderate study is that of O. Cullmann, *Jesus and the Revolutionaries* (New York, 1970).

70. See Daniélou, pp. 315–56.

71. Actually, during the Hasmonean possession of the high priesthood, from John Hyrcanus to the seizure of the Temple by Pompey in 63 B.C., the high priesthood and the kingship were formally identified.

72. See D. Stanley, "Kingdom to Church," *Theological Studies* 16 (1955), pp. 1–29; see also *idem, The Apostolic Church in the New Testament* (Westminster, Md., 1965), pp. 5–37.

73. Thus the obvious opposition, reflected in numerous New Testament passages, to the Judaizing tendencies of a powerful faction within early Christianity.

74. However, one must guard against a tendency to take too negative a view of the developments during the Jewish (i.e., post-Babylonian Exile) period; see the balanced cautions of H. Renckens, *The Religion of Israel* (New York, 1966), pp. 305–12.

75. See W. Davies, *Paul and Rabbinic Judaism,* 2d ed. (London, 1962), pp. 58–85, where the author indicates the highly nuanced attitude of Paul towards the Jewish community and the Torah.

76. Though the existence of the Epistle to the Hebrews would seem to indicate that some elements of early Christianity wished either to embrace or to parallel the structures of Jewish priesthood. See C. Spicq, *L'Epître aux Hébreux* (Paris, 1952), vol. 1, pp. 222–52.

77. Acts 6:7. See J. Schmitt, "Jewish Priesthood and Christian Hierarchy in the Early Palestinian Communities," in *Sacrament of Holy Orders,* pp. 60–74.

78. Schmitt, pp. 67–70; also G. Vermes, *The Dead Sea Scrolls in English* (Baltimore, 1962), pp. 45–51.

79. See J.-P. Audet, *Structures of Christian Priesthood* (New York, 1968), pp. 77–79, on the matter of priesthood in the first Christian decades.

80. See de Vaux, pp. 69–70; J. Pedersen, *Israel,* vol. 1–2 (London, 1963–64), pp. 33–38.

81. On the role of the Sanhedrin, see J. McKenzie, "Council," *Dictionary of the Bible* (Milwaukee, 1965), pp. 152–53.

82. See Vermes, pp. 16–28.

83. See G. d'Ercole, "The Presbyteral College and the Early Church," in *Historical Investigations,* vol. 17 of *Concilium* (New York, 1966), pp. 20–33.

84. See de Vaux, pp. 69–70.

85. See Schweizer, pp. 181–201; he indicates that New Testament evidence does not justify a distinction between charismatic and noncharismatic functions in the primitive church, but he also mentions the special continuity in social form between Jewish and Christian elders (pp. 200–201).

86. G. Bornkamm, *"Presbyteros," TDNT*, vol. 6, pp. 651–83. Perhaps the mention of Paul is misleading, for Paul's own letters do not use *"presbyteros."* On the other hand, it seems that recognized *presbyteroi* soon appeared in the Pauline churches and these could well be the leadership recognized and supported by Paul himself.

87. See H. von Campenhausen, *Ecclesiastical Authority and Spiritual Power in the Church of the First Three Centuries* (Palo Alto, Calif., 1969), pp. 76–123, for a careful discussion of "presbyter" in the New Testament and subapostolic writings. As he points out, it would be erroneous to see the presbyterate as an office; nor should one see "presbyter" as a precise function over against teaching or prophecy. There is evidence (both in the New Testament and in other first- and second-century writings) that *"presbyteros"* could overlap (or not overlap) with *"didaskalos"* or *"prophetes"* or *"episkopos,"* not in formal description of function but in the applicability of two (or more) of these terms to the same individual.

88. There seems to be a body of evidence that some in the primitive church were specially recognized (and to that extent designated) teachers. See K. Rengstorf, *"Didaskalos," TDNT*, vol. 2, pp. 157–59; also Schweizer, pp. 182–83, 197–98; von Campenhausen, pp. 60–62. However, we are here using the term in a broader fashion, referring to the fact that some members of the early communities functioned in a recognized way as teachers of their brethren; this could apply to those mentioned as *"presbyteroi"* or *"episkopoi"* or *"apostoloi"* as well as to those denominated *"didaskaloi."* Some recent scholarship on the Pharisaic movement and its influence on primitive Christianity opens up an area of investigation that may be of major importance for our understanding of the origins of Christian ministry: perhaps the Pharisaic rabbinate as known by Jesus and his early disciples was the prime model for the earliest Christian form of ministry. See esp. J. Pawlikowski, "The Minister as Pharisee," *Commonweal*, January 21, 1972, pp. 369–73; also J. M. Ford, "The Christian Debt to Phariseeism," *The Bridge*, ed. J. Oesterricher, vol. 5 (1970), pp. 218–30; and E. Rivkin, "The Internal City," *Journal for the Scientific Study of Religion* 5 (1966), pp. 225–40.

89. This is reflected even in Paul's view of his mission (see 1 Cor. 11:23) or in the very existence of the *Didache*, which seems to have been a manual to guide traveling apostles so that their teaching would correspond to the traditions of Christian faith (see J.-P. Audet, *La Didache* [Paris, 1958], pp. 119–20). The topic of tradition will be treated more extensively in chapter 8.

90. This, of course, is true even of Deutero-Isaiah, but it is more marked in Ezekiel's description of the role of the rebuilt Temple (e.g., from the Temple foundations flow the very waters of life for mankind). On the Jerusalem Temple as the symbol of Israel's focal position in creation, see Congar, *Mystery of the Temple*, pp. 90–100.

91. See Y. Congar, *The Mystery of the Church* (Baltimore, 1960), pp. 147–80.

92. Matt. 28:18; see Schnackenburg, *Church in the N.T.*, pp. 135–40.

93. See J. Bligh, "Development of Doctrine Within Scripture," *The Heythrop Journal*, vol. 11 (1970), pp. 408–20.

94. See H. Beyer, *"Diakonia," TDNT*, vol. 2, pp. 84–88.

95. See Schelkle, pp. 75–80.

96. *Ibid.*, pp. 81–83.

97. *Ibid.*, pp. 9–32.

98. See Schweizer's interesting discussion in "Charismatic and Non-charismatic Ministries?" (pp. 181–87); he argues against Harnack's separation of charismatic from administrative ministries (*Die Lehre der zwoelf Apostel,* Texte und Untersuchungen, 2 [1884], pp. 145–49). See also Schnackenburg, *Church in the N.T.*, pp. 123–26.

99. For three different views of Jesus' fulfillment of the various Old Testament "offices" (Messiah, Servant, Son of man, etc.), see V. Taylor, *The Names of Jesus* (London, 1953); O. Cullmann, *Christology of the New Testament* (London, 1963); and R. Fuller, *The Foundations of New Testament Christology* (New York, 1965).

100. For a fuller treatment of this point, see B. Cooke, "Christ's Eucharistic Action and History," in *Wisdom in Depth*, ed. V. Daues (Milwaukee, 1966), pp. 51–67. On

early Christianity's awareness of the presence to them of the risen Christ, see W. Marxen, *The Resurrection of Jesus of Nazareth* (Philadelphia, 1970); also R. Brown, *The Virginal Conception and Bodily Resurrection of Jesus* (New York, 1973), which is somewhat critical of Marxen's position.

101. On the New Testament view of Jesus as Servant, see W. Zimmerli and J. Jeremias *The Servant of God*, 2d ed. (Naperville, Ill., 1965), pp. 80–106; on Christian service, see Phil. 2.

102. John 13:35; see Schelkle, pp. 81–86.

103. See B. Cooke, *Christian Community: Response to Reality* (New York, 1970), pp. 134–40.

104. One of the aspects of soteriology that has been seriously neglected until recently and that is closely allied with contemporary interests in such questions as "Christianity and culture" or "Christian secularity" is the impact of Christian salvation not just on individuals but on the structures of human society. In this matter the notion of salvation (or grace) as transformation seems to offer intriguing possibilities; see Richard Niebuhr, *Christ and Culture* (New York, 1951); also J. Hartt's introduction to his *A Christian Critique of American Culture* (New York, 1967). Hartt highlights the need for confronting the question, but his book only gives preliminaries: it is a critical preaching of the gospel at American culture but not an attempt to see how Christianity and American culture could mutually infiltrate one another.

105. See J. Campbell, *The Hero with the Thousand Faces* (New York, 1949).

106. On this distinction between real and sacral time, see M. Eliade, *The Sacred and the Profane* (New York, 1959), pp. 68–113.

107. See the discussion of *anamnesis* in my *Christian Sacraments and Christian Personality* (New York, 1965).

108. It is precisely this distinctiveness (which is rooted in theological understanding of the *presence* of the risen Christ to the church) that was overlooked in Reformation/Tridentine controversies on Christian ministry, an oversight that influenced post-Reformation polemics until our own day.

109. See M. Weber, *Sociology of Religion* (Boston, 1964), trans. from the 4th German ed. (1956), in which charism is a recurring theme; *idem, Theory of Social and Economic Organization* (New York, 1947), pp. 358–59; and O'Dea, pp. 22–24.

110. The actual historical role of these disciples is often difficult to ascertain, since they tend to share in the legendary accretions that attach to the religion's founder himself.

111. See Wach, pp. 130–37. It is interesting to parallel this perpetuation of the religious founder with what is being done in Soviet Russia with the memory of Lenin.

112. See *ibid.*, pp. 19–24, 141–44.

113. *Ibid.*, pp. 49–53; O'Dea, pp. 60–71 (who studies it under the rubric of conversion).

114. See O. Cullmann, *The Early Church* (London, 1956), chap. 4; H. von Campenhausen, *Tradition and Life in the Church* (Philadelphia, 1968); R. Hanson, *Tradition in the Early Church* (London, 1963).

115. This point is dealt with more extensively in my "The Sacraments as the Continuing Acts of Christ," *Catholic Theological Society of America Proceedings* 16 (1961), pp. 43–68; on the notion of tradition, see also J. Geiselmann, *The Meaning of Tradition* (Montreal, 1966).

116. This more living form of moral teaching has received renewed attention in theological circles since World War II. One of the prime examples is B. Häring's *The Law of Christ* (Westminster, Md., 1961), which has had a major influence in redirecting Catholic moral theology.

117. See Wach, pp. 25–26, 39–44.

118. See "Priesthood," *Encyclopedia Brittanica* (Chicago, 1967), pp. 497–500.

119. See J. Jungmann, *The Early Liturgy* (Notre Dame, 1958), pp. 9–38.

120. On Paul's understanding of the notion of "Body of Christ," see Wikenhauser, *Pauline*

Mysticism, and Mersch, *Theology of the Mystical Body*, for a theological reflection on the New Testament notions.

121. This aspect of sacramentality will be treated extensively in chapter 27.

122. Quite recently the theme of eschatology has been the object of considerable theological study, to a large extent because of New Testament studies which discovered the prominence of this in the thought of primitive Christianity. Among the most recent developments are the so-called theologies of hope, such as J. Moltmann, *The Theology of Hope* (New York, 1967); J. Metz, ed., *The Evolving World and Theology* (New York, 1967); and R. Alves, *A Theology of Human Hope* (Washington, D.C., 1969).

123. See Cooke, *God of Space and Time*, pp. 107–12.

124. See Jungmann, pp. 13–18; Cooke, *Christian Community*, pp. 127–57.

125. See Wach, pp. 58–70; Pedersen, pp. 29–46.

126. See Fuller, pp. 125–31.

127. See Schelkle, pp. 59–86.

128. J.-P. Audet, "Esquisse historique du genre littéraire de la 'bénédiction' juive et de l' 'eucharistie' chrétienne," *Revue biblique* 65 (1958), pp. 371–99.

129. See H. Strathmann, "Martys," *TDNT*, vol. 4, pp. 489–501.

130. See *Constitution on the Church*, 12.

131. See Schelkle, *Discipleship*; also K. Rengstorf, "Mathetes," *TDNT*, vol. 4, pp. 441–61.

132. Schelkle, pp. 69–70.

133. *Ibid.*, pp. 82–83.

134. See A. Neher, *L'essence du prophetisme* (Paris, 1955), pp. 282–350.

135. See Zimmerli-Jeremias, pp. 25–36.

CHAPTER 2

Ante-Nicene Developments

Christianity is a community possessed, according to the Christian faith, with a unique vitality that stems from its animation by the Spirit of the risen Christ.[1] For this reason, the faith and experience and life forms of the New Testament communities, uniquely normative though they may be for future generations, can never be the static pattern for those future generations. As an eschatological reality the church is always coming into being, always new in a radical and sometimes unexpected fashion.[2] For that reason, the study of the historical evolution of Christianity must form an integral part of any study of the nature of the church, or of any element in it such as its ministry.[3] Because that evolution is organic, with a basic identity and mission gradually unfolding, the beginnings of the church do instruct us about its being and role, but they do not tell the whole story. Indeed, the fullest story to date is told by the present-day reality of Christianity; but to be understood adequately the church of today must be known in terms of the developments that explain its present existence.[4]

To divide that two-thousand-year history into certain periods (such as patristic, medieval, Renaissance and Reformation, etc.) is, of course, arbitrary, but for practical purposes it may be necessary to do so. To some extent the first period we will have to examine, that which stretches from the end of the first century to the Council of Nicaea in 325, does form a natural unity.[5] It embraces that period when early Christianity crystallized the institutional forms in which it would express the apostolic tradition, when it first had to

test and refine these expressions under the impact of persecution and heresy and intimate contact with secular culture, when it grew from a relatively small body of scattered communities into the powerful social entity that forced the attention and finally the respect of the Roman Empire.

These were particularly critical years, too, in the development of Christian ministry, that of the church's ministry to mankind and that of specialized ministry within the community. As the church grew in size, it was inevitable that there be a certain dilution of the commitment and enthusiasms of the early decades, and it proved increasingly necessary to devise methods, such as the formalized catechumenate, to safeguard and foster the spirit and insights upon which the community lived. Besides, this was the period in which the church realized increasingly the fact that it was meant to continue in historical existence for a long period, and this inevitably induced an attitude of "settling down." Whether one accepts fully or not the interpretation of H. Werner which stresses the "deeschatologizing" of Christianity at this point,[6] it is true that there is a shift of emphasis to the kingdom of God as it exists in the historical church. This inevitably changes people's view towards those offices within the community that are necessary to make an earthly "kingdom" run effectively! Ministry is still seen as having "community" as its goal, but the idea of this community is undergoing change.

To trace in detail the historical sequence of that second- and third-century development of Christian ministry is not our intent. There already exist a number of careful historical studies that attempt just this for the church as a whole, or more specifically for its ministry.[7] One thinks immediately of *The Apostolic Ministry* (produced by eminent Anglican scholars in the 1940s), or E. Schweizer's *Early Church Order* or von Campenhausen's *Ecclesiastical Office and Church Authority* or the writings of Jean Colson; or the treatment contained in Küng's *The Church* or the Fliche-Martin *Histoire de l'Eglise* or the new German *Handbuch der Geschichte der Kirche*. What may be more profitable than any attempt to add to this impressive list would be an attempt to isolate from this body of historical data some of the threads of development that help throw light on the actuality of ministry during this period and on the manner in which Christian faith viewed that ministry.

Social Evolution of the Church

Deeschatologizing

Living in the midst of one of the most turbulent periods of human history, and itself coming into increasing contact with secular society, the church of the first three centuries could not but be subject to forces of great social evolution.[8] But perhaps even more important than the forces that played upon it from outside was the fact that the human community which was the church was still in its early stages of self-discovery and self-establishment. Christians were still in the process of adjusting their eschatologically oriented faith to the exigencies of human history and to the task of bringing salvation to men in the concrete framework of that history.

One can perhaps make too much of the process of "deeschatologizing" which touched the first hundred years or so of Christianity's existence.[9] But without having to view the first Christians as unrealistic visionaries who sat around waiting for the imminent occurrence of the Parousia, and the next generation as slightly disillusioned realists who decided to make the best of the situation, it does seem that there was some need for Christians, around the turn of the first century, to adjust their understanding of the church's relation to history.[10] The essential direction of Christian life towards the fulfillment that would come only with passage through death and entry into "eternal life" remained: if no other evidence was available to us the symbolism of Christian baptism as it was understood throughout that period would witness to the basic Christian longing for the next life.[11] At the same time, the end of the world no longer seemed about to happen. The "final era" had dawned with the death and resurrection of Jesus,[12] but it was now uncertain as to how long this final epoch would last. While individual Christians might well pass from this life into possession of unending happiness in union with Christ,[13] the Christian community as a social reality could apparently now look forward to an extended historical existence.

Which raised the question: What was the role of Christianity in this continuing historical existence? Obviously, Christians were to preach the gospel and live it out in their daily activity, but what forms should this take as Christians found themselves confronted by a broad spectrum of cultural and social groupings? And as the activities of Christians took on new forms to meet the changing context, what forms should the community itself as a social entity adopt? It is not surprising, then, to see rather radical mutations in the social structures of Christianity between the time of the early Pauline Epistles and that of Cyprian or Origen. What is surprising is that there was, despite the multiplicity of forces affecting the church, the amount of social continuity that is demonstrated by the historical evidence. There was a clear line of identity, but this is far from the naive picture that sees all the social structures of Christianity as coming ready-made from some historical action of Jesus himself;[14] instead, early Christianity sees the abiding activity of the risen Christ through his Spirit as providing continuity for the church as it goes through historical change.

Ideal of Martyrdom

A clear indication of the limits that one must put on any contention that early Christianity became increasingly deeschatologized is the extent to which martyrdom became and remained an abiding ideal.[15] Luke's account in Acts of the vicissitudes undergone by Stephen, by the apostles, and by Paul witnesses to the emergence of that ideal by the time he wrote.[16] And the evidence of the next two centuries is too clear and abundant to need more than quick mention. Ignatius' letters,[17] the description of Polycarp's death,[18] Cyprian's letters,[19] the writings of such apologists as Justin[20]—all reflect the unquestioned and enduring conviction of early Christianity that this earthly life could not end more felicitously than in enduring suffering and death "for the name of Christ." This, more than anything else that one might accomplish in the course of one's Christian life, brought one to the realization of that initiation into Christ which began with baptism.[21]

As one reflects on this, it becomes clear that the position of martyrdom as the ultimate expression of Christian life made for a radical egalitarianism in early Christianity. While it was true that a large proportion of martyrs were leaders of Christian communities, *episkopoi* or *diakonoi*, there were many who occupied no previous position of eminence within the community. Some were even children. It is possible to see how this witness of martyrdom, open to all and even demanded of them when persecution confronted them, tended to limit or even challenge the kind of authority attached to officials within the early church. Probably the classic case was the struggle between Cyprian and the "confessors" in the Carthaginian community.[22]

Moreover, the prominence of this ideal of witness through death, clearly observable even to non-Christians who found it utterly perplexing, constituted a radical challenge to the various cultural contexts into which Christianity moved. This was a challenge felt by non-Christians, but perhaps even more impor-tantly by the Christian communities themselves. It served as a criterion by which they could judge whether they were still "not of this world" even though sociologically more and more involved in it.[23] The heroism displayed by many acted as a stimulus to the lofty ethical and spiritual ideals of the early church; but the sad experience of widespread defection, particularly in the Decian persecution, the first that really touched a large cross section of the community, led to painful evaluation of Christian life and institutions.[24] Out of this came sweeping modification of certain social patterns such as that of the catechumenate, and it affected the evolution of "office" within the church. Again, the judgment that was passed upon church leaders who failed to measure up in times of stress provides us with evidence regarding early Christian understanding about the role of these leaders.[25]

Merging of Two Structures

Coming more specifically to the evolution of institutional patterns in the ante-Nicene church, the evidence gathered by scholarly investigation seems to point to the coalescence of the somewhat divergent patterns that marked the apostolic communities, a coalescence that is already well advanced by the time of the pastoral Epistles.[26] Drawn from the heritage of Judaism, the presbyterate seems to have been a prominent agency for directing and nurturing the life of early communities, particularly those which more directly owed their origins to Jewish Christianity.[27] In these communities in their first decades of existence the governance of the teaching, liturgy, and shared social life of the group was entrusted for the most part to a group of "elders."[28] Apparently, these were not necessarily the oldest members of the community[29] but rather those who had some credentials, such as age and experience, association with the original disciples of Jesus, being the first converts to Christianity in the group, which indicated a right to leadership.[30] If and when an apostle or a recognized prophet visited the community, he exercised a superior but transitory authority.[31] However, the ordinary day-by-day direction of the community's Christian life rested with the corporate leadership of the presbyterate.

Another pattern, which seems to have been more common in the Hellenistic communities, derived from the practice of men like Paul who, having established a community, left some designated person in charge.[32] Or, if he did not himself appoint someone to provide for the community, he encouraged the Christians themselves to select someone who would bear this responsibility.[33] Associated with these *episkopoi* but subject to them were the *diakonoi*, appointed to help carry out such aspects of community care as providing for the poor or assisting in worship.[34] As convergence of these patterns began, *episkopoi* did not replace the presbyters but worked along with them. Very likely the chief leader of the community was picked from the presbyterate and in many instances even selected by it.[35] The impression one gets is that the presbyters acted as a corporate counseling, or even judicial, body;[36] but the executive role of directing the community rested with the *episkopos* assisted by the deacons.[37]

These elements rapidly developed into the tripartite structure which is indicated by the Pastorals,[38] sharply described in the Ignatian letters,[39] and firmly established throughout the church by the end of the second century.[40] Yet, it would be an anachronism to see the bishop-presbyter-deacon pattern as three levels of one pastoral office, with the bishop possessing the totality and delegating much of it to presbyters and somewhat less to the deacons. For the most part, the situation in the early churches seems to have been one in which it was the deacons who were most closely related to the bishops and totally dependent upon him for their authority;[41] whereas the presbyters, though receiving some of their functions (particularly in liturgy) by delegation from the bishop,[42] retained a certain autonomy in setting policy for the life of the community. While the precise office exercised by *episkopoi* only gradually came to be defined (and then inadequately), it seems that from the beginning they were looked upon as "officials" (as were the deacons in their own way), whereas the presbyters were not. At least, this is the situation well into the second century.[43]

At the same time that this coalescence of originally distinct patterns of polity was occurring, there was a second merging of "offices" within early Christianity: that of itinerant and residential ministries. In the early decades, traveling apostles and prophets were largely instrumental in founding Christian communities and in nourishing their faith. The *Didache* bears witness to the eminent position of such visiting leaders, to their role in worship and in teaching,[44] but also testifies to the need to pass some judgment on the authority and honor claimed by such men.[45] As the local churches became more stable, they increasingly provided and depended upon members of their own community, not only upon *episkopoi* and the presbyters but upon others who acted as teachers and prophets. One thinks, for example, of the role played by Hermas in the second-century Roman community. However, the influence of visiting teachers and prophets did not completely fade out of the picture—the role exercised by Origen in the third century shows this quite clearly. By this time, though, such teaching is considered proper to members of the clergy,[46] and the clergy is under the authority of the monarchical episcopate.[47]

Not only did the itinerant ministry tend to vanish as its functions became unnecessary or were absorbed by resident ministers, but the "offices" of prophet and teacher, originally quite distinct from the *episkopos-presbyteros-diakonos* structure, were increasingly taken over by the episcopacy.[48] Again, the process is not total, for both teachers and prophets are in evidence well beyond Nicaea. Yet, the third century provides no examples of prophets with the influence and autonomy of Hermas, nor of teachers with the independent status of Clement of Alexandria.[49] Already, at the beginning of the second century, Ignatius lays claim to prophetic endowment for the bishop in the performance of his role,[50] and one finds the same claim being made by as administratively oriented a bishop as Cyprian in the third century.[51] And the *Didascalia* indicates that at least in the Syrian church of the third century the episcopacy has laid quite exclusive claim to the office of authoritative teaching.[52]

By the end of the pre-Nicene period, the episcopacy has clearly taken over full authority for the direction of church life. They do not personally exercise all the roles, but official authority in the church is seen to be vested in them; theirs is the special divine guidance that safeguards the faith and effectiveness of the church; they are the ones from whom comes, by way of delegation, whatever responsibility and authority is exercised by others.[53] Governance of church life, even in its most spiritual aspects, is by Nicaea the almost total preserve of a distinct group, the clergy which finds its focus and source of power in the episcopacy.

Functional Evolution

A Community Holy and Unified

One could view the increasing possession of authority by the early episcopacy as a manifestation of that tendency to seize increasing power which is so often characteristic of those in official position. While it would be naive to exclude all such human weakness from the bishops of the early church (and certainly men like Tertullian were not loath to level such accusations!),[54] the historical evidence points rather to such increased power being a response to the needs of an expanding Christianity.[55]

In the earliest stages of its existence, the church, consisting as it did in relatively small and closely knit communities, could depend on strongly personal and charismatic direction. This could, and generally did, provide for safeguarding the accuracy and growth of faith and for nurturing unity based on love. Within a short time, however, the rapid growth of Christianity and its increased contact with elements in the surrounding culture

set up new demands. Even the New Testament literature indicates the tensions and differences of view that arose as Christians attempted to understand in more detail the content and implications of the revelation that had come in the Christ-event.[56] In that situation of the primitive church, the Twelve or those closely associated with them could resolve many of the emergent problems. But such a solution could not last beyond the end of the first century; provision had to be made by those who bore responsibility for the churches.

All the evidence points to the concerted effort of those in authority to preserve unity within each community and within "the great church." Beginning with Paul himself, the moral catechesis and exhortation given the Christian communities stresses the evil of dissension and disruption.[57] This clearly reflects the manner in which the leadership of the early church saw itself charged with the task of preserving this unity of the one Body of Christ. And since the two great threats to this unity were erroneous teaching and sinfulness in Christian life, it was inevitable that the episcopacy increasingly concern itself with maintaining unity of belief and purity of life. Rather than demonstrating a selfish quest for power and influence, this development testifies to the manner in which the early episcopate measured its responsibilities and established its identity of office in terms of the needs of the church.

As H. von Campenhausen has stressed in his study of early church authority,[58] early Christianity was soon confronted and perplexed by the problem of sin within the community. Unquestionably, the church was to be a community of "saints," living a life of ethical purity and unblemished spiritual dedication. Such was undoubtedly beyond ordinary human attainment, but Christians were linked with Christ himself through baptism and filled with the spiritual power of his own Spirit; the work of their perfection was, then, the work of God himself.[59] What, then, to do with members of the community who gravely betrayed their Christian role, in whom apparently the Spirit was not allowed to work? Was it proper, or even possible, for them to remain as members of the Body of Christ?

Though the exact nature of the procedure during the first two centuries is unclear, there is definite evidence that from the very beginning Christian communities both excommunicated and reconciled gravely sinful members.[60] New Testament literature attests to the origins of this Christian claim to deal with grave sin, a claim that is grounded in Christ's granting of the power to "bind or loose."[61] By the time of Tertullian, the decisive activity in such cases has clearly resided with the episcopacy for some time;[62] and the bishops' assertion of the right both to exclude and to reconcile sinners is justified by the developing notion of apostolic succession.[63] However, the practical process of dealing with the reconciliation of sinners, reflecting in their regard the mercy of Christ, without at the same time endangering the spiritual idealism of the church by moral laxity, seems to have done more to shape penitential discipline than any theological speculation on the episcopal office.[64] Theological discussion there was, on the effect of grave sin and on the "power of the keys," but insofar as this influenced episcopal exercise of authority it seems to have been a case of the theology being a justification for practical judgment already made rather than speculative grounds for decisions yet to be made.[65]

Formal Teaching

Several factors demanded increased organization of and control over the process of teaching. Large numbers of converts to Christianity confronted the church with the need of providing a careful process of catechumenate preparation for baptism and a continuing catechesis. This need became painfully evident at times of large-scale defection, as in the Decian persecution. And while the task now exceeded the possibility of the bishop handling it personally, the supervision of such educational programs became clearly the responsibility of the bishop.[66] He watched over the formation of the catechumens. It was primarily his function, as Justin already indicates in the middle of the second century, to form the community's understanding through the Eucharistic homily.[67] Throughout the pre-Nicene period there were teachers who functioned probably with some approbation of the community and its episcopal leadership but not precisely as delegates of the bishop.[68] Yet, by the third century the principle seems quite well established that instruction regarding the faith is reserved to the clergy, and therefore under the bishop's guidance.[69]

Some such official judgment on the explanations of Christianity being given the faithful was needed because there quickly developed a potentially dangerous diversity of religious teaching. This was much more than a difference of acceptable interpretations; the type of "insight" expounded by the various forms of Gnosticism implied a radical negation of Christianity as the New Testament communities understood it.[70] The essential heritage of Christian revelation was in danger of being lost; Christian communities were consequently in danger of ceasing to be communities of faith in the true mystery of Christ; and the episcopacy found it necessary to assert its communal faith, grounded in continuity with apostolic teaching, as a criterion that could safeguard the authenticity and integrity of the community's belief.

Emergence of "Clergy"

In the earliest decades of Christianity the functions of Christian ministry seem to have been for the most part a less than full-time occupation. Even some apostles who gave up a settled situation of employment and journeyed from community to community did, as Paul indicates about himself,[71] spend part of their time in other work. This situation was one, however, that started to disappear as a common pattern as soon as the size of Christianity and the complexity of its community life developed. Increasingly, the responsibilities of bishops and deacons tended to absorb their full attention; more and more of the presbyters were drawn into this same kind of full-time ecclesiastical employment.[72] By the end of the third-century there is, at least in the more populous sections of the Christian world, an established pattern of clergy who are already seen as "official" Christians in contrast to the remainder of the faithful.[73]

While the open recognition of the Constantinian period did not yet exist, non-Christian civil officials are already dealing in the third century with the "officialdom" of the Christian church. Such ecclesiastical officers are given the "honor" of special attention during times of persecution, being singled out for imprisonment and death.[74] They are also the ones with whom Roman officials deal on matters of property, etc.[75] Granted that this is a viewpoint on the structures of the Christian community taken by outsiders, it still reflects to some extent the image that the Christian community must have projected. All indications are that the dichotomy between clergy and laity, which would become more evident in later centuries, already existed in identifiable form by the beginning of the fourth century.[76] At least in this one vital element of church structure, the so-called Constantinian revolution intensified an already existent pattern rather than initiating it.

Continuity of Structure

Missionary Orientation of Communities

Even with the gradual and increasing appropriation of official functions to established clergy, it must not be forgotten that there continued to be broad participation of Christians in evangelization and in the internal nurture of the church's life.[77] Nowhere in the literature of the early Christian church is there indication of an organized campaign, under the direction of official church leadership, to obtain converts to Christianity.[78] There is every indication that, on the contrary, the remarkable spread of Christianity during the early centuries of the church's existence was the result of widespread "unofficial" activity on the part of laity as well as clergy.[79]

Christianity remained essentially a missionary community: the gospel had been committed to the entire people, the responsibility of witnessing to it was the task of every Christian —by his words and by his life. The supreme witness, of course, was to be granted the privilege of facing death "for the name of Christ." While persecution generally tended to concentrate on the leadership of the church, it was not limited to those occupying official positions. Thus, when it was a question of giving fullest implementation to that very function which pertained most centrally to the role of the Twelve,[80] that of bearing witness (*marturein*) to the mystery of Christ's life and resurrection, all members of the church could participate with equal "validity."

Sacramental Practice

If the entire community's sharing in missionary witness to the gospel indicates the basic continuity in the early church's purpose and finality, the relative homogeneity of liturgical life, from one century to another and across the increasingly complex geographical span, is a striking evidence of the unity and continuity of external structures. Despite the elements of expansion and development, which changing social conditions within the church dictated, there is an immediately recognizable identity between the baptism and Eucharistic action of the New Testament communities and that found in the *Apostolic Tradition* of Hippolytus or reflected in the writings of Cyprian.[81] This would seem to indicate a priori an unavoidable continuity in "official" functions: if, as New Testament texts indicate, the infant church thought of itself as a community existing for the purpose of worship;[82] and if, as is logical and attested to by early historical witness, those entrusted with the well-being of the community would have had a guiding function in this worship; and if the fundamental understanding and implementation of such worship actions remained constant, then this basic function of church leadership would have remained the same throughout these first few centuries. However, there was greater diversity in the earlier stages regarding those who could act as liturgical leaders. The *Didache* gives clear evidence that visiting apostles and prophets were considered proper "celebrants" for the Eucharist,[83] and that the role of resident *episkopoi* as liturgical leaders followed from the fact that one could not rely on such apostles or prophets being present in a community with any regularity.[84] On the other hand, the letters of Ignatius witness to a context in at least a fairly good-sized section of the early-second-century church where the *episkopos* is the *leitourgos* by the very nature of his role, and where the very existence of the Eucharist and of baptism is viewed as dependent upon him.[85] Justin also seems to reflect a situation where the bishop is the established celebrant.[86] Really, when one examines the first two centuries of Christian liturgy, what one sees is a clear continuity in the liturgical functions that Christian sacramental life requires, but development as to the "officials" who exercise these functions. Until well into the second century, perhaps even the third, one cannot say with assurance that throughout the "great church" the authority to function as liturgical leader is seen to be vested only in the episcopate.[87]

Apostolic Succession

Central to the continuity of Christian faith and life, and to the continuity amidst evolution of ecclesiastical office, was the notion of apostolic succession.[88] It was the original group of Jesus' disciples, especially the Twelve, who had been the privileged witnesses to and interpreters of the Christ-event. What they believed in, the saving death and resurrection of Jesus who was therein revealed as Messiah and Lord, was the indispensable object of faith upon which the internally unifying belief of early Christianity depended. If the Christian community of the second or third century was to lay claim legitimately to identity as Christian, then its faith had to agree essentially with that of the early apostles. Origen in apostolic teaching, or at the very least congruence with that teaching, functioned quite explicitly as a norm for es-

tablishing canonical New Testament writings[89] and for judging the orthodoxy and credentials of those who laid claim to the role of teacher within the community.[90] Thus Irenaeus could justify his own explanation of Christian belief by pointing out that he had received it from Polycarp who himself had received it from John.[91] There is abundant and clear evidence that the idea of "apostolic succession" (or, closely allied with it, that of "apostolic tradition") exerted important influence on the thought and life of the early Christian centuries. What is not so clear is that which we will have to examine more carefully later: in what manner is this "apostolic succession" understood? It is altogether possible (as we will try to show) that underneath the surface continuity there took place an unrecognized but critically important evolution of meaning.

Changes of Attitude

"Settling Down"

Inseparably linked with the evolving understanding of the eschatological nature of Christianity, but more subtle than any explicit ideas about the nature of the church, was the attitude of "settling down."[92] This came in stages: as the second and third generations of converts came into the church without the Parousia having occurred,[93] as the individual communities became larger and able to rely on their own internal resources and leadership, as Christianity became increasingly important and accepted as a part of the larger social scene (even when such recognition took the form of persecution), and finally as it receives full recognition as a powerful social entity with the Constantinian era.

Such a "new" attitude of accepting the prospect of a long historical future for Christianity and of accepting the identity of a stable and structured social reality had inevitable and basic implications for Christian attitudes towards the functions of ministry within the community. It could not but shift emphasis to the "official" and institutionalized types of ministry which promised the kind of stability and defined pattern that more charismatic activities could not supply. This is not to say that second- and third-century Christianity lost the notion of being a Spirit-filled community; but the Spirit was providing for the needs of the church in its new existential situation by working increasingly through the more structured agencies of the church's life.[94]

Montanism and Gnosticism

Such attachment of the Spirit's workings to the role of the clergy was in large part an answer to the perplexing but all-important question: Just where and how is the Spirit of Christ manifest in the church's life? From the beginning it was assumed that the Spirit did not speak exclusively through those (like the *episkopoi* or *presbyteroi*) entrusted with the pastoral care of the communities. There was a manifestation of the Spirit through prophets and teachers which was so important that, for a time at least, these constituted recognized ministries within the church.[95] Quickly, however, there arose the need for distinguishing the true from the false, among both prophets and teachers.[96] This need became acute in the second century, when Gnostic teachers claimed an ultimacy for their "new gospel" and Montanist prophets claimed the same final authority for their rigoristic understandings of Christian life. While neither prophets nor teachers vanish totally from the scene in mainstream Christianity, Gnosticism tends to make autonomous teaching suspect and Montanism tends to discredit the prophetic voice in the church.

Both prophecy and teaching are, however, intrinsic to the life of Christian faith in community. They did not pass out of existence but rather were more and more assumed to be part of the episcopal office and charism.[97] There is very early evidence of bishops seeing themselves as supreme teachers of the faith within their communities;[98] to some extent, even the Pastorals point in this direction.[99] And both Ignatius and Cyprian testify to episcopal claims to possess prophetic inspiration as part of the Spirit's support of them in

their pastoral function.[100] There is not yet a claim to exclusive possession of prophetic and instructional authority by the bishops; but by the fourth century it seems assumed that the highest level or fullest sharing in these functions does pertain to the episcopacy, and for that reason the episcopate can pass judgment on the acceptability of other prophecy or teaching within the church.[101]

Images of the Church

One thing that bears careful study is the imagery that began to attach to the church during this period.[102] Even the use of the image of "body," which unquestionably contains a strong element of continuity with the Pauline understanding of the church and of its various ministries,[103] begins to reflect a certain process of personifying the church.[104] Much more clearly does the image of "holy mother church" indicate the extent to which the church is assuming a dimension other than that of the experienced community in which the Christians are active. "The church" is starting to be viewed as an entity to some extent apart from and beyond the people who make it up, a living abstraction with an identity and essence and destiny of its own, a sacred personification that is the object of Christ's own love and sanctifying activity and that in turn watches over the baptized "children of God" entrusted to its care.[105] By the fourth century we are already beginning to find evidence of the church being viewed as the kind of "moral person" with which the technical abstractions of legal codes can deal;[106] but this view of the church as a "legal personality" (which assumes ever greater importance as we move into the Middle Ages) has already been prepared for by the emergence within Christianity itself of the view of the church as a "sacred personality."

When one puts together the psychological overtones of an image like that of "mother church" and those attached to the image of shepherd as used in Scripture for the pastoral office[107] and as then attached to the episcopal-presbyteral-diakonal ministry,[108] one can begin to see the impact this will have on the way the laity will view their own role in the church and their relationship to those in positions of official leadership. The spiritual care that one would expect from a mothering church is what one expects from a shepherding hierarchy. In thinking of the church as "mother" the Christian would think of the church as distinct from himself, as set over against him, and as doing for him precisely what he has come to understand as the task of the episcopacy.[109] In the realm of imagery, attitude, and implicit understanding we are, then, on the verge of identifying the church with its clerical ministers.[110] Within this context, a new "official" meaning can be read into the Pauline rhetoric of "palingenesis," which uses the imagery of begetting to describe the event of conversion and discipleship,[111] or into the Petrine Epistles in which baptism is described as new birth.[112]

Emergence of New Ideas of Ecclesiastical Structure

The "Great Church," a Civil Reality

Along with these changing attitudes and images, which exerted a subtle but powerful influence on Christians' understanding of the church and its ministries, there also developed a number of explicitly expressed ideas that both reflected the evolving ministry of the church and contributed to that evolution. One of the more influential of these was the notion of "the great church."[113] It is true that the early Christian communities had a clear sense of identity with one another. There was just one Lord, one gospel, one baptism.[114] Yet, by and large, the notion of "church" attached to the individual community; and even the more general perspective of Ephesians cannot too easily be used to support the application of "church" to the entire community of believers.[115]

Within a relatively short time, however, the notion of a worldwide community, of a spiritually unified people of God, came to explicit expression and common acceptance. Constant interchange between the churches by visits and letters, the quest for a universal agreement in such liturgical matters as the date of Easter, the assembly and acceptance of a common body of sacred writings, the gradual emergence of certain more important centers (such as Rome and Alexandria) which in turn were closely related to one another—all of this contributed to the understanding of "the church," the *ekklesia katholike*.

What contributed to, or at least accompanied, this "discovery" of the universal church was the increasing extent to which non-Christian elements of society, particularly the Roman government, had to deal with the church as an unavoidable reality. Not only was there within a given location, such as Rome, an identifiable group of Christians, there was also an identifiable link with believers in other places. The very notion of a general persecution supposes a recognition of a widespread religious group, the church.

Apostolic Tradition

We have already mentioned the need that was soon felt to apply some criterion in discerning true from false prophecy, true from false catechesis. It seems to have been an unquestioned assumption that in some fashion the teaching of the Twelve, the *didache ton apostolon*, must provide an abiding yardstick for orthodoxy. Not only was teaching, written or oral, assessed by virtue of its origin in apostolic teaching or because of its conformity (or nonconformity) to such clearly apostolic teaching, but this notion of apostolic tradition, i.e., of instruction and witness coming down in a line of succession from the first followers of Jesus, was formulated into a principle to which the episcopacy could appeal to vindicate the authenticity of their teaching.[116]

Within a relatively short time, though with some hesitation as to the exact limits (e.g., Hermas and Barnabas), the collection of writings we know as the New Testament obtained recognition as canonical writing.[117] And studies in the history of the New Testament text leave no doubt that the criterion for inclusion in this corpus of normative literature was the fact (or at least belief) of derivation from apostolic teaching.[118] We see this attribution to apostolic origin working not only with the accepted canonical literature but also in the names attributed to credal or liturgical collections—as *Didache apostolon, constitutiones apostolicae, paradosis apostolon.* However, it was primarily with reference to the books of the New Testament that the teachers of the early church applied the notion of apostolic tradition, and then used these writings as a basis for their exposition of Christian faith. The use of some New Testament texts as guides to teaching antedates such formal appeal to tradition, and probably antedates the final formulation of the text itself and its acceptance as canonical—one thinks of the writings of Clement of Rome or Justin, or even Irenaeus.[119]

However, the understanding of "tradition" was not limited to the preservation and exposition of canonical writings; it was applied to the activity of bishops and other teachers of the faith. One must be careful in evaluating (first of all, in observing!) this phenomenon of the early church. In the earlier stages of this process, it seems quite clear that a given bishop would appeal to the pedagogical fact that he himself had been carefully instructed by his predecessor, who in turn had been instructed by one of the Twelve or at least by one of their original disciples.[120] Thus, the appeal was to a linear transmission of understanding through teaching rather than to a guarantee of trustworthiness because of possession of an office (the episcopacy) by way of traceable linear descent. In such a context, others in the community could equally lay claim to possession of apostolic tradition; but the episcopal "descent" offered a clear and accessible instance of such a link with the Twelve, thereby certifying not only the faith of the *episkopos* but that of the community he headed.[121] H. von Campenhausen seems quite accurate in linking the emerging notion of "authority attached to ecclesiastical office as such" with the exercise of judgment against sin rather than with the exercise of the teaching ministry.[122]

Authority of Office

This leads us to a critically important element in our investigation of ministry in the pre-Nicene church. Granted that authority did attach to those who occupied ecclesiastical office (and most importantly the office of bishop), what was seen to be the source and nature of this authority? Did it derive from the minister's possession of knowledge (which he might have gained by learning from the apostolic tradition, or from special inspiration of the Spirit), of holiness, or of other gifts such as that of skill in governing; and was it therefore proportionate to the intrinsic "quality" possessed? Or, on the other hand, did the episcopal authority derive precisely from the social reality of "office" (granting, of course, in this view that the authority was bestowed upon the office by Christ himself), and even function somewhat independently of the qualifications of a given incumbent in the office? This question has never been answered with satisfactory clarity or conviction, though it has come to the surface repeatedly during the last two thousand years and has served to divide Christians into opposing ecclesiastical camps. The evidence of early Christian documents seems to indicate that there was progression from "quality" to "office."

NOTES

1. See H. de Lubac, *Splendour of the Church* (New York, 1956), pp. 55–86; H. Küng, *The Church* (New York, 1967), pp. 150–203.
2. Though the need for change in the church has become inescapably clear, there is still considerable reluctance to admit that this change may be more than a superficial adjustment to the times. See, e.g., the open-minded but cautious and limited approach of J. Newman, *Change and the Catholic Church* (Baltimore, 1965); or the

hostility and fear aroused (at least in some circles) by a book such as Y. Congar's *Vraie et fausse reforme dans l'Eglise*, 2d ed. (Paris, 1968).

3. On the role of church history in theology, see H. Jedin's introductory essay in the *Handbook of Church History* (New York, 1965), vol. 1, pp. 1–56.

4. This is particularly true of the present-day church's faith and doctrine: the intrinsic understanding of Christianity possessed by today's Christians must be seen against the background of its historical evolution.

5. For bibliography on this period, see *Handbook of Church History*, pp. 459–505.

6. M. Werner, *The Formation of Christian Dogma* (London, 1957).

7. Some helpful books (in addition to those mentioned in the text) are: J. Daniélou and H. Marrou, *The Christian Centuries*, vol. 1 (London, 1964); W. Clebsch and C. Jaekle, *Pastoral Care in Historical Perspective* (Englewood Cliffs, N.J., 1964); H. Niebuhr and D. Williams, *The Ministry in Historical Perspective* (New York, 1956); J. Bartlet, *Church-life and Church-order During the First Four Centuries* (Oxford, 1943); R. Grant, *The Apostolic Fathers* (New York, 1964), vol. 1, pp. 141–73; P. Carrington, *The Early Christian Church* (Cambridge, 1957).

8. See C. Cochrane, *Christianity and Classic Culture* (London, 1944).

9. See the perceptive criticism of Werner's thesis by J. Pelikan, "Beyond Bellarmine and Harnack," *Theology Digest* 16 (1968), pp. 302–3.

10. See L. Goppelt, *Apostolic and Post-Apostolic Times* (London, 1970), pp. 108–51; he views the adjustment of early Christianity to its historical situation as a struggle against secularization.

11. See J. Daniélou, *The Bible and the Liturgy* (Notre Dame, 1956), pp. 35–113.

12. On the link of this notion with early Christian celebration of Sunday as the Lord's Day and the fulfillment of Sabbath, see *ibid.*, pp. 222–61.

13. This is the view in the famous account of Polycarp's martyrdom, or in Ignatius of Antioch's letter to the Romans.

14. Thus, the oversimplified use of "institution by Christ" as applied to the church or its institutions, or the uncritical denomination of certain elements in the church's external structure as *de jure divino*. For a more critical understanding of such expressions, see the companion articles of E. Schillebeeckx, "The Catholic Understanding of Office in the Church," and G. Lindbeck, "Lutheran Doctrine of the Ministry," *Theological Studies* 30 (1969), pp. 567–87, 588–612.

15. See H. von Campenhausen, *Die Idee des Martyriums in der alten Kirche* (Göttingen, 1936).

16. Acts 6:8—7:60; 12:1–17; 21:27—24:27. Situating historically the witness of Acts to the Christian ideal of martyrdom depends, of course, on the position one takes with respect to the dating of Luke-Acts; on this still unresolved question, see J. O'Neill, *The Theology of Acts*, 2d ed. (London, 1970), pp. 1–47, who suggests an early second-century (between 115 and 130) dating.

17. Particularly that to the Romans, with the oft-cited passage 5.3–6.

18. See J. Quasten, *Patrology* (Westminster, Md., 1950), vol. 1, pp. 76–79, on the authenticity and content of the *Martyrium Polycarpi*.

19. Cyprian's most detailed treatment of martyrdom, though it is a gathering of material rather than a finished literary work, is found in the treatise *Ad Fortunatum de exhortatione martyrii*. See Quasten, vol. 2, pp. 361–62.

20. *Trypho* 110.

21. Thus Tertullian (like Hermas before him) sees martyrdom as fully wiping out sin; only the martyrs pass directly from this life to glory: *De resurr. carnis* 43.

22. See K. Baus, *Handbook of Church History*, vol. 1, pp. 330–32.

23. *Epistle to Diognetus* 5–6.

24. See H. Lietzmann, *The Founding of the Church Universal* (London, 1953), pp. 166–70; Baus, pp. 222–26.

25. See Cyprian *Epist.* 59. 10; 65. 1; 67. 6.

26. See E. Schweizer, *Church Order in the New Testament* (London, 1961), pp. 83–86; also Grant, pp. 141–73. Grant's early dating for the Pastorals ("not long after A.D. 70," p. 155) allows little time for such a coalescence.

27. See J. Daniélou, *The Theology of Jewish Christianity* (London, 1964), pp. 346–56; J. Schmitt, "Jewish Priesthood and Christian Hierarchy in the Early Palestinian Communities," *The Sacrament of Holy Orders* (Collegeville, Minn., 1962), pp. 60–74; H. von Campenhausen, *Ecclesiastical Authority and Spiritual Power in the Church of the First Three Centuries* (Palo Alto, Calif., 1969), pp. 76–123.

28. This is the pattern in Jerusalem, most likely also in Rome where Hermas attests to the important role of *presbyteroi* in the early second century (and the earlier letter of Ignatius to the Romans had made no mention of the *episkopos*), and it spread quite quickly to the Pauline churches. While there is no mention of *presbyteroi* in Paul's letters to the Corinthians, the letter of Clement to the Corinthians presupposes the established institution of *presbyteroi*.

29. See Goppelt, pp. 185–86.

30. *Ibid.*; see also Schmitt, pp. 60–74.

31. See Daniélou, *Jewish Christianity*, p. 356. The *Didache* also attests to the special credentials and authority of the visiting apostle, but the residential group that functions in the normal circumstances is not described as *presbyteroi* but as *episkopoi* and *diakonoi (Didache* 15. 1–2.)

32. See 2 Cor. 8:16–20; Phil. 1:1. It is not clear how the *episkopoi* and *diakonoi* of Phil. 1:1 came to possess their role, but the passage from 2 Cor. would seem to indicate that Paul took an active part in establishing the leadership of the communities he founded.

33. Recognition of the various charisms (1 Cor. 8:18ff.) would seem to imply establishment of regular resident leadership, i.e., of *episkopoi*. On the Pauline approach to order within the communities of early Christians, see Schweizer, pp. 89–104; von Campenhausen, *Ecclesiastical Authority*, pp. 55–75.

34. Prior to the Pastorals there is no Pauline clarification of the function or status of *diakonia*, though the linking of *episkopoi* and *diakonia* in the opening lines of Philippians would suggest the episcopal-assistant role that we know from other early testimony. Though the origins of the diaconate are not clear (the Acts cannot be appealed to as evidence, except with careful qualification; see Schweizer, pp. 70–71), all the early testimony indicates their activity in works of mercy and as liturgical assistants. See *1 Clem.* 40. 2–5; Hermas, *Pastor, Vis.* 3. 5. 1; Ignatius *Phil.* 4; *Magn.* 6.

35. This was the contention of Jerome (*Com. in Tit.* 1. 5; *Epist. ad Evangelum*); and seems a normal process of historical evolution.

36. See G. d'Ercole, "The Presbyteral Colleges in the Early Church," *Historical Investigations*, vol. 17 of *Concilium* (New York, 1966), pp. 20–33.

37. See Goppelt, pp. 187–91; Schweizer, pp. 198–203; and von Campenhausen, *Ecclesiastical Authority*, pp. 76–103. The divergence among these three scholars, each of whom is quite measured and careful in his conclusions, indicates the impossibility of arriving at definitive conclusions about the early Christian situation of ministry.

38. Schweizer, pp. 83–88, argues for a coincidence of *episkopos* and *presbyteros* in the Pastorals. See 1 Tim. 3–5.

39. See *Magn.* 6. 1.

40. See Tertullian *De praescriptione* 41; *De baptismo* 17. 1.

41. Thus, in the ordination ceremony of Hippolytus' *Apostolic Tradition* the deacon is "ordained for the service of the bishop" (9. 2), and the *Didascalia* details the fashion in which the deacon serves as the bishop's immediate assistant.

42. See d'Ercole, pp. 29–33. He stresses the historical importance of the more permanent type of functional delegation that begins with Cyprian, a development that undermines the collegial nature of the presbyterate.

43. Though Hermas mentions the prominent position of the *presbyteroi* in the community (*Vis.* 2. 4. 2), presbyters are not included in the listing of offices in *Vis.* 3. 5. 1.

44. *Didache* 10. 7. See J.-P. Audet, *La Didache* (Paris, 1958), pp. 432–33.

45. *Didache* 11. 8–10.

46. See von Campenhausen, *Ecclesiastical Authority*, pp. 238–64.

47. This is quite clear from the synodal activity of the bishops, which is already well established in portions of the church by the beginning of the third century. See Baus, pp. 352–55.

48. See Grant, pp. 172–73.

49. Even Origen, despite his international recognition, was fitted into the clerical structures.

50. *Phil.* 7; *Trall.* 4–6.

51. *Epist.* 16. 4; 66. 10.

52. *Didascalia*, chaps. 8, 11.

53. See Cyprian *Epist.* 66. 8; 33. 1.

54. See Tertullian *De pudicitia* (a work of his Montanist period), chap. 21.

55. Thus, Cyprian's insistence that the bishop (and also the presbyter and deacon) exists for the sake of the community; see von Campenhausen, *Ecclesiastical Authority*, pp. 268–69.

56. See the Pauline-Petrine tension reflected in Acts 15:1ff.

57. Thus, the concern for unity is found in the earliest Pauline letters (e.g., to the Corinthians), in the "body of Christ" teaching of Ephesians, and in the exhortations of the Pastorals; and *1 Clem.* and Ignatius' letters bear witness to the continuance of this concern into the second century.

58. *Ecclesiastical Authority*, pp. 213–37.

59. Rom. 8; see also the *Epistle to Diognetus*.

60. See B. Poschmann, *Penance and the Anointing of the Sick* (New York, 1964), pp. 5–13.

61. Matt. 16:18; 18:18; John 20:23. Of these texts, Matt. 16:18 became the most utilized text in patristic writing about penitential reconciliation, but its first clear citation occurs with Tertullian. See Poschmann, p. 48.

62. Even his Montanist attack upon episcopal power to forgive sin testifies to the established practice of his day.

63. See von Campenhausen, *Ecclesiastical Authority*, pp. 235–37.

64. This is particularly clear in Cyprian's adjustment to the specific needs of the situation he encountered; see Poschmann, pp. 52–62.

65. See von Campenhausen, *Ecclesiastical Authority*, pp. 284–92. He sees in the political thinking of Cyprian a critical deviation in Christian understanding of the church.

66. This is the situation reflected in the *Apostolic Tradition* of Hippolytus at the beginning of the third century.

67. *Apology 1* 67. This is assuming that one can identify the regular president of the Eucharistic assembly with the *episkopos*.

68. See Baus, pp. 229–31.

69. See von Campenhausen, *Ecclesiastical Authority*, pp. 238–64.

70. See Daniélou-Marrou, pp. 55–66.

71. 1 Cor. 9:1–18; 2 Cor. 11:7.

72. This is part of the redefinition of presbyter that takes place in the third to fifth centuries: presbyters become regular individual celebrants of the Eucharist, instead of the earlier custom of collegially celebrating with the bishop; presbyters begin to function as regular pastors of outlying communities; and the early synodal statements indicate that the presbyter in such situations (and soon the presbyter as such) is being viewed as the bishop's delegate and assistant. See d'Ercole, pp. 31–33.

73. Thus, canon 3 of the Council of Ancyra (314) draws a clear distinction between those *ek tou klerou* and *alloi laikoi*, and much the same mentality is reflected in canon 27 of the Council of Elvira (around 305). Interestingly, though presbyters, deacons, and

laity all shared in the proceedings at Elvira, the decrees come out in the name of the bishops: *episcopi universi dixerunt.*

74. See Baus, pp. 222–28.

75. As in the judgment of Emperor Aurelian regarding Paul and Domnus (in 272); see Carrington, vol. 2, p. 473.

76. As early as the beginning of the third century, Tertullian could speak in his *De exhortatione castitatis,* canon 7: "Differentiam inter ordinem et plebem constituit ecclesiae auctoritas, et honor per ordinis concessum sanctificatus."

77. So the participation (already referred to in n. 73) of laity in the Council of Elvira.

78. "The bearers of the Gospel were primarily the congregations and the enthusiasm of individual Christians; there is no indication of a central direction and organization of missionary work. The names of the missionaries are for the most part unknown." (Baus, p. 211.)

79. One of the important elements in this lay activity was the zealous work of women in spreading knowledge of the gospel and in nurturing the life of the early Christian communities. This was in addition to the activity of those women who belonged to the *ordines* of deaconess, widow, or virgin. See Daniélou-Marrou, pp. 239–40.

80. See H. Strathmann, "Martys," *Theological Dictionary of the New Testament* (hereafter referred to as *TDNT*), vol. 4, pp. 489–95.

81. See B. Neunheuser, *Baptism and Confirmation* (New York, 1964), pp. 38–41, 53–60.

82. In chapter 27 we will examine more carefully the *kind* of worship envisaged by primitive Christianity.

83. *Didache* 10. 7.

84. *Ibid.* 15. 1–2.

85. *Smyrn.* 8. 1–2.

86. This, of course, depends upon the interpretation of "president" (*proestos*) in *Apology 1* 67. See T. Jalland, "Justin Martyr and the President of the Eucharist," *Studia Patristica* 5 (1962), p. 85: ". . . It seems hardly possible to deny that Justin means 'the bishop.' . . ." So also L. Barnard, *Justin Martyr: His Life and Thought* (Cambridge, 1967), p. 133, sees the president as a "permanent officer of the church—the 'ruler of the brethren'—whose function included leading public worship, the celebration of the Eucharist and the administration of Church finances."

87. Certainly episcopal celebration (or episcopal delegation of a presbyter as celebrant) was seen as the normal pattern, but there is some evidence that in extraordinary circumstances (e.g., the Carthaginian church during the Decian persecution) a presbyter might take it upon himself to celebrate without episcopal consent or knowledge.

88. For a recent discussion of apostolic succession, indicating the reconsideration that is now being given this term, see *Apostolic Succession,* ed. H. Küng, vol. 34 of *Concilium* (New York, 1968).

89. See F. Schroeder, pp. 391–95 in vol. 2 of *New Catholic Encyclopedia* (New York, 1967); also, O. Cullmann, "Die Tradition und die Festlegung des Kanons durch die Kirche des 2. Jahrhunderts," *Das Neue Testament als Kanon,* ed. E. Käsemann (Göttingen, 1970), pp. 98–108. The essays in this collection give an excellent picture of the various issues relative to the formation of the New Testament canon that are under present-day theological discussion.

90. See Justin *Apology 1* 10. 61 and *Didache* 11. 1–2.

91. See Eusebius *Hist. eccl.* 5. 20. 5–7.

92. "It would be one-sided to regard the Church in the pastoral epistles only as an institution established on earth and settling down for a long time; a 'spiritual welfare institute'; but it is true that the eschatological tension is fading, the 'civic' virtues are insisted on, the conflict with heresies causes difficulties, and a more rigorous order and discipline are becoming apparent." (R. Schnackenburg, *The Church in the New Testament* [New York, 1965], p. 101.)

93. See O. Knoch, *Eigenart und Bedeutung der Eschatologie* (Bonn, 1964), pp. 449–58.

94. The struggle with Montanism illustrates this: both Catholics and Montanists were laying claim to being the authentic expression of the indwelling Spirit. On the early Christian sense of the presence of the risen Christ to the community, see W. Flemming, *Zur Beurteilung des Christentums Justins des Martyrers* (Leipzig, 1893), pp. 32–33.

95. See *Didache* 10–13 ("prophet" and "apostle" are not always distinguishable, e.g., in 11:1–6); Hermas, *Pastor, Vis.* 3. 5. 1; *Mand.* 11.

96. *Didache* 11. 8–10.

97. See Grant, pp. 172–73.

98. This is clearly the implication of the Ignatian letters, of Irenaeus, and somewhat later the *Didascalia*. However, there was an accompanying development of teaching along an autonomous, nonofficial line in the second and third centuries; see von Campenhausen, *Ecclesiastical Authority*, pp. 192–212.

99. See *ibid.*, pp. 106–19.

100. See above, nn. 50, 51.

101. This is reflected in the increased synodal activity of the episcopate at the beginning of the fourth century.

102. See P. Minear, *Images of the Church in the New Testament* (Philadelphia, 1960); J. Daniélou, *From Shadows to Reality* (London, 1960), and *The Bible and the Liturgy* (Notre Dame, 1956); and H. Rahner, *Greek Myth and Christian Mystery* (London, 1963).

103. On the Pauline usage of "body," see A. Wikenhauser, *Pauline Mysticism* (New York, 1960); L. Cerfaux, *The Church in the Theology of St. Paul* (New York, 1959).

104. See Cyprian *De catholicae ecclesiae unitate* 4–5.

105. *Ibid.*, 6: "Habere non potest Deum patrem qui ecclesiam non habet matrem." See also K. Delahaye, *Ecclesia Mater* (Paris, 1964).

106. See Baus, pp. 416–25.

107. See J. Jeremias, "Poimen," *TDNT*, vol. 6, pp. 487–89.

108. *Ibid.*, pp. 497–502.

109. See Y. Congar, pp. 9–10 in his introduction to Delahaye, *Ecclesia Mater*; as Congar points out, the communal sense of "church" was still dominant in the early patristic centuries but gradually gives way to the more juridical understanding.

110. It is interesting in this light to examine the views (until recently quite common in Catholic theology) that the episcopacy is the generating principle for the church (see, e.g., Delahaye, p. 217). Most theologians have tended to put this in terms of spiritual paternity, and common Catholic usage of the term "Father" for parish priests would seem to be another manifestation of this mentality. However, Cardinal Journet in his *Church of the Incarnate Word* (New York, 1955), pp. 93–95, makes a detailed case for the maternal function of the episcopacy in the life of the church.

111. See P. Gutierrez, *La paternité spirituel selon S. Paul* (Paris, 1968).

112. 1 Pet. 1:3–12.

113. See Baus, pp. 150–52.

114. Eph. 4:4–6; 1 Cor. 1:10–16.

115. Although, obviously, the application in Ephesians of such notions as "the body of Christ" to the community of believers implies a profound unity among all those who believe in Christ and are baptized. See J. Fitzmyer, *Jerome Biblical Commentary* (Englewood Cliffs, N.J., 1968), vol. 2, pp. 825–26.

116. See R. Hanson, *Tradition in the Early Church* (London, 1963), pp. 94–117.

117. See the essays of O. Cullmann, "Die Tradition und die Festlegung des Kanons durch die Kirches des 2 Jahrhunderts," and H. von Campenhausen, "Die Enstehung des Neuen Testaments," in *Das Neue Testament als Kanon*, pp. 98–108, 109–23.

118. See R. Brown, *Jerome Biblical Commentary*, vol. 2, pp. 525–26.

119. *Ibid.*, pp. 530–31.

120. See the letter of Irenaeus (to Florinus) contained in Eusebius *Hist. eccl.* 5. 20. 5–7; and *Adv. Haer.* 3. 3. 1.

121. This seems to have been the mentality behind the action of Hegesippus in going to Rome and Corinth, to find the true doctrine in contrast to Gnosticism. See Quasten, vol. 1, p. 285.

122. *Ecclesiastical Authority*, pp. 214–15.

CHAPTER 3

The Patristic Period

The eight centuries that separate the Council of Nicaea from the dawning of the medieval renaissance in the twelfth century marks a tremendous change in the social, intellectual, and spiritual pattern of the church's life, although, significantly, not nearly as great a change in its external liturgical activity. Actually, the period we are considering could logically be divided into two, for there is a great deal that separates the fourth to sixth centuries from what follows it, for one thing the more separated development of East and West from the seventh century onward. Yet, in the realm of Christian ideas and imagery (and of its refinement in theology) the entire eight centuries can justifiably be referred to as "patristic."[1]

Not only is there value in clarifying and honoring this strong continuity between patristic and medieval periods, but it is also most illumining to see the radical differences that separate the Western church of Gregory VII from the church of Athanasius and Basil and Ambrose. This change is critical to any study of the historical evolution of the idea of Christian ministry. At least in theory there is no loss of the notion that the ministry (bishop and lower clergy) exists for the sake of the *edificatio corporis Christi;* but as the sociological reality and the understanding of this *corpus* evolves, so also the role and notion of the ministry evolves.

As we begin to study this period it is good to note what Y. Congar stresses in his *L'ecclésiologie du Haut Moyen Age*: one must distinguish between the inner "mystery" reality of the church and its sociological externalization, and concomitantly between the develop-

ing understanding of these two aspects.[2] The two understandings do not grow in perfectly parallel fashion, nor do they even grow consistent with one another. But both must be taken seriously by the theologian. To quite an extent one is here faced with the distinction between the *faith* of Christianity (individual and community encounter with the mystery of Christ) and the Christian *religion* (the expression of this faith experience in given cultural and institutional forms).[3] These two can and must be distinguished, but they are inseparably intertwined and interacting. To the historian of religions they form one complex process of evolution; to the Christian theologian (who proceeds within the context of faith) they represent the one organic process of the growth of the church (the Body of Christ)—the process in which God still reveals himself to men of Christian faith.[4]

For understanding modern Christian views of ministry, the centuries between Nicaea and Hildebrand are of great importance. As this period ends in the beginnings of twelfth-century renaissance, one is on the verge of a magisterial formulation of Christianity both in thought and in institutions. That formulation has had a governing influence on the practice and thought of Christianity up to the present moment. Much of present-day thinking about Christian ministry is still cast in categories fashioned in the twelfth to fourteenth centuries, or framed in reaction to these categories, and it is therefore vital to study the process by which these categories came into existence.

Period of Great Councils

In many ways, the fourth and fifth centuries, despite the bitter controversy with which they were marked, were the golden age of the episcopacy. Emerging from the period of persecution as the unquestioned leaders of the Christian communities, grounding this leadership in the ideas developed by Cyprian and Irenaeus and the *Didascalia*, the bishops of that period clearly dominate the life of the church, and immensely enrich its intellectual heritage.[5]

This was a period of rapid and basic evolution in the social existence of the church. The Edict of Milan had created a new context for Christian existence; large-scale conversion introduced greater complexity into church organization; increasing absorption of cultural traditions and forms brought with it a pluralism of religious and theological expressions of the gospel—a source of enrichment but also a danger to Christian unity. Prominent as it was, the episcopacy found itself at the very center of this change.

New Relation to Civil Powers

To quite an extent the Christian communities of the first couple of centuries had existed as islands in the midst of a cultural and political world that was oblivious and at times hostile to Christianity.[6] Even during the "great" persecutions of Decius or Diocletian, Christians as a group were not an element of obstruction or opposition to the administrators responsible for the smooth operation of the Roman Empire.[7] Nor did they seek to be. It seems quite clear that Christians advocated acceptance and support of the Roman authorities as long as that did not entail acts of idolatry, that they did not see themselves as basically opposed to the civil authority, and certainly not in the position of exercising any domination over it.[8]

With the reign of Constantine, all this changes rapidly. Although with short-term reverses (such as the rule of Julian), the Christian church passes from rejection to official toleration, and from toleration to involve-ment. Almost immediately, bishops find themselves in the position of part-time functionaries in the civil sphere. There are the special assignments given by the emperor to bishops because of their prominence and acknowledged ability and influence.[9] There are also the regular functions, such as presiding over episcopal courts which now receive full civil recognition.[10] Moreover, with the rapid growth of the church, ecclesiastical activities and disputes begin to have a noticeable impact on the well-being of the civil society; consequently, civil authorities work increasingly with bishops to guarantee tranquillity within the church.[11] And increasingly the relation between the church and civil society comes to the fore as a theological question.[12]

Emergence of Important Episcopal Sees

This is the period when the metropolitan sees acquire considerable prominence and the patriarchates emerge.[13] Several of them (Alexandria, Rome, Antioch, Carthage) had already staked their claim to importance. These preserve their eminence and are joined by others—Milan, Caesarea, and especially Constantinople. Situated as they often were in the cities that were long-standing cultural and political capitals, these principal bishoprics inherited the local traditions, loyalties, and animosities. Thus, the theological differences between Alexandria and Antioch were to some extent a Christianized version of the age-old conflict of Egypt with Mesopotamia. The ultimately important conflict, however, that between Rome and Constantinople, was not of this kind; it was grounded instead in the attempt of Constantine and his successors to make the city truly "the new Rome," to give it religious preeminence by a specious claim to apostolic credentials, and so set it over against the Roman bishops' claim to primacy among the episcopal sees.[14] The period of the great councils will end with the acknowledgment at Chalcedon that "Peter speaks through the mouth of Leo"; but the gesture is ambiguous, for the same council (in its famous 28th canon) recognized the preeminence of Constantinople in the east.[15]

Perhaps one of the most important changes of this period is the subtle shift in imagery applied to the church, and derivatively to the episcopacy.[16] The church is now seen as an officially identifiable and accepted social entity, an organization with official administration to which the civil administration can relate legally, economically, and politically. Increasingly, the political model of society is applied (quite unconsciously) to the church and at least partially to the bishop. So, also, the image of the high priest of the Old Testament exercises an observable influence.[17]

Allied with this shift in imagery is the theological construction of an "ecclesiastical cosmology." The roots for such a world-embracing view of the church's function can be found in Ephesians or Colossians, in Irenaeus' use of Paul's *anakephalaiothesis*, in the *logos* theology of Clement and Origen. However, those deserve to be called "Christic cosmology," for the function of the church in creation or history is only vaguely sketched. But with Augustine's *City of God* and Pseudo-Denis' *Divine* and *Ecclesiastical Hierarchy* we find two highly developed explanations of the structure and functioning of the world, explanations that place the church firmly at the heart of happenings in the world.

Both of these writings were destined to have a major influence on ecclesiology (even on political theory), but the impact of Augustine's work was unbroken and more far-reaching.[18] From Augustine was drawn in large part the consequent patristic and medieval emphasis on order, though this notion is prominent also in the Dionysian writings; as a matter of fact, it is rooted in the Neo-Platonic thought common to both authors.[19] In this view, everything has its proper place, perfection consists in occupying one's place with fidelity and humility, and the notion of the church as hierarchical is cast in the image of a multilevel society.[20]

Evolution of Episcopacy (Presbyterate)

One of the most striking features of the fourth and fifth centuries is the extent to which the episcopacy was prepared to move aggressively into the post-Nicene situation and exploit its opportunities. In so doing, the episcopacy realized its potential as it had not been able to previously, but this development was in marked continuity with the preceding two centuries.[21] The same cannot be said for the presbyterate. Increasingly it loses the relative independence and initiative it had possessed, it loses its role as chief council for the church and the bishop (except for some residue in its part in electing a bishop), and it loses its corporate identity and function (except in the large cities in solemn liturgical functions).[22] Instead, presbyters are ordained as helpers for the bishop (what was previously true of the deacons, see Hippolytus' *Apostolic Tradition*), tend increasingly to be given individual assignments as "little bishops" caring for branch communities, and become part of the bishop's charge and "burden" rather than fellow members who selected him to head their "college."[23] True, some of these developments are more marked in the succeeding period, but they are definitely in evidence in the fourth century and more so in the fifth.

Unquestionably, the presbyterate (along with other elements in the community) is overshadowed by the episcopacy during these two centuries. One reason for this was, quite simply, the fact that there were many great bishops. They were gifted men, many of them well-educated, quite a number endowed with considerable natural leadership, some possessed a high degree of Christian sanctity. Not unimportantly, many of them were politically powerful both within the workings of the church (which was becoming rapidly politicized in its operations) and with the civil rulers. In several instances, Ambrose in Milan is a classic instance, bishops wielded power and influence far beyond what flowed intrinsically from their episcopal authority. It would be a mistake, however, to see this as a move by the bishops into the realm of civil politics and temporal power.[24] Some of this there was, and generally for the sake of protecting Christians from oppression or exploitation; but for the most part it was a question of the extraordinary moral power exerted by these men upon their contemporaries.

To a surprising degree, the bishops of this period, despite their expanding involvement in various types of administration, retained the primacy of preaching in their ministry. Not only do bishops preach—no other historical period has had a comparable group of great preachers (Ambrose, Augustine, Cyril, Basil, Gregory Nazianzus, Chrysostom)—but they insist that it is their special prerogative to preach.[25] If presbyters do preach it is by way of delegation or appointment from the bishop, as with Chrysostom in Antioch.[26]

The responsibility of teaching is seen to flow from two principles: (1) as successors of the apostles and entrusted with the tradition that comes from them, it is the bishops above all who are charged with the preaching of that gospel to the world; and (2) as shepherds of their people, they must care for them and "not hesitate to lay down their lives in order to give them the gospel."[27]

In general, the lines of development in religious formation continued from the third century.[28] For the laity the principal agencies of such formation were the catechumenate and then (after baptism) the homily of the Eucharist.[29] There do not seem to have existed for the people (already quite sharply distinguished from the clergy) any programs of what might be called "school education" in the faith.[30]

However, such more intensive efforts to educate men's understanding of the faith did develop for the clergy and in varying degrees for monks.[31] Augustine's establishment of a regular routine of life and continuing education for his clergy cannot be considered typical,[32] but it indicates the episcopal awareness of doing something to form the clergy (presbyters particularly) for their task of explaining the faith to the people.[33] In various ways, bishops did try to provide such training for their presbyters, often conducting the formation themselves.[34] Again, among monastic establishments the pattern of faith formation is erratic; but Basil clearly envisages such in his monastic legislation, and the monastery of Lerins gains eminence during this period and provides a number of eminent and well-educated bishops for the fifth-century church.[35]

Apparently, the bishops of these two centuries considered the pursuit of theology to be an intrinsic part of the episcopal function.[36] It is not clear whether they thought of theology as officially reserved to them (and perhaps delegated to others under their guidance), or whether they thought they were to function normatively in theological investigation. There is one strong reservation that has to be made, however, regarding this last statement: unquestionably the bishops of this period saw themselves corporately (and in some instances, like Cyril of Alexandria, individually) charged with preserving orthodoxy of belief and therefore with opposing any misleading or false explanations of Christian faith. Thus, while they did not formally develop any theory of their role in the theological enterprise, in actuality their synodal and conciliar judgments did regulate the course of theological speculation.

Few periods in the church's history can challenge the fourth and fifth centuries so far as theological and doctrinal ferment is concerned. With the great councils of Nicaea, Constantinople, Ephesus, and Chalcedon as focal points, much of the church was embroiled in bitter and divisive polemics about the doctrines of God, Christ, grace, and sin. And in this period of astonishing theological debate and development, practically all the outstanding theologians are bishops. One can point to Prosper of Aquitaine, a lay theologian who was consulted by presbyters, monks, and bishops on doctrinal issues (around the middle of the fifth century);[37] but he is quite definitely the exception. And the coincidence of theologian with bishop was not accidental: functioning as theologians was seen by such bishops as Augustine, Hilary, or Chrysostom as a necessary part of their episcopal function. How else could they preserve their flock from the contagion of error?

If these two centuries are the period of

great individual bishops, it is also a period of greatly increased corporate activity of the episcopacy. Alongside the four great councils, themselves preceded and followed by a number of smaller synodal meetings in various parts of the church, there developed a regular pattern of regional synod meetings.[38] While the need to deal with suspected doctrinal aberrations played a large part in many of these meetings, they were also concerned with the basic governance of the church's life —clerical behavior, liturgy, church property, etc. The disciplinary canons of these synods provide us one of our most valuable witnesses to ecclesiastical life and structure; this they do because they played such a basic role in the governance of the church. They were not only the equivalent but actually the beginnings of canon law.[39]

Thus, despite the individual eminence of so many bishops of this period, the increasing pattern of regional synods indicates the extent to which the collegial nature of the episcopacy was appreciated. One can also see how this corporate reality of the episcopate was taken for granted if one reflects that in the sixth century both Justinian and Roman bishops (e.g., Gelasius) can assume the unified corporate existence of the *sacerdotium*. In the fourth and fifth centuries there is still great insistence on the prerogatives of the local church and its bishop; but there is also a strong awareness of the *catholic* church and of the corporate unity of its priesthood.

It is interesting to notice that this period, which sees the bishops increasingly caught up into administration and increasingly acting "officially," also sees a rapid crystallization of their ceremonial role in Christian liturgy.[40] Now the name *sacerdos* is applied to them frequently and properly; there are enough texts to indicate that the *sacerdotium* was seen to extend to lower clergy (at least to the presbyters),[41] but the view of the bishop as *the* priest is so widespread that one can take for granted in texts of this period that *sacerdos* (when used without further qualification) is referring to the bishop.

What is much less clear is the mentality that lies behind this denomination of the bishops. Apparently there is a considerable shift in view from the first two centuries, when there seems to have been reluctance to use *hiereus* or *sacerdos* of Christian ministers. There seems little doubt that fourth- and fifth-century use of *sacerdos* has primarily in mind the ritual function of the bishop in the Eucharist, secondarily his role in other sacraments.[42] He is the *leitourgos*, and in the post-Constantinian movement of Eucharistic liturgy into larger and more splendid quarters the ceremonial role of the bishop became more observable.[43] Like the high priest of the old Jerusalem Temple he is now offering "the clean oblation" in a new temple situation; it is not surprising to see more and more comparisons of the Old Testament high priests to the bishops (and other Old Testament priests to Christian presbyters).[44] Yet, the priesthood possessed by Christian clergy is that of Christ, a priesthood "according to the order of Melchizedek." While in this period only Christ and not the ordained Christian minister is paralleled with Melchizedek, the overtones touch the bishop whose priesthood is a share in that of Christ.[45] One of these overtones relates to the fact that Melchizedek was both priest and king, as also was Christ, a fact that is not overlooked in the rash of fourth- and fifth-century references to Melchizedek.[46]

Although *sacerdos* applied to the episcopacy refers to a fundamental office or *dignitas* that embraces more than ritual function as *leitourgos*, it certainly reflects the prerogative and responsibility of the bishop in liturgical matters. One finds the episcopal function already described in the classic terms of "ministry of word and sacrament": "Nor are we bishops for our own sake, but for the sake of those to whom we minister the word and the sacrament of the Lord."[47] Yet, it is also worth noting that ministry of sacrament, particularly of Eucharist, is viewed as a ministry of Christ in the strict sense, i.e., the action of the sacrament is the action of Christ himself who acts through the external agency of the ordained minister.[48]

What is true of *sacerdos* as applied to the bishops extends, *mutatis mutandis*, to the role of presbyters and deacons in the sacramental liturgies. With Eucharistic concelebration the basic pattern in all the larger communities, with the presbyterate sharing in the imposition of hands for presbyteral ordinations, the collegiality of bishop and presbyters in the one Christian priesthood was clearly evidenced. While the bishop is the high priest of the church, the presbyters assist and surround him as did the Old Testament priests for the high priest of the Temple.[49]

Increasingly, of course, presbyters are found in situations of autonomous activity; as the number of Christians grows rapidly and as evangelization increasingly touches the rural areas and smaller villages, presbyters are established as resident pastors for these outlying communities.[50] Such communities retain a fairly close bond with the "mother church" and the pastor with the bishop whose representative and "extension" he is.[51] Yet, by the very nature of the situation, he grows more independent in his activity, providing for his flock what the bishop did for the urban community (instruction, celebration of sacraments, counsel in Christian living, and a good example of the latter).[52] So, too, is applied to them in their liturgical and homiletic activity the notion of "ministers of Christ"; they make possible (and present) for their people the priestly mediation of Christ himself.[53]

Despite the collegiality that existed in liturgical celebrations, this period saw (as we suggested earlier) an increasing movement away from the earlier Christian pattern of including the bishop within the presbyteral collegium. Already firmly established is the view of the presbyters as part of the "lower clergy."[54] They are less colleagues and more assistants, something that is required practically because of the size of the community rather than something that belongs intrinsically to the structures of Christian community. As the bishop's assistants, they are under his charge and guidance and supervision.[55] The image of their relationship is clearly vertical rather than horizontal, a verticality that will find its final expression in the papal primacy as viewed by Gregory VII, Innocent III, and Boniface VIII.

Yet, their subordination in rather complete fashion to the bishops did not receive total acceptance, either practically or theoretically, from the presbyters. Letters of some of the bishops to or about their presbyters indicate some claim to more autonomy on the part of presbyters, even in formulating appropriate liturgy for their people; synodal canons reflect the same.[56] And, of course, the most famous and influential formulation of presbyteral counterclaims is that of Jerome.[57] Actually, Jerome's own position is quite nuanced. He recognized as legitimate the episcopal domination of his day, but claimed that it was not so in the primitive church where a truly collegial presbyterate was the pattern.[58] Prescinding from the accuracy of his exegesis and the loss in transmission of some of the nuances of his presentation, Jerome was read in later centuries as espousing the position that a bishop was nothing more than a priest with the added power of ordaining other priests.[59] Chrysostom says just that. "By the act of extending the hand alone are they superior, by this alone do they seem to surpass the presbyters."[60] This will have its theological repercussions later, when the theologians of the Middle Ages will refuse to see episcopacy as an order distinct from the presbyterate; rather, they see it as the "fullness," or as the presbyterate "unleashed."[61]

What, then, was the function of the bishop as the fourth- and fifth-century fathers envisaged it? For Chrysostom, the bishop was teacher and spiritual father, protector and exemplar and high priest.[62] For Gregory Nazianzus the episcopal function is reflected in the eulogy preached for his father: the pastor who teaches his people and protects them from error, who cares for them in their needs, provides them with the sacraments of baptism and penitence, leads them in the celebration of the Eucharist, and inspires them by his own example of holiness.[63] For Basil, the bishop is to be a builder of the temple of God, a vinedresser who cares for the vineyard of the Lord, a cooperator with God (*theou sunergos*) who is totally dedicated to this work. And then, a bit more specifically, he is a doctor who cures the ills of men's souls by the knowledge of Christ's teaching, a shepherd who feeds his people with the word of God.[64] For Augustine, the bishop was the *dispensator verbi et sacramenti*; but he was also to bear the "burden" of his people, the need to instruct and correct and console and support them; he was also the one charged with preserving the unity of the church and the integrity of its faith.[65] Part of the function of preserving peace and unity was the act of judging. This dealt not only with strictly ecclesiastical matters but meant the conduct of a regular court for any case that was brought before him. Based on the Constantinian recognition of episcopal judgment as valid in civil judgment, this activity consumed a great deal of time (a fact that many bishops, Augustine, Ambrose, and Basil among them, bemoan).[66]

One aspect of the bishop's function as understood in the fourth and fifth centuries might be underlined: that of healer.[67] It is perhaps not surprising to find this role stressed, for Christ's own ministry was one of preaching and healing. In the patristic period (on into Gregory I), however, the healing is described not in a prophetic context (as is the case in the Gospels) but in a medical one. Moreover, there is a gradual shift in emphasis from the healing that is effected by the word of the gospel complemented by episcopal admonition or encouragement, and the healing effected through the discipline of penance and reconciliation, to the miraculous healings recounted of bishops in the legendary "biographies" that now begin to describe the great fathers of the church.[68] Quite apart from any critical judgment on the factual basis of these accounts of healing, they reflect the association of "healing" with the role of the bishop, and the belief that such healing attaches charismatically to the sanctity of the bishop.[69]

Evolution of Monasticism

Monasticism is a topic too vast, both in its historical evolution and in its nature, to be examined in this study.[70] Yet, for several reasons it cannot be completely ignored. Priestly life and ministry took certain specifically different forms in monasticism (and still other forms in later expression of "religious life") and these are a part of the historical data for a theology of Christian ministry and priesthood; the ideals and life-style of monasticism wielded major influence upon the understanding and practice of all clerical life (from the fourth century to the present day); and many of the great bishops whose thinking about their office helped shape the church's understanding of the episcopacy were drawn from monasteries, and came to the episcopal office with an outlook on Christian community and its leadership drawn from the monastic community and its abbot.

While the fourth and fifth centuries do not see as strong a monastic influence as that which will come with Gregory I, the Celtic missionaries, the Carolingian reforms (especially under Louis the Pious and the Council of Aachen in 816), or Gregory VII, they do give us in the East the great Basil, bishop and simultaneously the father of Eastern monasticism, Gregory Nazianzus, whose own contemplative bent finally led him to flee the episcopacy, Athanasius and Cyril of Alexandria, both closely allied with Egyptian monasticism and deeply touched by it; and in the West the influential role of Lerins, the adaptation of monastic patterns to training and communal life of "secular clergy" by bishops like Augustine, the involvement with part-time monasticism of prominent ecclesiastics like Jerome and Rufinus.

One thing to be noted about this period is the relatively close working relationship between the monks and the episcopacy.[71] While important monastic centers, like Lerins or the monasteries of Pachomius, possessed a certain autonomy because of their prominence and the moral leadership of their abbots, there was nothing like the "exempt status" of monasteries and religious orders that is found in the Latin church from the tenth century.[72] The monks in a given region are part of the church entrusted to the bishop of that region; however, in the East the monks seem to have been the special concern (and support) of the principal metropolitans.[73] In any event, monks come under the direction of the bishop and are cared for by him. This is the "proper order of things" described in Pseudo-Denis' *Ecclesiastical Hierarchy*, and probably reflects quite faithfully the situation that he (a sixth-century bishop) knew.[74]

A special question arises regarding the existence and function of presbyters within monastic communities. In principle, the monasticism of this period is a form of lay life, though there was no intrinsic opposition to clerics deciding to pursue the monastic life, as quite a few seem to have done. Once in the monastic situation, an ordained minister seems not to have exercised his ministerial functions except to the extent that his monastery might require it for its own liturgy.[75]

Considerable discussion has gone on regarding the *presbyteroi* mentioned in the monastic rule of Basil.[76] What seems to be the situation is this: Among those who entered the monastery and were already in presbyteral orders, some would gradually establish themselves as eminent in virtue and prudence and would then be designated as "official spiritual fathers" of the monastery. Their function consisted in giving corporate counsel to the abbot, preaching to (and otherwise instructing) the monks, and providing spiritual guidance for those who needed it.[77]

The Struggle of Imperium and Sacerdotium

Just thirty years after Chalcedon, Justinian was born. It was he who crystallized the imperial view of the church as an element within the divinely ordained state. But, when Justinian was still in his early teens, Gelasius I (492–96) had already laid down a clear opposing position, distinguishing the spheres of temporal and spiritual authority,

and claiming for the latter not only independence but even superiority.[78] The situation of discussion is very clear, i.e., the issues are clear-cut and the positions taken are not accommodation to solution of practical problems. Justinian argues within the framework of the Roman claim to primacy (he accepts a primacy for Rome in doctrinal matters), and Gelasius (as well as his successors who were contemporaries of Justinian) accepted the temporal sovereignty of the Byzantine *basileus*; moreover, both Gelasius and Justinian were theologically inclined and so tried to deal with basic theory and not just practical solutions.

Upon reflection it is quite surprising to find the meaning that is already attached to the term *sacerdotium* in the writings of Gelasius. It is at once the corporate reality embracing primarily the episcopacy of the church but implicitly extending beyond that to all the clergy, and also the spiritual power embodied in this group.[79] It is a generic reference to the complex societal function fulfilled in complementary fashion by the various "orders" of the clergy, the function of consecrating and spiritualizing human society, and thereby contributing to its justice and peace.[80] Actually, as Gelasius (and his successors) see it, the guidance provided by the *sacerdotium* would suffice for human society were it not for "original sin"; because of sin, the *regnum* is needed to help carry out the insight and regulation of the *sacerdotium*.[81]

It is interesting to speculate how the notion of *sacerdotium* might have developed if there had not been the conflict between the bishop of Rome and the emperor (and patriarch) in Constantinople, but this is futile; the concrete reality is that this controversy was the historical context in which the opposing theories were hammered out, that of Gelasius and Nicolas in Rome and that of Anastasius and later Justinian in Constantinople. What is highly significant, both for the period of the sixth to the eighth centuries and for the later Middle Ages, is the acceptance by both sides of the typically Hellenistic notion of the *basileus*, that is, of authority deriving by special divine endowment according to a vertical image, and the abandonment of the traditional Roman notion of democratic origin of authority, based on natural law and the consent of the governed.[82] Not only will the East preserve this understanding by acceptance of the Justinian Code with its canonization of the absorption of the *sacerdotium* by the *basileia,* but in the West the position of Charlemagne will be understood to quite an extent in this same context. As the Carolingian kingdom crumbles, the position of Christian *basileus* will be claimed by medieval popes from Gregory VII through Innocent III to Boniface VIII.[83]

Interestingly, an aura of sacrality does not disappear from the *sacerdotium* as this shift of "priesthood" from service at the altar to governance of society takes place; but it is the sacrality of the "divine kingship" rather than that of the Servant Messiah, the mystery of effective rule and authority rather than the unique mystery of Christ's death and resurrection. Actually, what is fascinating and quite amazing is not that such a shift to concentration on power and authority should have taken place, but that so much of the earlier ideal of Christian ministry was retained. One can look quite cynically at Gregory the Great's use of the phrase *servus servorum Dei* and see in it a subtle but powerful claim to have universal charge of the church, but Gregory himself and those who succeeded him in the papacy did preserve a considerable bit of the scriptural ideal of *servus*.[84]

One notion that unquestionably fed into the idea of a distinguishable group of men who constituted a key social force, i.e., the *sacerdotium,* was the clear distinction between clergy and laity. Within the church this was influenced by the situation of the clergy, at least from deacon on up, being a full-time occupation, by the increasing separation of clerics from others in their living quarters (often resembling monastic life), by the civic and political exemptions (e.g., from taxation) granted by Constantine and consequent Roman law, and by the gradually increasing discipline of clerical celibacy.

Pseudo-Denis in his *Ecclesiastical Hierarchy* reflects the view of his day that Christian priesthood was not basically a function but a different (and superior) level of *being* Christian—actually, in his philosophical view, that very superiority in existence was the key to the function of "illumining" those below.[85] The clergy were the "spirituals" in Christian society.

In the Byzantine emperor's view of the relation between *sacerdotium* and *imperium,* as we find it formulated in Justinian's code, the *sacerdotium* is under the ruler, who had supreme authority and responsibility for human society (since he is God's vicar on earth, his will embodied divine law).[86] The *sacerdotium* performs for society the important task of providing for men's spiritual well-being; thus they assist the *basileus* whose great responsibility this is, and who for this reason is most concerned (as Justinian often stated) about the level of sanctity and learning in the clergy.[87] This, obviously, gives the emperor a basis for total involvement and control of the church's life, and the history of Byzantine Christianity testifies to this danger.

At the time of Gelasius and the controversy over the deposition of Acacius, the need to assert the church's independence from imperial dominance was already clear, hence the position taken by Gelasius. At the time of Justinian this became even more apparent (what with the pro-Monophysite meddlings of his wife, and Justinian's own illusions of providing the church with his theological guidance) even if the bishop of Rome had to be imprisoned in order to grasp these theological insights! So, the Latin-speaking part of the church, increasingly free (after Justinian's abortive campaign to reestablish the old Roman Empire in the West) from actual imperial presence in the West, began a concerted effort to free itself from the embrace of the emperor.[88]

Part of this strategy was to ally the papacy, which by this time had considerable prestige in the midst of the confused situation of barbaric invasion and rule, with the new Teutonic rulers. A turning point in this procedure occurred when Pope Stephen II appealed to Pepin to be his protector.[89] This was of considerable immediate importance; but a more lasting and far-reaching action was the conscious papal effort to tie the notion of "Christian" to that of "Roman."[90] It will be several centuries before Roman Christianity is identified as "the church" (even in the West); but the groundwork for this is firmly laid by the eighth-century popes.

However, this is jumping ahead of ourselves historically. As the sixth century ends, with Gregory I as bishop of Rome, relations between Rome and Constantinople are not yet so exacerbated. Gregory himself was well-acquainted with the Constantinople situation, having spent several years there in diplomatic work; and he was not unaffected by the Byzantine notion of the *basileus*. Moreover, he was quite sensitive to the prerogatives and pretensions of ancient (or not-so-ancient) metropolitan sees, and with diplomatic shrewdness refused the title "ecumenical patriarch" not only for Constantinople but for himself, though subtly claiming primacy through the title *servus servorum Dei*.[91] He was more aware than most of his more-or-less immediate successors of the catholicity of the church and yet, by the very prestige that his pontificate gave to the church of Rome, he was an important part in the process of Romanizing the Western church. Rome was looked to as a pattern for belief,[92] for liturgical practice,[93] for ecclesiastical administration,[94] for effective clerical organization, and for sanctity. Gregory was active in fighting to reform the morals of the clergy, not just in Rome but in other portions of the church. The moral leadership he exercised in life has continued unbroken through his writings, particularly by his *De cura pastorali*.[95]

Missionary Extension of Roman Influence

Another source of widening Roman influence was the initiative taken by Gregory, and aggressively continued by his successors, in evangelizing areas of Europe as yet untouched, or only lightly touched, by Christianity. The most famous and most successful of Gregory's efforts in this regard was the mission of Augustine to England.[96] This resulted not only in a flourishing church in England but in an outpost of Roman influence. The see of Rome enjoyed immense prestige and popularity in the English church: Rome was the "mother church" whose daughter was English Christianity, and Gregory himself was venerated (as we can see from the writings of Bede) as the father of England's faith.[97] As the Roman influence spread (and it takes a dramatic leap forward in the eighth century under Gregory II and the missionary work of Boniface), so did the Roman understanding of the episcopal and presbyteral office, expressed in the decretals of the Roman bishops (going back as far as Siricius in the late fourth century), the liturgical books of the Roman church, and the pastoral and moral writings of Gregory.

Despite the accelerating social upheaval of the late patristic period (Teutonic invasions in Europe and Africa, the first impact of Islam, Monophysite and Nestorian schism in the East) the basic elements of episcopal activity remain what they were in the preceding two centuries. Naturally, things differed quite drastically between Constantinople and England as Augustine first began to evangelize there. But there was baptismal catechesis to provide, the liturgical celebrations to lead, formation to be provided for the clergy, instruction to be given the faithful (chiefly through the Eucharistic homilies), the needs of the poor to be filled, complaints to be heard, and (increasingly) the temporal goods of the church to be administered

What does seem to shift somewhat is the extent to which bishops are themselves the immediate pastors, and the extent to which this immediate *cura animarum* is entrusted to presbyters whom the bishop supervises. Certainly in some areas we already see emerging as one of the more time-consuming activities of the bishop his travel from one small community to another to keep in contact, to look over the activity of the local presbyter (especially his liturgical activity), and to administer Confirmation.[98] Then, too, we see (again, more noticeably in the larger episcopal sees) the clear presence of an episcopal curia.[99] This takes on complicated proportions in Constantinople, where in addition to local administrators there is a sizable "diplomatic corps" of representatives from important churches, to say nothing of a number of bishops who prefer residence in the capital to their own less cultured and less influential see cities.[100] Yet, even in less prominent episcopal sees one finds a group of officials assisting the bishop.[101]

Already the bishop is becoming, in actual practice, more the "father of the clergy" than the "father of the community"; and in dealing with civil authorities, which in some instances is a major portion of his role, he is much more often concerned with affairs touching clergy.[102] Obviously, this is by no means an exclusive thing—the bishop still has considerable contact with the people and preaches regularly to those who frequent his episcopal church—but it is an increasing development. This means that to an ever increasing extent the bulk of pastoral activity lies with the presbyters. It is they who baptize, provide the preparation and follow-up for baptism, celebrate liturgy for their people, console the afflicted and bury the dead, try to keep peace and harmony in the community, and lead the sinners to penance and reconciliation.[103]

Unquestionably, the most influential theorizing on the episcopal role in the sixth and seventh centuries is provided by Gregory's *Cura pastoralis*, though in its own ecclesiastical and cultural sphere the impact of Justinian's code should not be underestimated. Mention could also be made of Isidore of Seville's *De ecclesiasticis officiis*, but Isidore himself was strongly influenced by Gregory.[104]

Taking the *Cura pastoralis* as a guide, we can see the strong emphasis that is placed on the function of preaching/teaching.[105] At the same time, this teaching role is combined with the image of the physician entrusted with the *cura animarum* (and one is tempted to add *vulneratarum*). The bishop (or presbyter) is to admonish the people, leading them to repentance and conversion, reminding them of the "four last things," and stimulating them with edifying (and imaginatively legendary) accounts of pious Christians of bygone days. In contrast to the effort to create theological accuracy in the people's understanding which one finds in the sermons of Leo I or Cyril of Alexandria or even in the "pastoral concern" of Justinian, one finds a fostering of credulity in order to obtain better moral behavior. Even Scripture is caught into this effort, as the tropological meaning is stressed and the Bible tends to become a collection of moral precepts or aphorisms and of edifying examples of virtue.[106]

Closely connected with this homiletic "healing of souls" is the healing connected with penitential discipline. In the sixth century we are not yet under the impact of Celtic missionary practice, the classic exomologesis is still the prevailing discipline in most of the church, but the use of Penance is becoming more widespread and central in Christian thinking about salvation.[107] Increasing stress is being laid on the episcopal possession of "the power of the keys," though this shades off into questions of external church discipline (excommunication, etc.)[108] and into the question of relative power of *sacerdotium* and *regnum*. The episcopacy (and to quite a degree the presbyterate) is viewed as opening up for the people the "gates of heaven," through overcoming original sin in baptism and personal sin in Penance. It is also viewed as fortifying Christians by Confirmation (already described in terms of *robur*), by the word of the gospel, and by the Eucharistic body of Christ.[109] Already the church is described by Gregory as an army engaged in battle with the forces of evil,[110] a notion that will be emphasized later by Gregory VII on the eve of the Crusades.[111]

As for the liturgical role of the bishops and presbyters, one can find an implicit theorizing in the ordinals and sacramentaries originating in this period.[112] Without our having to distinguish, if possible, the precise contribution they made to the sacramentaries that bear their names,[113] it is clear that Gelasius and

Gregory I were influential in shaping the Roman liturgy for all later generations.[114] Thus the sixth-century view of *sacerdos* exerts a lasting influence on Latin Christianity's notion of Christian priesthood and ministry. This view is one of the celebrant as the mediator between the people and God; he is the sole agent (or at least only the attending clergy assist) of the sacred action which he does on behalf of the assembled people.[115] By the eighth century the *laos* has been reduced to almost total silence[116] and the canon is said quietly, for only the celebrant really needs to know what is being said, or needs to express his sacrificing intent.[117] The celebrant is the high priest offering sacrifice on behalf of the people rather than the *leitourgos* of a sacrificing community; he is the sacred actor performing the mystery rite, rather than the prophetic herald of the redeeming gospel of Christ's death and resurrection.[118]

Apparently, during this period the relationship between bishops and their presbyters was quite good. At least we do not find the open opposition that marked, for example, the situation of Hincmar and many of his clergy in the ninth century. Yet, the *Statuta ecclesiae antiqua* seem to reflect a certain presbyteral reaction against episcopal control in the Gallic church of the fifth century,[119] and it is more than likely that a certain tension existed between the rural clergy and the episcopal church in the city.[120] One of the touchy points is the attempt by conscientious bishops to reform the morals of the clergy.[121]

Feudal Christianity

In this somewhat ill-defined historical period, with the East and the West developing quite separately and under different pressures, with the West on the way to the Middle Ages but not yet there, with alternating periods of political unification and organization and of disarray and confusion, the church (though obviously quite deeply touched by these social developments) is the most abiding and stable

influence. This is particularly true of Rome and the other prominent episcopal sees, and of monasticism.

Ministerial patterns and clerical life-style were still quite fluid, though shaped by well-established roles in sacramental liturgy and considerable attempt to regulate clerical dress, employment, celibacy, recreation, etc.[122] For one thing, it was still a common pattern in many areas for the clergy to live in community with the bishop in the cities, and to go out into the countryside on "apostolic expeditions."[123] Increasingly, however, presbyters take up residence in country parishes, with the result that both their ministerial activity and their way of life become more autonomous and, in many instances, less disciplined.[124] Demarcation between episcopally governed and monastic ministry is quite vague: in some instances there is practically a merging of the two; in other cases there is the beginning of tension between the two structures, a tension that will become acerbated in later centuries.[125]

At the same time that it was providing a principle of continuity, the church was undergoing fairly radical alteration in its sociological reality and in its self-image. This period, the eighth and ninth centuries, sees the clear emergence of the idea of the *societas christiana*.[126] In its own way a variation on the Justinian notion of the *basileia*, it is rather an application of the Augustinian vision of the *civitas Dei*.[127] To some extent the viewpoint is logical in a context where everyone is now Christian or at least baptized. There is a total "material" if not "formal" coincidence of the church and human society; so instead of the Gelasian vision of two "parallel powers" coexisting and interacting,[128] the early Middle Ages and especially the papacy of this period develops the notion of one society whose spiritual element (or soul) is the clergy.[129] Animation and direction of this Christian society comes from the pope to the bishops to the other clergy to the people.[130] Civil government is needed to enforce the Christian way of life and justice; but this is due to the sinfulness of men and not to any essential need that is rooted in human nature.[131]

In speaking of the *societas christiana* and its basic coincidence with the church, one must not forget that these centuries maintained a fairly clear tradition about the church being the body of Christ, with Christ alone as its head and high priest and king.[132] True, this was complicated by the imagery connected with the risen Christ being "up there" at the "right hand of the Father," an imagery whose latent problems will surface in the Eucharistic controversies of the ninth and eleventh centuries,[133] but for the moment this complication was not keenly felt. As a matter of fact, one reason that it was not felt more may well have been the increasing emphasis on the clergy, particularly the pope, as being mediator or vicar for Christ. Without any denial that Christ is the head of the church, the popes of this period began to refer to themselves as the head of the body,[134] something that we would not have found in Leo I or before him, though occasional usage of "vicar of Christ" goes back as far as Gelasius.[135]

What is important in a Christian society is that the society be governed by the will of God. This will is reflected in the laws of behavior that have been transmitted through Scripture, or through the traditional teaching of the church.[136] One finds the latter in the writings of the great fathers, the decrees of the earlier councils and synods, and the traditions and decrees of the church of Rome.[137] This period sees an increased production of these Roman decretals and the collection and collation of previous decretals, a body of ecclesiastical precedent which can be appealed to in support for a certain desired course of action or for guidance in decision.[138]

The ascendancy of Charlemagne and his coronation as Holy Roman Emperor in 800 form the center of developments within these two centuries. Many of the latent political and social forms of the Merovingian period take on more obvious realization now. Concretely, the *societas christiana* finds a unified governmental structure to correspond to its unified sacerdotal organization. The Car-

olingian rule provides a stimulus in a number of important areas of ecclesiastical life: urging better intellectual formation of the clergy, imposing a certain amount of liturgical unity on the basis of the Roman rite, resuscitating regional synods and helping to enforce their regulations.[139]

The imposing personal authority of Charlemagne did much to bring about unity and stability; it also brought the threat of imperial interference in ecclesiastical matters. Charlemagne certainly did involve himself in ecclesiastical maneuverings; he had no choice, for these were intermeshed with secular politics, and at times they even threatened his own political position. Apparently, even the crowning of Charlemagne by Leo III was not the expression of a sudden charismatic urge (as is sometimes recorded), but a carefully calculated political move by the pope (without any previous knowledge or agreement on Charlemagne's part).[140] However, Charlemagne did preserve ecclesiastical forms even when he exerted pressure. Leo III, for example, was forced to submit to trial, but by an ecclesiastical court (and it is an indication of the "exaltation" already achieved by the bishop of Rome that the bishops of this synod state that, according to tradition, the pope is beyond judgment for none is his peer).[141]

One of the most important contributions of the Carolingian court was the opportunity and stimulus it provided for the development and distribution of a fairly homogeneous liturgy, based on the Roman patterns. A key figure in this liturgical unification (and purification) was Alcuin, tied in double fashion to Roman traditions because of his English origin (the English church being always close psychologically to Rome at this period) and his Benedictine training.[142] This Carolingian liturgical reform played a major part in the deepening and purifying of Christian life in the early Middle Ages, and unquestionably did much to instruct ordinary Christian (and clerical) understanding of the sacraments and of ministry.[143]

During these centuries, under the impulse of Frankish social customs and law the patterns of feudal life begin to establish themselves in Europe, though there is great fluidity in societal structures, both civil and ecclesiastical, until the great organizational period of the twelfth and thirteenth centuries. There is widespread development of Christian communities in nonurban contexts: in country "parishes," in small towns on their way to becoming cities, in conjunction with the feudal manor, or in some dependence on a monastic foundation.[144] Apart from the last, where ministration would be provided by the monastery, there developed the "country parish" type of clergy.[145]

Generally quite poorly equipped to perform their homiletic or sacramental ministry, these presbyters were to some extent a clerical reality different from clergy in the time of Chrysostom or Augustine. Though quite distinct by "law" and the prevalent theory about their sacerdotal character,[146] and recognized as distinctive because they possessed the sacred powers of consecration and absolution,[147] these men were not as much a "class apart" as clerics were in many other historical or social situations. In their little communities they were very much a part of the life of the people, identifying much more with it than with their clerical counterparts in the episcopal city, and caught up in the structures of emerging feudal society.[148] This is a large part of the problems in this period of investiture and clerical marriage. Both threaten the sacral "apartness" and freedom of the clergy.

It would be a mistake to envisage the ecclesiastical situation, however, as one of disarray, marked by the abandonment of old patterns and the lack of new established patterns. One needs only to read the *De clericorum institutione* of Rabanus Maurus in the mid-ninth century to realize how much of the classic pattern of clerical orders was preserved and how sharply the essential lines of authority and function were still drawn.[149] Actually, a difference in top-level organization was taking place as the office of archbishop took over the more ancient position of metropolitan,[150] and as abbots (though as such not technically part of the hierarchy of Orders)

began to exercise a function paralleling that of influential bishops.[151] But this did not much affect the functioning of the church on its broad-based "lower levels," and it was worked out in theoretical continuity with the metropolitan-patriarch tradition.[152]

However, one must draw attention to a distinction: the structure described by Rabanus Maurus is that intrinsic to the orders established through liturgical ordination; it is not necessarily the organizational order that was emerging from the official activity of the early medieval church.[153] The organizational order was increasingly a matter of authoritative management of ecclesiastical business, and a distinct "hierarchy" within the church was coming into existence and gradually receiving recognition, a hierarchy of administrative *jurisdiction* rather than of strictly sacerdotal authority. This development was somewhat dubiously grounded in Christian origins; often enough it was grounded in the "traditions" of false decretals and similar forgeries.[154] To some extent this seems to have been one of the factors that forced development of the (theologically questionable) distinction between *potestas ordinis* and *potestas jurisdictionis*.[155] This very distinction reveals a mentality which sees the church as something other than the sacrament of Christ, at least partially so, for it requires an authority in addition to that attached to sacramental existence. This seems to be the mentality associated with the notion of *societas christiana*, not only viewing the church according to a political model but actually identifying it with that model.

Though the details are not as clearly observable as they will be in the eleventh century and thereafter, the idea of the episcopacy that emerges in the Merovingian and Carolingian periods is already affected by an episcopal-papal tension (into which flows a monastic-episcopal tension) and by a presbyteral-episcopal tension. Partially this is due to the convergence of several streams of thought about the episcopacy; partially it is simply the result of the sociological evolution of the church and of its ecclesiastical structures at this time. The movement towards the un-challenged monarchy of the Roman see was a departure from the great patristic period (fourth and fifth centuries) that was so clearly an episcopal epoch;[156] and it is not surprising that this evolution did not take place unchallenged.

One of the most respected traditions about episcopacy was that stemming from Cyprian, a tradition that stressed the collegial authority and responsibility of the bishops.[157] This African tradition, which in Cyprian's case did take some account of a special prerogative of the Roman church[158] (this was more fully acknowledged by Augustine[159]) apparently persisted in Spain after the Vandal annihilation of the Carthaginian church.[160] Spain's episcopacy had a tradition of a close working-relationship with Rome, at least as far back as Hosius of Cordoba, and at the time of Gregory I this was further strengthened by Gregory's personal friendship with Leander.[161] Leander passed on his admiration for Gregory to his younger brother, the celebrated Isidore of Seville, and acquainted him with the writings of Gregory. Despite this link with Rome, which would predispose one to expect a propapacy attitude in Spain, it would seem that some of the Cyprianic tradition about episcopal-papal relations passed through Isidore to the Middle Ages and men like Hincmar of Reims.[162] It is interesting to note that the texts supporting papal prerogatives to which later popes appealed are to be found in the *Pseudo*-Isidorian texts.[163]

Whereas this Cyprianic tradition stresses the fundamental collegiality and coresponsibility of the episcopacy, though it leaves room for a Roman primacy *within* the episcopacy, the tradition tnat stems from Leo I is based on a *vertical* image of the source of authority. Authority was given by Christ to Peter and through him to the other apostles, so the pope receives the supreme authority which he then mediates to the episcopacy.[164] This position is intimated quite clearly in Leo I, more so in Gelasius I and in Gregory I (though the latter, with his Byzantine experience, seems more circumspect in the claims he makes, even though they are the same claims!), and expressed without any hesitation by Nicholas I (858–67) and the popes of the ninth century after him, especially John VIII.[165]

One of the most subtle, yet critical, influences on the notion of the episcopacy was that of monasticism, which by this time in the West was largely identical with Benedictine monasticism. As we intimated earlier, the ideal of pastoral ministry sketched by Gregory in his *Cura pastoralis* had a decisive influence on medieval understanding of the sacerdotal role (episcopal or presbyteral). Yet, upon examination, the ideal of the *rector populi* described by Gregory has striking resemblance to the ideal of the abbot described in the Rule of Benedict.[166] To some extent, which is hard to measure, the monastic life-style became (through writings like those of Gregory) the ideal for all in the church who aspired to "the higher gifts." And this meant the clergy!

Probably the most startling case of monasticism "absorbing" Christianity occurred in Ireland.[167] So strong was the domination of the monastic foundations that they overshadowed the established hierarchy. In some instances bishops became little more than chaplains for a large monastic foundation, functioning under the jurisdiction of the abbot or abbess.[168] The influence of these great monastic centers of learning and asceticism spread quite rapidly to Iona (and Lindesfarne) and then with Columbanus to the Continent. During the Merovingian period, the houses established by Columbanus thrived and exerted a major and salutary influence; it seems that, as in Ireland, such monasteries as Luxeuil and Fontaines served as centers for spiritual revival and particularly penitence, centers to which the people of the surrounding areas would come for the penitential observances that would free them from eternal damnation.[169]

The exact influence of this Celtic monasticism is hard to measure. Certainly, it helped restore a level of learning and culture to the clergy, and certainly, too, preserved the ideal of moral integrity and ascetic pursuit of sanctity. But perhaps the most important influence on the practice and theory of the priestly ministry was the importation of the Irish discipline regarding the sacrament of penance which stressed the confession of sins and the absolution given by the priest.[170] This was quite a departure from the classic discipline of the exomologesis, and despite strong opposition from official church decrees it gradually became the pattern for the sacrament (in the twelfth century).[171] Moreover, it made recourse to the sacrament a much more frequent thing (which it helped encourage by great emphasis in preaching on sins and the need for penitence) and thereby changed the view of people as to what priests were expected to do. Connected with this emphasis on priest-confessors was the subtle deemphasis of the episcopacy, characteristic of the entire Celtic undertaking in Europe.

The more durable form of monasticism in the West was that begun by Benedict of Nursia. In time it absorbed into itself the Celtic foundations on the Continent.[172] Its influence on the episcopacy (and presbyterate) was of considerable importance, for one reason because so many bishops were drawn from monasteries, especially in times of attempted church reform. Benedictine monasticism tended to integrate better with the episcopal pattern; however, its ties were traditionally strong with the bishop of Rome, and in the ensuing struggle between the papacy and episcopacy the great Benedictine houses (particularly Cluny) proved to be valuable support for the papacy. One could question the accuracy of transferring the ideal of monastic life to the life of the clergy in general, yet this was done. Because bishops and abbots were considered as ecclesiastical peers, it was natural to expect of both a similar level of "holiness"; and when "reformers" emanated from monasteries to restore to the life of the clergy the sanctity appropriate to it, it was natural that they should understand this ideal of clerical life and behavior according to their own monastic training and ideals. The only problem with this is that monastic life, at least in its essence, is a form of nonministerial exis-

tence, and it is questionable whether the church as a whole is meant to become monastic.

During the great patristic period, regional synods and general councils had become prominent as the guiding principle for ecclesiastical (and particularly clerical) life. To some extent the role of these synods declined during the Merovingian period, but they were energetically rejuvenated by Charlemagne and played a decisive role in the church of the ninth century.[173] But alongside them, and as basis for their own deliberations, the tradition of past episcopal, synodal, or papal decisions played an ever increasing role.

Informally gathered together into different collections, a mixture of authentic proceedings of synods or decretals of popes and of forged and specious documents (like the Donation of Constantine), these "authorities" were appealed to as foundation for any course of action taken by bishop or pope.[174] As one examines these "sources" it does not seem that the notion of Christian ministry or priesthood differs from one collection to another—except in the question of authority, especially the relation of episcopal to papal authority. It is on this point that the ninth century sees an ever sharper formulation of the Roman position under Nicolas I and John VIII, and opposed to it the cogent argumentation of bishops such as Hincmar of Reims, who are espousing a more "horizontal" view of the episcopal college.[175]

Though the "political" voice of the presbyters during this period was limited to opposing the practical decisions of a given bishop, and at times appealing over his head to the pope, as happened with Hincmar,[176] they were gaining a subtle triumph regarding the understanding (and theology) of priesthood. Whereas in an earlier age the term *sacerdos* was practically a proper denomination for the bishop, it now becomes increasingly associated with the presbyter.[177] Theological and polemic discussion of the episcopal role, because of the accelerating Roman claims, centers more and more on the jurisdictional and authoritative aspects of the bishop's activity, trying to establish what is proper to him in this sphere.[178] As a result, the right to preach, teach, celebrate the Eucharist, and forgive sins is no longer associated that properly with the episcopal office but with the priesthood which the presbyter (and also the bishop) possesses by virtue of ordination. The liturgical formulae for presbyteral and episcopal ordination, retaining the formulations of a past age, preserve the episcopacy's claim to being the "basic priestly order."[179] But in common understanding, and in theological discussion, the notion becomes more and more common that a bishop is "a priest with the additional power to ordain priests." One tries to distinguish the bishopric from the presbyterate by saying that the bishop has the fullness of what the presbyter has, and one asks the question (more commonly with a negative response): Is episcopacy an order distinct from that of presbyter?[180]

In such discussions the influence of Jerome's position seems to have been quite important. So, also, the *Statuta ecclesiae antiqua* seem to have wielded a noticeable influence.

Not that it is unique to this historical period (for it had begun at least as early as the late second century), the Old Testament notion of priesthood wielded a considerable influence on the manner in which priestly office and ministry were viewed.[181] Comparing the statements of Isidore of Seville with those of Rabanus Maurus (to take them as examples of the beginning and end of the period we are studying) does not seem to indicate any substantial difference: Christian priesthood is not only like Old Testament priesthood, it actually finds its origins in the latter.[182] It is quite different, however, for Christ was a priest according to the "order of Melchizedek." Granted this difference, bishops trace their origins from the high priests, priests from the other priests, deacons from the Levites—and another "lineage" sees the bishops deriving from the apostles, the priests from the disciples, the deacons from the deacons of Acts.[183]

Such reference to Old Testament priesthood gradually emphasized the idea of the priest as "offering sacrifice," and the power to consecrate the Eucharist elements takes on increasing centrality in thought about the priestly office.[184] Whereas discussion about the episcopacy's possession of "the keys" tends to center on exegesis of Matthew 16:18 (and related texts) and the claim to the grant made to Peter and the other apostles,[185] discussion about the presbyteral power to absolve sin tends to derive this power from the more ultimate and greater power of Eucharistic consecration—since they possess the greater power, *a fortiori* the lesser.[186]

The Period of Roman Ascendancy, Gregory VII

Throughout much of the tenth century there was little to indicate that the general movement of ecclesiastical history was in the direction of papal supremacy. After the fairly strong pontificates of the ninth century, the decay and disarray of the Carolingian structure, and even more so of the ecclesiastical situation in Rome, seemed to threaten the very existence (to say nothing of the moral authority and eminence) of the Roman see. However, the eleventh century saw a dramatic about-face; the reforming impetus of Cluny began to touch Rome itself; and the remarkable impact of Hildebrand pushed through a radical reform in the church itself and, beyond that, in the whole of emergent medieval society.

As the patterns of human life—economic, social, and political—were shaped more and more by the feudal system, the church itself was deeply affected in its institutional aspects. Technically, according to laws and grants, the clerical class and ecclesiastical institutions were an autonomous element in society. Practically, as manor lords obtained a "chaplain" to provide for the spiritual needs of the people, as bishoprics and abbatial positions were given by powerful princes to men who would pledge fealty to them, as benefices became a desirable source of income, the ministers of the church became ever more an intrinsic part of the feudal structure and not the dominant part.[187] Clergy tended to become either feudal serfs or feudal lords. What else could one be in the one reality which was the *societas christiana?*

The extent to which appointment of bishops was controlled by powerful temporal rulers (who generally made their appointments on the basis of financial or political considerations), and the extent to which ordinary presbyters were reduced to practical serfdom as part of the lord's entourage of "servants," posed a serious threat to the church's mission and internal health.[188] It was in grave danger not just of coming under secular control but of becoming a secular entity. To take but one small element, the "manor priest" had no freedom to exercise his own initiative in evangelizing the people who surrounded him; instead, because "saying Mass" did not take all his time, he was often employed in some other capacity as well, such as clerk, or manager of the stables.[189] In such a threatening context, one can see the symbolic importance of clerical celibacy, why it was so widely ignored in practice, and why reformers focused on it. Celibacy was a sign of the "sacral apartness" of the clergy, who therefore should not become like ordinary people, and it also provided a greater freedom from financial enchainment to the feudal lord.

Secular domination of the ecclesiastical institutions, particularly of the clergy, could proceed as far as it did because of the almost total inefficacy of the papacy in the tenth century. Actually, sincere Christians of that age did not ask, "How can we be saved by Rome?" but, "How can we save Rome?" By the end of the century, however, things had already started to change for the better; the impact of Cluny is increasingly felt, the first of a series of reforming popes, Gerbert (Sylvester II), is on the papal throne. By mid-century the movement of reform is in full swing, supported by many strong and influential figures, like Peter Damian, but dominated by the crusading zeal of Gregory VII, both before and after his reign as pope.

Gregory VII's efforts were directed principally to freeing the church from the lay investiture which threatened to shackle it.[190] Above all, he worked to reclaim for the church the selection of its bishops. However, in the struggle to keep the secular power out of spiritual affairs Gregory proceeded by way of exalting the authority and power of the papacy. One needs only to read through the *Dictatus papae* to see how absolute was the claim of Gregory to papal preeminence, both in the church and in human society as a whole.[191]

The papal claim to immediate jurisdiction over all Christians was exercised practically by Gregory VII, who had no hesitation in intervening in matters of dispute in any diocese.[192] More than that, he revoked some of the traditional rights of bishops;[193] and to carry out his reform measures, which not all the episcopacy favored, he sent his own legates (with plenipotentiary powers) into various key spots.[194] It was the action of an absolute monarch, which was what Gregory VII claimed to be,[195] though it must be granted, from the best evidence we have, that it was motivated by no selfish search for power but only by total dedication to the reform of the church.

Since the Latin church's understanding of Christian ministry will, from this point forward, be strongly influenced by the consolidation of Rome's claims to ultimate and uncontested authority, it is necessary theologically to examine the sources of these claims. By itself, this examination does not settle the issue, at least if one is willing to admit the church's power to develop historically whatever is required for the fulfillment of its evangelical mission. But such a study will at least put us in a better position to evaluate the hierocratic view of the Roman church developed by medieval European Christianity.

First of all, it should be remarked that Gregory VII was no innovator as far as the theory of papal authority is concerned. Long before his reign as pope, actually long before the eleventh century, the position of absolute papal authority had been worked out theoretically; Gregory VII was the one who was able to implement concretely what had been the Roman position on the topic for many centuries.[196] Leo I, Gelasius, Gregory I, Nicholas I, John VIII—all had added their bit to developing the position that all authority had been given to Peter, and since the pope functioned as Peter's vicar this same power belonged to him.[197]

To a great extent, the doctrine of absolute Roman authority was a Roman doctrine, resulting chiefly from statements on the topic made by bishops of Rome. Certainly, there had been from earliest times a recognition of a preeminence, even in some sense of a "primacy," attaching to *the* apostolic see.[198] Rome was looked to as an exemplar Christian community, as one whose faith was guaranteed by the promise made to Peter (Luke 22).[199] But the shift of this to an exercise of legislative and judicial governance over Christian moral behavior and ecclesiastical practice is something the earlier centuries had not known, and that the portions of the church outside immediate Roman influence did not readily admit as something pertaining to essential (or even correct) Christian teaching.[200] That is why it was centuries after its explicit and detailed formulation that the Roman view was finally imposed on the Latin church by the administrative zeal and firmness of Gregory VII, and after him Urban II and Innocent III.[201]

This is not to say that the Roman position was wrong but only to point out that it became "traditional" through the traditions of the Roman see. Yet it would be incorrect to assume that these "Roman traditions" were produced solely by Roman decree. A large portion of the traditional statements appealed to by the popes were decrees of their predecessors, but there were also a considerable number of other statements that helped make up the developing canonical tradition: canons of synods and councils, judgments of fathers of the church (Augustine, Ambrose, Jerome, etc.).[202]

One of the constant elements in this hierocratic argumentation is the appeal to Matthew 16:18, the gift of "the keys" to Peter.[203]

It is interesting to trace the exegesis of this text (interesting, too, the way in which it gradually eclipses Luke 22, which had also been commonly applied to the Roman prerogatives in earlier centuries).[204] The argument never loses sight of the text's application to the context of penitential reconciliation (or excommunication), but its application is extended far beyond this to embrace all authority, all judgment.[205] Considerable attention is also given to the text "Behold, here are two swords . . ." from the time of Gelasius onward, though it is only with Bernard of Clairvaux that one encounters the explicit theory of the "two swords."[206]

Appeal to the fathers is based on the notion of *"auctoritas"* as it was already beginning to emerge and to influence "theological" reasoning. For one thing, a writer was considered to have "authority" in proportion as he was ancient, closer to the time of Christ.[207] One finds some of the fathers treated practically as "word of God" along with Scripture, something that finds no "critical" appraisal or justification until Anselm of Canterbury and Abelard.[208] Moreover, the selection of fathers (and even of the writings of those fathers) was very limited; many of the most influential and important writings of the patristic period were unknown throughout much, if not all, of the Middle Ages.[209] Augustine, of course, was most influential; but Gregory I and Isidore, Jerome, Cyprian, and Ambrose also figured frequently in patristic citation— and commonly the citations were drawn from the *catenae* and *florilegia* of the day.[210]

Increasingly, the appeal was made to the evolving canonical tradition; but this, too, was selective. There was a fair amount of contrariety in canonical judgments over the centuries; even the papal decretals did not always seem to be perfectly consonant. And it was not until the *Decretum* of Gratian in the twelfth century that some harmony was established in the midst of this vast and partially contradictory material, just as Abelard attempted the same thing for patristic texts in his *Sic et non*. But in the meantime some criterion was needed to decide what was truly tradition and what was not, and in this situation Rome and its traditions served as the touchstone.[211] Thus, in the collections that prevailed and that guided the hierocratic theory which prepared for Gregory VII, those documents were retained that agreed with the Roman position.

As one might expect, there was not wholehearted acceptance by the episcopacy of the Roman view, and one must be careful in reading their acknowledgment of Roman primacy not to read it in the light of Vatican I. Even one as well-disposed towards Rome as was Isidore of Seville does not treat the pope as having jurisdiction over him—it is the Pseudo-Isidorian writings to which Roman apologists later appeal![212] Again, at the height of the Carolingian period, Hincmar illustrates the position of genuine episcopal respect for Rome with an accompanying resistance to Rome's abolition of long-standing episcopal prerogatives.[213] Even in the midst of the Hildebrandian campaign, when it required considerable stamina to risk the excommunications and other sanctions that emanated with easy frequency from the Roman curia,[214] bishops (like William Bona Anima, archbishop of Rouen) did resist the pope's abrogation of episcopal rights.[215]

It is difficult to measure the degree of episcopal agreement or disagreement with the theory and policy of the "reforming" popes in the eleventh century. After all, they were not given an invitation to pass theoretical judgment upon the theological validity of the papal view; they were given the alternatives of complying with the papal directives or facing serious reprisal. What was being invoked, at least partially, was papal *power* rather than the intrinsic Christian authority attaching to the bishop of Rome.[216] If this were not so, it is difficult to see why in the practical order the discipline imposed by Gregory VII did not come into effect centuries earlier. The Roman hierocratic theory was already worked out. The authority intrinsic to the Roman pontiff obviously does not vary (this is implicit in the Roman see's own claim to its authority being *de jure divino*), but

what was lacking earlier was the *power* needed to implement the theory.[217]

Humanly speaking, it is difficult to see how the Roman ascendancy of the eleventh century and thereafter could have occurred without Western monasticism. Not only was some of the most effective papal leadership, like Hildebrand, drawn from monastic life but the influential monastic institutions (such as Cluny and its affiliates) were a source of considerable support for the pope.[218] Already, many of these monastic establishments were more closely linked to the pope than to the local episcopacy by virtue of their exempt status.[219] Moreover, prominent abbots exerted considerable moral leadership in the society of that day, and they along with the monastic houses that ministered in many ways to the people threw their support behind the papal position.[220]

The Sacerdotal Office

Despite the ever increasing involvement of the higher clergy, especially the pope, with the secular aspects of medieval life, it would be a mistake to think that the episcopal (or presbyteral) office was looked upon as chiefly a societal eminence. On the contrary, it was regarded as essentially a religious responsibility; the function of a bishop or presbyter was the *cura animarum*.[221] To some extent the understanding of this *cura* has changed from some earlier historical periods; there is a more paternalistic tone, more exhortation to "law and order" through fear motivation, more of the notion of providing for people's spiritual needs through regular "services" performed for them (Mass, burials, confessions, etc.). But in the light of practice the sacerdotal role can still quite legitimately be called "ministry of word and sacrament."

Although not a new idea to be applied to the ministry—since it has New Testament roots, finds fairly frequent mention in the great patristic period, and is prominent in Gregory I—the ideal of "healing" is a central category for thought about the ministry. To quite an extent it is tied in with an increasing theological and popular concentration on man's sinfulness, and is probably affected, too, by the disturbed and raucous social conditions.[222] It acts to interpret the basic *ministerium verbi et sacramenti*.

Gregory's *De cura pastorali* devotes a large portion of its pastoral advice to directions for effective preaching, but all of this preaching is cast in the context of admonishing sinners to amend their ways and convert.[223] No other piece of writing can begin to compare with it for the influence it wielded on medieval thinking and practice about the pastoral office,[224] so it is not surprising to find moral teaching and admonition dominant in the preaching of these centuries.

Despite the fact that this period saw the gradual shift from the discipline of the exomologesis, which stressed the salvific function of penance, to that of confession and absolution, it was also a period when men's need for appeasing God for their sinfulness became almost an obsession.[225] The role of the priest (for he rather than the bishop now became the ordinary minister of penitential reconciliation) was more and more seen as one of applying to the sinner the healing that came from God through Christ.[226] Unfortunately, in this process the earlier awareness of the intrinsic function of penance as "righting things" in the personal attitudes of the person gave way to a more automatic notion of the operation of sacramental absolution. Yet not totally so, for the texts bear constant witness to the fact that the minister of the sacrament is meant to exercise discretion in handling the penitent; one of the two "keys" is that of discrimination in judgment.[227]

Perhaps because of the difficulties of life during this period, the Christian life was more and more described as a struggle, a war. This, of course, was far from being entirely new. Pauline imagery encouraged it, and some of the great fathers (such as Basil) had spoken of the Christian as the *miles Christi*.[228] But towards the end of this period it becomes a commonplace to speak of the church in this world as *ecclesia militans*.[229] For this struggle of life against the powers of evil and sin, the Christian needs strengthening, and

here again the ministry of sacraments is seen as a strengthening. Confirmation is *the* sacrament of fortifying, its effect is described as *robur*,[230] the sacrament of anointing fortifies the Christian for his last and decisive encounter with Satan,[231] and the Eucharist feeds the Christian on his pilgrimage with the food that gives him the strength of Christ's own sacrifice.[232]

Another of the notable aspects of the thinking of this period about the function of the ordained ministry is its emphasis on the *eschatological*. Christian thinking, in general, was turned very much to the "next life"; there was sharp emphasis on "the four last things" (perhaps to some extent under the impact of Gregory the Great).[233] The Christian people, and each individual Christian, was a pilgrim on the way to the heavenly homeland, and it was the role of the clergy to lead them there.[234]

Central to the episcopal and presbyteral task of leading the faithful to the heavenly kingdom was their possession of the "power of the keys." Christ had entrusted these originally to Peter and the Twelve; so now their successors in the papacy and episcopacy exercised this power principally though not exclusively in the sacrament of penance. It is interesting to note, however, that the common opinion at this time seems to be that any ordained minister to whom a Christian community was entrusted for care, thus, not only a bishop with his diocese but also a parish priest with his flock possessed "ordinary power" of penitential absolution.[235]

Christian pastors were not only meant to help rid people from their sinfulness post factum but they were also responsible for giving their people the kind of instruction and exhortation that would guide them along the paths of virtue.[236] This instruction should come in sermons and other formal instruction, but it should also come informally from the clergy's own example of Christian living. In the writings of the great "reformers" of this period, the sad lack of such edifying behavior is a recurrent theme.[237]

As we mentioned above, one notices a much

more common use of the military image. Gregory VII in particular is fond of this way of describing the efforts of good Christians: it is a battle for the cause of truth and virtue against the threatening forces of evil by which he feels surrounded.[238] Life is a crusade; the church on earth is "the church militant." Thus, it is not surprising that just at this time the preaching of the Crusades against the "infidel" could have such a popular appeal.[239] And if the community as a whole was the army of Christ, then of course the clergy were the leaders of that army, the pope first and foremost.

Probably the notion most commonly associated with the ministerial function, at least in popular thinking, was that of officiating in the ritual of sacrament. This was seen in terms of providing for the people the help that they needed from these sacraments: the remission of original sin in baptism, the strengthening against evil in confirmation, the freeing from the results of sin in Penance, the grace and strength of Christ's Eucharistic body.[240] While there was not yet much theological sophistication in their understanding of sacramental actions, they saw the minister's role as definitely *ministerial*, i.e., he was acting as intermediary for Christ. In Christ's name, and in his stead, the ordained minister dispensed salvation through the sacramental rituals.[241] By and large the mentality is quite close to what will soon be described in terms of the technical *"ex opere operato."* Much of the clarification of this point, as well as continued emphasis on it, came through the discussion of the efficacy of sacramental actions performed by unworthy, excommunicated, or schismatic ministers.[242]

Any understanding of the role of the ordained minister during this period depends greatly on the understanding by Christians of the action of the Eucharist. In the tenth and eleventh centuries, triggered by the controversy between Radbertus and Ratramnus and centering around the disputed opinions of Berengarius, there was heightened interest in giving some more thorough theological explanation of the Eucharist.[243] This did not result in any new formulations of the celebrant's role in Eucharist, but it did give increased meaning to the already existent formulations.

To present it in simplified fashion: the Eucharist was looked upon as a sacred action, a situation of the church's commemoration of the mystery of salvation, an act of worship of God which the church militant shared with the angels and the church triumphant.[244] Already, the Eucharist had acquired a considerable aura of awesomeness, and the notion of "mystery" as attached to it carried strong overtones of the "hidden and unfathomable."[245] At the same time, the celebration of the liturgical year was the core of people's reflection upon the events of Jesus' earthly life and death which kept alive an atmosphere of human familiarity with Christ.[246]

Though they lacked an accurate understanding of the resurrection of Christ,[247] and were unconsciously the heirs of a strong anti-Arian reaction which tended to locate the risen Christ "up in heaven" and to stress his divine aspects,[248] Christians of this period had in connection with the Eucharist a strong conviction of the presence of Christ.[249] One can see this quite clearly in the strong reaction against any suggestion that the Eucharistic body of Christ was not "the *real* body."

All of this touched the understanding of the priest's role: he was the "sanctified person" who alone could stand in the sacred precincts of the altar; he was the one who because of the "character of Orders" could change the bread and wine into the body and blood of Christ; he was the one who offered the sacrifice (a notion that was most inadequately understood) which the people watched;[250] he was the one who distributed the saving body of Christ to the community at Eucharist and in viaticum. These things he could do because he was specially empowered by his ordination.[251] There was a vague insight into the fact that he acted ministerially; there is a latent notion of "instrumentality" that will come to theological refinement in the thirteenth century; but the celebrant of the Eucharist is looked upon as "God's man" who has special powers of action to provide for the church rather than as the sacrament through whom Christ himself acts in sacrament.[252]

As the notion of *societas christiana* became more firmly fixed in the mentality of medieval society, it was inevitable that the clergy be considered more and more as part of the officialdom of this society. True, they were distinguished from secular officials, but they constituted a body of functionaries that paralleled that of civil government.

Influenced by the Augustinian notion of "order," which is reinforced during this period by the translation of Pseudo-Denis's *Ecclesiastical Hierarchy*, Latin Christianity in the tenth and eleventh centuries viewed human society as one basically unified structure.[253] By divine ordination the clergy were located on the higher rungs of the ladder, and within the clergy the bishops above the presbyters, presbyters above the deacon.[254]

Greater eminence and greater endowment (which presumably goes with higher "location" in the Dionysian world) brings with it a greater responsibility. So, we can notice increasingly that the bishops and presbyters are viewed as the *active* portion of the church; they are the ones who are to provide for the salvation of the people, who *receive* salvation.[255] Thus the initiative for the development of the church's life and for the implementation of its evangelical mission are quite exclusively reserved to the higher clergy. The laity are expected not to decide but to accept the decisions of their clergy. All of this is more and more expressed in terms of a growing body of official law and approved custom.[256] The "law of the church" is the law of God, and salvation will come by observance of this law.[257]

This situation is, of course, not new; it begins as far back as the sociological distinction of clergy from laity, but it becomes more and more accentuated. Nor is the situation fully formulated into clearly structured procedures and patterns of organization; that will happen in the next two centuries. But in the tenth and eleventh centuries we are observably at the beginnings of the highly organized ecclesiastical (and clericalized) world of the High Middle Ages. It is in this world that the *sacerdos* is *the* mediator of salvation. It is in such a view of Christianity that one finds the word "church" used as a designation for the clergy.[258]

An indication of the manner in which bishops, and particularly the bishop of Rome, are looked upon as "officials" is provided by the episcopal courts which roughly paralleled the secular courts of the higher nobility, and by the extent to which higher ecclesiastics were prominent in these royal courts.[259] Occupants of important episcopal sees were, of course, men of considerable prestige, and they logically surrounded themselves with advisers and assistants. Moreover, they possessed considerable wealth, dealt with the other wealthy elements in the society of their day, and generally behaved in a princely fashion, even if they were distinguished as "princes of the church."[260] We are not, of course, at this historical period dealing with the power and worldliness of the later "prince bishops"; but the basic pattern is already in evidence.

NOTES

1. See Y. Congar, *L'ecclésiologie du Haut Moyen Age* (Paris, 1968), p. 106.

2. *Ibid.*, pp. 86–90.

3. This distinction has always been recognized to some extent; only very recently, however, have theologians begun to develop a "theology of religion." See H. Schlette, *Towards a Theology of Religions*, vol. 14 of Herder, *Quaestiones disputatae* (New York, 1966).

4. Vatican II, *Constitution on Divine Revelation*, 7–8.

5. On the structure and function of the fourth- and fifth-century episcopacy, see J. Gaudemet, *L'Eglise dans l'Empire Romain* (Paris, 1958), pp. 322–67. A good short summary of ecclesiastical patterns from 350 to 450 is given in F. Hoare, *The Western Fathers* (London, 1954), pp. x–xix.

6. See J. Daniélou and H. Marrou, *The Christian Centuries* (London, 1964), vol. 1, pp. 81–89.

7. The motivations for the persecutions, particularly for the harsh measures under Diocletian, are difficult to discern. See *ibid.*, pp. 231–35.

8. One sees early reflections of this attitude in Paul's letters (e.g., Rom. 13:1–7) and in Justin's *Apologies*. For other instances, see Gaudemet, pp. 21–22.

9. E.g., Constantine's use of Hosius of Cordoba; see J.-R. Palanque in A. Fliche and V. Martin, *Histoire de l'Eglise depuis les origines jusqu'à nos jours* (Paris, 1935—), vol. 3, p. 33.

10. On the Constantinian recognition of the *audientia episcopalis*, see Gaudemet, pp. 230–45, and the consequent modification of this Constantinian grant. For this and other decrees regarding the church (up to the time of Justinian), see P. Coleman-Norton, *Roman State and Christian Church*, 3 vols. (London, 1966).

11. Perhaps the most prominent early instance of this was Constantine's role in convoking the Council of Nicaea. See C. Hefele and H. Leclercq, *Histoire des Conciles* (Paris, 1909), vol. 1, pp. 403–27.

12. Already by the end of the fifth century the famous Gelasian distinction of the royal *potestas* and the sacred *auctoritas* has emerged. See Gelasius, *Ad Anastasium imp.*, *P.L.* 59. 41.

13. See Gaudemet, pp. 377–407.

14. G. Bardy and J.-R. Palanque in Fliche-Martin, vol. 3 (1950), pp. 290–91.

15. See K. Morrison, *Tradition and Authority in the Western Church* (Princeton, 1969), pp. 66–68.

16. It is instructive to compare the images used of the church in the patristic literature of the fourth and fifth centuries with New Testament images studied by P. Minear in his *Images of the Church in the New Testament* (Philadelphia, 1960). Throughout, the influence of Paul seems paramount. His use of the military metaphor (e.g., 1 Thess. 5:8) is picked up by Basil, for example, who refers to the Christian as soldier of Christ (*Praevia institutio ascetica* 1; *P.G.* 31. 621). Much more often, however, it is the metaphor of "bride" or "body" that is used: Theodoret of Cyr and Origen (and in a limited fashion Gregory of Nyssa) give an ecclesiological interpretation to the Canticle of Canticles, and this notion of the church as "spouse" remains constant into the Middle Ages (see Congar, pp. 77ff.). Not all the use of New Testament imagery is rooted in Paul, however: to refer again to Basil, he calls the bishop a shepherd (*Epist.* 197) and a custodian of the vineyard (*Epist.* 161). And Jesus' acts of healing narrated in the Gospels certainly influenced the frequent patristic characterization of the bishop as a physician.

Somewhat less biblical is the increasingly prominent image of the church as "mother." This is thoroughly studied (and brought into relationship with other early Christian use of imagery) by K. Delahaye, *Ecclesia Mater* (Paris, 1964).

When one comes to the impact of the political model there is question not only of literary use of a figure but of translation into practical forms of ecclesiastical activity. For example (as F. Dvornik points out in his *Early Christian and Byzantine Political Philosophy* [Dumbarton Oaks, 1966], vol. 2, p. 608): "When ecclesiastical problems, such as the baptism of heretics, forced the bishops of Africa to meet for discussion, their gatherings gradually came to resemble the meetings of the Roman senate." For a brief review of the historical process by which the church came to be viewed according to civil forms, see P. Eyt, "Vers une église démocratique," *Nouvelle revue théologique* 91 (1969), pp. 600–604. As we will see later, this way of thinking was fortified by the city image drawn from Augustine's *De civitate Dei*. This Augustinian influence can be noticed as early as Leo I (*Epist.* 162).

17. Interestingly, it is at this time that one finds a good deal of discussion about Mel-

chizedek as the type of Christ's priesthood (for a listing of several references, see J. Lecuyer, *Le sacerdoce dans le mystère du Christ* [Paris, 1957], p. 89); the overtones of "kingship" in this discussion seem to anticipate some of the episcopal (papal) claims of later centuries. It is also important to note how often, when faced with a practical question of ecclesiastical practice, the tendency of these centuries (observable as early as Tertullian) is to look for an Old Testament precedent (or Old Testament legislation). For example: faced with the problem that their *basileus*, a quasi-priestly figure who functioned somewhat as a cleric in liturgy, was ecclesiastically a layman, Byzantine theologians found a solution in the fact that the emperor was heir to David and Solomon and to their priesthood. See Dvornik, pp. 643–44.

18. See C. Dawson, "St. Augustine and His Age," *Monument to St. Augustine* (New York, 1930), pp. 15–77; see also the essays in the same volume by E. Przywara and M. Blondel.

19. For references to Augustine's use of "*ordo*," see S. Grabowski, *The Church: An Introduction to the Theology of St. Augustine* (St. Louis, 1957), p. 96. Augustine was not, of course, the first to emphasize this notion in thinking about the church; "*ordo*" is already prominent in Tertullian's thinking (see P. Van Beneden, "Ordo: Ueber den Ursprung einer kirchlichen Terminologie," *Vigiliae Christianae* 23 [1969], pp. 161–76). What one does find in Augustine is the combination of Roman interest in law and organization with the Neo-Platonic cosmology. The presence of this latter element makes it quite easy for mainstream Augustinian thought to absorb the Dionysian cosmology at a later date.

On the use of "order" in Pseudo-Dionysius, see R. Roques, *L'univers dionysien* (Paris, 1954), p. 177. As with Augustine, Pseudo-Dionysius was influenced by earlier patristic writing, in this case by the Alexandrian and Cappadocian fathers, particularly by Gregory of Nyssa. See W. Völker, *Kontemplation und Ekstase bei Pseudo-Dionysius Areopagita* (Wiesbaden, 1958), p. 82.

For a broader discussion of Augustine's notion of the church, see J. Ratzinger, *Volk und Haus Gottes in Augustins Lehre von der Kirche* (Munich, 1954): prior to his study of Augustine, he examines the notion of the church in Tertullian, Cyprian, and Optatus.

In such a world-view of a divinely guided cosmic order, in which the church functions as the great sacrament (see Congar, pp. 11–12), the unity of the church is stressed as a major episcopal objective. "We should, in truth, be the most monstrous of all men if we exulted over the schisms and divisions of the churches, and did not esteem the union of the members of Christ's body as the greatest of blessings" (Basil *Epist.* 156. 1). This emphasis on membership in Christ's body as the truly Christian dimension of unity is profoundly expressed by Athanasius: commenting on *3 Cont. Arianos* 22, L. Bouyer says: "En d'autres termes, l'unité des chrétiens est essentielle à leur salut, tel qu'il a plu à Dieu de le réaliser, car ils sont sauvés par le fait que le Verbe incarné les a tous 'portés' en lui. Ce n'est pas seulement par le Christ qu'ils sont sauvés, c'est à la lettre dans le Christ, et leur salut n'est que l'effet de leur unité avec lui et en lui que son incarnation réalise en germe et que la vie de l'Eglise ne fait qu'épanouir." (*L'incarnation et l'Eglise* [Paris, 1943], p. 117.)

20. Certainly the Neo-Platonic strains in Augustine's thought related order and unity most closely, and the unifying force that brought about order was ultimately the One. So, it was most logical for those who were deeply influenced by Augustine to look for the church to achieve unity through a single unifying principle, the pope.

21. See Gaudemet, pp. 322–23.

22. *Ibid.*, pp. 368–74.

23. On the early steps towards parish priests, see *ibid.*, pp. 374–77. For an excellent and extended description of the life of the clergy in Augustine's diocese, see F. Van der Meer, *Augustine the Bishop* (London, 1961), pp. 225–34.

24. Perhaps the most flagrant instance of such episcopal involvement with civil affairs was in Alexandria, under Dioscorus (in mid-fifth century). Athanasius, one of Dioscorus' great predecessors in Alexandria, had himself stressed the important leadership that should be exercised by the important metropolitan sees, but that was

rather a question of religious and moral impact. See K. Hagel, *Kirche und Kaisertum in Lehre und Leben des Athanasius* (Leipzig, 1933), pp. 1–11.

25. "L'annonce de la Parole a conservé, pendant toute la période de la Patristique primitive, sa place prépondérante par rapport à toute autre activité médiatrice de l'Eglise" (Delahaye, p. 221). On preaching as an episcopal prerogative, see Gaudemet, p. 342.

26. See Gaudemet, pp. 593–94.

27. See K. Baus, "Wesen un Funktion der apostolischen Sukzession in der Sicht des heiligen Augustinus," *Ekklesia*, ed. by the theological faculty of Trier (1962), pp. 137–48.

28. Basil *Moralia* 80. 15 (*P.G.* 31. 865). It is interesting to notice the relation between *successio apostolica* and *cura animarum* in early patristic thinking about the episcopate. Already in 385, Pope Siricius links succession from Peter as bishop and succession from Paul in his *cura omnium ecclesiarum*, thereby claiming a primacy for Rome.

29. See J. Jungmann, *Handing on the Faith* (New York, 1959), pp. 1–11; G. Sloyan, "Catechetics," *New Catholic Encyclopedia* (New York, 1967), vol. 3, pp. 220–21.

30. *Ibid.* Both authors indicate the lack of adequate historical study of religious instruction during this and the ensuing period. One might think of the *didaskalion* in Alexandria as an exception to the lack of "school education" in the faith, but apparently there existed in Alexandria two agencies, the regular catechumenate program and a "theological institute" (this latter being the school that was graced by the teaching of such men as Origen and Didymus), neither of which was directed to further formation of faith for the ordinary Christian after baptism. See A. van Roey, "Alexandria, School of," *New Catholic Encyclopedia*, vol. 1, pp. 304–5.

31. One must understand "intensive" quite relatively; the procedures for education of clergy and monks were still very rudimentary and there is no question of schools until the sixth century. See Gaudemet, pp. 588–91. At the same time, one must not underestimate the influence of a center like Lerins, whose training was already producing excellent bishops and preachers for the fifth-century church. See Fliche-Martin, vol. 4, p. 403.

32. See Van der Meer, pp. 199–234.

33. Though preaching and teaching are still in this period a properly episcopal function, presbyters are increasingly utilized as delegates of the bishop.

34. For example, Ambrose's *De officiis ministrorum* testifies to his involvement in educating his clergy. On the informal nature of formation of clergy during this period and the gradual emergence of episcopal schools (in the sixth century), see H. Marrou, *A History of Education in Antiquity* (New York, 1956), pp. 334–36.

35. See *ibid.*, p. 335.

36. For example, at the end of the first book of his *De trinitate* Hilary of Poitiers prays for divine help in studying carefully "the writings of the prophets and apostles" (*P.L.* 10. 48–49), and then at the beginning of the eighth book he stresses the need for the bishop to be both *bonus* and *doctus* (*ibid.*, 236–37).

37. See P. de Lettre's introduction to *Prosper of Aquataine, Defense of St. Augustine*, vol. 32 of *Ancient Christian Writers* (Westminster, Md., 1963), pp. 3–20.

38. See Gaudemet, pp. 214–20.

39. "Dès les premières années du IVe siècle, les conciles d'Elvire, d'Arles, d'Ancyre, de Néocésarée, de Nicée jettent les bases de la législation canoniques et leurs dispositions reprises dans les collections canoniques survivront bien au delà de notre periode. L'antériorité chronologique de la législation conciliare est certaine." (*Ibid.*, pp. 214–15.)

40. Not that there is any substantial change from their liturgical activity in the preceding century, but this is the period when many of the basic liturgies were formulated.

41. Leo I (*Epist.* 6. 6 [*P.L.* 54. 620]) applies the *dignitas officii sacerdotalis* to both presbyters and deacons. The application to the deacons is a bit unexpected (Hippolytus'

Apostolic Tradition had explicitly excluded the deacons from the *sacerdotium*); it may reflect the increasing power of the deacons, against which Jerome and others protested.

42. Typically, Chrysostom speaks of the power of the priest who can beget men to new life (*On the Priesthood* 3. 5. 188), who can free men from those bonds which touch his very soul (3. 5. 183), who can help ward off greater evil by imposing penance (3. 6. 195). But the priest's loftiest dignity is connected with his Eucharistic role: "When the priest has invoked the Holy Spirit and performed that most awful sacrifice, and constantly handled the Lord of all, where indeed shall we rank him? What the purity and what the piety that we shall exact of him? . . . There ought to be nothing purer, nothing holier, than the soul which receives so great a spirit" (6. 4. 232). For leading patristic "theologies of priesthood," see R. Gryson, *Le prêtre selon saint Ambrose* (Louvain, 1968); J. Pintard, *Le sacerdoce selon Augustin* (Paris, 1960); R. Connolly, *The Liturgical Homilies of Narsai* (Cambridge, 1909). Homily 32 of Narsai (pp. 62–74), who taught at Edessa and Nisibis around mid-fifth century, is a precious patristic treatise on priesthood.

43. From the third century, specialized church buildings are already used in both West and East (see J. Zeiller in Fliche-Martin, vol. 2, pp. 435–37); in the fourth century these buildings became more pretentious (see P. de Labriolle in *ibid.*, vol. 3, pp. 430–36).

44. In the West, e.g., Ambrose *De Sacramentis* 4. 1 (*CSEL* 73, pp. 46–47) and *Epist.* 59 (to the church of Vercelli); Leo I *Epist.* 4 and *Epist.* 12 (where he gives Old Testament bases for clerical celibacy); and in the East, Chrysostom *On the Priesthood* 3. 6 and Narsai *Hom.* 32 (Connolly, pp. 62–63).

45. On patristic references to Melchizedek, see G. Bardy, "Melchisédech dans la tradition patristique," *Rev. biblique* (1926), pp. 496–510, and *ibid.* (1927), pp. 25–45; and R. Galdos, "Melquisedec en la patristica," *Estudios ecclesiasticos* 19 (1945), pp. 221–46.

46. See E. Scheller, *Das Priestertum Christi* (Paderborn, 1934), pp. 138–39.

47. Augustine *Contra Cresconium* 2. 10. 12 (*P.L.* 43. 474).

48. See Leo I *Sermo* 5. 2–4. (*P.L.* 54. 153–55).

49. This is already clearly expressed in the *Didascalia* 8–9.

50. See Gaudemet, pp. 376–77.

51. The Council of Orange (canon 10) recognizes still the bishop's *gubernatio* over all the churches built in his diocese.

52. See Gaudemet, pp. 376–77.

53. So, Ambrosiaster applies the term *"vicarii Christi"* (in *1 Epist. ad Timothy* 5. 19 [*P.L.* 17. 506]).

54. Even the *Statuta ecclesiae antiqua*, which has a propresbyteral viewpoint, reflects the extent to which the episcopacy actually controls in monarchical fashion the direction of the church. See C. Munier, *Les Statuta Ecclesiae Antiqua* (Paris, 1960), pp. 192–98.

55. Ambrose's relations with his presbyters was a classic example; see F. Dudden, *The Life and Times of St. Ambrose* (Oxford, 1935), vol. 1, pp. 131–32. For an excellent description of the contemporary situation in the African church, see R. Crispin, *Ministère et sainteté* (Paris, 1965).

56. See Carthage II, canons 3, 9 (*Mansi* 3. 869, 871); and Carthage III, canons 24, 32, 36 (*Mansi* 3. 884–85).

57. See *Epist. 146, Ad Evangelum* (*P.L.* 22. 1192–95). See also L. Sanders, *Etudes sur saint Jerome* (Paris, 1903), pp. 296–344.

58. *Epist. 146, Ad Evangelum* (*P.L.* 22. 1193–94).

59. He does say explicitly (*ibid.*, 22. 1194): "Quid enim facit excepta ordinatione Episcopus, quod Presbyter non faciat?"

60. In *Epist. 1 ad Tim., Hom.* 11 (*P.G.* 62. 553).

61. So, e.g., Bonaventure *Breviloquium* 6. 12. 13. The variety of views on this topic will be discussed in chapter 30.

62. See J. Quasten, *Patrology* (Westminster, Md., 1950), vol. 3, pp. 459–61.

63. *Hom.* 18.

64. *Moralia* 80. 15–19 (*P.G.* 31. 865–67).

65. An excellent summation of the bishop's functions is contained in the sermon preached by Augustine, probably for the ordination of a bishop; for the Latin text, see *Miscellanea Agostiniana*, vol. 1, pp. 563–75. See also Pintard, p. 371, n. 1.

66. See Dudden, pp. 121–22.

67. The image of physician is common in patristic descriptions of the episcopal function (e.g., Chrysostom *On the Priesthood* 3. 6), but more often in the sense of "physician of souls." (Is there any trace of "office" of healer?)

68. One of the earliest (and most influential) of these was the *Life of St. Martin* written by Sulpicius Severus around the year 400. For a detailed discussion of the literary genre, dating, etc., of this work, see J. Fontaine in the introduction to *Sulpice Sévère: Vie de saint Martin* (*Sources chrétiennes* 133), vol. 1 (1967). It may well be that Sulpicius Severus lays emphasis on Martin's identity as an ascetic rather than as bishop; this would only indicate the extent to which the episcopal and ascetic ideals have overlapped by this time. See Daniélou-Marrou, p. 447: "It is the bishop, above all, who is the typical saint of this period."

69. Prescinding from the historical accuracy of the wonders recounted in these writings, the appearance of these edifying biographies fits logically into the mainstream of traditional Christian thought: as early as *1 Clement* and Justin one can find the view that tradition is concerned (among other things) with preserving the heroic examples of Christian life and thus providing incentive to imitation.

70. On the origins of monasticism, see Daniélou-Marrou, pp. 269–79.

71. See Gaudemet, p. 344.

72. On the beginnings of this exemption, see F. Kempf, *Handbook of Church History* (New York, 1969), vol. 3, p. 295.

73. This was particularly true in Egypt where the pattern had been set by the relationship between Antony and Athanasius.

74. See Völker, pp. 78–80.

75. See D. Knowles, *Christian Monasticism* (New York, 1969), pp. 9–36; J. Leclercq, "On Monastic Priesthood According to the Ancient Medieval Tradition," *Studia Monastica* 3 (1960), pp. 137–55.

76. See P. Humbertclaude, *La doctrine ascétique de saint Basile de Césarée* (Paris, 1933), pp. 139–55. Much the same interpretation is given by M. Murphy, *St. Basil and Monasticism* (Washington, 1930), pp. 45–51.

77. Humbertclaude, p. 152.

78. *Ad Anastasium imp.* (*P.L.* 59. 41).

79. See Dvornik, pp. 804–8.

80. See W. Ullmann, *The Growth of Papal Government in the Middle Ages* (London, 1955), pp. 22–26.

81. Thus, as Isidore of Seville says (*Sententiae* 3. 51. 4; *P.L.* 83. 723), secular princes have power so that "quod non praevalet sacerdos efficere per doctrinae sermonem, potestas hoc imperet per disciplinae terrorem."

82. See Dvornik, vol. 2, pp. 848–50.

83. *Ibid.*, p. 850.

84. On Gregory's use of *servus servorum Dei*, see H. Küng, *The Church* (New York, 1967), pp. 470–71.

85. See Roques, pp. 280–81. It may be significant as a reflection of the solidified clergy-laity dichotomy that 1 Pet. 2:9 now begins to be applied to clerics (Isidore *De eccles. officiis* 2. 4. 4 [*P.L.* 83. 780]).

86. See Dvornik, pp. 717–23.

87. *Ibid.*, p. 816.

88. See Kempf, pp. 3–7.

89. *Ibid.*, pp. 21–22.

90. See Ullmann, pp. 61–69.

91. See F. Dudden, *Gregory the Great* (Oxford, 1905), vol. 2, pp. 224–26.

92. On Rome's prestige as a principle of unity, see Fliche-Martin, vol. 4, pp. 366–67.

93. See J. Jungmann, *Mass of the Roman Rite* (New York, 1951), vol. 1, pp. 59–66.

94. In Gregory's day, Rome still possessed a body of men who had inherited the traditions and training of governmental administration, and so the church could draw upon this skilled labor, as the popes did for administering their holdings and for devising legal theories to justify their actions. See H. Moss, *The Birth of the Middle Ages* (Oxford, 1935), pp. 131–33.

95. See Congar, pp. 13–15.

96. On the novelty and significance of this mission, see D. Knowles, *The Christian Centuries* (London, 1969), vol. 2, p. 9.

97. See Bede, *Ecclesiastical History of the English People*, ed. B. Colgrave and R. Mynors (Oxford, 1969), 2. 1.

98. See Gaudemet, pp. 341–43.

99. If one can judge from the antideacon attitude and statements of Jerome and Ambrosiaster, deacons seem to have been prominent in such curial positions and to have gained considerable influence.

100. See Daniélou-Marrou, p. 392.

101. This is reflected in canon 26 of Chalcedon (*Mansi* 7. 367) which stipulates that each bishop is to appoint a cleric as *oeconomus* to assist him in administering the goods of the church.

102. It is noteworthy, however, that teaching (preaching) is still stressed as basic to the episcopal function. See Isidore *De eccl. officiis* 2. 5. 17 (*P.L.* 83. 785). That episcopacy itself is seen as a function: "episcopus . . . nomen est operis, non honoris" (*ibid.*, 2. 5. 8 [*P.L.* 83. 782]).

103. One can see this reflected in the legislation of regional synods, in episcopal correspondence with presbyters, and in two anonymous writings: the *Statuta ecclesiae antiqua* and the *De septem ordinibus*. See Munier, pp. 192–97.

104. A helpful study of the influences that affected Isidore (among them the influence of Gregory) is J. Fontaine's two-volume *Isidore de Seville et la culture classique dans l'Espagne visigothique* (Paris, 1959). Though his emphasis is on the literary achievements and cultural outlook of Isidore, Fontaine does draw attention to attitudes of Isidore that would have important implications for his understanding of ministry (though Fontaine is not interested in drawing these implications). For example, he stresses the contrast between Isidore's positive view of secular culture and Gregory's negative and apocalyptic view, which would certainly affect the way in which each would see the task of the Christian pastor.

105. This will be studied in more detail in chapter 10.

106. See B. Smalley, *The Study of the Bible in the Middle Ages* (Oxford, 1952), pp. 32–35.

107. However, by mid-seventh century there are clear indications of the new approach to Penance, indications also that it is becoming ever more difficult to insist on a discipline of public penance. See B. Poschmann, *Penance and the Anointing of the Sick* (New York, 1964), pp. 122–38.

108. So, e.g., the letter of Gregory II to the Byzantine emperor in 729 (quoted by Ullmann, p. 46): "We derive our power and authority from the prince of the apostles, Peter, and we could, if we wished, pronounce judgment upon you. . . ."

109. However, much of the older patristic view of Christian initiation and exomologesis persists. See B. Neunheuser, *Baptism and Confirmation* (New York, 1964), pp. 161–80.

110. *Moral* 31. 10.

111. See Gregory VII *Epist. 21, Ad Herimannum* (*P.L.* 148. 594).

112. On these books, see Jungmann, *Mass*, pp. 60–66.

113. Jungmann leans somewhat to an actual link of the *Gelasianum* and the *Gregorianum* to Gelasius and Gregory. *Ibid.*, pp. 62–63.

114. *Ibid.*

115. One can see this reflected in the Roman stational liturgy of the seventh century (see *ibid.*, pp. 67–74). Even though there is much more sense of community participation than in the Carolingian (and later) Eucharistic liturgy, the moments of actual participation by the attendant faithful have been reduced to bringing the gifts, receiving Communion, and exchanging the greeting of peace. The people no longer answer the prayers, and a choir has preempted the singing.

116. This was particularly true in the Frankish church, where Latin was retained in the liturgy, though the ordinary faithful could not readily understand it. "Thus in the Carolingian empire the Mass-liturgy, so far as understanding its language was concerned, became a clerical preserve. A new kind of *disciplina arcani* or discipline of the secret had developed, a concealment of things holy, not from the heathen—there were none—but from the Christian people themselves." (*Ibid.*, p. 81.)

117. *Ibid.*, p. 82.

118. *Ibid.*, pp. 82–83.

119. Munier, *Les Statuta Ecclesiae Antiqua* (Paris, 1960). As Munier points out (pp. 192–97), the author of the *Statuta* is definitely in the propresbyteral tradition of Jerome and Ambrosiaster, but is much more temperate in his attempts to control the monarchical activity of the episcopacy than is the (also anonymous) Gallican *De septem ordinibus*.

120. See Gaudemet, pp. 376–77.

121. The *Statuta* lays upon the bishop the responsibility for the morals of his clergy (canon 102), but it also provides for a synod resolving disputes between bishop and clergy (canon 59).

122. See Knowles, *Christian Centuries*, vol. 2, pp. 7–15, 27–55; W. Cannon, *History of Christianity in the Middle Ages* (New York, 1960). Evolution of ecclesiastical patterns was somewhat different in Ireland and England from what it was in Frankish and Mediterranean areas, though a considerable amount of English and Celtic influence was brought to the Continent by evangelizing monks, particularly by Boniface. On the English developments, see M. Deanesly, *The Pre-Conquest Church in England* (London, 1961).

123. See W. Levison, *England and the Continent in the Eighth Century* (Oxford, 1946), pp. 104–6.

124. See J. Russell, *A History of Medieval Christianity* (New York, 1968), pp. 70–71.

125. Boniface himself is a good illustration of the situation: himself a monk, abbot-founder of Fulda (which he cherished as his "home"), he was also archbishop and most influential in bringing about an orderly episcopal structuring of the Frankish church; at the same time he helped lay the foundation for later conflict between bishops and monasticism; this he did by obtaining "exemption" for his abbey at Fulda. See Levison, pp. 78–93.

126. Though this particular term is characteristically that of Gregory VII, similar expressions are found earlier: Isidore uses the form *"civitas regis magni"* (*Quaest. in Vet. Test.* 1. 7 [*P.L.* 83. 393]), Nicolas I uses *"societas fidelium"* (*MGH Epist. 6*, Epist. 29, p. 296), and John VIII uses *"respublica christiana"* (*MGH Epist. 7*, Epist. 150, p. 126). On the understanding of *societas christiana* as it developed in the thought of Gregory VII, see Ullmann, p. 271.

    Though this kind of secular political language certainly reflects a growing influence of the political model in medieval thought about the church, there remained many other images (as Congar stresses in his *Ecclésiologie*, pp. 73–127): Rabanus Maurus, for example, calls the church, *mater, corpus Christi, sponsa Christi* (*De cleric. institutione* 1. 1 [*P.L.* 107. 297]); an anonymous canonical text of the ninth century, in dealing with ecclesiastical grades, makes a sharp distinction between the external aspect of the church and its inner reality as *congregatio fidelium* (R. Reynolds, "A

Florilegium on the Ecclesiastical Grades in CLM 19414: Testimony to Ninth-Century Clerical Instruction," *Harvard Theological Review* 63 [1970], p. 256). Christ was, of course, consistently seen to be the "head" of this *societas christiana*, but the understanding of this gradually shifted as the word *"corpus"* (even as used in the term *"corpus Christi"*) was affected by developing medieval notions of societal structures. On early medieval understandings of Christ as head, see Congar, pp. 112–13.

127. On the influence of Augustine's *De civitate Dei* on medieval thought, see N. Figgis, *The Political Aspects of Saint Augustine's "City of God"* (London, 1921), pp. 81–100.

128. See Gelasius *De anathematis vinculo* (*P.L.* 59. 108).

129. Though the idea of the priesthood of the faithful is still quite strong, there is an increasing separation of laity and clergy (see Congar, pp. 92–98). Moreover, the laity are distinguished not only from clergy but from those in monastic life: "Sunt tres ordines in Ecclesia . . . laicorum, monachorum et clericorum" (Rabanus Maurus *De clericorum institutione* 1. 2 [*P.L.* 107. 297]). This special dignity of the clergy was reinforced by the civil privileges of the clergy (interestingly reinforced by the "Donation of Constantine"; see B. Pullan, *Sources for the History of Medieval Europe* [Oxford, 1966], p. 10), but reinforced also by theological evolution. For example, Rabanus Maurus applies 1 Pet. 2:4 to the clergy (col. 298).

130. The pope-to-bishop element in this picture represents, of course, the Roman hierocratic theology, which was not completely accepted by the hierarchy of this period. Moreover, the picture was further complicated by the claims made for Charlemagne as protector of the *populus Christianus*, as a "new David" (i.e., a somewhat priestly king), etc., and his actual mode of inserting himself authoritatively into ecclesiastical affairs. On this complicated interaction of Carolingian civil and ecclesiastical institutions (and theories about these institutions), see W. Ullmann, *The Carolingian Renaissance and the Idea of Kingship* (London, 1969).

131. On the manner in which the royal theology of Hincmar of Reims placed the king under the episcopacy and made the temporal authority the instrument for carrying out the ethical teaching of the church, see *ibid.*, pp. 111–34.

132. See Congar, pp. 112–13.

133. On the post-Arian exaltation of the figure of Christ and its effects on Christian faith and liturgy, see J. Jungmann, *Pastoral Liturgy* (New York, 1962), pp. 1–63.

134. See Congar, pp. 194 (n. 41) and 216.

135. See Ullmann, *Papal Government*, pp. 27–28; Ullmann shows how this early employment of the term must not be taken in too technical a sense. On p. 39, he points out how Gregory I extends the term to the function of the entire *sacerdotium*.

136. It is significant that this point of view is quite different from that reflected in the imperial theology of Justinian, where the *basileus* is the incarnated will of God, and continues to stand in tension with the attempts of Charlemagne and (later) Gregory VII to assume a position not unlike that of the Byzantine *basileus*. As K. Morrison says, speaking of the eighth-century Franks: "Among them tradition took precedence as an authority over papal discretion" (*Tradition and Authority in the Western Church*, p. 167).

137. See *ibid.*, p. 213.

138. *Ibid.*, pp. 214–28; Knowles, *Christian Centuries*, vol. 2, pp. 140–43.

139. See E. Ewig, *Handbook of Church History* (New York, 1969), vol. 3, pp. 95–118.

140. *Ibid.*, pp. 92–94; Knowles, *Christian Centuries*, vol. 2, pp. 62–63.

141. See Ewig, pp. 90–92.

142. See G. Ellard, *Master Alcuin: Liturgist* (Chicago, 1956).

143. Not all the instruction coming from the Carolingian liturgists was an unmixed blessing. Apparently it was Alcuin who applied allegorical understanding to the Eucharistic action, and this allegorical approach was developed in detail in the *De ecclesiasticis officiis* of Amalar (Alcuin's disciple) which became extremely influential in shaping people's notions about the Eucharist. See Jungmann, *Mass*, pp. 87–91.

144. On the complicated development of parish structures, the problem caused by the

spread of proprietary churches (which in many instances left the selection of pastor to the secular landlord), and the impact of Germanic law on these developments, see Kempf, pp. 258–64.

145. See Jungmann, *Handbook of Church History*, vol. 3, pp. 307–12; also J.-B. Mahn, "Le clergé séculier à l'époque asturienne (718–910)," *Mélanges Louis Halphen* (Paris, 1951), pp. 453–64; and G. Prevost, *L'Eglise et les campagnes au Moyen Age* (Paris, 1892).

146. The various treatises on ecclesiastical grades from the eighth and ninth centuries make it clear that "*sacerdos*" is regularly applied to the presbyter, that it reflects his sacred character, and that it is linked with his act of offering sacrifice. See Reynolds' "A Florilegium" (Reynolds himself does not have as his purpose to draw attention to this, but the texts he quotes contain these elements).

147. On the shift of emphasis in this period to the Eucharistic celebrant as "cause of the Presence," see Jungmann, *Mass*, pp. 83–84.

148. See M. Bloch, *La société féodale* (Paris, 1940), vol. 2, pp. 99–111.

149. *De clericorum institutione* 1. 1–7 (*P.L.* 107. 297–302).

150. See Kempf, pp. 286–90. As we will see later, at the heart of this change was a shift from the primacy of episcopal collegiality to the primacy of papal authority. See also E. Amann in Fliche-Martin, vol. 6 (1947), pp. 26–27.

151. Kempf, pp. 270–79.

152. Thus, Rabanus Maurus simply equates archbishops and metropolitans, "Ordo autem episcoporum tripartitus est, id est, in patriarchis, archiepiscopis, qui et metropolitani sunt, et episcopis" (1. 5, col. 300).

153. On ecclesiastical structures during the Merovingian and Carolingian periods, see O. Dalton, *The History of the Franks by Gregory of Tours* (Oxford, 1927), vol. 1, pp. 260–317; also Amann, pp. 26–27, 82–83.

154. See Knowles, *Christian Centuries*, pp. 128–45; Ewig, *Handbook of Church History*, vol. 3, pp. 168–70.

155. As we show in greater detail, this shift to emphasis on jurisdiction is one of the key evolutions in Christian thinking about ministry. However, as Congar points out (pp. 16–17 in his introduction to Delahaye, *Ecclesia Mater*), this is also a basic shift in the view of Christian anthropology and soteriology. By the time that the Gregorian reform has established itself (in the late eleventh century) this juristic manner of viewing the church, its minstry, etc., is clearly dominant; in the Merovingian and even Carolingian periods we are still in a transitional situation, but the growing importance of this manner of thinking is quite apparent.

156. Not that this ascendancy of Rome was established during the Carolingian (much less the Merovingian) period. True, Charlemagne did much to link the religious renaissance in his realm with the teaching, liturgy, and institutions of the Roman church; however, he did much to perpetuate (and even extend) the already prevalent practice of temporal rulers appointing bishops. The decline of election as the basis for the selection of the episcopacy began not with papal interference but with secular intervention. Moreover, Charlemagne acted according to what he believed was his God-given right and responsibility; for example, writing to Gherbald, bishop of Liege, he says, ". . . Episcopo cum universis tibi omnipotente Deo et nostra ordinatione commissis in Domino salutem" (*MGH, Capit.* 1, p. 245). See R. Aigrain in Fliche-Martin, vol. 5, p. 369; Amann, pp. 82–83.

Moreover, this was a period when, particularly in the Frankish territory, much of the advance of the church's life was due to strong bishops such as Agobard and Hincmar and Rabanus Maurus, who not only acted with a clear sense of their episcopal responsibility and autonomy but expressed the same in the treatises they wrote on ecclesiastical offices. See A. Mignon, *Les origines de la scolastique* (Paris, 1895), vol. 2, pp. 210–14.

157. See Cyprian *De cath. eccl. unitate* 5 (*CSEL* 3, 213–4).

158. On the dispute regarding the relevant text (*De cath. eccl. unitate* 4), see Morrison, pp. 25–27.

159. However, a certain ambiguity still remains in Augustine's view of the Roman see. See Morrison, pp. 108–9; for a somewhat different approach to Augustine's view, see Congar, p. 139.

160. Probably the exile of many prominent bishops and monks during the years of Vandal persecution (many of these exiles settled in Spain) accentuated the infusion of African traditions into the Spanish church; however, there had been for centuries before this a constant interchange between Africa and the Iberian peninsula. Cyprian corresponded regularly with members of the Spanish episcopate. See Fontaine, *Isidore de Seville*, vol. 2, pp. 854–59.

161. Dudden, *Gregory the Great*, vol. 1, pp. 155–56, 411–13.

162. See Congar, p. 141. Congar cites Bede (who is often instanced as an example of devotion to Rome) as one of the most striking proponents of the Cyprianic view.

163. On the origin and nature of *Pseudo-Isidore*, see Ullmann, *Papal Government*, pp. 80–84.

164. See P. Batiffol, *Cathedra Petri* (Paris, 1938), p. 86.

165. On the absolute claim made by John VIII, see Ullmann, *Papal Government*, p. 219.

166. *Ibid.*, pp. 40–41.

167. See Knowles, *Christian Monasticism*, pp. 28–33. For a lengthier treatment, see J. Ryan, *Irish Monasticism*, 2d ed. (Shannon, 1972).

168. See Ryan, pp. 167–90; also, Leclercq-Vandenbroucke-Bouyer, *The Spirituality of the Middle Ages*, vol. 2 of *History of Christian Spirituality* (London, 1968), pp. 39–40.

169. See H. Daniel-Rops, *The Church in the Dark Ages* (New York, 1959), pp. 212–18.

170. Poschmann, pp. 24–34.

171. P. Anciaux, *The Sacrament of Penance* (New York, 1962), pp. 61–68.

172. On the background of Benedict and the Rule, see D. Knowles, *The Monastic Order in England* (Cambridge, 1941), pp. 3–15.

173. Much of the impetus for this "revival" of episcopal synods was provided by Boniface in mid-eighth century; see Amann, pp. 26–27.

174. See Mignon, pp. 210–11; also, C. Munier, *Les sources patristiques du droit de l'Eglise du VIIIe au XIIIe siècle* (Strasbourg, 1957), pp. 206–9. Of these texts Munier says (p. 207): ". . . Nous tenons là, nous semble-t-il, une source précieuse, encore mal explorée, capable de nous renseigner sur les aspirations profondes du clergé médiéval et sur l'idéal de la société chrétienne."

175. See Congar, pp. 164–77.

176. See E. Duckett, *Carolingian Portraits* (Ann Arbor, Mich., 1962), pp. 202–58.

177. As early as the eighth century in the listing of ecclesiastical offices in the *Collectio Hibernensis*, "*sacerdos*" is used as a distinctive term for the presbyterate: "Episcopum decet judicare et interpretari et consecrare et consummare et ordinare et baptizare et offerre; sacerdotem autem oportet offerre et benedicere et bene praeesse, praedicare et baptizare" (cited by Reynolds, p. 240).

178. Perhaps in reaction to this increasing emphasis on the bishop as administrator, the *Statuta ecclesiae antiqua* stresses the pastoral virtues desired in a bishop. See Munier, *Les Statuta Ecclesiae Antiqua*, p. 193.

179. See D. Power, *Ministers of Christ and His Church* (London, 1969), pp. 70–78. An indication of the continuity of liturgical texts for ordination: the same formulae for priestly ordination and episcopal consecration are used in the Roman Ordinal around 750 and in the Gregorian, Gelasian, and Leonine Sacramentaries; see M. Andrieu, *Les Ordines Romani du Haut Moyen Age* (Louvain, 1931), vol. 3, p. 569, n. 3.

180. See A. McDevitt, "The Episcopate as an Order and Sacrament on the Eve of the High Scholastic Period," *Franciscan Studies* 20 (1960), pp. 96–148. McDevitt quotes A. Landgraf to the effect that the explicit question of the episcopate's being a distinct order was not formulated until early scholasticism; this is true provided one uses "order" in a context of sacramental power, but in earlier texts the usage is different. Rabanus Maurus, for example, in *De clericorum institutione* 1. 4–5, does treat of

episcopate as a distinct order, but he is speaking in a sociological context; later (5–6), in discussing the sacerdotal functions of bishops and presbyters, he places the two groups on a more equal base (using the distinction that becomes classic: *"sacerdotes primi et secundi ordinis"*).

181. See Y. Congar, "Two Factors in the Sacralization of Western Society During the Middle Ages," *Sacralization and Secularization in the History of the Church* (New York, 1968), pp. 28–31.

182. Isidore *De eccles. officiis* 2. 5. 1; Rabanus Maurus *De cleric. inst.* 1. 4.

183. See Rabanus Maurus, 1. 5–7.

184. See IV, 8–9 (p. 254) in the text of the florilegium studied and edited by R. Reynolds in the article cited above (n. 126); this passage indicates that by the ninth century or earlier the *consecratio sacrificii* was viewed as the basic sacerdotal action.

185. See Congar, *Ecclésiologie*, pp. 138–51.

186. Actually, the "power" to absolve sins seems to have grown more out of the basic pastoral responsibility of caring for those entrusted to one in a given community. It is good to remember, also, that there was a strong tendency to see the priest's act as declaratory; see P. Anciaux, *La théologie du sacrement de pénitence au XIIe siècle* (Louvain, 1949), pp. 38–41.

187. See A. Dumas in Fliche-Martin, vol. 7, pp. 220–90.

188. In many ways, the heart of the problem was the benefice system; on the multiple influences leading to the creation of this system and its evolution within feudal structures, see Kempf, pp. 258–79.

189. See A. Dopsch, *The Economic and Social Foundations of European Civilization* (London, 1937), pp. 289–302.

190. For differing interpretations of this conflict, see *The Investiture Controversy*, ed. K. Morrison (New York, 1971), pp. 1–67.

191. For example: "Quod solus Romanus pontifex jure dicatur universalis. . . . Quod ille solus possit deponere episcopos vel reconciliare. . . . Quod illi licet imperatores deponere. . . . Quod a nemine ipse judicari debeat. (*P.L.* 148. 407–8.) On the source and character of the *Dictatus*, see Kempf, pp. 368–69.

192. Gregory, however, was no innovator in this regard. Movements to reform, spearheaded by Roman reformers, particularly Gregory's immediate predecessor Nicholas II, had almost of necessity to oppose and interfere with the irregular procedures of many dioceses. See Kempf, pp. 351–66.

193. See A. Fliche in Fliche-Martin, vol. 8, pp. 84–89.

194. *Ibid.*, pp. 89–95.

195. See Ullmann, *Papal Government*, pp. 271–97.

196. *Ibid.*, p. 271.

197. This progression will be studied in detail in chapter 22.

198. For a cataloging of early witness to Roman preeminence, see G. Glez, "Primauté," *Dictionnaire théologie catholique*, vol. 13, cols. 262–89.

199. Irenaeus *Adv. Haer.* 3. 3. 2. The Petrine promises apply to the Roman church because Peter continues as Rome's bishop, acting through his vicar (the present incumbent in the Roman episcopacy); see Leo I *Sermo* 3. 2–3.

200. Even a strong ally of Rome, like Isidore of Seville, held that the bishops all had equal power, just as the Twelve had equal power with Peter, though he was granted it first; see *De eccles. officiis* 2. 5. 5–6.

201. This is not to suggest that no further theoretical delineation of the papal position took place: on the contrary, the rise of canon law as a discipline in the twelfth century led to an impressive body of legal writing on papal prerogatives. See Ullmann, *Papal Government*, pp. 359–446.

202. See Munier, *Les sources patristique*, pp. 206–8.

203. See Congar, *Ecclésiologie*, pp. 138–51.

204. On the interrelated use of these two texts, see E. Dublanchy, "Infallibilité," *Dictionnaire de théologie catholique*, vol. 7, cols. 1639–55.

205. On the linked emergence of penitential discipline and official jurisdiction in the third and fourth centuries, see H. von Campenhausen, *Ecclesiastical Authority and Spiritual Power in the Church in the First Three Centuries* (Palo Alto, Calif., 1969), pp. 265–92.

206. See Y. Congar, "L'ecclésiologie de S. Bernard," *Saint Bernard: Théologien*, ed. J. Leclercq (Rome, 1953), pp. 168–71.

207. On late patristic and medieval use of *"auctores,"* see M.-D. Chenu, *Toward Understanding St. Thomas* (Chicago, 1964), pp. 126–34.

208. On Abelard's key role in developing critical theological use of sources, see M. Grabmann, *Die Geschichte der scholastischen Methode* (Freiburg, 1911), vol. 2, pp. 199–221.

209. *Ibid.*, pp. 54–94.

210. See Chenu, p. 139.

211. See Ullmann, *Papal Government*, pp. 361–65.

212. Contrary to Isidore himself, who is a mediator to the Middle Ages of the Cyprianic tradition on episcopal prerogatives, *Pseudo-Isidore*, while exalting the hierarchy, gives clear jurisdictional primacy to Rome. "The primacy of the Roman Church is, next to ecclesiastical freedom from lay jurisdiction, the most vital principle with which *Pseudo-Isidore* operates" (*ibid.*, p. 182).

213. See Congar, *Ecclésiologie*, pp. 166–77.

214. For a listing of prominent archbishops and bishops excommunicated and/or deposed between 1076 and 1080, see Fliche, pp. 96–97.

215. William refused to accede to Gregory VII's demand that all archbishops come to Rome to receive the pallium from him personally; William's position was strengthened (as in other matters was Lanfranc's in England) by Gregory's need to follow a conciliatory policy with William the Conqueror. See *ibid.*, p. 87.

216. This is not to pass judgment on Hildebrand's personal motives, for he does seem to have acted out of love for the church; but even Kempf, who stresses Gregory's religious motivation (pp. 370–74), admits that Gregory's actions mark a turning point in the exercise of papal power.

217. Even Gregory VII was frustrated in his attempts to assert full authority; such success came under later popes, reaching its zenith in Innocent III.

218. See H. Cowdry, *The Cluniacs and the Gregorian Reform* (Oxford, 1970).

219. Exemption touched upon two basic elements: the property of the monasteries was part of "the patrimony of Peter and Paul" and so was protected from incursion and freed from taxes, etc.; and the monks were not subject to the jurisdiction of the local bishop. On the most important instance of exemption at this time, that of Cluny, see Dumas, pp. 341–64.

220. Conversely, the papacy of this period, particularly Urban II (himself a former Cluniac monk), generally supported monastic institutions in their disputes with bishops. See Fliche, pp. 223–26.

221. Linked with this was the enduring notion, despite the obvious human determinants of episcopal selection, that men were called to priestly positions (beginning with the pope) by the Spirit. See Congar, *Ecclésiologie*, pp. 114–16.

222. See Daniel-Rops, pp. 529–48.

223. The character of this admonition is paternal (rather than fraternal): the basic word used by Gregory to designate the admonishing preacher is *"rector."*

224. See Dudden, *Gregory the Great*, vol. 1, pp. 238–40.

225. One factor that needs further study in this regard: the extent to which the Augustinian tradition (dominant throughout the late patristic and medieval periods) in linking original sin so closely to "concupiscence" transmitted a basically negative attitude towards human actions.

226. One finds throughout this and the subsequent period a constantly repeated comparison between the priestly act of penitential absolution and the Old Testament healing of leprosy and Jesus' act of raising Lazarus; the comparison comes from Jerome and is transmitted through Gregory I. See Anciaux, *La théologie*, pp. 38–39.

227. Thus Gregory I (though his view leans towards the declarative view of the minister's act of reconciliation): "Causae ergo pensandae sunt et tunc ligandi et solvendi potestas est exercenda; videndum est quae culpa praecesserit et quae sit poenitentia secuta post culpam, ut quos omnipotens Deus per compunctionis gratiam visitat, illos pastoralis sententia absolvat. Tunc illa vera est absolutio praesidentis, cum interni arbitrium sequitur judicis." (*In Evang.* 2, hom. 26. 5–6.)

228. *Praevia institutio ascetica* 1.

229. To some extent this was influenced by the interchangeability of feudal and ecclesiastical terminology (see Fliche, p. 114), but it goes much beyond this: Christian life was viewed as a battle—Gregory VII tells Herimann of Metz that he is "fighting in the front lines." C. Thouzellier, "Ecclesia militans," *Etudes d'histoire du droit canonique* (Paris, 1965), vol. 2, pp. 1407–23.

230. On the evolution of this notion as confirmation becomes increasingly separated from baptism, see J. Fisher, *Christian Initiation: Baptism in the Medieval West* (London, 1965), p. 134.

231. By the ninth century there seems to be clear emphasis on anointing having spiritual as well as bodily healing power; and there is a clear shift towards anointing *before death*. See C. Ruch, "Extrême onction," *Dictionnaire théologie catholique*, vol. 5, cols. 1970–85.

232. This notion had, long before the period we are studying, been attached to *viaticum*, the administration of the Eucharist to a dying Christian to fortify him for the journey into the next life. On the mixed roots of this practice, see G. Grabka, "Christian Viaticum: A Study of Its Cultural Background," *Traditio* 7 (1953), pp. 1–43.

233. Both Gregory's *Moralia* and his *Dialogues* (especially the fourth book) enjoyed widespread popularity in subsequent centuries as sources for belief about "the four last things." Gregory's presentation has been criticized, and with considerable justification, for its fanciful and legendary character. However, Gregory's impact in this respect was not only upon popular credulity, for, as F. Dudden remarks (*Gregory the Great*, vol. 2, p. 437), ". . . his dogmatic teaching about the future state determined the doctrine of the medieval theologians."

234. The view of life as a pilgrimage was reinforced by the widespread practice of religious pilgrimage, one of the key features of medieval life. An interesting anthropology of pilgrimage as a universal phenomenon is provided by V. Turner, chap. 5 ("Pilgrimages as Social Processes"), in *Dramas, Fields, and Metaphors* (Ithaca, N.Y., 1974), pp. 116–228. Turner's treatment, however, takes little account of the distinctive motivations of medieval pilgrimage.

235. As late as the Fourth Lateran Council, in the law of annual confession, there seems to be the assumption that power of absolution comes with ordinary pastoral office, for it is connected with confession to one's own pastor: "Omnis utriusque sexus fidelis, postquam ad annos discretionis pervenit, omnia sua solus peccata saltem semel in anno fideliter confiteatur proprio sacerdoti. . . . Si quis autem alieno sacerdoti voluerit iusta de causa sua confiteri peccata, licentiam prius postulet et obtineat a proprio sacerdote, cum aliter ille ipsum non possit absolvere vel ligare." (Lateran IV, canon 21 [*Mansi*, 22. 1007].)

236. An indication of the extent to which doctrinal clarification and direction of Christian behavior were linked, with the latter often the dominant influence, is the degree to which, by the latter part of this period, theology and canon law were intertwined. Indeed, the canonical collections had become a basic *locus theologicus*, a situation that continued in the next two centuries and deeply influenced the development of the scholastic method. See J. Leclercq, *Saint Pierre Damien: Ermite et homme de l'Eglise* (Rome, 1960), pp. 218–20.

237. See Dumas, pp. 465–82.

238. So, in his letter to Herimann of Metz (*Epist.* 21).

239. On the background and gradual emergence of the idea of a crusade to reconquer "the holy places," see J. Brundage, *The Crusades* (Milwaukee, 1962), pp. 1–23; S. Runciman, *A History of the Crusades* (Cambridge, 1962), vol. 1, pp. 3–105.

240. Interestingly, when the priestly functions in sacraments are listed in early texts (such as the *Statuta* or the anonymous Gallican *De septem ordinibus*) the role of ministers in penitential practice is not mentioned; see Munier, *Les Statuta Ecclesiae Antiqua*, pp. 195–97. This remains true of Rabanus Maurus *De clericorum instit.* 1. 4–6, where the respective roles of bishops and presbyters is discussed; but earlier (1. 2), when treating globally the role of the clergy, he says they should administer sacraments ("*sacramenta populis dispensat*") and a bit later, though not clearly under the rubric of administering sacraments, he says that clerics are chosen by God "ut judicent inter justum et injustum, et discernant inter sanctum et profanum inter pollutum et mundum . . ."—which points, though not exclusively, towards penitential judgment. When we come to Gregory VII, however, in his listing of the priestly powers of saving people, the power of absolution is placed alongside baptizing, confirming, and consecrating at the Eucharist—and all these powers are rooted in the promise of Matt. 16:18. *Epist.* 21 (*P.L.* 148. 598).

241. See Peter Damian *Liber qui dicitur gratissimus* 2–3 (*P.L.* 145. 101–2).

242. "Le problème de l'efficacité des sacrements en rapport avec la valeur morale du ministre qui les administrait, a été d'une importance capitale pour le développement de la doctrine sacramentelle. Les très nombreuses et violentes discussions ont obligé les théologiens catholiques à préciser et à exprimer plus clairement la foi traditionnelle. . . ." (Anciaux, *La théologie,* p. 117.)

243. See B. Neunheuser, *Eucharistie in Mittelalter und Neuzeit* (Freiburg, 1963), pp. 15–24.

244. See Congar, *Ecclésiologie*, pp. 108–13.

245. This is reinforced by the allegorical understanding of the Eucharist that becomes dominant from the Carolingian period onward; see Jungmann, *Mass*, pp. 86–91.

246. On the evolution of the liturgical cycle during this period, see Jungmann, *Handbook of Church History*, pp. 304–19.

247. This lack became quite evident in the disputes (from ninth century onward) about Eucharistic "real presence." In assessing this deficiency, we must not overlook the patristic and medieval notion of the unity between the divine and earthly celebrations of Eucharist; but even this needs to be appraised in the light of the allegorical mentality, which was applied not only to reading Scripture but to "reading" all human experience and especially liturgical actions.

248. See Jungmann, *Pastoral Liturgy*, pp. 1–58, on the effects of the anti-Arian reaction on liturgy and popular spirituality.

249. At the same time, there was a mixed development of understandings and attitudes towards Christ: there was increasing loss of appreciation for the resurrection, and a tendency to emphasize the divine in Christ and to focus on his "divine presence"— but accompanied by a growing stress on the earthly life and death of Jesus. See Jungmann, *Handbook of Church History*, pp. 315–19.

250. On the progressive removal of the people from Eucharistic activity, particularly during "the liturgy of sacrifice" (the Canon), see Jungmann, *Mass*, pp. 81–92.

251. See Rabanus Maurus *De cler. instit.* 1. 5–6; however, the idea persists that it is the Spirit, who acts invisibly along with the human minister, who is the principal agent of sacramental sanctification; see Peter Damian *Liber qui dicitur gratissimus* 2–3.

252. However, in the dispute about simoniac ordinations, there was need for those who espoused the effectiveness of such ordinations to stress the action of Christ (the Spirit) in sacrament. Thus, as we saw (preceding note), Peter Damian sees Christ (the Spirit) as the chief agent and the human minister as a canal through whom sanctification passes to the faithful in sacraments. See Leclercq, *Saint Pierre Damien*, pp. 231–34.

253. See J. Figgis, "Respublica Christiana," in *Essays in Modern History*, ed. I. Christie (London, 1968), pp. 1–24.

254. This is crystallized in the *Ecclesiastical Hierarchy* of Pseudo-Dionysius; see R. Roques, *L'univers dionysien*, pp. 176–86. On Pseudo-Dionysius' role in reinforcing the hierarchical view of things that was already prominent in Augustinian thought, see Congar, *Ecclésiologie*, pp. 105–6.

255. In the preface to Delahaye's *Ecclesia mater* (pp. 8–14), Congar indicates the key shift in the notion of the church as maternal: instead of denominating the community as font of new life, the stress is placed on the jurisdictional elements of church discipline and the church becomes *mater et magistra*. Interestingly, Gregory VII, who applies the phrase to Rome (he also calls the Roman church *mater et caput*), speaks of priests as being *fidelium patres et magistros* (*Epist.* 21).

256. Congar, *Ecclésiologie*, p. 10, sees this development as "le fait le plus important de cette histoire des doctrines ecclésiologiques; il marque la ligne de clivage entre une ecclésiologie de style et d'esprit patristiques et une ecclésiologie de type juridique."

257. This juridical soteriology is reinforced in the development of scholastic theology by the fact that in their early stages medieval theology and canon law emerge together and the early canonical collections serve as *loci theologici*.

258. See Congar, *Ecclésiologie*, pp. 92–98.

259. On the intertwining of feudal and ecclesiastical administrative structures and the resultant tendency to pick bishops and abbots from the nobility, see Kempf, pp. 270–79.

260. See Dumas, pp. 220–49.

CHAPTER 4

Ministry in Medieval Culture

Crystallization of Church Organization

In the period that extended from the beginning of the twelfth century to the Council of Constance (1414–18), the evolving institutionalization of medieval Christianity came to full flower and then rapidly began to disintegrate. While our specific interest is the formalization of ministerial structures and procedures that occurred during this period, this cannot be adequately separated from what was taking place in medieval life as a whole; for medieval life was one fabric woven out of ecclesiastical and secular threads. As in other aspects of ecclesiastical structure, this period is critical in formalizing the various offices in the hierarchical ministry, though it can scarcely be thought of as innovative in this regard.[1]

One of the basic reasons for the conscious formalizing of ecclesiastical structures during this time was the flourishing state of legal studies. In the eleventh century, the great legal centers in Italy, particularly Bologna and Padua, began to exert their influence through their graduates. These legal studies embraced both canon and civil law, and reintroduced into European thought and political life the impact of classic Roman law.[2]

The appearance in the early twelfth century of Gratian's *Decretum* was a milestone in legal studies, for it was the first thorough sifting and compilation of the legal traditions then being followed.[3] For this reason, it formed the foundation of a most important tradition of legal thought, the Decretists.[4] Side by side and with these canonists, who used the *Decretum* as their point of depar-

ture, were the Decretalists who focused rather on interpretation of the various decretals of the popes which came out in increased volume during this period.[5] While one cannot speak of "canon law" in the sense of the twentieth-century codification, the law of the church had reached a new level of unification and clarification which reflected the emerging uniformity of ecclesiastical structures and further effected this uniformity.

For many centuries already the clergy had been explicitly set off from the rest of the people; the Middle Ages pushed this even further and fostered what amounted to a "distinct clerical world." Clerics of various kinds were increasingly numerous, and when one added to them the considerable number of monks and friars this made up an appreciable portion of the populace.[6] Theoretically, at least, they had their own society, with its special privileges, and courts.[7] But to some extent this was theoretical because the structures of feudal existence reached out to include them. A bishop, for example, was often the sworn vassal of a king or lord.[8] It must also be kept in mind that there was a great cleavage between the clergy (bishops and the better educated and influential priests who worked in the cities) who functioned in the "power spots" of the church's life and those who lived and worked with the common people in small towns and rural situations. These latter were close in attitude and lifestyle to the faithful whom they served, which is why clerical celibacy was often ignored in this context and why these country pastors were as anticlerical as their flock.[9]

Reading through G. LeBras' masterly exposition of church institutions in the Middle Ages,[10] one cannot escape being impressed by the complex organizational reality which had come into being. Yet, the more one looks at it the more conscious one becomes that practically all of this growth is organizational and administrative in nature. It is essentially the proliferation of ecclesiastical bureaucracy; underneath the mass of legislation and custom and structures the main lines of authority are not much different than they have been for many centuries, and the basic offices in the clerical hierarchy retain practically the same definition they always had.[11] Apart from the increased influence of papal legates and the conciliar currents that come to expression in the Council of Constance, there is practically nothing ecclesiastical that is truly innovative.[12] The creative thrust in the church's life was felt in other directions, such as new religious communities, popular religious movements, theology, and mysticism. Indeed, the bureaucratic refinement of already existent structures reminds one of the top-heavy administrative development which in any society heralds the approach of decline and dissolution.[13]

The Exclusion of "Secular" and "Feminine"

Though it took many centuries for the damage to become apparent, the church's ministry and the church as a whole was deeply hurt by the insularity and exclusiveness that developed among the clergy during this period. The twelfth century opens as a period of almost unprecedented creativity and "openness," yet, for a variety of reasons, perhaps most basically a lurking fear of the dangers connected with some of these "new things," a negativity developed with regard to "secularism," to "pluralism," and to women.[14]

One of the basic sources of the vitality that manifested itself in the twelfth century was the exposure of Western Europe to a host of new ideas and experiences. The contact with the East in the Crusades was one of the principal, though not the sole, causes of this intellectual awakening.[15] These "new ideas" were philosophical, scientific, mathematical,

legal, and medical. They were basically "secular" yet having some threatening theological overtones.[16] In spirit this new approach to knowledge was more critical, more down-to-earth, more experimental and directly verifiable, less allegorical, less credulous, and therefore less "spiritual." To a monastic and clerical culture grounded in Augustinian emphasis on the spiritual, suspicious of the material and bodily, searching for the hidden revelation in Scripture and in the world (the *vestigia Dei*), this new "naturalism" in knowledge seemed not only inferior but even a bit impious. When its methods were applied to theology, as in Abelard and later Aquinas, it presented a real danger.[17]

So, in various ways, the thrust of secular knowledge was diverted from the church's thought life (e.g., the lack of real impact of Thomas Aquinas' thought in the areas of his greatest contribution)[18] and unofficially "excommunicated." It was increasingly isolated from contact with Christian thought during the consequent centuries and it grew into the modern secular thought that has seemed superficially to be in conflict with Christian faith and revelation.[19] What this meant to the church's thought, and for many centuries to come this meant almost exclusively "the clergy's thought,"[20] was an impoverishment of major proportions. Though the feed-in of creative impulse during the twelfth century was sufficient to stimulate the major theological constructs of the thirteenth and fourteenth centuries, the latter part of the fourteenth century is already manifesting that introverted activity by which theology became more and more complicated in its discussion of increasingly abstract topics and isolated in its own world without influence from or upon the life of the Christian people.[21]

A second species of impoverishment, less commonly noticed than the one we have just discussed, came about because of the almost total exclusion of women from influential positions in ecclesiastical or secular society. Again, this is not the case at the beginning of the twelfth century; indeed, there are some indications that women were coming into increased prominence during the twelfth century and early thirteenth century.[22] Yet, by mid-thirteenth century there are clear signs of the masculine suspicions and intolerance that one finds so dramatically expressed a bit later in the trial of Joan of Arc.[23] What is difficult to say is whether this antifeminism is the logical outgrowth of much earlier currents of thought (e.g., the negativity towards women present in much monastic literature) or is rather an aspect of the wave of intolerance that came in as reaction to Albigensianism, the Waldenses, and like movements and which expressed itself also in a resurgent anti-Semitism.[24] Whatever its roots, the relegation of women to doubly second-class status in the church (they were not only laity, they were not even lay*men*) was so effective that it remained almost unchallenged to the present day.[25]

The great symbol of clerical freedom from taint by either secular life or women was clerical celibacy. Because of celibacy, the clergy were in a more spiritual, and therefore superior, form of Christian life.[26] To them, and also to men and women members of religious communities, was open the possibility of evangelical perfection (i.e., Christian sanctity) which was closed to "ordinary Christians."[27]

There is sufficient evidence that the discipline of celibacy, finally imposed as obligatory (the sign of which was the canonical proscription of clerical marriage under penalty of invalidity),[28] was far from universally observed.[29] In many regions, common-law marriage of priests (and not a few bishops) was taken for granted by both clergy and their people.[30] Moreover, the popular literature of the age, while some of its emphasis on clerical crudeness and rapacity and promiscuity should probably be seen as exaggeration or even invention, indicates a rather sad state of sexual behavior on the part of many monks, friars, and secular clergy.[31] In the lives of both clergy and laity there was an unhealthy focus on sexuality as the key area of morality.[32] Yet, strangely enough, in this period of theological summas that treat almost every imaginable topic, one looks in vain for any theological explanation of clerical celibacy.[33]

In treating the preceding historical period we indicated how necessary it was to keep in mind both sides of the church—its external form which becomes complicated by innumerable historical influences, and its inner "mystery" reality—and to realize that both of these aspects of the church remained part of people's thinking about the church. This caution is just as applicable to the Middle Ages. There is real danger that one will become so absorbed in observing the externals of the church in this period that one will forget that Christians of that age still thought and spoke of the church as "the Body of Christ" (a commonplace assumption in all the theological writing of the period which discusses Christ's "grace of the Head"),[34] or as "the Spouse of Christ" (characteristic of Cistercian spirituality, but not limited to it).[35] It is worth recalling that these centuries never doubted that the supreme expression of the church's life came not in political or intellectual triumphs but in the celebration of the Eucharist. ". . . Actus nobilissimus in Ecclesia simpliciter est consecratio Eucharistiae. . . ."[36]

Bishops and priests were still looked upon as "physicians of souls," particularly in the penitential exercise of the keys.[37] And the resurgence of preaching, encouraged by strong legislation on the obligation of bishops and priests in this regard, indicates the extent to which the idea of the bishop (and priest) as minister of the word was still prominent.[38]

While it was not true that the Middle Ages was a clericalized society, the historian could well receive that impression because of the large numbers of clergy of all varieties. Actually, at many points during this period the large number of priests caused social and economic problems as well as problems for orderly ecclesiastical life.[39] In many instances, sufficient care was not taken to certify the qualifications demanded by church law for ordination; thousands were ordained without much ado about their intellectual or moral credentials.[40]

One of the problems came because of the "*vagantes*," the wandering priests, many of them monks without monastery or friars without convent, who lived off the credulity of the uneducated masses of Christians, fostering superstition for their own financial gains. It would be a mistake to exaggerate this situation or to see such unscrupulous clerics as typical, but the literature of the age indicates that they were far from uncommon.[41]

Though not as scandalous a situation, the large number of Mass-saying priests attached to benefices or to manor houses was an anomalous expression of the ministerial vocation.[42] Obviously, such utilization of ordained ministers emphasized almost exclusively the "transubstantiating power" of the priest, though in some instances these men were also on hand to hear confessions. But the notion of ministry of word, of pastoral service to a community, was almost totally lacking.

Practically all these wandering clerics and private family chaplains were poorly trained, even by the modest standards of clerical education demanded in those centuries.[43] There were, of course, many bishops and priests who were well-educated both in theology and in secular disciplines. This was, after all, the period when the great medieval universities developed out of the cathedral schools, which itself testifies to the encouragement of learning in some ecclesiastical circles.[44] But the ordained clergy was really two quite disparate groups: these well-trained priests and bishops (and monks and friars), and a large group of priests who were minimally educated at best.

The middle of the fourteenth century saw the series of extrasevere plagues which wiped out large portions of Europe's populace. In many areas life was literally brought to a complete halt, towns were deserted, farms abandoned; a fear-filled apocalyptic spirit haunted the people. Some analysts of the clerical decline of these pre-Reformation centuries are fond of attributing this decline to the decimating of the clergy during the "Black Death," but it is not clear that more clergy than laity were wiped out by the pestilence.[45]

What may be more important, though hard to determine, was the orientation that social conditions at this period gave to the need of ministration, and therefore to the task of ordained clergy. For one thing, the preaching on the popular level was dominated even more than usual by the "four last things" which Gregory I had already emphasized.[46] People were looking for magic cures with which to counter the constant threat of the plague; negatively, their constant state of fear projected itself into suspicions of the kind that began to produce phenomena like the burning of witches.[47]

This was a period overshadowed by death, and it colored the life of the church and its ministry. Celebration of death had already become prominent in liturgy: masses for the dead, celebration of All Souls, etc.;[48] now death became practically an obsession for large portions of the populace.

Establishment of Forms of Latin Liturgy

Though the imposition of a uniform liturgy upon the Latin church did not come until the post-Tridentine action of Pius V (in 1570), the Eucharistic liturgies upon which his *Missale romanum* would be based were already in wide use during the thirteenth century, especially those of the mendicant orders.[49]

Under the irresistible influence of allegory, the standard interpretation of the Eucharist was highly allegorized with each detail, such as the priestly vestments, having its special "hidden" meaning.[50] Moreover, the basic theme of this allegory was the passion and death of Christ, for the Eucharist was understood almost exclusively in relationship to Calvary.[51] One can see this reflected in the theological questions of the Middle Ages: How can Christ still be offering sacrifice if he is still not suffering? Or does the eating by the faithful constitute some kind of mystic immolation for Christ?[52] As Jungmann points out,[53] scholasticism of the Aristotelian variety, beginning with Albert, took a more realistic approach to the action of the Eucharist, one that took seriously the sensible reality of the action, instead of reducing it to a "screen" as allegory did; but this had practically no effect on popular thinking about the Eucharist. One finds in Gabriel Biel's treatise on the Eucharist a lengthy allegorical explanation of each detail of the Mass.[54]

Eucharist was looked upon as epiphany, as somehow having saving power of a well-nigh magical kind, a power that would work on all who saw "the Sacrament."[55] Hence, the popular frenzy to see the host, the attempt to view as many elevations of the Mass as possible, the introduction of the elevation of the consecrated elements which very quickly became the central attraction of the entire Eucharistic action, and the extension of this moment in the exposition of the Blessed Sacrament, the benediction of people by the consecrated host in a monstrance.[56] Most explanations of the manner in which Christ was "present beneath the appearances" were crassly quantitative and materialistic. Popular fancy, with its legendary tales of miraculous appearances of Jesus (often as a child!) in the host, went far beyond the materialism of this inadequate understanding of transubstantiation.[57] The metaphysical subtlety of Aquinas' theology of Eucharistic change was far beyond the capacity of the age to comprehend; had it been understood it would have been considered heretical or at the very least "dangerous."[58]

One can see by one liturgical detail, which took place in this period, just how far thinking about the Eucharistic action had drifted from what it had been in the primitive church or the period of the fathers. The so-called Preface, which invited the people to share in the great Eucharistic prayer and then began that prayer, is now considered as the final stage of the offertory liturgy rather than as intrinsic to the Canon.[59] This makes it clear that the Canon is no longer viewed as the great prayer of benediction over the gifts, as the evangelical proclamation of the ever present mystery of Passover of Christ, as the pentecostal moment of unifying the assembled community through the gift of the Spirit.

Rather, it is the uniquely powerful action of the church (in which its ministers had power even over the body of Christ) whereby from ordinary bread the "food of angels" is provided for the spiritual strengthening of Christians.[60] This action centers, of course, in the very brief moment of the consecration (and the accompanying elevations); its words are the "form" of the sacrament.[61] The other prayers from the "Te igitur . . ." to the "Per ipsum . . ." were reduced to ancillary ceremony and complicated by such things as the introduction of long listings of saints.[62]

All of this inevitably influenced the manner in which the role of the Eucharistic celebrant was understood. He was, above all, the agent of the change at the consecration, though theories differed drastically as to how he functioned as agent.[63] There seems scarcely a trace of a prophetic function of proclaiming the gospel.[64] What is universally held is that this power of consecrating the Eucharistic elements is considered the basic power associated with Christian ministerial priesthood, the supreme sharing in the priesthood of Christ himself.[65]

All of this formed an integral part in the doctrine of sacraments which, at least in its formal theological expression, became explicit in the twelfth and early thirteenth centuries. This was a theology formed out of the basic stream of Augustinian thought as it came through Gregory I and Isidore, the basic medieval view of the symbolic character reality, the statements about sacraments in the canonical collections (see the large and theological section of Gratian's *Decretum* on sacraments), and the Aristotelian explanation of essential structure (matter and form) and causality.[66]

Inadequate as this medieval theology of sacraments was, for it failed to explain with any satisfaction the central fact of *symbol*, it completely dominated later thinking about sacraments. After the mid-fourteenth century one finds no new approaches to sacramental theology until well into the twentieth century.[67] Given the fact that, at least in Roman Catholic thought, ministerial priesthood was directed essentially to administration of sacraments,[68] it is not difficult to see how this stagnation of sacramental theology was one of the reasons for the undeveloped state of thinking about ministry.

Papal Supremacy

Vatican I, with its statement about papal primacy and infallibility, may represent the ultimate in formalized emphasis on the bishop of Rome; but the zenith of actual effective papal power occurred during the two centuries that stretch from Gregory VII to Boniface VIII. *Sacerdotium* was triumphant, as its source and supreme example, the pope, was the acknowledged head of Christendom; men of the stature of Urban II, Innocent III, and Innocent IV lived up to this billing.[69]

While no pope of the twelfth century attains the eminence of Hildebrand or of Innocent III, a series of popes built upon the firm foundation of the late eleventh-century reform and gradually asserted Rome's prerogatives in the face of determined opposition from temporal rulers like Henry of England.[70] History has given more attention to such twelfth-century figures as Anselm of Canterbury, Thomas à Beckett, Bernard of Clairvaux, and John of Salisbury—who were not popes. But a series of fairly strong, if not outstanding, popes gradually increased the influence and prestige of the Roman see, often through the dedicated support of men like those named above.

The period of papal ascendancy really begins with the reign (and the word is appropriate) of Innocent III. If the basic purpose of Christian ordained ministry is to form Christian community, Innocent exemplifies the ultimate in one approach to this goal: the approach of using sovereign power.[71] In a medieval Europe that saw itself as one *societas christiana*, one *corpus Christi*,[72] the pope, since he claimed the *plentitudo potestatis* as vicar of Christ and earthly head of this body which is the church,[73] quite logically saw himself charged to use his absolute authority in whatever manner was appropriate to the task of unifying Christendom, preserving it

from its enemies, and bringing it to peace. Even in the thirteenth century, no pope managed to implement unchallenged his claim to all authority, but Innocent III came quite close.[74] The stage had been set for him through Barbarossa's defeat in the conflict with Alexander III near the end of the twelfth century, and Innocent rapidly asserted his power over European life. One can interpret his maneuvers as sheer power politics since they certainly occurred in the arena of political and diplomatic struggle; yet Innocent does seem to have sincerely sought the advance of God's kingdom and the glory of the church as he understood them.[75] He was one of the most effective and dedicated reformers of the clergy in the church's history: the decrees of Lateran IV, which marked the highpoint in his campaign to purify the church's life, mark out a comprehensive and farsighted plan to nurture the understanding and commitment of regular and diocesan clergy and through them of the whole Christian people.[76] For all his insistence on clerical prerogatives, especially those of the papacy, Innocent seems to have been quite attuned and open to new currents of ministerial vitality and new forms of ministerial activity even among the laity; thus his encouragement of the Franciscan movement and the Dominican friar preachers.[77]

The ministerial revolution begun by the friars under Innocent III continued into the thirteenth century, as did the papal dominance. Yet, the problems against which the Fourth Lateran had been directed did not vanish; rather, by century's end they had become even more marked, and by the fifteenth century the need for reform applied most acutely to the papacy itself. And though Innocent IV did manage finally to overcome Frederick II, the all-embracing authority of the popes was more and more questioned. Their exercise of power was ineffective, until the crucial confrontation between Boniface VIII and Philip of France revealed the papal inability to back its claims and so prepared the way for the Avignon captivity and the Western Schism.[78]

In attempting to assess the historical attempt to unify Christian Europe by ecclesiastical power, some mention must be made of the growing importance of town and city life from the thirteenth century onward.[79] Towns tended to be independent in spirit, reluctant to accept restrictions on their autonomy, and hostile to much that characterized feudal society. Conflict between the evolving bourgeois class, which controlled these towns, and ecclesiastical overlords (bishops or abbots) was quite common; and while the pattern was not uniform the institutional church tended to cling to the feudal structures in which its privileges and power had taken shape.

With Boniface, the papal fortune encountered a sudden and drastic reversal.[80] Papal overextension and the rapid rise of national monarchy, particularly in France with Philip the Fair, led to the debacle of Vienne (with its unjust condemnation of the Templars forced upon the Holy See), to the Avignon captivity, and finally to the tragedy of the schism that divided Latin Christendom into two and then three opposed camps.[81] Historically, the transition from Boniface VIII to the Council of Constance is a fascinating study in political and social dynamics; theologically, it is a period of intense writing about the nature of the church and its authority, most specifically about the papacy.[82] The great body of this writing about the papacy remains still to be studied adequately;[83] it is both quantitatively vast and qualitatively uneven, ranging from vituperative political invective to serious and balanced theological analysis, with all varieties of polemic and piety inbetween. It provided a rich mine for the pro- and antipapal controversialists of the Reformation period.[84]

The schism presented Western Christianity with one of those *in extremis* situations, where foregone conclusions are challenged by the need to continue in existence.[85] In the situation of the late fourteenth and early fifteenth centuries, the need to restore a basic unity to the church drew theologians and canonists to an examination of their previous teaching. A large portion of Christian thought came to espouse the conciliarist position: that a council of the universal church was the ultimate authority, though in the normal functioning of the church the pope was supreme ruler.[86] The circumstances of this schism and reunion at Constance are, naturally, unique, but the principles of the discussion have unfortunately dropped into a theological limbo. Only recently has attention again been drawn to the existence of a conciliarist theology distinct from that rejected by Vatican I.[87]

The Crusades

Few historical phenomena are harder to appraise than are the crusades of the Middle Ages. First begun in the late eleventh century and extending into the thirteenth century,[88] these "holy wars" were directed principally against Islam but found other targets in enemies closer to home, such as the Albigensians.[89] One can view them as simple perversions of religion, a "baptizing" of cruelty and conquest, and certainly much supports such a thesis.[90] Yet, one can also find some justification for the thesis that they were an attempt to divert the barbaric aggressiveness of medieval warlords from internecine strife, and to give some sublimation to these aggressive instincts.[91] However they are to be evaluated, they had considerable effect on the tone of medieval life and on the institutions of both civil and ecclesiastical life, the ministry included.[92]

The application of military imagery to the Christian life was not original to the medieval church. Paul himself uses it,[93] one can find fairly frequent use among the Fathers,[94] and before the twelfth century it has already become normal to refer to the church on this earth as *ecclesia militans*.[95] But with the crusades and the "canonization" of the ideal of chivalry, military activity provides more than a comparison, a source of appropriate metaphor. Actual warfare, "for the faith," now becomes a respected and advocated Christian ideal parallel to the ascetic or monastic ideal.[96]

What might be considered the ultimate in this development is the wedding of the military and the clerico-monastic in the military orders, and the Knights Templar.[97] It does something to the notion of the priesthood when ordained ministers live a life of committed military service, when the bishops or popes who send them into battle with liturgical blessing are themselves seen to be leaders in this great Christian battle.[98] One cannot but be perturbed, too, to see how this literal militarism is directed, with great conviction of "serving God," against those suspected of heresy. One is reminded of the monastic "strong-boys" who broke into the incipient council of Ephesus in 449 and turned it into the "Brigandage."[99]

Not that the crusades were the only stimulus to contact with the East; but they did accelerate it. Not only were a relatively few merchants or diplomats or scholars involved in this contact with new places, new art, new languages, and new peoples but a fairly large-scale exposure to this other, more cultured and somewhat exotic, world resulted from the crusades and opened up Europe to new currents of creativity.[100] And beyond Constantinople stretched the vast expanse of Asia which missionaries explored as far as China in the thirteenth and fourteenth centuries.[101] The proximate knowledge of this whole non-Latin world gave an orientation to the Christian mission of evangelization as the Latins understood it. Even the theologian's efforts could be specified by this objective, as the *Summa contra Gentiles* testifies.[102]

Humanly speaking, the crusades were a great boon to the medieval popes in their effort to establish their position of eminence in medieval society. From the beginning, the crusades were essentially sponsored by the pope. It was he who commissioned such men as Bernard to preach the crusade; it was he who sent out the official "call"; it was he who gave the crusaders the special blessings and indulgences that fortified them in their choice.[103] The pope was the leader of the crusade. The mightiest of princes served in the pope's army in this Christian war; even

Frederick II found himself unable to avoid this.[104] Ecclesiastically, this had its ramifications. During the crusade the men involved were more directly under the pope's direction and blessing and this helped strengthen the idea of the pope's "immediate jurisdiction" over all Christians.

Expansion of Religious Orders

Much of the story of the church in the Middle Ages is the story of organized religious life, particularly of the new religious foundations that sprang up in those centuries. The reform that prepared for the ecclesiastical flowering of the twelfth to fourteenth centuries was to a great degree the product of such great monastic reformers as Peter Damian and Hildebrand. But the continuation of this healthy impulse was dependent upon the renewal of monastic life itself, for it was affected profoundly (and seldom to the good) by increasing size and wealth and secular influence.[105] Fortunately, such reform was forthcoming in the twelfth and thirteenth centuries though it quickly abated from the fourteenth century onward, and thus prepared for the fifteenth- and sixteenth-century cry for reform.

Much of the most important reform took place within monasticism as such. New foundations of Benedictine rule, influenced by the achievements of Cluny, came into being as attempts to recover the pristine vigor and spirit of Benedict.[106] One of the most exciting and widespread reform movements within monastic life was the Cistercian adaptation of Benedictine rule. Rigorous in its asceticism, yet profoundly humanistic in some of its spirituality (particularly in its acceptance of affectivity as positive good and its "rediscovery" of the humanness of Christ), the Cistercian movement exercised a strong attraction for young people throughout twelfth-century Europe.[107] Cistercian monasteries became centers of intense Christian life, Cistercian monks (like Bernard of Clairvaux himself) were influential preachers, and not a few bishops were drawn from Cistercian houses.[108]

While the Cistercian movement was basically a "reform" of already existent monasticism, the new mendicant groups that sprang up towards the end of the twelfth century marked a shifting orientation in dedicated community life. Though still tied to basic monastic forms of community existence, the communal singing of the divine office, obligatory penitential practices (such as special fasting and abstinence), and membership in a specific convent (though not with the monastic vow of stability), these new groups began in dramatic fashion the redirecting of dedicated life towards apostolic action.[109]

The best known, largest, and most influential of these new groups were the Franciscans and the Dominicans. To discuss the new "philosophy of religious life" which underlay their appearance is not our purpose here, nor is it to analyze and appraise the conflict that arose almost immediately in Franciscan circles.[110] Rather, it is to note that the rise of these new groups introduced on the stage of medieval Europe a new variety of "priest," the friar, who was neither monk nor secular presbyter.

Friars were, of course, as varied as any other group. Many of them attained eminence as scholars, particularly in the sacred sciences. The majority of the theological "greats" of the thirteenth and fourteenth centuries were Dominicans or Franciscans.[111] Many of them were preachers and missionaries of great skill and effectiveness, and they brought about a great purification and resurgence of Christian faith in many parts of Europe. Many of them possessed holiness of a high order, and generally speaking the mendicant convents of the High Middle Ages were sources of great spiritual power for the church.[112] Unfortunately, for the church as a whole and for the religious orders themselves, their very success and rapid growth in size and influence brought with it many problems. Making due allowance for rhetorical exaggeration and prurient interest in clerical misdoings, the popular literature reflects the decline of idealism that set in, the exploitation by wandering friars of the gullibility and credulity of the uneducated masses of the people, and the socio-economic problem that such "mendicants" became,[113] and the picture painted by nonecclesiastical writings is confirmed by the canonical regulations of the late Middle Ages.[114]

Theologically, what the rise of the mendicant friars questions is the intrinsic relationship between episcopacy and presbyterate. While it is true that such friar-priests were dependent upon the episcopate for priestly ordination, and while a certain *modus vivendi* was worked out historically, the religious communities, and especially the new foundations that were encouraged and "approved" by the pope, operated in a manner that transcended diocesan boundaries or control.[115] The medieval popes fortified this tendency, for it gave them a powerful ally in their desire to establish their primacy vis-à-vis the episcopacy.[116] This raises a question which has never been satisfactorily answered: Can there be, and should there be, a segment of the *sacerdotium* which functions apart from episcopal control, though in close fraternal cooperation with that episcopacy?[117] And a further question: If the previous question is answered affirmatively, need such "freer" expressions of priestly life and ministry be tied to ecclesiastically constituted and approved (i.e., Roman-controlled) religious communities? Obviously, the very notion of the presbyter as essentially "bishop's delegate" is what comes up for questioning. One wonders if this very question was not in the air during the Middle Ages. Perhaps it helps explain the widespread influence of Jerome's ideas on the theological explanation of bishop-presbyter relations.[118]

The picture of new religious-order forms of priesthood would not be complete without a brief reference to such influential groups as the Carthusians and Praemonstratensians. In much different fashion (the Carthusians with their rigorous and intellectual dedication to contemplation; the Praemonstratensians with their corporate impact on liturgical developments, as well as on preaching and teaching) these groups contributed a major share to the flowering of Christian thought and dedication in the Middle Ages and to raising the level of clerical ideals and life.[119] Yet, in their own way they represent a further expression of the "autonomous" groups of ordained men; one wonders how appropriate it is to say "ordained ministers" for a contemplative group like the Carthusians.[120]

Though Christianity had always been characterized by a missionary orientation, the Middle Ages saw an important directing of such missionary effort to far-distant "foreign missions." This was largely the effort of the new religious communities; Franciscan missionaries were active as far away as the Mongol imperial capital of Peking.[121] Since these new religious foundations were specially allied with the papacy, the pattern of direct Roman control of such mission areas became more fully entrenched.[122] Actually, a new principle of ecclesiastical procedure was coming into existence: the "assigning" to a religious community of apostolate responsibility for a certain geographical area.[123] Although this is always considered a temporary stage, with the hope that an indigenous hierarchy will eventually take over, it does represent certain anomalies (at least in the matter of church jurisdiction) while it exists.

Resurgence of Preaching

Already referred to briefly, the resurgence of preaching was one of the most notable aspects of the surge of Christian vitality in the twelfth and thirteenth centuries.[124] This drew renewed attention to the ministry of word, to the need to feed the faith of the people with the word of the gospel, and to the need to prepare ministers for this all-important function. One can see this evangelical impulse not only in the increase of preaching both quantitatively and qualitatively but also in the number of treatises on the "art of preaching" which appeared increasingly during the Middle Ages.[125]

One of the forces at work in this renaissance of preaching was the new social situation brought about by the medieval developments in city living.[126] This rise of the city in the Middle Ages is admittedly a fact of major

socio-economic importance; ecclesiastically, it meant the possibility of more concentrated and effective religious formation. Obviously, the great bulk of the Christian populace still lived on the land or in small villages; but as the cities grew in size and influence they attracted many of the better-educated, became centers of cultural and religious evolution, and with the increasing development of cathedral schools and universities the cities where these were located became centers of ecclesiastical training and the source of episcopal appointees.[127]

This "urbanization" of medieval Europe undoubtedly changed to some degree the understanding of the priestly function, since the better educated and (at least structurally) more influential clergy were oriented to priestly functioning within the needs and potential of this city context.[128] Moreover, there seems to have grown up an increasing dichotomy between the urban clergy and those in rural or manoral situations. Some of this had, of course, existed for many centuries, but the increasing influence of the city now accentuates the cleavage.

Themselves the expression of awakened interest in effective evangelization, the new mendicant foundations were in the vanguard of the preaching movement. Not being involved in the administrative tasks of caring for parishes, they could direct more of their attention to direct evangelical activity. Moreover, their organized community life provided the context for more careful training of men for the various kinds of ministerial action, particularly for that of catechizing and preaching; and the continuity of their community life could bring into existence traditions of preaching.

Rise of Cathedral Schools and Universities

One of the most important social and cultural developments of the Middle Ages was the rising importance of the universities, which grew to quite an extent out of the cathedral schools that had gained considerable eminence by the end of the twelfth century.[129] In itself, this was not a priestly ministry; yet, the early stages of the development were almost totally dominated by clergy. Such involvement in schools, particularly in the "sacred sciences," was seen as part of the normal activity of some of the priests and bishops.[130]

The influential cathedral schools of the twelfth century grew out of the much older practice of providing education, primarily but not exclusively to clerics, in connection with the bishop's church.[131] In the twelfth century, such cathedral schools as Chartres and Reims became influential centers for the development of theological and canonical thought, and some of the leading scholars in these schools, e.g., Yves of Chartres, were influential in shaping the medieval notion of the *sacerdotium*.[132]

Along with these "secular clergy" schools, a number of monastic schools exerted key influence on the emerging medieval notion of the church and its ministry. Bec in Normandy and the convents of St. Genevieve and St. Victor in Paris were responsible for producing some of the period's most important thinkers, and they became centers for developing "theological traditions." Of these, the Victorine School, Hugh, Richard, and others, was probably the best known and exerted most influence (as a school) on later theological developments.[133]

Already towards the end of the twelfth century, and increasingly thereafter, the new universities took over the intellectual (and theological) leadership in medieval society and in the church.[134] It is wrong to lump them together as a homogeneous phenomenon, for the individual institutions had a distinctive character and approach to learning. They reflected the distinctive cultural (and national) outlook of their geographical location, this despite the genuinely international and cosmopolitan character of the medieval university. This is not the place to delineate these differences but only to note that such differing perspectives explain partially the differing viewpoints of these university faculties on the nature and function of Christian ministry and ecclesiastical authority.

Medieval Christian faith is often depicted as extremely credulous and superstitious, and no doubt there was much of this, especially among the mass of people who were devoid of any education.[135] Yet, the Middle Ages witnessed one of the most remarkable "rationalizations" of faith in the history of religions. This was due partially to the more general intellectual renaissance, but it was also due to the continuing viewpoint of the "official church" that learning and investigation about the faith should be encouraged.[136] This was not an unmitigated attitude of enthusiasm for learning; there were always voices that spoke against the application of profane knowledge to the sacred truths of faith.[137] But the twelfth century was marked by an enthusiastic openness to knowledge, and this impulse carried on into the next two centuries, despite the growing apprehension about "heresy" which was rooted in the appearance of the Albigensian threat.

Both exegesis and theology had been cultivated in the monastic schools of the early Middle Ages, but the twelfth century saw a flowering of such study. Already existent theological thought, generally circulated in *catenae* and *florilegia*, was gathered together, systematized, and evaluated (as in Abelard's *Sic et non* and Gratian's *Decretum*).[138] By the end of the twelfth century well-organized synthetic works are in existence, particularly Peter Lombard's *Sentences*, Hugh of St. Victor's *De Sacramentis*, and Gratian's *Decretum*, which provide both structure and sources for the compendious writings of the thirteenth- and fourteenth-century theologians and canonists.

From the point of view of the history of theology, and also for the insight it gives us about the way in which the theologian was seen to be engaged in the ministry of the word, it is important to note the emphasis laid on exposition of Scripture. *The* key activity of the master of theology was the *explicatio sacrae paginae*; the Middle Ages produced lengthy and frequently profound commentaries on the biblical texts. All the great systematic theologians, Alexander of Hales, Bonaventure, Thomas Aquinas, Albert, Duns Scotus, produced biblical commentary.[139] Bernard of Clairvaux and Denis the Carthusian testify to the flowering of biblical commentary within the more traditional context of monastic formation. In addition to the explanation of the scriptural texts, there also developed a formalized theory of exegesis, the "senses of Scripture."[140] Implicitly contained in such theological discussions of exegesis, of *sacra doctrina*," and of theology one can see some reflection of the role that medieval theologians considered themselves to play in the transmission and clarification of the word of God,[141] a role which they would probably have considered intrinsic to their sacerdotal function.

Complementing the technical clarification of faith by the theologians, medieval development of contemplation (both the actual flourishing of contemplatives and the formulation of the theory of contemplation) formed an important part of *fides quaerens intellectum*. It would be artificial to separate the two developments, though they can be distinguished: practically all the great twelfth- and thirteenth-century theologians saw contemplation (ultimately on the level of mysticism) as the stage beyond and prepared for by systematic exegesis or theology. This is clear from a "rationalist" like Anselm of Canterbury[142] as well as from a "symbolist" like Hugh of St. Victor;[143] it is as true of Thomas Aquinas[144] as it is of Bonaventure,[145] though their views of the manner in which systematic study and contemplative insight interrelate might be quite different.

Not all contemplation and mysticism was the outgrowth of deepened intellectual grasp of faith. Francis of Assisi is a case of outstanding and authentic contemplative insight apart from any particular theological formation. As a matter of fact, he could be considered an exponent of the position that such formal theological study was unnecessary, perhaps even a hindrance.[146] However, not all the "contemplatives" who emerged during the Middle Ages, especially in the fourteenth and fifteenth centuries, were as genuine as Francis. Yet, the mystic and the saint enjoyed great respect and influence; they were looked

to for guidance (especially when the *sacerdotium* failed in these respects, as it did during the Schism[147]) and they became increasingly a counterprinciple to the "established" authority of official ecclesiastics.[148]

Heresy and Inquisition

The Middle Ages witnessed remarkable success in clericalization of the church and in establishment of papal authority, and at the same time the emergence of those forces that would challenge profoundly this clerical and papal domination. Among these latter was the appearance of innovative Christian thinking and activity outside clerical circles. This presented a challenge both to Christian lifestyle and to the understanding of Christian faith.

In a form that was scarcely Christian, a parallel challenge presented itself at this very time in Albigensianism.[149] What this movement might have become as it settled down is difficult to say; there are indications that it was already losing some of its virulence and danger at the very time the anti-Albigensian crusade was launched.[150] At any rate, its tenets presented a radical problem for both church and society. Heresy, which surely had not been unknown in previous centuries, now assumed a new image. An element of fear began to enter the church's reaction to new ideas and movements, and the open attitude of the twelfth century gradually gave way to the restrictive mentality associated with the Inquisition.[151] The result of this combination, intrinsic development (the cultural movement to what we know as "the modern world") versus official restriction, was inevitable: the religious explosion of the sixteenth century, and the not-yet-healed rift between "secular" and "religious" which marked modern history. For Christian priesthood this had a special element of tragedy: sociologically and intellectually, Christian ministers (unless they wished to be classified as rebellious or even schismatic) were placed on the side of reaction against the forces that would to a large extent shape the modern world.

NOTES

1. For a detailed study of the various ecclesiastical offices in this period, see G. LeBras, *Institutions ecclésiastiques de la Chrétienté médiévale*, vol. 12 of A. Fliche and V. Martin, *Histoire de l'Eglise depuis les origines jusqu'à nos jours* (Paris, 1935—).

2. See H. Rashdall, *The Universities of Europe in the Middle Ages*, ed. F. Powicke and A. Emden (Oxford, 1936), vol. 1, pp. 87–141. See also LeBras, pp. 242–43.

3. See D. Knowles, *The Christian Centuries* (London, 1969), vol. 2, pp. 227–28; G. LeBras, C. Lefebvre, J. Rambaud, *Histoire du droit et des institutions de l'Eglise en Occident*, vol. 7 (*L'âge Classique 1140–1378: Sources et théorie du droit* [Paris, 1965]), pp. 52–129.

4. See LeBras-Lefebvre-Rambaud, pp. 275–92; A. Forest in Fliche-Martin, vol. 13, p. 181; L. Boyle, *New Catholic Encyclopedia* (New York, 1967), vol. 4, pp. 711–13.

5. See Boyle, *New Catholic Encyclopedia*, vol. 4, pp. 704–7; and C. Duggan, *ibid.*, pp. pp. 707–11.

6. By the late Middle Ages they constituted about a tenth of the populace; see E. Iserloh, *Handbook of Church History* (New York, 1965), vol. 4, p. 567.

7. See E. Watson, *Cambridge Medieval History*, 2d ed. (Cambridge, 1966), vol. 6, pp. 529–58.

8. See A. Dumas in Fliche-Martin, vol. 7, pp. 220–49; the feudal arrangements described by Dumas as operative in the tenth and eleventh centuries continued to be largely applicable to the next few centuries. However, an important variant in clerical situation comes into being with the thirteenth- and fourteenth-century growth of cities and the evolution of the urban parish; see Iserloh, pp. 566–70.

9. See G. Homans, *English Villagers of the Thirteenth Century* (New York, 1966), pp. 382–90; E. Faral, *La vie quotidienne au temps de Saint Louis* (Paris, 1938), pp. 41–53.

10. See above, n. 1.

11. The evolution of understanding during the late patristic and early medieval period regarding the episcopate and the papacy that is traced by Y. Congar, *L'ecclésiologie du Haut Moyen Age* (Paris, 1968), pp. 131–317, and by W. Ullmann, *The Growth of Papal Government in the Middle Ages* (London, 1955), is really achieved (and even fundamentally implemented) by the time of the Hildebrandian reform and is crystallized into legal forms by the twelfth-century development of canon law.

12. As we will see, the conciliar views are intrinsically of far-reaching importance for the structuring of the church, but they had little practical effect on the institutional development of the medieval church.

13. In this regard, the reflections of A. Toynbee in his *Study of History* (see the abridgment of D. Somervell [London, 1946], vol. 1, pp. 244–532) are a stimulating, if not always acceptable, guide to analysis of ecclesiastical developments.

14. On the twelfth-century renaissance, see M.-D. Chenu, *Nature, Man, and Society in the Twelfth Century* (Chicago, 1968); on the changing climate, compare the two chapters in *Handbook of Church History*, vol. 4, pp. 104–12 (on the lay movements, popular spirituality, etc., early in the twelfth century), both chapters by H. Wolter.

15. On the influence of the crusades as part of a larger evolution of European culture, see C. Haskins, *The Renaissance of the Twelfth Century* (New York, 1957), pp. 12–16; for a brief description of the many current influences that prepared for the cultural awakening of the twelfth century, see Knowles, pp. 235–86.

16. Theological worries about the intrusion of secular thought in the specific form of dialectic had already arisen in the eleventh century; see J. de Ghellinck, *Le mouvement théologique du XIIe siècle* (Bruxelles, 1948), pp. 66–78.

17. On Abelard, see Forest, pp. 100–114; on Aquinas and the condemnation of 1277, see E. Gilson, *Christian Philosophy in the Middle Ages* (New York, 1955), pp. 235–46, 381–83, 402–27.

18. See Gilson, pp. 426–27.

19. For a somewhat uneven but stimulating discussion of the early stages of this development, see G. Lagarde, *La naissance de l'esprit laïque* (Louvain, 1956).

20. Throughout the Middle Ages, education, having developed out of the parish (cathedral) and monastic schools, remained under ecclesiastical domination with, of course, the universities striving for autonomy in their own operation. Automatically, then, theology was totally developed and taught by clerics.

21. The famous decree of condemnation of Archbishop Stephen Tempier (in Paris) in 1277 already presaged this theological introversion, as did also the almost simultaneous action of Robert Kilwardby, the archbishop of Canterbury; see F. Van Steenberghen in Fliche-Martin, vol. 13, pp. 320–24. Recent studies in the late medieval centuries, such as H. Oberman's *Harvest of Medieval Theology* (Cambridge, Mass., 1963), have helped to offset an excessive denigration of late medieval theology (which marked much earlier study of this period). But the fact remains that partisan polemic divided the various theological schools one from another and diverted them from the intrinsic enrichment of theology that could have occurred through greater interaction with the evolving currents of humanistic thought.

22. See Wolter, pp. 108–9.

23. Basically, this antifeminism was neither new nor restricted to ecclesiastical circles. For example, the last section in one of the most famous books on courtly love (Andreas Capellanus, *The Art of Courtly Love*, trans. J. Parry [New York, 1941], pp. 187–212) contains a listing of those weaknesses and vices that are proper to the nature of women—a monument to male chauvinism; and as eminent a humanist as John of Salisbury has, in his *Polycraticus* (bk. 8, chap. 11), a view of woman that is almost as negative as that of Jerome, from whom much of it is borrowed.

24. Probably, it is both. Obviously, the task of studying and reevaluating the view taken of women throughout human history, a task as massive as it is urgent, has scarcely been touched. One can get some notion of the complexity just of the religious aspects of this task by comparing the differing views of D. de Rougemont, *Love in the Western World*, rev. ed. (New York, 1956), M. D'Arcy, *The Mind and Heart of Love* (London, 1945), A. Nygren, *Agape and Eros* (London, 1957), and C. S. Lewis, *The Allegory of Love* (Oxford, 1936), regarding the evolution of Christian thought regarding the nature of love (and marriage) and of woman's role in it.

25. While women certainly have not enjoyed ecclesiastical equality in the Reformation churches, their position has probably been most negatively viewed in the Roman Catholic situation. This is quite clearly reflected in the *Codex Iuris Canonici*.

26. This is the view later canonized by Trent (session 24, canon 10): "Si quis dixerit . . . non esse melius ac beatius manere in virginitate aut caelibatu quam fungi matrimonio, anathema sit."

27. Even Thomas Aquinas, who insists in the beginning of his treatment on "Christian perfection" (*Summa theol.* 2–2, q. 184, a. 1) that charity is the basis and measure of all Christian holiness, still sees the observance of poverty, celibacy, and ecclesiastical obedience as necessary for growth in charity, and a vowed commitment to such observance as necessary to place one in the "state of perfection" (*ibid.*, qq. 184, 186).

28. First Lateran Council, canon 21; Second Lateran Council, canons 6–7.

29. Perhaps the clearest indication of this was the constant effort of medieval popes and councils to enforce the discipline upon the clergy.

30. See Homans, p. 390; Faral, pp. 41–53.

31. Faral, pp. 48–49.

32. Granted the need to overcome much of the barbarism of life and attitudes that had been inherited from the recent past (a barbarism that manifested itself also in violence, drunkenness, and cruelty), the medieval view towards sexuality was directed not so much towards refining relationships between the sexes but rather to freeing man from the despiritualizing power of carnal existence. If one accepts the position espoused by the mainstream of patristic and medieval spirituality that progress in Christian virtue involves liberation from carnality, concentration on sexuality is logical since sexuality is the natural symbol of man's bodiliness. Yet, it is a testi-

mony to the power of authentic Christian insights to endure among antagonistic cultural influences that medieval thought (as represented by such diverse personalities as Abelard, Bernard of Clairvaux, Bonaventure, and Thomas Aquinas) saw love as the key and crown to Christian virtue.

33. The question seems to have been thoroughly relegated to canonical justification.

34. See Thomas Aquinas *Summa theol.* 3, q. 8.

35. However, in Bernard of Clairvaux (unquestionably the leading figure in Cistercian theology) it is more often the individual Christian soul that is thought of as the spouse of Christ. On Cistercian thought, see J. Leclercq, *History of Christian Spirituality* (New York, 1968), vol. 2, pp. 187–220; on the spiritual theology of Bernard, see Forest, pp. 133–41, and E. Gilson, *La théologie mystique de Saint Bernard* (Paris, 1934), esp. pp. 142–62. On Bernard's reference to the church as bride, see Y. Congar, "L'ecclésiologie de Saint Bernard," *Saint Bernard: Théologien*, ed. J. Leclercq (Rome, 1953), pp. 136–41: ". . . Pour S. Bernard, l'épouse est-elle l'Eglise ou l'âme individuelle aimant Dieu? Elle est, pour lui, tout cela car cela, pour lui, est le même chose" (p. 141).

Bernard applies the bridal imagery to the ordained ministry (they are the *amici sponsi*) and uses this as a basis for insisting that Christian ministry is to be loving service; see Congar, "L'ecclésiologie de St. Bernard," pp. 171–72. This theology receives a slightly different application in Bonaventure: the ordained (and particularly the bishop) as Christ's vicar is wed to the church; see H. Berresheim, *Christus als Haupt der Kirche nach dem heiligen Bonaventura* (Bonn, 1939), pp. 265–66.

36. Duns Scotus, *Ox.* 4, dist. 24, q. unica, n. 7.

37. See Lateran IV, canon 22; also A. Landgraf, *Dogmengeschichte der Frühscholastik* 3–1, p. 138 (in n. 68 he cites Praepositinus: "Sacerdos justificat ministerio, sicut phisicus sanat ministerio"). However, the actual understanding of the ordained minister's function in Penance was controlled by the position one took in the controversy as to whether the penitential absolution was declarative or effective; see B. Poschmann, *Penance and the Anointing of the Sick* (New York, 1964), pp. 156–93.

38. See, e.g., Lateran IV, canons 10 and 11.

39. This was, of course, tied in with the feudal-medieval structures of ecclesiastical landholding, support of clergy, ecclesiastical exemptions from taxation, etc.; for a brief description of these structures, see Watson, pp. 528–58.

40. Heroic efforts were made by strong and dedicated church leaders to correct this situation, for example, the reform measures of Innocent III which led up to Lateran IV, but the very minimal requirements demanded of parish clergy as late as the fourteenth and fifteenth centuries reflect the continuance of the problem. See Iserloh, pp. 575–76.

41. Isidore of Seville already complains of this problem (*De eccles. officiis* 2. 3. 1); it was considerably acerbated in the later Middle Ages by the decline of discipline in the mendicant communities.

42. On the development of the private Mass during the medieval period, see J. Jungmann, *Mass of the Roman Rite* (New York, 1951), vol. 1, pp. 212–33.

43. Lateran IV (in canon 27) decrees "severe punishment" for those who "presume to ordain ignorant and unformed men" to the priesthood; but the continuing cries for reform of the clergy in the ensuing three centuries indicates the enduring problem of a sizable group of uneducated clergy.

44. To keep a balanced view, one must remember that the existence of much ignorance, incompetence, and immorality among the medieval clergy was accompanied by a massive effort on the part of medieval ecclesiastics to educate, sanctify, and minister to the needs of the Christian people. See, for example, the efforts of Gerson (in the early fifteenth century) to deepen the Christian formation and better the human lot of clergy and laity alike—described by E. Delaruelle in Fliche-Martin, vol. 14, pp. 837–60.

45. The impact of the Black Death on the decline of religious orders is somewhat easier to establish. Not only was there a high rate of death in most religious communities

but the regular pattern of community discipline was disrupted, many monks and friars fled the monasteries and were reluctant to return, and there was often a short-sighted attempt to fill in losses by enlisting ill-suited and uneducated recruits. See Iserloh, pp. 581–82.

46. This was coupled with an increased emphasis on moralizing sermons, which marked the late Middle Ages. Such preaching, i.e., concentration on moral conversion stimulated by fear of hell (or desire of heaven), was importantly complemented by the development of the religious theater; see Delaruelle, pp. 605–28.

47. *Ibid.*, pp. 821–35; on the origins and evolution of the witch craze (which came to full expression in the sixteenth and seventeenth centuries), see H. Trevor-Roper, *Religion, the Reformation, and Social Change* (London, 1967), pp. 90–192.

48. See A. Cornides, *New Catholic Encyclopedia*, vol. 1, p. 318, and vol. 12, p. 384.

49. However, the Mass liturgy text upon which the 1570 *Missale Romanum* was most immediately based was the *Missale secundum consuetudinem Romanae Curiae*; see Jungmann, pp. 133–36.

50. See *ibid.*, pp. 86–92, 107–18.

51. *Ibid.*, pp. 115–16.

52. Such thirteenth-century theologians as Thomas Aquinas (*Summa theol.* 3, q. 80 and q. 83, a. 1) treat such questions with considerable theological sublety; but not all discussion of the matter was on this refined level. For a careful appraisal of distorted views of the Eucharist during this period, see F. Clark, *Eucharistic Sacrifice and the Reformation*, 2d ed. (Oxford, 1967).

53. *Mass of the Roman Rite*, pp. 113–14.

54. Gabrielis Biel, *Canonis Misse Expositio*, ed. H. Oberman and W. Courtenay (Wiesbaden, 1963), vol. 1.

55. Jungmann, pp. 107–20.

56. *Ibid.*, pp. 120–23.

57. See Clark, pp. 56–72.

58. See E. Schillebeeckx, "Transubstantiation, Transfinalization, Transignification," *Worship* 40 (1966), pp. 324–38.

59. Jungmann, vol. 2, pp. 101–6. The idea that the Canon of the Mass began with the prayer *"Te igitur"* was supported by the silent recitation of the Canon by the celebrant.

60. See the hymn *"Lauda Sion"* composed in the thirteenth century for the Corpus Christi liturgy.

61. Thomas Aquinas *Summa theol.* 3, q. 78.

62. On the development of the various elements of the Canon, see Jungmann, vol. 2, pp. 147–274.

63. The difference of these points of view was essentially a matter of different explanations of sacramental causality (which in turn was rooted in differing philosophical viewpoints); see B. Leeming, *Principles of Sacramental Theology*, 2d ed. (London, 1960), pp. 283–345.

64. However, a strong *didactic* element is preserved (though the direction in which the teaching developed was not always authentically evangelical) through the stress on allegorical understanding of the Eucharistic action. The Mass is seen as an epiphany, somewhat like (though much more profound and filled with mystery) the late medieval passion plays (on these latter, see Delaruelle, pp. 614–28).

65. It is worth noting here that throughout medieval theology a distinction is made between the *sacerdotal* action of consecrating the elements and the *ministerial* action of distributing Communion, e.g., Hugh of St. Victor *De Sacramentis* 2. 3. 10, and John of Paris *De potestate regia et papali* 12.

66. See de Ghellinck, pp. 449–510; N. Haring, "Berengar's Definitions of *Sacramentum* and Their Influence on Mediaeval Sacramentology," *Medieval Studies* 10 (1948), pp.

109–46; and "A Study in the Sacramentology of Alger of Liège," *ibid.*, 20 (1958), pp. 41–78.

67. The views of Reformation and post-Reformation theologians on sacraments will be studied later, and some judgment will have to be made at that point as to whether they provided any positive input into understanding of sacrament. As for Roman Catholic thought, a comparison of B. Leeming's *Principles of Sacramental Theology* (certainly one of the most perceptive and thorough pre–Vatican II treatments of sacraments) with the classic questions handled by Thomas Aquinas, Bonaventure, and Scotus indicates the extent to which theological discussion remained within the same borders for several centuries.

68. As distinguished from preaching, service to the faithful, etc. This distinction was heightened by reaction to the Protestant emphasis on preaching and to the various Protestant criticisms of Catholic teaching about the sacrificial nature of the Eucharist and of Eucharistic ministry.

69. On this full-blown hierocratic postion, see Ullmann, pp. 442–46.

70. See A. Fliche in Fliche-Martin, vol. 8, pp. 199–426.

71. See Wolter, pp. 136–82.

72. On the manner in which "body of Christ" became understood increasingly in sociological and political terms, and on the struggle between pope and king to be "head" of this body, see Congar, *Ecclésiologie*, pp. 262–307; also Ullmann, *Papal Government*.

73. On the twelfth- and thirteenth-century use of "*plenitudo potestatis*," and particularly on Bernard of Clairvaux's important role in applying this notion (as well as "vicar of Christ") to the medieval papacy, see B. Jacqueline, "Bernard et l'expression '*plenitudo potestatis*,'" *Bernard de Clairvaux*, ed. by monks of Notre Dame d'Aiguebelle (Paris, 1953), pp. 345–48; also Congar, "L'ecclésiologie de Saint Bernard," pp. 159–61.

74. The one prominent defeat of Innocent III concerned his dealings with Philip Augustus of France; see Wolter, pp. 152–53.

75. See Knowles, pp. 290–91.

76. See H. Schroeder, *Disciplinary Decrees of the General Councils* (St. Louis, 1937), pp. 242–89.

77. See H. Daniel-Rops, *Cathedral and Crusade*, Image edition (New York, 1963), vol. 1, pp. 177–95.

78. See Knowles, pp. 333–37.

79. See J. Clapham, *Cambridge Medieval History*, vol. 6, pp. 473–504; and H. Pirenne, in *ibid.*, pp. 505–27, a general treatment of the rise of cities in the Middle Ages. On the situation of the church in these emergent urban situations, see Iserloh, pp. 566–70.

80. Actually, the political entanglements of the papacy with Anjou, the wrangling within the College of Cardinals (during the final two decades of the thirteenth century), and the unwillingness to face up to the problems confronting the papacy (which was epitomized in the election of Celestine V) prepared for the conflicts of Boniface's reign. Yet, it is during the years of Boniface's rule that the effective opposition to the papacy was crystallized, particularly in the conflict with the French.

81. See K. Fink, *Handbook of Church History*, vol. 4, pp. 291–344, 401–25.

82. See Delaruelle, pp. 491–528.

83. Important studies have been made in large segments of this literature: e.g., those by B. Tierney (*Foundations of the Conciliar Theory* [Cambridge, 1955]) and W. Ullmann (*Medieval Papalism* [London, 1949]) in canonical thought; by J. Leclercq on John of Paris (*Jean de Paris et l'ecclésiologie du XIIIe siècle* [Paris, 1942]), F. Oakley on d'Ailly (*The Political Thought of Pierre d'Ailly* [New Haven, 1964]), and H. Oberman on nominalist thought (*Harvest of Medieval Theology* [Cambridge, Mass., 1963]).

84. See L. Willaert in Fliche-Martin, vol. 18, pp. 340–87.

85. See Fink, pp. 401–26.

86. No one statement can justifiably generalize the conciliarist position, since there was

a wide range of conciliarist opinions; see M. Wilks, *The Problem of Sovereignty in the Later Middle Ages* (Cambridge, 1963), pp. 455–523.

87. E.g., H. Küng, *Structures of the Church* (New York, 1964), esp. pp. 268–341; and B. Tierney, *Foundations of the Conciliar Theory*. Tierney's work is especially valuable because it traces the manner in which the conciliar theology develops out of mainstream currents of medieval canonist thought.

88. For a brief description and appraisal of the crusades, see Knowles, pp. 213–17.

89. One of the most enduring of these crusades was the struggle to reconquer the Iberian peninsula from the Muslims; see Fliche, pp. 482–85.

90. For example, the Fourth Crusade (fostered by Innocent II) fell under the venal domination of Venice, was first diverted to conquer Zara for the doge, and then involved in civil strife in Byzantium, in which latter adventure the crusading army ended up sacking and despoliating Constantinople. See Wolter, pp. 154–58.

91. J. LaMonte, *The World of the Middle Ages* (New York, 1949), pp. 334–36; C. Wood, *The Age of Chivalry* (New York, 1970), pp. 94–107; for a yet more positive appraisal, see C. Dawson, *The Formation of Christendom* (New York, 1967), pp. 208–9.

92. See H. Taylor, *The Medieval Mind* (New York, 1919), pp. 331–35.

93. 1 Thess. 5:8; 2 Cor. 10:3–5.

94. For example, Basil (*Praevia institutio ascetica* 1) calls the Christian a soldier of Christ, and Chrysostom (*On the Priesthood* 4. 4) uses the metaphor of a military campaign to describe the role of the pastor.

95. In his *Ecclésiologie*, p. 125, Congar stresses the fact that in the Carolingian period there was not yet this mentality of *ecclesia militans* regarding the earthly segment of the *communio sanctorum*; certainly he is right in emphasizing the dominance of the eschatological-mystery outlook during this period, but one does find explicit mention of the church as a force in battle. For example, Alcuin (whom Congar is discussing, *loc cit.*) speaks of the priest as "dux exercitus Dei et rector castrorum illius" (*Epist.* 112) and the context is explicitly one in which Christians are joined together to do battle with the devil.

96. This is reflected in the sermons preached for the crusades, and also in the figures of Roland and El Cid; see Daniel-Rops, pp. 356–62.

97. See F. Kempf, *Handbook of Church History*, vol. 3, pp. 464–65.

98. The call to the crusades was essentially a summons by the pope to heroic religious service; throughout the period of the crusades, the ultimate leadership of the crusade is acknowledged as a papal prerogative.

99. Perhaps the most striking case was the military undertaking of Simon de Montfort against the Albigensians; see Wolter, pp. 162–66.

100. See Daniel-Rops, pp. 433–83; J. Thompson, *Economic and Social History of the Middle Ages* (New York, 1959), vol. 2, pp. 428–39.

101. See Knowles, pp. 343–44.

102. See *Contra Gent.* 1, chap. 2; M.-D. Chenu, *Toward Understanding Saint Thomas* (Chicago, 1964), pp. 288–96.

103. This was the pattern, carefully established by Urban II for the first crusade (see Fliche, pp. 279–308), which set the precedent for future crusades.

104. See Wolter, pp. 188–98.

105. See Knowles, pp. 435–41.

106. See Fliche, pp. 427–45.

107. *Ibid.*, pp. 445–57.

108. See Wolter, pp. 12–16.

109. See Knowles, pp. 338–44.

110. See D. Knowles, *The Religious Orders in England* (Cambridge, 1956), vol. 1, pp. 114–26, 171–93.

111. See Van Steenberghen, pp. 233–336.

112. See Wolter, pp. 182–83.

113. On the late medieval decline and reforms of the mendicants, see Delaruelle, pp. 1065–100.

114. See Lateran V, session 11, "Supernae majestatis praesidio" (H. Schroeder, pp. 505–6; *Mansi* 32. 944–47.)

115. This became a prominent factor from the Cluniac movement onward. Prior to that time one does not find the large-scale and centralized direction of religious communities which consequently present a challenge to episcopal control, though the monastic evolution of the Irish church (and its offshoots) had earlier threatened to overshadow the episcopal organization of church life.

116. Gregory VII developed considerably the policy of granting exempt status to monastic institutions and this became a cardinal principle of papal ecclesiastical politics in the succeeding centuries. "Il [the bishop] perd notamment tout pouvoir de contrôle sur les réguliers qui, par exemption, relèvant directement du pontife romain: Gregoire VII, de plus en plus, considère toutes les questions d'ordre monastique comme étant de son ressort exclusif . . ." (Fliche, p. 88).

117. Such fraternal cooperation is, of course, the ideal; historically, there has been almost continuous friction, abetted no little by the friction between papacy and episcopacy. Apart from these pastorally important practical matters, the underlying theological question is that of the relationship of the episcopal *collegium* to the presbyteral *collegium*—which is more basic?

118. Jerome's influence is most noticeable in the theological tendency to view episcopacy and presbyterate as one priestly order. One cannot but wonder whether religious orders with their monastic and mendicant expressions of ordained presbyters were not largely responsible for keeping alive during the Middle Ages this question of episcopal-presbyteral relationship.

119. On the Carthusians, see Y. Gourdel, *Dictionnaire de spiritualité*, vol. 2, cols. 705–35; on the Praemonstratensians, R. Cornell, *New Catholic Encyclopedia*, vol. 11, pp. 737–39.

120. Whether in response to this kind of question or not, the Carthusian theologians did develop a theory according to which the celebration of Eucharist as such (even apart from any participating community) was the most basic and important action of apostolic ministry. See Gourdel, cols. 715–18.

121. On medieval missionary expansion to the Far East, see S. Neill, *Christian Missions*, vol. 6 of *Pelican History of the Church* (London, 1964), pp. 118–34.

122. For centuries before this the papacy had been importantly and immediately involved in the evangelization of new lands—as with Patrick, Augustine in England, Boniface in Germany, but the medieval missionary efforts of mendicants and canons regular involved the utilization by the papacy of structured, basically nonepiscopal, and enduring effort that was directly under its control. Eventually (in the post-Reformation period) this develops into the Roman Congregation for the Propagation of the Faith.

123. Administratively such division of effort according to assigned regions seems logical, but the history of missionary effort has been gravely marred by religious communities wrangling jealously over their rights to exclusive activity in a given part of the world.

124. See M.-D. Chenu, "Moines, clercs, laïcs au carrefour de la vie évangélique (XIIe siècle)," *Revue d'histoire ecclésiastique* 49 (1954), pp. 59–89.

125. See T. Charland, "Les auteurs d' 'artes praedicandi' au XIIIe siècle," *Etudes d'histoire littéraire et doctrinales du XIIIe siècle* (Paris, 1932), vol. 1, pp. 41–60; also, *idem*, *Artes Praedicandi* (Paris, 1936).

126. On the evolution of the urban parish in the later Middle Ages, see Iserloh, pp. 566–78.

127. On the effect this had in the English hierarchy, see D. Knowles, "The English Bishops, 1070–1532," *Medieval Studies*, ed. J. Watt, J. Morrall, and F. Martin (Dublin, 1961), pp. 288–91.

128. Actually, the early centuries of the Middle Ages had seen an evolution of clerical

life away from urban patterns and in the direction of feudal structures, while the latter part of the Middle Ages witnessed a movement back to increased influence of urban life on episcopal/presbyteral activity and life-style. See Watson, pp. 528–58. As this increased urbanization of European life took place in the late Middle Ages, the relationship between church and town was very mixed and ambiguous: cities were centers of reform under Gregory VII but they also became quite quickly centers of anticlericalism and sometimes of heresy. Higher ecclesiastics were hostile to the rights claimed by the emerging bourgeosie, many ecclesiastical writers looked upon cities as concentrations of evil and temptation. See Thompson, pp. 682–85.

129. See H. Rashdall, *Cambridge Medieval History*, vol. 6, pp. 559–601.

130. On the church's involvement in educational work during the patristic and medieval periods, see E. Power, *Main Currents in the History of Education* (New York, 1962), pp. 188–244.

131. See E. Ryan, *New Catholic Encyclopedia*, vol. 3, pp. 248–49.

132. On Yves' writings about *sacerdotium*, see A. Mignon, *Les origines de la scolastique* (Paris, 1895), vol. 2, p. 214. On the twelfth-century development of cathedral schools, see P. Delhaye, "L'organization scolaire au XIIe siècle," *Traditio* 5 (1947), pp. 211–68.

133. See Forest, pp. 120–33.

134. See Van Steenberghen, pp. 193–96.

135. Still, one must be cautious in attributing superstition to the Christians of those centuries; for one thing, there was a notable concentration of devotion on Christ (due at least partially to the widespread influence of Bernard of Clairvaux and Francis of Assisi) and on the celebration of the liturgical mysteries. On the religion of the laity in the twelfth and early thirteenth century, see D. Knowles, *Christian Centuries*, vol. 2, pp. 259–65.

136. Thus, Lateran III legislates (canon 18) that each cathedral church have a master who teaches gratis clerics and poor students; this is repeated by Lateran IV (canon 11).

137. See de Ghellinck, pp. 66–78.

138. *Ibid.*, pp. 52–65, 113–66.

139. On thirteenth-century commentary on Scripture, see B. Smalley, *The Study of the Bible in the Middle Ages* (Oxford, 1952), pp. 264–355.

140. On the evolution and complexity of medieval theories of biblical exposition, see H. de Lubac, *Exégèse médiévale* (Paris, 1959–64).

141. See, e.g., Thomas Aquinas *Summa theol.* 1, q. 1.

142. See *Proslog.* Proemium.

143. See *De sacram.* 1. 4. 30.

144. See *Summa theol.* 2–2, q. 180.

145. *Itinerarium* 1. 1–6. On medieval theories of contemplation, see vol. 2 of *Dictionnaire de spiritualité*: J. Leclercq (cols. 1936–48), J.-M. Dechanet (cols. 1948–66), P. Philippe (cols. 1966–88), and F. Vandenbroucke (cols. 1988–2001).

146. See Knowles, *Christian Centuries*, pp. 338–53.

147. See Delaruelle, pp. 509–12.

148. There was already some uneasiness (even on the part of men like Gerson and d'Ailly who were basically sympathetic to the prophetic voice in the church) about the role of mystics in the guidance of Christian faith and life; but the strong repudiation of this role comes in the post-Reformation period.

149. See Wolter, pp. 98–104; Knowles, *Christian Centuries*, pp. 365–74.

150. See F. Hayward, *The Inquisition* (New York, 1966), pp. 19–32; W. Wakefield, *Heresies of the High Middle Ages* (New York, 1969), pp. 32–36.

151. For a slightly different, though complementary analysis, see G. Leff, "Heresy and the Decline of the Medieval Church," *Religious Dissent in the Middle Ages*, ed. J. Russell (New York, 1971), pp. 99–114.

CHAPTER 5

Ministry in the Age of Reform

Although the conclusion of the Council of Constance promised the advent of a new era, one in which reform of the church (beginning with the top) might seriously be undertaken, the hope was short-lived. Constance was followed by a reassertion of papal dominance; the series of councils that was intended to carry out the unfinished agenda of Constance saw the weakening of the conciliarist forces. By the end of the Council of Florence (in 1439) the hope that serious reform would be effected by such councils had substantially evaporated.[1] Much of Rome's regaining of power was accomplished by political and less edifying elements of the Italian Renaissance, and Rome gave little promise of reforming itself much less leading a general reform of the church. So, the period between Constance and the outbreak of the Reformation was marked by continuing and clamorous cries for "reform in head and members." And the cries grew more desperate as repeated failures at reform suggested that the task might be beyond accomplishment.[2]

At the heart of this demand for reform was the observable need of the common people for truly dedicated ministration to their spiritual well-being. Although the fourteenth and fifteenth centuries do mark a decline from the creative religious awakening of the twelfth century and its continuation into the thirteenth, the general state of things in the ministry was probably not much worse than it had been at many times in the past. Still, life for the common people was quite hard and coarse; the plague had done nothing to alleviate this situation, the moral education and ethical refinement of the common folk was minimal, and the level of most clerical life and activity was not much better.[3] Unquestionably, there were many exceptions to the view of clerics provided by *The Canterbury Tales* or *Piers Plowman*,[4] to say nothing of Boccaccio, but it seems clear that there was widespread neglect of the religious formation and guidance of the general populace.[5]

The problem does not seem to have been one of a lack of priests; men like Thomas More actually advocated a lessening of their numbers, so that better quality might be secured.[6] Rather, the majority of the clergy were ill-trained for preaching, relatively innocent of any accurate theological understanding of the faith, and were routine functionaries in the sacraments.[7] Catechesis was often lacking, attendance at the Eucharist was perfunctory and few received Communion, the sacrament of penance was neglected except *"in extremis,"*[8] and superstition was not only widespread but actually fostered by many who exploited the credulity of the uneducated people.[9]

Much of the demand for reform came from the prominent theological faculties or from churchmen connected with them. At the Council of Constance the official leadership role of such theological faculties reached its zenith,[10] and while this same eminence was not maintained in the following decades, the prestige and influence of theological faculties carried into and beyond the Reformation.[11] It was at such university faculties and among those closely associated with them that was to be found the best educated clergy, a fairly high portion of whom were dedicated to the internal vitality of the church. It was they who were in the best position to see the reforms that needed to be made and to lead the fight for their adoption.[12]

Absorption with other questions, such as the dispute on papal prerogatives (which did indirectly influence thought about ministry), kept the theologians from developing any new approaches in understanding Christian ministry. For the most part, they simply repeated explanations of ministry and priesthood that had been developed in the Middle Ages. Wyclif's ideas, which questioned the whole notion of sacerdotal "power" deriving from official designation and ordination, still found some circulation in England, and through Hus had exerted considerable influence on the Continent.[13] But in theological circles they had failed to challenge seriously the views developed in the twelfth and thirteenth centuries, which centered around the explanation of the "sacramental character" of Orders. This failure is the more significant in the light of the rising tide of Donatism and the widespread concern with the problem of the sacramental effectiveness of "the wicked priest."[14] Probably of greater ultimate importance was the widening influence of the "nominalism" associated with the thought of such men as Ockham and Biel.[15] For the moment it did not directly challenge the classic medieval understandings of Christian ministry, but did so implicitly by the manner in which it demanded a radical reconsideration of the realities of grace and faith and salvation and sanctification, with which Christian ministry was presumably occupied.[16]

Common Understanding of "Priesthood"

Without adverting for the moment to technical differences of opinion that distinguished the views of one theological school from another,[17] we can describe the general understanding of "priesthood" that was commonly accepted in this immediate pre-Reformation period. For the most part, it was the result of gradual dissemination of the technical theological understandings achieved during the twelfth and thirteenth centuries,[18] allowing, of course, for the tendency of popular understanding to "materialize" reality and to give credence to magical and superstitious interpretations of religious happenings.[19]

The priest, by virtue of his ordination, was considered to possess certain special powers which enabled him to perform effectively in the work of "saving souls." The most important and basic of these powers was that of changing the bread and wine of the Eucharistic celebration into the body and blood of Christ; it was possession of this power that made a man a priest. Next in importance was the power of freeing men from their sins by penitential absolution, which found a certain extension in baptism and final anointing. These were the "standard powers" that were explained by classic theology and by popular instruction, and that were possessed *objectively* by the ordained minister (i.e., independent of his virtue or sin)[20] so as to guarantee the effectiveness of sacraments needed by the faithful. And what the ordinary priest possessed, the bishops possessed in fullness; they alone could ordain new priests, they fulfilled baptism by confirmation, and ultimate jurisdiction in conscience matters rested with them, since only they could excommunicate.

Popular belief and the activity of many clerics emphasized another "power," not entirely divorced from the two just named but somewhat nebulous and hard to define. This was the power to bless: to bless men and animals in order to heal them or to avert harm, to bless food and other inanimate objects so that they would better serve human needs, to bless various "charms" that would help ward off evil. This found expression in many official church ceremonies of blessing,[21] and official blessings for a wide range of objects have found a place in liturgical books up to our own day. It also found expression in some dubious practices such as the selling of relics, to which, of course, the salesman often ascribed great powers.[22] Other charismatic individuals (and kings) could attach blessings or curses to persons or things, but that was by virtue of some special quality that was found in them, whereas the power of blessing exercised by priests was believed to flow from their endowment with power at ordination.[23]

The power attributed to the ordained minister was only part, though probably the most important part, of his separateness from the ordinary. Although popular testimony to the avarice and sloth and lewdness of many of the clergy makes it clear that they could be all too "ordinary" at one level of their existence, they continued to be the distinct and superior caste of society which earlier centuries had gradually established and explained. One of the things that must be kept in mind is the deep division between the relatively smaller number of educated priests (who dealt with the higher levels of society, were quite cosmopolitan in their outlook, and were relatively affluent) and the bulk of country pastors. These latter were much closer to the people, both in their outlook and their life-style, and probably in many instances were more pastoral and less ecclesiastical. It is interesting to notice that Chaucer (who himself was a courtier and man of letters) pictures the priestly ideal exemplified in such a country pastor, whereas it is the well-to-do monk and the mendicant friar who embody much of the "evils" of the clergy.[24]

Even men like Thomas More, who were themselves the clear superior of most priests in theological learning and sincere Christian life, and who were maturely aware and critical of clerical shortcomings, still accepted the superior status of clergy within the structured life of the church.[25] Such a stratification of the church into "agents" and "those acted upon" had been confirmed by many centuries of legal precedent and theological justification: such was the *de iure divino* order of the Christian community.[26] The roots of opposition to this view of intrinsic clerical superiority had already been laid in the thought of Ockham and Marsilius of Padua,[27] but Ockham himself could not ultimately break with the hierarchical view of the church. He even conceded a "plenitudo potestatis qua papa praeeminet et praefulget."[28] For men in the

fourteenth and fifteenth centuries who desired reform, the practical course of action lay not in questioning the validity of the lay-clergy dichotomy but in discovering means of leading the ordained to an authentic fulfillment of their vocational ideal.

In pre-Reformation Europe the world of ecclesiastical institutions offered its own possibilities of professional occupation, advancement, and success that paralleled those of "secular" society. A man could aspire to a career in the church or in the world; if he chose the former he became professionally ecclesiastical, part of "the church." As the age of Reformation dawned, church and state were two organized and roughly parallel "governments" (not really, as is sometimes stated, two "societies") living together in uncertain detente.[29] The notion of the one *societas christiana*, which had dominated European thought for half a millennium, was growing dim and soon to be dissolved in the religious divisions of the sixteenth century. As a result, the clergy could no longer claim to be relevant for human life because they were the "soul" of this *societas christiana*; much anticlerical criticism dealt with them as a social and economic problem, and questions were inevitably raised about the nature and effectiveness of their spiritual ministration.

The Quest for More Authentic Liturgy and Catechesis

Almost every age in the church's life has seen a certain discontent with the insufficiency of religious formation and the imperfections of liturgical formulation. But there are some periods when this is felt more critically, and the late fifteenth and early sixteenth century time is one of these.[30] No doubt, some of this discontent was attached to the movement of Europe into the "modern world," to the increased sophistication of human understanding about man himself and the world in which he lived, to the beginnings of a critical sense which with the spread of printing and reading would reach down into the attitudes of the middle class, and to the emergence of an increasingly independent bourgeoisie that no longer saw human betterment as something that might hopefully come as an act of "salvation" by God. But it was also due to the slow adaptation of the official church to the changing patterns of human behavior and attitude. It was a reluctance to honor the diversity of vernacular languages and emerging national cultures,[31] a relative inability to grasp the fact of the final demise of the Roman empire,[32] and even more importantly a lack of understanding (quite excusable and by no means limited to church) that the fundamentally aristocratic and feudal patterns of classical and medieval civilization were being displaced by a "new world" of democratic aspirations and social structure in the next five centuries.[33]

Central to this ferment in the religious life of pre-Reformation Europe was the question of faith. The earlier centuries of Christian belief, of course, had not been ignorant of the basic problem of faith and of its relation to human reason and understanding.[34] This is clearly evidenced by the fact that the central thrust of the Augustinian current of theological thought, which in its various forms was the dominant stream of theology from the fifth through the sixteenth centuries, could be well summarized in Anselm's succinct definition *fides quaerens intellectum*.[35] Again, the incessant exhortations of church leadership advocating better preaching and more adequate instruction of the faithful honored the principle that believers should acquire a better understanding of the faith they professed.[36]

Despite such official urging and legislation, the level of theological understanding among the faithful and even among the bulk of the clergy was minimal. Even more telling was the fact that such ignorance was regarded as something to be expected even though it was not ideal. It was really sufficient that theology be possessed by "the church" (i.e., the influential clergy) which could then provide direction for the common body of Christians. The ordinary Christian should not be bothered with "theological sophistry," but left to his simple adherence to the church's doctrine and worship.[37]

Given the state of religious understanding among the mass of the people, it is surprising that their appreciation of the Eucharist was as profound and authentic as it was. Abuses there unquestionably were (such as the undisciplined multiplication of votive masses celebrated for stipends, the increase in private masses at the expense of public masses with participating congregations, or the "magical" power attributed to masses said in certain numbers or sequence); but the basic problem seems to have consisted in the laity's inability to share in the Eucharistic action, to a large extent because of the use of Latin. Quite literally, the people assembled on Sunday to "hear Mass"; the elevation of the host was the high point of the action as far as popular interest was concerned; reception of Communion was quite generally limited to the Paschal Communion.[38]

Yet, there was one aspect of the church's preaching and instruction and liturgy which (at least in better pastoral practice) worked in subtle fashion against the decline of people's faith and the routine performance of liturgy: There was unquestioned agreement that Christians should have a deeper "devotion" to Christ.[39] In this devotion, emphasis was laid not on theological understanding but on simple adherence and love; while this was often mixed with some false understanding and folklore, it did deal essentially with the reality of salvation. To this extent it represented a very real level of insight, one which could in the long run challenge the excessive abstractions of formal theology and the vacuity of overly formalized religious practice. By the very fact that the church never did relinquish this attempt to bring the faithful to some personal relationship to Christ, it prepared the problem of faith that confronted it at the end of the Middle Ages. In proportion as Christians did possess a genuine personal attachment to Christ, they wished to make this relationship more conscious and significant in their lives.[40]

Thus, it would be a mistake to see the upheaval of the Reformation period as other than a basically religious movement, even though cultural and social and political forces played an important part.[41] The widespread and profound heritage of religious faith possessed by Europe at the end of the Middle Ages cried out for some solution to the discontent with the state of ecclesiastical ministration.[42] There was a widespread awareness of the need for ministry of word and sacrament, a criticism of the absence of such ministration, and inevitably therefore of those who were meant to provide such ministry but who had drifted into another (more organizational and "political") approach to the pastoral office.

Reformation, 1517–1560

Despite the strong undercurrents of discontent and struggles for reformation, the surface of church life at the beginning of the sixteenth century seemed relatively calm and unified. Then, with remarkable suddenness the dammed-up forces of change swept over Christian Europe. In a couple of decades the splintering of the church (at least as a sociological reality) was an accomplished fact. In a religious upheaval without precedent in Christian history, there emerged a pluralism of doctrine and polity which has constituted the world of European Christianity and its derivatives until our own day.

Unquestionably, the role of Martin Luther as a catalyst in this upheaval was of major importance. Yet neither he nor any of the other great reformers can truly be said to have caused the split of the church. The centrifugal forces at work in European society in general, and in the church in particular, were both strong and largely unidentified. It is difficult to see how the process of division could have been reversed, if, indeed, it would have been a basically good thing to do so. These forces would erupt with revolutionary violence in "secular society" in mid-seventeenth century;[43] the religious "revolutions" of the Reformation period both anticipated and helped bring about this more general dissolution of medieval and Renaissance social structures.[44]

In the ecclesiastical disruption that occurred in the first half of the sixteenth century the principal dynamism was religious. This raises some grave questions for Christianity. The intrinsic nature of Christianity, at least according to the faith that is reflected in the New Testament writings, is to be a unifying force among men. Yet, fidelity to Christian faith was given (and sincerely given) by all parties as the reasons for separating from one another in the Reformation period; and this same fidelity, often magnified to fanaticism, found expression in the bitter religious wars that disrupted and impoverished Europe. Correlatively, it raises a basic question for Christian ministry: faced with this divisive appeal to "fidelity to Christian faith," what is to be the role of Christian ministers who are meant to function as agents of Christian community?

Results of the Western Schism

Much has been written about the schism that split Latin Christianity from 1378–1417 and about the disastrous economic, social, and religious effects that resulted from it. One of the most far-reaching, though unrecognized, religious results was the weakening of the papacy as a symbol of unity.[45] For centuries prior to the schism there had been a developing image of Rome as the center of Christian unity, an image that came to full dominance with Innocent III and that was a key element in the thirteenth-century consciousness of Christendom. With the schism, the very experience of Latin Christianity as a unified reality was threatened; but Christians on all sides of the schism did still maintain a common sense of membership in the one church. However, the papacy could no longer act as a symbol causing this consciousness of community. It was the focus of disunity rather than of unity. Besides, as the schism stretched on, people gradually developed the experience of Christian life and even the institutional activity of the church continued despite the ambiguous existence of that which had been thought to be the source of that life and activity. It is difficult to maintain the notion that the papacy is indispensable as a criterion for orthodoxy and as a channel of salvation when for decades the bulk of Christians could not look to it for either. Though the papacy quite rapidly reestablished its position in the power politics of the latter half of the fifteenth century, it was quite another thing to reinstill into the corporate imagination and memory of Europe an effective image of the *supreme* pontiff.[46]

Despite a mounting clamor for "reformation in head and members," it seemed that the task was almost too vast to be accomplished. What was particularly discouraging was the reluctance of the papacy to face candidly the need of "cleaning up the mess" in Rome itself. For more than a century, many of the most eminent members of the church, such as Gerson and Nicholas of Cusa and Erasmus, had attempted to foster an effective reform movement but with relatively little lasting result.[47]

Since the heart of the problem was the decadence of clerical life and activity, "reform of the church" meant "reform of the clergy." And throughout Europe there was widespread and often bitter anticlericalism. This resentment and criticism of the ecclesiastical "establishment" touched both diocesan and regular clergy, for if bishops and parish clergy were remiss in their pastoral ministry and less than edifying in their personal behavior, the religious orders were also in general need of reform at the same time that they constituted a serious economic burden on the people.

Thus, the fifteenth and early sixteenth centuries saw a mounting discontent with the "official church," and it is little surprise that the Reformation spread with such rapidity. Yet, there are many indications that European Christianity could still have been kept from definitive splintering if positive and straightforward moves towards reform had been initiated in the decade or two after 1521.[48] In the beginning, the cry of the reformers was not for division from Rome but for reform of the church. It is even possible that the opposing doctrinal views would not have crystallized into seemingly irreconcil-

able positions and reciprocal charges of "heresy" if official church response to Luther had not been put into the framework of heresy charges as early as 1518.[49] However, such charges and countercharges became the pattern of those decades; by the time the Council of Trent finally got under way in 1545 to provide some doctrinal clarification and initiate the long-delayed work of reform, the moment for decisive action to heal and reunify was already past. By then the religious division of Europe was an accomplished fact.[50]

One of the obvious aspects of the religious division of Europe in the sixteenth century was the diversity, even opposition, of credal formulations. Underlying this division of creeds was a source of divisiveness with which the church must deal in each period of its history. As the cultural and social patterns of men evolve historically, the formulations of faith (linguistic, liturgical, social) must evolve concomitantly if that faith is to provide understanding for life. At points of more drastic cultural change this need for reformulations of faith is correspondingly greater and the shift from the medieval-Renaissance to the modern world was one of those historical points.

It is good to note that the divisiveness caused by the gap which developed in the fifteenth and sixteenth centuries between the existent religious formulations and the new formulations required by cultural evolution sprang in considerable degree from authentic Christian faith. At least as far back as the twelfth century there had been manifest attempts to translate Christian faith into new patterns, attempts whose partial success and partial repression comprise a good part of the church's history for the past millennium. A study of those efforts indicates that for the most part they were initiated and fostered by men and women of religious vitality who wished Christian faith to find realistic embodiment in a changing world.

For a variety of reasons, these attempts to "modernize" Christianity did not keep pace with the process of Europe's emergence in the modern period. At the beginning of the sixteenth century the futility of trying to "keep new wine in old bottles" was keenly felt even if only vaguely recognized. It is part of the tragedy of this historical period that the official church had taken from as early as the thirteenth century a negative, judgmental attitude towards these attempts at reformulation, instead of exercising positive leadership in the creative search for new forms. Thus, the thrust of the Christian community towards reformulation of its life was deprived to some extent of the "conservatism" that is required by the dialectic of historical change. At the Council of Trent, the force of Catholic tradition was directed towards stemming the currents of change associated with the Reformation rather than towards merging with and intrinsically transforming those currents. And, obviously, to the extent that it drew back from involvement with the forces of change in the modern world, the Catholic church was impoverished and in danger of allowing its emphasis on "the traditional" to become inflexibility.[51]

One of the major sources of diversification in doctrinal formulation was the pluralism of theological opinion that characterized the beginning of the sixteenth century. We have suggested that the Reformation was essentially a religious movement, which is not the same as saying it was a theological movement. In the case of the Reformation and the Catholic response, theology's role was of capital importance. Most of the Reformers were theologians of better-than-average ability, the various religious stances of Reformation communities were in large part crystallized through theological discussion and dispute, theological faculties were deeply involved in the movements of "reform" and "counterreform," and the religious attitudes of the classic reformers were quite quickly translated by them into formal theological positions. This rapid movement to theology is perhaps best observed in Lutheranism, where the religious sensitivity of Luther was complemented not just by his own theological competence but by the theological genius of Melanchthon.

Now, having indicated that differing religious insights found expression in distinct and often opposed theological positions, we must draw attention to the other side of the coin. Religious attitudes are to some extent prepared for and grounded in theology, and the difference of one theological school from another is largely a matter of diverse philosophical presuppositions. So, beneath the broad spectrum of religious views that appears in sixteenth-century Europe there is the complicated diversity of theological opinion that characterizes the decline of medieval scholasticism; it is something that is reflected by the extent to which Reformation theological polemic continues the classic disputes of late medieval theologians, and to some extent the classic jealousies of opposing schools of theology.

To distinguish accurately the various lines of force that link the religious views of an individual or group with certain theological positions, and beyond that with certain philosophical principles, is almost impossible.[52] Rather than attempt that, our present objective is simply to recall that such lines of force do exist, and that theologians, conscious of it or not, do minister in a particular manner to the religious mentality of a community. Since the theologians of the Reformation period were almost all clerics (or the Protestant equivalent, once the Reformation got under way), "doing theology" was part of their understanding of what it meant for them to carry on ministry. Not only the content but the style of their theological work gives us some understanding of what ministry meant to them. When one remembers the contentiousness of so much theological discourse during this period, one wonders whether the men involved thought of themselves as "defending the orthodox truth" or as "ministering to the unity of Christian believers." The first of these two seems clearly to have dominated and to have set the tone for the religious attitudes of the various Christian communities as they faced other communities with credal formulations somewhat different from their own. In the situation where "controversial theology" rules, there is a certain premium set on division: separation from those "who are in error" is considered a virtue; attempts to transcend such divisive theology are often viewed as treasonable disloyalty.

When we mentioned that the reformulation of Christian faith lagged behind the secular developments of fifteenth- and sixteenth-century Europe, it was not to condemn the ecclesiastics of that day. To a great extent no one could be blamed, because it was almost impossible to ascertain clearly the cultural developments to which one should "adapt" Christianity. Even with the historical vantage point which we enjoy it is difficult to look back to that period and determine the cultural dynamics that were operative. Where, for example, does one situate late fifteenth-century "humanism"? Is it a reaction against, even a reversal of, the attitudes that underlie medieval culture? Or should one see it as a later stage in the cultural awakening of the twelfth century which marked the advent of the High Middle Ages?

However, though it may be impossible to make precise the influence of these nonreligious forces on the happenings of the sixteenth century, and though one may wish to stress the essentially religious nature of the Reformation, there is no doubt that these other factors contributed in major fashion to the divisiveness that prepared for the Reformation and determined to no small degree the nature of the division which did ensue. And even though we obviously cannot pretend an essay into sixteenth-century cultural history, some brief mention of the cultural and political situation is important for our study because in the Reformation-period discussion of ministry both educational work and political leadership are mentioned as forms of Christian ministry.

Misleading as such broad labeling is, the use of "humanism" and "scholasticism" to refer to two opposed trends in fifteenth- and sixteenth-century Europe does point to a basic cultural conflict underlying the religious divisions of that period.[53] As the sixteenth century dawned, the humanist movement had spread north from Italy and was a powerful force in university centers throughout Europe and at Oxford and Cambridge in England. However, when it found expression in "new" critical methods applied to Scripture, return to study of the early fathers of the church, and a movement away from the allegorical and syllogistic methods, this humanism encountered a strong opposition from the proponents of the "scholastic method." What this latter meant depended very much upon the loyalties of a given university to a particular "school of theology." For example, at Oxford it meant adherence to the thought of Duns Scotus, whereas at Erfurt the favorite "doctor" was Ockham. One cannot couple "humanism" with the Reformation, nor "scholasticism" with Catholicism. A large portion of the most influential humanists were and remained Catholic, and the ideals and methods of humanist scholars had a major impact on Catholic education and theology, whereas, on the other side, the continuing influence of scholastic thought on Reformation theology is quite evident. Nowhere are the ambiguities of this situation more apparent than in the person and career of Erasmus.[54] Regarded in his own day as the leader of northern European humanism, accused by many of being a catalyst in the Reformation though himself remaining a Catholic, an ardent advocate of reform within the church and a bitter critic of clerical evils and theological sophistries, Erasmus found himself gradually drawn into criticism of Luther whom he had earlier supported, and his later years saw him opposing both reformers and humanists. Eminent as a scholar, his great dream was the renovation of European life by a sincere return of men to the simple teaching of the gospel; this dream and his friendship he shared with men on both sides of the Reformation controversies.[55]

Without understanding the adjective in a pejorative sense, we can say that the humanism of the fifteenth and sixteenth centuries was clearly divisive; inevitably so, since it pulled at least some men away from the intellectual and cultural patterns of the previous period. It was the "modernism" of its day, representing the wave of new thinking that is a challenge to the established order. What is important from the precise viewpoint of our study is that the ministry of the word was itself understood in relation to the positions on this issue: on the one hand seeing the role of preacher and teacher to safeguard the faithful from these "innovations of doctrine," on the other hand wishing to use these new insights to bring people back to the simple teaching of the early church and free them from the confusing subtleties of "scholasticism."

As Europe moved out of the Middle Ages and into the modern world, there was quite understandably more than usual political ferment. Nations were coming into existence, but the important city-states that had come into prominence towards the end of the thirteenth century were more powerful than ever and quite autonomous in their political and economic life. Alliances were constantly shifting as governments maneuvered for control not only of Europe but of the foreign lands whose wealth had been opened up by the new wave of exploration. All this had a considerable effect on the Reformation coming into existence and upon the way in which it was accepted or rejected in different parts of Europe. The effect was so strong that some analysts of this historical period attribute the Reformation most basically to such "secular" causes.[56]

One of the political happenings that may have had a special link with the religious division of European Christendom was the demise of the Holy Roman Empire. While the latter-day Christian continuations of imperial Rome had a checkered history, the role of the emperor as a symbol of Christendom's basic unity remained fairly constant, even when his effective political power was negligible. And throughout this process the idea of the unity of the church was almost inseparable from the idea of Europe united symbolically under the emperor. The sixteenth century saw the last attempt to give viability to this notion of Holy Roman Emperor by Charles V and Philip II, a heroic but ultimately doomed attempt. As this symbol of allegiance to "Rome" faded, it became easier to think of the possibility of denying allegiance to ecclesiastical Rome.

Yet, when all is said and done, the secular influences upon the genesis of the Reformation seem secondary. The principal sources of the religious division of Europe were religious, and one is inclined to agree with Lortz's judgment: "As we now look back at the entire shifting process . . . at the movement away from the Church which is traceable since the Thirteenth Century, we see, particularly, the widespread radical discontent with the clergy, the theological vagueness, and the lack of religious strength."[57]

Attempts to Preserve Unity

Strong and widespread as the movements towards effective reform were, and important as the centrifugal forces were in both political and religious society, the first half of the sixteenth century saw repeated attempts to preserve unity and avoid a definitive split in Christian Europe. Just prior to Luther's move, the Fifth Lateran Council (1512–17) provided the last pre-Protestant opportunity to accomplish a genuine reformation of the church; but, in large part because of the skillful maneuvering of Leo X, the council was rendered impotent.[58] Then, when the storm did break, the Diet of Worms in 1521 tried for an easy early solution; again in the Augsburg diets of 1530 and 1555, Charles V tried for a peaceful reunion of Christendom. Only the last of these three diets resulted in some peace, but at the price of Charles recognizing the split between Protestant and Catholic lands within his own empire as an accomplished fact.

These were the more official attempts; there was also a host of meetings, discussions, debates, and exchanges of letters all aimed in one way or another at bettering understanding, or at least clarifying differences of understanding, and perhaps achieving some form of union. Some of these concerned Catholic-Protestant differences and some of them dealt with the widening differences within Protestantism. To a large extent these failed as completely as the imperial diets; the divisions in European Christianity became more widespread and more fixed.

In its own sphere of influence, the Council of Trent proved to be a more effective instrument of unification although it came into being too late to affect the split between Catholicism and Protestantism, and in its spirit and enactments was not calculated to heal that split. Both in the establishment of doctrinal unity and in the initiation of genuine institutional reform, the influence of Trent upon subsequent Roman Catholicism can scarcely be exaggerated. Only with Vatican II did the Roman Catholic church give official indication of becoming something other than a Tridentine form of Christianity.

Since the fostering of Christian community is unquestionably one of the basic functions intrinsic to ministry within the church, a study of ministry must ponder the reasons why the attempts to prevent the fragmentation of Christian community in the sixteenth century failed. These sixteenth-century failures were not new: Wyclif and Hus had both agitated for reform but their attempts were compromised by their deviant doctrinal teachings;[59] Gerson and Nicholas of Cusa agitated just as strongly, and while they could not be accused of heresy they were regarded in papal circles as less than trustworthy because they represented northern Europe. Cajetan accused Luther of being a "Gersonist."[60]

True, these earlier attempts were concerned more formally with reform and not with reunification, whereas the sixteenth century, once the Reformation movement was in full swing, was confronted with the precise problem of unity. However, it may be instructive to notice that the same response by higher ecclesiastics, particularly the papacy, to the threat of disunity characterized both the pre- and post-Reformation periods. Against the possibilities of "schism" implicit in the accusations and suggestions of Wyclif, Hus, Cusa, and Gerson, the papacy reacted with a greater insistence on centralization and univocal doctrinal formulation. In the sixteenth century,

this was again the strategy of both papal and imperial powers. The attempts of Charles V in this regard were frustrated, for he was unable to impose a clearly Catholic formulation of faith upon his Lutheran territories; the attempts of the papacy were more successful, for the Tridentine structuring of the Roman Catholic church represents a long step forward in the papacy's reassertion of absolute authority.

One cannot say that this emphasis on centralization and identical formulations of faith was the reason that attempts at reunification failed. It may well be that the disruptive forces at work in sixteenth-century Europe were simply too strong to be stemmed. Yet, a reading of the history of that period indicates that this introverted policy contributed to the bitterness of the divisions and to a widening misunderstanding of one another's real theological positions.

Under the surface there lurked a divergence of opinion regarding the nature of the church's unity at any given point in history, and its unity from one historical period to another. To oversimplify the question, the Reformers stressed the internal and functional aspects, the Catholic position emphasized the visible and structural aspects. Consequently, their attempts to attain or preserve the unity of the church had somewhat different objectives.[61] This was further complicated by the fact that the men and women of the sixteenth century were too close to the confusing and explosive happenings of those years to discern clearly the roots of their divisions, and so be able to overcome them.[62]

Although the European church at the beginning of the sixteenth century knew a greater diversity of pastoral forms, particularly in the liturgy, than did the Catholic church after Trent, there was a relative homogeneity of religious practice, and therefore of ministerial activity, throughout the church. With the rapid spread of the Reformation there ensued a short period of considerable confusion and disorder; there was a general movement towards emphasis on preaching services, but no agency to bring about some order in worship or church discipline. Before long, however, there began to emerge a variety of patterns within the Protestant areas and a clearer demarcation between Catholic and Protestant communities and practices.[63]

One of the most notable immediate effects of Luther's ideas and example was a movement in many areas towards the congregationalism which remained an ideal for the great reformer. Theoretically, each individual community was to exercise judgment in doctrine and discipline, call pastors and teachers, provide for community discipline, and manage finances and the care of the poor. This meant that the pastor was charged specifically with the preaching and administration of sacraments and so empowered by the calling community. In practice, much of the direction and control of Lutheran congregations was provided by the territorial princes or by the city council of the free cities, either directly or through appointed superintendents.[64]

Like Catholicism before it, the Lutheran movement had to proceed with two quite different groups of pastors; some were well-educated and because of their university backgrounds quite prepared for the emphasis on the preaching office, but many others were ill-trained for effective ministry. Understandably the former gravitated to the courts, or universities, or ministry in the towns, while the rural ministry was committed to the latter.[65] What these town or rural pastors did was not too different from the activity of their Catholic counterparts, except that there was relatively more stress on teaching than on sacramental ritual. The married status of these Reform pastors lent a different tonality to their ministrations and often forced them to undertake some supplementary employment. There was no place in the new Lutheran approach for the nonpastoral minister; the individual whose ordination found no expression other than "saying Mass." With the closing of monasteries and convents, religious-order clergy (still so prominent in Catholic areas) disappeared as a ministerial form in Lutheran territories. Still, in the ordinary parish situations, there was a good deal of

continuity between Lutheranism and the Catholicism that preceded it. This was even more true in Scandinavia than it was in Germany.[66]

While the Lutheran reform, even in its confessional stage, maintained an undefined attitude towards the structure of ministry, keeping "pastor" as the one basic office,[67] other Reformation churches established a more detailed ministerial order. The ministerial structure envisaged by Martin Bucer and implemented in Strasbourg did not eventuate in a lasting church order, but it is important because of the influence of Bucer on the Continent and in England. Like Luther, Bucer stresses the basic office of pastor and (perhaps even more than Luther) the active ministry of the entire community.[68] He provides for the three traditional offices of bishop (or superintendent), presbyter (or pastor), and deacon, and adds the office of "elder";[69] but "bishop" for Bucer means neither the traveling superintendent of the Lutheran situation, nor the higher ecclesiastic of the Catholic church.[70]

Bucer's reform of Christian community life and worship was much influenced by the social and political situation of Strasbourg. So, too, the reform movement inspired by Zwingli was deeply affected by affairs in Switzerland and especially in Zurich; not only was the procedure of his reform measures intertwined with the civil management of Zurich, but his religious reforming spirit is inseparable from his political activism. This would seem to indicate that increased involvement in political and social affairs marked the activity of ordained ministers in the "Zwinglian Reformation"; actually, the Swiss Reformed movement turned more exclusively to ecclesiastical activity under Zwingli's son-in-law and successor, Bullinger.[71]

As we read today about the way in which the introduction of Zwingli's reform measures was carried out by the city council, this control of church life by city officials might strike us as a Reformation innovation. Actually, some such civic direction of ecclesiastical forms and activity goes back to the rise of the cities in the thirteenth century, and to the accompanying assertion of power by the bourgeoisie.[72] What was probably most noticeably new about the Zwinglian reform in its early stages was the gradual elimination of images and most music (including the organ) from church services, the "simplification" of Eucharistic liturgy to a Communion service (which actually involved a radical shift in understanding the Lord's Supper and "ministry of sacrament"), increased emphasis on religious instruction (especially instruction in Scripture), the sociological changes accompanying the abolition of clerical celibacy and the disestablishment of monasteries and convents, and the break with higher church authority.[73] The form of ministry definitely shifted from "ministry of sacrament" to "preaching of the word," and the framework of ministry becomes not so much the parish as the Christian city-state.

This non-Lutheran reform movement finds its fullest and most influential expression in Calvin. Without for the moment going into the underlying theological views, we can notice the restructuring of ministry accomplished by Calvin.[74] In a given Christian commonwealth (such as Geneva) the principal ministerial officials are the "pastors," for it is they who are the ministers of the gospel; the central role of preaching is unquestioned, and everything else is supportive of this basic ministerial task. Closely allied with preaching, though having its distinct importance, is teaching; and a distinct group of "teachers" is commissioned to provide accurate instruction to the community. It seems presumed that these men have some theological formation. These pastors and *doctores* constitute a clerical reality in Calvinism; but in addition to them the *elders* and *deacons*, who are laity, provide for government of the community, for care of charitable activities, and for general assistance to the pastors. Thus, the pastoral ministry as such tends to be very intellectualized in Calvin's community. Both pastor and doctor are meant to concentrate on understanding and communicating the word of God,[75] and a fair amount of the task previously carried on by parish pastors is assigned to chosen members of the laity.

If considerable continuity of ministerial patterns characterized the passage from Catholicism to Protestantism in Lutheran territories, this was even more marked in the English situation. The very nature of the Reformation in England was, of course, conducive to such continuity. It was not, in the first instance, a passage to Protestantism, but an assertion within existing structures and doctrines of the autonomy of the church in England and of the ecclesiastical jurisdiction of the crown. Moreover, the clergy (higher and lower) kept on doing pretty much what they had been doing before Henry VIII's break with Rome; for the most part the ecclesiastical and civil structures within which they operated persisted with relatively little change. There was, of course, a group within England that was carefully striving to move the country towards Protestantism; in the time of Henry VIII this was spearheaded by Thomas Cromwell and, less aggressively, by Cranmer. Under Edward VI, the movement towards Protestantism was much more marked, and the changes in worship and doctrine formulated to a large extent under Cranmer's direction made it possible to withstand the temporary setback of Mary Tudor's reign. These changes appear in reconfirmed fashion under Elizabeth.[76]

The history of the Church of England has been, from its origins, characterized by a tension between Catholic and Protestant polarities in both doctrine and worship, with one or the other position dominant at a given time. So also with the understanding of ministry and the manner in which preaching or "Eucharistic service" was stressed in the worship service;[77] but for the most part, especially in the early decades of the English Reformation, there was a general sense of continuity with the pre-Reformation English church in both faith and religious practice, except for the obvious changes wrought by the suppression and despoliation of the monasteries and convents and by the break with the authority of Rome.[78] One of the clearest indications of the way in which the common man's view of the clergy stressed continuity with the pre-Reformation situation is the unbroken tradition of anticlerical criticisms of the church and of laity dislike of clerical pretensions; apparently, the structures of the church had not been that thoroughly "reformed."[79]

With rare exception, the activity of the Council of Trent was one of confirming or at most clarifying what was traditional in Catholic teaching and practice and structure; it was seen in Catholic circles as a defense of orthodoxy against the evils of heresy and schism. With regard to the exercise of ministry, it did finally enact some effective reform measures against the widespread neglect of ministerial responsibility, it legislated for careful preparation of the ordained, and it established more sharply the domain of episcopal control over ministry. But it advocated no real changing of ministerial patterns; and the emphasis (theoretical and practical) on the cultic-priest identity of the pastor was intensified in reaction to Protestantism. Symptomatically, the practice of a priest celebrating the Eucharist with no attendant congregation was defended rather than challenged.

Yet, by its reform legislation and by the stimulus it gave the Catholic Reformation, Trent did help bring about a qualitative betterment of ministry within the Catholic communion. Episcopal absenteeism and possession of multiple offices began to disappear; seminaries were gradually established and started to produce a large body of candidates for ordination; preaching was revived in many places and catechizing became more widespread; administration of both dioceses and parishes became regularized and pastoral care more dependable. Clearly, Trent was not the only, perhaps not even the principal, agent in this process; but it certainly was a major influence.[80]

In subsequent chapters we will examine more carefully the attitude of Trent towards ministry of the word, ministry of sacrament, service in the world, and ecclesiastical authority—all of which were seriously reexamined by the theologians of the Reformation—

and the role Trent played in crystallizing Catholic thought and practice in these various aspects of ministry. Now, we can make the preliminary generalization that the Council of Trent was defensive rather than creative in its approach to Christian ministry; that it relied upon reassertion of centralized authority to respond to the movement towards doctrinal, liturgical, and pastoral reformulation; that it tended to situate ministerial activity in the Catholic church within the Latin spirituality of southern Europe; that it linked the effectiveness of ministry to the *ex opere operato* effectiveness of ecclesiastical jurisdiction and the *ex opere operato* power of sacramental ritual.

Sixteenth-Century Theological Views on Ministry

Before 1517, but much more so afterwards, the sixteenth century was a time of intense and widespread theological activity. Obviously, a fair amount of this theological ferment was a direct result of the Reformation controversies. A good bit was also an effort by the established theological "schools" (Thomistic, Scotist, etc.) to give a systematic Catholic answer to the issues raised by the Reformation, or an effort along the same lines by Protestant theologians such as Melanchthon or Beza or Calvin. But a considerable portion of the theological productivity of this century flowed from the inner renewal of theology. This renewal itself was nourished by the expansion of libraries, the use of printing, the development of scriptural exegesis and positive theology.[81]

Because Christian ministry was so much a point of contention in Reformation controversy, theological discussion of ministry is frequent and quite divergent. However, certain themes or problems are consistently present and provide some coherence to a complicated body of opinion. The first of these themes is "return to sources," specifically to the New Testament.

Stimulated by the development among humanist scholars, particularly Erasmus, of clearer textual and exegetical methods, and by the religious desire to "get back to the gospel," both Protestant and Catholic scholarship achieved a major development of scriptural studies in the sixteenth century. Logically, then, reflection on the nature of Christian ministry would have been influenced by the example of ministry in the primitive church; because of their relatively more exclusive emphasis on Scripture, the Reformers would have been expected to draw more heavily on this New Testament source. Such was the case: Bucer, for example, certainly based his reinstitution of "elders" upon the existence of such elders in the early church;[82] Calvin uses the primitive Christian ministerial order as the prescriptive norm for any later structuring of Christian ministry.[83]

However, while Catholic theology and Catholic reform measures did not reach back to recover external ministerial structures in the way many of the Reformers did, Catholic controversialists did develop a detailed argumentation from New Testament texts to show that the ordained episcopacy and presbyterate as it existed in the Catholic church was the sole legitimate successor of the primitive Christian ministry. Special stress was laid, of course, on the "divine institution" of the papal primacy and the Petrine origin of Roman authority,[84] while Catholic theologians laid greater stress on the legitimacy of post–New Testament developments in the church's life and structure. Both Catholic and Protestant polemicists accept the assumption of a direct institution by Christ himself of the essential elements of the church, and the need of preserving whatever is in this way *de iure divino*.

Up to our own day, the matter of papal primacy in doctrine and ecclesiastical jurisdiction has been a major source of division between Roman Catholicism and the other Christian churches. This was the case from the beginning of the Reformation, and in no place is the defense or rejection of papal prerogatives more clearly felt than in the theology about and practice of Christian ministry. Catholic theologians remain very much within the classic medieval framework of *potestas ordinis* and *potestas jurisdictionis*

when they discuss the various ministerial offices in the church. The Council of Trent itself witnessed a decided division of opinion regarding the respective powers and authority of papacy and episcopacy; only the compromise "solution" developed by Laynez and de Soto averted a crisis in the council.[85] But Trent in its eventual outcome represents an eclipse of the conciliar position that had been prominent from before the Council of Constance. Post-Tridentine theology moves towards the unmitigated papalism of Vatican I, though not without strong opposition from "Gallican" theologians.[86]

Needless to say, Reformation theology rejected the Roman claims to primacy, but this rejection took different forms according to diverse Reformation positions on authority within the church. These forms ranged all the way from the Erastianism of the Church of England to the unmitigated congregationalism of the radical Reformation. To put it another way, some Reformation theologians saw authority coming to the ministry "from above" but through channels other than the pope; others saw the authority as residing in the community and being delegated from them to appointed ministers; others saw ministerial authority as coming immediately through charismatic designation by the Spirit. They are united in their rejection of the jurisdictional claims of the papacy.

One of the basic differences between Catholic and Protestant understandings of Christianity is their attitude towards cult. We have indicated earlier how the emphasis on a cultic approach to Christian sacraments, particularly the Eucharist, gradually developed and along with it an understanding of the ordained bishop (and presbyter) as a cultic personage. By the thirteenth century, at least in some theologians (e.g., Bonaventure), the cult dimension of Eucharist and the priestly action of "confecting the Eucharist" were so exalted that they were distinguished from the "ministry of sacrament" even when this administration of sacrament was the Eucharistic distribution of Communion.[87] What the Reformers did was to drive still further the wedge between these two. They retain the administration of sacraments (*ministerium verbi et sacramenti*) but reject a cult priesthood that is qualitatively distinct from the basic priesthood of the Christian community. This is, of course, too broad a generalization. Anglican and Lutheran worship is relatively more "cultic" than is Calvinistic or Zwinglian worship; but there is agreement in rejecting the Roman Catholic theology of cult and priesthood.

Behind this movement away from a cultic emphasis in Christian worship and ministry lies a critical divergence in soteriology. Whereas the Catholic church stated its basic position by stressing at Trent the *ex opere operato* effectiveness of sacramental ritual, Protestant theology stressed the process of faith being aroused and nurtured by communication of God's word. Unquestionably, some of the Reformation reaction to "the Mass" and to "Mass-saying priests" was triggered by and directed against the abuses and superstition that had grown up in the fourteenth and fifteenth centuries; but the issue is intrinsically much more radical, for it deals with the manner in which salvation is (or is not) mediated through the action of the church and its ministers.

Catholic theological defense of the cultic emphasis in Eucharist and ordained ministry was immediate and unmistakable. Without denying the importance of the ministry of the word, Trent places clear primacy on the priestly act of offering sacrifice. The decree on the sacrament of orders begins with the clause "Sacrificium et sacerdotium ita Dei ordinatione coniuncta sunt. . . ."[88] And post-Tridentine Catholic theology is consistent in its focus on "offering sacrifice" as the most proper action of the ordained minister. It is difficult to find a more sharply defined stress on the cult role of the ordained priest than that which characterizes the theology of Bérulle at the beginning of the seventeenth century.

One of the principal religious forces in the sixteenth-century reform (both Protestant and Catholic) was anticlericalism. One of the more important aspects of this anticlericalism was a rejection of the paternalistic clerical precept "believe and do what we tell you" and a reassertion of individual belief and conscience judgment. The theological translation of this religious impulse was the development of a doctrine of "justification by faith" and insistence on the Spirit's guidance of the individual believer as he encounters the word of God. Awareness of the basic role of personal faith was not new to this century; patristic and medieval theology assume that salvation comes with faith in Christ. Still, the sixteenth-century reform movements do represent a challenge to doctrinal and ethical conformism and a step towards relatively greater individuality in Christian life. This is true of Luther's sermons and of the *Spiritual Exercises* of Ignatius Loyola.

Yet, such emphasis on individual judgment is dangerous, and it did not go uncontested. Churchmen and theologians, both Catholic and Protestant, struggled to establish operative norms for Christian belief and practice. This was seen as essential to social and church unity, and therefore a basic task of those entrusted with pastoral ministry in the church. Apart from some elements of the radical Reformation, neither Protestants nor Catholics looked for the Spirit to direct the faith and life of Christians without the instrumentality of official ministerial guidance. And quite universally, the theologians of the past four centuries, both Protestant and Catholic, have worked to justify a given ministerial structure instead of developing a theology of the Spirit's function in the church. Obviously, though, such a developed theology of the Spirit, which would necessarily involve a clearer theological understanding of the individual Christian's faith and conscience, must be a presupposition for any adequate explanation of ordained ministry. Creation of this pneumatology is part of the "unfinished business" of the Reformation.

The Crystallization of Reform

At the end of the sixteenth century, the religious division of Europe by the forces of the Protestant Reformation and Catholic reaction to it was accomplished. The seventeenth century would witness a crystallization of the respective positions, both structurally and doctrinally. This is the century of Protestant scholasticism, of the Caroline Divines, of the Jesuit-Jansenist controversy, of Bérulle and Francis de Sales and Bellarmine; but it is also the century of Richelieu and Oliver Cromwell and Gustavus Adolphus. By and large, the century is one of conflict and upheaval—economic, social, political, religious, and intellectual. What precise role religious faith and polity played in all this, to what extent it affected or was affected by the general divisiveness of the European scene, is impossible to determine; but religious motivations and convictions were unquestioningly of major importance. What is clear is that the "holy war" attitudes that accompanied the Thirty Years' War or the English Civil War, and that characterized the polemical theology of this century, intensified the opposition among various religious groups, further split the "soul" of Christian Europe, and so enfeebled both Protestantism and Catholicism that they were ill-prepared to deal with the grave challenge to faith and religion which came with the emergence in this century of "the Enlightenment."

From one point of view, the seventeenth century represents a monumental failure of Christian ministry. If a primary purpose of ministry is to establish and nurture community within the church so that the entire church can then be an instrument of unity among all men, then the fragmentation and hostilities of Europe in this century testify to ministry's failure. Yet, by and large, this growing division among Christians was not deliberately sought; indeed, there were serious attempts to preserve and intensify whatever unity did exist in the various groups, and there were even some attempts to work towards a reunification of Christianity. But the failure to fashion religious community seems to have been grounded in false (or at least unrealistic) ideas about the kind of unity that was possible and desirable, and ultimately in an inadequate understanding of "unity" as a "mark of the church." Unification was re-

peatedly sought by means of a formulation of Christian faith to which everyone in a given situation would assent (under duress, if that was necessary); when such tactics proved a glaring failure, the "solution" that emerged was the development of tolerance for the deviants who refused the official formulation. This was the response of political pragmatism rather than of religious insight, though clearly it was a great improvement over fratricide "in the name of God."

One of the basic challenges to Christian unity in the seventeenth century was a constant emphasis on individualism in religion. This individualism had been strong for several centuries, and it had issued in many of the "private" reform measures of the fourteenth, fifteenth, and early sixteenth centuries. After repeated frustration by official reluctance to reform the institutional aspects of the church, this religious individualism gave the Reformation much of its impulse. To quite an extent, however, the classic Reformation churches became (in the latter half of the sixteenth century, and more so in the seventeenth century) as monolithic, abstract, and organizational in their approach to the unity of Christian faith and practice as was the Roman Catholic church. Thus, both Catholicism and Protestantism saw the rise of "Pietist" movements which were an attempt to provide a more personalized, affective form of belief and worship.[89]

One could read this thrust towards individualism as a continuing search for personally meaningful religious experience, which in considerable measure it was. And it could be seen as another reflection of failure on the part of the churches' official ministers. Yet, it is important to recall that the impetus for much of this movement came from ordained ministers. Recalling this makes us cautious about any judgments passed upon some generalization called "the clergy" or "ordained ministers" at this period. The split in attitudes and understandings which occurred in the fourteenth to seventeenth centuries and beyond was a split within the ranks of the ordained. But the movements towards betterment of ministry were spearheaded by ordained ministers, not a few of whom (such as Ximenes de Cisneros, Charles Borromeo, or Francis de Sales) were firmly committed to perpetuating ecclesiastical institutions. Perhaps the most valid judgment we can make on the official ministers of the church, both Catholic and Protestant, is that they lacked the historical perspective (inevitably so) or the prophetic insight which would have allowed them to understand and then intelligently minister to the forces of change that were reshaping Europe and Christianity. Even this judgment we cannot make without qualification; for prophets there were (as we will see) who heralded and helped bring into being a new age.

While nonreligious factors surely played a large part, the ups and downs of Britain's history in the seventeenth century were formally connected with disputes among religious parties: the Anglican church and its monarchist allies dominating the scene until about 1640; then a rising influence of Puritanism that culminated in the Civil War (1640–49), the execution of Laud in 1645 and Charles I in 1649, and the dictatorship of Oliver Cromwell; then the restoration of Stuart monarchy and Anglicanism as the established church in 1660; and finally, towards the end of the century, the final overthrow of the Stuarts by a coalition of Protestant dissenters. However, the dissenters did not at that point replace the Anglican church in its official position of establishment but merely obtained freedom for their own religious practice.[90] Moreover, the central issue of religious dispute had to do with ministry—the conflict between episcopal or presbyterian polity. Beneath this explicit issue lay the unresolved question of the relative Catholicism or Protestantism of the Church of England, a strong current of anticlericalism that reacted against the power and affluence of the Anglican episcopacy, and a neo-Pelagianism that found expression in Puritan asceticism.[91]

There is no doubting the Protestant character of the Presbyterianism that by the end of the century was firmly entrenched in Scotland and an important minority in England, nor of the sects (which actually represent more radical Protestantism than Scotland's modified Calvinism). The Protestantism of the established Church of England was harder to define. William Laud could declare before his execution that he had always "lived in the Protestant religion as established by law in England";[92] but he was considered much too "Catholic" by his Puritan executioners. Not only among Puritans but within the Anglican church there was strong feeling that Laud was not Protestant enough; his attempts to impose a more "Catholic" liturgy met with unbending opposition. There was strong support for retaining sacramental ceremonial, but also sizable opposition to such liturgical emphasis, with emphasis on preaching as the alternative.[93] Throughout the seventeenth century this polarization of the Anglican church around sacramentarian or evangelical views of ministry continued; by the end of the century there seems to be a more or less peaceful coexistence of the two positions.

Despite the setback to Laud's policies which came in the years of Cromwell's ascendancy, the general theological positions he and other Caroline divines developed became the "classic theology" of the Anglican church. Already in the latter part of the sixteenth century, John Whitgift in his debate with the radical Puritanism of Thomas Cartwright had written in defense of a ministry of sacrament and of episcopal authority.[94] But it was Whitgift's contemporary, Richard Hooker who (in his *Ecclesiastical Polity*) laid the foundations of Anglican ecclesiastical self-identity, and sketched out a *via media* between Rome and Presbyterianism.[95] On this foundation, the Caroline divines, among whom Lancelot Andrews, Jeremy Taylor, and Laud himself were probably the most influential, worked out the Church of England's theological understanding of and justification for the English Reformation. Theirs was an ecclesiology of clear episcopal, but nonpapal, authority; an explanation of ministry that stressed preaching but maintained the basic importance of sacraments; a desire to move towards reform in the church, but a concomitant determination to preserve historical tradition.[96]

Unlike Great Britain where the seventeenth century was dominated by controversy about the nature of Christian ministry, the territories where Lutheranism was established (principally Germany and Scandinavia) saw little formal change in understanding of ministry. For one thing, the very breadth of the basic Lutheran understanding of "pastor" made it capable of adaptation to varying ministerial needs and interests. Perhaps more importantly, by the time the seventeenth century dawned, the foundation of confessional unity was established. The Formula of Concord in 1577 brought unity after the theological disputes of the preceding half-century.[97] As a result, seventeenth-century Lutheranism in its internal life develops quite placidly; this is the century of "orthodoxy," the period in which Lutheran scholasticism flourished and in which the organic unity of Lutheran doctrine is clarified.[98] It is also a time when the structure of Lutheran community and worship attained increased uniformity.[99] Despite the suffering and disruption connected with the Thirty Years' War, Lutheranism attained new unity and stability.

Yet, because of the emphasis on preaching, catechizing, and doctrinal orthodoxy (i.e., on "word" directed to faith) in "establishment Lutheranism," the exercise of ministry was exposed to the same danger of rational abstractness which beset Lutheran theology. As a result, much of official Lutheran ministration failed to provide precisely that stimulation and guidance of personal faith which had been such an important element of the early Reformation.[100] Liturgical celebration, too, became more fixed and formalized; the result was a tension between emphasis on the religious response of the individual and the unified (i.e., official) response of the church.[101]

About the middle of the seventeenth century, in response to the increased rationalization and establishment of Lutheranism, Pietism became an influential current in Protestantism and an important influence on the theory and practice of ministry.[102] Its beginnings are associated with Philipp Spener and his disciple Hermann Francke, whose little groups, gathered for discussion on Scripture (*collegia pietatis*), gave the movement its name. Pietism, because it is antiformulary, is ambiguous as a movement; it extends from those who remained within official Lutheranism and Calvinism to those more radical groups like the Moravian Brethren. In its more radical forms, Pietism's stress on the "inner word" and "inner light" led to a rejection of church structures and established ministry. In its more moderate forms, it was a reform within the Reform, a catalyst for improvement of Lutheran and Calvinist ministry but also an abiding attempt to compensate for the drift of Lutheran theology towards rationalism.[103]

In comparison with Lutheranism, Anglicanism, and Roman Catholicism, which in the latter part of the sixteenth and into the seventeenth century enjoyed considerable "geographical stability," Calvinism (in its various forms) had a more disturbed and migratory existence and its theory and practice of ministry had a more diverse history. One place, of course, where the Reformed tradition found abiding support and continuous institutional existence was Switzerland. By 1566 the Zwinglian and Calvinistic wings of Swiss Protestantism came together in acceptance of the Second Helvetic Confession.[104] Given the normative role of this confession during the ensuing decades, its fairly lengthy treatment of ministry is an important source for our study.[105] Taken in itself, the description of the ministerial role is quite general. It denies any real division of power within the ministry (bishop, presbyter, pastor are all names for the minister), stresses the ministry of preaching and teaching, but adds other functions such as administration of sacraments, comfort of the sick, and the preventing of schisms. However, the Zwinglian tonality of the confession becomes clearer as one proceeds to the explanation of the Lord's Supper, of sacraments, and of the ministers' role in these.[106]

In France, the Calvinist communities flourished openly from mid-sixteenth century, held their first nationwide synod in 1559, managed to survive the Saint Bartholomew massacres of 1572, and finally attained a measure of toleration in the Edict of Nantes (1598). For about a half-century, the Huguenot church could function "above ground" with structure and pastors in evidence, but suppression began to mount under Richelieu and Louis XIV until the Edict of Nantes was revoked in 1685 and French Calvinism had to go underground.[107]

Granted the modifications necessitated by their frequently endangered existence, the structure of the Huguenot community follows closely the Geneva pattern: the pastor and the elders from the local consistory, which is in charge of discipline within the community; "doctors" where they do exist have a special role in guiding the religious instruction, and the principal function of the pastor is "simple scriptural preaching." Celebration of the Lord's Supper is limited to a few times each year, and the regular worship service focuses on the sermon. Above all, the pastors of Calvinist communities in those troubled circumstances were leaders of their flock, encouraging and strengthening them in the face of persecution. The measures taken against them by the government is an indication of their effectiveness. However, not all the leadership was clerical; many of the most influential Huguenots, men like Coligny and Mornay, were laymen. Elders (i.e., laymen) formed half the membership in the regional and national synods that guided the French Reformed church in those decades.[108]

For a time Calvinism seemed to be making some notable headway in eastern Europe, but the rising power of the Hapsburgs and the success of the Counter-Reformation fully checked Calvinist expansion in that region, although a sizable Reformed influence remained in Hungary.[109] In Germany, Calvinism had considerable and varied influence on the beliefs and practice of Lutheranism, but its own proper sphere of influence was concentrated in the Rhineland. It was here, at the University of Heidelberg, that the influential Heidelberg Catechism was produced

in 1563 and quickly became the basis for preaching and catechetical instruction in the Dutch and German Reformed churches. For this reason, it is a priceless witness not only to the centrality of teaching in the Calvinist exercise of ministry at this time but also to the manner and spirit of that ministry.[110]

In the Low Countries, the situation of Calvinism in the seventeenth century was one of freedom and of theological development. At the same time, an important deviation from classic Reformed views occurred: the movement of Arminianism gained increased influence and counted such prominent men as Grotius in its ranks, and a Calvinist brand of Pietism developed in advance of the German Pietism of Spener.[111] Both these movements meant a split from the theory and practice of ministry as found in the orthodox Calvinists, a greater emphasis on the priesthood of all believers, and a tendency (particularly in Arminianism) towards a "secularization" of Christian life.[112]

Along with Switzerland and Holland, Scotland had a Calvinist church that was already well-entrenched in the seventeenth century, a church that was thoroughly committed to Presbyterianism.[113] As elsewhere in the Calvinist world, the ministerial role concentrated on preaching and teaching. The worship service centered around the sermon, the Lord's Supper was infrequently celebrated (and then with a homiletic rather than cultic emphasis), and care of discipline was shared by pastor and elders.[114] Towards the end of the century, the persecution connected with the Restoration in England severely tested the Presbyterianism of the Scotch church; but the attempts to impose an episcopacy failed and the primate, John Leighton, to whom the task of effecting a compromise between Episcopalianism and Presbyterianism had been entrusted, retired in failure.[115]

From one point of view, the Roman Catholic understanding and practice of ministry in the century and a half after Trent stands in unchanged continuity with the late medieval period. Trent introduced no new theological insights, but continued to insist on the cultic identity of the ordained and on the jurisdictional nature of his mediatorial role. Yet, the reform measures legislated by Trent and then undertaken in the post-Tridentine church altered noticeably the practical conduct of ministerial activity in Roman Catholicism. This did not happen suddenly, for implementation of Trent's reforms was a difficult and slow process; but the year 1700 saw an attitude towards ministerial reform quite different from that of the year 1500, and there were already clear signs that a significant revitalization of clerical life and activity was in progress.[116]

In part, this revitalization of ministry was due to the vigorous measures taken by post-Tridentine popes to carry out the prescriptions of the council.[117] In part, it was the result of the surge in religious community life (reform of already existent orders and the foundation of many new and highly effective groups of men and women);[118] in part it flowed from the charismatic leadership of such men as Charles Borromeo, Francis de Sales, Vincent de Paul, Philip Neri, Ignatius Loyola, or Pierre de Bérulle;[119] in part it was a response to the challenge of the Protestant Reformation. But perhaps most importantly it was the effect of the seminary training of candidates for ordination. Bishops and religious orders alike saw the focal importance of such careful training, and seminary programs for both regular and diocesan clergy became gradually more widespread.[120] Despite certain obvious drawbacks (which history would reveal), this system of seminary training gradually produced a corps of dedicated men capable of implementing the ministerial ideal sketched by Trent in its disciplinary decrees.

What came with Trent and the post-Tridentine reforms was a general "tightening up" and homogenizing of the Roman Catholic church, and particularly of its clerical life and activity. Slowly the evils of episcopal and presbyteral "absenteeism" and of multiple possession of benefices diminished, though they were far from overcome by the beginning of the eighteenth century. Liturgical uniformity was achieved by imposing the Roman missal and sacramentary on Catholics throughout the world, and by establishing the Congregation of Rites to watch over liturgical activity in the church.[121] Preaching was improved, religious education was imparted in a more systematic fashion, theology flourished in numerous university centers[122]—and all this was monitored for orthodoxy by the Holy Office.[123]

Because so much of the anti-Catholic polemic (and, in some instances, persecution) was directed against the notion of the Eucharist as "an act of offering sacrifice" and the use of "priest" to denominate the ordained minister, Catholic insistence on the cultic identity of the ordained became even more pronounced. Along with this, there was a decided and successful effort to develop the prayer life of the clergy. This objective was, of course, unassailable and in continuity with the most solid traditions of the ministerial ideal. To some extent, the orientation given to the spiritual life of men engaged in the active pastoral ministry was more suited to monastic contemplatives. It reflected the way in which the church, particularly on its official levels, was growing out of touch with the modern world. At the same time, the purpose of theological seminaries was not infrequently seen in devotional rather than intellectual terms,[124] and this at the time when the Enlightenment was beginning to exert a major impact on Europe.

Understandably, the post-Tridentine church tends to give the impression of introversion. Shaken to its roots by the Reformation, the Roman Catholic church quite naturally turned its attention inward, to clarification of its own self-understanding, to purification and defense of its faith and worship, and to structuring more effectively its institutional existence. In theology, one notices the advent of extensive treatises *de ecclesia*, which stress the claims of the Roman communion to be "the one true church of Christ"[125] and which give disproportionate attention to the papacy. The establishment of the Holy Office and the Index of forbidden books reflects the "siege mentality" of church officials in the face of the divergent beliefs of Protestantism. Yet, in appraising such institutions great caution is required. Even if one disagrees with such a negative and restrictive approach to new ideas and plurality of opinions, the motivation behind such defensive measures was often a genuine pastoral fear that the faith of the mass of the people would be endangered by "heresy" and therefore needed to be protected from it.[126] What does seem quite clear is that the episcopacy and presbyterate of the post-Tridentine church directed their attention to diverting evil from their people, to regaining those "lost to the church" by the Reformation, and to fostering the inner strength of the church by increasing uniformity.

Religious isolationism was not, however, the entire picture. These were the years when Roman Catholic missionaries carried the gospel, quite literally, "to the ends of the earth." Certainly, there was an exploitation of such missionary efforts by the secular rulers whose financial aid made such evangelization possible. With the exception of some exceptional pioneers in "missiology," there was too much identification of Christianity with European cultural translation of Christianity in the gospel that was preached; but this remarkable story of men such as Xavier and Ricci is one of immense and self-sacrificing dedication to the task of bringing men to "the new life in Christ." Willaert is probably a bit too lyrical when he says: "If history one day describes the unification of mankind, it will have to point to this period as the most decisive step since the Son of Man proclaimed that all his brothers are sons of the same Father."[127] But the importance of this mission expansion is hard to overestimate. Even in the domestic development of the church, the existence of this missionary expression of ministry was influential, for such missionary activities were viewed as extensions of the same ministry that was being exercised "at home" and thus the clearly outgoing and apostolic character of missionary ministry colored the church's understanding of ministry in general.

NOTES

1. See J. Gill, *The Council of Florence* (Cambridge, 1959), p. vii, who points out that Florence's definition of papal primacy dealt a death blow to conciliarism and that the council (despite prevalent outcries for reform) did not pass a single reform decree. See also J. Dolan, *History of the Reformation* (New York, 1965), pp. 105–45.

2. See R. Aubenas, *New Cambridge Modern History* (Cambridge, 1961), vol. 1, pp. 76–94; H. Jedin, *A History of the Council of Trent* (New York, 1957), vol. 1, pp. 117–38.

3. See J. Lortz, *How the Reformation Came* (New York, 1964), pp. 88–100; Lortz makes the tragic judgment about this pre-Reformation period: "Healthy religious elements are much more in evidence, incomparably much more, in the piety of the people than in the ranks of the clergy" (p. 100).

4. See C. Dawson, *Medieval Essays* (Image Book ed.; New York, 1959), pp. 212–40, who indicates the manner in which Chaucer and Langland reflect the two strata of fourteenth-century English society (the educated and cosmopolitan upper class, and the common man) and how each with deep Christian faith criticizes the abuses in the church.

5. At the same time, the fourteenth and fifteenth centuries were a period of great religious activity, at times reaching almost feverish intensity, as in the apocalyptic responses to plague. See L. Spitz, *The Renaissance and Reformation Movements* (Chicago, 1971), pp. 47–49.

6. See P. Hughes, *The Reformation in England* (New York, 1951), vol. 1, p. 86; also, Aubenas, pp. 90–92.

7. See A. Fliche and V. Martin, *Histoire de l'Eglise depuis les origines jusqu'à nos jours* (Paris, 1935—), vol. 1, pp. 875–76.

8. See *ibid.*, pp. 870–75, which stresses the legalistic conformism to external regulations which characterized people's religious attitudes at this period. However, to take just the one symptom of infrequency of Eucharistic Communion as an example, J. Jung-mann's discussion of this phenomenon (*Mass of the Roman Rite* [New York, 1951], vol. 2, pp. 359–67) as something which can be traced as far back as the patristic period should warn us against too facile a condemnation of the pre-Reformation period.

9. This evil is mentioned by Trent in its reform decree on preaching, and in its "mirror for preachers" (which was contained in the preliminary draft of the decree but dropped from the final form) it exhorts preachers to avoid contention, curious tales, reports of visions, etc. See *Concilium Tridentinum*, vol. 5, pp. 73, 75. See also, Fliche-Martin, vol. 14, pp. 821–35. An interesting facet of this nurture of credulity by fanciful preaching is indicated by H. Trevor-Roper in the chapter on the European witch craze in his *Crisis of the Seventeenth Century* (London, 1956). Trevor-Roper contends that late medieval homiletic emphasis on the kingdom of Satan and on the activity of devils was an important root of this witch craze.

10. Specifically in question was the leadership of the faculty of Paris, especially of d'Ailly and Gerson. It is indicative of the rapid shift in ecclesiastical affairs after Constance that the leading theologian of the abortive Council of Basel (just fifteen years later) was Torquemada, whose *Summa de ecclesia* had such far-reaching effect upon all later theological defense of the supremacy of the pope.

11. See L. Willaert in Fliche-Martin, vol. 18, pp. 183–220.

12. It was not accidental that so much of the reforming thrust of Protestantism came out of the universities. This was intertwined with the influence of Renaissance human-ism which we will discuss later.

13. See Fliche-Martin, vol. 14, pp. 945–1030.

14. Biel, for example, discusses the matter but does not really confront it. See H. Ober-man, *Harvest of Medieval Theology* (Cambridge, Mass., 1963), pp. 220–22.

15. A helpful guide in obtaining a unified picture of late medieval nominalism (which tends to be an amorphous movement) is the article by H. Oberman, "Some Notes on the Theology of Nominalism with Attention to Its Relations to the Renaissance," *Harvard Theological Review* 53 (1961), pp. 47–76.

16. See P. Vignaux, *Justification et prédestination au XIVe siècle* (Paris, 1934); Oberman in his *Harvest of Medieval Theology* differs somewhat from Vignaux's analysis, esp. on p. 177 where he claims that "Biel's doctrine of justification is essentially Pel-agian"—which, of course, has radical implications for any theory of Christian min-istry.

17. These differences will be studied in chapter 30.

18. For a summation of these medieval views of priesthood, see A. Michel, "Ordre," *Dictionnaire théologie catholique*, vol. 11, cols. 1293–1315.

19. Even though, as we mentioned earlier, the late Middle Ages saw a good deal of credulity, one must be careful to put this into context. The touchstone of genuine Christian insight in any historical period is the view taken of the Eucharist; and it is important to examine the correctives of careful historical scholarship to the view that the pre-Reformation situation was a hotbed of Eucharistic heresy. In this regard, see F. Clark, *Eucharistic Sacrifice and the Reformation*, 2d ed. (London, 1960), esp. pp. 63–72.

20. This, of course, was disputed by Wyclif, as mentioned earlier.

21. Some of these, such as the blessing of the oils on Maundy Thursday or the consecra-tion of altars, were considered of such importance that they were reserved to the episcopacy.

22. See Fliche-Martin, vol. 14, pp. 822–25.

23. See E. Mangenot, "Benediction," *Dictionnaire de théologie catholique*, vol. 2, cols. 632–39.

24. See *The Canterbury Tales*, trans. into modern English by D. Wright (London, 1964), pp. 3–9. Chaucer's description of the poor parson is at once a tribute to the sincere pastors of his day, an exhortation to clergy to fulfill their office, and a reflection of

the view that Christians of his day had as to the intrinsic ministry of the ordained, a view, incidentally, that is very evangelical: "He taught the Gospel of Christ and His twelve apostles: but first he followed it himself" (p. 9).

25. See Hughes, pp. 86–88.

26. On the late medieval development of this position, particularly among the papalist thinkers, see M. Wilks, *The Problem of Sovereignty in the Later Middle Ages* (Cambridge, 1963), pp. 50–63.

27. See *ibid.*, pp. 84–117.

28. *De imperatorum et pontificum potestate*, chap. 10 (ed. C. Brampton [Oxford, 1930], p. 23).

29. See Aubenas, pp. 76–94; also Wilks, *The Problem of Sovereignty*, who examines the theories about the relation of these two governments.

30. This is reflected positively in the numerous attempts to initiate meaningful reform, attempts which for one reason or another were not able to move the church's officialdom to serious action. See Jedin, pp. 139–65; Dolan, pp. 146–98.

31. This seems to have been the deeper issue under the dispute over "Communion under both species." After all, this could have been handled as simply a matter of liturgical discipline and not allowed to evolve into a doctrinal dispute and schismatic movement.

32. It is interesting to notice the way in which, at this period, the imperial and papal interests (which had so often been in opposition) tend to come together against the rising power of the various princes. See R. Laffan, *New Cambridge Modern History*, vol. 1, pp. 194–219.

33. In the slow struggle by which basic human rights and equality would assert themselves in the next five centuries in the face of absolutist rulers, there is an intriguing dialectic of political and religious thought which moves from an emphasis on obedience (to both civil and ecclesiastical authority) to an emphasis on freedom. Central to this dialectic is the discussion of toleration; see M. Tooley, *New Cambridge Modern History*, vol. 3, pp. 480–506.

34. See E. Gilson, *Reason and Revelation in the Middle Ages* (New York, 1938).

35. *Proslogion*, Proem. (ed. F. Schmitt [Edinburgh, 1916], vol. 1, p. 94).

36. See, e.g., the decree of Lateran IV (*Mansi* 22. 998–99).

37. Even Gerson, who was a reforming pioneer in religious education, seems to have shared this view: see Fliche-Martin, vol. 14, pp. 856–57.

38. See *ibid.*, pp. 741–52; also, F. Vandenbroucke in *History of Christian Spirituality* (London, 1968), vol. 2, pp. 489–99; and Clark, pp. 56–72.

39. This was the basic orientation of the *devotio moderna* which had such a widespread influence in the pre-Reformation centuries; see Fliche-Martin, vol. 14, pp. 911–42. It found expression in Erasmus' dream of reform for the church.

40. See Jedin, p. 152, where he points out how the improvement of the situation in Germany helped trigger the outbreak of the Reformation in that country.

41. See H. Hillerbrand, *Christendom Divided* (New York, 1971), pp. 283–306.

42. In this light, careful attention should be given the judgment of E. Léonard in the introduction to his *History of Protestantism* (London, 1965), p. 4: ". . . The Reformation, far more than a revolt against Catholic faith, was its culmination and its full flowering."

43. See Trevor-Roper, pp. 46–89.

44. Since our concern in this historical review is to discover the actual implementation of Christian ministry, it is fascinating (and perhaps theologically important) to think of the manner in which the religious reformers of these centuries, both Protestant and Catholic, ministered to the changes taking place in human society and served as initiators into the experience and "mythology" of the modern world.

45. The theological correlative, the so-called conciliar theory, will be studied in chapter 23.

46. See the remarks of C. Davis, "Küng on Infallibility," *Commonweal* 93 (1971), pp.

445–47, regarding the unifying symbolic function of the papacy for Roman Catholics today.

47. See Dolan, *History of the Reformation*.

48. Between 1517 and the Diet of Worms in 1521, the "Luther affair" was for the most part a matter of church (and civil) authorities dealing with an individual whose questionable views were becoming more and more widespread; after Worms one can begin to speak of "the Reformation" as a movement. See H. Hillerbrand, *Christendom Divided* (New York, 1971), pp. 27–28.

49. *Ibid.*, pp. 8–16, 28–45.

50. Perhaps nothing reflects better the foot-dragging in official circles (both ecclesiastical and civil) than the historical account of the difficulties surrounding the opening of the Council of Trent. See Jedin, pp. 197–581.

51. To indicate the presence of this problem for sixteenth-century Catholicism is not to suggest that it alone among Christian churches has had this difficulty; in the sixteenth century, however, it is the official response of the Catholic church to the Reformation that best illustrates the problem.

52. In a limited fashion we will attempt in chapter 31 to trace the influence of the theological understandings of ministry and priesthood; but the synthetic history of theology, into which any such fragment should be fitted so that it can be corrected by perspective, does not yet exist. For the history of Roman Catholic theologians and theological schools, the relevant volumes of the Fliche-Martin *Histoire de l'Eglise* (particularly L. Willaert's treatment, in vol. 18, of the period 1563–1648) are quite helpful. One can also profit much from such analytic studies as Vignaux's *Justification et prédestination au XIVe siècle* and H. Oberman's *Harvest of Medieval Theology*, but there are too few of such books.

53. On this conflict and its relationship to the Reformation an immense literature exists, since every history of modern Europe and every study of the Reformation must to some extent advert to it. Some helpful sources are: H. Enno van Gelder, *The Two Reformations in the Sixteenth Century* (The Hague, 1964); L. Spitz, *The Renaissance and Reformation Movements* (Chicago, 1971); H. Lucas, *The Renaissance and the Reformation*, 2d ed. (New York, 1960); *New Cambridge Modern History*, vol. 1, pp. 50–126; J. Lortz, *How the Reformation Came* (New York, 1964), pp. 65–90; and Fliche-Martin, vol. 14, pp. 911–1030.

54. See B. Hall, "Erasmus: Biblical Scholar and Reformer," *Erasmus*, ed. T. Dorey (London, 1970), pp. 81–113; J. Huizinga, *Erasmus of Rotterdam* (London, 1924).

55. See Hall, p. 110; Dolan, pp. 275–78; Spitz, pp. 295–98.

56. One of the most influential of these secular interpretations of the Reformation was that of Preserved Smith, especially in his *The Age of the Reformation* (New York, 1920). An interesting reversal of this trend is found in G. Swanson, *Religion and Regime* (Ann Arbor, Mich., 1967), where from a sociological viewpoint he studies the manner in which basic religious attitudes underlay the political and social movements that accompanied the Reformation.

57. Lortz, p. 107.

58. See Jedin, pp. 117–38; it is symptomatic of the tragic frustration of reformers within the church that Jedin entitles an earlier chapter in this same volume "Victory of the Papacy over the Reform Councils."

59. On the reform attempts and heresy of Wyclif and Hus, see Fliche-Martin, vol. 14, pp. 911–1030.

60. On the reforming efforts and failures of Gerson and Cusa, see Dolan, pp. 146–98.

61. On Luther's position, see *ibid.*, pp. 293–95. Linked with the failure of governmental attempts to effect the reunion of European Christendom was the waning influence of Roman and canon law in the sixteenth-century international scene; see G. Mattingly, *New Cambridge Modern History*, vol. 3, pp. 165–70.

62. Even today we continue to find it difficult to discern the genuine nature and causes of the Reformation. See Hillerbrand, pp. 283–306.

63. See W. Pauck, *The Heritage of the Reformation*, rev. ed. (Glencoe, Ill., 1961), pp. 101–43.

64. See Spitz, pp. 352–53.

65. See Pauck, pp. 139–41.

66. *Ibid.*, pp. 103–10; also T. Parker, *New Cambridge Modern History*, vol. 3, pp. 83–85.

67. See E. Schlink, *Theology of the Lutheran Confessions* (Philadelphia, 1960), pp. 238–51. To quite a degree the traditional office of bishop was retained functionally in the superintendents, even though these were not considered to be a high order.

68. See J. Courvoisier, *La notion d'Eglise chez Bucer* (Paris, 1933), pp. 98–99.

69. Courvoisier, pp. 101–2, argues that Bucer never speaks of "lay elders" and rather uses "elder" as equivalent to "minister"; J. van de Poll, *Martin Bucer's Liturgical Ideas* (Groningen, 1954), pp. 69–70, cites texts which seem to indicate that some elders were laymen. What does seem clear is that the elders as a group were charged with the general discipline of the community, and that some of the elders were not commissioned as ministers of the word.

70. See van de Poll, p. 69.

71. See Spitz, p. 395.

72. See E. Iserloh, *Handbook of Church History* (New York, 1965—), vol. 4, pp. 566–70.

73. On the Zwinglian reform, see Léonard, vol. 1, pp. 139–45; E. Rupp, *New Cambridge Modern History*, vol. 3, pp. 96–103; Hillerbrand, pp. 60–64.

74. See J. MacKinnon, *Calvin and the Reformation* (New York, 1962), pp. 257–61; R. Caswell, "Calvin's View of Ecclesiastical Discipline," pp. 210–26 in *John Calvin*, Courtenay Studies in Reformation Theology (London, 1966); W. Niesel, *The Theology of Calvin* (Philadelphia, 1956), pp. 199–202.

75. See Spitz, pp. 425–27.

76. On the introduction of Reformation into England, see G. Elton, *New Cambridge Modern History*, vol. 2, pp. 226–50; also, Hughes, pp. 349–69.

77. On English Protestant views of ministry and worship ceremonies, see C. and K. George, *The Protestant Mind of the English Reformation* (Princeton, 1961), pp. 320–62.

78. "The English Reformation was an affair of state, and apparently while Thomas More, John Fisher, Anne Askew, Thomas Cranmer, Nicholas Ridley, and others died for their particular understanding of the faith, most parish priests went on doing whatever was expected of them by whoever was in power" (U. Holmes, *The Future Shape of Ministry* [New York, 1971], p. 66).

79. See J. Cooper, *New Cambridge Modern History*, vol. 4, pp. 535–37.

80. For a brief appraisal of the results of Trent, see Dolan, pp. 400–406. A detailed account of the ecclesiastical institutions of the Catholic church as affected by Trent is given by L. Willaert in Fliche-Martin, vol. 18, pp. 15–95.

81. See Willaert, pp. 173–77.

82. See van de Poll, pp. 69–70.

83. See Niesel, pp. 200–201.

84. See Willaert, pp. 331–60.

85. In essence the compromise was this: bishops and priests received with ordination the power to dispense grace (*potestas ordinis*). This power came directly from God, but they need a community upon which to exercise their power of orders, and they are given authority over such a community (*potestas jurisdictionis*) through the pope who possesses from God the *plenitudo potestatis*. See *ibid.*, pp. 338–39.

86. *Ibid.*, pp. 361–424. This will be studied in greater detail in chapter 25.

87. The genesis of this distinction will be studied more carefully in chapter 30.

88. *Concilium Tridentinum* 9, p. 620.

89. On the overall development of religious thought in this period, see G. Mosse, *New Cambridge Modern History*, vol. 4, pp. 169–201. On the rise of Pietism in the

Reformation churches, see R. Wilken, *The Myth of Christian Beginnings* (New York, 1971), pp. 123–27; and A. Whiteman, *New Cambridge Modern History*, vol. 5, pp. 145–48.

90. For a brief summation of this century in English church history, see Léonard, vol. 2, pp. 28–358; his treatment has the advantage of distinguishing between Puritanism and Presbyterianism (particularly in the case of Cromwell) and of paying attention to the role of the dissident sects in the movement towards toleration. See also, Trevor-Roper, pp. 345–467; J. Cooper, *New Cambridge Modern History*, vol. 4, pp. 531–84; and D. Ogg, *New Cambridge Modern History*, vol. 5, pp. 301–29.

91. At first sight, the alliance that developed between the Puritans and pentecostal groups such as the Quakers seems strange; yet, they were all expressions of the religious individualism of which we spoke earlier, and thus logically formed a common front against what they considered religious authoritarianism.

92. See Léonard, vol. 2, pp. 305–6.

93. See C. and K. George, pp. 320–41, 348–63.

94. On the dispute between Whitgift and Cartwright, see J. Marshall, *Hooker and the Anglican Tradition* (Sewanee, Tenn., 1963), pp. 18–34; also R. Dawley, *John Whitgift and the Reformation* (London, 1955), pp. 133–48.

95. However, Hooker's ideas (and specifically on the matter of ministry) stood much closer to Roman than to Calvinist theology, so much so that he clearly prepared for the "branch theory" and the Tractarian movement of the nineteenth century. See Marshall, pp. 41, 52–55.

96. On Andrewes, see M. Reidy, *Bishop Lancelot Andrewes* (Chicago, 1955); on Taylor, see F. Huntley, *Jeremy Taylor and the Great Rebellion* (Ann Arbor, Mich., 1970), pp. 1–30, and H. Trevor Hughes, *The Piety of Jeremy Taylor* (London, 1960), pp. 17–44. In chapter 32 we will have occasion to examine more carefully their theology of ministry.

97. See J. Pelikan, *From Luther to Kierkegaard* (St. Louis, 1950), pp. 24–49.

98. A detailed exposition of this age of orthodoxy and the leading theological positions of this period is given by R. Preus in *The Theology of Post-Reformation Lutheranism* (St. Louis, 1970); see also E. Léonard, "L'orthodoxie luthérienne en Allemagne au XVIIe siècle," *Etudes théologiques et religieuses* (1960), pp. 29–46.

99. See C. Bergendoff, *The Church of the Lutheran Reformation* (St. Louis, 1967), pp. 123–38.

100. However, one must be careful in attributing blame for the increasing aridity of Lutheran ministry of the word to the orthodox theology of the seventeenth century; see the remarks of Preus, pp. 15–24, but also J. Pelikan, pp. 76–83.

101. See F. Kalb, *Theology of Worship in Seventeenth-Century Lutheranism* (St. Louis, 1965), pp. 155–71.

102. See Bergendoff, pp. 153–69.

103. Pietism, as we mentioned, is not a clear-cut religious teaching, and this is not confined to Lutheranism in the seventeenth century (or thereafter). It finds various expressions both within and outside the established Protestant churches—and also within Catholicism. See Mosse, pp. 169–201.

104. On the movement of Swiss Reformed thought towards this common confession, the struggle between the positions of Beza, Farel, Bullinger, and the relation of this to Calvin's own teaching, see Léonard, *History*, vol. 2, pp. 1–11; for the text of the Second Helvetic Confession, see A. Cochrane, *Reformed Confessions of the Sixteenth Century* (London, 1966), pp. 220–301.

105. Actually, the confession's view on ministry is contained not only in its chapter 18 (which is devoted entirely to that topic) but in the following chapters on sacraments, the worship service, catechizing, burial of the dead, etc. (chaps. 19–28). In chapter 31, we will examine more carefully the theological position represented by these chapters.

106. This Zwinglian triumph over Calvin's own understanding of Eucharist (and there-

fore of ministry) was due to the fact that it was Bullinger who composed the confession. See Léonard, *History*, pp. 9–11.

107. For a brief summary of this history, see J. McNeill, *The History and Character of Calvinism* (New York, 1967), pp. 241–54; more detailed and analytic is the treatment of Léonard, *History*, pp. 95–171, 359–448.

108. See McNeill, p. 246. On the national level, there was considerable tension and dispute: at issue was the autonomy of the individual communities vis-à-vis the authority of regional and national synods; a lesser issue was the function of the deacons who in the early stage of French Calvinism were used as curate-assistants to the pastors. See Léonard, *History*, pp. 108–9, 132–42.

109. *Ibid.*, pp. 280–89.

110. For the text of the catechism, see Cochrane, pp. 305–31. An interesting testimonial to the enduring importance of this catechism is Karl Barth's popular commentary, *The Heidelberg Catechism for Today* (Richmond, 1964).

111. See McNeill, pp. 262–67.

112. See Whiteman, pp. 146–48.

113. For a brief period in the sixteenth century there was question of introducing some modified episcopacy, and apparently Knox himself was not absolutely opposed to it as long as episcopacy was not seen as a higher order, but sentiment against episcopacy was strong enough to turn the Scotch church irrevocably towards Presbyterianism. See McNeill, p. 305.

114. *Ibid.*, p. 300.

115. See Léonard, *History*, pp. 335, 340–41.

116. For an overall picture of post-Tridentine developments, see P. Janelle, *The Catholic Reformation* (Milwaukee, 1949), pp. 252–367; a more analytic treatment, with attention concentrated on the inner spirit of the Catholic reform, is given by Willaert in Fliche-Martin, vol. 18.

117. See Willaert, pp. 37–64.

118. *Ibid.*, pp. 95–167.

119. See Janelle, pp. 263–302.

120. For a short history of this development, see J. Ellis, "A Short History of Seminary Education," *Seminary Education in a Time of Change*, ed. J. Lee and L. Putz (Notre Dame, 1965), pp. 30–41.

121. See Jungmann, vol. 1, pp. 135–41.

122. See Willaert, pp. 181–220. These elements of the ministry of the word will be studied more fully in chapter 12.

123. *Ibid.*, p. 56.

124. See Ellis, p. 40.

125. See Willaert, pp. 315–448.

126. The theological question of the intrinsic appropriateness of these approaches to the nurture of faith will be discussed in chapter 32.

127. Willaert, p. 448.

CHAPTER 6

Ministry in the Modern Church

Despite the efforts in the late seventeenth century of Leibniz, Bossuet, and others to effect some kind of Christian reunification, the dawning of the eighteenth century saw the religious divisions of Europe hardened into doctrinal, devotional, and political patterns. Italy and the Iberian peninsula were solidly in the Roman Catholic camp; Poland and the German Hapsburg territories after some flirtation with various forms of Protestantism (chiefly the Reformed tradition) had become strong Roman Catholic areas; France still had an important Reformed community, but Catholicism was clearly the established church and pragmatic tolerance of the Calvinist community declined after revocation of the Edict of Nantes; much of Germany, especially in the north, was staunchly Lutheran (though touched in some areas with Reformed influence). Reformed Protestantism was dominant in Switzerland and Holland, ran into difficulties as a strong minority in England (where the Church of England was enjoying the fruits of the Restoration), and found wide acceptance in Scotland.

Temporal monarchs, ethnic prejudice, economic interest, and cultural tradition were major factors in nurturing the internal unity of each of these regions and in fostering their divisions from one another. However, much of the credit (or blame) for establishing the dominance of a given religious position in one or other situation rests with the ordained ministry. It was to a large extent the religious leadership of countries like France or England, working generally in close cooperation with secular rulers, that sought to solidify the faith and practice and particularly the legal prerogatives of its particular church. And in the climate of post-Reformation Europe that meant an unrelenting opposition to the "heresy and schism" represented by other religious groups. It was not that religious leaders sought the fracturing of the church as an end in itself; they would all have rejoiced in the reunification of Christian Europe, if that could be accomplished by others recognizing their error and being converted to truth. Unquestionably, there was in all this a mixture of motivations: churchmen who enjoyed the affluence and prestige of their positions were concerned about safeguarding their vested interests. But the controlling impulse was still religious, even though it sometimes drifted beyond religion into fanaticism.

Seventeenth-century theology had seen a golden age of orthodoxy in almost all the Christian churches, a period in which detailed clarification of confessional understanding was achieved. By the end of the sixteenth century the outburst of religious sentiment and insight that had characterized the Reformation (and the first reactions to it), an outburst that took variegated and rapidly evolving expression, had become "dogma." The key confessional documents (apart from the Westminster Confession) of the Reformation churches and the decrees of Trent were produced by 1600. By the end of the seventeenth century, these dogmatic statements had been thoroughly utilized as *loci theologici*, and the doctrinal positions of the various churches had been attacked and defended about as thoroughly as was possible. Post-

Reformation theology as such could do little more after 1700 than become repetitive and sterile, and consequently incapable of transcending the doctrinal divisions of European Christianity; creative impulse would have to come (as it did) from outside the context created by the Reformation.

At first glance, it would seem that the ordained ministry of the Christian churches had betrayed the basic purpose of their office, the formation and preservation of Christian community, for they were a key influence in keeping Christianity divided. Yet it probably would be more fair to say that their perspective grew more limited. They were interested in fostering the community of the faithful but they no longer identified this community with "the great church." Instead, in the congregationalist wing of Protestantism the emphasis was placed on the local community and its relatively autonomous cohesion and fidelity to the gospel. In churches (such as the Lutheran or Anglican) where there was a large-scale organized polity, it was the confessional and regional (national) unity of Christian belief and practice which provided the horizon for ministerial activity. Roman Catholicism was somewhat of an exception: its official view (particularly that of the papacy) was still that of a worldwide and all-embracing church. Its effort was to bring about the *return* of those in heresy and schism to the true church, to evangelize those who had not yet heard the gospel, and eventually to bring all men under its saving influence. However, even this official Roman thrust towards supranational and supraregional Christian community was effectively countered by strong "Gallican" movements which more than once threatened to break Roman Catholicism into a number of national churches.[1]

In several ways the history of the Christian churches from the seventeenth to the twentieth centuries is most instructive concerning the achievement of religious community. It demonstrates both the strengths and weaknesses of the "techniques" which practically all the churches assumed to be basic to fostering unity: homogeneity in confessional formulations of faith (whether doctrinal or liturgical) and centralized organization of community structure. These two approaches did bring about increasing unity within the various politico-religious camps during the sixteenth and seventeenth centuries; this was the age when absolute monarchical rule found its climactic expression in Louis XIV. However, already in mid-seventeenth century events in England forecast the coming challenge of absolutism on the Continent: in 1645 the archbishop of Canterbury (Laud) was executed and in 1649 King Charles I was deposed and put to death. With the eighteenth century, the hope that monolithic conformity to religious (and/or civil) legislation and doctrinal formulation could attain genuine Christian community, even when such conformity was implemented by carefully enforced central control, begins to appear as an illusion.[2] Though only more radical groups, like the Socinians, were beginning to speak about the positive advantages and desirability of credal and doctrinal pluralism within the religious sphere,[3] more and more regional or national governments were being driven by pragmatic considerations to deemphasize or even abolish the establishment of one religious group, and to allow a pluralism of religious faiths and practices within the one civil community. This has been a very slow process, and the task of disestablishing Christian churches is still unfinished in the latter half of the twentieth century.[4] However, there has been a gradual and considerable departure from the idea that religious community can be created by imposition (whether ecclesiastical or civil) of unified structure and practice.

As the Christian churches have been pushed by historical forces towards some acceptance of pluralism, those in official positions of leadership have experienced considerable anxiety precisely because they saw themselves charged with fostering the genuine belief of the community. It is obvious that a community based on faith must somehow preserve unity of faith; in striving for unity of faith, then, the various churches' leaders were doing what is proper to ordained ministry. What was not perceived until well into the twentieth century, except by a handful of farsighted people in the eighteenth and nineteenth centuries, was that such unity of faith might be compatible with a pluralism in doctrine and polity.[5]

Community of Historical Experience

While the divisions within Christianity have been unavoidably clear for the past four centuries, and for most of that time the differences between the churches have been stressed rather than their underlying unity, there were really many things they shared—if for no other reason than that they were involved in the same evolving and turbulent history of modern Europe.

In the centuries after the Reformation the churches had two major tasks: to work out intrinsically the implications in doctrine, liturgy, and polity of the positions taken in the sixteenth century, and to respond to the challenge presented by modern secularity. These tasks are intertwined, and though individual churches worked them out in their distinctive fashion and according to different timetables, there was a basic pattern of response to history that is found in each of the various groups. The strong reforming and religious impulse of the sixteenth and early seventeenth centuries is succeeded by a period of moralistic rationalism. This latter, however, is quickly countered by one or other form of evangelism or "pietism." But as this evangelical movement loses its thrust (by the early nineteenth century), and neither it nor a theology that has continued to be excessively rationalistic can revitalize faith, there is the attempt to "return to sources" to find direction and stimulus. This reappropriation of tradition in its more authentic form works hand in hand with the movement towards innovation that gains momentum in the nineteenth and twentieth centuries; in its misunderstood form, i.e., a frightened "crisis" mentality that clings to what is inadequately considered "traditional," it works against such innovation. A considerable portion of the history of Christianity in the nineteenth

and twentieth centuries was fashioned by this conflict between "modernism" and "traditionalism."[6]

Already at the beginning of the eighteenth century the Cambridge Platonists were arguing for a thoroughgoing reformulation of Christian faith, one that could cope more directly with the modern emphasis on "use of reason."[7] Nor were they alone: Bossuet in the late seventeenth century (especially with his *Exposition de la doctrine catholique*, 1671) and Mohler in the early nineteenth century are but two examples of men who were striving to break out of the pattern of post-Reformation polemic.[8] However, the need for reformulation touched much more than theology or official statements of doctrine. There was growing need to explain the gospel in ways that would touch the minds and hearts of the new groups of socially disadvantaged that emerged with the industrial revolution. Hence, the new and important movements of evangelism, above all, that of the Wesleys in the eighteenth century. Accompanying this was the need to devise more appropriate forms of community structure and more flexible approaches to ministry, although ecclesiastical officialdom was slow to grasp the presence of this need, and attempts to create such new forms often resulted in the formation of new churches or sects and the further splintering of an already divided Christianity. Liturgy was also in general need of refashioning. In the more fluid situations of Christian worship, as on the American frontier, there was a prayer-and-sermon meeting and very little of what ordinarily would be considered "liturgy"; in the more established contexts there was a loyal consistency in repeating established patterns of worship, patterns which (particularly in Roman Catholicism) carried with them several layers of inherited but meaningless "artistic" embellishment.

Not just the churches but the whole of modern European life witnessed an irresistible and growing movement against unquestioned and uncontrolled exercise of authority. The overthrow of the Stuarts in England, the violent rejection of French absolutism in the Revolution, the wave of revolts in 1848 are but the more dramatic evidences of an attitudinal force that had been gathering strength long before the Reformation or the Enlightenment, and which now proved strong enough to challenge successfully (though with more than one setback) the basic power structures of civil and ecclesiastical society.

So intimately linked had church and state become in most of the countries of Europe that opposition to absolutist authority of civil rulers was seen as a religiously deviant attitude and opposition to ecclesiastical authority was viewed as a threat to the good order of the body politic. At least, this was the case until well into the nineteenth century, and in some residual situations until well into the twentieth. When the power of absolutist rulers is thought to be "of divine right," when the king is accountable therefore to no one short of God, the rejection of such a sovereign authority cannot but have overtones of "rebellion against the will of God." This is intensified whenever a voluntaristic philosophy of law prevails (i.e., that the ultimate norm for interpreting the binding force of any law is the will of the lawgiver), for the will of the kingly legislator becomes the final criterion short of the divine will itself. Indeed, it is the "vicar" of the divine will. No European code of law incorporated this mentality as unequivocally as had Justinian's code in the sixth century; yet the mentality is clearly voiced in Louis XIV's "L'état, c'est moi."

Given the abuse of absolutist power in the seventeenth and early eighteenth centuries, the revolt against such monarchical authority in the eighteenth and nineteenth centuries was not surprising. And because the very source and nature of monarchical authority was being questioned, the authority of church officialdom was brought under scrutiny. In many instances, this was not so much a challenge to their "spiritual" authority, for there seems to have been little if any question about the pastoral authority of the ordinary "lower level" clergy; rather, it was a challenge to the power exercised by the higher clergy in the public arena. But once the question had been raised about the legitimacy of the power which the higher clergy wielded in political, social, and economic matters, it was inevitable that the questioning should extend to the authority they claimed in strictly ecclesiastical matters. Having linked the understanding and justification and support of their own "monarchical" authority to the secular monarchical structures of Europe, the higher clergy of those churches that enjoyed "establishment" and that functioned in a more or less Erastian situation were now caught in the attacks against absolutist monarchy. Religious monarchism, particularly in the Roman Catholic church, has managed to outlast civil monarchies; but its authority, too, has been increasingly attacked.

This attack has taken many forms, not all of which have been altruistic attempts of modern "liberals" to free men from the supposedly confining shackles of religious despotism. Anticlericalism, which had been a major force for many centuries, became even more bitter in some circles as, for example, in the eighteenth-century *philosophes*; there was unquestionably the desire in some quarters to destroy utterly Christianity, not to reform it. Eighteenth- and nineteenth-century ideologues who criticized and opposed the power exercised by churches over the thought and life of men were not above trying to substitute their own ideology as the "new religion." The eighteenth and nineteenth centuries witnessed open warfare between church officialdom and "modern rationalism," each seeking to control the minds of men.[9]

Not all the anticlericalism nor all the attacks on church authority were to be found outside the churches, nor for that matter outside the clergy. While all the churches experienced some of this, the most striking instance may be the presbyterianism that developed in the lower clergy of France in the eighteenth century and was associated with the Richerist movement, which found expression in the Civil Constitution of the Clergy (in 1790), and which was an important element in the ferment leading up to the Revolution.[10] Rooted in the Gallican theories of Edmond Richer, an early seventeenth-century canonist at the Sorbonne, but going beyond him in its emphasis on the prerogatives and autonomy of the lower clergy,[11] eighteenth-century Richerism became both a theological exaltation of the presbyterate and a practical effort to better the economic, social, and political situation of the lower clergy.[12] This "revolt of the curés" reached its zenith in 1789 when the parish clergy outnumbered the bishops in the Estates General 208 to 46. What might have been the result of this new possession of power in a calmer situation is impossible to say; as it was, France was already rushing towards the upheaval of the Revolution, and the Constituent Assembly's framing of the Civil Constitution of the Clergy and its imposition on all office-holding clergy in France led to a disastrous division within the clergy, the church, and the country as a whole.[13]

But that which revealed most tellingly the extent to which criticism of religious authority had advanced was the questioning of the Bible itself as authoritative source of religious truth. Attempts to devise some techniques for handling Sacred Scripture as literature go back at least as far as Abelard's *Sic et non.* The humanists of the fifteenth and sixteenth centuries, though not initiating lower criticism, had securely established its role in study of the Bible. However, all this had functioned within a calm assumption of the "inspiration" of the biblical text; throughout the period of Reformation dispute about the nature and sources of faith it was taken for granted that the Bible was unique "word of God." In the eighteenth and nineteenth centuries, scholarly examination of the Bible emphasizes the fact that it is "word of man" (though many of the scholars who dealt with it critically accepted it religiously as "word of God"), and as such must itself be subject to the analysis and criticism proper to literature.[14] Clearly, the last word on the religious authority of the biblical text is not yet spoken in the latter half of the twentieth century; but the autonomous ultimacy of the

Scriptures as authoritative Christian teaching has now been rejected by all but the most fundamentalist of Christian groups, and such notions as "inspiration" and "revelation" as applied to the Bible have been increasingly questioned by biblical scholars who themselves are believing Christians.[15]

Ambiguous though it is, the term "dechristianization" does point to a process that has been a severe challenge and perhaps even a dire threat to the Christian churches. Opinions may differ as to whether it represents decline or revitalization, but the abandonment of formal Christian religious belief and practice by a sizable portion of the population in those countries that had traditionally been considered "Christian" is one of the major religious phenomena of the past three centuries.[16] Nor is it a simple phenomenon: it includes the large-scale "loss of religion" among the masses who became the industrial proletariat; it includes also the antireligious (i.e., anti-Christian religion) spirit of much of the Enlightenment; it includes the increasing divorce of the state from religious influence; and it includes the dwindling impact of Christian moral teaching upon the operational ethics of European society. This dechristianization has tended to occur in waves, a period of widespread reaction against religion followed by a fairly general movement of "conversion" which in turn gave way to another period of hostility to religion.[17] And, if one can risk such a generalization, it seems that the waves have become slowly flattened out over the past two-and-a-half centuries. The hostilities between the two opposing camps (i.e., the Christian churches, most prominently the Roman Catholic church, and the forces of anti-Christian secularism) have slowly become less bitter, and greater appreciation for the merits of the "enemy position" has developed. Each group, as it has become more conscious of the complicated dynamics of modern civilization, has grown less inclined to blame the other for "the evils of the age." This is not to say that dechristianization has become less of a challenge to the churches, for it is not clear whether this less hostile climate reflects a gradual capitulation of Christianity to "the modern world" (or vice versa) or a more profound rapprochement.[18]

While much of Europe's dechristianization was directed against the ecclesiastical establishment, the clergy—particularly the higher clergy—were themselves touched by, and sometimes active in, this move towards secularity. Clergy were prominent in the early stages of the Masonic movement, in the antimonarchical (and antiecclesiastical) ferment of the French Revolution, and in the various modernist movements which attempted to harmonize the churches and modern civilization. But in the eighteenth century the more radical and dangerous dechristianization was the irreligious and worldly attitudes and behavior of many clergy. Not that their lives were openly scandalous (though some were); they were just not particularly Christian.[19] In the nineteenth century there was an increasing "conversion" of clergy to a more dedicated life-style, increasing involvement in properly religious activities, but increasing lack of contact with Europe's emerging social structures.[20] There are many things to suggest that since the mid-nineteenth century the nature of secularization as it threatens the clergy has shifted from "worldliness" to the intellectual sphere, and its influence is roughly correlative with the level of education available to a given group of clergy. To express it in cliché terms, there has been for well over a century and in all the churches a contest between "modernism" and "traditionalism" for control of the ideas and attitudes of the ordained ministry.[21]

The series of revolutions that has stretched from the mid-seventeenth century up to the mid-twentieth century reflects the radical change in social structure that has taken place in modern Europe and more recently in the entire world. This has created for Christianity and for its ordained ministry, both of which are meant to be committed to the goal of serving men in society, a somewhat new and fluid context of activity. Within the Christian churches, because they are part of this modern world and because their outreach is directed to men and women in this modern world, a new set of needs for ministry (or at least more acute expression of old needs) has arisen.

Population changes have been a major factor. In the nineteenth century, the population of Europe increased threefold; the increase in other regions of the world, particularly in North America, was even greater. This meant a much larger number of Christians, at least nominally such, for whom ministry was to be provided. Moreover, much of this population expansion converged increasingly on developing urban centers in Europe and North America. Not only did population increase in unprecedented fashion but large masses of people became mobile as never before in history, moving from agrarian to urban settings, but also moving from continent to continent in large-scale immigration.

Patterns of European Christianity, and more specifically of Christian ministry, had not been fashioned to provide for such circumstances. Recruitment of the clergy became not only a matter of finding enough young men willing to make sincere Christian ministry their career but also a question of finding those who would be willing to work where many of the people were going: into deprived urban situations or as immigrants to far-off lands. Besides, the training for candidates to the ministry, even though as a broadly organized endeavor it was a post-Reformation phenomenon, was generally out of date and not well suited to preparing pastors for the evolving world of the eighteenth to twentieth centuries.

Part of the problem lay in the fact that new kinds of poverty and oppression came with the modern age; industrialization brought with it the concentrations of men and women into slum areas, where the abysmal living conditions were but one element of the exploitation to which they were subjected. Economic overlords, supported by the civil structures (even the laws), ran roughshod over masses of people, and the reaction against such criminal oppression came into being very slowly. Whereas in an earlier age the laws regarding the poor were a safeguard of their intrinsic human rights and provided for their basic livelihood,[22] the debtors' prisons of eighteenth- and nineteenth-century England reflected the way in which laws were employed to fortify the interests of the rich. Thrust into the urban ghettos or fleeing such destitution by immigration to strange lands, millions of people were dislocated and exploited. How much sympathy there was for such disadvantaged persons is hard to assess, but one of the great problems was that there were no structures, civil or religious, in which such sympathy—if it did exist—could effectively be expressed. Heroic efforts were made by individuals and by groups,[23] but the problem was (and is) of such proportions that only a basic restructuring of societal and religious institutions can adequately cope with it.

Clearly, such a situation requires a radical reassessment of the notion of Christian ministry. If "service" is to be the characteristic of Christian ministration to the world, and characteristic of the specialized ordained ministry within the church, the conditions of modern industrialized and urbanized life call for a new approach to service. Even if one leaves aside for the moment the service to human needs and concentrates exclusively on the ordained ministry's service to individual Christian faith, new needs have arisen in recent centuries. To take but one: it is basic to genuine faith that a person identify himself as a Christian; but men and women unavoidably find their personal identities from the circumstances in which they live, to which they react, and in the midst of which they make their basic life decisions. Thus, the church structures (or lack of them) that existed in deprived urban areas or among immigrant groups (or, for that matter, in the agrarian situations where a great bulk of the Christian people still lived) provided the kind of Christian identification these people possessed.[24]

Again, the dechristianization that was taking place on all levels of society demanded some response. More fundamental than the anticlerical attacks on vested church interests, which is a fairly constant historical phenome-

non, was the challenge to the very world-view upon which Christianity was apparently based. The reaction to Galileo in the late sixteenth century had betrayed the extent to which "traditional" Christianity felt threatened by a new cosmology and a new anthropology. The fear has persisted, though with a slow abatement, as the modern world has created this new vision of man and his world. To a large extent, the task of relating Christian faith to this modern view of reality which no longer accepted a hierarchical world has rested upon the ordained ministry, who operated for the most part in hierarchical structures. Moreover, it was primarily to the clergy of the various churches that there fell the task of relating Christianity to the movement towards freedom which has slowly gained momentum in modern times.[25] The specific issue to which the ordained ministry (and in particular the higher clergy) has had to address itself is that of freedom within Christianity itself— the retention or modification of "traditional" authority structures, advocacy of freedom of conscience or of submission to authoritative teaching, and emphasis on law or liberty in religious practice. If there is increased personal freedom and autonomy in religious faith and life, the guidance of Christians in the formation of adult conscience becomes a major activity of the ordained ministry.[26] In this context, one of the glaring needs of the modern ministry has been to confront the set of values that has come with industrial productivity, values that have often (and quite glibly) been condemned by religious spokesman as "materialistic," values that have been influential in shaping the attitudes and activity of most people.[27] And relevant to all these issues is the fact that formal education has gradually passed out of ecclesiastical control during the past three centuries; "secular education" is taken for granted today in most places in the world.

Still another factor of major importance in the modern evolution of Christian ministry is the worldwide extension of Christian evangelizing in modern times. Missionary effort has always been with the church; the fifteenth and sixteenth centuries already saw a large-scale missionary undertaking in Asia, Africa, and the Americas. However, there was a great upsurge of such evangelization in the nineteenth century, as Protestant communities (most of them really for the first time) now became involved in "foreign missions."[28] It has been in the missionary situations, where the need for adaptation to indigenous cultures, for clarification of catechesis, for relevance of liturgy has been greater—or at least more apparent—that much of the impetus for structural reform of the church has originated.

Mention should be made, finally, of a development whose importance and far-reaching implications only very recently have been appreciated. This is the growing assumption by civil government of responsibility for people's social needs. While the process is at different stages in different portions of the world, it is already clear that provision for such things as health care and basic economic well-being and education and cultural opportunity will (and probably should) pass increasingly into the public domain. Private agencies to care for the poor, the aged, and the handicapped may continue to have some purpose; but most likely they will exist only to complement the civic structures which take care of, or work to eliminate, these social ills. Formally church-sponsored activities will vanish in many areas that had been considered the proper sphere of religious "acts of charity," and there will no longer be need for ecclesiastical organization and direction of such activities, functions that had absorbed a good deal of the time and energy of ordained ministers. Instead, a new objective of ordained ministry has emerged: to participate in the Christian formation of the entire Christian community, so that all its members can share creatively in civic structures and in the "secular" attack on social ills.

Alternative Soteriologies

Rooted as it is in one or another theological understanding of salvation, the exercise of Christian ministry has been radically challenged by the prominence in modern life of a number of alternative (and, at least to all

appearances, non-Christian) soteriologies. Relatively little notice of these secular doctrines of salvation was taken by Christian theologians; they were absorbed in their own interconfessional (or intraconfessional) disputes about "grace," "justification," "faith vs. good works," etc. Roman Catholic theology, to take the most prominent example, devoted an incredible amount of time and intellectual energy to acrimonious debate about "efficacious grace," "scientia media," "divine foreknowledge," and allied topics. In part, the theological concentration on these topics was due to the momentum generated by polemic —in this instance the Reformation controversies about justification and predestination, and the refinement of those debates in the Jansenist controversy. But it was also in part, and perhaps greater part, a reflection of the anthropocentric tendency of modern thought. It is precisely this anthropocentric approach to salvation which characterizes the secular currents of modern thought and places them in opposition to religious teaching about salvation by God.

Obviously, there can be no question here of analyzing or even describing these secular soteriologies; they comprise what can be globally named "secular humanism" and together they account for a large portion of the history of modern European thought. The negative side of the challenge which this humanism presented to the Christian theology of salvation was the blunt presentation of the "God-problem," not just the theoretical agnosticism regarding the divine which one finds in Kant's *Critique of Pure Reason* but the pragmatic atheism of Marx or Nietzsche which sees "religion" and "God" as a hindrance to true human development. The positive side of the challenge lay in the various gospels of human achievement which were preached by the Enlightenment, the Romantic movement, nineteenth-century liberalism, and the theories of human betterment through economic or psychological or cultural methods.[29] For the most part, the impact on Christian ministry of both positive and negative aspects of the challenge was more deeply felt in Protestantism than in Roman Catholicism. For one thing, Catholic theological seminaries in the nineteenth and twentieth centuries provided an effective shield to protect prospective clergy from "dangerous" currents of modern thought.

Without attempting the impossible task of determining the manner in which the existence of these alternative soteriologies influenced Christian ministry, we can mention two areas in which important reorientations of thought and activity have gradually occurred. The first of these touches upon the shift of emphasis from "detachment" to "involvement" in both popular and theological thinking about the "ideal Christian." As far back as the Gospel of John and throughout its history, Christian thought about "the world" has been a dialectic between "entry into" and "separation from." This has expressed itself not only in the classic option between contemplation and action but within each of these two: Christian contemplation can be seen as a process of discovering the divine by way of freeing one's religious understanding from earthly elements or by way of discovering that the created world is a sacramental revelation of the divine. Christian activity (as a share in the action of salvation) can be either "world-affirming" or "world-negating." For most of the patristic, medieval, and Reformation periods the "detachment" element in the dialectic was dominant, although a gradual shift towards "involvement" is observable as early as the twelfth century. In the modern period, however, the stress on "involvement" has gained strength and become dominant in the post–World War II world.

Even a quick glance at the history of Christian spirituality during the past nine centuries reveals the presence *within Christian thought* of forces pushing Christian prayer and life into closer relationship to the world.[30] However, there have always been forces outside the formal religious structures of Christianity that have been working to draw Christians closer to their world; such forces have been increasingly effective in the eighteenth to twentieth centuries. One of the clearest and most important reflections of this activist impulse of modern life and thought is Marx's notion of *"praxis,"* which is really a secular "spirituality of involvement." Man, in the Marxist view, can realize himself and achieve his destiny only in his creative relationship to the world, in work that is truly what it should be; more than this, it is only in this practical working out of the man-world relation that man attains an insight into "truth" about himself and his world.[31] At least until very recent times, this Marxist demand for human involvement in the world had little direct influence on Christian theories of spirituality; yet it contributed, as did many other nonreligious influences, in creating a context of attitudes in the midst of which modern Christians have become more conscious of the positive desirability of involvement in the world.

It should not be thought that more recent impetus towards such involvement came only from outside the church. On religious grounds Lammenais anticipated and probably influenced Marx and Engels with his *De l'esclavage moderne* (1839);[32] Albert Ritschl, in the latter half of the nineteenth century, propounded a widely influential doctrine of salvation through social involvement;[33] and the ideas and projects of Isaac Hecker were suspect in many circles (at the turn of the century) because of their strongly activist emphasis.[34] However, it is worth noting that such men generally encountered a good deal of opposition from ecclesiastical officialdom.

In a second important area the general evolution of modern thought created a changed background for understanding Christian ministry: the sciences (physical, social, and behavioral) in particular have taught that the *development* of human potential and the achievement of human destiny will come not through unquestioning *submission* to authoritative teaching but through *discovery*. Unfortunately, the basically valuable elements in this position were often accompanied (particularly in the eighteenth and nineteenth centuries) by attacks on all nonscientific ways of knowing, and unnecessary hostilities developed between modern scientific thought and the religious teaching of the various Christian groups. Thus, for a variety of reasons, the full impact of modern emphasis on discovering truth has been very lately felt in Christian theology and religious education; it is still quite suspect among large segments of the Christian people. Quite obviously, a shift in emphasis to intelligent discovery of faith's meaning demands a shift in the objectives governing the ministry of the word, and therefore a shift in the recruitment and training and structuring of the ordained ministry, just as does the shift in stress from "detachment" to "involvement."

Emphasis on "Personal" Religion

In the final essay of his *Theology of Vatican II*, Bishop Christopher Butler comments on the manner in which the council marks an important acceptance of the "subjective" elements of Christian faith and life.[35] As he points out very briefly, this is a tardy (though perhaps somewhat understandably tardy) acceptance by official Catholic teaching of modern "personalism." Taking "personalism" in the broad sense of giving attention to and placing special value upon human consciousness and affectivity and freedom and dignity,[36] there seems good justification for saying that the past few centuries have seen a growing development of this point of view. Not that the modern age has been the first to notice that men and women are persons, but the implications of human personhood have been better understood, more consciously accepted (or rejected), and more explicitly employed as the ground of decision and action. At the same time, social and economic developments in the modern world, urbanization and industrialization, for example, have constituted an unprecedented threat to people's personal dignity and fulfillment, and for that very reason have drawn attention to the personal aspects of human experience.

These developments have been allied with the concentration of attention on "personal religion" which characterized much late me-

dieval and Renaissance humanism and much of the Reformation. This fifteenth- and sixteenth-century reawakening to the importance of the individual Christian's life of faith became somewhat dull in much of Protestantism and Catholicism during the seventeenth and eighteenth centuries, as religion became increasingly "established," as doctrine hardened into new "scholastic" systems, and as Erastian church-state relationships tended to convert ministers into public functionaries. Against this impersonalization of Christian faith there were waves of reaction: the important developments of Pietism within both Lutheran and Reformed traditions, the evangelical resurgence that came with the Wesleys and Methodism, the theological emphasis on religious experience that one attaches to such names as Schleiermacher and Ritschl, the fostering of a close personal relationship to "the human Christ" which characterized the spiritual direction of the "French school" and at least one wing of Jesuit use of the *Spiritual Exercises*, the "Great Awakening" in the American colonies.

One of the common features of these varied reactions was the reliance on less formalized approaches to faith; even if, as was more the case in Catholicism and less in Protestant Pietism, the established structures of religious practice were not abandoned, the nurturing of genuine personal faith was undertaken somewhat independently.[37] This led to another common feature: the formation of small communities of dedicated believers in which a strong spirit of fellowship emerged; this acted as a force for social equalization, a quiet but important negation of class barriers within the church.[38]

Anthropocentrism increasingly characterized modern philosophy as it moved from Descartes through Spinoza and Locke and Hume and Rousseau into Kant and nineteenth-century idealism, and this inevitably had repercussions on religion. Above all, it focused attention on the individual believer and on the extent to which he "made his own God." Especially since Kant, modern thought has concentrated on the "subjective" element in human knowing, on the manner in which human thought constructs its own object of consciousness—with obvious implications for religious consciousness. What forms the object of study and criticism by nineteenth-century "atheistic" philosophers (Feuerbach, Marx, Nietzsche, and others) is not the divine in itself—they profess agnosticism in its regard—but rather man's idea of the divine.[39] Since much of this philosophical thought presupposes or "proves" that human thinking about a "real God outside man's mind" is either impossible or illusory, there was a strong reaction in traditional Christian religious and theological circles. Negatively, this was a loud condemnation and a lasting suspicion of modern "liberal" thought; positively, it took the form of a "fundamental theology" (or "apologetics") that was developed as a prolegomenon to and justification of Christian faith. All this began to shift considerably the orientation of the ministry of the word: there was often much more attention given, in what purported to be teaching of Christian doctrine, to matters that were essentially philosophical than to what strictly concerned Christian faith.[40]

Professional Activity of Modern Clergy

One of the remarkable features about the ordained Christian ministry in modern times is the durability of its institutional forms. Despite the constant social ferment of the past three centuries, even despite the radical attempts to reinstitutionalize the church and its clergy that came with the French Revolution or the *Kulturkampf* or the *risorgimento*, the external forms of clerical life-style and the patterns of ministerial activity have until very recently remained noticeably constant. An indication of the extent to which such continuity was a deliberately chosen goal is the fact that the clergy, especially the higher clergy, were prominent in the various "restoration" movements that followed each new wave of revolution. Even when ordained ministers were agents of change, as were the Wesleys in mid-eighteenth-century England

and their spiritual descendants in mid-nineteenth-century America, they introduced no really new elements of ministerial activity.

As the seventeenth century ends, the split in the ordained ministers in Europe between upper and lower clergy was probably greater than it had ever been. To some extent this was mitigated during the eighteenth century. In France, the lower clergy became more vocal and organized and by the end of the century had become a major political force; in Germany, the slowly rising level of clerical education bettered somewhat the status of the ordinary pastor; in England, the continuance (even increase) of plural possession of benefices kept the stratification of clergy quite pronounced; in Scotland, the clergy were generally respected but kept poor by the General Assembly; in Italy and Spain, the situation remained static, though in neither was the upper clergy as completely identified with the aristocracy as it was in most of Europe. By and large, the ordinary parish clergy remain relatively poor (in some instances, painfully poor) throughout the eighteenth century. This economic condition translated itself into their social identification: they were not part of society's elite.[41] However, a fairly important differentiation was developing between the German and Scandinavian areas on the one hand and France, England, the Iberian peninsula, and Italy on the other. In the latter group of countries the "middle class" that was now challenging the power of the aristocracy was more a financial bourgeoisie, a group into which the clergy did not fit; but in the region east of the Rhine and north of the Alps the "middle class" which more and more controlled affairs was largely composed of civil servants and professional men, a group into which the clergy tended to be drawn.[42]

At least on the surface, the eighteenth century was ruled by aristocracy. In England and Roman Catholic countries, the bishops (and abbots where religious orders had not been suppressed) lived and moved in these aristocratic circles. Heirs to the benefice system that had already worked such havoc in the church, they were financially comfortable and often quite wealthy. In England, there was a great deal of political manipulation and exploitation of the benefices, plural possession of beneficed offices was a prevalent practice, and promotion to the episcopate opened the way both to prestige and to wealth.[43] Not only were French bishops identified socially with the aristocracy but they were also almost exclusively drawn from aristocratic families. On the eve of the Revolution, only one bishop was a commoner. Most of them were relatively wealthy: a bishop in a less important diocese enjoyed an income twenty times that of a curé, and most of the prominent bishops had an income three hundred times that of a curé. Many bishops conscientiously administered their sees, but many of the more favored and politically implicated were nonresident. Many of them still ruled as feudal lords in their own territories and enjoyed a certain immunity from national laws and taxation. Many of them lived as princes surrounded by their court or at the court of princes.[44] Probably the most corrupt usage of church wealth in France concerned the abbatial appointments in monastic institutions. More than half the revenue of each of the great abbeys (which had acquired immense holdings over the centuries) went to a titular absentee abbot, who often was not even ordained.[45]

In Spain and Portugal the higher clergy were less aristocratic and less worldly than they were in either France or England and although they were not as wealthy as their French counterparts there was still a wide economic gap between them and most of the parish clergy. Monks and friars formed a large percentage of the countries' clergy; their manner of life was generally edifying and their influence on the religious life of the country of major importance. However, they possessed considerable corporate wealth and so became the object of expropriation and "reform" by ambitious civil rulers.[46] Still, despite the efforts of powerful politicians, such as Pombal in Portugal, to bring their countries into the world of modern thought and organization, the cultural climate on the Iberian peninsula remained religious in a way

that was no longer true of the rest of Europe. And in this context, churchmen in general and members of religious orders in particular enjoyed a unique respect and moral persuasiveness.

For the most part, the activities engaged in by higher and lower clergy were as different as their social status. Bishops, abbots, and their immediate clerical associates were essentially administrators, involved in taking care of financial matters, ecclesiastical organization, and affairs of state. Because of the Erastianism that characterized church-state relations in most places, many bishops were as much high-level functionaries in the government as they were ecclesiastical rulers. The late seventeenth and early eighteenth centuries had at least seen occasionally the phenomenon of a prominent episcopal preacher—Tillotson in England, Bossuet and Fenelon in France; even this becomes rarer as the century progresses. Certainly, if the higher clergy kept some notion of themselves as the pastors of the Christian people, this was in terms of a distanced overseeing of ecclesiastical structures and operations rather than any immediate pastoral care of the ordinary Christian; bishops were not in the same social community with the bulk of the ordained clergy, to say nothing of the bulk of Christians.

The overall religious spirit of Europe in the eighteenth century has been described as one of "dispirited moralism,"[47] and this describes fairly accurately the approach to ministry on the part of most of Europe's lower clergy. Spain and Portugal are somewhat an exception, for there the fervor of crusade and the medieval symbolism of Christendom remained strong. But elsewhere the advance of secularization had concentrated men's "religious" attention on natural ethic, or perhaps only on social respectability, and dimmed the idea of mystery. In England one can point to the Wesleyan revival or on the Continent to continuing expressions of Pietism as evangelical exception to this somewhat pessimistic appraisal; but that is what they were—exceptions. In most places the local pastor became more and more a public functionary; he continued to preach and instruct and conduct religious services, but these were increasingly perfunctory and lifeless.[48] For the most part, he was a good man, often with human failings and eccentricities but still respected and even at times loved by the people with whom he lived in close daily relationship.[49] What seems to have been lacking was a vital Christian *faith*. It was only in somewhat oppressed situations of religious practice, as among the dissenting groups in England or the Catholics in Ireland, that the ministry escaped the dullness of routine.[50]

Shaken to its roots by the Revolution which had ended the eighteenth century and the *ancien régime* and had led to the bitter and destructive division between "juring" and "nonjuring" clergy, caught in the antagonistic polarities of "progressive" and "reactionary" parties and thus unable to take a clear position of repudiating or fostering the principles of the Revolution, Christianity in nineteenth-century France illustrated in striking and painful fashion the struggle of the church, and particularly its ordained ministry, to relate to "the modern world."[51] For the most part, the effort of the Catholic church was one of reconstruction after the shattering experience of the Revolution. That reconstruction was clearly intended, particularly by the majority of the bishops, to be a *restoration*. Though there was this nostalgic looking back to the days of broad episcopal power and privileges, the bulk of the French hierarchy were still royalist. Though the rebuilding of the French Catholic church was carefully and successfully undertaken during the century, there were basic and important changes. The Gallican church of Bossuet and Louis XIV was dead. In a sense, it had already been replaced by the concordat between Napoleon and Pius VII, but it took several decades before Ultramontanism dominated the French church, as it did by the end of the century. All this meant a drastic shift in the position and role of the bishops. Their financial situation was approximately that of well-to-do professional men. While they were still a force of considerable moral leadership, they

were not enmeshed formally in the political structures of the country. Increasingly they became a reactionary force in French society, and a reciprocal antagonism developed between "the church" and much of the intellectual and social leadership of France. Ecclesiastically the growing Ultramontanism weakened their former corporate identity and focused each bishop's attention on the affairs of his own diocese. One of the most promising developments in the nineteenth-century episcopacy was its recruiting of membership from all levels of French society and, for the most part, on the basis of merit; thus, to some degree, the identity of the church with the aristocracy was weakened. More importantly, the "spiritual" level, and to a lesser degree the theological level, of the French hierarchy was clearly raised over pre-Revolution days.

All this did not mean the end of the cleavage between higher and lower clergy. For the most part the diocesan clergy were recruited from the peasant class, the sons of bourgeois families being more inclined to enter a religious congregation. Their education, carried out for the most part in minor and major seminaries, whose emphasis was on training devout priests rather than on intellectual formation, ill-equipped them for dealing with the social and cultural and intellectual developments of their day. So, they were good-living, for the most part very poor, doomed in many instances by their training and by the purely nominal Christianity of so many of their parishioners to a routine performance of ministerial tasks. The suffering and shock of the Revolution had brought many of the aristocracy back to a more sincere faith. The same thing happened to many of the well-established middle-class families after the outbreaks of 1848. But the new middle class and particularly the lower class, both urban and rural, became increasingly dechristianized and in their politics republican. By and large, the diocesan clergy was reactionary in its political views and, particularly in the latter half of the century, quite often worked vigorously against republican influences. In some of the traditionally Catholic areas (Brittany, for example) this accorded well with the political conservatism of the populace, but in many portions of the country the clergy were seen as a symbol of a blind clinging to the past.[52]

Though still very much a minority, the Reformed clergy in France received public acceptance with the Revolution and became a definite force in the development of France from the Third Republic onward. Since it had been the Revolution that provided them with greater freedom, the Reformed pastors were generally more sympathetic with the liberal and "secular" developments in nineteenth-century France. This accorded quite well also with the more democratic tendencies of their ecclesiastical polity.

But the Reformed community, too, was caught in the "liberal-conservative" tensions of the century. In this case, the two views were a "traditional" emphasis on orthodox dogmatics which was supported by a fairly rationalistic theology and an opposing emphasis on individual religious faith and conscience. This latter position, which was partially due to Wesleyan influence coming by way of Geneva, found wide acceptance among both ministers and people and helped stimulate a genuine religious revival in mid-century.[53]

Italy remained relatively untouched until the mid-nineteenth century by the currents of dechristianization that had for more than a century been challenging the Christianity of northern Europe. As a result, its clergy was generally apathetic in the midst of a social context that was firmly Christian. Both diocesan and regular clergy were numerous, relatively poor, and provided in their seminary training with an education that was with rare exceptions superficial and out-of-date. Thus, the bulk of Italy's clergy were ill-prepared to deal with the "modern world" when it assaulted Italian society and the Italian church after 1848. There were exceptions, such as Don Bosco in Turin or Cardinal Riario Sforza in Naples, but the general picture was one of lethargy: sacramental liturgy was perfunctory and religious fervor was more often aroused by devotional practices of various kinds, religious instruction was routinely given if at all, and preaching was widely neglected. Many ordained priests were not assigned to nor involved in active apostolate.[54] When the forces of modern secularity did begin in the late nineteenth century to threaten the church's hold on Italian Catholics, the common reaction of both higher and lower clergy was to retreat to a defensive and polemical position. In this, the papacy from Pius IX onward (with some exception being made for Leo XIII) set the pattern.

In Germany and Austria, the history of the Catholic clergy in the nineteenth century is largely one of bitter struggle against the attempts of the civil government to place the church under complete state control.[55] Much of the struggle centered on the relative roles of church and state in education, including the education of the clergy. The most intense stage was reached in Prussia with the passage in 1873 of the "May laws" which implemented a change in the Prussian constitution and permitted Bismarck's government to regulate education, appoint or dismiss clergy, and interfere in all ecclesiastical affairs. This high point of the *Kulturkampf* continued until 1878 when the election of Leo XIII gave the Prussian government an opportunity to back off from this disastrous policy which had proved unworkable and an increasing embarrassment to Bismarck's party. Despite the arrest and imprisonment of a number of prominent bishops, the deposition of several others, and the arrest and removal from their parishes of hundreds of priests, the resistance of the Catholic community to government control of religion had only been strengthened. Moreover, under the courageous leadership of Catholic laity, particularly Mallinckrodt and Windthorst, the Center party had opposed Bismarck in the *Reichstag* and gradually brought about a realignment of political power in the government itself. Gradually the persecution of the Catholic community abated until by century's end the *Kulturkampf* was at an end.

Somewhat the same pattern of struggle between the Catholic church and a government that sought to place religion under complete civil control took place in other portions of Germany and in Austria.[56] After the overthrow of absolutist rule in 1848, Josephenism ceased to be an important force in the Austro-Hungarian Empire and for about twenty years the church was able to function with relative autonomy and lack of interference. But from 1867 onwards the government again undertook a campaign to bring ecclesiastical affairs under its control, and. as in Germany the basic issue was control of education. In Austria there . was no prominent lay movement in support of the official church (as happened in Germany), nor any of the widespread sense of "fighting for one's faith" which German Catholics had experienced during the *Kulturkampf*. Instead, the struggle with the anticlerical government in Austria was carried on almost exclusively by the bishops, who were able to achieve a basic *modus vivendi* which safeguarded at least the externals of Austria's traditional Catholicism.

Protestant churches were in quite a different political situation in the German-speaking world, and so also the problems facing their ordained ministers and the developments within their ministerial activity were different from those of the Catholic clergy.[57] In general, continental Protestantism in the nineteenth century was more deeply touched and modified by "liberal" currents of thought than was Catholicism; much of the Catholic struggle over the educational issue was rooted in a fear of and opposition to the dangers of "liberalism." Liberal Protestantism, on the contrary, became a major development in continental theology and infiltrated down into popular attitudes.[58] Thus, while emphasis on teaching and preaching was common to the ministry of both Catholic and Protestant communities, the content of Catholic instruction remained very constant in contrast to an important "secularization" in much of Protestant teaching. Liberal Protestantism did not go unchallenged, however. There was a strong reaction of orthodox Protestant thought, particularly in Lutheran circles. Very significantly, neo-Lutheranism developed a sacramentalism that has endured in sections of both continental and American Lutheranism up to the present.[59] Clearly, where such a sacramental emphasis was found, the identity and activity of the ordained ministry was shifted somewhat in the direction of Catholic thinking and practice.

In England, the nineteenth-century revitalization and reorientation of ministry is in large part the history of the Oxford movement and its influence. Despite the Evangelical movement, which still had considerable influence in the early nineteenth century, the Church of England was in the doldrums. Religious practice and pastoral ministry were for the most part desultory, there was widespread dissatisfaction with the church, and anticlericalism was rampant. And, in the minds of the Tractarians at least, much of this was rooted in the clergy's ignorance of the true nature of the church and of her ministry.[60] Though the tracts that Newman, Keble, Froude, and others composed were neither creative in their theology nor innovative in their approach to ecclesiastical polity, they had lasting impact because of their religious depth. Basically, the Oxford movement was a reassertion of the church as a mystery, as the possessor of divinely given truth and authority and power to save. Neither this position nor the other elements of Christian faith emphasized by the Tractarians were new to Anglican theology, yet the attention drawn to them by the Oxford movement "seriously altered the accepted patterns of Anglican thought and practice."[61] Along with the Evangelical thrust of the previous century, but with more influence at the very heart of the Anglican church, the Oxford movement swung the balance away from identification of the Anglican clergy as functionaries of the government and towards their identity and activity as pastors. Moreover, in its emphasis on deepened Christian spirituality and on more careful pastoral training for prospective clergy, the Oxford movement helped to prepare a large body of clergy better equipped for a ministry of word and sacrament.[62] One of the key elements in the Tractarian vision of the church was the centrality of the Eucharistic action, an action which they explained as involving both the presence and the sacrifice of Christ.[63] The "Cambridge movement" was more responsible for the external aspects of liturgical renewal,[64] but it was the Eucharistic theology of the Oxford Tractarians that moved a large segment of the nineteenth- and twentieth-century Anglican clergy to think of their ministry in more "priestly" terms.[65]

Clearly, the Anglo-Catholicism that stemmed from the Tractarian movement did not represent the whole of the Anglican church in the nineteenth century, but it did become an increasingly prominent element within the church and altered basically the attitudes and activity of the entire Anglican ministry. Besides, the nineteenth century in England saw a rather vigorous development among the dissenting communities. Somewhat surprisingly, since their traditions were so strongly evangelical, there were evidences of growing stress on liturgical aspects of ministry that would be more apparent in the next century.[66]

For the Roman Catholic community in Ireland, the nineteenth century was almost an "emergence from the catacombs." Persecuted and driven underground by the Penal Laws, the church and particularly its clergy would very likely have declined seriously in the eighteenth century had it not been for the welcome given Irish bishops, priests, nuns, and seminary students by Catholics on the Continent. Most importantly, Irish colleges to train candidates for ordination were established in various European centers. This not only gave the suppressed Irish church a continuing corps of pastors, but the group of men who did return to Ireland were well-educated, cosmopolitan, and alert to the currents of modern thought and life. In this way Irish Catholicism was preserved from the isolationism that might easily have resulted from its persecution.[67]

This changed radically, however, with the French Revolution and the rise of Napoleon, for the greater number of Irish colleges on the Continent were permanently closed. Fortunately, the Penal Laws had been eased enough to permit the beginnings of seminary training in Ireland itself, and in 1795 St. Patrick's College, Maynooth, was established. But the precious contact of Ireland's clergy with the thought and life of continental Christianity was lost, the intellectual outlook of Irish priests became gradually more insular, and the relationship of Ireland's episcopacy to the outside world became increasingly focused on Rome.

Working out relations with the papacy was, of course, an important task of the Irish church as it reorganized itself in mid-century after the Catholic Emancipation Act. Most importantly, the method of selecting bishops and the assignment of pastors and their curates had to be regularized. In mid-nineteenth century some recognition was given to the diocesan clergy's voice in selecting their bishop: they could recommend three candidates, from among whom the new bishop was generally picked by Rome. Gradually, however, this was changed until in 1925 Ireland was brought under the regulations already applied to several other countries whereby the recommendation of candidates was left to the bishops and the selection to Rome. As for the appointment of pastors and their curates, the *concursus* (or competitive examination) required by Trent for pastoral appointments was bypassed and selection was left entirely to the bishop's judgment, and appointment of curates was also made directly by the bishop (contrary to the general church law prior to 1917, which gave the pastor the right to appoint his curate).[68]

Obviously, the political situation, even after the Emancipation Act, preserved the Roman Catholic clergy from any identification with the English government; but if they were not official functionaries the bishops and priests were definitely public figures. They constituted a large portion of the educated populace, they had been a rallying force for the people during the days of persecution, and they remained the principal leadership of the Irish Catholics throughout the nineteenth and into the twentieth century. They were relatively poor, being dependent upon the free-will offerings of their congregations. They placed great stress on education, and much of their effort in the period of Irish reconstruction was devoted to providing adequate schooling for their people. However, their principal functional identity was "cultic" in a broad sense: though the Eucharistic action remained basic in their activity and in the religious life of the Irish people, there was as in continental Roman Catholicism of the period a strong development of devotional piety to the Sacred Heart, to Mary, and to various saints. The pastor was generally the leader in these devotional exercises and chaplain to pious groups dedicated to fostering them.

Because so many of them left Ireland in the nineteenth and twentieth centuries for such places as the United States or Australia, either accompanying groups of immigrants or recruited by bishops in countries that could not yet supply their own clergy, the Irish clergy were widely influential in shaping the identity, function, and life-style of Catholic priests in the twentieth century. To a large degree they were responsible for the establishment of the Catholic church in these "frontier" situations, for they were unquestionably a major principle of unification (often *the* major principle) among the immigrant groups.

In North America, the evolution of the activity and life-style of ordained ministers was basically parallel to the evolution in Europe, since the two regions shared a common history; yet, the American experience (religious and otherwise) was quite distinctive in many respects, and inevitably there developed distinctive attitudes towards Christian ministry and distinctive patterns of ministerial activity. This distinctiveness was more evident in the Protestant churches, since their American development was less controlled by "mother churches" in Europe.

For a number of reasons, the Roman Catholic community and its ordained ministry in particular remained very much tied to Europe

and very much influenced by developments in the European church.[69] First of all, the Catholic church was a late arrival on the scene. Although Catholic missionaries and explorers and small settlements of Catholic colonizers were very early participants in the settling of North America, the Catholic presence on the continent remained relatively minor until shortly before the middle of the nineteenth century when the waves of immigration began. This stream of immigration from Catholic countries continued into the twentieth century, which worked to keep the Americanized immigrants in close contact with the "mother country," somewhat tenacious of their ethnic culture, and wary of too quick adjustment to the new situation. By and large this attitude was abetted by the clergy, for they feared that loss of traditional Catholicism would accompany loss of ethnic identity; hence their own approach to ministry remained what it had been in Europe. Moreover, the rapid numerical growth of American Catholicism demanded an accompanying increase in the numbers of ordained clergy. Since the newly established dioceses and parishes in the United States and Canada were not yet able to provide their own clergy, a steady stream of European-born and European-trained priests came to minister to American congregations. Even when North America began to provide its own ordained ministry it took some time for adequate educational facilities to be established, with the result that candidates for ministerial activity in America were trained for that work in European seminaries. When seminaries were set up in North America, they were fashioned according to European models, staffed by men who were trained in Europe, and guided by regulations coming from the Vatican.[70]

Finally, Catholicism in the United States and Canada was very much touched by the influence of Rome. In part this was due to the fact that American Catholicism remained under the direction of the Congregation for the Propagation of the Faith until 1908, and therefore the evolution of its pastoral ministry was the object of vigilant Roman watchfulness.[71] In part it was a manifestation of the Rome-centeredness that increased in the entire Catholic church in the years after Vatican I. In part it resulted from the increasing influence of canon lawyers in the administration of American dioceses and from the Roman influence on North American seminaries. This Romanization of American Catholicism was not effected without a struggle. Almost all the United States' hierarchy vigorously opposed the establishment of an apostolic delegation in 1893.[72] However, until World War II, there was no "American identity" (either U.S. or Canadian) strong enough to weld the wrangling immigrant groups into a unified church; the strongest common tie was the allegiance to the pope. At the same time, there had been progressive organizational unity achieved through such agencies as the series of plenary councils of Baltimore in the nineteenth century and the National Catholic Welfare Conference in the early twentieth century.[73]

Because of the ghetto mentality that was strong among American Catholics until around mid-twentieth century, the ordained ministry tended to identify strongly with the Catholic faithful and not too strongly with the non-Catholic American life around them. But there was strong insistence on the civic loyalty of American Catholics.[74] One instance of this was the absorption of Catholic clergy in maintaining the parochial school system, and a relative lack of interest in the evolution of public education. This meant that the Catholic priest remained in close contact with his congregation, something which was facilitated by the fact that the vast bulk of candidates for ordination came from the working-class and so could identify sociologically with the Catholic populace which was concentrated in the lower income brackets. Fidelity to church law and official doctrinal formulation, regularity in performance of religious services, common-sense administrative ability, "good example" in moral behavior— these were the attributes that were expected of the Catholic priest, and that to a high degree did exist.[75] Probably more than any-

thing else, this pastoral performance of basic ministerial tasks explained the striking development of American Catholicism; it found expression both in the strengths and in the weaknesses of the Catholic community at mid-twentieth century.

Like the Catholics, the Protestant communities in North America derived their attitudes towards Christian ministry and the basic patterns of ministerial activity from their European roots. There was, moreover, a continuing input from Europe of evolving theological thought and of new movements of evangelization and pastoral care. One thinks immediately of Whitefield's preaching and the beginning of Methodism in the American colonies, or of the influence of Philip Schaff in the Mercersburg movement, or of the role played by Walther in the formation of Missouri Synod Lutheranism. Beyond such evident instances, there was a broadly based interchange that enriched the North American churches and before too long began to enrich European Protestantism with America's Christian thought and experience.[76]

This enrichment of Europe's heritage by American Protestantism could happen as quickly as it did because the understandings and exercise of Christian ministry that were brought to North America were quickly altered by the different social conditions, the different need for support and "protection" on the part of institutionalized Christianity, and the different opportunities for evangelization. Besides, a considerable portion of the colonizers and immigrants who came to North America were in one form or another "dissidents" religiously as well as politically; they were quite open to the kind of adaptation of ministry, in life-style and in patterns of activity, which the evolving course of the American experience seemed to demand.[77]

One of the political developments that very early influenced the function of Protestant ministry in the United States was the disappearance, with the revolt against English rule, of legal establishment for any church. Instead, there was by law a governmental neutrality towards all religious communities which did not, however, prevent the Protestant ministry from continuing to exercise unofficially the role they would have had in a theocratic system of using the pulpit to provide "prophetic" guidance for public policy.[78] To quite an extent, Protestant ministers were able to exert influence in the public sphere without drawing criticism for interference in secular matters, for their popular image was a mixture of religious and civic leader, which accorded well with the quasi-religious character projected onto the American way of life.[79]

Despite the movement towards organization and centralization, which became prominent in the latter part of the nineteenth century, American Protestantism was characterized by strong individualism, emphasis on local congregational autonomy, and stress on personal religious experience and freedom of conscience. This brought splintering of "traditional" churches and a proliferation of sects, which obviously fostered the development of diversity in ministerial practice. Actually this diversification expressed itself for the most part in details and not in basically new approaches to pastoral care or to evangelization. At the same time, there slowly developed a generic "Protestant" identity, which created an informal bond among churchgoers who were not Roman Catholic.[80] So, in the small towns and the countryside it was common for the one or two churches, whether Baptist or Congregationalist or some other church, to be frequented by all the Protestants despite what their earlier denominational adherence might have been. In this context, the Protestant minister was essentially a preacher; he also handled baptisms and marriages and burials, he counseled and consoled, directed religious instruction, and organized parish activities of one kind or another.[81] He commanded respect as a religious and ethical leader but also as a prominent citizen. His life-style and socioeconomic level depended somewhat on the particular denomination to which he belonged. Some older well-established churches drew more affluent membership, whereas other groups such as the Baptists in many

places were comprised of economically poorer communicants.[82]

This, of course, was the picture of the settled congregation situation which moved westward with the nineteenth-century American expansion. A step ahead of this was the frontier, with its own élan and its own characteristics; the frontier with its pioneering spirit and fluid social structures and its special human and religious needs; the frontier which was an experience the European churches did not know and which helped shape the theory and practice of ministry in North America; the frontier which brought into existence three patterns of ministry that did much to form American Protestantism and give it its characteristic spirit of "revival."[83]

The first of these patterns was the ministry of the circuit rider, the itinerant preacher who went continuously from one station to another, preaching, encouraging, or correcting as the situation demanded, and providing direction for the lay leaders who guided the congregation in his absence.[84] It was the Methodists who most successfully employed this means of bringing the gospel to the widely dispersed frontier populace, though other churches also had their traveling preachers and missionaries. And among the Methodists, the circuit rider was more generally ordained and was a representative of some higher church direction.[85]

Somewhat different was the second pattern, which was found among the Baptists particularly; this was the emergence of lay preachers from the local situation.[86] A local congregation would form around a man who felt "called" to preach; his continuing to do so would depend upon the approval of that community. He might even be invited as visiting preacher to some neighboring group, and years later he might then get a more formal ordination. There was an alternative pattern: a licensed preacher might be sent out by a local community as its missionary, and it would be his task to gather people by his preaching and bring into existence a new congregation.

The third pattern was the wilderness camp meeting.[87] Begun by the Presbyterians, it was quickly adopted by other groups. Eventually it became most prominent among the Methodists and Baptists. These gatherings, combined religious and social events, often attracted people by the thousands and became a major instrument for conversion and renewal. Even when the camp meeting as such became less popular with groups such as the Presbyterians and Congregationalists, they continued in modified form in the various "renewal weeks," "revivals," and Bible camps which became a standard element in American Protestantism.

Thus, a large portion of the Protestant ministry in the United States came into existence informally, was exercised in local congregations that grew spontaneously or in grass-roots revival movements, and was only loosely connected (if at all) with the institutionalized clerical structures of the classic Reformation churches. In many instances, where preachers operated without ordination and often as a Sunday task added to their regular occupation, the dividing line between clergy and laity tended to vanish. As American Protestantism moved further into the twentieth century, as the frontier became part of history, and as urbanization increased, the forms of ministry became more institutionalized and officially controlled; but the eighteenth- and nineteenth-century waves of "revival" and the spontaneity of frontier ministry continued to influence the American understanding of Christian ministry.[88]

As the nineteenth century ended, the situation and role of the ordained ministry were being dragged into currents of radical change; but for the moment this was not apparent. On the surface the old forms seemed to have weathered the storms of revolution and irreligion; even anticlericalism seemed to be a bit weaker.

Religion was definitely on the upswing; the tally sheet on the nineteenth century could list a spectacular increase in church membership as well as an internal reawakening in the churches. As always, there were some voices raised to warn against "the evils of the times,"

but a sense of confidence marked the early decades of the twentieth century. Numerical growth continued, the foreign missions flourished, the education of clergy and their financial stability reached a new high, and more young men were attracted to the ministry. For the most part the churches enjoyed a greater measure of freedom to carry on their own affairs, and more and more lay men and women were becoming active in church organizations of one sort or another. It would take World War II, prepared for by the Spanish civil war and the rise of Nazism and followed by the collapse of European colonialism, to alert the ordained ministry of the various churches to the fact that a radically new world was emerging around them, a world in which shoring up old structures and procedures of readjusting them might prove to be completely ineffective.

One of the factors that affected Christian ministry in ambiguous fashion was the increasing disestablishment of the church. Official disestablishment did not occur in France until 1905, in Germany until after World War II, and in other countries (such as England, Spain, or Scandinavia) it has not yet happened. The latter part of the nineteenth century had already seen the gradual dissolution of the link between church and state, a development that accelerated in the twentieth century. Less slow to vanish, even though it has been under constant attack from secularizing forces, was the cultural establishment of one or other form of Christianity in a given country or area as, for example, the cultural establishment of Protestantism in the United States; but its days, too, seem numbered.

All this gave ministerial activity a freedom from nonecclesiastical interference, but the obverse was also true. Nonecclesiastical institutions have increasingly declared themselves free in their conduct from any Christian interference. Religious activity became more and more divorced from public life. Governments have often continued to encourage some practice of religion, even favoring it by privileges, especially to clergy, and exemptions, for religion was expected to foster civic morality in an "establishment" situation. But the churches were to carry on their activity, even their support of civil authority and society's mores, in the isolation of their own religious sphere. What they were not expected to do was to interfere in "worldly affairs," economic or social or political. Thus, the sphere of activity proper to the ordained minister became "the church," which itself was being separated not just from the state but from human society in all its non-religious activities. It was in this socially irrelevant ecclesiastical structure that the ordained minister was to "do his thing" and he received his social respectability from so doing. He could even be quite socially active, but such activity was to consist in fostering those Christian "works of mercy" (hospitals, orphanages, homes for the aged) which helped civil society absolve itself of responsibility to its less fortunate members.

Christian communities that were the minority, or at least the "dissenting church," in a given country (such as the Reformed in France or the Catholics in Ireland) felt this adjustment to "nonestablishment" less keenly, but the problem touched them, too. The divisions between "established" and "dissenting" became less important and less an influence on their respective clergies. All ecclesiastical institutions were being relegated to the periphery of society by the process of dechristianization. Much more noticeably than, for example, in mid-nineteenth century, the social status and identity of ordained ministers from the different churches became quite homogenous; so, too, granting the divergence of viewpoint on the precise nature of preaching and teaching and worship, did the activity undertaken by clergy of the various churches. There were obvious differences such as the imposed celibacy of Roman Catholic clergy or the heavy involvement of some communities (particularly the Roman Catholics) in parochial schools, but ordained ministers came to be looked upon as a *professional* group parallel to physicians or lawyers whose function was to take care of people's religious needs. In general, they were among the better edu-

cated in a given region, but their intellectual formation tended to be quite narrow like most professional training and specialized, for seminary training in denominational colleges and seminaries was now the standard preparation for ordination.

For the most part, ordained ministers in the early decades of the twentieth century were relatively well-trained and dedicated practitioners, socially respectable and dutifully committed to their pastoral tasks. But also for the most part they were unimaginative, at a time when the mounting crisis of Christianity demanded creative reconsideration of the structures and activity of the church. Dechristianization was a widely recognized phenomenon. The inadequacies of the parish approach to pastoral care in many contexts of industrialized society became increasingly evident; the outlook and human potential and Christian needs of the laity were being transformed by the technological and social forces at work in the world. Yet, ministerial activity retained much of the pattern it had acquired in the second half of the nineteenth century.

One unmistakable feature of ministerial activity in the early twentieth century was its organization. Some degree of organization is, of course, inevitable in an enduring society, and the various churches had their respective forms of polity long before the twentieth century. But that special emphasis on large-scale organization which so marks the modern world found a specific expression in the churches, even in communities such as the Baptists where local autonomy was a cardinal principle of church polity. No place was this more evident than in the United States. The quest for organized effectiveness brought increased structural unification. This brought a number of modifications to ministerial activity. Some ordained ministers became typical "organization men," in charge of denominational bureaus of various kinds; planning and direction of various church programs (catechetics, liturgical worship, adult education, etc.) came from regional or national offices. As regional or national church groups of one sort or another came into existence, the ordinary pastor found himself involved with the local chapter. Centralization was a general tendency, but it reached its zenith in the Roman Catholic community where directions came from the various Vatican bureaus to the episcopates of the world and fashioned an incredible identity of view and practice in hundreds of millions of Catholics. It was a church, at least on the surface, according to the mind of Vatican I.

This does not mean that ordained ministers were reduced to mere cogs in an ecclesiastical machine. There was at least as much individual dedication and initiative as one could find in most periods of history. This became evident when the aftermath of World War II brought forth the ferment in ministerial ranks which we experience today. But something does happen to a religious community when a corps of administrative technicians, as distinguished from the kind of authoritative leadership proper to a religious community, comes into controlling position. New types of relationship and evaluation come into existence (e.g., the "efficient manager" is promoted to pastoral responsibility); and while "ministry of word and sacrament" continues to be the theoretical description of the ministerial function, a somewhat different job description actually governs the activity of ordained minister.

Underneath all this, the increased professionalism, the organized efficiency, and the many successes of Christian ministry in the decades before World War II, there was great ferment and much anguished questioning. The very advances of the church, particularly in education and scholarly development of biblical studies and history and theology, in involving laity more actively in the life of the church, in moving towards liturgical revitalization, and in probing the possibilities of Christian reunion, had made more apparent the chasm between the ideal and the real in the postmodern world. But it was World War II that brought things to a head. How the war is to be situated in the history of *Realpolitik* or world economics or man's cultural evolution is for experts in those fields to judge; in the religious development of Christianity (indeed, it may well be that we can say "in the religious development of mankind") there is every indication that the experience of that war, with what immediately preceded it and resulted from it, is a watershed. What exactly ended with it, we cannot yet see with clarity; what began with it we can only imagine and dream about, and then hope or dread.

NOTES

1. An indication of the intense nationalist struggle against the ultramontanist viewpoint is provided by the concerted and bitter opposition to the Society of Jesus, opposition which finally led (in 1773) to the suppression of the order.

2. This is not to say that it was clearly seen as illusory by men of the eighteenth century; indeed, up to the present time uniformity and centralization of power are still considered by many as apt means of obtaining religious unity.

3. See E. Wilbur, *History of Unitarianism* (Boston, 1945), esp. p. 5, where he describes the three leading principles of the movement that eventuates in Unitarianism.

4. The United States provides, of course, a unique situation of nonestablishment according to law. However, even here there has been a subtle but important evolution away from cultural establishment of Protestantism as the official religion and towards a genuine and open pluralism. See F. Littell, *From State Church to Pluralism* (Chicago, 1962).

5. It is interesting to reflect that the classic post-Reformation discussion of the "four marks" of the church often stressed the link between unity and catholicity, but always in the direction of insisting that one could not properly speak of a religious

group being *catholic* unless it was *one*. There was not yet the realization that perhaps it could not properly be unified unless it was intrinsically catholic.

6. A detailed analysis of this historical progression as exemplified in the English situation is given by H. Davies in his *Worship and Theology in England*, vols. 3 and 4 (Princeton, 1961). See also, A. Vidler, *The Church in an Age of Revolution* (London, 1961), pp. 12–14. An interesting study of the influence exerted by the crisis mentality in these religious developments is given by K. Swart in his *The Sense of Decadence in Nineteenth-Century France* (The Hague, 1964).

7. See G. Cragg, *The Church and the Age of Reason*, rev. ed. (London, 1970), pp. 67–71.

8. Both Bossuet and Mohler were influenced by the French Jesuit François Veronius who in the early seventeenth century had broken from the distorting kind of polemic that had marked so much of the theological controversy of the preceding century. See F. Heyer, *The Catholic Church from 1648–1870* (London, 1969), pp. 37–38.

9. See R. Palmer, *Catholics and Unbelievers in Eighteenth-Century France* (Princeton, 1939), esp. pp. 179–81.

10. For a detailed description of this movement, particularly its connections with Jansenism, see E. Préclin, *Les Jansénistes du XVIIIe siècle et la Constitution civile du Clergé* (Paris, 1929). See also A. Goodwin, *New Cambridge Modern History* (Cambridge, 1961), vol. 8, pp. 686–90; and J. McManners, *The French Revolution and the Church* (London, 1969), pp. 15–18. His remarks earlier (pp. 10–13) about the nature of French anticlericalism give a good insight into the temper of the French Catholic church in the eighteenth century.

11. See Préclin, pp. 10–12.

12. See McManners, pp. 15–18.

13. See *ibid.*, pp. 19–79.

14. Spinoza, in his *Tractatus Theologico-Politicus* of 1670, had already anticipated many of the questions and critical positions of the later biblical criticism; the extent of his influence on these later developments is hard to determine, but a number of the German university centers where the new criticism flourished were also centers of interest in Spinoza's philosophy.

15. For a short account of the emergence of modern biblical scholarship, see R. Grant, *The Bible in the Church* (New York, 1960), pp. 118–75; and the essays by E. Carpenter ("The Bible in the Eighteenth Century," pp. 89–124) and G. Lampe ("The Bible Since the Rise of Critical Study," pp. 125–44) in *The Church's Use of the Bible*, ed. D. Nineham (London, 1963).

16. On the catalytic position of the French Revolution in the dechristianizing process, see B. Plongeron, *Conscience religieuse en Revolution* (Paris, 1969), esp. pp. 176–77; on the French situation later in the nineteenth century, see Swart, pp. 181–92. On the broader picture of European nineteenth-century liberalism and its opposition to Roman Catholicism, see R. Aubert, *Le pontificat de Pie IX*, vol. 21 of A. Fliche and V. Martin, *Histoire de l'Eglise depuis les origines jusqu'à nos jours* (Paris, 1935—), esp. pp. 224–61, 373–401.

17. What is hard to determine, of course, is the classification of specific influences as Christianizing or dechristianizing. The evangelical effort of the Wesleys quite clearly belongs on the Christianizing side, but the impact of Schleiermacher or Hegel, for example, is much more difficult to situate. Each thought of himself as fostering Christianity, each has been accused repeatedly of being a major influence in the loss of true Christian faith, each considered the other a threat to genuine Christianity.

18. Though limited to France, and therefore to a large extent to Catholicism, the two volumes of A. Dansette's *Religious History of Modern France* (New York, 1961) are an excellent guide to the nineteenth- and twentieth-century conflicts (and attempts at harmonization) between the church and modern secular society. A broader but less detailed picture is provided by the relevant essays (by J. Walsh, N. Sykes, D. Thomson, A. Cobban, and R. Greaves) in vols. 8–12 of the *New Cambridge Modern History*.

19. See Cragg, pp. 202–8; Vidler, pp. 34–39, 12–14.

20. See Vidler, pp. 90–95; Dansette, vol. 1, pp. 353–62.

21. It is interesting and perhaps quite significant that in late nineteenth-century Catholicism the American church became some kind of symbol of this modernist threat: this is the case of the Leo XIII's letter *"Testem benevolentiae"* (1899) which condemned the supposed heresy of Americanism. For an account of this strange case of ecclesiastical excitement over a "phantom heresy," see T. McAvoy, *The Americanist Heresy in Roman Catholicism* (Notre Dame, 1963).

22. See B. Tierney, *Medieval Poor Law* (Berkeley, Calif., 1959).

23. In a later chapter we will discuss the important formation of such groups (especially the Roman Catholic religious congregations) to provide for these needy.

24. In this regard, it is interesting to reflect on the manner in which, among the Roman Catholics who formed a large portion of this urban and immigration poor, the symbol of the pope acted as a principle of community identification.

25. An interesting discussion of this movement in the nineteenth century, and of the extent to which it itself became a religion, is given by B. Croce in the early chapters of his *History of Europe in the Nineteenth Century* (London, 1934), pp. 1–58. See also J. McManners, *Lectures on European History, 1789–1914* (Oxford, 1966), esp. pp. 400–420.

26. As we will see in chapter 13, in discussing patterns of preaching and catechetical instruction, the ministry of the various churches has been slow to break out of the pattern of stressing unquestioning acceptance of church officialdom.

27. At present, however, there are indications of some important shift in the value structure of persons in practically all portions of the world, a phenomenon which (if true) must be part of any present-day reflection on ordained ministry. See pp. 58–81 in my *Theology in an Age of Revolution* (New York, 1971).

28. See J. Dillenberger and C. Welch, *Protestant Christianity* (New York, 1954), pp. 166–78.

29. On the rise and decline of these various theories, and their interaction with Christian thought, see C. Dawson, *Progress and Religion* (London, 1945).

30. To identify and relate these forces would be, in effect, to produce an adequate theology of Christian history. Some indication of the immensity of this topic can be gained by studying the lengthy article (cols. 1634–2193) in the second volume of the *Dictionnaire de spiritualité*; the almost totally Roman Catholic orientation of this article can be supplemented by L. Bouyer's *Orthodox Spirituality and Protestant and Anglican Spirituality* (London, 1969). A recent and interesting attempt (though limited to Roman Catholic developments in its treatment of modern times) to present the historical evolution of the action-contemplation dialectic is T. Gannon and G. Traub's *The Desert and the City* (New York, 1969).

31. On Marx's idea of *praxis*, see H. Marcuse, *Reason and Revolution* (London, 1941), pp. 312–22; J.-Y. Calvez, *La pensée de Karl Marx*, 7th ed. (Paris, 1969), pp. 152–57, 372–404; R. Garaudy, *Marxism in the Twentieth Century* (New York, 1970), pp. 82–100.

32. See H. Schenk, *New Cambridge Modern History*, vol. 9, pp. 116–17.

33. See Vidler, pp. 106–11.

34. See McAvoy, pp. 110–28, 179–90.

35. C. Butler, *The Theology of Vatican II* (London, 1967), pp. 159–89.

36. It may well be misleading to use the word "personalism," but no better term seems at hand. As we have seen, "individualism" can be and often is employed to indicate the interest in the individual Christian's faith and conscience and relation to God, an interest that is characteristic of many of the great Reformers and specially characteristic of the Radical Reformation. Yet "individualism" carries connotations, and with some historical justification, of a lack of appreciation for community, especially in its structured forms. The classic terminology of "subjective/objective" is at least as confusing; indeed, the understanding of these words in various modern philosophers is so diverse

that a person with a neo-scholastic background will completely misunderstand a Kantian use of "objective."

37. See Dillenberger-Welch, pp. 122–40; J. McNeill, *History of the Cure of Souls* (New York, 1951), pp. 180–91, 210–17, 229–86; Cragg, pp. 100–106.

38. See Cragg, pp. 101–6.

39. See J. Collins, *God in Modern Philosophy* (Chicago, 1959).

40. One of the by-products of this apologetic development of fundamental theology was a further dislocation of questions about the relation of philosophy and theology, indeed of all questions about the relation of natural and supernatural—a dislocation that is still with us.

41. See C. Kunstler, *La vie quotidienne sous Louis XV* (Paris, 1953), pp. 306–7; W. Bruford, *Germany in the Eighteenth Century* (Cambridge, 1968), pp. 251–54; J. Lindsay, *New Cambridge Modern History*, vol. 7, pp. 269–73; Cragg, pp. 96–99, 120–28, 230–33.

42. See Lindsay, pp. 58–62.

43. See Cragg, *The Church and the Age of Reason*.

44. *Ibid.*, pp. 202–4.

45. See McManners, *French Revolution and the Church*, pp. 9–11.

46. See Cragg, pp. 229–33; R. Herr, *The Eighteenth-Century Revolution in Spain* (Princeton, 1958), pp. 29–34.

47. Vidler, pp. 12–13.

48. See Bruford, pp. 251–56; Kunstler, pp. 305–7; Davies, vol. 3, pp. 52–75.

49. See McManners, pp. 11–13; Cragg, pp. 128–33.

50. See W. Brock, *New Cambridge Modern History*, vol. 7, pp. 245–46; J. Brady and P. Corish, *History of Irish Catholicism* (Dublin, 1971), vol. 4, pp. 49–75; Cragg, pp. 133–36. One of the most striking instances of religious revival in the eighteenth century was the "Great Awakening" that took place in the American colonies. See A. Heimert, *Religion and the American Mind* (Cambridge, Mass., 1966).

51. See Dansette, esp. vol. 2, pp. 3–28.

52. On the dialectical movement of French religious and social ideas in the nineteenth century, see Swart, pp. 46–192.

53. See Dansette, pp. 23–28; see also E. Léonard, *Histoire générale du Protestantisme* (Paris, 1964), vol. 3, pp. 371–86, who passes a more negative judgment on the nineteenth-century history of French Protestantism: "En somme, le protestantisme ne s'est pas adapté à la France nouvelle. S'il fallait résumer d'une phrase l'histoire du protestantisme français au XIXe siècle, on pourrait dire que sa faiblesse essentielle résida dans ses querelles ecclésiastiques" (p. 386).

54. See Aubert, pp. 72–75.

55. See *ibid.*, pp. 137–51, 384–95; J. MacCaffrey, *History of the Catholic Church in the Nineteenth Century*, 2d ed. (Dublin, 1910), pp. 278–318.

56. See Aubert, pp. 132–36, 392–95; MacCaffrey, pp. 327–42.

57. See esp. Léonard, pp. 249–422.

58. On the nature and evolution of liberal Protestantism, see Dillenberger-Welch, *Protestant Christianity*, pp. 179–231.

59. See Léonard, pp. 306–11, who judges this development somewhat negatively, as downgrading individual religious experience: "Ainsi, le néo-luthéranisme s'oriente vers la seule nécessité des formulations correctes d'une doctrine correcte, au détriment des convictions et de la foi personnelles—dogmatisme; il insiste sur la puissance de l'autel, sur la valeur des services liturgiques, sur l'efficacité de l'agenouillement pour la prière—ritualisme" (p. 307).

60. See Vidler, pp. 45–55.

61. E. Fairweather, *The Oxford Movement* (Oxford, 1964), p. 8.

62. See J. Moorman, *History of the Church in England* (New York, 1954), p. 375.

63. See the passages from Wilberforce's *Doctrine of the Eucharist* (1853), reprinted in Fairweather, pp. 362–67.

64. Less famous than its counterpart at Oxford was an influential high church group at Cambridge which for the most part paralleled and supported the Oxford Tractarians. See J. White, *The Cambridge Movement* (Cambridge, 1962).

65. See Fairweather, p. 12: ". . . In the long run their doctrine of the eucharistic sacrifice and presence inevitably led to sweeping changes in liturgical usage."

66. On these free-church developments in nineteenth-century England, see Davies, vol 4. We will study more at length the American evolution of ministry in these various dissenting churches, for it was in the United States that they gained greatest strength and influence.

67. See C. Giblin, "Irish Exiles in Catholic Europe," vol. 4, pt. 3, of *History of Irish Catholicism* (Dublin, 1971).

68. See T. Cunningham, "Church Reorganization," vol. 6, pt. 7, of *History of Irish Catholicism*, pp. 11–15.

69. For a brief description of the evolution of U.S. Catholicism, see J. Ellis, *New Catholic Encyclopedia* (New York, 1967), vol. 14, pp. 425–48; on Canadian developments see G. Carrière, *ibid.*, vol. 3, pp. 2–9. Longer treatments are given by T. McAvoy, *A History of the Catholic Church in the United States*; D. de Saint-Denis, *L'Eglise catholique au Canada*, 6th ed. (Montreal, 1956); and W. Bull, *From MacDonnell to McGuigan* (Toronto, 1939). Though not intended to be a history of all aspects of U.S. Catholic priesthood, the recent volume edited by J. Ellis, *The Catholic Priest in the United States* (Collegeville, Minn., 1971) is a unique contribution to understanding the U.S. Catholic priesthood.

70. See Ellis, "The Formation of the American Priest," in A. Greeley, *The Catholic Priest in the United States* (Washington, D.C., 1972), pp. 3–110.

71. Perhaps the most striking and strange manifestation of this watchfulness was the condemnation in 1899 of "Americanism"; see McAvoy, *Americanist Heresy.*

72. See R. Trisco, "Apostolic Delegation in the U.S.," *New Catholic Encyclopedia*, vol. 1, pp. 690–93.

73. See McAvoy, *History*, pp. 192–302.

74. On the complex history of Catholic clerical attitudes towards and involvement in U.S. society, see D. O'Brien, "The American Priest and Social Action," in *Catholic Priest in the U.S.*, pp. 423–69.

75. Though there was a prevalent assumption (within Catholic circles) that seminaries provided a superior level of education, intellectual interests were not strong among the Catholic clergy during most of this period. However, as the twentieth century progressed there was a quiet development of scholarship (mostly in the sacred sciences), particularly though by no means exclusively among the members of religious communities whose specialized undertakings required advanced education. See M. Gannon, "Before and After Modernism: The Intellectual Isolation of the American Priest," in *The Catholic Priest in the U.S.*, pp. 293–383. However, this developing intellectualism was still marked by one of the characteristic traits of U.S. clergy, the tendency to identify with European thought rather than with the American intellectual heritage.

76. In church polity, the various churches in the U.S. were early forced to make certain nationalistic adjustments because of the War for Independence and the separation of church and state provision of the Constitution. See W. Sweet, *The Story of Religion in America* (New York, 1950), pp. 189–204.

77. *Ibid.*, pp. 44–116.

78. See H. Bosley, "The Role of Preaching in American History," *Preaching in American History*, ed. D. Holland (Nashville, 1969), pp. 17–35.

79. On the intermingling of Protestantism and the evolution of American institutions and experience, see M. Marty, *Righteous Empire* (New York, 1970). See also J. Wil-

son, "The Status of 'Civil Religion' in America," *The Religion of the Republic,* ed. E. Smith (Philadelphia, 1971), pp. 1–21.

80. See W. Herberg, *Protestant—Catholic—Jew* (New York, 1955), pp. 113–40, 250–54.

81. On the somewhat new status that came to the local minister in the American situation, see Marty, pp. 72–73.

82. See K. Latourette, *Christianity in the Revolutionary Age* (New York, 1958), vol. 3, pp. 86–91.

83. The classic study of the frontier situation was W. Sweet's *Religion on the American Frontier,* 4 vols. (New York, 1931–46); for a shorter treatment, see his *Story of Religion in America,* pp. 205–42.

84. See T. Miyakawa, *Protestants and Pioneers* (Chicago, 1964), pp. 45–58.

85. *Ibid.,* p. 49.

86. *Ibid.* There are interesting parallels between the ministerial evolution of primitive Christianity and the frontier practices of community validation of a minister's charism and of sending out "apostles" to form other communities.

87. See C. Johnson, *The Frontier Camp Meeting* (Dallas, 1955).

88. See Latourette, pp. 13–14.

CHAPTER 7

Ministry as Formation of Community

Differing views on the nature of Christian ministry and priesthood are grounded in differing soteriologies. This is clear from a study of history. Dependent upon the manner in which Christians look upon the action of God in Christ and upon the church's role in that action, they understand the function of Christian ministry. On the surface, proponents of opposed theologies of ministry support their respective positions by appeal to the New Testament evidence or to historical precedent or to the concrete needs within the church for ministration; but such appeal is inevitably colored by the soteriological perspective of each group. Consequently, no workable unity of opinion about Christian ministry, which could make a reunited Christian church possible, can exist unless it is the expression of a basic agreement about the reality of Christ's redeeming action.

Obviously, one cannot talk in terms of some definitive explanation of Jesus of Nazareth and his saving role, for it is increasingly apparent that theological reflection on Jesus as Christ and Lord has now moved in largely uncharted post-Chalcedonian directions. What we must do is understand as sharply as possible the real issues and differentiate clearly the various approaches to explaining the salvific function of Jesus. We must learn to delineate the implications for an understanding of Christian ministry of each approach, and then to examine the possible complementarity or irreducible opposition of these differing views in the hope of discovering a pluralism of insights that is compatible with the unity of faith that is needed if

the church is to be truly one and catholic.

It is no surprise that today's theology is wrestling in a manner that is quite disturbing to many in the church with the age-old question: Who is Jesus of Nazareth? Basically, responses to this question are attempts to give some meaning to "incarnation" as applied to Jesus. It is undeniable that the mythic elements in our understanding of the reality which John's Gospel calls "the Word becoming flesh" must be recognized, critically evaluated, and perhaps eliminated from our Christian language and understanding. It is also undeniable that the uniqueness and ultimacy of Christ and Christianity, a uniqueness and ultimacy that in some sense has always been an element of Christian faith, will vanish if Jesus the Christ is not "divine" in some proper and unparalleled sense. If one interprets the title "Son" to mean nothing more than an incomparable congruence of Jesus' attitudes and behavior with the divine design for mankind, and the title "Word" to mean only an unparalleled eminence of prophetic charism, then he should recognize that he is reducing Christianity to a humanistic moralism and the Fatherhood of God to a metaphor. Now there is certainly nothing wrong, as a matter of fact there is great value, in humanistic moralism or in the metaphorical aspects of God's fatherhood; but neither takes serious account of what the New Testament literature and centuries of Christian faith have meant by the *mystery* that has been revealed in Jesus of Nazareth.

Even if one takes the Johannine and Chalcedonian statements about the Incarnation of

Jesus quite literally, there is still a broad spectrum of understanding corresponding to phrases such as "true God and true man," "hypostatic union," "Son of God become man." One of the most basic differences might be expressed by the terms "static" and "dynamic." Historically, most of the theological and dogmatic explanation of the Incarnation has been quite "static." It has concentrated on the two elements in Christ, the divine and human "natures," defending and explaining the integrity and propriety and consequences of each in Christ, and on the union of these two elements in the one person (the Son, the second person of the Trinity). Particularly in Latin theology, such thought about the Incarnation has been "structural." Theological students have had to be warned against thinking about "two parts making up a whole" or about the two natures of Christ being simply juxtaposed. What added to the static understanding of Incarnation was the relatively static understanding of "divine immutability"; the Incarnation could in no way change or affect the divine element in Christ.

Without caricaturing the static quality of centuries of "structural" thought about the Incarnation, and recognizing that the enduring insights of this Christology must be retained in any "higher synthesis" that future theology may produce, it seems quite clear that we must probe more deeply into the dynamic aspects of the Incarnation. We must investigate the effect of God on man and of man on God in the incomparable union of the two in Christ. We must study the presence of divine salvific power in the existing and activity of this man Jesus, and reflect on the manner in which Jesus the man is "word," the unique created "translation" of God's own Word. The search must continue for an understanding of the role played by Christ, the Logos enfleshed, in the evolution of the created universe.

It is not a new insight that the resurrection of Jesus is a key to any understanding of him that one may possess. Christianity's earliest faith, from which all Christian belief and practice evolved, was essentially a faith in the risen Jesus who is Christ and Lord. Yet, the history of Christian theology and belief during the past century has highlighted the centrality of the Resurrection. These decades have seen innumerable attempts to "prove" or "disprove" the reality of Jesus' resurrection, interpret its nature as historical or transhistorical, explain it as "myth" or extrapolation of subjective expectations, examine its role in Christian faith and life, and see it as a symbol of the positive meaning of human experience or as the continuing personal influence of Jesus himself in his "new" context of human existence.

Clearly, if one believes that resurrection means that the historical Jesus passed through death into the new and ultimate state of human life which constitutes the fulfillment of created personality, this sets up a context of theological reflection that differs radically from the one that is grounded in the view that "resurrection" has no such "objective reality" but is rather a manner of expressing the unique importance of Jesus and his teaching. If one starts with the faith that Jesus of Nazareth still *is* humanly (however much that "humanly" may be transformed by the state of resurrection), and if one can dispel the illusion that he "has gone up to heaven and will only come back to earth on the last day," this opens up the possibility of explaining Christianity as a redeeming presence of this risen Christ to a community of believers and through them to all mankind. Resurrection then appears not just as the "proof" of Jesus' claims and promises, nor as some "meritorious cause" of men's salvation, but as the ever present source of new life. Moreover, the Father who in this context raises Jesus from the dead is not one who needed to be appeased by the obedient death of Jesus. He is the God who so loved the world that he sent his only-begotten Son to give men unending life, the God who knows no Sabbath but works to redeem the entire course of human history through the sacramentality of the risen Christ.

Jesus' mission is, then, one into whose fullness he entered only with his Passover. In the supreme statement of his Servanthood which occurred in his death and resurrection, he becomes the Christ and the Lord; he gains that full possession of the Spirit which enables him to minister to and transform human existence by that Spirit. Resurrection means not the peaceful result of Jesus' redeeming act but in fuller measure the continuation of his saving activity. However, even if one accepts such a belief about the continuing dynamic reality of the risen Christ, there can be basic differences of opinion about the nature of his saving action; one can think of him as dispensing (or being the instrument of his Father's dispensing) "grace," a mysterious inner energy that elevates man's nature to the level of the "supernatural"; or one can think of him working as the "word," influencing men's consciousness and motivations and thereby their activity; or one can think of him as working behind the scenes, carrying on a war against the powers of evil that strive in hidden fashion to deprive man of his God-given destiny; or one can think of him as continuously reconciling men to his Father by his unending worship and glorification. Without for the moment trying to assess the relative accuracy of these different points of view, it is quite clear that the understanding one has of Christian ministry will be affected basically by his view of the risen Christ.

A slightly different way of discovering the soteriological differences that underlie differing views of ministry is to examine the various meanings of "salvation." Much of classic theological discussion has driven a wedge between *creation* and *redemption*. Redemption is seen as the activity that God had to undertake after men destroyed the "initial plan" of creation; or redemption is viewed as the work of restoring creation to its primeval integrity; or creation is looked upon as a preliminary stage in God's activity in the world, a substratum for his personal activity in the work of redeeming mankind. As a result, "God the creator" is studied in separation from "God the redeemer." Yet, contemporary theological discussion, triggered at least partially by modern scriptural studies, has come to question this separation. Instead, the one process of the universe's evolution is seen as simultaneously creative and redemptive. One can speak of the Christic dimension of evolution, or one can talk of created reality in its ongoing development as sacramentalizing the dynamism of God's Spirit, or one can deny the validity of distinguishing "sacral" and "secular," or one can say that the "hermeneutic" of Christian interpretation of the world should treat that world as sacrament and not as allegory. These are but complementary ways of viewing "creation" and "redemption" as coextensive.

Another polarity that controls much theological consideration of salvation is that of *community* and *individual*. Historically, emphasis has shifted back and forth from one to the other. Most postmedieval religious thought has tended to consider "salvation" in individualistic terms. More recently a reaction has set in, both in theology and in the attitudes of people in general, against such a "save *my* soul" mentality. In some instances this has resulted in an excessive attention to the social dimension at the expense of the individual, but a more promising development is the growing realization that the polarity of community and individual need not imply an opposition of these two elements but rather an enriching interdependence. Individual humans cannot be liberated and brought to genuine personal fulfillment unless the social structures in which they are involved are "saved"; on the other hand, any attempt to foster the evolution of genuine and fruitful human community is doomed to failure unless the individuals who comprise the community develop their personal potentialities. Participation by Christian ministry in the work of "salvation" is, obviously, forced to honor this reciprocal influence of individual and community in order to be truly effective.

Yet another "opposition" that has played a major role in Christian thinking about salvation is the relation between man's soul and body. Enough has been written in recent years about the influence of "Platonic" anthropology on Christian ideas and attitudes;

actually, much of this effort to blame Greek thought for dichotomizing man and bequeathing to succeeding centuries of European history an excessively spiritual view of human nature needs to be carefully evaluated. Be this as it may, there is no avoiding the historical evidence which indicates that for many centuries the Christian notion of salvation was linked with liberation of man's soul from the impediment of his body; one spoke regularly of "saving my soul." Christian faith honored verbally the teaching of Genesis that the material world was created good and the teaching of John's Gospel that the Word became flesh; but little was done to make the implication of such scriptural teaching an intrinsic and positive element of soteriology. Perhaps more importantly, the linking of "spiritual" with "soul" (i.e., nonbodily) overshadowed the critically important link of "spiritual" to the Holy Spirit, and therefore obscured the specifically Christian understanding of "sanctification."

Closely allied with this historical emphasis on freeing man's soul from the "down-pull" of the body was the prominence of concern about sin, a concern that at times became unhealthy and obsessive. Evil took on identity as a personal force roughly parallel in power to God though, of course, one always stated the superiority of God and his salvific action. This force not only attacked man "from outside" but worked as a destroying element within man's own inner being. Evil activity was rooted in this inner sinfulness and witnessed to a man's being dominated by sin; on the contrary, good actions (or the absence of evil actions) evidenced the triumph within a man of the powers of good. Such emphasis on sin or lack of sin focused religious attention on the ethical and tended to reduce faith to moralism. One must guard against simplistic historical judgments in this regard. From its beginnings Christianity was seen to be a way of life, and it would be an emasculated faith that did not express itself by translating the Christian law of love into daily behavior since moral idealism is intrinsic to the gospel. Yet Christian faith maintains that "salvation"

transcends correct ethical behavior, it condemns as "Pelagian" the notion that man's own good actions can bring him to his destined goal of union with God, and (at least from time to time) it states the primacy of Spirit rather than laws.

Examination and evaluation of these various historical understandings of "grace" and "salvation" take on new importance in the contemporary situation of the church and its theological reflection. The reason is that alternative soteriologies, at least apparently nonreligious and certainly not formally Christian, have come to prominence in the modern world. Expressions of an historical evolution of thought and experience that is centuries-old, these secular theories of human salvation present a radical challenge to present-day Christianity's claim to have a unique and ultimate path to life. Therefore they radically challenge the very existence of anything like a Christian ministry. "Secularization" is not a new phenomenon in Christian history; much less is it a fad that has fascinated the liberal fringe of the church these last few years and that will soon be forgotten as attention returns to the essential issues of Christian faith. Secularization is an essential issue; it has been a continuous and unavoidable challenge since the inception of the church. If anything is new in our present situation it is the realization within the church that the matter cannot be solved authentically by divorcing Christianity and "the secular." This realization has been and is one of the most powerful influences in forcing a reconsideration of Christian ministry.

If a particular understanding of the risen Christ and of "salvation" is integral to one's soteriology, so also is the view one has of the church and specifically of the church's role in the process of Christ saving mankind. This will touch upon the manner in which one understands the relationship between "internal" and "external" aspects of the church; but inevitably a discussion about Christian ministry and its soteriological role must draw attention to the external aspects, the institutionalization, of the Christian community. And perhaps most basically it must face the question: What difference does it make whether a certain agent of salvation or a certain course of saving activity is "official"? It seems difficult to countenance the notion that the divine saving action is tied to the exercise of jurisdictional power within the church; yet centuries of Christian faith have seen this as a correct reading of "Whatever you bind on earth will be bound in heaven. . . ." In this context, obedience to the church which has usually meant obedience to church officials and to the laws they have enacted is equivalently obedience to God, and therefore the condition for achieving one's destiny.

Certainly, one cannot dismiss the real function of the Christian community and its official leadership in the work of salvation; to do so would be to reduce the church to a parasitic and introverted existence. Yet, it seems self-evident that the leadership of the Christian community should be helping the members of that community to develop their own personal integrity and autonomy, and to grow in their own capacity to form conscience judgments appropriate to the situations of life. These leaders should not presume to be the conscience of the Christian people, providing a detailed listing of "do's" and "don'ts" that will eliminate people's need to make their own critical choices. Again, it seems quite apparent that the leadership of the church should be encouraging people to confront maturely the realities of their world, which means facing the presence of evil and the tension of "worldly" values with the viewpoint of the gospel. Certainly, this requires prudent preparation of Christians for what is a difficult and challenging task; it also requires guidance and counsel during the actual conduct of Christian life. But it does not imply the kind of paternalistic protection from reality which denies to people the opportunity to exercise their Christian responsibilities.

History indicates, however, that it is all too easy for church officials to drift into such a paternalistic understanding of pastoral care and for the bulk of Christians to accept, even welcome, such an approach. Hidden in this situation is a theological understanding of "salvation" which sees the Christianization of the individual as an almost magical process, a process in which his own activity is merely a condition that must be fulfilled so that God will bless and sanctify him as a reward. Accompanying such a view of salvation is an interpretation of "mediation" (obviously, mediation by those in official positions) that has consistently bothered thoughtful Christians through many centuries. It is an interpretation that stresses both in doctrine and religious practice the need for ordinary Christians to reach God *through* the activity of church officials. Whether this view be right or wrong it is quite clear that it conditions basically the manner in which one thinks about the role of the church's ordained ministers.

"Models" of the Church

Not completely separate from the implicit soteriologies we have been discussing, but distinct and important enough to merit special attention in any discussion of Christian ministry and priesthood, are the "models" according to which Christians have viewed the church. What lies behind the importance of these models is the controlling influence of sense experience and imagination on all levels, even the most "rational," of human consciousness. Historically, a number of models (military, political, medical, etc.) have shaped Christian understanding of the church; often, several models have been simultaneously operative at a given point in history, or for that matter in the consciousness of an individual Christian. To describe them, however briefly, will aid us in clarifying and appraising the various ways in which Christian ministry has been understood.

One of the most basic, but also one of the most elusive, models for the church is that of the "moral entity." Whether one uses an image such as "holy mother church" or not, there is a certain personification of the church as a protecting or directing agent that acts upon Christians and to whom Christians are to relate themselves in loyalty and devotion. This "moral entity" is not identified with the Christians who make up the church, not even in their corporate Christian existence; rather, it has a certain identity of its own. This identity is real and powerful in the consciousness of Christians, so real and powerful that the bulk of Christians have lost for many centuries the sense of themselves being the church: "the church" is this other reality to which they are related through faith and religious practice. While this mythic figure of the church first took on historically the character of "sacred personality," it quickly assumed characteristics of "legal personality." The church came to be identified increasingly with its governing structures, an identification made both by rulers and by the ruled. It is both interesting and instructive to study the manner in which ordained ministers (particularly those in administrative activity) have often felt a greater concern about this "mythic church" than about the Christian people who are the church.

Another model which inevitably affects one's notion of the church is the cosmological myth that is prevalent in a culture at a given historical period. One possibility is that one views the church as an integral component of the cosmic geography; the other possibility is that the church in its structure is paralleled to the structure attributed to the cosmos. There are instances of both possibilities in the history of the church. Perhaps the clearest instance of this sort of thing, and certainly one of the most influential, was the Dionysian image of the stratified (hierarchical) church fitting into the larger stratified structure of the created universe. And as an instance of the manner in which attributes drawn from the cosmic myth are transferred to one's understanding of the church we might cite the recurrent (and futile) hope of "restoration." This dream of going back to the "good old days" before the French Revolution, or before the Reformation, or before the "Catholicizing" of the primitive church is closely linked to the view that there exists some ideal structure for the world and the church, that this ideal guided God in creating the world and in instituting the church, that man in his capitulation to evil has turned away from this ideal structure, and that we should work to restore things to the way they once were and really ought to be. Quite evidently, such a view of the world and of the church is radically incapable of confronting the evidence that has driven modern thought to an evolutionary understanding of man and the world.

Still another model that has exerted major influence on Christian thinking about the church is the political model. Christianity is not, of course, unique in transferring to religion the images drawn from man's political activity; many other religions have imagined that the "heavenly city" was conducted along the same lines as the "earthly city." Still, the application of the political image to the Christian church has had a major impact on the historical evolution of ecclesiastical institutions and of theology about the church. And this kind of "politicizing" of Christianity was carried still further as the church acquired for many centuries the dubious privilege of being the "established religion."

Connected with this political model is the long-standing argument about the nature of authority in the church. Is it permanently determined by divine institution to be monarchical, or can it adjust in certain historical situations (such as the twentieth century) to a more democratic form of governance? Actually, the Christian community may not be faced with such an "either/or"; it may well be that the course of action open to us is not a shift from one political model (monarchy) to another (democracy) but entirely away from a political model. There is enough evidence, both scriptural and historical, to suggest that such a shift would not only be permissible but even highly desirable.

Since mankind's political activity has almost always included the conduct of war, it is not surprising that the military model has colored Christian notions about the church. The Christian community is God's army, pledged to waging for him a holy war against the forces of evil; the ordained ministers of the church are the officers in that army. Historically, it has not always been clear whether Christians in a given context were fighting God's wars or whether they were enlisting God to fight with them in their own wars. But there is no question about the prominence and powerful influence of the image of "crusade." Such an image may have attached to it a certain glamour and overtones of heroism, but its application to Christian life in the church is more than dubious. It carries with it the isolationist connotations of the church being a fortress that protects Christians on the inside from the evils of the outside world and from which these Christians sally forth to demolish "the heathen and the infidel."

The incompatibility of the fortress image of the church becomes quite clear when we bring it into conjunction with a New Testament passage such as Ephesians 2:14, which speaks of Christ as "our peace, who has . . . broken down the dividing walls of hostility." Such incompatibility is less clear when we come to the monastic model; it also has implications of "walls," implications of "retreat from the world," and implications of stratification within the Christian community. But it is not clear whether such implications are intrinsic to formally dedicated religious community life or whether they have somewhat accidentally accrued to it in the historical evolution of religious orders. This much seems clear: such dedicated Christian communities have been and still are seen as attempts to live Christianity more intensely. Therefore, they should logically serve as models for Christian life as a whole, though at the same time the life of the community as a whole is a norm for what the dedicated religious communities should be. Historically, the application of the monastic model depended upon the actual structure and conduct of monastic communities, which were not always ideal and to some extent at least were rooted in truncated soteriology. Moreover, the application of the monastic model to the church as a whole was to some extent a negative one. The monastic ideals and way of life were not meant for "ordinary" Christians, the laity were nonmonks and therefore not intended to pursue Christian contemplation, just as they were

nonclerics and therefore intended to be receptive rather than active members of the church. The "walls" of the monastic model have existed not only between the monastery and the world but between the monastery and the rest of the church.

The use of one or another model is probably unavoidable in the Christian's thought about the church, but an awareness of the distortion that such use introduces into our understanding should lead to two conclusions. First, if some model does promise to be helpful as an aid to formulating Christian insight about the reality of Christian community existence, then we should use it critically, knowing that we are involved with metaphor and must therefore be careful not to over-apply the metaphor. Second, and more important, we should let the Christian community be what it is and not try to categorize it as something else. Our starting point in probing its deeper reality must be our experience of being the church, an experience that we try to understand as accurately as possible by the use of "scientific" methodologies (whether sociological, or psychological, or phenomenological, or some other) and by studying the centuries-long experience of Christians before us. This experience, both immediate and vicarious, should provide our basic image of the church. Such use of our own experience of participation in the Christian community as *the* model for understanding the church is, of course, precarious. Our particular experience (of liturgy, Christian service, etc.) may not be adequate; it may even be traumatic and misleading. But only if our view of the nature of Christianity is grounded in our own experience can membership in the Christian community be interiorized and become part of the living faith of individual Christians.

The Theology of Ministry

If the "experiential" model is to be basic to our understanding of the church (and elements in it such as its ministry), an historical-descriptive method by which one gains knowledge about the present reality of the church through recapturing as far as possible the experience of Christianity's origin and evolution must play a central role in an ecclesiology. However, even if one attempts to pursue this method as objectively as possible, it is impossible to do so without theological presuppositions—more specifically in this case, without one or other of the soteriological stances we described earlier. There can be widespread agreement that the church finds its origin in the death and resurrection of Jesus of Nazareth, but at the same time widespread disagreement as to the meaning of such a statement.

Taking the soteriological viewpoint that "resurrection" means that Jesus of Nazareth continues to live and work as Christ and Lord and that he is constantly present to the Christian community in a variety of ways, then the "originating" of the church through the death and resurrection of Christ is an ongoing historical process. One can, obviously, single out the temporal beginnings of this process and refer to that as "the origin of the church"; but it would be a mistake to limit to that brief period of history Christ's input into the existence of the Christian community. To take seriously the presence of Christ to the church or the animation of the historically evolving church by the Spirit of Christ is to admit that terms such as "institution by Christ" or *de jure divino* cannot be limited to the earliest decades of Christianity. Not just the first community of his immediate disciples but the church in its entire historical development comes into being under the impact of the risen Christ and his Spirit.

Without taking any particular theological interpretation of either Christian faith or the church, it seems apparent that the Christian community is dynamically constituted by a shared faith in Christ, by a shared experience of his continuing presence. This is ultimately the distinctive characteristic of the church, that which differentiates it from other religious or social groupings. Yet, in any given historical situation the sociological reality of the church does not correspond totally to this a priori judgment. The common unifying at-

titude, to the extent that there is one, is a mixture of religious and ethical and social viewpoints in which the specifically Christian point of view can be overshadowed by opinions that are either unrelated or opposed to the basic traditions of Christianity. Not infrequently, the mentality of the Christian church has drifted towards a legalistic and moralizing view of Christian community existence. Absorption with external structures and practices has drawn attention away from the unifying activity of Christ's Spirit. Even more paradoxically, the critical role of Jesus as unique mediator between man and God has been professed verbally but not honored practically. A critical aspect of this has been the way in which classical trinitarian theology has largely bypassed the historical reality of the man Jesus. The basic problem with such views is that they thwart the authentic existence and evolution of the church. They tend to make it a religious group committed to a "revealed message" rather than a community formed by shared devotion to a person.

But if one does retain the insight of Christ's presence to the church and his continuing gift of the Spirit, an insight that has never been completely absent from Christian consciousness, it is possible to speak meaningfully of the church as "the extension of Christ in history," not in the sense that Christians are the successors of Jesus but in the sense that they are a sacrament through which he can still make himself redemptively present to human history. Retention or loss of this insight has played an important role in Christian understanding of ordained ministry. It has been quite common to speak of ordained ministers as "legates of Christ" or "representatives of Christ" or even "vicars of Christ." But these and similar designations can be understood within the context of the entire church embodying and sacramentalizing the presence of Christ, or they can express the idea that the ordained ministry "carries on" for Christ here below, since he himself has gone up to heaven. The latter view, which is patently grounded in an image of Christ "going up to heaven" in his resurrection and ascension, has had incredible influence on centuries of Christian thinking and has been the source of no end of theological and ecclesiastical conflict.

One of the less happy developments in the church's self-understanding was the gradual limitation to the ordained clergy of the notion of actively representing Christ. Though intrinsically it was the entire community that was body and sacrament, the bulk of Christians (the laity) was early reduced to passivity within the life of the church. This passivity found expression in the laity's role (or lack of role) in liturgy, in the retreat of laity from active evangelical witness, and most basically in the laity's Christian self-image. Fortunately, in more recent times there has been some recovery of the understanding that the entire Christian community is the body of Christ, sharing in Christ's prophetic-priestly role, "ordained" in baptism to evangelical witness, to concerned service in the world, and to Eucharistic worship of the Father in union with Christ.

During the centuries-long evolution of the church one of the critical objectives of Christians, and especially of church officials, has been the preservation of genuine unity. However, though the effort to achieve or maintain a true community has pervaded the church's history, the understanding of the unity that would be desirable has been drastically different from one historical period to another or from one group of Christians to another. In the twentieth century, as we struggle to clarify our goals in the effort of ecumenical reunion, we are living through one of the clearest instances of such differing views of "desirable Christian unity."

From the beginning of Christian history there has been the recognition that sin and error are divisive influences and that they must be curbed if the Christian community is not to fragment. Without disagreeing with this basic insight into the need for some discipline in Christian doctrine and behavior, one can disagree with the manner in which such discipline has often been sought. There has been a recurring ecclesiastical policy that the key to the solution lies in increased centralization of authority and administration and in monolithic formulation of doctrine, submission to this formulation being obtained through the centralized church government. Such an approach has had short-term success, particularly when Christians have believed their salvation to be conditioned by ecclesiastical jurisdiction. But it does not take account of the legitimate pluralism that exists in Christian insight and conscience, a pluralism that is not only unavoidable and therefore tolerable but that is positively desirable because it is an expression of the catholicity of Christian faith.

It would be presumptuous to suggest any ready and simple solution to the problem of obtaining genuine unity of faith without jeopardizing individual belief and freedom of conscience. Yet, it is clear that two elements must be part of any realistic and viable solution. There must be some form of "spiritual direction" that can guide Christians as they form their own understandings and conscience according to the most authentic insights and traditions of Christianity, and as the ground for such practical spiritual direction there must be a developed pneumatology which can aid the Christian community (and its individual members) in the perennial and difficult task of "discerning the Spirit." No amount of threat or coercion by ecclesiastical officials, no amount of doctrinal decrees, can substitute for these two elements in obtaining genuine unity of faith within the church.

In the complex dialectic that constantly brings into being a living community such as the church, the inviolability of individual faith and freedom must interact with the corporate understanding and decisions of the community, and both individual and corporate faith of Christians at any given time in history must resonate creatively and compatibly with the faith of earlier Christian generations. This raises the whole question of "tradition," its nature, its limits, and the instruments of its operation. As in so many other questions that we have mentioned, there can be no hope of giving a definitive response, but it does seem that "tradition" and allied notions such as "apostolic succession" must relate most basically to the Christian community as a whole. Certain agencies, for example, the episcopacy, may have a specific function relative to the preservation, development, and transmission of Christian faith; however, the process of tradition is not confined to any such agency (or group of agencies) but rather involves the complementary activity of the entire church.

For most of the church's history, the problem of fostering the appropriate kind of unity within the church has been aggravated by the intertwining of ecclesial and civil interests and structures; the effort to maintain the unity of the church has often been inseparably mixed with efforts to achieve political unity. Church and civil governments have frequently depended upon one another for support; each has expected the other to use its power to preserve the situation in which authority is respected and laws observed and unity thereby preserved. For many centuries this interpenetration of the civil and the ecclesiastical was linked with the notion of the *societas christiana*, the view that there was the one Christian people with two complementary leaderships, civil and ecclesiastical rulers. Ideal as this notion of a unified society might seem, and it has not yet died for those who dream of a "restoration," both historical experience and theological analysis indicate that it is unworkable and undesirable. To give just one basic reason: the kind of unity proper to the Christian church, a unity that is grounded in genuine communication of faith among Christians, cannot possibly come by law and government either civil or ecclesiastical. There is no easy way to achieve the unity of the church, precisely because it is, and is meant to be, a living and evolving reality. Some tension among "competing" groups and goals and insights and values is inevitable and, if confronted positively and resolved in a spirit of genuine charity, a source of creativity and enrichment. Unification of the worldwide church is desirable, but it should not be achieved in a manner that destroys the

healthy autonomy of the local Christian community. Considerable pluralism in theological opinion, in liturgical expression, in styles of spirituality, even in doctrinal formulation, can be a sign of catholicity; but it must be accompanied by the basic agreement about faith and life which permits men and women to identify with one another as Christians. Or again, institutionalization is unavoidable and appropriate external structures can enable a community of people to express their corporate existence and achieve their corporate goals; but structures tend always to grow rigid and self-perpetuating, and so the church must always work to maintain flexibility in faith formulas and religious practices.

As one reflects on the historical evolution of the church and on the extent to which a truly fraternal community in faith has characterized that evolving experience, it becomes clear that one of the enduring divisions within the church has been that between clergy and laity. Perhaps it would be better to modify that judgment and situate the division between rulers and ruled, for in many situations the lower clergy have tended to identify with the people and form a community with them rather than with the ruling group in the church. On the other hand, those in positions of power and authority have consistently identified with one another in a special fashion and formed a "community of rulers" within the larger community of believers. Quite early in the church's history, this special status of the ruling group within the church was canonized as being "of divine institution"; and even when, as in the Protestant Reformation, there were groups that refused the authority of these rulers and formed their own Christian communities some form of division between clergy and laity quickly arose in these communities.

Without denying the obvious need for leadership in any community of human beings, nor the fact that different persons in the church will have quite different degrees of commitment to Christianity and consequently different degrees of involvement in and responsibility for the activity of the church, we can say that the understanding of authority in the life of the church must be basically changed, that there is no place in the church for "rulers," and that the clergy/laity division was to a large extent a deviation from the authentic ideal of Christian community and no theological justification can be found for allowing it to continue. This does not deny the intrinsic need for specialized ministries in the church, nor the need for certain individuals to be officially ordained for one or other of these ministries. What it does deny is the equation of designated (ordained) ministry with either "superior status" or "ruling."

Origin of Christian Ministry

It is not enough to criticize past views of Christian ministry, nor does it suffice to say what that ministry is not. Some attempt must be made to grasp more positively the nature and function of ministry within the church. Theological investigation of this question cannot, of course, proceed profitably in an a priori manner, so a quick analysis of the actual origin and evolution of Christian ministry (which we have studied at length in the preceding chapters) will be helpful.

All Christian ministry finds its origin in the salvific ministry of Jesus himself; throughout history, Christian theology is united in recognizing this principle. There has also been agreement on the principle that all authentic Christian ministry involves a participation in Christ's own ministerial mission and power, but there has been considerable disagreement as to the nature of this participation. If one adopts, as we have done, the view that Jesus in his risen life as Christ and Lord remains actively present to and operative through the Christian community, then "participation in the ministry of Christ" means an ongoing cooperation between Christ and the community in the work of establishing the kingdom of God, i.e., achieving the destiny of mankind. And in this view, Christ's "institution" of Christian ministry begins in his own undertaking of ministerial activity and continues in sharing this with his disciples. "Institution by

Christ" is not limited to some point of beginning but implies a constant historical association of Christ and Christians in the tasks of ministerial service.

The very fact that Christian ministry is participation in Christ's ministry should warn us against driving too large a wedge between "ministry" and "priesthood." The heart and culmination of Jesus' own ministerial service to his fellow humans undoubtedly came in his death and resurrection, which is also his supreme act of priestly sacrifice. By way of anticipation, we might here suggest that Jesus' "priesthood" and "priestly sacrifice" have to do more with his *being*: in his being the risen Christ he *is* sacrifice, whereas his "ministry" has to do with the *activities* of service that flow from this priestly-sacrificial way of being.

Historical studies of the church's origin have made it quite clear that one must abandon the notion that Jesus himself described and established a structure for the primitive Christian communities and then designated certain disciples (especially the Twelve) to fill these designated positions of community governance. It does seem that he formed a small group of followers, who could and did provide central leadership for the community of believers which came into existence with the Easter event. But it was left to these disciples to provide prudently for the structural needs of the early Christian communities. This they did by assessing the particular requirements of a community that was constituted by faith in the risen Christ, and either adapting already familiar instrumentalities (such as groups of governing elders) or devising new means, for example, their own Christian catechesis, to meet these requirements. Granting the essentially extraordinary context of their community existence, granting also the directive impulse coming from the Spirit, the approach of the early Christians and their leaders to the establishment of ministries was quite pragmatic. They attempted to provide the kinds of ministration that were needed to establish and maintain the kinds of community which would nurture faith and hope and charity. This pragmatic approach continued over the centuries to characterize the evolution of structures in the church, more specifically the evolution of ministry. Changes and innovations were made in the light of the needs that arose, and then theological reasoning was devised to justify these new patterns.

One of the clearest manifestations of this pragmatic approach is provided by the manner in which residential ministries succeeded itinerant ministries. While the early communities were being founded and stabilized, the role of the traveling apostles was of critical importance. It was such an apostle who initially evangelized a group; it was he who remained with them for a time and helped them to come into existence as a Christian community; it was he, or some co-worker, who kept in contact with the infant community and periodically visited it to check on its development and to help solve whatever problems had arisen. As these communities became more self-sufficient, however, the role of the itinerant ministry gradually gave way to the activity of leaders within the community itself.

Yet, if it is incorrect to think of Christ personally establishing various ministerial offices for the church and assigning functions and authority to these various offices, it is equally incorrect to think of these various ministerial functions as originating through purely natural processes. At least if one is to take seriously the faith viewpoint of Paul's letters to the Corinthians or of the Acts of the Apostles (to take but two examples), one must see behind the observable emergence of these ministerial functions the action of the risen Christ and his Spirit. To put it another way, ministerial role is the expression of charism. Not only such manifestly "charismatic" activities as prophecy are rooted in this empowering by the Spirit, but also regularized teaching and structured governing. This means that one cannot simply contrast "charism" and "institution" in the life of the church. Institutions themselves are meant to be the organs through which the Spirit-animated community expresses its life, and whatever charisms are granted to individuals are given for the sake of the unity and vitality of the institutionalized church.

Yet, there is a certain inevitability about the process in which societal functions and roles lose their flexibility and become overly formalized. The history of Christianity reflects this in the rapid clericalization of ministry, the early and persisting association of "power to minister" with "occupying an office," and the identification of ministerial function with "full-time professional occupation." That same history reflects also the persistent suspicion of the "charismatic," a suspicion that is partially justified and partially unjustified. It is justified because of the frequency of supposed "charismatics" who in many cases prove a seriously disruptive force in the community, and it is unjustified because the distrust of the charismatic is to some extent a fear of the new and the unknown and a reluctance to alter already established patterns of action.

Today we are faced with the possibility and the need to pay renewed respect to the action of the Spirit in the community, and specifically to respect the Spirit's charismatic designation of Christians for special ministerial roles. Discovery of such designation is not easy; it is part of the perennial problem of the discernment of spirits in the church. Yet, to ignore such action of the Spirit is to "sin against the light" and to presume that the human direction of the church is more trustworthy than the divine. Moreover, since the discernment of spirits is something that involves the entire church, not just its official leadership, the entire community must in ways appropriate to a given instance participate in the discovery of the charisms granted to individuals or groups for the sake of the church. Public acknowledgment of these charisms and therefore of the designation of Christians to certain ministerial functions will constitute the essence of "ordination."

History has bequeathed to us a question concerning the charisms of ministry that is basic to our entire discussion of specialized ministries, a question to which we may be able to give no satisfactory answer but one that still must be faced honestly. The question: Is there one basic "pastoral charism" of which all the other charisms (prophecy, teaching, healing, etc.) are elements and which, if given fully to any one person or group, contains in preeminent form all the other charisms? Very specifically the question pertains to the office of bishop and to the historical evolution in which the episcopacy absorbed into itself the other ministerial functions of the church. Most present-day discussion of Christian ministry, even by those who do not subscribe to episcopacy as a necessary or even worthwhile element of church polity, seems to presume that there is some one generic reality called "ministry" which can find differing expressions. Yet, there is increasing evidence that this presumption must be challenged, and that we must rather think of distinct ministries which derive their being from the rich charismatic endowment of the Christian community and not from some supreme pastoral office or charism. Taken in this context, the tension that can arise among those possessing diverse charisms will be healthily and productively resolved, not by one ministerial group passing judgment on the others but by the faith and charity of the community as a whole.

Even if there were one charism that included implicitly all the others, this would not according to the theological viewpoint of the New Testament be the charism of "governing" (*episkopein*) but rather that of prophecy. Jesus himself is theologically described in the New Testament writings as Messiah (i.e., kingly in some ideal fashion) and priest ("according to the order of Melchizedek") and prophet; but it is his prophetic function that acts to reinterpret basically the other two functions. So, too, in the earliest Christian decades there was some recognition of prophets as leaders in worship and in direction of the community. However, it seems more accurate to consider the various charisms as flowing from the prophetic character of the church rather than from the "office" of a special prophetic group in the church.

It may well be that episcopacy came to be considered as the depository and source of all other ministerial functions in the church because charism came to be associated with "office." Naturally, the special spiritual empowering connected with episcopacy was thought of as something that happened to the man who was consecrated bishop and not as something that happened to an abstraction called "the episcopal office." Yet, one can think of this special power as being granted to a man precisely because he comes to occupy this office, or as something that is granted to a man who then (because he is Spirit-empowered) is appointed to the office. Historically, it was the first of these two alternatives that became dominant and in many situations almost exclusive, with the result that all charismatic functions in the church came to be thought of as "offices." In this context of "official" ministerial roles it is easy to see how the idea arose of a hierarchically arranged order of ministries in which power flowed downward from the preeminent office of bishop (or pope). Later we will examine more carefully the nature of authority within the church, and therefore this attachment of "spiritual power" to an office; yet in doing this we will not be resurrecting the Donatist problem. Rather, we will suggest that the "objective power" attached to the activity of those ordained for sacramental ministry derives from performing an action as a sign of the church's faith. Because a man through his ordination possesses public recognition as a witness to the church's faith he is enabled to act as a "word" of the church; but the effectiveness of his action comes from that action being the church's *word* and not from some other power that is attached to the office which the man occupies.

However one may wish to evaluate what happened, the historical evolution of Christian ministry was one in which the "pastoral office" absorbed the other ministerial functions. In its earlier stages the collegial character of this pastoral ministry was quite marked; both the episcopacy and the presbyterate were considered to be possessed and exercised corporately, the presbyterate evidencing more the collegiality within a given community, the episcopacy testifying rather to the bond among the communities. When one reflects on this early historical situation and on what evolved from it a number of questions arise. One basic question that has far-reaching practical implications is whether the episcopacy is the basic *collegium* to which the presbyters are then associated, or whether the presbyterate is the basic *collegium* within which the episcopacy has a special role. This question cannot be answered by appealing to history because, as we have seen, the situation became hopelessly confused: pastoral ministry especially as exercised by bishops, was quite early identified with priesthood and so for many centuries the *sacerdotium* (including bishops and presbyters) was looked upon as the fundamental *collegium*. Moreover, the basic identification of a person as a member of the *sacerdotium* came not from his community association with other "priests" (though this was certainly an important factor) but from his possession of the power to consecrate the Eucharist. However, this sacerdotal community involving both bishops and presbyters does not stand in historical continuity with the early presbyterate; rather, it is a broadened participation in the episcopal *collegium* and its function. As for the presbyterate which the early Christian centuries knew, it seems gradually to have disappeared from the life of the church and to have found only partial rebirth in the role of "elders" in some Reformation communities. This may appear to be a strange judgment about the historical evolution of the presbyterate, since the word "presbyter" as a designation for pastors who are not bishops remains in continuous usage up to the present and is used to refer to the bulk of ordained ministers in the church. The presbyterate does not seem to have disappeared. However, the presbyterate in this more recent sense, i.e., those ordained ministers who regularly and ordinarily exercise the pastoral function, is quite a different body from the early Christian presbyterate. The latter was not a group assigned to certain ministerial functions. One or other "presbyter" might undertake some ministry, but

this was not consequent upon his being presbyter; the word *"presbyteros"* was not a functional term such as *"episkopos"* or *"diakonos."* Rather, the *presbyteroi* within a community acted as a corporate leadership, seeing that the necessary ministries were provided but not necessarily exercising these ministries themselves. To be a presbyter did not mean to be an assistant to the bishop, or the bishop's delegate, or a "lesser bishop"; it meant being a member of this group which acted quite autonomously though (at least ideally) in harmony with the bishop. It was the deacon, not the presbyter, who was the bishop's man. Before long, however, the presbyters were co-opted into permanent assistance to the bishops; the corporate function and identity of the presbyterate diminished and then disappeared; presbyters became deacons with fuller powers, though they often preferred to think of themselves as bishops with lesser powers.

What is important theologically about this development is not the way in which ministerial authority and official leadership passed into the hands of the bishops, but rather the fact that the episcopal function came to be understood as the epitome of ministry and the model for any understanding of ministry. A theology of the presbyterate could only be a lower level application of the theology of the episcopacy. In Roman Catholicism the problem grew still more acute as papal primacy came to the fore, for now the entire *sacerdotium* tended to be seen extending and implementing the pope's own role; he was the supreme pastor whose office and activity were the model and source of all other pastoral ministry.

Evolution of episcopacy, papacy and presbyterate, in the form that it actually took, was a major factor in shaping Christian understanding of both ministry and priesthood; but it was not the only factor. Legal thought and its crystallization in church legislation was another important influence on the developing Christian notion of ministry. As communities continue in existence for some time, and particularly if they become large and widespread, as happened with the church, some attempt to order and direct their activities by formulated laws is natural. In Christianity, this emerging body of laws (from synodal and conciliar canons, episcopal and papal decrees, etc.) dealt to a large extent with the behavior of clerics and with the relationships among various levels of the ordained ministry.

Intrinsically, laws should be the reflection of life; but once formulated, laws tend to shape the attitudes and institutions of a society. So it has been with the church, particularly in Latin Christianity and its post-Reformation derivatives. In practical decisions about the desirable or permissible life-style, social status, and pastoral activity of ordained ministers, there has been a consistent practice of appealing to church laws as a norm. In many instances where no formulated law existed the appeal has been to custom as a not yet legislated but most important criterion. Seldom has there been a conscious effort to make these practical decisions by trying to discern the movement of the Spirit in the community, a movement that by definition is the ultimate inner law of the church's life. One principal reason that this discernment of the Spirit has not been more prominent has been the assumption that these church laws represent the will of God, and the Spirit would certainly therefore not move the church except according to these laws. As a matter of fact, one can discern the Spirit precisely by consulting the laws.

In such a context, a definite shaping of Christian understanding of ministry according to legal models occurred. The image of "the good cleric," the patterns of acceptable and effective ministry, the social status of the various levels of the ministry, even the theology of the ministerial role, were fashioned by the mentality proper to canon lawyers. This was by no means a completely undesirable development. Good laws can enshrine the better values and higher ideals of the church, and a considerable amount of the legislation regarding clerics was aimed at elevating the self-understanding, sense of responsibility,

and religious commitment of ordained ministers. However, the dangers of such legal definition of ministry are that laws appropriate to one situation will be perpetuated (perhaps on the questionable philosophical presupposition that laws reflect the nature of an institution, and natures are basically unchanging) and act as a barrier to genuine historical evolution; that this legal definition may be considered *the* definition rather than as a reflection of only one facet of ministry; and that conformity to law may be looked upon as the key to ministerial effectiveness. History indicates that these dangers are only too real, though they are not unavoidable.

Another major influence on the historical evolution of Christian ministry was monasticism (using that term broadly to include later types of religious communities). Unquestionably, the spiritual and ascetic ideals of monasticism have done a great deal to fashion the religious outlook and behaviors of the ordained ministry; but the most important impact has come through the development of characteristically monastic forms of ordained ministry within monasticism itself. Actually, it is a bit misleading to speak of monastic forms of "ordained ministry" because one of the anomolous aspects of this development was that monks were ordained to ministry particularly in the earlier centuries without any prospects (or desire) of exercising ministry apart from private celebration of the Eucharist. This inevitably shifted the understanding of ordination and concomitantly of ministry. Fulfillment of ordination did not come through pastoral activity but through the worship of personal prayer and sanctity and the celebration of Eucharist.

However, the impact was not all one-sided. The existence of large numbers of ordained ministers within monasticism gave an increasingly apostolic thrust to monastic communities, and the evolution of religious orders during the past thousand years has been a steady movement in the direction of "the active life." As this happened, it became clear that organized community life could provide for many ordained ministers an advantageous base for effective ministry. There was the obvious help given by personal support within the community. More than this, the continuity of practice and traditions within a religious community from one generation to another, plus the relative stability of members, made more careful training, spiritual and theological, possible. Perhaps most radically, though quite implicitly, monasticism provided, or at least was capable of providing, a context in which the authentic charismatic impulse could be discerned, nourished, and defended against institutional repression.

Reflecting on this last point, one cannot but wonder whether monasticism is meant to be a charismatic counterpoise to overly monarchical control of Christian ministry by the episcopacy. The centuries of struggle by the episcopacy to gain control over religious orders might suggest this. At the same time, one cannot but be bothered by the fact that monasticism like the ecclesiastical hierarchy has been dominated by the notion of paternalistic government and allowed itself to become part of the "clerical establishment," whereas genuine nurture of charism demands a basically fraternal approach to community existence. It may well be, and many developments in present-day Christianity support the view, that the fundamental abode and safeguard of the charismatic element is the church as a whole. Perhaps the emphasis in our day should be placed on helping the entire people of God to discern, cherish, and then give expression to the movement of the Spirit in its midst. Out of the people there will no doubt arise, as religious communities have seen in past centuries, certain more intense group manifestations of the Spirit's directing presence; but these groups (as well as religious orders already in existence) will preserve their vitality and perform their true function in the church's life only if they resist clericalization and remain open and alert to what the Spirit is doing in the whole church.

Historically, monasticism had much to do with shaping the notion of "the priestly role." The more obvious aspect of this influence concerned the ordination of monks whose only ministerial function would be the private celebration of the Eucharist; this played a large part in fostering the not-too-happy practice of ordaining Mass-saying priests. The less obvious but perhaps more important aspect touched upon the gradual coincidence of the ideals of "the good priest" and "the good monk." This meant an emphasis on the clerico-cultic in monastic life which was not completely in accord with the original thrust of monasticism and very likely not in accord with the true mission of monasticism in the church. It meant an emphasis on the ascetic and contemplative aspects of the ordained minister's life, an emphasis which tended to overshadow the essentially pastoral orientations of the ministerial vocation and within the ministerial activity to give too exclusive a priority to cultic celebration.

The historical evolution of ordained ministry points to several tasks that confront today's church if it is to develop ministry in a manner appropriate to the needs of people and to the intrinsic mission of Christianity. Among the theological tasks none is more basic than the development of a theology of vocation, which will clearly be difficult because this is part of the larger task of developing a less inadequate pneumatology. Yet, until such a deepened understanding of the Spirit's activity in the church is applied to the specific question of the call to specialized ministry, we will be ill-prepared to decide what ministries should be maintained or initiated, what changes should take place in these ministries, and who is called to undertake these ministries. All the Christian churches are today facing a host of problems regarding "vocation to the ministry," and various analyses of these problems are being made and various suggestions to solve them are being given. Much of this can be valuable but none of it can be far-reaching unless we become clearer than we now are about the basic reality of "vocation to ministry."

One of the most basic issues in an understanding of the church's ordained ministry is the relationship between that ministry and the ministry of the Christian community as a whole. Historically, this matter has been discussed under rubrics such as "the priesthood of all believers," "the apostolate of the laity," or "the laity's participation in the mission of the hierarchy." All these terms are misleading. As we have already suggested and will examine more carefully in another chapter, the priesthood possessed by the Christian people as a whole is not exactly the same as their common ministry, though the two realities are inseparably linked. The corporate ministry of the church is not an "apostolate of the laity" (understanding "laity" as nonclerics, which is the common usage up to the present) but a commission that pertains to all baptized Christians including those also designated for specialized ministries. This common ministry of the community does not derive from the special ministerial function of the bishops; instead, the episcopacy is one of the special ministries that exist to sustain and nurture the corporate ministry of the church.

What we wish to discuss now is that broad area of ministry (actually it involves a number of distinguishable ministries) in which all the members of the church share. Obviously, this is a sharing in Christ's own redemptive mission, which is simultaneously his continuing worship of his Father. All Christians are to be of service to their fellow humans in all that pertains to making life's experiences more truly human and enriching. Beyond this they are to be of service to one another in all that pertains to deepening their corporate experience of Christian faith and hope and love. Basic to this service is the witness, carried out corporately and individually, to the risen Christ and to his Father. Fitted to the specific needs and opportunities of divergent historical situations, and obviously finding one type of implementation within the Christian community itself and another type when directed to those who do not yet believe in Christ, this evangelical ministry is a primary right and responsibility that flows from baptism itself. One could express this same truth by saying that the entire community possesses the Spirit of prophecy, though in some this prophetic Spirit may work more intensely or more obviously.

Because this common witness to the gospel belongs to the entire community, it is the community and not the hierarchy that is in the first instance the heir to the "apostolic succession" and the bearer of the "apostolic tradition." Again, it is the loving dedication of all Christians and of the community corporately that is meant to find expression in those activities which effectively better the human condition, and which in so doing sacramentalize the saving presence of God's own love. Even in the realm of worship, it is the people as a whole that offers that unique Christian sacrifice which embraces their entire personal activity and finds its supreme symbolic moment in the Eucharist.

For such widespread Christian ministry to be effective, indeed, for such a ministry to exist, a number of specialized functions (or ministries) must support and guide and vitalize the community itself, and certain other functions must carry out specific elements of the church's corporate mission in the world. It is apparent that the social unification and the unified activity of the church will require, as does any grouping of human beings, some appropriate leadership. Since leadership is not to be confused with administration, there must also be in the church some individuals who organize the communities' life and activity into effective unity. Because the church is meant to be *community* in the deepest personal sense, i.e., a truly open sharing of faith and life, there can be no place for those radical disparities between rich and poor, powerful and weak, which so patently corrode the brotherly unity of mankind. So there must be effective *diakonia* which can minister to the needs of the socially disadvantaged and bear witness to the basic equality of all members of the church.

Precisely because the church is a believing community and destined to give prophetic witness to that faith, there is need for widespread formation of people's religious understanding. Teaching is a ministry upon which the well-being of the church depends. Correct understanding and deepened insight are basic requirements if the Christian community is to understand itself and its role in the world; but part of that understanding and insight involves the elusive and undefined (but critical) process of "discerning the Spirit." So there is needed a specialized function that for the moment we can simply call "spiritual direction." Powers of discernment, accurate understanding of the faith, genuine fraternity based on shared faith and common concern, all these are weakened and threatened by the enigmatic presence of *evil* in the church, evil in the attitudes and behavior of individual Christians, evil in the structures and corporate outlooks of the church. So, there must be a constant ministry of healing the Christian community from its own self-inflicted wounds, so that it can be a healing agent in the wider world of men.

Specialized Ministry

Later we will treat at greater length such key ministries as preaching, teaching, liturgical leadership, government, and healing. At this point, we examine some of the more general questions about ministry, and give preliminary suggestions about the manner in which the needs of the Christian community, and beyond that the needs of all men and women, can be tended to by various ministries.

First of all, it does seem preferable to think in terms of *ministries* rather than of some all-embracing function and charism called "Christian ministry." Historically, despite the official absorption of all the diverse ministries into the official pastoral office, some autonomous expressions of these various charisms have generally existed in unofficial, and sometimes "underground," fashion. This has often made for tension and division; those exercising such ministries have often been repressed, condemned (sometimes justly, but often unjustly) as divisive and heterodox. The potential of such ministerial activity to unify and further the life of the community has been negated. Quite clearly, there is no advantage in having a helter-skelter proliferation of "ministries" in the church. What is needed is a straightforward recognition of the fact that the Spirit has given throughout history and still gives at the present moment a

plurality of gifts which exist in autonomy and complementarity. What unifies and orders these charisms and passes judgment upon their genuineness is the community as a whole and the one Spirit working in the community.

Since the ground of these charisms, and of the ministries that spring from them, is the living, evolving reality of the church, it seems reasonable that new ministries will come into existence as the life of the church develops in history, and that ministries which effectively served the church's needs in an earlier historical period might cease to have a purpose and should disappear. What should serve as the norm for creating, retaining, modifying, or abolishing ministries is the need of the church at a given time: what is needed to foster its own inner life, and what is needed to make its ministry to the world more effective. One might object that this conflicts with the principle classically appealed to for retaining certain offices in the church, namely, that certain offices are of divine origin because they were instituted by Christ himself and cannot therefore be altered by human decision. However, the objection is ungrounded and based on a superficial understanding of the church and of "institution by Christ." If one accepts the belief that the church is truly the body of Christ and animated by his Spirit, then the risen Christ himself and his Spirit remain involved in the developing historical life of the Christian community, and no element of the creative unfolding of the church's being can be seen as purely human and not "instituted by Christ." Certainly, this requires a delicate and faith-filled appraisal of the church's historical development, so that one can discern what is of Christ and his Spirit and what is not; but the burden and risk of such a task is part of the price for retaining the vitality and flexibility of the church.

Secondly, it might be good to draw the obvious distinction between the ministries that exist to provide for the church's service to the world and the ministries that exist to nurture the church's own internal well-being. In trying to determine the appropriate ministerial activities *"ad extra"* one becomes very conscious of the need to proceed pragmatically, to learn from experience, and to submit one's preconceived ideas and projects to be judged by the criterion of eschatological effectiveness: Is establishment of the kingdom of God being helped or hindered? One also becomes conscious of the fact that establishment of God's kingdom is an enterprise in which many who are not Christians are also engaged, even though they might not view their endeavors to better human life in those terms. And one becomes distrustful of the "religious imperialism" which presupposes that Christians have answers about man's destiny whereas others have questions and, at best, inadequate answers.

Rather, genuine Christian ministration to the world is grounded in an honest sharing by Christians of the basic questions facing men and women. This does not mean that Christians can irresponsibly neglect enriching human understanding by the insights of their faith, for example, in contributing to the ethical judgments of society; but it does mean that they cannot arrogantly presume that the situation is not one of mutual learning in which their own Christian faith will be clarified by the sincere human insights of their fellow humans.

One of the basic problems that will always bother Christian ministration to the world is the extent to which the Christian community can and should identify with human society, with its values, with its mythologies, and with its structures. History indicates the grave risk that comes with naive identification: doctrine can be formulated according to the cosmology prevalent at a given point in history without critical awareness of the inadequacy and relativity of this cosmological framework; the church's own structures can become dangerously entangled with the structures (and therefore with the goals and processes and values) of political governments; Christians and the church in its corporate activity can be caught up in the cultural values and prejudices of a given historical situation to the point where they lose much of the vision that is proper to Christian revelation. On the other hand, the Christian community cannot legitimately hold itself aloof from the rest of mankind. The very finality of the Incarnation which is extended into the church is one of identification with the human condition in order to transform it. "Sanctification," whether of the individual or of society, can take place only from within; Christianity must better human life by itself being an intrinsic part of that life.

What all this seems to say is that Christians must immerse themselves in the processes of their society, must remain open and alert to all the creative elements in those processes, must be zealous for the advance of all that is truly human; but in so doing they should be maturely critical of the forces at work in their society, helped by the insights of their faith to evaluate these forces, and stimulated by their Christian hope and love to seek unselfishly the genuine good of all men and women. It also means that the church's relation to "the world" and its ministration to the human condition should be considered more from the viewpoint of individual Christians and less (if at all) from the viewpoint of "the official church." For too long the question of Christian involvement in the life of mankind has been distorted by the controversies over church-state relations, as if the heart of the matter consisted in the cooperation or opposition of two officialdoms. At our point in history we have definitely broken out of that old pattern, though an obvious residue of the church-state mentality remains with us. The question we face goes much deeper, for we must ask to what extent the Christian community's service to the world should be carried on through groups or activities that are formally Christian.

With such a shift in Christian thinking about service to human society, the centuries-old clerical appropriation of control over such service makes little sense. Instead, the effective effort to better human life and to lead all men and women to their destiny belongs to the entire community, and individual members of the church are to translate their own faith into whatever course of service seems desirable. Some of this will be done individually, some will be done in cooperation with fellow Christians, some will be done in cooperation with fellow humans who do not share the Christian faith. In any case, Christians are to exercise their own initiative, undertake responsibly but autonomously whatever needs to be done, receive guidance from whatever agencies within the church exist to provide guidance, but resist the attempts of church officials to control their activity.

With such a shift of ministerial responsibility from church officials to the community as a whole, a number of basic and rather evident problems arise. Most fundamentally, we are faced with an immense task of formation and stimulation. Most Christians are neither prepared nor willing to undertake the evangelical and diakonal implications of their faith and baptism. But even when such formation and motivation is achieved, there remains the problem that most people have limited time and energy and resources and find it difficult (if not impossible) to commit themselves to the "extra" projects that Christian evangelization and service demand. Perhaps part of the answer lies in reconsidering the ministerial function of "apostle," i.e., one who is sent out from a community as its full-time "professional" legate, sustained by that community, psychologically, economically, and religiously, and responsible to that community for the integrity of his faith and the conduct of his ministry.

When we turn our attention to the church's ministry *"ad intra,"* and confine ourselves for the moment to general consideration, there seem to be two principal objectives that such ministry must achieve. It must provide for the organic development and unity of the Christian community; and while this undoubtedly implies attention to the institutionalized aspects of the church's being, it must focus on the deeper task of fostering the faith and hope and charity that are the very life process of the church. Secondly, it must prepare the community for its mission of evangelization and service to the world and, intertwined

with this, for an authentic celebration of Eucharistic worship.

Whether we consider ministry within the church or ministerial service of the church to mankind, a basic tension or dialectic in ministerial activity must be confronted: ministry must deal with persons, since the fulfillment of persons is the purpose of society, and since any real betterment of society will be grounded in the attitudes and activity of the persons who make up that society. On the other hand, some structures and processes are necessary if men are to live in society and develop as individuals, and these structures and processes have great power to shape the lives and personalities of people. Every important reform movement within Christianity has had as its ultimate purpose a deepening of Christian spirituality, i.e., a transformation of people, and has recognized that without this any change of institutional patterns is superficial and ephemeral. At the same time, effective reform movements have also seen the need to renovate the structural aspects of the church. Clearly, we are faced with a "both/and" situation rather than an "either/or"; yet there is a certain ultimacy about the need to change persons, and the prophetic voice in both Old and New Testaments, though unequivocally committed to social reform, is most basically a call to "conversion."

Within the church itself this raises the entire question of preserving or altering the institutional aspects of the church. It is a poorly kept secret that the ordained ministries of the several Christian churches are deeply divided today as to whether the stress in ministerial activity should be placed on preserving or on changing. Though this is but one manifestation of the fundamental tension between continuity and discontinuity in the Christian community's life, and this basic tension will exist as long as the church remains in history, we can make this tension not only bearable but positively creative. One element in such a positive approach to change is correct understanding of what continuity and discontinuity really mean when one is dealing with Christianity. This involves a "debunking" of some false fears about change, a rejection of such stereotyped classification as "radical" or "liberal" or "traditional," and insistence that preservation of tradition is utterly different from maintenance of the status quo.

When we turn our attention outward, to the question of preserving or changing the structures of human society, we discover one of the most exciting and potentially important areas of reflection about the future of Christian ministry. Just as advances in science have brought us to the point where men can look forward to a new and creative role in the evolution of the physical universe, so we have the power today to shape economic and political and social forces and create a society truly appropriate to man. Direction of the course of human history can be, as never before, a consciously planned and freely chosen endeavor in which all men can participate. As yet, this is but an ideal, but it is a realizable ideal if men but wish it. In the realization of this ideal the Christian community could play a decisive role.

What this suggests regarding Christian ministries is that they can be, and probably should be, viewed as agencies that work to nurture the authentic unfolding of the historical process. In the last analysis, it is the entirety of the historical experience of mankind that is to bear witness to the redeeming power of the risen Lord and to the faithful love of his Father. It is the historical process in the totality of its manifold interactions and forces that shapes the consciousness and activities and growth (or deterioration) of men and women, which is to say that it is concretely the process that we name "redemption" or "salvation." It is this unfolding sequence of movements and institutions and personal lives that is meant to explicate the "Christ mystery," to give expression to the humanly transformative power of the death and resurrection of Christ. And the task (i.e., ministry) of Christians is to exercise creatively the faith and hope and charity which they share in community, and thus contribute to the truly human (and Christic) evolution of history.

This dictates the need to relate Christian faith at any given point in history to the prevailing world-view and the basically formative social movements. One can understand such activity as an imperious Christian attempt to pass judgment upon the understandings and motivations of the rest of mankind, but such is clearly not the real intent. Rather, there is the question of an organic interpenetration and enrichment of Christian insights and "secular" understanding, of "secular" quest for the betterment of man and Christian endeavor to establish the kingdom of God.

Considering this broad, really all-embracing, need for Christian ministration to the development of human history, we can raise one last general question: Should these various ministries to human society be carried on by individual Christians acting as responsible citizens guided in their understandings and values by faith, or by official and organized activity of the church? Does the institutional church as such have a role to play in the evolution of society's structures and processes? There is no easy answer and certainly no a priori answer; but we are unquestionably moving away from officially Christian activities undertaken by officially constituted Christian organizations and moving instead towards active involvement of dedicated Christians in cooperative ventures with non-Christians. And as this trend develops, it will have increasing effect on the evolution of specialized ministry within the church, for there will be less need for direction and sustenance of church organizations and more need to form Christians for effective participation in "secular" activity.

Turning, then, to a preliminary discussion of the various specialized ministries in the church, we might logically begin by analyzing the function of leadership in Christianity. Several recent studies on the nature of Christian priesthood and ministry have focused on leadership as the fundamental function of Christian ministry. For several reasons, however, this focus must be questioned. First, this position remains within the context of "clerical" ministries, and links leadership too closely to office. Granted that it would be desirable to have those in official positions exercise more imaginative leadership, leadership is by no means to be identified with those occupying official positions. Part of the present discontent with ecclesiastical exercise of authority is the false presupposition that one should expect to find Christian leadership primarily and almost exclusively from those who occupy ecclesiastical office.

Actually, leadership is not a specific function, much less an office. It is a broader and more basic reality, a capacity to inspire and direct and support a social group as it moves towards some goal. One can justifiably refer to it as a charism, in the sense that it is a special and relatively rare endowment which gives an individual the power to influence the decisions and actions of others; but in any given instance, it is composed of a number of qualities which particularly fit the needs of a given situation. What would equip a person to exhibit leadership in one context would be completely ineffective in another context.

Christian leadership, i.e., the leadership that one exercises precisely as a Christian and for the most part in relation to his fellow Christians, is as distinctive as are the goals towards which it is directed and the means of attaining those goals. Yet, as one reflects on the nature of leadership and on the manner in which being Christian can contribute to leadership, a remarkable coincidence becomes apparent: Faith and hope and charity, which are the life process of the Christian community, deal with the very qualities that a leader must possess. Leadership involves a *vision* of the goal to which a group should be guided, an understanding of the task the group is being asked to perform. Christian faith gives such a vision and understanding, not for some particular goal or task, but for human life as a whole. Leadership involves the capacity to *motivate* people, so that they will effectively seek the proposed goal. Christian charity, because it is the intensification of human love, provides the most basic of all motivational power. But a group that envisages a goal and truly wishes to attain it must still be *encour-*

aged to persevere amid the difficulties that are encountered in reaching the goal. A true leader provides such encouragement by instilling in the group some of his own hope.

Obviously, this is but a hasty and oversimplified sketch of the convergence of the charism of leadership with the Christian transformation of a person which we call "faith, hope, and charity"; but even this quick analysis should lead us to conclude that a person exerts Christian leadership precisely by being Christian more intensely, by the depth of his faith and hope and charity. This does not deny the importance of certain other qualities that might help a Christian to lead his fellows, but the heart of his leadership activity will consist in sharing his own faith and hope and love.

To some extent, there is an overlap of this fundamental Christian leadership with the function of "witness" that we will probe more thoroughly in another part. The faith and hope and charity of a Christian cannot have an impact on other Christians unless they are manifested, for only then can they inspire others and serve as an example to be followed. Yet, the heart of the Christian leadership we are describing lies in *being* Christian; it is an "ontological prophetism" which is more radical than the prophetic activity that flows from it. Such persons are "possessed" by the Spirit of Christ in the most personal levels of their human existing; they are "consecrated," not in some unintelligible ritual way but by the fact that their consciousness is absorbed in the Christ-mystery and thus "set apart" and Christianized. Those who meet such Christians encounter a presence of the Spirit and can themselves become more intensely inspired, which is another way of saying that such Spirit-filled Christians act sacramentally on their fellows, or of saying that they act as instruments of grace for others.

Clearly, this kind of leadership is not something that derives from an office or that is limited to those possessing office; it is something that is open to any Christian who desires to live his faith with greater intensity. Those in the community who exert this kind of leadership do not fill any specialized function, but they do bear a striking parallel to the *presbyteroi* of the primitive church. As we pointed out earlier, "*presbyteros*" was not really a functional term (as was, for example, "*episkopos*") and seems rather to have denominated that group within the community which exerted the type of radical Christian leadership we have been describing. If we are to seek in today's Christianity a group that is comparable to the early Christian presbyterate we will, then, make a mistake in looking for it in terms of one or other group of ordained ministers. If some wish to retain the use of the word "presbyter" to denominate a specialized pastoral ministry in the church, there is no great value in fighting over names and such an application of the term "presbyter" can be justified by the historical migration of that term (which we described in the earlier part of our study). What is important is that we recognize and accept leadership from that group of Christians within the community whose profound communal faith and sensitive Christian conscience are intrinsically though "unofficially" normative for the community.

Unquestionably there will be (at least one would certainly hope so) considerable overlap in the exercise of leadership and the exercise of specialized ministries within the community; but it is important to insist on the fact that important leadership can be exerted by men and women who have no special ministerial function. There is also considerable overlap among the specialized ministries themselves, not only in the sense that a single person might be involved in more than one ministry (for example, he might be both teacher and theologian) but also in the sense that many of the lines of distinction between ministries cannot be sharply drawn. Prophecy, for example, is certainly a service, and service itself gives prophetic witness. Yet, the attempt to absorb all the various ministries into the episcopal function seems unjustifiable, and (as our historical treatment indicated) other ministries, such as prophecy and teaching, continued to exist with a certain

amount of unofficial autonomy. One cannot but wonder whether the attempt to reduce all these diverse ministries to one office was a cause of the false opposition that developed between "evangelical" and "sacramental" understandings of Christian ministry. In the context of a single office the intrinsic dialectic between different aspects of Christianity which distinct but cooperating ministries can maintain tends to be lost and one element becomes dominant while the other is obscured.

Actually, if there is one ministry that might lay some claim to being *the* basic ministry it is not that of governing (*episkopein*) but that of prophecy. In the Gospel descriptions of Jesus' own mission and ministry, it is his prophetic identity and function that are stressed. Moreover, behind this stress of the New Testament writers there seems to lie Jesus' own human conviction of his ministry as being essentially prophetic. Yet, when one moves from Jesus' own exercise of prophetic ministry to prophetism in the church, it is difficult to define a specialized prophetic function. It is the entire church, individually and corporately, that is meant to bear prophetic witness to Christ and to his Father. When one looks for the institutionalization of such prophetic witness in an enduring "office," what one encounters is discipleship, but this too pertains to the entire community. The yet deeper theological understanding of discipleship leads one to the notion of the church as sacrament of Christ, which also applies to the whole church. Unquestionably, there are some individuals in the community who either regularly or only on rare occasions speak out with special charisms to provide guidance and encouragement. But it is highly dubious whether this kind of prophetic activity should be institutionalized in any fashion; it should be a recognized ministry and respected as a gift from the Spirit to the community, but there is neither the need nor any genuine possibility to make it an officially established ministry.

Teaching is another matter, for it deals with the constant need of a religious community to educate the belief of its members. There is a good bit of prophecy in the best religious teaching, as evidenced by the fact that the founders of the great world religions spent most of their public careers teaching. Yet, there is the distinctive activity of instruction, of clarification and correction of understanding already possessed by people, of spelling out in diverse historical contexts the implications of the basic religious tradition. Teaching certainly contributes towards religious certitude and commitment, but its particular contribution deals with accuracy of understanding and depth of insight. For that reason, effective teaching is rooted in the teacher's own knowledge and insight; neither personal conviction nor holiness nor official status can substitute for that required understanding. On the other hand, if a man or woman has clear and deep understanding of the faith and some basic ability to communicate, no official designation is needed to make that person a teacher in the church. There might well be some benefit in giving community recognition and support to some teachers, so that a continuing ministry of effective teaching can be provided.

While any attempt to give a detailed understanding of faith involves some theological reflection, the progressing faith life of the church requires a serious and "professional" pursuit of theology by men and women who thereby perform a specific ministry to the community. Theology can be done by those in the church who are teachers or administrators or pastors or none of these, but it is a distinct activity with its own intrinsic norms and principles and goals. For that reason, theological research and reflection should be considered a distinct ministerial function, and the right and responsibility to exercise this function is proportionate to the theological expertise of an individual. As such, it is not dependent upon jurisdiction or official approval or occupation of some office.

Quite different is the role of "cult official." Actually, though we have grown accustomed to giving strong cultic connotation to "Christian ministry," the very notion of cultic min-

istry presents problems in Christianity. Early Christianity had no shrines, and on principle was opposed to such specialized locations for the worship of God, and therefore had no place for "shrine custodians." At the same time, Christianity did have from its origins a pattern of worship, but a pattern whose character was so distinctive that it is misleading to apply to it any generic term such as "cult."

For reasons that are not entirely clear (reasons we attempted to evaluate in the historical portion of our study), the *episkopos* quite quickly emerged in the early church as a cult minister, and before long bore the title "priest" which the primitive church assiduously avoided. However one may wish to assess this historical development, the simple fact is that effective liturgical celebration requires a unique type of leadership. It was inevitable that some institutionalization of this cultic role occur quite early in the church's history. One may wish to disagree with the fashion in which this role evolved in the church's history and with the gradual monopoly of sacramental activity by clerics, and he may wish to describe the function of the liturgical leader as one of forming a worship community. But whichever view one takes, it seems quite clear that there is a need for a distinctive ministry which is not reducible to any of the other ministries in the church.

One of the elements that strengthens this irreducibility of cult leader to some other ministry is the persistent tradition that in some fashion the liturgical celebrant "makes things sacred." Without espousing any magical understanding of this consecratory function, and without admitting that this view of cultic ministry stands in basic opposition to an evangelical emphasis in liturgical ministry, one can and must account for the centuries of belief that God "uses" the minister of sacrament to sanctify the people. It does not help to drive a wedge between the notions of "cult priest" and "administrator of sacraments" and to admit that the Christian minister is the second but deny that he is cult priest. As we will see later, in the concrete reality of

Christian worship and sacraments, such a distinction is meaningless. Instead, what is needed is a more creatively theological understanding of *ministerium sacramenti*, an understanding that will in turn open up a much more evangelical understanding of cult and priesthood.

Among the most ancient functions of ministration within the Christian community is that of governing, an obvious need in any enduring social group but one which takes special form in Christianity because of the uniqueness of the church as a community. Though governing is in itself only one form of ministry, the role of governing as it developed historically into the episcopal office became identified with the totality of Christian ministry. Others (specifically presbyters and deacons) might also carry on one or other ministry, but they did so by participation in the episcopal role and because of delegation from the episcopacy. Because of this historical evolution, it is difficult to examine in itself the function of governing and detach it from the connotations of all-embracing ministry that have become associated with the episcopal office (or, in parallel fashion with the "pastoral office" in nonepiscopal Christian traditions). To appreciate how intrinsically complicated this question is, one need only recall the difficulties faced by the great Reformers of the sixteenth century when, having rejected the ecclesiastical structure of Roman Catholicism, they strove to provide within their respective communities for the ill-defined reality of *disciplina*.

Precisely because our attempts to clarify the nature of the pastoral office require us to distinguish the function of governing from all the other ministries with which it has been historically confused, it would be precipitous to do more at this stage in our discussion (when we have not analyzed those ministries in depth) than raise a number of the relevant questions. Historically the episcopal office has involved both the exercise of ministries such as preaching and teaching and sacramental leadership, and supervision over others who performed these functions, with a general

evolution towards increased supervision and relatively less actual ministerial activity. This supervision became increasingly authoritative and for centuries the idea has prevailed in the Catholic tradition that the bishops (and preeminently the pope) have jurisdictional control over all ministry, as a matter of fact, over all aspects of the church's life. Inevitably, the justification or criticism of this historical exercise of power raises all the questions about authority which we will study in a later part.

One of the basic questions that must be asked in a present-day examination of the pastoral office is whether the charism of governing that is given certain men or women for the sake of the church is to be identified with administrative skill or with possession of an administrative position in the church. Competent administration of church affairs is clearly desirable, but such administration is not to be confused with leadership or even with governance, and it does not of itself involve the possession of whatever authority is proper to the church as a community. For one thing, we must clarify the justifiable scope of administration in the church: How many of the numerous social, economic, and educational ventures, which today demand such large-scale administrative staffs, should continue as part of the Christian church's ministerial activity? How much of the corporate economic activity and possession of lands and buildings, which again necessitates large-scale administration, is really compatible with the church's being and mission? And to move into more clearly religious activities, how much of the centralized direction and control of religious education and liturgical service is necessary or desirable?

Supposing we could quickly define the proper scope of administrative activity in the church, we would still be faced with the question Who should be doing such administration? There has been enough criticism of the overinvolvement of bishops and pastors in routine administration to suggest that such activity is not really proper to either bishop or pastor and that their historical absorption in such tasks was largely a matter of undertaking what no one else was doing. But until it is made clear that these church officials as such have neither the authority nor the responsibility for such administration they will not feel free in conscience to relinquish this portion of their present ecclesiastical burden. And if bishops (and their equivalents in non-episcopal communities) are not ultimately responsible for effective administration of church affairs, who is? Should the community delegate such responsibility to a group of leaders (like the early Christian presbyterate) who in turn would appoint or hire competent administrators for various needs? Or should some new form of diaconate be established to provide a continuing group of administrative personnel to which the community could entrust its affairs? Or should we avoid deciding upon any particular pattern and recognize the responsibility of each local Christian community to provide prudently whatever procedures and personnel its needs require? There is no simple response to these questions, but what is important to assert is that these are real options and are not ruled out by episcopal claims to monarchical authority.

One of the most ambiguous terms used in explanations of the episcopal and presbyteral role is "the pastoral office." Grounded in the biblical imagery of the shepherd providing for his flock, the term can indicate that the one who holds this office is to do everything for his people that their spiritual well-being demands. Clearly, we are right back with the idea of an all-embracing ministerial post. The bishop is seen as both "pastor of the people" and "pastor of the pastors of the people." Practically, this has meant providing for all the needs of a parish or a diocese.

There has been an enduring insistence in all the Christian traditions that the heart of this pastoral activity is "the ministry of word and sacrament"; but in the concrete realities of church life, involvement in the tasks of ecclesiastical government has generally meant that a man (particularly a bishop) has little if any opportunity to be a minister of word and sacrament. Over the course of the centuries there have been innumerable suggestions as to

how this practical problem of opposing "pastoral" responsibilities could be solved, and today we are seeing once more a widespread discussion about the priorities that should be honored in episcopal or pastoral activity. But might it not be that the basic presuppositions of the discussion should be challenged, and that the opposition between the task of governing and the ministry of word and sacrament vanishes when we discover that there is no appropriate manner of governing a Christian community other than by the ministry of word and sacrament?

Another basic problem in understanding "governing" as it applies to the church is the falsifying application of a "political model." In ordinary political activity, effective government implies legislative, executive, and judicial activity on the part of public officials. Yet, officials in the Christian church function in that unique situation where Christ alone is the lawgiver, where the prophetic voice may well be the most authentic channel of Christ's directives to the community, and where the sacramental liturgies are meant to be the richest and most ultimate expressions of Christian law. In a very fundamental and real sense, it is the word of God that is meant to govern the Christian community, and the human function of governing is one of enabling the directive power of that word to shape the corporate behavior of the community. So, again we seem to arrive at the centrality of the *ministerium verbi et sacramenti*. Any further insight into the nature of governing as we find it in a Christian community must depend upon our deeper investigation (in later chapters) of the ministry of the word and the ministry of sacrament.

Historically, the ministry of healing has found its most clearly recognizable form in the penitential practice of the church, where the power to forgive sins was claimed as one of the key elements of episcopal authority. Other forms of healing did go on. There was, over the centuries, the dedicated commitment of many Christians to caring for the sick and invalid; there was the consoling and counseling that guided and encouraged many with spiritual ills; there were the various forms of peacemaking that attempted to heal the ills of families or neighborhoods or nations. Such activities, though undertaken as conscious expressions of Christian faith and love, were not seen as distinct ministries and for the most part came under clerical control as soon as they began to acquire any structured existence.

More recently, and especially in the decades after World War II, the important ministerial character of such activities as psychological counseling has become clear, with the result that many ordained ministers have been attracted to such activity. There has been relatively little suggestion that such kinds of healing are in themselves a ministry, completely apart from their being conducted by clerics. Yet, as we reflect on the broad range of activities that in today's world can contribute to the healing of individual humans or to the healing of mankind's social existence, it is quite clear that we are dealing with a diversified but intertwined group of ministries. The classic sacramental ministries of reconciling penitents and anointing the sick begin to converge as we grow more conscious of the extent to which sin is mixed up with psychological problems and more conscious that the symbolic healing effects of anointing should apply to the sick, including the mentally sick, and not just to the dying. Our consciousness of sin and culpability has moved in recent decades from an overconcentration on individual misdeeds to a rediscovery of the radical malice of social sins; we are much more aware of the corporate culpability we share, and aware of the reconciliation and healing that is needed in this sphere. Even within the area of medical practice there is increased interest in psychosomatic healing, a greater awareness of the interaction of mental states and organic activity.

What all this says to us is that the effective healing of men and women is a complicated ministry, one which involves the cooperative interaction of professionally trained people in many fields such as medicine, psychology, social sciences, theology, social work, politics, and education. It is precisely in such a venture, where vibrant Christian faith and hope and love could be a key element in the dynamics of "reconstructing" human persons and their society, that much of the redemptive mission of Christ and his church will be achieved. And it is precisely in such activities that "ordination" to ministry can result only from a man or woman's recognized qualifications and not from any official appointment. However, it may well be that we will see the desirability in the years ahead of giving some kind of community recognition to those who are so endowed, in order that their ministerial activity can be more effective.

Quite another type of ministerial function which demands reconsideration in today's Christianity is that of the apostle. The role of the Christian who was sent out from an established Christian community, in order to preach the gospel and bring new communities into being, was understandably prominent at the beginning of the church and understandably faded as the church became more settled. The need for such itinerant ministry vanished as resident ministers supplied the needs of the faithful, and "apostle" lost its identity as a distinctive ministry. Yet, at each point historically that Christianity has discovered new frontiers for evangelization, men and women have been sent out as missionaries (i.e., apostles) to bring into being the established Christian communities which would render their missionary presence no longer necessary. One thing, however, about these later exercises of apostolic ministry needs careful appraisal: Quite early in the church's history and from that point onward, such missionaries were clerics or under clerical direction. This meant that to a large extent the activity of these cleric-apostles was one of transplanting geographically the kind of clerical ministry they had exercised and for which they had been trained in their home country. There have always been voices calling for recognition of missionary evangelization as an activity quite distinct in its character from the ministry of word and sacrament carried on "back home"; but until recently there has been relatively little attention paid to such voices.

Today, indeed, the question we face is

much broader than that of missionaries going off to foreign lands; for one thing, such missionary frontiers have all but vanished. The new frontiers of Christianization are everywhere in the world; the form that evangelization must take will be drastically different from the past. The "apostle" must deal with a new and modern version of "pagans" and "infidels"; he must go wherever the existence of evil betrays the absence of God and a consequent threat to human well-being, or where a burst of human creativity and idealism manifests the workings of the Spirit. Basically, all Christians are meant to be involved in such apostolic activity in the human milieu where they are situated. However, Christian communities may wish to commission certain individuals as their representatives, as their apostles to particular social situations or groups of people, to undertake tasks of evangelization that would require special training and full-time attention. And if such an apostolic ministry were to come into being its viability and effectiveness would depend upon its distinctiveness and autonomy vis-à-vis the present ordained ministry of the Christian churches. Compromise solutions, such as a worker-priest movement, laudable though their motivation and objectives may be, will not do; they will always remain half-measures.

While the preceding listing of specialized ministries is by no means exhaustive, it may well have proved exhausting. So we will draw attention to only one more ministerial function that is critically important in today's Christianity—the ministry of spiritual direction or formation of conscience, though these two are not completely identical. At the basis of this ministry is the need for all Christians to develop the capacity of deciding in any given set of circumstances the course of action that is most compatible with their relationship to Christ. Today, when there is a new awareness of the prophetic and diakonal mission of the entire Christian community, there is even greater need for such formation of Christian ability to make prudential choices. The concrete Christian judgments about economics and politics and art and social rela-

tionships can only be made "in the marketplace," by Christians who are engaged in political life or in commercial undertakings or artistic creation; the ability to translate the insights of Christian faith into realistic practical judgments is one that must be carefully nurtured.

The task of such conscience formation is unquestionably one of the most important ministries in the church today. Yet, there is a felt absence of this ministry. Many dedicated Christians complain that they are unable to find such spiritual guidance, and many seek such help wherever they can find it—not infrequently from ill-trained and unreliable "guides." Their complaint is not new in the church. Treatises on the development of Christian spirituality in ordained clergy or in members of religious orders have always stressed the need for regular spiritual direction, but the demand for competent directors has always far outstripped the supply of such men. At least part of the problem has been the widespread assumption that such direction could be given only by men with presbyteral ordination; this meant that a large reservoir of potential spiritual guides, both men and women, was left untapped. In the church of today, means must be found to discover and to train those Christians who have the potential for this crucial task.

If there is one basic conclusion that can be drawn from this first part of our study, it is that decisions about the retention, change, abolition, or inception of ministries in the church must be governed by the evolving needs and opportunities of the church. At the same time, such pragmatic decisions are not to be based upon purely human considerations; rather, since any genuine ministry in the church is rooted in the charismatic impulse of the Spirit, our decisions about ministry must be always a discernment of the Spirit. Theological insight into the nature and historical reality of Christian ministry cannot by itself provide such discernment, but it is an indispensable element. So, we will essay a more detailed examination of certain key aspects of ministry.

Selected Bibliography

Formation of Community

Any history of Europe and North America provides general background; the following treat the matter of Christian ministry more directly:

Bouyer, L., Leclercq, J., and Vandenbroucke, F. *History of Christian Spirituality*. 3 vols. New York, 1963–69.

Chadwick, O., ed. *The Pelican History of the Church*. 6 vols. Harmondsworth (Eng.), 1961–64.

Daniélou, J. and Marrou, H. *The Christian Centuries*. Vol. 1. New York, 1964.

Fliche, A., and Martin, V. *Histoire de l'Eglise depuis les origines jusqu'à nos jours*. Paris, 1935—.

Jedin, H., ed. *Handbook of Church History*. New York, 1965—.

Jungmann, J. *The Mass of the Roman Rite*. 2 vols. New York, 1955.

Knowles, D. and Obolensky, D. *The Christian Centuries*. Vol. 2. New York, 1968.

Latourette, K. *A History of the Expansion of Christianity*. 5 vols. New York, 1937–45.

Le Bras, G., ed. *Histoire du Droit et des Institutions de l'Eglise en Occident*. Paris, 1955—.

Niebuhr, H. R. and Williams, D., eds. *The Ministry in Historical Perspective*. New York, 1956.

PRE-NICENE CHRISTIANITY:

Daniélou, J. *The Theology of Jewish Christianity*. London, 1964.

Küng, H. *The Church*. New York, 1967.

Schweizer, E. *Church Order in the New Testament*. London, 1961.

PATRISTIC AND MEDIEVAL CHRISTIANITY:

Chenu, M.-D. *Nature, Man, and Society in the Twelfth Century*. Chicago, 1968.

Congar, Y. *L'ecclésiologie du Haut Moyen Age*. Paris, 1968.

Crespin, R. *Ministère et sainteté*. Paris, 1965.

Knowles, D. *The Monastic Orders in England*. 2d ed. Cambridge, 1963.

POST-MEDIEVAL CHRISTIANITY:

Dansette, A. *Religious History of Modern France*. 2 vols. New York, 1961.

Davies, H. *Worship and Theology in England*. 4 vols. Princeton, 1961.

Dolan, J. *History of the Reformation*. New York, 1965.

Jedin, H. *History of the Council of Trent*. Vols. 1 and 2. New York, 1957, 1961.

Leonard, E. *A History of Protestantism*. Vols. 1 and 2. London, 1965, 1967.

Spitz, L. *The Renaissance and Reformation Movements*. Chicago, 1971.

**PART
TWO**

Ministry to
God's Word

CHAPTER 8

Ministry of the Word
in the New Testament

Starting with the premise that any study of ministry in Christianity must take its beginning with the New Testament evidence about the ministry of Jesus and then the ministry of the Twelve, we discover that the notion of "witness" is basic to both. Jesus is the supreme witness to the saving act of divine love; the Twelve are the privileged witnesses to Christ's own witness of death and resurrection.[1] However, it immediately becomes clear that this topic merges into the question of the ministry of the word of God, and we are confronted with the earliest stage of the church's traditional emphasis on this ministry of the word, an emphasis which at least in the theoretical order continues throughout Christian history.

Witness

Christianity, like Old Testament Israel before it although in its own unique fashion, is a community of believers in an event: the saving event of the death and resurrection of Jesus who is the Christ.[2] The notion of "witness" takes on several levels of meaning in Christian understanding, because this event is actually a complex social reality. It is not just the historical happening of Jesus and his redeeming death, nor even that coupled with his continuing saving action as the risen Lord, but all this finding expression in the evolving process of mankind's salvation which is effected by the Christian community acting as the body of Christ.[3]

"Witness" applies to the testimony given by Jesus or by the early Christians or by Christians today. It is testimony to their consciousness of the action of God in their lives. It applies to the disciples' testimony of their experience of Jesus in his historical existence as well as to their experience of him as the risen Lord. It applies to the continuing activity of those in the church who have exercised the function of retaining and expressing the apostolic witness. It applies to the entire community's witness to the traditions of earlier Christian faith which it accepts in its own profession of belief.

Such witness involves a ministry of word, for it is in and through the words and lives of those who so bear witness that the word of God's saving love is brought to men. But it becomes even more clearly a ministry of the word of God when we begin to see that the very "event" to which witness is given is a *speaking*. What is happening in the Christian community is God's self-revelation which he continues to speak in his own Word-become-flesh, Jesus who is now gloriously risen and living on in his church which manifests him and his Father to the world.[4] The church is meant to bear witness to what it itself is as event, to what God is saying in and through it, including what he has said through previous generations. This the church does by speaking its own faith and the faith of previous believers which it cherishes as its own inherited tradition.[5]

Such a ministry of God's word is basically prophetic; it is a "speaking for God," a bearing witness to the divine intent and divine action.[6] New Testament texts indicate that the early church saw this prophetic aspect of its own identity as well as of the identity of Jesus.[7] All four Gospel traditions depict Jesus in his public ministry as a prophetic figure, going about bearing testimony to the divine vocation of men to the kingdom.[8] Acts and the Pauline letters make it clear that the early communities saw themselves as filled with the prophetic Spirit, and saw their role as one of spreading the word of God's salvation in the Christ.[9]

In the Christian context, "prophecy" takes on the precise application of the preaching of the gospel (Matt. 4:23). To prophesy is to evangelize, to be a herald of the gospel, to bear witness to the death and resurrection of Jesus who is Messiah and Lord.[10] The prophetic role of heralding the coming divine act of salvation which is highlighted in the opening chapter of Deutero-Isaiah is consciously appropriated to itself by early Christianity, as is clear from the use of Isaiah 40 at the beginning of each of the synoptic Gospels.[11] Like Jesus himself before them, and the Old Testament prophets before him, the early Christian apostles exhorted men to that "conversion" which consists in accepting the saving act of the Lord in "his day" (Acts 2:38; 13:23–41).

While much can be gained by a detailed study of the New Testament use of "prophecy" ("*propheteuein*" and derivatives), the characteristic parameter of Christian thought on the topic is clarified by the cluster of words connected with "bear witness": "testify," "evangelize," "herald," etc. The Johannine writings contain the most extensive and most theologically sophisticated use of the notion of "witness";[12] but already the early epistles of Paul reflect an established usage of the term "witness" in a specialized Christian sense. Paul describes his own preaching to the Thessalonians as a *martyrion* (2 Thess. 1:10). In 1 Corinthians 2:1 he seems to extend this idea: again referring to his preaching, he gives as the object of that preaching *to martyrion tou theou*; literally this would mean "the testimony of God," and in the context it seems to be an application of the notion of witness to the activity of Jesus himself.

Yet, it is necessary to be cautious of such a translation, because Paul also conveys the notion of the Resurrection's being God's witness to his Christ, somewhat the way in which God bears witness to lesser heralds such as Paul (Rom. 1:9). Christian faith in Christ bears witness to the justice of God, that justice to which law and prophets formerly testified (Rom. 3:21). By the very nature of faith, all believers in the community share in this witness to God; all exercise a prophetic function.

Throughout Paul's use of the term *"martyrion,"* whether he is applying it directly to the Christian mystery or whether he is using it in a more "profane" sense, as when he "testifies" to the virtue of Epaphras in Colossians 4:13, the notion of "legal witness" seems always somewhat present. The term is used for anything that involves a solemn attestation to something as true—Paul's teaching, Paul's conscience, the gospel, God himself (Gal. 4:15; 2 Cor. 1:12; 1 Cor. 1:6; Rom. 3:21). One is reminded of the scenes from Acts in which Peter or Stephen or, on several occasions, Paul himself bears solemn witness before officials of Judaism or Rome regarding the truth of the gospel. The tradition carries on into the apologists of the next century. One is reminded, too, of the sworn testimony to one's promises that is connected with the Old Testament scenes of making or renewing the covenant between Yahweh and Israel. However, it is apparent from Paul's exhortations to the early churches that witness extends to much more than these "official" situations of martyrdom; the whole of Christian life is meant to be a witness to the saving action of God in Jesus Christ (Rom. 15:7–13).

As we already mentioned briefly, the Gospel traditions depict Jesus as engaged in a ministry that is basically prophetic, and there is abundant evidence in all four versions that Jesus is explicitly viewed as the fulfillment of Old Testament prophecy. He is at one and the same time the greatest prophet who realizes fully the prophetic ideal, especially as it is compressed in the Deutero-Isaian figure of "the Servant," and he is the messianic figure who inaugurates the eschatological fulfillment "foreseen" by the Old Testament prophets.[13]

The prophetic proclamation of the gospel, the announcement that the awaited "day of the Lord" has indeed come, is begun by Jesus himself in his public preaching about the kingdom (Matt. 4:17); it is continued in the evangelical activity of primitive Christianity as we have it reflected in the pages of Acts.

It is, however, in the Johannine literature that we find a complex and explicitly developed theology of Christian witness.[14] Indeed, it is hard to find a theme that is more basic to the theological construct of the Johannine writings than "witness." What is more, the Johannine writings make explicit the link between "the word of God," "prophecy," and "witness." That is, the Christian act of bearing witness to Christ is a prophetic act of communicating the word of God.

Actually, the notion of "witness" is applied to a wide range of human and divine activity. What is very interesting, however, is the fact that practically every usage of *"martyrein"* and its derivatives deals with witness to Christ. John the Baptist witnesses to him (John 1:15, 32, 34); the Father witnesses to him (John 5:32); Jesus' own works bear witness to his mission from the Father (John 5:36);[15] and the Old Testament witnesses to Christ (John 5:39). While the Spirit already bears witness to Jesus during his earthly ministry, it is above all in the post-Resurrection situation that this Spirit witness will reach its full expression (John 15:26), a witness that will work through the disciples themselves (John 15:27). Thus the very production of John's Gospel is such a witness (19:35; 21:24), as is the prophetic communication of the message of Revelation (Rev. 1:9–10; 22:16). Revelation 2:13 and 11:3, 7 refers to the preaching of the gospel as witness, but even more so the giving up of life for Christ (12:11; 17:6).

The one exception to this use of *"martyrein"* to denominate the witness to Christ is the application of the notion to Christ's own activity. Jesus himself is the great and faithful witness, obviously, to his Father. This is the way in which the Gospel of John depicts him in his prophetic activity (as, of course, the other Gospels also do); he is sent by the Father to say what he says and to do what he does. Much of the fifth chapter of the Gospel is a discourse devoted to this "justification" of Jesus' ministry. The sixth chapter takes us a step deeper into the mystery of the prophetic sending from the Father. Jesus is the life-giving word sent into the world by the Father so that men may have eternal life through faith acceptance of this word. In everything he says and does, but supremely in his death and resurrection, Jesus bears witness to the loving Father; this is the first title given him in Revelation: he is the "faithful witness" (1:5).

Thus, Jesus' own ministry, which is the source and paradigm for all ministry within the church, is seen in the New Testament writings as one of prophetic witness. However, the Johannine viewpoint sees this same ministry continuing in the church; the same Spirit of prophecy that worked in Jesus during his earthly life lies at the root of the church's evangelical activity. This is not, of course, a notion that belongs only to the Johannine perspective. In the Lucan writings Jesus himself is filled from the moment of his conception by the prophetic Spirit (Luke 1:35) and enters upon his public ministry in the fullness of this Spirit (Luke 4:14); the Christian community itself begins with the pentecostal outpouring of the prophetic Spirit (Acts 2). However, it is in the Johannine Gospel and Epistles that we find explicitly stated the belief that the Christian witness to Jesus' death and resurrection is the action of the Spirit. In the "last discourse" the witness given to Christ by the Spirit and by his disciples is immediately linked (John 15:26–27). It is clear that the reference is to the post-Resurrection testimony of the Spirit, for it is stated that this witness will be given after Jesus sends him from the Father. Yet, this Christian witness can function only in the realm of faith; the very act of belief is a witness to Christ, and such belief obviously underlies any proclamation one makes to others. In the last analysis, one can only testify to his own belief. The prophet is the only ultimate proof of the truth of his message. This seems to be the dimension of witness to which the First Epistle of John points when it speaks of the Spirit (along with the water and blood) bearing testimony to Christ, a testimony which must be received in faith. It is this experience of faith, of eternal life that comes with the Spirit of truth, that witnesses to the saving power of the risen Lord and to his identity as the Son of God (1 John 5:5–12).

It does not seem to be a stretching of the Johannine viewpoint (although, obviously, it is a theological rearrangement of ideas) to see the Spirit as first bearing witness to God in the human consciousness of Jesus, simultaneously bearing witness to Jesus' own unique prophet identity, and then bearing witness, both to Jesus' prophetic veracity and to the Father who sent him, through the preaching and deeds of Jesus. And in the case of Christians, the Spirit witnesses within their own consciousness and faith to the reality of the death and resurrection of Jesus, to the fidelity of the Father who sent him, and to their own identity as prophetic witnesses to Christ and as sons of the Father. This would seem to be the mentality that is reflected in the text of Revelation 19:10: "I am a fellow servant of yours and of your brothers who possess the witness (*martyria*) of Jesus. . . . The witness of Jesus is the spirit of prophecy."[16]

This, then, would seem to be the understanding possessed by the early church: Jesus himself, filled with the Spirit of prophecy and conscious of his own prophetic role, bore witness in his public ministry of word and deed to the event of salvation. This event, which basically he himself was, was already taking place in his ministry but would reach its eschatological stage with his own final act of witness, his death and resurrection. Though no longer visibly active, the risen Lord continues his prophetic witness to the saving love of his Father; this he does by communicating to his disciples his own prophetic Spirit. Filled with this Spirit, the early Christians go out to proclaim the gospel so that this saving word of God can bring eternal life to men. The ministry of the church is, like that of Christ himself, essentially a ministry of the life-giving word of God. Though more noticeable exercise of this prophetic activity is manifested by certain leaders, preeminently by the apostles but also by others gifted with special charisms, the prophetic function belongs to the entire community; it is a prophetic people (Acts 2:15–33).

Having examined this basic reality of Christian witness and seen that it involved a ministry that can be termed "prophetic" in the fullest sense and which belongs to the entire community (see Phil. 1:7, 14), we can more accurately approach the question: Was there a "prophetic office" in early Christianity, comparable to the "office" of *episkopos* or *presbyteros*?[17] On New Testament testimony alone, it seems that one can draw the following conclusions:

(1) There definitely were some individuals within the community who were referred to as "prophets." In some instances, this seems to have been a fairly permanent situation for the individuals concerned (Acts 15:32; 21:10); in other cases, there seems to be some evidence that the special charism of prophecy was a temporary gift, provided for a given occasion (1 Cor. 14).

(2) At the same time, there seems to have been some overlap in the view of the prophetic and the apostolic "office." Paul, for one, definitely thinks of his ministry, which he insists is basically that of preaching the gospel (Gal. 1:11), as the expression of a prophetic vocation (Gal. 1:15).

(3) In any event, the special prophetic gift is provided for the sake of the community (I Cor. 14:4). For that reason, it is to be preferred to other charisms like the gift of tongues and should be sought for in prayer (14:1, 12). While the manifestation of tongues can serve as a sign to nonbelievers, the gift of prophecy is a sign provided precisely for believers; it is meant to help form their faith (14:22), and its use is to be governed by the common good of the faith community (14:26–32).

(4) The Pastorals, explicitly 1 Timothy

4:14, seem to indicate that by the stage of development they reflect there is some intrinsic connection between the charism of prophecy and the charism that is provided an *episkopos* with the imposition of hands.

Closely linked with the function of prophecy in early Christianity, though not exactly identical with it, is the reality of discipleship.[18] Without repeating all the elements in this basic Christian reality, which has been quite thoroughly studied by Schelkle,[19] it will be necessary to draw attention to some elements which bear importantly on the questions of ministry.

It is clear in the New Testament writings that the early followers of Jesus thought of themselves as his disciples. The twelve and a small group beyond them had been privileged to have Jesus as their immediate master, and the Gospel traditions indicate that much of Jesus' time and energy was devoted to the formation of this select group. Even during the days of Jesus' public ministry, but much more so in the time after his resurrection, these disciples bore witness to their master by perpetuating his teachings and by living according to his counsels.

Discipleship was, however, something that was not reserved to those who had known and followed Jesus in his public life. All those who accepted the Lord Jesus in faith were committed thereby to being his disciples.[20] They were to adhere to the teachings of Jesus as these were transmitted to them by the apostles and other teachers in the community. More than that, they were to model their lives on the example of Jesus, even to his death and entry into new life.[21] This was a most intimate kind of imitation, for they had been engrafted onto Christ in the mystery of baptism, they formed one body with him and lived by his very life.[22]

Such an acceptance of Christian discipleship by successive generations requires within the community some activity of recruiting, forming, and maintaining men and women for such a view of life and pattern of behavior. Ordinarily in a group of people, one would expect the task of so developing a group of disciples to be that of the teacher, for

teacher is the ordinary correlative of disciple. In Christianity, the formation of men and women as disciples is to quite an extent achieved through teaching. Yet, the situation is different from any other because, in a very true and important sense, only Christ himself is the teacher in Christianity (Matt. 23:8, 10).[23] The treatises on Christ the Teacher in later centuries[24] testify to the abiding conviction of this special role of Christ himself as the correlative to Christian discipleship. What this points to (and the New Testament literature confirms it) is the fact that the Christian "teacher" who successfully leads men to discipleship does so by his own witness of discipleship. By his own instruction he can clarify the nature of "the following of Christ"; by his exhortation he can attempt to convince others of the benefits of so following Christ.[25] But it is only when he witnesses by his own life to the truth of what he advocates, only when he himself is truly a disciple of Christ, that he can say, as Paul does, be "imitators of us and of the Lord" (1 Thess. 1:6).

While no technical precision is provided for this function of "giving example," Paul sees it as constituting a most basic element of his apostolate.[26] In the Synoptic traditions the extensive treatment given to the conditions of discipleship indicates the central position it held in early Christian catechesis.[27] While such fidelity to the teaching and example of Jesus was expected of all the baptized, and all were to exhort one another to follow this example, it seems to have been specially expected of those who occupied positions of leadership in the community. It is central to the credentials demanded for the *episkopos*-presbyter of the Pastorals (1 Tim. 3:2–7; Titus 1:6–9), and for Simon Peter in the Johannine account of his commission by the risen Christ (John 21:15–19, which ends with the command "Follow me").

There is considerable overlap between the notion of prophetic witness and the witness expected of the Christian "good example." The prophetic word is exhortation to conversion, as is that of the Christian who encourages others to discipleship. True prophetic witness involves more than the words of the prophet; it catches up the whole person of the prophet at times even leading him to perform strange symbolic actions.[28] On the other hand, discipleship includes a proclamation of the risen Lord whom the Christian is following.[29]

Yet, there is also an important difference. While the prophet cherishes the authentic traditions of the faith community, his witness is essentially to the *present* event of God speaking through him and directing the people towards a future course of action; his message is necessarily eschatological, necessarily a call to conversion. Discipleship, especially in the Christian context of the presence of the risen Christ to the community, does not lack the element of present call to a changed pattern of behavior, but by its very nature it tends to look to what the "master" has already done; it demands in some fashion or other a "tradition" of behavior. Obviously, there is no reason that the two functions cannot come together in the same person, as they certainly did in Paul; the two are certainly meant to interact in the life of any Christian community. But it is important to distinguish them, so that both continue to exist, so that discipleship not become mere social custom, so that prophecy retains the wisdom already communicated through the word of God.

In discussing Christian discipleship we have inevitably drifted into the topic of Christian witness to the community's faith traditions. We must be careful not to lose sight of the early Christian insight that it, the Spirit-filled community through which the risen Christ continued his saving action and his worship of the Father, was the *event* of revelation; it was the mystery (Eph. 5). Yet the first Christians looked on the historical life and teaching of Jesus as a unique moment in that event and on his death and resurrection as the very summation of that event. For that reason, Christian witness must point to what happened. And since its only link with the past stages of the Christ-event is through the faith of past generations of believers, the community must guard the traditions of that belief and bear

witness to them from one generation to another.[30]

The faith of the primitive Christian communities, forged as it was in the first stark awareness of the resurrection of Jesus and shaped by the immediate witness of the Twelve, is a privileged window onto the mystery of Christ. It contains an immediacy of experience which could not possibly occur again. Thus the record of this earliest Christian faith, retained in the rich diversity of its various traditions, was gathered into a canon of sacred writings.[31]

While there is no conscious reflection upon the nature of the process of witnessing to faith traditions within the infant church, the existence of the New Testament literature is the evidence that they did so witness. Actually, the word *"paradosis"* very quickly became a word with accepted technical meaning, perhaps as early as Paul's first letter to the Corinthians.[32] And the missionary envoys, the apostles, who went out from communities like Jerusalem to evangelize the Mediterranean world, were expected to expound not just their own personal faith but that of the community which had sent them.[33] This they did by teaching the new Christians their own creed and also their liturgical usages. Thus tradition was from the beginning given expression through "Scripture" and "sacrament."

All the elements of the New Testament writing indicate that some members of the early church enjoyed a special role in this process of witnessing to the community's developing faith traditions: the Gospels by their accounts of the "commission" given to the Twelve (Matt. 28:18), and in a particular way to Peter (Matt. 16:18; John 21:15-19), Acts with its narration of the evangelization undertaken by individuals like Paul and Barnabas, Paul's own letters with their references to his own apostolate and to that of others. It is less clear just who and in what official capacity was responsible for such special witness. Inevitably it fell to some extent on anyone in the community who was in a position of some leadership, even parents with regard to their children. The traveling apostles who brought the faith to new places and there helped establish communities were clearly recognized as special witnesses.[34] It seems, too, that the earliest converts of such apostles thereafter played a special part in guiding the community's faith; it seems that such men were considered among the *presbyteroi*.[35] Where they existed, the *episkopoi* were charged with bearing witness to the authentic tradition of faith. Certainly this is a recognized "episcopal" function by the time of the Pastorals (Titus 1:9; 2:7–10).

Actually, once we move past the first stage of evangelization and conversion, in which the apostle holds a unique position, all of the people in the community must have shared to quite an extent in the responsibility of bearing witness about the faith which they themselves had *received*. This they did to one another as they prayed together, celebrated sacramental liturgy (baptismal or Eucharistic), or discussed the teaching of Jesus or the apostles or their own understanding of the realities of Christian life. This they would also do whenever they brought the good news of Christ to non-Christians. As we have already seen, such "missionary" endeavor was something shared by all Christians in the early centuries. This does not say that all shared equally in shaping Christian faith by witnessing to the community's traditions; all shared somewhat in this, but leadership did immediately emerge to give direction and some unity to the process of tradition.

Teaching

Given the kind of community that was formed in early Christianity, teaching in one form or another inevitably played a major part in that community's internal activity. And, both from a priori judgment on the nature of the situation in early Christianity and from the evidence of New Testament texts, we must say about teaching what we have just remarked about witness: to some degree each member of the community func-

tioned as a teacher, but a select group immediately emerged as "official" teachers.

There is no more hope of disengaging from one another the concrete functioning of witness and teaching in early Christianity than there is of separating prophecy and discipleship in an apostle such as Paul. In any action of genuine teaching there is always some witness to the teacher's own interests and enthusiasms and ideas. Clearly, this becomes much more operative when there is a question of teaching that takes place in an area of special personal impact, as would exist preeminently in the teaching of religious faith.

Having said this in the hope of avoiding the pitfall of trying to distinguish more sharply than the evidence will allow the various ministries of early Christianity, it is still important to distinguish, if the New Testament texts so allow us to do, a function of "teaching" that goes beyond a simple and summary act of proclaiming that Jesus is the risen Lord. Some basis for making such a distinction is provided by the New Testament language: "*kerygma*" (and the words related to it, along with allied words such as "*martyria*" and "*evangelion*") is not the same as "*didache*" (to which we might join "*katechein*"—it seems that the noun "*catechesis*" is not used in the New Testament). Studies on this verbal usage[36] indicate that "*kerygma*" refers rather to the stage of first proclamation of the gospel; it is aimed at bringing faith into existence and leading to conversion and entry into the community.[37] "*Didache*," on the other hand, denominates that ensuing process of extending the believer's understanding of the faith he has embraced. It adds further information about the person and activity and teaching of Jesus, more detailed instruction about life in the Christian community, its meaning and its demands, and lengthier explanation about the significance of baptism and the Eucharistic assembly.[38]

This suggests teaching activity that demands of the one exercising it a wider range of information, an insight into the meaning of the Gospel, an ability to clarify and explain details of Christian language and life that are not necessary in the witness. One can be truly convinced of the truth of the gospel, deeply attached personally in faith to Christ, and have an understanding of Christianity that is accurate, but at the same time be without knowledge of many of the details of Christian belief and practice and without any theological sophistication. Such a person can witness, sometimes in strikingly effective fashion, to his own faith and to the reality of Christ, but he is incapable of serving as a teacher of Christian doctrine.

Adequate and effective religious education cannot be reduced to "giving witness." In our own day this has been a mistake made by some who were searching for more exciting catechetics. There must be a teaching ministry, in which accurate information and insights are imparted, in which ungrounded opinions about the reality and meaning of Christ and Christianity are replaced by well-grounded understanding.[39] Apparently, from the very beginning of Christianity, such "rationalization" of the Christian message and way of life was undertaken for two purposes: to make Christianity more intelligently meaningful for those of the faith, and to defend Christian claims against skeptics or opponents. Even the New Testament writings, which are essentially catechesis, are at the same time the early Christian church's "apologetic."

Using the New Testament texts as our basic window into the earliest Christian ministry of teaching, we can reconstruct to a limited extent the content and method of this instruction. At the very beginning and apparently for some decades, it was quite informal. For the most part, it would have been carried on in the gatherings of the small and closely knit communities, especially in the gathering for the "breaking of the bread." Immediate disciples of Jesus, if they were present, enjoyed a privileged role in such teaching; or, in their absence, someone taught who had been converted and instructed by such apostolic teaching.[40]

Exactly how certain individuals came to exercise recognized authority in teaching is not clear; there is no "office" of teacher. There is a recognized *role* or *function*; this is even seen (in some instances at least) as a special gift from the Spirit for the good of the community (1 Cor. 14:26). It is easy enough to see how the persons who had been closely associated with Jesus himself would be recognized as particularly qualified to instruct others about his person, his deeds, and his teaching. So, also, there is evidence that the earliest converts in a given community then instructed others who were attracted to the gospel and baptized.[41] No doubt, some of the converts to Christianity were more educated and better equipped to grasp the nature and implications of the Christ-event, and so naturally would have been looked to as teachers. One group that fits this picture were the Jewish priests who embraced the gospel. Certainly there were such, perhaps fairly numerous (Acts 6:7). Almost inevitably they would have received recognition from their fellow Christians, particularly in Jewish-Christian communities, as specially competent to understand and explain the gospel. Very likely they would have been prominent in the group leadership, the *presbyteroi*, that figured so importantly in primitive Christianity.[42]

There is very little evidence of individuals being formally designated to teach. Acts describes the manner in which some, as Paul and Barnabas, were selected to go out as apostles (Acts 11:22–26; 13:1–3); perhaps the tenth chapter of Matthew (the mission of the disciples) reflects this same aspect of early Christianity. It seems quite clear that the major Christian communities, and particularly the "mother church" of Jerusalem, sent out emissaries to evangelize. Such apostles were engaged not only in the first preaching of the gospel and the establishment of a nucleus community but in the work of follow-up, in furthering teaching and encouragement. Paul's letters are an instance of this sort of thing, and the *Didache* provides contemporary nonbiblical testimony for the same pattern.[43] As a matter of fact, there is good likelihood that the *Didache* was intended as a manual or guidebook for the instruction to be given by such visiting apostles.[44] If so, it testifies to the practice, and also the "content" of such teaching.

While the *Didache* (presuming that one can follow Audet's dating of 70 A.D.) can provide some valuable information, it is the New Testament texts themselves that give us an explicit picture of the content and orientation of early Christian teaching. Roughly, this teaching deals with two main topics: the event of God's saving revelation in Jesus, and the "new way" of life that follows from this event. This twofold character of the catechesis is clearly illustrated by the Epistle to the Ephesians, in which the mystery of Christ is explained in the early chapters and the implications of this for Christian living are treated in the second half of the letter. One sees a reflection of it also in the structure of the Matthean Gospel, where the deeds and teachings of Jesus are presented in juxtaposed form in each of the "five books" of the Gospel.

One thing should be noted, for it could have important implications for the later understanding of ministry. The teaching about Christian life and its implications, though it inevitably touches upon "ethical" matters, is not an attempt to formulate an ethic; rather, it is exhortation and counsel to live out an ideal that is based in the death and resurrection of Jesus, an ideal of life that is the external expression of the Spirit's working within the community.[45] For this reason, the "minister" of such teaching would have to be gifted with authority that derived from more than "clear and distinct ideas." For one thing, it seems that he would have to be able to say, as Paul did, "Be imitators of me, as I am of Christ" (1 Cor. 11:1). Thus, the element of "good example" which we discussed earlier (when dealing with discipleship) played an important part in early Christian teaching.

How early the function of teaching devolved upon the "governmental leadership" of the Christian communities is impossible to say.[46] However, the *Didache* indicates that *episkopoi* and *diakonoi* should be designated, so that they can function in the absence of prophets and teachers.[47] This would seem to say that the day-by-day task of instruction would have fallen to their lot. Again, in the Pastorals we can see evidence for the fact that by the end of the first century the community leaders, the *episkopoi*, were responsible for the teaching of the community (1 Tim. 3:2–3; 4:6–11). This is not to say that the involvement of *episkopoi-presbyteroi* in teaching was viewed as their function alone, or something that derived from their office in the community; it was rather a logical implication of their role in the community. It would be quite difficult to envisage a situation in which responsibility for the well-being of a faith community and leadership in that community would not include some form of teaching. As a matter of fact, in trying to reconstruct the evolution of ministry in early Christianity, it is difficult to say whether "teaching" began as a more or less independent function that was then progessively claimed by an emerging hierarchy, or whether it was first seen informally as pertaining to the *episkopoi* and only "delegated" by them to others as the communities became larger and more complex.

One of the most instructive pieces of evidence in this matter must be the development of first-century thought and imagery about Peter. Without retrojecting notions of "primacy" onto the biblical writings, it does seem that Peter is depicted as an ideal for those in positions of responsibility in the early communities. Consequently, it is significant for our study to note that by the time the New Testament literature was completed the *symbolic* function of Peter (prescinding from the questions of his actual historical activity) included witness, shepherding, and safeguarding accuracy of faith. However, it also seems significant that such Petrine functions are linked to his being a privileged recipient of revelation, rather than to any special governing position he occupied within the early community.[48]

A group of people that forms a community shares certain common ideas and objectives, certain attitudes, and a certain spirit. Inevitably, because this is the manner of human consciousness, these are linked with certain key images and symbols which in a subtle but powerful way give both structure and justification to the community consciousness.[49] At the same time, such images and symbols, communicated from one generation to another (often subconsciously), provide an extremely important agency of continuity within the group[50]—which is another way of saying that any human community lives according to one or another "mythology," a partial or total world-view that is cast in an imaginative framework.[51]

Early Christianity was no exception. As a matter of fact, the New Testament literature provides a fascinating instance of the manner in which the "new" and radically unexpected event of Christ's death and resurrection demanded of the early Christians a reevaluation of their previous religious and cultural mythologies. This is not the occasion for a detailed study of the unique character of the Christian "mythology," its rooting in the historical facts and therefore realistically imaginable aspects of the Christ-event, its intrinsic fulfillment of Old Testament symbolisms, and its expression in the enactment of Christian sacrament. Such study is only in its early stages;[52] but enough has been done to indicate the basic need of early Christianity to initiate its new members into the mythology, the image-world proper to the gospel and to Christian life.[53]

Nothing is clearer in the New Testament texts than the early church's awareness of initiating its new members into the mystery of Christ's death and resurrection. Basically, of course, this was seen in terms of baptism, which was entry simultaneously into the believing community and into the death and resurrection of Christ.[54] But baptism was only the beginning; the "entry into Christ" was a progressive process that found its fulfillment only in the eschatological union with the risen Lord. Such deepening entry into union with the risen Christ was undoubtedly associated with the celebration of the Eucharist. The catechesis distilled into chapters 13–17 of John's Gospel makes this clear. But

this celebration of mystery in symbol was linked with progressive instruction as to the meaning of this symbolism, so that psychologically the individual and the community as a whole were introduced more deeply into the life of faith in Christ. This utilization of word in primitive Christian sacramental liturgy is one of the principal sources of the New Testament literature.[55]

There is nothing that would point clearly to an official group entrusted with the instruction that would have been part of Christian initiation.[56] The evidence of New Testament texts is varied: it is the deacon Philip who functions in this regard for the emissary of the queen of Ethiopia (Acts 8:26–39); Paul's epistles are in many portions an explanation of the baptism which the faithful had received, a clarification of the implications of that entry into Christ (Rom. 6:3–11), and an exhortation to live out faithfully the commitment of baptism (Gal. 3:23ff.). For that reason they may point to a special apostolic role in initiating people into the "Christian myth," though it is interesting to notice that Paul lays no claim to the right to baptize (1 Cor. 1:14–17). The attribution of the two Petrine Epistles to Peter, and the fact that they are to quite an extent catechesis bearing on baptism, may indicate some tendency to see baptismal instruction as the proper responsibility of the leader of the community.[57] The fact that the commission of Matthew 28:18 to baptize and to teach is addressed to the Twelve may point in this same direction, but actually such evidence, though suggestive, is far from decisive.

What we seem to find in the early decades of Christianity is a lack of that religious situation in which some special sacred group is entrusted with a secret tradition, a hidden myth, which they communicate only in a celebration of "mystery." Elements of such a mentality can be found in some Rabbinic circles,[58] in some of the esoteric Jewish sects of the day,[59] in Gnosticism,[60] and in the Near Eastern mystery religions;[61] but it is quite foreign to the New Testament Christian communities, even explicitly disowned by Paul in his letter to the Corinthians (1 Cor. 1:18—2:16). The Christian mystery is essentially something revealed, something to be proclaimed to the whole world. Thus, no special group is needed to guard some higher truth that must be hidden from the masses. The gospel is the heritage of the entire people and each Christian has the responsibility of cherishing and proclaiming it. In this regard it is important to note that the key celebration of "mystery" in Christianity was clearly the Eucharist, and this action was viewed in the early decades as an act of proclamation.[62] If there is a group especially responsible for the traditional faith and religious understanding of Christianity, and increasingly such a group emerges in the early church, then it is to function in constant and open discourse with the entire community and with the objective of extending and deepening the community's knowledge and capacity to evangelize the world. Ultimately, in the view of early Christian faith, it is the Spirit who gives insight into the "Christ myth" and the Spirit is given to all the people (John 16:13–14).

Oracle

One of the most intriguing passages in the New Testament literature is the short remark in John's Gospel that Caiaphas prophesied about Jesus without being aware of it, "being high priest that year" (John 11:51). If nothing else, the text reflects the belief of early Christians that God still continued to utilize some men as oracles, as situations where humans could come into some more direct contact with the divine and receive a communication from the divine. And that such an oracular role is to be found within the Christian community is a constant presumption of the New Testament writings.[63]

It does seem, however, that the function of oracle as it is found in the church of the first decades is thought of in terms of prophecy rather than of priesthood, as priesthood was known to either Judaism or the pagan religions of the time. This would, of course, have been a logical development of the Old Testament understanding of prophecy; the prophet (especially the charismatic prophet) of Israel was one in whom the people were confronted with Yahweh's demanding word: "Thus says the Lord God. . . ." It is this same prophetic office to which the entire Christian people succeeds, though certain individuals within the community apparently possess specialized prophetic gifts.

It is interesting to note that the notion of "oracle" is never attached to a place in early Christianity; instead, it is the people that provide a context in which men contact God, the people who are the Temple of God in which his Spirit dwells.[64] Of its very essence the Christian community is a "moving oracle"; it is a missionary people, constantly moving out in order to provide occasion for all men to come into contact with the Father of our Lord Jesus Christ (Matt. 28:18–20).

Those within the community who function in special ways as prophets seem to do so intermittently and under occasional direct impulse of the Spirit, rather than by virtue of some official designation.[65] Early Christian communities prayed for guidance through such inspired utterance, and they record that they were so guided (Acts 13:1–3). As far as the texts indicate, anyone could receive such charismatic powers of communicating God's word to the community. Some, like the Twelve, seem to have been recognized by the community as particularly designated by the Spirit for this function (Acts 2). Genuine prophecy existed for the sake of the community, to form and direct its life and faith (1 Cor. 14:3–5), and the community had the right and responsibility of distinguishing true from false prophets (1 Cor. 14:29–33, 37–38). However, it is clear that the community did not designate prophets (a fortiori, no one—not even the Twelve—officially appointed prophets); the Spirit alone did that. The community merely recognized what the Spirit had done.[66]

The distinct impression that one receives in reading the New Testament literature is that the early Christians were imbued with the reality of "the word of God." This word was not a reality of the past, recorded in the sacred literature of Israel. Nor did it terminate with the word spoken through the historical teaching and passion of Jesus, focal though that was. The Father who sent Jesus as his own incarnated Word continued to speak to the disciples of Christ, continued to make his will known in direct fashion, continued to make his presence tangibly felt through the words of his prophets. More basically, he continued to speak to men through the words and life of his new chosen people to whom he imparted his own Spirit of prophecy.

If, however, the Christian people was a privileged agency for communicating God's word to men, it was only because God's own Word incarnated still dwelt in the midst of the church and united it to himself as his Body. As a matter of fact, the only word that Christianity really has to speak to men is Christ in the mystery of his death and resurrection (1 Cor. 1).

It would be an obvious anachronism to ask Does primitive Christianity see the church as "sacrament of Christ"? This notion is scarcely emerging into explicit expression in contemporary theological discussion.[67] Yet, if one asks the question in slightly different fashion (Is the Christian community seen as a situation where the saving presence of the risen Christ and his Spirit touches men and transforms their lives?) it does appear that one can answer affirmatively. The Christian community's role of preaching the gospel to all men is not like any other kind of proclamation. Not only are Christians bringing a message about his saving action but they are also establishing his presence to the consciousness of men so that Christ himself can save those who receive him in faith. Their word to men is really Christ's own word, for they are his body: just as his own love finds expression in their loving concern for one another and for all men (1 John 4).

It is here that we are touching on what has always been (and still is) one of the most puzzling aspects of Christianity. If the action of Christ in his death and resurrection is all-sufficient as salvation, then what contribution can be made by Christians to the salvation of mankind? Christ alone is the Word that brings unending life; but it is in the proclamation of the gospel by the Christian people that men come into contact with that saving Word. This seems to be quite explicitly the response of early Christianity to that question (Rom. 10:14–17). What this seems to say is that the understanding of the community as prophetic is deepened by the realization that the community is this as Christ's own Body. Thus we have a radical unification of word and sacrament: the church is sacrament precisely insofar as it is word.[68] This is why, though early Christianity does not explicitly theologize about it, the supreme sacramental expression of the community's faith and life and being is also seen as its supreme prophetic proclamation, "As often as you eat this bread . . ." (1 Cor. 11:26).[69]

If there is one thing that is indisputable about New Testament thought on Christian ministry it is that this ministry finds its source and focus in the ministry of Christ himself.[70] Moreover, Christ's ministry, and therefore that of the church, is basically a mystery of the communication of the word of God. Christ's ministry of the word operates on several levels. There is the sensible level of his own historical public ministry of preaching; there is the inner power of his word to give life and healing to those who receive his word in faith; there is the unparalleled utterance of the Father's redeeming love for man that takes place in the death and resurrection; there is the radical ministry performed by the very human existing of Jesus, as in the mystery of incarnation it serves to give expression and "outlet" to his identity and redemptive role as God's own Word.

It is, of course, the Johannine tradition that develops most explicitly and extensively the theology of Jesus as the Word.[71] On the other hand, if one were to undertake a thorough investigation of this topic it would be necessary to probe carefully the Synoptic presentation of Christ as the fulfillment of Old Testament prophecy, a fulfillment that reaches unique proportions in a text such as the parable of the unjust custodians of the vineyard (Matt. 21:33–46); the Lucan theology of Christ as the *doxa theou*;[72] or the Pauline usage (which is not unique to him) of the imagery of light.[73]

Sufficient study has been done on this theme, however, to indicate without doubt that the first-century church has an explicit and quite highly developed theology of Christ's function as the Word of God, and that this stood at the center of their soteriology. More than that, it stood at the center of what men thought of Christianity as a reli-gion, for this word of God in Jesus, while it was a word of power and life, did not work magically but only in conjunction with the faith and free cooperation of men. This implies some critical aspects of early Christianity's view of ministry: Since it is the ministry of the word that is sharing in Christ's own ministry, it does not work magically nor through enslaving *imperium*; rather, it must work through persuasion and exhortation and attraction, for it can be effective only to the extent that it elicits the free response of men's faith and conversion.[74]

NOTES

1. See H. Strathmann, "Martys," *Theological Dictionary of the New Testament* (hereafter referred to as *TDNT*), vol. 4, pp. 489–504; O. Cullmann, *Christology of the New Testament* (London, 1963), pp. 30–50.

2. This theme is developed at length in J. Leuba, *L'institution et l'événement* (Paris, 1950).

3. See Strathmann, "Martys"; also the article "Witness" in J. McKenzie, *Dictionary of the Bible*, which contains a good synthetic listing of the New Testament uses.

4. For a technical discussion, historical and theological, of "revelation," see R. Latourelle, *Theology of Revelation* (New York, 1966).

5. See E. Schillebeeckx, *Revelation and Theology* (New York, 1967), vol. 1, pp. 33–56.

6. See G. Friedrich, "Prophetes," *TDNT*, vol. 6, pp. 828–61.

7. See Phil. 1:14–18; also Friedrich, pp. 841–50.

8. See Vatican II, *Constitution on the Church*, 35; also B. Cooke, *The God of Space and Time* (New York, 1970), pp. 192–98.

9. See A. Richardson, *Introduction to the Theology of the New Testament* (New York, 1958), pp. 103–20.

10. See Friedrich, pp. 854–55.

11. Matt. 3:3; Mark 1:3; Luke 3:4. All quote Isaiah 40:3.

12. See Strathmann, pp. 495–502.

13. See Cullmann, pp. 13–50; Richardson, pp. 125–41.

14. See R. Lightfoot, *St. John's Gospel* (Oxford, 1956), *passim*; F. Mussner, *The Historical Jesus in the Gospel of St. John* (New York, 1967), pp. 35–39.

15. It is interesting to notice that 5:38 says that because the people will not accept this witness to the Father, nor the witness of Jesus' works, they "do not have his word abiding with you."

16. The Jerusalem Bible translates: ". . . All your brothers who are witnesses to Jesus. . . . The witness Jesus gave is the same as the spirit of prophecy"; and in a footnote: "This is the word of God to which Jesus testifies and which is implanted in every Christian, and which inspires the prophets." This interpretation seems to negate the explicit statement of the text: "*he marturia Iesou estin to pneuma tes propheteias.*"

17. See E. Schweizer, *Church Order in the New Testament* (London, 1961), pp. 186–87; also H. Küng, *The Church* (New York, 1967), pp. 396–98.

18. See K. Rengstorf, "Mathetes," *TDNT*, vol. 4, pp. 441–59.

19. See K. Schelkle, *Discipleship and Priesthood* (New York, 1965).

20. *Ibid.*, pp. 9–16.

21. *Ibid.*, pp. 16–32.

22. Rom. 6:3–8; 1 Cor. 12:12–13; Eph. 4:11–16.

23. See Cooke, pp. 159–73.

24. E.g., Clement of Alexandria's *Paedagogus* or Augustine's *De magistro.*

25. See Schelkle, pp. 79–86.

26. *Ibid.*, pp. 69–70.

27. *Ibid.*, pp. 9–29.

28. On symbolic actions of Old Testament prophets, see J. Lindblom, *Prophecy in Ancient Israel* (Oxford, 1962), pp. 165–73.

29. See Schelkle, pp. 59–86.

30. For examples of the extensive recent discussion of "tradition," see R. Hanson, *Tradition in the Early Church* (London, 1962); H. von Campenhausen, *Tradition and Life in the Church* (London, 1968); Y. Congar, *Tradition and Traditions* (New York, 1967).

31. On the formation of the New Testament canon, see R. Grant, *The Formation of the New Testament* (New York, 1965).

32. See F. Büchsel, "Paradosis," *TDNT*, vol. 2, pp. 172–73. 1 Cor. 11:23; 15:3ff.

33. See J.-P. Audet, *La Didache* (Paris, 1958), pp. 116–20.

34. See Schweizer, pp. 194–97.

35. However, we are here in the realm of conjecture. While the Pauline letters indicate that the initial converts of a church often played a special leadership role, Paul never employs the term *"presbyteros"* and there is no evidence of a presbyteral structure in the early Pauline communities. See H. von Campenhausen, *Ecclesiastical Authority and Spiritual Power in the Church of the First Three Centuries* (Palo Alto, Calif., 1969), pp. 55–83.

36. See G. Auzou, *The Formation of the Bible* (St. Louis, 1963), pp. 319ff.; L. Hartman, "Preaching," *Encyclopedic Dictionary of the Bible*, cols. 1901–6; C. Dodd, *The Apostolic Preaching* (New York, 1962).

37. G. Friedrich, "Kerusso," *TDNT*, vol. 3, pp. 707–17.

38. See K. Rengstorf, "Didaskein," *TDNT*, vol. 2, pp. 144–48; see also the articles "Preaching" and "Teaching" in *Dictionary of the Bible.*

39. For amplification of this theme, see J. Hofinger, *The Art of Teaching Christian Doctrine*, 2d ed. (Notre Dame, 1962); also, the essays in *Modern Catechetics*, ed. G. Sloyan (New York, 1963), and *Pastoral Catechetics*, ed. J. Hofinger and T. Stone (New York, 1964).

40. See H. Riesenfeld, *The Gospel Tradition and Its Beginnings* (London, 1957).

41. See von Campenhausen, pp. 66–68.

42. On the influence in primitive Christianity of convert Jewish priests, see J. Schmitt, "Jewish Priesthood and Christian Hierarchy in the Early Palestinian Communities," *The Sacrament of Holy Orders* (Collegeville, Minn., 1962), pp. 60–74.

43. See Audet, pp. 116–20.

44. *Ibid.*, pp. 248–52.

45. See R. Schnackenburg, *The Moral Teaching of the New Testament* (New York, 1965), pp. 42–53; also W. Grossouw, *Spirituality of the New Testament* (St. Louis, 1961), pp. 35–46.

46. It would not be hard to imagine that church leaders (*presbyteroi, episkopoi, apostoloi*) all performed various tasks of teaching, though there were designated teachers in at least some of the communities; the question that faces us is: When and for what reasons was teaching seen to be the proper responsibility and prerogative of the administrative leadership?

47. *Didache* 15. 1.

48. See the important study *Peter in the New Testament*, ed. R. Brown, K. Donfried, J. Reumann (Minneapolis, 1973), esp. the conclusions, pp. 157–68, which use the

notion of trajectory to describe the early Christian evolution of understanding about Peter.

49. For an excellent review of the various theories about the role of symbols in society, see H. Duncan, *Symbols and Social Theory* (New York, 1969), and *Symbols in Society* (New York, 1968). On the more limited topic of symbols and religious community, see M. Eliade, *Patterns in Comparative Religion* (New York, 1958), and W. Lynch, *Christ and Apollo* (New York, 1960).

50. See Duncan, *Symbols in Society*, pp. 44–46.

51. One must be careful not to mistake an implication of "the unreal" in the use of myth; rather, myth tends to be an imaginative formulation of the insight into the "more ultimately real." See M. Eliade, *Cosmos and History* (Torch ed., New York, 1959), pp. 34–48; and G. Van der Leeuw, *Religion in Essence and Manifestation* (Gloucester, 1967), vol. 2, pp. 413–18.

52. Which is not to deny the pioneering work done by such scholars as P. Minear, W. Lynch, A. Farrer, F. Dillistone, and H. Rahner.

53. An interesting question arises at this point: Is there a proper Christian mythology, *the* myth, into which Christians must be initiated? Or is it part of the task of each generation to explain *critically* the inherited mythologies, and to devise other and still inadequate myths to accompany the intelligible content of faith without fundamentally perverting it? And is it not the task of theology, which in this instance must guide the community's teaching, to carry on this work of de- and re-mythologizing?

54. Rom. 6:1–11; Gal. 3:27–29. See also J. Giblet, "Baptism—The Sacrament of Incorporation into the Church According to St. Paul," in *Baptism in the New Testament* (Baltimore, 1964), pp. 161–88; and D. Mollat, "Baptismal Symbolism in St. Paul," in *ibid.*, pp. 63–86.

55. See D. Stanley, *The Apostolic Church in the New Testament* (Westminster, Md., 1965), pp. 91–194; B. Vawter, "The Johannine Sacramentary," *Theological Studies* 17 (1956), pp. 151–66; C. Moule, *The Birth of the New Testament* (London, 1962), pp. 11–32.

56. However, the "apostolic" criterion for New Testament canonicity may reflect the "official" approach to initiation catechesis.

57. For a brief review of opinion regarding the relation of the Petrine Epistles to early Christian baptism, see J. Elliott, *The Elect and the Holy* (Leiden, 1966), pp. 6–13.

58. See G. Scholem, *Major Trends in Jewish Mysticism*, 3d ed. (New York, 1954).

59. G. Bornkamm, "Mysterion," *TDNT*, vol. 4, pp. 815–17.

60. See K. Smyth, "Gnosticism in the Gospel According to Thomas," *Heythrop Journal* 1 (1960), pp. 189–98.

61. See C. Barrett, *The New Testament Background* (London, 1956), pp. 91–104.

62. 1 Cor. 11:26. See J.-P. Audet, "Esquisse historique du genre littéraire de la 'bénédiction' juive et de l' 'eucharistie' chrétienne," *Revue biblique* 65 (1958), pp. 371–99.

63. For example, the type of direct Spirit guidance of the communities through special charisms (such as prophecy) to which the Pauline Epistles attest.

64. On the Pauline use of this figure, see Y. Congar, *The Mystery of the Temple* (London, 1962), pp. 151–72.

65. Though the *Didache* would seem to indicate a community recognition of the charism which established a prophet in something like a permanent position or "office." See Schweizer, pp. 142–45, who points out also how this *Didache* pattern differs from that of the Pauline communities.

66. See Küng, p. 396.

67. One of the few who has developed the notion is O. Semmelroth. See his *Church and Sacrament* (Notre Dame, 1965), and his earlier *Die Kirche als Ursakrament*, 2d ed. (Frankfurt, 1955).

68. See K. Rahner, *The Church and the Sacraments* (New York, 1963), and *idem*, "Word and Eucharist," *Theological Investigations* (Baltimore, 1966), vol. 4, pp. 253–86.

69. This may be why the *Didache* seems to take it for granted that prophets are logical celebrants for the Eucharist. See *Didache* 10.7 which says that it should be granted to prophets *eucharistein*; the reference to prophets in 13.3 as "your high priests" may well be confirmative, but it does not conclusively relate to early Christian worship.

70. See H. Beyer, "Diakoneo," *TDNT*, vol. 2, pp. 84–87; Schelkle, pp. 16–45; and *Constitution on the Church*, 18–21.

71. See R. Brown, *The Gospel According to John* (New York, 1966), vol. 1, pp. 3–37.

72. See H. Conzelmann, *The Theology of St. Luke* (New York, 1961), pp. 171–206; the Lucan treatment of Jesus' *doxa* is intertwined with the view of Jesus' *exousia* and *dynamis* (all three are manifested in Jesus' ministry), yet Conzelmann tends to reserve the notion of Jesus' *doxa* to the risen state of Christ (p. 203).

73. Within the almost universal religious utilization of "light" as symbol, it would be necessary to make precise the Christian (and more limited, the Pauline) use of this symbolism. Some notion of the philosophical depths of this task can be gained by reflecting on J. Macquarrie's remarks in his *God-Talk* (New York, 1967), pp. 192–211. The question that arises, and its implications for Christian theology and faith are obvious, is: What is the extent to which proper names for Christ as divine (e.g., Word, Son, Light-from-Light) are truly "proper" and the source for theological inquiry into the unique identity of Jesus?

74. Though it itself does not draw the conclusion, early Christian theology implies a basically new approach to the question of God as creator and to the understanding of "providence." Already the Old Testament literature had seen creation as a mystery of *salvation*; in its notion of "second Adam" the New Testament theology continues and "christologizes" this Old Testament view. However, it does not develop the role of man in the creation of history and of the world, nor does it explicate the creative freedom left by God to man to determine the precise evolution of the future, though the biblical eschatology opens onto both these questions. Today's theology is faced with the immense task of investigating the church's (and mankind's) ministry of God's word as this word works (in conjunction with human freedom) to shape the world towards its eschatological fulfillment.

CHAPTER 9

The Word in the Ante-Nicene Church

Despite the rapid and in some aspects radical evolution of Christian faith and life in the first decades of the church's existence, the essentially evangelical character of Christianity remains dominant into the second century and for quite some time thereafter. Christian communities exist for the purpose of manifesting the gospel and preaching it to all who will listen; the gospel is still new enough to be startling, still fresh enough to have avoided institutionalized dullness. Both community life and doctrine are still simple enough, so that the gospel itself is not obscured or overshadowed. Christianity still remains almost totally a witness to the Christ-event.

Central to the evangelical approach to Christian existence was the function of witness.[1] It was not the special genius or role of the Christian community to develop or preserve a philosophical or even a religious tradition. Paul had already made this clear to the Corinthians.[2] Rather, it was to bear witness to the supreme event in human history, the definitive divine intervention that brought about man's salvation. Jesus himself was, of course, the first and greatest witness. The New Testament literature had already indicated this, and the early patristic writings continue this view. In the basic "Christian apologetic" that extends from Justin through the third century, Jesus is presented as the one who by his words and deeds bore witness to the salvific fidelity of the God who had predicted salvation through the Old Testament prophets.[3] Clearly, it was in his death and resurrection that Jesus bore the ultimate witness. This event itself is the great procla-

mation of the "good news," a word that is at once "the light of the world" and a word of power that frees and enlivens.[4]

Logically, then, there is nothing that a Christian can say that is able to bear witness in the way his own death for Christ's sake would do.[5] The assimilation to Christ and consequent reflection to men of Christ's own word can take no higher expression than the Christian's own martyrdom. One can see the intimate relationship in the thinking of early Christianity between "witness" and death suffered for the gospel from the very fact that the word "witness" (*martyr*) is gradually appropriated as the name given such heroic Christians.[6] By the time of Cyprian there is a thoroughly developed ideal of martyrdom, an explicit recognition that it constitutes the highest ideal of Christian perfection;[7] in the East, the *Didascalia* attributes to martyrdom the remission of sin.[8] But the praise and appreciation of this highest witness to Christ is found in less theologically developed patristic writings as early as the letters of Ignatius to the Romans[9] and the account of the martyrdom of Polycarp.[10]

Not all Christians were called by circumstances to proclaim the gospel by their own death, but all were called to proclaim the gospel in some form. They all belonged to a people commissioned to evangelize and endowed with the Spirit of prophecy. So, alongside the ideal of martyrdom there developed the ideal of heroic Christian life, a "daily martyrdom," as witness to the gospel. It is to such practice of lofty ethical principles that Justin and the other apologists can appeal to counteract the calumnies directed against the early churches.[11] It is this witness of "good example," which Paul had already indicated as especially appropriate to the leadership in the community, which gradually evolves into the ascetical ideal that will find extended expression in the historically influential writings of Basil and Augustine.

If the community bore witness to the mystery of Christ by its willingness to face death "for the sake of the gospel" and by its day-by-day living out of the ideal of conduct preached and lived by Christ, it also bore witness by guarding and proclaiming the traditional belief that originated with the apostles.[12] This was a living tradition, closely bound up with those who occupied positions of teaching in the community. But from the earliest decades of the second century there is evidence that it was specially related to the New Testament Scriptures as to its privileged expression. And this even before the final crystallization of the text and the early collections of canonical writing.

Ignatius and Clement of Rome already indicate dependence upon some form of the New Testament writings.[13] With Justin the dependence upon developed New Testament texts is already much clearer,[14] and by the time of Irenaeus (at the end of the second century) there is explicit appeal to the traditions of belief contained in the major New Testament writings.[15] By the beginning of the third century the pattern is established: the exposition of Scripture is the essence of explaining the apostolic tradition. Clement of Alexandria will work in this framework,[16] Origen even more so;[17] the African tradition from Tertullian[18] through Cyprian[19] to Augustine[20] will appeal to the Scripture texts as the apostolic tradition to which orthodox doctrine must conform. In the Roman sphere of influence the writings of Hippolytus continued the approach of Irenaeus,[21] though the most valuable extant work of Hippolytus (which significantly bears the title of *Apostolic Tradition*) deals with the transmission of apostolic faith and practice in the Christian sacramental liturgy.

It would be a mistake to confine the thought of these pre-Nicene centuries on the topic of "tradition" to the Scriptures, central though these were.[22] The traditional faith is that which began with the apostles, has been handed down from one generation to another, particularly by "lineages" of teachers (e.g., John to Polycarp to Irenaeus), and finds expression in the teaching of the bishops, the writings of the New Testament canon, and the ceremonies of Christian liturgy. On the other hand, there does not seem to be in orthodox Christian circles a notion of "hidden traditions," a special body of truths not contained in the New Testament writings but committed to the bishops or some other group for semi-secret transmission.[23] Such a notion is at home in the esoteric atmosphere of Gnosticism but foreign to the Christian notion of revelation and evangelization. The purpose of the Christian community, its mission given to it by its Lord, is to preach the gospel to every creature. It is not the right of the church to hide any portion of the faith of the apostles.[24]

What we seem to see, then, in these centuries which immediately follow the apostolic epoch, is the conscious and expressed intent of the church to continue what the apostles began. These latter had been the great witnesses and teachers of the mystery of Christ; it was the obligation of later Christian generations to see that this same witness and teaching was given in unadulterated form to men. And since it was the New Testament writings that preserved this apostolic catechesis and witness, the handing on of apostolic tradition consisted very largely in exposing faithfully the New Testament texts.

If the entire Christian community has this function of evangelizing according to the authentic traditions of apostolic faith, can one ascertain a specific function in this regard that is reserved to a specially designated and "official" group or individual? Certainly there is no limitation of the supreme witness of martyrdom or of that of exemplary Christian life —these can be expected and even demanded of any Christian. However, the evidence indicates that Christians of the second and third century expected more of their leaders in these respects than they did of others; possession of "office" did bring with it greater responsibility to set a good example for others.[25] After all, this is a presumption as old as the Pauline writings and explicitly expressed in the Pastorals.[26] But it is a presumption that is critically important for the study of the authority attaching to "office" in the Christian context. Is such authority grounded in the intrinsic leadership of one who sets the example, or in the office itself? And if such example is not given, does the individual occupying such an official position still possess effective authority in the faith life of the people? The question will reoccur frequently in the church's history.[27]

Nor can we extract from the historical evidence the conclusion that active evangelization was the proper function of such as bishops and presbyters. On the contrary, one of the reasons for the rapid expansion of Christianity in those centuries seems to have been the commonly accepted responsibility of all Christians to evangelize.[28] Unquestionably, many of those who were bishops or presbyters or deacons felt a particular responsibility to be active in evangelization; and, as the situation became more complicated by both larger numbers and increasing institutionalization, the *organized* tasks of evangelizing and catechizing fell upon the designated leaders of the churches.[29]

Granted the greater burden of responsibility in the ministry of the word that rested upon church "officials" in the second and third century, it is difficult to discover anything in this regard that is specifically reserved to them.[30] Before making any clear negative judgment, however, it is necessary to study more carefully the understanding of "witnessing to tradition" as this touched bishops, presbyters, teachers, and deacons.

Just prior to the beginning of this period, the *Didache* had stated that no prophet or apostle should be listened to if he preached a doctrine contrary to that outlined in this apostolic handbook.[31] Here we are at a stage where no body of New Testament Scriptures yet exists to provide a norm. With *1 Clement* we are still in this beginning phase and while it would be superficial to deny to Clement the notion of "handing on" doctrine the emphasis is on preserving and transmitting the edifying example of holy life.[32] It is the same emphasis to which Justin makes allusion in telling how the "homilist" exhorts his hearers at the Eucharist to follow the good example described in the "memoirs of the apostles."[33]

Ignatius is clearly involved in transmitting the understanding of the gospel that he has received from the apostolic generation, but there is no clear reference to a consciousness of "apostolic tradition."[34] Rather, it is later in the second century when, most likely to meet the need of distinguishing orthodox doctrine from the teaching of the Gnostics, a theory of apostolic tradition is consciously appealed to by Clement of Alexandria[35] and Irenaeus.[36]

The combination of these two writers is interesting, for one is a prominent bishop whereas the other was a teacher who apparently was quite independent of all ecclesiastical control.[37] For Clement, tradition was inseparable from the reality of the church itself;[38] the purpose of the Christian church was to propose for men the gospel which could lead them to true understanding and their destiny. Only one ultimately was the Teacher, the Word who had become man,[39] and hence it was the role of the Christian teacher to communicate to others the wisdom that had been handed down to him.[40]

Clement himself does not seem to have fitted into any particular stream of tradition within Christianity. He did not, as is sometimes supposed, belong to any "succession" of teachers at the *didaskalion* of Alexandria and as such inherit a "school tradition" like those that later characterized the thinkers of Alexandria or Antioch.[41] Nor did he, as a bishop of his day might have done, appeal to descent from one of the Twelve as basis for his teaching authority. Rather, as a learned man he had a respect for the wisdom of the past, and this found special expression in his Christian faith that the revelation given in Jesus Christ and handed on through the apostles, especially through the Scriptures, must be safeguarded and transmitted in its purity.[42] Thus the witness to Christian faith and doctrine is not specific to an office like *episkopos* but belongs to every Christian proportionate to his level of insight and understanding.[43]

As might be expected, the viewpoint of Irenaeus focuses on the function and responsibility of the bishop. "Tradition" is not a sharply defined notion for the bishop of Lyons, but in general it refers to the body of revealed truth that came to the church from the apostles. It can refer specifically to the kergyma of the apostles or it can denote the faith of Christians.[44] For the most part the term is used in an "objective" sense; it is the revelation given by Christ and perfectly handed down by the apostles.[45] What makes the apostles an object of veneration is not their endowment of special charismata, nor their possession of official authority, but their fidelity in witnessing to Christ.[46]

On the other hand, when Irenaeus sees that the episcopate in the church performs a special role in safeguarding the traditions of faith, he attributes this to a special grace given them because of their apostolic succession.[47] "The action of the Spirit in teaching the truth falls in a special way on the episcopate, that is, on the bishops who are gifted, by virtue of the apostolic succession, with the charisma of truth. This is the reason why those who want to be guided by the Spirit and obtain a perfect knowledge of the truth, must read the Scriptures under the guidance of the Church's presbyters."[48] The bishops' function seems to be largely one of preserving, fostering, and transmitting the truth of apostolic tradition.[49] And while there is no statement that limits tradition to Scripture, there is generally the association of Scripture with the objective apostolic tradition, and no indication that there is any "revelation" contained in some other source.[50]

Though he does in one place say that this apostolic tradition is preserved and transmitted by the *successio presbyterorum*, the im-

mediately succeeding passage indicates that the bishops are principally (if not exclusively) intended by this term.[51] And it would seem that two factors contribute to the authoritative witness of such *episkopoi*: the fact that they had heard the faithful witness of their episcopal predecessor who himself had heard it from his predecessor, and so on back to one of the apostles or disciples of Jesus; and the special gift of the Spirit to help them be faithful in their witness to truth.[52]

Tertullian's *De praescriptione* contains much the same view as that contained in Irenaeus. The Catholic church is to be followed, for she alone has the authentic Scriptures, the doctrine of the apostles, and the apostolic succession.[53] The more that he leaned to Montanism, however, the more Tertullian set the Church of the Spirit in opposition to the Church of the Bishops; the witness to truth comes from the "spiritual" man rather than from the bishop.[54] However, the very dispute in question testifies to the central position of the "ministry of the word" in the activity of the entire church and specifically of its "ordained ministers" at the end of the second century.

With Cyprian there does seem to be a definite shift to emphasis on the administrative and cultic aspects of the bishop's role.[55] This is not surprising when one considers the need to keep his diocese united despite the disrupting influences of the Decian persecution, the challenges to his episcopal authority from the "spirituals" in his church, the disputes over the nature and effectiveness of sacramental actions, and the critical problem of adjusting penitential discipline in the face of the "lapsi" and their need for reconciliation.[56]

Cyprian sees the bishops as the ones responsible for the retention of authentic faith.[57] This comes through in his praise for the church of Rome.[58] He himself obviously felt responsible for the careful instruction of his flock. However, if we can put it in terms of a more recent distinction, Cyprian seemed more concerned about matters of church discipline than about questions of doctrine.[59] His short treatises and letters indicate that his instruction, which he did see as a direct responsibility of his episcopal position, consisted largely in practical counsel and exhortation to virtuous life, in which the notion of following good example, particularly that of Christ, is prominent.[60]

Written at about the same time, the *Didascalia* provides a view of the teaching and practice of the Syrian church, and especially a detailed clarification of the episcopal function.[61] We find reflected in this document a situation where the monarchical episcopate is fully in control, where it has completely absorbed into itself any previously independent functions or ministries.[62] Among these all-inclusive functions of the bishop, that of witnessing to the apostolic faith seems to hold the primary place.[63] The unity which the bishops are meant to preserve is threatened by schism in doctrine; therefore let the bishops and their subordinate clergy be careful to teach the people the same doctrine. Bishops are to be "mediators between God and the believers, receivers of the Word, preachers of it, evangelists of it, knowers of the Scriptures and of the Word of God, witnesses of his will. . . ."[64] Yet, it must be mentioned that in this same passage the application of the word "priest" to the bishop does not seem to denominate his teaching function as such. Another interesting feature is the way in which the "deacons," not the "presbyters," are consistently associated with the bishop in his functions and specifically in that of imparting doctrine to the people.[65]

At Rome in this same period there seems to have been much the same view that the bishops were the privileged witnesses to the true gospel, and this because of their succession from the apostles. The view of Irenaeus is continued by his disciple Hippolytus.[66] Whatever may have been the exact nature of his disputes with the bishops in Rome at his time, it seems that he expected of them a fidelity to apostolic teaching.[67] However, Hippolytus himself is an interesting testimonial to the fact that at Rome during a considerable period of time there were a number of "independent theologians," not all of them orthodox. And one gathers the impression, though not on any definite textual evidence, that such teaching was not under episcopal control nor did it require any episcopal approval.[68] Rather, it seems to continue a "tradition" that goes as far back as Justin Martyr.

Independent or not in the "official" status of his teaching, Hippolytus (who was a presbyter) placed the greatest stress on conformity to apostolic tradition—both in doctrine and liturgy.[69] The whole tone of his *Apostolic Tradition* conveys such desire to retain the truth of the apostolic church. The document is, of course, a precious reflection of the clerical situation in Rome at the end of the second century, with all the major "orders" clearly in existence and their functions distinguished.[70] And, in the context of our present chapter's examination of the ministry of the word, it is surprising to find in the "commission" implied in the prayer consecrating the new bishop no mention of ministering to the word except the general phrase "feed your holy flock."[71] An interesting fact that may have some relation to this is witnessed to by Origen. When he came to Rome to visit he heard the sermon of a certain presbyter, Hippolytus—thus, preaching was carried on by presbyters.[72]

However, we also know from Hippolytus that the bishop "oversaw" the instruction of catechumens, though most if not all of the actual instruction was delegated to others,[73] and that the bishop performed the final exorcisms and examined the candidate's knowledge of the basic creed. So also in the initiation ceremony's final phase, the communion of the Eucharist, he is the one who gives the liturgical explanation of the mystery.[74] Moreover, it seems that there was a regular program of continuing doctrinal formation for the clergy that took place when these met with the bishop for prayer.[75]

It would seem, then, that third-century Rome was a fairly flexible situation regarding the ministry of the word. The bishop was *the* witness to apostolic tradition and foremost teacher, but others shared in this, either as

presbyters "delegated" to preach and cate-
chize or as "unofficial" teachers (with more or
less approval of the bishop and presbyterate).
Much of the episcopal teaching consisted
apparently in guiding the moral behavior of
the community.[76] In this it followed the
widespread point of view of these centuries.
Lucian of Antioch, Lactantius, and Arnobius
—who represent quite a diversity of backgrounds—all see salvation as being accomplished essentially through the teaching and
example of Christ;[77] and we have already
seen much the same emphasis in Clement of
Rome and Clement of Alexandria, as well as
Cyprian.

Teaching

It is impossible to indicate the line of division between the witness to the Christ-event
and the doctrinal instruction given for the
formation of faith. Yet, in the continuum of
activities that stretches from episcopal witness
(to which, as we will see later, the celebration
of Eucharist must really be joined) to the
ordinary explanations of Christian faith and
practice which one Christian gives another,
there are in each historical period some things
that are restricted to certain functionaries,
though the areas of restriction and the officials
involved change from one period to another.
The pre-Nicene period was uninterested or
unable to draw any sharp distinctions in this
regard.[78] What was universally important
for Christians of this epoch was the fact that
Jesus himself had taught, that he had commissioned his disciples to teach, that these disciples had in turn been succeeded by others in
the teaching function, that true teaching was
critically important for Christianity. Since it
was a community based on true faith, this
unity of faith was being frequently threatened
or disrupted by those who taught false doctrine.[79] This was a period of intensive and
widespread teaching, of true and false teachers competing for a following among Christians, the period in which the great "schools"
of Alexandria and Antioch emerged and
gained prominence and prepared for the pa-

tristic flowering of the fourth and fifth centuries.[80]

And no one man gained more renown as a
teacher, and deservedly so, than Origen of
Alexandria.[81] He is an important historical
witness to the ecclesiastical attitude towards
teaching. He himself occupied a position of
unparalleled teaching authority, not because
of official position (even his presbyteral ordination was impugned by his own bishop in
Alexandria) but because of his theological insight.[82] At the same time, Origen himself
believed that all teaching of the faith should
be done by clergy.[83] Teaching should, then,
come under episcopal governance of some
kind; but bishops themselves were not necessarily the most authoritative teachers.

This, of course, was not universally accepted. Already there were bishops who assumed that the episcopal position somehow
gave them a charism akin to infused knowledge.[84] But one aspect of common belief
underlay all pre-Nicene discussion of this
matter, the belief that Christ himself, working
within the consciousness of Christians as "the
light," was the true teacher.[85]

One thinks immediately of the great Alexandrians, influenced as they were by the combined influence of Platonic, Philonic, and
Johannine doctrines of the divine Logos.[86]
Clement, for example, in his *Paedagogus* develops the theme that Christ is the teacher
who indicates for men the true path that leads
to the light that is life;[87] he is the divine
Logos that has been guiding men through
every period, especially during the Old Testament period, and supremely now after his
manifestation in human form.[88] Jesus has
given us the rules for perfect life, he has provided the model for this by his own earthly
life, and he has made it possible for us to
follow this teaching and model by freeing us
in his death from the sin that would block us
from contemplation.[89] Origen, too, will insist that Christ alone is *the light*; but the
church, as in special fashion the teacher
within the church, reflects this light as the
moon does the sun.[90] The whole of Christian life is seen by him as intellectual and

moral education, as gradually increasing illumination which, however, depends upon constantly increasing moral purification.[91] Christian teachers of virtue and truth are of key importance in such a view of Christianity, but Origen would always insist that Christ alone is *the* teacher.[92]

There is the widespread assumption, too, that the "inner illumination" effected by Christ and his Spirit works in conjunction with the apostolic teaching as this is preserved in Scripture. Moreover, this tends to go beyond just the apostolic witness of the New Testament and include also the Old Testament, seen as a preliminary stage of the revelation of Logos and Spirit.[93] The Christian teacher, whether he be bishop or not, can do nothing better. Actually he can do nothing other than present to the believer the text of the Bible and lead him to its understanding.[94]

One of the most clearly attested situations of teaching in these centuries was the catechumenate training. The need for instruction prior to baptism, particularly in those centuries which still took very seriously the intelligent commitment made in baptism, was universally felt and provision was made for it very early in the church's existence.[95] While the pre-Nicene epoch gives us no detailed documentation to compare with the baptismal catecheses of Ambrose, or Cyril of Jerusalem, or Theodore of Mopsuestia, we do have clear though brief descriptions of an organized catechumenate as early as Origen[96] and Hippolytus.[97] In their own way, the Petrine Epistles may also be a witness to the early church's doctrinal formation of the newly baptized.[98]

Practice seems to have varied as to whether the bishop himself or some delegate did the actual instructing of the catechumens. Such diversity of practice is indicated by the fourth-century texts, but there never seems to be any question but that the direction and supervision of the catechumenate training is the province of the bishop.[99] He, too, is the principal "celebrant" in the baptismal initiation which completes the catechumenate formation by the unique catechesis of liturgical event. However, in this instance also, much of the actual ministry of the liturgy is carried out by presbyters and deacons.[100] When we realize that early Christianity saw such an occasion as a proclamation of the mystery of Christ's death and resurrection, a celebration of the Christian community's consciousness of being incorporated into its risen Lord through the waters of baptism, we can see that the bishops were the ones entrusted with communicating to the neophyte the "myth" by which the religious community existed. To speak in such terms of the bishop in early Christianity is not to impose categories from contemporary religious anthropology; it is quite clear from the language used to describe the baptismal ceremonies that the bishop was looked on as a "mystagogue."[101]

Again, it is quite clear that the need for continuing formation of baptized Christians' understanding of their faith was immediately recognized and provided for. The very existence of the New Testament literature, growing as it did out of the various oral traditions of the first century, gives clear evidence to such catechesis. Less clear is the agency to which this catechesis was entrusted.

Whether and in what way the Twelve (and others who were called "apostles") carried on such teaching is not clear, but very early there is reference to the *didache ton apostolon*.[102] Whether the early *episkopoi* and *presbyteroi* also taught, and to what extent, is much less clear. The lack of clarity is connected with the existence of two other ministries, prophecy and teaching, whose distinct existence can be traced well into the second century. The *Didache* speaks of teachers (*didaskaloi*) who are distinct from the prophets, who occupy a position that is of recognized dignity (apparently for the moment at least as esteemed as *episkopos* or *presbyteros*). If no teacher is present in a community, *episkopoi* and *presbyteroi* are to fill this function. But it is not clear from this text whether one can apply this to more than their liturgical function, since the word used for the "ministry" of the prophets and teachers in this instance is *"leitourgia."*

Hermas indicates quite explicitly the early second-century existence of teaching as a distinct ministry in the Roman church.[103] It may be that teachers were selected from among the presbyters, but there is no clear sign of this. It is clearer that they occupied a position of community approval and were to some extent tested by the community, for there were also "false teachers."[104] Though the precise nature of his relationship to *episkopoi* and *presbyteroi* cannot be determined, Justin certainly exercised a recognized and respected position as a teacher.[105] We know that he established a school at Rome, but there is no indication what relationship his role there bore to the *didaskaloi* to whom Hermas refers. Though it is not a conclusive indication, the absence of "teacher" from the list of "consecrated functions" in the *Apostolic Tradition*'s description of the ordination liturgy would seem to indicate that by the early third century a distinct teaching ministry had ceased to exist in Rome.[106]

Despite the prominence in second-century Alexandria of three great teachers, Pantaenus, Clement, and Origen, the precise function of such teachers in the ecclesiastical structures of the Alexandrian church is not clear.[107] Apparently, they functioned in the training of catechumens, but their activity clearly extended far beyond this. The very nature of the writings of Clement and Origen indicate that they were addressing themselves to a theologically sophisticated audience. Their teaching was listened to by bishops as well as others; even bishops prided themselves on being their disciples and friends.

Origen himself believed that teaching in the church belongs to the clergy, and he was eager to obtain ordination as a presbyter.[108] Clement, on the other hand, seems never to have been a part of the official ecclesiastical structures in Alexandria.[109] Even in the case of Origen, it does not seem that he relies upon his clerical status to give any authority to his teaching. Rather, this came from his theological genius and his fidelity to apostolic tradition.[110] Yet, von Campenhausen[111] feels that with Origen the fusion of presbyteral and teaching offices has been accomplished; he criticizes Daniélou for "being too tentative when he sees in Origen only the beginning of a fusion of the 'visible hierarchy of the presbyters' with the 'invisible hierarchy of the doctors.' "[112] One wonders, however, about the accuracy of von Campenhausen's position: in the passage in Origen's commentary on the *Canticle*[113] where he parallels Solomon's beneficence to the Queen of Sheba and Christ's endowments of the church, he seems to distinguish the "teachers" from the ecclesiastical orders of bishop, presbyter, and deacon. The teachers are the "pourers of wine" who prepare the Word of God and doctrine (the text uses the verb *"miscent"*) for the people so that they may bring joy to the hearts of their auditors.[114]

To the extent that Origen did bring together the "clerical position" and the role of teaching, a basic question is raised. Does this mean that the accuracy of the teaching or its intrinsic impact on auditors is affected by the ecclesiastical office possessed by the teacher? Or, on the other hand, does it mean that the effectiveness of the official function is reliant upon the "spirituality," theological competence, or pedagogical skill of the officeholder? Certainly, some of the nonepiscopal disciples of Origen in later centuries (particularly among the monks) opted for the second alternative.[115] And, the rising importance in Eastern monasticism of the "spiritual director" and the authority attributed to him, which demanded blind obedience on the part of his disciples, are part of this same view.[116]

Clement of Alexandria seems to be entirely on the side of the intrinsic role of teaching. Whatever authority the teacher possesses comes from the fact that he already is far advanced into the realms of illumination and contemplation, and is therefore able to serve as a guide for others.[117] There is no hint that some of these effective teachers might function because of a special charism given them by virtue of an ecclesiastical role. With Origen there does seem to be some shift towards a more clerical mentality. The situation seems to be one in which the distinct ministry of "teacher" as it appears in 1 Corinthians, the *Didache*, or Hermas no longer exists. Yet, though it no longer is one of the formally recognized ministries, teachers do function as an acknowledged factor in the life of the community, and such teaching is already viewed as pertaining specially to clerics.

When we examine the situation at this same time in either Syria or Africa the absorption of the teaching ministry into that of the *episkopos* seems total and final. The *Didascalia* leaves no doubt but that it is the bishop who is "to sit in the church and teach and admonish"; apparently, deacons share with the bishop in teaching but do so entirely under his direction. It is noteworthy, though, that such teaching seems to be described chiefly as moral exhortation and admonition, and was closely associated with the bishop's role as "judge."[118]

Tertullian is definitely on the side of attributing the teaching role to the bishops, until his movement towards Montanist beliefs when, of course, he emphasizes the prophet's role as authoritative teacher in the community. The intrinsic questions raised by this "conversion" of Tertullian to Montanism will have to be examined when we discuss prophecy, but there does not seem to have been any insistence on Tertullian's part that "teachers" as a distinct group in the church have a special ministry.[119] With Cyprian there is no obscurity: the bishop is the teacher in his church. The only other agency to which the bishop's teaching might have to submit or be accountable is the corporate reality of the episcopal college. Though he does not lay claim to it in just those words, Cyprian acts in accord with Irenaeus' statement that the bishops possess a *charisma veritatis certum*.[120]

As one reflects on the disappearance of the distinct ministry of "teacher," or rather its absorption into the episcopal function (if not actually embodied in the bishop, at least controlled by him), he searches for the reasons behind this historical evolution. Certainly, if an individual (or a group, e.g., a presbyterium headed by an *episkopos*) is charged with the pastoral care of a community of be-

lievers, the preservation of purity and unity of faith is a critical part of his function. Yet, the question should arise: Does such an *episkopos* as officeholder preserve this purity and unity, or does the truth defend itself—and if the latter (which seems patently true) is not an educated and honest teacher more effective than an uninstructed and perhaps prejudiced bishop? To some extent this issue was handled by the unique role of Scripture; it, rather than a given bishop or teacher, was the norm of faith and the "food" for that faith. Scripture was the "apostolic tradition," and it was now taken for granted that the apostles were at once the chief pastors and the privileged teachers of the church.

One thing that certainly does not become clarified during this period, and is not raised as an explicit question for many centuries, is the function of the "theologian" in the church's life. Theology is simply included under the category of "teaching." The assumption of special episcopal competence in this regard is an indistinguishable element in the assumption of his supreme teaching prerogative.[121] The fact that practically all the prominent theologians for several centuries were bishops helped confirm this view. This had some definite advantages in that theological competence was often a consideration in the choice of a bishop (at least for a more influential see) and in that many bishops felt a responsibility to obtain or deepen their theological understanding.

Perhaps the increasing danger of Gnosticism was part of the reason for the decline of a distinct teaching ministry in the second and third centuries. Gnostic teachers were unquestionably a menace to the orthodoxy and unity of Christian belief.[122] And in the last analysis their misleading sophistries could not be answered by appeal to another pedagogical endeavor, to another "system of thought" which also claimed to be Christian. The truth or falsity of Gnosticism could only be determined by confronting it with the criterion of the "objective reality" of the Christ-mystery. This is what the bishops in particular tried to do, by claiming to present in unadulterated form the "apostolic tradition," the witness of the apostles themselves to the death and resurrection of Jesus.[123]

In such a situation, subtlety of theological understanding does not appear as the prime requisite. Rather, the emphasis is on "faithful witness"; and since such fidelity is contingent upon one's access to reliable tradition about Christ, the bishops are clearly in a privileged position because of their apostolic succession.[124] The factual reality reflected in this episcopal witness to the apostolic witness must be the basis for all teaching in the church, whether carried on by the episcopacy or by other teachers. But, in a context of threat to orthodox faith, it is natural that bishops should be regarded as especially trustworthy teachers and as responsible for evaluating other teachers in the community.[125]

Prophecy

If the distinct ministry of "teacher" has been very nearly absorbed into the episcopacy by the end of the third century, another vital ministry of the word, that of prophecy, has even more clearly disappeared as a recognized and distinct function in the Christian community. There were, after all, prominent teachers who continued to exist alongside the bishop within the clergy and even outside the clergy. But prophets seem to have completely vanished from the scene, to be replaced by charismatic bishops or ascetics.[126]

In the second century, prophetism continues to be prominent for some time. Justin speaks often of the Spirit as the Spirit of prophecy, and repeats the New Testament belief (e.g., Acts 2) that the prophetic Spirit of Old Testament Israel passes over into the Christian community as a whole.[127] But Justin is also aware of "special" prophets within the church and of the community's need to distinguish between true and false prophets, a problem to which both the New Testament literature and the *Didache* had testified earlier.[128]

Obviously, Hermas is a striking example of the continuation of Christian prophetic min-

istry into the second century.[129] Here clearly is an instance of a man who occupied a recognized function within the community, not by virtue of any "appointment" or even because of native intellectual ability or education but because of the extraordinary prophetic gifts he received. He is not just a free-lance charismatic, but one whose prophetic endowment is given for the sake of the community; he is instructed to present his visions to "the presbyters."[130] He is aware of the need to distinguish the true from the false prophet.[131] The very fact that he discusses this point (as do others like Justin) would seem to indicate that the ministry of the prophet was not a "continuous" function (much less an office) like *episkopos* or *didaskalos*, but that a prophet might be endowed for a given occasion or need and function for a relatively short time.[132]

For some reason, however, the Christian prophet seems to have been eclipsed by the end of the century. Both Athenagoras and Clement of Alexandria, for example, will speak of the prophets who are "witnesses of our ideas and beliefs, men who have spoken out under divine inspiration about God and the things of God."[133] But a closer examination of the texts indicates that the prophets of whom they are thinking are the Old Testament prophets. The apologetic support of prophetic witness to which these men are now turning is not the voice of prophecy within the church but that from the Old Testament. The very notion of prophecy has tended to shift to "prediction," specifically the predictions about Christ which find fulfillment in his life, death, and resurrection.

No doubt the fate of recognized prophets within the church was related to the rise of Montanism, but the causal relation is less easy to determine. Some historians would tend to see a movement such as Montanism as a reaction against an excessive administration control of the church and an attempt to preserve the prophetic voice.[134] Such they would see as the underlying motivation in Tertullian's espousal of the Montanist position.[135] On the other hand, whether or not Montanism can be classified under "enthusiasm," an example of the recurrent tendency to seek some "newly revealed religion," it does seem that contemporaries of the movement did view it with a certain alarm.[136]

What Montanism did accentuate was the need to crystallize the community's norm of orthodox faith. Without such a criterion, the church would be in great difficulty when it attempted to judge the right of a movement like Montanism to speak as a compelling Christian voice. Since the apostolic succession of the bishops was a critical element in the norm that was formalized, i.e., apostolic tradition, it is not too surprising that the episcopal office began to absorb the prophetic function. After all, if the bishops judge prophetic utterance this presupposes an insight into faith not only comparable but even superior to that possessed by the prophet. That would seem to imply one of two conclusions: either the Spirit does not provide any worthwhile guidance to the church through prophetic inspiration, or the bishops are beyond all others the special recipients of such inspiration.

It is interesting, then, to note that Cyprian in the third century lays explicit claim to the kind of direct divine guidance ordinarily associated with the prophetic charism.[137] Nor was he the first. Almost a century earlier Irenaeus had spoken of the charism of truth attached to the bishop's teaching.[138] Admittedly, this probably applied chiefly, if not exclusively, to the specific episcopal function of conveying the gospel. But it does seem to refer to a special pneumatic endowment, an unusual guidance or illumination above that provided to all Christians.[139] However, upon reflection it is difficult to see what an authentic prophetic gift would be other than a special ability to grasp the inner meaning and applicability of the gospel.

One of the elements in this evolution away from the prophetic ministry is the development of the ideal of "the Christian Gnostic," an ideal that is inseparable historically from that of the "dedicated ascetic." If such a role as that explicated by Clement of Alexandria, continued in the Alexandrian fathers, carried out into oriental monasticism, and institu-

tionalized in the "rules" of Basil, Augustine, and later Benedict is developed in the life of the church, it is difficult to see where prophecy is needed. The "mystic" has replaced the New Testament prophet. However, the further question must be asked: Is the professional ascetic, monastic or otherwise, to be that readily equated with the authentic mystic? Is the "spiritual athleticism" of the kind that fed into Pelagianism to be recognized as either manifesting or "demanding" the Spirit? Is there not something that has to be watched when "true Christianity" as exemplified in some of the famous ascetics emphasizes the denial of what constitutes daily Christian existence for the bulk of the people of God? Is there not danger that this is a loss of the fundamental sacramentalism of creation and human life, a loss of the "identification principle" of the Incarnation, a loss of Paul's "whatever you do, do all for the glory of God?"

Where, then, does the prophetic voice go? Certainly, there were great bishops who possessed preeminently the prophetic gift with which the Spirit endows the church. But for the most part it was the development of "religious life," monasticism and its later variants, which gave expression to prophetic charism in the life of the church. Yet, two problems were indigenous to this evolution: (1) of its very nature the prophetic charism cannot be institutionalized; and (2) the vocation of dedicated Christian apostolate and prayer was too often interpreted according to a cosmology and anthropology which may have been radically inimical to the soteriology and optimism of the New Testament. As a result, the "secular" was increasingly left outside the impact of the gospel, and man's historical existence, which in Old Testament prophetism and New Testament kerygma had been the very matrix of God's continuing revelation, was neglected as Christians searched for the *leges aeternae* which would tell them the will of God.

The Eucharist as Proclamation

For modern Christians, whose orientation to Christian liturgy has been so different from that of pre-Nicene Christians, it is extremely difficult to appreciate the evangelical understanding of Eucharist possessed by these early Christians. A clear indication of this divergence of view is the long-standing Catholic-Protestant controversy on evangelical versus liturgical emphasis in interpreting Christianity, a controversy that becomes utterly meaningless when one begins to grasp the deeper reality of the word of God and of the Eucharist: at the deeper level they coincide, they are mutually interdependent for their existence in the church.[140]

Contemporary scholarship, converging studies in New Testament and in liturgical history in particular, has highlighted the evangelical character of the early Christian Eucharist.[141] Exegetical studies of the sixth chapter of John, for example, have moved beyond the controversial-theology stage in which Catholic scholars insisted on the chapter as referring to the Eucharist and Protestants insisted that it dealt with the word.[142] Instead, there is increasing agreement that the basic religious truth that is meant to be conveyed by the passage is the mystery of God's communication of his word to men in Jesus of Nazareth, but that this very reality involves the Eucharistic communication in the body of Christ.[143] The scholarly advances indicate the extent to which confessional presuppositions had imposed a foreign mentality on the New Testament community whose traditions of faith are reflected in John 6. The dichotomy of word and sacrament would have been quite unintelligible to them.

When one turns to the nonbiblical literature, beginning with the *Didache*, historical studies of liturgical texts point to the continuation of the same mentality. Granted the difficulty of interpreting the *Didache* passages which may or may not give us some elements of primitive Eucharistic practice, it seems that Audet's study makes an excellent case for the fact that *eucharistein* is basically an action of proclamation, an action of praise of God for his *mirabilia* and particularly for his work of salvation in Christ.[144] This is, of course, not surprising when one recalls Paul's words to

the Corinthians ". . . You proclaim the Lord's death. . . ."

Second-century references to the Eucharist, as in Justin, see it regularly as fulfillment of the prophecy of Malachias, where the notion of the praise of God is uppermost. If it is a sacrifice, it is precisely a sacrifice of praise.[145] This is reflected in the name which early designates what later centuries would call the "*anaphora*" or the "canon"; it is called the "benediction."[146] And the name "Eucharist" itself conveys much more of the notion of public acknowledgment and praise than it did of anything like "expiatory sacrifice."[147]

Much more needs to be said on this topic, but even this little can indicate how such a viewpoint on the Eucharist (as on other liturgical actions) affects quite radically the understanding one would have of "ministry of sacrament." The Eucharistic celebrant functions as a proclaimer of the very mystery that is being celebrated; he is the agent of God's sacramental revelation of himself to the assembled Christians who profess their faith (as Justin emphasizes) by their "Amen" to the Eucharistic prayer.[148] One can readily see in such an understanding of the Eucharistic action how logical it was to view the "prophet" as the appropriate celebrant of liturgy, as the *Didache* does.[149] The Eucharistic celebrant was really saying in effect: Hear, O Israel, the word of the Lord.

We know, too, from the *Apostolic Tradition* of Hippolytus (and the later baptismal catecheses of Ambrose, Cyril of Jerusalem, and others confirm it in greater detail) the manner in which the liturgical celebration of Christian initiation served as the catechetical climax of the catechumenate training. Moreover, the assembly of Christians for the Eucharistic celebration was *the* occasion for the continuing catechetical formation of their faith.[150] Such instruction of their faith was intrinsic to the action, a clarification of the very mystery they were enacting and the very word they were therein hearing; it was not something extra brought in to profit by the fact that people were present. What was most instructive was the very action itself, and the purpose of the homily was to indicate the "revelation" contained in that particular day's liturgy, to draw from it the lessons appropriate to the assembled community.

Thus, as early as Justin we have the evidence that the "leader" of the Eucharist (probably already in Justin it is the *episkopos*; and certainly by the end of the second century it is clearly the bishop who is Eucharist celebrant) is the one who comments on the readings of the day.[151] The vast body of episcopal homilies (which comprise a large portion of Migne's *Patrologia*) testifies to the continuation of this tradition throughout the early life of the church. It would be an interesting study to investigate the extent to which the bishops who preached these homilies saw themselves as functioning in a prophetic role,[152] which, at least to some extent, they really were.

NOTES

1. H. Strathmann, "Martys," *Theological Dictionary of the New Testament*, vol. 4, pp. 489–508.

2. 1 Cor. 2:6–7.

3. See W. Shotwell, *The Biblical Exegesis of Justin Martyr* (London, 1965); B. Lindars, *New Testament Apologetic* (London, 1961), pp. 251–86.

4. See J. Daniélou and R. du Charlat, *La catéchèse aux premiers siècles* (Paris, 1968), pp. 76–78.

5. On the early Christian ideal of martyrdom, see H. von Campenhausen, *Die Idee des Martyriums in der alten Kirche*; H. Delahaye, *Les origines du culte des martyrs* (Bruxelles, 1933).

6. See H. Leclercq, *Dictionnaire d'archéologie chrétienne et de liturgie*, vol. 10 (1932), cols. 2360–66.

7. See E. Hummel, *The Concept of Martyrdom According to St. Cyprian of Carthage* (Washington, D.C., 1946), pp. 129–32.

8. *Didascalia*, chap. 20 (Connolly ed., pp. 176–78).

9. Rom. 5:3–6.

10. See J. Quasten, *Patrology* (Westminster, Md., 1950), vol. 1, pp. 76–82, on the authenticity and historical importance of the *Martyrium Polycarpi*.

11. See W. Flemming, *Zur Beurteilung des Christentums Justins des Martyrers* (Leipzig, 1893), p. 46.

12. On tradition in the early church, a treatment that takes open but critical account of the volume of recent writing on the topic is that of R. Hanson, *Tradition in the Early Church* (London, 1962).

13. See R. Grant, *The Formation of the New Testament* (New York, 1965), pp. 77–102.

14. *Ibid.*, pp. 131–37.

15. *Ibid.*, pp. 151–56; also J. Ochagavia, *Visibile Patris Filius* (Rome, 1964), pp. 180–205.

16. Grant, pp. 162–75; however, as Grant indicates, there is still some flexibility (or confusion) as to what pertains to the authentic New Testament canon.

17. Both Clement and Origen respect extrabiblical traditions (liturgical and ecclesiastical), but see the biblical tradition as central and normative. See R. Hanson, *Origen's Doctrine of Tradition* (London, 1954), pp. 178–81.

18. See Hanson, *Tradition in the Early Church*, p. 111.

19. *Ibid.*, p. 99.

20. See E. Portalie, *Guide to the Thought of St. Augustine* (Chicago, 1960), pp. 118–24; a lengthier treatment is provided by A. Polman's *The Word of God According to St. Augustine* (Grand Rapids, Mich., 1961).

21. For two opposing views as to the identity of the *author* Hippolytus, see Quasten,

vol. 2, pp. 163–66, 198; and P. Nautin, *Lettres et écrivains chrétiens* (Paris, 1961), pp. 203–7.

22. See R. Hanson's discussion of the relation between the rule of faith and the Scriptures in the early church in *Tradition in the Early Church*, pp. 102–17.

23. *Ibid.*, pp. 22–35, where Hanson examines the evidence for a *disciplina arcani* in the second and third centuries and establishes its relative tardiness and its independence from implications of "esoteric and secret teaching."

24. The only pre-Nicene father to claim any secret tradition is Clement of Alexandria; see Hanson, *Tradition in the Early Church*, pp. 26–27, who sees this as an indication of Clement's close links with Gnostic circles.

25. This is a presupposition of the epistolary exhortation (directed to presbyters and deacons, as well as fellow *episkopoi*) of Ignatius or Cyprian.

26. 1 Tim. 3:1–13; Titus 1:5–9.

27. More careful attention to this question will be paid in chapter 27.

28. See K. Baus, *Handbook of Church History* (New York, 1965), vol. 1, p. 211.

29. See D. van den Eynde, *Les normes de l'enseignement chrétien dans la littérature patristique des trois premiers siècles* (Gembloux, 1933); Daniélou–du Charlat, *La catéchèse aux premiers siècles*.

30. Perhaps the first official role to emerge was that of giving the Eucharistic homily, a function that Justin attributes to the president of the Eucharistic assembly. However, the link of Eucharistic celebrant with the prophetic function in the *Didache* implies that early homiletic activity may have been linked more with charism than with office.

31. *Didache* 11. 1–2.

32. *1 Clem.* 7. 2. See R. Reynders, "Paradosis, le progrès de l'idée de tradition jusqu'à S. Irenée," *Recherches de théologie ancienne et médiévale* 5 (1933), pp. 161–62.

33. *Apology 1* 67.

34. Rather, it is the *presbyteroi* who are compared with the apostles: *Magnesians* 6; *Philadelphians* 5.

35. In Clement's case, it is obvious that "apostolic tradition" is not something attached to teaching office but more broadly applied to the entire life of the church. "Eglise et Tradition se confondent pour lui en une seule réalité vivante et présente" (C. Mondésert, *Clément d'Alexandrie* [Paris, 1944], p. 117). Clement is not so much interested in apostolic succession (in the usual sense of that term) as in a succession of teachers. See Hanson, *Tradition*, p. 158.

36. With Irenaeus there appears to be more link of apostolic tradition with episcopal office. See W. Schmidt, *Die Kirche bei Irenäus* (Helsingfors, 1934), p. 73: "Das Amt ist keine göttliche Stiftung, auf sich selbst gestellt, sondern es soll der Wahrheit, der apostolischen Tradition, dem Kerygma dienen, es vermitteln, es schutzen." See also Ochagavia, p. 207: "The action of the Spirit in teaching the truth falls in a special way on the episcopate, that is, on the bishops who are gifted, by virtue of the apostolic succession, with the charism of truth. This is the reason why those who want to be guided by the Spirit and obtain a perfect knowledge of the truth, must read the Scriptures under the guidance of the Church's presbyters."

37. Though there has been a long tradition that Clement headed the Alexandrian catechumenate (the statement goes back to Eusebius and finds expression in contemporary scholars, e.g., Quasten, vol. 2, p. 5); it seems, in the light of modern research, that the school of Alexandria with which Clement was associated was quite independent of the catechumenate program. See M. Spanneut, *New Catholic Encyclopedia* (New York, 1967), vol. 3, p. 943; he bases his position on the work done by J. Munck in *Untersuchungen über Klemens von Alexandria* (Stuttgart, 1933).

38. See Mondésert, p. 117.

39. This is the theme of the first book of the *Paedagogus*.

40. *Paedagogus* 1. 12.

41. See *Stromata* 1. 11.

42. See R. Tollinton, *Clement of Alexandria* (London, 1914), vol. 2, p. 207: "Clement's high estimate of 'tradition' is a particular aspect of his veneration for the past." See also Mondésert, pp. 118–20.

43. One finds traces early in the Alexandrian tradition of the notion of a spiritual adviser whose authority comes internally and not by way of office or appointment, although his intrinsic qualifications of wisdom and sanctity may receive community approbation.

44. See Hanson, *Tradition*, pp. 41–46; Van den Eynde, p. 158.

45. "Normally, Irenaeus does not understand by 'tradition' the oral communication of the apostolic teaching. For him tradition is primarily an objective thing: the teaching of the apostles. Except for the first chapter of the third book of the *Adv. Haer.*, he finds 'tradition' both in the Scripture and in the oral teaching of the apostles. With regard to tradition's content, this is neither richer nor poorer than the content of Scriptures." (Ochagavia, p. 207.)

46. *Ibid.*, p. 184.

47. *Adv. Haer.* 4. 40. 2; 4. 42. 1. See Hanson's discussion of these passages, *Tradition*, pp. 159–62.

48. Ochagavia, p. 207.

49. See Schmidt, pp. 70–87.

50. See Hanson, *Tradition*, pp. 44–46.

51. *Adv. Haer.* 3. 2. 2—3. 3. 1.

52. *Ibid.*, 3. 3. 3.

53. See R. Hanson's discussion of the meaning of apostolic succession in Tertullian and Irenaeus, *Tradition*, pp. 157–62.

54. See Quasten, vol. 2, p. 331.

55. See von Campenhausen, *Ecclesiastical Authority and Spiritual Power in the Church of the First Three Centuries* (Palo Alto, Calif., 1969), pp. 265–73.

56. See Quasten, vol. 2, pp. 341–43.

57. *De unitate ecclesiae* 5.

58. *Epist.* 59. 14.

59. Thus, for example, in *ibid.*, 45. 3 (writing to Cornelius): "Hoc enim vel maxime, fratres, et laboramus et laborare debemus ut unitatem a Domino et per apostolos nobis successoribus traditam possumus obtinere curemus. . . ." See also *ibid.*, 59. 14. This seems to be accompanied by a different approach to the notion of apostolic succession. Just as earlier writers viewed the matter in terms of passing on understanding from one generation to another (therefore a succession in knowledge), so now, if the emphasis shifts from teaching to administration, apostolic succession would involve a transfer of governing power from one episcopal generation to the next.

60. See Quasten, vol. 2, pp. 344–66.

61. Eight chapters, 4–11, are devoted to the bishop.

62. For example, the listing of episcopal functions in chap. 8: "Therefore, bishops, you are priests to your people and Levites who serve in the house of God . . . priests and prophets and princes and governors and teachers and mediators between God and the believers, receivers of the Word, preachers of it, evangelists of it, knowers of the Scriptures and the Word of God, witnesses of his will, who bear the sins of all men and who will give account concerning all men. . . ."

63. When describing the bishop's dignity, the primacy seems to go to his "kingly priesthood," but when describing the bishop's function, attention centers on his ministry of the word (including the example he gives to his flock).

64. *Didascalia*, chap. 8.

65. See R. Connolly, *Didascalia Apostolorum* (Oxford, 1929), pp. xxxviii–xii. It is in-

teresting to reflect on the minimal involvement of presbyters in ministerial activity that is described in the *Didascalia* (which probably reflects a third-century Syrian community), to compare it with the prominent ministry of John Chrysostom as a presbyter in Antioch just about a century later, and to question how this increased ministerial role of the presbyterate developed.

66. See J. Daniélou and H. Marrou, *The Christian Centuries* (London, 1964), vol. 1, pp. 150–51.

67. *Ibid.* In part, the hostility of Hippolytus to Zephrinus and Callistus may be linked with his defense of the Old Roman presbyteral traditions and prerogatives and his objection to the rising influence of the deacons.

68. See *ibid.*, pp. 106–8.

69. See Baus, pp. 246–47.

70. See *The Apostolic Tradition*, ed. G. Dix, reissued and updated by H. Chadwick (London, 1968), 2–15. Of the minor orders only that of lector is considered.

71. *Ibid.*, 3.

72. See Quasten, vol. 2, p. 163.

73. *Apostolic Tradition* 16–19.

74. *Ibid.*, 23.

75. *Ibid.*, 33.

76. However, their approach to ethical behavior was specifically Christian; see Daniélou–du Charlat, pp. 125–55.

77. See G. Bardy, *Recherches sur Saint Lucien d'Antioche et son école* (Paris, 1936), pp. 155–56.

78. Perhaps because so much of the ministry of the word was concerned with first evangelization or with the formation of the catechumens. As the need to distinguish true from false teaching became more acute and discussion of a rule of faith became more explicit, there developed an increased distinction between "witness" and "teaching," although those two terms were not always applied in making the distinction. See Hanson's discussion of the rule of faith, *Tradition*, pp. 75–129.

79. The period remains one of mixed private and official teaching. One finds clear reference in Hippolytus' *Apostolic Tradition* to the teachers who directed the catechumenate, but there were a number of schools (particularly in Rome) established by individuals on their own initiative and under their own direction. The doctrinal deviaton of some of these latter, e.g., the schools of the Marcionites, probably played a major role in diminishing the importance of "teacher" as a distinct ministry in the church of the third and fourth centuries.

80. See Baus, pp. 229–60.

81. See *ibid.*, pp. 234–40, and the selected bibliography on pp. 484–85.

82. The danger, even error, of some of Origen's views is quite apparent in the light of history, but the scope of his genius and the importance of his role as pioneer of Christian theology is undeniable. For a brief appraisal of Origen and his historical influence, see H. Crouzel, *New Catholic Encyclopedia*, vol. 10, pp. 767–74.

83. See J. Daniélou, *Origene et son temps* (Paris, 1948), pp. 57–63. It is not clear whether this attachment of teaching to the clergy was due to personal conviction on Origen's part or whether it was due to the fact that that was the situation in the Alexandrian church of his day. What is clear is Origen's insistence that his own teaching role was one carried on within the church; it was intrinsically ecclesiastical (even if not necessarily clerical). See M. Harl, *Origene et la fonction révélatrice du Verbe incarne* (Paris, 1958), pp. 355–57.

84. Within a few centuries this will be expanded in popular belief, with the accounts of how certain legendary figures (e.g., Martin of Tours) received special visions and revelations, along with other extraordinary powers.

85. Unquestionably, the influence of the Johannine prologue was basic in fostering this point of view.

86. See J. Lebreton in A. Fliche and V. Martin, *Histoire de l'Eglise depuis les origines jusqu'à nos jours* (Paris, 1935—), vol. 2, pp. 225–48.

87. *Paedagogus* 1. 7.

88. *Ibid.*; see also *Stromata* 6. 15. 122.

89. On Clement's stress on Christ's teaching as salvific, see H. Marrou, introd. to *Clement d'Alexandrie, Le Pedagogue*, vol. 70 of *Sources chrétiennes* (Paris, 1960), p. 29: "L'oeuvre de Jesus présente un triple aspect: il nous a donné à la fois les règles de la vie parfaite, par les préceptes formulés dans son enseignement, le modèle, par l'example de sa propre vie terrestre, la possibilité enfin, en nous libérant de la servitude du péché par le sacrifice sanglant de la crois.

   "De ces trois aspects, le chrétien d'aujourd'hui soulignera plus fortement le dernier; c'est celui pourtant sur lequel Clément insiste peut-être le moins: chez notre Alexandrin, comme plus tard aussi chez Origène, la valeur proprement rédemptrice de la mort du Christ prend moins de relief que les autres fruits de l'Incarnation: révélation, inauguration et don de la vie nouvelle."

90. *Hom. in Gen.* 1. 5–6; see also *Com. in Joan.* 1. 25. See H. Koch, *Pronoia und Paideusis* (Leipzig, 1932), pp. 62–78.

91. "Das Leben in der Kirche wird somit fur Origenes eine ständig fortschreitende moralische und intellektuelle Erziehung" (Koch, p. 89).

92. See Harl, pp. 77–78.

93. This results in a basic "Christologizing" of the Old Testament texts. See B. Fischer, "Le Christ dans les Psaumes," *Maison-Dieu* 27 (1951), pp. 86–109; also H. de Lubac, *Exégèse médiévale*, vol. 2 of pt. 1 (Paris, 1959), pp. 671–75.

94. See Hanson, *Tradition*; in his treatment of oral tradition and the rule of faith, he shows how teaching about Christian traditions dealt more and more exclusively with the Scriptures. By the time of Origen, with the text of Scripture well fixed, the homily can become the basic literary form for preaching; see T. Parker, *The Oracles of God* (London, 1947), p. 15.

95. See J. Jungmann, *New Catholic Encyclopedia*, vol. 3, pp. 238–40.

96. *Contra Celsum* 3. 51.

97. *Apostolic Tradition* 16–20.

98. However, see the cautions of J. Kelly, *Epistles of Peter and of Jude* (London, 1969), pp. 15–23, regarding some of the liturgical interpretations of the Petrines.

99. See H. Leclercq, "Catéchèse," *Dictionnaire d'archéologie chrétienne et de liturgie* (Paris, 1903ff.), vol. 2, cols. 2554–66.

100. Hippolytus *Apostolic Tradition* 21–23.

101. The "mystagogical catechesis" of Ambrose, Cyril of Jerusalem, and others indicates that the instruction of the newly baptized focused on the liturgical experience itself and that the bishop's role was one of making this experience intelligible—before, *during*, and after.

102. As used in the *Didache*, it seems quite clear that the apostles in question were not the Twelve; rather quickly, however, the "teaching of the apostles" refers to the original disciples of Christ, and its content is considered coextensive with the New Testament writings.

103. See L. Pernveden, *The Concept of the Church in the Shepherd of Hermas* (Lund, 1966), pp. 146–49.

104. *Ibid.*, p. 147.

105. Daniélou-Marrou, pp. 90–91.

106. Against such a conclusion stands the clear reference to teachers who function officially in the instruction of the catechumens: *Apostolic Tradition* 16; later (19) the text states that such teachers can be either clergy (*ekklesiastikos*) or laity (*laikos*). Perhaps this indicates that one should not look too exclusively to the ordination ceremony as a criterion of the recognized ministries within the community. As early as Hippolytus the ordination may be concentrating on the more limited sphere of liturgical ministration.

107. See Spanneut, pp. 943–45.

108. See von Campenhausen, *Ecclesiastical Authority*, pp. 248–49.

109. *Ibid.*, pp. 197–98.

110. After all, Origen was already internationally established as an eminent teacher before his ordination to the presbyterate.

111. *Ecclesiastical Authority*, pp. 250–64.

112. *Ibid.*, p. 256, n. 119.

113. *In Cant. Cantic.*, bk. 2 (*Die griechischen christlichen Schriftsteller* [Leipzig, 1897ff.], vol. 8, *Origen*, pp. 118–21).

114. *Ibid.*, p. 120.

115. See von Campenhausen, *Ecclesiastical Authority*, pp. 260–64. One difficulty in trying to discuss such questions as they pertain to the early centuries of the church lies in attempting to assess the extent to which the notion of jurisdiction is applied to the activity of church officials. This matter will be studied more carefully in chapter 21.

116. See I. Hausherr, *Dictionnaire de spiritualité*, vol. 3, cols. 1007–51.

117. See von Campenhausen, *Ecclesiastical Authority*, pp. 202–7.

118. *Didascalia* 5: "Bishop, strive to be pure in your works, know your proper place, that you are appointed in the semblance of God Almighty and that you hold the place of God Almighty; thus, sit in the Church and teach, as one having power to judge sinners in the place of God; for to you bishops it is said in the Gospels that what you bind on earth will be bound in heaven."

119. The tendency of his *De Praescriptione* is to stress the official teaching role of the bishops; at the same time, Tertullian himself was certainly acting in a prominent teaching role, and it is not clear that he was a cleric. In any event, Tertullian's explicit statements about the autonomous teaching role of those who are not bishops date only from his Montanist period.

120. On this phrase of Irenaeus and its historical use, see L. Ligier, "Le charisma veritatis certum des évêques," *L'homme devant Dieu* (Paris, 1963), vol. 1, pp. 247–68.

121. Though not involving a notion of infallibility, this view of teaching competence and authority attaching to an office (at this point in history the episcopate) is the ground for future developments in the idea of infallibility.

122. As M. Harl points out (pp. 78–80), Gnosticism took the emphasis on Christianity as a revelation, a teaching, and pushed it to the extreme by equating knowledge with salvation. Moreover it reserved the true understanding to a Gnostic elite, and, as always happens historically, such snobbish pseudointellectualism was countered by a rise of antiintellectualism.

123. This centered, of course, in the appeal to the New Testament Scriptures; see Hanson, *Tradition*, pp. 75–129.

124. Prior to Cyprian, however, there is no clear indication that this apostolic succession is viewed in terms of succession in office.

125. The unmistakable insistence (at the end of the pre-Nicene period we are now studying) of Athanasius on the primacy of Christ as teacher and on the Scriptures as containing the apostolic witness makes it clear that the role of the bishop was considered to be one of guarding the true Christian faith expressed in the Scriptures. See J. Roldanus, *Le christ et l'homme dans la théologie d'Athanase d'Alexandrie* (Leiden, 1968), pp. 244–49.

126. Later we will have to examine the question as to whether prophetic gifts and activity are essentially distinct from the grace and message of the mystic; should the Christian contemplative be seen as the continuation or replacement or absorption of the prophet? For a careful study of this matter, see J. Lindblom, *Prophecy in Ancient Israel* (Oxford, 1962), pp. 1–46.

127. *Apology 1* 6; 13. *Trypho* 91.

128. *Trypho* 82.

129. See Daniélou-Marrou, pp. 115–21.

130. *Vis.* 2. 4.

131. *Mand.* 11. 13.

132. See Pernveden, pp. 149–51.

133. Athenagoras *Embassy for the Christians* 7. See Clement *Strom.* 2. 12. 54.

134. To some extent von Campenhausen espouses this position; see *Ecclesiastical Authority*, pp. 181–92.

135. *Ibid.*, p. 190.

136. See R. Knox, *Enthusiasm* (Oxford, 1950), pp. 25–49.

137. See *Epist.* 16. 4.

138. *Adv. Haer.* 4. 40. 2.

139. As Hanson indicates (*Tradition*, p. 159, n. 4), it seems quite clear that Irenaeus' original phrase was *"charisma aletheias"* (the Latin text has *"charisma veritatis"*).

140. One of the finest contemporary expressions of this coincidence is the essay "Word and Eucharist" of K. Rahner, *Theological Investigations* (Baltimore, 1966), vol. 4, pp. 253–86.

141. See, e.g., the studies of O. Cullmann and J. Jeremias on the primitive Christian Eucharist; or the essays in *The Liturgy and the Word of God,* Martimort *et al.* (Collegeville, Minn., 1959).

142. For a short listing of some of the more recent and important studies, see D. Crossan, *The Gospel of Eternal Life* (Milwaukee, 1967), p. 75. To this list should be added P. Borgen, *Bread from Heaven* (Leiden, 1965).

143. See J. Dunn, "John VI—A Eucharistic Discourse?" *New Testament Studies* 17 (1970–71), pp. 328–38; Dunn plays down the Eucharistic implications. By contrast, see E. Kilmartin, "The Formation of the Bread of Life Discourse," *Scripture* 12 (1960), pp. 75–78.

144. J.-P. Audet, *La Didache* (Paris, 1958), pp. 372–402.

145. *Trypho* 41; *Apology 1* 13.

146. See J. Jungmann, *The Early Liturgy* (Notre Dame, 1959), pp. 43–49; E. Kilmartin, *The Eucharist in the Primitive Church* (Englewood Cliffs, N.J., 1965), pp. 154–59.

147. See C. Moule, *Worship in the New Testament* (London, 1961), pp. 41–43; Moule draws from the important article of Audet in *Revue biblique* 65 (1958), pp. 371–99.

148. *Apology 1* 62.

149. *Didache* 10.

150. See H. Riesenfeld, *The Gospel Tradition and Its Beginnings* (London, 1957), pp. 22–23.

151. *Apology 1* 67.

152. From one point of view, there is an unbroken view on the part of the bishops (and their delegates, as such functions as preaching become increasingly delegated to presbyters) that they speak for God. What changes in the course of history is the understanding of *how* they speak for God—as a sacrament, or a mouthpiece, or an envoy, or a substitute. One of the important elements in this changing mentality is the application (which we will examine in chapters 21 and 22) of the text "Whatsoever you bind . . ."; and one of the prevalent readings of this text in later centuries maintained that God stood behind any official statement. Implicitly this means that possession of office becomes equated with prophetic charism.

CHAPTER 10

The Word in the Patristic Period

By the time of Nicaea the role of the bishop as *the* teacher in the community is firmly established. The only challenge to it comes, if the bishop of a given city is suspect in his doctrine, from fellow bishops or from some other Christian (generally a cleric) who reports the suspect bishop to his fellow bishops.[1] Or, if a challenge does arise from a nonepiscopal source, as it does with Eutyches in the fifth century, it is answered by the official judgment of the episcopacy.[2]

Moreover, teaching is seen throughout the period we are studying as central to the bishop's function.[3] The question is not whether the ministry of the word is basic to the episcopal role; this is taken for granted. Rather, the differences we note in this period touch the meaning that one attaches to "ministry of the word," and the seriousness with which episcopal practice corresponds to the theoretical recognition of the importance of teaching.

Another general point might be mentioned. By the time of Nicaea the distinction between proclamation of the gospel and teaching has disappeared, and with it any trace of an independent function of "teaching" in the church.[4] Others than bishops do teach, and we find teaching exercised by even larger numbers of presbyters as the membership of the church swells. But such teaching is derivative from and ancillary to the teaching of the bishops themselves; it remains under their direction and subject to their authority.[5] In the twelfth century we begin to see traces of autonomous theological activity (which will become critically important in the thirteenth and fourteenth centuries); but the only thing

like this to which one could point in the preceding period is the polemic of the "imperial legists" against the popes of the eleventh century.[6]

Connected with this practical fusion of preaching and teaching (to which must be added quite early "legislating") is a development fraught with great significance for later developments in the church. To a very great extent, the prominent theologians of these centuries are bishops. Moreover, they consider the activity of theology an intrinsic part of their episcopal teaching. Obviously they do not hold this view explicitly, for there is not yet any distinctiveness given to Christian theology.[7] But when they do attempt to describe their activity as teachers, part of this activity is what a Christian theologian is meant to do; or, if they do not describe their activity, they act in this way.[8]

One might cite Hilary of Poitiers as an early example; Athanasius would certainly be another.[9] Even Ambrose, whose own temperament and the needs of whose church dictated a pastoral rather than a theological tone in teaching, describes his teaching role as one of trying to expose the implications of Scripture.[10] Augustine, of course, functions as theologian even in his most homiletic teaching; this despite the fact that his highly influential statement about the role of the Christian teacher (in his *De doctrina christiana*) stresses the simple exposition of Scripture.[11]

Instances could be multiplied. What is important to note, though, is the manner in which theological activity has been absorbed without challenge into the episcopal office.

Resulting from this, an authority is given theological conclusions made by bishops (and particularly the bishops of Rome) which is not distinguished from the authority of their proclamation of the word of God. Ambrose, for example, will speak of his episcopal office as one of *doctor*, distinguish it from that of apostle or evangelist or prophet or *pastor* (he is referring back to 1 Cor. 12 or 14), and then add that it is the *necessitudo sacerdotii* which imposes on him this *officium docendi*.[12] So, also, the *Didascalia* derives the all-embracing teaching authority of the bishop from his office as high priest.[13]

There is little that one might call "theologizing" in the episcopal, and particularly papal, teaching of the Latin church after Gregory the Great and Isidore of Seville.[14] However, there is an increased amalgamation (and confusion) of (a) episcopal proclamation of the word, (b) previous theological conclusions, and (c) legislative activity. As one can see from Gratian's *Decretum*, this legislative activity, as it entered into the formation of canonical traditions, included a good mixture of what was really theological speculation.[15] Hence, we find the situation where some theological opinions are authoritatively imposed as part of ecclesiastical legal judgment.[16] What becomes increasingly confused is the meaning of "tradition" as that is applied to the starting point of theology. Who really are the *auctores* with which the orthodox Christian theologian must work in developing further his own insight into the realities revealed by God in Jesus Christ?[17] More basically, the very notion of *auctoritas* is confused,[18] and we are still living with that confusion. Perhaps most basic, and this is what later theologians such as Abelard will wrestle with, is the subordination of the authority intrinsic to truth itself to the judicial authority possessed by one occupying an office in society.[19] This can happen because the office in question (i.e., of the bishop or pope) is one of leadership in a faith community, in a society based on authoritative teaching of a suprarational truth.[20]

To untangle this skein of intertwined "teaching" functions, as we observe it historically or try to describe it analytically, is beyond the scope of this present work. Achievement of this goal can only come with the writing of an adequate history of Christian theology, something no one has seriously attempted.[21] However, to gain greater clarification in the one limited area of the theology of ministry and priesthood, this present work tries to divide the episcopal function of teaching from the function of judging and both of these from the function of witness.

As already observed, throughout the eight centuries we are now studying, one can find statements that speak of the ministry of the word as basic to episcopal responsibility. What is impressive, however, is the practical illustration of this in the activity of the bishops. Particularly in the first half of this period, preaching or teaching of various kinds occupied a large portion of a bishop's time and energy. There was less tendency in the earlier centuries to "farm out" preaching and teaching to presbyters or other delegates; there was instead a tendency to look on such preaching and teaching as a properly episcopal prerogative, one which is somewhat grudgingly extended to others, and then always in a clearly subordinate and dependent role.[22] One thinks, for example, of the great deference paid to his bishop by Chrysostom during the time when, still a presbyter of the church of Antioch, he was commissioned by the bishop to give most of the catechumenal instructions. When he says at one point in these conferences, "Next time, your teacher will come . . ." the reference is quite clearly to the bishop.[23]

Episcopal teaching could and did take many forms. In the well-established and large Christian communities, which were already numerous by the fourth century, there was little, if any, opportunity for the bishop to exercise *kerygmatic* proclamation of the gospel to nonbelievers.[24] Yet, wherever expansion of Christianity took place, as it did in the missionary activity of a Patrick, or an Augustine in Britain, or Cyril and Methodius among the Slavs, or Boniface in northern

Europe, we find bishops engaged in activity much like that of the apostles of Christianity's first decades.

For the most part, however, the episcopacy of these post-Nicene centuries is engaged in forming the faith of the already converted. This could mean the instruction of the catechumens, or homiletic instruction of the faithful gathered for Eucharist, or providing formation of the clergy. The great body of homiletic literature that has come down to us from the patristic period bears ample witness to both the constancy of episcopal preaching and the high quality it often possessed.[25]

For a variety of reasons, a gradual shift in activity took place in the life of the episcopacy. Not that the ministry of the word ceased entirely to be a concern of bishops; but from the seventh century we do not find it occupying as much of the bishop's time as previously.[26] True, the exhortations to preaching that are enshrined in such writings as Gregory's *Pastoral Care* or Julian Pomerius' *Vita contemplativa* continue to keep the ideal of effective preaching before the minds of medieval bishops and presbyters. But in many portions of the church preaching was badly neglected and a felt need for more communication of the saving word began to develop. It was into this vacuum that the friar preachers would move in the late twelfth and thirteenth centuries.

It would be a mistake to read history as if for several centuries the ministry of the word was seen as basic to the episcopal office, and thereafter it gradually came to be considered as of lesser importance. The view that it is essential to episcopal and presbyteral ministry continues throughout the centuries. What does evolve, or at least changes, from one historical period to another and from one cultural situation to another is the understanding of what ministry of the word is. To a great extent, the view one takes about communication of the word depends upon his soteriology; this is quite logical, since the word is meant to be a saving and life-giving force, and one should preach and teach in a manner calculated to bring about salvation.

One can see salvation as basically a work of "illumination." This is the point of view we generally associate with the Alexandrian theology which starts with Clement and Origen and continues into the period we are now studying with Athanasius and Cyril.[27] Here the function of Christ as Logos is uppermost; as such he is the unique teacher, the Light of the world, the bearer of the only saving truth.[28] However, the truth involved is not some esoteric theory or metaphysical insight. It is a practical truth that shapes and nurtures man's life as a spirit. Christ, the Logos, is the first and unparalleled Image of the "unspeakable" God; men are meant by their imitation of him to become lesser likenesses, and in proportion as they do so to reach "godliness," to become truly spiritual, and thus reach their destiny.[29]

In such a soteriology, the ministration of the church and particularly the ministry of the word is aimed at bringing the Christian to contemplative communion with the divine. There is a strong element of ethical exhortation, for advance in "illumination" is conditioned by one's moral purity; but the sharing of understanding and insight is more ultimate. As far as possible, the teacher or preacher wishes to lead his Christian hearer into the mystery revealed in the Logos become man.[30]

This viewpoint, though characteristic of Alexandria, was not limited to that church nor even to its immediate neighbors. Ambrose of Milan was strongly influenced by the Alexandrians,[31] and through him Augustine was also touched by this Logos soteriology. However, in Augustine its coincidence with his philosophical attraction to neo-Platonic thinking led to a highly developed theology of salvation.[32] In Augustine's cosmology, the entirety of divine action upon creation can be subsumed under the notion of "illumination"; at the center of this creative-redemptive activity of God one finds Christ, the Logos incarnate, the *Magister internus*.[33]

So, again, despite a strong ethical interest on the part of both Ambrose and Augustine, the word of God that is communicated by preaching or teaching is sacramental. In this word the mystery of divine revelation still continues; in this word of the preacher (and in their day that meant the bishop) the Word himself speaks.[34] And the emphasis on what we might call doctrinal content is quite marked. It forms the basis for the moral reform that the preacher also seeks, but even this greater purity of life is hoped for as a step to deepened understanding.[35]

The viewpoint of Hilary of Poitiers is harder to classify. For him the ministry of the word is central to the bishop's task of providing for the flock entrusted to him,[36] but does not seem to be cast in the context of "illumination." Rather, it is a question of encouraging, strengthening, converting, and feeding the life that comes with faith.[37] Salvation would seem by implication to be achieved by faithful correspondence to the dictates of the divine will which the word of revelation conveys. And it is the role of the minister of this word to provide it accurately and truthfully, so that people's needs are fulfilled.[38]

Another way of regarding the word of God is that it is a word of healing and therefore of salvation. This aspect of the word becomes particularly important when the reality of man's "injury" by sin is stressed. This is not necessarily separate from the stress on illumination, for sin can be (and often is, particularly in neo-Platonic thought) thought of as "darkness." But in many of the patristic thinkers the consciousness of man's affliction by sin leads them to think of the pastoral office as one of healing. The bishop (or by extension the presbyter) is the "physician of souls" and his task is described as the *cura animarum* in this healing context.

Gregory of Nazianzus so describes the episcopal function of imparting the word, as do Augustine and Basil.[39] But it is with Gregory I that the notion of bishop-physician finds its fullest and most influential formulation. As the *Pastoral Care* stresses repeatedly, the role of the preacher or teacher is to exhort sinners to turn from their evil ways.[40] Gregory gives detailed instructions as to the best

manner of dealing with people of differing temperaments or in differing circumstances; each is to be corrected discreetly and thereby effectively.[41]

Of course, connected with this physician role of the bishop and its concomitant notion of salvation as sickness/health is the view that sees salvation being achieved through moral behavior. As a matter of fact, this second view is the basis for the first. Sickness is a figure of speech to describe immorality; the purpose of the minister of the word is, in nonfigurative language, to direct people to correct moral actions. It is not accidental that the same Gregory whose homiletic theory, expressed in the *Pastoral Care*, wielded such impact on medieval understanding of the pastoral role, is also the author of the *Moralia* (Commentary on Job) which feeds into medieval formulation of moral theology and into the tropological interpretation of Scripture.[42]

Though it is never formulated into an explicit soteriology, one of the most prevalent theories of salvation is that of ethical achievement. Or perhaps it would be more accurate to say that its explicit formulation, by Pelagius, never obtained official acceptance. Yet, in its more subtle forms, the tendency to reduce Christian living (and therefore salvation) to acceptable ethical behavior is present throughout the church's history.[43]

In this perspective, the role of one who is in a leadership position in society tends to be seen as that of lawgiver or judge. For a society whose notion of human excellence consists in conformity to law, to an enunciated code of acceptable morality, the function of the custodians and interpreters and enforcers of the laws is of utmost importance. In a later chapter we will discuss at length the evolution during the patristic period and early Middle Ages of the judicial role of the episcopacy. For the moment, however, we can notice how such an understanding of the bishop's role interprets his ministry of the word. He is to appeal to that revealed word as to a code of behavior; he is to explicate its laws and in their light pass judgments on men's actions.[44] Unfortunately, this can lead to the situation where Scripture is used as a source of justification for the judicial or legislative decisions of church rulers. One needs only to examine the "exegesis" of Scripture contained in the decretal literature of this period to see what happens to the word of God in this framework.[45]

It would be an error, however, to think that these centuries lost all sense of the mystery of the word and drifted instead into a purely moralistic or political version of Christian faith. Certainly, there were unhappy driftings in these directions; but more basically there remained an awareness of the activity of Christ immanent in the church. This activity was intimately associated with the preaching of the word and with the words of sacramental blessing and consecration. As we will see in more detail when studying the ritual function of Christian priesthood, it was a commonplace to say (as Augustine did), "When the bishop baptizes it is Christ who baptizes."[46] But in terms of a ministry of the word, it is interesting to note that it is the *word* of the minister through which Christ himself acts in sacrament.[47]

Here we touch upon an evolution, as yet scarcely distinguishable but destined to assume major importance in Christian thinking. One is already beginning to draw a line between the word (whether in preaching or in sacrament, but particularly in the latter) as effective in a manner proper to word, i.e., by its power of psychological transformation, and the word as possessing some instrumental effectiveness by its "objective meaning." While not exactly the distinction *ex opere operato/ ex opere operantis*, it is the beginnings of such a mentality.

Probably the Donatist controversy played a key role in this whole matter. If one was going to maintain in the question of rebaptism (or reordination) that essential effectiveness attached to baptism administered by a schismatic, then one must answer the objection How can one give the Spirit if he himself does not possess that Spirit?[48] The same objection will arise several times in later centuries, more generally in the case not of a

schismatic but of a gravely sinful minister. And the only possible response lies in attributing some causative power to the "objective significance" of sacramental action and word.

What begins to emerge very early in this discussion is the notion that the unworthy minister must "intend that which the church intends." That is to say, the sign he places must be that which the church wishes placed; and because it is this sign, it is the church's sign and bears the meaning and intention of the church.[49] Which implies, even in the case of the orthodox and saintly minister, that the effectiveness of a minister of the word (sacramental or otherwise) comes most basically from his office, from the fact that he is speaking officially, as one ordained to speak in this recognized position.[50]

The Bishop's Role

Throughout the period we are studying, the bishop's role was seen as one of possessing the saving word and being entrusted with safeguarding and transmitting it.[51] Already there is some shift from the ante-Nicene period. During those earlier centuries, the episcopacy was viewed more as the corporate heirs of a sacred tradition. The true understanding of Christian faith came to them by their apostolic succession; during the centuries after Nicaea, on the contrary, importance attached increasingly to the episcopal *office*. By virtue of occupying this office a bishop or presbyter was charged with the responsibility of imparting the word.[52]

Naturally, the precise understanding of this official responsibility varied accordingly as one or other of the views of salvation we have just examined was espoused. Chrysostom, Gregory of Nazianzus, and Augustine would see themselves as charged with illumining the minds and guiding the consciences of their people, leading them to truth and love.[53] Hilary of Poitiers would see himself as the steward entrusted with distributing the life-giving word that would nourish the faith of the community.[54] Gregory the Great would see the minister charged with the task of healing the spiritual ills of men by admonishing them for their sins and encouraging them to follow examples of true Christian behavior.[55]

But whatever the variations of their understanding of how the word of God was meant to function in the lives of men, the bishops in these centuries never lost sight of the centrality of the word in Christian ministry. They themselves consistently preached and taught and the Scriptures formed the unchallenged basis for their preaching. Moreover, there is constant evidence of their concern for the formation of presbyters, so that they could effectively (or at least not disastrously) communicate the word to their people.[56] No doubt the unsettled situation of the "barbaric invasions" and the poor conditions for clerical training led in many instances to a neglect of preaching. Yet, the writings of such men as Caesarius of Arles or the repeated canons of synods like that of Saint-Jean-de-Losne (673) indicate that the theoretical understanding of the ministry of the word's importance remained explicit and clear.[57]

There is, then, a noticeable continuity in affirmations about the centrality of preaching in the sacerdotal function. Moreover, there is little distinction (if any) between the activities of preaching and teaching, though monastic centers of learning and teaching are coming into existence. There is even less distinctness accorded theology; it remains implicit in the episcopal (and presbyteral) teaching activity. What does shift notably during this period between Nicaea and the twelfth century is the content and orientation of the teaching.

Scripture, of course, retains an uncontested position as *the* word that must be communicated to the faithful. All preaching consists in proclaiming it; all teaching is an attempt to clarify its meaning and implications. But recent studies in patristic and medieval use of Scripture (Smalley, DeLubac, McNally, etc.) indicate the great variation that existed in the manner that Scripture was utilized and its meaning "discovered."[58]

Because Scripture does convey a way of life, it contains a great deal of guidance for practical Christian behavior. As a result, any expositor of Scripture will find himself to some extent in the area of ethical teaching. Yet, in the post-Nicene centuries there is a sharp increase of emphasis on the Scriptures as a source of moral exhortation.

One need only compare the approach to teaching contained in the *De doctrina christiana* of Augustine, or Ambrose's letter to Constantius,[59] both of which stress simple exposition of the Scripture text, with the viewpoint of Gregory I in his *Pastoral Care*. As Batiffol remarks: "Gregory, we repeat, was a moralist. In his sermons he seeks to make his people conform to the Christian system of morals, in his *Regula pastoralis* he examines the conscience of the bishops, and in his commentary on Job he has especially in view the monks who are listening to him. His purpose, in explaining the Scriptures to them, is to instruct them in their vocation. . . ."[60]

Gregory was not alone. His close follower, Isidore of Seville, not only carries on the Gregorian moralism but adds to it a strong element of Stoicism.[61] And the continuation of this moralizing emphasis is witnessed to by Alcuin[62] and Rabanus Maurus[63] in the ninth century.

By the very pressure of large-scale conversion to Christianity, the bishops of the post-Nicene church were compelled to delegate much of their preaching/teaching responsibility to their presbyters. Here one notices a clear change from the situation of Augustine or Ambrose or Chrysostom or Basil, where the "lower clergy" were empowered to preach or teach but (at least in the cities) under rather close episcopal supervision, to the situation of Merovingian times and thereafter when the bulk of the faithful were in country "parishes" and instructed by presbyters who were relatively and at times obstreperously autonomous.

More and more, the preaching/teaching role of the episcopacy finds its principal expression in guiding the instruction provided by the presbyters. This is particularly true in the tenth and eleventh centuries and thereafter. One can find a reflection of this in the increasingly complex structure of the diocese and the division of labor among deans, archpriests, etc.[64] And as this trend increases, the bishop's role in the ministry of the word shifts increasingly in the direction of supervision and judging, or of providing guidance and formation through synods or "handbooks."[65]

In such a development, one can ask what was happening to the "sacramental dimension" of the bishop's proclamation of the word. No doubt, a fair amount of the connotation of "apostolic succession" still attached to the bishop's teaching from his *cathedra* during the Eucharistic liturgy. Yet, the *cathedra* itself had a significance for Ambrose or Augustine quite different from that it had for Hincmar or Hildebrand. By the time of these latter, particularly for Hildebrand, the bishop's *cathedra* had more than a little overtone of political rule. It is hard to think of Augustine or Chrysostom, or even Leo I or Gelasius, claiming what Gregory VII does in the *Dictatus papae*: "Quod solus possit uti imperialibus insigniis."[66] Indeed, a rather radical alteration occurred in the sacramental signifying connected to Orders!

Early Christianity had possessed a somewhat distinct ministry of teaching, but this was very rapidly absorbed (along with prophecy) into the episcopal function. At the time of Nicaea there is certainly no explicit prohibition of teaching by others than the bishops.[67] But it seems to be increasingly taken for granted that teaching of the faith should be done within episcopally directed circumstances, which practically means that it is to be done by clerics.

However, at the very time when, in the incipient "diocese-parish" pattern of ecclesial life, teaching becomes a clear clerical prerogative, another situation develops which will bring forth an evolution of teaching essentially independent from direct episcopal control though accidentally brought under that control historically. This independent context for Christian teaching was monastic life.

Long before there was anything resembling the monastic school developments that one associates with Columban and Theodore of

Canterbury and Alcuin, the role of the "spiritual father" was already one of a teacher,[68] so much so that "schools of spirituality" developed out of the traditions of teaching cherished in the Thebaid or the Syrian desert or Lerins.[69] Some of the great monastic mentors, such as Basil, were also bishops; but this was accidental to their role as teachers of monastic life.

Benedict, though he produced no volume of writing and conducted no formal schooling program, must be counted as one of the great teachers of monasticism, indeed of western Europe.[70] His rule is a most influential bit of teaching and the monasteries founded on his principles quickly developed into the most potent educational force in Europe. Not all the teaching went on in monasteries for there was teaching carried on by many bishops for their clergy, and by the Carolingian era it was recommended for each "parish" that it have a school attached to the local church.[71] But it was the monasteries that had the wealth of manpower, the continuity of traditions and personnel, and the facilities of libraries which could permit serious study and scholarly communication.

Thus the eminence in seventh-century England of Canterbury and Lindisfarne and Jarrow, and on the Continent of Saint Gallen and Luxeuil and Bobbio.[72] But these themselves drew from earlier centers of monastic learning and instruction in Ireland or Italy or southern France.[73] Perhaps the most renowned and influential of these was the monastic community of Lerins.[74]

Cathedral schools continued to exist throughout this period, and not a few maintained a high level of instruction. Yet the fact that they were staffed by canons, whose financial situation was often precarious, gave them less stability and continuity than the monasteries.[75] Still it is important to note the existence throughout these centuries of a sizable group of ordained presbyters devoted basically to educational work. However, the field of learning from the sixth century onward is increasingly dominated by the monks. And it is from this monastic movement that there emerges the reform impulse that strengthens both the intellectual and spiritual life of the Western church, and particularly of its clergy.[76]

In this way, apart from any theory that provided for an expansion of the notion of *magisterium*, a nonepiscopal (and increasingly clerical) agency came into focal prominence in the pedagogical activity of the church. There was not, certainly, any claim to supersede the episcopacy but just the opposite; even the Celtic developments remained well within the notion of apostolic tradition and succession as controlling norms for faith and doctrine.[77] Concretely, however, the thrust of doctrinal evolution and communication tended to pass into what was not even (at least in its pure forms) a clerical context of Christianity.[78]

For the most part, this deep involvement of monasticism in the life of learning did not cause conflict with the episcopacy in the centuries prior to the twelfth century. Actually the conflict comes with the simultaneous emergence into prominence of the universities and the mendicant orders. But the seeds of conflict were already planted—the ecclesiastical aspect of conflict (i.e., papal/antipapal polemics) enhanced by the Roman alignment of the religious orders and by their exemption from episcopal control,[79] and the deeper intellectual aspect of conflict fortified by the "pious" monopoly of Christian tradition by institutionalized religious life.[80]

As far as the teaching of the "sacred disciplines" is concerned, the period between Nicaea and the twelfth century is totally dominated by clerics or monks. This is true both in the West and in the East.[81] Religious education and theology became quite quickly the preserve of the clerical establishment (including the monks), and remained that way throughout the Middle Ages.

One striking exception must be made, though in its own setting it is scarcely an exception: the emperor Justinian. With the well-known results that were close to catastrophic for the church, Justinian insisted on functioning as official theologian and forcing

his opinions in the Three Chapters controversy.[82] Later Byzantine rulers attempted at times to impose some doctrinal position on the Eastern church, as Zeno with the *Henoticon*,[83] but none of these really attempted to exercise a role of teacher. Instead, they attempted politically to favor one or other camp in a dispute which they were interested in seeing settled for the sake of unity in their realm.

Much more important in its ultimate implications was the emergence towards the end of the tenth century of centers of legal study.[84] While many of the prominent professors and students of law at Bologna or Padua were clerics, an increasing number of laymen frequented these schools.[85] Before long a sizable corps of trained legists began to play a prominent part in discussion of ecclesiastical authority and related topics. This was unavoidable at a time when church-state relations were so confused and intertwined; but what it meant was that reflection about the nature of the church was being done by men whose background and training was almost exclusively legal in orientation. Eventually this will find expression in the writings of Marsilius, Jacques of Viterbo, and Jean de Jandun.[86] But in the tenth and eleventh centuries there is no trace of this later, starkly antiecclesiastical doctrine; instead, there is one unified development of law that involves both ecclesiastical and civil legislation.

By the time of the great fourth- and fifth-century councils, the "mystery" dimension of the church's reality was already a theologically refined element of Christian thought.[87] And, despite the increasing emphasis on external institutional aspects of the church and the concomitant increase of political models as bases for thinking about the church, the notion of the church as mystery remains dominant throughout the eight centuries we are studying.[88]

Probably no author of this period worked out more systematically the role of the bishop as "initiator into mystery" than did Pseudo-Denis;[89] but the understanding of the episcopal function in this manner was by no means unique to him. Both in their descriptions of the bishop's role in the initiation of new members into the Christ-mystery and in their own conduct of this initiation rite (and its preparatory and ensuing catechesis), a number of the great bishops of this period give us valuable insight into this aspect of the episcopal ministry.[90]

Unique as it is among the religions of man's history, and unique as is the reality of its initiation ritual, Christianity had to provide two elements intrinsic to any religious initiation: an introduction to the community's "myth" (i.e., its cherished and traditional explanation of the meaning of reality and of human life) and a symbolic confrontation with the "mystery reality" itself.[91]   In Christianity there is a first and decisive stage in both of these elements; there is a catechumenate instruction and then the baptismal initiation. But there is also a continuing initiation: further catechesis becomes a permanent part of one's Christian life and the entry into "mystery reality" is meant to grow deeper through continued participation in Eucharistic liturgy.

No less than Cyprian or Irenaeus, the bishops of the fourth and fifth centuries considered themselves the guardians of authentic apostolic tradition.[92]   Really, this is the backdrop for the bitter controversies connected with the great trinitarian and Christological councils.   Gathered at Nicaea or Ephesus or Chalcedon, the bishops did not speak of themselves as formulating new theological insights (though they were doing this); rather, they tell us in the proemia to their doctrinal decrees that they intend only to express the faith contained in the New Testament writings and defended by the fathers of the church who have preceded them.[93]   They have come together in order to guarantee the orthodoxy of Christian faith, an orthodoxy that is preserved by fidelity to apostolic tradition.[94]

What we find in communal statements at councils we find also in the writings of individual bishops of that period.   Athanasius, writing to Serapion, speaks of the "original tradition and faith and teaching of the cath-

olic church, which the Lord gave, the Apostles proclaimed, and the Fathers preserved," a tradition without which the church could not truly be called "Christian."[95]   His contemporary Hilary of Poitiers appeals to the faith of the apostles, especially of Peter, as the norm for the accuracy of his own trinitarian teaching.[96]   Ambrose, Augustine, Basil, Gregory of Nazianzus, Chrysostom, Leo, Cyril of Alexandria—all insist on their dependence upon apostolic tradition and their intent to act as faithful guardians of this truth.[97]

But it was not enough to preserve intact the apostolic teaching; it was the proper role of the bishops (even when, as they increasingly did, they delegated the task to presbyters or deacons) to convey this "word of God."   We have already seen the manner in which this was carried out through their preaching and other forms of teaching.   A special look, however, should be directed at the instruction given the catechumens, for here we find in sharp focus the notion of introducing men and women into the understanding of Christian mystery.   Much of the other teaching tends to pass into doctrinal and especially moral explanation, but in the baptismal instruction we can see clearly the effort to instill into the minds and imaginations of the neophytes the Christian "vision," the understanding upon which they can ground their basic faith relationship to the risen Christ and the Father through their Spirit.[98]

As one examines the classic witnesses to this imparting of "Christian myth," the baptismal catecheses of Ambrose[99] or Augustine[100] or Theodore of Mopsuestia[101] or Cyril of Jerusalem,[102] one is struck by the prominence of the explanation of scriptural typology and the application of this typologically to the life of the Christian.[103]   The very use of this symbolic explanation highlights the extent to which this catechumenal instruction instilled the notion of Christianity as "the mystery hidden for centuries, but now revealed to us in Christ Jesus" (Eph. 3:9).   Though they do not preserve for us the catechumenal instruction as such, the explanations of baptism provided by Damascene in the East and Gregory I and Isidore in the West indicate how prominent the explanation of baptismal typology remained throughout the patristic period.[104] It might be worth noting, however, that the latter two stress much more the ethical aspect of this typology.[105]

Throughout the early patristic period it is clearly the bishop who is charged with providing the understanding of Christian mystery to the initiates. This is particularly true of the mystagogical catechesis which immediately followed the initiation ceremony. For the most part this seems to have been given by the bishop himself when this was possible (i.e., in the city situations). Even in the prebaptismal catechumenal instruction the bishop played an active part: he was in charge of this training, directed its program if he himself did not actually give the instruction, came from time to time to teach the group (and probably to bless them), and himself conducted the scrutiny before their admission to the ceremony of initiation.[106]

All the evidence indicates that the basic pattern of Christian initiation described in the *Apostolic Tradition* of Hippolytus continues to be followed throughout these centuries.[107] And what is clear in this ceremony is the principal role of the bishop. He himself is not the immediate agent at each step of the initiation. Deacons or deaconesses perform the prebaptismal anointings, presbyters apparently do the actual baptizing; but this is done in the presence and under the presidency of the bishop. It is the bishop who seals the baptism by the "confirmational" chrismation, and it is he who as celebrant of the Eucharist leads the neophytes into the final stage of their initiation, explaining to them the significance of the communion in the body and blood of Christ.[108] Thus, the entire local church transmits to the new Christians the mystery of Christ's death and resurrection, but it does so under the leadership of the bishop.

What begins in the initiation ceremony continues throughout the life of the Christian; he is increasingly introduced into the mystery of Christ.[109] At the center of this process stands the celebration of the Eucharist, linking him with the historical event of death/resurrection and with his eschatological achievement of full union with Christ and the Father. As part of his ministry of the word, the bishop (or presbyter, as "parishes" develop) celebrates the Eucharist; for it is still seen during this period as a unique occasion for the imparting of the word, it is the proclamation of the mystery by Christ himself.[110]

Though, as we noted, the explanation of baptism given by Gregory I and Isidore still retains the elements of typology found in the earlier patristic texts, there is already evident a shift in the understanding of baptism. To quite an extent the notion of mystery is gone, and even the understanding of mystery is shifted from that of "saving event" to that of "hidden significance."[111] The same change of viewpoint is observed in the exegesis of Scripture as one increasingly loses the "history of salvation" notion and emphasizes the allegorical and moral meanings.[112] This trend, already observable in Gregory and Isidore, becomes intensified at least partially through the influence of their writings.

It would not be fair, however, to lay the major responsibility for this shift in thought about baptism at the door of Gregory and Isidore. Rather, a number of factors probably played an influential role in altering the earlier understanding of Christian initiation. Perhaps most important was the sociological situation, which prevailed from about the seventh century onwards, in which practically everyone in the Christian areas of the world was Christian. The *societas christiana* was, at least from Carolingian times onward, synonomous with human society in western Europe. In such a context, though there was no theological teaching that baptism was unnecessary and the practice of baptism was universally accepted as entry into the church, there was inevitable cultural acceptance of the fact that one was a Christian "by birth." Having been born into this *societas*, his baptism was a foregone conclusion. Naturally, such a view is intrinsically linked with the practice of infant baptism, a practice which itself tends to obscure the nature of baptism as a conversion to Christ through acceptance in faith of the mystery of his death and resurrection.[113]

Again, the rapid diffusion of Christianity and (particularly in the West) the increasing numbers of Christian communities in rural areas tended to eclipse the role of the bishop in baptism, and along with this the solemnity of the action. Baptism is no longer reserved for the ceremony of the Easter or Pentecost vigil, nor is it performed with the entire congregation present.[114] The bishop does retain a tenuous connection with the Christian's initiation (in the West), because the confirmational anointing is reserved for him; but this has the negative effect of breaking the unified notion of Christian initiation, unnaturally separating baptism and confirmation, and eventually downgrading the appreciation of baptism itself.[115]

Another important factor in obscuring the understanding of baptism as mystery was the concentration of attention on original sin that followed from Augustine, the Pelagian controversies, and the general Latin trend towards moralizing.[116] Whereas in the pre-Nicene period it is practically impossible to find statements that baptism "remits original sin" (though the theological equivalent is present: entry into the new Christian epoch of history),[117] this becomes after the fifth century an increasingly important explanation of the effect of Christian initiation.[118] In this perspective, the role of the minister of baptism is that of "applying the merits of Christ's death" or of "curing and correcting" the sinfulness of the baptized.[119]

One of the very curious aspects of the development of doctrine during this period is the manner in which baptism and faith remain firmly linked with one another in all theological and catechetical discussions, even though the actual practice of baptism is taking it further and further away from being a profession of faith.[120] To some extent this may tie in with the fact that in the early medieval theology of faith (e.g., Anselm of Canterbury), there is a tendency to see faith as a moral rather than an intellectual act, a presupposi-

tion to the understanding of Christian mystery rather than as the first initiation into the intelligibility of that mystery.[121] Of course, this is part and parcel of the mentality that begins to develop in ninth- and tenth-century theology: asking how the sacraments cause their effect, and in answering turning towards the idea of instrumentality rather than the effectiveness of personal experience of mystery. In this perspective, the one most capable of explaining Christian initiation is no longer the "initiator" (the bishop) but the theologian. The minister of baptism becomes not so much a *leitourgos* as the official administrator of the grace-causing sign. Baptism ceases to be (not in its intrinsic liturgical reality, but in people's understanding) what every Christian sacrament is meant intrinsically to be: proclamation of and response to the gospel.[122]

The Bishop as Example

Perhaps no element in the history of Christian theology of ministry is more consistent than the idea that the bishop (and relatively the other clergy) is meant to be an example of Christian virtue. This is a constant theme in the letters of the great bishops of the patristic and early medieval period as they write to fellow bishops or to other clergy; it is expressed in such treatises as Gregory's *Cura pastoralis* or Chrysostom's *On the Priesthood* or Pseudo-Denis' *Ecclesiastical Hierarchy*, and it is the presupposition for a great portion of the canonical literature that results from synods or episcopal (papal) decree.

At first glance, then, it would seem that there is little if any development in understanding this facet of the episcopal function. Yet, there does seem to be a subtle and perhaps significant shift in view. In the pre-Nicene epoch one seems to be still in the context of Paul's approach—to be a disciple of mine as I am of Christ. That is to say, the bishop can point to his own behavior as a model for his flock because he is the heir of a tradition of discipleship, a way of life has been handed down to him by those who learned it (eventually) from the Master himself.[123] Shortly after Nicaea we find this same mentality reflected in Athanasius who to justify his own flight from his enemies points to the examples of others, especially Christ, who at times prudently hid out from their enemies.[124]

Shortly, however, a different point of view comes to the fore; the bishops (and according to their order, the other clergy) are to be an example of virtue because that is what is appropriate to the more exalted rank they hold within the Christian society. The most conspicuous exposition of this mentality is found in the *De hierarchia ecclesiastica* of Pseudo-Denis;[125] but this viewpoint is not that different from other Eastern theologians of the late fifth and early sixth centuries, especially those strongly influenced by Neo-Platonism. In the West, too, even prior to the introduction of Denis' thought in the ninth century (through the translation of Erigena), much the same mentality of exemplary sanctity attaching to bishops because of the office they occupied grows out of the Augustinian notion of "order" which itself is rooted in a Neo-Platonic cosmology.[126]

Alongside the notion of clerical holiness there developed that of monastic perfection. This latter can very appropriately be termed an ascetical ideal, for it is clearly the view that perfection must be achieved through a process of careful and unrelenting self-discipline.[127] In the more orthodox explanation of this ascetic spirituality, the Christian element is preserved by insisting that the goal to be achieved in all this is charity, that without this charity all the rest could be pride and self-delusion.[128] And the more orthodox views also insist on the need for divine assistance, for grace, if one is to achieve the level of perfection appropriate to a Christian ascetic.[129]

This is not the place to enter into a careful appraisal of the advantages and drawbacks of this ascetical ideal. The unquestionable greatness of some of the individuals who lived their lives according to this ideal indicates the contribution it can make to Christian perfec-

tion. On the other hand, the many instances of extremism and "spiritual athleticism" which suggest masochism or psychological exhibitionism rather than the gospel, and the affinity of much of this ascetic movement for Pelagianism, indicate that one must be somewhat critical in giving support to the idea of asceticism as the road to Christian perfection.[130]

Be that as it may, the ascetic replaced the martyr as the ideal Christian even before the period of persecutions had come completely to an end.[131] And during the fourth and fifth centuries there was a rapid and widespread development of cenobitic and monastic life, the situation in which this ascetic ideal was formulated, promulgated, and cherished.[132] Quite quickly, too, the adherents of this way of life appropriated to themselves the notion of *true* Christian spirituality. They alone were living fully the life of the spirit, apart from material concerns or bodily joys.[133]

If such ascetic life is the ideal fulfillment of the Christian vocation, and if the bishops are meant to be the examples for their people of Christian living, then it follows that they must be par excellence "spiritual men" according to the ascetic ideal. This we find advocated in truly edifying and attractive form by Gregory of Nazianzus, by Augustine, by Pomerius, by Gregory the Great, to name but a few.[134] Yet, even these men, themselves examples of truly great Christian holiness, were conscious of a tension between this ideal drawn from monastic life and the practicalities of their episcopal role. More than once they complain, at times almost in desperation, at the unresolvable opposition between the active and contemplative life.[135]

Pseudo-Denis adds another element to the picture, one which will have a subtle influence on later thinking about bishops and other clergy despite its obvious variance from experience. In the hierarchy of people within the church, he arranges them according to their relative approximation to the divine, i.e., according to their degree of spirituality. And in this hierarchical ordering of the church's membership the clergy are situated by the very ontological reality of their office above all laity, even the laity in religious life. Thus, by being bishop a man is constituted in a situation of holiness; the bishop is not only a seeker after perfection, he is in the state of perfection because he is the one who must communicate this to those below him in the church. The bishop is "light," so that he can illumine his flock—first the other clergy, then the monks, then the "ordinary faithful."[136]

This emphasis on good example as an intrinsic part of the ministry of the word reinforces in Christianity the importance attached in any religious community to the moral behavior of the "priesthood."[137] Placed in a position of leadership (by their possession of the apostolic tradition, by their liturgical role, and increasingly by their sociological position), the clergy, particularly the bishops, were expected to reflect in their lives the holiness of Christ himself; they were to exemplify for others the *imitatio Christi*.[138]

What this meant among other things is that the clergy became increasingly a separate class in Christian society; they were not "ordinary people." They were above the laity not just in the dignity of their functions within the community but in the very nature of their membership in the church.[139] This finds its ultimate expression when the popes begin to refer to themselves as the "head" of the church. This does not imply a denial of the role of Christ himself as the head of his Body,

but that he exercises his headship through the pope who is his vicar.[140]

From as early as Leo I, one finds references to the distinction between the *ecclesia discens* and the *ecclesia docens,* but this becomes a commonplace assumption from the time of Gregory I.[141] Moreover, the viewpoint represented by Pseudo-Denis moves this distinction into the ontological order. There are two spheres of Christian being and holiness, one could almost say that there are two kinds of holiness, two kinds of "being Christian." This historical period sees the clergy gradually appropriating to themselves the role of "active Christians," whereas the laity are more and more cast in the role of the "recipients of salvation."[142] Finally, in the eleventh century we find the word *"ecclesia"* being used to refer to the clergy and particularly the episcopacy[143] (a usage that is still with us, even after the correctives of Vatican II!).

During the latter half of the period we are studying, the thrust to establish and preserve the moral standards of the clergy reduced itself to the fight against simony and the struggle to establish the discipline of clerical celibacy.[144] Sociologically the two were closely linked; they were part of the attempt to gain for the church that freedom from "secular influences" which would permit it to carry on its task of salvation. It is an interesting note, however, that in such statements about the "freedom of the church" what is meant is the freedom of the higher clergy.[145]

NOTES

1. E.g., in the case of Paul of Samosata; see J. Daniélou and H. Marrou, *The Christian Centuries* (London, 1964), vol. 1, pp. 208–18.

2. On Eutyches, his opinions and influence, his synodal condemnation in Constantinople, and the events leading up to the Council of Chalcedon, see C. Hefele and H. Leclerq, *Histoire des conciles* (Paris, 1909), vol. 2, pp. 512–66.

3. So Athanasius in *Festal letter* 39 (cited by J. Roldanus, *Le christ et l'homme dans la théologie d'Athanase d'Alexandrie* [Leiden, 1968], p. 245); Ambrose *De officiis* 1. 1. 2–3; or Chrysostom, who devotes two of the six chapters of his little treatise on the priesthood to preaching. On the attitude from Gregory I through the Carolingian period, see Y. Congar, *L'ecclésiologie du Haut Moyen Age* (Paris, 1968), pp. 72–73.

4. This is clearly reflected in the extensive development of the homily during the patristic period; see W. O'Shea, *New Catholic Encyclopedia* (New York, 1967), vol. 7, pp. 113–15.

5. Chrysostom, for example, in his famous sermons on the statues will frequently refer to the bishop as "our teacher" (e.g., *Hom. de stat.* 3. 2); see also Ambrose *De officiis* 1. 2.

6. See K. Morrison, *Tradition and Authority in the Western Church* (Princeton, 1969), pp. 292–306.

7. On the historical evolution of theology in the church prior to the twelfth-century renaissance, *Dictionnaire de théologie catholique*, vol. 15, cols. 341–63. As Congar points out (col. 345), it is not until Abelard that we find the word "theology" used somewhat the way we would use it.

8. The very process of preaching a homily, i.e., a simple but accurate clarification of Scripture as used in sacrament, involves an important element of theologizing.

9. Hilary *De trin.* 8. 1–2.

10. *De officiis* 1. 1. 3.

11. *De doct. christ.* 4. 4. 6.

12. *De officiis* 1. 1. 2.

13. *Didascalia* 8.

14. There were exceptions in these centuries between Gregory I and Gregory VII, such as Agobard and Rabanus Maurus, but theology was more and more being done in monastic circles. Rabanus himself was abbot of Fulda before becoming bishop.

15. This is particularly noticeable in the section of the *Decretum* that deals with the sacraments, which, incidentally, becomes one of the principal sources for medieval treatises on the sacraments.

16. Later we will have occasion to study the obverse, i.e., the manner in which canon law operated as the source of speculative theology.

17. See P. Smulders, "Le mot et le concept de tradition chez les pères grecs," *Recherches de science religieuse* 40 (1952), pp. 56–60; B. Studer, *Die theologische Arbeitsweise des Johannes von Damaskus* (Ettal, 1956), pp. 57–60.

18. On late patristic and early medieval use of "*auctoritas*," see M.-D. Chenu, *Toward Understanding Saint Thomas* (Chicago, 1963), pp. 126–39; and J. de Ghellinck, *Le mouvement théologique du XIIe siècle* (Bruxelles, 1948), pp. 477–99.

19. See de Ghellinck, pp. 163–75; Chenu, pp. 140–50. However, it must be noted that the discussion in the late patristic and early medieval period was not directed explicitly to the conflict between the authority of office and the authority of knowledge; rather, the question was one of determining the extent to which reason and dialectic could pass judgment upon the meaning and authority of traditional texts.

20. Obviously, this entire matter is colored by the view that one takes with regard to the nature of faith, revelation, and mystery, and unresolved questions about these notions will continue throughout medieval theology and into the confessional conflicts of the Reformation period.

21. Such a history would be quite distinct from the histories of dogma, of which a number have been produced, for it would trace the evolution of the method of doing theology. Fortunately, several important studies have been made of specific stages in the development of Christian theology (Chenu, de Ghellinck, Grabmann, Congar, etc.) and a large number of thorough monographs on the method of individual theologians also exist, so the synthetic historical study is now possible.

22. See F. Dudden, *The Life and Times of St. Ambrose* (Oxford, 1935), vol. 1, pp. 131–32 (esp. p. 132, n. 2). By the time of Isidore, however, preaching is recognized as an intrinsic function of the presbyter; see *De eccles. officiis* 2. 7. 2: ". . . In confectione divini corporis et sanguinis consortes cum episcopis sunt, similiter et in doctrina populorum, et in officio praedicandi."

23. *Baptismal instruction* 11. 18 (as arranged in P. Harkins' translation in *Ancient*

Christian Writers, vol. 31; it is listed as instruction 3 in the Papadopoulos-Kerameus series).

24. In reading the descriptions of their preaching function that are given by Ambrose, or Leo I, or Augustine, or Hilary, one sees that they point to the postkerygmatic situa-ation (i.e., one or other stage of catechesis) as the one in which they are involved.

25. See Daniélou-Marrou, pp. 301–8.

26. One can see the increasingly supervisory responsibility of the bishops reflected in the Justinian Code (*C.I.* 1. 3. 41) and in the prescriptions of the successive Carolingian reforms (see E. Ewig, *Handbook of Church History* [New York, 1969], vol. 3, pp. 70–117).

27. See Roldanus, pp. 244–49.

28. Cyril *In Joan.* 11. 4; Athanasius *Epist. ad Serap.* 1. 31–32.

29. Cyril *In Joan.* 11. 10.

30. See Roldanus, pp. 246–47.

31. See S. Greenslade, *Early Latin Theology* (Philadelphia, 1956), p. 176.

32. On the various aspects of this soteriology, see the series of essays in *Augustinus magister* (Paris, 1956), vol. 2, pp. 737–986.

33. See R. Jolivet, "La doctrine augustinienne de l'illumination," *Mélanges augustiniens* (Paris, 1931), pp. 52–172.

34. See F. Schnitzler, *Zur Theologie der Verkundigung* (Freiburg, 1968), p. 168: "Der Leitgedanke in den verschiedenen Ausserungen des hl. Augustinus über die Predigt ist die Gegenwart Gottes: Gott ist gegenwartig im Wort der Schrift und im Wort der Predigt; er ist gegenwartig im Prediger und im Horer."

35. See A. Polman, *The Word of God According to St. Augustine* (Grand Rapids, Mich., 1961), pp. 123–76.

36. *In Matt.* 27. 1.

37. *Ibid.*: ". . . Doctrinae opportunitate et veritate infirma confirmet, disrupta consolidet, depravata convertat, et verbum vitae in aeternitatis cibum alendae familiae dispendat. . . ."

38. See also *De trin.* 8. 1–2.

39. Augustine *Epist.* 169. 3–4; Basil *Moralia* 80. 16; *De cura past.* 3. 25. See also Chrysostum *On the priesthood* 4. 3.

40. See esp. 3. 25 for the metaphor of healing.

41. The whole of part 3 is devoted to such homiletic counsel.

42. See B. Smalley, *The Study of the Bible in the Middle Ages* (Oxford, 1952), pp. 32–35.

43. There are several facets to this tendency: one of them is the temptation of semi-Pelagianism which, at least as far back as Cassian, is difficult for asceticism to avoid (see O. Chadwick, *John Cassian* [Cambridge, 1968]); another is the strong and endur-ing impact of Stoicism, especially its ethical elements (see R. Wenley, *Stoicism and Its Influence* [New York, 1963]).

44. To some extent, of course, this is inescapable in any practical application of the gospel, and as such is standard homiletic practice as early as Justin (see *Apology 1* 67).

45. See de Ghellinck, pp. 52–65; on the canonistic exegesis of Scripture, see H. de Lubac, *Exégèse médiévale* (Paris, 1959), vol. 1, pp. 542–43.

46. *In Joan.,* Hom. 6. 7.

47. *Ibid.,* 80. 2. Interestingly, we have here a clear convergence of ministry of the word and ministry of sacrament.

48. This was precisely the question posed by the Council of Carthage in 255; see Cyprian *Epist.* 70.

49. See B. Leeming, *Principles of Sacramental Theology,* 2d ed. (London, 1960), pp. 435–61.

50. This could, of course, be understood magically, as if the words and actions of the minister had some automatic power. Or again, it could mean that official status puts

one in the position of being an instrument that God uses in the sacrament's causality. However, neither of these interpretations imposes itself: the statement could also be understood in a sacramental sense, i.e., the minister is really sacramental of the presence of the church (and of its tradition coming down from the apostles) and of the presence of Christ, both of which can then operate through this sacramentalizing ministry.

51. See, e.g., Julianus Pomerius *De vita cont.* 15–20.

52. On the pre-Nicene view, see K. Delahaye, *Ecclesia mater* (Paris, 1964), pp. 220–29; on the post-Nicene notion of responsibility for preaching as grounded in office, see Ambrose *De officiis* 1. 1. 2–3; Augustine *Enar. in Ps.* 126. 3; Isidore *De eccles. officiis* 2. 5. 16–17.

53. On the strong moral implications of teaching, see E. Fleury, *Saint Grégoire de Nazianze et son temps* (Paris, 1930), pp. 124–27.

54. *In Matt.* 27. 1.

55. *De cura pastorali* 3. 25.

56. Early in the sixth century there existed a number of schools for training presbyters, and the spread of this practice was stimulated by synodal legislation prescribing education as prerequisite for ordination. See Daniélou-Marrou, pp. 440–44.

57. See R. Aigrain in A. Fliche and V. Martin, *Histoire de l'Eglise depuis les origines jusqu'à nos jours* (Paris, 1935—), vol. 5, p. 377.

58. See Smalley, *Study of the Bible;* de Lubac, *Exégèse médiévale;* C. Spicq, *Esquisse d'une histoire de l'exégèse latine au moyen âge* (Paris, 1944); R. McNally, *The Bible in the Early Middle Ages* (Westminster, Md., 1959).

59. Augustine *De doct. christ.* 4. 4. 6; Ambrose *Epist.* 15.

60. P. Batiffol, *St. Gregory the Great* (London, 1929), p. 126.

61. See J. Fontaine, *Isidore de Seville et la culture classique dans l'Espagne visigothique* (Paris, 1959), vol. 2, pp. 698–705.

62. Alcuin *De virtutibus et vitiis* 6: "Sacerdotis est in pace populum Dei admonere quid debeat agere: populi est in humilitate audire quae monet sacerdos."

63. Rabanus Maurus *De clericorum institutione* 3. 28: "Debet igitur divinarum Scripturarum tractator et doctor, defensor rectae fidei ac debellator erroris, et bona docere, et mala dedocere; atque in hoc opere, sermone conciliare aversos, remissor erigere, nescientibus quid agere, quid expetere debeant intimare. . . ."

64. See F. Kempf, *Handbook of Church History* (New York, 1969), vol. 3, pp. 259–79.

65. See J. Jungmann, *Handbook of Church History,* vol. 3, pp. 307–12.

66. The *Dictatus Papae* is inserted between letters 55 and 56 in Migne *P.L.* 148. 407–8.

67. This is the implicit presupposition of conciliar judgment upon theological or doctrinal teaching. Actually, the role of temporal rulers in the convocation and conduct of councils (beginning with Constantine's interest in Nicaea) indicates that they were thought to share some responsibility for the orthodoxy (or at least the unity) of teaching.

68. See I. Hausherr, *Dictionnaire de spiritualité,* vol. 3, cols. 1008–18; and G. Bardy, *ibid.,* cols. 1062–83.

69. See L. Bouyer, *Spirituality of the New Testament and the Fathers,* vol. 1 of *History of Christian Spirituality* (New York, 1968), pp. 303–94.

70. On the somewhat nebulous evidence regarding Benedict, his life, activity, etc., see C. Peifer, *Monastic Spirituality* (New York, 1966), pp. 47–53. There is also a good bit of doubt as to the exact origin of the Rule of Saint Benedict. Its really important influence dates not from the time of Benedict of Nursia but from the ninth century and Benedict of Aniane. See Bouyer, pp. 512–22.

71. See Daniélou-Marrou, pp. 442–43.

72. It was from this earlier flowering of monastic scholarship that the Carolingian renaissance was able to draw its moving impetus, through such monastic teachers as Alcuin and Rabanus Maurus. See Ewig, pp. 70–78, 115–18.

73. See D. Knowles, *The Christian Centuries*, vol. 2, pp. 118–20.

74. See Daniélou-Marrou, pp. 426–29.

75. See Kempf, pp. 332–34.

76. This reforming impetus found expression in the Carolingian developments under Charlemagne and Louis the Pious, but more so in the great Cluniac reforms of the tenth and eleventh centuries.

77. See D. Knowles, *Christian Monasticism* (New York, 1969), pp. 25–44.

78. Insistence on the essentially *lay* character of monasticism as such is important for theological reflection on church institutions; practically, however, monasticism became rapidly clericalized (esp. in the West). Choir monks were ordained and the entire monastic movement became sociologically a part of the clerical world. See *ibid.*, pp. 37–40.

79. This became explicit and prominent with Cluny in the tenth century; see Kempf, pp. 326–27.

80. As we suggested earlier, there is a critically important aspect of Christian history that needs detailed investigation and analysis: the manner in which the nonascetic elements of Christian thought and life, especially the ordinary life-style of lay Christians, were denied status as part of the pursuit of Christian perfection; the evolution of this ordinary Christianity in movements of thought and activity that remained somewhat apart from the classic schools of spirituality, since these latter dealt with participation in monasticism or its derivatives; and the connection of this lay Christian development with the roots of much of modern secularistic humanism.

81. See Y. Congar, *Dictionnaire de théologie catholique*, vol. 15, cols. 346–62; D. McGarry, *New Catholic Encyclopedia*, vol. 5, pp. 112–14.

82. See Daniélou-Marrou, pp. 365–67.

83. *Ibid.*, p. 367.

84. See H. Rashdall, *The Universities of Europe in the Middle Ages*, ed. F. Powicke and A. Emden (Oxford, 1936), vol. 1, pp. 87–141.

85. *Ibid.*, pp. 142–67.

86. See G. Sabine, *History of Political Theory* (New York, 1956), pp. 287–304.

87. Irenaeus' link of Christology and ecclesiology in his explanation of "recapitulation" represents already in the second century a sophisticated analysis of the church as participant in the mystery of Christ.

88. See Congar, *Ecclésiologie*, pp. 73–90.

89. See R. Roques, *L'univers dionysien* (Paris, 1954), pp. 296–97.

90. See J. Daniélou and R. du Charlat, *La catéchèse aux premiers siècles* (Paris, 1968), pp. 58–67, 173–226.

91. On the basic patterns of religious and societal initiation, see M. Eliade, *Rites and Symbols of Initiation* (New York, 1958).

92. See Morrison, pp. 38–74; Y. Congar, *Tradition and Traditions* (New York, 1967), pp. 42–50.

93. See, e.g., the profession of faith by the Chalcedonian bishops (*Mansi* 6. 951–60.)

94. On the fourth- and fifth-century understanding of apostolic tradition, see Congar, *Tradition*, pp. 42–64.

95. *Epist. 1 to Serapion* 28.

96. *De trin.* 6. 32–39.

97. See Congar, *Tradition*, pp. 42–48.

98. See Daniélou-Charlat, pp. 103–21.

99. *Saint Ambrose: Theological and Dogmatic Works*, trans. R. Deferrari, vol. 44 of *Fathers of the Church* (Washington, D.C., 1963), pp. 5–33 (*De mysteriis*) and pp. 265–328 (*De sacramentis*).

100. *St. Augustine: The First Catechetical Instruction*, trans. J. Christopher, vol. 2 of *Ancient Christian Writers* (Westminster, Md., 1946). Actually this work, the *De*

catechizandis rudibus, was intended to deal with the precatechumenate training, but it reflects Augustine's approach to later catechesis also.

101. *Théodore de Mopsueste: Homélies catéchétiques*, trans. R. Tonneau (Vatican City, 1949).

102. *The Works of St. Cyril of Jerusalem*, trans. L. McCauley and A. Stephenson, vols. 61 and 64 of *Fathers of the Church* (Washington, D.C., 1968, 1970).

103. For a study of patristic use of typology, see J. Daniélou, *The Bible and the Liturgy* (Notre Dame, 1956); also Daniélou-Charlat, pp. 209–26.

104. Isidore *De eccles. officiis* 2. 21–25; John Damascene, *De fide orthodoxa* 82 (4. 9); Gregory *Moral.* 4. 3.

105. See B. Neunheuser, *Baptism and Confirmation* (New York, 1964), pp. 176–80.

106. See the "protocatechesis" of Cyril of Jerusalem (McCauley-Stephenson edition, vol. 61, pp. 69–84) which indicates a continuous involvement of the bishop in the catechetical formation and then in the baptism; in other places, as in Antioch at the time of Chrysostom, much of the catechumenate training was delegated to another, but the bishop came from time to time to inspect and bless the catechumens.

107. See Neunheuser, pp. 107–80.

108. For a detailed description of the solemn initiation rites at the time of Augustine, see F. Van der Meer, *Augustine the Bishop* (London, 1961), pp. 347–82.

109. This progressive initiation is reflected (and implemented) in the yearly cyclic celebration of the major liturgical feasts, centering on the Easter vigil.

110. See Isidore *Etym.* 6. 19. 38; as this text is cited by Ratramnus in his *De corpore et sanguine Domini* 40 and 43 (*P.L.* 121. 145–46) it contains a more explicit reference to the word working in Eucharist than is contained in the *P.L.* text of Isidore.

111. Much of this is involved in the Latin evolution of the word *"sacramentum"* as replacement for the Greek *"mysterion."* The early stages of this evolution have been fully studied, particularly since the magisterial work of J. de Ghellinck and his associates, *Pour l'histoire du mot "sacramentum"* (Louvain, 1924). Relatively little has been done on later stages of this development, though intriguing suggestions and insights are contained in such works as Congar's *L'ecclésiologie du Haut Moyen Âge*; but the existence (in the twelfth century) of a writing such as Hugh of St. Victor's *De sacramentis* and the influence it exerted on later theological developments indicates the need to clarify the use of "mystery" in the late patristic and early medieval theologians.

112. Augustine's approach to the presacramental catechesis still preserves the saving-event approach (see Daniélou-Charlat, pp. 249–62) and the explanation of the deeper meaning is basically typological; but Gregory's and Isidore's emphasis on the moral teaching of the Scriptures leads them to stress the allegorical meaning. See McNally, pp. 53–61.

113. Another element that enters the picture is the focus on remission of sin through baptism, and the accompanying development of the doctrine that infants dying without baptism are beyond salvation. See Neunheuser, pp. 176–80.

114. Already in the time of Gregory I, while Easter is seen as *the* occasion for baptism, it can be celebrated on a major liturgical feast (see *ibid.*, p. 177); moreover, because of the danger of their being deprived of salvation, newborn infants should be baptized at once without waiting for a solemn occasion of baptism (Gregory *Moral.* 9. 21).

115. On the separation and relationship of baptism to confirmation, see G. Dix, *The Theology of Confirmation in Relation to Baptism* (Oxford, 1946), pp. 21–30; A. Hamman, *Le baptême et la confirmation* (Paris, 1969), pp. 194–204; W. Breunig, "Baptism and Confirmation: The Two Sacraments of Initiation," *Adult Baptism and the Catechumenate*, vol. 22 of *Concilium* (New York, 1967), pp. 95–108; J. Fisher, *Christian Initiation: Baptism in the Medieval West* (London, 1965), pp. 1–100.

116. On the development of patristic and early medieval theology of original sin, see A. Gaudel, *Dictionnaire de théologie catholique*, vol. 12, cols. 406–32; N. Williams,

The Ideas of the Fall and of Original Sin (London, 1927), pp. 246–391; C. Baum-gartner, *Le péché originel* (Paris, 1969).

117. See Daniélou-Charlat, pp. 192–99.

118. See Neunheuser, pp. 167–84.

119. In the earlier stages of the development of the notion that baptism remits sin, this was integrated with the notion of baptism as illumination, particularly in the Greek fathers. This emphasis on illumination continues throughout the Greek patristic period (see *ibid.*, pp. 161–75) but becomes less prominent in the West, where more attention is placed on cleansing and healing.

120. A key element in this shift was the move to the declarative form of the actual baptizing, replacing the earlier situation where the neophyte's own profession of faith accompanied the triple immersion. However, the ascendancy of this declaratory form is difficult to explain, since the Roman liturgy throughout the period of Gregory I maintained the triple immersion and the accompanying profession, and this was again imposed as the accepted practice by Charlemagne. See P. de Puniet, *Dictionnaire d'archéologie chrétienne et de liturgie* (Paris, 1903ff.), vol. 2, cols. 297–344.

121. Anselm *Cur Deus homo* 1. 1–2.

122. In this respect, it is enlightening to examine the treatment of baptism in Peter Lombard's *Sentences* (Lib. 4, dist. 2–6) and see the manner in which baptism as "enlightenment" has completely vanished and faith is being discussed as the cause of justification. As a result, Lombard raises the question (dist. 7): What symbolism can baptizing have if the person who is baptized is already justified by faith and charity, and therefore the baptism cannot symbolize the remission of sin?

123. This is very much the orientation towards tradition that one finds in *1 Clement*, in the early Alexandrians, or in Irenaeus.

124. *Apologia pro fuga sua* 15–22.

125. See W. Völker, *Kontemplation und Ekstase bei Pseudo-Dionysius Areopagita* (Weisbaden, 1958), p. 58.

126. However, the Roman civil use of *"ordo"* also played a major role in the application of the word *"ordo"* to ordained ministers in the church; see P. Gy, "Notes on the Early Terminology of Christian Priesthood," *The Sacrament of Holy Orders* (Collegeville, Minn., 1962), pp. 98–103.

127. This is clearly, almost frighteningly, illustrated by the *Apothegmata Patrum*, trans. O. Chadwick in *Western Asceticism* (Philadelphia, 1958), pp. 33–189.

128. See, e.g., the *Rule of St. Benedict* 9, where, in the listing of the degrees of humility (i.e., of monastic perfection) the goal is charity; or Cassian *Conference* 11 (the first conference of Abba Chaeremon), trans. in *Western Asceticism*, pp. 246–57.

129. See Chadwick's discussion of this question in the disputed case of Cassian: *John Cassian*, pp. 110–62.

130. One of the necessary distinctions that needs to be made (and more often than not has been overlooked) in this matter is between asceticism and heroism. The ascetic approach to Christian living is but one means of living Christianity in heroic fashion, and Christian tradition has always been insistent that charity and not ascetic self-denial is the ultimate and more solid criterion of authentic Christianity. An interesting study of this same basic issue in a more modern context, namely, the phenomenon of Puritanism, is provided by M. Walzer, *The Revolution of the Saints* (London, 1966).

131. See M. Viller and M. Olphe-Galliard, *Dictionnaire de spiritualité*, vol. 1, cols. 964–68.

132. *Ibid.*, cols. 968–76; also Bouyer, pp. 303–530.

133. One of the subtle but critically important shifts in thought and language is that from spiritual as implying the influence of the Holy Spirit to spiritual as implying opposition to matter and body. Even when the patristic writers (many of them under the influence of Greek philosophical thought) ground their explanations in Pauline texts about spirit and flesh, they actually equate this with the dialectic of spirit and matter.

134. See Fleury, pp. 124–27; Pomerius *De vita cont.* 15–19; Gregory I *De cura past.* 2. 2–6.

135. One of the classic attempts to provide a resolution of this perennial tension between the active life and contemplative life was that of Gregory the Great; see C. Butler, *Western Mysticism* (London, 1922), pp. 212–41.

136. See Völker, pp. 58, 78–83.

137. On the complex relationship between "saint" and "priest" in Christianity, see W. Stark, *Sociology of Religion* (New York, 1969), vol. 4, pp. 98–211.

138. See Leo I *Sermo* 5. 1–4; the good example to be given by the bishops is grounded in and extends Christ's own role as *exemplar*: *Sermo* 25. 6.

139. Thus Gratian's principle (which he claims to get from Jerome): "Duo sunt genera christianorum" (*Decret.* 7. 12. 1). See also Y. Congar, *Lay People in the Church* (Westminster, Md., 1956), pp. 1–12.

140. Leo I (in his five sermons *In die natali*) already applies this notion of headship to the Roman see, but it is not clear how precisely he attributes it to himself, though the sermons do deal with his role as the occupant of the Petrine see. However, the personal application of the notion to the pope seems to have been established by the Carolingian period (see Alcuin *Epist.* 173, 174) and to have been consciously appealed to by Nicholas I (see Congar, *Ecclésiologie*, pp. 206–26).

141. See, e.g., the quote from Alcuin in n. 62 above. On the link in Leo's thought between the roles of official teacher and liturgical initiator, see M.-B. de Soos, *Le mystère liturgique d'après Saint Léon le Grand* (Munster, 1968), pp. 100–103.

142. This is reflected quite clearly in the gradual monopoly of liturgical activity by the clergy; see Congar, *Ecclésiologie*, pp. 95–97.

143. See W. Ullmann, *The Growth of Papal Government in the Middle Ages* (London, 1955), pp. 292–97.

144. See Kempf, pp. 339–45, 370–85.

145. See Ullmann, pp. 294–95.

CHAPTER 11

The Word in the Middle Ages

The twelfth and thirteenth centuries deserve in many ways to be called a period of renaissance. In the history of Western culture they were a period of creativity—in social forms and law, in art and music and literature, in science and philosophy and theology —whose influence upon our modern culture is still strongly felt.[1] In no area is this more true than in that of religion. If this high medieval culture was anything it was the expression of a widely accepted and vibrant faith.[2]

"Medieval" when applied to Christianity still tends to have in many circles the connotation of "overpoweringly ecclesiastical," with overtones that the faith of the common people was more superstition than genuine faith. To deny the all-pervasive influence of the church, of its official personnel, of its institutional (and particularly liturgical) forms, would be contrary to the evidence we possess. As we saw in the previous chapter this was the period when a notable crystallization of those forms took place, but it was the period of their coming to full flower, not yet the period of their stagnation or dissolution.[3]

The surge of Christian life during the High Middle Ages, which then so quickly dissipated its vitality in the tragedy of the Western Schism, was thoroughly evangelical.[4] Much of this period was one of religious revival, when the gospel was heard afresh and when it inspired conversion and dedication and heroism in many men and women. Some of this heroism was expressed in ways that were to a large extent futile or misguided, such as the Crusades; but one cannot deny that this pe-

riod produced a large number of Christianity's finest minds and saintliest people.

No historical movement of this kind comes to be ex nihilo and the evangelical awakening of the High Middle Ages was no exception. Monasticism, which had been the principal source of the Gregorian reforms of the eleventh century, was one of the most important fonts of the twelfth-century renaissance.[5] This applies both to the basic Benedictine institutions, particularly those of the Cluniac reform, and to the Cistercian movement that came into quick and impressive prominence in the twelfth century.[6] A large portion of the men who initiated and shaped the twelfth-century developments were monks—Anselm of Canterbury, Bernard of Clairvaux, Hugh of St. Victor, even Abelard from time to time.

Moreover, the monastic life and the spirit of Benedict's rule had deeply fashioned these men who in turn communicated this to the age in which they lived. While it may not have actively fostered scientific exegesis of the Bible, the monastic life with its constant utilization of Scripture for prayer and reflection, with its thoroughly Christian theory of contemplation which saw the *lectio divina* as the necessary prelude to faith response, bred into the sincere monk a deep reverence for the word of God.[7] To quite an extent the monastic culture was a biblically rooted culture, and it was the vitality of the word of God that periodically revitalized the monastic institutions, as it did in the twelfth century.[8]

The older monastic forms, even with the far-reaching reforms initiated by the Cistercians, could not give adequate expression to the religious creativity of the period. A number of new ways of dedicated life emerged, the most important of which were the communities of mendicant friars, particularly the Franciscans and the Dominicans.[9] Though rooted in the same urge to rediscover and live out the ideal of primitive Christianity in poverty and simplicity of life, the Franciscans and Dominicans were quite distinct in their orientations (even more so before external pressures and internal "confusion" brought to the Franciscans a pattern of life and activity somewhat alien to Francis' own vision).[10] More oriented to the academic life, the Dominicans were dedicated to more formal situations of preaching and teaching. They saw the need for intellectual defense of the faith, and committed themselves to the development of theology; they were from the start *defensores fidei* against some of the heresies that threatened the purity of Christian faith.[11] To the Christianity of the High Middle Ages they provided many of its greatest preachers and theologians as well as many of its greatest bishops. Franciscan life also produced a large number of first-rate theologians and preachers and churchmen, but this was accidental to its own genius. In its spirit, in the lives of its earliest members, and in a persistent current of Franciscan thought and life, the order is committed to a simple and total living-out of the ideal of Christian poverty and love.[12] Nor was it meant to be a way of life isolated from men. While it did retain a great deal of the practices of monasticism, as did all religious foundations of that period, Franciscan life was intended to reach out to others in good example, in concerned service, and in catechetical formation.[13]

Largely under the impulse of the new mendicant groups, preaching became more popular and of better quality. Not that the level of preaching was uniformly high; a large portion of the diocesan clergy remained dismally untrained and a considerable portion of the monks and friars of various kinds were not much better educated.[14] Much popular preaching consisted in exhortation to practices (veneration of relics, etc.) that were only slightly above the superstitious, or in imparting pious stories of "miracles" that appealed to the popular credulity.[15]

As medieval civilization evolved, and particularly as cities with the cathedral at their center[16] came into greater prominence, a situation emerged where provision for better preaching could be more easily made.[17] Many of the great theologians or churchmen of these centuries were also distinguished preachers and intensely interested in fostering the quality of preaching. Besides the Dominicans, quite aptly called Friars Preacher, and Franciscans such as Bonaventure or Alexander Hales, there were outstanding preachers like Gerson who were influential in advocating and exemplifying careful and effective ministry of the word of God.[18]

Not all the people, or even the majority of them, lived in the larger towns or cities. And because the rural clergy for the most part were ill-equipped for the ministry of the word and often totally negligent of it, the faithful in the rural areas were still quite deprived of religious instruction.[19] As a partial response to this widespread need, competent preachers particularly from the mendicant orders went out on "home missions," preaching intensely for a short period of time, inciting the people to faith and repentance and a return to regular participation in sacraments, and then moving on to another location.[20]

These "parish missions" became one of the most potent forces for nurturing and correcting the faith of the common people; they have endured until well into the twentieth century when, really for the first time, they began to decline. And the names of saints who labored heroically in this apostolate are among the best known in Latin Christianity: Vincent Ferrer, Bernardine of Sienna, Anthony of Padua, etc.[21]

Although it is difficult to sort out the extent of theology's interaction with the revitalization of preaching, it may be significant that the role of Christ as the Word is emphasized in the soteriology of a number of medieval theologians, thus bringing to the fore again the theological orientations of Clement and Origen.[22]

Both Bernard of Clairvaux and Bonaventure are noteworthy for their development of this theme.[23] All medieval theologians, of course, spend a fair amount of attention on the Word in their treatment of Trinity and Incarnation; but what is characteristic of Bernard and Bonaventure is the extent to which they use the identity of Christ as the Word as the key to their soteriology.[24] Logically, such a theological position should as a corollary lead to emphasis on ministry of the word as central to the church's apostolic efforts.[25]

The Theologians

One of the most significant developments in the evolution of Christian ministry during the High Middle Ages may be the emergence of the theologian. Some manner of theology is inevitable in a community of believers, for it is basically nothing other than the attempt to understand what it is that one believes. So, theology does not begin with the twelfth century. Yet, in the twelfth century (and in the succeeding two centuries) theology came of age as a self-aware and disciplined way of human thought. Theologians, individually and in "schools," became a major force in the church's life.[26] If the patristic period was one of great bishops, the Middle Ages is a period of great theologians.

This development seems to be of considerable import for a history of Christian ministry. Increasingly, as the twelfth and thirteenth centuries unfolded, it was nonbishops who came to prominence as masters of theology,[27] though they were all clergy. Moreover, in the case of the mendicants, who gradually won the right to profess theology publicly in the universities, there was no question of their functioning as theologians by way of sharing the bishop's role.[28] True, some monks had always been engaged in theology; some of them, such as Rabanus Maurus or Radbertus or Peter Damian, attained some prominence and influence, but theologians as

a group had never wielded the concerted influence one finds in the Middle Ages.

There was some questioning of the role and rights of the theologian, but this generally occurred in very specific contexts and was limited to specific practical issues, e.g., the question as to whether theologians had the right to examine the prerogatives of the pope,[29] or whether religious order men had the right to teach in the university.[30] For the most part, theologians gained increasing prestige and influence. At the time of the Council of Constance, a faculty of theology (such as Paris) was looked to for guidance and leadership.[31] And the major theological writings of this period (the *Summa* of Aquinas is the best-known example) provided the basic "authority" for the theological and dogmatic developments of the immediately consequent centuries.[32]

To locate such theological activity within the spectrum of Christian ministry is not easy. It seems clear that the men engaged in such theological effort looked upon this as an intrinsic part of their function as ordained ministers.[33] One thing that would indicate this is the limitation of professional theology to clerics.[34] Though taking place in the university, theology was still very much an ecclesiastical activity.

However, it is not certain whether we are faced with an element of the episcopal office that splintered off and became more and more autonomously exercised by men who intrinsically should have been seen as delegates of the episcopacy; or whether there is a resurfacing at this time of the ministry of teaching, which was apparently an autonomous ministry in the primitive church; or whether there is a function, demanded intrinsically by the life of the Christian community as it matures in its faith, that can be reduced neither to the episcopal role nor to the function of the teacher. Concretely, the question is muddied by the fact that some bishops were theologians, not a few theologians were selected to be bishops, most canonists considered themselves to be theologians (though not all theologians considered them such), and many of these self-appointed theologians became bishops or acted as bishop's officials. Practically all theologians were also teachers (Aquinas claimed the theologian's right to teach),[35] and many men taught theology without being theologians.

The theologians of this period did not provide a clear answer to these questions. Probably they could not. For one thing, the social presupposition that theologians had to be clerics would have kept them from distinguishing "theologian" and "cleric," and therefore from freeing theology from its ecclesiastical overtones. What these centuries do provide is the concrete reality of theology coming to prominence and contributing in vital fashion to the evolution of the church and its faith, i.e., the concrete life experience of church ministry which we can study theoretically today.

One of the interesting and important aspects of the rise of the theologians was the extent to which they felt beyond judgment by the episcopacy of their day.[36] One of the most revealing facts is the manner in which current magisterial statements of the church were overlooked as a theological source. The two chief authorities from which they work are Scripture (to which they closely link the Fathers) and reason.[37] This tendency became more pronounced as the theologians increasingly distinguished themselves, even to the point of a certain hostility, from the canonists.[38]

Clearly, such a challenge did not go unanswered. The bishops (particularly the pope) reasserted their prerogative of passing judgment on the theologians. This they did through condemnation issued by individual prelates (as the condemnation of Thomist teaching by Tempier in 1287),[39] or more importantly by councils (as in the case of Abelard's trial at Sens, or Lateran IV's condemnation of Joachim of Flora).[40]

Most of the great names in medieval theology with which people are familiar come from the period of theology's emergence into prominence, i.e., up to about 1275. But it was in the immediately subsequent period (late thir-

teenth century until the Council of Constance) that theological faculties, such as that at Paris, wielded their greatest influence in ecclesiastical affairs. Theological faculties, quite logically, became a court of appeals on theological issues because, presumably, they were made up of experts on such matters. Then, with the confusion about official magisterial teaching that accompanied the Western Schism, the theological faculties were one of the few compelling voices on doctrinal issues.[41]

This does not mean that they were accepted as a final criterion; the amount of controversy in which they were embroiled indicates the opposition often raised against the positions taken by a given theological faculty or theologian.[42] But it was seemingly taken for granted that theologians constituted one of the voices of responsible faith that must be heard, even by the bishops. At the Council of Constance this seems to have been the context in which men like Gerson, speaking for major theological centers, could wield determining influence in guiding the conclusions of the council.[43]

Preaching

We have already indicated that this period of the twelfth to fourteenth centuries was one of evangelical awakening, of an important revival and development of preaching. This preaching took many forms, all of them somewhat intertwined. There was, of course, the traditional preaching that went on in connection with the celebration of the Eucharist;[44] there was also the occasion devoted exclusively to a sermon, as in "parish missions";[45] there was the instruction given the monks in their monasteries or to the friars in their convents;[46] there was the constant teaching imparted by art, by the statuary and glass in the cathedrals, by illuminated prayer books;[47] there was the more sophisticated *lectio sacrae paginae*, the commentary on Scripture which was still the major function of the recognized Master of Theology.[48]

It is notable that "ministry of the word" is

still universally viewed as somehow basic to the role of the episcopacy, though by this time many bishops have drifted out of the custom of regular preaching. Eadmer's *Historia Novorum* reflects a common understanding when it says: "The plough (which must cultivate the fields of the Lord) in England is drawn and directed by two oxen superior to all others, the King and the Archbishop of Canterbury, the former by the exercise of justice, the latter by teaching divine doctrine and by the exercise of the magisterium."[49] The Fourth Lateran Council, insisting on the episcopal obligation to provide the people with the essential food of the word, is practical enough to legislate that the bishop, if he is unable to take care of this ministry of the word himself, must at least see that other competent men are appointed to provide for it.[50] The council does not seem to espouse the opinion—which one does find in some writers, medieval and more recent—that episcopal consecration confers theological insight. In listing the reasons that the bishops might have to utilize others, the conciliar decree says: "ne dicamus defectum scientiae. . . ."[51]

Moreover, the teaching of the bishops was considered normative for Christian belief and life, though the exact fashion or limits of this normative function were not satisfactorily clarified.[52] Before the twelfth century the at least apparent contradictions present in the traditional *auctores* (fathers of the church, decretals, etc.) were already bothering thoughtful people. Gratian's *Decretum* and Abelard's *Sic et non* are the pioneering efforts in the twelfth century to bring some order into this situation, canonically and theologically, and to establish some criteria for evaluating and (if necessary) selecting among these historical *auctores*.[53] The questions raised by these two men, essentially hermeneutical questions, continue to be discussed throughout the Middle Ages and are quite naturally intertwined with the various explanations given of "the senses of Scripture."[54]

In the patristic period the ministry of preaching was the treasured prerogative of the bishops, only occasionally or under pressure of necessity delegated to some other. In the late patristic and early medieval period, preaching became the common prerogative of all those entrusted with pastoral care, bishops and presbyters alike, though the bishop was seen to have some greater responsibility and therefore some supervisory role. In the High Middle Ages, preaching is extended to the diaconate, not by way of exception but as something that belongs properly to the diaconal office. It is not clear how much exercise of this preaching function actually belonged to deacons at this period, but in the theological explanation of the sacrament of orders the office of preaching is now stated as proper to the deacon.[55]

The Middle Ages was by no means the first period in church history to become aware of the need to prepare clergy for the function of preaching. Yet, for many centuries this formation had been most informal if it existed at all, and was dominated by a very few "handbooks," the most influential being Gregory's *De cura pastorali*.[56] Now, as in the whole area of religious instruction, there occurs a much more extended and sophisticated attempt to develop training for prospective or already operative preachers. Much of this is linked with the twelfth- and thirteenth-century flowering of the cathedral schools and universities, which had its impact also on intensifying the scholarly level of the older monastic schools.[57]

Knowledge is basic to effective preaching. It is a tribute to the official *magisterium* at this period that it insisted on the need for careful intellectual formation of clergy, though the very repetition of this insistent legislation indicates the continuing need. Lateran IV, for example, in its eleventh canon insists that each metropolitan church must have attached to it a theologian who can explain to the priests and others the meaning of Scripture and other things that are needed for the *cura animarum*.[58]

Basic to this entire endeavor was the careful interpretation of Sacred Scripture, for there is an unchallenged assumption that it is the Scripture that must be explained to people.[59]

And when one examines the commentaries on Scripture from this period (e.g., those of Denis the Carthusian, of Thomas Aquinas, of Bonaventure, of Albert) one is far removed from the pious credulity implicitly recommended by Gregory I. This is even more true when one studies the sophisticated theories of exegesis proposed by these men, or by others, such as the Victorines or Abelard.[60]

An indication of the extent to which the "pure science" theories about exegesis which the theologians produced affected the practice of preaching is the proliferation in the thirteenth century of opuscula *De arte praedicandi*."[61] These treatises, more in the area of "applied science," give us a reflection of what preaching actually was, but more importantly (from a theological interest) they indicate what theologians of that age thought about the objectives and modus operandi of the ministry of the word.[62]

Though there was an important and welcome impact of theology upon preaching, the close link of preaching with morality (always prominent in Christian preaching, but much accentuated in the Gregorian tradition) was by no means severed. Since the objective of preaching was to instill good morals into the faithful, the morality of the preacher was not only desirable but necessary.[63] First of all, the example of the preacher speaks as loud as do his words; unless he himself is a man of exemplary Christian life, his exhortation to the people will fall on deaf ears. Secondly, good moral life is a prerequisite if the preacher is to have those insights into faith which should form the foundation for his preaching.[64] It is interesting to note how, at this point, the traditional explanation of the need for virtue as the condition for contemplation (Clement and Origen) is made part of the "theology of preaching."[65]

Despite the welcome purification of preaching from superstition which the influence of theology effected, the orientation of preaching to the people was not essentially towards understanding but towards good behavior. In privileged circles (e.g., preaching in monastic communities) the objective might well be understanding and contemplation, but it was taken for granted that the "common folk" neither needed nor were capable of such. Sufficient for them was effective exhortation to behavior in accord with the laws of God and of the church, which largely coincided![66]

Yet, without denying this absorbing moralistic attitude, or even denying the extent to which Stoic and even semi-Manichean points of view encroached upon the teaching of the Gospels, an important corrective to our understanding must be mentioned. Medieval preaching (and connected with it, medieval liturgy), for all its defects, did lead the faithful to genuine devotion to Christ. We of a more critical culture may not find the forms of devotion to Christ very appealing and we may question the large-scale emphasis on devotion to the saints and angels. But the fact remains that a deep and touching affectivity, even tenderness, characterizes the attitude of Christians towards Christ during these centuries. Much of this is due to the writings and influence of Bernard of Clairvaux (as expressing the Cistercian tradition), of the Victorines, of Francis of Assisi, and other great Franciscans like Bonaventure, etc.[67] But we can see how much sifted down into the attitudes of the people if we read the hymns they sang, or even the popular songs and literature of the time.[68] While it was not formulated as a precept alongside other moral dictates, nor preached in that fashion, such attachment to Christ may well have been the most profound and most truly Christian moral attitude of the medieval world.[69]

One gets a frightening glimpse of the way in which moralistic preaching could be abused when one reads in the *Defensor pacis* (of Marsilius of Padua) in the fourteenth century that the purpose of the priesthood is to exhort people to act in such a way as to reach their destiny.[70] In itself this sounds innocent enough, but when one couples it with Marsilius' basic position that the church and its ministry should form a "department of government," keeping people religious so they will be politically submissive,[71] one sees the danger (which was more than once realized under so-called Christian rulers) of converting the preaching of the gospel into exhortations for "law and order."

One phenomenon of this medieval period, which perhaps has not received sufficient attention, was the emergence of lay preachers.[72] Not only does this exercise of a preaching ministry by laity find expression in off-beat developments of the day, it also lies at the origins of the Franciscan movement, even though that was quite quickly "sanated" by papal approval and by the ordination to the priesthood of the friars. What seemed to lie behind such developments was a simple and incontrovertible attitude. If one's brother would be aided by having the gospel preached to him, Christian love would seem to dictate that one preach that gospel. This attitude seems to have been prevalent during those centuries of the early church, when the bulk of evangelization was carried on by laity. But by the Middle Ages such activity on the part of the laity had long since come to be viewed with suspicion. Preaching is the prerogative of the *ecclesia docens*, and the faithful are the *ecclesia discens*; moreover, preaching stems from the possession of authority, all of which ultimately flows from the "keys," and such authority obviously has been given only to the bishops and their "substitutes."[73]

It may well be that this distrust of non-authorized preaching was also linked with the fear of heresy which comes to the fore at this time as a result of the discovery of Albigensianism. In an age that felt it had to protect its faith through the establishment of the Inquisition, it is not surprising that explanation of the faith by unauthorized and untrained persons was suspect.[74] Not all emergence of lay leadership was treated with harsh repression; in many instances it was effectively smothered by "elevating" it to official clerical status, as in papal approval of new religious communities where it could also be effectively policed.

NOTES

1. See M.-D. Chenu, *Nature, Man, and Society in the Twelfth Century* (Chicago, 1968); C. Haskins, *The Renaissance of the Twelfth Century* (New York, 1957).

2. This raises the question of the relation between faith and secular culture. The fact that many of the roots of our modern world can be traced back to these centuries of pervasive faith should warn us against quickly opposing faith and secular humanism. At the heart of this question lies the relation between faith understanding and philosophy; and one of the most perceptive treatments of this relation in the medieval centuries can be found in E. Gilson's *Spirit of Mediaeval Philosophy* (New York, 1936).

3. Much of the difficulty in appraising the vitality or appropriateness of ecclesiastical forms in the High Middle Ages lies in the mixture of social dynamics that characterized the general cultural situation of that time. The economic and political and social movements and structures and conflicts that have made up modern Europe were already appearing in the twelfth and thirteenth centuries (even more so in the fourteenth and fifteenth centuries) although they were overshadowed and to some extent suppressed by the forces and institutions of a matured feudalism. In Christianity, too, powerful currents of religious creativity and insight were flowing under the surface of officially approved doctrinal formulations and officially controlled patterns of religious behavior. To some extent at least, this was why the repeated efforts at church reform failed. What the situation demanded was not reform in the sense of purifying the already present institutions of Christianity or of returning to the simplicity and fervor of primitive Christianity but rather the creative reexpression of Christianity through a positive employment of the new forces at work in society, forces which were to quite an extent the outgrowth of Christian faith.

4. See Chenu, pp. 239–69.

5. See D. Knowles, *The Christian Centuries* (London, 1964), vol. 2, pp. 155–97; A. Fliche in A. Fliche and V. Martin, *Histoire de l'Eglise depuis les origines jusqu'à nos jours* (Paris, 1935—), vol. 8, pp. 427–61.

6. See H. Wolter, *Handbook of Church History* (New York, 1965—), vol. 4, pp. 11–22, 39–43.

7. See J. Leclercq, *The Love of Learning and the Desire for God* (New York, 1961), pp. 65–138.

8. However, it is good to insist (as Leclercq points out, *ibid.*) that the constant recourse to the Scriptures was inseparable from monasticism's retention of the patristic traditions of biblical explanation and from the liturgical employment of the Bible. This interplay of the three sources of monastic contemplation is clearly illustrated by the pattern of the Divine Office whose recitation was so basic a part of monastic life.

9. On the origins of the Franciscan movement and order, see J. Moorman, *History of the Franciscan Order* (Oxford, 1968); on the beginnings of the Dominican order, see P. Mandonnet, *St. Dominic and His Work* (St. Louis, 1944).

10. On the shift in orientation that occurred within the Franciscan order even during Francis' lifetime, see D. Knowles, *The Religious Orders in England* (Cambridge, 1956), vol. 1, pp. 114–26.

11. See Mandonnet, pp. 69–95, 156–92.

12. See F. Vandenbroucke, *The Spirituality of the Middle Ages* (London, 1968), pp. 283–314.

13. See Wolter, p. 181.

14. On the plight of preaching in the early twelfth century, see R. Ladner in Mandonnet, pp. 120–37.

15. See Vandenbroucke, pp. 243–57; he rightly stresses that the focus of popular devotion during these centuries was the figure of Christ, despite the somewhat superstitious elements of belief connected with saints, devils, etc. See also J. de Ghellinck, *L'essor de la littérature latine au XIIe siècle*, 2d ed. (Brussels, 1954), pp. 388–93, 403–11.

16. See E. Power, *Main Currents in the History of Education* (New York, 1962), pp. 235–37.

17. The increasing urbanization of Europe in the Middle Ages was unquestionably a major influence in the evolution of preaching. Not only did the city draw the better educated clergy and educational facilities provide for better training of preachers, but the city populace itself gradually began to demand a more sophisticated and careful form of preaching and (particularly in university centers) a scholastic form of sermon developed in addition to the traditional homily. On the rise of urban parishes and the shift in preaching, see E. Iserloh, *Handbook of Church History*, vol. 4, pp. 566–78; also T. Parker, *The Oracles of God* (London, 1947), pp. 17–19.

18. On Gerson's influence on the betterment of preaching, see E. Delaruelle in Fliche-Martin, vol. 14, pp. 848–60; also J. Connolly, *John Gerson: Reformer and Mystic* (Louvain, 1928), pp. 152–64.

19. On the disputed question of the extent and quality of medieval preaching see G. Owst, *Preaching in Medieval England* (Cambridge, 1926), pp. 1–47.

20. Rather quickly, the increasing size and influence of this group of unattached preachers brought about conflict with the episcopal/presbyteral structures of pastoral care; see Knowles, pp. 180–93. While this conflict has its tragic aspects, it is theologically important because it points to unresolved polarities in the understanding of Christian ministry.

21. See Delaruelle, pp. 636–56.

22. On the influence of Origen on twelfth-century monastic thought (esp. on Bernard of Clairvaux), see Leclercq, pp. 118–38. However, the emphasis on Christ as Word was certainly transmitted to the Middle Ages through other channels in addition to Origen. Very likely the central Augustinian current of thought would have been even more important than Alexandrian patristic theology, since a stress on Christ as Word is characteristic of Augustine's soteriology; moreover, the allied notion of illumination is central to Augustine's thought (as it is also to that of Pseudo-Dionysius).

23. See J. Bougerol, *Introduction to the Works of Bonaventure* (Paterson, N.J., 1964), pp. 163–68; J. Bissen, *L'exemplarisme divin selon Saint Bonaventure* (Paris, 1929);

A. Gerken, *Theologie des Wortes* (Dusseldorf, 1963); E. Gilson, *The Mystical Theology of St. Bernard* (New York, 1940), esp. chaps. 3 and 4, where he treats the role of the Word in the spiritual union of the soul with God.

24. As Y. Congar points out (in "L'ecclésiologie de S. Bernard," *Saint Bernard: Theologien*, ed. J. Leclercq [Rome, 1953], pp. 149–50), Bernard resembles Origen in emphasizing the relation between the individual soul and the Word; thus his approach to soteriology is quite psychological.

25. Both Bernard and Bonaventure were, of course, famous in their day as preachers. On Bonaventure's approach to preaching, see Bougerol, pp. 135–51.

26. On the twelfth-century development of theology, see A. Forest in Fliche-Martin, vol. 13, pp. 9–190; J. de Ghellinck, *Le Mouvement théologique du XIIe siècle* (Bruxelles, 1948).

27. In large measure this was due to the rise of university faculties and to the involvement of the mendicants in these faculties.

28. In a university such as that at Paris, for example, the theologian received his *licentia docendi* from the chancellor (who was historically the successor of the chancellor of the cathedral church who had given the permission to teach in the cathedral school), but his effective acceptance as a master was a matter of acceptance by the magisterial guild. See H. Rashdall, *Cambridge Medieval History*, 2d ed. (Cambridge, 1966), vol. 6, pp. 562–65. This did not mean that the theological faculty operated outside ecclesiastical structures but rather that it enjoyed a privilege analogous to the exemption granted religious orders; see M.-D. Chenu, *Toward Understanding Saint Thomas* (Chicago, 1964), pp. 18–22, and his *La théologie au douzième siècle* (Paris, 1957), p. 217.

29. See Ockham, *Brevil.* 1. 1–2; A. Hamman, *La doctrine de l'Eglise et de l'état chez Occam* (Paris, 1942), pp. 26–32.

30. See Chenu, *Saint Thomas*, pp. 340–42.

31. See L. Loomis, J. Mundy, and K. Woody, *The Council of Constance* (New York, 1961). Both Richental's *Chronicle* and Fillastre's *Diary* (the two principal documents translated by Loomis in this volume) mention the active role of the theologians; and they make it clear that they participated not only in virtue of their individual personal expertise but also as representatives of the theological faculties from which they came. See also J. Morrall, *Gerson and the Great Schism* (Manchester, 1960).

32. This is due in large part to the formation of theological schools in the late thirteenth and fourteenth centuries; see F. van Steenberghen in Fliche-Martin, vol. 13, pp. 305–36.

33. See Chenu, *Saint Thomas*, pp. 44–50.

34. See Chenu, *La théologie*, p. 359.

35. Godfrey of Fontaines, faced with the need to think through his role as a theologian vis-à-vis episcopal judgment as represented in the condemnation of 1277, says that the theologian, though he receives from the episcopacy the office of public teaching, has the obligation to teach the truth because he shares the responsibility of the episcopal office. See P. Tihon, *Foi et théologie selon Godefroid de Fontaines* (Paris, 1966), pp. 228–31.

36. As K. Fink mentions (*Handbook of Church History*, vol. 4, p. 451), " . . . since the High Middle Ages the universities, Paris at their head, had assumed the tasks of the *magisterium ordinarium*." Yet, there was considerable difference between an opinion such as that of Ockham who (*Dialogus* 1. 5) emphasizes the basic role of theology in deciding orthodoxy and the pope's dependence upon theologians in this regard; and the more moderate view of Gerson who does insist that a theological view should be judged on its intrinsic worth, i.e., the validity of its insights and theological reasoning (*Conclusiones octo de jure episcoporum*, p. 177 in *Jean Gerson: Oeuvres complètes*, ed. P. Glorieux [Tournai, 1965], vol. 5), but also admits the episcopal power to judge orthodoxy: "Ad episcopos spectat quod damnare possint errores in fide et bonis moribus . . ." (*ibid.*, p. 178).

37. See M.-D. Chenu, *La théologie comme science au XIIIe siècle* (Paris, 1957). He shows in conclusive fashion how the two poles of creativity and conflict in twelfth- and

thirteenth-century theology were a renewed interest in and reverence for Scripture and the attempt to utilize philosophical reasoning in probing the meaning of Scripture.

38. Most theologians were not as formally critical of and hostile to canonists as is Ockham (e.g., in the first book of his *Dialogus*). Yet the distinctiveness of theology's and canon law's treatment of common topics (e.g., the nature of the church) became more apparent as theology's utilization of philosophy increased in the thirteenth century and thereafter, and the natural alignment of canonists with those more conservative elements in the ecclesiastical establishment whose fear of and opposition to theological rationalizing came to a head in the Paris and Oxford condemnations of 1277 caused a growing rift between the two groups of scholars. The extent to which this rift developed (at least in some circles) can be seen in d'Ailly's attacks on the canonists; see M. de Gandillac in Fliche-Martin, vol. 13, pp. 503–4.

39. See van Steenberghen, pp. 320–23.

40. See Wolter, pp. 47–48, 170.

41. The widespread confusion of thought (Salembier in his *Great Schism of the West* [London, 1907], pp. 109ff., calls it "anarchy in doctrine") did not come from the schism alone. The apocalyptic currents fostered by the Black Death, the diverse movements allied with emergent humanism, attempts at reform of church and society—all contributed to the problem. See Delaruelle, pp. 885–1130.

42. On the contention among the various theological schools and most importantly between the *via antiqua* and the *via moderna*, see de Gandillac, pp. 351–512. The doctrinal credibility of the universities was further weakened by their becoming embroiled more and more in both national and ecclesiastical politics; see Delaruelle, pp. 459–86.

43. See Fink, pp. 455–68; also Morrall, pp. 94–123.

44. See Owst, pp. 144–94.

45. See Delaruelle, pp. 636–56; one of the most interesting and prevalent situations for such extraliturgical preaching was that of the "preaching cross," generally erected in a cemetery; see Owst, pp. 195–221.

46. See Leclercq, pp. 206–20.

47. And perhaps most effectively by religious theater; see Delaruelle, pp. 605–28.

48. See Chenu, *Saint Thomas*, pp. 233–63.

49. *Historia Novorum* (Rolls series ed., p. 36), cited by M. Charlesworth, *St. Anselm's Proslogion* (Oxford, 1965), p. 18.

50. Lateran IV, canon 10 (*Mansi* 22. 998–99).

51. *Ibid.*, col. 998.

52. Probably the root of this normative function lay in the fact that preaching and teaching were considered part of the *cura animarum* and the responsibility for this *cura* rested primarily on the bishops; see J. Leclercq, "Le magistère du prédicateur au XIIIe siècle," *Archives d'histoire doctrinale et littéraire du moyen âge* (1946), pp. 105–47.

53. See de Ghellinck, *Le mouvement théologique*, pp. 472–99.

54. For a magisterial treatment of medieval development of "the senses of Scripture," see H. de Lubac, *Exégèse médiévale* (Paris, 1959–64), vols. 3 and 4.

55. See Hugh of St. Victor *De sacramentis* 2. 3. 10; Guido de Orchellis *Tractatus de Sacramentis*, chap. 8, 124.

56. On the influence of Gregory, see de Lubac, vol. 2, pp. 538–48.

57. See Power, pp. 230–68.

58. *Mansi* 22. 999.

59. See Chenu, *Nature, Man, and Society*, pp. 270–330.

60. See de Lubac, vol. 3, pp. 287–435; vol. 4, pp. 263–325.

61. See T. Charland, *Artes predicandi* (Paris, 1936); Delaruelle, pp. 629–34. Along with these treatises on preaching there were also commentaries and other aids to the use of Scripture and collections of pious *exempla* to illustrate various virtues or vices. See Owst, pp. 279–354.

62. See Owst, pp. 309–54, on the variety of objectives and styles in preaching. As preaching tended, especially in the later Middle Ages, to become more complicated and abstract, there were strong voices raised to restore it to evangelical directness and simplicity; one of the most important of these was Gerson (see Delaruelle, pp. 838–54), who represents the impulse of the *devotio moderna*.

63. E.g., Hugh of St. Victor *De sacramentis* 2. 3. 11; or Alexander of Hales *Quaest. disput.*, q. 29 (*De officio praedicationis*): "Triplex est praedicatio; quaedam quae est simplex narratio articulorum contentorum in Symbolo; et hanc potest etiam anus habere, quae potest docere iuniores hos articulos et dominicam orationem. Est alia praedicatio, scilicet expositio intellectus litteralis in doctrina quae est secundum pietatem; et haec est annexa Ordini presbyterorum vel diaconorum, et ad eos pertinet. Est alia praedicatio, scillicet expositio intellectus tropologici, allegorici vel anagogici; et haec pertinet ad eos qui habent officium cum scientia. Immo, quod plus est, semper propter reverentiam officii oportet habere vitae meritum. . . . Debet ergo habere vitae meritum quoad idoneitatem, et hoc ad exemplum." (Quaracchi edition, vol. 1, pp. 518–19.)

64. *Ibid.*, pp. 523–24: "Docere tamen duplex est: unum generale, et sic non exigit nisi purgationem intellectus. Secundum vero quod transumitur ad officium pastoris exigit perfectionem et munditiam vitae et doctrinae, et maiori indiget purgatione . . . Similiter in praedicatione exigitur duplex eminentia, scientiae scilicet et vitae; unde exigit purgationem intellectus practici in ipso praedicante."

65. Logically so, since many of the great preachers (and theorists of preaching) in the Middle Ages saw preaching as intimately linked with contemplation. For example, Nicholas of Cusa (himself a dedicated preacher) teaches that contemplation is superior to action, since the former deals with the love of God and the latter with the love of men, but makes an exception for preaching and teaching which presuppose and draw from contemplation. See E. Vansteenberghe, *Le cardinal Nicolas de Cusa* (Paris, 1920), p. 154.

66. Along with such moralistic preaching, there was considerable circulation (especially from the thirteenth century onward) of manuals that exhorted the faithful to good moral behavior. See Vandenbroucke, pp. 344–47.

67. See H. Daniel-Rops, *Cathedral and Crusade* (Image ed., New York, 1963), vol. 1, pp. 50–64. It is not accidental (and quite important for an accurate assessment of medieval Mariology) that these same men made major contributions to a deepened understanding and appreciation of Mary's soteriological function.

68. William Langland's *Piers Plowman* is an obvious example; so also are the fourteenth-century poem *The Pearl* and Richard Rolle's *Meditations on the Passion*. For these and other selections, see R. Loomis and R. Willard, *Medieval English Verse and Prose* (New York, 1948).

69. See Vandenbroucke, pp. 243–54.

70. *Defensor pacis* 1. 6. 4–9 (ed. C. Previte-Orton [Cambridge, 1928], pp. 23–25).

71. See Iserloh, pp. 359–63; M. Wilks, *The Problem of Sovereignty in the Later Middle Ages* (Cambridge, 1963), pp. 96–117: "But if Marsilius' society is still in a sense a Christian society, there has been a profound change of emphasis. The society does not exist for a Christian, religious end, but the Christian religion is permitted to flourish in the society for the purely secular end of internal security." (P. 113)

72. Unfortunately, much of this lay preaching was associated with heretical or suspect groups, and consequently any preaching by laity was ruled out officially in orthodox circles. See Wolter, pp. 101–7.

73. A number of currents ran counter to this attempt to restrict preaching by episcopal control, and they grew in importance as the Middle Ages progressed. The papacy itself contributed to this by the exemptions granted the mendicant orders; a wide range of reform movements (from the Waldensians to the Lollards to the Hussites to the *devotio moderna*) proceeded autonomously despite various types of ecclesiastical opposition; and preachers in university churches shared the liberty possessed by university faculties.

74. See Wolter, pp. 208–16.

CHAPTER 12

The Word in the Reformation Period

Sloganistic description of Protestantism and Catholicism has characterized the former as "evangelical" and the latter as "sacramental." There is some truth in this, because the Protestant Reformation certainly gave great impetus to the ministry of the word, and explicit emphasis on preaching has marked the Protestant churches of the past four and a half centuries. However, there is a false implication in this distinction of the two traditions. On the one hand, there is the presumption that preaching had practically vanished prior to Luther; on the other hand, the presumption that Protestantism completely abandoned sacraments and settled for preaching alone. Both presumptions are contrary to historical fact.[1]

The fact of the matter is that preaching had received a major infusion of life in the twelfth century when the ideal of evangelical activity by both laity and clergy found expression in a number of new forms (among them the mendicant orders) and preaching was carried on widely in both home missions and foreign mission lands.[2]

With the widening influence of the mendicants, the foundation of the universities, and increasing numbers of priests, the thirteenth century witnessed a relatively high level (both qualitatively and quantitatively) of preaching. This carried on into the fourteenth century; great itinerant preachers like Vincent Ferrer and Bernardine of Siena lent prestige to the ministry and impetus of popular preaching.[3] Towards the end of the fourteenth century and into the fifteenth, the influence of the *devotio moderna* became more widespread and worked to reanimate all

Christian instruction (including preaching). At the same time such men as Jean Gerson, one of the great preachers of the Middle Ages, were exerting a major influence on fifteenth-century development of preaching.[4] Another development indicates that preaching was recognized as important and fostered in a practical way: in southern Germany and in Switzerland in the fifteenth and early sixteenth centuries, it was fairly common for wealthy citizens to endow a preachership, not only in cathedrals but in smaller town churches.[5]

Thus, the late medieval picture of popular preaching was not as bleak as it is sometimes painted; however, many signs pointed to the fact that the pastoral ministry of the word was in decline. Even if one does allow for rhetorical excess in the attacks of Wyclif on preaching in late fourteenth-century England, there seems to have been considerable basis for his criticism. The perpetuation of his views in the Lollards of the fifteenth century indicated that not all was well in the instruction of the faithful.[6] Perhaps the decline of preaching was more apparent in England, where the parishes suffered greatly from pastoral neglect;[7] but things were not much better on the Continent, where the same root of the problem, the benefice system, was causing irrevocable harm to the pastoral ministry.[8]

However, the infrequency of preaching in the ordinary parish context may not have been the most serious aspect of the problem. Rather, it was the content and style of so much of the preaching and the obvious discrepancy between the sermonizing and the behavior of so many of the preachers. In the pulpits of cathedrals and university chapels the scholastic type of sermon seems to have been relatively effective, but in other situations the rather abstract approach of a sermon (as distinguished from a homily) did little to arouse the faith of the people. Indeed, if one can trust even a portion of contemporary critique of preaching, there was uncontrolled use of allegorizing, and little communication of accurate understanding. As a result, credulity instead of genuine belief was often enough instilled into the faithful.[9]

At the same time, one must be cautious in passing judgment on the overall quality of preaching in the fourteenth and fifteenth centuries. Sermon manuals from that period (which were widely used throughout Europe) and the texts of sermons that were actually preached point to a great esteem for preaching, an appreciation of the role of Scripture as basis for all preaching, a fundamental care for accuracy of faith, and a concern that the sermon instill Christian attitudes and lead to more Christian behavior.[10] From our twentieth-century vantage point we may well criticize the fancifulness and superstition of much late medieval preaching. But it is good to remember that many voices were raised at that time against such abuses; for example, the great preacher Bernardine of Siena openly attacked such things as the credulous use of relics.[11]

Indeed, the more one examines the state of preaching in the century or so before the Reformation the more one wonders if the acerbity of criticism is not itself a sign of the trend towards improvement. Generally, protest against social evils depends upon improvement of those evils sufficient to make people aware of what the ideal situation might be. Whether or not one can speak of "improvement," there was certainly a widespread interest in bettering preaching. One cannot argue too strongly from official legislation on the point (for the existence of laws generally indicates their need and not necessarily their implementation); but it is instructive to read the decree on preaching (*Supernae maiestate praesidio*) of the Fifth Lateran Council,[12] published less than a year before Luther's posting of his theses in Wittenberg. By demanding examination and approval of all who were involved in preaching, by establishing standards (of knowledge, prudence, and edifying behavior) for such approval, by insistence that preaching be directed to explanation of Scripture and be in conformity with orthodox Christian tradition, the decree reflects the positive understanding of the ministry of the word possessed by the bishops at the council. It would seem that the neglect of good preaching which did exist (the neglect of good liturgy was at least as extensive) was due not to a theoretical denigrating of the ministry of the word but to the general negligence of pastoral ministry that was so intimately bound up with the evils of the benefice system and with the decline of religious orders. Those in the fifteenth and early sixteenth centuries who were agitating for "reform in head and members" placed the revitalization of preaching high on the list of their demands. Gerson, for example, had insisted at the Council of Reims in 1408 that preaching was the primary pastoral duty and that prelates were not justified in simply delegating this task to mendicants.[13]

Despite the fact that a reform movement, with appropriate emphasis on fostering effective ministry of the word, was already in existence, the activity of the great sixteenth-century Protestant reformers certainly fixed attention on the evangelical apostolate of the church. What differentiated them, and increasingly so as the polemics of the sixteenth century developed, from non-Protestant reformers was their insistence on the primacy of preaching. The preeminence of the preaching of the word in the "pastoral theology" of Luther and Bucer and Melanchthon and Calvin and Zwingli is too well known to need amplification. Nor is there need to draw attention to their common insistence on the use of Scripture as the basis for preaching.

However, some mention should be made of different emphases among these men. While Calvin certainly agreed with the biblical orientation insisted upon by Luther, his own bent was more in the tradition of scholastic exposition. To some extent one sees the distinctive attitudes of one trained in law as opposed to one trained in Scripture, though, of course, both men had solid formation in the scholasticism of the day and were clearly influenced by it. Moreover, it is interesting to notice the key position given by Calvin to *doctores*, i.e., to trained theologians. Their role is not just that of directing evangelical efforts along lines of depth and accuracy; it is also, and very importantly, that of contributing to the understandings that should guide the governance of a *civitas christiana*.[14] Thus, for Calvin the *doctores* seem to constitute an officially recognized ecclesiastical and civil office.[15] Luther, on the contrary, lays more stress on the basic responsibility and right of all the baptized to exercise the ministry of the word, because of their share in the priesthood of Christ.[16]

In the question of relative emphasis in the word/sacrament polarity, Luther (whose own religious attachment to the Eucharist was quite enduring)[17] and even more so Bucer (who had been much involved in the liturgical reforms at Strasbourg that accompanied the "Reformation" in that city)[18] were inclined to link liturgy to preaching and to insist on the evangelical possibilities of the liturgical actions themselves.[19] Zwingli, by contrast, undertook in Zurich a carefully planned campaign by which the city council gradually moved against sacramental practices and placed emphasis almost exclusively on the preaching service.[20]

Central to any discussion of how this "evangelical challenge" was met in Catholic circles is the question How appropriate is the idea of Counter-Reformation? As we saw, there was strong agitation for a reform of preaching long before 1517, and this carries straight into the reform measures of the Council of Trent. What this reform would have been, how strong or what shape it would have taken, without the shock provided by the Protestant Reformation is impossible to say. Unquestionably the Protestant presence and its attacks upon the "decadence of Rome" was a

stimulus; moreover the polemical theology that emerged in response to Protestantism was an important influence in shaping post-Tridentine Catholic preaching. Yet, much of what was done in improving preaching was in continuity with the creative elements of medieval thought and life and did not come into being as reaction to Protestantism. In a sense, the Reformation served the purpose of shaking the church out of its late medieval lethargy, so that within Catholic circles much of the demanded reform could be initiated by Trent and then carried out in subsequent decades.

In any event, a broad-based resurgence of preaching with stress on both frequency and accuracy pervaded the Catholic church in the sixteenth and seventeenth centuries. Such prominent preachers as Peter Canisius, Philip Neri, and Francis de Sales were influential in the post-Tridentine resurgence of Catholic life; but there was also the host of lesser-known priests and bishops who in parish situations or as traveling missionary preachers strove to purify the faith and behavior of the people, to fend off the attacks of "heresy," and to win back to the church of Rome those who had "strayed into the errors of the Reformers."

Perhaps the best quick insight into the post-Reformation Catholic approach to preaching can be gained by examining the Council of Trent's decree on preaching.[21] The decree itself, which quite significantly combines directives for the teaching of Scripture and for preaching, was a key element in the Tridentine reforms that did so much to shape the Catholic church in the subsequent centuries. Moreover, the conciliar discussions prior to the final draft and promulgation of the decree are very instructive on the state of preaching at the time of the council, on the way in which the neglect of good preaching was linked with other needs for reform, and on the mentalities towards the ministry of the word which prevailed at that time among theologians and ecclesiastical officials.[22]

When presented to the council in April 1546, the preliminary draft of the decree was preceded by a short listing of abuses: the bishops and curates do not preach; many of the religious clerics who do preach are not legitimately appointed, nor well educated, nor of edifying life; and there is a crowd of wandering preachers, many of them unordained and pretending to be clerics and religious who are spreading error and credulity by their doctrinal ignorance, and misleading the simple faithful by their fables, reports of "miracles," and false predictions about the future.[23] There was no dispute about the existence of these evils, but a great deal about the remedy. The reform of preaching was inseparably linked, intrinsically and in the conciliar debate, with the question of episcopal and presbyteral residence, with the entire matter of Scripture studies (which itself raised the question of a radical reform of theology), and with episcopal control of the regular clergy. As a result, the decree is a mixture of basic principles about the preaching office, practical directives for revitalizing the office of "prebend,"[24] prescriptions about the teaching of Scripture in various situations, and procedures for more effective episcopal control of preaching.

Foremost among the principles enunciated is that of pastoral responsibility for ministry of the word, a responsibility that rests first upon the bishops. Speaking of *praedicatio evangelii* (as distinguished from the more technical *"lectio"*), the decree says: "This is the principal task of bishops" (*hoc est praecipuum episcoporum munus*).[25] Secondly, the scriptural base of this preaching is clear: the bishops are to preach or to see that others preach "the holy gospel of Jesus Christ."[26] However, this evangelical orientation of preaching becomes a bit hazy when the decree goes on to say a bit later that the objective of the regular parish preaching is to feed the people with salutary words, teaching them what they must know for salvation, telling them clearly and briefly what vices they should avoid and what virtues they should acquire in order to avoid eternal punishment and gain heavenly glory.[27] The moralizing emphasis is unmistakable. Actually, in the heated conciliar discussions that had preceded

this decree, the principles for use of Scripture (which, of course, would govern both training in Scripture and homiletic use of Scripture) and the relative roles of Scripture study and scholasticism in theology had been debated;[28] but this is bypassed in the final decree.

As for the frequency of preaching, the decree makes it clear that at a minimum preaching should be provided for the faithful on Sundays and major feast days, and penalties are laid down for neglect of this task.[29] Responsibility for punishing such neglect, whether it take place in churches committed to diocesan or regular clergy, is placed squarely on the bishops.[30] Finally, by its insistence on careful training in Scripture in monasteries, convents, and schools, the decree provides for the formation of capable ministers of the word. Though its existence did not guarantee its implementation, the decree provided quite specific guidelines for the reform of teaching and preaching in the Catholic church, and a canonical basis for the reforming efforts of post-Tridentine bishops and popes.[31]

As one looks at the development of the sixteenth-century notion of ministry, there does not seem to be real disagreement between Catholics and Protestants (nor within each group) about the fundamental importance of the preaching of the gospel. Rather, the disputes centered more around the degree of exclusivity one gave to ministry of the word and around the elements that were embraced by this term "ministry of the word." To oversimplify the picture, one might say that there was common agreement among Catholics and Protestants that the ordained minister should proclaim and explain the word of God to his people; but there was disagreement (not all of it polarized along Catholic-Protestant lines) as to which other essential function, if any, he had.[32]

Catholics, of course, identified the ordained minister principally under the category of "priest," with explicit reference to his power to officiate effectively ("to confect") as Eucharistic celebrant and to exercise the "power of the keys" in sacramental absolution.[33]

They did not deny that the man so ordained for sacramental activity should also explain the word of God to the faithful,[34] but they saw this as preparatory and dispositive of the action of God that took place in conjunction with the sacramental ritual. The Catholic tradition did not, then, shift from emphasis on the notion of "priest" in the post-Reformation years; if anything, it concentrated even more on this identification of the ordained minister.

Luther, and the two Reformers who were closest to him in their own thinking, Melanchthon and Bucer, maintained an important role for the sacraments of baptism and Lord's Supper. The church exists where the word of God is preached and the sacraments duly celebrated.[35] However, all three reacted against the somewhat superstitious popular view of the priest-celebrant and against the theological notion of the "sacramental character of Orders." All three emphasized the priesthood of all the faithful and, while recognizing the vocation and role of the designated celebrant, held that the radical empowering for ministry came with baptism;[36] all three, in their descriptions of the pastoral function, stressed the ministry of the word.[37] Thus, though these three men might with some justification be considered the "liturgical wing" of the Reformation, there is an observable evangelical evolution in their thought: from viewing the ordained minister as a sacral figure performing cultic mystery to viewing him as one whose sacramental action gave expression to the basic function of communicating the word of God.

This tendency to find the ordained minister's identity and function in terms of "word" rather than "sacrament" was still more pronounced in Calvin and Zwingli. Probably, Calvin should not be too closely grouped with Zwingli since he stands at least as close to Luther. Calvin still maintains a prominent role for sacrament, and therefore for ministry of sacrament, that is distinct from its homiletic function.[38] However, in Calvin's writings the ordained minister scarcely appears as a cultic personage; he is above all a teacher of the gospel way of life, a preacher of repentance, and liturgical activity is supportive of this function.[39] With Zwingli the anti-liturgical swing is more complete; it is here that one encounters the view that is sometimes (and falsely) attributed globally to the Reformers, namely, that the effectiveness of the Lord's Supper comes solely in terms of the didactic functions it performs by reminding the faithful of the saving action of Christ.[40]

As a summary reaction of Catholicism to this shift in the function of the ordained from "priest" to "preacher," one can cite the twenty-third session of Trent, which dealt with the sacrament of orders, unfortunately in very truncated fashion.[41] Severely delimiting the context of discussion and without relating the condemned "heresy" to any particular person, the first canon of the decree (reiterating in more succinct form the initial paragraph of the decree) says:

> If anyone should say that in the New Testament there is no visible and external priesthood; or that there is no power of consecrating and offering the true body and blood of the Lord and of remitting and retaining sins, but only the office and ministry of preaching the Gospel; or that those who do not preach are not priests; let him be anathema.[42]

Explicitly this canon merely rejects the claim to exclusivity on the part of the ministry of the word. Yet, the earlier paragraph of the decree which parallels it (chap. 1, which begins, "Sacrificium et sacerdotium ita Dei ordinatione coniuncta sunt . . .") clearly stresses the "offering of sacrifice" rather than the ministry of the word.[43]

Since its purpose was to reiterate the cultic role of the ordained, which was under attack by the Reformers, this Tridentine decree cannot exactly be faulted because it does not deal positively with the ministry of the word. As a matter of fact, the disciplinary measures that were promulgated at the same session of the council insist on episcopal (and presbyteral) residence, on careful clerical education, and on responsible screening of candidates for ordination, so that the ministry of the word can be more effectively implemented.[44] However, in the centuries after Trent, when theological students approached a study of the sacrament of orders, and in the ordinary procedures of the "thesis method" gave this conciliar text as their primary piece of "revealed data" from which to proceed, the decree of Trent did its own bit to concentrate attention on the cultic element in Christian ministry.

Thus, the positions were taken and the Protestant emphasis on the abuses connected with Catholic sacramental views and the Tridentine emphasis on the elements it judged needed condemnation laid the groundwork for the false antinomy between evangelical and sacramental. Yet, one wonders if these two traditions of emphasis were not crystallized less by theology, even the lopsided "controverse-theology" of the consequent years, than by the pastoral practice of the two groups. There was pretentious use or pretentious rejection of liturgical vestments, the decoration or purposeful bareness of church buildings, the relative infrequence of the Lord's Supper in many Protestant communities, and the relative neglect of Bible services in Catholic churches. All this fed into the "pastoral preparation" of seminarians in the two camps, into the identity they formed of themselves as pastors, into the priorities they then honored in their pastoral work.

The Role of "the Word"

Despite the differing emphases we have just discussed, the Reformation and Tridentine understandings of the centrality and implementation of the ministry of the word do not seem that far apart. In its "anathemas" the Council of Trent actually had to formulate for condemnation a position that only Zwingli among the classic Reformers (and perhaps not even he) could have accepted as his own. But there was a considerable difference between Catholic and Protestant understandings (and, for that matter, among Protestant understandings) about the manner in which the word of God functioned as a saving force.

To put it more technically, the underlying questions were soteriological. Up to a point, this was recognized at the time (the attention given the matter of "justification by faith" indicates this) but soteriology had been insufficiently developed in medieval theology, with the result that the sixteenth-century thinkers saw neither the depth nor exact nature of the questions that were surfacing. In a later chapter, we will have to examine this matter in terms of "sacramental causality," but at this point it is appropriate to glance briefly at the Reformation and Tridentine "theologies of preaching."

Sixteenth-century discussion of the effectiveness of "the word" deals almost exclusively with its correlation to faith. It is easy enough to see the radical importance of the proclamation and explanation of the word of God, if one views the arousing of faith as purely a natural psychological happening, i.e., a persuasive explanation of Christian teaching leading to understanding and acceptance. Obviously, in such a context everything depends on homiletic and didactic competence.

However, no one in the sixteenth century looked at the matter in such a "naturalistic" manner. Catholics and Protestants alike had inherited a belief that the word of God was a special force that worked in the minds and hearts of men; it had some kind of autonomous power of its own that could lead to salvation even when it was transmitted by a less than adequate preacher. Moreover, in both Catholic and Protestant views one can notice a divergence from earlier Christian theology: in patristic thought the action of "the word" in the consciousness of Christians was the action of the Word, i.e., of Christ himself; in the subsequent centuries "the word" (whether in its proclaimed form or in its scriptural form) somehow acquired a distinct force.[45] Wyclif insisted on this transforming power of the word, which the words of the priest by themselves could not possess, power to melt hearts and overcome sin and bridge the gap between God and men.[46] Wyclif's insistence on this point passes through Hus into the thought of Luther.[47]

Luther himself, of course, placed faith at the very heart of man's justification and salvation; faith was brought into existence by the power of the word accompanied by the Spirit.[48] Yet, the difference between Luther's thought and that of the Middle Ages lies not in the discovery of faith's importance (for that is assumed in medieval soteriology), nor in the emphasis on the word, but in his insight into the distinction (in the message of Scripture) between law and gospel, his realization that Christ as savior is the essential content of the Bible.[49] Even here, one cannot claim complete novelty for Luther's view. The *devotio moderna*, to which Luther among others was heir, had already redirected attention to the figure of Christ;[50] but there is certainly a swing away from a moralistic approach to preaching. Without detracting from Luther's contribution, it does seem to be pastoral rather than theological; it has to do with *what* the word of God says to men rather than with the *manner* in which the word acts.

In Bucer there is a comparable emphasis on the power of the word, but in line with Bucer's concentration on the *community* aspect of the church, the word is looked upon as an assembling force. Not just that, of course, because in the word that he directs to people through the ministers who are his instruments Jesus exhorts men to spiritual development, proclaims pardon, attracts disciples to himself, leads them to divine life in baptism, and teaches them to observe his commands.[51] Actually, as Bucer talks about the manner in which Christ uses mediators (i.e., ministers) to convey his teaching to men and to forgive and save men, it is difficult to say whether he considers Christ as himself constantly present in this process or rather as being "in heaven" and reaching men on earth through his word and his Spirit. It is the second of these two views, however, that better fits Bucer's description of the pastor acting "in the place of Christ" (*vice Christi*).[52]

Melanchthon's understanding of the church and its ministry is very functional and governed by the model of a school.[53] The "true church" exists where one can find the continuity of authentic teaching and where, consequently, authentic faith can exist. Certainly this does not rule out the importance of pastoral proclamation of the word, but it does shift attention to the didactic and even theological aspects of the ministry of the word. Melanchthon's descriptions of the teaching of the gospel are clearly within the context of faith in the power of God's word; yet, there is less hint of the "sacramentality" of this word than there is in the writings of Bucer or Luther, and relatively greater stress on accuracy of understanding.[54]

It would be difficult to imagine a greater emphasis on ministry of the word than one finds in Calvin: not only is the preaching of the word mentioned first in any of his treatments of the church's ministry but the ministry of sacrament and the care of discipline are discussed in relation to the function of the word.[55] But the preaching of the word itself has just one guiding objective, to bring the hearer to faith, to acceptance of and incorporation into Christ. In this union with Christ (and only in this way) the believer can profit by the salvation which Christ effected in his suffering and death.[56]

How all this fits together into a soteriological explanation of the ministry of the word is, however, difficult to ascertain. At the end of the second book of the *Institutes* (chaps. 15–17), Calvin presents what is a brief systematic soteriology; in it, the work of Christ is discussed under the classic headings of prophet, king, and priest. Significantly, very little is said of Christ's prophetic office and there is no hint that Christ continues his prophetic or revealing work in the life of the church. Indeed, it would be surprising if we did find such, for Calvin teaches in other places that the Christian ministry of the word functions as a *witness* to Christ and to what he has done for men, since Christ himself is no longer among men.[57] The minister of the word is the ambassador of Christ and speaks for him.[58] Yet, at the same time, there is in Calvin's view an unmistakable sacramentality in the preaching of the word. This word is salvific and life-giving because it is accompanied by the power of Christ's own Spirit; in authentic preaching of the word, God makes his saving presence known to believers.[59] What one wishes for in Calvin (but in the context of sixteenth-century theology has no right to expect) is an explanation of the manner in which hearing the word of God in faith brings about incorporation into Christ. Without this clarification, the functional explanation of ministry must remain incomplete.

Despite his more exclusive emphasis on the preaching of the word (as contrasted with administration of sacrament), Zwingli adds nothing to theological insight about the manner in which salvation comes through the power of the word. If anything, there is less attribution of power to the word itself, less of the sacramentality of the word than one finds in Luther or Calvin. Instead, there is greater emphasis on the action of the Spirit, which seems to go hand in hand with his identification of preaching as a prophetic function.[60] Much the same is found in the varied teaching of the "radical Reformation," i.e., a relatively greater stress on the action of the Spirit and of the "inner Word," though on this point there was considerable controversy, not just between classic Reformers such as Luther and "spiritualists" like Karlstadt but among the radical reformers themselves.[61]

When one turns from the Reformation theologians to the decrees of Trent, one is conscious of a style and outlook that is quite different. Above all, the approach to the questions of faith, preaching of the word, conversion, and salvation seems grounded in a different set of soteriological presuppositions. Whether this involves a substantive opposition of Trent to Reformation thought on the topic of the ministry of the word remains to be seen.

Though it cannot be thoroughly appraised apart from the earlier decree on original sin nor from later decrees on the sacraments, Trent's discussion and decree on justification stands at the heart of Catholic response to Reformation teaching about salvation. This was recognized at the council itself. The debates during the sixth session which produced the decree on justification were the most heated and most detailed of any in the council, and Roman Catholic theology since Trent has used this decree as its chief guide in relating itself to Reformation thought.[62] The decree on justification moves within the framework of a theological ontology in which salvation is effected by means of a God-given power, sanctifying grace, which works within man to transform him into a son of God. Grace is not the Spirit, though caused by the Spirit; grace is not faith, though faith is the inseparable condition and expression of grace. Rather, grace is a fundamental reorientation ("renovation") of the spirit of man which constitutes his justification by God.[63]

Even though the key passage in the decree (chap. 7) is a scholastic analysis of grace in terms of its causes, the decree as a whole is descriptive in style and traces the "history" of a person's justification. It is as part of this process (which extends from the first prompting of the Spirit in the consciousness of a man up to its fulfillment in "glory") that the preaching of the word should fit. It does fit into Trent's description, but receives only the briefest of mention in the one phrase *fidem "ex auditu" concipientes* (chap. 6); instead, it is the psychological dynamic correlative to preaching that is described by the decree. Thus, Trent has no theological explanation of the ministry of the word, and were it not for the serious attention paid to the reform measures (residence of pastors, training of preachers, etc.) related to preaching, one would be tempted to think that Trent considered the matter unimportant.

It would be a mistake, however, to take the statements of Trent as a sufficient indication of the Catholic attitude towards ministry of the word in the sixteenth and seventeenth centuries. After all, the great Catholic surge towards reform was spearheaded by eminent preachers (Bellarmine, Borromeo, Canisius, Francis de Sales, Lawrence of Brindisi, to mention but a few) who obviously felt that ministry of the word was critically important. Moreover, two of the most influential theologians of this period, Bérulle and Suarez, place considerable emphasis on the ministry of preaching.

Bérulle, whose theology is very much controlled by the notion of the incarnational sending of the Word[64] and by the "spiritual cosmology" of Pseudo-Dionysius,[65] sees all authentic preaching as grounded in "mission." Fundamentally this is Christ's own mission, but this is extended through the apostles and their legitimate successors to all who are properly sent to proclaim the gospel.[66] Thus, the power of the preaching of the word is grounded in the mission of Christ himself, and only preaching which is so grounded possesses divine power and authority.[67] Unquestionably, Bérulle's viewpoint is typical of post-Tridentine stress on "apostolic succession," but it is a relatively dynamic explanation of this succession, one which could open out into a "sacramental" view of preaching. Moreover, the intrinsic link of preaching with the mystery of the Word-become-flesh quite clearly gives preaching a central role in Christian ministry.

Suarez, explaining the various ministries that were appropriate to the Society of Jesus, begins with a fairly long section on preaching.[68] Though jurisdictional questions dominate the treatment and the mentality tends to be legalistic on the whole, the basic importance of preaching (and more specifically of a qualitatively high level of preaching) is assumed throughout. One of the interesting features of Suarez' explanation is his contention that preaching can be delegated (by the bishop or, a fortiori, by the pope) to one who is not ordained,[69] because, properly speaking, preaching is not a sacred ministry.[70] Not only does this reflect the extent to which the ministry of the word has been divorced from the cultic approach to priesthood (just as it has been in Protestant circles, for quite different reasons), but it shows quite clearly the extent to which the notion of "authoritative teaching" has become dominant. One really gets the impression in reading a passage of this kind (which is immediately reminiscent of the disciplinary decree on preaching of

Trent) that preaching, no matter how much good it would accomplish, can be rightfully undertaken only if one has proper ecclesiastical jurisdiction. The irony of the situation is that Ignatius Loyola, the founder of the order to which Suarez belonged, was himself jailed by the Inquisition for daring to preach as a layman.[71]

Yet, one must be cautious in appraising such an authoritative mentality too critically. A very real problem existed for both Catholics and Reformers (and for that matter is still unresolved): even if one does respect the power of the word of God to make itself manifest, and respects also the right and freedom of a Christian to share in the ministry of this word, how does the Christian community guard against falsifications or misunderstandings of this word? How is direction to be given, so that "another gospel" is not preached, so that the theologically unsophisticated are not led astray by every opinion that is voiced; and upon whom does the responsibility for such direction rest?

The questions we have just raised were intertwined with the sixteenth-century controversies on the relation of Scripture and tradition.[72] Clearly, the disputes about Scripture and tradition were grounded in concern for genuine Christian faith. Theologically, the question was one of finding criteria for genuine Christian faith and preaching of the word: what norms could be used to authenticate (or criticize) preaching and teaching? But the question was not originally presented this way by the Reformers; instead, it was posed in more pastoral terms: people need simple and direct exposure to the word of God in the Bible rather than explanations of complicated doctrinal issues; people need to be told the simple message of the gospel.[73]

Enough study has been done in recent years to destroy the old simplistic notion that Protestants chose Scripture instead of tradition (a misreading of "sola scriptura") and Catholics did just the opposite.[74] For most of the Reformers, the validation of their role as ministers of the gospel was grounded in the notion of *functional* succession from apostolic witness, which necessarily implies doctrinal continuity and therefore some kind of ecclesial tradition.[75] On the other hand, the Council of Trent itself was careful not to adopt the "two fonts theory" (i.e., that Christian revelation is contained partially in Scripture and partially in tradition) which unfortunately became prominent in post-Tridentine Catholic theology.[76]

Still, the differing emphases of Catholics and Protestants in the sixteenth century, the former giving more weight to "the teachings of the church" and the latter confining themselves more to the content of the Bible, did give a distinct orientation to preaching and religious instruction.[77] Nor did the succeeding centuries bring the two positions closer together. Just the opposite, for the tendency to stress "doctrine" in Catholic preaching grew stronger as theology (which, of course, controlled seminary formation of future preachers) focused increasingly on an apologetic ecclesiology. Where the two traditions did agree was in their emphasis on moral exhortation as an incentive to conversion and as a guide to a disciplined way of life.

Where the Scripture-tradition polarity may have had more influence on the various understandings of "ministry of the word" was in the preacher's understanding of what he was doing in the pulpit. Though such generalizations always need qualification, it does seem that the Catholic preacher thought of himself more as the instrument of the church, officially designated to teach authoritatively the orthodox traditions of the church, whereas the preacher in the Reformation tradition was more inclined to think of himself as the instrument of the Spirit, called to proclaim the saving and converting word of the gospel. In other words, the sixteenth- and seventeenth-century theologies of preaching were a part of the various ecclesiologies that developed in that period.

Foreign Mission Expansion

Simultaneously with the religious upheavals within European Christendom, there took place the most widespread and large-scale missionary activity that Christianity had witnessed up to that time. This was almost exclusively a Roman Catholic venture. The Reformers were not particularly interested in such expansion (their interest centered more on the "purification" of Christianity as it existed in Europe) and the important involvement of Protestantism in mission work was still some time in the future.[78] As missionaries went to the newly discovered regions of the Americas, to the Orient, which was being "rediscovered" by the new trade routes, and to a lesser degree to Africa, a vast endeavor of evangelization was launched.[79] Somewhat ironically, at the very time when Catholic theologians in Europe were engaged in polemics against Protestants who claimed too important or too exclusive a role for the ministry of the word, Catholic missionaries were involved in an apostolate which, very much like the apostolate of the first Christian century, was largely a ministry of the word.

Missionary endeavors of the sixteenth and seventeenth centuries raised, however, a new and most important aspect of the ministry of the word: the whole question of adapting the gospel to indigenous culture.[80] Christian evangelization had had to face this problem from its beginnings, but the solution was worked out implicitly and unconsciously, and for that reason somewhat imperfectly.[81] More explicit confrontation of the problem came with the evangelization of the Slavic peoples initiated by Cyril and Methodius,[82] or with Spanish Christianity's encounter with Visigothic and then Moorish culture.[83] For the most part, however, the rapprochement of Christianity with the various European peoples that were evangelized in the late patristic and early medieval periods just happened; and modern studies have made us question the extent to which Europe was thoroughly converted to Christianity.

In the sixteenth century, however, with the imaginative efforts of such men as DeNobili in India and Ricci and Schall in China, a new phase of "missiology" began to emerge.[84] Tragically, the deeper issues underlying the controversies between these missionary pioneers and their opponents were not appreciated, or perhaps they were seen but were pushed aside by a European chauvinism that still identified Christianity with medieval Christendom. The issues raised by these imaginative and farsighted missionaries remained with the church. Twentieth-century attempts at missiology have still not given a satisfactory response.

Basically, of course, the theological questions about the relation of Christianity to "secular culture" which missionaries encountered in their sixteenth-century evangelization of foreign lands were the same questions that their contemporaries in Europe were facing in the discussions about Christianity and renascent humanism, questions that are perennially present to the church. Really, one wonders whether there would have been a Protestant Reformation as we have known it historically, if the appreciation for cultural pluralism in religious forms (which one finds in a man like Matteo Ricci) had been dominant in sixteenth-century Europe and the subtle antagonisms between Teutonic and Mediterranean culture had not fed into the religious controversies of Catholics and Protestants to the extent they did. Because of the basic importance of this matter for an accurate understanding of the ministry of the word, it might be good to state the two opposing theories of missionary work (even though briefly):

On the one side, the essence of missionary work consisted in the baptizing of neophytes, even if their preparation was minimal. At least, according to this view, the Spirit was at work in the souls of these baptized, and millions of souls were being saved from perdition. Moreover, this meant that the Eucharist could now be offered among these people, and the Eucharist had its own irresistible efficacy. Then, after a few generations the faith would become more deeply a part of the culture of the people. Christianity would at that point become a more conscious and appreciated part of the people's life. It is not clear how well such a missionary theory distinguished the process of becoming culturally Christianized from that of becoming Europeanized. At the heart of such a theory of missionary effort is the belief in the *ex opere operato* effectiveness of sacramental acts.[85]

Without denying the hope of ultimately converting people to full Christian life, those who advocated an adaptation of Christianity to indigenous cultures stressed the need for the gospel to be heard authentically by men and women of varying cultural traditions. Without putting it in those exact words, they were concerned that the gospel be authentically preached and correctly heard, something that could not happen in Asia or Africa or the Americas if Christianity is expressed only in European cultural forms. Moreover, these men were distrustful of mass baptisms unless they were preceded by genuine understanding and free acceptance of the gospel. They feared that a superficial form of "Christianity," accepted by the masses in a mixture of superstition and enthusiasm and fear, could be a barrier to the conversion of the educated classes and to the more ultimate conversion of the culture as a whole.

Catechizing

One of the phenomena that characterized the activity of both Catholics and Protestants during the period of the Reformation was a widespread use of the catechism method. Catechizing was not, of course, a sixteenth-century innovation; catechesis in one form or another is as old as Christianity, and the New Testament literature itself is in large part the product of catechesis. Even the question-and-answer method which we have come to associate with catechisms was in existence for centuries before the Reformation.[86] While practically all of the simple handbooks of faith produced in the Middle Ages were intended for adults (chiefly for the clergy), Gerson in the early fifteenth century pioneered in providing for the religious instruction of children.[87] About the same time the Brethren of the Common Life were beginning to give some catechetical formation in the schools they established.[88] Slightly later, both the Waldensians and the Bohemian brethren produced catechisms in the question-and-answer form.[89]

Still, the Reformation and the Catholic response to it brought the use of catechisms into a wholly unprecedented prominence. The felt need of both groups (Protestants and Catholics) to inform the simple faithful about "the true doctrine" and about the errors of the opposition, the impact of printing and the adoption of paper as material for books, and the example of the earlier question-and-answer manuals all worked together to make this an age of catechisms.

Much of the credit for the rapid spread of Reformation ideas should probably be given to the popularly written and broadly circulated summaries of "Reformed thought."[90] Not all of these were catechisms in the strict sense. Some, such as Luther's justly famous Large and Small Catechisms, were, but many others were in the long-standing tradition of broadsides and tracts. One can get some impression of the immense literary productivity of those decades by glancing at the forty-two volumes of the *Corpus Reformatorum*. In many ways, this development makes it clear that writing has by the sixteenth century come into its own as a major element in the ministry of the word; so has formalized catechetical instruction, both in schools and in home or parish situations. The catechism is the great instrument by which this was achieved.[91]

Use by the Reformers of the catechism raises some interesting questions about their practical understanding of the ministry of the word. Part of the strength of Reformation thought lies in its stress on direct contact with the word of Scripture; yet, religious formation grounded in mastery of catechism answers seems to run counter to this basic principle. A doctrinal or credal manner of thinking about the mysteries of Christianity, rather than a scriptural mentality, emerges from this kind of instruction. Moreover, if one examines the style and content of Luther's or Calvin's small catechisms it is more reminiscent of scholastic theology than it is of the Bible.

Faced with the impressive success of the Reformers' catechisms (within a few decades, more than one hundred thousand copies of Luther's catechism were circulated) Catholics began to produce their own catechisms.[92] The first wave of these, beginning with 1530, even though produced by such eminent figures as Peter de Soto, Johannes Gropper, and Michael Helding, did not enjoy great success. Success came with the catechisms of Canisius and Bellarmine.[93] Peter Canisius produced three catechisms between 1555 and 1559: a large compendious work, more a Summa than a catechism and written in Latin (actually entitled *Summa doctrinae christianae*), intended for the clergy and widely used by them; a very brief catechism for children (with only fifty-nine questions); and a medium-sized catechism intended for youths. It was this third volume, written originally in Latin but almost immediately translated into German, which dominated Catholic catechetics in the German-speaking world for more than two centuries. Canisius died in 1597. By that time his medium-sized catechism had seen 134 editions and his *Summa* 82 editions. In the following year, under commission from Clement VIII, Robert Bellarmine published his catechism. It was widely used in Italy and then enjoyed worldwide circulation because it was prescribed for foreign missions by Propaganda. Compared with the catechisms of Canisius, Bellarmine's work is more scholastic in tone and more closely allied with the catechetical formulations of the Middle Ages, whereas Canisius had attempted to keep his formulations as biblical and patristic as possible within the question-and-answer framework.[94] Interestingly, Bellarmine himself remarked that he would not have written his catechism if at that time he had known the catechism of Canisius; he would simply have translated the latter into Italian.[95] Paralleling the catechetical influence of Canisius in Germany and Bellarmine in Italy, other Jesuits (Auger in France, Astete and Ripalda in Spain) produced catechisms that were widely used in other portions of Europe.

Mention must be made of the so-called Catechism of the Council of Trent, the *Catechismus Romanus*.[96] Like the *Summa* of Canisius, it was intended for pastors as a guide to the catechetical work they would do with children and adults. Its basic approach is doctrinal and its aim was to give a clear guide to orthodox understanding and explanation of Christian belief. Until the present day, this volume has been proposed by Roman authorities as a norm and source of catechetical formation in the Roman Catholic church.

Jesuit Schools

If the attitude towards ministry of the word in the post-Tridentine Catholic church tends to emphasize catechetics, it is in large part due to the influence of the Society of Jesus in the sixteenth and seventeenth centuries. From its inception, the society undertook catechetical instruction as one of its principal activities: teaching catechism was one of the "experiments" through which the novice in the order had to pass;[97] the professed members of the order made specific mention of catechetical work with children in the solemn vows that bound them to the Society;[98] and careful instruction in Christian doctrine was prescribed as part of the training of students in Jesuit schools.[99] Jesuit schools became centers of catechetical activity; not only novices and student members of the Society engaged in the teaching of catechism, but "extern students" as well were extensively used to provide catechetical instruction for children in the vicinity of the school.[100]

Despite their great influence in post-Tridentine catechetics, the Jesuits had no monopoly in this work; other religious communities, both the older orders and the religious congregations established in the sixteenth and seventeenth centuries, shared in this work. The legislation of Trent on the instruction of adults and children (which gradually found implementation) points to widespread catechetical activity in the parish context. Where the Society of Jesus may well have made its most distinctive contribution to the ministry of the word was in schools. While the in-

volvement of Jesuits in conducting schools for students other than candidates for the order was somewhat accidental, and outside the original apostolic objectives of Ignatius and his earliest companions, educational work quickly became one of the principal apostolic activities of the Society of Jesus. Jesuit colleges quickly sprang up in many cities throughout Europe (in the British Isles, of course, the penal laws against Roman Catholics prevented any open activity of the order), and the effectiveness of these schools drew both enthusiastic praise and bitter criticism. However, friend and foe alike agree in the historical judgment that Jesuit schools were a major force in shaping the post-Tridentine Catholic church and modern Europe.[101]

In evaluating theologically the role of Jesuit schools and studying the manner in which they fitted or did not fit into the Christian ministry of the word, it should be noted that whatever the social or political or personal dynamics were in a particular situation the order always looked upon its schools as an apostolic venture. Without prejudice to the intrinsic demands of academic formation, and these schools were in the forefront of humanistic training of young Europeans in the seventeenth and eighteenth centuries, the ultimate purpose of Jesuit schools was to serve the church. The *Constitutions* governing the Society's life and activity states clearly: "The masters should make it their special aim, both in their lectures when occasion is offered and outside of them, too, to inspire the students to the love and service of God our Lord, and to a love of the virtues by which they will please Him. They should urge the students to direct all their studies to this end."[102]

Thus, an aspect of presbyteral ministry that had long existed in institutions such as the medieval cathedral schools that were taught by the cathedral canons finds somewhat new and heightened expression: Many of the Jesuits engaged in teaching were at best marginally concerned with what would classically be considered "pastoral" tasks. Ministry to the students of these Jesuit colleges did, of course, include regular preaching and ready availability of sacraments, but certainly this could be (and was) provided by a relatively small portion of the staff. Unquestionably, there was also some exercise of ministry in the day-by-day guidance and counseling of the students by their teachers which would have been linked with the formal catechetical instruction provided for the students at each level of their schooling.

Yet, for many members of the order, involvement with educational work led them to full-time research and writing in profane as well as sacred sciences. The compatibility of such nonministerial work with the sacerdotal ordination of these men was not clear; most likely this theological problem about the nature and limits of "priestly ministry" did not bother people too much until more recent times. Clerical involvement in educational work had been for many centuries a cultural assumption. Yet, the larger question always loomed in the background (and was part of the controversy about "Christian humanism" which surfaced in the fifteenth to seventeenth centuries): to what extent, in Christian educational ventures of this sort, is the entire educational effort part of the ministry of the word?[103]

The "Spiritual Exercises"

One of the principal instruments of the Catholic reform movement was the *Spiritual Exercises* of Ignatius Loyola, which has remained a constant element of Catholic life for the past four centuries. A sizable body of literature, some of it explanatory, some polemic, some homiletic, has grown up around this small volume and the spirituality connected with it. It is not our purpose here to review this literature nor to give any analysis or appraisal of the Ignatian *Exercises*, but only to advert to the role played by the *Spiritual Exercises* in making prominent in modern Catholic priestly activity the tasks of "giving re-

treats" and of "spiritual direction," and to suggest the reorientation they caused in Roman Catholic ministry of the word.[104]

That the practice of "making retreats" is a relatively widespread phenomenon in the modern Roman Catholic church (and to some extent in other churches as well) needs no proving. Jesuits have had no monopoly on the work of directing such retreats, but they have played a leading role in this form of ministry, and the Ignatian *Exercises* have been a guide and a catalyst for the retreat movement. Because the concrete reality of any given retreat is very much dependent upon the "retreat master," and the interpretation of the *Spiritual Exercises* so diverse (if indeed, Ignatius Loyola's little book is even used as the basis for the retreat), it is impossible to use the text of Loyola's *Exercises* as sufficient indication of the manner in which this book changed Catholic understanding of the ministry of the word.[105]

Still, in one form or another (often, unfortunately, in an adulterated and watered-down form) the Ignatian *Exercises* played a major role in the formation of seminarians and priests, i.e., of ministers of the word. This came through the "annual retreat" many of these men made (which in not a few cases was their only opportunity to deepen or to "recover" their prayer and theology) and through the fact that the *Exercises* were often preached as a "parish mission" and thus provided an exemplar for other preaching.[106] There is another fascinating element, which further study may prove to have been quite important. The *Exercises* involve a viewpoint on soteriology that is very biblical, which perhaps did much to prepare for our modern rediscovery of "the word of God" as a present and dynamic mystery: a practical approach to soteriology that coincides very largely with the desire of the great Protestant Reformers to bring faith to life through genuine conversion.

NOTES

1. Yet this neat stereotyping fits well into the post-Reformation polemic theology which understood neither the evangelical nature of sacrament nor the sacramental nature of the word, and consequently did not see that Scripture and sacrament are inseparable parts of one mystery of the word of God.

2. See M.-D. Chenu, *Nature, Man, and Society in the Twelfth Century* (Chicago, 1968), pp. 204–28, on the revolutionary nature of this evangelical movement.

3. See A. Fliche and V. Martin, *Histoire de l'Eglise depuis les origines jusqu'à nos jours* (Paris, 1935—), vol. 14, pp. 636–52.

4. *Ibid.*, pp. 840–60.

5. See G. Rupp, *Patterns of Reformation* (London, 1969), p. 6.

6. See Fliche-Martin, pp. 978–85.

7. An indication of the absence of preaching is the fact that church legislation imposed on the pastor or vicar the obligation of preaching four times a year. See *ibid.*, p. 653.

8. On the decline of the latter half of the fourteenth century, see *ibid.*, pp. 885–910; on the benefice system and its impact on the decline of preaching, see *ibid.*, pp. 295–313, and also E. Iserloh, *Handbook of Church History* (New York, 1965—), vol. 4, pp. 570–80.

9. See E. Delaruelle in Fliche-Martin, pp. 629–36.

10. See Fliche-Martin, pp. 629–54.

11. *Ibid.*, p. 646.

12. *Mansi* 32. 944–47.

13. See Fliche-Martin, p. 849.

14. See W. Dankbaar, "L'office des docteurs chez Calvin," *Regards contemporains sur Calvin* (Paris, 1965), p. 124.

15. *Ibid.*, pp. 124–25.

16. So, e.g., in "Concerning the Ministry" (*Luther's Works*, vol. 40 [Philadelphia, 1958], pp. 21–22). Though one must make the distinction cautiously, Calvin tends to be more of an intellectual aristocrat in dealing with the ministry of the word, while Luther is more of an egalitarian.

17. This comes through quite clearly in his magisterial treatise of 1528, "Confessions Concerning Christ's Supper" (*Luther's Works*, vol. 37 [Philadelphia, 1961], pp. 161–372).

18. See E. Rupp, *New Cambridge Modern History* (Cambridge, 1961), vol. 2, pp. 109–11.

19. See W. Stephens, *The Holy Spirit in the Theology of Martin Bucer* (Cambridge, 1970), pp. 179–84; J. Pelikan, *Spirit Versus Structure* (New York, 1968), pp. 113–30.

20. See E. Payne, *New Cambridge Modern History*, vol. 2, pp. 100–102.

21. In the fifth session, June 17, 1546 (*Concilium Tridentinum* 5, pp. 241–43).

22. On the discussions leading up to the final form of the decree, see H. Jedin, *A History of the Council of Trent* (London, 1961), vol. 2, pp. 99–124.

23. *Concilium Tridentinum* 5, p. 73.

24. *Ibid.*, p. 241. The council was here going back to canon 11 of Lateran IV, which prescribed that each cathedral have attached to it a teacher of Scripture who could help train the clergy; but it is significant how much of Trent's statement has to do with the financial arrangements of this office.

25. *Ibid.*, p. 242.

26. *Ibid.*

27. ". . . Pascant salutaribus verbis, docendo ea quae scire omnibus necessarium est ad salutem, annuntiandoque eis cum brevitate et facilitate sermonis vitia, quae eos declinare, et virtutes, quas sectari oporteat, ut poenam aeternam evadere et coelestem gloriam consequi valeant" (*ibid.*).

28. See Jedin, pp. 117–19.

29. *Concilium Tridentinum* 5, pp. 242–43.

30. *Ibid.*, p. 243.

31. For a brief description of these reform activities, see P. Janelle, *The Catholic Reformation* (Milwaukee, 1948), pp. 252–332.

32. In chapter 31 we will try to show that the Reformers did not make the option "ministry of the word" instead of "ministry of sacrament," but distinguished within "ministry of sacrament" between *celebration of cult* and *administration of sacrament* and opted for the latter.

33. See Trent's decree on the sacrament of orders (*Concilium Tridentinum* 9, pp. 620–21); both the beginning of the decree and the first of the appended canons stress these two powers of the ordained.

34. Though in its final canon on Holy Orders (*ibid.*, p. 621), Trent is careful to indicate that actual involvement in the ministry of the word is not essential to ordained priesthood.

35. And Christian ministry was meant to provide these two; see Augsburg Confession, art. 5, 1–2, *Book of Concord* (Philadelphia, 1959), p. 31. For Bucer, see his treatise on the sacraments in reply to I. a Lasco (J. Pollet, *Martin Bucer: Etudes sur la correspondance* [Paris, 1958], vol. 1, p. 286). In this passage he seems to treat the preaching of the word as preparatory to sacrament: ". . . Quam [fidem] Dominus nonnumquam simul inspirat hominibus, cum eius sacramenta praebentur; aliquando ante ad auditum Evangelii sacramentorum perceptionem praecedentem."

36. For Luther, see W. Brunotte, *Das geistliche Amt bei Luther* (Berlin, 1959), pp. 46, 60, 76, 82–85; on Bucer see J. van de Pol, *Martin Bucer's Liturgical Ideas* (Groningen, 1954), pp. 66–73; on Melanchthon see W. Maurer, *Der junge Melanchthon* (Göttingen, 1969), vol. 2, pp. 311–12. Obviously, the position of any one of these three on the difficult question of the relation between ordained ministry and the priesthood of the faithful cannot be simply described; some attempt to examine this more carefully will be made in chapter 31.

37. For Luther, see Brunotte, pp. 94–95. For Melanchthon, P. Fraenkel, *Testimonia Patrum* (Geneva, 1961), pp. 154–57. On Bucer, see J. Courvoisier, *La notion d'Eglise chez Bucer* (Paris, 1933), pp. 99–102.

38. Though clearly inseparable from this homiletic function; see J. Boisset, *Sagesse et sainteté dans la pensée de Jean Calvin* (Paris, 1959), pp. 116–17. Calvin, like Luther, says that the church exists "where the Word of God is truly preached and heard, and where sacraments are administered according to Christ's institution" (*Inst.* 4. 1. 9).

39. See L. Schummer, *Le ministère pastoral dans "l'Institution Chrétienne" de Calvin* (Wiesbaden, 1965), pp. 5–8.

40. This is developed at some length in his *Commentary on True and False Religion* (see *Zwingli-Hauptschriften*, vol. 10, German trans. and ed. F. Blanke [Zurich, 1963], pp. 30–36).

41. See *Concilium Tridentinum* 9, pp. 620–22.

42. *Ibid.*, p. 621: "Si quis dixerit, non esse in novo Testamento sacerdotium visibile et externum, vel non esse potestatem aliquam consecrandi et offerendi verum corpus et sanguinem Domini, et peccata remittendi et retinendi, sed officium tantum et nudum ministerium praedicandi Evangelium, vel eos, qui non praedicant, prorsus non esse sacerdotes: anathema sit."

43. *Ibid.*, p. 620.

44. *Ibid.*, pp. 623–30.

45. This same process occurred in thought about sacraments, as we will see later. It indicates that the basic question is one of the underlying soteriology, a soteriology that tries vainly to cope with the false presumption that Christ is "in heaven" and therefore made present to Christians through some substitutional medium.

46. See T. Parker, *The Oracles of God* (London, 1947).

47. On the process of this link from Wyclif to Luther, see Iserloh, pp. 443–48.

48. See H. Sasse, "Luther and the Word of God," *Accents in Luther's Theology*, ed. H. Kadai (St. Louis, 1967), pp. 47–97; also G. Ebeling, "Faith and Love," *Martin Luther*, edition "Internationes" (Bad Godesberg, 1967), pp. 69–79.

49. See Sasse, pp. 60–62.

50. See Iserloh, pp. 437–43.

51. See Courvoisier, pp. 98–100.

52. Talking about the effect of ordination, he says: "Significat iam tradi ei potestatem ut vice Christi Ecclesiam doceat et gubernet . . ." (*Scr. A.*, p. 543 [art. 45]; cited by van de Poll, p. 66). See also W. Stephens, pp. 84–85 (esp. the passages cited from Bucer) and pp. 173–212.

53. See Fraenkel, pp. 132–34.

54. To a great extent, this difference between Melanchthon and Luther is based in the one being a teacher and the other a preacher; see M. Rogness, *Philip Melanchthon* (Minneapolis, 1969), pp. 60–64.

55. See Schummer, p. 54.

56. See W. Niesel, *The Theology of Calvin* (Philadelphia, 1956), pp. 26–30, 120–25.

57. See *ibid.*, p. 35.

58. See Schummer, pp. 48–51; also J. Boisset, *Sagesse et sainteté dans la pensée de Jean Calvin* (Paris, 1959), pp. 115–17.

59. See Niesel, pp. 36–39.

60. See the tenth item in Zwingli's confession of faith presented to Charles V prior to the Diet of Augsburg (1530) in *Zwingli-Hauptschriften*, vol. 11, ed. R. Pfister (Zurich, 1948), pp. 286–87.

61. See G. Williams, *The Radical Reformation* (Philadelphia, 1962), pp. 816–28.

62. For a description of the discussions on justification at Trent, see Jedin, pp. 166–96, 239–316.

63. *Concilium Tridentinum* 5–2, pp. 792–97.

64. See A. Ingold, *Dictionnaire de théologie catholique*, vol. 2, col. 799.

65. For a study of the influences on Bérulle's thought, see J. Dagens, *Bérulle et les origines de la restauration catholique* (Paris, 1952).

66. *De la mission des pasteurs* (the first of his three discourses against the Reformed), *Oeuvres complètes*, p. 68.

67. *Ibid.*, p. 69; Bérulle's point is, of course, that Protestant preaching is not so grounded in Christ because they do not have legitimate succession from the apostles.

68. *Opera omnia* (Vives ed.; Paris, 1860), vol. 16, pp. 968–84.

69. *Ibid.*, p. 972.

70. ". . . Praedicationem proprie non esse ministrationem sacram . . . cujus signum est, quod propter illam, ut supra dicebamus, nec specialiter consecrantur ministri, neque etiam aliquae peculiares caeremoniae per se necessariae sunt; neque etiam ordinatur ad aliquam mysticam significationem, sed solum ad moralem et spiritualem fidelium utilitatem, ideoque ex ratione sua non postulat sacrum locum in quo fiat [he is defending the Jesuit practice of preaching in "profane" places], sed tantum accommodatum et opportunum ad utilitatem et aedificationem audientium" (*ibid.*, p. 979). Thus, the "authority" to preach seems grounded entirely in the *potestas jurisdictionis*.

71. W. Bangert, *A History of the Society of Jesus* (St. Louis, 1972), pp. 12–13.

72. For a description and analysis of these controversies, see G. Tavard, *Holy Writ or Holy Church* (New York, 1959); also, Y. Congar, *Tradition and Traditions* (New York, 1967), pp. 139–76.

73. See H. Hillerbrand, *Christendom Divided* (New York, 1971), pp. 39–40. He maintains that the very simplicity of the early Reformation teaching was responsible in large measure for its success.

74. See G. Moran, *Scripture and Tradition* (New York, 1963); J. Geiselmann, *The Mean-*

ing of Tradition (New York, 1966); R. Brown, "Tradition as a Protestant Problem," *Theology Today* 17 (1961), pp. 451ff.

75. Among the Reformers, it was probably Melanchthon who most explicitly worked out this matter in his theory of scholastic succession. See Fraenkel, pp. 133–39.

76. See J. Geiselmann, "Das Konzil von Trient über das Verhältnis der Heiligen Schrift und der nicht geschriebenen Traditionen," *Die mundliche Ueberlieferung*, ed. M. Schmaus (Munich, 1957), pp. 125–206; also, E. Stakemeier, "Das Konzil von Trient uber die Tradition," *Catholica* 14 (1960), pp. 36ff.

77. The situation in England seems to differ somewhat from that of continental Europe. On the level of pastoral care (including preaching) the Reformation seems to have brought less discontinuity with previous practice. Yet, here too the influence of the Reformation-style preaching is clearly observable; see J. Blench, *Preaching in England in the Late Fifteenth and Sixteenth Centuries* (Oxford, 1964), esp. pp. 71–112.

78. For a brief history of Christian missionary activity, see S. Neill, *Christian Missions*, vol. 6 of *Pelikan History of the Church* (London, 1964).

79. Missionary contact with the Far East and with Africa was not, of course, entirely new; as early as the thirteenth century the mendicant orders had reached as far as China, but there was no lasting result of these ventures.

80. See Neill, pp. 118–29.

81. On the early Christian "solution," see A. Cochrane, *Christianity and Classical Culture* (London, 1944).

82. See D. Obolensky, *The Christian Centuries* (London, 1964), vol. 2, pp. 19–26.

83. A key phase in the early development of this Spanish experience is analyzed by J. Fontaine in his *Isidore de Seville et la culture classique dans l'Espagne visigothique* (Paris, 1959).

84. V. Cronin has written two popular volumes which describe the creative missionary endeavors of these men: *A Pearl to India: The Life of Roberto de Nobili* (New York, 1959) and *The Wise Man from the West* (London, 1955), on Matteo Ricci. For a more extensive study of the early missionary efforts in China, see A. Rowbotham, *Missionary and Mandarin* (Berkeley, Calif., 1942). It would be valuable to investigate the influence upon the pioneering missiological theories of these men of the humanistic ideals adopted by the early Society of Jesus.

85. More recent opinion is quite critical of this approach, but it should not be dismissed out of hand, for much of the Christianity of the past millennium and a half developed out of such beginnings.

86. On pre-Reformation history of catechetics, see G. Sloyan, "Religious Education: From Early Christianity to Medieval Times," *Shaping the Christian Message* (New York, 1958), pp. 3–37. See also E. Mangenot, "Catéchisme," *Dictionnaire de théologie catholique*, vol. 2, cols. 1895–1968; this article is a mine of information on the historical evolution of catechisms.

87. See Fliche-Martin, vol. 14, pp. 845–47.

88. *Ibid.*, pp. 928–30.

89. See Sloyan, p. 36.

90. An indication of the amazing rapidity with which the ideas of the Reformers spread: in 1519 Luther's words are already circulating in France and Spain. See F. Spooner, *New Cambridge Modern History*, vol. 2 (1962), pp. 212–13.

91. On the Lutheran and Calvinist approaches to religious education, see R. Ulich, *A History of Religious Education* (New York, 1968), pp. 107–25.

92. See J. Jungmann, *Handing on the Faith* (New York, 1959), pp. 19–23. Positive direction along these lines was given by Trent (in session 24, the fourth of its reform canons) which prescribed regular catechetical instruction for children (*Concilium Tridentinum* 9, p. 981).

93. See Jungmann, pp. 21–25.

94. See *ibid.*, pp. 22–23; also G. Sloyan, "Catechism," *New Catholic Encyclopedia* (New York, 1967), vol. 3, pp. 227–28.

95. See J. Brodrick, *Saint Peter Canisius, S.J.* (London, 1935), p. 250, n. 2.

96. On the origin and nature of this book, see Jungmann, pp. 23–24; Sloyan, pp. 228–29; Mangenot, cols. 1917–18.

97. *Constitutions of the Society of Jesus*, trans. G. Ganss (St. Louis, 1970), *General Examen* 4. 14 (p. 97).

98. *Constitutions* 5. 3. 3 (Ganss ed., p. 238).

99. *Ibid.*, 4. 7. 2 (Ganss ed., p. 199).

100. See Jungmann, p. 25.

101. The story of reaction to the Society of Jesus is a long and complicated one. Various reports on it tend to be deeply affected by the religious or theological convictions of the reporter. To some extent the order inherited the hostility of the secular clergy towards religious communities that had been prominent since the Middle Ages. It also incurred no little dislike from other religious orders which looked upon the new order and its success as a threat to their long-established rights, and its close alliance with the papacy made it less than acceptable in many quarters. On the other hand, members of the order did at times become involved in some dubious political maneuvering and financial schemes, which made it possible for enemies of the order to magnify these misdeeds and create the myth of "the scheming Jesuits."

102. *Constitutions* 4. 16. 4 (Ganss ed., p. 224).

103. The question remains unanswered (at least in satisfactory form) in our own day, as is clear from the endless (and often fruitless) discussions about the nature and purpose of "the Catholic university." For some present-day attempts by Jesuits to clarify this as it pertains to their universities (and incidentally to face one facet of the "hyphenated priest" question), see J. Donohue, *Jesuit Education* (New York, 1963); G. Ganss, *Saint Ignatius' Idea of a Jesuit University* (Milwaukee, 1954); and *Christian Wisdom and Christian Formation*, ed. B. Cooke, G. Klubertanz, and B. McGannon (New York, 1964).

104. In chapter 31 we will discuss at greater length the theology of priesthood contained in Ignatian spirituality and the impact it had on later development of Catholic thinking about ministry. On the sources and influence of the Ignatian *Exercises*, see O. Evennett, *Spirit of the Counter-Reformation* (Cambridge, 1963), pp. 43–66.

105. On the more limited topic of how the *Exercises* influenced the Jesuits and their ministry of the word, see J. De Guibert, *The Jesuits: Their Spiritual Doctrine and Practice* (Chicago, 1964).

106. Such use of the Ignatian *Exercises* was contrary to their purpose and nature. According to the intent and usage of Ignatius Loyola himself (and of his early disciples), the *Exercises* were to be made on an individual basis (i.e., with the retreat master directing only one retreatant) for a period of about one month, and with the objective of arriving at a basic decision regarding one's future role as a Christian. Even the compressing of the *Exercises* to the eight-day retreat made annually by many clergy and religious is a modification of their original form. In parish mission and weekend retreats, where the compression was much greater, what often happened was that only the "First Week" of the *Exercises* (which is more doctrinal or systematic in tone and consists in reflection on the purpose of life, final reward or punishment, Christian use of the world) was preached; and the second, third, and fourth weeks of the *Exercises*, which are strongly biblical and Christological, were ignored. Such missions are much more in the spirit of Gregory the Great than of Ignatius Loyola.

CHAPTER 13

The Word in the Modern Church

Though the type of sermon preached in the late seventeenth and early eighteenth century might not appeal to twentieth-century hearers, that period was in many respects a golden age of preaching. Much of the Reformation and immediate post-Reformation stress of communication of the word of God still endured. There had been, it is true, a movement away from the directness and simplicity which were the ideal if not always the practice of the Reformation. In both Catholic and Protestant communities, post-Reformation "scholasticism" and the sophistications of Baroque influence had their impact on the style of preaching. On the other hand, for more than a century the Protestant insistence on the evangelical character of Christian ministry had created in people a sense of the centrality of preaching, and this had led to better preparation of clergy for this pastoral function. So, by the mid-seventeenth century there was widespread interest in and appreciation of good preaching, and a flowering of sacred oratory in both Protestant and Catholic churches.[1]

There were differences, of course, from one Christian church to another—indeed, from one community to another within a given church. In general, the Reformation churches laid relatively greater emphasis on preaching. More of the minister's time and attention was directed to preparing what was the principal, in some instances almost the only, element in the worship assembly. Even within the Reformation churches there was wide variation, dependent upon the extent to which a liturgical tradition was maintained or

regained—as happened in the Church of England and in much of Lutheranism. Again, there is considerable variation in style (and, as we will see later, in content) between sermons given in a "pietist" context and those given in "established orthodox" contexts.

In general, though, there was respect for good preaching and in the ordinary local community the pastor apparently considered his preaching as a major responsibility. There were at hand a number of helps: manuals on preaching, suggested sermon outlines, printed sermons of outstanding preachers of the age (which he could use as models or, in obvious or subtle fashion, plagiarize).[2] The local pastor did not command the same attention as did the famous preachers of this period, but the efficacy of his preaching was an object of much interest and concern. There is already widespread discussion of the need for more direct and simple preaching in order to meet the needs of the mass of the faithful in the various churches. This effort to free preaching from complicated literary devices and rationalistic sophistries, to make it simpler and more practically effective, continues from the seventeenth into the eighteenth and nineteenth centuries and remains an objective of twentieth-century Christianity.

In Roman Catholic homiletics,[3] the influence of Vincent de Paul's "little method" on seventeenth- and eighteenth-century preaching and training of seminarians was critical in preserving normal preaching from excessive sophistry. Fenelon's *Dialogues on Eloquence*, published posthumously in 1717, continued this emphasis in France; in Italy, Ludovico

Muratori, Alphonsus Ligouri, and Vincenzo Strambi all campaigned for simplicity and practicality in preaching.[4] Treatises on preaching which abounded from the seventeenth century onward tended to criticize complicated and high-flown sermons and to advocate a return to a simple and earnest style. At the same time, the simplicity that was urged was not necessarily that of direct evangelical proclamation; instead, it dealt with a clear argument for a good ethical decision, or a clear explanation of a point of doctrine, or a clear attack on some erroneous opinion. An appropriate biblical text might be used as a springboard for the sermon, but it generally did not control the content of the sermon. Already in the late eighteenth century J. M. Sailer realized the need in preaching to integrate Scripture with doctrinal and ethical elements. His *Vorlesungen aus der Pastoraltheologie* (1788) was widely influential in German-speaking Catholicism, but it was not until the early 1900s that there was a move, led by Bishop von Ketteler, back to the preaching of a homily rather than a sermon in the Eucharistic liturgy.

Protestant preaching would presumably be freer of sophistries and literary conceits because of the Reformation emphasis on unobstructed presentation of the gospel. However, the presumption is not justified by historical practice. Lutheran preaching was, indeed, tied to explanation of the scriptural pericopes assigned to the Sundays and major feasts of the year, but this "evangelical" preaching was quickly systematized.[5] Seventeenth-century sermons rather rigidly followed the five elements that Hyperius had emphasized in his *De formandis concionibus sacris* (1553): instruction, reproof, exhortation, correction, encouragement—a good sermon was expected to contain these five applications of the biblical text. Moreover, this was accompanied by the move within Lutheran orthodoxy towards a (somewhat un-Lutheran) stress on law, which gave an impetus to moralistic preaching. The very fact that the Sunday sermons had to deal with the same scriptural texts year after year made it difficult to avoid repetition, so

there was a natural tendency to shift towards a topical framework for the sermon; but routine seems often to have killed inspiration. Against such dull and patterned preaching Spener in the late seventeenth century urged more simple and direct proclamation of the word, and this continued to be the thrust of Pietist preaching in the following centuries, though witness to personal faith and focus on religious experience sometimes assumed an importance that overshadowed the scriptural word itself. Throughout the eighteenth century there was conflict between Pietist currents within Lutheranism and the shift in other quarters towards a rationalism linked with the Enlightenment; and one can read as a victory for the Pietist position the revival of popular preaching in the nineteenth century. However, the key role of Schleiermacher in this nineteenth-century revitalization of European Protestant preaching should warn one against such easy explanation. His approach to the development of homiletic theory was rigorously theological, but the kind of preaching he advocated and practiced was not abstract and rationalistic.[6] In any event, the nineteenth century did see in continental Lutheranism a revival of preaching that was marked by a return to Scripture. Interestingly, there was a reorientation of Lutheran preaching in the United States also, though the dynamics of the situation seem to have been different. The search for denominational identity (which affected all the immigrant communities) and the controversies about doctrine within American Lutheranism seem to have been the principal sources of the nineteenth-century shift from ethical to doctrinal emphasis in preaching.[7] As it moved into the twentieth century, Lutheran preaching continued to preserve a common tradition of the importance of the ministry of the word. But the actual practice of preaching was differentiated by a tension between evangelical and liturgical emphases, between "liberal" and "orthodox" theologies, between doctrinal and Pietist objectives.

English preaching in the seventeenth century was inevitably touched by the sharp divisions that disrupted the country's life, for those divisions were most basically religious and preachers exercised determining influence on the attitudes and movements of that age.[8] Though most religious histories of England concentrate on the series of great preachers (such as Andrewes, Taylor, South, and Tillotson) whose public impact was so apparent, the sermons given by local pastors (whether Anglican or Puritan) were a major factor in shaping the attitudes of the common people. Given the temper of the times and the turbulence of public affairs, it is not surprising that much of this popular preaching was polemical and partisan.[9] Joined with this was a large measure of denunciation of moral evil; apparently behavior on all levels of English society left much to be desired. Sermons tended to be long and tedious; their method was topical and analytic rather than evangelical. Yet there was not only acceptance of but even interest in much of this preaching, perhaps because of the conviction and earnestness of so many of the preachers, perhaps also because much of it dealt with the actual life experience of the audiences. Like continental preaching of the period, the sermons tend to have a considerable amount of rhetorical conceit and fairly complicated thought content; but in the latter half of the century there is an evolution towards greater clarity and simplicity which one can notice in comparing the sermons of Donne or Jeremy Taylor with those of South or Tillotson.

But if the Anglican pulpit of the Restoration, as exemplified in Tillotson's sermons, was characterized by greater directness of style, its Latitudinarian theology was a long step towards the rationalism of the eighteenth century, and its strong ethical emphasis heralded the moralizing of eighteenth- and nineteenth-century sermons.[10] Actually, the eighteenth-century decline of preaching in established pulpit situations in England (both Anglican and Dissenting) was quite marked. Sermons tended increasingly to be discourses or essays, more often on topics of morality; preachers appealed to reason rather than to faith, for there was a general desire to accommodate religion to the deistic spirit of the age; the ministry of the word became perfunctory, lacking in spirit, and out of touch with people's needs.[11] Counteracting the aridity and religious emptiness of so much of this "official" preaching, the Methodist revolution that was led by the Wesleys and Whitefield "transformed the pulpit and also the religious life of England and North America."[12] However, the enthusiasm of this revival movement was long looked at askance in traditional church circles, and it was not until the end of the century and the influence of Charles Simeon that evangelical preaching gained a position of respect in England. Simeon trained thousands of young men at Cambridge in preaching; he consciously worked to combine the clarity and straightforwardness of Latitudinarian preaching with the fervor and emotional impact of evangelism, and so helped fashion part of the future of English preaching.[13]

The impact of the evangelical movement continued into nineteenth-century England, and it was one of the forces behind the spiritual revival that came with the 1830s. However, it found no theological deepening to accompany its zeal and ethical earnestness; it tended increasingly to be anti-Catholic and antiliberal; and it did not flourish as did Methodism (and the evangelical movement in general) in North America. Rather, the spiritual initiative passed to the Tractarian movement. It was not only the published tracts but the sermons of the Oxford and Cambridge groups that roused the slumbering English church.[14] Newman's sermons, for example, combine a religious intensity with a limpidity and grace of style, and they continued to be read and to wield their influence well into the twentieth century. Unquestionably, the Tractarian movement was strongly intellectual, even academic, in its orientation; much of the influential preaching associated with it took place in university pulpits. Yet, an important element of the movement was the evangelization of the poor in the slum areas of England's large cities.

Important as the Tractarian development

was, it formed but one part of the overall resurgence of preaching in Victorian England. The nineteenth century, much like the seventeenth, was a period of great interest in and influence by preachers. More so than the seventeenth, it witnessed a broad variety of sermon techniques and contents, from Newman's classic illumination of Christian doctrine to Spurgeon's rousing exhortations to conversion.[15] Though personality differences explained partially the rich diversity of preaching styles, the manner of preaching was largely the result of the theological posture adopted by the community to which the preacher belonged; the diversity in preaching reflected the diversity of views about the purpose of preaching, a diversity that continued into the twentieth century in England.

Given the widely different theologies and attitudes of the churches and sects that belonged to or derived from Calvinist Protestantism, and given the dominant function of preaching in the ministry of all these communities, it becomes practically impossible to trace a history of Calvinist preaching. Such a history would be, as in no other sphere of Christianity, a history of the total evolution of the church. For it is the sermons preached by Scottish Presbyterians or exiled Huguenots or American Methodists on the frontier (to name but three situations) that reflect more than anything else the changing fortunes and beliefs of Reformed Protestantism, its broadening multiplicity of understandings, and the consequent splintering into a number of separate religious groups. Moreover, the basic emphasis within the Calvinist tradition on the local community's autonomy implies a relatively greater independence of a local preacher in the style and content of his sermons.

Nonetheless, the Calvinist communities of the seventeenth to twentieth centuries have experienced the same religious challenges and stimuli as have the other Christian churches, and Calvinist preaching has had to react to these same forces. There was the political pressure exerted on the churches, the impact of rationalistic thought and of the broader phenomenon of modern dechristianization, and the new evangelical impulse which reacted against this rationalism.[16] The last-named had the most obvious influence on Reformed Protestant preaching, particularly in the Methodist and Baptist communities in America. To a great extent, the rapid development of Protestantism in nineteenth-century America was a part of the wider resurgence of evangelical Protestantism; both in North America and in Europe the pulpit was the principal agent of revitalization. More in Calvinist than in Lutheran congregations (and still more than in Anglican or Roman Catholic communities), the worship service and the pastoral ministry centered on the sermon.

At the same time, probably because it was not linked with ministerial ordination to cultic activity (as in Roman Catholicism), ministry of the word was more frequently exercised by laity in the communities of the Calvinist tradition, particularly in evangelical communities in North America. This was not the general practice, however, in established congregations, for the function of preaching was highly respected and not lightly undertaken. Particularly in the evangelical movements of eighteenth- and nineteenth-century Britain and North America, the pulpit was not only the integrating principle of the Protestant community but also the source of important social and political change.

Despite the recurrent infusion of life from movements such as the Methodist revival, ordinary parish preaching in modern times has been quite generally routine, unimaginative, and uninspiring. Bishop Dupanloup, no mean preacher himself, could make the bitter remark in 1830: "Thirty thousand sermons every Sunday in the churches of France —and France still has the faith!" No church has had a monopoly on this problem; no church has escaped it. It is quite obviously grounded in the immense difficulty of providing large numbers of truly competent ministers of the word, somewhat less obviously grounded in the institutionalized and repetitive patterns that tend to be imposed on parish preaching. Not surprisingly, then, the more vital expressions of preaching in the seventeenth to twentieth centuries have occurred in "outreach" situations.

Most prominent and probably most influential among these instances of preaching carried on outside an established pulpit situation was the field-preaching of Wesley and Whitefield.[17] Wesley himself was apparently quite reluctant to violate the regulations that forbade unauthorized preaching; but the spiritual needs of people took precedence in his mind, and so he endorsed preaching outside the parish pulpit and (when circumstances dictated it) preaching by lay people. What was important was that authentic preaching of the word be done.[18] If the Methodist practice of bringing the ministry of the word to people wherever they were had a transforming effect on English Christianity, its effectiveness was even more manifest in America. The Methodist circuit rider, making his way from place to place and preaching in a log cabin or a barroom or in the open air, was a familiar figure on the American frontier. This approach to evangelization made the Methodist church the most successful in following the westward flow of population.[19] However, the Methodists had no monopoly on evangelism. Particularly in the United States, a number of evangelical churches were formed in the nineteenth and twentieth centuries, and the general technique and spirit of Wesleyan preaching became part of the overall heritage of American Protestantism. Revival meetings of one sort or another were to be found in all the churches of the Calvinist tradition, but the old frontier revival sessions became "domesticated" as the membership of the various churches moved up in the social and economic scale. The tent-meetings moved into permanent housing, regular Protestant parishes now had an annual revival session of a week or two, and modified revival sessions were held in denominational colleges.[20]

Closely intertwined with the increased influence of evangelism within the Protestant community was the involvement with foreign missionary work which flourished from the end of the eighteenth century onward.[21] In its earlier stages a dominantly European undertaking, for North America itself was for some time a prime object of such missionary effort, the evangelization of the mission countries rested more and more upon the human and financial resources of American Protestantism. While the churches more directly touched by the Wesleyan influence were leaders in this missionary endeavor, the Lutheran and Anglican and Reformed churches both in Europe and North America also undertook large-scale commitments to the work of foreign missions.[22] Much of the activity of the missionaries was concerned with bettering the material situation of people (building dispensaries, schools, etc.), and though it was unquestionably bound up to some extent with colonial imperialism this missionary expansion was essentially a ministry of the word, a work of evangelization.

Roman Catholicism had its parallels to the "outreach" preaching of the Reformation churches. Itinerant preachers, going from parish church to parish church for "special" sermons, or preaching to people wherever they could be gathered, had been common long before modern times. But such activity became more prevalent and was importantly fostered by religious communities. The Redemptorists, the Passionists, the Vincentians (among others) were formed for just such work, and older orders, such as the Jesuits and Capuchins, continued to be prominent as "home missionaries."[23] The parish mission became a regular feature in the life of Catholic parishes. While its content was somewhat more doctrinal, its style somewhat more didactic, and its spirit somewhat less "enthusiastic" than its Protestant counterpart, it did serve much the same purpose as a revival session.

In the foreign mission fields, too, Roman Catholic activity, which had anticipated Protestant involvement by more than two centuries, became more extensive in the nineteenth and twentieth centuries. The burden of missionary effort that had rested chiefly on the Mediterranean countries during the earlier stages was increasingly assumed by the northern European countries and a bit later by the American church.[24] Evangelization inevitably played a major role in the missionaries' activity during the early stages of work in a given mission, but there generally followed quite quickly the establishment of pastoral patterns much like those of the country from which the missionaries came.

The Role of Prominent Preachers

It can be a mistake to base a history of Christian preaching solely on the activity of those preachers whose fame and published sermons preserve their names for history. Unquestionably, there was a great difference in manner and in effectiveness between the court sermons of Bossuet or the Notre Dame discourses of Lacordaire and the Sunday sermon preached in an ordinary parish. Yet, it was the famous preachers of each age who set the styles and whose sermons served as models; if they themselves did not write instructions on preaching, their sermons served as guides for those who did.

One factor made the impact of prominent preachers immeasurably greater in modern times: printed publication of sermons. In the seventeenth century and into the eighteenth, more sermons were published than any other kind of literature, and sermons were widely read for their religious content and for their literary style.[25] This meant that the sermons of Andrewes or Tillotson or Bourdaloue or Bossuet not only reached in their own lifetime a much wider audience than those who actually heard them, but that they continued to be read and to influence preaching technique long after their author's death. Such publication of sermons became, really, a somewhat distinct form of the ministry of the word, closely allied to the writing of expository or hortatory essays. It reflected, too, the double aspect under which the sermon could be viewed: it could be seen as a piece of literature and, as such, shaped according to the precepts of grammar and rhetoric; or it could be seen as an instrument to excite and form

Christian faith, and from this perspective it was to be governed by a theological understanding of soteriology. Modern theories of homiletics have treated the sermon under either or both of these headings. The publication of sermons, however, which often entailed an improvement of the sermon after its actual delivery, has tended to lay stress on the literary refinement.[26]

Printing the sermons of prominent preachers meant that it was much easier for others to imitate their style, even to plagiarize them quite effectively. It also meant that more careful criticism of sermon methods and content was possible, for critics could deal with a widely known text. For the preacher in question it meant a somewhat different point of view in preparing his sermons: though his actual delivery of a sermon was directed to a specific and fairly limited audience (to which presumably he was directing it), the published sermon was intended for a much wider and differentiated reading public. Influencing this latter group could not but have been a controlling objective in the preparation of the sermon.

Perhaps nothing indicates more clearly the changes within the style and content of preaching in modern Christianity, nor shows more unmistakably the decline in preaching's influence in the twentieth century, than the history of these prominent preachers. One can trace the manner in which literary sophistries connected with Baroque culture complicated the style of preaching in the sixteenth and early seventeenth centuries, how the development of orthodox "scholasticism" in the seventeenth century emphasized the analytic and "intellectual" element, how this passed into the trend towards rationalistic moralizing in the eighteenth century. And all the time there was a countercurrent urging greater simplicity and directness and evangelical proclamation. With the evangelical revivals of the eighteenth and nineteenth centuries, balanced by continuing "rationalism" in nonevangelical circles, the dialectic between pietist, nonconformist preaching and established institutional preaching becomes more evident; there is also more conscious effort to bring the best elements of each approach into a homiletic synthesis, as in the teaching of Charles Simeon.

One can also trace the declining influence of great preachers as symptomatic of the wider decline of preaching. There have been great preachers in the nineteenth and twentieth centuries: Newman and Lacordaire, Moody (who, incidentally, was a layman) and Finney, Schleiermacher and Brooks and Lombardi are but a few of the names that come immediately to mind. And it would be temerarious to suggest that their skill and performance was inferior to preachers of an early age. Yet, there was a gradually lessening impact of such preaching on public opinion and life; there was less reading of sermons as people turned to other "prophets" for analyses and solutions to society's problems. By the mid-twentieth century the "great preacher" was still around, still honored in church circles (though much less influential even there), but practically unnoticed in the larger picture of human life.[27] To some extent at least, preaching has been diminished in its influence by the general dechristianization process. "Religion" has been relegated to its own detached sphere of irrelevance and with it the voice of the preacher.

The fact that preaching in the mid-twentieth century no longer exerts the influence it possessed in the seventeenth and eighteenth centuries does not by itself argue that the quality of preaching has become inferior. One reason for being hesitant about any such judgment is the training in preaching that has been a standard part of seminary (divinity school) education, which should indicate a reasonably good level of preparation for the mass of ordained preachers.

Inclusion of courses in homiletics in the seminary's curriculum has been, however, an ambiguous practice. In some instances it has been rhetorical theory, in other cases it has been training in forensics; in some curricula homiletics has been handled as part of "pastoral theology" (itself an ill-defined area), in other curricula it has been treated distinctly.

But significantly, in practically all instances prior to 1950 the courses in preaching were separated (along with other "practical" courses) from the teaching of Scripture and history and theology. Obviously, the content of preaching was to be drawn from these other more "theoretical" fields of study, but the structuring of seminary curricula fostered the notion that there were two discrete ways of thinking about the Christian faith, one proper to the theologian and the other proper to the preacher.[28]

Not surprisingly, the actual implementation of seminary training in preaching has been as diverse as the views held by different Christian churches about the nature and purpose and importance of preaching. The very fact that one is dealing with a pastoral competence that involves both "science" and "art" means that the personal factor, both in seminary teachers and students, is critical and the structured elements of instruction are secondary. About the only thing that seems common to all the churches is a history of discontent with seminary training for preaching, which is reflected in endless discussions about "making seminary training more practical," and "professional versus academic education."

The Increase of Religious Education

Catechetical formation, particularly of children, which had become prominent during the seventeenth century, continued into the modern world as one of the principal exercises of the ministry of the word. Alike in Catholic and Protestant communities, the instruction of children by use of the catechism was assumed to be one of the basic pastoral tasks; the understanding that most modern Christians have had of their religion has been largely the product of such catechetical training. Like preaching, and for many of the same reasons, religious education has tended to drift into unimaginative routine, into memorization of rather abstract notions and acceptance of certain precepts of religious or ethical behavior. Against such desiccation of catechesis there has been a strong tradition of protest and reaction, repeated attempts to devise a more vital approach to religious education, and a gradual development of a "theology of catechesis." At least in Roman Catholic circles, the twentieth-century evolution of catechetics has outstripped and set the pace for the development of pulpit preaching.

Catechetical instruction in Roman Catholicism has been, until World War II, dominated by the Council of Trent with its objective of imparting orthodox doctrinal information and by the emphasis on moralism which has been broadly characteristic of modern Christianity.[29] The Catechism of the Council of Trent, though not truly a catechism nor ever used as such, was a basic outline of doctrine that had been intended as a guide to preserve unity of teaching in the post-Tridentine church. It was not that widely used in catechetical practice and was the first in a series of modern attempts to achieve some form of national or international homogeneity of religious teaching. Actually, in the seventeenth century the usage of the catechisms of Bellarmine, Canisius, Auger, and Ripalda was still widespread; and in many places there was no great distinction in method between catechizing adults and catechizing children. Most of the catechizing was done in a parish context—with obvious adjustments being made in England and Ireland because of persecution—generally on Sunday afternoon. Involvement in catechetical work increased in the eighteenth century. There were a number of attempts to break away from an excessively doctrinal and "intellectual" formulation of catechetical instruction, to introduce more of the Bible and of history, to form the entire person and not just the mind (or the memory). However, the procedure remained essentially one of committing to memory, hopefully with some understanding, a series of abstract doctrinal formulations.

Already in the eighteenth century, catechetical formation was being more exclusively given to children, which tended to accentuate the learn-by-rote character of religious instruction. This becomes even more the case

in the nineteenth and twentieth centuries, when "catechism" is thought of as something proper to children, usually attached to preparation for their confirmation or First Communion. There were serious attempts to devise more effective methods of educating the faith of children, one of the most admired and copied of which was the method of Saint Sulpice.[30] Theologians of the stature of Sailer and Hirscher worked for a deeper integration of Scripture and sacred history with the doctrinal elements in religious education, but the overall theological climate was not yet prepared for this, and what tended to result was the standard catechism format plus ancillary study of "Bible history." Another development worked to reinforce this "intellectualized" approach to religious formation: more religious instruction of children was now being given in a school situation rather than in the parish church; "religion" became another class along with mathematics or language or history, and unavoidably took on more of an academic tonality.

Agitation for change in catechetical procedures mounted in the latter half of the nineteenth century and finally erupted in the twentieth century, spreading from Germany and the Low Countries to France and then to the English-speaking countries. Perhaps the most basic shift in mentality that one notices in this twentieth-century catechetical revival is the emphasis on formation of faith according to the psychological needs and potential of the child rather than an emphasis on doctrinal information. But along with such pioneering efforts at change there has been a strong party urging adherence to the "traditional" approach. This has been linked (though not confined) to efforts by national hierarchies to impose a uniform catechetical text, especially the Baltimore Catechism in the United States. Such efforts were quite successful until World War II; it is doubtful if such uniformity can again be achieved.

Considering this modern catechetical effort as an expression of the ministry of the word, several observations seem appropriate. As the number of children to be catechized multiplied, it became logical to utilize others than ordained ministers to perform this function. One of the most important instances of this use of laity as catechists occurred in the mission fields, where the native lay catechist was an indispensable agent in the evangelizing of his own people.[31] Again, the fact that so much religious instruction came to be handled in Catholic parochial schools by non-ordained teachers who occupied a semiofficial ecclesiastical position makes one wonder if the ancient ministry of teaching has found a new modern form. Allied with this is the tantalizing question: How much of the teaching of "profane" disciplines that takes place in conjunction with formal religious instruction in parochial schools is really part of "religious instruction"? This question, which has been long discussed in the context of justifying the existence of parochial schools (as opposed to extraschool programs in religious instruction), takes on new dimensions with current theological reflection on Christianity and secularity. Finally, the continuing discontent with a catechetical formation divorced from Bible and liturgy may well be an important indication that the ministries of word and sacrament cannot be separated from one another and still remain life-giving. This may be a salutary lesson at a time in the church's history when the increased literacy and educational level of Christians, plus the modern communications media, might suggest up-to-date techniques in mass information about Christianity, techniques which would, however, be more removed than ever from the experience of enacted word in liturgy.

Catechetical instruction, both of adults and of children, had been one of the most effective instruments of the Reformation. It continued to be an important part of Protestant church life in modern times, though going through much of the same ups and downs as preaching. One of the important features of the evolution of religious education within the Reformation churches has been the involvement of these churches in the emergence of the educational system in northern Europe and America. Much of what had become by

mid-twentieth century a "secular" system of schooling originated in denominational institutions; those earlier denominational schools were conducted for explicitly religious purposes, with religious instruction an intrinsic part of the curriculum.

But religious instruction formed an important part also of parish life, as well as of ecclesiastical concern. One of the most striking implementations of this concern was the nineteenth-century development of the Sunday school movement, particularly in the United States.[32] Providing catechetical instruction on Sunday, both to adults and to children, was not new; but the increasing secularization of public schools in the United States highlighted the importance of the Sunday catechizing, and a highly organized effort with training programs for Sunday school teachers, church-wide (or even interchurch) councils on religious education, and centralized offices for educational materials and curricula was mounted by the Protestant communities in the nineteenth and early twentieth centuries. Allied with this catechetical effort was the large-scale dissemination of religious literature by the various Protestant communities, which established for the purpose their own publishing houses.

In many cases, especially in the lengthy Sunday services that occupied Protestant congregations for several hours, it was difficult to say where the sermon left off and religious instruction began. An indication of this intertwining of preaching and religious education was the influence on Henry Ward Beecher and Phillips Brooks, two of the nineteenth century's leading pulpit orators, of Horace Bushnell's *Christian Nurture*, which was the century's most important piece of American Protestant writing on religious formation.[33] The exact nature of what was being done in the pulpit became yet more vague when lectures (sometimes on religious topics, sometimes on timely topics of the day) rather than sermons were delivered; a practice that was not totally absent from any of the churches (Catholic or Protestant) in recent centuries, but which was more common in "liberal" Protestant communities. Ministry of the word has become in the modern church a far-ranging function.

Apart from a large-scale utilization of printing and the formation of centralized organization to further religious education, modern Christian preaching and catechetics have not been noticeably innovative prior to World War II. Modern advances in sociology and psychology helped make the churches more aware in the nineteenth and early twentieth centuries of the relative inadequacy of their efforts at evangelization and catechesis. To a limited extent some of these nonreligious areas of knowledge have been utilized in religious education, but for the most part this touched upon pedagogical techniques rather than upon the content and governing purpose of preaching and instruction.

An important qualification of this last statement must be made. The stress on ethical instruction and exhortation when it found expression in the liberal wing of Protestantism produced an approach to preaching and religious education that focused on the psychological development of the individual. To situate better this point of view (for it was not an isolated phenomenon) and to evaluate more accurately its validity may well be close to the heart of our study of the ministry of the word in modern times. The reason is that the "liberal theology" that lies at the root of this understanding of ministry is a soteriology that challenges all the classic understandings of Christianity. Obviously, "liberal theology" is a broad term denominating a rather amorphous movement of religious thought away from classic formulations and denominational limitation; it embraces thinkers as diverse as Newman and Emerson and Schleiermacher and Bushnell. It ranges from an attempt to probe more deeply the traditional Christian beliefs about "grace" and "faith" and "salvation" to a complete reduction of Christianity to "being a good human being." This "liberal theology" intersects strangely with other elements of modern Christianity. Quite clearly it is a further statement of that interest in man (particularly man in his in-

dividual autonomy) which we associate with Renaissance humanism; it is certainly linked with the Reformation's interest in personal faith; it is quite compatible with the pietist and evangelical stress on such personal faith and religious experience. Yet, it repudiates the narrow fundamentalism which characterizes so much of pietism and evangelism, it is linked philosophically with the rationalism that dried up so much personal faith, and it tends often to flourish better in well-established ecclesiastical situations than in more charismatic (and supposedly, therefore, freer) contexts. What seems central to this way of thinking is the idea that man must work out his own salvation, for it consists essentially in becoming human. Differences within this way of thinking appear when one asks about the nature and extent (if any) of "supernatural" help required by man to achieve this goal.

All this is reminiscent of the arguments about faith and good works, of the controversy regarding predestination and human freedom, of the dispute between Barth and Bultmann. The increasing man-centeredness of modern thought has made soteriology the point of focus in religious reflection, and this has found expression in the modern ministry of the word.[34] In the sixteenth century there had been a clear challenge to the view that salvation could come through adherence to institutionalized patterns of religious behavior or through external membership in a Christian community. Personal faith and conversion were emphasized, and this caused a marked upsurge in the quantity and quality of preaching and catechizing. By the seventeenth century, indoctrination in "orthodox" confessional formulations of faith has become a dominant objective; preaching and religious instruction become more didactic, less evangelical, often quite profuse and complicated. But protest against such abstractness and "impracticality" is prominent. There are demands in both pietist and "establishment" circles that preaching be simplified and governed by the individual Christian's needs. Leading a man to living faith and salvation, rather than simply instructing him, is stressed as the purpose of ministry of the word. However, emphasis on the practicalities of Christian life leads in the eighteenth century to stress on ethics rather than on doctrine; again pietist and "establishment" practice converge in this regard. This is reinforced by the rationalistic developments of the century, for as discourses on secular topics tend to replace biblical preaching a concentration on the ethical is almost unavoidable. The eighteenth century became a time of moralizing, and even the evangelical revivals were aimed at conversion to more Christian behavior.

By the nineteenth century the rationalistic impetus was somewhat spent, the force of evangelism increased, the Romantic movement displaced the classicism of the eighteenth century, and there was a revival of biblical preaching. Yet, there was an enduring moralistic emphasis in preaching and religious education, and the thematic form remained dominant in sermon structure. Preaching became more markedly confessional and "religious" in the dogmatically oriented churches. Explicit reaction against "liberalism" became a major concern. Roman Catholic preaching, for example, tended to be quite ecclesiastical. There was stress on the role of the Catholic church as the unique instrument of salvation, stress on the teaching that salvation came through obedience to the teaching and governance of the Catholic church, stress on Catholic tradition as the norm of orthodox belief, and stress on the fact that this traditional faith and practice was threatened by the forces of modern liberalism. However, the sharpest attacks on liberal theology came from the fundamentalist groups in the evangelical wing of Christianity —one of the clearest examples was the controversy over evolution.

As the nineteenth century ended there were increasing signs that neither "liberalism" nor "traditionalism" was about to vanish, but signs also that neither of them (nor indeed the opposition between them) was a static reality. What men began to suspect was that these were but symptoms of the profound

changes taking place in the entire fabric of modern society, and perhaps most deeply in the religious outlook and behavior of mankind. This was a frightening prospect and the religious establishment tended to fear not just for the safety of Christianity's institutional structures but for the spiritual welfare of the ordinary, theologically unsophisticated believer. "Modernism" was considered a dire threat in most of the Christian churches until well into the twentieth century; this created a defensive attitude towards traditional teachings and correlatively a defensive (and self-defeating) posture in preaching and religious education. But the forces of change were irresistible; this became evident first of all in progressive theological circles, then in the twentieth-century catechetical renewal, and then to a limited degree in the revival of biblical and liturgical preaching. By mid-twentieth century the Christian ministry of the word had come to a crossroads; the crisis that faced it was unavoidable and absolutely radical. But it took World War II and what accompanied it to force upon the Christian churches an awareness of that crisis.

The Ministry of Theologians

An adequate description of the ministry of theologians in modern Christianity would necessarily incorporate a detailed study of the evolution of theological opinion since the sixteenth century. The contribution of theologians (as theologians) to modern Christian faith and life came precisely through the development and dissemination of their theological views. Without undertaking this task one might still examine more generally the function played by theologians in recent centuries, and so gain some insight into the manner in which theological activity was (or was not) considered a ministry of the church.[35] One can argue, of course, about applying the term "theologian" to one individual rather than to another. A man caught up entirely into evangelical activity may well in his sermons and catechetical instruction be a more profound and creative theologian than a university professor of theology. However, there are always in the various churches some individuals who are considered "professional theologians" (though they may also be active in other spheres) and who as such play a particular role in the church's life. Actually, the role they were expected to play in modern Christianity was multiple.

In the sixteenth century, each of the various Christian communities made a number of basic options (in doctrine, polity, liturgy) which were pretty well crystallized into confessional doctrine by the century's close. However, there remained the task of expanding and explicating these relatively brief statements of faith (whether from the Formula of Concord, or the Council of Trent, or the Heidelberg Catechism), of providing background for their understanding through examination of their historical roots, of forging them into a coherent synthesis, of indicating their relevance for the emergent society of modern Europe and America. This was the task to which European theologians addressed themselves in the seventeenth century, creating in the process a variety of scholastic traditions, many of which remained influential until mid-twentieth century.

Such clarification of Christian belief was stimulated, even demanded, by the questions that were posed by the Reformation. These questions were not, of course, exhaustively answered by the end of the seventeenth century, despite a monumental theological achievement. As both the Reformation and the Council of Trent found expression during subsequent centuries in doctrinal teaching and religious practice and ecclesiastical institutions, there were countless questions to be answered and differences of view to be reconciled. By itself, this might well have provided a continuing need for theological clarification of confessional belief; but the need was heightened by the confrontation of Christianity with the modern "secular world," which brought into question the entire meaning and purpose of Christianity. It was further intensified by the late nineteenth- and twentieth-century moves towards some form of Christian

reunion. For the most part, even in churches where higher ecclesiastics or agencies such as synods controlled the process of official doctrinal clarification, the actual work of providing such clarification was considered proper to professional theologians and was undertaken by them.[36] If others, like bishops, undertook such doctrinal clarification it was not because they denied that this was properly theological activity but because they thought of themselves as theologians, which in not a few instances they were.

Since the theologian's role was so clearly situated within his own confessional community and was finalized by the internal well-being of that community, the theologian often found himself cast as a *defensor fidei*. He was to demonstrate the truth of the views held by his church and the theological validity of the religious practices in which it was engaged. In practice this implied that he was to prove false those opinions that were opposed to or opposed by the officialdom of his church. Some of these opposing views came from other Christian communities or from dissidents within his own community; another kind of opposition came from secular sources such as civil governments trying to establish control over education or agnostic thinkers attacking religion. But whatever the source of the "attack," the theologian was to be supportive of his church's official teaching. There were instances when a theologian failed to act in this way, when he even "went over to the other side"; but this was considered a betrayal of the function entrusted to him.

Though only the Reformed tradition tended to look on theologians as exercising a distinct ministerial office, all the Christian churches looked upon the man designated for theological work (e.g., by appointment to a theological faculty) as occupying a position of special trust. More so, if he was appointed to a teaching post in a seminary, but not only in that case, he was selected on the basis of his ecclesial stability as well as because of his theological expertise. To some extent this requirement of confessional allegiance was altered, particularly in the United States, as "union" or nondenominational seminary faculties (or university divinity faculties) emerged in the late nineteenth century, but even here a certain fidelity to "Protestantism" was expected. Roman Catholicism, especially in the century following Vatican I, provided the most obvious illustration of theologians who functioned within ecclesiastical structures as auxiliaries to church officials and who were expected, if they wished to retain ecclesiastical approval and therefore the possibility of continuing theological activity, to agree with and defend the opinions of those officials. The unhappy professional history of many prominent Catholic theologians who were subjected to prejudiced criticism, removed from teaching positions because their opinions were "dangerous," and accused of heterodoxy and disloyalty reflects the understanding (at least in official circles) of the theologian's function which prevailed in the nineteenth and twentieth centuries. However, not all the theological "witch-hunting" went on in the Roman Catholic church. Heresy trials and official condemnation of deviant theological opinion can be found in other communities as late as the mid-twentieth century.

Paradoxically, it was in fulfilling this role of preserving, explaining, and defending their confessional traditions that the more creative theological minds of the nineteenth and twentieth centuries were forced out of their confessional confinement as they began to discover Christian tradition. This came slowly because it involved the emergence of modern Scripture exegesis, a massive effort to recover the thought of the early church fathers, thorough investigation into the history of Christianity, and an exposure to the divided theological thought of the many post-Reformation "traditions." And it came painfully because it required the abdication of cherished confessional prejudices and the abandonment of many supposedly certain theological views. This effort, undertaken by men who (at least for the most part) were convinced believers and committed to enlivening the faith of their coreligionists, was often looked upon as an attempt to undermine Christianity. What has

been at the bottom of this tension between progressive theology and other elements in the Christian churches has been the understanding of "tradition"; it is not accidental that mid-twentieth-century theology saw a large-scale reconsideration of this notion.[37] As the real nature of Christian tradition is better understood, the particular function of theologians within the Christian community will be more apparent, for it is undeniable that the activity of theologians should be one of making that tradition more intelligible.

Post-Reformation Christianity was marked by a continuing upsurge in formalized clerical training. Seminaries for training ministerial candidates in theology and other knowledges related to pastoral work became a standardized institution of church life. The nineteenth and early twentieth centuries saw a large-scale expansion of seminaries as the spectacular population growth in Europe and the waves of immigration to North America demanded an enlarged corps of ordained ministers, and as the increasing secularization of university education either drove theology out of the university curriculum or (at least to those church officials interested primarily in "confessional" preparation) made it unsuitable for training future pastors. A variety of patterns developed: the completely detached and self-sufficient training through minor and major seminary education (characteristic of the Roman Catholic situation), or the divinity school thought of as professional training complementary to regular undergraduate university work (a common American Protestant practice), or a university faculty in theology attended by students who lived in church-sponsored residences (seminaries) where they received pastoral training to supplement their academic university study (as in many places in Germany and Britain).[38]

By and large, no matter what the precise pattern, the theological formation of these ministerial candidates was entrusted to a group of church-approved professors, and within each church these appointed instructors of divinity students were looked upon as the "official theologians." However, the theological activity of these men tended for the most part (though, fortunately, in some instances not exclusively) to be governed by the objectives which the church had in maintaining seminaries or divinity faculties. Allowing always for the unusual professor or student who can rise above the system, the purpose of these seminary courses was indoctrination, the method one of high-level catechetics, and the atmosphere relatively antiintellectual. Seminary professors were expected to prepare their students to fit into church structures and procedures, to carry out responsibly the duties of ordinary parish ministry, to preach and teach according to confessional guidelines. In their seminary teaching, these theologians acted as appointed delegates of higher church officials and generally were controlled, in one fashion or another, by these officials.[39] Thus, theology became as clericalized as it had ever been; it was carried on by clerics, in clerically controlled institutions, for the purpose of training more clerics.

However, there persisted in theological circles the notion that theology was in some fashion a body of professional knowledge (a bit like medical or legal knowledge), and that some theologians at least ought to be about the business of developing that body of knowledge by research and reflection. And in some instances, as in certain university faculties particularly in Germany or with the Mercerburg group in the mid-nineteenth century or in a few houses of study conducted by Roman Catholic religious orders for the training of their own members, there was enough autonomy and sufficient convergence of genuine theological activity to bring about theological advance. This internal development of theological understanding and methodology, which by mid-twentieth century had swelled to a major theological movement throughout the Christian churches, will certainly be seen by later historians of Christianity as an important ministry of modern professional theologians to the life of the Christian community.

If Christian ministry has as one of its principal objectives the fostering of Christian community, then progressive modern theology has clearly performed a ministerial function. One cannot easily ascertain the causes of such phenomena as the twentieth-century ecumenical movement; but scholarly theological research in Scripture, patristics, history, liturgy, and systematic theology was certainly one of the elements that made the churches discover their community, clarify and question their differences, and move towards unity. Moreover, theologians have been prominent in stimulating and guiding the progress of ecumenism; their activity in this regard, much of which only trained theologians could do, may well indicate part of their proper ministry within the church.

NOTES

1. Writing of the English scene, J. Downey, *The Eighteenth-Century Pulpit* (Oxford, 1969), p. 3, says: "In the Seventeenth Century pulpit oratory achieved a pre-eminence which has not since been equalled. . . . No other age has produced so many astute and articulate preachers as the Seventeenth Century. . . . This indeed was the golden age of English pulpit oratory."

2. On the Lutheran situation, see H. Wyman, *Encyclopedia of the Lutheran Church* (Minneapolis, 1965), vol. 3, pp. 1942–43; on France, see J. Connors, *New Catholic Encyclopedia* (New York, 1967), vol. 11, pp. 693–96; on England and Scotland, see G. Cragg, *The Church and the Age of Reason*, pp. 65–71, 91, and I. Simon, *Three Restoration Divines* (Paris, 1967), pp. 1–73.

3. See the article of J. Connors cited above, n. 2; also H. Dressler, *New Catholic Encyclopedia*, vol. 11, pp. 684–89.

4. The influence of their ideas extended far beyond Italy, since Ligouri as founder of the Redemptorist congregation and Strambi as founder of the Passionists shaped the thinking and practice of two of the most important groups of preachers in the modern church.

5. For a brief history of Lutheran preaching, see Wyman, pp. 1942–47.

6. See F. Winter, *Die Homiletik seit Schleiermacher bis in die Anfange der 'dialektischen Theologie' in Grundzugen* (Göttingen, 1969), pp. 11–21; see also Cragg, pp. 254–55; and L. Brastow, *Representative Modern Preachers* (New Haven, 1904), pp. 1–48.

7. See W. Poovey, *Encyclopedia of the Lutheran Church*, vol. 3, p. 1950.

8. On English preaching in the seventeenth century, see E. Darzan, *History of Preaching* (New York, 1912), pp. 136–85.

9. "It was a century of violent theological and political upheaval, and the sermons of the period reflect its varying opinions and emotions as no other literary remains of the time can be said to do; for the sermon . . . was a pronouncement of views held by an appreciable number of contemporary Englishmen, and the sermon has come down to us stamped with the sincerity of conviction or urgency of appeal of strong-minded individuals or of the great theological parties which were then struggling for supremacy in England. For the century in question the sermon, besides its strictly religious function, took in large measure the place of the journalistic press at the present day, and enjoyed the enormous influence, reinforced by a tremendous sanctity of authority, of a modern broadcasting company." (W. Mitchell, *English Pulpit Oratory from Andrewes to Tillotson* [New York, 1962], p. 3.)

10. See Cragg, pp. 70–80.

11. See H. Davies, *Worship and Theology in England* (Princeton, 1961), vol. 3, pp. 65–74.

12. *Ibid.*, p. 143.

13. See Downey, pp. 228–29.

14. See Vidler, *The Church in an Age of Revolution* (London, 1961), pp. 49–55.

15. See Davies, vol. 4, pp. 282–348.

16. See J. McNeill, *History and Character of Calvinism* (New York, 1967), pp. 353–425.

17. On the style and influence of these two preachers, see Downey, pp. 189–225, who says of Wesley's impact: "No other English sermons, not even those of Donne, Tillotson, or Butler, have enjoyed such widespread attention and influence" (p. 225); see also D. Marshall, *Eighteenth-Century England* (London, 1962), pp. 244–51; Davies, vol. 3, pp. 143–83; A. Lawson, *John Wesley and the Christian Ministry* (London, 1963). A. Outler in the introduction to *John Wesley* (New York, 1964), pp. 3–33, gives a more theological appraisal of Wesley's preaching.

18. See Lawson, pp. 20–37.

19. See W. Sweet, *The Story of Religion in America* (New York, 1950), pp. 218–21.

20. *Ibid.*, pp. 345–47.

21. See J. Dillenberger and C. Welch, *Protestant Christianity* (New York, 1954), pp. 166–78.

22. See S. Neill, *Christian Missions*, vol. 6 of *Pelican History of the Church* (Harmondsworth, 1964), pp. 243–396.

23. See A. Baillargeon, *New Catholic Encyclopedia*, vol. 9, pp. 937–38.

24. See Neill, pp. 397–449.

25. Mitchell, pp. 3–11.

26. There is a need to study further the relative influence of rhetorical and theological viewpoints on the evolution of preaching, especially the manner in which literary ways of thought and expression entered into the kind of theologizing that took place in sermons. Some work in this regard has been done by literary scholars, e.g., W. Fraser Mitchell's *English Pulpit Oratory*, but practically nothing by historians of theological method.

27. To some extent the judgment must be changed a bit for the United States. There has been the same gradual decline, but the timetable has been retarded. The line of important preachers stretches at least as far back as Jonathan Edwards and the Great Awakening in the early eighteenth century; preaching continued to be an important force in shaping public opinion during that century and the following one. The struggle over abolition of slavery illustrates this. The end of the nineteenth century saw perhaps the greatest number of illustrious preachers in the country's history.

Here, too, decline in public influence set in, but some decades later than in Europe, perhaps because the cultural establishment of religion disappeared more subtly than the legal establishment of religion in Europe.

28. On seminary training in theology and its relation to the crisis in preaching, see D. Grasso, *Proclaiming God's Message* (Notre Dame, 1965), pp. xvi–xxxii.

29. On the history of modern Catholic catechetics, see G. Sloyan, *New Catholic Encyclopedia*, vol. 3, pp. 229–31; J. Jungmann, *Handing on the Faith* (New York, 1959), pp. 19–64; J. Crichton, "Religious Education in England in the Penal Days," *Shaping the Christian Message*, ed. G. Sloyan (New York, 1958), pp. 63–90; and, also in this last-named volume, J. Colomb, "The Catechetical Method of Saint Sulpice," pp. 91–111.

30. See Colomb, "The Catechetical Method of Saint Sulpice."

31. One of the questions, however, that needs to be asked about this situation is whether or to what extent the formal selection and commission of these mission catechists constitutes a form of ordination. The same applies more recently to those professionally trained men and women who are officially charged with religious education.

32. See M. Taylor, *Religious Education* (New York, 1960), pp. 17–23; Sweet, pp. 253–55.

33. On Bushnell's influence, see W. Hudson, *Religion in America* (New York, 1965), pp. 175–78.

34. An interesting reflection of the evolution of modern preaching which we outline briefly here is found in B. Dreher, *Die Osterpredigt von der Reformation bis zur Gegenwart* (Freiburg, 1951); in terms of the Easter preaching he traces the progression from Reformation emphasis on Scripture, through Baroque sophistication of form, rationalistic moralizing, etc.

35. The literature on modern developments in theology is immense, but a thorough synthesis of these developments remains to be written. Studies such as Tillich's *Perspectives on Nineteenth and Twentieth Century Protestant Theology*, ed. C. Braaten (New York, 1967), or Barth's *Die protestantische Theologie in 19. Jahrundert*, 3d ed. (Zurich, 1960) are obviously limited in scope; moreover, they raise the almost insoluble question about the extent to which theology is to be extended to or distinguished from modern philosophical thought. Any number of careful studies of individual theologians or of theological movements have been undertaken, such as Geiselmann's work on Mohler or Kasper's study of Schrader or Preus' book on Lutheran orthodoxy; they still need to be brought together into a more comprehensive history of modern theology. In the meantime, they act as sources for and a salutary corrective of any attempt at such a history.

36. However, there was wide divergence from one church to another (e.g., Swiss Reformed Protestantism and Roman Catholicism) and from one historical situation to another within a church (e.g., French Catholicism under Louis XIV and French Catholicism during and after Vatican I) regarding the extent to which such theological statements acted normatively or were themselves judged for orthodoxy by church officials.

37. See, e.g., Y. Congar's *Tradition and Traditions* (New York, 1967—the French edition appeared a few years earlier); or G. Tavard, *Holy Writ or Holy Church* (London, 1959); or the essays in *Die mundliche Ueberlieferung*, ed. M. Schmaus (Munich, 1957); or R. Hanson's *Tradition in the Early Church* (London, 1962). For a brief study of the gradual evolution of Roman Catholic thought on tradition in the latter nineteenth and early twentieth century, see J. Mackey, *The Modern Theology of Tradition* (London, 1962); the book emphasizes the formative influence of Franzelin's theology of tradition, and can be profitably complemented by W. Kasper's study of Franzelin's confreres, Schrader and Passaglia, *Die Lehre von der Tradition in der Romischen Schule* (Freiburg, 1962).

38. See K. Latourette, *Christianity in a Revolutionary Age* (New York, 1958), vol. 2, pp. 98–100 (on Germany) and pp. 284–93 (on England); on Catholic seminaries, J. Ellis, *Seminary Education in a Time of Change*, ed. J. Lee and L. Putz (Notre Dame, 1965), pp. 30–81, and S. Poole, *Seminary in Crisis* (New York, 1965), pp. 30–55.

39. Trent's prescription that the bishop was to be in charge of seminary training for his diocese governed Roman Catholic practice and became part of canon law; see Poole, pp. 56–65.

CHAPTER 14

Theological Reflections on

God's Word

Though ideas may differ as to what exactly is meant by "ministry of the word," history indicates that there has always been in all the various Christian traditions an acknowledgment that a certain primacy attaches to the preaching and explanation of the word of God. At the same time, history shows us that there is a recurring alternation between periods when the ministry of the word becomes perfunctory and falls into neglect and periods of reforming reaction against such neglect. The mid-twentieth century saw the flowering of just such a movement to vitalize the ministry of the word. However, two factors may make this most recent evangelical awakening distinctive. First of all, it has been stimulated by the technical biblical studies of the past century or so, and so combines scholarly depth with popular awakening. Secondly, it coincides with the development of a new rapport between Christianity and "secularization."

The more that technical and popular studies treated "the word of God," the more it became apparent that some basic clarification was needed: What precisely is this "word of God" which Christians hope to discover and then communicate? To quite an extent, the widespread usage of the past had assumed an identity between the Bible and the word of God; most of the Reformation and post-Reformation controversies about the scope of Christian ministry had worked on this assumption. Yet, our more recent attempts to explain the manner in which the Scriptures nurture Christian faith and life, the manner in which this scriptural word of God works as a re-

deeming influence in human history, have forced us to abandon the simple equivalence of the Bible and the word of God.

Since it is obvious that words can operate as words only when there is some process of actual communication between persons, the text of the Bible by itself cannot be word of God; it can function as word only when it is being used to convey some understanding to a believing individual or community. In any such context of actual communication, the insight into God and the world and the believer himself that the Bible can give is conditioned by the already present consciousness and experience of the person who hears the scriptural word. Unless that consciousness and experience had already spoken about "God," at least in some implicit fashion, a basic receptiveness to the scriptural words as word of God would be impossible. Somehow human experience and Bible together form "word of God."

Clearly, the issue is not nearly that simple; anyone familiar with the extensive scholarly writing about "history as revelation," about hermeneutics, about revelation as a continuing historical process knows the complexity of this matter. Yet, if one draws from the soteriological stance that we sketched in part one, it does seem possible to present a coherent explanation that takes account of the principal conclusions of modern research and reflection. The basic principle is that God reveals himself progressively throughout history and precisely in the historical process. The notion that somehow Christian revelation stopped with the end of the apostolic period must be corrected. Revelation being a matter of divine self-revelation to the consciousness of humans, it is obvious that it is in the conscious experience of humans as the historical evolution of man takes place that the revelation occurs. Moreover, if one takes seriously the Christian belief in the universal providential governance of God, the life experience of all humans be they formal believers or not is part of this revealing process, though a fuller divine self-communication is possible in the context of formal religious faith.

One can then understand by the "word of God" that revealing word-event which is mankind in its historical evolution towards the eschaton. But to view this unfolding of human experience as revelation one must, of course, have belief in some kind of personal presence to men of a self-giving God, a presence that at least implicitly challenges men to view themselves and all reality with new insight. Since the meaning that life's experience is meant to reveal to us is obscure and ambiguous if we have nothing but that experience to guide our understanding, a special revelation is given us in the Christ-event and prior to that in the event that is Old Testament Israel. Because it transmits to us that word of God which was the faith-filled historical experience of Israel and primitive Christianity, the Bible can throw light on that word of God which is our own experience; as a matter of fact, because it interprets and therefore alters this experience, it becomes an intrinsic element in this present-day word, but it does so according to the way it is understood.

This implies that the "word of God" is a continuing divine self-revelation. Like any process of communication that is enduring and progressive, the word of God to man is characterized by both continuity and discontinuity. There is basic constancy in the "divine message," but this is the constancy of personal fidelity not the constancy of unchanging formulations; there is a pattern to "providence" which is reflected in the biblical theme of promise-and-fulfillment, yet this is not a question of eternal divine ideas or of a predestined blueprint. There is also basic

and genuine evolution in human affairs, and the unexpectedness of the future means also that the word of God possesses always a character of radical "newness." Our human capacity to grasp and appropriate the word that God speaks to us can (and hopefully does) develop as history progresses and so the extent of communication from God to men can grow. But there is something more than this. Within the word of God itself there is growth and change; God does not keep on saying exactly the same thing over and over.

If this last point be true, it has considerable importance for the ministry of the word. It implies that changes in the ministry of the word should never be just expedient adjustment to circumstances; rather, they should be the result of listening to the divine presence in a given situation. Prudential judgment, theological reasoning, and historical tradition should all guide the actual exercise of the ministry of the word, but they cannot substitute for the discernment of the Spirit's action in men's lives, that action which speaks creatively of the gradual "filiation" of men and their world.

However, if the entire course of mankind's historical evolution is the basic word-event in which the divine reveals itself to men, then (for Christians) the unique word-event which reveals the meaning of everything else is Jesus of Nazareth in his historical experience and death and resurrection. He is the incarnation of God's own proper Word; he is God speaking humanly by being humanly. Everything Jesus is and does as man, and preeminently his death and resurrection, *speaks* the saving presence of God among men and provides the key to understanding the entire mystery of salvation as it stretches through human history. Thus, Christian theology of salvation cannot avoid being strongly evangelical; that is, Christian soteriology must be basically a theology of the word of God. At the same time, because it is the very reality of Jesus as a man that both makes God uniquely present and proclaims that presence, Jesus is in the truest sense the unparalleled sacrament of God. "He who sees me, sees the Father."

In trying to give some clarification of the manner in which Jesus, the incarnated Word, speaks salvifically to men, Christian theology has tended to stress either the "external" action in which Jesus by his teaching and actions functions as the ideal which Christians can follow or the "internal" action in which Jesus functions as the "inner light" to illumine men's minds and to give them an insight into truth. Actually, both elements must be respected and subjected to reflective study. For Christians, Jesus (in both his historical life and in his resurrection) epitomizes in himself the new law and the ultimate revelation of the divine; but he also works in the depths of men's believing consciousness, sharing in mysterious fashion his own understanding of the divine by communicating to them his own Spirit of sonship.

One can see this complex function of the risen Christ as realizing in transcendent fashion many of the elements that have traditionally been associated with "priesthood." There is a most profound kind of acknowledgment of and witness to God, i.e., authentic *worship*; there is clearly a *mediation* and *reconciliation* between the divine and the human, which finds its culminating expression in men and God sharing a common Spirit; there is an announcing of God's great deeds in a context of special presence, i.e., the *oracular* role of priesthood. But the priesthood Jesus exercises is radically prophetic; it cannot be otherwise, for he is Word, and the entire finality of the Incarnation (which is another way of denominating the priestly mission of Jesus) is that Word *as such* be enfleshed.

In the Christian community the mystery of Jesus as sacrament of the divine saving presence is taken a step further, because this community of believers is the body of Christ. Just as for each of us, the bodily aspect of our humanness situates us in space, provides organs of communication, gives externalization and expression to our personal conscious existing, and thus makes presence to one another and human community possible, so in analogous fashion the church provides that location in space and time, that external

manifestation, those organs of communication, which enable the risen Christ to be present to men and to fashion with them a unique divine-human community.

It is the entire being of the Christian community which is, then, a word of witness to the presence of Christ and of the Father in their Spirit. But the being of the church must be manifested by what the church does, and the prophetic dimension of the church's being must, obviously, be manifested primarily by what the church says. Among the words the church speaks "for God," giving utterance to the prophetic Spirit which animates it, the word of Scripture enjoys a privileged position. While the Spirit of Christ finds expression in all the words of the church, the word of Scripture is specially "inspired"; it enjoys special status as "word of God." This is what Christianity has always believed about the Bible; but it is much more difficult to explain just what this special character of Scripture is.

Certainly, the revelatory function of the scriptural word is secondary or derivative in the sense that it formulates and expresses that faith experience (of primitive Christianity and of Israel before it) in which most basically the divine self-communication occurs. It was the experience of Jesus and of themselves as believers in the risen Christ that was the basic "word of God" to the first generation of Christians, and it is this initial Christian experience that has spoken in normative fashion to all later Christians. In a sense there is a parallel between the originating experience of Christianity and the initiating prophetic experience of an Isaiah or a Jeremiah. It constitutes a radical "intrusion" of God into human consciousness, granting an initial gift of grace and insight which contains potentially the entire vocation of that group or individual. So, Christianity goes back incessantly to that first stage of its mission, to that first definitive and somehow all-embracing moment of grace, to understand what it is that it has become, whether it has been faithful to or negligent of that divine call, and to what it is still being called. In its use of

Scripture the church speaks again to itself the words it used in giving inspired utterance to its first awakening to the grace of Christ; in so doing, it is awakened again, inspired again, renewed in faith and hope, because the indwelling Spirit still speaks through those words.

Both by theological reasoning and from historical experience we can testify to the community-forming power of the Bible. Historically, the Scriptures, when faithfully and carefully utilized by Christians, have been a privileged instrument for nurturing both faith and charity. Historic monasticism with its insistence on the regular *lectio divina* as the foundation for prayer and evangelical revivals with their stress on an appreciative return to Scripture as the font of effective preaching are but two of the examples of how deepened Christian community resulted from exposing faith to Scripture. Every important movement of spiritual renewal in the church's history has involved a "return to Scripture."

This power of the Bible can, though erroneously, be viewed in a somewhat magical light as if there dwelt in the very text an effectiveness that worked automatically when the text was read or heard. In actuality, the notion of *"ex opere operato"* must be applied as carefully to Scripture as to sacramental liturgies. In both instances the key notion is "sacramental." The Bible is not an autonomous spiritual force but rather part of that mystery of presence by which God reveals himself in Jesus Christ, his Word, and in that community of faith which as the Body and Sacrament of Christ continues to speak prophetically the presence of this incarnate Word. The Scriptures exist as saving word of God when and because they are spoken by the Spirit-filled believing community and are therefore word of Christ who is sacramentally operative through that community.

Scripture and liturgical ceremony form, then, one conjoined reality of the church giving expression to its own sacramental function of making Christ redemptively present to men and women throughout history. The ritual actions that have come to be named "sacra-

ments" because they speak in special fashion of the mystery of Christ continuing to transform human experience by his death and resurrection are "word of God" in the fullest sense. Moreover, in these sacramental actions, which of their very nature are "enacted words," the spoken word has always been seen to play the key role. It is the spoken word that specifies the precise significance (i.e., sacramentality) that the action is meant to bear, and so it is the spoken words that have traditionally been called the "form" of the sacrament. Yet, the words of sacramental ritual are much more than clarification; they are words of power, words of "ontological command." And the reason for this is that they are sacramental word; they are the word of the risen Christ who, because he is the creator Word incarnated, cannot speak other than with creative effectiveness.

Scripture and sacramental ritual do not exhaust the church's mediation of the word of God, for the Christian community's very existence among men is an essential part of this word. By its faith, this community establishes a privileged matrix for the revealing presence of God; by bearing witness to this faith, the community performs an irreplaceable oracular function. Concomitantly, the love for their fellow humans which Christians express in their devoted service to all men and women is sacramental word in which God's own saving love is made present. One can distinguish, for purposes of more accurate analysis, the *prophetic, diakonal,* and *cultic* aspects of the church's role; in reality they coincide.

The Objectives of Ministry of the Word

One of the striking features in the history of Christian ministry is the persistent stress on the primacy of "ministry of the word." Even when such verbal insistence was not translated into dedicated practice of this ministry, the criticism and cries for reform reflected the recognition that this ministry was basic to the well-being and mission of Christianity. More specifically, even when a large portion of the episcopacy had been distracted by other activities from actual involvement in preaching and teaching, theological and official explanations of the episcopal role still mention the ministry of the word as basic to the bishop's task. Given this undeviating insistence on the importance of the ministry of the word, it would be good to determine the purpose that Christian ministry of word is meant to achieve so we can better see how it should be exercised in today's world.

"Ministry of the word" can refer, of course, to the Christian community's communication of the word of God to non-Christians or to the sharing of that word within the Christian church. The first of these two is in a sense more ultimate, since the Christian community has been given the gospel in order to preach it to "every creature." Obviously, there is need to foster the community's understanding of God's word, so that its own corporate faith deepens and so that the individual faithful enter more deeply into the Christ-mystery. But even this internal development of the church is directed towards more effective implementation of the church's mission of witnessing to the gospel of the risen Christ.

Formal evangelization is the most evident aspect of this mission. Such explicit proclamation of the "good news" that salvation from evil and death has come in Jesus' own death and resurrection has been the task of the Christian apostle from the earliest decades of Christianity. And the obvious purpose of such evangelization is to let all men know about salvation in Christ, so that they will be led to faith in and union with this Christ. Those who do come to faith through such preaching of the gospel will by that very fact become part of the community of believers. But winning new members to the church's ranks is not the ultimate purpose of that preaching; the church is meant to win men and women for Christ and not for itself. This might seem to be an unnecessary and subtle distinction, but history teaches us that it is of great importance in preserving the true perspective in the church's apostolic endeavors.

When Christian apostles bring the gospel to a group of men and women who have had no previous contact with Christianity, it is very often (as a matter of fact, almost always) impossible to speak immediately about the mystery of God's revelation in Christ Jesus. Christian revelation is of its very nature a "transignification," an injection of new meaning into the historical experience of men and women, and so a certain level of true understanding of and reaction to this basic experience is required before the gospel can be heard for what it is. Recent study in missiology and catechetics has drawn attention to this preliminary stage of basic social and cultural preparation for the gospel, and the term "preevangelization" has become a common way of referring to activity preparatory to actual preaching of the gospel.

No matter what term one uses to describe it, it is clear that the Christian "apostle" must address himself in a given situation to the values and points of view and attitudes and beliefs which people already possess and which open or close them to hearing the gospel. It may well be that the situation is such that the confrontation with this already present human "wisdom" will last throughout the apostle's lifetime and that the formal preaching of the gospel will have to wait for his successors. Even when the situation is such that formal evangelization can appropriately and fruitfully take place, the task of preevangelization is never finished. Though a given group of people be quite thoroughly converted to faith in the death and resurrection of Jesus, there remain always elements in their motivations and outlook on life which hinder a completely honest listening to the paradoxical wisdom of the Christian message. And so the tasks of evangelization and preevangelization must continue together and reinforce one another.

What this means in practice is that any contribution to the evolution of authentic human wisdom is a contribution to that "transignified" insight into human existence which is genuine Christian faith. Thus, the task of preevangelization can be accomplished by dedicated Christians who are conscious that their efforts to advance human culture are part of that task; but it can also be accomplished quite effectively by devoted "humanists" who have neither knowledge of the gospel nor desire to serve it. It is in this arena that a crucial and thoroughly genuine common effort can unite Christians with all those men and women who seek the advance of human understanding and freedom. The Christian's participation in this common effort can be his formally Christian "apostolate," though he never speaks in formally Christian language and never acts through formally Christian structures.

When one turns from the Christian community's ministry of bringing the word of God to the world, and concentrates on that ministry of the word which must take place within the community, he sees that essentially the same tasks must be performed, though at a somewhat more advanced stage. No matter how long Christianity exists and flourishes in a given situation, there is always need for a continuing effort that combines preevangelization, evangelization, and catechesis. There are always some outlooks and prejudices and goals that are inimical to Christian wisdom but that Christians still cherish and from which they need to be converted; there is always need to preach the gospel to Christians, so that their faith is challenged to correspond ever more honestly to the word that God is actually speaking in Christ; there is always need to provide instruction about the intrinsic meaning and contemporary relevance of Christian faith, so that belief be more accurate and realistic.

Without addressing ourselves for the moment to the question whether specially designated (ordained) ministry or ministries is required, it seems clear that there is large-scale and multifaceted need for ministry of the word within the Christian church itself. Moreover, this ministry has both individual and corporate dimensions. There is need to form the individual Christians in a faith that is basically a personal involvement in the Christ-mystery, and therefore "subjective" in the truest sense of that term. There is also the need to foster a genuine community in

faith, which implies some form of "objective" expressions of faith that can provide means of communicating faith and norms for safeguarding the accuracy of the individuals' faith. Certainly there has been, and perhaps must always be, a tension between these two poles. It is part of the tension between "charismatic" and "structured" to which Paul's first letter to the Corinthians already bears witness. But the tension need not be antagonism; it can be creative challenge in both directions, with individual faith experience keeping the external expression from becoming static and empty, and the external expressions keeping the individual faith from becoming isolated and drifting into religious fantasy.

Ministry to the faith of individuals in the church must unquestionably be much more than imparting information about Christian doctrines and practices. It must consciously foster genuine human freedom and mature capacity to make the moral judgments that apply Christian insights to a given set of circumstances. In one way or another, the ministry of the word within the church has conversion as an objective, but this in no way implies that preaching and teaching are to be moralizing exhortation, because the desired kind of conversion is that organic evolution of motivations and decisions that grows out of deepening insights into the Christian implications of one's own life experience. As far as is possible at a given stage of history, the ministry of the word in the church, and very specifically that function which has been called the *"magisterium,"* must avoid the temptation to tell Christians what detailed course of action is "the will of God," for such a course of ministerial activity tends to deprive people of their own right and responsibility to make mature decisions and it tends to reduce the gospel and the action of the Spirit to legislation.

Much as human freedom and the right to gain maturity must be respected, there is also need to face realistically the fact that men and women are often less than mature and that they abuse their freedom. And so the ministry of the word must take account of the mystery of sin. Though the church is Spirit-filled it is still a church of sinners. In this context, the ministry of the word is directed to healing sin not only in the immediately apparent sense of preaching conversion from sin but also in the much more complex sense of communicating those insights and attitudes which can dispel or counteract the ignorance and prejudice and errors and fears which are both the ground and the residue of people's sins. One of the most important moments in this process of healing Christians' moral evils is that of presenting them inescapably with the fact of their sinfulness. The ministry of the word must do this both on the individual level and on the corporate level: there is negation of love on the part of individual Christians, there is negation of love on the part of communities (including the church); both negations are opposed to the gospel's command of love and should be challenged by that command. It should be remembered, however, that love itself is the only ultimately effective challenge to denial of love; it is God's own word of love in the risen Christ and his Spirit that overcomes evil (which is most radically the denial of love), and authentic Christian ministry of the word must concentrate on ministering to this divine word of love rather than on denunciatory sermonizing or fear-inducing teaching.

Since the gospel which Christianity proclaims is basically the risen Christ himself, God's own Word to men incarnated, Christian ministry of the word is ordered fundamentally to discipleship. Throughout the history of theological discussion about the ministry of the word one finds the axiom that Christ himself is *the* teacher of men and women, and that response to the gospel means to become his disciple. Whatever forms, then, the ministry of the word may take in the church, it must somehow bring about that encounter between the believer and Christ's own magisterial activity which will nurture this master-disciple relationship. Master-disciple relationships there may well be among Christians themselves, as in varying circumstances some proclaim the word and others

hear it; but all such relationships are meant to be sacramental of the more ultimate master-disciple relation between Christ and the hearer of the word. There is an abiding truth to the gospel dictum "Call no man master," a truth which the minister of the word must always respect.

Though "mystery" in its Christian usage (also in its Old Testament usage) means "that which has been revealed" and not "that which has been hidden," the revelation of God in Jesus Christ is so profound and rich in implication that the entire historical experience of mankind will not suffice to explain it. For this reason, the Christian church has an unending task of reflecting upon the word that God speaks to men and of then clarifying a bit further the understanding that Christians have of this word. This means that teaching is an intrinsic and enduring need of that faith community which is the church. The aim of such teaching is personal understanding of and relationship to Christ and the Father; the aim cannot be a submission to church formulations, whether doctrinal or legal, valuable though these may at times be. Authentic Christian teaching is an increasing initiation into an experience of mystery, the mystery of one's own life being united with the life of the risen Christ in response to divine love.

Genuine Christian faith can neither originate nor grow in isolation; its genesis and development must come in a community of believers. Fostering such a community in faith must, then, be a goal of the church's intrinsic ministry of the word. This community (and it might be good to note that "community" should be understood with emphasis on the action of "sharing a common faith" rather than on the structured group) has both a geographical and a historical character. There must be a community among Christian believers throughout the world at any given time, and there must be a community of faith from one historical period to another. Somehow, there must be a "common word," one gospel, that is heard by believers throughout space and time and that acts to bring about their unity in faith. Obviously, the one word that is capable of achieving this is God's own Word, the risen Christ; but the difficulty comes in "enabling" the faith encounter between this risen Christ and the individuals who comprise the church. Such an enabling is the purpose of preaching and teaching within the church, and the need for effective ministry of the word grows more acute as the church grows larger and more dependent upon such activities to nurture a living community of faith.

Maintaining an essential continuity in faith and life from one Christian generation to the next is without question necessary if the Christian community is to preserve its identity throughout history. So, there has never really been much dispute about the fact that "apostolic tradition" must be preserved. The disputes have arisen over the meaning of this "apostolic tradition." Is it equivalent with the New Testament Scriptures? Or are there unwritten traditions that have been transmitted through other media? What are the limits within which an evolution of the primitive apostolic teaching can occur? etc. . . . Certainly, if one wishes to keep a basic community in faith with the earliest Christians, the nuclear elements of their belief must still be present in his own faith, though he live centuries later. At the same time, there is an unavoidable dialectic between these nuclear elements of traditional faith and the ever changing historical developments that make each generation's Christian experience a new thing. For this reason, it is hopeless to ground the continuity of Christian faith and tradition on so-called traditional formulations or institutions. Even the Scripture itself as a written document is incapable of safeguarding the true continuity of Christian faith. Were Christianity ever to become simply a "religion of the book" it would lose that eschatological openness to new life which is at the very heart of its faith. Indeed, what is normative for later centuries of Christian faith is primitive Christianity's unique experience of faith; that experience is the word through which the Christ-event is spoken. All genuine Christian experience is a word to other believers, but the experience of Jesus' death and resurrection possessed by his earliest disciples was unrepeatable in its immediacy. It was an initiation into the death and resurrection of Christ by way of historical experience; it was not, as all later Christian faith must be, an initiation by way of sacramental symbol. For that reason, it is normative for the understanding of all such later sacramental initiation. To preserve an essential community of experience between the apostolic generation and a group of Christians living centuries later in an utterly different cultural milieu may demand in the later community a linguistic or liturgical formulation that would have been almost totally alien to Jesus' immediate followers. No one will question the delicacy and danger of this adaptation of Christian faith to divergent cultural contexts; it is one of the most critical tasks in the ministry of the word. Yet, it is unavoidable. Not to do this is gradually to empty the meaning out of doctrinal and institutional and liturgical formulations.

All ministry of the word within the church should be directed to the goal of forming community in faith. Yet, views can differ as to what such community is and how it is to be achieved, and so tensions, even bitter disputes, develop among Christians dedicated to this same goal. One such tension that seems built-in is that between individual insight (be it prophetic, theological, or mystic) and institutionalized formulation. The first stresses life and fears ossification of faith; the second stresses stability and fears chaos. And so they both ask, How can we foster individual freedom in faith and still avoid heresy?—which may well be the wrong question. It is not a question of the limits of Christian freedom but rather a question of the truth or falsity of what claim to be charismatic understandings. There are no limits to Christian freedom of thought as long as one preserves fidelity to truth. Unfortunately, innovative Christian theologians have frequently been charged with "doctrinal disloyalty," which at times was not very carefully distinguished from "heresy," because their views were upsetting. But the real issue at stake was the truth or falsity of their views; it was on this that judgment should have been clearly passed and until that issue was clarified, it was unjust to burden them with vague charges of "disloyalty" and give the impression that they were divisive of Christian community. It is more than possible that the new though disturbing insights' they transmitted were the very means of renewing vital Christian community in faith, something not really new in the prophetic tradition.

The Various Ministries of the Word

One thing is perfectly clear from what we have been saying. The goals of Christian ministry of the word are broad and diverse. Moreover, the more one ponders the history of the past two millennia of Christian faith and life the more it seems that we must once more honor a multiplicity of distinct and autonomous ministries. After all, because the Christian community as a whole is prophetic and sacramental, its entire existence is a ministry of the word. Yet, as is true of all complicated living realities, it must maintain and express its life force and activity through a multiplicity of distinct but interacting organs.

As we will see, the various ministries of the word overlap and depend upon one another; but no one ministry (for example, the pastoral/episcopal) includes all the others. If one adopts a monarchical "model" for thinking about the Christian community, a model in which the absolute ruler is everything in society preeminently, then an absorption of all ministries of the word into one office can seem logical. Actually, this is what did happen historically. However, the use of this monarchical model is highly questionable, not because we should substitute for it a "democratic" model, and therefore decentralize by dispersing roles and responsibilities, but because any understanding of Christianity by means of a political model is questionable. Certainly the New Testament literature would suggest that an "organic" model is much less misleading; some New Testament passages as well as theological reflection indi-

cate that authentic Eucharistic experience may provide the most ultimate model available to us.

Instead of giving some monarchical priority to one ministry (the episcopacy) and viewing it as the source of all other ministry of the word, it seems more accurate to grant such "fullness of power" to the community as a whole, and obviously, in a more ultimate sense, to the Spirit of Christ that animates this community. Rather than thinking of the church originating from the Spirit dwelling in the episcopacy, it seems more accurate to think of the episcopacy as a functional expression of the community's Spirit-filled life; thus, in that subtle imaging which controls our thinking about the church, we will reinsert the episcopacy (and *mutatis mutandis* the rest of the clergy) into the community instead of having them occupy some mediational status halfway between God and the church. This is not to deny a proper mediational function to the episcopacy, but it is one of many such functions, all of which are elements of that immanent activity by which the community preserves and nurtures its own life. It is the community that is primary; it is the community that is the Body of Christ that lives by faith in him; it is the community that has the basic prophetic responsibility of safeguarding and living and communicating the gospel; "tradition" is a process that involves the whole corporate life of the church and the lives of all its individual members.

At least to some extent, the loss of an understanding of this ministerial primacy of the Christian community as a whole was linked with the growth and worldwide expansion of the church. Before long, practical considerations dictated a transfer of responsibility and authority to a "ruling group," and the primacy of responsibility for the community's well-being was seen to abide in an office (the episcopacy) that was given directly by God for the sake of the church. This view, quite different from one which sees the episcopacy as a charismatic expression of the Spirit-filled community, played a major role in setting the clergy in general, and the episcopacy in particular, over against the other members of the church.

It may well be that such a development, during a historical period when the media of communications were quite limited, was needed to safeguard the indefectibility of the worldwide church. Today, however, there are many indications that we can and should reinstate the local Christian community as the basic effective unit for ministry of the word. Theologically it is quite clear that all the members of this local community share the responsibility of prophetic witness by word and example to one another and to their fellow men. On the smaller scale of this local scene, it is feasible to think of all the members sharing in this ministry of the word. Logically, as circumstances demand it, certain individuals will more appropriately undertake particular aspects of this ministry. They will do so by virtue of the Spirit's "urging," an urging that the community discerns to be consonant with its faith and therefore a genuine function of its corporate life. The faith and hope and charity of the community will continuously provide support and guidance for the designated minister as he carries out his specialized function.

To advocate such a reemphasis on the local community and to recognize that any community of Christians possesses a large measure of autonomy in its shared life of faith is not to suggest that the local community should develop in isolation from "the great church." Rather, it is to view that worldwide church as a community of communities. Moreover, it is to take seriously the prophetic priesthood of the Christian people, a priesthood that is to be understood corporately, and to recognize that the corporate experience and corporate exercise of this priesthood can occur (with rare exceptions) only on a local level. (By way of parenthesis, we might remark that "local" in this present discussion should not be understood in too narrow a geographical sense. Geographical proximity will still play a major part in human grouping for the foreseeable future, but the increased mobility which has so notably altered the dynamics of human communities in general will unquestionably have its impact on the establishment of Christian communities.)

Having made these preliminary remarks, we can now begin to examine in detail the various ministries of the word, keeping in mind that they not only complement one another but overlap, and that it is altogether possible for one man or woman to be involved in more than one of these ministries. Certainly, in a community that exists because of shared faith in an event, one of the key ministries must be that of witness. The entire community, since it is itself part of the event of God's salvation in Christ, witnesses to God's saving love. The community's very existence is a revelation of the divine self-giving, for the Spirit of prophecy in the community is the most basic witness to the risen Christ and to the fidelity of the Father. In sending this Spirit into the church, Christ himself continues to bear witness. Every Christian shares in this basic witness, by his life and particularly by his death and passage into new life, and if he should be put to death because of his Christian faith, his dying would participate eminently in Christ's own witness. Significantly, martyrdom, which was the original ideal of Christian existence, was open to all Christians and because of this radical egalitarianism it acted as a unifying ideal; on the contrary the "ascetic" ideal which for the most part replaced it has been a divisive force in the church.

Martyrdom is profoundly evangelical, for it proclaims the mystery of death and resurrection as nothing else can. However, Christian life as well as Christian death is meant to bear witness to the transforming power of Christ's Passover; the witness of truly Christian behavior, of "good example," belongs to every member of the church. Each Christian should from observing the lives of his fellow Christians be able to obtain insights into his own Christian life and guidance for his own Christian decisions. Most importantly, each Christian is meant to share with others his own faith in Christ; he is meant to let them know that he believes and what it means for him to believe. Obviously the manner and extent of such intimately personal witness will depend upon the relationship one bears to other members of the community; but such witness in faith to Christ is at the very heart of Christian community. It *is* "Christian community" understood in the active sense. In speaking of the prophetic witness of Christian life, it might be good to insist that no specific life-style can lay claim (as both the clerical and ascetic life-styles have) to being *the* exemplar of Christian behavior. It is certainly true that leadership within the community entails the witness of truly Christian living, but it has been a mistake to link leadership in the church too closely to possession of official status.

All we have said so far indicates that the ministry of witness is shared by all in the church. But is there, in addition, a more specialized witness that requires the existence of a recognized group of witnesses? The answer seems to be clearly affirmative, because the individual local communities need to be linked with the other communities that are separated from them geographically and with those other communities that are separated from them in time. Someone or some group must be in the position to witness to a given local community the faith of "the great church" today (and vice versa) and to witness to the essential continuity of faith over the centuries (i.e., to the apostolic tradition). Because they are in this "link" position, unifying the communities into "the great church," those who perform this function must do so collegially. In unique fashion they should share their faith with one another, so that each can bear witness in his own community to this communal faith and so that each can enrich this communal faith with the particular insights of his own community. Besides, as history proceeds and new members replace those who have died, these new members can be initiated into the collegial faith of this group of special witnesses, and can share in the collegial function of passing on that witness to Christ's death and resurrection that began with the Twelve. This group of Chris-

tians, as a corporate entity, embody and sacramentalize within the church the presence of the apostolic testimony to the Christ-event.

Almost indistinguishable from the function of witness is that of prophet. This is particularly true when one is speaking of the Christian community as a whole, for this entire community is prophetic and it exercises its prophetic role by bearing witness to its risen Lord. However, within this general prophetism and for its sake there exists a special charism of prophecy. Charismatic prophecy is not restricted to Old Testament times; though we have largely lost sight of the fact, prophecy reaches its fulfillment in Christ and in the Christian period of history. Genuine prophets there have been, there are, and there will be in the church. The problem the Christian community always faces is to discover and nurture them, to distinguish the genuine from the false, to accept them despite the challenge they always present. In our own day there is a critical need to reinstate the prophetic voice in the counsels of the church, but to do this, we must understand more accurately what Christian prophetism is, and here the theologian can be a support to the authentic prophet.

Certainly, one of the elements in the prophetic charism is the ability to discern the movement of Christ's Spirit in the community and beyond that in the rest of mankind. To discover the impulse of the Spirit, to distinguish it from other "spirits" that move men's minds and hearts, to interiorize that Spirit as the very nucleus of its life of faith, is basic to Christian existence. It is as basic as hearing the word of God, for "word" and "spirit" are distinct but inseparable manifestations of God. The special prophetic gift involves, then, increased sensitivity to the Spirit's impulse, an increased awareness of which courses of Christian action resonate compatibly with that Spirit and which actions do not.

The prophet is able to say to the community, "It seems good to the Spirit. . . ." Though he is not the recipient of foreknowledge about the future nor able to make clear and infallible predictions, the genuine prophet can bear witness to the Spirit's "message" to the community about the manner in which that future should be fashioned; he can give guidance for the community as it faces decisions. To quite an extent, the role of the prophet and the role of the true contemplative overlap: the true contemplative possesses that more profound insight into "the mind of Christ" which allows him or her to speak for Christ to others in the community. However, the prophetic charism does seem to have an element that is not necessarily found in the contemplative: the irresistible drive to proclaim the word given to him. The authentic prophetic gift involves a special ability to grasp not just the inner meaning but the here-and-now applicability of the gospel. This explains at least part of the prophet's traditional unpopularity with certain segments of the community. He is action-oriented; he is not content with theoretical acceptance of his insights. His prophetic impulse demands that these insights be translated into decision and action. The heart of the prophetic message is always "Convert!"

Yet, as one tries to ponder the lesson of Christian history, the relation between the "prophetic" and the "contemplative" vocations seems ambiguous, perhaps because it is intrinsically so, perhaps because extraneous factors have clouded the reality of one or the other. At least to some extent, prophetism was replaced by, or found expression in, the ascetic movement. It was assumed that the ascetic, having broken with the spirit-clouding entanglements of ordinary human existence and become thoroughly detached from emotional involvements and cares about "the world" was therefore closer to God, more capable of spiritual vision, more filled with the Spirit, and therefore able to guide the community along lines of genuinely Christian behavior.

Undoubtedly, there is much truth in this assumption; a large measure of detachment is needed to make decisions that are faithful and hopeful, genuine discipline of spirit is required to continue the work of creating a world by bringing order out of chaos. But "Christian detachment" is freedom of spirit in the midst of involvement with life. The discipline proper to Christian existence is that flowing from a mastering love of God and men. One cannot but ask of the classic ascetic tradition a most basic question: Is not advocacy of retreat from the "ordinary" life of Christians a denial of the basic sacramental character of creation and a denial of the special sacramental character of the church? By way of contrast, it is the function of the prophet to live detached in the midst of his people, sharing the same life experience that is theirs but set apart because in this experience he perceives and is overpowered by the word this experience speaks because of the sacramental presence of a revealing God.

Since the authentic prophet is specially possessed by the Spirit of Christ, no man or woman can arrogate to himself or herself the prophetic function, nor can the community of itself designate certain individuals and expect them to receive the special charism. The Spirit alone designates prophets, but the community does have the right and responsibility of judging those who claim to be prophets and of discerning the true from the false, and in so doing the community is itself guided by the Spirit. No set pattern can be devised for such discernment, but there are many things to suggest that "monasticism" or "religious life" (using those terms generically to refer to the enduring historical tendency of devoted Christians to group in communities) has as its most basic finality the safeguarding and fostering and evaluation of prophetic charism in the church. Not that prophetism is limited to such groups, but that their corporate insight and strength can nurture prophetism wherever it exists.

Few ministerial activities in the church illustrate better than does preaching the overlap of specialized ministries. The widespread need for competent preachers would suggest that not all preachers possess the specialized prophetic charism, though preaching is proper to the prophet and some measure of the prophetic gift would seem most appropriate to the preacher. However, preaching is itself a diversified activity; in some instances it converges more with the ministry of teaching, in other instances with the ministry of sacramental celebration. Clearly, the preaching of the homily in the Eucharistic celebration needs to be given special status, for it is an intrinsic part of the celebrant's role of proclaiming understandably the transforming word of the liturgical action. The celebrant's homily (or, if he shares it with others, his synthesizing of the homily) is meant to serve the word that any given liturgy should speak to the Christians who celebrate it. All preaching is ultimately directed to Eucharistic celebration, but preaching is limited neither to the occasion of liturgy nor to the content and style of the homily. There can be many other situations in which the faith of the community can be nourished by a proclamation of the gospel that is more didactic than the prophetic message but more prophetic than simple teaching. Such preaching needs to be directed to Christians and to non-Christians, according to the needs for preevangelization, evangelization, or catechesis. Its predominant purpose can be to inform, to exhort, to motivate, or to encourage; but none of these goals will be absent from genuine preaching.

Preaching, liturgical or extraliturgical, does not seem to be as patently or simply charismatic as prophecy. Even in the case of the preacher who clearly has the special prophetic charism and function, effective preaching involves a certain element of art, i.e., of humanly acquired proficiency. And in the case of the preacher who has no special prophetic endowment, insights gained from theological study and from reflective human experience can complement the basic prophetism of Christian faith and equip a person to nurture the faith of the community through preaching. Liturgical homilies as creations of the art of liturgical leadership (which we will examine later) would ideally be more rooted in prophetic charism, since liturgical leadership is ideally a prophetic function; practically they must depend a great deal upon the developed artistry of the homilist.

Who has the right and responsibility to preach? Bracketing for the moment the question of the liturgical homilist (since this is part of the question about the right to be liturgical celebrant), it would seem that any Christian who has the ability through clear insight, or deep conviction, or rhetorical persuasiveness to move a group of fellow Christians to more lucid and more personal faith has some right and some responsibility to do so. There is, certainly, a need for the community to provide "certification" for preachers, a certification that in many instances can be quite informal and implicit, so that talented demagogues do not preach "some other gospel." But this does not mean that preaching as such is linked with office or with any kind of jurisdictional authority.

In the very early church, one of the most prominent ministers was the apostle, whose function was that of transient pioneering as a herald of the gospel. His was the task of bringing communities of believers into existence by his proclamation of the gospel, of nurturing the earliest stages of their corporate existence, and of leading them to self-sustaining Christian life. Having then prepared the way for and perhaps even himself trained a resident and more permanent group of ministers, his task was finished. It could be debated whether this ministry, at least as a distinct reality, survived historically beyond the very early Christian centuries. Clearly, there has been a constantly recurring pattern of men going out to "mission lands" to begin the work of evangelization and to establish the church in yet another part of the world. However, in many instances at least, such activity often became a process of transplanting to a strange geographical setting the same Christian activity the missionary had known in his home country; his ministration would be essentially the same whether he was in the mission country or in his land of origin.

Without attempting any judgment on past practice, we can profitably reflect on what "apostle" as a distinct ministry could be in today's church. There still do remain some geographical areas in the world where no contact with Christianity has been made, and some "missionary" endeavor in these areas will be needed. However, the principal "mission field" for Christian apostles today and in the foreseeable future lies in frontier situations that are sociological and cultural and intellectual rather than geographical. Within any of the economically and technologically developed countries, where one can find millions of church-going Christians and large-scale institutional foundations of the church, there are uncounted millions (both inside and outside the church) who have never had the opportunity to hear the gospel. Moreover, in these same countries the basic patterns of economic and political and social behavior are quite untouched by the impact of Christianity. In the so-called third world the situation is quite different but no less divorced from deep Christian influence. As a result, there is need for a massive evangelizing, a preaching of the gospel that will have to be much different from anything in the past, for it must be directed to people and societies as they actually are with all the cultural pluralism and seething change and social upheaval that characterize today's world.

For several decades there has been an emerging consciousness in all the Christian churches that this situation demands something new, and that somehow the laity (i.e., the nonclergy) who are part of this turbulent world must be the point of contact and the instruments of evangelization. Undoubtedly, this long overdue recognition that a basic prophetic function belongs to the entire Christian people should be encouraged; but it may be a mistake to leave the sensitive task of evangelization to some vague ambiguous development called "the lay apostolate." For one thing, a most important distinction must be made between the task of evangelization (the formal preaching of the Christ-mystery) and the task of establishing the kingdom of God. Evangelization is for the sake of the kingdom, and the establishment of God's kingdom is a much broader endeavor that involves anything that contributes to the betterment of men and women as personal beings. No Christian is free of the responsibility to

seek the kingdom of God in all he does, but it may well be that formal evangelizing, if and when it is appropriate, requires Christians with a special charism and specialized preparation.

There are many indications that such "apostles" would perform an essential ministry in today's Christianity. Selected by a local community (on the basis of the person's capabilities and dedication) to proclaim the Christ-mystery in "frontier" situations, such as the communications media, or urban development, or the academic community, these persons would be supported (psychologically and financially) by the sending community and so enabled to devote themselves full-time to this task. Because of the delicacy of such evangelization—which must avoid any religious imperialism, which would need to combine genuine openness to the religious and cultural views of non-Christians with an insight into the unique values of Christianity, and which would need to adapt flexibly to evolving circumstances without compromising basic principles of faith—it would obviously demand special talents and training that was aimed specifically at the task to be undertaken. Like the apostolate of early Christianity this ministry would be intrinsically temporary and transient, even though a given "apostle" might spend his entire adult life in the same situation. Designation (ordination) for this apostolate would be task-oriented; it would not be initiation into a "clerical" group, and it would cease when the task was completed.

Actually, more and more of such apostolic ministry is being undertaken by dedicated Christians on a "private" basis, but it does not have the formal recognition and support that would give it stability and encourage new recruits. To reconstitute such an "apostolate" in the church would do much to break down the clergy/laity division, for it would be essential to the success of these apostles that they find total social identification with the Christian community from which they come and with the human community to which they are sent, that they be free from the temptation to introduce "official" Christian structures into the situation to which they are sent (if such structures are appropriate, they will emerge organically), and that they represent no human interests other than those of the people to whom they are sent.

History indicates clearly that the ministry of teaching has always been recognized as critically important to the vitality and continuity of Christianity; either it receives status as an autonomous ministry, as it did for a time in early Christianity and in certain later developments like Calvinism, or it is seen to be a primary element in the pastoral/episcopal function. No great reflection is required to see the need for continuous teaching on many levels. There must be widespread informal teaching (conversation among Christians, attitudes and practices learned in the family circle, liturgical arts, etc.), and there must be more structured forms of catechesis arranged by the local community or by agencies of "the great church."

Two basic questions must be answered if we are to decide whether teaching is a distinctive ministry: In what is a Christian's right (and responsibility) to teach grounded? Is there any teaching in the church whose authority derives from an office (such as the episcopacy)? Fundamentally, these are the same question, but for several reasons it might be helpful to confront the same issue from two slightly different perspectives. Like all teaching, teaching within the church about the meaning of Christianity must be grounded in and receive its authority from the possession of knowledge. Intellectual insight and understanding have their own authority; nothing can substitute for this and nothing else can intrinsically validate it. If a person possesses true knowledge about the Christ-mystery, and to the extent that he or she possesses such knowledge, that person can and should speak with authority in the community.

Christian teaching is distinctive, of course, in that all those who teach are meant to enable the risen Christ and his Spirit to form Christians' consciousness. Though the teacher can and should be a witness to his own faith at the same time that he teaches, there is a distinctive function that teaching fulfills consequent to witness. This is the function of clarifying the exact meaning of the revelation that has occurred in Christ, and the function of expanding and deepening people's understanding of this revelation. Since it is aimed at accurate knowledge of Christianity, teaching presumes such accuracy of understanding in the teacher. If such accuracy be absent no amount of religious or rhetorical skill or ecclesiastical power can supply for it.

Can there be, then, any activity of teaching in the church that derives its authority from ecclesiastical office? Taking "teaching" strictly, as distinct from witness, the answer to that question appears to be negative. Certainly other ministries (particularly the pastoral ministry, which we will examine in a moment) involve some teaching, but whatever element of authority attaches to such teaching is still grounded in the possession of knowledge. What needs to be stated unequivocally is that no one in the church *by virtue of possessing jurisdiction* has authority to teach or to pass judgment on the teaching of others. The notion of authoritative teaching, if by this one means that the truth of a person's teaching derives from his occupying some office, is basically false; it is a dangerous confusion of two very different kinds of authority.

When one looks carefully at developments within the Christian churches in the past few decades, it seems quite clear that we are already quite far advanced in reestablishing a distinct ministry of teaching. As interest in religious education has grown, and ordained clergy have been too few to provide for the demand, catechetical instruction has passed increasingly into nonclerical hands, even to some extent to nonclerical control, though the struggle for control is far from settled. Not only are increasing numbers of nonclerics receiving technical preparation for religious education, and then with differing degrees of autonomy engaging in this work, but many of these men and women have received community recognition as "accepted teachers," a recognition that bears definite resemblance to a commissioning (i.e., ordination) for a specific ministry. Historically and theologically it is not this development towards an autonomous ministry of teaching, a development that admittedly must be governed by the community's careful selection and training of teaching personnel, that needs to be justified; what needs to be justified, if it can be, is the amount and type of control exercised by church officials over religious education.

Closely related to teaching, to witness, to spiritual guidance, and to preaching, though distinct from all of them, is the ministry of theology. Theology itself is not a simple function. As a discipline of knowledge it does not have a single methodology, and consequently it has a multifaceted contribution to make to the Christian community's faith and life. Theology should, with all the scientific precision afforded by sociology, historical methodology, literary criticism, and other developed branches of scholarship, sharpen Christian understanding about the exact nature of the Christ-event. Theology at any given point in history must criticize the formulations (linguistic, liturgical, or institutional) of faith provided by earlier generations, since such formulations are inevitably inadequate and limited by cultural and historical context. But theology must also go beyond this and suggest alternate formulations that can complement, and to some extent correct, the statements of the past. This entails a cautious and constant demythologizing and remythologizing, which is not a denial or denigration of the past but an organic absorption of the past into an ever expanding corporate consciousness. In each age of the church's life, theology accomplishes this distinctive function by allowing Christian faith in all its traditional formulations and the prevalent human "wisdoms" of that age to interact dynamically in the thought life of theologians and so produce a "new" synthesis.

Though in more recent centuries it has been somewhat obscured, the consensus of theologians is a most important normative principle for the faith of the Christian community, precisely because it has the intrinsic authority of a corporately possessed and corporately monitored body of educated understanding. Like other scholarly procedures, theology has its basic principles of discovery and reasoning and insight, principles that any individual theologian must honor if he is to function responsibly; should he fail to do so he is subject (as are scholars in other disciplines of knowledge) to the professional criticism of his peers. This criticism is particularly important because only his scholarly peers can adequately judge the contribution made by a given theologian. It is not, however, the only norm against which theological thought must be judged. Since its starting point is the Christian faith of the community, authentic theological reflection must not negate the controlling insights of that faith. Put more positively, this means that living theology is part of the corporate life of Christian consciousness, and as such it must constantly interact with the various expressions of that consciousness—Scripture, sacramental liturgy, Christian service to the world, doctrinal formulations, Christian prayer, preaching. To remain intellectually alive and faithful to their role in the church, theologians must listen to the word of God as it is spoken to the Christian community to which they minister. It is their specific contribution to safeguard accuracy of understanding in the community's hearing of that word.

For completeness' sake, we might make brief reference to the function of writing. However, such literary expression of Christian faith would seem to be a modality of one of the other functions we have already discussed, prophecy or theology or teaching or witness. In the practical order, there is a clear need to discover and support those in the community who can write with skill and precision, for much of the thought life of the church is shaped by such writing. Moreover, the function of writing should here be understood in the broad sense of embracing all use of communications media, all literary or artistic forms that can translate and nurture the understandings and attitudes of the believing community.

No ministerial function in the community is more central, more complex, or more ultimate than that of liturgical celebrant. This flows from the fact that the church is of its essence a Eucharistic community. Later we will have occasion to reflect extensively on other aspects of this liturgical ministry, but within our present context of studying the ministry of the word it is appropriate to look at the liturgical celebrant as minister of the word. That he is such should be quite apparent. Once one has said that Christian liturgy is sacramental, it is clear that the ministry of the word is involved, since sacrament is a specially rich and effective form of word.

In discussing the sacramental ministry of the word, it is important to distinguish the experience of the sacrament itself from preparatory instruction about its meaning and from follow-up explanation about its implications. Both these latter two are important, and much of the "catechetical" impact of the sacramental action will depend upon them. But the sacramental experience itself is meant to make a unique and irreplaceable contribution to the growth of Christian understanding, precisely because it is *immediate experience* of the Christ-mystery being enacted. And it is within this reality of the sacramental liturgy acting as experienced event/word that there is a special function to be performed by a designated, publicly recognizable liturgical leader.

This liturgical leader ministers to the sacramental action, i.e., to the community as it celebrates in sign its Christian faith, by being a sacrament within a sacrament. Though he himself does not cease to act as a member of the assembled community and to be part of the corporate symbol which that community is, the celebrant sacramentalizes in special fashion the presence of the risen Christ *in his own sacerdotal action*. Because he is known by the assembled group of Christians to be a member of the ordained liturgical ministry, the celebrant symbolizes that corporate reality and through it "the great church." Thirdly, the celebrant symbolizes the unity in faith of the assembled Christians, and his words and actions are representative of that corporate faith. Thus the celebrant "speaks forth" Christ, the entire church, the corporate litur-

gical ministry, and the local community in its act of worship. The celebrant is a word, clarifying the experienced event of sacramental action, so that it can more effectively function as a word and so shape the community's faith.

Liturgical ministry is, then, a matter of shaping a community of faith and worship in the very act of worship. Obviously, the role of the celebrant is not to do the act of sacrament for the people, replacing their action by his own and thereby reducing them to spectators. Rather, the celebrant is to help bring into being, in the very act of corporate liturgical celebration, a living liturgical community. His ministry is to that community, understanding "community" in the active sense of "the sharing of faith." To accomplish this is difficult. It demands a real art of liturgical leadership; it involves not only the direction and integration provided by the homily but also the creation of a unifying atmosphere, the fostering of a sense of the reality of Christ's presence, and the sharing of the celebrant's own faith and hope with his Christian brothers and sisters.

Such a task requires training, because it is an art. But it also demands a charism, an endowment of the Spirit, and the charism in question overlaps to a great extent with the charism of prophecy. Since the liturgical celebrant as a special sacrament of the presence of the risen Christ speaks for Christ, functions *in persona Christi*, acts as Christ's vicar, he is clearly in a prophetic role. And just as the word of genuine prophecy is always effective and not merely didactic, so the words of liturgical celebration have power to vitalize faith and form community, a power that is rooted ultimately in the fact that the risen Christ who speaks through the celebrant is the creator Word incarnate. Selection and approval of liturgical celebrants by the community cannot, then, be a random and arbitrary matter; nor can ordination for this function be given to everyone who professes a genuine desire to exercise it. Essentially, the only legitimate procedure of a community in selecting, training, and designating (i.e., ordaining) liturgical ministers is to remain alert to the Spirit's selection of apt candidates, a selection that will be manifested through the grant to certain Christians of the requisite "charisms," the gifts of nature and grace that fit a person for this particular ministry in the church. Having discovered persons so endowed, the community can then enable them to acquire appropriate formation and then through ordination give that public recognition of their charismatic role which will enable them to act in the sacramental manner we described earlier. Only the Spirit can give the charisms in which functions like liturgical ministry are grounded, but we must be careful not to overlook the extent to which the Spirit in granting charisms to individuals works in and through the community as a whole.

There would seem to be, then, a number of ministries—prophecy, witness, teaching, theology, liturgical leadership, preaching—that are basic to the church's life and each of which has a certain autonomous identity. But if this is so, what is the role of the ministry of pastoral overseeing, the ministry which historically swallowed up all these other ministries and laid claim to being all of them in preeminent fashion? Put in slightly different words, this is the question of the origin, nature, and limits of the episcopacy. Is it a distinctive ministry existing in complementarity to the ministries we have described, or are all these other ministries only facets of the episcopal (pastoral) ministry and obtain some independent existence only as functions delegated by episcopacy?

In attempting some answer to this question, which is one of the most critical questions about Christian ministry, it helps to keep distinct four areas of activity: leadership, organization, administration, and service. Of these leadership is quite distinct from the other three because it does not point specifically to a certain function but rather to a much more general and subtle influence that some individuals exert upon a group. The distinction is perhaps of key importance in our present discussion, for it may help us clarify the position and role of the presbyterate. In the very

early church, *presbyteroi* denominated the corporate leadership of a community and did not refer to any specific ministerial function (much less to any office). Historically, the role of this corporate leadership of the community diminished and then vanished; and those referred to as *presbyteroi* became the episcopacy's delegates and assistants, so much so that the earlier role of the deacon as the bishop's assistant was rendered unnecessary and disappeared. This raises the question Is there not a need to reinstitute a recognized corporate leadership in the church (both locally and on the larger scale) that would somewhat resemble the primitive Christian presbyterate? This question emerged in the sixteenth century, received a partial response in some of the Reformation churches, but perhaps needs broader consideration today.

However, our principal purpose in mentioning the matter here (after having treated it more fully earlier) is to indicate that community leadership and presbyterate *as such* do not involve a ministry of the word though an individual presbyter might well under some other title have such ministry. And, apart from the obvious fact that any of the ministries of the word that we described is a service to the community, neither organization nor administration nor service (which may be elements in the function of "overseeing" the community) include intrinsically a ministry of the word. So, it would seem that episcopate, at least insofar as it is concerned with "governing," is not a ministry of the word.

Still, the historical tradition linking ministry of the word to the episcopate is too primitive and too persistent to be this easily dismissed. Actually, what seems to have happened is that the important ministry of collegial witness, beginning with the collegial witness of the Twelve and continuing historically through their collegial successors, became very early a ministry appropriated to the episcopacy. No matter how one wishes to relate (or not relate) the functions of *episkopein* and *martyrein*, the episcopate of the church has inherited historically the special witness role of the Twelve; some collegial continuation of this corporate apostolic witness seems an indispensable ministry of the word in the church.

It would be a mistake to limit "apostolic succession" to this episcopal college. The entire church bears the mark of "apostolicity"; the entire Christian community is the bearer of the apostolic tradition. Yet, there is a special role this episcopal college fills. It bears witness to the present community of faith within "the great church" and so binds to one another the local communities of believers. And it bears collegial testimony to the enduring historical presence of the apostolic witness within the church and to the church's fidelity to that witness. In this function the episcopal college stands in historical continuity with the Twelve's function of collegial witness to the death and resurrection of Jesus. To say this is not to say that the function of the Twelve was itself the forerunner of the "overseeing" function attached to the *episkopoi* of the early church and thereafter to the episcopacy; but it is to say that the collegial witness of the Twelve was substantively normative of primitive Christianity's faith, and that this normative function continues in the episcopacy and as far as we can see must continue in some such collegial witness. What does not seem to be necessary is that the group performing this special ministry of collegial witness be the group in charge of governing the social existence of the community.

Understandably, any role of "taking care of the Christian community," whether it is seen in terms of basic leadership or in terms of "office," will mean some involvement in teaching, either actual teaching or seeing to it that accurate and adequate teaching is provided. Thus, the pastoral office (whether the episcopacy or its equivalent in non-Catholic traditions) has always included religious teaching. What is important theologically is that the basic power or authority of such teaching and the basic pastoral right and responsibility to so teach are rooted in the "pastor's" possession of understanding and not in his possession of office or status within the community. There is no "grace of office" that provides the

pastor with correct theological insights to guide his teaching.

Even less can the "pastor" as such claim to exercise the ministry of theology. By virtue of its special witness within the community, the episcopal college can legitimately claim a certain normative role regarding theology; its collegial witness is one of the principles from which theology must proceed and to which its conclusions must essentially conform. But this does not mean that the episcopal college (or any of its individual members) can therefore claim theological expertise, or pass judgment on the methodological procedures of theologians.

Positively, the "pastor's" special ministry of the word consists in his being a link between the local community and other Christian communities. As a representative of the pastoral (episcopal) college's faith, which itself resonates with the faith of all the various communities, the pastor's faith witness is normative for his local community. The pastor, in his own faith, bears witness to the genuine faith of his own community, to the faith consensus of the pastoral (episcopal) college, and to the correspondence of these two. Thus, there is a particular appropriateness in such a pastor functioning as celebrant of sacramental liturgy, since he can aptly sacramentalize the faith of the celebrating local community and of "the great church." But there does not seem to be any particular appropriateness in joining the functions of "link" and "governor."

Historically and intrinsically the ministry of the word is associated with the good discipline of the Christian community, for it is God's word that is meant to direct Christian behavior, individual and corporate. And, in varying fashions and degrees, the maintenance of such discipline has been regarded as part of the pastoral (episcopal) function. If such responsibility for the community well-being does rest with the pastoral (episcopal) college, it is a delegated responsibility. The fundamental responsibility rests with the community as a whole and must ultimately be carried by the entire community. Basically, any attempt to overcome abuses of behavior within the community is a matter of fraternal correction, and fraternal correction is an obligation resting on all Christians, though it rests more heavily on those who have greater social influence within the community (the presbyterate?). Moreover, in authentic fraternal correction, it is the word of God (and not the conscience judgments of the "admonitor") that alone can pass judgment on any Christian's actions; fraternal correction seems to coincide with "witness." So, if there is a special ministry of the pastoral (episcopal) college to the discipline of the Christian community, it consists precisely in that group's collegial witness to the gospel.

Before we finish our discussion of the various ministries of the word, something needs to be said about revising the explanation of "magisterium," i.e., the normative teaching within the church. Probably the need to reconsider this idea applies more acutely to the Catholic tradition, but in one way or another it touches all the Christian churches. In the light of historical and theological reflection, there seems no justification for appropriating "magisterium" to one group or one ministerial function, even that of teaching. Instead, "magisterium" is the interaction of various kinds of teaching (prophecy, preaching, teaching, liturgical celebration, etc.), each of them normative in a somewhat different fashion. The entire Christian community shares in this magisterium, by the church's corporate reality as sacrament, and by individual members exercising one or more teaching functions. Thus, the classic division of members of the church into *docens* and *discens* (teachers and taught) needs to be revised: in various and complementary ways all members of the church are both *docens* and *discens*. The witness of the episcopal college teaches the entire community but so also does the experience of Christians living their faith in family and business and social involvement. The technical clarifications of theology must be listened to by bishop and factory laborer, but the theologian must himself learn from the Eucharistic liturgy that he celebrates along with bishop and factory worker. Everyone in the church must learn from all the others and must help form the faith of all the others.

In conclusion, it appears that "ministry of the word" is many ministries. Although they are intimately related and even overlap, no one ministry (specifically the episcopal/pastoral) is the source of the others. Rather, all of them flow from the basic prophetic and sacramental nature of the Christian community itself, that is, from the indwelling presence of the incarnated Word and of the Spirit. It is the people of God that is the revelation, the word of God; the various ministries we have described are organs by which this believing community nurtures and expresses its prophetic existence. Whatever need there is for a particular ministry of the word is rooted in a basic need of the community as word. This is the principle that must guide us today in our practical examination of ministry of the word.

Selected Bibliography

Ministry of the Word

A number of works cited below deal with ministry in a somewhat broader fashion, but do provide a concentration on the ministry of the word; this is obviously true of works by theologians in an evangelical tradition.

EARLY CHRISTIANITY:

Daniélou, J. and du Charlat, R. *La catechèse aux premiers siècles.* Paris, 1968.
Grant, R. *The Formation of the New Testament.* New York, 1965.
Hanson, R. *Tradition in the Early Church.* London, 1962.
Schelkle, K. *Discipleship and Priesthood.* New York, 1965.

PATRISTIC AND MEDIEVAL CHRISTIANITY:

De Ghellinck, J. *Le mouvement théologique du XIIe siècle.* Bruxelles, 1948.
Leclercq, J. *The Love of Learning and the Desire for God.* New York, 1961.
McNally, R. *The Bible in the Early Middle Ages.* Westminster, Md., 1959.
Morrison, K. *Tradition and Authority in the Western Church.* Princeton, 1969.
Neunheuser, B. *Baptism and Confirmation.* New York, 1964.
Owst, G. *Preaching in Medieval England.* Cambridge, 1926.

Smalley, B. *The Study of the Bible in the Middle Ages.* Oxford, 1952.

POST-MEDIEVAL CHRISTIANITY:

Blench, J. *Preaching in England in the Late Fifteenth and Sixteenth Centuries.* Oxford, 1964.
Brunotte, W. *Das geistliche Amt bei Luther.* Berlin, 1959.
Congar, Y. *Tradition and Traditions.* New York, 1967.
Dankbaar, W. "L'office des docteurs chez Calvin." In *Regards contemporains sur Calvin,* pp. 102–26. Paris, 1965.
Downey, J. *The Eighteenth-Century Pulpit.* Oxford, 1969.
Lawson, A. *John Wesley and the Christian Ministry.* London, 1963.
Mitchell, W. *English Pulpit Oratory from Andrewes to Tillotson.* New York, 1962.
Neill, S. *Christian Missions.* London, 1964.
Rogness, M. *Philip Melanchthon.* Minneapolis, 1969.
Rupp, G. *Patterns of Reformation.* London, 1969.
Schummer, L. *Le ministère pastoral dans l' "Institution Chrétienne" de Calvin à la lumière du troisième sacrament.* Wiesbaden, 1965.
Sloyan, G., ed. *Shaping the Christian Message.* New York, 1958.
Ulich, R. *A History of Religious Education.* New York, 1968.
Williams, G. *The Radical Reformation.* Philadelphia, 1962.

PART THREE

Service to the People of God

CHAPTER 15

The New Testament Ideal of Service

Earlier in this study we laid down the principle that one must start with the reality of Jesus' own role and function and use it as the criterion for what we may wish to call Christian "priesthood" or "ministry" rather than trying to fit it into some already possessed definition of religious ministry or priesthood. If such procedure be correct, then one must take seriously the early church's characterization of Jesus as "the Servant," a characterization that seems rooted in Jesus' own identification of himself in this manner.[1]

One of the most notable features of the New Testament Christology is the manner in which the various mediatorial functions occurring in Old Testament thought are brought together in Jesus: Son of man, Messiah, Prophet, Servant.[2] Of these, none is more basic and interpretative of the others than is that of Servant, which is quite clearly used in reference to the Servant hymns of Deutero-Isaiah.[3] This means that Jesus' ministry was viewed as service, not just any kind of service but precisely that which would realize the expectations expressed in the Old Testament Servant ideal. It would also indicate that whatever view the primitive church had of the priesthood of Christ would also be controlled by Jesus' Servant function.[4]

This Servant role applied not only to Jesus himself but also to his disciples, as we see reflected in passages such as Philippians 2. Just before going on to the famous passage (Phil. 2:6–11) that describes Jesus' glorification through fulfillment of his Servant role, Paul exhorts the Philippian church: "Let that mind be in you which was in Christ Jesus. . . ."

Again, there is considerable evidence in the New Testament texts that the explanation of the Servant ideal was part of primitive Christian baptismal catechesis.[5] And the critically important passage in Matthew 20:28 lays down the Servant role as proper to leaders in the Christian community.

Semantically, the case for placing "service" close to the center of Christian ministry is strengthened by the New Testament use of "*diakonia*."[6] It is the word that is used basically for "ministry." Besides its primary meaning of "serving the needs of people,"[7] it is used for "service of the word" (Acts 6:4), for "service of the spirit" (2 Cor. 3:7), for the "service of justification" (2 Cor. 3:9), and for the overall task of the *episkopos* (2 Tim. 4:5). This indicates that the task of Christian ministry was interpreted in terms of "serving others." Yet, while the secular meanings of "*diakonia*" would thus have been present in Christian usage, they would have been reoriented by association with the Isaian Servant passages. The explicit interrelation of these two spheres of meaning occurs in Matthew 20:28 where *diakonia* of both Jesus and the apostles is described in reference to the fourth Servant hymn.[8]

Since "*diakonia*" in New Testament usage has this wide application, embracing both common "secular" ministrations and the spiritual ministries proper to Christian faith, life, and worship, it is somewhat artificial to devote a section of our study to "service" in distinction from our treatment of the ministry of the word, or of sacrament. Yet, with awareness that "service" does extend to these other ministrations, that the Christian community needs to be served by the word and sacrament, we can profitably concentrate on the notion of "taking care of the community." Actually, this more general idea of "doing what is necessary to provide for people's needs" is central to both Old Testament and New Testament exhortations regarding the responsibilities of leaders. Because of this, the Christian ethic contains a strong emphasis on social responsibility, and this despite its equally strong eschatological character.[9]

Having said this, one must be careful not to reduce the Christian notion of service to nothing more than the concerned care for one's fellow man that can be found in the dedicated humanist. It accepts that latter ideal as a genuine good, incorporates it into its own ethos,[10] and then goes an important step further. What, then, is the specifically Christian kind of service, particularly as it pertains to the role of the community's leaders?

Shepherds of the People

The New Testament "job description" of community leadership is not cast for the most part in detailed specification of tasks (though the Pastorals already have a bit of this), but in figurative and imaginative language. Among these images of leadership a special position is occupied by the figure of "the shepherd." Building on the Old Testament usage of this image, particularly as found in prophetic passages such as the thirty-fourth chapter of Ezekiel, the early Christians interpreted the function both of Jesus and of the community's leaders as "shepherding." Jesus himself, and he alone, could lay claim to being *the* shepherd; he alone could claim the flock as his own possession (John 10). But those who were his disciples and charged with taking care of the flock for him also exercised a shepherding function.[11]

In examining the New Testament passages where the shepherd image is used and in attempting to determine what specific functions fall within this role, one must never forget that involved in the connotations of the

image are its links with the biblical notion of Messiah (Ezek. 34), with the Jewish priesthood,[12] and with the role of Moses.[13] More immediately the passages point to feeding (John 21:16), guarding from danger (John 10:11), leading to a goal (pasture or sheepfold) (John 10:16), and liberating from oppression (John 10:9–10). In the classic passage, John 10, the protection and fostering of the life of the flock will be achieved by the Shepherd's giving his own life for their sake (John 10:11). Here, quite clearly, the shepherd image is brought into relation with the fourth Servant hymn.[14]

Such passages indicate that the specific meaning to be given the function described by the shepherd imagery is dependent upon the specific nature of the community which is "the flock"; the shepherd is to provide whatever is required for the life of the flock. Moreover, later shepherds of the Christian community are to provide for it as does Jesus himself, for he is the model shepherd, the example for his disciples. Actually he remains the great shepherd (Heb. 13:20).

Jesus' disciples are both flock and shepherd; they are part of that flock of which he is the good shepherd, but they are to help take care of his flock and so share in his own pastoral task. To his close disciples he tries to communicate some of his own pastoral concern for the people who "wander like sheep without a shepherd" (Matt. 9:36). To Peter he gives the commission to feed the flock (John 21:16). And the early Christian community's understanding of itself as "the flock of Christ" (Acts 20:28) would inevitably have had implications of the community leaders being "shepherds."

There is practically no explicit application of the term "shepherd" to a group of functionaries in the early church.[15] However, there are two passages which may give us some insight, though one must be careful not to overread them. In 1 Peter 2:25 there is reference to "the shepherd and overseer [*episkopos*] of your souls." The referent in this passage is clearly the risen Christ and one could not argue from this passage to the conclusion that the *episkopos* of the early church was looked on as a shepherd. Yet, this text is roughly contemporaneous with the Pastorals which themselves tend towards the Ignatian view of the function and authority of the *episkopos*.[16] To apply this term to Christ along with the term "shepherd" would seem to reflect the view that Christians of this period had of the *episkopos*. In the second passage, Ephesians 4:11, where a listing of various ministries is given, we find "shepherds and teachers" linked together not so much as two distinct groups but rather as two names for the same group. If this is so, and the grammatical construction of the Greek would seem to indicate it, then it would point to teaching as the key activity of "the shepherds" in the community and give us an interesting insight into early Christianity's view of "the pastoral office."

Behind the figure of shepherd/flock lies the notion of assembling, of gathering together, of forming the *ekklesia*. The shepherd must be solicitous about the life of each of the flock, but his task is to keep the flock unified, to resist the forces that would tend to disperse the sheep. No doubt the New Testament passages that speak this way about the ministry of Jesus himself are written against the background of the Old Testament messianic passages that refer to the Israelites driven into exile and diaspora and then reunited in the day of the Lord.[17] But they are also written in the context of the early church with its need to keep the various communities unified internally and with one another.

The various ministries share this common objective of preserving the unity and vitality of the people. This is Paul's point in writing to the Corinthians (1 Cor. 12:1–31). Genuine charisms work to unify, not to divide; for this reason love is the greatest of the charismatic gifts, for its essence is to be a bond of community (1 Cor. 13). Love is the very heart of Christian service, of Christian ministry.[18]

While the nurturing of community is a service of great value to each of the individuals in the group, it is important to notice that in the New Testament perspective *diakonia* is directed to community as such, though, obviously, it is also directed to the individuals (such as the poor) who need care.[19] Thus, high priority is placed on the preservation of community when there is question of the *diakonia* shared by all members of the church (Eph. 4:11–13) and when there is question of the special *diakonia* of those entrusted with the care of the group (1 Cor. 12). This priority on preserving unity remains throughout the centuries a characteristic of official ecclesiastical concern.

Healing

Jesus' own public ministry was one of serving his fellow Jews through teaching and healing. These two elements of his activity complemented one another both in the Gospel narrative and in the actual conduct of his public life. His word was a word of healing, and the acts of healing themselves spoke of the divine saving intent which he implemented. The word he speaks, and more so the Word he is, must be believed in as a word of salvation or it says nothing at all; it is a word that must be received in faith, in order to be effective.

At this point the ministry of the word and the ministry of service come together. The word of the gospel, though profoundly instructive, is more than instruction, it is lifegiving.[20] Even more than the word of Old Testament prophecy, the word spoken in the mystery of Christ, whether uttered by Jesus himself or by his disciples, is a word of power.[21] Yet its effectiveness must not be seen as functioning in the realm of the near-magical; it possesses power precisely *as word*, as communicating truth to the consciousness of men.[22] It illumines minds, provides insight, moves the heart, leads to conversion, catalyzes decision, and thereby alters the course of human lives and the evolution of human society.

Always, however, the effectiveness of the word is blocked by a certain amount of negativity, by some evil. The human person and the overall human situation need healing.

Man is somewhat sick and disoriented and crippled.[23] Man needs salvation; this is the persistent lesson of revelation, in both the Old and the New Testaments, a lesson only grudgingly admitted by men. Even when the need for some help is recognized it is still difficult to believe that salvation can come by the "good news" of Christ. This is why the credibility of this gospel must be conveyed by the word of healing action as well as by word of instruction.

This healing action, of Christ and of his disciples, is meant to touch the whole man, body and spirit.[24] Nor is this to be understood in the sense that it touches the body as well as the soul. The anthropology of the New Testament is such that salvation cannot come to one aspect of man without simultaneously affecting the rest: "He could work no miracles, because they did not believe."[25] Throughout the gospel description of the "wondrous deeds" of Jesus, healing of bodily ill and salvation from sin are intrinsically linked.[26] Part of this linkage might be attributed to the medical mythology of the day which attributed physical ills to "evil spirits" and saw physical healing therefore as "dispelling the demons";[27] but there is the more profound link, grounded in the insight that the power of evil is one, just as the being of man is one, and the healing creative power of love is one.

Christian service is intended, then, to provide for the healing of man in the bodily aspects of his existence. Christ himself healed and pointed to such healing as proof of his mission from God, as sign that he was "he who was to come" (Matt. 11:2–6). He sent his disciples out to heal and provided them with the power to do so. However, it would be superficial to see such healing as occurring only in "miraculous" fashion. Even during the specially charismatic period of Christianity's inception much of the healing activity of Jesus and of early Christians operated through the ordinary channels of trying to correct social patterns, encouraging the "haves" to share with the "have-nots."

But it is in salvation as healing man in his spiritual level that Christian ministry has something unique to offer, something not possessed by dedicated humanism. Though dedicated men can do much for the spirit of their fellow men, they cannot share with them the life-giving Spirit of the risen Christ, the Spirit of love which drives out nonlove, the source of all evil. This power over sin, proper to the agent of divine justification, is claimed for Christ himself as Lord and Son of man (Luke 5:20–25; Rom. 8) and in secondary fashion for his disciples (Matt. 18:18–20). In a later chapter we will study carefully the kind of judgment involved in the church's claim to forgive sin, but we might note here the element of healing that is involved in this kind of service.

What deserves considerable attention is the constant link in biblical thought of bodily healing and forgiveness of sin. To put it in more modern terminology, the bodily healing seems to be sacramentally effective of the spiritual salvation. We might well ask the question: Is there perhaps an element of New Testament insight that we have overlooked, the fact that working to heal the bodily ills of men is an intrinsic element in saving them from the power of sin? Is there, really, any ministry in the church that is purely spiritual? Is it not erroneous to confine the activity of the ordained minister to some supposedly "spiritual realm" in contradistinction to the "secular" needs of mankind?

Reconciliation

When we apply the notion of healing to the social existence of man, we are in contact with the biblical category of "reconciliation."[28] One can see how basic this ideal is in New Testament thought about salvation when one recalls that the opposite notion, "alienation," is the most basic scriptural designation for sin.[29] If sin is alienation of man from God, of man from his fellow man, of man from his true self, then salvation must consist in healing each of these three cleavages; it must involve a three-fold reconciliation.[30]

Because of the mysterious power of evil, the

priestly ministry of building community must be one of achieving reconciliation. The work of Jesus himself was clearly seen in this light by the New Testament writers, perhaps most explicitly by Paul.[31] Christ's ministry, particularly the supreme service of his death and resurrection, accomplished the reconciliation of men to his Father; it broke down the barriers of division between Jew and Gentile, between social and economic classes, between men and women (Gal. 3:28). In his death he has absorbed into himself the hostilities that divide men and he has destroyed them (Eph. 2:16). As risen Lord he establishes peace by being "corporally" the bond of unity; all men are meant to be joined to him in one body (Gal. 3:28).[32]

For Christ's disciples, too, the task of reconciliation is a key part of their ministerial service: "Blessed are the peacemakers." True, the words for "reconciliation" are infrequent in New Testament writing (*"apokatallassein"* is found only in Ephesians 2:16 and Colossians 1:20; the cognate is *"katallage"* in Romans 5:10–11 and 2 Corinthians 5:18–19), and refer essentially to Christ's role. Yet, much of the activity described or reflected in the New Testament activity of the early Christians in general or of early church leadership in particular, is really reconciliation in one form or another.

Paul's exhortation to the churches he founded always includes a strong urging to work for unity within the group, to heal whatever divisions have arisen within the community. Acts reflects the deep concern of the early apostles and presbyters to heal the rift that developed over the Judaizing problem. The prophetic task of proclaiming the advent of the kingdom and the need for *metanoia* was basically one of trying to reconcile men to the Father through Christ.

The fifth chapter of 2 Corinthians (the only passage that explicitly categorizes the ministry as "reconciliation") describes the work of God in Christ, the "making all things new," as one of reconciling men to himself. In achieving this reconciliation he has given to apostles such as Paul a "ministry of reconciliation." The manner in which this ministry operates seems indicated by the clause in verse 19: "he has placed in us the word of reconciliation."

Thus, the ministry of reconciliation, the ministry of service to those alienated from God and from one another, coincides at its deepest level with the ministry of the word. This is not surprising, but it does highlight the prophetic essence of the ministry in the church or, what is practically the equivalent, the evangelical nature of mediation in the church. Moreover, the coincidence of the ministry of reconciliation with that of the word and of service points to the community perspective of Christian ministry. The process of establishing reconciliation is the process of establishing or strengthening community.

Discussion of the notion of *diakonia* in the first-century church naturally raises the question of the origin of deacons.[33] While it is clear that some such recognized function did exist quite early, the very fact that *diakonia* is such a broadly applicable term in primitive Christianity makes it very difficult to delineate the precise nature of the diaconate in the early Christian decades.

For a long time, popular explanations of the diaconal office used Acts 6:2–6 as a reference to the inception of deacons in the church. More careful scholarship, however, has brought into question such an identification of the seven chosen to minister to the Hellenistic Christians with those otherwise called "deacons" (as in Phil. 1:1).[34] Their task is referred to as *"diakonein"*; but the term *"diakonos"* is not applied to them individually or as a group, though Acts describes the activities of two of them, Stephen and Philip, at some length. While their task is first placed in the context of assistance to the Twelve in Jerusalem (Acts 6:2–6), which would be parallel to what we know of the early diaconate in other contexts, the role they actually exercise is more like that of presbyters or even apostles.[35]

There were, though, other situations in which *diakonoi* were designated (by what process is not clear) to work with the *epis-kopoi,* most likely to take special care for the material welfare of the community. Such would seem to be the case with the *diakonoi* of Philippians 1:1 and 1 Timothy 3:8, and perhaps also with the "fellow workers" men-

tioned a number of times by Paul (e.g., Rom. 16:21). However, the evidence is extremely slim, and there is no first-century evidence that points to a special role of liturgical assistant which second-century texts attribute to the deacon.

NOTES

1. See A. Richardson, *Introduction to the Theology of the New Testament* (New York, 1958), pp. 303–4; T. Manson, *The Servant Messiah* (Cambridge, 1961), pp. 110–13; V. Taylor, *Jesus and His Sacrifice* (London, 1959), pp. 281ff.; J. Jeremias, "Pais theou," *Theological Dictionary of the New Testament* (hereafter referred to as *TDNT*), pp. 698–713. For an opposing view (i.e., one that denies such self-identification on the part of Jesus), see R. Fuller, *Foundations of New Testament Christology* (New York, 1965), pp. 102–31.

2. See V. Taylor, *The Names of Jesus* (London, 1953), pp. 25–35; J. Jeremias, *New Testament Theology* (New York, 1971), pp. 272–99.

3. See Jeremias, pp. 698–713.

4. This relationship between "servant" and "priest" will be discussed more thoroughly in chapter 27.

5. See Y. Tremel, "Baptism—The Incorporation of the Christian into Christ," *Baptism in the New Testament* (Baltimore, 1964), p. 202; Richardson, pp. 338–41.

6. See H. Beyer, "Diakonia," *TDNT*, vol. 2, pp. 84–88.

7. See H. Liddell and R. Scott, *Greek-English Lexicon* (Oxford, 1901).

8. A. Jones, *Gospel According to St. Matthew* (New York, 1965), pp. 226–27; R. Gundry, *The Use of the Old Testament in St. Matthew's Gospel* (Leiden, 1967), pp. 39–40.

9. See R. Schnackenburg, *The Moral Teaching of the New Testament* (New York, 1964), pp. 144–51.

10. See C. Dawson, "The Kingdom of God and History," in *The Dynamics of World History* (New York, 1956), pp. 265–80; a more detailed study is contained in *idem, The Formation of Christendom* (New York, 1967).

11. See K. Schelkle, *Discipleship and Priesthood* (New York, 1965), pp. 33–45.

12. See J. Jeremias, "Poimen," *TDNT*, vol. 6, pp. 487–89.

13. *Ibid.,* p. 489.

14. R. Brown, *St. John* (Garden City, N.Y., 1966), vol. 1, p. 398.

15. Except the use of *"poimainein"* with *"episkopoi"* in Acts 20:28.

16. See C. Barrett, "The Ministry in the New Testament," *The Doctrine of the Church,* ed. D. Kirkpatrick (New York, 1964), pp. 60–63.

17. E.g., the relation between John 10 and Ezek. 34; see E. Hoskyns, *The Fourth Gospel* (London, 1947), pp. 366–67; Brown, pp. 397–98.

18. See C. Spicq, *Théologie morale du Nouveau Testament* (Paris, 1965), vol. 2, pp. 781–815.

19. Beyer, pp. 87–88; Schelkle, "Their [the apostles'] ministry is ministry to the salvation of God's people, and in this their concern for salvation is directed mainly to the totality of the elected people, not to individuals" (p. 33).

20. G. Kittel, "Lego," *TDNT*, vol. 4, pp. 117–18; Richardson, pp. 159–66.

21. Kittel, pp. 106–7; on the historical power of the word see H. Urs von Balthasar, *Word and Revelation* (New York, 1964), pp. 9–86.

22. Kittel, p. 119; pp. 134–39 in J. Bonsirven, *Theology of the New Testament* (Baltimore, 1963); J. Connolly, *Human History and the Word of God* (New York, 1965), esp. pp. 205–89.

23. See P. Schoonenberg, "The Sin of the World," *Man and Sin* (Notre Dame, 1965), pp. 98–123.

24. The central symbol of this integral salvation is the resurrection of the body; on the reality and the myth of this bodily resurrection, see K. Rahner, *Theological Investigations*, vol. 2 (1963), pp. 203–16; S. Ogden, *Christ Without Myth* (New York, 1961).

25. Mark 6:5; see J. Robinson, *The Body* (London, 1963), on New Testament anthropology.

26. See L. Monden, *Signs and Wonders* (New York, 1966), pp. 106–30.

27. See J. Bonsirven, *Palestinian Judaism in the Time of Jesus Christ* (New York, 1964), pp. 38–41; *idem, Le règne de Dieu* (Paris, 1957), pp. 67–70; C. Guignebert, *The Jewish World in the Time of Jesus* (New York, 1959), pp. 99–105.

28. See Richardson, pp. 215–17.

29. E. Beaucamp, "Péché," *Dictionnaire de la Bible, Supplement*, vol. 7, cols. 439–54.

30. Perhaps one should, to remain faithful to biblical thought, add a fourth element of alienation/reconciliation: that of man in relation to his world.

31. Our present discussion could well be supplemented by a study of New Testament understanding of "peace" (*eirene*); see W. Foerster, *TDNT*, vol. 2, pp. 411–20; D. Stanley, *Christ's Resurrection in Pauline Soteriology* (Rome, 1961), pp. 224–28.

32. While the Pauline texts do not explicitly mention the breaking down of barriers between clergy and laity, one can question whether one can draw such a conclusion from theological reflection on a number of New Testament texts. The Parable of the Good Samaritan involves a criticism of priestly separatism and sanctity laws; Jesus himself belonged to the laity in liturgical celebrations; moreover, Jesus' own ministry developed increasingly in tension with the established Jewish priesthood.

33. On *diakonos*, see Beyer, pp. 89–93; H. Küng, *The Church* (New York, 1967), pp. 399–401; E. Schweizer, *Church Order in the New Testament* (London, 1971), pp. 198–201. For a lengthy study of the various aspects (historical, theological, pastoral) of the diaconate see K. Rahner and H. Vorgrimler, *Diaconia in Christo* (Freiburg, 1962).

34. See Küng, pp. 400–401.

35. See H. von Campenhausen, *Ecclesiastical Authority and Spiritual Power in the Church of the First Three Centuries* (Palo Alto, Calif., 1969), p. 771; Küng, p. 401.

CHAPTER 16

The Patristic Period and the

Early Middle Ages

On the basis of the New Testament literature, we know that before the beginning of the second century the Christian community possessed a theologically sophisticated ideal of "service," as applied both to Christ himself and to Christians, and specifically to those who occupied positions of ministry within the church.[1] In the New Testament perspective, as we have seen, that which dominated the reality of "service" in Christianity was the death and resurrection of Jesus. This was his supreme act of Servanthood in fulfillment of Isaiah 52–53 and Christians in baptism were assimilated to this ideal by "mystery entry" into Christ's death and risen life.

As the practicalities of community existence became more complicated, which they had already begun to do by the opening of the second century, the ideal of "servant" inevitably began to be interpreted by other notions, particularly as it was applied to those in charge of the communities. Here, two other notions were increasingly dominant and tended to overshadow the notion of servant. These were "king" and "shepherd," obviously closely linked with one another, since both in Israelitic and in nonbiblical literature "shepherd" was a standard figure for kingship.[2] Both of them were drawn from the Old Testament traditions, both of them inevitably colored by cultural understandings at any given point of history, both of them thoroughly reinterpreted by New Testament theology, though it is questionable how thoroughly this was understood by some later rulers of the church. Two others come in later: "physician" and "spiritual father."

One would expect "shepherd" to be used immediately of those who succeeded to the kind of responsibility for the church that the apostles had enjoyed,[3] since the image of shepherd is explicitly applied to Peter and indirectly to the other apostles. Moreover, the prominence in New Testament writings of Jesus' function as shepherd would have colored early Christian thinking about the role of those who acted as his ministers in caring for the community.

Probably, in the context of administrative activity and supervisory responsibility, it was inevitable that "shepherd" increasingly acquired overtones of "ruling," i.e., of its kingship connotations. Yet, in the light of the strong New Testament polemic against the attribution of any such regal status to Jesus, much less to his disciples, it is a bit disappointing that such a development happened. Jesus was king, but his was a kingship "not of this world"; his entry into possession of effective rule came with resurrection, for his kingdom is ultimately an eschatological reality.

Increasingly, in a process whose exact dynamics are extremely difficult to define, a regal interpretation of episcopal ministry came into existence in the church. The idea of monarchical episcopate came to be taken quite literally; and while the biblical aspects of Servant and Shepherd were appreciated by many of history's bishops, heroically appreciated by not a few, the official understanding of *"sacerdotium"* particularly as it applied to the bishops drifted further and further away from the ideal of Matthew 20:25–28. Among the many influences that helped bring about this change of viewpoint, two can probably be singled out as functioning precisely in the theological realm, in the evolution of the idea: the impact of the Old Testament notion of priesthood, and the influence of the secular notion of ruler, particularly the Byzantine notion of *basileus*.[4]

However, it would be a mistaken oversimplification and an injustice to so many of history's bishops, presbyters, and deacons, to suggest that a civic notion of kingship and administrative rule completely replaced the gospel ideal of shepherding service. To avoid such a onesided misreading of history, this present chapter will table for the moment the question of the "secularization" of the ministerial role and will consider the manner in which the basic ideal of ministerial service found expression as the life of the church unfolded.

Shepherd of the Flock

Certainly, by the time of the *Didascalia* in the East and of Cyprian in the West, the bishop has appropriated the biblical image of shepherd.[5] In both instances, the bishop is seen as sharing his concern and responsibility with assistants, either presbyters or deacons; but he alone is truly the pastor of the flock entrusted to him.[6] The duty and authority of the bishop is grounded in the commission given to Peter, and while the text that is ordinarily appealed to by such bishops as Cyprian is Matthew 16:18 there could not have been lacking some connotative reference to John 21's "Feed my lambs; feed my sheep."[7]

Already at the beginning of the third century, the prayer for the ordination of the bishop which is contained in the *Apostolic Tradition* lists "to feed your holy flock" as the first of the purposes for which the Spirit is invoked upon the ordinand.[8] And a century earlier, as is attested by 1 Peter 5:2, the commission of John 21 is extended to the *presbyteroi* who are told to "shepherd the flock of God that has been entrusted to you." This seems to give us a clear line of application of the image of shepherd: from Christ to Peter

(and the other apostles?) to those responsible for the care of the community in later generations.

Though there is little second-century evidence that church leaders, whether *presbyteroi* or *episkopoi*, were called "shepherds,"[9] there is no reason to doubt that the people continued to be thought of as the "flock of Christ" and those in charge as exercising a pastoral care. However, it might be worth noting in Clement's introduction to his *Paedagogus* the use of a comparison (which, admittedly, in his thinking applies to the Christian teacher and not necessarily to the clerical ministry) which will become increasingly important in the theology of Gregory I, that is, the comparison of the Christian teacher or bishop to a physician, which figure then absorbs into itself the scriptural references to the healing effected by the shepherd.[10]

Thus, the image of the leaders of the community as the shepherds of the people remains explicit and basic throughout the ante-Nicene period and straight into the Middle Ages. While more specific elements of the episcopal or presbyteral function, such as the ministry of the word or of sacrament, receive varying interpretations and emphases in differing circumstances, the "pastoral" responsibility seems to be a constant though often ill-defined duty of taking care of the needs of the Christians within a given community. The understanding and fulfillment of the pastoral office thus depends historically on what those in this office at a given time judge to be for the good of their flock. Hence, it is always correlative to the soteriology of a given era, whether it is apocalyptic or incarnational, "spiritual" or "secular" in emphasis, correlative to the notions of "grace" and efficacy of sacraments.[11]

Unquestionably one of the critical elements in such overall care of the Christian people is the direction or government provided by those in authoritative positions.[12] How much and what kind of social direction is needed by a group is very much conditioned by contingent historical factors. Without passing negative judgment on the evolution that did take place, it seems quite clear that the pastoral office especially as exercised by the episcopacy came to be seen more and more in terms of "ruling."[13] One can see the crystallization of this development in the *De cura pastorali* of Gregory the Great. The term that most regularly designates the bishop in this guide for the pastoral office is "rector."[14] And the unparalleled influence of this pastoral handbook on the medieval ministry is well-established historical fact.[15]

Much of this government of the Christians, as individuals and as communities, naturally took place through the ministry of the word. As we saw in the previous chapter, this same *De cura pastorali* of Gregory is largely taken up with instructions to the preacher or teacher. But it is one thing to educate people to an understanding of the principles of Christianity, from which they can with initiative and mature judgment draw their own prudential conclusions; it is another to urge people to observe the teacher's judgments about the implications of the gospel. Gregory's advice to "rectors" is constantly in terms of admonishing rather than informing their auditors.[16] Thus, even the ministry of the word is directed to proclaiming precepts, to promulgating law in its more detailed "positive law" aspects.

Obviously, this is not something entirely new with Gregory. The New Testament literature itself, precisely because it is instruction about a "new way," is filled with practical directives. This continues throughout the patristic period, and as "intellectual" an interpreter of Christianity as Clement of Alexandria sees the making of law as a basic element in the function of the Christian teacher.[17] However, there is a question of emphasis that is difficult to isolate but most important in its implications: Does one urge a specific course of action on the basis of unquestioning obedience motivated by eschatological reward/punishment (sometimes the reward is not even eschatological)? Or does one communicate an understanding of faith from which personal decision emerges? Obviously, the emphasis shifts even further when the sanction suggested or imposed for noncon-

formity to the practical directives of the "teacher" is some penalty which this teacher has power to implement through his own agency or that of a supportive temporal power. Hopefully, we will be able to analyze this critical problem area more systematically in the next part, when we study the function of the minister (bishop or presbyter) as judge. One must be careful, then, not to read the term "ministry of the word" in a univocal sense in various historical circumstances. Different interpretations of Christian ministry are not distinguished (for the most part) by their acceptance or nonacceptance of ministry of the word as essential, but by their understanding of this term.

Care for the Indigent

One area of ministerial service has always been recognized and shouldered by the leaders of the Christian communities. This is the care for those in temporal need: the poor, the orphans, the widows.[18] One may perhaps, in today's complex civilization, disagree with the manner in which this task is performed. One may also judge the behavior of church leaders in many historical contexts where perhaps they were themselves part of the "establishment" that exploited the poor, or were at least unwilling to challenge the exploitive establishment. But one must admit that the bishops and presbyters of the church have consistently been aware that care for the poor is a ministry intrinsic to Christianity.

Obviously, such care for the needy is demanded by the New Testament writings themselves; this was in direct continuity with Old Testament exhortation. Moreover, there is abundant testimony that the earliest Christian communities honored this teaching by providing for the weak and poor in their midst. Acts speaks of a sharing of goods, though how widespread this was is hard to determine. And we know from both Acts and Paul's letters of collections taken for the needy. Justin's brief references to the Eucharistic gathering let us know that this was a common context, probably the principal context, for collecting goods to distribute to the needy.[19]

One thing the church never lacked in these early centuries was poor and needy members. If nothing else, the afflictions connected with the persecutions that came periodically until well into the sixth century always left a number of Christians destitute and dependent upon charity.[20] Hence, there was a constant need to attend to such poor, and the leaders of the church would logically have seen this as part of their pastoral care.[21]

We know that beginning with the primitive church the responsibility of providing for the needy rested on those in charge of the community. Acts tells how this task was commissioned to men who had this responsibility as their chief function. Deacons apparently continued to play a special role in administering such help to the poor, but their role always seems to be one of aiding the *episkopos* upon whom the ultimate responsibility rested.[22] This is particularly noticeable from the third century onward; at this point we can observe quite clearly the situation in which the church possesses an increasing amount of goods which have been donated for works of charity.[23] The bishop is the sole responsible guardian of these goods. The earliest Roman laws touching on church property and the earliest synodal canons both reflect this situation, though they make it clear that the bishop has no possession of these as his personal property.[24]

During the patristic period and early Middle Ages, episcopal involvement in such charitable works found expression, as we already suggested, in three contexts. The first, the time of persecution, dominated the early centuries but lasted long after Constantine's termination of the "classic" Roman persecutions. One of the most common penalties inflicted upon Christians was the confiscation of their goods; thus many were left quite destitute and dependent upon the charity of their brethren.[25] To this was added the perennial needs of groups such as widows and orphans who in the social situation of those times were

without ordinary means of support.[26] In the West the persecutions shade off into the second context, the "barbaric invasions." As a matter of fact, it is often difficult to state which of the two phenomena one is dealing with in the fourth to eighth centuries: so many of the invading armies had already been converted to Arianism and severely afflicted the populace that would not accept Arianism.[27] Be that as it may, the devastation that accompanied the increasing inroads of the Teutonic peoples from the north brought much of the populace to a level of severe indigence.[28] In such sore straits, the poor looked to the episcopacy (and also increasingly to the monasteries) for help.[29]

The third context was due not to catastrophes such as invasion but to the increasingly important civic status of bishops. For a number of reasons, not the least of which was the Roman imperial procedure of dealing with the Christian populace through the bishop, the episcopacy quickly attained a role in society parallel to that of higher officials or nobles.[30] As such, their approach to the service of the poor became one of establishing and sustaining and directing fairly large-scale social agencies such as hostelries, orphanages, and hospitals.[31] Basil's vast efforts in Caesarea are a prominent example,[32] and the Code of Justinian reflects a situation of well-developed ecclesiastical organization of charitable works.[33] In the West the developments along this same line were retarded by the incursion of the northern peoples, but by the late Merovingian period the bishops are prominently involved in the evolution of necessary social institutions.[34]

Administrative Involvement

Much of the bishop's time and energy was apparently absorbed with people's problems, a fact that many bishops, such as Augustine, bemoan. Not only was there the necessary watchfulness for the needy, presiding over the ecclesiastical judiciary, and acting as informal delegate of the civil ruler on occasion, but there was also the basic administration of the

Christian community, a task that became more complex as small local churches grew into large dioceses with numerous clergy and monks.[35]

Since an earlier chapter has described the administrative growth of the episcopal and presbyteral functions as a response to the priestly objective of preserving unity in the people of God, we can briefly allude to such administrative tasks insofar as they translated the notion of *diakonia*. From the time of Paul onward, one of the principal governing tasks of the church's leaders was to reconcile differences within the community. These could take the form of disagreement, jealousies, misunderstandings. No doubt, these were the bulk of the "cases" that bishops and presbyters had to handle.[36]

Another more serious threat to unity within a given church, or at times within the church as a whole, was the rise of "heresy" and schism. Apart from the obvious threat to unity of faith which erroneous doctrines constituted, they also occasioned intense controversy and bitterness. It is quite amazing how utterly unrestrained and un-Christian can become the reaction of "defenders of the faith" when they are confronted by a real or imagined "heresy." History gives sad testimony to the fact that the rancor associated with doctrinal controversy establishes more of a barrier to later reconciliation than do the doctrinal differences themselves.

This, then, was an important arena of church governance, associated with though not completely identified with the ministry of word: to safeguard the community from such divisive influences, and, if they did occur, to work for a reunified Christian community. One immediately thinks of the efforts of an Augustine to heal the divisions of the Donatist controversy, or Ambrose dealing with the Arian problem in Milan, or the Cappadocians striving to reunify the Near East that was torn by controversy on the homoousion/homoiousion issue.

Constantine's decree in 313[37] (shortly before the so-called Edict of Milan), ordering the restoration to Christian communities of the properties taken from them, gives clear proof of the fact that Christian communities already possessed considerable material goods, gathered for the most part, it is true, to provide for charitable activities of various kinds. Yet, the frequent reference to ecclesiastical property in synodal canons,[38] and even more so in official decrees of the Roman government,[39] would seem to indicate that a certain amount of conflict arose in the administration of this property.

Inevitably, the bishop was in charge of such material goods, and even if he delegated much of its administration, as was often the case, he still bore the final responsibility.[40] It is interesting to read some of the letters of Gregory I and to discover not only the extent of papal holdings but also the amount of attention that this busy administrator had to pay to such material concerns.[41] Granted that the problem was probably more acute in Rome because of the greater influence and wealth of this see, the same thing existed to some extent in practically every diocese. What goods a given church possessed belonged to that community and was intended for the needs of its people; the bishop or presbyter was the steward entrusted with the care of this wealth.[42]

One of the negative results of the new situation that followed Constantine's recognition of Christianity was the increasing involvement of church leadership in state affairs.[43] Even apart from the instances where a civil ruler would utilize the services of a prominent bishop or presbyter to expedite some of his own business,[44] the leaders of the church were in more or less constant interchange with civic authorities.[45] This touched upon the arrangement of Christian property rights,[46] the question of clerical freedom from civil service and taxation,[47] and the involvement of bishops in judicial proceedings.[48] Constantine himself had given recognition to judicial proceedings by the bishop as equivalent to civil court action.[49]

The more numerous Christians became, the more complicated were the relationships between the various Christian communities and the civic structures with which they interacted. Nor could sharp lines be drawn. If a given city or region was predominantly Christian, the bishop as leader of his people would at times be drawn into conflicts and crises that were not religious in nature. One thinks immediately of the famous case of the "desecration" in Antioch of the statues to the emperor, and of the bishop's embassy to appease the emperor who was threatening dire punishment to the city's inhabitants.[50]

Then, too, there was business of various kinds that had to be carried on between bishops, or bishops with their presbyters or with the monks residing in their dioceses. Already by the time of Cyprian one is aware how much of this routine business is occupying the time and energy of the bishop.[51] It has increased measurably by the time of Ambrose and Augustine,[52] and by the time of Gregory I has become a threat to the "more spiritual" aspects of the bishop's task.[53] Naturally, not all the bishops (much less the presbyters who worked with them in the cities or the presbyters who were in charge of the country communities) had the complicated diplomatic dealings that were part of ecclesiastical life in sees like Rome or Carthage or Constantinople.[54] But there are indications that the bishop or presbyter became very early, certainly as early as the mid-fourth century, a public personage with all the unformulated demands on his time and attention that that implies.[55]

Ministry of Hospitality

From its origins, early Christianity held hospitality in the highest esteem, as a basic service that all Christians should extend to one another and to others in need.[56] Traveling apostles or prophets received, of course, a special welcome from the early communities; but New Testament writings and other very early documents such as the *Didache* exhort the Christians to receive with open service any brother or sister who needed shelter. Nor did the prescriptions that were laid down to prevent freeloaders from exploiting such charity indicate any disillusionment with or abandonment of this hospitable attitude.[57] On the contrary, the very fact that rules were provided to prevent such exploitation testify to the manner in which Christians felt bound by the obligation of providing hospitality.

Quite naturally, the leadership of a church would play a prominent part in extending such charity to visitors. When the churches remained quite small, this constituted no particular burden. But as Christianity grew, the number of Christians traveling from one place to another was such that the informal provision no longer sufficed. Hence, there developed in many cities the practice of bishops providing a hostel (or hostels) for travelers.[58] Even when monastic houses began to supply such shelter, as they were already doing in Constantinople in the fifth century,[59] hostels maintained by bishops still continued to increase in size and numbers.[60] Along with such other charitable activities as orphanages, hospitals, and homes for wayward girls, they became a regular part of the church's confrontation of social needs by its own works of mercy.

Thus, there was an ever increasing range of activities through which the bishops and other clergy of the patristic period translated their *diakonia* of the community. Naturally there was some danger of this becoming bureaucratically enlarged and impersonal, but the letters and sermons of bishops from Cyprian in the third century to Hincmar of Reims in the ninth century are a clear testimonial to the deep episcopal concern for the human needs of their people, a concern which they regarded as a responsibility of their office.[61]

Healing

Difficult though it is to determine the objective facts connected with healings, either in the New Testament period or in the centuries that immediately followed, some attention to healing must belong to any discussion of Christianity's ministry of service.[62] Given the extent to which emphasis on healing marks the Gospel accounts of Jesus' own ministry, it would be presumptuous to say that the first-century church saw healing as incidental. Moreover, Acts retains the tradition that certain healing powers passed into the apostolate of the early church, and Matthew 28:18 attaches to the kerygmatic commission a certain wonder-working guarantee.

Practically all the second- and third-century accounts of "miracles" are connected with reports of martyrdom.[63] Yet, one cannot but wonder about the practice (to which the Epistle of James refers) of bringing in the presbyters to pray for and anoint the sick. Was this connected with the hope that actual physical healing might result? Or was it intended to strengthen psychologically and spiritually the sick member of the community?[64] Or, again, what was the ministry of healing that is reflected in the fact that the list of *ordinandi* in the *Apostolic Tradition* of Hippolytus contains "healers"?[65]

During the second and third centuries there seems to have been very little special healing. From the fourth century onward, one begins to encounter more accounts of it. The emphasis is on the healings attached to burial places of the martyrs; it quite quickly extends to the wonders worked by renowned ascetics.[66] Before long, shrines like that of St. Martin at Tours become places of pilgrimage and wonder-working.[67] This process was abetted considerably by popular writings such as those of Gregory of Tours.[68] Probably the most influential work in this regard was the *Dialogues* of Gregory the Great, whose impact on popular credulity in the Middle Ages is inestimable.[69]

Though a large proportion of the famous figures to whom were attributed healing powers—if not in life, then after their death and "canonization"—were bishops, there does not seem to have been an association of such healing with official ministry as such. Rather, the power to heal seems to have been considered the result and the manifestation of extraordinary personal sanctity. One who was exceptionally free from the power of evil was able to overcome the influence of evil, even its physical aspects, in others.[70]

Actually, the healing that was more basically associated with the special ministry of episcopate and presbyterate pertained to the "spiritual" rather than the bodily order. Working on the presupposition that man was ill because of the heritage of sin, wounded by the attacks of "the evil one," many patristic writers speak of the need fulfilled by one who is "the physician of souls." The term is already found, though not often, in Clement and Origen of Alexandria. Ambrose and Augustine in the West and Chrysostom and Gregory of Nazianzus in the East all develop the idea. Gregory the Great makes much of it and transmits it to later centuries.[71]

Certainly, part of the overtones of such imagery is the episcopal ministry connected with baptism and penance. But the image extends beyond the episcopacy, especially in the East (and in movements like Celtic monasticism that were strongly influenced by the East) where the "spiritual director" is involved in helping heal his disciples from their sins and faults.[72] The ability to heal "spiritually" is dependent upon the "physician's" own possession of the understanding and sanctity he wishes to transmit to his charges.[73] Yet, it would not be accurate to say that there is no special relationship to the episcopal and presbyteral ministry. There seems to remain a faith in the power of the word as an instrument of healing. To the extent that some of the ministry of the word pertains specifically to the community's specially designated ministers, those ministers have a responsibility to heal men's wounded spirits by that word. Actually, what one finds in the patristic writing is frequent stress on the fact that the bishop or presbyter, precisely because he had the commission to give the healing word to others, must himself live according to that word and be a perfect instrument of its transmission.[74]

In the next chapter we will have occasion to discuss the thought of Pseudo-Dionysius on ecclesiastical officials, but it might be well to recall here the extent to which his situation of bishops and priests in a higher "rank" is an ontological ranking which defines their capacity to heal and sanctify and teach.[75] Just as their insight is meant to illumine those below them on the ladder, so their sanctity should work to heal the faithful beneath them.[76] The importance of Pseudo-Dionysius' writings is that, though he alone sketches such a detailed and defined picture of Christianity as a hierarchical reality, his thought sharpens a point of view that was basic to all those in the patristic period who were influenced by Neo-Platonic thinking on "illumination," "hierarchy," "order," etc.[77]

Before leaving our discussion of the attitude of the premedieval church to ministry of service, it might be well to examine the question of Christianity's view of "the secular" during this period. As we have already seen, the New Testament literature gives us relatively little direction in this important question, largely because the infant church had not yet confronted the larger context of its historical existence. But it is precisely in the period we are now discussing, between the end of the first century and the Hildebrandian reforms, that Christianity had to discover and enunciate its role vis-à-vis the other elements of human existence.

For the most part, the relationship church/world remains ambiguous and uncertain, despite quite a number of unmitigated and outspoken denunciations of "the world."[78] There is one or another form of stress on the eschatological, ranging from that proper to the New Testament writings (which see the end of history accomplished already in the resurrection of Christ) to the fearsome descriptions of the "four last things" which mark Gregory's *Dialogues*.[79] There is, moreover, the "holy disdain" of everything temporal and bodily and earthly that develops in conjunction with much of the ascetical theory and practice of those centuries.[80]

Yet, Christianity never gives way to the negativity towards the material creation that characterized Gnosticism and even more so Manicheism.[81] Material goods and the temporal needs of men may not be highly evaluated by the preachers and teachers of those centuries but if men were in need and pain,

the dictates of Christian charity were quite clear. As Origen stated it, the church was the inn to which the Good Samaritan, Christ, could bring the needy of the world for help.[82] More by Christian instinct than by reasoning from some of the world-negating ascetic principles that they explicitly stated, the great leaders of Christianity during those years worked to better the life situation of their people.[83]

On the other hand, the very detachment from the things of this world, at least for those who aspired to Christian perfection, that was inculcated into people was designed to dissuade them from the kind of commitment to "secular" social structures which would have eventuated in profound social change.[84] The remarkable thing is (as we will have to examine in detail later) that such "secular" implications of Christianity did develop; but they did so "outside the walls," not only unencouraged by official Christianity but generally looked down upon as inferior and occasionally opposed.[85] Actually such development took refuge in the resurgence of lay responsibility, though now it occurred apart from "the sacred" and continued to drift further away until it eventuated in what was (until very recently) pejoratively called "modern secularism."[86]

Part of the confused attitude towards the church/world relation was the position taken by the Roman bishops from Leo I onward on the question of *sacerdotium* and *imperium*.[87] The two alternatives are posited by Gelasius[88] (the *imperium* is an instrument of the *sacerdotium*, since the latter really implies the plenitude of power over men) and Justinian[89] (the *sacerdotium* is the instrument of the *imperium*, since the latter implies the plenitude of power). If one takes seriously such papal claims, it follows that the church through its official leadership is responsible for the temporal common good, responsible for establishing those forms of human social existence which would most benefit men and women in a given historical situation. Such responsibility the episcopate never shouldered, at least during the period we are discussing.

It contented itself with striving to keep the Justinian alternative from being implemented in such fashion that it, the church, would lose its own proper freedom.[90] It is with Hildebrand and the emergence of the medieval papal power that this question will come to a head, though it does not then find a true solution.

NOTES

1. This is evidenced by Matthew 20:25–28 and by the Gospel accounts of Jesus' baptism and transfiguration. See J. Jeremias, "Pais theou," *Theological Dictionary of the New Testament*, vol. 5, pp. 700–717; K. Rengstorf, "Doulos," *ibid.*, vol. 2, pp. 270–79.

2. For example, the classic chapter 34 in Ezekiel, or Homer's regular use of *"poimen laon"* (shepherd of the peoples) for Agamemnon.

3. We have already discussed the question as to whether and in what sense the Twelve were really "apostles," and whether and in what sense one can speak of an "apostolic office." Whatever the historical reality might have been, by early in the second century the Twelve are assumed to have been *the* apostles and to have been the first bearers of the pastoral responsibility.

4. We have discussed the impact of Old Testament ideas of priesthood in chapters 2 and 9, and will study the influence of the Byzantine idea of *"basileus"* in chapter 22.

5. *Didascalia*, chap. 7; Cyprian *Epist.* 61.

6. See *Didascalia*, chaps. 9 and 11, which discuss the cooperation of bishop and deacons; and Cyprian's many letters to his clergy, in which he talks about the various ministerial needs of the community, for which the presbyters and deacons must provide in Cyprian's absence.

7. See Cyprian *De ecclesiae unitate* 4.

8. *Apostolic Tradition* 3. 4.

9. However, Ignatius' use of the image in *Phil.* 2 (he simply uses the word "shepherd" to refer to the *episkopos*) seems to indicate that this usage was common. Obviously, the image of shepherd is prominent in Hermas, but it is not applied to church leaders. On early symbolisms for the church and its ministers, see H. Rahner, *Symbole der Kirche* (Salzburg, 1964).

10. *Paed.* 1. 1–5.

11. This points up the necessity of accurate theological understanding, and therefore of careful theological formation, in those who exercise such ministry.

12. It might be good to reiterate the falsity of contrasting "charismatic" to "institutional" when speaking of ministries in the early church, for governing is itself a charism (1 Cor. 12:28). See E. Schweizer, *Church Order in the New Testament* (London, 1971), pp. 181–87.

13. There is the further question (which we try to treat in the theological portion of our work) about the nature of ruling in Christianity. Is there, for example, any real place for *jurisdiction* in the conduct of the Christian community?

14. The whole of part 1 in the *De cura pastorali* is devoted to discussing the nature of governing in the church, the necessary qualifications, etc., which makes it clear that Gregory saw the episcopacy as essentially a task of government.

15. See H. Davis, introduction to *St. Gregory the Great: Pastoral Care*, Ancient Christian Writers Series (Westminster, Md., 1950), pp. 9–14.

16. In part 3, which gives detailed instructions about preaching, the dominant word is *"admonere"*: how to admonish slaves and masters, how to admonish the wise and the dull, how to admonish the impudent and the timid, etc.

17. This is grounded, of course, in Christ, the primary teacher, being himself the new lawgiver and the new Law; see *Paed.* 1. 7–12.

18. See W. Telfer, *The Office of a Bishop* (London, 1962), pp. 158–86.

19. *Apology* 1 67.

20. Cyprian *Epist.* 12.

21. *Ibid.* 7.

22. See Telfer, pp. 165–76.

23. See K. Baus, *Handbook of Church History* (New York, 1965), vol. 1, pp. 352–53.

24. See Telfer, pp. 175–81.

25. Eusebius *H.E.* 6. 41.

26. Justin (*Apology 1* 67) mentions that the Eucharistic collections support the widows and orphans.

27. See L. Schmidt, *Cambridge Medieval History*, 2d ed. (Cambridge, 1966), vol. 1, pp. 312–22.

28. This was further complicated by the drastic shift in economic and commercial patterns that came with the confrontation of Teutonic and Roman institutions; see P. Vinogradoff, *Cambridge Medieval History*, vol. 1, pp. 542–67.

29. On the extensive financial undertaking this involved for bishops of the more important sees, see F. Dudden, *Gregory the Great* (Oxford, 1905), vol. 1, pp. 295–320.

30. See J.-R. Palanque in A. Fliche and V. Martin, *Histoire de l'Eglise depuis les origines jusqu'à nos jours* (Paris, 1935—), vol. 3, pp. 437–88.

31. See Isidore of Seville *De eccles. officiis* 2. 5. 18–19; R. Aigrain in Fliche-Martin, vol. 5, pp. 368–69.

32. See J. Daniélou and H. Marrou, *The Christian Centuries* (London, 1964), vol. 1, p. 328.

33. *C.I.* 1. 3. 41; trans. in P. Coleman-Norton, *Roman State and Christian Church* (London, 1966), vol. 3, pp. 1018–19.

34. In fact, in the late Merovingian period certain cities have been handed over to bishops to govern; see C. Pfister, *Cambridge Medieval History*, vol. 2, pp. 142–45.

35. This was particularly true of the more important episcopal centers such as Rome; see H. Moss, *The Birth of the Middle Ages* (Oxford, 1935), pp. 132–33.

36. See F. Van der Meer, *Augustine the Bishop* (London, 1961), pp. 129–264; F. Dudden, *The Life and Times of St. Ambrose* (Oxford, 1935), vol. 1, pp. 117–24.

37. See Eusebius *H.E.* 10. 5. 15–17; Coleman-Norton, p. 28.

38. See Council of Carthage in 421, canons 9 and 10 (*Mansi* 4. 450); Council of Hippo, canon 9 (*Mansi* 4. 442).

39. See Coleman-Norton, *Roman State and Christian Church.*

40. By the early Middle Ages the term *"episcopatus"* came to denominate not just the episcopal office or the episcopal see but also the material goods of the church that were under his administration. See A. Dumas in Fliche-Martin, vol. 7, pp. 220–21. See also Justinian's legislation on the administrative responsibilities of bishops, which concentrates on care of ecclesiastical property; *C.I.* 1. 3. 41 (Coleman-Norton, pp. 1018–19).

41. See Moss, pp. 131–33.

42. Thus the bishop was not free to dispose of this property: "Ut episcopus matricis non usurpet quid fuerit donatum ecclesiis quae in diocesi constituta sunt. Ut episcopi rem ecclesiae sine Primatis concilio non vendant. Ut presbyteri rem ecclesiae sine conscientia episcopi non vendant." (Council of Hippo, canon 9 [*Mansi* 4. 442].) So, also, the Justinian legislation referred to above (n. 40) forbids alienation of church property by the bishop.

43. For an appraisal of the turning point under Constantine, see Baus, pp. 426–32.

44. E.g., Constantine's use of Hosius of Cordova. See V. C. de Clerq, *New Catholic Encyclopedia* (New York, 1967), vol. 7, pp. 153–54.

45. For an account of Ambrose's activity in this regard, see Dudden, *St. Ambrose*, pp. 115–26. Despite Ambrose's prominence as a metropolitan in a key city, his activity was quite typical of bishops of his time.

46. See Telfer, pp. 178–86.

47. This had begun with Constantine; see Eusebius *H.E.* 10. 7; Coleman-Norton, p. 44.

48. See Dudden, *St. Ambrose*, pp. 121–22.

49. See *Cod. Theod.* 1. 27. 1.

50. The details of this agonizing experience of the Antiochean populace and of their bishop's role in obtaining some clemency are provided by John Chrysostom's twenty-one "Homilies on the Statues."

51. Cyprian's letters to his church, and especially the frequent letters to his clergy, were indeed written during the circumstances of persecution, but they do reflect the kinds of administrative detail he had to handle. Much the same picture is conveyed by the *Didascalia*, which makes it clear that the entire practical administration of the church is the care of the bishop, though he delegates much of it to the deacon.

52. See G. Bonner, *St. Augustine of Hippo* (London, 1963), pp. 121–27.

53. Dudden, *Gregory the Great*, pp. 242–51.

54. On the early (i.e., fourth-century) development of the centralized administration of the prominent metropolitan sees, see J.-R. Palanque in Fliche-Martin, vol. 3, pp. 437–88.

55. Understandably, but not too happily, the Constantinian recognition of the church quickly changed the social status and social behavior of the higher clergy; see H. Chadwick, *The Early Church* (London, 1967), pp. 160–65.

56. See. J.-P. Audet, *Structures of Christian Priesthood* (New York, 1968), pp. 55–66.

57. *Didache* 11–13.

58. The Justinian Code (*C.I.* 1. 3. 41) presumes the existence of a hostel (along with hospital, almshouse, orphanage, and nursery) as a common element in the property to be administered by the bishop.

59. In the West, care of the poor and hospitality for travelers was a basic principle of monastic behavior. See *Regula S. Benedicti* 53. 30–31; D. Knowles, *The Monastic Orders in England*, 2d ed. (Cambridge, 1963), pp. 479–86.

60. See G. Schnurer, *Church and Culture in the Middle Ages* (Paterson, N.J., 1956), vol. 1, pp. 488–89.

61. One of the most touching of these testimonies is Gregory of Nazianzus' funeral oration for his father, in which he describes his father's daily pastoral concern for his congregation.

62. While not all healing involves the miraculous, the question of miracles (their nature, possibility, etc.) is tied in with any discussion of a special gift of healing; on the theology of the miraculous, see L. Monden, *Signs and Wonders* (New York, 1966).

63. Actually, the earliest accounts of the martyrs are quite free of the legendary details about miraculous preservation from wild beasts, fire, etc.—such details are added a bit later. What the earlier accounts of the martyrs do stress is the extraordinary fortitude of the Christians in facing torture and death, e.g., in the account of Polycarp's death, or in the account of the martyrdom of Perpetua and Felicitas.

64. See B. Poschmann, *Penance and the Anointing of the Sick* (New York, 1964), pp. 234–41.

65. *Apostolic Tradition* 15. The text states that hands are not laid upon such a healer, but there is recognition of some special charismatic ministry.

66. See H. Leclercq, *Dictionnaire d'archéologie chrétienne et de liturgie* (Paris, 1903ff.), vol. 10, cols. 2432–58; Sulpicius Severus, *Vita B. Martini*, chaps. 16–19.

67. See Gregory of Tours, *De miraculis S. Martini*; Daniélou-Marrou, pp. 318–19.

68. For a listing and brief description of Gregory's writings, see H. Beck, in *New Catholic Encyclopedia*, vol. 6, pp. 798–99.

69. See E. Duckett, *Gateway to the Middle Ages: Monasticism* (Ann Arbor, Mich., 1961), p. 175.

70. As credulity in such healing power developed, so did a fear of witches, which is just the other side of the coin: the power of those who were somehow linked with the forces of evil to do harm to others.

71. Basic to this usage is the notion of Christ as physician; for early Christian reference to Christ as *"medicus,"* see R. Arbesmann, "The Concept of *Christus Medicus* in St. Augustine," *Traditio* 10 (1954), pp. 1–28.

72. This is already quite thoroughly developed in Origen; see H. von Campenhausen,

Ecclesiastical Authority and Spiritual Power in the Church of the First Three Centuries (Palo Alto, Calif., 1969), pp. 250–62. On the role of the spiritual director, see I. Hausherr, *Dictionnaire de spiritualité*, vol. 3, cols. 1008–60.

73. Hausherr, cols. 1023–32.

74. This is a constant theme in Gregory's *De cura pastorali*: the admonition furnished by the pastor in his preaching is aimed at healing the sinner. On the theme of salvation as a healing from evil, see Alcuin *Epist.* 112. In this instance, however, the healing is discussed in terms of the confession of sins and sacerdotal absolution rather than with reference to the healing influence of preaching.

75. See R. Roques, *Dictionnaire de spiritualité*, vol. 3, cols. 264–86.

76. *Ibid.*, cols. 270–75; see also Roques, *L'univers dionysien* (Paris, 1954), pp. 176–77; and W. Völker, *Kontemplation und Ekstase bei Pseudo-Dionysius Areopagita* (Weisbaden, 1958), pp. 78–83.

77. On the Neo-Platonism of the fathers, see R. Arnou, *Dictionnaire de théologie catholique*, vol. 12, cols. 2258–392. On the influence of Pseudo-Dionysius, see A. Rayez, *Dictionnaire de spiritualité*, vol. 3, cols. 286–429.

78. On this ambivalent relationship, see H. Marrou, *Saint Augustin et la fin de la culture antique*, 4th ed. (Paris, 1958); and C. Cochrane, *Christianity and Classic Culture* (London, 1944).

79. For a brief summation of Gregory's eschatology, which had such a marked impact on medieval thought and imagery, see Dudden, *Gregory the Great*, vol. 2, pp. 430–37.

80. See L. Bouyer, *Spirituality of the New Testament and the Fathers*, vol. 1 of *History of Christian Spirituality* (New York, 1963), pp. 422–54.

81. It could not do so, of course, if it remained faithful to the opening chapters of Genesis or to the prologue to John's Gospel. In many ways the temptation (if one can call it that) which endangered Christian orthodoxy was not so much the Neo-Platonic view of matter as evil as it was the Christianized version of the Stoic spiritual athlete, i.e., the ascetic who was capable of heroic denial of the ordinary claims of human bodiliness and feeling.

82. *Hom. Luc.* 34.

83. This is a good example of the theology at two levels which is important to bear in mind in historical study of Christian thought. The pragmatic translation of Christian insights into necessary social structures or religious practices can and did at times represent a more accurate theologizing than some of the verbal formulations.

84. Thus, monastic abandonment of "the world" became quite quickly the ideal path of achieving true Christian life, and development of theology about Christian perfection was almost totally confined to reflection on a monastic approach to Christian life.

85. One reflection of this was the attitude of the church towards civic service in the post-Constantinian era. The principal interest seems to be that of obtaining and preserving exemption for Christian clergy from the general civic responsibility of accepting public office. Even prior to the fourth century, Cyprian had enunciated the principle that the ordained should never be involved in secular affairs (*Epist.* 1).

86. On the late medieval and modern aspects of this development, see G. Lagarde, *La naissance de l'esprit laïque* (Louvain, 1956). However, as we will see, a major breakthrough in lay involvement in both church and worldly affairs came with the twelfth-century resurgence of European culture; but it was gradually repressed.

87. This will be examined in detail in chapter 22, pp. 444–51.

88. On the somewhat ambiguous position of Gelasius, see F. Dvornik, *Early Christian and Byzantine Political Philosophy* (Washington, D.C., 1966), vol. 2, pp. 804–9. As Dvornik points out, the main thrust of the Gelasian statements was to deny *sacerdotium* to the Byzantine emperors.

89. See *C.I.* 1. 3. 41 and 1. 4. 34.

90. This is not to say that bishops were inactive in providing for their people's needs; indeed, church officials increasingly assumed responsibility for education, care of the sick, even civic administration, as the older Roman structures collapsed (see Daniélou-Marrou, pp. 435–48).

CHAPTER 17

Medieval Structures of

Church Service

As medieval society came into existence, the church's role of service underwent considerable change. Most basic to this change was the complete coincidence of the constituencies of ecclesiastical and civil society. There was just the one *societas christiana*. This meant that the church (and increasingly "the church" meant the clergy, with special emphasis on the higher clergy) found itself involved in establishing and maintaining those basic needs of any society: order, unity, provision for the indigent, law, and justice.[1] At the same time, the church's own religious activity demanded ever more complicated organization. Perhaps it might be more accurate to say that a highly complicated ecclesiastical world came into existence and that a considerable portion of clerical time and energy was spent in making this structure function in somewhat unified and effective fashion. When one reflects upon the early medieval period, the fragmentation of European society in the period of the Teutonic invasions, the quick dissolution of the unity achieved by the Carolingians, the overlay and interaction of Teutonic and Roman law, the rich but confusing diversity of liturgies and religious folklore and vernacular languages, there can be no question but what the later medieval unification of Europe (with all its deficiencies and fragility) is a most impressive achievement. That the ordained ministers of the church were at the very heart of this achievement is undeniable. No matter how one evaluates theologically the medieval understanding of Christian ministry, the ecclesiastical activity of those centuries does translate a certain view

of Christian ministry and priesthood, one in which service to people is a dominant element.[2]

Church Administration

Since the superiority of the spiritual over the bodily (the "eternal" over the temporal) was an unquestioned value judgment of these centuries, it followed that the church's most important task was to make available to the faithful the necessary means to their salvation. This meant the provision of some rudimentary instruction about the faith, opportunity for reception of the necessary sacraments, and regular religious services in which they could fulfill their obligation to worship God. To provide all this, a complex and somewhat disjointed administrative structure emerged.[3]

Parishes

As the patristic period gives way to the early Middle Ages, the system of baptismal churches which finds its origins in the Latin countries and in Roman legislation is already in conflict with the proprietary churches which are supported by (if not grounded in) the usages of Teutonic feudal society. The ancient baptismal churches had been directly under the bishop, their ministers were supplied and directed by him, and they had the traditional right to the Sunday Mass, to burial, to baptisms and weddings.[4] During the seventh and eighth centuries these baptismal churches were merged in rural areas of

Italy, Gaul, and Spain into a system of large parishes. At the same time, the Germanic areas produced increasingly the opposing structure of the "proprietary church." This was a system in which the church building with its attached properties was the focus, in which control (including the appointment of the church's pastor) lay in the hands of a "proprietor," and in which the proprietor profited from the income of church properties.

Needless to say, the episcopacy reacted strongly to this secular infringement on the functioning of church life, and a compromise of sorts was worked out under Charlemagne. The church building was still held by the proprietor, but the priests of a given proprietary church were made subject to episcopal jurisdiction, and a certain financial independence of these priests was guaranteed in exchange for religious services rendered in the church.[5] As these proprietary churches thus became more incorporated into episcopal structures (at least in regard to their "spiritual" functioning), and large parishes proved inadequate to provide for the increasing rural population, more and more small parishes emerged and succeeded for the most part to the juridical rights of the old baptismal churches.[6]

In rural situations, then, the presbyters found themselves in a semicontractual situation. Through a compromise arrangement of their ecclesiastical and temporal overlords, these clergy were provided for financially in exchange for their performance of the pastoral tasks. In the cities, a somewhat different evolution occurred: the collegiate chapters were attached to the cathedrals or other larger churches. From the time of Louis the Pious (specifically his reform of 816–817) these chapters were composed of canons, the monastic communities being clearly distinguished from them. Their function was to provide for the liturgy, the school, the material possessions of the church, and the care of souls. In exchange, again a semicontractual arrangement, they were provided an income. This income, at first collegially held, gradually developed into part of the benefice system and

was quite eagerly sought in the later Middle Ages.[7]

During the later Middle Ages a multiplicity of patterns is still found in the parish structure. In rural areas the system of the patronage supported the position of powerful proprietors, but in other instances rural communities themselves administered their own church. Still other churches (with their benefices) came into the possession of monasteries, and in some cases churches belonged to families or to pious fraternities. In all of these, however, there is a certain basic similarity in the powers, responsibilities, activity, and way of life of the parish clergy. In charge of the parish is the pastor whose function it is to provide for the cultic worship in his church (Mass on Sundays and on other established occasions) and for the administration of sacraments, the instruction of the faithful, and the establishment of peace and order in the community.[8] Often, he is the only literate person in the parish (or at least he is presumed to be such). This and his sacred character give him a position of prestige. On the other hand, the rural pastor is generally quite uncultured, being drawn from the peasant or artisan classes, and lives (often in disregard of clerical celibacy) much like his parishioners.[9]

Dependent upon the extent of his responsibilities, the pastor could provide assistance for himself by recruiting a vicar and a sacristan (who was a cleric). In some instances, the vicar worked under the pastor, his position was viewed as preparation for becoming a pastor, and he was without established situation within the diocesan clergy. But in the later Middle Ages there seem to have been increasing instances in which the pastorate (and, of course, the accompanying income) of a given parish was held officially by an individual or a "corporation" (such as a monastery) who did not perform the pastoral responsibilities but hired a vicar to act as the actual pastor.[10]

As the Middle Ages progressed, the parish became an ever more clerically populated situation. In the century after the Carolingian reforms one would still find (in general) one pastor providing for a given parish. By the thirteenth century a parish would involve not only the "parish church" with its pastor and his assistants but a number of other founded chapels (established by rich families, or by pious confraternities) with a corps of "chaplains" who were only loosely connected with the parish church. Sometimes these chaplains helped with the care of souls and the liturgy, but sometimes they competed with the pastor by holding their own services and administering sacraments. In addition, if the parish contained the castle of some noble, the castle had its own chapel and chaplain to provide for the family.[11]

Towards the end of the thirteenth century quite a different pattern is clearly emerging. With the rapid growth of cities, the life of the church is once more gravitating back to the urban parish. Now, however, there are numerous parishes in such cities as Cologne or Lubeck, some under the bishop and others conducted with various exemptions from episcopal control by religious clergy. Not only are clergy numerous but their numbers plus their large-scale property holdings and claims to exemption from taxation make them a heavy burden on the populace. As a result, the bourgeoisie work to free themselves from the bishop's political control and to bring all the various institutions of the city (schools, hospitals, and parishes) under their own control. This meant in many cases that municipal governments administered the property of the churches and even appointed pastors for the various parishes. A strong link between the clergy and bourgeoisie came into being since most of these appointees came from bourgeois families.[12]

Diocesan Structures

The more strictly ecclesiastical or spiritual aspects of the early medieval episcopate tend to be overshadowed by the investiture struggle, which came to a head during the Gregorian reforms of the eleventh century,[13] and by the constant involvement of the episcopal office in the benefice system.[14] All this points, of course, to the role of the bishop as a public dignitary who often possessed considerable power and wealth since he was a member of medieval aristocracy, an associate or competitor of princes. Yet, the essential activity of the medieval bishop still had to do with *ministerium verbi et sacramenti*, though his precise function in this ministry was increasingly one of supervising the activity of the lower clergy. Even this supervisory role, requiring as it did the visitation of the various parishes of the diocese, participation in regional synods, and officiating as ecclesiastical judge, became too large a task. For a time, the somewhat ill-defined office of *chorepiscopus* (roughly like an auxiliary bishop) was utilized, with these "assistant bishops" functioning in the rural areas; but by the end of the tenth century this institution had been abandoned.[15] The more lasting means of handling this need for "decentralization" was the deanery system, which began as early as the seventh century and with some modifications continues to our own day. Acting as the bishop's delegate, though he generally was elected by the pastors and vicars of the deanery with the bishop's approval, the dean helped to provide education, stimulation, and adjudication for the parish clergy. Naturally, he was expected to keep a watchful eye on the accuracy of doctrine and on the moral behavior of the clergy.[16]

While the bishop's jurisdiction applied more directly to such things as penitential discipline and administration of ecclesiastical properties, it also found expression in his service to the needy. Precisely because the goods of the church were in large measure committed to his stewardship, it was his task to see that the traditional Christian duty of *diakonia* to the neglected members of society was fulfilled. Moreover, he had the nebulous but important task of seeing to it that the general state of medieval society—economic, social, moral, military, and intellectual—was such that it could foster true human development and "growth in grace." It is instructive to discover the extent to which great bishops of these centuries were committed to bettering the entire social fabric of their society, something which they apparently saw as intrinsic to their position as bishops.

To handle these many tasks, the bishop not only delegated much of his responsibility to such agencies as the deanery but also gathered around him a group of trusted associates. Actually, one can distinguish two groups of assistants who tend to balance one another in power and influence. The more ancient of these is the cathedral chapter, whose most eminent member, the archdeacon, was a person whose power often approximated that of the bishop himself. Often enough, though he was appointed by the bishop, the archdeacon worked in tension with (even opposition to) the bishop, as did also the chapter.[17] Though both archdeacon and chapter remain powerful, actually the chapter probably reached the zenith of its influence in the thirteenth century.[18] The episcopal "chancery office" assumes greater importance from the twelfth century onward.[19]

Papal Government

If the average bishop felt a responsibility for the overall well-being of the entire populace and way of life in his diocese, and spent most of his time directing in administrative and supervisory fashion the activity of others, this was *a fortiori* true of the popes who (by their own statements) bore the *cura omnium ecclesiarum*. Already by the time of Gregory I the pope was not only engaged in doctrinal, liturgical, and disciplinary affairs far beyond the bounds of his own diocese, he was also in communication and sometimes controversy with temporal rulers of both East and West. Moreover, he had the administrative charge of the ever increasing material possessions of the Roman church, the "patrimony of St. Peter." Inevitably this meant a growing staff of officials, secretaries, and assistants of various sorts. Increasingly powerful in this Roman governmental structure is the College of Cardinals. However, compared with the mushrooming of Roman bureaucracy in the twelfth and thirteenth centuries, the administrative setup prior to the Gregorian reform was relatively simple.[20]

Supreme pontiff, possessed of the *plenitudo potestatis* over all Christians, head of the papal state and thus exercising powerful political and economic control, a twelfth- or thirteenth-century pope was the most influential ruler of medieval Europe.[21] To organize and expedite the mounting burden of official papal business, a rapid expansion and reorganization of the Roman curia took place in the twelfth century. The resultant power and autonomy of curial officials began to raise protests from such eminent critics as Bernard of Clairvaux and John of Salisbury.[22] However, such protests did nothing to slow down the rapid expansion of curial offices and business. Fortunately, the legal and administrative genius of thirteenth-century popes brought about a streamlining of curial structures and procedures, and so kept the burgeoning bureaucracy from becoming unmanageable.[23] Yet, the very size and complexity of the Roman curia in the thirteenth century "made it clear how extensive the practical direction of the Church by the Pope had become. Weighed down by all the weaknesses of large bureaucracies, but also distinguished by astonishing achievements in tribunal, *camera*, and chapel, the Thirteenth-Century Curia was one of the most impressive phenomena of Church life in the High Middle Ages."[24]

All this might well give the impression that the medieval popes were monarchs of unchallenged power. In a sense this was true, at least after the triumph of the Gregorian reforms, but at least three forces acted as counterpoises to papal absolutism. The first of these, the attempts of the laity to rediscover an effective voice in both secular and ecclesiastical life (which found its most prominent but by no means isolated expression in the claims and actions of medieval kings), was quite effectively sidetracked by reiterating the papal claims to be supreme teacher, judge, etc., *de jure divino*.[25] But the other two, the medieval "ecumenical" councils and the College of Cardinals, were at least partially of papal creation, and so drew themselves upon the power and prestige of the papacy, at the same time that they presented a challenge to that power.

Both the emergence of a conciliar movement (which finds focus in the later Council of Constance) and the power struggle between popes and the College of Cardinals are complex ecclesiastical phenomena,[26] and even an abbreviated description of their structure and procedures goes beyond our topic of ministry. However, the increasing power of the cardinals (who at this period are claiming a share in the *plenitudo potestatis* of the Roman see) and the manner in which this was often an obstacle to genuine ministerial service to the Christian faithful do bear brief examination. It is a natural tendency for branches of government, or any other organization, that are established as "service departments" to become ends in themselves, with the result that those who were meant to be served find themselves subordinated to the well-being of the "service department." It is also a natural development that persons or agencies that become powerful and prestigious arouse envy and hostility. So, it is not surprising to find that for centuries, actually for as long as the College of Cardinals has been prominent, there has been a steady current of criticism directed against the Roman curia, most specially against the cardinals involved in it, charging that the Roman bureaucracy failed to serve the true needs of the members of the church. One can, of course, dismiss some of this criticism as ignorant, spiteful, or malicious; but much of the criticism has been voiced by men and women who were recognized for their competence and sanctity. As a result, the historical evidence raises the question: To what extent or in what ways can complex administrative structures implement the basic Christian responsibility of *diakonia*?

Religious Communities

In any discussion of "service" in medieval Christianity, the activity of organized religious communities looms large. Much of the task of helping people "bear the burdens of this life while preparing for the next" was carried on by these groups. Before going on,

however, to examine the service contributions of these communities, it is necessary to ask, How was the very formation and existence of such communities a service?

Obviously, the orderly, purposeful sequence of activities in the monastic community served the needs of the monks or nuns, providing them with a "guaranteed" means of expressing their faith and of fulfilling their Christian obligation of giving worship to God. As a by-product, the liturgical functions of the monastery provided the context of worship for many of the Christian faithful who lived near the monastery. Then, too, the monastic communities performed for the Christian people as a whole the unparalleled service of praying to God and thus winning his favor and blessings for mankind. And in a subtle way, the monastic community provided a model of Christian living that could serve as somewhat of a guide to other Christians. However, it does not seem unfair to say that the emphasis in monastic communities (and the clear theoretical justification for their existence) was found in "service of God," the liturgical *opus Dei*, rather than in "service of men."[27]

Both the communities of canons (such as the Augustinians or the Praemonstratensians) and the mendicant orders were more explicitly directed to serving the faithful, though the structures of their life remained basically monastic. Even more clearly oriented to the needs of the medieval Christian populace were the Mercedarians and Trinitarians, established to help the enslaved, the various military orders (Hospitallers, Templars, etc.), and a number of orders founded for hospital work. In these communities (and, in less formally organized and binding fashion, in any number of pious fraternities) men and women could find the context in which effectively to serve their fellow man. The proliferation of such religious foundations could create an impression of uncontrolled "religious joining," and it did actually lead in the twelfth and thirteenth centuries to tightened controls by the papacy over the establishment of new groups; but it also bears testimony to the widespread dedication of medieval Christians to the service of the needy.[28]

Social Apostolate

One who investigates the involvement of the medieval church, and more specifically of the medieval clergy, in the social issues and problems of that period must be careful not to draw hasty theological conclusions about the sphere of properly Christian *diakonia*.

Leaving aside our theoretical questions about the proper spheres of civil and ecclesiastical institutions in dealing with men's social needs (questions which to a large extent have become clarified for us quite recently because of such societal occurrences as separation of church and state), we cannot but be impressed by the extent to which the medieval church, and particularly its ordained ministers, was involved in caring for these needs. Superficial reading of medieval history can leave the impression that ecclesiastical activity was directed exclusively to preparing Christians for "the next life." Unquestionably, emphasis was laid on the hereafter (such is intrinsic to Christian faith and hope!); but one observes also an ever mounting effort to make the "waiting period" of this earthly life as humanly decent as possible. It does not seem accidental that the great evangelical revival in the twelfth century is accompanied by the social and cultural renaissance that points to modern civilization. Unfortunately, ecclesiastical officialdom became suspicious both of the nonclerical elements in the religious revival and of the "secular" elements in the cultural renaissance. This led to the result (among others) that Christian interest in improving the human situation tended to be channeled into the "works of mercy" undertaken by pious groups under clerical direction.[29]

Education

From the dawn of the Middle Ages through to the time of the Reformation, education—profane as well as sacred—was a major undertaking of the church. Indeed, until the twelfth century the educational institutions were almost totally conducted by clerics. During this period, the monastic schools (in Ireland and Britain as well as on the Continent) were the principal depositories and communicators of culture. Even when a temporal ruler lent his support and resources to education, as happened in the Carolingian renaissance, the staffing and direction of the court school had to be drawn from Europe's monasteries. However, the monastic schools were not alone in the field; quite a number of important episcopal sees could boast of an excellent cathedral school in which a solid foundation in the liberal arts prepared for study of the sacred sciences. Instruction on all levels was apparently a clerical monopoly: monks in the monastic schools, canons in the cathedral schools.[30]

After the cultural decline of the tenth century, a relatively few institutions (monastic schools such as Bec and Sankt Gallen, cathedral schools at Reims and Chartres and Cologne) provided the forward thrust that eventuated in the renaissance of the twelfth century. In this twelfth-century flowering of medieval life and thought there was a continuing impact of monastic learning and culture. Rupert of Deutz, Suger of Saint-Denis, William of Saint-Thierry, and Hugh of Saint-Victor are but a few of the illustrious names in monastic circles. But the creative initiative passed increasingly to the cathedral schools and (especially in Italy, where the direction was nonclerical) to the urban schools.[31] It was out of these urban schools, in an evolution that has been often described, that the medieval universities came into being.[32] Even though these universities marked a new step in the direction of "secular education," the ecclesiastical influence was still very strong. For example, the licensing of professors in Paris was under the control of the chancellor (the official of the cathedral chapter who was charged with supervision of the university). Little by little, however, the university faculties established their independence; episcopal involvement and jurisdiction became formalities.[33] This did not mean that the climate of the university was less ecclesiastical. Most of the students were clerics, and (except for Bologna) the professors were to be clerics; besides, many students lived a type of community life in hostels provided by the wealthy or by religious communities.[34]

Actually, the thrust towards secularization of education does not seem to have come from the desire of academicians, either students or faculty, for autonomous control of their institutions, though this was certainly a factor. Rather, in the late medieval development of cities and the concomitant emergence of a powerful urban bourgeoisie there was a widespread reaction against clerical domination. Basically it had to do with economic and political power as cities strove to free themselves from episcopal government and the burden of clerical exemption from taxation, but it quickly widened (in the fourteenth and fifteenth centuries) into a campaign for control of parishes, hospitals, and schools. But even as schools passed into control by the city, clerics continued in great numbers as teachers in these schools.[35] So it was that from beginning to end of the Middle Ages the task of teaching was carried on by monks and diocesan clergy, and such teaching was apparently considered an appropriate expression of the ordained minister's special call to service in the church.

Hospitals

Extensive as it was, the involvement in education was not the only important clerical contribution to the advance of medieval society. Also of major importance was the establishment and maintaining of hospitals and other shelters for the sick, indigent, and travelers. In some instances a group of dedicated laity conducted a shelter for travelers, which then developed into a permanent operation and the group into a recognized religious community—as with the famous Alpine hospice of St. Bernard.[36] Similarly, a hospital would be established, often financed by some rich nobleman, and this led to the foundation of an order. Such was the origin of the famous Order of Hospitallers which later evolved into a military order, at which point the hospital work was almost entirely turned over to the brothers in the group.[37] In many cases, hospitals were conducted by pious confraternities of one sort or another which never

did develop into formal religious communities; such foundations became quite numerous as European urbanization accelerated. On the other hand, in the outlying colonial regions it was chiefly the Praemonstratensians, Cistercians, and Teutonic Knights who provided the hospital care.[38]

Along with this rapid development of new forms of hospital care (from the twelfth century), there was an expansion of already existent institutions. In many places, bishops had had provisions of a kind for the sick; these were now expanded. Monasteries had always had a tradition of hospitality; the hostels attached to the monastery became increasingly a shelter for travelers, though in many instances it was the wealthy and the nobility who stayed at these monastic hostels.[39] Hospital orders, both military and nonmilitary, increased in number in the thirteenth century; and other groups, both canons regular and mendicants, became more and more involved in work with the sick and needy.[40]

Once urbanization accelerated in the thirteenth century, the institutions of religious groups proved inadequate to the increased medical needs of the populace, and municipalities assumed an increasing proportion of hospital direction. However, even in this growth of municipal hospitals, the ecclesiastical authorities were involved in providing for the spiritual welfare of the patients; in many instances the civil administrators committed the actual hospital work to confraternities or hospital orders. Thus, to the end of the Middle Ages there was widespread involvement in hospital care on the part of ordained ministers.[41]

Parish Works of Mercy

From the earliest formation of Christian communities and throughout the process of their development into some form of "parish," the individual or group charged with the care of the community functioned in a vaguely defined area of "helping people in time of need." This could involve financial difficulties, sickness, family disputes, or death. One of the most consistent activities of pastors was to console and fortify the dying, provide Christian burial and prayers for the deceased, and counsel and comfort the bereaved family.

As the ecclesiastical structures of the parish developed in the late patristic and then medieval periods, it was the rector (pastor) of the parish church who was legally responsible for such tasks. In those situations where a system of vicars functioned as the actual implementation of parish ministry, the vicar was expected to provide regularly for the needs of the faithful. Often enough, though, the service provided for the people was inadequate or totally lacking; in these situations the mendicant friars often made a major contribution. The mendicants were particularly effective in their work among the masses of people who began moving into cities towards the end of the Middle Ages, effective enough to arouse the ire of bishops and diocesan clergy who resented the many exemptions granted these religious by the pope.[42]

When it came to provision for the indigent within the parish, it was assumed that Christian charity would motivate the pastor and the more prosperous members of the community to provide for such needy brethren. However, it was not left entirely to such assumption. The church law of the Middle Ages encouraged clergy and religious to be hospitable to the poor, but it also legislated for relief to be given the poor out of parish funds. Such laws are not always honored by observance; but there is good evidence that parish poor relief was a common reality in the thirteenth and fourteenth centuries. Abuses and neglect there were, but "the poor were better looked after in England in the thirteenth century than in any subsequent century until the present one."[43]

"Supervision" of the Secular

Even in the Middle Ages when religious and secular attitudes and even institutions were so intertwined, the ecclesiastical establishment could not directly legislate for civil behavior. However, since the *sacerdotium* was the soul of society, it was clearly expected to provide the ethical impetus which would keep civil institutions from exploiting people. This the ecclesiastical institution tried to do, formally and informally, and with a fair amount of success. The pattern set by Ambrose in his confrontation with Theodosius was imitated by more than one medieval bishop or pope. In some instances there was unquestionably a power struggle involved, but even in these cases the bishop or pope in the case was convinced (or at least so claimed) that he was defending the church's right to protect people from bad princes.

While the more attention-gathering aspects of the dialectic between *sacerdotium* and *regnum* took place on the level of bishops and popes with kings and princes,[44] on the lower levels of the clergy a less obvious but widespread monitoring of "secular" attitudes and activities occurred. Preaching by pastors, curates, monks, or friars evaluated the policies (political and economic) of public officials.[45] Ecclesiastics dealing with the more influential members of medieval society (as, for example, the monks in an affluent abbey playing host to prominent guests) would certainly have had the occasion to convey attitudes on public policies. However, there is indication that clerics did not always espouse a more "spiritual" point of view. Even so, the economic and social behavior of clerical or monastic groups (e.g., the new approach to agricultural economy by the Cistercians) provided models for appropriate Christian behavior in these spheres.[46]

Contribution to Cultural Development

To detail the clergy's immense contribution to medieval culture would be a practical impossibility,[47] but some advertence to this contribution is necessary in a study of the "service" ordained ministers performed in the Middle Ages. Ecclesiastical personnel on all levels were deeply involved in the process of humanizing the rather barbaric populace out of which modern Europe was formed. Being the better educated (in many situations, the only educated) members of society, the monks and diocesan clergy were the educators and the custodians of Europe's cultural heritage. Monastic communities (e.g., Cluny) were centers of artistic development and the very existence of Europe's great Romanesque and Gothic cathedrals testifies to the episcopal support of the arts. Traces of Jerome's distrust of profane culture continue throughout the medieval centuries, as in the Cistercian return to "primitive simplicity"; but the creation of medieval humanism was very largely accomplished by the church's ordained ministry.

Theological explanation of such clerical involvement in cultural development as activity proper to Christian ministry becomes a bit easier when one realizes the focal cultural impact of the liturgy in medieval life. Granted all the pastoral inadequacies of the liturgy, and they were many, the medieval celebration of liturgy was central to the lives of the people and the raison d'être for much of their art and architecture and music. Symbolisms loomed large in the consciousness of medieval men and women—all creation was a symbol of God;[48] the Mass was believed to be the greatest of symbols, for it made Christ really present.[49] So, from one point of view, the responsibility of the ordained ministry to provide for Christian cult was the very thing that led him to foster humanistic culture. Had there not been the increasing shift to emphasis on cultic activity in Christian thinking about ministry, it is hard to imagine how medieval culture could have evolved as it did.

NOTES

1. Actually, there is an important evolution in this regard. As the Middle Ages work towards their climax in the late twelfth and thirteenth centuries there is an increased provision of social needs by the ecclesiastical establishment. But in the late medieval period the agencies of secular society increasingly take over this task (which is properly theirs), with a resultant crisis in the thought and action of the church—which is not totally resolved by the twentieth century.

2. To quite an extent, this service aspect of Christian ministry finds little clarification in explicit theological reflection about ministry and priesthood, except for discussion of the minister as dispensing sacraments and canonical prescriptions about the pastor's responsibilities for the *cura animarum*. Thus, it is the *praxis* of these centuries that may provide our most important theological source.

3. Our attempt to describe official church organization and activity is heavily indebted to the Gabriel LeBras volume (vol. 12) in the A. Fliche and V. Martin *Histoire de l'Eglise depuis les origines jusqu'à nos jours* (Paris, 1935—), which is a magisterial treatment of medieval ecclesiastical institutions.

4. See F. Kempf, *Handbook of Church History* (New York, 1969), vol. 3, p. 263.

5. *Ibid.*, p. 261.

6. *Ibid.*, pp. 263–64.

7. *Ibid.*, pp. 264–66.

8. For relevant statutes detailing the pastor's obligations, see LeBras, *Institutions ecclésiastiques . . .*, vol. 12 of Fliche-Martin, pp. 406–7.

9. *Ibid.*, pp. 410–12; J. Moorman, *Church Life in England in the Thirteenth Century* (Cambridge, 1945), pp. 59–67.

10. This practice seems to have been especially widespread in England; see Moorman, pp. 38–51. However, the fact that Lateran IV had to deal with it (in its canon 29; see *Mansi* 22. 1015) as a problem indicates that the practice was not limited to England; it was one of the chief evils of the benefice system.

11. See LeBras, pp. 420–23.

12. See E. Iserloh, *Handbook of Church History*, vol. 4, pp. 566–70.

13. See Kempf, pp. 351–403.

14. *Ibid.*, pp. 270–74.

15. *Ibid.*, p. 268.

16. See LeBras, pp. 428–34.

17. *Ibid.*, pp. 376–94.

18. Cathedral chapters sent representatives to the Fourth Lateran Council (1215) and the First Council of Lyons (1245). See H. Wolter, *Handbook of Church History*, vol. 4, pp. 168–95.

19. *Ibid.*, pp. 396–403. One can quite easily see the parallel between these medieval chancery officials—chancellor, *officialis*, vicar general—and the officials in a present-day Roman Catholic chancery office.

20. See Kempf, pp. 279–85.

21. On the extent and instruments of this papal power, see LeBras, pp. 305–27.

22. See Wolter, pp. 30–34.

23. *Ibid.*, p. 262.

24. *Ibid.*, p. 267. For a detailed description of this thirteenth-century Roman curia and its functioning, see LeBras, pp. 348–62.

25. See LeBras, pp. 328–33.

26. Some aspects of these will be studied in chapter 23. On the rising power and structure of the College of Cardinals, see *ibid.*, pp. 340–48.

27. See C. Peifer, *Monastic Spirituality* (New York, 1966), pp. 504–17.

28. See Wolter, pp. 172–87.

29. Such a statement is not made in criticism of the immense good accomplished in this way, not only in medieval times but up to our own day. It seems quite clear that much, if not most, of the social need of those centuries would have been ignored if the institutions of the church had not taken the initiative. The question is, however (if one is asking theological questions about the nature of Christian ministry): What elements of this activity were proper to Christian *diakonia* only because of a temporary deficiency (or incapacity) of civic institutions?

30. On the educational scene in the ninth and tenth centuries, see E. Ewig, *Handbook of Church History*, vol. 3, pp. 115–18.

31. See Wolter, pp. 39–50. On educational developments in England during the twelfth century, see R. Southern, *Medieval Humanism and Other Studies* (Oxford, 1970), pp. 158–80.

32. See Wolter, pp. 95–97; also B. Tierney and S. Painter, *Western Europe in the Middle Ages* (New York, 1970), pp. 330–36; and F. Powicke, *Ways of Medieval Life and Thought* (Oxford, 1949), pp. 149–229.

33. See Tierney-Painter, p. 333. This does not run counter to the statement of F. Powicke in *The Christian Life in the Middle Ages* (Oxford, 1935), p. 88: "The development of education involved at every step co-operation with the Church, and in general, though not always, submission to the rules and practices gradually devised under the direction of popes, councils and bishops. Similarly, the traditions of teaching were derived from ecclesiastical education and only gradually became free."

34. See Wolter, p. 250.

35. See Iserloh, pp. 566–70.

36. Kempf, p. 460.

37. *Ibid.*, pp. 464–65.

38. See Wolter, p. 184.

39. See Moorman, pp. 353–56.

40. See Wolter, pp. 184–87.

41. See *ibid.*, p. 187.

42. See *ibid.*, p. 570.

43. B. Tierney, *Medieval Poor Law* (Berkeley, Calif., 1959), p. 109. Though dealing specifically with laws concerning care of the poor, this volume is a valuable guide to medieval conditions of the poor and of attitudes towards them; for one thing, it indicates how basically Christian the social attitudes of the period were.

44. This will be treated more fully in chapter 23. For a succinct presentation of the church-state controversy, see D. Knowles, *The Christian Centuries* (London, 1964), vol. 2, pp. 198–209, 329–37.

45. At the base of any such clerical judgments upon society lay the evolving moral theology of the Middles Ages. In the matter of moral judgments upon economic activity, much of medieval reflection centered on the question of usury and the need for a difficult adjustment of perspective on this point as Europe moved into a commercial culture. See Tierney-Painter, pp. 224–27.

46. See H. Pirenne, *History of Europe* (New York, 1956), pp. 236–37; C. Brooke, *Europe in the Central Middle Ages* (London, 1964), pp. 69–72.

47. See the bibliographies on the church and medieval culture in Tierney-Painter, pp. 377–78, and Knowles, p. 485.

48. So, Hugh of St. Victor will entitle his twelfth-century compendium of theology *De sacramentis* and find it quite appropriate to study all created reality under that rubric.

49. There has been considerable negative appraisal of medieval superstition about the Eucharist. Certainly, there was much superstition and credulity in popular belief just as there was in the mythologies of ancient religions; but scholars have become much less quick in assessing these ancient myths as naive, and the same kind of caution needs to be applied to angelology and belief in miracles.

CHAPTER 18

Reformation and Post-Reformation

Evolution

Any analysis of the church's "service to the world," when it deals specifically with the betterment of the social and economic situation, must treat of two levels: the more evident one of Christians' involvement in works of mercy (such as hospitals, orphanages, etc.) and the less apparent impact of the church on the evolution of social institutions. This distinction becomes increasingly important (and difficult to apply) as the medieval world gives way to the modern era, as feudalism very gradually fades, and as absolute monarchs and powerful bourgeois groups complement one another in shaping modern Europe. Some measure of the radical shift taking place under the surface was the reversal of the mentality concerning the relative roles of church and state in this matter. In the classic medieval view of the *respublica christiana*, the temporal power played the role of implementing in the realm of politics and economics and social structures those insights of social morality that were taught by "the church." The state was the instrument to carry out the policies of the church. In the church-state pattern that was already prominent in the fifteenth and becomes dominant from the sixteenth century, the church is meant to serve as an instrument of the civil government in inculcating and enforcing (spiritually!) morality and good order. However, on the surface level of works of mercy, there was considerable continuity in the church's *diakonia*. In the cities, where the rising bourgeoisie assumed increasing control of civic and even ecclesiastical structures, the traditional ecclesiastical undertakings of hospitals and hospices and schools quite often

came under the power of city councils, but actual involvement in the management of such enterprises remained largely clerical.[1] In the nonurban pastoral situation, whether in small towns or strictly rural areas, the role of the ordained ministry remains consistently one of trying to provide some solace and help for the people of the parish, especially for the needy. Yet, it seems clear that in all too many instances in the late Middle Ages and into the period of the Reformation, this care of the socially oppressed was neglected; instead, the privileges of the clergy (particularly their exemption from taxation) and the abuses connected with the benefice system contributed in no small measure to the economic and social burden that rested on the common man. The widespread and sharply voiced anticlericalism of the age seems to have had considerable foundation.[2]

The Church and Renaissance Humanism

The relationship between Renaissance humanism and the Reformation, indeed the very definition of Renaissance humanism, is too complicated a matter to admit of clear description; yet, the issue at stake—the reciprocal influence of religious and cultural forces in late medieval and early modern Europe—touches importantly the question about the ministry that Christianity is meant to exercise to "the world"; so, some discussion of it is unavoidable.[3] Christianity's role in the development of culture had been an underlying question that deeply affected the evolution of Latin Christianity throughout the Middle Ages and into the period of the Reformation. Nor had this been a new question for the medieval church. It had confronted primitive Christianity, had deeply troubled some of the great church fathers (particularly Jerome), and had been operative in the forces that led up to the great twelfth-century awakening of European culture. It was this cultural revival in the twelfth century that once more brought the question to the fore in various forms: the worry about Aristotelian "infiltration," the tendency of song and literature to develop in anticlerical contexts, the confrontation of civil and ecclesiastical systems of law.

Quite clearly, the modus vivendi between Christianity and "secular" culture that had been worked out in the Middle Ages, productive as it had been, involved many drawbacks and inadequacies. Above all, it produced a worldliness of attitude and life-style among higher ecclesiastics that by the late Middle Ages threatened the spiritual vitality of the church. So, the oft-repeated cry of fifteenth and sixteenth centuries: "Reform in head and members." In evaluating the reform spirit that swept the church in these centuries, one must ask how much of this cry for reform voiced a fear of the new forms that the church might take under the influence of humanistic "modernism." There was in some circles (as there is in every age) a reactionary hearkening back to "the good old days." Yet, this is more than ordinarily hard to evaluate in the sixteenth century, especially when it finds expression in the Reformation's desire to recapture the community life of primitive Christianity.

Another thing that makes it hard to clarify the sixteenth-century situation is the ambivalent stance of both Protestantism and Roman Catholicism. Neither took a "pure" position in favor of progressive movement into the modern world or, on the contrary, for retention of age-old traditions. Catholicism would foster the new art and literature, yet cling to Latin in its liturgy. It would be suspicious of democratic theories of government and scientific discoveries, yet it helped develop the very institutions of higher learning whose gradu-

ates became leaders of democratic and scientific thought. Protestantism on its side embraced the vernacular languages in translations of the Bible, in catechetics, and in liturgy. But it often shied away from Renaissance and Baroque art, the great exception being the development of church music. It emphasized individual religious autonomy, yet generally fostered for itself the status of "established religion," despite the attendant dangers of civil domination.

Still, nebulous though it was, the church's attitude to Renaissance humanism was an important component in the intellectual and religious atmosphere of the fifteenth and sixteenth centuries. It gave expression to the perennial question of the church being "in the world" but "not of the world." Into its content flowed the Augustinian tradition's distrust of the bodily and material, the medieval notion of the *respublica christiana*, the allegorical-symbolic view of the material world (as expressed, for example, in the Victorines), Cistercian and Franciscan traditions with their "spiritualized" rediscovery of the human side of Christianity, and an undercurrent of "secularity" that had been gaining forces since at least as early as the twelfth century. There was fear in the early sixteenth century that Christianity's religious heritage might be lost as the church succumbed to a renascent paganism. And there was no end of criticism of higher clergy, especially of the pope, for being too much "of the world." Yet, no one doubted that the church had a real role, ill-defined though it might be, in shaping the social and cultural patterns of human life. No one suggested that the church should restrict itself to an isolated "religious" sphere and leave the main current of human activity untouched by its influence—this suggestion would come somewhat later.[4]

In the historical context of the late Middle Ages, to ask the question about the church's involvement with civic, economic, and cultural affairs was equivalent to asking about the clergy's involvement (especially the higher clergy). By this time the equivalence of "the church" with the hierarchy and their immediate associates was common and accepted. Such equivalence was challenged by the Reformers with some success; but apart from the Radical Reformation the same identification of "church action" with "clerical action" became common in Protestantism.[5] There was the enduring outlook in both Roman Catholicism and the Reformation communities that those in official leadership positions in the church were responsible for preserving a Christian perspective in economic, political, and social life.

Charitable Works

Quite apart from intentionally fulfilling its pastoral responsibilities, the medieval church had been a principal agent in the development of those economic and social patterns which were the foundation of modern Europe. Despite the gospel teaching about detachment from wealth, the ordained ministers of the medieval church became very much involved in economic matters, and even the monastic institutions (which theoretically honored a commitment to evangelical poverty) became a major factor in Europe's financial evolution. Clearly, such absorption in economic activity led the medieval clergy away from primary attention to their spiritual responsibilities; from this point of view, it is easy enough to pass a critical judgment upon it. What is more difficult to assess is the contribution that the medieval church made to the evolution of Europe's economic structures, a contribution that prepared the way for modern capitalism.[6]

No doubt, such economic activity was often enough defended by the churchmen involved in it as something which the practicalities of life demanded of them, something undertaken for the well-being of "the church." No doubt many of them were quite sincerely distressed by the extent to which such financial matters deterred them from attending to what was more proper to Christian ministry. Yet, the situation was basically deplorable, more than a little rapacity (individual and corporate) tinged the attitudes of ecclesiastics in financial affairs, and the anticlerical criticisms of the later medieval centuries are directed frequently at this target.

With considerable justification, much of this criticism of "money-hungry ecclesiastics" was directed at monastic and conventual institutions. Not only had these religious communities grown affluent and amassed some of the largest holdings of wealth in Europe, but their members had assumed a comfortable (in some instances even luxurious) style of life which diverted funds from that performance of charitable works which had been a monastic tradition.[7] This did not always mean that less alms were being given the poor, but the amounts provided to assist the needy in an earlier age were quite insufficient in the fifteenth century as poverty became more widespread. And while expropriation or heavy taxation of monastic properties by civil powers did enter the picture in some instances, the basic problem was still the attitude of the monks and friars and of the professional lay administrators who in many cases actually handled the monastery's finances.

The increased poverty of the fifteenth century outstripped also the parish structures which earlier had provided for the needy. With both church and state competing for the diminishing financial resources of Europe, and with increasing drains on church finances by an expensive ecclesiastical bureaucracy, there was no possibility of augmenting the official provision for works of mercy on the local level.[8] More and more of the burden of caring for the poor, establishing hospitals, and the like was assumed by secular rulers or by other prominent citizens or by pious organizations established for that purpose. Accompanying this partial but important retirement of the clerical establishment from control of charitable works was a gradual movement of the church's official teaching on economic morality away from the earlier teaching on usury and just price to a position more accommodated to the economic practices of Europe's merchants and financiers.[9]

During the sixteenth century, in those areas where the Roman Catholic influence remained dominant, there was a resurgence of interest in charitable works, stimulated by the challenge and criticisms of the Reformation, by the reforms undertaken by Trent (in particular the reforms regarding episcopal residence and religious orders), and by the needs of the poor which became aggravated by wars and the growing economic depression. Increasingly, however, new patterns of charitable activity were being established. Men and women in high position, whether political rulers or wealthy bourgeoisie, undertook projects to aid the needy. To quite an extent the service to the poor performed by prelates, including charitable enterprises of the papacy, now fitted into this social structure. Pious organizations to provide for society's disadvantaged were established (or, as in the case of some of the Third Orders, reestablished), and in several instances these groups then developed into formally constituted religious congregations. The old established religious orders found a new commitment to their traditional exercise of charity. Even more importantly, a number of new religious foundations came into being with the express purpose of providing for one or more "work of mercy." These "active orders" (as distinguished from the more monastic and contemplative orientation of the older religious communities) represented an important new stage in the evolution of religious communities within the Catholic church. Their role in the reform and pastoral development of the modern Roman Catholic church was critically important.[10] It was often through such groups that wealthy Catholic laity (or in some cases, secular princes or local governments) found a means of exercising their own charity, by giving financial support to the hospitals or refuges or schools that these religious congregations conducted. Thus, much of the direction of charitable work, which had been moving out of ecclesiastical and into secular structures, now began to return to the clergy—but to clergy who were very often "clerical specialists" in one or other aspect of pastoral care.

In the areas of Europe where the Reformation gained control, provision for the needy rested more on civil authorities for several reasons. First of all, the total suppression of monasteries and convents eliminated an important social agency, and the expropriation of this monastic property by civil authorities tended to make them the logical substitute. Secondly, the Reformation churches tended (obviously, in somewhat differing fashion) to include the secular ruler within the divinely called ministry of the church, granting him a quasi-episcopal (i.e., supervisory) function with regard to the Christian people.[11] Thirdly, the increasing complexity of economic and social problems and the absence within Protestantism of any centralized ecclesiastical force comparable to the papacy meant that only the secular power could muster unified large-scale action against social problems.[12]

Luther himself had urged, for example in the *Leisniger Kassenordnung* of 1523, that the Christian community on the local level should assume the care of the poor and needy; social duties were part of the community's Christian responsibility. He even detailed a structure in which each community would elect "guardians" to manage the community's treasury and provide for the needy. They were even to function in certain circumstances to counteract the imposition of unjust prices on goods needed by the ordinary person.[13] However, Luther's idealistic hopes that communities would assume such charitable works were not realized. In more than one instance this was grounded in the lack of the financial resources to do so; but in many cases it seems that the people were only too willing to let the civil authorities assume the responsibility. In its early stages, Lutheranism was inclined to be an "individual" religion without noticeable church involvement in social problems. And the growing Erastianism of Lutheran polity only confirmed this tendency to leave economic and social matters to civil rulers.

Matters were quite different in early Calvinism, particularly in Geneva where the views of Calvin could find rather full implementation. In the structure of a covenanted community, where ministers and laity participated in the governing bodies of the commonwealth which directed political and economic and social affairs, there was no "outside" secular government to whom the care of the poor could be shifted. Unavoidably, the believing community had to take a stance on social problems and undertake measures to provide for the needy; unavoidably, the actual involvement in such social and charitable enterprises rested specially on the ministers and on the deacons.[14] Importantly, the main thrust of clerical participation in this effort was directed at the control of economic and social activity according to religious principles; for example, there was stringent regulation of the financial transactions in Geneva. Thus, the involvement of ordained ministers in the "ministry of service" dealt with an institutionalized attack upon social evils rather than simply with individual works of mercy.

However, this system of a tightly cooperative "spiritual-temporal" government, in effect a theocracy where moral theological opinion was translated into civil law, proved difficult to implement in Geneva and impossible in places like France where the political government was strong and largely hostile. In the Low Countries the Calvinist religion and social ethic found a congenial reception, but it was Calvin's more open attitude to money-handling (which, of course, in his own mind was inseparably linked with close community control) rather than his stress on governing public behavior by gospel principles that made him attractive to the commercial and industrial interests.[15] Actually, it was in seventeenth-century Puritan settlements in New England that Calvin's own social ideals came closest to realization.

Sixteenth-century England presented a complex picture of provision for the poor. Some of it was carried on by monasteries, some in the parish structure, some by wealthy individuals, some by guilds, some by local civic communities. Things become no better with Henry VIII's suppression of the English monasteries. No doubt there was much to be desired in the care these institutions had given to the needy; but when, in a period of four years, all orders of monks and friars were dissolved and their properties expropriated by the crown, a vacuum was created and not quickly filled.[16] Henry did not devote the wealth gained by this dissolution of the monasteries to providing for the indigent; instead, he issued orders that parish and borough officers should see to it that the poor were aided financially and kept from begging. Moreover, these officials were not to divert any regular funds to this purpose, nor to levy any taxes; rather, they were, in cooperation with the clergy, to solicit alms from people for this purpose. This dependence on voluntary contributions continued under Edward VI and Mary, and collection of such funds is made the responsibility of the local clergy.[17] Such reliance on voluntary alms proved impossible. Inexorably, the civil authorities were forced to take over the various charitable institutions and to finance them by property taxes. Demand for a consistent national policy and poor law increased, and finally, in 1572, a comprehensive poor law was enacted.[18] But its provisions for the actual situation were not adequate; probably its implementation was uneven. However, the law's very existence was a clear indication of the extent to which the state had assumed control of (if not always operative responsibility for) poverty and allied social problems.

The Seventeenth Century

Already in the fifteenth century it had been apparent that the medieval structures of provision for the needy were basically inadequate. By the seventeenth century, despite the attempts at some readjustment, the situation in most places had reached the point of explosion. Renaissance rulers had managed to squander much of the available economic resources. Wars in particular had drained the treasuries of most governments. The Thirty Years' War at the beginning of the seventeenth century made matters just that much worse, for it further impoverished the very classes of needy people that the civil rulers were increasingly incapable of helping.

Apparently, the large numbers of wandering beggars which had been a major social problem ever since the period of the Black Death became even more of a menace to orderly and safe conduct of society. Laws to curb vagabonds and begging in general were already common throughout Europe in the sixteenth century; now they become even more extensive and harsh. Thus, provisions for the needy in the form of hospices, orphanages, etc., were not just the expression of Christian charity or of human concern; often they were part of an attempt to avoid social chaos.[19] Tragically, the handling of this social problem of the poor was mixed with the handling of criminals; there was an increasing tendency to consider many of the needy as criminals, for they were "lazy, shiftless, and unwilling to work," and a considerable part of the legislation directed to the indigent had to do with forcing them to work. Laws and prisons did help curb the social and economic threat of the poor and the urban criminal, but there was no effective curb on the soldiers who, in one war after another, roamed over the countryside and sustained themselves by pillage and imposition on the already overburdened peasant class.[20]

Christian Ministry to the Poor

In England, the attempts to deal with this complex situation reflected the Erastian context of state-church relations. Increasingly, the poor laws of the early seventeenth century established a centralized governmental provision for the indigent, one which touches the problems of both urban and agrarian poor. To a large extent, the actual implementation of these legal prescriptions was left to the parishes and carried out by parish officials (churchwardens and overseers).[21] There is no question but what the ordained clergy were acting as agents of the civil government; but one cannot deny to this activity all notion of *Christian* ministry. In any event, the provision for the poor seems to have functioned reasonably well until the disruptions of the civil war in mid-century and the ensuing official apathy which was not effectively dispelled

by the Restoration. To some extent, the lapse of official care of the poor in the latter half of the century led to an increase in private philanthropy; it also led to municipal plans (such as the Bristol plan, approved by law in 1696) of organizing the poor into work forces, thereby "training them in the Christian attitude of hard work."[22] Both these developments constitute a further removal of care of the poor from church ministration.

On the Continent, Protestantism continued along the lines established in the sixteenth century, with care of the poor being ever more relegated to civil authorities in those situations where Protestantism was the established religion. In persecuted minority situations, which chiefly concerned the Calvinist community in places like France, there was understandably no outreach ministry to the needy of society in general, nor was there generally much sharing in whatever provisions were made for the needy by the secular government. There was, however, an intramural caring by the minority group for its own poor that constituted one of the more strictly religious forms of social welfare. Some of this same smaller-group provision for the needy was fostered in Pietist circles, particularly when (as in the case of the Moravian Brethren) Pietism expressed itself in distinctive community structures.

In countries within the Roman Catholic sphere of influence, many of the same problems concerning the poor and oppressed existed, though the move towards urbanization and capitalism was not as rapid in the Iberian peninsula. However, in Catholic areas the institutional structures for dealing with the indigent had been less disrupted in the sixteenth century, and so more of the attempts to care for the disadvantaged of society were carried on through ecclesiastical activity. It is not easy, though, to denominate all of this as Christian ministry to the poor, because some of the higher ecclesiastics who were active in this regard were doing so as public administrators. The largesse distributed to the poor by wealthy churchmen paralleled the philanthropy of wealthy bourgeoisie in some Protestant areas, i.e., it was fulfillment of public responsibility.

One manifestation of concern for the poor was unquestionably grounded in religious motivations, and was exercised quite independently of state-church alliances. This was the continuing activity of religious congregations that had been established for such charitable work, and the establishment of a number of new groups for this same purpose. France provided the prime example of such organized commitments to care of the needy; to quite an extent it was the concomitant of the spiritual revival of the early seventeenth century in France, and the most notable figure was Vincent de Paul.[23] However, Vincent de Paul, influential though he was, was not alone in France, nor was France alone in Catholic countries. The period witnessed a truly remarkable flowering of the post-Tridentine revival of religious orders and congregations.[24] One of the dominant forces working in this revival was a widespread desire to provide some succour for the oppressed of society.

From the point of view of a history of Christian ministry the most significant aspect of this seventeenth-century establishment of new religious communities may well be the fact that a large number of them were groups of women. There had been in earlier centuries any number of religious orders, monks and friars and canons regular, which had a branch for women; but these were all essentially contemplative establishments, and though the women who belonged to these communities were to some extent incorporated in popular thinking (though never in church law) to "the clergy," they were never identified functionally with Christian ministry. Now, in the post-Tridentine church, the major development of "active" groups of women religious meant that these women began to share in many of the activities associated with Christian ministry, and did so by virtue of a certain official recognition and delegation. Though there was never any question of ministerial ordination for them, nor of admitting them to pulpit preaching,

much less to officiating in liturgy, their functional identity within the Catholic community was somewhere between "clergy" and "laity." Theologically their precise position in the Christian community, as distinct from the laity on the one side and from the ordained clergy on the other, may be difficult to define; but in the actual life of the church in modern times they have been a critically important agent of service.

The Eighteenth Century

Beginning with the Restoration in England and ending with the French Revolution, both illustrating the linkage of civil and ecclesiastical "establishments," the eighteenth century is a good point at which to reflect on the church's (i.e., the clergy's) role in causing or alleviating the social problems of the modern world. Essentially, this is a question of the support provided by the higher clergy (and by official church policies and pronouncements) to the political and economic power structures that oppressed a large portion of Europe's population. Such support began earlier than the eighteenth century and continues into the twentieth, but capitalism (and its attendant social problems) was already dominant in most of eighteenth-century Europe and before the end of the century was being reshaped by the industrial revolution. The official attitudes of the churches to this socio-economic phenomenon are quite instructive about the prevalent understanding of the church's role in the world.

Official Church Attitudes

One of the basic changes that occurs in this move from medieval to modern economic and social patterns is the emergence of a new group of poor. Previously, the indigent for whom Christians' charity should provide were those who could not work (the aged, orphans, etc.); now, the indigent are predominantly workers. They are the exploited masses of people who, both on the land and in urban production, by their loss of freedom and by the depressed economic level at which they were forced to live, provided the base for European capitalism's accumulation of wealth. In an earlier age, the church had faced the problem of exploitation through unjust prices and usury, and it had developed a teaching about the criterion of justice in such dealings. In the modern age, a new element of social teaching was needed, some norm for the determination of just wages. More than that, there was need for Christian witness to the basic human dignity and rights of the men and women who made up the industrial and agricultural proletariat.

Such witness was critically necessary, since preservation and development of property had become the primary social objective of "respectable people." The attitude of the upper classes was expressed in the mid-eighteenth century by the eminent jurist Gladstone when he described the purpose of the state as the protection of property.[25] Stable ownership of property was the principle of society's stability; consequently, social rights (both active and passive) were based on possession of property—without property a man was an "unperson," politically and legally and socially.[26] The vast majority of persons were clearly subordinated, even by law, to property.

Any number of explanations can be offered for the emergence of this inhuman set of values. What is most difficult to explain is the manner in which Christianity (at least at the level of church officialdom) found itself supporting a viewpoint that is so radically opposed to the teaching of the New Testament. Unquestionably, part of the answer lies in the prevalent church-state relationship of the period, in which the church was willing to support governmental policies in exchange for the privileges attached to being the established church. No doubt, also, institutionalized oppression can be easily overlooked (in any society or historical period) by those who are not its victims; and support of it and profit from it can be so subtle and implicit that men can be quite active in such exploitative institutions and simultaneously (and sincerely) active in works of charity to aid those

impoverished by these institutions. Then, too, the church was not obstructed in its works of mercy by either the state or moneyed interests; instead, in many instances there was considerable subsidization of church charities by governments or rich individuals. Thus, the official church could be active in charitable activities but effectively removed from the arena of prophetic judgment upon social and political and economic institutions.

One of the components in this multivalent church-state relationship was the reluctance (or inability) of the official church to recognize and support the rising currents of democratic thought and action—though exception to this statement must be made for some of the churches in the Reformed tradition and in the Radical Reformation. Ironically, much of the theoretical basis of this democratic movement was the outgrowth of insights and values fostered by Christianity and developed by many of its greatest theologians; and the fundamental principles and expectations of this democratic current were thoroughly compatible with the gospel. Yet, the rise of democratic hopes and ideals was met by established interests—civil and ecclesiastical—with more than a little suspicion.

Thus, with the best will in the world—and this was often the case with sincere churchmen who were truly "pastoral" in their outlook but hopelessly out of touch with the evolution and deeper social needs of the modern world —the official church grew increasingly distant from the people it was meant to serve. The obverse of this picture was the growing dechristianization and alienation from the church of large masses of Europe's population.

Strangely, in this link between the church "establishment" and the secular "establishment," influential members of the higher clergy (both Catholic and Protestant) were often enough supporting the policies of men whose religious outlook was at best agnostic and whose sworn purpose in some instances was the destruction of the church. One cannot but wonder about the self-identity as "ordained minister" that was possessed by higher ecclesiastics who functioned in the established-church situation. Did they see themselves as officials in one of the most important (really, the most important) agencies that provided for people, as providing for the citizens' spiritual needs? One suspects that they did to quite an extent, and that the actual situation resembled more the plan of Marsilius of Padua in which the church would function as a department of the government than it resembled the early Christian ideal of a community in which all were basically equal and brothers. One suspects, too, that the dominant objective of most churchmen was that of preserving and fostering the established church structures rather than that of witnessing prophetically to the death and resurrection of Christ—and probably for the bulk of them an oversimplified identification of the interests of the church-as-institution with the interests of God enabled them to pursue their goal with truly religious zeal. The purpose in describing this mentality is not to condemn nor even evaluate it but to suggest that it influenced the manner in which the role and nature of episcopacy (or its equivalent) was understood in this period.

Pastoral Care of the Poor

Though the official church, Catholic and Protestant, continued throughout the eighteenth century to align itself with the economic and political "establishment," there were some efforts to bring the church's concern to the disadvantaged of society. One of the most striking of these was certainly John Wesley's apostolate to the poor—in many ways a very well-rounded apostolate for he not only went to them in their own life context to evangelize them but he also undertook a number of practical projects to alleviate their need, and he worked for social reform.[27] Another impressive instance was the continuing work in Europe and in foreign missions of Roman Catholic religious communities: providing education for the poor (as well as the more prosperous), conducting hospitals and shelters of various kinds, and in general caring for the bodily and spiritual needs of society's disadvantaged. Still another element

was important—as became evident in the grouping of forces on one side or the other at the time of the French Revolution: this was the identification (economic, social, and psychological) of the lower clergy with the poorer classes of society, whose poverty and antagonism to the "power structure" they often shared.[28] Finally, though it is hard to determine the extent to which it was a Christian impulse, some mention must be made of the philanthropy that flourished in the eighteenth century. There is no doubt but that it was rooted to some extent in the humanistic emphases of the Enlightenment, to some extent in the awakened sensitivity to social ills that marks the later decades of the century, and to some extent in proprietary and paternalistic concern for the well-being of society; but the frequent exhortation in the sermons of this century to undertake such philanthropy indicates that at least part of the motivation was religious, and that such charitable undertakings were seen as properly Christian responsibilities.

Nevertheless, the lot of the poor in the eighteenth century was utterly out of line with human dignity. In England, it was becoming more and more apparent that the administration of the poor laws through parish structures was ineffective, the system of workhouses failed, the fate of debtors in prison was a public disgrace—yet in many ways England in the eighteenth century was a leader in seeking some solution to the problem of the poor.[29] It should be stressed, since our particular interest is in studying "Christian service to the poor," that the prevailing attitude of English society towards the indigent concentrated on putting the poor (including children) to work, so that they would cease being a social and economic problem.[30] This mentality of "solving a social problem" was present in much of Europe, for in the eighteenth century there was widespread fear in the upper levels of society of the mob violence which could, and periodically did, erupt from the discontent of the oppressed. More often than not the exhortations to involve the poor in hard work had religious overtones, for stress on hard work as virtue and as the road to human fulfillment was characteristic of much ethical preaching, and not just in the Puritan tradition.[31] In the efforts to provide some education to the children of the lower classes, the objective of preparing them to be useful and productive economically was paramount.[32]

Another form of pastoral care, which in theory was not denied to the poor and uneducated but which generally benefited a relatively small group that was drawn from the better educated and socially established strata of society, was "spiritual direction." Under this broad term one can situate the more specialized guidance of prayer and conscience that was found, for example, in the Bérullian circle in the seventeenth century; or the kind of counsel and guidance of life that would have occurred quite naturally wherever a pastor was in concerned contact with his parish; or the wide range of practice regarding confession of sin, not just in Roman Catholicism but in the Reformation churches as well.[33] The natural link of such activities with religious instruction is obvious, particularly in the area of formation of conscience. For the most part the attitudes that characterized religious education, such as indoctrination or emotional stimulus to conversion, in a given group characterized also the "spiritual direction." There was also a natural link to the pastoral practice of "visitation," whether to the sick and infirm and aged, or to the homes of parishioners to encourage and counsel faithful members, or to win back those who had drifted away, an activity which often absorbed a good deal of a zealous pastor's time.

From Napoleon to World War II

The American and French revolutions of the late eighteenth century signaled one of the characteristics of the nineteenth and twentieth centuries: the increasing split of church and state. Though the full separation was long in coming, the former close if not always cordial working relationship on many things in the social order was more fre-

quently replaced by competition and even hostility. At least part of this opposition between church and state was rooted in the efforts of increasingly centralized and powerful national governments to gain control over the lives of their citizens. For obvious reasons, the focus of such struggle was the management of educational institutions. Broader provision by secular authorities for social needs and a continuing contribution by private philanthropy raised the question about the church's (and more specifically about the ordained ministry's) responsibility for service to the poor.

Yet, the last century and a half probably saw the ordained ministers of the various Christian churches more involved in the social apostolate than ever before. One reason for this certainly was the increase of organization, especially large-scale organization, in dealing with social needs. Ordained ministers were logical choices in many instances to help direct the social agencies or philanthropic projects conducted under church sponsorship, even occasionally for those under other auspices. Thus, many of the clergy found themselves involved in supervisory roles in schools, homes for the aged, hospitals, etc.; and some participation in public or private (as well as religious) ventures of social betterment became a normal part of the ordinary pastor's role. Whether this reflected an accurate "theology of Christian ministry" or not, it did reflect a continuing popular assumption (which clergymen themselves shared) that the church should be particularly interested in caring for the disadvantaged and for society in general, that Christians had a responsibility of alleviating the hardships of the needy, and that the clergy as leaders in the Christian community should take a more prominent role in this regard.

Education

Of the many services undertaken by the church over the centuries, none has been more extensive and enduring than that of providing education. During the Middle Ages, the church's role in education was clearly dominant, not only in the monastic, cathedral, and chantry schools, but also in most of the municipal schools that began to come into existence around the twelfth century.[34] The later medieval period saw some shift away from this clerical monopoly as more schools were conducted for nonclergy and by nonclergy. The religious perspective in schooling (i.e., greater religious understanding was the final goal of all learning) no longer governed all education. Indeed, in some circles of humanist influence in late fifteenth and early sixteenth centuries there was an antireligious tone to educational endeavors.[35] On the municipal level, schools came increasingly under full control of the town officials, and in some cases wealthy laymen or groups (particularly in the guilds where they were influential) endowed schools and entrusted them to professional teachers who were not ecclesiastics.[36]

This movement towards the secularization of education, though not yet very far advanced, was reversed in the sixteenth century. Both the great Reformers and the leaders of the Roman Catholic response to the Reformation recognized the key importance of education. Many of them were intensely active in fostering educational advance; the shape of modern education was deeply affected by religious educators such as Sturm and Melanchthon or by the Jesuit *Ratio studiorum*. Yet, the efforts of such men was for the most part directed to educating the elite in society. They were not alone in this, for most other educational efforts at this time, for example, the "public schools" in England, had this same elitist orientation. About the only formal education given the lower classes of society was in religion, particularly its ethical aspects.[37] The exception was in Holland where, though the Reformed church became dominant, the municipal authorities retained control of the schools, and where a broad base of education for the masses was provided.[38]

During the seventeenth and eighteenth centuries, there was a slow movement to extend education to the bulk of the populace. Such Christian educators as Francke or Comenius

or La Salle were prominent in fostering this evolution. But the idea of universal education was not widely accepted in most of Europe until late in the eighteenth century. Then, due to a number of influences, probably most importantly the move towards national control of education, the ideal of providing for all children the education that would permit them to participate profitably in society became a controlling principle of educational efforts.[39] This was accompanied, at the end of the eighteenth and the beginning of the nineteenth century, by a major transition from church to state control of education,[40] a transition that had been foreshadowed by the suppression of the Society of Jesus in 1773. However, this immense entry of civil government into education did not cause the end, nor even (despite some temporary setbacks, like the *Kulturkampf*) the diminution, of ecclesiastical involvement in educational work. Just the opposite happened. As education began to be spread to the general public, the demands for educational opportunity steadily increased and more schools (private, parochial, and public) came into being; some religious groups, worried about the secularizing influence of public education, worked to establish their own parallel school system; and in more than one instance the dominant religious leadership (for example, the Protestant ministers in the United States) continued to be involved in one way or another in the conduct of public education.

In no place was the role of the churches in education more evident than in the United States. Because of the key role of the churches (and especially their ordained ministers) in the colonial period, and the concern of church leaders about the immigrant groups that came from Europe, clergy of the various churches were prominent in establishing, sustaining, and directing schools at every level. Until almost the end of the eighteenth century, it was taken for granted that elementary schools existed to provide the elements of religion and the three R's (particularly reading); and the notion still predominated that higher educational institutions should be under religious control.[41] At the turn of the century, and then with increased momentum in the nineteenth century, the movement for public education asserted itself until it slowly became the dominant pattern, even on the university level.[42] However, private schools under denominational direction and parochial schools also flourished; in particular, as the immigration of Roman Catholics began to assume major proportions from the 1830s onward, a large-scale commitment to education gradually brought into being a Catholic school system extending from kindergarten to university.[43] However, Catholics were not alone; some other groups continued to conduct private academies or parochial schools, though with the increasing emphasis on public elementary and secondary schools as "the American pattern," the formal Protestant sponsorship of schools shifted to the college level.

Throughout this modern educational development, much of the time and effort and resources of the "official" church was spent in this area of service. For many ordained clergy this constituted one of their more important activities and was one of the key elements in their professional self-identity. By and large, ordained ministers did not themselves do the actual teaching in such schools (except for the formal religious instruction that was given), but they did often function as directors and supervisors and so were looked upon as professional educators.

Other Charitable Works

The awakened sensitivity to the needs of the oppressed groups in society and the wave of philanthropic activity that marked the later eighteenth century carried on into the nineteenth century. When incorporated into the Christian ethic, such philanthropy was seen as part of the "stewardship" over material goods that God had entrusted to men. And although there was increasing centralization of social services in the hands of regional or national governments, even in a country like Spain where the church had traditionally

taken care of this, there continued to be large-scale church activity in the care of the sick or the aged or orphans or the indigent. Charitable societies of various kinds flourished, and parishes quite normally had a local branch of one or other of these groups. Yet, such undertakings, institutionalized under church direction, often tended to be quite introverted and limited to providing for needy members of the church group itself. This was understandable at times, particularly in the newly arrived immigrant groups in North America or Australia. However, it took a long time for nineteenth-century Christianity to become aware of the need to confront the widespread indigence and oppression that accompanied the growing industrialization of Europe and America.[44]

One thing is worth remarking about such organized movements to perform works of Christian charity. Although clergy were often involved in the initiation of such endeavors, or in their ongoing direction, participation in such service to the needy, and even controlling direction of such service, was seen as something quite proper to the laity. However, there was often a noticeable drift towards clerical control of such enterprises, with the laity relegated to the task of raising the necessary funds; but when this did happen, it seems to have been a question of administrative centralization rather than of theological principles. In Roman Catholicism in the United States, the issue of the laity's sharing in control of the parish's undertakings was complicated by the problem of "trusteeism" among the immigrant communities,[45] a problem which unfortunately obscured for a long time the role of lay Catholics in the United States.

Generally speaking, clerical control of charitable undertakings tended to be more pronounced in Roman Catholicism because most of the burden of carrying on these works rested on the religious communities (especially the communities of women) and these communities were under episcopal or papal control. Particularly in the United States, the diocese came to be the controlling unit for support and direction of most charitable undertakings. The well-being of this diocesan structure of charitable institutions has become a major preoccupation for many modern Catholic bishops.

Christian Transformation of Social Structures

Although great social reformers of the eighteenth and nineteenth centuries saw the need *on Christian principles* to confront the institutionalized economic and social evils of the modern world, the official levels of the various churches were reluctant to move in this direction. On the practical level, one can see how churches that still existed in an "established" context or that were trying to preserve privileges, etc., inherited from such establishment or that operated through concordat arrangements with civil governments would hesitate to question the basic structures of the civil society to which they were allied. Moreover, in reflecting on the violent reaction of many liberal French Catholics against the social reform ideas of Lammenais or Ozanam,[46] one realizes how radically such reform challenged the social presumptions of the upper classes and how difficult it was for Catholics to realize the implications of the late eighteenth- and nineteenth-century revolutions and to abandon the dream of a "restoration." During this period, the papal attitude (which was increasingly formative of Catholic opinion on an international scale) was noticeably reactionary. The "Syllabus of Errors" reflected the withdrawal of Pius IX after 1848 to a conservatism on social issues that continues into the twentieth-century papacy, with some opening to more progressive ideas under Leo XIII.

However, the movement towards deeper social reform could not be thoroughly blunted. Both clergy and laity were found among the Roman Catholic figures who worked to change the enslaving structures of nineteenth-century industrialization. By early twentieth century, priests in France were becoming engaged in activities of social change and therefore diminishing their previous involvement with charitable or pious undertakings,[47] but those who did so were a small minority and were quite severely criticized by their clerical confreres. Earlier than this in Germany there was considerable effort, theoretical and practical, devoted to attacking the economic and social exploitation of the working class; probably no figure was more prominent in this development than Archbishop Ketteler.[48] In other countries also there were signs before the turn of the century of an awakening social Catholicism; even in England where the Catholic church was only reestablishing itself, the hierarchy under Manning's leadership was taking a strong stand against economic and social oppression.[49]

England, too, witnessed some Christian reaction against the deplorable conditions of the poor and the working class. Both the Tractarians and the Methodists were prominent in this reaction, but the Tractarians did little to work for fundamental change, despite their fruitful apostolate among the urban poor in many places. The Methodists, on the other hand, led by the prophetic insistence of Hugh Price Hughes that Christianity was a social gospel, rallied the nonconformist churches to work for a moral transformation of English society, though much of their attention was directed to drink, gambling, and sexual immorality.[50] However, it was in the United States that the preaching of the "social gospel" became most prominent and its influence most deeply felt in Christian activity.[51]

In its early stages, the evolution of American religious reaction to the economic and social structures connected with industrial capitalism was almost entirely a Protestant phenomenon, though before the turn of the century the Roman Catholic and Jewish communities were making substantial contributions to development of American social conscience. This is not the place to attempt an analysis or assessment of a very complex socio-religious process; rather, we might indicate very quickly the key role played by ordained ministers, so that we can then reflect on the intrinsic theological issues. Certainly, one of the components in the process was the assumption by the Protestant establishment in the United States that theirs was the God-given task to bring forth on American soil a truly Christian society, and that within this (by law disestablished) theocracy the prophetic voice of the preacher was to act as the conscience for society.[52] Another was the position of the ordained minister vis-à-vis the successive waves of colonizers or immigrants. By and large, the religious pastor acted as a leader in the group, remained close to them and aware of their social needs. He did not have (at least, not as much as his European counterpart) the baggage of historical links with the economic and social "establishment." The rather extraordinary success of the churches in retaining the religious affiliation of the immigrants was an important influence on the development of the American social ethic. Still another was the important role of clergymen in education, whether this was through formal schooling, or through denominational publication of books and journals, or through crusading movements of various sorts, for the emphasis on Christianity's responsibility for the social order was transmitted through these agencies.

From the beginning, the involvement of ordained clergy in such secular issues raised questions, as it did in Europe also. There was question about the appropriateness or even the right of religious preachers to evaluate and criticize the practices of business and industry and politics, since these were areas of secular activity and "had nothing to do with religion." Thus, more clearly in the United States than in Europe, the separation of church and state was linked with the separation of religion from the rest of life: religion was a good thing for people to have, it was even part of the social respectability one should maintain, but it existed in a world of its own and was irrelevant in the marketplace. On the surface, the rising impact of "the social gospel" in the beginning decades of the twentieth century would appear to be a reassertion of Christianity's relevance. The question that remains to be answered theologically is the extent to which this represented the transformation of social attitudes

by Christian faith or, on the contrary, the reduction of Christianity to social concern.

But if ordained ministers were criticized in many circles for speaking out against social abuses, they were even more condemned if they "interfered" by activity in social movements. Much of the controversy in this regard centered on the emerging labor movement and on the prominent support given it by many of the clergy. Granting the fact that much of the opposition to such clerical involvement in social activity came from vested interests who saw their continuing profit-through-exploitation threatened, or from ecclesiastics who worried about what might happen to church institutions if the wealthy or powerful in society withdrew their support, a major issue lay under the surface. In a world where it had become evident that Christianity's relationship to the developing course of human society could not (and should not) be worked out in terms of some interaction of church and state, what reciprocal influence (if any) should there be between Christianity and human society, and in what manner (if at all) should the institutionalized aspects of Christianity, especially its ordained ministry, function in this regard?

Unquestionably, one of the most important developments concerning Christianity's relationship to human society has been the increasing role of laity in the various social undertakings of the churches, and in translating Christian attitudes into political and social activity. This "reentry" of the laity into the active apostolic functions of the church has been most dramatic in Roman Catholicism, particularly after World War I, but it has applied to some extent to all the churches. It has raised obvious questions about the meaning and applicability of a doctrine of priesthood of all believers, about the precise limits of the ministry of ordained clergy. To what extent do such clergy have a role that is proper to them and not to all baptized Christians? What about the relationship between clerical and lay Christian activity in social reform activity? It has also raised the less apparent question about the fundamental role of Christianity in history. It is all well and good to talk about the lay person as the one who carries Christianity out "into the world," and to say that this is his particular sphere of activity; it is far from clear what these statements mean in terms of actual life situations and of the present-day social institutions of mankind.

NOTES

1. See E. Iserloh, *Handbook of Church History* (New York, 1969), vol. 4, pp. 568–70.

2. See G. LeBras in A. Fliche and V. Martin, *Histoire de l'Eglise depuis les origines jusqu'à nos jours* (Paris, 1935—), vol. 12, pp. 571–84. However, it is important to recall that the late fifteenth and early sixteenth centuries saw a large-scale expoliation of church property by the secular power. Henry VIII's moves against the English monasteries was one of the more spectacular instances, but by no means isolated. Moreover, many of those who profited greatly from exploiting the benefice system could scarcely be called clergy; rather, temporal rulers who had gained control over appointment to such benefices used them as rewards for their own political favorites. And in many ways the lower clergy were more the victims of these evils (to which must be added the papal exactions of money) than any other group. See D. Hays, *New Cambridge Modern History* (Cambridge, 1961), vol. 1, pp. 12–14; and R. Aubenas, *ibid.*, pp. 85–88.

3. An indication of how far afield this question could lead us (though it might well be with great profit) is provided by H. Enno van Gelder's thesis that Renaissance humanism itself constitutes a distinctive and profoundly influential religion and that it, rather than the Protestant Reformation, represents the radical new thing on the religious scene. See his *The Two Reformations in the Sixteenth Century* (The Hague, 1961). Though it obviously needs to be assessed critically, the thesis takes on new interest in the light of very recent theological discussion about Christianity and secularity.

4. Probably the thinker whose view had come closest to this radical irrelevance of the church was Marsilius of Padua (in the fourteenth century) whose *Defensor Pacis* was destined to have major influence upon those who in later centuries wished to subordinate the church to the state. See G. Sabine, *A History of Political Theory*, 2d ed. (New York, 1950), pp. 292–304; and W. Ullmann, *Principles of Government and Politics in the Middle Ages* (London, 1961), pp. 276–79.

5. One might expect less of this in the Calvinist tradition, where the episcopal principle has been less operative, but, as Troeltsch points out (*The Social Teaching of the Christian Churches* [London, 1956], vol. 2, pp. 628–32), the sermons preached by Reformed pastors, voicing the view of the church on correct Christian social activity, often played a major role in political decision.

6. See J. Gilchrist, *The Church and Economic Activity in the Middle Ages* (London, 1969), pp. 122–39; he criticizes the Weber-Tawney thesis (about the Calvinist rooting of capitalism) for neglecting the religious forces already at work in the medieval world.

7. See *ibid.*, pp. 97–98.

8. *Ibid.*, pp. 92–98.

9. See M. James, "The Effect of the Religious Changes of the Sixteenth and Seventeenth Centuries on Economic Theory and Development," *European Civilization*, ed. E. Eyre (London, 1937), vol. 5, pp. 5–18.

10. On the renewal of religious communities within the Roman Catholic church, see L. Willaert in Fliche-Martin, vol. 18, pp. 99–164.

11. See J. Figgis, "Respublica Christiana," *Essays in Modern History*, ed. I. Christie (London, 1968), pp. 18–21.

12. At a later stage in its development, Protestantism became much more organizationally unified (particularly in the United States) in its social endeavors; but in the sixteenth

century, apart from England where there was more carry-over of the preceding episcopal structure, the congregational approach to Christian life characterized the Reformation churches.

13. See H. Koenigsberger and G. Mosse, *Europe in the Sixteenth Century* (London, 1968),
pp. 131–33. Also S. and B. Webb, *English Poor Law History* (London, 1927), vol. 1,
pp. 31–32; they indicate the influence of this plan of Luther's on the municipal ordi-
nances of several cities, most notably Ypres. Luther continued the late medieval
teaching on the just price and usury. He was much more reluctant than Calvin to
come to grips with the increasing commercialism of Europe, though Calvin, too, was
deeply interested in combating the exploitation of people by excessive interest rates.
See James, pp. 30–55.

14. See *Instit.* 4. 3. 9.

15. See James, pp. 50–55.

16. See G. Elton, *New Cambridge Modern History*, vol. 2, pp. 236–37.

17. See Webb, pp. 44–47.

18. *Ibid.*, pp. 54–59.

19. See H. Trevor-Roper, *The Crisis of the Seventeenth Century* (New York, 1968), pp.
1–89; J. Neveux, *Vie spirituelle et vie sociale entre Rhin et Baltique au XVIIe siècle*
(Paris, 1967), pp. 742–45; Webb, pp. 60–62; P. Zumthor, *Daily Life in Rembrandt's
Holland* (London, 1962), pp. 248–65.

20. See D. Ogg, *Europe in the Seventeenth Century*, 8th ed. (London, 1961), pp. 14–21.

21. See Webb, pp. 52–95.

22. *Ibid.*, pp. 95–125.

23. It is a bit paradoxical, though theologically quite significant, that much of this devotion to works of charity was linked with the spiritual teaching of Bérulle, a teaching
that stressed priesthood (in a strongly cultic and "supernatural" sense) as the source
of all human salvation. See chapter 31.

24. See Willaert, pp. 127–65.

25. See Ogg, pp. 515–17.

26. "What we now call personal status was assessed in relation to ownership, usually of
freehold land, so that the societies of the Ancien Régime may be said each to have
had a hard core, consisting of the privilege or monopoly derived from possessions,
round which there was formed an increasingly large zone of men without property,
and therefore without rights. In Blackstone's description, these rightless men provide the manual labour necessary for the subsistence of the state. He might well
have added two important facts about them, first, that they were a great majority, and
second, that they were mostly obliged to sacrifice themselves in war by enforced service.
The civilization which Blackstone had in mind was a very high one; it was made
possible only by this organization of humanity. Throughout, the disagreeable word
slavery is avoided." (*Ibid.*, p. 516.)

27. See G. Cragg, *The Church and the Age of Reason,* rev. ed. (London, 1970), pp. 141–52.

28. See A. Cobban, *New Cambridge Modern History*, vol. 7, pp. 228–30.

29. See D. Marshall, *The English Poor in the Eighteenth Century* (London, 1926), esp.
pp. 246–54.

30. *Ibid.*, pp. 15–27.

31. See R. Douglas, "Talent and Vocation in Humanist and Protestant Thought," *Action
and Conviction in Early Modern Europe*, ed. T. Rabb and J. Seigel (Princeton, 1969),
pp. 261–98. Earlier in the article (pp. 261–80), he discusses the Renaissance humanist
development of the ideal of work as a good in itself.

32. See Cragg, pp. 130–31.

33. For a historical review of these activities in the various churches, see J. McNeill, *A
History of the Cure of Souls* (New York, 1951).

34. See E. Power, *Main Currents in the History of Education* (New York, 1962), pp. 230–68.

35. *Ibid.*, pp. 269–307.

36. See F. Eby, *The Development of Modern Education*, 2d ed. (New York, 1952), pp. 37–39.

37. In defense of the elitist context of education, it should be noted that the elite in question were not always the aristocratic or the rich; the Jesuits, for example, insisted on establishing free schools that were endowed and asked no tuition, so that no capable student would be refused admission because of poverty. See J. Donohue, *Jesuit Education* (New York, 1963), pp. 194–95.

38. *Ibid.*, pp. 120–25.

39. See Power, pp. 373–78.

40. See Eby, pp. 361–93 (on the transition in Europe) and pp. 394–410 (on the transition in the United States).

41. See R. Butts, *A Cultural History of Education* (New York, 1947), pp. 372–81.

42. On the evolution of the American educational system, see N. Edwards and H. Richey, *The School in the American Social Order*, 2d ed. (Boston, 1963); Eby, pp. 546–69.

43. See Power, pp. 465–67.

44. See A. Vidler, *The Church in an Age of Revolution* (London, 1961), pp. 90–95.

45. See J. Ellis, *American Catholicism*, 2d ed. (Chicago, 1969), pp. 45–49; he points out that the basic problem was the attempt by some lay trustees to preempt the episcopal appointment or dismissal of pastors, an attempt that was often linked with the nationalism of immigrant groups.

46. See A. Dansette, *Religious History of Modern France* (New York, 1961), vol. 1, pp. 252–64.

47. *Ibid.*, vol. 2, pp. 289–90.

48. See E. Hales, *The Catholic Church in the Modern World* (New York, 1958), pp. 195–96; also F. Heyer, *The Catholic Church from 1648 to 1870* (London, 1969), pp. 169–73.

49. See R. Aubert, *Le pontificat de Pie IX*, vol. 21 of Fliche-Martin, pp. 486–97.

50. See Vidler, pp. 143–45.

51. For a brief introduction, see J. Dillenberger and C. Welch, *Protestant Christianity* (New York, 1954), pp. 232–54; and R. Handy's introduction to *The Social Gospel in America* (New York, 1966), pp. 3–16.

52. See M. Marty, *Righteous Empire* (New York, 1970), an excellent introduction to the development of American Protestant attitudes on the relation of religion to society.

CHAPTER 19

Theological Reflections on Human Need

In post–World War II writing about Christian ministry no word has appeared more often than "service," and by now it has become a commonplace that ordained ministry should be seen in terms of service. However, this still leaves open the question as to the kind of service that is appropriate to the church. "Service" can range from strictly cultic activity ("serving the altar") to governmental activity as a "public servant." But how far does the qualification of service as "Christian" properly extend? It is a question that must be answered with some precision if we are to avoid vague generalities in talking about Christianity's role in today's world or about the more precise role of specialized Christian ministries.

Recognizing the fact that the ministries of word and sacrament qualify as "service," we can here prescind from them and concentrate our discussion on the broad range of activities associated with such phrases as "bettering the human condition" or "caring for the needy." In this area, the notion of "ministry" is much less parochial, for there is question not only of the entire Christian community working for the advance of all their fellow humans but of Christians cooperating with non-Christians in a common endeavor to better the world. Since loving concern for all men and women is the most basic precept of the Christian ethic, the entire church is *diakonal*. Delegation of special service functions to some within the community, if such delegation seems an effective way of helping people, does not free any member of the church from the continuing obligation of caring for others.

Obviously, the poor and oppressed and disadvantaged are to be found within the Christian community as well as outside, and so Christian service must be directed to this need. As a matter of fact, Christian service to "the poor" has historically been directed primarily to helping the needy within the church. What is somewhat new in our present-day context is the added emphasis on Christian responsibility for the whole human situation. What is even newer is the shift in mankind's social patterns and social attitudes, a shift that has made "service" a complex international endeavor to achieve justice and dignity and equality for all men and women.

During the later patristic period and into the Middle Ages, the lack of adequate civic provision for the needy caused the church to move massively into this area. Towards the end of the Middle Ages this trend began to be reversed, and very slowly humanistic philanthropy and civic institutions started to care for economic and social welfare. In today's world, this process of civil society undertaking basic social responsibility is still far from complete: religious groups and philanthropic foundations still carry on large-scale social welfare programs. But there is increasing awareness that the burden must move from such "private" agencies; the peoples of the world must, through the basic processes of their political and social life, guarantee justice and equality and opportunity for all.

This trend promises a major change in Christian involvement in social welfare. As governmental agencies of one kind or another handle the problems of poverty and employment and sickness and old age and education, there will be less need (if any) for church-sponsored efforts. It seems clear that for some time to come identifiably Christian social agencies will be needed to complement the social programs of secular society. But the ultimate achievement of the common good for all mankind can come about only through national and international political action, for only such effective worldwide effort can come to grips with the forces that presently cause economic and social deprivation. Clearly, this assumption of social responsibility by civil governments should be encouraged by the church, even if it means eliminating many official church projects. What is important is that the work be done, not that the church get the credit for doing it.

Tensions have arisen for centuries between church-sponsored and state-sponsored efforts in this "service" area, particularly in the field of education, though it must be admitted that in many instances the struggle was not to see who could better serve the people but to see who could more effectively control them. Such tensions have given the impression at times that the trend towards increased public provision for the common welfare has been an antireligious development. Certainly there are instances when the advocates of such public activity have been personally motivated by animosity to a specific form of religion or to religion in any form, but the basic evolution seems to coincide with rather than oppose the finality of Christianity. Christianity exists to help establish the kingdom of God; basic elements in this undertaking are the achievement of justice and equality and dignity for all men, and any movement towards these goals brings the kingdom of God closer to its realization.

Historically, much of the modern movement to provide through secular public agencies for the welfare of all members of society found its origin in the twelfth-century resurgence of the Christian laity. Though its attempts to establish an increased role for nonclerics in the church's own internal life were abortive, this lay movement found ever increasing expression in the task of organizing the patterns of Europe's economic and social and political activity. Admittedly, many elements in the structuring of modern Europe and its offshoots bear little mark of this initial religious impulse; but religious motivation has continued to be one of the most important forces in public decision and public endeavor. One of our needs today is to recognize the presence of this religious motivation, to make it correspond authentically with genuine Christianity, and to channel it into dedicated concern for justice and peace.

Perhaps it sounds strange to express it this way, but it may well be that Christianity today will best serve its diakonal mission by fostering the secularization of care for the needy. The justification for such a view lies not just in the fact that only the massive power of international governmental cooperation can cope with the problems of the disadvantaged in our world; it lies also in the church's history of gradual disestablishment during the past couple of centuries. This change to nonestablished status is a second basic shift in the church's service role, a shift that has been gradually but drastically altering the approach to Christian service, a shift that is closely linked with the move from church-sponsored to state-sponsored welfare activity which we have just discussed.

Official establishment of a particular church as *the* approved form of religion for the citizenry seemed to have many advantages, for the church as well as the government. Specifically in the matter of social welfare activity, the church found it advantageous to have the government encouraging citizens to support the church's charitable undertakings, even at times making generous subsidies to these good works. Ecclesiastical projects and their accompanying bureaucracies were not threatened; often they were strengthened and nurtured by this public approbation. Governments for their part were quite happy to shunt off responsibility for society's disadvantaged, to pay as little as possible for some solution to social problems, and to have these problems be considered a matter of concerned

Christian "charity" rather than a matter of basic social justice.

At least from the church's side, these advantages were largely illusory. The dependency status of the established church meant that it was subservient to the economic and social "power elite" who oppressed and exploited the poor and caused the very social problems with which the church's charitable endeavors were striving vainly to cope. Moreover, the status of "establishment" stripped the church of its prophetic character, deprived it of the power to challenge the unjust policies of the politico-economic establishment, and actually trapped it into giving symbolic approval for these policies. Disestablishment has been a necessary condition for the church's reassertion of her prophetic and diakonal functions in the modern world, and though this disestablishment is not yet complete it has advanced far enough for the Christian community to be once more a force for justice and peace.

Such changes of the context in which Christians must render service to their fellow men raise basic questions about the church's *diakonia* in the world. If more and more of the effective structured attack on social problems should be handled by public agencies, if the church is no longer to act in the field of social welfare as formal or informal instrument of civil governments, what role is the church to play? What form should its service take? Some answers appear quite clear, others can be nothing more than hypothetical solutions that experimentation and experience will have to test.

One clearly essential role of the Christian community will be that of converting its own members, and through them others, to "hunger and thirst after justice." Fundamental betterment of the human situation depends ultimately on people. Society's institutions and structures and processes are vitally important to the struggle for social justice; but these societal forms are only as effective as the men and women who utilize them. There will be justice when men and women decide to act justly. The most basic need is the con-

version of people, especially those people who have some opportunity to influence the centers of power in society. Christians could make no greater contribution to domestic and international peace and justice than that of leading men and women to adopt those values and make those choices in which such peace and justice are rooted.

Anyone familiar with the prophetic tradition of the Old and New Testaments will immediately see that such a call to conversion by today's church would be nothing new—this has been the prophetic message at least as far back as Amos. Recognizing that link should, however, alert us to some of the difficulties that Christians will encounter if they decide to bear witness against the injustices in today's world. Prophets of old were accused of being unrealistic, of disturbing social equilibrium, in some instances of disloyalty and treason. Much the same is likely to happen today. In the backwash of "disestablishment," the church will still be looked at suspiciously if it criticizes rather than supports the politico-economic establishment (for should not religion be a support for "law and order"?). On the other hand, the church, having opted for disestablishment, will be told that it has nothing to say to the business of public life, that it should "mind its own business," which presumably means providing some form of irrelevant worship service for religiously inclined people.

Granting, though, that the Christian community has such a prophetic role, and that it has no choice but to face its implications, this still leaves us with the question whether the church in its institutionalized expressions should enter directly into social reconstruction. If one understands this question in terms of the clericalized ecclesiastical structures which we have so often identified with "the church," then it is not clear that there is any proper role for the institutional church apart from the prophetic witness we have just described. However, this in no way says "no" to the need for corporate social activity by concerned groups of Christians. If they share a common vision of what human life should be and a common concern to see that all men and women share such a life, it is only natural that Christians should work in organized fashion to overcome social evils.

Among the various "services" with which Christians should be concerned, education seems to be a special case. Obviously, no easy identification can be made of the church's role in this regard. The continuing, often contentious, debate on the issue indicates its complexity. That the Christian community should make some provision for educating the faith-understanding of its members cannot be contested. The problem arises as one realizes that all human knowledge (and therefore all education) has a bearing on the manner in which Christians understand their faith. Can the church provide for the mature faith of its members without providing the other educational components (history, literature, science, etc.) which impinge on faith? But even beyond this, does not the Christian community, out of its concern for the true common good of all mankind, have the responsibility to see that truth is sought and preserved? And might such a responsibility demand, even with an honest honoring of cultural and intellectual and religious pluralism, that Christians maintain some academic structures to preserve and develop those insights and values which they consider basic to truly human development? Without such an effort, a critically necessary element in the pluralistic interplay of religious and cultural viewpoints could be neglected and disappear.

A third shift in the context of Christian service today concerns the need to structure the institutional patterns of human society in such a way that "the good life" is made available to all men and women. Christians have certainly had an important impact on social institutions in past centuries, but the governing mentality in Christian service to the disadvantaged was that of "performing the works of mercy." Though admittedly it is a bit of a caricature to describe it this way, the effort to feed the poor and clothe the naked became for the most part a matter of "picking up the pieces," of compensating for the evils caused by economic and social and political processes, rather than of altering the processes that caused the evil. When all of society is considered a Christian community (as it was in the Middle Ages or in some Reformed communities), this approach of repairing the damage caused by society can gradually become a built-in part of the economic and social processes themselves. But this cannot happen in an industrialized society where not only a given church but all religion has been quite thoroughly disestablished.

It is not our purpose here to describe or analyze the complex developments in finance, production, distribution, communication, and technology that shape our present and will shape our future, developments that are linked with a frightening acceleration of injustice in the world. Suffice it to say that Christian conscience is faced with the inescapable conclusion that something basic needs to be done, and done very soon, to reverse the destructive exploitation of the many by the powerful few. This in no way implies that technology be opposed, that sensible material progress be halted; what it does imply is that justice and respect for human dignity and human development must begin to govern the evolution of economic, industrial, social, and political activity. In some appropriate and effective fashion, these controlling institutional processes must be made to serve people rather than to impoverish and enslave and degrade them.

Unless Christians, individually and corporately, commit themselves to the task of redirecting the institutions of our society, any other expression of the church's diakonal mission must be either hypocritical or illusory. What makes the Christian responsibility so much heavier is the fact that the traditionally Christian nations are the ones whose exploitative economics and insatiable lifestyles and technological arrogance are responsible for most of the problem. Granted the immensity of the problem—or perhaps better the immensity of the opportunity, for technology also offers unprecedented possibilities of overcoming poverty and ignorance and disease—if Christians' service to their fellow man is to have real meaning in today's world, it must become an enlightened and unrelenting effort (in cooperation with all other concerned people) to bring into being those economic and social and political institutions that will work for the genuine betterment of all human beings.

Concomitant with this effort to reorient the institutions of society, the need for many of the traditional "works of mercy" will continue, at least for some time to come. There is no either/or option that Christians must make: either the works-of-mercy approach or the change-of-institutions approach. It is just that the latter is more basic and of mounting importance in our contemporary situation.

Moreover, it is important that concentration on the works of mercy not impede the needed change of social institutions. "Charitable institutions" can be the means of isolating and hiding society's problems and sins, much in the way that prisons have done, and thus leaving potentially responsible Christians complacently unaware of the grave social injustices that surround them. What we are saying is that Christian "service" today involves a corporate obligation of the Christian community to work for the common good of all men and women, and to do so by every effective and feasible means. It is not possible, nor would it be desirable, to delineate the particular actions that Christians should take; practical decisions must be made according to differing circumstances, principles and hopes will have to be translated into policy and strategy. What will be important, and here we can touch upon some universal elements, is that correct insights and attitudes govern these decisions. For example, provision of such things as medicare and unemployment compensation must be seen as systematized ways of giving people what is due to them in justice, and not as means by which society takes care of its "social problems." Christianity can make a major contribution to the establishment of justice in the world if it will only instill in Christians authentically Christian attitudes towards all their fellow human beings.

Besides these three "sociological" shifts in the situation of Christian *diakonia*, there has been a fairly basic reorientation of the theology that relates to Christian service. More precisely, theological reflection on the nature of "salvation" has focused on eschatology, on the relation of Christianity to "the secular," on the social and psychological aspects of reconciliation; and this has somewhat altered our understanding about the kind of "service" that Christians should render to one another and to all their fellow humans.

Eschatology is not, of course, a new notion for Christianity; but what is quite new is the extensive reflection upon the manner in which "eschatological" is a basic (one is almost tempted to say "constitutive") characteristic of Christianity. This reflection is part of the larger modern consideration of history and evolution and cosmic finality, but it has its own proper roots in the Christian belief about the risen Christ and his "second coming." And precisely because it is grounded in this which Christians see as the unique saving event, Christian eschatology coincides with Christian soteriology and has a controlling influence on a theology of Christian ministry.

Perhaps we can sharpen our discussion by looking at the relation between "eschatology" and "involvement." If one thinks of "eschatology" only in terms of some end-time, if he sees no intrinsic evolution of history towards this final fulfillment, if he equates "eschatological" with "apocalyptic," then it is hard to see how involvement in bettering the human situation can be a valued element of the Christian ideal. It would be better to hold oneself apart from the world and devote one's energies to preparing for the "real life" beyond. If, on the other hand, "eschatological" implies that the historical experience in which we are engaged, imperfect and incomplete though it obviously is, is part of the process of mankind evolving towards its goal and that it is making an intrinsic contribution to that evolution, involvement in the world becomes an indispensable aspect of the church's diakonal mission.

There is considerable evidence that Christian understanding of the church's eschatological character has moved significantly towards the second of these two views, i.e., towards the idea that our historical existence is intrinsically valuable and part of the process of establishing the kingdom of God. For Roman Catholics there was a dramatic indication of this in Vatican II's statement on "The Church in the Modern World"; but other religious groups have witnessed a similar shift to emphasis on the here-and-now. And the conclusions for a Christian understanding of "service" are apparent: Christian service should be directed positively and unstintingly to making the world a fit place for humans to become persons.

Without rejecting this genuine appreciation for all created reality, the Christian community still faces a basic question. To what extent can it identify with "the world"? Clearly, there has always been a conflict between the values espoused by Christianity and the values of many of those who control the patterns of human life; that conflict is obvious today, and it is likely that this conflict will remain as a basic dynamic in human history. Christianity must challenge the value systems that subordinate people to material advance, or to the acquisition of power, or to national pride, or to any other "god." For the church to identify with the outlook of the "power elite" that still continues to manipulate human life for its own purposes would be a fundamental betrayal of the gospel. But the fact that they cannot accept these value systems that devalue men and women does not mean that Christians should not be as much a part of their times as any other group of people. Unless they truly share the questions and hopes and labors of their contemporaries they will be incapable of the empathy that is an indispensable part of any human service.

Fundamentally, the answer to this question and one's whole understanding of Christianity's relation to the world rest on the view that one takes of Christ's relation to "the secular." This reduces itself to the interpretation that one gives to the Christian belief in "the Incarnation." No matter what metaphysical or symbolic explanation is offered for the mystery of the Word becoming flesh, it is clear that the unique presence of the divine in Jesus represents an incredibly profound identification of God with the human situation. Incarnation implies divine consciousness embodied in the human awareness of Jesus. It implies unlimited divine love at the source of Jesus' human motivation. It implies that Jesus' human experience was in some sense a matter of God experiencing human history. And it implies that that human experience translated divine wisdom into a form that men can use to guide them in shaping their history. Depending upon the extent to which one wishes to give a "realistic" interpretation of Incarnation, these implications have more or less depth.

Like all humans, Jesus had a life experience that was individually his and unrepeatable; unlike many humans, in his life experience he was very much "his own man." His own insights and principles and choices determined the manner in which he affected and was affected by the elements that entered into his experience. In his case this kind of mature self-determination was immeasurably deepened by the divine level of his personhood. However, what is important for our present discussion is the fact that he opened up completely to experiencing his own historical situation. There is no indication that Jesus avoided any context of experience that would challenge either his self-identity or his idealism; indeed, the texts of the Gospels would seem to suggest that the opposition which his public ministry aroused forced him to a searching reappraisal of his saving mission. No matter how unique one sees the human awareness of Jesus to have been, it was a consciousness that evolved in interaction with the basic life experiences of a man of his time and place.

This would seem, then, to be the key to the question of Jesus' relation to "the secular," a relation that continues on but achieves a qualitatively new level in his resurrection. Jesus as the Christ is redeemer of the entire created world "from within"; in his human interaction with the historical situation he is the sacramental presence of divine wisdom and divine love and provides in his own human psychological existence for the translation of this wisdom and love into concrete and relevant expression. Without the impact of experience gained through intimate involvement in the human condition, there would not have been that basic reality of *being human* which Jesus shared with other men and which he transformed. Without his own unique consciousness and love there would not have been the transformation of this experience and of the human condition.

As far as can be ascertained from the evidence of the New Testament writings, and theological reflection on the intrinsic nature of Incarnation would support the conclusion, Jesus did not feel himself alienated from the realities, human or other, that he experienced. The only alienation he experienced was from sin, i.e., from the denial of truth and love, wherever he encountered it. His insight and wisdom challenged from within the human and religious traditions he inherited, but did so in the very process of giving deepened assent and expression to those traditions. His own human experience gave unprecedented depth to both secular and Jewish experience and values, and reacted against the negative and degrading elements in both.

Christ's transformation of "the secular," i.e., of the entire fabric and context of human existing, was more radical than any adjustment or creation of social structures. It provided a new rooting for innovation in patterns of individual and social life; or, to view the matter eschatologically rather than genetically, it gave a new finality to men's historical experience. Insights, motivations, and decisions lie at the source of all changes that men make in their behavior; Jesus initiated a new epoch in mankind's structuring of its historical career by communicating his own unique wisdom and love. To the extent that other men and women accept and interiorize Christ's views and spirit, what mankind is and does will be profoundly altered.

At the heart, then, of Jesus' own attitudes and activity, radically transformative and challenging though they were, one finds a great reverence for all that is, for all that is true, for all that is good, for all that is beautiful. Few things about the historical Jesus come through more clearly in the New Testament literature. And his reverence for all that came from the creative beneficence of his Father found special application to men and women: old and young, prominent and obscure, rich and poor, all were honored by him because of their personhood. For Jesus (at least as far as the New Testament writings will allow us to judge) there was no idea of "secular" which could be applied pejoratively or even neutrally to the persons and things in his world. On the other hand, he was painfully aware that this world was still in transit towards its fulfillment, that mankind was a pilgrim on its way to the Father, and that while this pilgrimage was still in progress there was much in the consciousness and activity of men and women that needed to be purified and redirected and intensified by the truth and the love he brought into the human situation.

Beginning with Jesus himself, Christianity is a "humanism"; it is a movement to bring to fullest realization all that is most properly human in men's lives. By introducing into history an intensified form of the very influences that shape men and women as persons, Jesus respected the goals sought by all honest humanists and made these goals attainable. To spell out this statement in detail would necessitate a full theological discussion of "grace"; but it is enough to allude to such a transforming power of grace in order to see the manner in which Christianity is most truly a humanism. Christian spirituality in its historical expressions has not always honored such a humanistic approach to man's salvation; more than one bit of negativity has crept into Christians' attitudes towards man (and especially woman!). But it does seem that theology and faith today can justifiably defend Christianity's profound compatibility with the authentic developments of "secular humanism." Christianity differs from secular humanism by insisting that man must be *saved*. Without the special divine intervention in Jesus, mankind's destiny to become fully human cannot be realized; to become increasingly free, man needs to be liberated by God in Christ.

Such a theological perspective on the relation between the Christ-mystery and "the secular" is bound to have important implications for a theology of Christian ministry. For one thing, it immediately denies Christianity any ministerial monopoly and points to some sharing of "ministry to the world" by Christians and all others who work to better the human situation. On the other hand, it indicates the area in which Christians can and must make a distinctive contribution to the betterment of the world, namely, that of influencing the viewpoints and motivations of people. Upon Christians in a special way rests the responsibility of preserving and developing mankind's most truly human traditions, the heritage of insights and values and principles from which any progressive building of the future must draw. But to fulfill this responsibility, Christians must embody, and in a sense re-create, this living tradition in the life experience they share with their contemporaries. Only in this way can the often-mentioned goal of "relevance" be attained and Christians join forces uncompromisingly with secular humanists.

An integral part of any Christian effort to better the human situation is the attempt to overcome strife and divisions among men. This "ministry of reconciliation," a facet of Christian sharing in the work of redemption that has received a good deal of attention in recent theological writing, is meant to extend beyond mere elimination of conflict and to work for a harmony and a peace that are grounded in justice. Actually, as one reflects on the various kinds of alienation that afflict mankind, he becomes conscious of the need to break down barriers between classes of people (rich and poor, men and women, etc.), but he becomes aware also that these barriers exist because individual men and women are alienated from their genuine selfhood. A man must be reconciled with himself if he is truly to be reconciled with his brother and with God, and for this he must be healed.

Soteriology has quite logically, then, drawn attention to the sociological and psychological aspects of healing that constitute a large part of mankind's salvation. The distintegration of human affectivity and the substitution of illusion for reality in human consciousness, basic psychological ills that flow directly from man's sinful condition, must be healed by the integrating influence of human and divine love and by the orderly clarity of truth. If men are thus healed and become honest knowers and courageous lovers, genuinely communal effort to overcome social alienations becomes possible. In actual practice, the two processes of psychological and social reconciliation must go along simultaneously, but the healing of men and women in their inner life has a certain causal priority.

Clearly, all this has much to say about the nature of Christian ministry. The ministries of word and sacrament must be directed to the various needs for reconciliation. Christians must seize every opportunity to overcome those elements of alienation that stand in the way of Christianity's basic goal, the formation of human community. One unavoidable responsibility of all Christians is to remove from the Christian community itself any elements of alienation. This is not to say that some flat homogeneity should characterize the church; a healthy diversity of theological opinion and of prayer and of life-styles is part of the richness of Christianity. But such catholicity is quite other than those jealousies and class distinctions and power struggles and "pious hatreds" that so often split the church into warring camps. Basically, the church's effectiveness is sacramental—it causes by being—and healing its own divisions will be the most important contribution to bringing peace and unity to the rest of mankind.

Since the particular focus of our study is on Christian ministry, it might be appropriate to say a word or two about the clergy/laity division within the church. Without overdramatizing the elements of opposition in this division, for a great deal of loving concern of each group for the other has been the more prominent characteristic of this relationship, it does stand as one of the major barriers to formation of a Christian community in which all have basic equality and dignity as brothers and sisters of Christ. There are many aspects to this question which we have already mentioned or will mention later; here we might concentrate on the significance of Jesus' own religious situation and on his attitudes towards the clergy/laity division within Judaism that he knew.

First of all, there seems to be considerable significance in the fact that Jesus, who clearly came to be the intrinsic fulfillment and most perfect exemplification of Israel's destiny and religious calling, did not belong to the priestly class and functioned in Judaism's liturgy as a "layman." A Christian theologian would have to say that Jesus' participation in any given Temple ceremony was qualitatively superior to the participation of the high priest, which challenges any claim to intrinsic religious superiority based on occupation of official religious position. Moreover, the Parable of the Good Samaritan reflects quite unmistakably the teaching of Jesus that the specialized precepts of priestly activity (which kept the priest from assisting the robbed and beaten man) are subordinate to the basic responsibilities of human life, and therefore that those with priestly function cannot justifiably absolve themselves from involvement with ordinary life which is as properly theirs as it is the layman's. Again, Jesus represents a fundamental challenge to the entire clerical structure of his day. By a process that is not denial but sublimation, he replaces Israel's entire liturgical system and its sacerdotal personnel, and the process in question is his totally nonclerical living, dying, and rising. Thus, in Christianity one can enter most profoundly into an imitation of Christ without any participation in official clerical activity. It is most difficult to avoid the conclusion that Jesus and Christianity in its early decades were purposely intent on abolishing any separation between "official" and "ordinary" Christians.

Reflection on the exemplary role played by Jesus in the "ministry of service" leads us in-evitably to the most profound facet of such ministry: Jesus' realization of Isaiah's ideal of the Suffering Servant. The very difficulty that scholars face in trying to determine the individual or corporate identity of the Servant as described in Isaiah 52–53 indicates how inseparably the individual and social elements of service are linked in Israel's understanding. When one deals with the New Testament identification of Jesus as this Servant, the passage in Isaiah is clearly given an individual interpretation but without loss of its corporate dimension, because Jesus in his salvific action of service acts as the source and head of the Christian community. This means that the church in its mission of service must continue to implement this same mysterious ideal of serving one's fellow men by giving one's life for them.

Understanding the manner in which Jesus was and is Isaiah's Suffering Servant is, then, quite important for understanding the Christian's ministry of service, for no Christian can claim to fulfill his basic vocation to service unless in some fashion he shares in Jesus' Servant role. What seems critical in interpreting Jesus' own function as the Servant is to see it operative in his entire Passover, i.e., both in his death and in his resurrection. Linking the suffering and death of Jesus to the Servant figure is not too difficult. Although the effectiveness of vicarious suffering is mysterious, one can see Jesus' death as a supreme expression of that love which lies at the root of his saving activity, and it is this love that overcomes the evil that afflicts his brethren. It is somewhat more difficult to see the Suffering Servant ideal fulfilled in the resurrection of Jesus, but it is all-important that this link be established, for it is as the risen Lord that Jesus not only continues to be Servant but receives the full power to serve other humans by the gift to them of his own life. In a very true sense, Jesus enters into the fullness of his ministry of service with his entry into risen life.

The ramifications of this interpretation of Jesus as Servant are numerous and important. For one thing, it places at the very root of all Christian service the personal gift of oneself to others; it forces us theologically to clarify what it means to give ourselves and our life to others, and what it means to be the instrument for giving Christ himself and his life to others. Again, without in any way diminishing the key role of love-unto-death in the process of salvation, an insight into Christ's risen role as Servant draws attention to the life-giving aspect of love. Christ was not only willing to face death because of his love, he willingly passed over into new life so that he could share with others that new and fuller life. So, too, *living* rather than *dying* stands at the center of Christians' service of the fellow humans.

Like the other elements of contemporary soteriology, this theological reflection on Jesus' ministry as Servant does not dictate immediate and obvious conclusions in the practical order. What all these theological understandings do provide is a point of view, a basic attitude, from which today's Christians, individually and corporately, can assess the world in which they live and decide how most effectively they can better the life of their fellow humans. The actual judgments cannot take place in theological detachment; they can be made only in the arena of practical life situations.

Specialized Ministries of Service

The fact that practical judgments about the service that Christians should undertake is so much conditioned by circumstances makes it difficult to distinguish and describe specialized ministries of service. This is particularly true if one is speaking of the community as a whole in its service to mankind, for this consists in doing whatever people need. However, there are a few fairly distinct kinds of service that form a constant part of the church's diakonal mission to the world. Within the Christian community's own corporate life a number of ministries of service are needed to provide for the well-being of individual Christians and of the community as a whole. Obviously, a given Christian may

exercise more than one of these ministries, for many of these ministries complement one another or complement some of the ministries of word and sacrament we discussed earlier. However, it is helpful to keep the various functions distinct, so that their purpose is not obscured and their existence is not threatened.

One basic service internal to the community's own life is stewardship of the community's material possessions. Few functions in the church's life have been so influential (for good and evil), few have been so coveted, and few have been the object of more criticism. Today, as part of the attempt to prune the church's life of elements that are inconsistent with its evangelical and diakonal mission, there is widespread debate about the extent to which the church should possess material goods. Granting the fact that churchmen and institutions within the church (e.g., religious orders) have often become wealthier than was appropriate, and that there is a genuine need to stress evangelical poverty as an individual and corporate ideal, the Christian community must have some possessions in order to undertake effectively its various ministries. Realistically, then, someone must provide for the community the service of caring for these possessions: providentially anticipating the economic needs of the community and gathering whatever resources will be needed, seeing to it that existent properties are cared for, dispensing resources as they are required by the community's ministerial activity.

What may appear to be a prosaic and quite "unspiritual" activity is really a key influence in maintaining (or endangering) the distinctively Christian character of the community's existence and activity, and for that reason it is important to see this ministry as grounded in charism. History makes it clear that the church's attitude towards material wealth is an important aspect of its witness to the gospel, that the handling of possessions within the church determined the extent to which the church alleviated or aggravated economic and social injustice, and that greed and avarice and excessive concern about church properties have been major influences in dividing Christians one from another and in keeping them from fulfilling their responsibility of caring for the poor of the earth. Thus, it is most important that those who exercise stewardship over the Christian community's property be animated with faith and charity in performing this service.

This does not imply that such care of the community's possessions is an office, or that an individual need necessarily perform it. There would seem to be a number of different ways of arranging for this need, dependent upon the practical exigencies of a given situation. What is important is that the handling of the church's material possessions be seen as a function that is intrinsic to the church's evangelical and diakonal mission, and that decisions about the acquisition or disposition of wealth be made in this perspective. Whoever fulfills this need performs an indispensable service to the Christian community.

Quite different from this ministry of stewardship, which deals with things for the sake of persons, is the ministry of healing, which deals directly with men and women. Healing is, of course, a very broad reality. It extends both to the church's ministration to mankind and to the church's internal needs for ministration, since the ills that need healing are to be found in people and institutions inside and outside the church. Moreover, there is a wide spectrum of activities that can fit under the canopy of "healing": physical medicine, psychological therapy, spiritual direction, sacramental anointing, forgiveness of sins, and the reuniting of opposing social groups. Consciousness of this qualitative diversity forces us to speak in the plural of "ministries," though the exact lines of distinctions are not clear and probably cannot be sharply drawn. The function of the surgeon can quite easily be distinguished from that of the spiritual director; but it is not that easy to say where the proper task of the spiritual director ends and that of the psychological counselor begins. Again, it is hard to say when the term "Christian" can be properly and distinctively applied to some of these service roles.

Part of the problem in establishing some lines of distinction lies in the very real link between these forms of healing. Somehow they do form a continuum, and it is the nature of this continuum that theologians must study seriously, a task they have just begun. The evidence of the Gospel narrations of Jesus' own ministry points explicitly to some intrinsic link between bodily healing and forgiveness of sin, a link which in the biblical perspective is grounded in the basic unity of evil. Again, the evidence of recent developments in Christian sacramental practice and understanding indicates a continuum of healing. Increasingly, enlightened counseling of men and women in the sacrament of penance has dealt with the roots of whatever patterns of sinful behavior were disclosed. Since such roots always involve some element of psychological disorder, penitential healing and psychological therapy are now seen to verge upon one another and sometimes to overlap. On the other side, the sacrament of anointing, which for centuries had been treated as a sacrament for the dying, is now being applied to cases of serious sickness, and it is not unlikely that it may soon be extended to psychological sickness, at which point a clear continuity between the sacraments of penance and anointing will be visible, a continuity that has been vaguely glimpsed in the traditional teaching that the sacrament of anointing could somehow supply for confession and absolution if (obviously in the case of the dying) these were impossible.

In a way, the continuum we are trying to understand is easily understood. Men and women are afflicted by evil in all its many forms, physical and psychological and moral, individual and social, and so there must be a process of healing the wounds that evil has inflicted. What is not easily understood is the manner in which the healings that are directed against the various manifestations of evil influence one another. Yet, such an understanding is basic to any intelligent structuring of ministries of healing.

Any ministry of healing must deal with man as a whole, even though it may concentrate on one facet of his being. Man is not body *and* soul. Man is an incarnated spirit, an intelligently animated corporeal being; he is body spiritually and spirit bodily. Again, man's individual and social existence cannot be divorced; man must exist socially in order to develop his individuality, and his capacity to participate in society will rest upon his own integrated individuality. Thus, the various functions that we can point to as ministries of healing are interdependent and their effective service of mankind demands that they consciously relate to and interact with one another. But there are also distinctions that need to be drawn in the practical order (as, for example, between spiritual direction and psychological counseling), because the achievement of distinct goals demands distinct expertise on the part of the "healer."

From one point of view, all that the Christian community does in its various ministries of word and sacrament and service contributes to the healing of mankind; all positive fostering of life can be viewed as "preventive medicine." And for a number of good reasons, our present-day reflection on Christian ministry might be well advised to stress this approach of nurturing life rather than to focus on man's wounding by evil and consequent need for healing. However, Christian faith is realistic in its recognition that man does need healing. If nothing else made this clear, the inescapable reality of death would, and Christian faith has always insisted that death is to be confronted straightforwardly, and Christian ministry has always dealt with the

wounds inflicted by death: to help heal the dying person and to help heal those bereaved by death. Precisely because death is so paradigmatic in human experience and the critical turning point in man's life, development of theological understanding about ministration to Christian death may be the key to developing a less inadequate theology of the ministry of healing.

A number of other ministries of "service" could be studied, but one in particular demands some special attention: the ministry of governing. In any situation, political or social or religious, governing is a service to the common good of the community in question. In the context of Christianity the basic biblical ideal of "service" is a normative principle for understanding and exercising the ministry of governing. During the past decade there has been a chorus of voices insisting on the "service" character of church government, so there is no great need to stress the idea that governing must be viewed in the church as a ministry of service. However, because governing does imply authority of some kind it is far from clear how governing is to be understood as "service." After all, an autocratic dictator could quite sincerely believe that he was serving his fellow men by giving them the benefits of his absolutely monarchical rule.

Consequently, it may be better to postpone a thorough discussion of the ministry of governing until part four, in which we can more carefully examine the nature and appropriateness of authority and jurisdiction in the church.

Selected Bibliography

Service to the People of God

EARLY CHRISTIANITY:

Audet, J.-P. *Structures of Christian Priesthood.* New York, 1968.

Conzelmann, H. *History of Primitive Christianity.* New York, 1973.

Goppelt, L. *Apostolic and Post-Apostolic Times.* London, 1970.

Jeremias, J. *New Testament Theology.* New York, 1971.

Monden, L. *Signs and Wonders.* New York, 1966.

Tyson, J. *A Study of Early Christianity.* New York, 1973.

PATRISTIC AND MEDIEVAL CHRISTIANITY:

Gilchrist, J. *The Church and Economic Activity in the Middle Ages.* London, 1969.

Moorman, J. *Church Life in England in the Thirteenth Century.* Cambridge, 1945.

Poschmann, B. *Penance and the Anointing of the Sick.* New York, 1964.

Powicke, F. *Ways of Medieval Life and Thought.* Oxford, 1949.

Schnurer, G. *Church and Culture in the Middle Ages.* Paterson, N.J., 1956.

POST-MEDIEVAL CHRISTIANITY:

Dillenberger, J. and Welch, C. *Protestant Christianity.* New York, 1954.

Edwards, N. and Richey, H. *The School in the American Social Order.* 2d ed. Boston, 1963.

Ellis, J. *American Catholicism.* 2d ed. Chicago, 1969.

Hales. E. *The Catholic Church in the Modern World.* New York, 1958.

Koenigsberger, H. and Mosse, G. *Europe in the Sixteenth Century.* London, 1968.

McNeill, J. *A History of the Cure of Souls.* New York, 1951.

Marshall, D. *The English Poor in the Eighteenth Century.* London, 1926.

Ogg, D. *Europe in the Seventeenth Century.* 8th ed. London, 1961.

Power, E. *Main Currents in the History of Education.* New York, 1962.

**PART
FOUR**

Ministering to
God's Judgment

New Testament Concepts of Judgment

In the light of the overall history of Christian ministry, the role of judge assumes major importance. Tied in with it is the nature of the authority possessed by those occupying office in the church. Some of the most basic developments in the exercise of Christian ministry are linked with the evolution of thinking and practice regarding the judicial aspect of episcopal ministry.

Thus, again, we must risk artificiality and even a certain distortion by focusing in somewhat isolated fashion on the element of judgment in Scripture, especially in the New Testament texts. Any intelligent human action and particularly any thoughtful social activity involves judgment, not just upon material factors but upon human ideas and motivations and responsibility. And, to single out just one clear example, the prophetic function in a religious society like Old Testament Israel or the early Christian community involves a large element of critical judgment of human behavior.

But this very centrality of judgment in a religious community raises a critical problem. Who possesses judgment, on what authority, and of what kind? Can a man subject any of his fellows to his religious judgment? Can he discern religious truth as it applies to another, or pass judgment upon the religious sincerity or genuineness of another? In an earlier age, the answer to such questions might have seemed relatively clear, as ecclesiastical institutions and those responsible for them seemed divinely established for the very purpose of passing such judgment.[1] But in our own day we have become increasingly conscious of the

inadequacy of human activity in such matters. We are not even clear anymore as to what constitutes heresy, which would seem to be a much more objective area than the judgment of moral guilt.[2]

At first glance the New Testament literature is no great help. As a matter of fact, it almost seems to rule the whole question out of court; judgment belongs to God alone and to the risen Lord into whose hands he has given judgment.[3] This divine monopoly pertains to judgment upon the truth of faith and revelation, to judgment upon the value and correctness of human behavior, and to judgment upon sin that takes final expression in the death and resurrection of Jesus. Thus, there seems to be no judicial function remaining for men; all they can properly do is give expression to the judgment of God.

This is all true, but, of course, we are again facing that enigmatic situation which is of the essence of mankind's religious behavior, indeed of its total existence. From one point of view God does everything, man is totally dependent; yet, human activity is not just illusion, it does somehow contribute to a joint divine-human effort. Christianity sees the key to this question in the salvific economy which centers in the mystery of Jesus Christ, in the enfleshment of God's own Word.[4]

Specifically, in our present question, all judgment belongs to Christ. In the reality of expressing himself in his Word existing humanly, and in that human experience finding ultimate statement in death and resurrection, God passes creative judgment upon the world and man without depriving man of his freedom and existential autonomy. It is clear that we are here in contact with the classical problem of providence. If judgment is left solely in the divine and no intrinsically effective judgment belongs to man, there can ultimately be nothing but predeterminism.[5]

True, it does not add a great deal to the clarity of our understanding to place the "solution" in the human freedom of Jesus, for this raises its own questions. But there may be some value in defining the problem more accurately—if nothing else, it may make clear how Christological every Christian understanding of reality must be![6]

Our purpose, however, is not to write an exhaustive exposition of New Testament thought about judgment, but only to see what kind and what extent of judgment enters into ministry in the life and thought of the New Testament community. Consequently, our treatment of judgment as it belongs to Christ will be limited; we will deal with it only to the extent that this is required for grasping the character of Christian ministry.

Judgment on Truth

By the very fact that God reveals himself supremely in Jesus who is his Word, and by the fact that the preaching of the gospel is the announcing of this revelation, the existence of Christianity and its preaching of the "good news" is a judgment on truth. All human understanding, more directly in those elements that touch upon man himself, is altered to some extent, that is to say "judged," by the insights that come with Christian revelation.

The question, however, that is critical for a community that believes such a revelation is: Who can act with authority to judge the accuracy of the community's understanding of this revelation? Who or what is the norm of faith, the criterion of orthodoxy? Who if anyone is authorized to judge another's understanding of the gospel?

Here it is clear that some authoritative role was played by the Twelve and certain other privileged witnesses to the mystery of Christ's death and resurrection.[7] Individuals among

them laid claim to their prerogatives because of their own experience, Peter appealing to his experience on the mountain (2 Pet. 1:18) or his experience of the risen Lord (Acts 2), or Paul appealing to his experience of the risen Christ on the road to Damascus (Acts 26:9–18; Gal. 1:15–17). As a group, the apostles and presbyters at Jerusalem felt empowered to determine the formulations of faith that were to guide the early evangelization and catechesis (Acts 16:4). The Epistle of James indicates that only a few should presume to exercise this role of teacher, for they themselves will receive a stricter judgment (James 3:1).

The very existence of the New Testament literature attests to the importance given to the apostolic tradition, and to the increasing role it played as a norm of Christian belief. To receive acceptance as a credible element of faith, an element of teaching apparently had to possess some relation to the experience or teaching of the Twelve.[8] This does not become an enunciated principle until well into the second (or third?) century,[9] but it is already operative in the early decades. Thus, there was constant judgment on anything that appeared innovative—"even if a messenger from heaven should come preaching . . ." (Gal. 1:8).

To quite an extent the entire community participated in the judgment on the truth of teaching. It would seem that both those who occupied the ministry of teaching and those who functioned as prophets needed the approval of the community. And Paul tells the Corinthians to be discriminating in their attention to men who claimed to be prophetic (1 Cor. 14:37–38).

Imparting the Spirit of Truth

One subtle but important way by which the Christian community was to pass judgment on truth was by communicating the Spirit. Christ's Spirit is the Spirit of truth, bearing witness to the truth of the Christian gospel (John 15:26). This is effected by his illumination of men's minds and hearts whereby they are given insight into truth. His also is the guidance that directs men of good faith to a course of action that leads in truth to God and the achievement of the Kingdom.

Thus, to share with others the Spirit is to place their understandings and attitudes under judgment, for the Spirit within them will inevitably witness to truth and challenge their false views. One wonders in reading the earliest literature of Christianity to what extent such a truth-evoking gift of the Spirit was seen as central to the "ordination" of ministers by the imposition of hands.[10] In such a gift of the Spirit there would be no infusion of ideas, no charismatic gift of language or prophetic utterance; instead, there would be an internal power of awareness which would "sense" the incompatibility of certain notions with the gospel of Christ. One could cling to error only by "resisting the Spirit."

One aspect of judgment was clearly prominent in the early Christian decades: the validity of a man's teaching was approved or disapproved by his own deeds. In the eleventh chapter of Matthew, which raises the question of the acceptability of Jesus' "wisdom," Jesus himself points to his deeds as the judgment upon his prophetic teaching. "Wisdom is justified by her deeds." Again, the principle of the Sermon on the Mount is clear: "By their fruit you shall know them" (Matt. 7:20). The Johannine tradition preserves the same "pragmatic" criterion regarding Jesus' own teaching: "If you do not wish to believe in me, at least believe in the works I do . . ." (John 10:38).

Paul repeatedly appeals to his own dedicated activity as a reason for accepting his teaching and ministry, and he warns his Christians to beware of those who would try to profit personally from an "apostolic vocation."[11] While unselfish devotion to apostolic work does not in itself guarantee the accuracy of the teacher's message, the absence of such disinterested activity does tend to throw suspicion on one's teaching.

Judgment on Behavior

While it saw quite clearly the vital need of judging the truth of the teaching to which Christians were exposed, the early church seemed more concerned with judgment on the behavior of its members. Or perhaps, in the light of the actual New Testament texts, it would be more accurate to say that the early church was interested in having its members avoid passing judgment on one another. One of the most repeated precepts in the moral exhortation one finds in the Gospels and Epistles is "Judge not."

Judgment upon the culpability of men's actions belongs only to God. Even in the case of this divine judgment, there are interesting texts that indicate that the New Testament writers, Paul in particular, saw that evil passes judgment on itself. God's judgment is simply the revelation of the intrinsic worth of a man's deeds (Rom. 2:2–11). Actually a man passes condemnation upon himself by what he does (Gal. 5:10). Paul is particularly strong in his statements that Christians should avoid imposing their own conscience judgments upon others; all should feel a genuine freedom to do what they sincerely believe to be true, though they owe it in charity to take account of the weakness of some of the brethren who might misunderstand and be hurt by their actions (1 Cor. 10:23).

At the same time, because it was a social reality, early Christianity required some agencies of judgment within its early communities. Apparently, some special prerogatives along this line were recognized for the Twelve. A text like that in Matthew 19:28 would seem to touch on this: "When the Son of man comes in his glory you will sit on twelve thrones judging the twelve tribes of Israel." Practically the same saying is found in Luke 22:30. However, any attempt to apply such texts to the social situation of primitive Christianity must be very cautious. The text in Matthew is clearly eschatological in context and closely allied in its language to the eschatological judgment parable of 25:31,[12] and Luke's location of the saying in the midst of the narration of the Supper could well give the text a Eucharistic tonality.[13]

Paul can repeat that Christians are not to judge one another (Rom. 14:10–13), which apparently applies to individuals taking it upon themselves to so judge. Yet, he also makes it clear to the church of Corinth that it should provide for someone from the community to act as judge of differences that arise among members, rather than taking such problems to pagan tribunals for judgment (1 Cor. 5:22—6:8). The whole tone of this latter passage would lead us to think that it was the common pattern of early Christian communities to handle all their judicial needs within their own group, without recourse to civil courts. There is no indication of precisely who acted as judges, though it probably involved the *episkopoi* and the *presbyteroi*.[14]

Matthew 18:18, among other passages, points to the community's power to excommunicate from its midst those who betrayed their membership or were considered a danger to the faith of the others. It is not clear, however, to what extent the idea prevailed that such "excommunication" involved also a judgment upon the moral state of the individual in question.

The bulk of community judgment on behavior occurred *ante factum*, through its ethical teaching and its "legislation." God himself was seen to be the authority behind all law; even civil rulers were to be respected and obeyed as ministers of God in his lawgiving activity (Rom. 13:1). Christ was, of course, the privileged emissary. He came not to judge in the sense of condemning (John 3:17ff.; 12:47) but to bring the light of truth which, if a man rejects it, passes judgment on him. He is the light come into the world and this is the light that is the life of men; if they reject it, it follows intrinsically that they remain in darkness and death. No judge need pass such a sentence upon them (John 1:4–5; 3:19–21). By the very fact that he speaks truth, Jesus judges the truth or error of those who hear him (John 8:28).

Though they never lost sight of the fact that there is really one lawgiver in Christianity (James 4:12; Matt. 23:8), the Twelve, along with other apostles and presbyters of the early decades, did feel it was their function to legislate practically for the needs of the communities. Theirs was the role of determining the policy of evangelization, of

baptizing, of religious observance. To them also fell the function (or at least to the apostles and presbyters of the mother church in Jerusalem) of "decreeing" the formulations of early Christian faith (Acts 16:4). And Paul, in writing to the Corinthians, gives decisions on a number of "cases of conscience" that had apparently been submitted by them. One thing that must not be lost sight of is the New Testament belief that in such activity the early leadership was acting along with and under the special guidance of the Spirit: "It has seemed good to the Holy Spirit and to us" (Acts 15:28). Community decision in the New Testament period was clearly a process of "discernment of the Spirit," and it might be good to bear in mind the essential role of prophetic charism in this process.[15]

It is an essential element of prophetism (as we know it in a biblical context) that it be judgment, judgment on the activity of those to whom the prophet addresses himself, judgment upon the meaning of the community's religious understandings and traditions, judgment upon the present situation to which the prophet and the community must respond with practical decision.[16] Such prophetic judgment obviously plays a major part in the New Testament description of the activity of Jesus and of his disciples. Jesus' own critical judgments extends to the whole spectrum of life as he knew it in the Jewish theocracy, reaching even to the most treasured precepts of the Law. His teaching was not only a matter of interpretation, as Rabbinic instruction was meant to be; it was also the imparting of a new evaluation of life, a new insight into the meaning and responsibilities of human existence (Matt. 5:21–22).

Much of this same charismatic grounding for the exhortation, condemnation, and "legislation" carried on by early Christianity's leaders explains their assertion of authority in preaching and the community's acceptance of their activity.[17] While Christians are not to judge one another (Rom. 14:10–13), this seems to pertain to their "private" relationships with one another. Paul certainly exercises an effective judicial role in his condemnation of the incestuous Christian at Corinth (1 Cor. 5:3). And as a regular part of his continuing instruction of the Christian communities he judged the orthodoxy of faith and the prudence of Christian judgments; this he did, not as an executive or judicial "official," but as a prophet. But if the prophet can judge the community, the community has a role in passing judgment on the prophet as true or false, for the whole community had a basic prophetic gift.

One of the most instructive passages regarding the prophetic basis for early Christian exercise of judgment is found in the scene after Jesus' cleansing of the Temple (Luke 20:1–8). Challenged to defend his action and to assert by what authority he had acted, Jesus refuses a direct response but instead asks the priestly authorities about their view of John the Baptist: Did he act by prophetic authority or not? The implication is clear: if they would recognize John's charisma as prophet, then they would be capable of recognizing his own prophetic function as John's fulfillment. In other words, the text seems to assert quite clearly the early Christian view that Jesus' own authority in his public ministry came as an aspect of his prophetic mission. He occupied no official position in the Judaism of his day; he neither claimed such nor sought it. Yet, his authority surpassed and challenged that of Jewish officialdom, for it proceeded immediately from the Spirit of God.

Judgment on Sin

To say that the early Christian communities and their leadership saw the intrinsic need for authoritative judgment upon behavior that would endanger the good of the community is one thing; it is another thing to say that they believed that some in their midst possessed the authority to affect the internal culpability of men. Clear and correcting teaching, prophetic exhortation, edifying example—all would obviously have their power to change the state of soul of a sinner, and these did so in those who needed it. But

the claim that is made (or at least seems to be made) in the New Testament literature is more than that; it is the claim to forgive sin.

The claim is already a startling one when it is made for Jesus in his public ministry; the reflection of such a "scandal" is found in the scene of the healing of the paralytic (Matt. 9:1–8 and par.). Here the claim to have power over sin is sharp and unmistakable and "proved" by the wonder of healing that Jesus works. The implications of such a claim are recognized, yet in later scenes of his ministry Jesus is repeatedly described as forgiving the sins of men. One aspect of these narratives might well be emphasized: although the forgiveness of sin is an act of judgment, and its reality depends upon Jesus' *exousia*,[18] it is in the context of healing.[19] Against the background of Old Testament thought this should not be too surprising. The act of judgment on the part of Yahweh had always been essentially one of healing his people from their sins; it was judgment in the sense of making them just.[20]

However, the claim to lead the sinner out of his sins to life, to lead him from darkness to light, is made by Christ's disciples (Acts 26:16–18). They see this grounded in a commission from Christ himself, as described in the authority granted to Simon Peter at Caesarea-Philippi (Matt. 16:18–20), or the more broadly applicable promise of Matthew 18:18–20, or the grant of power over sin given to the Twelve on Easter night (John 20:23). It would, naturally, be anachronistic to understand such texts in the light of the later evolution of the sacrament of penance. Probably (in the understanding of early Christianity) much of their applicability lay in the freeing from sin that took place through conversion and baptism.[21] Paul's frequent statements to his converts that they have been freed from their sins seems to refer to this baptismal liberation. On the other hand, it would be exegetically unjustified to confine the New Testament statements about the "power of the keys" to baptism. While these texts do not refer specifically to a postbaptismal ritual of reconciliation from sin, they open up a basic ministry of effectively freeing men from their sin which could, and actually did, develop into both the sacrament of baptism and the sacrament of penance.[22] However, as we will see, such a development did not take place without considerable division of opinion, even bitter controversy. But the point of the controversy was not precisely the episcopal power to forgive grave sin after baptism but rather the prudential advisability of such "lax" practice.[23]

One thing that deserves mention in this context, though its exact meaning and applicability is difficult to establish, is the New Testament insistence that Christians be merciful to one another, that they be forgiving, that they not pass condemnatory judgment upon one another (e.g., Luke 6:36). Such an ethical exhortation is easy enough to understand, even though its ideal is difficult to realize. What is more difficult to understand is the link which is mentioned in a number of texts between a Christian's forgiveness of his fellows and his own forgiveness by God (e.g., Matt. 6:12). Such mercy towards others seems to be *the* means of obtaining divine forgiveness for one's own sinfulness. It would seem to suggest, though it would be presumptuous to draw too definite a conclusion, that in the early Christian decades forgiveness of post-baptismal sin was effected by the sinner's own internal reconversion. There is little if any indication that there was any intervention in this process by the pastoral ministry, except by way of exhortation to repentance.[24]

What one does find as a prominent part of the liberation from sin is the effective preaching of the gospel.[25] The word of the gospel is creative and salvific; it leads to *metanoia* and the new life of baptism and faith. Justification comes with faith, as both Romans and Galatians insist (Rom. 1:16–17; Gal. 3:11), and there can be no faith in Christ without the preaching of the gospel. In saying this, we are back with the prophetic aspect of ministry, for such causing of *metanoia* is the precise objective of prophetic activity.

Like the Old Testament theologians, only

more so, early Christianity sees the prophetic word as a bearer of power and life.[26] The preached word of the gospel with its promise of forgiveness and new life is, then, truly the bearer of that new life. Conferring of life and defeat of death are two sides of the same reality, as are the bringing of light and the dispelling of darkness. So, in the very process of giving light and life the word of the gospel "remits sin"; but only, of course, if it is received in faith and implemented by active entry into the Christian community and the mystery of Christ.[27]

Ultimately, the only effective judgment against evil, and especially against human sinfulness, comes in the death and resurrection of Jesus. This it is which reveals the intrinsic evil of sin and the salvific power of divine love in final combat.[28] Sin is judged by having its true nature made known and by having its power broken definitively. Mankind's justification from its sin comes only in the sacrificial death of Christ (Heb. 9). The law of Moses is ineffective in achieving man's justification; this comes only with Jesus' death and resurrection (Acts 13:38; Rom. 10:5–13).

The Johannine perspective is particularly interesting in its identification of the process of judging with that of giving life.[29] This is not exactly unique to John but it finds there a more explicit and extended treatment.[30] The Incarnate Word is given judgment precisely because he is the one sent to give life to men (John 5:21ff.). Because he is the Word, the judgment he gives is not just his own but that of the Father who sends him. Thus, the life-giving judgment passed on man is nothing other than the saving mystery of the Word. To say that Jesus is supreme judge is to say that he has ultimate power over life and death; this he has because he is the very source of eternal life (John 5:26).

Forgiveness of sin, introduction into life, can only come, then, by bringing to bear on a man's life (or on the life of society) the power of the risen Christ. This is central to any ministry exercised within the church: to bring men, through word and example and sacrament, into saving contact with the risen Lord.

All salvation, all forgiveness of sin, must come through entry into the mystery of Christ (1 Tim. 2:5).

The Nature of Authority in the Church

From a theological point of view, it would be more valuable if the New Testament writings provided an insight into early Christianity's view of the kind of authority rather than if they gave a description of the various "offices" that were exercised in those early decades. Understanding the nature of the authority that is appropriate to Christianity itself as a community, it would also provide us with a guide by which to assess the actual exercise of authority which occurs in the twenty centuries of the church's history, and a guide to present-day exercise of authority within the church.

Fortunately, the New Testament evidence on this point is abundant and unmistakable. Paul's Epistles, which reflect his own unique authority as well as that possessed by various individuals within the communities he formed, attribute all authority to the risen Christ and see any other authority as a result of being sent by Christ to preach the gospel of salvation. Paul's mission is one of *diakonia*, a service of Christ and a service of his fellow Christians.[31] When some challenge to his apostolic authority did arise, Paul justified his own position and role by appealing to his direct delegation from the Lord (Gal. 1:11), to the correspondence of his teaching with the apostolic tradition (1 Cor. 11:23), to his possession of the Spirit (1 Cor. 2:10–16), and to his fidelity to the apostolic ministry (2 Cor. 11:22ff.).

In the Gospel traditions, three texts are of pivotal importance: John 18:37, Matthew 20:25–28, and Luke 22:25–30. The first of these, Jesus' declaration to Pilate, takes Christ's own authority (and therefore that of the church) out of the realm of ordinary political power ("My kingdom is not of this world") and situates it in the context of witness to truth. The authority belongs to truth itself and he who faithfully conveys the truth speaks with that kind of authority. This is the kind of authority proper to the prophet as well as to the teacher, and this text links us therefore with Luke 20:1–8 where Jesus, challenged by the priestly leadership to state the basis for his teaching authority, implicitly claims the authority of a prophet.

The second text, Matthew 20:25–28, pictures Jesus clarifying for his disciples the kind of authority that is proper to his kingdom,[32] again, not according to the model of civil rulers: "The Lords of the Gentiles dominate their subjects; but it is not so in my kingdom." And here again the authority is prophetic, but in terms of the full prophetic ideal contained in Isaiah 52–53: Jesus himself has authority precisely by serving others, even to the extent of giving his life for them.

Luke's version of this same saying occurs in the Supper narrative, thus introducing an important element of theological interpretation.[33] As in the text of Matthew, Jesus makes clear that political authority has no place in his kingdom, that those in leadership positions in the church are to be servants of their brethren; he appeals to his own exercise of authority as a model. But in this instance (i.e., the Lucan setting) the service he has just performed is the giving of himself through the bread-wine symbolism, the action which continued into his death and resurrection establishes the kingdom. The Eucharistic self-gift of Christ becomes, then, the norm for Christian exercise of authority.

Essentially the same conclusion emerges from Ephesians 5:23–27. The text is part of the Epistle's discussion of various authority relationships, a discussion whose entire content is governed by the introductory verse (5:21) which exhorts Christians to be subject (i.e., of service) to one another. In treating of the husband's authority in the marriage relationship, the Epistle invokes the example of Christ's own authority over the church, an authority which consists in his gift of self in death and resurrection. It is in this self-gift that Christ "becomes one flesh" with the church, functioning as head of the church which is his body.

NOTES

1. Of course there has always been a prominent group within the church that raised questions as to the extent that God was bound by ecclesiastical decisions. We will see the various forms of such questioning as we examine the history of ecclesiastical judgments.

2. See K. Rahner, "What Is Heresy?" *Theological Investigations*, vol. 5, pp. 468–512.

3. See F. Büchsel, "Krino," *Theological Dictionary of the New Testament* (hereafter referred to as *TDNT*), vol. 3, pp. 936–39; J. Guillet, *Themes of the Bible* (Notre Dame, 1961), pp. 82–89 (on judgment).

4. See E. Mersch, *Theology of the Mystical Body* (St. Louis, 1951), pp. 252–322.

5. See J. Macquarrie, *Principles of Christian Theology* (New York, 1966), pp. 219–25. L. Gilkey, *Maker of Heaven and Earth* (New York, 1959), pp. 163–207.

6. On the freedom of Christ, see Rahner, *Theological Investigations*, vol. 5, pp. 157–215.

7. See H. Strathmann, "Martys," *TDNT*, vol. 4, pp. 492–94; E. Schweizer, *Church Order in the New Testament* (London, 1961), pp. 194–97.

8. See H. von Campenhausen, *Ecclesiastical Authority and Spiritual Power in the Church of the First Three Centuries* (Palo Alto, Calif., 1969), pp. 21–54. Within the witness of the Twelve, some special function seems clearly to have been attributed to the role of Peter—as special recipient of revelation, as special confessor of the faith (culminating in his martyrdom), and as special guardian of true teaching. See R. Brown, K. Donfried, J. Reumann (eds.), *Peter in the New Testament* (Minneapolis, 1973), esp. pp. 162–68, in which they suggest the trajectory of New Testament thought and imagery about Peter and indicate that it flows open-endedly into patristic developments.

9. Justin *1 Apol.* 42. 4, 52. 12; Hermas *Sim.* 9. 17. 1; Irenaeus *Adv. Haer.* 3. 3. 4; see Y. Congar, *Tradition and Traditions* (New York, 1967), pp. 23–26.

10. 1 Tim. 4:6, 13–16; Schweizer, pp. 206–10.

11. So also the advice given by the *Didache* 11 regarding the need to distinguish true from false prophets.

12. A. Jones, *The Gospel According to St. Matthew* (New York, 1965), p. 221.

13. This Lucan relocation of the passage will be discussed at length in chapter 27.

14. See, however, von Campenhausen, pp. 69–74, where he insists on the unstructured and unofficial nature of judgment in the Pauline churches.

15. On the practical casuistic teaching in the early church, see C. Spicq, *Théologie morale du Nouveau Testament* (Paris, 1965), vol. 2, pp. 592–612, 667–72.

16. See B. Vawter, *The Conscience of Israel* (New York, 1961), pp. 13–18; J. Lindblom, *Prophecy in Ancient Israel* (Oxford, 1962), pp. 202–6, 346–60.

17. On the question of charismatic and noncharismatic ministries in the early church, see Schweizer, pp. 181–87.

18. See W. Foerster, "Exousia," *TDNT*, vol. 2, pp. 568–69; A. Feuillet, "L'*exousia* du Fils de l'homme," *Recherches de science religieuse* 42 (1954), pp. 161–92.

19. Matt. 9:1–8; Luke 7:47–50.

20. See Guillet, pp. 24–32, 47–82.

21. See A. Richardson, *Introduction to the Theology of the New Testament* (New York, 1958), pp. 341–50.

22. See B. Poschmann, *Penance and the Anointing of the Sick* (New York, 1964), pp. 6–19.

23. *Ibid.*, pp. 19–62.

24. *Ibid.*

25. See G. Friedrich, "Euangelion," *TDNT*, vol. 2, pp. 729–34; K. Schelkle, *Discipleship and Priesthood* (New York, 1965), pp. 67–72.

26. R. Schnackenburg, *The Church in the New Testament* (New York, 1965), pp. 35–40.

27. See E. Schillebeeckx, *Revelation and Theology* (New York, 1967), pp. 41–49.

28. See P. Schoonenberg, *Man and Sin* (Notre Dame, 1965), pp. 118–23; A. von Speyr, *Confession* (New York, 1964), pp. 47–59.

29. See R. Brown, *St. John* (Garden City, N.Y., 1966), vol. 1, pp. 218–21; R. Bultmann, *Theology of the New Testament* (New York, 1955), vol. 2, pp. 33–40.

30. See Guillet, pp. 88–89, 190–91.

31. On authority in the Pauline congregations, see von Campenhausen, pp. 65–75.

32. For a more detailed treatment of this and the following two texts, see B. Cooke, *Christian Community: Response to Reality* (New York, 1970), pp. 18–22.

33. See Richardson, pp. 315–17, who draws attention to Luke's emphasis on *diakonia*. It is doubtful, however, whether one can read the passage (as Richardson does) as Luke's account of the ordination of the apostolic ministry, the consecration of a new priesthood.

CHAPTER 21

Judgment in the Ante-Nicene Period

The New Testament literature, the Acts in particular, provides testimony that Christians in the early decades of Christianity felt themselves specially directed by the Spirit. It was the Spirit, since he was the Spirit of truth, who was able to discern truth from falsity in faith and in practical judgments. As we move into the second century, the very endurance and canonical recognition of this New Testament writing evidences the retention by the Christian communities of this view regarding their direction by the Spirit.

But this is far from being the only evidence. The early apologetes and particularly Justin look upon the church as a Spirit-filled community, guided by this Spirit of prophecy, and therefore true in its faith and conduct.[1] And certainly such a trust in and acceptance of the Spirit's direction lies behind the visionary experience of Hermas, a charismatic happening that occurs to him for the sake of the community's guidance.[2] However, what seems to be even more prominent in second-century thought is the abiding presence in the community of its risen Lord.[3] Since he is, as Ignatius stresses, the truth remaining with them and their supreme example of true living,[4] and since he is also the Logos, i.e., the very source of all truth and law, a basic theme of Justin's writings,[5] Christians have a unique possession of truth. "Whatever all men have uttered aright is the property of us Christians."[6]

One finds essentially the same viewpoint in Athenagoras,[7] in Theophilus (especially in his teaching on the Spirit's inspiration of both Old and New Testament writings),[8] and in the letter to Diognetus, though the last has no explicit mention of the Spirit.[9] It is with Irenaeus that one finds a more detailed and complex presentation of the church as the embodiment of the Christ-mystery (the mystery of "recapitulation," which stands at the center of Irenaeus' theology),[10] and of the church's possession of truth because of the continuing action of the Spirit in conjunction with the apostolic tradition.[11] In a different vein, though equally sophisticated, is the writing of Irenaeus' contemporary, Clement of Alexandria. Like Irenaeus, Clement disputes the Gnostics' claim to special insight into truth; instead, it is the sincere Christian who can make such a claim, because he has working within him the Logos, the true Light, the true teacher and lawgiver.[12] Clement speaks often enough about the Spirit, but it seems that in his view the Spirit is more connected with energy and life than specifically with truth;[13] truth is rather the province of the Logos, i.e., Christ. Judgment about what is and what should be depends upon him if it is to be true.[14]

Discerning the Spirit

We could continue through the third and early fourth century, showing the continuing belief in the inner direction of the church faith and life by the abiding presence of Christ and his Spirit. Hippolytus, Origen, Tertullian, and Cyprian—all clearly attest to this belief.[15] However, the question that is more specifically directed to our study of ministry is: If judgment of truth depends on guidance from the Spirit, who discerns true from false "inspiration"?

We have already noticed how the New Testament communities had to grapple with this question—unavoidably so, for it is a perennial problem that is present in every age of the church's existence. In the New Testament writings, however, and also in the *Didache*, the instructions for such discernment are left very general. The community is to discern the true charismatic from the false; the community, or a group (in one instance, the Twelve, in another, teachers and prophets) prays for guidance from the Spirit. Already some norms are emerging. Whatever comes from the Spirit cannot be a new gospel, but must conform to that preached by the apostles; whatever comes from the Spirit must foster peace and love and unity. But these are still quite nebulous. Who precisely decides that something does or does not conform to the apostolic teaching?

Second-century Christian understanding as to how the truth and the Spirit of Christ are to be discovered seems mixed. At the very beginning of the century one finds the situation reflected in the epistles of Ignatius; here the concord of truth and charity that makes of the community a unified body is clearly dependent upon the *episkopos*.[16] The presbyterate seems to be functioning as an instructing and policy-making group;[17] but the *presbyteroi* are to find their own unity and "orthodoxy" through their union with the *episkopos*, even if he possesses less experience than they.[18]

In Rome, if we can argue from Hermas, there does not seem to be (in the early part of the second century) a single *episkopos* who is looked upon as the privileged "discerner." Rather, Hermas is directed to take his visionary insights to the presbyters. Not just so that they can verify their authenticity but so that they can gain guidance from them, guidance for their own practical judgments about the community.[19] Before the end of the century, as we can see from the prayer for the consecration of the bishop in Hippolytus' *Apostolic Tradition*, the bishop is looked

upon as one with special possession of the Spirit for teaching and judgment.[20] Prior to Hippolytus is the evidence of his master, Irenaeus, who sees the *episkopoi* and the *presbyteroi* with them as endowed with some special guidance, so that they will teach with truth in the community.[21]

Clement's writings do not indicate a negation of this episcopal development in Alexandria, but they certainly represent a different emphasis.[22] For Clement, the discernment of truth is proportionate to one's growth in Christian "gnosis."[23] As one advances in holiness, through discipline and charity, one is increasingly "illumined" and consequently more able to grasp truth and to order life according to truth.[24] Clement clearly keeps certain "objective" criteria, particularly the apostolic traditions preserved in Scripture, as norms for true Christian faith.[25] Moreover, in at least one passage (which sounds like an anticipation of Pseudo-Dionysius) he refers to the orders of bishop-presbyter and deacon as possessing the very righteousness which goes along with illumination by the Logos.[26]

Origen, too, while stressing the need for authentic Christian teaching to remain within the context of the apostolic and ecclesiastical traditions, maintains that the clarification and "grounding" of the apostles' teaching belongs to those who have prepared themselves for the task by their love and pursuit of wisdom.[27] While this wisdom is certainly seen by both Clement and Origen as a charism, there does not seem to be a question of its belonging to any "official" group as the guarantee of truth that Irenaeus saw belonging to *episkopoi*.

If there is any figure in the pre-Nicene church that we should expect to justify his teaching and practical judgments on the basis of office, it is Cyprian. This he does, but it is also interesting to notice how he appeals to special insights from the Spirit to justify the judgments he has made.[28] It would be interesting to know if he thought such special guidance was a prerogative on which he could depend because he occupied the position of bishop. There seems little doubt, however, that he did consider bishops as the object of special direction by the Spirit, for the very integrity of Christian faith and life depended upon them.[29]

Tertullian's witness on this question is, of course, inconsistent. In his pre-Montanist stage he stressed institutional continuity with the apostolic teaching, as he does in his *De praescriptione*.[30] And in his *De baptismo* he urges agreement with the bishop as the basis for unity.[31] However, with his adherence to Montanism, possession of the prophetic charism became the unique index to truth of teaching and judgment.[32] This is already clear in the *Adversus Praxeam*[33] and more than anything else in his teaching provided the basis for his break with the Catholic church.

In the East, to the extent that we can depend upon the *Didascalia*, the picture seems to be one in which the Spirit's direction of the church, and therefore the discernment of this direction, centers almost exclusively upon the *episkopoi*. He is teacher, *leitourgos*, ruler, shepherd, prophet; he seems to be both institutionally and charismatically unchallenged, a true hierocrat, a spiritual monarch.[34]

Given, then, the diversity and evolution to which we have referred, what is it upon which the leaders of the church can pass judgment? First of all, it is upon the knowledge or understanding of their fellow Christians, upon their understanding of what Christianity is and of what it implies by way of practical application.

Obviously, the bishops and presbyters do not apply just their own understanding in judging the orthodoxy of their brethren's faith. They apply the norm by which their own faith is kept consonant with revelation, namely, the tradition of belief that has been handed on to them from the apostles.[35] And they form or, if it is necessary, reform the faith of others by proclaiming this apostolic teaching.

Christian understanding and life demand more, however, than a simple repetition of the apostolic catechesis, more even than a mere verbal presentation of the New Testament writings. This apostolic teaching must be applied practically in changing historical situations to the demands of individual lives and to the life of communities. Precise rules of behavior, accepted patterns of life, practical application of fundamental principles of morality—these are the concrete practical judgments that one cannot find as such in the apostolic teaching. And it is here, in the evolving process we have seen, that the bishops quickly assert their right and responsibility to pass judgment. The huge body of patristic preaching attests to this, and it flows through Gregory the Great into the medieval and modern developments of moral theology.[36]

This legislative function seems to have begun as pedagogical guidance in drawing conclusions from the gospel principles and then evolved towards the political function of decreeing rules. Allied with it was the judgment passed upon behavior that had already taken place. This dealt with two quite distinct realities. There was the need to adjudicate differences that arose among members of the Christian community, the sort of thing that is intrinsic to any situation where fairly large numbers of humans deal with one another over an extended period of time, and secondly there was the judgment passed upon the personal culpability of "sinners."

For a few decades, the presbyterate might have been quite prominent in the function of judging "cases" of conflict in a given church, but before too long this became the privileged role of the *episkopos*, though the presbyterate seems to have some rights to participate in such judgments, at least on a consultative basis.[37] The letter of Clement of Rome indicates that there was not at that point in Corinth a single community leader to settle the dispute that divided that church.[38] On the other hand, Cyprian asserts without qualification the episcopal claim to authority in disputes affecting the unity of the church.[39]

Such a development, in which the administrative leader of the community increasingly asserts the authority to pass judgment upon matters of social contention, is not at all surprising; he is responsible for preserving unity. More difficult to understand, unless it had some extraordinary grounding, such as a special commission from God, is the claim to pass judgment on the internal state of a man's conscience. Yet, the story in Acts of Peter's denunciation and punishment of Ananias and Sophira reflects the belief of the early church that such judgment could be passed (and quite effectively!), at least by some in positions of authority. And bishops in later centuries (who claimed a basis for their authority in the promise made to Peter, Matthew 16:16), found frequent occasions for rousing denunciation of well-known sinners.

One could, of course, argue that in the early centuries (and for that matter throughout history) the episcopal condemnation of sinners was precisely of those whose external behavior was a true scandal to the community. Such condemnation, therefore, did not constitute so much a judgment on the internal state of soul as upon the fact that the known behavior was a menace to the morals of the community. And in these instances one is faced not with a "condemnation of hell-fire" but with excommunication from the church. Granted the separability of these two notions in early Christian thinking (which is probably not possible) and granting also the relative lack of distinction between the state of excommunication and the state of sin, one still must take account of the bishops' role in the Christian discipline of exomologesis.

Despite the lack of clear evidence about its details, the very early practice of imposing penalties upon sinners and then reconciling them (with the clear implication that this involved forgiveness of their sins) is undeniably witnessed to by the bitter disputes it aroused.[40] As we piece together the evidence for this Christian practice of penance and consequent reconciliation, we can see that the bishop passed judgment at two points in the process. It was he who decided what penance was commensurate with the sin involved,[41] and it was he who officially reconciled the penitent at the end of the process.[42] Now, one could explain the first of these two acts of judgment

as one that was quite appropriate to the official leader of the community. As the one who was in good position to assess the gravity of harm done by the action, as the one charged with preserving unity and therefore justice in the group, as the one who was acquainted with the traditions and practice of "the grand church" in such matters, he could decide an appropriate penalty. But in the second act of judgment much more was at stake. Precisely because this action of reconciling (or not reconciling) the individual to the community was believed to be sacramental of his reconciliation with God,[43] the bishop was acting as the sacrament of the divine judgment, as the agent of a man's eternal salvation.

Despite the stupendous claim this is, it appears that the church from its inception made such a claim to free men from their sins by its sacramental activity, and that one of the forms that this claim took was the evolving discipline of the exomologesis.[44] Certainly the New Testament passages such as Matthew 16:18 and 18:18 and John 20:21 point to some such understanding. And certain it is, too, that well before the end of the second century we have evidence that the episcopate is exercising some such judgment. What we do not have evidence for is that, prior to Cyprian, such power to forgive sin is seen as attached to the episcopal *office*.[45] The closest we come to that is Tertullian's polemic as a Montanist, in which he maintains that such power to forgive sins belonged to the apostles because of their spiritual power rather than because of their official role, which would indicate that he is arguing against the claim of the episcopacy of his day to possess such power by virtue of their apostolic office.[46]

While it is not as difficult or critically important an instance of episcopal judgment as is that of the forgiveness of sin, the function of the bishop in early Christian baptism also bears on his exercise of judgment. Allowing always for the gradual emergence of the episcopate, as it does appear historically, it is connected with the preparation for and actual admission of candidates for baptism.[47] As the catechumenate comes into being, it is the *episkopos* who has principal supervisory responsibility for its conduct; it is he who makes the judgment as to formal admission to catechumenate formation, he who is in charge of the "course of instructions" provided which he probably in some instances gave himself (as did Ambrose in the fourth century), he who passed judgment upon the readiness of candidates for baptism.[48]

Sources of Authority

The evidence seems to point quite clearly, then, to the fact that those in leadership positions in the church, and specifically the bishops, functioned increasingly as judges. Naturally, the question arises: On what grounds did they lay claim to this function in the church? Which leads to the somewhat broader question: What was the origin and the nature of the authority claimed by the episcopacy of the pre-Nicene church?

In modern times there has been considerable discussion in Roman Catholic circles about the nature of a "priestly vocation," argument as to whether this vocation was constituted by the inner call of the Spirit or by the external call from the church that came with ordination.[49] Through this discussion has run a consistent popular belief that one is called to the ministerial life of the church by some inspiration from God. Such belief apparently extends all the way back through Christian history to the earliest centuries of the church, and probably stands in continuity with 1 Corinthians 12–14. But where it seems that early Christian attitude and practice were at times different from that of more modern times was that the early Christians looked for those already endowed by the Spirit with those gifts that would indicate their aptitude for episcopal, presbyteral, or diaconal functions—and then recognized this by ordaining the man.[50] More recently, men have been ordained with the assumption that the Spirit will follow through with the endowments needed for the function to be performed by the man. Not infrequently, this

has even involved a naive expectation of gifts of sanctity and knowledge, the "grace of vocation."[51]

While we cannot assume a common pattern of selecting *episkopoi* in the first few centuries (indeed it is some time before we can assume a common pattern of monarchical episcopacy), the practice of election by the people of a given church seems to have been quite widespread.[52] True, Paul's own practice and the directives of the Pastorals indicate an appointive process[53] (which, as we will see shortly, was honored partially even in the instances of popular election), but as early a witness as the *Didache* speaks of selection of *episkopoi* and *presbyteroi* by the members of a given community.[54] Clement's letter to Corinth refers to the apostles' designation of certain men in each community to act as leaders, and to their instruction that such men be succeeded by others designated for this purpose. He does not state sharply the process of this later designation, but he does add that it is done "with the consent of the whole church" (which can obviously refer only to the local church).[55]

What seems to develop quite quickly is that established communities elect their own *episkopos*; but in the case of evangelizing new areas and establishing new communities, the *episkopos* is designated. (This certainly pertains to cases like Patrick's being sent to Ireland.) There seems to be a fairly universal pattern of the election of *episkopoi* by the end of the second century, and except for emergencies (such as designation of bishops in time of persecution and dispersal of a church) this continues well into the early Middle Ages, and in some instances much later.[56]

It is unclear how *presbyteroi* and *diakonoi* were chosen, though the most likely guess is that it resulted from a process of joint decision (or least advisement) on the part of the *episkopos* and his presbyterate.[57] There is early evidence, however, that an *episkopos* was able, if he wished, to ordain *presbyteroi* and *diakonoi* on the basis of his own decision. The ordination of Origen to the presbyterate would be a case in point.[58]

The fact that the members of a given Christian community selected their bishop does not imply that they thereby bestowed authority on him. Rather, it was probably envisaged as the recognition by the community of the leadership that the Spirit had provided by his endowment of a given individual with virtue and understanding.[59] In any event, at a very early stage of the episcopacy's development, as far back actually as we have evidence of episcopate as such, it was recognized that the process of his designation was not completed until he had received the acceptance, approval, "ordination" of at least one (and preferably more) of his fellow bishops.[60] This came in the ritual of the "laying on of hands," and was seen as a reception into the ranks of the collegial reality that was the episcopacy of "the great church."[61]

Of the two realities, election by the people or consecration by episcopal colleagues, the latter was the essential. At least from the late second century onward there is no indication that a bishop could obtain and exercise his position except after ordination by a fellow bishop.[62] With the laying on of hands came not only the designation to episcopal function and the authority to exercise it, but the gift of the Spirit for its responsible fulfillment.[63] As a member of the episcopal college, the bishop shares in the special guidance provided to this group for the sake of the church,[64] shares in the authority that this group has as the heir to the apostolic college,[65] and shares in a concern for the whole church.[66]

Until Augustine's "solution" to the problem of reordination of schismatic baptisms and ordinations, there was uncertainty in the early church regarding the dependence of episcopal or presbyteral authority on the individual's personal sanctity.[67] After all, as Cyprian argued, how could one give the Spirit if he himself did not possess the Spirit?[68]

This would seem to reflect the mentality of the pre-Nicene church in laying stress on the "internal" qualifications for ministry. One must be careful not to impose on those centuries the view that authority, specifically episcopal, derived from the office as such.[69]

Perhaps one cannot exclude such a point of view entirely (and to this extent von Campenhausen may overstate his case in denying the notion of "office" to Christian thinking about ministry prior to Cyprian),[70] but it certainly is true that these early centuries saw the authority of a minister as largely derived from "interior" factors.

As a member of the episcopal college, as a "successor of the apostles," a bishop inherited the apostolic tradition of belief.[71] This centered, of course, on the New Testament writings which were entrusted to him to preserve and communicate in their purity.[72] But it also involved a continuity of living understanding of Christianity, by which the Scriptures themselves were inevitably interpreted. Very importantly it involved the inheritance of episcopal and presbyteral life and practice, the example of how to live as Christian and of how to minister to the community's needs.[73] We have the beginnings of the process by which, lacking anything like seminary formation, ministerial "know-how" was passed on by informal instruction, example, and apprenticeship.[74] Thus, in addition to apostolic tradition in the strictest and narrowest sense, there would have been episcopal traditions of homiletics, liturgical ceremony, catechetical formation, and community organization.[75] Proficiency in such was certainly a factor in the authority which a bishop was able to exert over his people.

Even more important was the minister's own sanctity, the example of his Christian life.[76] Much of the bishop's (or presbyter's) ministry of the word consisted in telling his people about the practical (i.e., moral) implications of the gospel;[77] the bishop's own life spoke more eloquently than his words, a fact to which the writers of this period often allude.[78] Beyond the matter of good example was something more profound. The minister of the community was even more so the minister of Christ, the instrument through whom the risen Lord and his Spirit worked for the salvation of men. As such, his ministerial effectiveness was very obviously conditioned by the extent to which he himself possessed this Spirit, i.e., allowed himself by his moral attitudes and behavior to be possessed by this Spirit.[79] A man of holiness was a man of power, power in some instances so great that he is able to "work miracles." Such Spirit-power is not limited to bishops or other clergy; indeed, this period already attests to ascetics whose heroic detachment from the unspiritual gives them unusual powers over evil.[80] Yet, such possession of holiness and the Spirit is particularly appropriate to bishops, for it is they who communicate the Spirit in Christian initiation and ministerial ordination, it is they who "call down" the Spirit in the midst of the Eucharistic assembly.[81]

This ante-Nicene period of the church's life is one in which the awareness of the Spirit as the Spirit of prophecy is still quite strong.[82] Hence, to say that the ordained ministers of the church, and particularly the bishops, are specially endowed with the Spirit is partially equivalent to saying that they are meant to be endowed with the charism of prophecy. As we saw earlier, the ministry of the word as it was viewed during this period clearly contains overtones of prophetic proclamation. And both Cyprian and the *Didascalia* make specific claims to prophetic powers of the bishop.[83]

Authority by Apostolic Succession

Perhaps the most important quality of the ordained minister, above all of the bishop, was his "orthodoxy," his possession of and fidelity to the gospel of Jesus Christ.[84] Obviously, this was critically necessary for one who is intended to preserve unity of belief in a community which exists as such because of its common faith. And, as we have already seen, the touchstone for the authenticity of a bishop's teaching was his claim to apostolic succession.

Earlier we had occasion to examine the extent to which apostolic succession could be appealed to because it implied a continuity of knowledge—an apostle instructing his disciple, who in turn instructs his own disciple. Thus, the tradition of apostolic faith was

carefully and faithfully transmitted; the teaching of the latest member of this chain deserved credence because of his intrinsic correspondence to the faith of the apostle who stood at the beginning of the chain.[85] But, the question also has to be faced: Did they envisage an "apostolic office" as such, the establishment (either by the infant church or by Christ himself) of an official position in the Christian community which was occupied in the first instance by the apostles, and was then occupied later by their legitimate successors?[86]

For one thing, the pre-Nicene church (including even its most monarchically minded *episkopoi*, such as Ignatius and Cyprian) saw the role and function of the early disciples (and above all, of the apostles) as unique and unrepeatable.[87] If they had successors (and in the broad sense it is obvious that they did, since the social entity that began with them continues in historical continuity after their death), these could never occupy the same position the apostles did. There could be only one "founding generation," only one generation of immediate witnesses to the life, death, and resurrection of Jesus, only one group whom the Master himself had taught. Thus, there could be no question of anyone later exercising the "apostolic office."[88]

However, what one does find stated explicitly is the tradition that the apostles, having established the earliest communities, gave directions that *episkopoi* and *presbyteroi* should be appointed to succeed them in caring for the churches.[89] Thus, there is some notion of an enduring function in a community. However, the formalizing of this function in political terms, i.e., as an office in a society, seems to have happened first in the African church.

Already in Tertullian, perhaps because of his propensity for legal terminology and categories of thought, one finds traces of this understanding of episcopal "office."[90] However, it is worth noting that in his *De pudicitia* (perhaps his last extant work), he seems to limit apostolic succession to *doctrina* (*disciplina*) as a basis for governing and to reserve *potestas* like that of the apostles (e.g., in forgiving sin) to the charismatics in the church.[91] Without passing judgment on Tertullian's own position on the question, the fact that he discusses the matter in these terms indicates that the idea is already current that some *potestas* may attach to the *episkopos* because of his succession from the apostles.

This cast of mind is very congenial to Cyprian, who is largely responsible for crystallizing a "political" understanding of the episcopal office, which is then transmitted to the post-Nicene church through Augustine, Leo, and Isidore.[92] However, Cyprian's own view (as well as that of his disciples) of episcopal authority must be examined in terms of another basic question: Even granting that episcopacy is an office and its occupant has the authority appropriate to that office, does such authority come through the office itself (by one or other kind of "lineal descent") or directly from God on the occasion of occupying the office? Or, to put it another way, is the *de jure divino* authority to which bishops will appeal the result of an original grant of authority (to an apostle) to which they are heirs, or the result of a power given directly to each succeeding generation (a vertical rather than horizontal grant of authority)? It would seem that the second alternative (the direct grant from God) is more dominant. This in turn seems linked with another idea: that Christ himself abides with his church, working actively and authoritatively through his ministers.[93] Actually, then, it is he who is functioning "officially" "behind the scenes," and the bishop is acting as Christ's sacrament.[94]

One final aspect of ministerial authority in the pre-Nicene church needs to be examined: What was the nature of the authority that attached to ministry? In a later age, we could ask this simply of the episcopacy, since by that time other "orders" are considered to derive all their authority from the bishops; but this cannot be done for the early church. For a time, at least, the presbyterate has a somewhat independent even though subordinate authority, an authority not derived by delegation from the episcopacy.[95] One finds evidence for this as late as Hippolytus, where grounds such as confession of the faith in persecution can dispense with ordination to the presbyterate.[96] And Cyprian himself complains about the assumption of authority by presbyters, which he sees as unfounded but which may not have been viewed by them as such.[97]

To dwell on this presbyteral authority for a moment, it seems that various factors gave some individuals an eminence in the community. This might be age and experience, or observable fidelity in faith and Christian practice, or endurance of persecution, or (in the instance of newly founded communities) being among the first converts in a given church, the "first fruits" of the Spirit's action in that community. With such recognized eminence came extra responsibility for the faith and life of the community, a certain implicit grant of authority to participate effectively in providing for the community, and the right to be listened to by the *episkopos* if such existed in the community.[98]

In the early church, such presbyteral authority was not the result of episcopal delegation. However, this body of responsible Christians was the most logical group upon which to draw if there was need to supply in the absence of the *episkopos* for those functions which were more properly his, such as providing baptism and Eucharist. When they functioned in these substitute capacities, the *presbyteroi* would have been sharing in the bishop's authority; yet it is interesting, and perhaps important, to recall that for many centuries it is the *diakonoi* and not the *presbyteroi* who are referred to as the ministers of the bishop.[99]

One thing that is not clear but that is basic to any historical study of the evolution of Christian priesthood is whether or not the notion of "priestly office" attaches primarily to the presbyterate and thereby to the *episkopos* as the preeminent member of the presbyterate. The historical data which indicates that the word *"hiereus"* or *"sacerdos,"* once it begins to be used of Christian ministry, applies for quite some time only to the bishop would seem to argue against the above suggestion.[100] However, it would be necessary to study whether this application of *"sacerdos"* to the bishop is not part of the process of re-Judaizing Christian thinking about priesthood and losing the primitive Christian insight into the unique ministry of Christ and of his church.

To go on, then, to the nature of episcopal authority prior to Nicaea, we can draw from our earlier description of the types of judgment exercised by *episkopoi* in these centuries. It seems that their authority was viewed as that proper to possession of truth (for they were privileged possessors of apostolic tradition), as that proper to those entrusted with care of a group (their pastoral role), to some extent as that proper to the prophet, and as that proper to one who ministerially conveyed God's own redeeming or damning judgment. Thus, it would seem that the political or societal aspect of episcopal authority is coming to the fore by the end of the pre-Nicene epoch, but that episcopal authority is still seen more as religious than as institutional power.

It is good, also, to notice the diversity of opinion in the early fourth century as to which religious element is most basic in the authority of the bishop. The *Didascalia* indicates the Syrian attitude as being strongly hierocratic (according to a Jewish pattern, perhaps through Essene influence). From the fact that the bishop is cultic high priest flow his other roles of prophet, king, judge.[101] In Alexandria, on the other hand, the role of the episcopacy (and of the other clergy) as conveyors of truth, preservers of orthodoxy, and spiritual guides seems to have prominence.[102] In Carthage and Rome, while the evangelical and cultic role of the bishop was certainly recognized, the governing of a religious community and the preservation of its unity and vitality seems to be uppermost in thought about the episcopal role.[103]

NOTES

1. Thus, in his *Dialogue with Trypho*, before going on to explain that the Christians are correct in applying the Old Testament predictions to Christ, Justin (chap. 82) says: "The prophetical gifts remain with us, even to the present time. You ought to realize that these gifts which previously existed among your nation have been transferred to us."

2. See *Pastor, Vis.* 2. 1.

3. It is significant, however, that by the end of the second century this awareness takes quite different theological forms—in Clement of Alexandria's stress on Christ as Logos and inner teacher, or in Irenaeus' development of the Pauline themes of Christ's headship and recapitulation.

4. On Ignatius' notion of "imitation of Christ," see J. Quasten, *Patrology* (Westminster, Md., 1950), vol. 1, pp. 70–73.

5. *Apologia* 2. 10 and 13; see also Quasten, pp. 209–10.

6. *Apologia* 2. 13.

7. *Apol.* 7.

8. See Quasten, p. 239.

9. See esp. chap. 11; one could make a case, though not conclusively, that *"charis"* has overtones of the Holy Spirit, particularly in the expression "the grace of the prophets" (*charis propheton*).

10. See E. Mersch, *The Whole Christ* (Milwaukee, 1938), pp. 227–42.

11. *Adv. Haer.* 1. 2; 4. 53. 1. See R. Hanson's discussion of the rule of faith, in *Tradition in the Early Church* (London, 1963), pp. 75–129.

12. *Paed.* 1. 7. 11; see also *Strom.* 7, although in this classic passage on Christian perfection there is more attention given to the ascetic elements connected with Christian *gnosis.* For a detailed study (and valuable bibliography) on Clement's idea of the

Christian gnostic, see W. Völker, *Der wahre Gnostiker nach Clemens Alexandrinus* (Berlin, 1952).

13. *Paed.* 1. 6; *Strom.* 7. 11. However, the Logos is also described by Clement as the *power* of God (*Strom.* 7. 2. 9). On the other hand, the Spirit is clearly the spirit of prophecy, the spirit of truth (*Strom.* 5. 13).

14. See *Strom.* 7. 2–3.

15. See Hippolytus *Apostolic Tradition* 3 (the prayer for consecration of a bishop); Origen *Contra Celsum* 1. 46; Tertullian *De virginibus velandis* 1. In Cyprian, one finds some of the mentality that Christ abides with the church, e.g., in the eighteenth chapter of his treatise on the Lord's Prayer; but for the most part, and particularly in what should be key passages (such as the *De unitate ecclesiae*), there is much more of the attitude that "Christ has gone up to heaven," and it seems that Cyprian's view is rather that Christians should dwell in the heavenly kingdom (even during their life on earth) than that Christ dwells with Christians on earth. However, Cyprian clearly and frequently refers to the church's guidance by the Spirit through Scripture.

16. *Eph.* 4.

17. *Magn.* 6. 1.

18. *Ibid.*, 3. 1.

19. *Pastor, Vis.* 3.

20. *Apostolic Tradition* 4.

21. *Adv. Haer.* 4. 26. 2.

22. See H. von Campenhausen, *Ecclesiastical Authority and Spiritual Power in the Church of the First Three Centuries* (Palo Alto, Calif., 1969), pp. 196–212. In *Strom.* 6. 13 Clement not only speaks of the grades of deacon, presbyter, and bishop, but seems to consider them as progressive steps towards "glory."

23. *Strom.* 2. 11–12.

24. *Ibid.*, 2. 19–20.

25. However, Clement still appeals (in addition to Scripture) to the unwritten traditions of the presbyters; see Hanson, pp. 42–43.

26. *Strom.* 6. 13.

27. *De principiis*, preface 1–3.

28. *Epist.* 16. 4.

29. *De ecclesiae unitate* 5.

30. See Quasten, vol. 2, pp. 271–72.

31. *De baptismo* 17.

32. See von Campenhausen, pp. 228–33.

33. *Adv. Prax.* 1.

34. "He (the bishop) is indeed the centre and pivot of the whole community. He holds the place of God in relation to his people. . . . In a word, the bishop within his province is supreme." (R. Connolly, *Didascalia Apostolorum* [Oxford, 1929], p. xxxviii.)

35. See Hanson, pp. 75–129.

36. On the compendious nature and historical influence of Gregory's *Moralia*, see F. Dudden, *Gregory the Great* (London, 1905), vol. 1, pp. 194–96.

37. The prayer for the ordination of presbyters that is contained in Hippolytus *Apostolic Tradition* 8 mentions the "spirit of counsel" that is sought for the presbyters so that they can share in governing the community.

38. On the contrary, it presupposes that the governance of the Corinthian church is the responsibility of the presbyterate. Significantly it is these *presbyteroi* to whom the famous passage in *1 Clem.* 44. 1–5 about "episcopal succession" is meant to apply.

39. In *Epist.* 3. 1, speaking of the right according to which Rogatian could have punished his deacon, Cyprian says: ". . . Cum pro episcopatus vigore et cathedrae auctoritate haberes potestatem qua posses de illo statim vindicari, certus quod

collegae tui omnes gratum haberemus quodcumque circa diaconum tuum contu-
meliosum sacerdotali potestate fecisses." Interestingly, Cyprian goes on to compare
the episcopal office with the authority and dignity of Old Testament priesthood,
much in the way that *1 Clement* had done a century and a half earlier.

40. See B. Poschmann, *Penance and the Anointing of the Sick* (New York, 1964), pp. 19–52.

41. This was the basic assumption behind the controversy about the lax policy of the bishops towards grave sin; see *ibid.*, pp. 38–52.

42. Referring to the bishop, the ordination prayer in the *Apostolic Tradition* of Hippolytus says: "By the high priestly Spirit he may have authority to forgive sins according to thy command, to assign lots according to Thy bidding, to loose every bond according to the authority Thou gavest to the Apostles . . ." (3, Dix trans.).

43. What is not clear from the early texts, as a matter of fact it remains a matter of controversy for many centuries, is whether the action of the church (and precisely the act of the bishop) in the reconciliation of sinners is petitionary, declarative, or causative. Does the church assure the penitent that his sins are forgiven, or does it act as God's instrument in this forgiveness?

44. See Poschmann, pp. 18–80.

45. See von Campenhausen, pp. 282–90.

46. This is the argument of his *De pudicitia*, in which the teaching on Christian reconciliation of sinners is in quite marked difference from his earlier (Catholic) *De poenitentia*; see Poschmann, pp. 39–49.

47. The second-century evidence, stretching from Ignatius' letters (e.g., *Smyrn.* 8. 2) to Tertullian's *De baptismo* (17–20), is quite clear on this point.

48. See K. Baus, *Handbook of Church History* (New York, 1965), vol. 1, pp. 275–81.

49. See the discussion of C. Schleck, *The Theology of Vocations* (Milwaukee, 1963), pp. 255–301. It is characteristic of the theological discussion of priestly vocation that prevailed for many centuries and practically up to the present moment that Schleck treats of the vocation of bishop and presbyter with reference to the vocation to religious community life, i.e., within the context of the so-called vocation to the state of perfection. The presuppositions of this long-standing viewpoint have been basically challenged by the fifth chapter (On the universal call to holiness) of Vatican II's *Constitution on the Church*.

50. One immediately thinks of striking instances, such as the selection of Ambrose for the episcopal office in Milan; but the pastoral Epistles indicate that the designation of men for ministerial functions should be based on the already present and proven endowments of the persons in question.

51. In the last half-century there has been an increasing (and healthy) reemphasis on the need for men to possess the necessary natural talent and training prior to ordination (see Schleck, pp. 295–99), but this has focused almost totally on ordination to the presbyterate and not on ordination to the episcopacy. Yet, serious questions arise about the bishop's "grace of vocation," for example, where does he obtain the intrinsic theological expertise that equips him for the role of supreme teacher of the diocese which bishops claim?

52. See P. Stockmeier, "Gemeinde und Bischofsamt in der alten Kirche," *Theol. Quartalschrift* 149 (1969), pp. 133–46.

53. E.g., Titus 1:5.

54. *Didache* 15. 1.

55. *1 Clem.* 44. 3.

56. See W. Telfer, *The Office of a Bishop* (London, 1962), esp. pp. 192–96. Though the clergy of a given church, or a group of leading clergy, take an increasingly prominent role in the selection of the bishop, the entire community retains (at least in many places) the right to approve or disapprove the candidate.

57. As D. Power points out in his *Ministers of Christ and His Church* (London, 1969), pp. 31–41, the presbyters were not thought of as derived from the episcopacy but as

part of the same *collegium* to which the bishop himself pertained; it is highly un-likely that the bishop by himself would have selected the presbyters. A somewhat different situation did prevail for the deacons, however, since they were "the bishop's men"; *Didascalia*, chap. 16, quite specifically refers to episcopal appointment of the deacons.

58. See L. Duchesne, *The Early History of the Church*, trans. from 4th ed. (London, 1965 reprint), pp. 251–52, on the controversy surrounding Origen's ordination and the reasons for the controversy.

59. This leaves open the question as to whether the episcopate emerged out of the early presbyterate, as Jerome contended.

60. *Apostolic Tradition* 2 speaks of more than one bishop being in attendance and lay-ing hands upon a new bishop, although only one bishop pronounces the consecratory prayer.

61. For a listing of relevant third-century textual witnesses, see A. Michel, *Dictionnaire de théologie catholique*, vol. 11, cols. 1245–46.

62. See Baus, pp. 347–50; also Telfer, pp. 64–106.

63. See Hippolytus *Apostolic Tradition* 2. 3–5.

64. However, as Hanson, pp. 157–62, points out, one must be careful not to read into second- and even third-century texts the notion that such guidance is attached to the office and results from ordination.

65. Though the link of the bishops to the apostles is much earlier, Cyprian (e.g., in *Epist.* 3. 3) seems to be the first one who thinks of the apostles as occupying an episcopal office in which they are succeeded by later bishops.

66. Cyprian *De ecclesiae unitate* 5.

67. Origen, for one, seems to have viewed episcopal authority as dependent on the bishop's sanctity; see von Campenhausen, pp. 254–64. The classic instance was Cyprian's view on rebaptism, but Cyprian seems also to have held that a bishop's immorality voided his ministry (*Epist.* 65. 2 and 67. 3).

68. *Epist.* 74. 4; on Cyprian's position in the rebaptism controversy, see B. Neunheuser, *Baptism and Confirmation* (New York, 1964), pp. 99–104.

69. It may seem like quibbling to insist that ministerial role and function were only gradually viewed as "office," since one can legitimately use the word "office" for any societally recognized and relatively permanent function. What is really at stake is the application of the political model to the Christian community, an application whose legitimacy is challenged by the New Testament literature. Yet, a case can be made (see L. Goppelt, *Apostolic and Post-Apostolic Times* [London, 1970], p. 198) that the application of this political model and some notion of offices in the church began with *1 Clem.*

70. So, von Campenhausen, pp. 265ff., may underplay the presence of the idea of "office" prior to Cyprian and lay too great stress on Cyprian's originality in this regard. The approach to the episcopal role in the *Didascalia* certainly seems to be strongly "offi-cial"; if so, this would seem to run counter to von Campenhausen's association of stress on office with the Roman tradition (p. 265).

71. See Y. Congar, *Tradition and Traditions* (New York, 1967), pp. 35–38. However, as Origen indicates in the preface to his *De principiis*, other responsible persons besides the bishops are special heirs of this tradition.

72. Congar, pp. 30–35; also Hanson, pp. 102–17.

73. This is already suggested in the criteria for presbyteral/episcopal selection in the Pastorals, and explicitly treated in *1 Clem.* 40–44.

74. The daily gathering of presbyters and deacons mentioned in *Apostolic Tradition* 33 may have been one of the occasions on which such instruction and formation took place.

75. See D. Van den Eynde, *Les normes de l'enseignement chrétien* (Gembloux, 1933), p. 158; also Hanson, pp. 130–86.

76. This is a recurrent theme in Cyprian's letters to his clergy and to fellow bishops.

77. Patterns for this moral instruction are already set in the Synoptic accounts of Jesus' teaching, in the Epistles, or in the Jewish Christian teaching of the two ways (as in the *Didache*); and *1 Clem.*, the Ignatian letters, and the *Pastor* of Hermas bear witness to continuation of this practical instruction in the early second century.

78. So, the stress of the Pastorals on the life-style and character of a candidate for *presbyter-episkopos*; the account of Polycarp's martyrdom; or Ignatius' use of unChristian behavior as a criterion to discern false teachers (*Eph.* 7–9). Ignatius' principle "It is better for a man to be silent and be a Christian, than to speak and not be one. It is good to teach, if he who speaks also acts" finds many parallels in patristic (and later) descriptions of the ministry of word.

79. Origen in particular stresses the need for the bishop (and presbyter) to be a "spiritual"; see von Campenhausen, pp. 251–64.

80. See D. Knowles, *Christian Monasticism* (New York, 1969), pp. 9–24.

81. *Apostolic Tradition* 3. 3–5; 4. 12; 22. 1.

82. Athenagoras *Supplication for the Christians* 10; Irenaeus *Adv. Haer.* 4. 5 and 4. 11; Origen *De principiis* preface 1–3. It is interesting to note, however, that the consecratory prayer for the bishop in the *Apostolic Tradition* speaks of the royal and priestly Spirit.

83. *Didascalia* 5; Cyprian *Epist.* 66. 10. These claims are the more significant because in neither Cyprian nor the *Didascalia* is the prophetic character of the bishop emphasized.

84. Tit. 2:1–10; Cyprian *De ecclesiae unitate* 5.

85. Clement *Strom.* 1. 1. 11.

86. This view, which comes to dominate Catholic theology of the episcopate for many centuries, is adumbrated in *1 Clem.* 42–44. What needs to be assessed is the extent to which *1 Clem.* is already introducing an element of fiction into his description of the apostle's role, and thus setting the ground for later references to the apostolic office. See Goppelt, pp. 177–83.

87. The very fact that the apostolic experience and witness remain the touchstone of authentic Christian faith indicates an abiding recognition of the apostolic uniqueness. This does not preclude, however, the possibility that a collegial group (e.g., the episcopacy) could at a later date in the church's life perform by its faith witness a unifying and vitalizing function analogous to that performed by the apostolic college for the first Christian generation.

88. This still leaves open the historical question as to the precise function exercised by the apostles in the primitive church. For two complementary and somewhat opposed views, see D. Stanley, "The New Testament Basis for the Concept of Collegiality," *Theological Studies* 25 (1964), pp. 197–216; and W. Schmithals, *The Office of Apostle in the Early Church* (Nashville, Tenn., 1969).

89. There is no evidence for this view prior to *1 Clem.*; see Goppelt, pp. 182, 199.

90. See von Campenhausen, pp. 225–37.

91. *De pudicitia*, c. 21.

92. On Cyprian's use of political terminology when speaking of the episcopacy see von Campenhausen, p. 274, esp. nn. 45, 46. Some of the range of Cyprian's view of the episcopacy can be seen in the *Epist.* 66. 5: ". . . Ecce iam sex annis nec fraternitas habuerit episcopum nec plebs praepositum nec grex pastorem nec ecclesia gubernatorem nec Christus antistitem nec Deus sacerdotem. . . ." Only two of the six terms used are clearly political, which should warn us against viewing Cyprian's outlook on his office as exclusively official.

93. It must be admitted, however, that there is relatively little in Cyprian's writings that reflects this "Christ abiding with the church" idea. See n. 15, above.

94. This point of view, which is still strong in the second century with Ignatius and Irenaeus and Clement of Alexandria, seems to fade somewhat in the third century

and even more so in the fourth and fifth centuries, perhaps because of the trinitarian controversies and the need to emphasize the transcendence of Christ as Son of God.

95. See Power, pp. 31–41; G. d'Ercole, "The Presbyteral Colleges in the Early Church," *Historical Investigations*, vol. 17 of *Concilium* (New York, 1966), pp. 20–33.

96. *Apostolic Tradition* 10. 1.

97. *Epist.* 16.

98. Cyprian, *Epist.* 14, writing to the presbyters and deacons of his church says: ". . . From the beginning of my episcopate, I determined to do nothing on the basis of my own opinion alone, without your advice and the consent of the people."

99. As we noted earlier, this is reflected in the ordination ceremony: only the bishop lays his hands on the deacon, whereas fellow bishops impose hands on a new bishop and fellow presbyters on a new presbyter.

100. An argument favoring the "insertion" of the bishop as priest within the presbyteral college is provided by the *Apostolic Tradition* which speaks of both bishop and presbyters as being ordained for priesthood (whereas the deacon is not so ordained), but the argument is not conclusive.

101. *Didascalia*, chaps. 8 and 9. On possible Essence influence on *episkopos*, see P. Benoit, "Qumran et le N.T.," *New Testament Studies* 7 (1961), pp. 276–96.

102. Not only is this view clearly espoused by Origen in the third century (see von Campenhausen, pp. 247–64), but it continues on in the fourth century with Athanasius' view that the church is the situation in which Christ himself continues his teaching work through the ministers of the church (see J. Roldanus, *Le christ et l'homme dans la théologie d'Athanase d'Aléxandrie* [Leiden, 1968], pp. 244–49).

103. However, as Cyprian's *De ecclesiae unitate* indicates, the emphasis in governing still rests on the bishops' teaching authority and we have not yet come to the more jurisdictional view that is found in Leo I (in the mid-fifth century).

CHAPTER 22

Judgment and Authority in the Patristic Period

With the ascendancy of Constantine and the public acceptance of the Christian religion, a new context of official church life rapidly emerged. The monarchical episcopate was by that time already solidly established. It had absorbed into itself practically the entirety of the ministry which it, in turn, delegated to different "orders." But the Constantinian approbation and the ensuing sociological changes in the various Christian communities directed the attitudes and activities of the episcopacy in ways which were to alter the very understanding of ecclesiastical office.

However, it would be a mistake to overemphasize the impact of the Constantinian influence; especially is it a vast oversimplification (though a somewhat fashionable one) to lay blame on this period for all the political and institutional developments that are seen as deviations from the original and simple pattern of the New Testament communities. Later in this part we will have to examine in greater detail an influence which was just as great and, if one is looking for something to blame, more disastrous to the New Testament vision of ministry: the influence of the oriental notion of *basileus*, the divine monarch, as we find it crystallized in Justinian's code.

As we have observed, the period that stretches from the Council of Nicaea to the beginning of the twelfth century is dominated by bishops, and increasingly by the bishop of Rome. With few exceptions, the most notable being some of the important monastic figures, such as Cassian and Benedict and Alcuin, the men who produced the ecclesiastical literature, law, liturgy, and institutions were bishops. Moreover, in the active give-and-take of those centuries that saw the disintegration of the old Roman power, the split of Latin and Byzantine Christianity, the waves of Teutonic invasion from the north, the schismatic loss of Egypt and the Near East, and the perilous advance of Islam, the bishops asserted prominent leadership for good or for evil. One must mention the exceptional situation of the Irish church and of those developments which emanated from it, particularly the influence of Irish monasticism on the Continent. However, even this was a temporary departure from the pattern, and gradually even the monastic dominance of the Irish pattern gave way to the traditional centrality of the episcopacy.[1]

For all practical purposes one can, throughout this period, consider the question of priestly authority by concentrating on the episcopacy. Whatever authority presbyters are seen to possess, whatever judgment they do exercise, stands in relation to the bishops. Presbyters are, as the prefatory prayer of the ordination ceremony says, "*cooperatores ordinis nostri.*"[2] Certain aberrations do occur, as in the practice of lay investiture, where selection and assignment of presbyters is not under full episcopal control; but such situations are just that, aberrations, and hence contribute little to an investigation of the intrinsic evolution of Christian priesthood.[3]

One thing that the Constantinian recognition of the church definitely did was to accentuate the character of episcopacy as an office, and therefore to throw the question of episcopal authority increasingly into this official context. The church was now seen as a social grouping, to some extent as a political entity, capable of political recognition as a legal and corporate entity that was capable of ownership, rights, and obligations. It was not just a community but an established and organized society; its organizational structures could be thought of, however inappropriately, in categories already familiar to secular political society.[4]

To deal with the church, Roman officialdom did envisage it according to its own patterns. Particularly, Roman politicians dealt with the leaders of the Christian churches as with their opposite numbers from another society, i.e., officials in another organized group. Legal formulations according to which the church lived, and which touched things as strictly religious as church councils, described ecclesiastical processes in secular legal terms.[5]

This does not mean that bishops (or other Christians) began to think of ecclesiastical office as no different from office in civil society. But it does mean that they did think of Christian ministry as "office." Often during the patristic period we find bishops exalting the priestly office over that of the temporal ruler; it is superior as the soul is over the body, or as heaven is over earth. In one form or another, whether that of the Gelasian "two powers" or the Justinian subordination of *sacerdotium* to *imperium*, the question is under constant discussion and is the source of constant turmoil. Basic to all this, however, is the presupposition that Christian priesthood and ministry (as found in the episcopate) is the kind of reality that can be so paralleled and compared with secular political authority.

Certainly, in the more influential episcopal sees, the authority attached to the *cathedra episcopalis*, the seat of authoritative evangelical proclamation and community judgment, came from apostolic foundation, historically justified or (as in the case of Constantinople) legendarily created.[6] During the golden age of the patristic period, from the fourth to sixth centuries, there does not seem to be any

notion that a bishop possessed the authority he had by any other agency than the office he occupied. The question already raised as to how one is to understand the claim to authority *jure divino* still remains unresolved. However, there does seem to be a more explicit theology of sacramental action, and therefore of Christ's presence to and action through his ministers.[7] While this clearly applies to the liturgical activity of the episcopacy (and the presbyterate also), it is not quite clear that this view carries over into the bishop's activity as a judge.

Some light may be thrown on the question by looking at the manner in which a man was seen to acquire episcopal authority. In the eight centuries that separate Athanasius from Hildebrand rather drastic changes took place in this regard. In general, three elements within the ecclesiastical functioning of the church enter into the selection of the bishop throughout this period: the voice of the members of the local church, the ordination of the candidate by the surrounding episcopate, and the approbation of "higher" ecclesiastical authority (such as the metropolitan).[8] One should add two other elements. The three just mentioned are seen in varying degree to implement and manifest the selection of the bishop by the Spirit;[9] and accidentally, though often quite effectively, civil authorities exercise their power to see that a given candidate is selected by the traditional ecclesiastical means.[10]

During the fourth and fifth centuries the voice of the local community was truly determinative, though not self-sufficiently so, in the selection of their bishop. There are occasions of a choice by acclamation, in which the entire people participated; such was, of course, the situation with Ambrose.[11] Apparently, however, the more common pattern was to have representatives of the church, both clergy and laity, carry on the actual process of choosing.[12] Even in instances where the incumbent bishop wished to groom a successor and have him become the next bishop, he wisely submitted him to the people in advance for their approval, as did Augustine.[13]

Increasingly, the development seems to be in the direction of the choice being made by the clergy of the church. The voice of the laity is one of approving the choice already made.[14] And even this seems to become narrowed into nomination by a group of the leading clergy. It is this kind of pattern which finds expression in Rome in the selection of that bishop by the prominent ministers (*cardinales*) of that city and its immediate environs.[15]

In the great apostolic sees, where awareness and jealousy of their prerogatives were particularly strong, the autonomy of the local church in the designation of its bishop was longer preserved. For one thing, the bishop of such a see was precisely the one who participated importantly in the alternative pattern, which was the selection of a bishop for a given see by the surrounding bishops, or in some instances by the metropolitan or patriarch, generally in consultation with surrounding bishops.[16] Already by the late fourth century this procedure is dominant in the Alexandrian and Antiochean-Constantinopolitan patriarchates, where influential metropolitans had the principal voice in the selection of their suffragants.[17]

In the West, the unsettled conditions for most of these centuries and the frequent result of poor communications apparently strengthened the pattern of episcopal selection by surrounding bishops, often, of course, with secular interference.[18] Increasingly, however, the bishop of Rome exercised patriarchal prerogatives in designating bishops; this was particularly true of the evangelizing activity of such popes as Gregory who would send out missionaries, consecrated as bishops, to establish an episcopate as soon as possible in the newly converted region.[19]

Paradoxically, the evil of "lay investiture," which became an increasing threat in the later centuries of this period, probably strengthened the trend towards centralization in selection of bishops. Because of the power and position possessed by many of the feudal lords and princes who took it upon themselves to designate the occupants of ecclesiastical positions, it took the prestige and authority of the papacy to win the church's freedom in the selection of its ministers.[20]

Realistically, one must admit that in the latter half of the period we are studying the actual designation of bishops (and pastors) was often done by secular powers. This was always subject, at least theoretically, to the approbation of appropriate church authority, but the freedom exercised in such "approbation" was often quite limited.[21] One might note in passing that the bishops so selected by powerful temporal rulers, though they were never viewed as obtaining spiritual authority from such temporal sources, certainly did gain much of their *power* of administration from such secular support. And even in something as specifically religious as a doctrinal judgment on the heretical or orthodox nature of a certain teaching, the effectiveness of such a judgment could be radically influenced by the support or opposition of the temporal power.[22]

Canons of the early fourth-century synods indicate that an established pattern of episcopal consecration is recognized.[23] While the preferred situation is that all the bishops of a given metropolitan area share in the ordination of the new bishop, at least three should participate in the ceremony. There is no clear evidence that the reality of the ordination is conditioned by the presence of three "consecrators"; ordination by a single fellow bishop is recognized.[24] But it does seem that they were interested in preserving a collegial sacramentality in the action. Episcopal consecration, where a candidate was being received into the episcopal community, whose corporate identity and function had already been emphasized by Cyprian,[25] was quite different in its orientation from sacerdotal ordinations where from the fifth century onward a bishop was seen as designating ministers to work with him in the shepherding of the local community.[26]

No matter how the nomination of the episcopal candidate had taken place, by community election, episcopal designation, choice by the metropolitan or patriarch (with or without pressure of temporal rulers), there was never any question of his being able to exercise episcopal functions or lay claim to episcopal authority prior to his sacramental consecration.[27] Once the *episcopatus* comes to mean in large part the economic holdings and responsibility of the bishop, the bishop-designate can lay claim to the jurisdiction necessary to carry on these temporal elements of his role even prior to his episcopal consecration.[28] However, even this was seen as an exceptional and temporary measure which was allowed because of practical demands.[29] And there is no evidence that any bishop attempted to exercise the principal episcopal ministries of word, sacrament, or ecclesiastical government without being ordained.

So much is clear. What is not clear is the manner in which this episcopal ordination was seen as the source of episcopal authority. One element was the official recognition from the rest of the episcopate that this individual occupied the *cathedra* and therefore the office that was apostolic in origin and authority.[30] Another element, as we can tell from the ordination formulae, was the gift of the Spirit, conferred upon the ordinand through the agency of his fellow bishops, the divine source of his episcopal authority and power.[31] It seems, too, that the ordination of the bishop was seen as an incorporation into the collegial body of bishops, a sharing in the dignity and responsibility and power which they corporately possessed.[32]

But did the consecrating bishop(s) confer authority on the new bishop in the ordination, acting as representatives for the entire episcopal body? In the West, from Leo I onward, it is the Roman contention, accepted by a large group of bishops, that the pope is the source of the episcopal authority; episcopal authority is essentially delegated authority.[33] Prior to Leo, and later in those situations where sections of the Latin church resisted Roman dominance, the source of authority seems to have been sought rather in the "apostolicity" of the see's origin.[34] Thus, one finds in the ninth century the widespread interest in tracing the foundations of a bish-

opric (such as Paris) back to an apostle or at least to an immediate link with an apostle (as Paris did in confusing the legends attached to two Denises, and claiming foundation by Denis the Areopagite).[35]

An entirely different source of authority came to the episcopacy with Constantine's decree that bishops could preside over courts, and that these courts would have full legal recognition.[36] From Paul onward, it had been the Christian custom to bring disputes among members of a community not to the civil courts but to the leadership of the community. This could suffice for maintaining tranquillity in the Christian community, but it had no standing in secular society and received no recognition if an aggrieved party carried his matter to a civil judge. Moreover, no sooner does the secular power show itself open to the existence of the church than elements within the church turn to this secular power to support their side in what are strictly ecclesiastical matters, as the Donatists did in appealing to Constantine.[37] Constantine shrewdly turned such matters back to bishops for judgment, but concretely they now were judging in a mixed context—they were also his delegated court. It is this sort of thing that he extends in his ruling that persons could carry their case to either a civil or an episcopal judge, that both court rulings had equal validity, and that both rulings would be executed by public power.[38]

Such a situation was bound to confuse thought about the source of the bishop's authority as judge. The range of things that the bishop was called upon to judge would stretch from settlement of wills and estates, to providing for an orphan child, to grievances people had against the lower clergy, to accusations of immorality leveled against one of his presbyters or deacons. In some of these instances he was clearly on the borderline of judging the sinfulness of some men and women. Certainly, in these latter cases the authority he exercised would come with the "power of the keys" and not from any civil grant. So, it would be quite logical to suppose that his authority to judge all the other cases was part of this same authority. All the civil law was doing was recognizing a situation which was beyond it.[39]

Part of the problem with this situation was that it may well have been a dangerous confusion of authorities, an exercise by ecclesiastics of activity that pertained properly to the civil sphere; but it did often prove a social good in that it gave protection to the poor and defenseless who could come to the bishop expecting the just hearing which they had little hope of obtaining from some of the civil judges. Not that it always functioned this way. Yet there is no question but that the bishop in this situation did have something the civil judge could not claim: he could urge justice and restitution not just on the basis of temporal sanction but under threat of punishment in the next life. The fact that one cannot say that such exhortation, when it did take place, was inappropriate to the bishop's ministry of the word indicates how confused were the lines of authority that the bishop was exercising.

Authority Derived from the Pope

Prior to Nicaea there is no evidence whatsoever that the bishop of Rome claimed to be the source of authority for his brother bishops, nor that any other bishop thought Rome to be the source of his authority.[40] There is some evidence that Rome has a certain preeminence, even that it is the guardian of orthodox faith in a special way.[41] But there is no evidence that the bishop of Rome is the source of episcopal authority. Nor can one refer to the notion, found in Cyprian, for example, that Peter is the head of the episcopate, that the authority granted to him is the beginning of all later episcopal authority, as an indication that a later successor of Peter in the see of Rome was considered to be the source of authority for his contemporaries.[42]

During the fourth- and fifth-century flowering of patristic thought there is great respect for the doctrinal and spiritual eminence of the Roman church.[43] Above all, from the point of view of evidence for Roman primacy,

there is the attestation at Chalcedon to the Petrine succession of Leo I: "Peter speaks through the mouth of Leo."[44] Yet, there is no evidence that the bishop of Rome plays any greater role in the selection and empowering of bishops in his own patriarchate than does any other patriarch; he plays no such role in other patriarchates. Nor does it seem that bishops within a given patriarchate, including that of Rome, felt that they derived their authority from the ruling patriarch.[45]

With the pontificate of Gelasius, at the very end of the fifth century, a new orientation of thought begins. At least to some extent in reaction to the claims of Byzantine rulers, Gelasius lays claim for the papacy to ultimate spiritual power. The *basileus* may have supreme authority in the temporal sphere, but even the *basileus* falls under the authority of the pope in "the kingdom of heaven."[46] Gelasius does not draw the conclusion from his claim as it would affect the origin of episcopal power, but the principle has been enunciated, and it is only a matter of time before the logic of the Gelasian view is made explicit.

The occasion and stimulus for such refinement comes with the events surrounding Charlemagne's rise to power and with the beginnings of "Christian imperialism" in the West. Gregory the Great had already (after Gelasius) asserted the primacy of Roman authority in the Western church; his use of the term *"servus servorum Dei"* reflected his claim to universal *cura animarum*, though he declined to use of himself the title *"patriarcha universalis."*[47] Moreover, his influence on Isidore of Seville (whose writings exercised such widespread effects) and his sending of Augustine to England (which made him the "father" of the later developments which sprang from this) laid the groundwork for later papal prestige and claims.[48] Then with the Carolingian ascendancy there came the need to give some further clarification of the relative claims of pope and king. As the latter claimed to be the possessor of God-given authority over all things imperial, so the pope was the possessor of God-given authority over all things ecclesiastical, most critically over all things episcopal.[49]

Such a claim to be the source of authority for the episcopacy of the West (which was all that practically concerned Rome for the moment) found support in the commonly accepted view that all apostolic and consequent episcopal authority stemmed from the grant of authority given to Peter.[50] Yet, prominent bishops of Carolingian times, Hincmar of Reims for one, acknowledged a primatial authority in the bishop of Rome but opposed the Roman claim to being the fountainhead of episcopal authority.[51] This opposition continued through the eleventh century, even under the reigns of Gregory VII and Urban II, though the bishops who at that time found themselves arrayed against the pope seemed to lack the incipient theology of episcopal collegiality which Hincmar possessed[52] and moved more in the realm of "power politics."[53] On the other hand, the papal "legists" and theologians had gradually developed a consistent hierocratic theory which embraced not just the ecclesiastical structures but the entirety of *societas christiana*.[54] All that was lacking by the beginning of the twelfth century was a metaphysical justification, a religious cosmology which would rationalize the claims already made by Rome on the basis of the "traditions" of the past.[55] Such will come with Innocent III.

One of the most fascinating aspects of episcopal claim to authority touches on the relation of a given church to its "founder," whether real or legendary. Undoubtedly, the most developed and important instance of this occurs in Rome, but Rome is not unique in this regard.

It is not just a question that a particular church, whether Rome or Constantinople or Tours or Campostello, lays claim to some special eminence because a great apostle (or later "apostle" such as Martin of Tours) established it. Rather, the church is still seen to be the church of this saintly founder; he still rules over it and cares for it, since the Lord has given him this church as his own charge unto the day of judgment. Thus, he is invoked as the heavenly protector of this church, and as the ultimate steward of this community (for whom the incumbent bishop acts as delegate) he still holds in trust even the material possessions of this church. The sign of his abiding presence and guardianship is the possession (so highly prized) of the saint's relics.[56]

One can see the kind of authority this reflects upon the bishop of a given church (or for that matter upon a parish priest who was fortunate to have some local saint attached to his church). The bishop is ruling along with and as the delegate of the heavenly patron. Compliance with the bishop clearly merits favorable response from this heavenly patron; properties willed to the patrimony of the saint is an especially powerful way of showing veneration of the saint and thereby gaining his favor.[57] Contrariwise, opposition to the bishop is more than an affair of earth; it has overtones of rebellion against heaven.[58]

All of this may sound a bit fanciful, but from Leo I onward one finds quite explicit statements of this kind in papal documents. Later we can examine these in greater detail, but here we might advert to the practice in other places. Apparently the earliest expressions of this viewpoint in many places had to do not so much with apostolic origin as with the abiding presence of a holy "wonder-worker."[59] Tours, where the burial place of Saint Martin became a place of veneration and pilgrimage, is a case in point.[60] It was not long, however, before the element of apostolic origin assumed importance. Most churches, of course, could find no basis even in legend for a link with one of the Twelve. So, they settled for foundation by and possession of a saint who was immediately linked with the apostolic age, as did Paris with Denis.[61] Or, as did the great sees of England and Germany, they grounded their claims through Augustine or Boniface in Gregory I, and therefore in Peter.[62] Naturally, this latter procedure strengthened immensely the prestige and influence of Rome. It also prepared in England for the bitter struggle between Canterbury and the English kings.

English lords found it difficult to accept the Petrine ownership of English lands and wealth.[63]

What this link between the local church and its heavenly patron makes clear is that in the period we are studying the church never ceased to be viewed, at least partially, in eschatological perspective. True, it became increasingly identified with the temporal as the notion of the one *societas christiana* became prevalent, but the inner or spiritual element in this *societas* was rooted in mystery, the mystery of Christ as head of the church, the supreme high priest who continued to express himself salvifically through the *sacerdotium*. The teleology of Christian society as a whole, but especially that of its priesthood, never ceased to be seen as extending into "the next life."

Doctrinal Judgment

At the root, then, of sacerdotal authority during this period, whether the authority be that of Rome, of the bishop, or even of the parish priest, lay the Christian faith. The sanction to which the *sacerdotium* could most ultimately appeal was that of eternal damnation. Unquestionably, this was far from being the only kind of sanction threatened by such popes as Gregory VII to bring recalcitrant kings or bishops to heel, but it was the underpinning of all sacerdotal judgment. From this it follows that the most basic area of judgment exercised by the episcopacy was that of doctrine. Unless they could pass judgment on the truth or falsity of a given explanation of man's salvation, they were in no position to threaten their "subjects" with the loss of that salvation.

We have already seen the responsibility for the ministry of the word which the great bishops of the patristic period recognized as their own, a charge which Gregory and Isidore passed on to the late patristic and medieval centuries. What concerns us here is not, however, the bishops' own preaching and teaching but their activity in passing judgment on the doctrinal views of others. That

they did so with assurance that such was their responsibility and power is clearly evidenced by the great councils that marked the early centuries of this period and by the innumerable lesser councils and synods that took place throughout the church, East and West, during these centuries.

One can give countless examples, from the well-known ones of Cyril of Alexandria and Augustine and Leo I to less famous ones such as Hincmar (with Gottschalk) and Agobard (with Felix of Urgel), of bishops who felt impelled by their office to pass judgment on the doctrinal errors of others.[64] What is, however, important is the consistent pattern in which they appeal for support and joint action to their fellow bishops, seeing doctrinal judgment as something that pertains collegially to the episcopate.[65] In most instances such individual discovery of "heresy" is carried to a synod of bishops for a corporate judgment.[66]

More than a few such synodal judgments on doctrine were directed at the teaching of some bishop, so it is quite clear that a bishop by himself was not considered the norm of orthodoxy; the episcopacy was. It does seem that one must make some exception in this regard for the bishop of Rome. Despite the attempts to subject Vigilius to conciliar control,[67] or the synodal judgments against Honorius and Formosus (in the ninth century),[68] or the "condemnation" of Gregory VII by the German bishops opposed to him,[69] such actions were widely considered to be contrary to both law and justice.[70] Throughout, even in secular affairs, but much more so in doctrinal matters, the bishop of Rome was considered beyond judgment by others, even by his brother bishops. Such was the view, accepted at least in the West, which the bishops convoked by Charlemagne to judge Leo III expressed to the emperor.[71]

Beyond the more formal judgments on doctrine passed by bishops when they gathered in synod, there was the continuing judgment involved in the direction that bishops were expected to provide for their clergy, particularly for those involved in teaching or preaching.[72] We find this expressed in the letters of bishops to their own clergy or to fellow bishops encouraging them to direct their presbyters and deacons.[73] It took form also in the "formation" of clergy, which the bishop was expected to oversee.[74] And from the sixth century in the West it was part of the reason for the regular episcopal visitations to the parishes of his diocese. On the occasion of this visit he was able to examine and, if necessary, correct the doctrinal views being propounded by the local presbyter.[75]

One of the interesting features of this episcopal judgment in matters of doctrine is the early manifestation, fortunately in not too many instances, of the belief that episcopacy confers power to discover truth, despite the theological ignorance of the bishop concerned. Epiphanius is a memorable instance of this.[76] One wonders to what extent this view was linked with the manner in which the *ordo episcopalis* is endowed with ontological supremacy in the Dionysian world of "descending illumination."

One of the most obvious situations where the role of bishops as judges found expression was in the episcopal courts.[77] These were of various kinds, some exclusively ecclesiastical in their business, others totally taken up with matters that would ordinarily be handled in civil courts, and some where the ecclesiastical and secular were hard to distinguish. This last became increasingly the case as the number of clergy grew considerably, and as the distinctions between church and state became increasingly blurred.[78]

Constantine's decree that episcopal courts could function equivalently as civil courts brought upon the bishops a heavy burden of judicial administration. Ambrose, Augustine, and Basil, to name but a few, complain about the time and energy consumed in hearing such cases.[79] Probably the bulk of the business in such courts dealt with disputes or grievances that could as well have been handled in civil courts, though they probably involved more and more cases where clergy were exercising their exemption from trial in civil courts. Even though many bishops saw the basic unrelatedness of such civil judgment to their functions proper to them as bishops, it is likely that "judge" became a prominent element of their self-identity.

It is not clear just what happened to such episcopal courts in the West as the political and legal situation of the Roman Empire gave way to the structures and procedures of feudal society.[80] Certainly, many bishops did act as judges in matters that were not strictly ecclesiastical in nature, but it is not evident whether they did this through legal recognition of their bishopric or through accidental acquisition of temporal power.[81] In the East, the Constantinian grant was incorporated into the Justinian Code. As long as this code was being applied the episcopacy continued to be involved in conducting episcopal court.

Probably a certain amount of the actual conduct of episcopal courts concerned itself with ecclesiastical matters such as peoples' grievances against a presbyter or the regulation of ecclesiastical property.[82] But it would seem that the more formal situation of ecclesiastical court as such was the synod or council.[83] Even the synods or councils that were convoked chiefly to deal with some doctrinal matter devoted a certain amount of their time to practical disciplinary questions. The disciplinary decrees of these episcopal gatherings are perhaps our best source of knowledge about clerical life throughout these centuries.[84]

Such synods, however, dealt only with matters of greater moment or with those that had aroused dispute. For the most part ecclesiastical discipline, more and more equivalent to regulation of *clerical* life and activity, was provided for by each bishop.[85] The need to form and guide the lower clergy was early seen to be a most important aspect of the bishop's pastoral care. Somewhat advanced for its day, Augustine's provision for communal life and formation for his clergy is a response to this duty. Not infrequently, the bishop found himself in the position of judge with respect to some of his presbyters and deacons, at times through the informal medium of epistolary correction, at times through more formal process of judgment and sanction.[86]

Such judgment was not imposed only on lower clergy, though they were the ordinary object of such episcopal scrutiny. Laity also, if they proved to be a scandal to the life of the community, had their actions judged and sanctioned appropriately by the bishop.[87] Here, of course, we are involved in situations which relate very closely to the discipline of penitence and forgiveness of sin.

No aspect of judgment was considered more properly the province of bishops than dealing with penance for and forgiveness of sins.[88] From Leo I onward (and he was anticipated to some extent by Cyprian, Ambrose, and Augustine) the basis for all episcopal and especially papal claims to authority was the "power of the keys" that was given to Peter.[89] This was essentially the power to loose or bind eschatologically, in the realm of sin or salvation. But it was given a much broader application, especially in the papal theology that develops from Leo through Gelasius and Gregory to John VIII and Gregory VII and Innocent III.[90]

This wider application of the power of the keys, coupled with the conflict between the Mediterranean discipline of exomologesis and the Celtic discipline of private confession and absolution, makes the history of the sacrament of penance somewhat fuzzy during this period, though no more so than in the preceding historical period. Obviously, there could be no question here of trying to summarize the historical studies of Anciaux, Rahner, Adam, Poschmann, Grotz, and Galtier (to name but a few), much less trying to evaluate their positions.[91] Instead, attention can be drawn to some aspects of this history that touch importantly on our attempt to discover what idea of their authority bishops during this period had.

Traditional Exomologesis

During the early portion of the period we are discussing, the pattern of exomologesis as we know it from the Nicene period seems to continue in both East and West.[92] In this process, the bishop functions in a prominent role at two points in the process: at the beginning in assigning penance to the culpable according to the gravity of their sin, and at the end in receiving them back into communion.[93] The first of these two instances is easy enough to interpret. There is some doubt as to how sins were confessed to the bishop at various points of history and how soon and to what extent sins of lesser gravity were confessed.[94] These are questions which are interesting from a historical point of view but which do not affect a theological understanding of the bishop's role as judge of penance to be performed.

Actually, the view of the great Alexandrian theologians Clement and Origen,[95] that such assignment of penance could be the function of a "spiritual father" who was not necessarily a bishop or even a presbyter, carried on to some extent in monastic life in the East.[96] In this practice, the authority of the spiritual guide lay not in any official position but in his skill as a spiritual counselor, his knowledge of what manner of penance would be most medicinal in a given person's case. Somewhat the same point of view is reflected in the continuing monastic practice both in East and West of manifestation of conscience.[97]

So, in the bishop's assignment of penance there is involved a judicial action which dictates a course of action and lays a specific sanction on the penitent. In the second spot of special episcopal involvement, the reconciliation of the penitent, the act of judgment is more profoundly sacramental. Acting in the name of the community he heads, but also acting in the name of Christ who promised Peter to ratify "whatsoever you loose on earth," the bishop (or his delegate) restores the penitent to communion with the church and with God.[98] The obverse of this act of reconciliation is, of course, the judicial action of excluding a person (to a greater or lesser degree) from the community. Interestingly, there never seems to be as much assurance about this excommunication effecting alienation from God as there was about absolution effecting reconciliation.[99] But there was enough fear of such an effect to make threat of excommunication a powerful weapon in the episcopal arsenal.

By the sixth century it is quite clear that the bulk of the ministry of reconciling sinners has been assigned to presbyters, particularly in the countryside.[100] In the West, the bishops continue to officiate personally in the exomologesis of their own church in the city, and in the East it seems that penitential discipline had been entrusted to certain designated presbyters as early as the late third century.[101] In the West, the designation of presbyters to receive people's confession of sin, assign penance, and then reconcile them probably helped prepare for the spread of private confession.

However, the spread of such private confession was largely the doing of the Celtic monks whose influence spread from northern Europe through Switzerland into Lombardy.[102] Confession of sins was looked upon as a saving ascetic exercise, one which could have much of its impact even if the confession was given to a lay person.[103] However, it does not seem that there was ever question of such a lay confessor conferring any absolution. It is even vague just what kind of absolution from sins was provided by the monk-priest confessors.[104] Yet, the expanding influence of this practice can be gauged by the widespread use of the "penitential books" in the seventh to eleventh centuries, and by the decrees of eighth- to eleventh-century synods demanding a return to the traditional discipline of the exomologesis.[105]

There is still evident throughout all this period a certain hesitation regarding the relationship between the "internal forum" and the "external forum"—or, which is not quite the same thing, the respective contribution to spiritual betterment and reconciliation with God of the personal attitudes and activity (e.g., penance) of the penitent and of the official (sacramental) actions of the episcopacy.[106] In the period of the great councils and great patristic figures there was quite limited use of the discipline of exomologesis,

limited, that is, to grave offenses.[107] As early as Basil and Augustine there is emphasis on ridding oneself of lesser sinfulness, but this takes place through manifestation of conscience (which may or may not involve sacramental confession) and prayer and ascetic discipline.[108]

Given the situation of graver sins, sins that in one way or another involved an element of excommunication, there was a recognized need for episcopal intervention to fix the penance, guide the period of penitence, and reconcile the penitent to the community.[109] But beyond this there does not seem to be any clear and universally accepted need for sinners to submit their culpability "to the keys." That repentance is necessary and that penance (including confession) helps counterbalance sin is recognized and emphasized, but the intervention of episcopal or presbyteral absolution does not seem to be seen as required.[110]

A drastic shift in view is expressed shortly after the end of the period we are studying. The law of mandatory confession of sin to a bishop or his delegated presbyter is enacted by the Third Lateran Council.[111] Here is the final step in the institutionalization of salvation from sin. The efficacy of the internal disposition of repentance is officially conditioned by its being linked with the external activity of the episcopacy. Religiously, of course, the critical question is: Can the claim be legitimately made that the divine judgment itself upon the penitent conforms to the ecclesiastical judgment of bishop or presbyter? To this the official answer is affirmative, based on the appeal to the Petrine power of the keys, "Whatsoever you bind upon earth. . . ."[112]

By the end of the eleventh century and the dawning of the great medieval period, it has become increasingly difficult to describe the nature of the bishop's authority. Perhaps one can apply the distinction that Congar uses quite effectively (though in a broader context) in his *L'ecclésiologie du Haut Moyen Age*, namely, that between the "inner mystery" and the "outer embodiment."[113]

There is a "mystery" aspect to the episcopal office as both clergy and laity view it during these centuries, and there is a sociological aspect to the bishop's identity and function. In the first of these, there is relatively little change of understanding, at least on the surface, for the theological formulations remain comparatively static.[114] In the second aspect, the authority wielded by bishops in the actual conduct of Christians' lives is correlative to the changing view of the church from a community situated in the midst of a political and social entity which is the Roman state to that of a *societas perfecta* which absorbs into itself the entirety of the social and political spheres. In the *societas christiana*, the notion of monarchical episcopate is taken quite seriously according to a political model. Though he is not *the* king, for that dignity belongs to the pope, the bishop is a lesser monarch within the religious society.[115] True, his approach to exercise of authority should be predominantly spiritual, for he pertains to the *sacerdotium* rather than to the *imperium*. Concretely, however, since the spiritual enjoys superiority and even supervision over the temporal, the bishop cannot (and does not!) divorce himself from what is taking place in the temporal sphere.[116] In varying degrees, dependent upon the talent and leadership qualities of the individual, bishops in the eleventh century actually exercise an authority that is a mixture of (a) what derives from their episcopal ministry of word and sacrament, (b) what is consequent upon their role as part of the ruling class in feudal society, and (c) the moral leadership that comes from the prestige of their office or from their learning or holiness or from their "political connections" (with God, the local "patron saint," the pope, or the king).

How different this is from the bishop at the beginning of this period. Here is the same recognized ministry of word and sacrament, the same possession of priesthood, the same claim to apostolic origin and tradition, but the sociological implications are drastically different. Great bishops of the fourth to sixth centuries unquestionably exerted influence on the political and social situations of their day, at times a decisive influence, and the list is long: Ambrose, Augustine, Basil, Cyril of Alexandria. It would be naive to deny that part of their influence came from their influential political connections. Occasionally, a great bishop would neglect such political fence-mending to his own detriment, as Chrysostom certainly did. But what is significant in these earlier centuries, and Chrysostom exemplifies it very well, is the fact that the bishop, if he was true to his own role, stood over against the political establishment; he might have to deal with it on the level of *Realpolitik*, but he was never part of it.

However, before long both in East and in West, the political power structure attempted to include under it the authoritative structures of the church.[117] In the East, the church never managed to free itself from the imperial embrace as formalized in Justinian's code.[118] In the West, the papacy carried on a centuries-long battle to free "the church" (read: "the clergy") from secular control. It won this battle by the twelfth century, but at the price of distorting its own self-understanding.[119]

Papal Authority and Judgment

Probably nothing gives us such an insight into the attitudinal and sociological changes that took place in this period between Nicaea and the Crusades as does the evolution of the papal office. Prescinding temporarily from theological judgment as to whether the essential nature of the "apostolic see" remained constant,[120] there is a marked difference between the role played by Leo I and by Gregory VII and a marked difference also in the manner in which each understood his office. This change in understanding of the papal office is critically important for a theology of priesthood, because the history of the word "*sacerdotium*" centers increasingly in these centuries on its application to the bishop of Rome and his authority and function.

Anything that was considered a basis for episcopal authority in other sees applied *a fortiori* to *the* apostolic see. There was never a question of challenging the episcopal authority of the bishop of Rome. As far back as Irenaeus, Rome was used as an instance of clear succession from apostolic origins.[121] Rather, discussion and controversy over the centuries has concentrated on the claim of this particular episcopal see to some kind of unique authority.[122] Examination of the sources of authority to which popes (and propapal polemicists) point to justify their claims is valuable theologically, not just as guides in accepting or rejecting these claims but also as a reflection of the Roman thinking on the kind of authority possessed by the pope.

Most basic, of course, to the Roman claim was the link with Peter and Paul.[123] By the time of Nicaea there is widespread acceptance of some privileged position of Rome as the "apostolic see." During the next two centuries there is a mounting consensus that Rome is a touchstone of orthodox faith because its bishop enjoys the benefit of Christ's promise to Peter: "Simon, Simon, Satan has sought you . . ." (Luke 22).[124] This early acceptance of Roman "primacy" reaches its high point at the Council of Chalcedon with the acknowledgment of the council fathers that "Peter speaks through the mouth of Leo."[125]

Certainly, no one before Leo I had laid claim more sharply to the preeminent position of the Roman see, nor more insistently grounded this claim in his own succession from Peter.[126] It should be noted, however, that the claim is basically one of authority in doctrinal matters. His demand to the council is that they adhere to the viewpoint of his *Tome*. This they must do if they wish to preserve the apostolic faith and with it the unity of the church.[127] There is no evidence of his claiming any administrative authority over any of the other great churches, much less any authority in the civil sphere.[128] He did act, however, as the patriarch of the Latin church, exercising both administrative and liturgical authority.[129]

From one point of view, it may not be correct to say that Leo I based his claims to authority on his succession from Peter. Rather, a number of texts seem to indicate that he thought of Peter as still present to and active in the church of Rome, and through it in the universal church. It is through the bishop of Rome (in this case Leo), his vicar, that Peter still continues his mission from Christ. Peter still occupies his office as primate of the apostles, still enjoys Christ's promise of authority and indefectibility in faith; he acts through Leo.[130] It is noteworthy that the bishop of Rome at this time lays no claim to being "the vicar of Christ" (that term will be used once by Gelasius but will not become an accepted reference to the pope until the twelfth-century use of the term by Saint Bernard); he thinks of himself as "the vicar of Peter."[131]

As we mentioned briefly before, part of the Roman bishop's claim on Peter was the fact of the apostle's burial in Rome. Already there stood the basilica, erected by Constantine, over the relics of Peter, a constant sign of Rome's special claim to be *the* apostolic see.[132] This factor will assume great psychological importance in centuries to come, when pilgrims from all parts of the Latin church will come to visit the apostle's tomb, and reinforce thereby their allegiance to the pope.

Fairly early in the history of the papacy, incumbent popes began to appeal to previous statements and decisions of the Roman church, issued by earlier synods or by their episcopal predecessors. Thus, there began to grow up a tradition of laws and customs (administrative, liturgical, disciplinary). Particularly important were the Decretals issued between the fifth and twelfth centuries.[133] Though never codified until the twelfth century, they were gathered together in different collections, added to by other decrees, either genuine or forged, and used as guides (or at least as justification) for ecclesiastical judgments.

By the time of Charlemagne and thereafter, this body of decretal literature is a major source of papal argumentation for the authoritative primacy of Rome, not just in the ecclesiastical sphere but in that of the temporal order as well.[134] The argumentative process used, while it is in the legal order, is not unlike the theological arguments from the Fathers. Interestingly, in the twelfth century Abelard will try to organize the one with his *Sic et non* and Gratian will do the same for the other with his *Decretum*.[135]

Greogry VII's letter of 1081 to Herimann of Metz makes it clear, however, that the argument from specific Roman traditions and legal precedent does not replace the basic appeal to New Testament texts about Christ's grant of authority to Peter.[136] This argument does not proceed the same way, though, that it did at the time of Leo I. Then it had dealt with the promise of truth in belief, now with Hildebrand it is an appeal to the power of the keys as the source for all-embracing social sovereignty.[137] Gregory VII is enunciating nothing particularly new; he is only reducing to practical application a hierocratic theory that began developing with Gelasius and crystallized as early as John VIII.[138]

It would be inaccurate stereotyping to say that Leo I had seen himself as supreme teacher and Greogry VII saw himself as supreme judge and lawgiver, but some such change of papal self-identity took place. Midway between them stands Gregory the Great, to whom Gregory VII looks back with reverence and by whom he is deeply influenced.[139] As we saw earlier, Gregory, who looks on himself as the chief pastor of the church, describes that pastoral office in terms that combine teaching and judgment. Above all else, the pastor (the term he uses most frequently is *"rector"*) is to admonish and by his admonitions to help heal sinful men.[140]

Not all the basis for the pope's increasing prestige and power was religious or theological. It is necessary to advert briefly to these other factors, since an awareness of them will help us assess the magisterial statements of Roman pontiffs during these centuries, and so determine to what extent they can or should ground our theological understanding of the episcopal or papal office.

No doubt, the political dominance of Rome during the early centuries of the church's exis-

tence gave additional prestige to the church of that city, a prestige that endured even when political Rome waned in power and influence. As a matter of fact, the political decline of Rome tended to increase the prestige of its bishop. When people have been accustomed to regarding a city as an international capital for centuries they do not immediately lose this point of view (this certainly was the case with Rome);[141] but no longer having an emperor and imperial government on which to hang these associations, at least some of this was attached to Rome's bishop, for after all he now made the city the religious capital of the church.

Complicated though it was by the danger of domination by the temporal power, the papacy's close association with Charlemagne (as with other temporal rulers) gave it a position of eminence among episcopates in the West, and a basis for resisting Constantinople's pretensions to equality as an apostolic see.[142] True, this very recognition by such temporal rulers was based on Rome's already present status as the patriarchal see of the Latin church; but its treatment by such rulers, either as foremost ally or foremost enemy, tended to reinforce in men's minds Rome's position of importance.

Lastly, Rome was blessed with a number of extremely competent and strong-willed bishops during these centuries, much more so than any other episcopal see. These men, such as Leo I, Innocent I, Nicholas I, Gelasius, and Gregory I, not only tended by temperament to insist upon and exercise whatever power or authority their responsibilities seemed to demand, and to enshrine all this in their correspondence and official decrees; but their strength and success in governing gained prestige for the papal office, prestige that was able to withstand even the dark days of the tenth century. Their contemporaries looked to them increasingly to pass judgment on all manner of things; this they did.

There is no need here to detail the history of doctrinal decisions made by bishops of Rome during these centuries; this has been done repeatedly in studies of the Roman see's

claim to infallibility.[143]   In this area, however, it seems that there was no evolution.
The most forthright and influential papal action in doctrinal matters during these eight
hundred years was that of Leo I in his intervention before and during Chalcedon.[144]
Actually, the only aspect of Christian belief in
which the popes after Leo exercised any doctrinal initiative was in developing a justification for the position of the Roman see. Apart
from that, they were involved in reacting,
generally at a geographical and cultural distance, to the increasingly sophisticated refine-
ments of Byzantine heresy, the countless attempts of Byzantine emperors and patriarchs
to find some acceptable brand of Monophys-
itism, or the iconoclast controversies.[145]   By
and large they did this not by entering into
the theological debate of the Byzantine court
but by insisting on adherence to the decisions
of Chalcedon, even to the point of excommunicating the emperor Zeno because of his
imposition of the heretical *Henoticon*.[146]   In
the West, too, their doctrinal activity was
largely that of responding to instances of supposed doctrinal aberration that were referred
to them or of giving approval to the acts of
regional synods (such as Orange II with its
condemnation of Semi-Pelagianism).[147]   It is
quite surprising that neither on their own
initiative nor at the behest of concerned bishops did the popes play any part in such doctrinal controversies as that over Gottschalk's
ideas on predestination or the ninth-century
debates about the Eucharist.[148]

There is never any questioning, in the
West, of the pope's power of ultimate judgment in doctrine, and very little clarification
of it. For the most part, discussion of his role
had shifted to other aspects of his authority.
Only towards the very end of the period we
are studying does the Roman council of 1050
(under Leo IX) with its judgment on Berengarius presage the renewed interest in doctrinal issues that will find expression in the
great thirteenth-century councils.[149]

Gregory the Great's *Pastoral Care*, the most
influential book in medieval clerical formation, stressed the moral concern the true pas-

tor should have, the admonition he should
direct towards erring mankind. And if this
burden of admonition weighed heavily on
every pastor of souls, none felt it more than
the bishops of Rome upon whom rested the
care of all mankind.[150]

Foremost in the concerns of the bishops of
Rome throughout these centuries was their
care for the moral and spiritual well-being of
the clergy. Upon this depended the spiritual
level of the entire church. Though there is
no lack of expressed concern for this clerical
integrity during the fourth and fifth centuries, it becomes a constant refrain in later
centuries when the pressure of many factors
caused a deplorable situation in a large portion of both higher and lower clergy, a situation which cried out for reform.[151]

As the period ends, Gregory VII uses sanctions such as deposition and excommunication
quite freely to remove from the episcopacy
those who refused to abandon their scandalous behavior or who refused to impose
his reform measures on their own clergy.[152]
Such actions depended upon acceptance of
the theory that the episcopal authority of
these deposed prelates was derived from the
bishop of Rome. It is not surprising, then,
that one does not find such drastic action in
earlier centuries when this papal theology had
not yet crystallized. In those earlier periods,
deposition of a bishop seems to have been
rather the prerogative of a regional synod, i.e.,
effected by judgment of his peers.[153]

Charged with the care for the moral well-
being of their flock, and for the popes from at
least as far back as Leo I this means the entire
church,[154] the bishop of Rome could not
overlook immoral behavior on the part of
leading figures in society. Or if it did seem
more practical not to denounce certain prominent sinners too directly, there was the need
to inveigh against the sins they committed.[155]
It does not seem that much public condemnation was ever directed against some of
Charlemagne's less than edifying practices.
On the other hand, at a time when it became
increasingly necessary to insist on the inviolability of Christian marriage, Lothair's open

attempts to divorce his wife Theutberga met with unrelenting opposition from Rome.[156]

Considering the jealousy with which ancient apostolic sees such as Antioch and Alexandria guarded their independence and prerogatives, it is amazing to find at an early date some instances of appeal to Rome to settle disputes between even the most powerful of these churches.[157] One cannot assume from this that such appeal, whether it comes from Athanasius to Liberius in the aftermath of Nicaea, or from Cyril of Alexandria and Nestorius to Celestine I a century later, or from John Chrysostom to Innocent, implies a recognition of Rome's authority to give determinative judgment.[158] Yet, it does establish a pattern of Rome's involvement in such disputes.

From Leo I, and even more so from Gelasius, we can begin to trace the evolution of Rome's claim to intervene, and with proper jurisdiction, in controversies between churches or even between elements within a given church.[159] We have here, quite clearly, the beginnings of the decretal tradition that the pope has immediate pastoral relationship to each Christian, as the bishop has to those of his particular diocese.[160] Foundation for such a claim is worked out very neatly by Siricius in the very first decretal. Combining Paul and Peter, Siricius applies Paul's concern "for all the churches" (2 Cor. 11:28) to the burden that Peter carries in the person of the pope.[161]

Once the papal claims to headship over the *societas christiana*, or at least over its spiritual element, began to crystallize, this logically brought with it the conclusion that the bishop of Rome had not only the right but the responsibility to watch over the entirety of Christendom and to intervene, if it seemed necessary, in disputes that were threatening the faith or morality of Christians.[162]

The Formation of Canonical Traditions

Though certainly not limited to decisions made in such dispute situations, the canonical traditions did arise partially from the responses given by popes or councils to concrete questions of doubt or debate.[163] It would be difficult to overestimate the importance of this body of legal literature which arose out of the judgments made by synodal meetings and by the Roman see. It began to form a detailed, though still amorphous, body of law to guide both the external management of the Latin church and the consciences of clergy and through them of the laity.

Study of this canonical literature, its history, and the principles of its internal evolution has quite recently come into its own as a recognized endeavor of great theological importance. Yet, the mass of material is so vast, and its interpretation so dependent upon a tangled skein of historical influences, that the bulk of the task still remains to be done.[164] In the meantime, any satisfactory theology of the church or of its ministry must remain to this extent an unrealized ideal.

One conclusion we can, however, quite safely draw from this body of canonical writing. It reflects increasingly the mentality that the bishops are meant to be judges, and the bishop of Rome preeminently so. The Decretals, for example, are nothing more or less than a collection of judgments that synods and pontiffs have made, a gradually developing pattern of legal precedent that can act as guide for future judgments.[165] By the time of Gregory VII it seems we can safely say that no element of the papal office is more prominent than that of judge; it may well be that we can extend this more broadly to the episcopal office in general.

One of the areas of judgment which the Decretals indicate as common and far-reaching was the church's sacramental liturgy. A glance at the table of contents of Gratian's *Decretum*, in which a considerable portion of the work deals with decisions on liturgical matters, indicates how much attention was paid to liturgical legislation in the preceding centuries.[166]

Clearly, this development is not new to the post-Nicene period. Ignatius of Antioch already asserts the "disciplinary" role of the *episkopos* relative to baptism and Eucharist;[167] and the *Didache* contains directions for liturgical practice.[168] However, this need not be seen precisely in the light of the *episkopos* (or his equivalent) acting judicially. It could be simply that, as the possessor of the apostolic traditions, he is teaching others the correct pattern of Christian worship. Hippolytus' *Apostolic Tradition* would seem to point still in this *didactic* direction, though no doubt the description of Eucharistic celebrations therein contained reflect a liturgical practice that is already quite conventionalized, most likely under the direction of *episkopoi* in various places.[169]

As we already saw, the early post-Nicene period was marked by numerous episcopal synods in various portions of the church, and quite early one notices references to regulation of liturgy among their disciplinary decrees.[170] This seems to mirror a situation of liturgical freedom on the part of local churches, or at least of patriarchal areas. No doubt, the liturgy of the Roman church had considerable influence as an example of orthodox belief, so much so that Ambrose felt compelled to explain why the church of Milan differed from Rome in its approach to the ceremony of the washing of the feet.[171] Yet, there does not seem to be question of Rome judging or regulating the liturgies of other churches.[172]

One begins to observe some moves in the direction of liturgical judgment on the part of Rome about the time of Gregory I, not so much in terms of controlling the sacramental practice of churches with developed traditions but rather in regulating the nascent liturgical life of regions being newly evangelized or re-evangelized. As such missionaries as Augustine went out from Rome, they brought with them the Roman liturgical traditions and texts. However, it seems that the first noticeable attempts at liturgical control come with the Carolingian period, seemingly at the urging of Pepin and Charlemagne rather than of the pope.[173] Yet, even here there seems to be respect for the principle of episcopal autonomy; there is more urging than legislation, and there seems to be little strict judgment in

liturgical matters (i.e., by Rome) prior to the eleventh century.[174]

However, one must be careful not to draw conclusions too rapidly in this regard. Instead, one must study carefully the rubrical regulation of Christian liturgy as this developed and was enshrined in the missals and sacramentaries and ordinals.[175] As the sacramental liturgies, and particularly that of Eucharist, became more formalized the attitude towards rubrics also changed. Though it is not clear when and in what manner there came into existence the rubrical obsession that marked Roman Catholic sacramental liturgy until very recently, it is quite clear that in the early Middle Ages the rubrics contained in the missals were already viewed as regulations rather than simply as suggestions.[176] In twelfth- and thirteenth-century theologians one finds questions posed regarding the effect on the very reality of sacraments if rubrics are not followed.[177]

It is in this context that one must view the impact of the various liturgical books that issued from Rome. Their influence was widespread and critical in the historical evolution of Western liturgy.[178] Perhaps more than anything else they were responsible for the emergence of a relatively homogeneous Latin rite and the eventual domination by the Roman rite. Yet, throughout the Middle Ages these Roman ritual forms never replaced the cognate liturgical patterns of the various local churches, e.g., the endurance of the Sarum liturgy, or religious orders.[179]

It is to a large extent, then, in terms of developments connected with the papacy that one must study evolution in the notion of "priesthood" during the period between Nicaea and 1100. In the church immediately after Nicaea the word "*sacerdos*" (*hiereus*) has scarcely gained recognition as a legitimate term for Christian ministry. It is applied almost exclusively to bishops and seems to denominate only their liturgical function. One must indicate, though, the viewpoint contained in the *Didascalia*, where the possession of priesthood by the bishops is seen as the source of didactic, prophetic, and regal authority. On the contrary, in the Latin (and increasingly Romanized) church of Gregory VII the term "*sacerdotium*" refers to the entire spiritual aspect of human society's regulation and activation, paralleling the *regnum* which handles the material aspect. In the East, an equally drastic though different development occurred, a development that can be seen clearly by examining Justinian's position on *sacerdotium* (*hierarchia*?) and *imperium* (*basileia*) and the antecedents and consequents of this position.

To help make intelligible this highly complex evolution of thought, and at the same time preserve theological accuracy in dealing with it, we might single out ten key spokesmen: Ambrose, Chrysostom, and Leo I (from the period of the great early councils); Gelasius, Justinian, and Gregory I (coinciding roughly with the sixth century); Nicholas I and Hincmar of Reims (from the Carolingian period); and finally Gregory VII.

Ambrose

While Dudden's insistence that Ambrose inaugurates the new relation between church and state that will characterize the Middle Ages seems to be an overstatement,[180] there is no question but that one can see a new social equality of ecclesiastical and civil rulers, each group functioning in its own sphere. There is a certain overlap in the practice of bishops serving as both ecclesiastical and civil magistrates, but Ambrose saw this as accidental to the episcopal office and complained of its imposition on his more properly spiritual tasks.[181]

Strictly speaking, the tasks of the bishop lay in the spiritual order, and Ambrose uses the term "priestly" in referring to these tasks. He does apply the term "*sacerdos*" to presbyters, and grants that they can be liturgical celebrants and even occasionally preach.[182] However, in his day "*sacerdos*" is still used properly of the bishop, and Ambrose conforms to this usage.[183] Though in one passage he says that the principal task of the priest is to see to the care of the church building,[184] his own episcopal activity as the principal priest

of the church of Milan dealt primarily with people: "In the fourth century, a bishop of Milan had many tasks to keep him occupied. He regularly assisted at the prayers of the faithful in the church. He had the principal role in the celebration of the Eucharist. He had to see that the catechumens were properly instructed for baptism, and he had to correct, assist, and console the penitents."[185] He also had to superintend the charities of his church, provide for the defense of the oppressed, and provide for the discipline of his clergy.[186]

Thus, the role of the *sacerdotium*, emanating from the bishop who is *the* priest, is seen quite exclusively in terms of formally religious activity. It does involve judgment in the activities of preaching, dealing with penitents, admitting candidates to baptism, and directing the clergy. The bishop is judge of his people, and is beyond judgment by them.[187] Unquestionably, Ambrose's own preaching contained judgment upon the morality of the nonecclesiastical world of his day. The affair with Theodosius is a clear example. And he states explicitly that Valentinian *as a layman* in the church has no right to pass judgment on the episcopacy;[188] but as yet he does not raise the question of the manner in which the *office* and *secular authority* of the civil ruler relates to the structures and activity of the church.

Chrysostom

Ambrose's contemporary, Chrysostom, seems at first glance to have been more deeply involved in the *sacerdotium/imperium* dialectic. His own constant conflict, once he became patriarch of Constantinople, with the imperial court, and his eventual exile and death seem to parallel the later career of Gregory VII. Then, too, his use of the body/ soul analogy when speaking of the relative dignity of ecclesiastical and civil authority sounds very much like the later papal descriptions of the *sacerdotium* as the "soul" of the *societas christiana*.[189]

Yet, as one examines the case more closely, it appears that Chrysostom's attitude towards the imperial authorities at Constantinople focused on the manner in which they (and particularly the empress Eudoxia) were a cause of scandal to the Christian community over which Chrysostom had pastoral responsibility. Certainly, when faced with the Byzantine court's attempts to depose him, John opposed this as an illegitimate interference of the civil power; but the very fact that his deposition by Arcadius in 403 was supposedly based on the Synod of the Oak and his exile under Eudoxia in 404 was justified on a technicality connected with the first deposition tended to obfuscate the issues. It could not be viewed purely as a conflict of temporal and ecclesiastical authorities; rather, it was disguised as an ecclesiastical procedure.[190]

Indeed, as one reflects on the dramatic situation when John was still at Antioch which followed upon the antiimperial rioting and dishonoring of the emperor's statue at Antioch, and upon the statements of Chrysostom on that occasion, one is aware that the attitude is not that of the classic *imperium/sacerdotium* controversy. Of course, the Antiochean patriarch Flavian (and Chrysostom, who was acting as his adviser) were representing a guilty and petitioning Antiochean populace.[191] However, the difference in tone between their words to Theodosius and the words addressed some years earlier by Ambrose to this same Theodosius is quite striking. And, in the third of his sermons preached to the people of Antioch during the critical days of Flavian's embassy to the emperor, Chrysostom tries to encourage the populace to trust in the patriarch's mission by assuring them that Flavian is also "a prince, indeed at a level superior to that of the kings of this world. . . . The priesthood is indeed royalty, the priest is a king." But immediately he goes on to indicate that all his power is a strictly spiritual and persuasive power, that the patriarch's justice and truth and goodness will make him irresistible to the emperor.[192] At its best, Chrysostom's position is like that of Ambrose, for Chrysostom, too, insists that the emperor must petition heaven through the priest and not vice-versa.[193]

Leo I

With Leo I, one is clearly in a more advanced stage of the discussion about the relation between *sacerdotium* and *imperium*, a stage at which one is now aware of competing jurisdictions.[194] Some years earlier, in 422, Boniface I had joined the notion of *"principatus"* to the apostolic see,[195] but, as Ullmann points out, it was with Leo I that "this monarchic form of government was given its permanent theoretical fixation."[196]

Basing his viewpoint on the grant of authority to Peter, Leo I speaks of his own exercise of *principatus*. True, the possessor of this power to rule is Peter himself, for the power of the keys was given directly to Peter and never withdrawn. But Leo acts as Peter's vicar, and in this capacity lays claim to genuine sovereignty.[197] An indication that Leo's use of *"principatus"* was not accidental, and that the implications were perceived by the emperors of his day, is the fact that the imperial documents assiduously avoid adopting the Roman usage and reserve *"principatus"* to designate the imperial sovereignty.[198]

One could, though, question whether the developing emphasis on sovereignty in Leo's thinking about the Roman episcopate was linked with his understanding of priesthood. Certainly, we could not say that he sees such sovereignty as intrinsic to priesthood, for in one of his letters he applies the *dignitas officii sacerdotalis* to presbyters and even to deacons,[199] and it seems quite clear that he did not see them as sharing sovereignty. But, like his contemporaries, his principal and proper use of *"sacerdos"* was to the bishops and here one finds *"rector," "antistes," "pontifex,"* and *"sacerdos"* as practically interchangeable terms for the bishop.[200] Thus, Leo can lay claim to *principatus* not because he (along with others) belongs to the *sacerdotium*[201] but because he is in a unique position in this priestly body. He is the vicar, the embodied presence as it were, of Peter who is the source of the entire *sacerdotium*; hence, all ruling power in the church passes through him.

While it may sound like a pedantic subtlety to make such a distinction, it does seem important to indicate that Leo I claims the primacy not for himself but for Peter.[202] He does not even claim it for the Roman see, in the sense that jurisdiction attaches properly to the office of Roman bishop as such. Rather, the underlying authority seems to be that granted personally to Peter by Christ, and Leo appeals to Matthew 16:18 in this context.[203] In the practical order, however, such distinctions make little difference. Leo I and his successors feel that they not only may but, as vicars of Peter, must use the *principatus* granted by Christ to the prince of the apostles. Whether monarchical power is properly and immediately theirs, or whether it abides more properly with Peter and beyond that with Christ himself, they act as monarchs and demand that their actions be accepted as authoritative.

Gelasius

Gelasius died just before the beginning of the sixth century, leaving his statements on imperial and ecclesiastical power as an ambiguous heritage to future generations. Gregory I is the last pope of that century, and the emperor Justinian who ruled from 527 to 565 dominated almost half of that century. Thus, a look at their views on *sacerdotium* and *imperium* should give us some insight into the evolution of those two notions. Even before becoming pope, Gelasius had given expression to his views on the imperial status (in his two tractates on the Acacian schism).[204] As pope, most of Gelasius' statements about priestly and imperial authority are made in the context of his disputes with the emperor Anastatius I. It was in a letter to this emperor that Gelasius makes his famous statement about the world being governed by the sacred authority (*auctoritas*) and the royal power (*potestas*).[205]

Whether or not Gelasius intended these two realities to be distinguished according to the old Roman understanding, in which "*auctoritas*" referred to the traditional prestige of certain established groups and "*potestas*" des-

ignated effective political power, the Byzantine court would very likely have understood Gelasius' usage in this way.[206] And the Gelasian claim, understood this way, should have caused the emperor no distress, for all true sovereignty attached to *potestas*. However, Gelasius' usage was not consistent. In his treatise *De anathematis vinculo*, speaking of Christ (who himself was both priest and king) as separating for the future the two roles, he parallels the two as powers (*officia utriusque potestatis*).[207] At this point, the door is open to all the controversy as to which *potestas* is superior and which derives from which. The impression that Gelasius intended the "*sacra auctoritas*" to imply more than eminent moral prestige, and that his use of "*potestas*" for the pope has implications of some genuine sovereignty, is strengthened by the manner in which he uses the term "*principatus.*" At the Roman synod of 495 (where, incidentally, Gelasius was the first pope publicly acclaimed as "vicar of Christ"[208]) Gelasius says that the apostolic see holds, by way of delegation from Christ, the sovereignty of the entire church (*totius ecclesiae principatum*).[209] It is quite clear that this is a spiritual *principatus*, one that is rooted in the power of the keys granted to Peter. Even though the emperor himself, as a Christian, is subordinate to the pope (significantly, Gelasius seems to take for granted the usage by which he refers to the emperor as "my son"), there is no indication that Gelasius sees the imperial power as in any way derivative from himself or as such under his control. On the other hand, and this was a definite challenge to Byzantine imperial claims, he denies to any secular ruler the title "*sacerdos.*"[210]

However one interprets the Gelasian usage of "*auctoritas*," "*potestas*," and "*principatus*,"[211] it seems quite clear that with Gelasius one can very correctly speak about the jurisdiction of the Roman see, even though this be "spiritual jurisdiction." The notion of officially effective judgment has become permanently a basic element in the idea of episcopal function; those who are preeminently effective in the church's dispensation of salvation are so because they are rulers. One cannot agree with Batiffol that it was Gelasius who "consecrated the word *principatus*,"[212] for Leo I had already done that. However, Gelasius may well be the one whom we credit with the attribution of *"principatus"* to the *office* of Roman bishop.

Gregory I

More flexible by disposition and seasoned by long diplomatic experience, particularly his long term as papal representative at the Byzantine court, Gregory I deals more discreetly with the imperial power. Even with other patriarchal sees, he is not as insistent as some of his predecessors on his primatial prerogatives. Yet, though it is not a pretentious title and though Gregory no doubt sincerely felt himself "servant" of his fellow Christians, the use of *"servus servorum Dei"* is in its own subtle way a claim to episcopal preeminence.[213] Moreover, Gregory clearly continued the Roman claim to *principatus*. In his dealings with the Latin Christian sphere, even with secular rulers, he was not loath to exercise this sovereignty. Basically, he stands in the line that leads from Leo and Gelasius to Gregory VII and Innocent III.[214]

Much of Gregory's own activity was that of a ruler, even to the extent of administering the considerable temporal possessions of the Roman see.[215] But what is more important for our purposes is the manner in which his most formal explanation of the episcopal office (in his *Pastoral Care*) utilizes *"rector"* as its most common designation for the bishop. And the jurisdictional overtones of this term become evident when the faithful are referred to as "subjects" (*subditi*). True, this governance of the bishop over his people was to be paternal; Gregory (himself a monk and biographer of Benedict) was strongly influenced by the ideal of monastic life and introduced much of the monastic outlook into his thinking about the *sacerdotium*.[216]

Gregory I did not contribute much, if anything, to the developing papal theory of hierocratic rule. However, he is the instrument that is uniquely effective in transmitting to the Middle Ages the rather highly developed thought that he himself had inherited. In pastoral theory, his *Pastoral Care* is the Vademecum for medieval bishops and priests. In conscience direction and the development of moral theology his *Moralia* are unparalleled in their influence. And because of his strongly legalist mentality, his various decrees form a substantial contribution to the developing body of canonical texts.

While Gregory was a gifted ruler and organizer, saw such activities as proper to his particular episcopal role in Rome, and looked upon spiritual ruling as basic to the *sacerdotium* (at least in its episcopal level), his *Pastoral Care* would indicate that he saw the focus of this ruling to lie in preaching. Moreover, this clear emphasis on the religious aspect of "ruling" found expression also in Gregory's involvement in liturgical developments.[217]

Thus, ministry of word and sacrament dominate Gregory's understanding of the function of the *sacerdotium*; such ministry is the contribution sine qua non of the priesthood to the *societas christiana*.

Justinian

If late patristic popes (such as Gelasius, Symmachus, and Gregory) introduce us into a view which sees human society, at least in the West, as a *societas christiana* over which king and pope rule with complementary power, Justinian presents the Byzantine alternative, a fully detailed plan for a Christian people that is unified, governed, and led to salvation by an absolute monarch-priest-theologian. For Justinian, who epitomizes the imperial theology that prevailed in Constantinople over the centuries, the *basileus* is the single figure at the head of Christian society. It is this sacred imperial personage who is the vicar of God among men; it is he who is the living embodiment of the divine will—and therefore himself above all human laws and institutions.[218]

In such a view the *imperium* lays claim to all *auctoritas*, *potestas*, and *principatus*. If other agencies, and specifically the *sacerdo-*

tium, exercise authority and power, they do so in subordinate fashion. Justinian himself took all this quite seriously, watching over the orthodoxy of doctrine (in which watchfulness he caused no end of confusion), the formation and selection and moral rectitude of the clergy, and the smooth functioning of ecclesiastical institutions. This he did because God had entrusted to him the care of human society in its totality; and because the spiritual health of this society was of paramount importance, he was especially concerned for the effective functioning of the church's ordained priesthood. It is this view of the all-powerful *basileus*, who uses the *sacerdotium* as his instrument in providing for the people, that is enshrined in the code of law that bears his name.[219]

Granted that the priests (both bishops and presbyters) were in a position subordinate to that of the *imperium*, what (in Justinian's world) were they to do for the salvation of men and in support of the imperial rule? Briefly put, they were to see to it that the people became truly Christian, an objective that ranked uppermost on the emperor's scale of values. This obviously meant that they were to instruct the faithful in sound doctrine. Ministry of the word was a primary concern, but it seems to give way somewhat to "ministry of the temple"—the priests are to see to it that the church to which they are attached is carefully tended, that the spiritual needs of their flock are provided for by regular liturgical services, and that they themselves pray constantly to win God's favor for the emperor and his people. "The business of clerics is the service (*leitourgia*) of God."[220] When the legislation forbids bishops to migrate to the capital and insists that they remain in their own home situation, the reason given is that they are meant to provide for proper worship of God in their churches.[221] After all, it would be incongruous if the pious faithful would flock to church to sing psalms and the clerics, who are ordained for this, would avoid doing so.[222] Priests (and deacons also) should be involved in prayer and fasting for men's salvation, and

should not mix in profane things.[223] This does not mean, however, that the clergy are not active in such things as works of mercy; just the opposite was the case. Besides, under Justinian and even more so under some of his successors there was considerable utilization of bishops in public administration.[224] In the last analysis, though, the emphasis on the sacral, cultic role of the *sacerdotium* is quite pronounced in the Justinian view.

Nicolas I

In Charlemagne, Latin Christianity had its *basileus*. In his own view (and in that of his courtiers) king and father, lord and priest, the governor of all Christians is charged with the care of the *civitas Dei*. Charlemagne so dominated his own lifetime that no real challenge to his interference in ecclesiastical matters was made. But scarcely a half-century after Charlemagne's coronation the notion of the one *imperium* was dead;[225] the papal claims were once more expressed by Nicolas I in his controversy with Lothar II (over the latter's attempts to divorce his wife Theutberga), in his quarrels with Hincmar of Reims, and in his unhappy handling of the "Photian affair."

Polemical discourse tends towards exaggeration, and since almost everything Nicolas said or wrote was in a polemical context, one might be tempted to take his statements with a grain of salt; it is difficult to find more absolutist statements of papal authority within the church. However, these views became part of the heritage of papal canonical tradition and were cited in the controversies of later centuries.[226] Moreover, Nicolas' own actions in excommunicating Archbishop John of Ravenna, bringing Lothar and the German bishops who backed him to heel, in imposing his own claims to jurisdiction upon Hincmar of Reims, and in condemning and "deposing" Photius indicate that he took seriously his own papal theology; they form part of the precedent of strong and forceful papal action. Whether these actions were justified by prudence and even (in some instances) by then-existent canon law is another question.[227] What is important is that these exercises of papal *power* (for circumstances allowed Nicolas to impose his will in these instances at least in the West) became part of the tradition of papal "authority."

Actually, in his theory of *sacerdotium/imperium* relationships Nicolas adheres quite closely to the Gelasian distinction. He made no claims to rightful interference in the affairs of civil government and did enter into controversy with civil rulers only when he felt that they as his subjects in the church were a public scandal. Within the church Nicolas' claims were absolute. Rome is the "mother church" and the pope the father for all Christians.[228] More than that, Rome is the epitome and source of all Christianity.[229] Nicolas both claimed and exercised the right of dealing directly with any member of the church. He deposed the highest-ranking bishops without any reference to episcopal courts or synods. In the Latin church, the force of circumstances (and some help from the Pseudo-Isidorean collection) made it possible for Nicolas to implement his claims, even though he met with bitter opposition from bishops like Hincmar. In his dealings with Constantinople it was a different matter. Nicolas' claims were absolute enough and his denial of Photius' position unmistakable; but the Byzantine Empire went its own way despite Rome, and the pontificate of Nicolas marks one of the key stages in the schism between East and West.[230]

Hincmar of Reims

Sharply opposed though he was to the sovereign ecclesiastical claims of the papacy (specifically Nicolas I), Hincmar himself provided some of the most important theoretical support for the developing papal theology. In exposing his views on the relative positions and functions of *sacerdotium* and *regnum*, Hincmar was thinking primarily of the corporate episcopate or of any individual bishop who found himself in conflict with the civil power. Papal theorists could use the same line of reasoning in claiming eminence for the pope.

John Scotus Erigena had just translated Pseudo-Dionysius Areopagita and Hincmar draws from these writings the picture of a completely ordered hierarchical society. With this he combined the notion of obedience as expressed by Gregory I: though men were basically equal, in the actual situation of life some were meant to be superiors and others subordinate to them; obedience was the acceptance of this order according to which the will of God was accomplished.[231] Thus, in civil society the king is placed in a position of eminence and all owe him obedience; he is the Lord's anointed, and his appointed task is to dispense justice to all.[232]

Apparently this set the king on a rung above the bishops, but such was not really the import of Hincmar's thinking. As he saw things, the consecrator is clearly superior to the consecrated; so, the bishop who anoints the king must be in some fashion above the king. More basically, the king was dependent upon the teaching of the episcopacy in his decisions about justice, for it was to them that the divine teaching about justice was committed.[233] The king was bound to exercise justice as the episcopacy understood it. At this point, one can see how the ministry of the word, particularly as that had been interpreted by Gregory I in terms of a *rector* admonishing his Christian *subditi*, becomes the basis for the claim of the *sacerdotium* to ultimate control of human society. Everyone, including the king, must follow their directives, for they speak on behalf of God.

Within the structures of church authority, Hincmar was a constant champion of the rights and sovereignty of regional bishops under their metropolitan; he resisted bitterly the effort of Rome to centralize all jurisdiction in the apostolic see. Though he recognized a primacy of Rome, Hincmar saw this Roman authority as something that was meant to function within the framework of the ancient law that governed the relationships of higher ecclesiastics.[234] This is not the place to discuss the validity of the conflicting canonical claims made by Hincmar and Nicolas. What is important for our theological purposes is the obvious assumption of both parties that exercise of jurisdiction is intrinsic to the episcopal function—they disputed only as to which of them had jurisdiction in a given instance.

Gregory VII

The claim to supreme power that is latent in the ecclesiastical role of teaching authoritatively about the truth and justice that should guide society, a claim that was made for the episcopacy by Hincmar, is made explicit in the late eleventh century by Gregory VII. In his case, obviously, the claim is made for the papal office. A few months after his election as pope he wrote to the people of Lombardy, "I have been placed in this position in order to proclaim truth and justice to all the world, especially to Christians, whether I wish to or not."[235] He, the pope, is to decide what constitutes truth and justice, and the temporal power exists to carry out his directives.[236]

In his famous letter of 1080 to Herimann of Metz[237] and in the *Dictatus Papae*[238] the statement of absolute papal supremacy is clear and insistent. The Roman see is of divine origin; only the pope is universal pontifex, only he can depose or reconcile bishops or transfer them from one see to another, only he can make new laws as the needs of the church require. He can judge all, even to the point of deposing the emperor, but he himself is above judgment. When one turns from these bold statements of the *Dictatus Papae* to the letter to Herimann there is a more pastoral tone. Because the power of the keys, which as Peter's vicar he exercises, extends to all men (even the king), the pope must be shepherd of all. Thus all must acknowledge his shepherding power and concern, for consciously to reject it is to range oneself among the damned. Moreover, since Rome is the "mother church" and the "head" of the entire church, her teachings and judgments are to be reverently accepted. There is no possibility of appeal from the judgment of Rome.[239]

Histories of the eleventh century generally give ample attention to Gregory's conflicts with the temporal power and his claim to superiority over all secular rulers. The bases for this were already established in earlier papal texts and actions: since the *sacerdotium* is the "soul" of the *societas christianae*, it is superior to the temporal power as is the soul to the body;[240] the pope is subject to judgment only by God;[241] the pope's jurisdiction dealt with the salvation of men's souls (including that of the king) which is an objective obviously superior to the purposes of the secular rule.

However, it is Gregory VII's attitudes and actions vis-à-vis his fellow bishops that chiefly concern us in this study, because it is this which reflects even more clearly the view of *sacerdotium* (or at least the papal view) in the late eleventh century. Gregory's reign as pope marks a clear erosion of the bishops' authority: his revocation of traditional rights of metropolitans (even beyond what Nicolas I had done with Hincmar and others), his interference in diocesan matters, and his increasing use of special papal legates to implement his policy in various regions were some of the ways in which he expressed his claim to universal jurisdiction.[242] Only the pope can depose bishops, a clear indication of his superior authority, because the power to depose is greater than the power to ordain.[243] It does not seem an exaggeration to say that Gregory saw himself as heading a spiritual battle against the forces of evil; he is commander-in-chief of the *ecclesia militans* and the bishops are the chief lieutenants in implementing the papal policy and discharging the pope's universal responsibility.[244] The source of such far-reaching authority is, of course, the power of the keys which passes through Peter to the other apostles, and so also through the vicar of Peter and the apostolic see to the successors of the other apostles.[245] So, from the pope to all the other members of the *sacerdotium* flows the power to save men: to snatch them from evil's power in baptism, to fortify them for their adult conflicts with evil through confirmation, to provide for them the body and blood of Christ (the loftiest power in Christianity!), to bind and loose.[246] Interestingly, there seems to be comparatively little emphasis on preaching as act of salvation. Perhaps because of the social circumstances and the precise needs of the moment, the stress is laid upon the exercise of "spiritual jurisdiction"; *sacerdotium* has more to do with kingship than it does with prophecy.

NOTES

1. See F. Kempf, *Handbook of Church History* (New York, 1969), vol. 3, pp. 221–24.

2. *Sacramentarium Veronense* (text given by D. Power, *Ministers of Christ and His Church* [London, 1969], p. 195).

3. To call lay investiture an aberration is not to suggest that participation of the laity in the selection of bishops and presbyters is an aberration; rather, such lay involvement in the choice of their ministers was (as we will see) the ancient tradition.

4. For a brief review of the process by which the church came to be viewed in civil forms, see P. Eyt, "Vers une église démocratique," *Nouvelle revue théologique* 91 (1969), pp. 600–604.

5. See J. Gaudemet, *L'Eglise dans l'Empire Romain* (Paris, 1958), pp. 9–47.

6. See H. Leclercq, *Dictionnaire d'archéologie chrétienne et de liturgie* (Paris, 1903ff.), vol. 15, cols. 1427–31. By the fourth century there is explicit teaching that the apostolic office is the source of all Christian ministry. Chrysostom, for example, sees the power of the apostles as the source of all other powers in the church—prophet, healing, governing, teaching, etc. The apostolic charism contains all the other charisms and is superior to them. (*De util. lect. script.* 3.)

7. So, for example, Leo I (*Sermo* 3. 2): ". . . Etsi multis pastoribus curam suarum ovium delegavit ipse [i.e., Christ] tamen dilecti gregis custodiam non reliquit."

8. See Gaudemet, pp. 330–41; A. Dumas, Fliche-Martin, *Histoire de l'Eglise* (Paris, 1935—), vol. 7, pp. 190–98.

9. See Y. Congar, *L'ecclésiologie du Haut Moyen Age* (Paris, 1968), pp. 114–15.

10. See Dumas, pp. 198–211; E. Voosen, *Papauté et pouvoir civil à l'époque de Grégoire VII* (Gembloux, 1927), p. 11.

11. See J. Dudden, *The Life and Times of St. Ambrose* (Oxford, 1935), vol. 1, pp. 66–74.

12. See Dumas, p. 192. There was, however, no universal pattern; the Justinian Code, for example (*C.I.* 1. 3. 41), prescribes that "a vote by the persons inhabiting the said city should be taken concerning three persons . . . so that from these the most suitable should be selected for the episcopate."

13. See F. Van der Meer, *Augustine the Bishop* (London, 1961), pp. 270–73.

14. See Gaudemet, p. 332.

15. On the origin and role of the *cardinales* in Rome, see K. Morrison, *New Catholic Encyclopedia* (New York, 1967), vol. 3, pp. 104–5; Dumas, pp. 154–59.

16. See Gaudemet, p. 333.

17. For example, Basil's appointment of Gregory of Nazianzus to the see of Sasima.

18. As with Charlemagne, this interference often consisted in direct appointment of bishops by the civil ruler; see D. Knowles, *The Christian Centuries* (London, 1969), vol. 2, pp. 32–33.

19. On the beginnings of this Roman influence on the appointment of bishops, see Gaudemet, pp. 333–34.

20. The dispute over lay investiture reflects the change that has taken place in the notion of ecclesiastical office. The office in question, whether that of bishop or pastor or abbot, was viewed largely in terms of its social and economic aspects and so regarded as something that should fit into the feudal structure of fiefs and benefices. See Kempf, pp. 270–79.

21. See Dumas, pp. 198–211.

22. This is clearly, sometimes tragically, illustrated by the role played by Byzantine emperors in the doctrinal disputes of the post-Chalcedonian period.

23. See Gaudemet, pp. 338–41.

24. The synod of Riez (439) does nullify a consecration in which there were only two consecrating bishops; but there were other "irregularities" as well—lack of consenting letters from other bishops of the province, lack of accord from the metropolitan, etc. On the other hand, the Irish practice until well into the Middle Ages was for a single bishop to function as episcopal consecrator.

25. *De eccl. unitate* 5.

26. See B. Botte, "Collegiate Character of the Presbyterate and Episcopate," *The Sacrament of Holy Orders* (Collegeville, Minn., 1962), pp. 75–97; also, Power, pp. 53–88.

27. For an interesting discussion of the relationship between the ceremonies of consecration and installation of a bishop, see W. Telfer, *The Office of a Bishop* (London, 1962), pp. 187–208. Separation of these two actions, clearly apparent in the case of consecrating an auxiliary bishop or in the transfer of a bishop from one see to another, raises basic questions about the nature of episcopacy: "Is it essentially the possession of more power (which the consecration of an auxiliary seems to indicate) or is it the leadership of a community (which the installation ceremony stresses)?

28. See Dumas, pp. 220–22; Kempf, pp. 258–79.

29. On the canonical discussions relative to the rights and role of the bishop-designate, a matter that was complicated by the early-medieval absorption of the episcopal office into the feudal structures, see R. Benson, *The Bishop-Elect* (Princeton, 1968).

30. The shift in the symbolism of the *cathedra*, from its earlier connection with preaching and liturgical leadership to the later accretion of reference to monarchical jurisdiction, reflects the shift in thought about the episcopal office. On the early history of the episcopal *cathedra*, see H. Leclercq, vol. 3, cols. 19–75.

31. See R. Beraudy, "Les effets de l'ordre dans les préfaces d'ordination du Sacramentaire Leonien," *La tradition sacerdotale* (Le Puy, 1959), pp. 81–94.

32. *Ibid.*, pp. 94–97.

33. See Congar, pp. 138–51.

34. In the non-Roman stream of thought, which was largely grounded in Cyprian's view as transmitted through Isidore, the episcopal authority was grounded in the grant given to Peter (Matt. 16:18), but this grant was seen as extended to the other apostles who then have equal power. "In Novo autem Testamento post Christum sacerdotalis ordo a Petro coepit. Ipsi enim primum datus est pontificatus in Ecclesia Christi. . . . Ille ergo ligandi solvendique potestatem primus accepit, primusque ad fidem populum virtute suae praedicationis adduxit; siquidem et caeteri apostoli cum Petro pari consortio honoris et potestatis effecti sunt, qui etiam in toto orbe dispersi Evangelium praedicaverunt." (Isidore *De eccles. officiis* 2. 5. 5.)

35. See Dumas, pp. 179–86.

36. *Cod. Theod.* 1. 27. 1.

37. See J. Daniélou and H. Marrou, *The Christian Centuries* (London, 1964), vol. 1, pp. 244–46.

38. See Gaudemet, pp. 230–33.

39. The obvious lack of precision regarding the nature and limits of episcopal and civil judicial power became apparent soon after Constantine, and a series of imperial decrees made more specific the area of recognized episcopal judgment; see *ibid.*, pp. 233–40. This post-Constantinian legislation laid greater stress on the bishop's role as a conciliator in disputed cases.

40. Probably the most disputed case is that of Cyprian, with much of the dispute focusing on the variant text traditions for *De ecclesiae unitate* 4 (see Quasten, *Patrology* [Westminster, Md., 1950], vol. 2, p. 352); however, even the "longer version" of this work seems to point to the symbolic function of Peter's primacy—he is the sign of

the episcopal unity—rather than to any jurisdictional superiority. The text states that it is Christ who extends to the other apostles the power he had first given to Peter; as a result they have the same status and power: "Hoc erant utique et ceteri apostoli quod fuit Petrus, pari consortio praediti et honoris et potestatis. . . ."

41. As, e.g., the correspondence between the two Dionysiuses (of Rome and Alexandria); see *ibid.*, pp. 239–41.

42. As already indicated (see above, nn. 34, 40), both Cyprian and Isidore of Seville (who is a key link between Cyprian and medieval theology) insist that the other apostles had equal position and authority with Peter.

43. See G. Glez, *Dictionnaire de théologie catholique*, vol. 13, cols. 276–94.

44. However, one must be careful not to read too much into this conciliar statement. There is considerable evidence that indicates that it was a somewhat hollow gesture that was contradicted by the council's rejection of practically all of Leo's instructions for the council. See K. Morrison, *Tradition and Authority in the Western Church* (Princeton, 1969), pp. 66–68. For an Orthodox study of the evidence for papal primacy in the fourth and fifth centuries, see J. Meyendorff, "La Primauté romaine dans la tradition canonique jusqu'au concile de Chalcédoine," *Istina* 4 (1957), pp. 463–82.

45. Isidore of Seville, for example, despite his great admiration and respect for Gregory I, gives no indication that he thinks his own episcopal authority to be derivative from or dependent upon the pope.

46. See F. Dvornik, *Early Christian and Byzantine Political Philosophy* (Dumbarton Oaks, 1966), vol. 2, pp. 804–9.

47. *Epist.* 5. 43: ". . . Si unus patriarcha universalis dicitur, patriarcharum nomen caeteris derogatur."

48. W. Ullmann (*New Catholic Encyclopedia*, vol. 10, p. 954) sees Gregory I, without conceding the theoretical claims of Roman primacy, turning pragmatically to the West and laying the foundations for papal dominance of Latin medieval Christianity.

49. Charlemagne himself pays constant tribute to the normative position of the Roman church (see W. Ullmann, *Growth of Papal Government in the Middle Ages* [London, 1955], pp. 110–11), but still asserts his authority over the episcopacy. In writing to Ghaerbaldus, bishop of Liege, he addresses him ". . . Ghaerbaldo episcopo cum universis tibi omnipotente Deo et nostra ordinatione commissis in Domino salutem" (*Capitularia* 1, p. 245; cited by E. Amann, in A. Fliche and V. Martin, *Histoire de l'Eglise depuis les origines jusqu'à nos jours* [Paris, 1935—], vol. 6, p. 82, n. 2). On Charlemagne's theocratic understanding of his own role, see Dvornik, vol. 2, pp. 848–49.

50. By the sixth century it is commonplace to consider the apostles as being the first bishops; for example, the Justinian Code (1. 3. 41) speaks of the apostles as having "accepted the episcopate from the Lord Christ our God."

51. See Congar, pp. 131–86.

52. *Ibid.*, pp. 166–77.

53. See Kempf, pp. 367–92.

54. See Ullmann, pp. 359–446.

55. See Dvornik, pp. 848–50, on the manner in which the development of this pontifical theocracy intensified and crystallized the split between Latin and Byzantine Christianity.

56. See Leo I *Sermo.* 4. 4.

57. See Dumas, pp. 220–21.

58. So Gregory VII in his letter to Herimann (*Epist.* 21): "Quis, rogo, in hac universali concessione ligandi atque solvendi a potestate Petri se exclusum esse existimat, nisi forte infelix ille qui, jugum Domini portare nolens, diaboli se subjicit oneri, et in numero ovium Christi esse recusat?"

59. On the origin and evolution of the cult attached to such shrines (and their relics)

and of pilgrimages to these shrines, see M. McCarthy, *New Catholic Encyclopedia*, vol. 11, pp. 363–65, and E. Labande, *ibid.*, pp. 365–68.

60. On the legends attaching to the dioceses of France, including Tours, see Leclercq, vol. 8, cols. 2357–440.

61. See Dumas, pp. 179–84; he describes the two competing traditions regarding the establishment of the Gallican church: the one (espoused by Sulpicius Severus and Gregory of Tours) that sees a third-century origin and the other that defends an earlier apostolic origin.

62. On the Rome-oriented attitude of the English and German Christians in the early medieval period, see Congar, pp. 149–51; also Leclercq, vol. 14, cols. 40–65.

63. The conflict over ecclesiastical poverty was heightened in England because of the large holdings of the monastic establishments which, with the increasing influence of the Cluniac reform, tended to have relatively strong links with the papacy. See D. Knowles, *The Monastic Orders in England*, 2d ed. (Cambridge, 1963).

64. On Hincmar and Agobard, see F. Cayré, *Précis de patrologie*, vol. 2 (Paris, 1930), pp. 377–78.

65. However, it is not always clear, as in the case of Cyril of Alexandria, whether the action of a given bishop is one of appealing to collegial episcopal responsibility or one of rallying allies to his own position.

66. As, for example, with the ninth-century disputes on the Eucharist and on predestination; see E. Ewig, *Handbook of Church History*, vol. 3, pp. 160–63.

67. See Daniélou-Marrou, pp. 366–67.

68. See Ewig, p. 156.

69. See Kempf, pp. 380–85.

70. The case that is much more difficult to assess is that of Honorius I. That is, the extent of his assent to monothelitism and the significance of his subsequent condemnation by later popes and by the Sixth Ecumenical Council (at Constantinople, 680–81). For a summary of the discussion on Honorius, which because of its implications for the question of papal infallibility has been heatedly debated for centuries, see H. Beck, *New Catholic Encyclopedia*, vol. 7, pp. 124–25; and E. Amann, *Dictionnaire de théologie catholique*, vol. 7, cols. 93–132.

71. The canonical principle *"prima sedes a nemine iudicatur"* had been in existence since the early sixth century, and it was Alcuin who urged its observance in the case of Leo III; see Ewig, pp. 90–92.

72. In the earlier patristic period more of this clerical formation was provided personally by the bishop (as witnessed, e.g., by Ambrose's *De officiis*). As the church in the West became more dispersed into the countryside, an increasing portion of clerical supervision and formation was handled by the deanery structure. See Kempf, pp. 264–70.

73. See Van der Meer, pp. 225–34; F. Dudden, *Gregory the Great* (Oxford, 1905), vol. 1, pp. 363–401.

74. Such episcopal efforts to provide clerical training, developing into the cathedral schools which paralleled and sometimes rivaled the monastic schools as centers of learning, provided the roots out of which grew the European universities. See F. Powicke and A. Emden, H. Rashdall's *Universities of Europe* (Oxford, 1936), pp. 26–34.

75. See J. Jungmann, *Handbook of Church History*, vol. 3, pp. 308–11.

76. See Quasten, vol. 3, pp. 384–96.

77. See Kempf, p. 267. On the Carolingian association of the bishops with secular judicial power, see Dumas, pp. 222–25.

78. See Ewig, pp. 165–68.

79. See Gaudemet, p. 233.

80. On the adaptation of episcopal structures to emergent feudalism, see Dumas, pp. 220–49.

81. By the end of the Carolingian period, however, the position and power of the bishop has been legally clarified; see Kempf, pp. 269–79.

82. This was particularly true of the ecclesiastical court held in conjunction with the bishop's visitation of a parish; see Jungmann, pp. 309–11.

83. As early as the beginning of the fourth century, the regional synod was recognized as the tribunal to which lower clergy could appeal against a judgment of their own bishop; see Gaudemet, p. 371.

84. This is particularly true of reform councils, such as the one held at Aachen in 816 under Louis the Pious (see Ewig, pp. 106–7). But even the doctrinally oriented councils, such as Chalcedon, convey in their disciplinary actions a considerable insight into clerical life and activity. For the disciplinary decrees of these councils, see H. Schroeder, *Disciplinary Decrees of the General Councils* (St. Louis, 1937).

85. Most of this would be handled during the episcopal visitation of the parish; however, a good part of this visitation was devoted to inspecting and arranging the economic aspects of the parish. On the complicated situation regarding parish property, income, and management as these related to bishop, secular lord, monastery, etc., in the early Middle Ages, see Dumas, pp. 265–90.

86. See Van der Meer, pp. 225–34.

87. Such judgment was on occasion directed against the highest levels of the laity, as Ambrose's action against Theodosius, or Nicolas I's condemnation of Lothar II; on the latter case, see Ewig, pp. 130–32.

88. See Congar, pp. 138–51; he points out how the power of the keys became increasingly the basic power connected with the *priesthood* of bishops and presbyters, even overshadowing to some extent (or perhaps more correctly subsuming) the power of Eucharistic consecration.

89. Though the three main currents of thought about episcopal and papal authority (Cyprian, Augustine, Leo) differed on the manner in which episcopal authority was related to the Petrine grant, all three grounded episcopal authority in this grant; see *ibid.*, pp. 138–46.

90. *Ibid.*, pp. 187–246.

91. For a listing of the works of these scholars (as well as many others), see the bibliographies at the beginning of chapters in B. Poschmann's *Penance and the Anointing of the Sick* (New York, 1964).

92. See *ibid.*, pp. 81–116; however, as Poschmann describes on pp. 110–13, there was an interesting and theologically significant exemption of clerics from the ordinary penitential discipline.

93. *Ibid.*, pp. 87–99.

94. *Ibid.*, pp. 97–98.

95. *Ibid.*, pp. 70–71.

96. *Ibid.*, p. 120.

97. In the West, the influence of Cassian (*Instit.* 4. 9) and the Benedictine *Rule* (4. 7) were paramount in establishing manifestation of conscience in religious life.

98. See Poschmann, pp. 96–99.

99. One reflection of this was the increasing tendency to grant Christian burial to sinners who had not gone through the public reconciliation; see *ibid.*, pp. 100–101.

100. On the earlier use of presbyters for handling the penitential discipline, see *ibid.*, pp. 97–98.

101. Poschmann (p. 98) sees this penitential ministry of presbyters as abruptly ceasing towards the end of the fourth century; however, Theodore of Mopsuestia bears witness to its continuation within at least one portion of the East. See Quasten, vol. 3, pp. 422–23; and G. Koch, *Die Heilsverwirklichung bei Theodor von Mopsuestia* (Munich, 1965), pp. 212–14.

102. See Poschmann, pp. 124–38. On private confession up to the time of Gregory I, see R. Mortimer, *The Origin of Private Penance* (Oxford, 1939).

103. Alcuin in his letter to the province of the Goths (*Epist.* 112) argues eloquently for

the salvific power of confessing, though he is speaking specifically of confession to a priest. On the practice of confessing to a layman, see Poschmann, pp. 141–42.

104. On the much-disputed question of Basil's inclusion of private confession in his *Rule*, see Quasten, vol. 3, pp. 234–36. In the West, a practice of ascetic confession of sins extended beyond monastic circles to pious laity; see Poschmann, pp. 120–22. However, in both situations (East and West) what seems to have been involved, at least in most instances, was the practice of manifestation of conscience to a spiritual father rather than the sacrament of penance.

105. Already in 589 the Third Synod of Toledo had found it necessary to decree a return to strict observance of the *exomologesis*.

106. See Congar, pp. 124–25.

107. See Poschmann, pp. 84–87.

108. The limitation of official penitential discipline, i.e., the formal *exomologesis*, to graver sins did not mean that there was no pastoral attention paid to the need for dedicated Christians to face their venial sins. Contrary to the contention of H. von Campenhausen (*Tradition and Life in the Church* [Philadelphia, 1968], pp. 138–39), there was not "exclusive attention paid to the struggle against gross sins by means of public ecclesiastical discipline," either during the patristic period or during the early Middle Ages. For a brief description of the variety of penitential practices in the patristic and early medieval church, see P. Anciaux, *The Sacrament of Penance* (New York, 1962), pp. 46–69.

109. *Ibid.*, pp. 49–52.

110. On the evolution of thought towards greater insistence on the priestly intervention, even in cases of lesser culpability, see Poschmann, pp. 147–49. Thus, as he points out (pp. 138–40), there is a noticeable move towards more frequent confession as something necessary.

111. On the implications of this move to mandatory confession of sins to a priest, see Ullmann, pp. 374–79. For one thing, it deemphasizes the healing role of the confessor (which Alcuin, for example, had stressed in his advocacy of confession to a priest) and lays greater stress on the officially effective power of the ordained; this will find even clearer expression in the thirteenth-century imposition of the indicative formula of absolution as mandatory.

112. This is not, of course, a new position: Chrysostom (to take but one example) insists unmistakably on the effective judgment of the confessor: "Priests can bind with a bond that pertains to the soul itself, and transcends the very heavens. Whatever priests do here on earth, God will confirm in heaven, just as the master ratifies the decisions of his servants." (*On the Priesthood* 3. 5.) At the same time, there is a strong tradition continuing as late as the eleventh century and appealing to texts of Jerome and Gregory I, which insists that the confessor's judgment is merely declarative of the judgment given by God. See P. Anciaux, *La théologie du sacrément de pénitence au XIIe siècle* (Louvain, 1949), pp. 39–41.

113. See pp. 61–127.

114. As in other aspects of theological thought, the early medieval centuries preserved and repeated the insights and formulations of the great patristic centuries (or at least a certain portion of those insights and formulations), particularly the heritage of Augustinian thought. So, the theological formulation of the episcopal office and function is largely repetition of the texts of Cyprian, Augustine, or Leo I.

115. As we indicate at the end of this chapter, there is a gradual shift of view (from Gelasius to Hildebrand) regarding the relationship between *imperium* and *sacerdotium*: what begins as a struggle to disengage priesthood from kingship, and so deny priesthood to the Byzantine emperors, ends with the claim that priesthood contains kingship in preeminent fashion.

116. Although argumentation is devised to justify such episcopal involvement in temporal affairs, as, for example, the use of the body/soul analogy to explain the relation of spiritual and secular power, the involvement preceded such theological reflection

and was basically a matter of response to concrete situations and needs. See Dumas, pp. 220–49. Another striking example of the manner in which concrete historical circumstances shape theoretical explanations of episcopal (or papal) authority is the shifting papal response to Byzantine political power from the fifth to seventh centuries; see Morrison, *Tradition and Authority*, pp. 77–152.

117. This was practically inevitable as there emerged, both in East and West, a Christian society in which the monarch saw himself as God's vicar who was charged with maintaining a truly Christian kingdom. See Dvornik, vol. 2, pp. 816–18, 848–49.

118. This became painfully evident during the iconoclast controversy; see H.-G. Beck, *Handbook of Church History*, vol. 3, pp. 26–48.

119. See Morrison, *Tradition*, pp. 205–91. One can sense the change in papal self-identity that has occurred if one compares, for example, the fourth of Leo I's sermons *De natali* (which speaks of the common kingliness and priesthood of all Christians, and of the abiding spiritual authority of Peter) with the *Dictatus papae* of Gregory VII.

120. Such a judgment would rest upon an understanding of the essential nature of the Roman primacy; it is not our purpose to propose and defend a position on this still-disputed point.

121. *Adv. Haer.* 3. 3. 2–3.

122. See Glez, cols. 276–302. As Congar has pointed out (p. 159), the emphasis until well into the medieval period was on the doctrinal rather than juridical primacy, and even this doctrinal authority was "plutôt une qualité religieuse que Rome doit au fait qu'elle est le lieu du martyre et du tombeau de Pierre et de Paul."

123. Significantly, as the attribute of primacy shifts from the church of Rome to the office of the pope the references to Paul as one of the fathers of the Roman church fade out and reference to Petrine authority becomes predominant. One of the few remnants of the older position is the annual liturgical celebration of the feast of Peter and Paul.

124. One of the critical questions that this early history raises is whether primacy attaches to the Roman church or to the pope. This question has once more come to the fore since Vatican II; see H.-M. Legrand, "Revaluation of Local Churches," *The Unifying Role of the Bishop*, vol. 17 of *Concilium*, ed. E. Schillebeeckx (New York, 1972), pp. 61–62.

125. However, see n. 44 (above) regarding the caution required in interpreting this conciliar acclaim of Leo I.

126. However, Innocent I had already claimed for the Roman see a wide range of authority, both in doctrinal and in disciplinary matters; see Gaudemet, pp. 440–41.

127. See C. Hefele and H. Leclercq, *Histoire des Conciles* (Paris, 1909), vol. 2, pp. 567–84.

128. However, he does not hesitate to intervene in disciplinary and jurisdictional matters when cases are appealed to him, as they quite frequently were. See Gaudemet, pp. 442–43.

129. See F. X. Murphy, *New Catholic Encyclopedia*, vol. 8, pp. 637–38.

130. *Sermo* 4. 4; see Gaudemet, p. 429.

131. This is true also of Gregory VII: "Gregory entirely operates with the Petrine commission; he does not say or imply that he was Christ-like or that he was Christ's vicar. . . . The Petrine commission was not yet conceived to constitute a vicariate of Christ." (Ullmann, p. 280.)

132. On the veneration of the tomb of Peter and the building of the Constantinian basilica, see E. Kirschbaum, *The Tombs of St. Peter and St. Paul* (New York, 1959).

133. See C. Duggan, *New Catholic Encyclopedia*, vol. 4, pp. 707–9.

134. See Congar, pp. 187–232.

135. See J. de Ghellinck, *Le mouvement théologique du XIIe siècle* (Bruxelles, 1948), pp. 62–65.

136. This letter, which is an excellent summary of Gregory VII's position, does argue from papal precedent, but the primary argument is drawn from the Petrine text:

because of the grant of authority given to Peter the authority of the Roman see is of divine origin and can be rejected only at the price of damnation.

137. Leo I (*Sermo* 3. 2): "Soliditas enim illius fidei, quae in apostolorum principe est laudata, perpetua est; et sicut permanet quod in Christo Petrus credidit, ita permanet quod in Petro Christus instituit. . . . Manet ergo dispositio veritatis, et beatus Petrus in accepta fortitudine petrae perseverans, suscepta Ecclesiae gubernacula non reliquit." Gregory VII (*Epist.* 21): "Numquid sunt hic reges excepti? Aut non sunt de ovibus quas Filius Dei B. Petro commisit? Quis, rogo, in hac universali concessione ligandi atque solvendi a potestate Petri se exclusum esse existimat, nisi forte infelix ille qui, jugum Domini portare nolens, diaboli se subjicit, et in numero ovium Christi esse recusat?"

138. See Ullmann, pp. 219–20; Congar, pp. 232–46.

139. See A. Fliche in Fliche-Martin, vol. 8, p. 62.

140. As described in the *De cura pastorali*, such admonition is the basic element in preaching, a clear indication of the extent to which preaching is directed to moral exhortation rather than doctrinal clarification. It is interesting that both Gregorys see themselves, the church, and all mankind beset with enemies. For Gregory I the principal imagery is medical (man is afflicted with wounds and disease, and so needs to be healed); for Gregory VII the principal imagery is military (man is engaged in a battle with the forces of evil, and so needs to be led in a crusade).

141. What helped support this was the continuing existence of a Holy Roman Emperor even though he did not reside in Rome. As we will describe later, the unifying symbolism of Rome continued to function in Europe until at least the sixteenth century.

142. See Knowles, *Christian Centuries*, vol. 2, pp. 61–79.

143. See E. Dublanchy, *Dictionnaire de théologie catholique*, vol. 7, cols. 1665–72.

144. See Hefele-Leclercq, pp. 567–84.

145. See Knowles, *Christian Centuries*, pp. 105–15.

146. Exactly what was the doctrinal position of the *Henoticon* is not clear. Certainly in the West it was considered heterodox, perhaps because of its derogatory references to Chalcedon, and it was given a definitely Monophysite interpretation by more than one Byzantine emperor or bishop; however, it was ambiguous enough that some bishops who subscribed to it remained in basic agreement with Chalcedon. See H. Marrou, *Christian Centuries*, vol. 1, pp. 357–58.

147. On Orange II, where the effective direction was provided by Caesarius of Arles, see C. Aherne, *New Catholic Encyclopedia*, vol. 10, p. 712.

148. See Ewig, pp. 158–63.

149. See Hefele-Leclercq, vol. 5, pp. 1040–55.

150. On the developing understanding of the idea of Rome's *cura omnium ecclesiarum*, see Congar, pp. 190–95.

151. The great reform synods during the Carolingian period did much to better the situation (see Ewig, pp. 70–78, 103–18), but the collapse of the Carolingian structures brought new problems for church discipline, problems which remained acute until the triumph of the Gregorian reforms in the late eleventh century.

152. See Fliche, pp. 63–83, 95–106.

153. There had been the exceptional case (in the dispute over the divorce of Lothar II) of Nicholas I's deposition (in 963) of the archbishops of Cologne and Trier; but this was recognized at that time as being an irregular canonical procedure and was implemented only because of the obviously weak moral position of the two prelates in their support of Lothar. See Ewig, pp. 130–32.

154. *Sermo* 5. 2.

155. One element that should come into our study at this point, if the material were available and manageable, is the role of the Roman see in the evolution of moral theology in the Latin church. One can, of course, point to certain obvious influences, such as the critical importance of Gregory I's *Commentary on Job*. However, much

of the development of moral instruction (listing of sins and their penalties, etc.) is connected with the history of the penitential books and of official reaction (generally quite negative) to their usage, and the role of Rome in this development is vague. See Poschmann, pp. 122–45; G. Le Bras, *Dictionnaire de théologie catholique*, vol. 12, cols. 1160–79.

156. See Ewig, pp. 130–32.

157. On the other hand, Dionysius of Alexandria served as a mediator between Rome and Antioch; see J. Daniélou, *Christian Centuries*, vol. 1, p. 210. And Irenaeus had intervened between Victor and the bishops of the East over the Easter issue; *ibid.*, pp. 105–7.

158. Rather, it seems to have been a case of seeking support from a respected and particularly important ally. However, it seems undeniable that the notion of Rome's primacy that was prevalent in the fourth and fifth centuries (and thereafter in the West) involved some idea of determinative judgment; even the twenty-eighth canon of Chalcedon implies this, otherwise its attempt to establish equal status for Constantinople would have been meaningless. See Congar, p. 159, who points out that as late as the ninth century understanding of Roman doctrinal primacy laid stress on the *exemplar* role of the faith of the Roman church.

159. See Marrou, pp. 425–26.

160. See Congar, pp. 190–91.

161. See Ullmann, p. 5, n. 4.

162. See Congar, pp. 191–205. W. Ullmann, *Medieval Papalism* (London, 1949), p. 58, points out how the principle enunciated by Nicholas I in a letter of 865 to Emperor Michael ("Jus habemus non solum monachos, verum etiam quoslibet clericos de quacumque diocesi, cum necesse fuerit, ad nos convocare") was later invoked by papal canonists to justify the pope's universal jurisdiction.

163. On the manner in which the Roman position gained importance in the canonical traditions and even acquired a certain precedence over patristic positions, see C. Munier, *Les sources patristiques du droit de l'Eglise du VIIe au XIIIe siècle* (Strasbourg, 1957), pp. 206–11.

164. Fortunately, this field of research has been blessed by a number of first-rate scholars (Le Bras, Munier, Gaudemet, de Ghellinck, Kuttner, Tierney—to name but a few); however, this study of legal institutions, though vast in itself, is but a part of the broader field of research into the sociological and anthropological aspects of Christian life and activity over the centuries.

165. One of the subtle but important aspects of this development is the basic understanding of law that acts as a presupposition for such an appeal to precedent. Though it would take a lengthy and much more careful study to prove or disprove the judgment, it does seem that this canonical tradition is grounded in a voluntaristic approach to law, one which sees the mind of the lawgiver as the ultimate ground for a law (and therefore also the ultimate criterion for its interpretation). This seems much more in accord with the kind of monarchical theory attached to the Byzantine *basileus* than it does with a theory that sees law as the expression of nature or with the ancient Roman tradition of law. See Dvornik, pp. 848–50.

166. In a sense, one can carry the evidence for a tradition of episcopal regulation of liturgy as far back as the Easter dispute between Victor and the bishops of the East (in the late second century); specific synodal regulations on liturgical practice are found already in fourth and fifth centuries (e.g., Carthage III, in 397, canon 23; or Mileve, in 417, canon 12). But it is in the Carolingian and post-Carolingian period, when there was a concerted effort to overcome the confusing diversity of liturgical practices, that one finds a much greater bulk of liturgical legislation.

167. *Smyrn.* 8. 2.

168. *Didache*, chaps. 7–10.

169. See Quasten, vol. 2, pp. 180–87.

170. Council of Arles (341), canons 8, 15–19; Council of Sardica (343), canon 15.

171. *De sacr.* 3. 1. 5.

172. However, Innocent I, Celestine I, and Vigilius did not hesitate to solve liturgical questions sent to them by inquiring bishops, and their responses reflect the attitude that in the West the Roman usage enjoyed some sort of normative role. See A. King, *Liturgy of the Roman Church* (London, 1957), pp. 438–42.

173. See Ewig, pp. 72–73.

174. Even though one finds some statements among early medieval writers that the popes should regulate liturgy (see King, p. 442), there was great diversity until the unifying reforms of Pius V in the sixteenth century, and prior to Trent the supervision of liturgical forms was still a matter of regional episcopal groups. See J. Jungmann, *Mass of the Roman Rite* (New York, 1951), vol. 1, pp. 92–138.

175. Incorporation of rubrical regulations into the sacramentaries and missals was very limited until more modern times, but there existed from as early as the eighth century collections of regulations, *ordines*, to direct the liturgical celebrations, and even prior to these there can be found collections of canons regulating the ritual for the sacraments. See King, pp. 181–83. However, beyond the existence of rubrics in the strict sense there was the direction of liturgical activity provided by the very structure of ceremonies contained in the sacramentaries, etc., and by the customs regarding liturgy that were transmitted (often orally) in less formal fashion.

176. On the emergence of the rubrical mentality with the reforms of Pius V, see Jungmann, *Mass*, pp. 141–42; and T. Klauser, *Orate Fratres* 23 (1948–49), pp. 154–60.

177. However, the rubrical directives in question touch upon the matter and form of the sacrament, for example, the discussion about the addition of water to the wine for Eucharistic consecration (see Peter Lombard *Sent.* 4. 11. 5).

178. See Jungmann, *Mass*, pp. 60–66; however, there is a tangled history of the Roman liturgical forms as they meet Gallican liturgies, mix with these liturgies, and then return to affect Rome's own liturgy. Jungmann traces this development, pp. 74–127.

179. See Jungmann, *Handbook of Church History*, vol. 3, pp. 300–307; for a detailed study of four of the enduring "local" liturgies, see King, *Liturgies of the Primatial Sees* (Milwaukee, 1957).

180. See Dudden, *St. Ambrose*, p. 496. Ambrose's position does not involve any notion of the relation of the emperor's authority to the grant of authority given the church (as is the case in Roman hierocratic theory from Leo I onward); rather, he is insisting that insofar as he is himself a member of the Christian community the emperor must accept the guidance of the episcopacy in the formation of his conscience.

181. See A. Paredi, *Ambrose: His Life and Times* (Notre Dame, 1964), pp. 135–36.

182. See *De Mysteriis* 6; *De officiis* 1. 152; *Epist.* 20; also Dudden, *St. Ambrose*, pp. 131–32.

183. See Dudden, *St. Ambrose*, p. 131, n. 8.

184. *De officiis* 2. 11. 111: "Et maxime sacerdoti hoc convenit, ornare Dei templum decore congruo. . . ." Probably this emphasis can be explained by the nature of the *De officiis* as a guide and exhortation for his clergy.

185. Paredi, p. 132.

186. See Dudden, *St. Ambrose*, pp. 117–26.

187. *Epist.* 5. 15; see H. von Campenhausen, *Ambrosius von Mailand* (Berlin, 1929), pp. 266–67.

188. *Epist.* 9.

189. See *In Epist. II ad Cor.*, Hom. 15.

190. See Quasten, vol. 3, pp. 425–28.

191. On details of this incident, see C. Baur, *John Chrysostom and His Time* (London, 1959), vol. 1, pp. 259–83.

192. *Ad pop. Antioch.*, Hom. 3. 2.

193. *Ibid.*

194. See Ullmann, *Papal Government*, pp. 7–10.

195. And even earlier (in 414), Innocent I, writing to Rufus of Thessalonica, had claimed universal authority.

196. *Papal Government*, p. 7.

197. Ullmann (*ibid.*, pp. 7–9) treats this claim as if it were purely a matter of jurisdiction attaching to the office of Roman bishop; but as we indicated earlier one must inject into the understanding of these claims the belief that Peter himself still continued to be present to the Roman church and to be active in carrying on his function through the Roman bishop.

198. See *ibid.*, pp. 9–10.

199. *Epist.* 6. 6.

200. *Sermo* 3. 1; 5. 1–2.

201. Indeed, he joins the notions of priestly and royalty in speaking of the Christian people: *ibid.*, 3. 1.

202. See *ibid.*, 4. 2.

203. *Ibid.*

204. See Dvornik, vol. 2, p. 804.

205. See *ibid.*, pp. 804–6.

206. *Ibid.*

207. *P.L.* 59. 108.

208. See *New Catholic Encyclopedia*, vol. 6, p. 316.

209. See *Mansi* 8. 181.

210. See Dvornik, p. 808.

211. For the most part, I have followed the interpretation of F. Dvornik (in his *Early Christian and Byzantine Political Philosophy* and *The Idea of Apostolicity in Byzantium*); this view is disputed to some extent by Ullmann (*Papal Government*, p. 25, n. 3), but in general their analyses are complementary.

212. P. Batiffol, *Cathedra Petri* (Paris, 1938), p. 89.

213. H. Küng, *The Church* (New York, 1967), pp. 470–71, eulogizes Gregory as being non-monarchical and pastoral in his outlook. Without appraising the personal humility or zeal of Gregory, who unquestionably was a great bishop, we must still ask whether his language and attitudes do not betray an evolution of thought away from primitive Christianity's idea of ministry, an evolution that in large part he inherited but which he crystallized for future centuries.

214. "Gregory I's *societas reipublicae christianae* (Regist. of his letters, 9, 67, p. 88, lines 5–6) over which the Roman church exercises its *principatus* unimpeded by considerations of a constitutional nature, is the prophetic vision of medieval Europe" (Ullmann, *Papal Government*, p. 37).

215. See H. Moss, *The Birth of the Middle Ages* (Oxford, 1935), pp. 132–33.

216. See Ullmann, *Papal Government*, pp. 40–41; however, it is not clear that one can draw elements from the Benedictine Rule to explain the outlook of Gregory (as Ullmann does in considerable detail, pp. 40–41): there is some doubt about Gregory's familiarity with the Rule. "There is no evidence, and little probability, that Gregory and his monks followed the rule of Benedict. . . ." (D. Knowles, *Christian Monasticism* [New York, 1969], p. 40.)

217. See Jungmann, *Mass*, vol. 1, pp. 63–65.

218. ". . . Justinian and his collaborators were thoroughly imbued with the spirit of Hellenistic political ideas. Only the designation of law animate is missing [from the Constitution], but Justinian makes up for it in the Novel of the year 536, 'On the Consuls.' . . . There he states: 'The imperial station, however, shall not be subject to the rules which we have just formulated, for to the emperor God has subjected the laws themselves by sending him to men as the incarnate law.' Thus, the *nomos empsychos* (living law) entered into the Code of Justinian which preserved it for

future speculation.   The victory of Hellenism was final.

"This marks the end of a long evolution.   The notion of the law animate, born of the old Oriental monarchism, nursed by the Greek rhetors and philosophers in the Hellenistic age, long resisted by the survivors of Roman republicanism, was finally adopted by the New Rome, Constantinople, and sanctioned by the Church. Its enshrinement in the Code of Justinian destined it to play its part in Byzantium, in the evolution of the medieval Papacy, and in the new era of political thought of the Western Renaissance." (Dvornik, vol. 2, pp. 722–23.)

219. On imperial domination of the priesthood, see *Cod. Just.* 1. 4. 34; 1. 3. 41. On Justinian's ecclesiastical policy and formation of the Codex, see A. Vasiliev, *History of the Byzantine Empire* (Madison, Wis., 1928), vol. 1, pp. 174–89.

220. *Cod. Just.* 1. 3. 4. On the ecclesiastical structures and the functions of the clergy in the Byzantine Empire, see E. Herman, *Cambridge Medieval History* (1967 ed.), vol. 4, part 2, pp. 105–33.

221. *Cod. Just.* 1. 3. 42.

222. *Ibid.* 1. 3. 41.

223. *Ibid.* 1. 4. 34.

224. *Ibid.* 1. 4.

225. See Ewig, pp. 128–31.

226. See Ullmann, *Medieval Papalism*, p. 58, for the manner in which Nicolas' letter of 865 to Emperor Michael was used by later papal canonists.

227. See Ewig, p. 131, on the canonical irregularity of the deposition of the archbishops of Cologne and Trier; and pp. 145–46 on the papal reversal of the episcopal tribunal (under Hincmar) which deposed Rothad, a papal intervention that was against existing canon law but which Nicolas justified by appeal to the False Decretals.

228. See Ullmann, *Papal Government*, pp. 201–2.

229. "Universitas credentium ab hac sancta Romana ecclesia, quae caput est omnium ecclesiarum, doctrinam exquirit, integritatem fidei deposcit" (*Monumenta Germanicae Historica* [Hanover-Berlin, 1826ff.], *Epist. 6*, Epist. 86, p. 447). "Suscepit ergo ac continet in se Romana ecclesia quod Deus universalem ecclesiam suscipere ac continere praecepit" (*ibid.*, Epist. 88, p. 478).

230. See Knowles, *Christian Centuries*, vol. 2, pp. 110–11.

231. In his *The Carolingian Renaissance and the Idea of Kingship* (London, 1969), W. Ullmann shows in detail how Hincmar combines these elements in the theory he works out relative to the anointing liturgy for the king.

232. *Ibid.*, p. 117.

233. *Ibid.*, pp. 117–19.

234. See Congar, pp. 166–77.

235. See Fliche, p. 63, for the background of this letter and an analysis of the mentality it represents.

236. See Ullmann, *Papal Government*, pp. 283–85.

237. *Epist.* 21 (*P.L.* 148. 594–601). Of this letter A. Fliche (*Gregoire VII*, vol. 2, p. 389) says: "Cette lettre est un véritable traité de politique ecclésiastique, où se cristallise la pensée pontificale."

238. *P.L.* 148. 407–8.

239. *Epist.* 21 (*P.L.* 148. 595). Later in the same letter, he makes the claim for the *sacerdotium* (which, of course, finds its *plenitudo potestatis* in himself): "Quis dubitet sacerdotes Christi regum et principum omniumque fidelium patres et magistros censeri?" And, to indicate clearly the response to this question, he refers to the words of Constantine to the Nicene fathers in which he said that the council was above his judgment.

240. Gregory refers also (in his letter to Herimann) to the simile of Ambrose: the *dignitas sacerdotalis* is superior to the *regia potestas* as is gold to lead.

241. On this opinion in pre-Gregorian writers, see Voosen, pp. 154–55.
242. See Fliche, vol. 8, pp. 84–95.
243. *Epist. ad Herimannum (P.L.* 148. 598).
244. See the beginning of his letter to Herimann.
245. *Epist. ad Herimannum (P.L.* 148. 594–96).
246. *Ibid.,* col. 598.

CHAPTER 23

Judgment and Authority in
the Middle Ages

In the short span of three centuries the hierocratic explanation of absolute papal authority came to its fullest expression and then faced its deepest challenge at Constance. These three centuries, the High Middle Ages, witness the high-water mark of sacerdotal influence (even control) over human society. The emphasis on authority and judgment in this influence is reflected in the fact that the bulk of theological writing (and as one might readily expect, of canonical writing) about the *sacerdotium* deals with the precise point of papal authority. The intrinsic nature of the priesthood and ministry receives very little attention in the great theological syntheses produced by these centuries.[1]

What this means is that lengthy treatises on ecclesiastical polity, rather than carefully developed ecclesiology, were the sources to which the fifteenth and sixteenth centuries had recourse (without much avail) when the very nature of Christianity was being questioned in the Reformation.[2] Without an adequate theology of Eucharist or ministry or ecclesial authority, Reformation and Counter-Reformation theologians had to turn to polemics and controversial writing.

In the twelfth century, however, things looked different from the fifteenth century. All Europe was awakening to a resurgence of intellectual and cultural and spiritual life. The papacy seemed to stand at the very heart of this movement as its source of guidance and vitality.[3] The longed-for reform of the church had come about to a considerable extent because of the efforts of Gregory VII and his immediate successors. Though they faced constant struggles with temporal rulers, the popes enjoyed increasing prestige as the true leaders of the transnational reality that was the *societas christiana*.[4]

Unsuccessful though they were, marked often by barbaric cruelty and pillage, or on the other hand by colossal failure, the crusades against the Saracens provided a natural context for the increase of papal power and prestige.[5] It was the pope who summoned the flower of medieval chivalry, even the barons and kings, to free the holy places from the grasp of the infidel. Thus, the pope was the conscience of Christianity, pointing out to men their neglected duty to end the impiety of Saracen rule in Jerusalem.[6]

Since the crusade was response to special divine vocation, its direction depended upon the voice that God used to summon his people to this holy war. That voice was the pope. In this capacity the pope was both prophet and high priest; he consecrated the men and the arms for battle, he promised, in God's name, eternal salvation to those who died fighting for the cross.[7]

Another source of support to the twelfth-century papacy as it worked to secure and increase its power was the cooperation of such great figures as Anselm of Canterbury and Bernard of Clairvaux. Though Gregory VII and Urban II decisively turned the tide in the investiture controversy, the fight continued, and England was one of the chief battlegrounds.[8] Gregory VII himself had managed to work things out satisfactorily with William after his conquest in 1066, but William's successors were less amenable to papal claims.

Fortunately for the papacy (though perhaps of less profit to the English church) a series of strong and competent archbishops of Canterbury—Lanfranc, Anselm, Thomas à Beckett—helped the popes assert their claims with dignity and win considerable prestige even when they could not always press their case effectively against the English monarchs.[9]

In his own way, Bernard of Clairvaux was of even greater support to the papacy. Not tied down to defending any claims in which he himself had a vested interest, bringing with him all the prestige and numerical strength of the vigorous Cistercian movement, looked upon by multitudes of people as a saintly and prophetic personage, Bernard's advocacy of the practically unlimited power of the bishop of Rome did much to shape twelfth-century ideas of the papacy and to secure the pope's influence in practical affairs.[10] Bernard seems to have been largely responsible for the common usage, from this point onward, of the term *"vicarius Christi"* for the pope.[11] It is a usage that reflects the manner in which the pope had ceased to be considered "bishop of Rome" and had become the "head of the church."

The twelfth century was the period in which canon law came into being as an organized discipline, and a great deal of the writing and commentary of the influential canonists of that century dealt with the rights and prerogatives and responsibilities of the Roman see.[12] While papal decretals did not yet come out with the frequency that will mark the reigns of the thirteenth-century popes, there was a marked increase in the decretal literature. The propapal wing of canonical opinion was well represented in the so-called decretalists who used these papal decrees as bases for legal precedent.[13]

As fairly typical of "theological" views on the papacy, Peter Lombard's *Sentences* reflect little direct treatment of the topic.[14] For the most part, it is assumed that the discussion belongs to the canonists and will be treated by them.[15] This very classification of the discussion has its own profound implications, namely, that the papacy (and presumably related realities) is the kind of reality that is appropriately studied in a legal context of thought.

If one can justifiably say that Gregory VII was himself no innovator in hierocratic theory but merely brought into existence the situation long advocated by his predecessors,[16] the same cannot be said of Innocent III. One of the ablest administrators and diplomats ever to occupy the see of Rome, he also brought into a consistent and fairly final form a juristic theology of the papacy.[17] Himself a distinguished canonist, his manner of thinking is markedly legal; yet he places the whole notion of the papacy and its role in a metaphysical framework much like that employed by Thomas Aquinas in his *Summa contra Gentiles*.[18]

Iron-willed in his implementing of the Inquisition, successful in arranging the Second Council of Lyons (with its attempt to reconcile the Orthodox), thwarted in his various crusading efforts, Innocent IV enjoyed a supreme papal power that was on the point of decline.[19]

Reflecting on the pontificate of Boniface VIII, one feels that he is faced with the last, and unsuccessful, attempt of the medieval papacy to preserve the absolute power attained with Innocent III. Fighting a courageous counterattack against nascent national monarchy exemplified in Philip of France, Boniface summoned all his resources, including his bull *"Unam sanctam"*; but in the end his successor, Clement V, submitted to the indignity of unwilling assent to the crimes of Vienne.[20]

This is a period of fervent and somewhat intemperate invective (a quality of ecclesiastical discussion that will continue unabated for several centuries), of polemics carried on in the midst of a fight-to-the-death struggle between pope and king; the theological discussions of papal authority produced at this time must be evaluated against this background. The value of the considerable volume of writing produced at this time is that it represents just about every conceivable position on the relation between church and state[21] from the unmitigated papalism of Giles of Rome,[22] through the temperate and balanced treatment of Jean of Paris,[23] to the extreme antipapal writings of Jean de Jandun[24] and Marsilius of Padua.[25]

Badly shaken by events at the beginning of the fourteenth century, the prestige and power of the papacy was further eroded by the tragic situation of the Avignon captivity and the Great Schism. Moreover, questions about the ability and responsibility of the papacy to provide for the church, and beyond that for Christian society, spread to a questioning of the role of the *sacerdotium* as a whole. Should not the secular officials, especially the king or emperor, bear the responsibility and therefore the authority to provide for the practical needs of society, even to the point of intervening in ecclesiastical affairs when that was needed, as in the healing of the schism?[26] To some extent at least this question coincided with the *"naissance de l'esprit laïque,"* the assumption by the secular elements of society of the responsibility for developing science, commerce, social structures, and education.[27] However, the notion of one *societas christiana* was so strong that there was no question yet of a radical distinction between church and secular society; rather, there emerged the classic modern problem of the relation of church and state within one geographical community.[28]

For the moment, the precise problem faced by late medieval Europe was the confusion and division of the schism. It is a witness to the deep grounding of the papal claims that the fundamental notion of the papal primacy survived this period.[29] The actual situation of schism made it clear nonetheless that in a time of such obvious inability of the papacy to solve its own problems there must be some other more ultimate source of resolution. For this, the theologians and canonists (or at least a large portion of them) turned to a general council.[30] There were, of course, some extreme antipapal positions, a heritage of the Boniface-Philip controversy, but the moderate and thoughtful conciliar position, espoused by such men as D'Ailly, Gerson, and Nicholas

of Cusa, was not a repudiation of papal primacy. Rather, it involved recognition of papal authority, monarchical authority, in the ordinary situations of church life; but it grounded that authority in the nature and needs of the Christian community as a whole, and so made it in emergency situations (like the schism) subject to the basic authority of the entire church.[31]

As scholars of the conciliar movement, especially Tierney, have pointed out, the position taken by the great conciliarists was no doubt stimulated by the situation of schism but grew out of basic principles already enunciated by many medieval canonists.[32] Perhaps most basic was the notion that the *sacerdotium* (i.e., the clerical ministry) exists for the sake of the church as a whole; its own nature and structure is shaped therefore by the needs of the Christian community.[33] It is interesting to see the manner in which the medieval canonical traditions, which were themselves grounded in patristic sources, gave expression to the basic New Testament position that Christian priesthood (beginning with Christ himself) is oriented to the formation of community.[34]

The basic question that emerges, however, is whether the official ministry (specifically the episcopacy) as the "source" of the church's continuing life is the normative principle for the way in which the church ought to evolve, or whether the Christian community and the needs it has to grow progressively and in pluralistic unity is the norm for the shape which the ministry should take. The late medieval form of conciliarism brought the second of these two alternatives to the fore after centuries of being obscured by increasing clericalism. Then, almost immediately after Constance, the papacy was able once more to establish the *sacerdotium* as normative of the church. Part of the concrete problem involved in this *sacerdotium*-as-norm position is that it has proceeded historically (both in practice and in theory)[35] not from an analysis of the intrinsic nature of priesthood and ministry but from the legal judgments and doctrinal decisions of popes.

Popes have been governed in their own understanding of the traditions they should follow by canonical legal precedent rather than by a theologically sophisticated understanding of evangelical tradition involving the continuing activity of the Spirit in the church.

Late medieval conciliarism embraces a wide range of views on the relation between the papacy and the church as a whole: from the moderate position of Gerson or Zabarella, which was the position adopted by Constance in its decree "Haec sancta," to the more limited conciliar emphasis of Nicholas of Cusa on the one side or on the other side Marsilius of Padua's radical subordination of the papacy.[36] Moreover, some of the key conciliar theorists who arrived at more or less common positions, Gerson and Zabarella for example, arrived at their conclusions by quite different routes. Zabarella's was that of a great canon lawyer who argued from canonical traditions in his attempt to resolve the *impasse* of the Schism; Gerson seems to have been chary of canonist reasoning, and inclined rather to support a position of conciliar precedence over papacy as a pragmatic pastoral solution to the intolerable situation of the Schism.[37]

Actually, the conciliarist position that was accepted by the Council of Constance did not deny to the pope a clear jurisdictional primacy, did not in fact argue against his *plenitudo potestatis*. What it did contend (and this is, of course, of great importance in any historical or theological study of papal authority) was that the pope received his authority from God through the church, and the church though delegating the *plenitudo potestatis* to the pope still continued to possess this *plenitudo*. Thus, Zabarella insisted that the plenitude of power rests fundamentally in the corporate body of the church and derivatively in the pope as the principal minister of that corporate reality.[38] One can confine this understanding to the jurisdictional order, and assert that this conciliar position (and its adoption by Constance) says nothing about the origin of the episcopacy's *potestas ordinis*. It does seem clear that the dispute about papal authority in the four-

teenth and fifteenth centuries was confined consciously to the *potestas jurisdictionis*.[39] However, if the reality of the distinction between *potestas ordinis* and *potestas jurisdictionis* is to be questioned, then the implications of the conciliar position and of Constance's decree "Haec sancta" touch the entire theology of ministry and priesthood. On the other hand, any hasty derivation of theological conclusions from the "triumph" of moderate conciliarism at the Council of Constance must be challenged by the countervailing action of the Council of Florence (only a quarter-century later) in issuing the decree "Laetentur coeli" whose affirmation of absolute Roman primacy seems absolute and unqualified.[40]

Theologically, the Council of Constance has not had the impact it should, though recently such scholars as Hans Küng and Brian Tierney have again directed attention to the council.[41] Part of the difficulty lies in the fact that the impulse of conciliarist thought weakened quickly once the practical problem of the Schism was solved by the election of Martin V. The conciliarist school itself began to break into factions; it had no sociological principles of unity and continuity as did the papacy in its curial structure. The project of regular general councils faded with the failure of Basel.[42] All of this has tended to associate Constance with dubious dogmatic developments, to throw its understandings into the background (as if it were an almost heretical tangent), and to remove it from the data that must be accounted for in a theology of church ministry.[43]

The Sacrament of Penance

Patristic and early medieval discussion of ecclesiastical authority had concentrated on the possession by the episcopacy or papacy of the power of the keys.[44] This had always, of course, involved the understanding that "the keys" pertained very specially to the church's ministry of forgiving sin; but a great deal of the discussion of the power of the keys had been directed to the persistent question of the relation between *sacerdotium* and *regnum*, i.e., to authority that was not specifically that concerned with the sacramental reconciliation of sinners.[45] Such wider application of the notion of the keys continues into the medieval theologians and canonists, but there is a much greater development of theology about the nature of sacramental confession and forgiveness, and the church's authority in this sphere.[46]

As in many aspects of the church's life and thought, the twelfth century marks a fairly drastic turning point in the history of the sacrament of penance.[47] Not that the rapid evolution of thought and practice which occurred in this century was entirely new. Yet, the century opened with the tension between the ancient discipline of exomologesis and the Celtic emphasis on individual confession and absolution still unresolved.[48] By 1200 the basis for all theological discussion is the assumption that the sacrament of penance is constituted by confession and absolution.[49] The performance of penance is by no means forgotten, but it is not seen as intrinsic to the *sacramental* action.[50]

From the beginning, the ancient discipline of penance and reconciliation had involved an act of judgment on the bishop's part, judgment about the penance to be imposed and judgment at the point of reconciliation. With the shift to a "sacrament of individual confession," which is established by the end of the twelfth century, the power and burden of judgment rests on every priest who hears confessions. This naturally raises many questions: How able are the majority of priest-confessors to make such judgments? To what extent is the actual process of forgiveness of sin by God tied to such sacerdotal judgments? Can priest-confessors actually free men from their sins, or only tell them that God has promised forgiveness to all who sincerely repent? Is such power to absolve sins limited exclusively to ordained ministers, or can one in emergency situations obtain forgiveness by confessing to a lay Christian? To what extent is one bound to confess his sins to an ordained

priest in order to obtain divine forgiveness? These questions are found discussed at length in the theologians and canonists of the twelfth century and reflect the extent to which the sacrament of penance was viewed as a situation of judgment.[51]

In thirteenth-century theological discussion of the sacrament of penance, the presupposition is that it is constituted essentially by the confession and contrition of the penitent and the absolving action of the ordained minister.[52] The opinion persists that in emergency circumstances there is some purpose in confessing to a layman if a priest is not available; but theologians are uncertain as to how the effectiveness of such action is achieved.[53] Yet there is increasing insistence on the absolving act of the priest-confessor.

There is universal agreement among theologians of this century that the absolution given by the priest pertains to the essence of the sacrament of penance.[54] For many—e.g., Thomas Aquinas, Bonaventure—it constituted the formal element of the sacramental sign, acting in conjunction with the penitent's contrition and confession.[55] For others, e.g., Duns Scotus, the priestly absolution absorbs into itself all the essential significance of the sacramental sign.[56] Discussion of the nature of the power of the keys which is used in the sacrament follows the lines already set in the previous century. The one key is that of discrimination by which the confessor distinguishes sin from sin, or guilt from innocence; the other key is that of freeing the sinner from his sin.[57] It is acknowledged that some confessors might lack the kind of knowledge and insight required for accurate judgment of sinfulness. Some theologians go so far as to say that ordination to the presbyterate confers some of this insight upon the ordinand, that this is part of the power of the keys given to him.[58] There is no common acceptance, however, of such "infused understanding," nor is there a common teaching as to just what effectiveness attaches to the priestly absolution. For some it touches guilt, for others eternal punishment for sin, and for others the temporal punishment.[59] In all events, whatever true absolving the priest does, he does *ministerialiter,* i.e., Christ does it in and through him.[60]

Another element that becomes explicit in theology at the end of the twelfth century and into the thirteenth is the distinction between internal and external forum.[61] This applies specifically to the sacrament of penance, and to the different authority of episcopacy and presbyterate in absolving sinners. Apparently, there is common agreement, theologically and canonically, that ordination to presbyterate (especially if it is ordination in view of pastoral work) confers power to absolve in the internal forum.[62] On the other hand, it is clear from centuries-long practice that excommunication is the prerogative of episcopacy, though traditional practice varied as to whether individual bishops or metropolitans or councils of bishops or only the pope could excommunicate. Power to judge effectively in this external forum was something that differentiated the authority of "priest of the first order" from "priests of the second order."[63]

This raises another aspect of the emerging distinction between jurisdiction and orders. In what had to do with the sacrament as such, with the internal forum, it was the power of orders that was at work and that was common to bishops and presbyters.[64] But in the external sphere of ecclesiastical jurisdiction, bishops and priests were no longer basically equals. Such authority belonged properly to the episcopal level, perhaps only to the papal, and could be exercised by presbyters only as delegates of the bishops.[65]

For the most part, fourteenth-century theology of the sacrament of penance continues the questions already posed in the preceding period. However, there is increased examination of the priest's absolution as being effective or merely declaratory. There are a number of thinkers during this century who seem to espouse the opinion that the judgment of the priest-confessor is merely declaratory— telling the penitent that he has been forgiven by God.[66] However, one must be cautious in so appraising these theological statements.

What some, at least, seem to be striving for is a clear and emphatic statement that it is Christ and he alone who is freeing the sinner from his guilt.[67]

An exercise of authority that attaches to the papacy at this time has to do with the approval and direction of religious orders.[68] Exactly how it came about is not clear, since monastic foundations had for centuries been established without papal or even episcopal approval; but by the thirteenth century it seems taken for granted that the pope can allow or disallow the inception of groups of dedicated Christians wishing to live in community. Intrinsically, such claims on the part of the pope seem to have no basis. Christians should be free to live Christianity more intensely, or in organized community fashion, if they wish. Yet, we find the Fourth Lateran Council (i.e., Innocent III) prohibiting the establishment of any new religious groups,[69] and at the same time, popes (Innocent III among others) granting their approval to such new foundations as the Dominicans and Franciscans and then directing and modifying the structures of the communities, as happened particularly to the Franciscans.[70]

Not only is such papal control over religious communities a new and widely influential exercise of ecclesiastical authority, but it further emphasizes the notion of the pope as source of church authority. It is not clear yet whether the notion has emerged that the authority exerted by religious superiors is derivative from the pope, whereas more ancient monastic practice would see the monastic chapter as the source of authority.[71] Yet, effectively the new religious communities do derive their autonomy and their legitimacy from the papal permission to exist as approved groups.[72] Whether or not an explicit theory exists of the authority exercised within communities being derivative from the pope, popes from this time onward act in that framework.[73]

Whether done by bishops or by the pope, this period saw several instances of the increasing tendency of Christian officialdom to pass judgment (generally quite negative) upon popular movements of piety or apostolic action. No doubt, some of this watchfulness over grass-roots developments sprang from the shock that accompanied the discovery of Albigensianism. But it seems to have been broader than that.[74] What it seems equally rooted in was the assumption, grounded in centuries of clerical monopoly, that any initiative or salvific activity in the church was to be exercised by the clergy. Laity (and most of these popular movements were predominantly lay) were the passive element in the church, the *ecclesia discens*; this was *de jure divino*, because the episcopacy traced its authority and distinctiveness back to Christ's commission to the apostles.[75] Once established, the Inquisition was a particularly effective watchdog over such emergent lay movements.[76]

Here one encounters a tension in the church's life that is as delicate and basic as any that can occur. History makes clear that the action of the Spirit, which is the very source of the church's vitality and historical evolution, has more than once manifested itself through nonclerical media. Many of the great religious movements that gave impetus and purification to Christian life began spontaneously, informally, on the grass-roots level. When these were authentic[77] they were guided by true understanding of the gospel. But at times there were messianic figures who were deluded, or at least deluding, and who began religious revivals which proved false and harmful to people. While not the only agency in the church which exists to discern the "spirit" in such movements, the episcopacy has traditionally borne this responsibility, and from medieval times the bishop of Rome has claimed ultimate responsibility in this regard for himself.[78]

Granted the fact that many scholarly studies of the medieval inquisition have been colored by the bias of religious polemic, it is difficult to find sufficient grounds to justify the establishment or the conduct of the Inquisition.[79] Apart from the justice or injustice of its actions, the historical phenomenon of the Inquisition raises several questions about the view of authority and priestly responsibility that must have been connected with it.

For one thing, it certainly drew strong attention to the function of judge. More specifically, the judge in question was the pope. The Inquisitors acted as his delegated agents, with his authority, under his control, and in his name.[80] It seems to have been an outgrowth of the appointment of special papal legates which became common practice at the time of Gregory VII.[81] And to that extent it seems to be an appropriation to himself of authority and responsibility that belongs intrinsically to the episcopacy of the region in question.[82]

A more basic question, though, concerns the precise capacity which these Inquisitors were thought to be exercising. Were they looked upon as funtioning in terms of the episcopal office, judging the orthodoxy of the accused against their own (i.e., the Inquisition's) possession of apostolic tradition? Or were they considered theological experts who because of their technical understanding of theology could evaluate the doctrinal and moral tenets of the suspected deviants? The question is not just academic. Being able to answer it would enable us to decide if already at this point the pope (and perhaps some other bishops also) was operating in the realm of theological judgment and demanding acceptance of his theological views on the basis of his papal (episcopal) authority.[83]

The Inquisition was closely tied to the idea of a crusade against domestic heretics, and much of its excesses and injustice were excused or defended on this basis. In this context, the Inquisition, and any comparable activity, puts itself in the position of judging not just the objective accuracy or error of a theological or doctrinal view but the religious sincerity and state of soul of the accused person as well.[84] Accused "heretics" are considered as likely criminals, instead of being the object of fraternal correction.

This was what the whole inquisitorial approach assumed. Instead of considering error its own "punishment" and trying to rescue a person from his plight, ecclesiastical courts of one kind and another tried to enforce truth by punishing those judged to be in error.[85] This took bloody form in the crusade against the Albigensians.[86] To some extent, given the concrete circumstances and the apparent threat to the very fabric of society (though the princes who led the war did not seem concerned about this danger to society until the popes promised them the booty of conquest, the lands of the conquered heretics), one can understand the popular reaction to this heresy.[87] But it is much more difficult to sustain some justification, or even excuse, for the execution of DeMollay at Vienne and of Hus at Constance.[88]

The number of large-scale councils, some of which (like Lateran IV) are sometimes considered worthy of inclusion among the ecumenical councils,[89] testifies to the vitality and overall unity of medieval church life, to the energy and power of the medieval popes, and to the ferment in life and thought which raised so many issues for conciliar consideration. Without passing critical judgment upon this evolution, it is important in studying the role of authority in the theological activity of the church to notice how the scope of conciliar decision is broadened out to touch theological opinion as well as dogmatic or doctrinal statements.[90] Obviously, conciliar statements have always contained a prominent element of theological interpretation of the gospel revelation. Moreover, medieval councils tried to avoid purely theological decision, or choice of one acceptable theological approach in preference to another also acceptable. Yet some medieval councils (even more so some regional councils of bishops) accuse or vindicate some theologian in an area of teaching that does not seem too directly *revelabile* or *revelatum*.[91]

Connected with the papal judgment passed upon popular religious movements of this period was the judgment passed by one or other form of inquisition upon those who were, or at least were reputed to be, gifted with special gifts of mysticism.[92] Mysticism as such was certainly not in bad repute; many of the great and recognized figures of the High Middle Ages were men of high-level contemplative endowment, Francis, Bernard, Aquinas, Bonaventure, to mention but a few. But more than a few supposed mystics were quite other than that. Some judgment was called for in many instances, lest people of simple and uneducated faith be led astray by psychotics or charlatans. What needs to be questioned is not the simple fact that some judgment was made but the context in which it was at times made (inquisitorial in the pejorative sense of the term) or the sanction used to implement the judgment.[93] Theologically, the much more critical question is: How does one relate to one another (i.e., which judges which), the charismatic manifestation of the Spirit in the authentic mystic, and the manifestation of the same Spirit in the charisma of episcopal office?

One of the forces that comes to maturity at this point in the church's life is the corporate and individual contribution of theologians. Theology had, of course, always been done to some extent in the church; but for many centuries it was an element in the ministry of the bishops or of the preacher or of the teacher. Now, in the Middle Ages, theology as a distinct area of intellectual pursuit (as well as background for preacher and teacher) attains its identity.[94] What this says about ministerial patterns in the church is not yet clear in the twentieth century, whether theological activity is part of the ministry of the episcopacy, or part of the ministry of the teacher (which itself has long ago lost formal recognition as an official *diakonia*), or whether the function of the theologian constitutes a distinct ministry which the evolving life of the church brought into being by its own internal need. In trying to answer this question, it is important to notice the extent to which theologians have exercised *judgment* in the life of the church, a phenomenon which is clearly observable from the twelfth century onward.

Almost any theological work produced in the Middle Ages judges favorably or unfavorably the positions taken by other thinkers on a given point. In many instances the judgment involves the basic acceptance or rejection of that position as orthodox. Obviously, in most of these cases the theologian is merely repeating a judgment made by earlier church authorities, councils, great fathers, etc. (i.e., the *auctores*).[95] But in certain other instances, he is deciding that either theological conclusions or philosophical presuppositions are incompatible with the faith. There is almost never a situation when a theologian is in the position of officially condemning the heresy of another thinker, though some of the Inquisitors were not far from such power; but one wonders to what extent their theological views influenced popes or councils that did so officially condemn heretics. It is hard to imagine the Council of Sens meeting to take action against Abelard if there had not been the previous decision of Bernard that Abelard was teaching contrary to the faith.[96] Yet, one cannot but wonder by what title such groups of bishops could accept the theological judgment of a man like Bernard, when they themselves did not understand the issues. They obviously were not making a theological judgment (of this they were incapable); what they seemed to be doing was trusting either the theological insights or the charismatic sanctity (and presumably therefore doctrinal accuracy) of Bernard.[97]

The picture is somewhat clearer (at least the intrinsic issue is clearer) when theologians pass judgment upon the theological accuracy and competence of other theologians. Here, there is no questioning of another's personal fidelity to faith and Christian tradition; instead, there is a judgment passed against his methodology or erroneous presuppositions or false information or illogical conclusions.[98]

Historical studies may well conclude that the area in which theologians most took to themselves the mantle of official magisterium was that of moral theology.[99] Rooted in compact sources, a relatively small body of patristic writing, more specially the *Moralia* of Gregory I and the *Sententiae* and *De officiis ecclesiasticis* of Isidore of Seville, medieval moral theology quickly became a highly detailed discussion of all the various aspects of human behavior: man's virtues and vices (down to the least subspecies of sin), the roots and remedies of these sins, and the laws of God and man and church that gave directives to man's moral behavior.[100] Thus, the great moral treatises of medieval theology drew upon Christian anthropology and canon law and the traditions of asceticism and spirituality that for the most part had been developed in monastic life over the centuries, but they also drew from Greek philosophy (particularly Stoicism) and medieval cultural mythology (i.e., in the view taken of woman's relation to man) and the secular ideals of feudalism and chivalry.[101]

Actually what happened, from the Middle Ages until our own day, was that moral theologians made those judgments upon human behavior which were then applied, generally with some human mercy but little prudential adjustment to circumstances, to homiletic and penitential judgments of people's sinfulness. Moreover, these very specific conclusions of moral theologians became the norm against which the accuracy of men's consciences was checked. Thus the theologian became a judge of men's culpability, a priori rather than post factum. What further complicated this confusion of functions was the historical fact that theologians in the Latin church were all clerics, so that theological activity came to be viewed as one of the proper functions of ordained ministers, or at least of some of them. Thus, theologians were often looked upon as functioning by way of delegation from higher ecclesiastical authorities and therefore as subject to their control.[102] This tendency was resisted in the late Middle Ages at such places as the University of Paris, where the faculty was powerful enough to insist on its autonomy.[103]

Admonition had long been considered one of the preacher's principal tasks. Gregory I had made it the chief objective of the preaching task as he outlines it in his *De cura pastorali*. With the great preachers of the Middle Ages and on towards the period of the Reformation, this public denunciation of the moral evils of the day retains its central position. Savanarola may have been more agitating a preacher than some others, but he was acting in a long-standing tradition of medieval preaching. However one may appraise such rhetorical activity, the fact remains that the role and the image of the ordained minister which is conveyed is that of judge.

NOTES

1. The classic locations for discussion of ministry and priesthood (e.g., in Thomas Aquinas) were the questions dealing with the priesthood of Christ (*Summa theol.* 3, q. 22) and (under each of the sacraments) with the minister of the sacraments (*ibid.*, qq. 67, 82). However, the treatment of the minister of the various sacraments tends to concentrate on the question, Who is the appropriate minister? rather than on the nature of the minister's activity. Treatment of Christ's priesthood is much richer in implication, since the ruling principle (as enunciated by Aquinas, q. 22, a. 4) *"Christus est fons totius sacerdotii"* points the direction for a detailed development of the theology of Christian priesthood; but this developed theology is no more than implied.

2. John of Turrecramata's *Summa de ecclesia* (1449) might be considered the first systematic ecclesiology and did have major impact on later developments in ecclesiology, but its purpose was to justify the monarchical claims of the papacy and its emphasis is therefore on political rather than theological issues and its argumentation actually proceeds more from political than theological principles. See A. Black, *Monarchy and Community* (Cambridge, 1970), pp. 53–84.

3. However, it is important to insist on the autonomous vitality of the *"vita evangelica"* movement, which in many respects was the dominant Christian element in the twelfth-century renaissance. See F. Kempf, *Handbook of Church History* (New York, 1969), vol. 3, pp. 453–65; M.-D. Chenu, *Nature, Man, and Society in the Twelfth Century* (Chicago, 1968), pp. 239–69.

4. This was accompanied by a marked centralization of church authority and organization. "L'événement majeur de l'âge classique fut la centralisation romaine. Cette unité législative, administrative, que n'avait pu imposer Grégoire VII, se réalise presque insensiblement d'Alexandre III à Jean XXII." (G. LeBras in A. Fliche and V. Martin, *Histoire de l'Eglise depuis les origines jusqu'à nos jours* [Paris, 1935—], vol. 12, p. 303.)

5. See Kempf, pp. 445–50.

6. See S. Runciman, *History of the Crusades* (Cambridge, 1962), vol. 1, pp. 106–13.

7. On the manner in which the carefully worded decrees of the Council of Clermont, which dealt with the armed pilgrimage as commutation for the penitential discipline imposed by the church, gave way to much broader promises of plenary indulgence, see Kempf, pp. 448–49.

8. See D. Knowles, *The Christian Centuries* (London, 1969), vol. 2, pp. 198–202.

9. See H. Wolter, *Handbook of Church History* (New York, 1965—), vol. 4, pp. 66–74.

10. Writing to Eugenius III (*De consid.* 2. 8), Bernard attributes to the pope a unique historical primacy: "Tu princeps episcoporum, tu haeres Apostolorum, tu primatu Abel, gubernatu Noe, patriarchatu Abraham, ordine Melchisedech, dignitate Aaron, auctori、ate Moyses, judicatu Samuel, potestate Petrus, unctione Christus." Moreover, he taught that the pope had a *plenitudo potestatis* that gave him immediate jurisdiction over each Christian as well as over all other bishops; see B. Jacqueline, "Bernard et l'expression 'plenitudo potestatis,' " *Bernard de Clairvaux*, ed. by monks of Notre Dame d'Aiguebelle (Paris, 1953), pp. 345–48. On the meaning of papal *plenitudo potestatis* in Bernard's ecclesiology, and also on Bernard's doctrine of the "two swords," see Y. Congar, "L'ecclésiologie de S. Bernard," *Saint Bernard: Théologien*, ed. J. Leclercq (Rome, 1953), pp. 159–75; and M. Pacaut, "L'opposition des canonistes aux doctrines politiques de Saint Bernard," *Mélanges Saint Bernard* (Dijon, 1953), pp. 187–93.

11. See W. Ullmann, *Growth of Papal Government in the Middle Ages* (London, 1955), pp. 426–37.

12. See C. Lefebvre, *L'âge classique*, vol. 7 of *Histoire du droit et des institutions de l'Eglise en Occident* (Paris, 1965), pp. 133–67.

13. *Ibid.*, pp. 292–324.

14. Ecclesiology as such was scarcely developed during the twelfth century, the principal exception being the second book of Hugh of St. Victor's *De sacramentis*; see Ullmann, pp. 437–46. In the thirteenth century, though there was still no systematic treatment of ecclesiology, theologians (and Thomas Aquinas in particular) made major contributions to the evolving understanding of the papal office and power. See *ibid.*, p. 444, n. 1.

15. Actually, the matter was handled by the canonists (see J. Watt, *The Theory of Papal Monarchy in the Thirteenth Century* [New York, 1965]), though it is good to remember that in the twelfth and early thirteenth centuries the lines were not as sharply drawn between theologian and canonist.

16. See Ullmann, p. 271.

17. See Watt, pp. 34–58.

18. *Summa contra Gent.* 4. 76.

19. On the understanding of the *plenitudo potestatis* of the pope at the time of Innocent IV, and the convergence of papal and theological views, see Watt, pp. 75–105.

20. See K. Fink, *Handbook of Church History*, vol. 4, pp. 291–304.

21. That is, every position on the church-state question in its classic form, i.e., as the relationship between two perfect societies. However, as we suggest in other places, this confrontation was grounded in the unjustified application to the church of the political model; the historical disputes over the church-state issue were rooted in the de facto evolution of ecclesiastical and civil institutions rather than in some intrinsic opposition between the Christian community and civil society.

22. Giles' *De ecclesiastica potestate* (1301) is perhaps the most complete theological argumentation for the *plenitudo potestatis* of the pope; on Giles' importance as the leading proponent of the papal position enunciated in Boniface VIII's *Unam sanctam*, see C. McIlwain, *The Growth of Political Thought in the West* (Cambridge, Mass., 1932), pp. 248–59. On the somewhat similar views of a most influential contemporary of Giles, Augustinus Triumphus of Ancona, see M. Wilks, *The Problem of Sovereignty in the Later Middle Ages* (Cambridge, 1963).

23. See J. Leclercq, *Jean de Paris et l'ecclésiologie du XIIIe siècle* (Paris, 1942), esp. pp. 121–23.

24. The leading Averroist at Paris, Jean de Jandun, was closely associated with Marsilius; he probably had considerable influence on the writing of the *Defensor pacis*, but does not seem to have been its coauthor. See A. Gerwirth, "John of Jandun and the Defensor pacis," *Speculum* 23 (1948), pp. 167–72.

25. See E. Iserloh, *Handbook of Church History*, vol. 4, pp. 359–63; G. Sabine, *History of Political Theory*, 2d ed. (New York, 1959), pp. 290–304. Though he is often paired with Marsilius as the opponent of the papal position, Ockham's view was more moderate. "Ockham's problem was the actual extent of the Pope's power; still more correctly and precisely, it was the actual limits of the papal power. This was the problem which inspired Ockham to write all his political works. . . . Ockham was a theologian who, for the benefit of the Church and for the love of peace between Church and State, tried to define the proper authority of the Church and its jurisdiction side by side with those of the State." (P. Boehner, *Collected Articles on Ockham* [St. Bonaventure, N.Y., 1958], p. 445.) See also Iserloh, pp. 363–68; and E. Jacob, *Essays in the Conciliar Epoch*, 3d ed. (Manchester, 1963), pp. 85–105.

26. This notion was, of course, not new: Justinian epitomized it in his actions and in his legislation, and Charlemagne took for granted his responsibility to oversee ecclesiastical affairs; but the widespread disarray caused by the schism (see E.-R. Labande in

Fliche-Martin, vol. 14, pp. 3–166) and the inability of ecclesiastical structures to re-establish order inevitably led to secular intervention.

27. See G. Lagarde, *La naissance de l'esprit laïque* (Louvain, 1956), vol. 1.

28. The continuity of this presupposition of one *societas christiana* can be seen in the sixteenth-century principle *"Cuius regio, eius religio,"* even though at that point Europe is being fragmented into many (and opposed) Christian societies.

29. See P. Ourliac in Fliche-Martin, vol. 14, pp. 203–92, on the triumph of the papacy after Constance. However, the basic reasoning for the papal claims shifted in the later medieval period from what it had been in the preschism period; on this shift and on the key role of Turrecramata in this new argumentation, see Black, esp. pp. 53–84.

30. See F. Oakley, *Council Over Pope?* (New York, 1969), pp. 33–55.

31. *Ibid.*, pp. 56–77; Wilks, pp. 455–523 (stresses the views of Augustinus Triumphus and Ockham); J. Morrall, *Gerson and the Great Schism* (Manchester, 1960).

32. See B. Tierney, *Foundations of the Conciliar Theory* (Cambridge, 1955), which F. Oakley (p. 79) rightly says "marked something of a turning point in Conciliar studies."

33. Even more basic to the conciliar theory itself was the "corporist" view that authority resided most basically in the body of the faithful; see Tierney, pp. 238–47.

34. However, there is a radical split in views (that is still unresolved today) as to whether Christ's unifying presence should be seen as touching immediately the community as a whole ("corporist" views, theological emphasis on the priesthood of the Christian faithful) or as touching immediately the episcopacy (papacy) and through it the Christian community (classic modern Catholic theology). On the thirteenth-century and fifteenth-century developments of this latter view, see G. Le Bras in Fliche-Martin, vol. 12, esp. pp. 305–27, 365–67; Watt, *Theory of Papal Monarchy*; and Black, pp. 53–84.

35. The theory in question is that of the pope's position, epitomizing in his jurisdictional judgments the will of God for the Christian people, very much like the function of the *basileus* in Justinian's legislation. A basic element in this theory is a voluntaristic approach to law, an approach in which the intent of the lawgiver is the ultimate criterion of legal interpretation. It would make an interesting study to see how much of this mentality lies behind sixteenth-century disputes about the relative primacy of Scripture or tradition.

36. See Oakley, pp. 56–77; P. Sigmund, *Nicholas of Cusa and Medieval Political Thought* (Cambridge, Mass., 1973); Morrall, pp. 112–23.

37. See Morrall, pp. 120–23; Jacob, pp. 7–15.

38. On the moderate conciliar position as understood by Gerson, d'Ailly, and Zabarella and as espoused by the Council of Constance, see Oakley, pp. 68–77.

39. See *ibid.*, pp. 70–71.

40. On this action of Florence, and on the subsequent evolution of conciliarist views, see *ibid.*, pp. 78–131, where the research and discussions of Jedin, Franzen, Küng, de Vooght, and Gill are discussed.

41. Tierney, *Conciliar Theory*; and H. Küng, *Structures of the Church* (New York, 1964).

42. See Ourliac, pp. 203–92.

43. An indication of this is provided by the Denzinger-Schonmetzer *Enchiridion symbolorum* (1964 ed.) which has fairly lengthy citations from Constance's condemnations of Wyclif and Hus and an excerpt from the decree on Communion under both species, but has nothing from either *Haec sancta* or *Frequens*, i.e., from Constance's treatment of papal authority.

44. See Y. Congar, *L'ecclésiologie du Haut Moyen Age* (Paris, 1968), pp. 138–51.

45. For a detailed study of this discussion, see Ullmann, *Growth of Papal Government*.

46. See B. Poschmann, *Penance and the Anointing of the Sick* (New York, 1964), pp. 145–93. As Anciaux points out (*La théologie du sacrément de pénitence au XIIe*

siècle [Louvain, 1949], p. 101), at the beginning of the High Middle Ages the notion of jurisdiction as applied to the sacrament of penance was formalized: "C'est à cette époque que s'introduit la notion de jurisdiction et la distinction claire et nette entre le for sacramentel et juridique de l'Eglise."

47. See Anciaux, esp. pp. 350–53 (which summarize the first half of the twelfth century) and pp. 604–7 (which summarize the second half).

48. See Poschmann, pp. 142–54; however, as Poschmann stresses (p. 145), the decisive contraction of confession, imposition of penance, and reconciliation into one act had come to be general practice about the year 1000.

49. Anciaux indicates the key role of Peter Lombard in crystallizing this position: ". . . La solution fondamentale du Maître des Sentences demeure la base de la conception théologique au sujet du pouvoir des prêtres dans la pénitence: ils déclarent la rémission accordée par Dieu, imposent la satisfaction ou remettent une partie des peines et réconcilient à l'Eglise" (p. 607).

50. As a matter of fact, a considerable body of opinion in the twelfth (less in the thirteenth) century saw the function of the priestly absolution as precisely one of freeing from the *punishment* due the sin. For example, the statement of the *Summa sententiarum* (tract. 6, chap. 11): "Apparet igitur quod solus Deus dimittit peccata vivificando per gratiam; et quod sacerdos dimittit, non intus vivificando, sed a debito futurae poenae absolvendo per eam quam injungit satisfactionem." Yet, as the final phrase of this citation suggests, there remained the notion (which continues on in medieval theology) that the penance performed by the penitent somehow affected, at least indirectly, the efficacy of the absolution, even though it was performed after the sacramental ritual was completed.

This problem seems to reflect the manner in which, as theologians focused more and more on the intrinsic definition of sacrament, the sacraments were increasingly seen as discrete ritual actions, separated off from the rest of life by their sacrality. The enduring element of sacrament (e.g., the sacerdotal *collegium* rather than the ordination ceremony) was obscured, and instead the *res et sacramentum*, explained as some intrinsic qualitative power, was made to provide the continuity of sacramental effectiveness.

51. And since twelfth-century developments in the theology of Penance focused on the necessary role of the priestly minister of the sacrament, this penitential judgment became an even more central function of the ordained ministers. ". . . L'administration de la pénitence était alors considerée parmi les fonctions principales des prêtres" (Anciaux, p. 121).

52. This is not to suggest that there was agreement regarding the manner in which sin was forgiven; see Poschmann, pp. 156–93, on the variety of views in this question.

53. The views of Albertus Magnus are interesting in this question. He speaks of a power of freeing others from sin that attaches to persons of special sanctity (*potestas ex vitae merito et suffragiis orationum*) and one that attaches to all laity in situations of necessity (*potestas ex unitate fidei et caritatis*); see F.-J. Nocke, *Sakrament und personaler Vollzug bei Albertus Magnus* (Münster, 1967), pp. 84–85. At the same time, he insists on the link between confession and official absolution: "Confessio enim ordinatur ad absolutionem; absolutio autem est effectus clavis; ergo ei qui claves non habet, non est confitendum" (*De sacramentis,* tract. 6, pars. 2, q. 2, a. 14). Throughout the thirteenth century some positive efficacy was attributed to confession to a layman. The first radical denial of its value came with Duns Scotus; see Poschmann, p. 188.

54. At the same time, the problem of the relation between the penitent's contrition and the external sign of penitential confession and absolution was widely disputed and remained unresolved throughout scholastic theologizing about the sacrament. Even in the highly systematized explanations of Aquinas and Scotus no adequate response is given to the critical question: If a person's own repentance (contrition) which involves some exercise of the virtue of charity has already gained an essential reconciliation with God, what intrinsic role do the subsequent confession and absolution of sins play in the forgiveness of his sin? See Poschmann, pp. 156–93.

55. Thomas Aquinas *Summa theol.* 3, q. 84, a. 3; Bonaventure *Brevil.* 10. 1–6.

56. See Poschmann, pp. 187–88.

57. Peter Lombard *Sent.* 4, d. 18, 2: "Claves istae non sunt corporales, sed spirituales, scilicet discernendi scientia et potentia judicandi. . . ." See Nocke, pp. 223–25.

58. Thus Peter Cantor (cited by Anciaux, p. 555): "Tertii dicunt et melius quod potestas ligandi vel solvendi est una clavis. Alia est debitum quoddam vel obligatio vel obnoxietas, qua sacerdos tenetur scire discernere qui ligandi qui solvendi, que propter adiunctum consortium vocatur scientia discernendi et hoc datur cuilibet cum ordinatur in sacerdotem. . . ."

59. For example, Alexander of Hales sees the confessor's activity as confined to the penalty due the sin, the power of the keys does not deal with the removal of guilt: "Ad removendum autem impedimentum quod est culpa, non est clavis necessaria, ut scilicet auferat eam, quia hoc facit Deus" (*Quaest. disp.* q. 61, disp. 1). Similarly, Bonaventure *Brevil.* 6. 10. 20–21; and on the contrary Thomas Aquinas sees the confessor's absolution as touching the forgiveness of sin itself (*Summa theol.* 3, q. 84, a. 1). On the difficulties attached to this latter view, see Poschmann, pp. 168–83.

60. "Postquam factus fuit mediator, tunc Christus et alii sacerdotes, qui vocati sunt in partem ministerii, sunt medii in reconciliatione" (Alex. Hales *Quaest. disp.* q. 56, disp. 2). "Cum igitur triplex sit potestas secundum triplex obstaculum, triplex est clavis. Prima, scilicet auctoritatis, a qua est; secunda, scilicet excellentiae, et haec est in solo Christo; et tertia est clavis ministerii, quae descendit a clave auctoritatis mediante clave excellentiae. . . ." (Bonaventure *Brevil.* 6. 10. 20.) See also Scotus *Oxon.* 4, dist. 14, q. 4; and dist. 19, q. unica; and Thomas Aquinas *Summa theol.*, *Suppl.* q. 18, a. 1.

However, it should be noted that the notion of "minister" varies quite markedly from one theologian to another. In Bonaventure, e.g., the juridical context is dominant, whereas in Aquinas it is rather a question of an instrumental cause of change in the penitent. Another observation might be made: the view of the minister of Penance as a representative of the church and the view of the sacrament as a reconciliation with the community seem to have faded into the background. Instead, there is a *verticality* of salvific effectiveness: either the effect of jurisdiction coming down from God, through Christ, through the pope and bishops, through the individual minister of the sacrament, to touch the penitent, or the effect of divine causation of grace, passing down *instrumentaliter* through Christ and the minister of the sacrament.

61. See Anciaux, p. 101.

62. So Bonaventure (*Brevil.* 6. 10. 28): "Utramque enim Dominus ipsi Petro contulit potestatem, et ligandi et solvendi in foro poenitentiali, et ligandi et solvendi in foro iudiciali. Prima potestas respicit ordinem, secunda praelationem." However, the exercise of this power requires jurisdiction; see also Thomas Aquinas *Summa theol.*, *Suppl.* q. 20, a. 2.

Lateran IV, canon 21 (*Mansi* 22. 1007), in prescribing annual confession of sin, states that only a penitent's *proprius sacerdos* has the jurisdiction to absolve. For a good reason another confessor can obtain permission from this *proprius sacerdos*. This seems to tie the jurisdiction for absolution not to the episcopacy (as distinct from presbyters) but to the pastoral charge in the broader sense.

63. Thomas Aquinas *Summa theol.*, *Suppl.* q. 22, a. 1.

64. Yet, there is always a certain hesitation in theological explanations. The penitential judgment seems to be of its nature a jurisdictional action, and the distinction between *potestas ordinis* and *potestas jurisdictionis* is not clearly applicable. This theological uneasiness may betray the inappropriateness of the political model for understanding the church, yet this inappropriateness was hidden (at least for the most part) by the increasing introduction of juridical understandings into the heart of soteriology (as in Anselm) and sacramental theology.

65. Thomas Aquinas *Summa theol.*, *Suppl.*, q. 22, a. 1.

66. See C. Feckes, *Die Rechtfertigungslehre des Gabriel Biel* (Münster, 1925), pp. 136–

37. Feckes stresses the nominalistic tendency to stress the externalism of sacramental actions and therefore the inclination of nominalist thinkers to favor the declaratory explanation of the confessor's absolution. However, even among those whose theology sees the action of sacraments as more intrinsically causative (e.g., the Thomistic school) the problem of explaining what, if anything, the penitential absolution effects in a person who comes to Penance with contrition can lead to an option for the declaratory position.

67. The dispute over the correct interpretation of Gabriel Biel's position is a case in point: Feckes (p. 80) claims that Biel basically espouses the declaratory position, whereas H. Oberman (*Harvest of Medieval Theology* [Cambridge, Mass., 1963], pp. 158–59) sees Biel as rather stressing the merely ministerial role of the confessor's absolution.

68. For several centuries before this there had, of course, been the papal granting of exemption to monasteries (beginning with the grant to Bobbio in 628)—which involved some implicit claim to papal authority over these institutions; and Rome's support of the Cluniac movement in the eleventh century was an important factor in the spread of Cluny's influence (see H. Cowdrey, *The Cluniacs and the Gregorian Reform* [Oxford, 1970], pp. 32–76). However, this did not concern the right of the monastic institution to exist, but rather dealt with its rights and privileges, particularly vis-à-vis the episcopacy.

69. Lateran IV, canon 13 (H. Schroeder, *Disciplinary Decrees of the General Councils* [St. Louis, 1937], pp. 254–55).

70. See J. Moorman, *History of the Franciscan Order* (Oxford, 1968), pp. 46–52, 176–87. The change introduced into the Franciscan movement by papal approval was more drastic, for Innocent III immediately absorbed the new group into the clerical sphere by giving tonsure to Francis and his first disciples. With the Dominicans the situation was somewhat different because Dominic and his companions were already ordained and chose the Rule of St. Augustine which had already become the common rule for communities of canons regular. Being ordained and wishing as such to exercise their apostolate, they more clearly needed to work out some arrangement with the jurisdictional structures of the church, which they did by first obtaining the approval of Bishop Fulk of Toulouse in 1215 and then winning the papacy's confirmation in 1216. See W. Hinnebusch, *History of the Dominican Order* (New York, 1966), pp. 39–50.

71. Lateran IV's imposition on all religious communities of the Cistercian structure of general chapters (Lateran IV, canon 12; see Schroeder, pp. 253–54) does seem to reflect Rome's authority over the jurisdictional patterns of religious communities; yet, closer examination of the decree indicates that the purpose was to insure monastic reform and that the procedure followed the lines of ecclesiastical provinces rather than of large religious communities as such. So, it does not really touch directly the question of the source of authority internal to such communities. In many ways, the legislation fashioned within the Dominican order during its formative years gives us the clearest picture of the medieval view about authority within religious communities. Within the order the highest authority is the general chapter, and its executive officer, the master general, is the one to whom the Dominican pledges his obedience (within the context of the rule) and whom he sees as linking him in obedience to Christ himself. (See Hinnebusch, pp. 128–33, 195–205.) Another instructive insight is given us by the Praemonstratensian Canons, who have never during their nine centuries of existence either sought or obtained papal approval.

72. In a sense, the question is tautological: to be an approved group, official approval was required. The real question is: Was the felt need to be an approved group grounded in a religious impulse and the desire to have legitimate authority functioning within the religious community, or was it grounded in the need to have the support of papal power against the opposition of bishops or princes?

73. This is reflected in the papal actions of granting basic dispensations from the legislation under which the religious orders were founded. Perhaps the most famous case was the Holy See's interventions in the Franciscan disputes about the form of poverty appropriate to the order.

74. See Wolter, pp. 98–112.

75. On the historical development of this view, see Y. Congar, *Lay People in the Church* (Westminster, Md., 1956), pp. 281–98. One of the notable features of the twelfth century was the emergence of laity into increasing prominence, even in strictly ecclesiastical activities such as preaching, and as monarchically minded a pope as Innocent III granted fairly broad ministerial functions to laity. However, this was quickly shut off as fear about deviant groups led to the "Inquisition mentality."

76. See A. Maycock, *The Inquisition* (London, 1926); M. Bévenot, "The Inquisition and Its Antecedents," *Heythrop Journal* 7 (1966), pp. 257–68, 381–93; and *ibid.*, 8 (1967), pp. 52–69, 152–68.

77. Judging such authenticity presents (and has always presented) a major problem for the Christian community, the problem of discerning the action of the Spirit in the church. History has forced enough reversals of appraisals originally made in such cases that we must question the adequacy of the procedures used, particularly the adequacy of grounding such judgments in monarchical jurisdiction.

78. The calling of general councils by the popes begins only with the twelfth century. These councils dealt with a wide range of ecclesiastical affairs, including judgment on current movements of thought and spiritual activity. Day-by-day watch over deviant developments, especially in doctrine, was largely handled by the Inquisition.

79. In the articles cited above (n. 76), Bévenot, while not approving the procedures of the Inquisition, attempts to soften judgment against the Inquisition by studying its origins and its compatibility with the times in which it was powerful.

80. See W. Ullmann, *Short History of the Papacy in the Middle Ages* (London, 1972), pp. 255–58.

81. Gregory VII had almost always selected as his permanent legates bishops from the country itself (see Kempf, pp. 372–73), but from the thirteenth century onward the Inquisitors were for the most part chosen from the mendicant orders.

82. In theory, the basic inquisitorial responsibility rested on the bishops (Lateran IV, canon 3) and the papal inquisition was to support rather than replace this basic episcopal responsibility for orthodox teaching. In actual fact, there was often considerable friction between the papal representative and the bishops of a given region as the papal inquisition gradually supplanted the episcopal process.

83. Actually, the appointment of mendicant friars to most of the inquisitorial positions seems to have been based on their possession (or supposed possession) of technical theological competence; being trained theologians, they would be able to judge the orthodoxy of the accused brought before them. There does not seem to have been any particular claim of popes to theological competence in connection with the Inquisition.

84. Though arguments about doctrinal positions marked many an inquisitorial session, the general thrust of the inquisitor's efforts was to obtain a confession of guilt and a statement of repentance. The penalty then laid on him was regarded as penance for sin rather than as simple judicial punishment. See Maycock, pp. 151–57.

85. This use of punishment, even death, to combat heresy was strongly supported by the development of legal theories, particularly in Gratian's *Decretum*, that regarded heresy as an attack on the common good of both church and state, that advocated a crusade against heresy, and that classified heresy with *maiestas laesa* (therefore punishable with death); see Wolter, pp. 102–4. Thus, the Christian task of fraternal correction is translated by the politico-military model of the church.

86. See Knowles, pp. 367–71; S. Runciman, *The Medieval Manichee* (Cambridge, 1960), pp. 138–47.

87. However, in southern France, where the Cathar (Albigensian) influence was greatest, there was widespread acceptance of its tenets by people on all levels of society and a tolerance, if not acceptance, by a large segment of the clergy. See Wolter, pp. 162–65.

88. On Hus, his background, teaching, and condemnation, see E. Delaruelle in Fliche-Martin, vol. 14, pp. 989–1029; on De Mollay and the destruction of the Templars, see K. Fink, *Handbook of Church History*, vol. 4, pp. 297–304.

89. Denzinger-Schonmetzer, for example, includes among the ecumenical councils the five Lateran councils, Lyons I and II, Vienne, and Constance.

90. One could contend that the expanded credal statements of Lateran IV or Lyons II are concerned with doctrine and contain little, if any, teaching on the level of theological opinion; however, Lateran IV's defense of Peter Lombard (see Denzinger-Schonmetzer, pp. 803–7) certainly passes over into the area of theological explanation.

91. Vienne's condemnation of Peter John Olivi's views on the multiplicity of substantial forms in man (see *ibid.*, p. 902) is a case in point.

92. Probably the most famous case of this kind was the trial of Joan of Arc, which has been the object of almost incessant dispute since its occurrence. Despite all the political factors involved, the heart of the ecclesiastical inquisition had to do with Joan's insistence on the authenticity of her religious experience—her "voices." See L. Fabre, *Joan of Arc* (London, 1954), pp. 276–323.

93. See Knowles, vol. 4, pp. 372–74.

94. On the maturation of theology in the twelfth and thirteenth centuries, see the two studies of M.-D. Chenu, *La théologie au douzième siècle* (Paris, 1957), and *La théologie comme science au XIIIe siècle*, 3d ed. (Paris, 1957).

95. On the medieval theologians' use of *"auctores,"* see J. de Ghellinck, *Dictionnaire de théologie catholique*, vol. 6, cols. 1739–44; and M.-D. Chenu, *Toward Understanding Saint Thomas* (Chicago, 1964), pp. 126–55.

96. See L. Grane, *Peter Abelard* (New York, 1970), pp. 106–62.

97. The same seems to have been true of Innocent II when the matter was referred to him. Without granting Abelard a hearing, he dispatched letters of condemnation to the archbishops of Sens and Reims, leaving Abelard's punishment to their discretion. "It must be assumed that Bernard's personal prestige had decided the issue" (*ibid.*, p. 151).

98. See Chenu, *Saint Thomas*, pp. 188–96.

99. At the present, there is nothing like an adequate history of moral theology; for a brief summation of the Roman Catholic development of moral theology, see B. Häring, *The Law of Christ* (Westminster, Md., 1961), vol. 1, pp. 3–33.

100. For example, in the *Summa theologica* of Thomas Aquinas the second part (of three parts), which itself is divided because of its bulk into a *prima secundae* and a *secunda secundae*, deals entirely with man's moral behavior and comprises more than half of the entire *Summa*.

101. See the six volumes of O. Lottin, *Psychologie et morale aux XIIe et XIIIe siècles* (Gembloux, 1940–69). On the naturalist elements that influenced the moral theology of the High Middle Ages, see Chenu, *Nature, Man, and Society in the Twelfth Century*, pp. 1–48.

102. As we will see, this becomes more pronounced after Trent, but already in the twelfth and thirteenth centuries such practices as papal granting of charters to university faculties tends to place such academic activity in the context of the ecclesiastical establishment.

103. Yet, the impact of the condemnations (at Paris and Oxford) of 1277, and the very fact that such condemnations took place, indicates the extent to which the theological activity of the universities was still considered to be under episcopal authority. See F. Van Steenberghen in Fliche-Martin, pp. 305–36.

CHAPTER 24

The Reformation Controversies

The post-medieval period, involving as it did the Reformation and the humanistic-scientific emergence of the modern world, is a good vantage point from which to study at more length the confusion between authority and power in the ministerial offices of the church. To some extent, the two realities must always coexist, for authority is meaningless if one does not possess the power to make his authority operative. Yet, there are many kinds of authority, each with its correlative kind of power, and in the history of the church a distorted understanding of the Christian community has come not only from mistaking power for authority but also (and more importantly) from misunderstanding what kind of authority and power is proper to a church which is the *sacramental* means of establishing the kingdom of God.

Although the discussion was moved into a church-state framework, the troubled relationship between secular rulers and the ecclesiastical establishment in the sixteenth and seventeenth centuries was heir to the patristic and medieval conflict of *regnum* and *sacerdotium*. The notion of a *societas christiana*, which had the clergy as its "soul," was fading quickly in these centuries. The two great symbols of this unified spiritual-temporal society, the papacy and the emperor, became increasingly less important for many portions of Europe; but the *societas christiana* still remained as a confusing assumption and ideal. Though elements of radical secularity were present in European thought from at least as early as the twelfth century, and in the matter of church-state relations found important ex-

pression in Ockham and Marsilius of Padua and Jean de Jandun in the fourteenth century, the notion of a radical distinction between church and state in human society that is basically secular did not really gain ground until the eighteenth century and is not fully accepted in our own day.[1]

In the attempt to free themselves from constraining secular power, first from the Byzantine rulers and then from the various rulers of medieval Europe, the popes insisted on the superior authority of the *sacerdotium* and insisted that the functions of this *sacerdotium* did not fall under the judgment of the *regnum*. Unfortunately, this position which could from one point of view be justified ends up as the claim that all authority (civil and ecclesiastical) has been given to the pope as the head of the *societas christiana*, and he delegates civil authority to secular rulers. Such a view served to intensify the notion of one society, and it also gave the impression that civil and ecclesiastical authority were quite similar in nature.

Because the implementation of ecclesiastical discipline, particularly the appointment and ordination of worthy bishops and priests, was in many instances hindered by secular rulers who illegitimately used various forms of power to accomplish a goal that lay outside their proper authority, medieval bishops and popes countered with use of power that was alien to the intrinsic authority of the episcopacy. By and large, the medieval papacy and episcopacy sought objectives within the sphere of their own proper function and authority. These were objectives such as the dissemination of the gospel, the elevation of men's moral behavior, the sincere practice of Christian virtue and worship, and the correction of erroneous understandings of faith. However, in working towards these goals they saw themselves as *rulers* who should enforce the law of God by whatever means proved effective: by threatening damnation, by cutting men off from salvation through excommunication (since *"extra ecclesiam nulla salus"*), by supporting those political figures who in turn would enforce (particularly on the clergy of their territory) the papal legislation, or in extreme cases by attempting to depose secular rulers who were judged to be a scandal to the faithful.

The episcopacy (and in growing measure the papacy) was armed with vast power: the power that flowed from possession of the keys to the kingdom of heaven and the social-moral power that gradually accrued to the episcopacy and papacy because of their central role in the development of medieval Europe. They could, then, intervene most effectively in the world of secular politics; and they did. This power was a means of obtaining from the secular ruler the freedom and autonomy of the church. It was also a means of securing from the ruler the kind of personal and official behavior that befitted a Christian prince, though this was often more an ideal than a reality. However, such power could be abused to further the personal prestige or wealth or secular power of bishop or pope. Abuses of this nature became particularly flagrant in the papacy of the fifteenth and early sixteenth centuries, unquestionably provided an important emotional element in the build-up to the Protestant Reformation, and seriously sapped the religious vitality of the pre-Reformation church. Yet, in the last analysis, such abuses precisely because they were seen as abuses may have done less harm than the sincere but misguided employment of secular power to enforce ecclesiastical decisions.

The danger of this latter course of action became very real for the church in the Reformation and post-Tridentine periods. In its efforts to reassert its power in the face of conciliar theories of church authority, the papacy after the Council of Constance turned to diplomacy and to support from secular monarchs.[2] However, the price it had to pay for the various concordats that guaranteed such support was to grant these secular princes a yet greater voice in church affairs, especially in appointments to rich benefices. In such maneuverings, the pope was becoming more and more just another monarch among the monarchs of Europe; it is symbolic that Frederick III was the last emperor to go to Rome for coronation (in 1452). "This heralded the *Ancien Régime*, in which royal authority, while still leaning on religious sanctions for its own support, claimed autonomy from the church."[3] Linked with this was the ecclesiology developed by Torquemada in conjunction with the Council of Basel. His *Summa de ecclesia*, which had a truly normative influence on sixteenth- and seventeenth-century Roman Catholic defense of the papacy, stressed as a basic premise the monarchical character of authority in the church.[4] Thus the Roman Catholic church, in the struggle between absolute monarchs and representative government which made up so much of the political history of modern Europe, was apparently situated quite clearly in the camp of monarchy.

But if the pope became, in the late medieval period, more and more a temporal sovereign, he was not alone in this among ecclesiastics. Throughout the Middle Ages, higher ecclesiastics functioned as counselors and administrators for secular rulers and in not a few instances (e.g., the prince-bishops of the German Imperial structure) bishops were themselves autonomous secular princes. Given the unified view of European society as Christendom that prevailed in those centuries, it was logical for a king or prince to seek competent and trustworthy officials from among the better educated, and that generally meant the higher clergy. However, this clearly involved the bishops concerned in a conflict of interests, diverted them from the careful fulfillment of their episcopal function, and created in them an understanding of their episcopal authority and power which scarcely flowed from evangelical principles. Wolsey and Richelieu were worthy successors of this tradition.

The danger of Erastianism emerging from such late medieval precedents was all too real, and it was intensified by the growing influence of the theory that religion should function as subordinate to and supportive of the secular state. Yet, in examining the period of the Reformation it would be a distortion to see the relationships between secular rulers and the various churches as varieties of Erastianism. Rather, it seems better to take the somewhat broader category of "established religion," and see how this applied to the different situations of church-state relations.

Though Protestantism cannot be seen as *the* cause of the established church phenomenon, the occurrence of the Reformation was responsible for formalizing this arrangement. While there had been various working relationships between the church and civil governments, there was no need to formalize the particular government's approval or tolerance of a given church as long as all Europe was one Christian church.[5] With the Reformation all this was changed. By the time of the Peace of Augsburg (1555) the principle *"cuius regio, eius religio"* is adopted; the prince as the "principal member of the church" has the responsibility of regulating the institutional life of the church. His ecclesiastical function begins to be viewed quite logically as derivative from his political authority.[6] On the Protestant side, this Erastian solution was adopted in the Lutheran sections of Germany, in Scandinavia, and in the Church of England, that is, wherever the state was headed by a monarch. On the Catholic side, a comparable situation prevailed under the Bourbon and Hapsburg monarchs, even when the official Roman theology did not accept the Gallican claims of these rulers to control ecclesiastical affairs. Somewhat different patterns were adopted in Switzerland and the Low Countries (and for a time in Britain) because the political structure was more representative and because Calvinism which was dominant there tended towards rule by a theocratic community. Yet, here, too, the privileged existence of one church was established by law.

Thus, across Europe, secular governments, whether one calls them "the most Catholic king" or "the Christian commonwealth," decide (with the support, or at least the acceptance, of religious leaders) how Christians are to practice their religion and therefore how Christian ministry is to be exercised. What this clearly implies is that the authority which operates in the church is derivative from the authority of the government. This implication is never fully accepted, because both Catholic theology's insistence on the autonomous sovereignty of the church and Protestant emphasis on freedom of conscience work against it. Instead, things move slowly but irreversibly towards increased separation of church and state.[7] However, this new situation reinforces the very misunderstanding of ecclesiastical authority which grew up in the centuries before the Reformation. Whether one derives secular political authority from ecclesiastical rulers or on the contrary derives the authority of church officials from secular governments, the model of the political society is operating in one's understanding of the authority that functions in the Christian community. As governments in the nineteenth and twentieth century have become increasingly secular, the inappropriateness of this model has become more evident.

Another aspect of this established church pattern needs to be mentioned. To some extent it is a process of decentralization, a centrifugal movement away from Roman domination and towards regional or national autonomy. The late Middle Ages already witnessed the beginnings of this tendency. The bitter conflict between Boniface VIII and Philip of France was a clear omen; the Avignon residence of the popes and the Western Schism intensified the anti-Roman attitude. And a part of the welcome accorded the Reformation in northern Europe was linked with a sense of liberation from Rome. In territories that remained united to the papacy, there was a certain check in this "away-from-Rome" tendency. For one thing, the Council of Trent was a major force in the reassertion of papal authority against the conciliarist views of the fifteenth century. However, one or other form of Gallicanism continues to exert great influence in the Catholic countries.[8] And, in the context of establishment, the secular governments lend their support to the Gallican aspirations of the nation's clergy. They expect in return that their ecclesiastics will support the government's political positions. In such a situation there is little doubt where the country's episcopacy obtains its power; the source of its authority is much less clear.

The inclination to side with the interests of their own nation rather than with those of the papacy was understandably strengthened in those higher ecclesiastics who functioned as part of the secular governmental structure, whether as officials or as members of the representative councils that shared in the task of government. Today we look upon such employment of higher clergy in governmental roles with a critical eye; but in those days it probably seemed a great advantage for the church (almost a need, in fact) to have bishops in such influential positions. However, because such ecclesiastics obviously had considerable impact on secular politics, secular rulers were deeply involved in the selection of bishops and increasingly demanded a determinative voice in this process. Clearly, such choices were made on bases that were not exclusively evangelical. Bishop-politicians with ambitions of rising in the secular power-structure could hardly be expected to foster the interests of the church to the disadvantage of the king.

With a foot in each world, bishops in an established situation could hardly be expected in concrete instances to distinguish accurately which kind of power they were exerting or what kind of authority they were exercising. With a given religion recognized as that established for the good of the realm, neglect or attacks against this religion could logically be viewed as detrimental to the state itself. So, bishops charged with the dual civil-ecclesiastical responsibility probably considered it quite logical to use civil power to enforce their ecclesiastical judgments. And, of course, the secular sovereign himself who wished unity and order in his realm saw no inconsistency in his enforcing religion by law and sanction.

In the Reformation period and thereafter, this intertwining of state and church authority was found principally in national situations where Gallicanism was strong; the papacy reacted consistently against the threat that this arrangement posed for the church's interests.[9] However, the use of secular power to implement ecclesiastical policies was clearly in line with the medieval papal understanding of the relation between *sacerdotium* and *regnum*. The latter existed to carry out instrumentally the Christian insights and policies of the pope and bishops, for it was these spiritual rulers who possessed the understandings of morality according to which human society should be governed. Bossuet's role as the tutor of the Dauphin fits admirably into this hierocratic view.

However, this problem was not confined to the Roman Catholic context; if anything it was more severe in the Reformation churches, for here a parallel to Gallicanism (whether Erastianism or hierocratic rule) could exist without the counterpoise of papal opposition. And the situation arose almost immediately for Protestantism. Luther was reluctant at the beginning to have princes interfering in religious matters, but by 1525 he is already stressing the duty of the secular authority to suppress, by force if necessary, any blasphemous religious practices (such as the Mass); by 1527 he encourages the Elector of Saxony to reorganize the ecclesiastical structure in his territory; by 1530 he urges secular rulers to compel people by civil law to attend the sermon and catechism.[10] In Switzerland the political and religious situation were both somewhat different, but the establishment of the Reformation in both Zurich and Geneva was the result of civic enactment (stimulated, of course, by the activity of men like Zwingli and Calvin). And in England, the very origin of the Reformation lay in the crown's assumption of ultimate control over the affairs of the English church. Laud's attempt in the early seventeenth century to enforce his ecclesiastical reforms by secular power makes it clear that Erastianism in the English church was not confined to kings grasping for power.

Somewhat more subtle, though equally prevalent, was the support that established religion gave the civil government. Since fidelity to the ruler and observance of the civil law were preached as basic Christian virtues in both Catholic and Protestant establishments, this religious teaching by the church moved the sanction of civil law into the sphere of Christian morality and "eternal damnation." Though this often constituted a distortion of Christian teaching and a prostitution of the church's power to guide men's consciences, it was quite widely assumed that ecclesiastical support would always be given to law and order. Those who functioned as ordained ministers comprised, then, a part of the establishment; in many cases they were committed to continuing and defending the status quo, and they often found their evangelical freedom limited by their dependence upon secular rulers. The clear exception to this was found in those who ministered to persecuted minorities; they were spared the paralyzing favor of the prince, though they quite often sought to obtain it.

It is the intrinsic nature of the Christian community that whatever authority is possessed by any human agency in the church exists only in dependence upon the faith of the baptized. This authority exists to foster faith; it should be accepted only because faith sees Christ acting through those who possess authority. But in the context of established state churches, the attempt was made to place the authority of Christian ministers, particularly that of higher ecclesiastics, within the bounds of political structures, to ground it in civil law, and to support it with the sanctions provided by that law. One of the drawbacks of this practice, apart from the fact that it was

wrong, was that it created or at least reinforced a false understanding about the genesis of ecclesiastical authority. Later, when ecclesiastical structures were freed from the embrace of political establishment and civil law could no longer be claimed as a source of ministerial authority, ecclesiastical officials still continued to think of their authority as deriving from law, though now it was from church law.[11]

Along with its challenge to prevalent understandings of salvation, interpretation of Scripture, and the function of sacraments, the Protestant Reformation presented a number of alternatives to the ecclesiastical polity with which the sixteenth century opened. The fifteenth century ended with men still somewhat aware of the uncertainties about the church's structure that had come from the Great Western Schism. Martin V and his immediate successors had quickly reasserted the Roman claims against the conciliarist position of the Council of Constance. The conciliarist forces had been increasingly disorganized at Basel and Ferrara, and almost completely ineffective at Florence.[12] However, if Rome had been dimmed as a symbol of institutional unity during the Schism, it was dimmed as a symbol of religious leadership by the decadence which marked the papal court during the latter half of the fifteenth century. Consequently, much of Europe had been disposed for the proposals of the reforms, and the new patterns of church polity established by the various leaders of the Reformation fitted in quite naturally with the emergent structures of civil government. As a matter of fact, much of the Reformation church structure grew out of and along with the sixteenth-century evolution of political institutions.

This is not the place to discuss in detail the various forms of ecclesiastical organization adopted by the Reformers, nor to suggest what underlying notion of ministry or priesthood these new forms translate.[13] Rather, our purpose at this point is to see what clarification of jurisdictional lines occurred in the Roman Catholic church because of the sixteenth-century crisis, what understanding of *potestas jurisdictionis* dominated the Roman response to the Reformation's challenge to its jurisdiction, and how this reflected the Roman understanding of ministry, especially episcopal ministry. Pivotal, of course, to any such investigation is the Council of Trent, which stands as a most important landmark in the history of Christian ecclesiastical structures. To a large extent, not only did it streamline and stabilize the ecclesiastical patterns that had emerged from the Middle Ages, but it froze them to such an extent that Catholics in the twentieth century are still living in a church which is Tridentine in organization.

Given the broad scope of Trent's doctrinal judgments and reform measures, it is highly significant that it produced no decree on the structure of the church nor on the authority of the pope. It is true that some of this is contained in the reform decrees about ministry and in the decree on Holy Orders, but the fundamental issue regarding ecclesiastical jurisdiction, the relationship between papacy and episcopacy, could not be resolved at the council and had to be left a somewhat open question, and so the entire matter of authority and power in the church remained unclear at the council's close. Against the Reformers' attacks on the evangelical origin of the Catholic bishops and priests, Trent could say that the hierarchy of bishops, presbyters, and ministers was instituted *divina ordinatione*.[14] But the council avoided taking a position on the source of episcopal jurisdiction, whether it came directly from God or was mediated through the pope. The bitter disagreement on this point, which finally surfaced during the last winter of the council (1562–63) could not be worked out in discussion. Even the compromise solutions of de Soto and Lainez, though they gained considerable following, failed to win sufficient support.[15] Not only the continuance of the council but also the unity of the Roman Catholic community seemed threatened by the controversy. Obviously, the conciliarist theories were not completely dead. Though the pope could not obtain from the council a definition of papal

primacy, he did manage to avoid a definition favoring conciliarism.[16]

If it could not resolve the pope-bishops relationship, Trent did bring some order into the episcopal-presbyteral relationship. This was achieved through its disciplinary decrees on preaching[17] and on clerical reform.[18] The decree on preaching placed the nurture and control of preaching, even that done by religious, firmly in the hands of the bishops. The decree on reform legislated against the ordination of "unattached" presbyters, conditioned presbyteral power to absolve sins upon episcopal approval, and laid upon the bishop the responsibility of approving (and, if necessary, training) candidates for ordination. However, it seems fair to say that the Tridentine decision about jurisdiction in these contexts was a practical pastoral judgment rather than an attempt to clarify theologically the nature of ecclesiastical jurisdiction.

Yet, Trent's approach to ecclesiastical jurisdiction already marks an emphasis that is different from that of the Middle Ages, an emphasis that will become increasingly clear in subsequent centuries. In the Middle Ages, the *potestas jurisdictionis* was certainly seen as touching the teaching authority of the ordained (the action of synods and councils in handling doctrinal issues testifies to this), but the emphasis was rather on the manner in which ecclesiastical authority functioned in the overall government of European society. This political arena was the scene of dispute between *sacerdotium* and *imperium* and it was at least partially the context of papal-episcopal controversy. It was in relation to the contest for power between pope and king that so much of the literature regarding papal authority came into existence. Now, as the Reformation raises the issue of large-scale heresy, the emphasis particularly in theological dispute shifts to the issue of authority in doctrinal matters. Increasingly the *magisterial* (i.e., teaching) authority of the bishops and particularly of the pope is stressed. To some extent, this shift of attention from the political to the magisterial is connected with the changing political structures of sixteenth-

and seventeenth-century Europe, and to the fact that relations between pope and princes are now resolved on the basis of diplomacy and concordat. But to some extent it is due to the fact that the Reformation period inherited the notion of an ecclesiastical authority called *"potestas jurisdictionis,"* which was distinct from the *"potestas ordinis,"* which was concerned with governing the social order of the church, indeed of all human society, and which pertained *de jure divino* to pope and bishops. And since this power of jurisdiction was assumed to be basic to the church's order, for it was of divine institution, churchmen and theologians and jurists had to find some place to locate it once its application to the political-social sphere became less relevant. A considerable part of this relocation consisted in emphasizing the official church as the authoritative teacher of Christians and to some extent of all men. A reflection of the manner in which doctrinal authority is being seen as jurisdictional, rather than as consisting in possession of theological insight, can be found in Trent's decree on preaching, and precisely in its description of the way in which bishops are to control preaching.

When one turns from the formulations of Trent to the theological writings of the Reformation period, one finds the same shift in emphasis. There are, of course, lengthy discussions about the relative jurisdictions of church and state in which the classic medieval developments of papal *plenitudo potestatis* are preserved and, sometimes with modification, defended; but the basic approach now to the authority of the episcopacy, and above all to the primacy of the pope, is in terms of the teaching office.[19] To a large extent, discussion of the papal teaching authority turns about the question of infallibility. But it is significant that propapal apologetes proceed in their argumentation from the pope's possession of primatial authority to that specific exercise of authority which comes in infallible doctrinal teaching. The idea of jurisdiction is basic to the idea of church teaching.[20]

While the first wave of theological defense of papal and episcopal authority was directed against Reformation views, the late sixteenth century saw a renewed controversy within the Roman Catholic community on the question of papal prerogatives. Such men as Eck and Cajetan, and then a bit later Pighius, Canisius, Stapleton, Cano, and Bellarmine, had worked out a position of papal absolutism which was not directed primarily at the conciliarist part within the Roman church but which did actually oppose that party and its alliance with nationalist sentiments. It was only a matter of time until these propapal views would come under attack by the proponents of Gallicanism, i.e., of the rights and autonomy of national churches. The very fact that "Gallicanism" is employed to denominate this phenomenon, which actually affected other countries (e.g., Spain and Germany), indicates the extent to which the doctrinal expression of this nationalist sentiment was formulated in France.

To obtain a clear picture of the ecclesiastical situation in France of the seventeenth century is well-nigh impossible, for the lines of allegiance to either Rome or France cross on different issues. For example, Louis XIV, who in 1681 convoked a general assembly of the French clergy to approve the Four Articles which are the charter of Gallicanism, allied himself with the popes in their opposition to Jansenism. Severe divisions existed within the French church itself. Jansenists and Jesuits (each group supported by influential allies) were engaged in a bitter dispute that would carry on into the next century. Not all the hierarchy sided with Bossuet, who drafted the Four Articles. The theological faculty of Paris, which had itself taken a strongly Gallican stand in 1663, now resisted Louis' imposition of the articles as theological teaching. The movement of spiritual revival that was associated with Bérulle, Olier, Vincent de Paul, and John Eudes, a movement that had profound effect on numerous clergy and laity, was generally quite ultramontane.[21] However, the Gallican articles of 1682 represented the thought of a goodly portion of the French Catholics as well as of the royal partisans; its anti-Roman brand of episcopalianism is a step towards the strong presbyterianism of eighteenth-century French lower clergy and the Civil Constitution of the clergy.

While it did not directly emanate in any new understandings of the nature of ecclesiastical jurisdiction, the power struggle between the religious orders and the episcopacy was an important element in the practical exercise of jurisdiction. For centuries a rather bitter contest had been waged by the episcopacy against the relative autonomy and competing influence of the religious orders. The controversy focused on the exemptions from episcopal control that had been given the religious foundations by the popes.[22] Clearly, the fight over exemptions was part of the struggle between papacy and episcopacy; understandably, the religious orders tended to side with the papacy, and the extension of the practice of exemption was (at least in many instances) a move by Rome to obtain powerful allies. Moreover, the theory and practice of jurisdiction flowing directly from the pope to the internal government and the ministerial activity of religious communities (and bypassing episcopal mediation) was a continuing proof of the papal claim to immediate authority over all Christians.

Though the victory was not complete (exemption did continue), Trent marks a definite gain in the episcopacy's campaign to control religious communities. While the internal government of houses of exempt religious continues under the immediate direction of Rome, clerical religious are placed under episcopal control in their pastoral ministry by the need to obtain diocesan approval for preaching and penitential absolution. Intrinsically, this arrangement makes quite good sense, for it honors both the episcopacy's responsibility to safeguard the ministry of word and sacrament and the religious community's right to direct its own internal affairs; by and large, it has worked out fairly well in practice. However, the centuries since Trent have seen a continuing tension, sometimes open, sometimes latent, between the episcopacy and religious orders.

One of the by-products of this tension between regular and diocesan clergy may be of considerable importance in the evolution of Catholic thinking about priesthood and ministry. Apparently there was a strong reaction on the part of leading diocesan clergy against the suggestion that the clerical-religious vocation was a higher call than that of the diocesan clergy. Very likely the consistent use by the popes of religious orders to help them implement the reform decrees of Trent did not help the situation. As a result, there was a determined effort to develop a spirituality of the secular priest, a spirituality that could be polemically defended as at least as lofty (and actually loftier) as that fostered by religious community life.[23] At the center of this movement was the so-called French School (Bérulle, Olier, Vincent de Paul, etc.), out of which developed the Congregation of the Missions and the Society of Saint Sulpice, which have played such a key role in seminary training from the seventeenth to the twentieth century.[24] In the next part we will have occasion to analyze this view of priesthood and ministry, its Dionysian roots, and its absorption of the ideals of monasticism into the ideal of pastoral ministry; but it helps somewhat in evaluating this theological development to see that it was partially stimulated by a struggle for eminence and influence within the clergy.

The notion of the bishop as a monarch is not new to the period we are studying, but the challenges of the Reformation once more drew attention to it; the notion figures prominently in post-Tridentine controversial theology. To some extent, the reform measure of Trent requiring episcopal residence may have been an influence, for it certainly draws attention to the bishop as governor of his diocese. Another influence may well have been the widespread discussion of monarchy among the political theorists of the day. The appeal by ecclesiologists like Torquemada to such theories as parallels for understanding ecclesiastical authority was certainly influential. At any rate, it is a presumption of post-Tridentine theology that the church is meant to be monarchic in its structure. It is a supernatural society whose authority must come from above; the only question is whether it is to be an absolute monarchy with all power coming through the pope, or whether it is to be more oligarchic.

It is clear from the literature of the day that much of the theological explanation of episcopal monarchy was in answer to various Reformation teachings about the priesthood of all believers. The emphasis of the Reformers on the basic priesthood of the Christian people was not a repudiation of ministry as a normal need of the community. On the other hand, the need for any distinction between the pastor who brought the word of God to his people and a higher ecclesiastic (whether he was called "bishop" or not) was not generally accepted; England, of course, was a unique situation. Thus, the cutting edge of Reformation criticism of Christian ministry struck at the Roman Catholic episcopacy, especially at its authoritative claims. It was in response to this attack that post-Tridentine controversial theology tried to bolster the case for bishops possessing monarchical jurisdiction within their dioceses.[25]

One might gather from this episcopal insistence on their divinely given authority that the attitude of bishops in the sixteenth and seventeenth centuries was autocratic and domineering. While there may have been some of this, it is also quite illuminating to read the panegyrics of Bossuet and to see how in the episcopal ideal that he proposes the authority of the bishop is linked with service and self-sacrifice. More than that, Bossuet insists that the real authority of such bishops as Francis de Sales, Charles Borromeo, or Thomas à Becket derived from their devotion to Christ and their untiring concern for the flock committed to them.[26]

Such words (from Bossuet or from others) were not just empty rhetoric without theological foundation; the sixteenth- and seventeenth-century debates about the nature and extent of ecclesiastical authority were always governed by the premise that Christ's own authority is the source and therefore the exemplar of all authority in the church. Both Protestant and Catholic controversialists argue from the threefold office of Christ as prophet, priest, and king. And if Bellarmine will see the monarchical authority of Christ extended into the monarchical authority of the episcopate, Calvin will speak of the authority that attaches to the pastor as the ambassador of Christ.[27] Though such emphases are often quite subtle and difficult to ascertain, there is little question but what the Roman Catholic polemicists laid greater stress than did their Protestant counterparts on the kingship of Christ, and did so in terms of arguing from that to the monarchical nature of the church. Obviously, all this is conditioned by the interpretation one gives to the kingship possessed by Christ; everyone will insist that Christ's kingship is essentially spiritual ("my kingdom is not of this world"), but at a time when the secular ruler is seen in his kingship to be expressing the kingship of Christ, the "political model" was bound to influence one's thinking about the kingship of Christ and of the church.[28]

It says something about the centrality of judgment in the notion of Christian ministry that both Catholic and Protestant officials during the period of the Reformation and thereafter were convinced that judging the truth or falsity of doctrinal statements was an essential part of their ministerial task—and this despite their fundamental division on the source of such authoritative discrimination. Recent studies have made it clear that the popular understanding of the Reformation's appeal to Scripture as the sole judge of faith needs serious modification. Often this had been presented as a simple polarity between Scripture and tradition, the Protestants claiming Scripture alone can judge the orthodoxy of a given doctrinal statement or theological opinion, the Catholics claiming a preeminence for tradition (i.e., ecclesiastical teaching).[29] At least some of the Protestant insistence on Scripture was more pastoral than theological; Luther, for one, was interested that sermons deal with the simple word of God rather than with "scholastic sophistications."[30] All the classic Reformers recognized a ministerial function of explaining Scripture according to an orthodox tradition; almost immediately confessional formulations developed within the Reformation churches as guides for understanding Christianity. Without minimizing the problem created by pre-Reformation exaggeration of the authority of official teaching (whether papal or conciliar), there is considerable justification for saying that the underlying tension at the time of the Reformation is not Scripture versus tradition, but authoritative teaching versus the charismatic individual as ultimate interpreter of Scripture. Who can provide better guidance in understanding the word of God, the bishop or the saint?[31] Without exactly raising the theological issue as such, the Council of Trent seems to have dealt implicitly with the basic problem when, in its reform decree on preaching, it places the preacher of the gospel (no matter how charismatic he may be) under the normative jurisdiction of the episcopacy.

Surprisingly (at least to twentieth-century Catholics, who have become accustomed to equating *magisterium* with episcopal and especially papal teaching), the Roman Catholic church at the time of the Council of Trent did not have an explanation of teaching authority that totally identified the *magisterium* with the episcopate, as most post-Tridentine theology did. Yet, it was taken for granted that the corporate voice of the bishops assembled in general council was the ultimate criterion of Christian orthodoxy. Trent was finally convoked in response to the demand for just such a corporate judgment. In the early stage of the Reformation, there was still enough trust in the role of such a council that the Reformers themselves might well have cooperated in such an assembly.

Quite clearly, the assumption that underlies the activity and decrees of the Council of Trent is the supreme authority of the episcopacy (involving, of course, the pope, but without specifying exactly his relation to the council) in doctrinal matters. The bulk of the doctrinal decrees of Trent are framed in language that is unambiguously that of dogmatic definition, though, clearly, not everything in these decrees was intended to be definition. This is reflected particularly in the manner in which each of the major declarations is followed by a series of canons, each of which summarizes a portion of the preceding decree and then judges as heterodox ("*anathema sit*") anyone who rejects this teaching. It is important to note that it is certain intellectual understandings and not precisely persons that are being judged by the council. While the dogmatic definitions are certainly intended to deal with the questions raised by the Reformers, they are not directed explicitly at any person but at heretical positions.

In addition to the collegial activity of the episcopacy at Trent, there is abundant evidence of individual bishops who by their efforts to work against the infiltration of Protestant ideas indicated their conviction that they had the right and the responsibility of passing judgment on views that were contrary to the faith. But there was also a noticeable hesitancy of many bishops to move against the Reformation ideas, for what reasons is difficult to say. Probably the most striking example was in England, where the bishops, having compromised themselves by their acquiescence in 1531 to the royal supremacy over the church, found themselves subscribing to the Ten Articles of 1536, then to the royal injunctions of 1538, and finally to the king's Book of 1543, each of them a step away from the old faith and towards continental Protestantism.[32]

Despite the disillusionment with the papacy that the Avignon captivity and the Great Western Schism had caused, and despite the Renaissance papacy's own sad need for reform, bishops as well as other Christians still looked to Rome in the early sixteenth century to initiate the needed reform of the church and to provide doctrinal clarification by convoking a council. So, within those portions of the church which did not follow the Reformers, the pope continued to exercise his supreme doctrinal authority throughout the Reformation and into the post-Tridentine period. It was papal action that first brought decisive judgment against Martin Luther; it was the popes who passed judgment against the sovereigns who claimed supremacy over the English church. During the Council of Trent the popes continuously worked through their legates to direct the progress of the council, and it was the popes who guided the post-Tridentine reforms of the church.

In the post-Tridentine church, the doctrinal position of the pope was at least as strong as it had ever been. Despite an enduring strain of antipapal sentiment and of conciliar theology, the explicit espousal of papal infallibility was gaining strength in theological circles.[33] Further support came from a development within theological methodology. The formal structuring of theological reflection on the basis of the various sources of data (loci theologici) was initiated in the sixteenth century by Melchior Cano and gradually became a basic pattern for theological analysis and exposition.[34] Both conciliar statements (which, of course, implicitly involve papal authority in Cano's view of the relation between council and pope) and papal teaching are high on the list of loci; only Scripture precedes them. Thus theologians within the Catholic tradition began to regard the papacy as superior to all other traditional auctores.

Much of the far-reaching impact of the Council of Trent was due to the energetic efforts of post-Tridentine popes in enforcing the council. In the area of doctrine, one of the chief agencies through which they worked for the safeguarding of orthodox teaching was the Congregation of the Holy Office, which had already been established in 1542 by Paul III to combat the teaching of the Reformation. Its function, which it possesses by delegation, of passing judgment in all matters of doctrine presumes the supreme judgmental authority of the pope himself. Its statements have force, not because of the clear faith or theological acumen of its members but because it participates in the pope's power of official teaching.[35]

Though they did not enjoy the key position of doctrinal judgment that they occupied at Constance, theological faculties still functioned until the middle of the seventeenth century as a major factor in the official teaching activity of the church. Moreover, the sixteenth and early seventeenth century saw a large-scale evolution of theological faculties both quantitatively and qualitatively. Paris, which had once had an almost unchallenged position as the most eminent of theological schools and as an informal arbiter of theological developments, saw its privileges threatened by the increased prestige of Louvain and Salamanca and Alcala and Coimbra. Even in its own backyard, Paris was challenged by the faculty of eminent theologians assembled at the Jesuit college of Clermont.[36] Yet, somewhat paradoxically, this widespread flowering of theology in the universities and in the houses of studies of religious orders was accompanied by a gradual disappearance of their role as official judges of theology. Erasmus could still speak of the faculty at Paris in 1520 as enjoying a ruling position in theology comparable to the sovereignty of the Roman see in the Christian religion.[37] And many of the theological faculties, to say nothing of important theologians acting in an individual capacity, played an important role in combating Reformation theology and in supporting the reform activity of the papacy. Still, "it is in the post-Tridentine period that one sees the Holy See profiting by the disagreements among theologians to diminish the doctrinal authority of the university and to reserve decisions to itself."[38]

If Roman Catholic theologians were losing the right to pass conclusive judgment on theological procedures and conclusions (and roughly parallel things were happening in Protestant circles, as for example the manner in which theological tensions in Lutheranism were solved by the Formula of Concord in 1580), there was at least one area in which their judgmental influence was informally expanding. This was in the evolution of moral theology, which in the Reformation period and thereafter takes on the position of an autonomous branch of theology and expands rapidly in the direction of casuistry.[39] Partially because the new manuals of moral theology were used in training candidates for the pastoral work of the confessional, partially because of the large-scale incorporation of canon law into sections of moral theology, the teaching of moralists exercised an increasing judgment upon the morality of people's actions.[40]

Judgment upon doctrinal orthodoxy was not new to the Reformation period, though it was somewhat new to excommunicate such a large mass of diverse heretics. What is new is the extensive judgment (as a doctrinal judgment) on matters of fact, judging that certain realities do or do not exist, for example, that Calvinist pastors do not effect genuine Eucharist when they celebrate the Lord's Supper.[41] This attempt to define fact, which comes close to absurdity in the interchanges between the Holy See and the Jansenists, has raised some serious theological questions about the proper sphere of dogmatic statements and about the whole question of authoritative teaching.

One of the areas in which this magisterial pronouncement on a factual situation assumes considerable importance is that of Christian priesthood and ministry. Even when there was no explicit statement to that effect, there was a growing assumption by Roman Catholic authorities that the ministry being exercised in the Reformation churches was an empty pretension.[42] After all, how could their ministry be valid? They had no possible means of obtaining the *potestas ordinis* since they had repudiated the only source of such power, the episcopacy with its legitimate apostolic succession.

On the surface, this could seem nothing more than another expression of the recurrent problem about reordination. However, in many respects the Reformation situation was quite different. It was not for the most part a matter of a hierarchy in schism (though this could to some extent apply to the English church), nor of ordaining bishops whose credentials were suspect because of simony or some other "invalidating" deficiency; rather, the Reformation confronted the Roman church with large communities of Christians who formally repudiated the need for an episcopacy linked by imposition of hands to the apostles, and instead functioned with a pastoral ministry that was independent of any delegation of power from Rome or the Roman Catholic episcopacy. And for most of the past four centuries the judgment passed on this Protestant ministry by the Roman Catholic *magisterium* has been that of nonexistence: the Protestant ministry simply could not be what it claimed to be, a divinely ordained instrument for the sanctification of the Christian people.[43]

Another area in which the notion of validity (and therefore of existence or nonexistence) was introduced was that of marriage. Prior to Trent, the church had legislated regarding Christian marriage, particularly against the practice of clandestine marriages. But the only instance in which it went beyond the normal impediments (consanguinity, age, etc.) which civil law recognized in declaring marriages invalid was that of priests who married. While it denounced the practice of clandestine marriages, which was the source of much confusion and injustice, it admitted their basic validity.

Trent's famous decree *"Tametsi"* in 1563 changed all this; it conditioned the validity of Christian marriages on observance of the external form which required that the marriage contract be pronounced before witnesses and in the presence of an ordained minister with proper jurisdiction. This decree proved insufficient, and a number of modifications had to be made over succeeding centuries, but the basic principle had been established by Trent.[44] What is notable is that the Roman church at this point not only decided which marriages were approved marriages, but went beyond that to declaring whether marriages did or did not exist.

Such church legislation about marriage proved to be an area of major conflict with civil governments, both church and state claiming to have jurisdiction in this matter. Apart from such contention, which was at least partially an aspect of a larger power struggle, there is serious theological question about the kind of power or authority the episcopacy or presbyterate exercises in this Christian sacrament. Certainly, it is not the *potestas ordinis*, since the couple themselves are the effective ministers of the sacrament. And if it is *potestas jurisdictionis*, it is far from clear who exactly is exercising jurisdiction, since the bishop or his delegate is only a witness and not an agent.

NOTES

1. Some interesting and stimulating reflections on the enduring importance of the notion of *"respublica christiana"* are contained in the article of J. Figgis, "Respublica Christiana," *Essays in Modern History*, ed. I. Christie (London, 1968), pp. 1–24.

2. See A. Black, *Monarchy and Community* (Cambridge, 1970), pp. 124–29.

3. *Ibid.*, p. 124.

4. See *ibid.*, p. 95. Significantly, Torquemada bases the claim that church government should be monarchical upon the political theory that authority resides in the prince. It is interesting to see the similarity between the political theories of Torquemada and those expressed two centuries later by Bossuet in his *Politique*.

5. An exception (and a forerunner of the Reformation-time practice) is the position of the Utraquists in fifteenth-century Bohemia. See A. Fliche and V. Martin, *Histoire de l'Eglise depuis les origines jusqu'à nos jours* (Paris, 1935—), vol. 14, pp. 1026–29.

6. See J. Lecler, *Toleration and the Reformation* (London, 1960), vol. 1, pp. 258–59. As Lecler points out, the phrase *"cuius regio, eius religio"* is not itself used in the Peace of Augsburg; instead, the equivalent *"ubi unus dominus, ibi una sit religio"* is found.

7. Interestingly, it seems to have been minority groups, living under some form of persecution, that developed the idea of church and state as two distinct societies; see Figgis, pp. 19–20. Figgis' view of the link between the Reformation grant of ecclesiastical authority to secular rulers and the continuing assumption of a *respublica christiana* is provocative enough to deserve quotation: "The campaign of the Reformers was just *une campagne laïque*. They were not attempting to take power out of the Christian society, but merely out of its clerical officials. All coercive power was to be vested in the prince, but in theory it was always the godly prince, 'most religious.' So long as they had him on their side, men so different as Laud and Luther felt that they were safe. The sixteenth century witnessed an undoubted victory of the secular over the ecclesiastical power; but it was not for the secular power as a society distinct from the Church, it was a victory for the temporal authority within the one society which can be called either Church or State according to the aspect prominent at the moment." (P. 21)

8. On the theological formulations of this Gallicanism, see L. Willaert, in Fliche-Martin, vol. 18, pp. 361–424.

9. Thus Alexander VIII issued his constitution *"Inter multiplices"* in 1690, condemning the famous Four Articles adopted by the Assembly of French Clergy in 1682. His predecessor, Innocent XI, had fought bitterly with the French hierarchy and Louis XIV over these articles but had delayed a formal condemnation because he feared a schism of the French church. See A. Whiteman, *New Cambridge Modern History* (Cambridge, 1961), vol. 5, pp. 135–39.

10. See Lecler, pp. 155–60. See also, R. Davies, *The Problem of Authority in the Continental Reformers* (London, 1946), pp. 57–62.

11. In this regard it is instructive to notice the progression that takes place in the thought of the Protestant churches about the genesis of ministerial authority. At the beginning they all start with an emphasis on the charismatic source of authority (i.e., the vocation of the Spirit, though they see some role of the community in calling the individual to ministry), but the role of *official* empowerment quickly comes to the fore. See Davies, *Problem of Authority*. His thesis is that for the great Reformers

ministerial authority flows from the word of God, but in each case his evidence leads him to the conclusion that the Reformers moved away from a charismatic and towards an institutional approach to authority.

12. See R. Aubenas, *New Cambridge Modern History*, vol. 1, pp. 76–94, on the papacy after Constance; also J. Gill, *The Council of Florence* (Cambridge, 1959), pp. 16–45.

13. An earlier chapter described the various Reformation structures, and chapter 31 will give a theological analysis of the views of ministry related to these structures.

14. See *Concilium Tridentinum* 9, p. 622.

15. Lainez' solution (which he had drawn to some extent from Cajetan and Torquemada) is worth mentioning because many later treatises *de ecclesia* repeat it: bishops and presbyters receive with ordination, and directly from God in the ordination, the "power of orders" by which they can dispense the merits of Christ; but they are incapable of exercising this ministry validly on a given group of Christians until they have received the "power of jurisdiction" which comes to them through the mediation of the pope. See Willaert, p. 338.

16. *Ibid.*, pp. 336–40. An intriguing instance of the enduring influence of the conciliarist position is provided by Giovanni Gozzadini. Although he was a very influential and favored official in the papal curia at the beginning of the sixteenth century, his work *De electione Romani pontificis* expounds an unmistakable conciliarist position. See A. Jedin, *Kirche des Glaubens—Kirche der Geschichte* (Freiburg, 1966), vol. 2, pp. 17–74.

17. *Concilium Tridentinum* 5, pp. 73–74.

18. *Ibid.*, vol. 9, pp. 623–30.

19. For a bibliography (up to 1960) on the doctrinal authority of the pope, see Willaert, pp. 340–42.

20. A brief but perceptive summation of fifteenth- and sixteenth-century theological discussion of papal doctrinal authority is given in *ibid.*, pp. 343–59. See also G. Glez, *Dictionnaire de théologie catholique*, vol. 13, cols. 316–28.

21. See Whiteman, pp. 130–39; Willaert, pp. 367–406.

22. See E. Iserloh, *Handbook of Church History* (New York, 1965—), vol. 4, p. 570; Jedin, pp. 360–66 (on the attempts at Lateran V to assert episcopal control over religious orders).

23. For a more recent statement of this position, see J. Heenan, *The People's Priest* (New York, 1952), pp. 1–6.

24. See Willaert, pp. 140–42; also H. Bremond, *Histoire littéraire du sentiment religieux en France* (Paris, 1925), vol. 3, which is still the classic treatment of the "French school."

25. To take but two theologians as an example: Soto, who was one of the first to react to Reformation thought and who participated importantly in Trent, clearly defended at the council the divine origin of episcopal authority and saw episcopacy as an order and a sacrament. See his *Instit. sacerd., De ordine*, lect. 4. Writing some decades later, Bellarmine, who insists that Christ established his church as a spiritual kingdom with Peter (and his successors) at the head, and who teaches that councils are subordinate to the pope, also insists that bishops are *de jure divino* true princes in their own dioceses and do not function as vicars of the pope. See *Recognitio, de summo pontifice* 5. 3.

26. See J. Truchet, *La prédication de Bossuet* (Paris, 1960), vol. 1, pp. 138–41.

27. See L. Schummer, *Le ministère pastoral dans l'"Institution Chrétienne" de Calvin* (Wiesbaden, 1965), pp. 78–82.

28. On the historical antecedents of this Christological approach to the discussion of secular and ecclesiastical authority, see J. Leclercq, *L'idée de la royauté du Christ au Moyen Age* (Paris, 1959). Perhaps it was a bit easier to view the kingship of Christ more spiritually in the situations where Christians did not see a king as symbolizing God's rule in their midst; see, e.g., B. Milner's explanation of Calvin's view of the

church as kingdom of Christ in *Calvin's Doctrine of the Church* (Leiden, 1970), pp. 164–79.

29. See G. Tavard, *Holy Writ or Holy Church* (New York, 1959), which deals precisely with the Reformation period; G. Moran, *Scripture and Tradition* (New York, 1963); Y. Congar, *Tradition and Traditions* (New York, 1967), pp. 139–76, 459–93.

30. See H. Hillerbrand, *Christendom Divided* (New York, 1971), pp. 284–87.

31. The words of Francis de Sales (cited by Congar, p. 333) seem relevant here: "Scripture has no need of a rule or an exterior light, as Beza thinks we believe; . . . still less do we wish for a judge between God and us, as he seemingly suggests in his epistles; it is between men such as Calvin, Beza, Luther and others such as Eck, Fisher and More that we want a judge; for we are not asking whether God understands Scripture better than we do, but if Calvin understands it better than St. Augustine or St. Cyprian."

32. See P. Hughes, *The Reformation in England* (New York, 1951), vol. 2, pp. 22–57.

33. See Willaert, pp. 350–59.

34. For a detailed explanation of Cano's methodology and his appraisal of the various *loci*, see A. Gardeil, *Dictionnaire théologie catholique*, vol. 9, cols. 712–39.

35. Mention of the Holy Office, which is direct heir to the Inquisition, raises the question of authoritative teaching and its relationship to freedom of conscience. From one point of view, responsible teaching authority in a religious community must be intolerant (it cannot say that what is false is true), and the sixteenth- and seventeenth-century papacy was not more marked by tolerance towards error than were the various Reformers. See J. Lecler, *Toleration and the Reformation*, 2 vols., which, though attending primarily to the matter of legal tolerance, provides much insight into religious attitudes on freedom of conscience during this period. For the papacy the matter of infringing on freedom of conscience by authoritative doctrinal judgment becomes an unavoidable issue in its dealings with Jansenism.

36. See Willaert, pp. 183–220.

37. In his letter of December 6, 1520, to Cardinal Campeggio: "Expectabatur sententia Parisiensis Academiae, quae semper in re theologica non aliter principem tenuit locum, quam Romana sedes christianae religionis principatum." He is speaking of the judgment asked of the Paris faculty on the teaching of Luther, and he is quite critical of the tone of the Parisian condemnation and in general of the Roman approach to handling Luther. (*Opus Epistolarum Des. Erasmi Roterdami*, ed. P. Allen [Oxford, 1922], vol. 4, p. 409.)

38. Willaert, p. 184.

39. See B. Häring, *The Law of Christ* (Westminster, Md., 1963), pp. 14–22, for a brief explanation of the genesis of the modern discipline of moral theology.

40. A most important aspect of this question, but one that is too subtle and complicated to discuss thoroughly in this book, is the employment of "probabilism" as a formal principle in the judgment of conscience. While there is the obvious danger of "theological triumphalism" on the part of moral theologians (who, if they form a "solidly probable" opinion on some topic, become an ultimate criterion of moral judgment), probabilism can also function as a safeguard against a too rigid and legalistic application of official church teaching in moral matters.

41. This tendency is not limited to Roman Catholic officials. Some of the Reformers would contend that God did not work through Roman Catholic ministers because of corruption, etc., in the Roman church. However, this attempt to apply faith to an a priori judgment on something's existence does not reach the point of formalization it acquires in Catholicism—the question is seriously raised as to whether papal infallibility covers statements about facts.

42. There is a clear reflection of this mentality in the first of Bérulle's three discourses against the Reformed; see *Oeuvres complètes du Cardinal Bérulle* (Montsoult, 1644), pp. 68–71. His argument is simple: How can one preach effectively if he is not sent by Christ; but the Protestants obviously are not sent by Christ (since they will not accept Christ's delegated representative).

43. At the present time, in Roman Catholic theological circles, there is serious reconsideration of the very notion of "validity." See K. McDonnell, "Ways of Validating Ministry," *Journal of Ecumenical Studies* 7 (1970), pp. 209–65; also K. Osborne, "Rethinking of the Special Ministry," *ibid.*, 6 (1969), pp. 200–217.

44. On the somewhat complicated history of this marriage legislation, see W. Loftus, *New Catholic Encyclopedia* (New York, 1967), vol. 9, pp. 276–80.

CHAPTER 25

The Exercise of Authority

in the Modern Church

By the beginning of the eighteenth century, one can already see quite clearly the centrality to modern European history of the problem of authority. The Reformation had, of course, already dramatized this problem, but the depth of the challenge to established authority became even more apparent with the execution of Charles I in mid-seventeenth century. As often happens in such instances, the reaction to the seventeenth-century revolutions was to insist as never before on the traditional bases of political authority. The divine right of kings was defended with unprecedented emphasis in the France of Louis XIV and the England of Stuart Restoration. But this attempt to repress questions about authority quite quickly collapsed, and the problem of authority surfaced in still more unavoidable fashion as evidenced in the American and French revolutions at century's end.

To interpret the evolution of modern thought concerning authority (which is equivalently the evolution of modern political theory) is, to put it mildly, a difficult and treacherous enterprise. However, one approach which seems to shed some light, and which complements interpretations that stress economic or military or sociological factors, is to study the manner in which spiritual power declined as the Middle Ages gave way to the modern era. There had been, from time immemorial, a certain aura attached to rulers; whether one wishes to characterize this quality as charismatic or magical or supernatural, it functioned as a basis and justification for the power exercised by such rulers. Such

claims to divine appointment had not always gone unchallenged. Interestingly, the challenge often came from priestly groups. And the rise to power of many a ruler came quite evidently through such natural events as military victory. However, the very possession of power tended to be interpreted as a sign of divine favor and of divine grant of authority. It remained for the modern era gradually to understand and to exercise power as a secular reality. Once the notion of power had been secularized, the philosophical and religious explanation of authority became an acute problem.

It does not seem accidental that this rapid evaporation of political rulers' claims to divine support is a post-Reformation phenomenon. The Reformation had been a shattering attack on the power and the authority of both the pope and the Holy Roman Emperor. Nor does it seem accidental that secularizing political theorists of the sixteenth and seventeenth centuries, such as Machiavelli and Hobbes, were influenced by the ideas of Dante and Marsilius of Padua who lived and wrote at the very time (early fourteenth century) when the claims to all-embracing authority made by Innocent III and Innocent IV were no longer being accepted and when popes were finding it necessary to support their exercise of power by political alliance. Nor is it accidental that polemicists on either side of the modern struggle between monarchical and popular sovereignty use argumentation which was developed at the time of the Great Western Schism and the ascendancy of conciliarist thought.

Modern European and American history has seen a growing rejection of any mythic understanding of power and authority, whether that power and authority be political or social or religious (or even artistic or scientific). Clearly, this is part of the much-discussed dechristianization of modern life, and the very ambiguity of this demythologizing of authority should warn us against too hasty a judgment on the process of dechristianization. Clearly, too, the postmedieval evolution of Christian thought and practice concerning religious authority cannot be viewed apart from the overall development of European thought about power and authority. Indeed, the question of the authority possessed by "God's chosen ministers" has been at the very center of this development.[1]

Societal Authority

Modern European history was a rapid sequence of power struggles: between monarchs and ambitious aristocracy, then monarchs and aristocracy in alliance against a rising bourgeoisie, then between a dominant bourgeois establishment (allied with whatever remained of monarchy and aristocracy) and the masses of people. And though political and economic and military power had always been intertwined historically, the relationships among these three shifted in the modern world, with the rich or the army exercising in many instances a somewhat hidden but very real control of political processes. At first, one is tempted to think that those involved in such behind the scenes control of political and social developments have made no claims to legitimate authority, because they have not followed one or other classical position of political theory. Interestingly, however, their claim to legitimate authority has been made on religious grounds. The rich exerted power in society and saw it as part of the stewardship over the world that God had entrusted to his predestined, and the military exerted power as part of conducting a holy war. And it was in the midst of these interacting and changing

centers of power that the Christian churches have struggled to understand and express the authority that is proper to the church and more specifically to its ordained ministers.

Not too happily, the officialdom of the church has generally found itself allied with the more monarchical or oligarchical side in any socio-political power conflict, though the lower clergy were often enough on the "populist" side.[2] Such link of the structured church with the secular monarch was quite clear in the Erastian situation of German Lutheranism or the Church of England or Gallican Catholicism. However, these post-Reformation situations had been prepared by the papal policy immediately after the Council of Constance, when, in the quite successful effort to regain the power lost during the preceding century, the popes had entered upon that concordat diplomacy which shaped Rome's relationships to other sovereign powers throughout the modern period. The significance of such concordats is that they situated the pope as one of several European sovereigns, maneuvering as they all were in the game of power politics, for the most part basing his actual power on the same secular elements upon which the others depended, and identifying himself as a monarch among fellow monarchs. Because of this self-identity, he felt threatened as did other sovereigns whenever any monarchical structure was attacked, and he had a vested interest in the defense of monarchical structures as such, though he might inveigh against unjust and exploitative activity of a particular monarch.

This particular form of papal claim to monarchical authority found theological formulation in the *Summa de ecclesia* of Torquemada (in the fifteenth century) which was the foundation for most post-Reformation defenses of papal primacy.[3] Since this theology insisted on the intrinsically monarchical character of authority in the church, bishops also stressed quite logically their own monarchical prerogatives, and so were part of the royalty surrounding the pope or the king. Though with somewhat different theological justification, the bishops of the Church of England were also part of the monarchical structure and social aristocracy. Thus, in continental Catholic countries and in England the church found itself allied to the parties of political absolutism and alien to the aspirations and endeavors of a growing republicanism.

Gradually, in the course of the nineteenth and early twentieth centuries, the Roman Catholic church was disestablished, concordat diplomacy proved a less effective way for popes to influence European politics (though concordats continued to be made with some governments up to World War II), the pope ceased to be really a temporal sovereign, and both he and the bishops have come to identify themselves as "monarchs" in a more exclusively spiritual sense. However, in large measure this development was one that was forced upon the papacy and the Roman Catholic episcopacy. The initiative in this political despoliation of the Catholic church was taken by civil governments, such actions were viewed within official Catholic circles as attacks of the powers of evil against the church of Christ, and what was hoped for and prayed for and worked towards in diplomatic maneuverings was some form of restoration. It has been only quite lately (around mid-twentieth century) that Roman Catholic officialdom and most of its theologians have begun to entertain the idea that these developments may well have constituted the liberation of the church and that a separation of church and state such as the one established by the United States Constitution might be quite compatible with the nature and the welfare of the church.[4]

In countries where the Reformed tradition became dominant, a somewhat different evolution took place; the communities in this tradition generally found themselves on the antimonarchical side of Europe's political struggles. However, because of their very early alliance with the urban bourgeoisie in such places as Switzerland and Holland, perhaps also because of the mutual acceptability (about which Weber and Tawney have theorized) of Calvinist theology and European capitalism, the Reformed churches often found themselves supporting the interests of the bourgeois oligarchy in its conflict with the working poor and other disadvantaged groups of society. This has raised considerable question in the twentieth century about the Protestant attitude towards the authority of secular governments, particularly in the United States where popular Protestant opinion has always assumed that "Protestantism" and "democracy" were allied from the origins of the nation, where the WASP establishment (which sociologically included Protestant ministers) identified its own ethos with the "spirit of America," and where (because the American way of life was in many ways the operative "folk religion") governmental authority was given quasi-religious respect.[5]

As the complexion of church-state relations and the understanding of their respective spheres of power and authority was drastically affected by the emergence of modern secularity, so, too, was the nature of modern anticlericalism. In an earlier age, even at the time of the Reformation, anticlericalism was almost totally a religious phenomenon. It voiced the discontent of people with the shortcomings (real or imagined) of the clergy; it was a protest on many occasions against clerical venality and economic exploitation of the poor; but it was fundamentally a criticism of the clergy's failure to fulfill what was assumed to be a critically necessary function in society, the pastoral ministry. Because it was this kind of attitude, it could easily be shared (and was shared) by many of the clergy themselves, who were not reluctant to rail against the pretensions and misconduct of fellow clerics.

Such intramural anticlericalism did not vanish in the modern church; in addition there appeared a new and powerful attack upon the ordained ministry. This attack, which came to prominence with the Enlightenment and its rejection of supernaturalism, was the focus of the broader assault on Christianity in general. Secular critics saw the clergy as symbolizing the irrelevance and antihumanism of institutionalized religion; it was the clergy who exploited the people, who kept them in ignorance and docile submission, who hypocritically kept in existence an ecclesiastical structure so that it could serve their own purposes. France had no monopoly on this brand of anticlericalism, but in no other country (even Garibaldi's Italy) was it more bitter or more influential in the political, intellectual, and social developments of the eighteenth, nineteenth, and twentieth centuries.[6] And whether one was dealing with the rationalistic writings of the Encyclopedists or Stendahl's *Le rouge et le noir*, the picture of the clergy given was one of a parasitical element in society, a group that was ignorantly and obstinately using the supposed authority of revelation to impose their own anachronistic ideas on the uneducated, a basic obstacle to the advance of civilization.

In assessing the nature of this secular anticlericalism and the validity of its criticisms of the ordained ministry, one is helped greatly by the history of France in the eighteenth and nineteenth centuries. What was actually taking place was a power struggle between two opposing religions, for the Encyclopedist movement (and its heirs) actually constituted a secular religion.[7] The movement had its own high priests, its own theologians (Diderot would say, for example of Voltaire, "loin d'être un philosophe, est un docteur en théologie"),[8] its own saints, even its own martyrs (e.g., Prades who was condemned in 1752 by the University and the Archbishop of Paris, by Parlement, and by the pope). And the tone of the Encyclopedists' attack on the Jesuit *Journal de Trévoux*, because it had the effrontery to point out shortcomings in the *Encyclopédie* (even though its scholarly reviews of the endeavor were basically quite favorable), illustrates the extent to which they expected their own teaching authority to be reverenced.[9]

The importance of this secularistic anticlericalism lay in the influence it had in shaping public reaction to the ordained ministry's claim to some form of authority, and consequently in determining the groups in modern society to which the clergy could effectively direct its pastoral ministry. Though the anti-Christian polemic extended beyond the clergy and brought under question the authority of the Scriptures and even the authority of God (if there was a God), the credibility of the ordained representatives of authoritative religious truth was the first line of attack. And this attack had another important effect, one that is difficult to describe and impossible to measure. Inevitably, the particular ministerial group under attack either reacted acceptingly (though not necessarily correctly or honestly) to the charges leveled against it and tried to accommodate its identity and behavior, or it reacted with self-justifying emphasis on the very things against which criticism had been directed. Both reactions could, and often enough did, betray an unrecognized uneasiness about the nature and bases of ministerial authority, and about the nature and bases of Christianity itself.

Ultimately, the authority possessed by the Christian ministry is derived from the authority of revelation; perhaps more accurately we should say that the authority belongs to that word of God to which he ministers. The power that is intrinsically linked with such authority is power which works to shape the consciousness and affectivity of men. This has always been true of Christian ministry in its nature, but often enough that ministry claimed authority and exercised power in other spheres. However, as post-Reformation Europe has emerged, the force of events has slowly compelled the ministry of the various churches to specify more carefully its authority and to exercise alien forms of power less often. One of the clearest reflections of this can be seen in post-Tridentine Roman Catholic theology of the papacy, where discussion quite clearly shifted to emphasis on the teaching authority of the pope.

This has coincided and clashed with the developments in modern European and American intellectual history.[10] One way of reading this history is to view it as a continuing quest for an adequate criterion of truth, a quest which in its early stage (Descartes would be the obvious example) overly identified certitude with truth and which in its latest stage may be in danger of overemphasizing authenticity to the detriment of accuracy. But throughout this evolution, no matter whether the stress was on reason (as in the eighteenth century) or feeling (as in the Romantic movement), the criterion for truth is sought *within* man—the logical consistency of his thought and the fulfillment of his psychological needs. Even the apparent exceptions to this, the pragmatism espoused by William James or by Marx, still make man's personal development the measure of truth.

To such ways of thinking, the appeal to some outside source, a God who has revealed mysteries to men, as the criterion for what is true or not true about human existence and experience is deceptive and fruitless. Above all, it seems a basic insult to human rationality to ground in religious faith, which by definition defies proof, the most important understandings about human life. This becomes yet more difficult when one is asked to accept these critically important truths on the authority not directly of God but of certain religious officials, who claim some special possession of these truths and some special appointment from God to transmit them. To those who did not view the activity of the Christian churches from the perspective of faith, the ministry of the word could easily have appeared as a misleading and obscurantist activity carried on by a self-appointed religious establishment. The responses of Christian communities (or of groups within a given community) to this radical criticism of authoritative religious teaching was quite diverse. In some quarters there was the tendency to reduce Christian teaching to little more than humanistic moralism; in other quarters there was a full-scale attempt to out-rationalize the rationalists and to provide a rational grounding for the act of faith; in still other quarters there was an increased emphasis on the God-given teaching authority of the ordained ministry, especially the higher clergy. A given church might well employ more than one of these counterattacks, as did the first Vatican council, whose two doctrinal decrees deal with the relation of faith to rea-

son and with the supreme teaching authority of the pope. But they were *counter*-attacks. Modern secular thought has been characterized (at least until the shattering experience of two world wars) by a somewhat naive but basically valuable faith in human reason and human goodness. Confronted with this mentality, the Christian churches (and very concretely the Christian preacher and teacher) had to make modern sense out of such doctrines as original sin, salvation, revelation, or supernatural grace.

In all this controversy about the relation of faith and reason (or science and religion), the ordained ministry of the Christian churches was deeply involved and its role in the modern world subjected to radical questioning. On the level of official church statements, on the level of theological utterance, and on the level of popular preaching or writing, ordained ministers rallied to defend the truth and the relevance of Christianity—but with great variation of response to the challenge of "science," as the reaction to Darwin's theories illustrated. For the most part, although there were important exceptions in most of the churches, the response of Christian leadership (administrative and theological) to modern scientific developments was defensive and quite negative,[11] and the Christian minister's preaching was an alien sound in progressive intellectual circles. Not only did there develop an almost unbridgeable gap between Christian teaching even in its more respectable theological expressions and the modern non-Christian intellectual, but Christian teaching, at least in its officially recognized formulations, ceased to make sense to many well-educated persons within the church. For many in this latter group, a genuine crisis of faith developed. Since World War II there has been some more sympathetic recognition of the true dimensions of this problem and some isolated attempts to take account of it in the church's ministry of the word.

Another way of viewing modern intellectual history is to see it as a key element in modern man's movement towards increased freedom. However one wishes to evaluate the various currents of modern thought as contributors or hindrances to the genuine acquisition of human freedom, there is no doubt that many important modern thinkers have seen Christianity both in its doctrine and in its practice as an obstacle to freedom, and there is little doubt that institutionalized Christianity has to some extent been an obstacle. Partly, this was linked to the alliance of the churches with the political-economic establishment, for there is a general reluctance of such establishments to encourage free expression of ideas that threaten the status quo. More radically, however, it had to do with the very nature of authoritative religious teaching, especially as distinguished from modern scientific exploration and discovery.

At the time of the Reformation, the question of ecclesiastical authority's function as a norm for Christian faith found expression in the controversies about Scripture and tradition, controversies that hid to some extent the underlying question: Was the official teaching of the church or the individual Christian's inspiration by the Spirit a more ultimate criterion? This underlying question did, however, find expression in the spirit of liberation from ecclesiastical restrictions that animated many of the sixteenth-century reform movements. To some extent, there was a retrenchment of this spirit by the seventeenth- and eighteenth-century development of confessional orthodoxies, but pietist and evangelical movements within both Protestant and Catholic traditions continued the emphasis on individual faith and religious experience. With the nineteenth and twentieth centuries there developed a more sophisticated theological discussion about personal and traditional faith, the broad range of the discussion being reflected in the difference between Newman and Schleiermacher (or in America between Bushnell and Nevin). Accompanying this, but by no means embracing all of it, was the emergence of liberal theology, which, however amorphous and fluid it might be in its teachings, did consistently stress the ultimacy of religious experience and personal insight rather than of authoritative church doctrines.[12]

Largely because of the papacy's success in controlling Catholic thought during the nineteenth century, a success that was grounded in the triumph of Ultramontanism, the development of liberal theology was largely a Protestant phenomenon, so much so that the term "liberal Protestantism" is often applied to it. However, the Modernist controversy at the beginning of the twentieth century revealed the presence of such liberal ideas in Roman Catholicism; the response of the papacy was quick and authoritative. It was not too clear exactly what it was that Pius X's "*Pascendi gregis*" was meant to condemn, but the cloud of modernism continued to hang over progressive Roman Catholic theology until Vatican II, if not later.[13] Though the emotional overtones of the modernist controversy and of subsequent theological disputes did not make it easy to discern the precise issues that were in question, the course of action taken by Roman Catholic officials, especially the Holy Office, towards progressive theological opinion reveals the understanding of their own teaching authority they possessed. *By virtue of their official position*, they passed judgment on theological opinions and demanded, as an act of religious obedience (*obsequium religiosum*), agreement with their own views. In the background, as justification for such procedure, lay Vatican I's decree on papal infallibility, although doctrinal judgments issuing from Rome in the late nineteenth and twentieth centuries were carefully phrased in order to avoid identification as infallible statements. At the same time, the accusation made against dangerous theological innovators was not exactly one of erroneous theological procedure; rather, it tended to be one of disloyalty and disobedience.[14] Significantly, for decades after the condemnation of Loisy, Tyrrell, and their associates, all those who taught theology in approved situations like seminaries had to pronounce each year the oath against modernism, a practice that quietly lapsed in recent years because of its obvious incongruity.

While the magnitude of the situation and the publicity given it made the Roman Catholic church's handling of dangerous doctrine the most prominent example of authoritative imposition of official theological opinion, it was not unique among the Christian churches. One immediately thinks of the refusal of church officials in fundamentalist communities to examine the results of modern biblical exegesis, even the more moderate results. But other more liberal churches have had their share of heresy trials and theological witch-hunting. It has taken all of them some time to discover the truth of Benjamin Jowett's remark: Doubt comes in at the window when inquiry is denied at the door.[15]

Claims to authority by the Christian churches have been increasingly disallowed, and concomitantly the churches' exercise of power has been curtailed, by the growing disestablishment of the churches in the modern world. This disestablishment has been most clearly evident in the political order where legal establishment of a given church has all but vanished; but the progressive cultural disestablishment has been just as real and in many ways more far-reaching. The most important and obvious symptom of this distancing of modern culture from institutionalized religion has been the gradual dominance of public education.

However, at the outbreak of World War II the process of disestablishment was not complete, even in the legal sphere. Ordained clergy, especially the higher clergy, continued to expect privileges and to play roles that derived from the earlier historical situation when they were effectively part of the ruling class and exerting almost monopolistic control over education. World War II was a sign, which took some time to read, that this old world order was dead, that there would be no "restoration," and that the ordained ministry would have to seek elsewhere than in the secular order for any claims to special authority in human society. One obvious move in this situation was that the clergy retreat to their denominational ghetto and concentrate on the "spiritual" authority which they possessed within their respective churches. Another obvious alternative was that the ordained clergy seek the moral authority that comes with being a respected public figure; they

could become paragons of public virtue. Neither alternative clearly characterized the clergy from any given church. As a matter of fact, these alternatives were not perceived explicitly as such; rather, they were positions into which men imperceptibly and almost unconsciously shifted, and an ordained minister could insist upon his spiritual authority when he acted within his own church and depend upon his public figure authority when involved in extrachurch affairs.

All this raised new problems for those exercising authority and power in the churches. As they were forced back to the spiritual sources of their authority to justify the power they enjoyed in ecclesiastical affairs, these spiritual sources came under closer scrutiny. In an earlier age, when the focus of dispute had been the claim of ordained ministers to authority and power in the temporal sphere, their claim to spiritual authority had gone relatively unchallenged. Even the Reformation challenge to the spiritual authority of Rome had concentrated on the charges of immorality and infidelity, and on the contention that Rome had therefore forfeited her spiritual authority. That some kind of official authority attached to the ordained pastor in his ministry of the word is a basic principle in all classic Reformation views of ministry. But in more recent centuries, the precise nature and extent of the authority exercised *within* church life by the ordained ministry has been brought under question by a number of factors: the evolution of biblical exegesis (which drew attention to a normative understanding of Scripture provided by non-officials), the increasing stress on personal faith (therefore, the individual conscience and the authenticity of religious experience as norms) that stands in tension with institutionalized church authority, and the movements towards some form of reunification of the divided Christian community.

At the same time, there are indications that some new lines of force may be developing within the Christian churches and between them and "the world." As its political clout and educational monopoly gradually evaporated, a church that had previously in an established context depended on these now found itself redirected towards moral leadership, service to those in need, and proclamation of the gospel. For no group within the church has this shift demanded more adjustment than it has of the ordained clergy: there are in the post–World War II decades indications that the job description of the ordained minister is undergoing basic change, and that the authority and power he will exercise in coming decades will be quite different from what it was for many centuries.

Papal Authority in Modern Times

As we have tried to indicate, the existence and activity of the papacy cannot be examined apart from the larger picture of Christianity in the modern world. The papacy does present the most evident and probably the most ultimate example of institutionalized Christianity faced with a challenge to its power and authority. So, some concentration on Rome's theory and practice regarding religious authority may help clarify the intrinsic issues. It may also have the side benefit of aiding ecumenical understanding, since the authority exercised by the bishop of Rome has been an obvious stumbling block to Christian reunion.

While its effective political power in the affairs of secular governments has steadily diminished, Rome's exercise of ecclesiastical jurisdiction (and concomitantly its exercise of a certain moral power in those countries with predominantly Catholic populations) reached unprecedented levels from mid-nineteenth century onward. Ultramontanism gained dominance over the Gallicanism of the seventeenth and eighteenth centuries, and was solidly entrenched by the proceedings of Vatican I.[16] Vatican I did not dissipate all remaining elements of Gallican sentiment, but the third chapter of the council's dogmatic constitution *"Pastor aeternus"* leaves no question about the completeness of the pope's jurisdictional primacy.[17] His authority extends not just to teaching but to discipline and govern-

ment (*ad disciplinam et regimen*); it pertains to all members of the church throughout the world; it touches all of them immediately, and no one may legitimately interfere with the pope's direct communication to these members; the pope is the one supreme pastor of the flock; he is the supreme judge, the last court of appeals in all ecclesiastical matters, subject himself to no judgment within the church. This description of the jurisdictional authority of the pope was incorporated into the code of canon law,[18] but what gives it its unique status as binding law within a faith community is the fact that Vatican I expressed it not in a disciplinary decree but as an explicitly intended proposition in a dogmatic constitution.

If the conciliar statement about the papal jurisdiction confirmed in solemn doctrinal fashion the most far-reaching Roman claims to ecclesiastical power, and in so doing laid the groundwork for a post–Vatican I period of unprecedented rule by Roman congregations, it was the council's definition of infallibility that drew (and still draws) more attention. It was in this decree that the emphasis on infallibility that one finds in post-Tridentine defenders of the papacy comes to fulfillment, though not without a considerable struggle among the council fathers at Vatican I. Without for the moment evaluating the method by which the definition on infallibility achieved council acceptance or the intrinsic meaning of the statement,[19] it is worth noting the jurisdictional mentality that colors the context of the definition: the section of *"Pastor aeternus"* which treats of infallibility follows immediately upon the one describing the jurisdictional primacy of the pope, and it begins with the statement that supreme teaching authority pertains to the primacy that the pope inherits from Peter. In the appeals to Lyons II and Florence as conciliar precedents, the texts cited deal with the Roman *plenitudo potestatis*. One reason given for the expediency of the definition is the modern challenge to the pope's authority. And in the heart of the decree the language of authoritative official teaching is prominent: a condition for a statement to be safeguarded by infallibility is that it be pronounced with the pope's full authority (*pro suprema sua Apostolica auctoritate*); another condition is that he say that it must be held by the entire church (*ab universa Ecclesia tenendam*).

Thus, the pastoral ministry is seen by Vatican I to find its most perfect expression in a supreme officeholder. By virtue of possessing this office, he has the authority and the responsibility of controlling the institutional life of the church at every level; he can (and in some sense ultimately does) pass judgment on the behavior of every member of the church; he can and should judge the orthodoxy of any formulation of Christian faith. For the most part, this view of papal power dominated the Roman Catholic church from Vatican I to World War II. There were some rumblings and a small-scale schism as a result of Vatican I, but there was negligible intramural contesting of papal absolutism. On the contrary, because of a sequence of relatively competent popes, the Holy See enjoyed rather wide popularity and prestige. Although only one papal pronouncement of the years since Vatican I involved the full implication of infallibility, Pius XII's definition in 1950 of Mary's Assumption, the aura of infallibility has tended to cling to papal statements in general and to give them an influence beyond their intrinsic doctrinal importance. Another feature of papal teaching, especially in the twentieth century (though Pius IX's "Syllabus of Errors" set an unhappy example), has been its condemnatory character. Unquestionably, papal encyclicals such as Pius XII's "*Mystici corporis*" (on the church as the Body of Christ) and "*Mediator Dei*" (on the liturgy) were milestones in the growth of popular understanding about the church; but even they were written to correct certain theological excesses. The papal role of condemning errors dominates such influential encyclicals as "*Humani generis*" (in 1950) and "*Casti connubii*" (in 1930) or the decrees of such Roman agencies as the Holy Office or the Biblical Commission.

Episcopal Power and Authority

As preparations for Vatican II advanced, and even more so as the actual sessions discussing the proposed Constitution on the Church began, it became apparent that Vatican I had left unclarified the precise role and authority of the episcopacy.[20] While Vatican II did not give a thoroughly satisfactory explanation of the relationship between papal and episcopal authority (since the critical text, the third chapter of the dogmatic *Constitution on the Church*, juxtaposes without intrinsic resolution the papal absolutism of Vatican I and the episcopal collegiality "discovered" by the fathers of Vatican II), it did reverse the trend of Vatican I by reinserting the bishop of Rome within the episcopal *collegium* and by altering the operative image of the bishop. That image, which had become dominant as a result of Vatican I, cast the bishop in the role of deputy to the pope, deriving authority from him (though Vatican I had not said precisely this), carrying out papal policy in doctrinal control and ecclesiastical management, and representing to the faithful of their diocese the pastoral concern and guidance of "the supreme Pastor."

Actually, such a complete subordination to the papacy was not characteristic of the entire modern period. During the seventeenth century there was a notable ascendancy of Gallicanism and in the eighteenth century the papacy's power (both inside and outside the church) was definitely on the decline.[21] It was only the shattering influences of the French Revolution and Napoleonic rule that opened up the possibilities for papal recovery of influence in the nineteenth century. One of the important factors in increasing papal power within church structures was the disestablishment of the church in "Catholic countries," for this restored to the pope the key power of appointing bishops and thereby influencing episcopal activity. Thus, the period between the two Vatican councils was atypical of the history of the church; most of that history has witnessed an unresolved contest between papal and episcopal claims to authority.[22]

If the authority-power relationship between pope and bishop shifted during the nineteenth century, so did that between bishop and presbyter. In general, there was a pattern of increasing episcopal control, though the causes and sequence of this growing control were quite different from one country to another. In France, it was the aftermath of eighteenth-century Richerism, of the revolution, and of the deep division caused by the Civil Constitution of the Clergy; in Ireland and England it was related to the reestablishment of normalcy after the years of Roman Catholic proscription; in North America it was part of the process of shaping a unified Catholic community out of the multiple and diversified immigrant groups.[23]

Though subordinated by law to the bishop of Rome, each bishop was also by law a monarch in his own diocese, possessing full jurisdiction in spiritual and temporal aspects of church life.[24] In actuality, the episcopal direction of church affairs, essentially a direction of the lower clergy, has been a combined exercise of religious authority and administrative power. By virtue of the promise of obedience made by the ordinand on the day of his ordination, compliance with the bishop's directives was made a matter of moral obligation; because of reliance upon the "faculties" granted by the bishop within his diocese, each ordained minister depended upon episcopal approval in order to preach or act as sacramental celebrant. By canon law the very validity of his absolution in the sacrament of penance and the validity of marriages to which he witnessed were conditioned on his having such "faculties." The bishops' control of pastoral assignments, which grew in proportion as secular governmental interference and secular control of the benefice system disappeared, gave them a powerful means of reward or punishment. Relations between bishops and priests who belonged to religious orders, particularly the exempt orders, were often strained and always a bit ambiguous; the bishop could not direct the seminary for-

mation of such men as he did for his own diocesan clergy, nor could he directly assign them to particular activities nor remove them, unless they were a public scandal or danger to faith. However, he did have a source of power because of his grant (or refusal) of the faculties for preaching and sacramental ministry, because religious orders were dependent upon bishops for ordination of their members, and because the financial well-being of a religious community could be effectively undermined by episcopal opposition.

Judgment on orthodoxy of teaching, on acceptability of liturgical practices, on matters of ecclesiastical discipline, and on the moral behavior of members of the church (lay and clerical), belonged to the bishops—always, of course, ultimately to the pope. However, most of the day-by-day conduct of the church's life was controlled on the local level by the designated pastor. Like the bishop he governed his parish by a mixture of authority and power. The ecclesiastical authority he possessed was delegated from higher levels; as the modern church became more centralized and the bishop's control of the diocese more absolute, the local pastor became increasingly the delegate of the bishop, appointed by him to carry out policy formulated at the diocesan level, and expected to carry out the particular job assigned to him. His power within the parish derived from this delegated authority. The faithful were taught that this authority, since it was divinely established, must be accepted by an act of religious obedience. But it also derived from the people's dependence upon him for preaching, teaching, and provision of sacraments, from the professional status he enjoyed in society, from the education he possessed (which was often assumed to be quite superior), and from the "charism" attached to his ministerial ordination and his membership in the clerical caste. Though the presbyterate made no formal claims to monarchical authority, as did the episcopacy and the pope, the exercise of authority on the local level tended to be monarchical. The pastor generally dictated the policies for conduct of the parish school, handling of parish finances, undertaking of parish activities and, of course, the liturgy and religious instruction. Many a wise pastor shared the planning and conduct of such activities with his parishioners, but the underlying understanding always was that the directive decisions were his prerogative, if he wished to make them. After all, ecclesiastical law made the pastor accountable for his decisions and actions to the bishop, not to his parishioners.[25]

NOTES

1. For a stimulating discussion of this link of secular and religious currents of thought about authority, see J. Cameron, *Images of Authority* (New Haven, 1966).

2. However, an important qualification needs to be added to this latter statement. As "the professions" (law, medicine, etc.) gain increasing prestige and a subtle power in modern society, and professional governmental bureaucrats grow in influence, and as ordained ministry is more often thought of as a profession and ministers are used as bureaucrats, the lower clergy incline much more to be supportive of the established order.

3. See A. Black, *Monarchy and Community* (Cambridge, 1970), pp. 95–96.

4. As late as the 1950s, John Courtney Murray (one of America's most eminent Roman Catholic theologians, who later was the chief architect of Vatican II's decree on religious freedom) was subject to repressive Roman scrutiny because of his scholarly, and quite moderate, attempts to give theological justification for the "new view."

5. Another contemporary example that highlighted the complexity of this matter and the extent to which the problem transcends confessional boundaries was the response of the churches in Germany to Nazism. In the light of later developments, the churches' developing crisis of conscience regarding the Nazi regime, and the postwar controversy about the Christian support of Hitler, it is interesting to read the remarks of P. Kosok in his *Modern Germany* (Chicago: University of Chicago Press, 1933): "Since in Germany membership in the church is almost coincident with citizenship, both the Protestant and the Catholic churches with their numerous auxiliary organizations can serve as a most important element in inculcating civic loyalty among the people. . . . Reaching into almost every branch of activity, the church through its auxiliary organizations comes to stand as a great—perhaps the greatest—auxiliary of the state. At a thousand points it co-operates until loyalty to the church in its many activities becomes almost undistinguishable from loyalty to the state and the nation. And the political and moral duty of the citizen to the state and nation becomes a religious one, invested with a halo of divine sanctity." (Pp. 189–203)

6. On the eighteenth century, see R. Palmer, *Catholics and Unbelievers in Eighteenth-Century France* (Princeton, 1939); on the nineteenth and early twentieth centuries, see A. Dansette, *Religious History of Modern France*, 2 vols. (New York, 1961).

7. ". . . The conflict was not simply between enlightened and backward thinkers. Nor was it a dispute between skeptics and men of faith. The work of the *philosophes* was not to destroy a faith; that would have been a barren accomplishment. The great work of the *philosophes* was to supply a new faith. . . ." (Palmer, p. 20.)

8. *Ibid.*, p. 119.

9. *Ibid.*, pp. 17–20.

10. On the question of religious authority vis-à-vis modern intellectual developments, see R. Davies, *Religious Authority in an Age of Doubt* (London, 1968); *Problems of Authority*, ed. J. Todd (London, 1962); G. Cragg, *Reason and Authority in the Eighteenth Century* (Cambridge, 1964).

11. See A. Vidler, *The Church in an Age of Revolution* (London, 1961), pp. 112–33; also I. Barbour, *Issues in Science and Religion* (Englewood Cliffs, N.J., 1960); and J. Dillenberger, *Protestant Thought and Natural Science* (New York, 1960).

12. See J. Dillenberger and C. Welch, *Protestant Christianity* (New York, 1954), pp. 179–

231. On the modern emergence of the authority of individual religious experience, see Richard Niebuhr, *Experiential Religion* (New York, 1972), p. 8.

13. For a brief description of the events connected with the papal condemnation of modernism, see Dansette, vol. 2, pp. 291–314. Somewhat lengthier treatments are given by B. Reardon, *Roman Catholic Modernism* (Stanford, Calif., 1970), who concentrates on the French developments; J. Ratte, *Three Modernists* (London, 1968), who studies Loisy and Tyrrell and Sullivan; and M. Ranchetti, *The Catholic Modernists* (London, 1969), who pays more attention than usual to the Italian modernists. For two earlier, somewhat divergent though complementary analyses of modernism, see A. Vidler, *The Modernist Movement in the Roman Church* (Cambridge, 1934), and J. Rivière's article in *Dictionnaire de théologie catholique,* vol. 10 (1928), cols. 2009–47.

14. This was reflected, too, in the way in which the relation of such suspect theologians to the Holy See was discussed as a "crisis of conscience versus law." One of the most celebrated and tragic cases of such conflict of personal conscience and ecclesiastical authority was that of Lammenais. See H. Laski, *Authority in the Modern State* (New Haven, 1919), pp. 189–280; Dansette, vol. 1, pp. 207–26.

15. Quoted by Vidler, p. 126. Jowett himself was no stranger to the problem, for as one of the leading liberal theologians in the Anglican church he was at the center of the controversies that divided the Church of England in the 1860s and 70s.

16. See R. Aubert, *Le pontificat de Pie IX*, vol. 21 of A. Fliche and V. Martin, *Histoire d'Eglise depuis les origines jusqu'à nos jours* (Paris, 1935—), pp. 262–367.

17. See Denzinger-Schonmetzer, *Enchiridion Symbolorum* (Freiburg, 1965), nos. 3059–64; for a description of the formation of this decree of Vatican I, see Christopher Butler's reedition of Cuthbert Butler's *The Vatican Council* (London, 1962); J. Hennesey in his *The First Vatican Council: The American Experience* (New York, 1963) concentrates on the attitudes and contributions of the American hierarchy at the council.

18. *Codex iuris canonici*, canon 218.

19. See H. Küng's recent *Infallible? An Inquiry* (New York, 1971) and the reactions to it.

20. A journalistic reflection of the centrality in Vatican II's proceedings of the "theology of the episcopacy" is given by H. Fesquet, *The Drama of Vatican II* (New York, 1967), pp. 144–47, 197–98. For a more theological description of the council's treatment of the episcopal office and particularly the question of collegiality, see C. Moeller, *Vatican II: An Interfaith Appraisal*, ed. J. Miller (Notre Dame, 1966), pp. 129–35.

21. See R. Greaves, *New Cambridge Modern History* (Cambridge, 1961), vol. 7, pp. 113–22.

22. Not that all tension between bishops and Rome vanished. There was considerable struggle on specific issues, for example, the posture of the American church vis-à-vis the laboring movement.

23. On the relationship between bishops and priests in the United States, see the thorough and balanced study of R. Trisco, "Bishops and Their Priests in the United States," *The Catholic Priest in the United States*, ed. J. Ellis (Collegeville, Minn., 1971), pp. 111–292; on the French situation, see Dansette, vol. 2; on Ireland (and Irish developments in Britain) see vols. 5 and 6 of *History of Irish Catholicism* (Dublin, 1971).

24. On the role and power of the modern Catholic episcopate, see the several articles under "bishop" in the second volume of the *New Catholic Encyclopedia* (New York, 1967), especially that of T. Faulkner (pp. 586–88) on the canonical status of the episcopacy.

25. See canons 872–74, 1094–95.

CHAPTER 26

Theological Reflections on Judgment

In the light of the reiterated New Testament precept that Christians are not to pass judgment upon one another, the prominence in Christian history of judgment as a "ministerial function" is difficult to explain. One simplified explanation would see the gradually increasing exercise of authoritative judgment as a manifestation of the human inclination to seek power; but while there is probably a certain element of such power-seeking in the history of ecclesiastical judging, this is not the basic cause. Instead, what seems to be the case is that judgment in some form (perhaps in several forms) is intrinsic to the life of the church, and that what is needed is not an elimination of judgment from Christianity but a discovery of the kind of judgment that is appropriate to Christianity, with the consequent practical decision to exclude inappropriate kinds.

First of all, judgment in some form is absolutely basic to human life, whether in individual activity or social existence. Judgment means the perception and acknowledgment of reality (i.e., the heart of human consciousness); it means the act of decision, which grounds all human activity. Sharing perceptions of reality and sharing decisions, through one or other form of communication, is the very essence of human community; without some such common judgments, human society would be impossible. So, it is apparent that judgment must play a prominent role in the life of the Christian community.

However, more than a priori human reasoning points to the importance of judgment in the church's life. Careful theological examination of the faith experience of Old Testament Israel and of Christianity indicates quite clearly the divine intent that men and women move towards increased freedom and responsibility, i.e., towards increasingly autonomous judgment. Moreover, it is precisely the autonomy of each Christian's self-judgment that rules out unjustified criticism (i.e., judgment) by others. Put in other words, there is a fundamental inviolability to the individual's conscience; in the last analysis only the person himself and God can evaluate the truth of the personal judgments that a person makes. Yet, such subjective judgment is obviously not to be capricious; to be honest and genuinely self-fulfilling it must relate authentically to objective reality. Individual conscience needs guidance; providing such guidance is a major part of the task of Christian ministry.

If we are to deal with judgment in the deeply effective sense, at the level where human consciousness and attitudes are challenged and freely changed, then it seems quite clear that only reality and truth themselves can pass judgment upon any person's ideas or decisions. Should a person alter his own understandings and convictions in response to the mere opinion or to the moral pressure of others, this would be a less than desirable situation. Instead, a mature person's state of awareness is one in which as a result of concomitant self-discovery and self-assertion he peacefully possesses a certain integrated perception of reality and a certain motivational structure, but remains fearlessly open to modifying his understandings and values as he grows in knowledge and wisdom. One can legitimately lead such a person to growth only by bringing him into closer relationship with reality, only by exposing him to truth; reality and truth will then pass judgment upon the adequacy of his present understandings and help produce a bettered state of awareness. Any real teacher knows that he will truly help a student not by confronting the student with his (i.e., the teacher's) understandings, but by using his own understandings to help the student come into contact with that reality which both teacher and student are striving to grasp; the goal is that reality, not just the teacher's view of reality, shape the mentality of the student.

In this process of leading men and women to a more enlightened insight into reality, and therefore to a freer decision about that reality's practical implications, the Christian gospel, the revelation of God in Jesus Christ, is meant to play a unique and ultimate role. At the heart of this revelation, which reaches its culmination in Jesus as the incarnating of God's own Word, stands the prophetic experience which consists essentially in the prophet being confronted inescapably and in mysterious immediacy by the personal presence of the divine. This reality of God, intruding upon and challenging the consciousness of the prophet, passes judgment upon all the prophet had been and done. In Christianity, the utterly unparalleled prophetic experience of Jesus as risen Messiah, mediated through the Christian community, makes present in human history the continuously challenging reality of the divine. Because of this presence of divine reality and divine truth, human history stands under constant and creative judgment.

Christians, individually and in community, participate in this judgment by bearing witness to the gospel, by attesting in their own faith to the actuality of this divine self-revelation in Christ. Apart from the genuineness of their own faith and the practical manifestations of this faith in their loving concern for others, Christians do not have other means of persuading people to accept the truth to which they bear witness. They cannot justifiably invoke any extrinsic sanction as a means of motivating people to believe; the only penalty appropriate to a willful rejection of truth is a person's deprivation of truth; in a very deep sense, sin is its own punishment.

This matter of Christians passing judgment upon their world only by their witness to the divinely given truth they possess in faith finds a special relevance today. After centuries of assumed responsibility to speak about the important issues of human life, and an accompanying assumption that the church's voice in such matters deserved attention, the church has found itself increasingly ignored by modern society. Civil institutions proceed in almost total independence of Christian teaching and ecclesiastical power. And Christian theology is hard-pressed to point out where, if at all, specifically Christian understandings should enter into the political prudential judgment. And the disestablishment of the church goes further. Contemporary human culture in general is evolving in a secularistic fashion that emphasizes the importance of autonomous human insight and creativity and that (apparently, at least) feels no need and leaves no place for Christianity's wisdom.

The actuality and profundity of this problem should not be evaded. Christianity today can no longer rely upon any extrinsic supports in its mission of bearing witness to God's revelation. In many ways, and for Christians this should be a source of hope, the church has its back to the wall in a manner that reminds one of Jesus in the crisis situation of his own public ministry. Confronted by the failure of his preaching and wonder-working to challenge effectively the religious presuppositions of Jewish leadership, Jesus had no alternative but to move on to the ultimate witness of his death and passage into new life. Only in actually dying and rising and sharing the Spirit of new life could he adequately manifest the reality of love's power to overcome death, adequately manifest the ability of human persons supported by God to face and overcome the power of evil, adequately indicate that authentic personal life can only be

Spirit-grounded life, adequately testify to the fidelity of his Father and the ultimacy of that Father's providential wisdom. So, too, Christians in their mission of sacramentalizing Christ's own act of witness cannot avoid the need to preach the gospel through their own passage into new life.

Divine revelation is meant to be as challenging as it is because it is an act of self-revelation; it is God's gift of self in a fully personal sense. In Jesus, this divine self-gift finds expression and embodiment in his own human gift of self to others, a gift of self that finds fulfillment in his risen ability to communicate the very Spirit of sonship in which his human existing and self-identification and activity are grounded. Christians have no other way of allowing the divine gift of self in Christ to pass through them and touch men's lives than by becoming in their own gift of self to others the symbol (sacrament) in which Christ's self-giving can become present. No more radical act of judgment could be performed by a Christian than to love, and in lovingly giving of himself to allow his own faith possession of Christ and his Spirit to interact with the consciousness of those he loves.

Within the Christian community itself, one of the most critical exercises of judgment is discernment of the Spirit of Christ; for, in fidelity to Christ, the church must strive to live by his Spirit, to make its own decisions an expression of the movement of his Spirit. Ultimately, it is this Spirit of truth that judges the inner reality of men's lives; this Spirit is the norm against which all human wisdom, and even more so all that lays claim to being Christian wisdom, must be evaluated. And so Christians must find the means of discovering the workings of the Spirit in their midst. Because it is a prophetic community, with a corporate prophetic charism that flows from Christ's own prophetic possession of the Spirit, the church does have in its faith awareness the medium in which the Spirit's action can be perceived. Yet, the art of discerning in particular situations the movement of Christ's Spirit, an art to which many ministries in the church must con-

tribute, is an art that the church is always acquiring and that it can never fully possess. The exercise of this art is the very essence of genuine Christian judgment, whether it be a judgment about the orthodoxy of a given formulation or practice, or a judgment about the Christian appropriateness of a certain course of action, or a judgment about the aptitude of a candidate for specialized Christian ministry.

In an activity that is so basic to the church's well-being, it is important to discover who (or which groups), and on what basis, can contribute to this discernment of the Spirit. Certainly, theological reflection can help sharpen the community's identification of the Spirit. Genuine holiness and prayer provide an element of resonance with whatever is truly of Christ's Spirit and a quasi-instinctive capacity to distinguish Christ's Spirit from other spirits. Of the various specialized ministries, the prophetic function is most specifically directed to aiding the community discern the Spirit; the ancient credal expression that the Spirit "has spoken through the prophets" seems to confirm this. The claim of certain official groups to be able to discern the Spirit precisely because they are official may be a bit more difficult to sustain.

Unquestionably, the entire community's faith experience must be consulted in the attempt to discover the Spirit's action. This means not only the entire community at any given moment of history but the entire community in its historical continuity. For this reason, the traditional faith and historical experience of Christianity must always be one of the sources of insight that shape the church's search for the presence of the Spirit in its life. That which is the key to the church's unity of faith and the community's most important link with tradition is the celebration of the Eucharist. And so the community's awareness of the Spirit coming upon it in conjunction with Eucharistic *epiklesis* is (or at least would be, if Eucharist were more evangelically celebrated) a privileged situation for discernment of the Spirit.

Another basic act of judgment in the

church is that exercised in the sacrament of penance, an action whose symbolic effectiveness is inseparable from the action being formally one of judgment. Yet, for the very reason that judgment functions by its very significance in the sanctifying action of this sacrament, it is theologically important to discover what meaning should be given to judgment in this case, and it is pastorally important to see that that meaning finds recognizable expression in the liturgical ritual. At the risk of oversimplification (for there can be no pretense here of giving a thorough theological explanation of Penance's sacramentality), it seems that judgment in this sacrament is equatable with reconciliation.

A few remarks may help justify this equation. First of all, it is quite clear that what is involved in any genuine reconciliation or remission of sin or absolution (or any other such term) is genuine conversion. Such a returning to God finds its origin in the divine call to repentance, and many human agencies (within and without the church) share in this process of redirecting the sinner and overcoming his alienation from God. Because this alienation from God always involves an alienation from self, and both of these inevitably take form within Christians' dealings with their fellow men, the process of conversion necessarily involves a sinner's relationship to the Christian community. It is within the community's reconciliation of the sinner that the divine reconciliation occurs; the community's forgiving concern acts sacramentally to make present Christ's own forgiving concern, and the church's formal sacramental act of reconciliation speaks effectively of God's reconciliation of the sinner to himself. However, it would be a mistake to distinguish the ritual act too sharply from the entire community action of reconciliation, which precedes and continues after the penitential ceremony. Reconciliation, which obviously implies some judgment against the foregoing alienation, is a continuing activity that the community as a whole must carry on with respect to each of its members; the liturgical action is the ritualized moment in this ongoing activity.

Again, it is worth remarking that only reconciliation and not the contrary notion of condemnation pertains properly to the sacramental action. Though scriptural and traditional texts join "binding" with "loosing" and "retaining sins" with "forgiving sins," the grant of power to the church which those texts describe, at least to the extent that they refer to something like the sacrament of penance, is clearly concerned with the loosing element in the polarity. No particular power is needed to leave a sinner in his sinful state, and no man can possess the power of keeping another in a state of sin. Moreover, the divine act which finds sacramental expression in the church's act is always one of reconciliation. God's act is never one of causative condemnation; human condemnation is always a matter of self-condemnation that involves a rejection of the divine reconciling overtures. Thus, the sacramental significance of the judgment in Penance is not one of deciding what culpability is present, nor one of deciding whether this culpability should be forgiven. Rather, it is one of proclaiming God's and the community's openness to reconciliation, an openness that existed prior to the sinner's desire for reconciliation and which now finds completion in the actual reconciliation. Prophetic proclamation of God's word constituted the stimulus to conversion throughout the process of reconciliation; in the penitential ritual it takes its fullest form.

Such a view of Penance as an act of mercy rather than as an act of discriminating judgment seems, however, to ignore a constant and central tradition regarding the church's power to "bind" as well as to "loose." Moreover, it seems to be wildly idealistic in supposing that the Christian community has no need to safeguard order and Christian behavior in its midst, and to do so by punishing as well as rewarding. Yet, this may point to the very issue that needs clarification: the various ministries of reconciliation (including liturgical celebration of Penance) are one thing, and caring for good discipline in the community is another. Though it is not completely satisfactory, the classic distinction between internal forum and external forum is helpful here. *Reconciliation* is essentially a healing process that affects a sinful Christian in his inner life of faith and charity; *discipline* is a community action of regulating the external behavior of seriously deviant members, so that it harms neither the corporate faith life of the community nor the individual faith of its members. Both are necessary, and there is some relationship between them (the fact that a Christian who is a disciplinary problem may also be in need of reconciliation); but it is a serious pastoral mistake (and a perversion of the basic sacramental significance of the act) to utilize Penance as a means of guaranteeing church discipline. Besides, in a Christian community the exercise of discipline itself should be a matter of fraternal correction rather than of judicial condemnation.

We have already intimated that the Eucharistic action has a unique role to play in the church's discernment of the Spirit. Actually, this is but one facet of the fact that celebration of the Eucharist is the supreme and ultimate law in the church, the privileged norm for making every judgment that the Christian community faces. It is this, because it is the continuing injection of the death/resurrection mystery (i.e., the concrete reality of the risen Christ himself) into the life experience of Christians; it is this reality of Christ's death and resurrection that is the ultimate judgment upon all human existence and behavior. Obviously, this gives the notions of "law" and "judgment" an interpretation that is far from common understanding; but it is the insight into this specifically Christian interpretation which must govern all exercise of judgment in the church.

Authority to Exercise Judgment

Since judgment and authority are such closely correlative realities, it is clear from what we have been saying that authority in the church must be radically distinct from the authority that functions in other human contexts. Perhaps we can come closer to an ac-

curate understanding of the kinds of authority that are appropriate to the Christian community by studying the grounds which justify the various kinds of judgment we have studied.

Since all judgment is a claim to understanding, it might be logical to begin by studying knowledge as a basis for authority. Obviously, the possession of knowledge is one of the most basic sources for human authority: a man has the right and responsibility to speak authoritatively about something in proportion as he has accurate understanding of it. Common usage testifies to this: we speak of someone as an "authority" in a given area of human knowing.

Within the specific range of knowledge that is proper to the church's existence as a community of faith there are several kinds of understanding that provide the grounds for speaking or acting with authority. One who has actually seen something happen can witness to the fact that it happened and (within the limits of human capacity to observe objectively) can describe the nature of the happening. If this witness passes on his firsthand knowledge to someone else, this second person can also speak about the event, but with somewhat lessened authority. This is basically the kind of authority that attaches to "apostolic succession" (whether one applies the term, in different fashion, to the community as a whole or to the episcopal *collegium*) or to "the apostolic tradition."

Another kind of understanding possessed by members of the church is that involved in religious experience, the understanding that is intrinsic to faith itself. Though the nature of this understanding may be difficult to describe, it does imply a distinctive kind of immediacy in knowing. The believer does not only know things *about* God, he knows *God*, an immediacy which links faith with the prophetic experience. Despite all the evident dangers of delusion that attach to this kind of highly subjective experience, Christian religious experience, especially when it is the shared religious experience of large numbers of mature and psychologically balanced people, possesses a certain authority to pass judgment upon verbal, liturgical, or institutional formulations that claim to express Christian faith.

Critical appraisal, methodic analysis, and systematic structuring of the understandings contained in Christianity's historical traditions and in the community's shared experience of Christian faith provides still another dimension of knowledge. This is the realm of theology; the understanding that results from careful theological reflection gives one a specific authority to judge Christian belief and practice. This does not imply that theologians are to lay claim to "the chair of Moses" and spend their time pointing out the inadequacies or errors of nontheologized Christian understandings. Instead, the theologians' task is to lead the way towards richer and more accurate formulations of faith. This is a task of creative *re*-mythologizing, but it necessitates a concomitant *de*-mythologizing, i.e., a judgment upon already existent formulations, which clearly implies that theologians as such have authority that is proper to them because of their theological knowledge.

Partially distinct from knowledge as a basis of authority is prophetic charism. One element in this charism is an unusual awareness of and insight into the divine presence and into the practical demands it lays upon Christians. This element coincides with the heightened faith consciousness ordinarily referred to as "mysticism." A second element, however, distinguishes the prophet from the mystic: the impulse to communicate to the Christian community (and perhaps to others also) the special word of God that has come to him; the prophet is not only *enlightened*, he is also *sent*. Quite clearly, then, one who has a genuine prophetic charism possesses a particular authority to speak to the community; he is an oracle through whom the Spirit of Christ finds expression.

Because the prophetic oracle involves a sharpened appraisal of the community's existential situation and an exhortation to deepened conversion, it is always an act of judgment. However, prophetism is character-istically eschatological: it is not primarily a criticism of the past (though that may be a necessary ingredient at a certain point in history) but rather a pointing to the future. In Christian prophetism this eschatological aspect is heightened, for the Christian prophet always speaks about the community's destiny to enter more deeply into the resurrection of its Head. So, the prophetic voice in the church is meant to awaken the community to new levels of life; it is a creative call to increased faith and hope and love. Like truth in general, the prophetic oracle does not need the support of any official reward or punishments, for it contains its own intrinsic sanction: the prophetic word is word of life; he who receives it will live, he who rejects it will die.

If the prophet is to pass judgment upon the community, the community must also pass judgment upon the authenticity of anyone who claims to have the prophetic vocation. This it can do, because the community itself is the fundamental abode of the prophetic Spirit, and any specialized expression of Christian prophetism occurs as part of the community's own vital evolution. Yet, discrimination between the true and false prophet is generally difficult; many a true prophet is verified by the community only after his death. In a sense, it could not be otherwise, since the genuine prophet is always one of those humans who lives very literally in the future. His insights and judgments are those that society as a whole will have some decades later, and society will have them because of the prophet. During his own prophetic ministry, the prophet may seem too deviant, too radical a challenge to the status quo, too irreverent towards that which his auditors erroneously identify as Christian tradition. However, if he be genuine, the prophet will be vindicated by history; his words will be seen as instruments for the Spirit-ualization of the church and of all creation.

Perhaps the prophet's fate need not be as painful (even tragic) as it has often been, for his charismatic authority *can* be recognized by at least some of his contemporaries. Precisely because the prophetic insights are not additions to the gospel but rather a deepened understanding of the gospel, the faith of those Christians who have been able (through study and prayer and truly sacramental experience) to acquire a more profound grasp of the Christ-mystery will resonate favorably with the prophet's message. This has happened in the past, but often there was no agency through which this congruence of faith could be expressed; there was a ruling assumption that only jurisdictional judgment by church officials could ultimately declare the genuineness or falsity of an apparent prophet. In the church of the future, could not organized religious communities or their equivalent provide the context within which the prophetic charism could be discerned, nurtured, and protected? This is not to say that the prophetic ministry would be exercised only by members of such communities—in some instances it might; instead, it is to suggest that religious communities might have a particular function of ministering *to* Christian prophetism.

Quite different from the authority attached to knowledge is the authority connected with *love*. Nebulous and ultimately impossible to define (as is love itself), the authority that friendship gives one to involve himself in the life of his friend is a very real and constructive force in human relationships. Without detailing all the dangers of abusing such authority (parental domination, selfish exploitation of friendship, etc.), we can concentrate on understanding the nature of such authority as it finds special expression in the Christian community. One can legitimately carry over into Christian charity all the characteristics of genuine human love that we know from our other personal relationships; for Christian charity assumes and transforms all these other forms of love, and does so by introducing into Christian experience the love relationship each Christian (and the community as a corporate reality) has with Christ. Thus, each Christian has added authority in dealing lovingly with his fellow Christians, for they are in special fashion his brothers and sisters.

Clearly, the kind of authority attached to Christian charity does not belong specially to, nor form the basis for distinguishing, any ministry within the church. Charity is at one and the same time the loftiest and the most universal of the charisms. Each Christian has the obligation to love all other men and women, therefore the right and responsibility (i.e., the authority) to do for them whatever mature love and concern dictate. Charity finds expression in all the church's specialized ministries, and it provides in each one of them part of the authority with which they function.

However, certain ministerial functions seem to translate more immediately or obviously the community's love. In many ways, the ministries of reconciliation that find their sacramental fulfillment in Penance draw heavily upon the authority of love; personal love is, ultimately, *the* reconciling force in human affairs, and in Christian reconciliation the force of divine love works sacramentally in Christian love. Again, fraternal correction within the church derives its authority from the love it expresses—which, of course, says a great deal about what fraternal correction is. Strictly speaking, fraternal correction is a duty that rests upon each Christian; yet, one cannot help wondering if the very delicacy of this task and the relative rarity of persons who can fulfill it fearlessly and lovingly do not point towards some special charism of fraternal correction. And if there is some such special gift of the Spirit, might it not be a critical element in the charismatic ministry of governing? If so, governing the Christian community is radically distinguished from ordinary administrative or management activity, and holiness (i.e., mature possession of Christian love) would be one of the attributes indicating a given person's aptitude for government within the church.

This brings us to the touchiest and most obvious kind of authority within the church, the authority that pertains to "office." Bracketing for the moment the question as to what function, if any, official authority is meant to play in a Christian community, we can study ecclesiastical office as we know it from history and from our own experience and inquire about its particular authority. Despite the obvious similarities of official activity in the church and official activity in civil society, there must also be a fundamental distinctiveness in both "office" and "official authority" when applied to the church; the church as a unique kind of community must have a correspondingly unique kind of authority operative in its official activity.

One of the ways of getting at the nature of any authority is to study its source. History does not give us any simple insight into the source of episcopal authority, taking episcopacy as the paradigmatic instance of ecclesiastical office. Bishops have been elected by their people, selected by cathedral chapters, designated by kings, chosen by the episcopacy (or by the metropolitan) of a given region, picked by the papacy. Moreover, Christian understanding has shifted as to what authority comes with selection and what comes with episcopal consecration. Certainly, episcopal consecration has always been seen as a necessary basis for the man to exert full episcopal authority, but how is one to view this consecration? Is it a grant of authority by the episcopacy to its new member, or is it the initiation into a corporate charism of ruling, or is it the occasion on which God gives directly to the new bishop the authority befitting an autonomous religious monarch, or does it bestow on the new bishop the supernatural powers ("the power of orders") that enable him to exercise the authority granted him by the pope? These do not exhaust the alternatives that have been offered historically as explanations of the source of episcopal authority, but they suffice to indicate the theological uncertainty that belies any unquestioned assumptions about the God-given authority of a monarchical episcopate. This does not argue against the authority of the episcopate (or the authority of equivalent or derivative offices), nor even against the episcopate having monarchical authority; it simply says that we are not yet clear as to what that authority really is or whence it comes.

Another way of discovering the nature of episcopal authority is to examine the activity of bishops over the centuries and to discern therein the kind of authority they were actually exercising. Again, this provides an ambiguous answer, because the self-awareness that bishops have had regarding the authority attached to their episcopal functions has been quite diverse from one historical period to another, despite the fact that there has been a strikingly consistent recognition that certain functions (such as preaching, Eucharistic celebration, or ordaining) were basic to the episcopal office. Moreover, the picture is complicated by the process of the episcopacy absorbing into itself all the various ministries of prophecy, healing, and teaching. As a result of this process, the episcopacy would logically lay claim to all the kinds of authority proper to these charisms, and the authority proper to office as such becomes less clear.

It is no great help to say that Christ himself is the source of all the authority possessed by the hierarchy (or by anyone else), and therefore the nature of the authority is that possessed by Christ as prophet, priest, and king (an addition that became classical in post-Reformation polemical theology). All this is quite evident and undeniable. The question is how one understands this according to one or other soteriology. If one views Jesus himself as having exercised some form of jurisdiction (or as possessing all jurisdictional authority, but deciding to exercise only that which pertained to the spiritual realm) and then having passed on this jurisdiction to a line of successors who act as his legates until he himself comes in final judgment, this is a fundamentally different viewpoint from that of the person who sees the risen Christ still exercising his redemptive function *sacramentally* through those who fulfill the ministry of governing.

Undoubtedly, one of the factors that reinforced the historical accretion of jurisdiction to the episcopal function was the characterization of the episcopal role as sacerdotal.

Throughout most of history there has been an interplay of kingship and priesthood in people's thinking. Both king and priest have been looked upon as occupying a sacral position and possessing some special sacred power and authority. Precisely because their authority came to them from their relationship to *the* sacred, this authority lay outside challenge by the laity. The extreme modern expression of this view was the "divine right of the absolute monarch" as advocated by a king, such as Louis XIV. However, for more than two centuries this image of the sacred king has been gradually fading from the consciousness of European man; political power has been increasingly secularized, although those possessing such power still strive at times to cloak themselves with the mantle of sacrality.

To quite an extent, the image of the sacred monarch has fared better in religious circles, particularly in Roman Catholic attitudes towards the papacy. However, recognition of the nonreligious nature of ordinary political authority was bound to raise the question about ecclesiastical authority: What exactly is the reason that it should be regarded as especially "sacred," if there is nothing sacred about monarchs as such? Does sacrality attach to ecclesiastical rulers because of their priestly character and function? If so, what is the nature of their priesthood and what, if anything, does this imply about the authority to rule? Or, to put it quite simply, does Christian priesthood say anything at all about kingship as a ministerial role in the church?

Obviously, the answer to that question depends upon our understanding of Christian priesthood, and so no adequate response can be given until we undertake an analysis of priesthood in the church, which we will do in the next part. Prior to that, however, we might discuss an issue that appears to underly all the intertwined and unresolved questions about ecclesiastical authority, namely, is the very notion of "jurisdiction" (i.e., authority that attaches to a societal office and that comes to a person precisely because he or she occupies that office) genuinely applicable to the

corporate life of the Christian community? Although a negative answer to this question raises many historical and theological issues (and will unquestionably arouse no little emotional response), it does appear that a negative answer should be given.

First of all, let it be clear that jursdiction and authority are not identical. It is impossible for any community to continue in existence and to act effectively unless some *authority* unifies its life and activity. The Christian community is no exception. As we have already seen, there are several forms of authority that are proper to the church's inner being, and some of these pertain in special fashion to one or other specialized ministry. Jurisdiction is a particular form of authority, and people's experience of that particular form of authority can be used as a model for thinking about other kinds of authority. Our question, then, is quite clear, though twofold: Does this particular form of authority which is jurisdiction belong in the church? And, is jurisdiction an appropriate way of conceptualizing the authority of those who exercise the charism of governing in the church?

Jurisdiction is exercised (as the word itself indicates) by "speaking the law," by carrying out one or more of the classical governmental functions of legislation, execution, and adjudication. Because it operates in the realm of law, jurisdiction deals with the direction and control of persons' external behavior and not properly with their inner consciousness. Jurisdiction cannot be satisfied with the extent to which negligent error and deliberate malice are their own intrinsic punishment; to achieve the societal common good, it imposes external sanctions as a deterrent to harmful behavior. The jurisdiction of a civil ruler is quite distinct from the authority of one who teaches social ethics. The teacher works out of the authority of his own understandings to lead a student to a similar understanding of the kind of behavior required by societal existence; the public official uses his authority to enact or carry out laws which enforce a particular pattern of behavior.

Jurisdiction is required in human society because it is not a community to which men and women belong by choice. The Christian community, on the contrary, is a community of those who freely accept faith in Jesus as Lord and Christ. They cannot be forced to believe, nor to live out the implications of that belief; the totality of their Christian activity, individual or corporate, is rooted in their own free decision. No external system of sanctions is relevant as reward for fidelity or punishment for infidelity. Fidelity itself involves communion with one's fellow believers and possession of God in personal friendship; infidelity involves excommunication and loss of that friendship. It appears, then, that there is no role for jurisdiction in the Christian community. Some profit may come from formulation of laws, but strictly speaking this would be a teaching function that provided guidance for Christians' prudential judgments rather than real legislation. The motivational thrust to follow the line of conduct described in such laws would come out of the individual Christian's own relationship to Christ, and not from the official's societal power to enforce his laws. There might also be profit in preserving a body of legal precedent. If one is to regard this with theological accuracy, it would not be legal precedent in the strict sense but would be a distillation of the church's historical discernment of the Spirit which would serve to enlighten the church's present need to discern the Spirit.

Even if there were no place for jurisdiction as such in the church, would it not be advantageous to use jurisdiction as a model for understanding more fully and practically that properly Christian authority which should govern the church? This is a more difficult question to answer, since it concerns the religious value of a particular metaphor. But history does indicate that "jurisdiction" has been a misleading metaphor. While Matthew 20:25 makes it quite clear that leaders in the church are not to exercise jurisdiction as do the "lords of the Gentiles," the history of ecclesiastical government often belies this gospel principle. Besides, describing the membership of the church by dividing those who possess the power of jurisdiction from those who are subject to this power has tended to obscure the radical freedom of spirit that should characterize each Christian's faith and conscience. And it has led to such anomalies as the statement that bishops or the pope are beyond judgment by the rest of the church. Moreover, metaphors do not function in isolated fashion; because their contribution to understanding comes from their connotation, they tend to cluster with cognate symbols and so historically the notion of jurisdiction has often been accompanied by implications of military or police action. The Crusades and the Inquisition are glaring examples.

It is impossible to unravel the complicated history of Christian thought about jurisdiction, but a major influence during centuries of that history was the distinction between "power of orders" and "power of jurisdiction," a distinction whose validity is widely questioned by theologians today. Presumably, for such a distinction to have had any meaning, power of jurisdiction would be a kind of authority other than that exercised by the Christian community in its sacramental activity. If one were to overlook the all-embracing sacramental nature and activity of the church, and reduce Christian sacraments to some isolated and relatively infrequent cultic ceremonies, and forget the profound inner link between word and sacrament, the notion of power of jurisdiction might make some sense. (Historically, of course, the emergence of emphasis on a distinct *potestas jurisdictionis* was closely tied to the medieval church's involvement in civil affairs.) However, these "if's" are theologically inadmissible. There can be no authority in the church which is not the expression of the community's sacramental character; all authority would be in the realm of *potestas ordinis*. Yet, even this way of speaking is undesirable, for in its actual historical usage "powers of orders" has been too closely tied to an understanding of Christian sacraments which introduced emphasis on the cultic to the neglect of the evangelical. At any rate, the entire discussion would probably be helped if we were to drop from usage this distinction between orders and jurisdiction.

One of the most dangerous misapplications of jurisdiction came in the area of teaching, in the idea that authority to teach was derived from office. The clearest (though by no means an isolated) instance of such application of jurisdiction to teaching has been the attitude and activity of the papacy. Interestingly, as the emergence of post-medieval political structures eliminated the papacy's ability to exercise jurisdiction in the socio-politico-economic sphere, ecclesiastical teaching was increasingly emphasized as the place where papal jurisdiction (guaranteed by infallibility) found expression. Though naturally not honored by Christians outside the Roman Catholic community, the pope's claims to very broad teaching authority *because of his office* were almost completely unchallenged within that community, at least until very recently. A number of factors—among them the application of historical and exegetical methodology to conciliar statements, Vatican II's challenge to the "pyramid" image of the church, the issuance of *"Humanae vitae,"* careful historical study of the background and climate of Vatican I—have led theologians in the last decade to reexamine the nature and scope of the pope's authoritative teaching. However, the question is more fundamental than the pope's teaching authority; the question is the very notion of teaching that is authoritative because it is official, that is, because of the *jurisdiction* possessed by the teacher.

Accepting the teaching authority that can attach to a group like the episcopacy because of a privileged collegial witness, accepting also the possession by the bishop of Rome of a special normative resonance with the orthodox faith of this episcopal college, one can still see no justification for grounding the truth of any statement made by pope or bishop in ecclesiastical jurisdiction. Membership in the episcopal college can give bishops (and pope) a share in the corporate charism of apostolic witness, and this witness has its own special authority in the church's life of faith; but this witness functions as truth to shape men's consciousness and not as positive law to control their behavior. There is, of course, nothing to prohibit bishops or pope from going beyond the function of expressing their collegial witness, but when they do engage in other teaching or theological reflection or prudential judging, their authority is as great as their understanding and no special weight attaches to their teaching because of official position.

Removing jurisdiction from the picture as a basis for authoritative Christian teaching may do much to complete the reconciliation between Christianity and modern scientific thought. Truth needs no support outside itself, if it be pursued with care and honesty. And without canonizing modern intellectual movements, for they, too, have had their share of blinding presuppositions and self-serving prejudices, the spirit of modern science has been one of open exploration and continuing discovery. The very notion of men and women attaining truth by accepting conclusions that have ecclesiastical jurisdiction as one of their premises appears (and is) inadmissible. But if the Christian community's endeavor to understand more accurately and profoundly the special truth committed to it became a completely free and fearless quest for knowledge, bound only by the reality of its object (as is science itself), Christianity could be recognized as a partner with science in the task of liberating human thought.

If the notion of jurisdiction has intruded into the church's ministry of the word, it has also had important influence on the ministry of sacrament, most specially in Roman Catholicism. More precisely, from medieval times on, the very reality of some sacramental actions (their validity) was conditioned upon the ordained sacramental celebrant having appropriate jurisdiction. The two key instances have been the sacrament of penance, where an ordained presbyter, no matter how skilled a confessor, no matter how sincere and keen his desire to help reconcile a fellow Christian to Christ, was not able to perform penitential absolution effectively unless he had diocesan faculties (i.e., appropriate grant of jurisdiction) from the bishop in whose territory he found himself; and the sacrament of marriage, where a marriage was considered nonexistent if the ordained celebrant who witnessed the marriage contract did not have the necessary authorization.

As is true of each of the other sacraments in analogous fashion, Penance is a prophetic and effective proclamation of God's saving word. Acting as the representative of the community which reconciles the sinner to itself and so sacramentally to Christ, the minister of the sacrament can be said to exercise judgment; but this judgment can be seen as one involving jurisdiction only if one understands the Christian community according to a political model. There are good, pragmatic reasons why some kind of control should be exercised over the selection of confessors and over their continuing ministry; there is intrinsic reason in the very nature of the sacrament of penance as a symbolically causative action that the celebrant must be seen as publicly representative of the reconciling community. But neither of these implies that the confessor performs on behalf of the church a *jurisdictional* act.

If it is difficult to see how the effectiveness of the confessor's action can be conditioned by a grant (or denial) of jurisdiction, it is much more difficult to see how ecclesiastical jurisdiction conditions the sacrament of Christian marriage. In a Christian marriage the ordained minister is not even the minister of the sacrament; he is merely a special witness. What takes place essentially is the personal commitment of two Christians to each other in response to the church's proclamation of belief in the mystery that links such loving self-gift to Christ's own self-gift to mankind. Absolutely no ecclesiastical jurisdiction can enter into the action these two people perform, since the right they are exercising is given them by nature and by their Christian faith. Their action of contractually beginning this sacramental relationship (as well as their continuing life together as a Christian couple) is an act of witness to the gospel, and this obviously implies that it be done in the presence of a Christian community that can receive this witness and in relationship to the church as a whole. Thus the ordained minister who witnesses the marriage does share in the action's sacramentality. But supposing that without knowledge of the marriage partners the attendant liturgical celebrant has no proper jurisdiction to witness their marriage, which canonically would invalidate the marriage: can one contend that this renders nonexistent the existing reality of the two persons' commitment to one another, and negates the witness they are giving to their fellow Christians? Quite clearly, a radical reassessment is needed with regard to the application of jurisdiction to Christian marriage. More radically, the very notion of validity needs thorough reexamination, a matter we will discuss at greater length in the following part.

Selected Bibliography

Ministry of Judgment and Jurisdiction

EARLY CHRISTIANITY:

Cooke, B. *Christian Community: Response to Reality.* New York, 1970.

Gaudemet, J. *L'Eglise dans l'Empire Romain.* Paris, 1958.

Spicq, C. *Théologie morale du Nouveau Testament.* Paris, 1965.

Telfer, W. *The Office of a Bishop.* London, 1962.

Von Campenhausen, H. *Ecclesiastical Authority and Spiritual Power in the Church of the First Three Centuries.* Stanford, Calif., 1969.

PATRISTIC AND MEDIEVAL CHRISTIANITY:

Anciaux, P. *Le théologie du sacrement de pénitence au XIIe siècle.* Louvain, 1949.

Benson, R. *The Bishop-elect.* Princeton, 1968.

Bevenot, M. "The Inquisition and Its Antecedents." *Heythrop Journal* 7 (1966), pp. 257–68, 381–93, and 8 (1967), pp. 52–69, 152–68.

Cameron, J. *Images of Authority: A Consideration of the Concepts of Regnum and Sacerdotium.* New Haven, 1966.

Cowdry, H. *The Cluniacs and the Gregorian Reform.* Oxford, 1970.

Dvornik, F. *Early Christian and Byzantine Political Philosophy.* 2 vols. Washington, D.C., 1966.

Morrall, S. *Gerson and the Great Schism.* Manchester, 1960.

Oakley, F. *Council over Pope?* New York, 1969.

Tierney, B. *Foundations of the Conciliar Theory.* Cambridge, 1955.

Ullmann, W. *The Growth of Papal Government in the Middle Ages.* London, 1955.

Voosen, E. *Papauté et pouvoir civil à l'époque de Grégoire VII.* Gembloux, 1927.

Watt, J. *The Theory of Papal Monarchy in the Thirteenth Century.* New York, 1965.

Wilks, M. *The Problem of Sovereignty in the Later Middle Ages.* Cambridge, 1963.

POST-MEDIEVAL CHRISTIANITY:

Black, A. *Monarchy and Community.* Cambridge, 1970.

Davies, R. *The Problem of Authority in the Continental Reformers.* London, 1946.

Lecler, J. *Toleration and the Reformation.* 2 vols. London, 1960.

Milner, B. *Calvin's Doctrine of the Church.* Leiden, 1970.

Vidler, A. *The Church in an Age of Revolution.* London, 1961.

PART FIVE

Ministry to the Church's Sacramentality

CHAPTER 27

Cult, Priesthood, and Ministry in the New Testament

One of the most striking features of the early Christian decades, as we find them reflected in the New Testament literature, was their apparently a-cultic character. This is the more notable when we recall that Christianity in its origins found itself surrounded by the sophisticated religious ritual of Judaism and the rich and varied cultic ceremonial of the Egyptian, Greco-Roman, and Syrian religions. Yet, Christianity never pretended to be other than a religion. It was more than an idealistic ethic: it was a religious community directed to the worship of God.

Closer examination does reveal, of course, a profound level of cult, but it is cult of a unique type.[1] To pretend that it stands in no continuity with the religious ritual of Israel, or that it was unaffected by the religions of the contemporary Mediterranean world would be unreal, for some such influence was unavoidable.[2] However, it is significant that such outside influences are more observable from mid-second century onward,[3] and that it is in its earliest decades that the church is least marked by an institutionalized ritual of worship.[4]

This has unavoidable implications for our examination of ministry in these decades. If there was not yet a developed cultic ritual that was characteristic of Christianity, it would be hard to sustain the view that cultic functions were central to Christian ministry in the primitive church. One must be careful not to assume that the appearances justify the conclusion that these first decades of Christianity were truly a-cultic; we will have to study the situation much more closely before making any evaluation. Yet, it is intriguing and perhaps significant that key cult terms, such as *"hiereus," "thusia," "thusiasterion,"* are scarcely used in the New Testament.[5] A very few times they are used to characterize what Jesus had done in his death and resurrection,[6] but never to describe any cultic activity of the early Christians.

The one exception would seem to be the Epistle to the Hebrews, which treats at length the sacrificial nature of Christ's death and resurrection. But even in this instance, one is struck by the purpose of applying such categories of thought to the saving action of Jesus. The author has in mind to point out the uniqueness of this priestly action. It cannot be subsumed under the Israelitic sacrificial ritual which it surpasses and renders ineffective, nor can it be supplemented or enriched by any further sacrificial actions undertaken by Christians. Hebrews would seem to lead to the conclusion that sacrificial cult is not only unnecessary but inappropriate in the Christian community. Christian sacrifice has been offered once and for all.[7]

Thus, in the light of the extended priestly theology of Hebrews we would have to be hesitant to draw any conclusions about priesthood in the church from New Testament statements about Jesus as priest. The fact of the matter is, however, that (apart from Hebrews) Jesus himself is not called *"hiereus."* No attempt whatsoever is made to relate him to Levitic lineage (on the contrary, his descent from David in the tribe of Judah is underlined). He is never described as taking any official role in Jewish ceremonial, aside from the commonplace occurrence of reading the scroll in the Nazareth synagogue. With the single but all-important exception of the Last Supper, he is not described as performing any cultic actions as substitution for the official liturgy of Judaism; rather, he encourages his contemporaries to participate meaningfully in these.

Several factors should warn us against hastily drawing theological insight from this negative evidence. First of all, the dramatic struggle which forms the public ministry of Jesus and leads to his condemnation and death focuses on the effectiveness of the then-existent Jewish priesthood: Is it to continue, or does Jesus herald its replacement by his own ministry? The New Testament writers (and the traditions they represent) are explicitly aware of this central issue of Jewish cult. In treating Jesus as the antithesis to the official priesthood they are necessarily categorizing his own ministry, even though implicitly, as somehow priestly.[8]

Secondly, the theological viewpoint behind the early chapters of Luke's Gospel, with their Midrashic account of the infancy of Jesus, is clearly involved with the reality and significance of the Temple in Jerusalem, and with Jesus' relationship to it.[9] And this view is carried throughout the Lucan corpus whose chiastic structure converges on the Temple: the Gospel leading up to Jesus' purification of the Temple and the disciples praying in it to glorify God for the resurrection/ascension of Jesus; and the Acts using the Temple as the spot from which the apostolic preaching of the gospel spreads outward to the world.[10]

Thirdly, the elements of dedication (which tends to coincide with the idea of sanctification), acknowledgment of the Father, victim-hood, and self-gift, when examined carefully in their application to Christ, are seen to bear on the unique New Testament understanding of worship and priesthood. While an exhaustive study of these notions as applying precisely to the priestly ministry and identity of Christ is not our present purpose, some brief look at these facets of the New Testament presentation of Christ is needed as back-

ground for understanding the primitive church's outlook on the priestly ministry as possessed by the community itself and by some of its leaders in a special manner.

In the Old Testament theology of sacrificial ritual to which Jesus himself and his first disciples would have been heir, the notion of "dedication" is central.[11] The chosen people are a people apart, singled out by Yahweh from all the peoples of the earth as his own.[12] He himself has dedicated them in covenant to be his servants who will express their dedication to him by their worship.[13] In the worship ceremonial itself, the offering is rendered holy, put aside as consummating this "removal from the profane" in actions like the holocaust, i.e., it is religiously dedicated.[14] This, of course, is meant to be a symbol of the people's own self-dedication and the consummation of this dedication by Yahweh's consecratory act.

It is precisely the human participation in the dedication of the victim that is reserved for the priesthood. Others, particularly the Levites, might help prepare the offering, including the killing of an animal intended for the sacrifice, but only the priest could stand at the altar and lift the gift to Yahweh and then place it on the altar.[15] Because of their special participation in this consecratory activity, the priests themselves were a select and dedicated portion of the people.[16]

Seen in this light, the New Testament description of Jesus as specially dedicated, both by his own decisions and by his Father's action through the Spirit, may well have cultic overtones. There is no doubt but that his death and resurrection are looked upon in relation to ritual sacrifice; this is the event that definitively and totally dedicates him to human salvation. Yet, this dedication already finds expression in the human life and experience that lead up to this hour. The baptism at the Jordan is a form of ritual expression of Jesus' dedication to his Messianic function. This dedication is reiterated and deepened in the Transfiguration, and it is notable that the description both of this scene and of the Palm Sunday entry into Jerusalem is colored by the Jewish liturgy of Tabernacles;[17] and Jesus speaks in anticipation of the need to sanctify himself for the sake of his brethren (John 17:19). Apart from any specific use of the terms "dedicate" or "sanctify," the entire career of Jesus as we have it described in the Gospels is one of dedicated service to men and dedicated fulfillment of his Father's will.

In biblical thought the notions of "dedication" and "victim" are very closely connected.[18] The precise thing that is done with a victim in an act of ritual is to put it aside as special, separated off for God, removed from the realm of the ordinary and profane. Men can do part of this victimizing, especially if they enjoy such an official function *jure divino*; but the final stage of the sacralizing remains a divine monopoly, for only God is capable of divinizing, of bringing something created somehow into his own realm of being.[19]

In New Testament thought Christ is both victim and the priest who performs the human aspect of the sacrificing act. In him the realities of priest and victim coincide, since his priestly act is one of self-offering.[20] Yet, his priestly role and authority reach their true expression only with the definitive sacrificial intervention of God. As Hebrews insists, Jesus becomes high priest and perfect victim only when he enters into the true "holy of Holies" by his resurrection (Heb. 5:9–10; 6:20; 9:14); if he were still in his earthly state, he would not be mankind's high priest (Heb. 8:4).

Clearly, the mystery of his death and resurrection is something that is not forced upon him; the notion of suffering associated with sacrificial victims, i.e., that something is simply done to them, does not find an exact equivalent in Jesus' case. He freely chooses to confront the mystery of death and new life; this is his obedience which would certainly not find the praise the New Testament gives it were it an attitude of fatalistic acceptance or grudging agreement. A passage such as the second chapter of Philippians clearly indicates the awareness of early Christianity that Jesus' own human decision was a key factor in the salvific efficacy of his death.

There is another aspect of Jesus' priestly act by which he dedicates himself as victim. The purpose for which he sets himself apart, the goal of his dedicated status, is not something apart from the historical life of mankind; it is precisely that historical life of men for whose transformation he gives himself in death and new life.[21] There occurs here a revolution in the meaning of "sanctity," "dedication," and "sacrifice" which is of utmost importance in understanding the nature of Christianity, and therefore of Christian ministry and priesthood.[22] These terms, as they find exemplification in Jesus as Christ and Lord, do not denote an achievement of human destiny through a process of abandoning the human for the heavenly. Rather, the redemptive action of Jesus, in placing himself in an irrevocable status of unending self-gift to men, is one of radical identification with men rather than of separation from them. As such, it is the ideal human translation (obviously, to be achieved only in the God-man) of the finality of the Incarnation itself.[23] This latter is certainly not an action of fleeing the contagion of creation and specifically of human life; it is a wedding of the divine with the human which finds its culminating expression in the nuptial gift of Jesus to men (Eph. 5:25).

All this in no way negates Christ's action as a priestly act of worship directed towards God. Christ is definitely *the* high priest (Heb. 3:1; 4:14), and it is in dying for men that he is this high priest (Heb. 2:17). However, it is only with his glorious entry into the true sanctuary that he fully assumes his function as celebrant of the heavenly liturgy. Christ's gift of himself to men is his self-gift to the Father; it is the perfect acknowledgment of the wisdom and love of the Father, for the Father has sent him to give himself to men (John 3:16–17). The same fifth chapter of Ephesians which so richly describes Jesus' death and resurrection as a marital gift of self to men (v. 25) speaks also of Jesus giving himself as an oblation and sacrifice to God (v. 2).

Christian Cult and Priesthood

So strong are the statements of Hebrews on the absolute uniqueness of Christ's priestly act that it is in a class by itself, that it is all-sufficient in its salvific power, and that its culmination in the heavenly liturgy is a lasting reality, that no room remains for anything that we might call cultic priestly activity on the part of Christians. And it seems that this is the way that the church in early decades thought; there is no place for *hiereis* in the church (or any place else for that matter) since there is one abiding *hiereus*.

But precisely because the priestly worship of Christ is a constant reality (Heb. 10:12–14), and because he abides with his brethren whom he joins to himself in his Body (John 15:1–11), the entirety of Christian existence is caught up into a cultic context, the whole of Christian life is meant to be an act of worship. There is a tendency to read New Testament statements which speak of Christian life as worship as if this were a figurative way of speaking; but it seems that such statements must be taken with strict literalness, even if that may require adjusting our notions of worship.

Paul, for example, will insist that every action of a Christian's life is to be one of acknowledgment of God: "Whatsoever you do . . ." (1 Cor. 10:31); he will tell his Christian converts that they themselves are to be a conscious victim offered to God (Rom. 12:1). This is not to say that ordinary human life by itself is worship; it becomes so in the Christian situation because of faith. Christian faith is a "liturgy and sacrifice" (Phil. 2:17), for it is the acknowledgment of God as he has revealed himself in his Son.

Special attention is paid the place of love and concern for one's fellow man. Hebrews 13:16 speaks of good works and the sharing of goods with one another as sacrifice. Paul tells the Philippians that the gifts given him are "an offering pleasing to God" (4:18). In the light of his general teaching on charismatic gifts of the Spirit being given for the edification of the Body and the praise of God, the preeminent position of charity in 1 Corinthians 13 takes on sacrificial significance.[24] Matthew 5:23–24 (Mark 11:25) underlines the intrinsic place of fraternal love in all genuine worship: "If you come to the altar to offer your gift and remember that your brother has anything against you. . . ."

In the Johannine tradition one can find a similar emphasis on love: if nowhere else, then surely in the "Last Discourse" where the theological reflection on the Passover of Jesus and its Eucharistic celebration stresses love for one another as the one command attached to the new covenant. However, there is another interesting and important emphasis in the Johannine writing: the witness to truth (which, of course, coincides with the Pauline view that the faith of the Christian community is a sacrifice).[25] At Jacob's well, Jesus tells the woman that the day is coming when the true worshipers of his Father will worship "in spirit and truth" (4:23–24); before Pilate, Jesus describes the purpose of his saving mission, and therefore specially of his death and resurrection, "for this have I come into the world, to bear witness to truth" (18:37). In the so-called priestly prayer after the Supper, Jesus prays that his disciples will be sanctified (which in the context seems justifiably open to the interpretation of "dedicated separation from the profane and belonging to God") by that truth which comes in God's own Word (John 17:14–19). Here, too, the theme is interwoven with the notion of love: the desired sanctification in truth will have the fruit of their fraternal unity. And it is this loving unity that will make manifest the Father's love for Christ and for men; it will be the very acknowledgment of God that is the heart of worship (17:23).

From such evidence it might seem that the early decades of Christianity were devoid of anything that might be called properly "cultic," that for some time the Jewish Christians continued to participate in the Jewish ritual, but that no characteristic Christian cult came into existence until later. Yet, any such sweeping conclusion is challenged by the evidence for the celebration of baptism and

Eucharist from the earliest days of the church. Acts 2, describing the event of Pentecost, indicates that the introduction of new converts into the community through baptizing as a rite was as old as the community itself.[26] There is no good reason to question this. It is entirely logical that some such social sign would have been utilized; baptizing (though not with the significance attached to Christian initiation) was a religious ritual already at hand,[27] and the earliest letters of Paul speak of baptism as a practice already in existence for some time and accepted unquestioningly by himself and his converts (1 Cor. 1:13–17).[28]

While the evidence regarding early Christian baptism is substantial and fairly detailed, it tells us practically nothing about the ministerial function of administering baptism, if, indeed, there was such a recognized function. True, it seems clear that the Twelve baptized (Matt. 28:18); so did Paul and other apostles such as Apollo (1 Cor. 1:12–17); so, too, did the "deacon" Philip (Acts 8:38). Paul's remarks to the Corinthians (1 Cor. 1) would seem to indicate that there was no reservation of baptizing to an official position; rather, it was generally the function of the "evangelizer" of a given group to fulfill his preaching by baptizing those who believed. Baptism is the "word of response" to the gospel; in the passages that do speak of a commission to baptize, this is always preceded by the mission to evangelize. The neophyte in his baptism proclaims Jesus as Messiah and Lord, bears witness to Christ and his Father and the Spirit.[29] In this context, baptizing would seem appropriately classified as part of prophetic ministry.

What seems important in the New Testament view of baptism is not the power or authority of the minister of baptism but the genuineness of the gospel whose acceptance it signifies. Baptism is not in the name of Paul, or Apollo, or of John the Baptist but in the name of Jesus who is the Christ and the Lord, and it is the power of this name that brings salvation.[30] Baptism initiates the person not just into the community of Christian faith but through symbol into the very mystery of Christ's death and new life (Rom. 6:3–5). Christian baptism, then, despite some surface resemblances to and even dependence upon similar religious rituals of first-century Judaism, was a unique act of cultic ritual.[31] Everything about it was specified by the reality of Christ's Passover: it was acknowledgment of that event as the gospel of salvation; it was acceptance of the risen Lord as savior and center of one's existence; it was entry into that community of faith in the resurrection which was in the deeper reaches of mystery the Body of Christ; it was praise of the Father who had fulfilled his *magnalia* in this supreme act of redemption; it was renunciation and liberation from sin, a conversion from the old to the new Adam.[32]

Cult Action of the Eucharist

While early Christian baptism deserves to be considered a cultic action, this designation can be applied even more readily to the Eucharistic celebrations of the first century. Scholarly investigation of the New Testament evidence regarding the practice and theology of the early Eucharist allows us to draw many conclusions with fair certitude; one of these seems to be that there is no clear New Testament indication about the ministry of liturgical leadership.[33]

What is clear is that no official of the early church, not even one of the Twelve, was looked upon as a cultic priest who offered sacrifice. In what may be the closest thing to a statement about the specific cultic nature of the Christian Eucharist, Hebrews 13:15 speaks of the Christian sacrifice as one of praise, a verbal sacrifice. Such sacrificial praise of God can be called "sacrifice" only because it is joined to and gives expression to the perdurable heavenly liturgy which the glorified Christ celebrates. Thus, the only priest who enters the picture is Christ himself.

Really, what the New Testament evidence seems to point to quite conclusively is the view that the Eucharistic breaking of bread is essentially an act of evangelic proclamation.[34] It is a "proclaiming the death of the Lord until he come" (1 Cor. 11:26). It is, as the Johannine perspective presents in theological detail, the continuing phase of the mystery of God sending his own life-giving word into the world, so that men can be led to faith, acknowledgment of the Father, and unending life (John 6).[35]

If this evangelical understanding of the Eucharistic celebration is consonant with the New Testament texts, the action of Eucharistic blessing is one of recognizing the saving act of God, of proclaiming his great deeds as these find culmination in Christ's death and resurrection, of expressing the conversion and dedication of life that are appropriate response to the gospel. Within such an action by a believing community, the leadership role becomes essentially a prophetic role. The liturgical leader is the one who publicly voices the blessing, the witness to God's saving action in Christ, the prophet whose own word carries the divine word of power and authority. In such a perspective it comes as no surprise to find in the *Didache* the testimony that prophets were considered normal celebrants of Eucharist in the earliest decades of Christianity.[36]

Some evidence would, then, point to a measure of liturgical leadership belonging properly to those who more officially acted as designated apostles and prophets. Less evidence, though still some, points in the direction of the regular community leaders (the *presbyteroi* or the *episkopos*) acting as the chief actor in Eucharist. A fair amount of evidence indicates that the Eucharistic assemblies were a key situation for uniting and forming the early communities. Instruction, exhortation, a certain amount of adjudication about community problems, provision for the needy—all these seem to have taken place (though perhaps not exclusively) in conjunction with the Eucharistic gathering.[37] Certainly, Paul sees the Eucharistic meal as an important agent for and expression of community; he castigates the Corinthians because they have betrayed this element of the action (1 Cor. 11). In such a situation, given the need for relatively frequent celebration of Eucharist, and most likely the rare presence of an apostle or prophet, it would logically have devolved upon those charged with caring for the community's good to see that the Eucharistic action was carried out, though such responsibility would not necessarily entail their own performing the role of celebrant. There would not necessarily have been *a* celebrant, or even a group acting in this capacity (as, e.g., the presbyters); but the precedent of the Jewish sacred meals with which they would have been familiar probably allows us to presume such a pattern of leadership in the early Christians' Eucharist.[38]

What distinguishes Christian celebration of Eucharist most sharply from other religious rituals of worship is the Christian belief, which inevitably controls their liturgical forms, that the risen Lord is present in their midst, himself celebrating the all-sufficient heavenly liturgy of redeeming sacrifice.[39] It is this heavenly liturgy which the Christian act of Eucharist reflects and expresses. Christians are a priestly people because they are the Body of him who is the one high priest; in joining their lives and persons to his sacrifice they are giving to the Father the worship that is his due.

One finds no trace in the New Testament literature of the notion that some designated minister has the function, at Eucharist or on any other occasion, "to make Christ present." Rather, wherever two or three are gathered in his name he is present among them (Matt. 18:20). The only thing that might conceivably point to this view, which becomes so central in later Christian thinking about the Eucharistic celebrant, is the notion that the presence of the risen Lord is connected with the invocation of his name.[40] But such invocation is certainly not reserved in early Christian prayer and worship to any individual in the community.

First-Century Christian Ministries

After reflecting on various facets of the New Testament view of ministry in this and preceding chapters, we can attempt a brief summation of the offices existent in the first-century church.[41]

Apostle

Many authors who treat the question of primitive Christian ministry begin, and rightly so, with a study of the role of "apostle."[42] Evidence from the New Testament makes quite clear that the role of apostle was centrally important in the early church, but relatively little is said about the exact nature of this role and about the persons who exercised it. We know that New Testament texts do not support a simple equation of "apostles" with the Twelve; actually, most of the traditional picture of the Twelve journeying about on apostolic missions is a product of later centuries. What the New Testament writings do state is that a number of others in the primitive church bore the title "apostle," the most prominent of them obviously being Paul. These writings do apply the notion of apostle to the Twelve, and the thesis that "apostle" was developed in the Pauline church and artificially applied to the Twelve rather late overlooks the centrality of *witness* in the apostle's activity.

What seems fundamental to the idea of apostle is the notion of "being sent to bear witness to the gospel." In the initial situation of the Jerusalem community, the Twelve apparently held some position of collegial guidance; they were the privileged witnesses to the life and teachings and Passover of the risen Lord. After the peace of their community's life was disrupted by the opposition of Jewish leadership, there was some missionary movement outward, certainly by Peter. Popular traditions see practically all the Twelve spreading out at this point to carry the gospel to distant lands; but actually there is surprisingly little New Testament mention of apostolic activity on the part of these immediate disciples of Jesus.

Whatever their precise activity, the Twelve, with their special credentials for gospel witness, would have formed a particularly respected center of apostolic activity, and so they would have merited the title in unique and unrepeatable fashion.

Yet, the Twelve were not alone as *apostoloi*. It seems that any well-established community felt the urge to send emissaries to preach the good news, to help form the newly baptized into viable communities, and then to help sustain them in their early years. Such a task for apostles is implied by Paul's letters (regarding his own activity and that of others like Barnabas and Apollos), by the descriptions of apostolic activity in Acts, and by such Gospel passages as Matthew 10:1—11:1 and Matthew 28:18–20.

If one can take Paul as the clearest instance, the key role of the apostle was the ministry of the word—evangelization and then catechesis. It is striking, as one examines the relevant New Testament uses of *"apostellein,"* that when God is the subject of this verb, the verb is complemented either by the infinitive *"kerussein"* or by the noun *"prophetes."* However, the apostle, though not a resident administrator, did have a certain plenipotentiary power which permitted him to instruct, legislate, judge, and appoint leaders with authority. All this seems to have come with the apostle's mission as emissary of Christ and the Spirit. Perhaps we can infer from this that the apostle also exercised leadership in the worship of the infant communities, but there is no clear confirming evidence for this (except in the *Didache*).

As one reflects on this ministry of the *apostolos*, it is difficult to differentiate it from the activity of the prophet. This prophetic character of the apostolic ministry is reflected also in the *Didache* picture of the apostle: a traveling emissary of the gospel sent out from a "mother church," prophetically witnessing to the word, guiding and shaping the early communities.

Apart from their presence at the Supper and at the post-Resurrection meals, there is practically nothing in the New Testament that might refer to a special role of the Twelve in early Christian worship. The same is true of others who are called *"apostoloi."* We can safely surmise that those who actually went out on apostolic missions did baptize, even though Paul says that this was not precisely his role. It would fit the overall picture of the New Testament writings if apostles did act as Eucharistic celebrants. But practically nothing exists as clear New Testament evidence for this. The *Didache* does grant "prophets" (which probably would include visiting apostles) a role of Eucharistic leadership, but there is practically no suggestion in first-century sources that overtones of cultic priesthood (as known, for example, to Judaism of that period) attaches to Christian apostleship.

Prophet

While apostles seem to have functioned in what was essentially a prophetic ministry—one could almost think of them (apart from the special collegial role of the Twelve in Jerusalem) as the traveling branch of the prophets—there were others also who were specially endowed with prophetic charism and ministry.[43]

Basically, all Christians were prophetic, each community was Spirit-guided and directed to prophetic witness. Yet, within the community some were recognized as possessing special prophetic gifts and a somewhat official function. Apparently, in some cases this was a temporary exercise of prophecy; but in other instances the person (e.g., Agabus) enjoyed a recognized and relatively permanent role as prophet. Apart from clear indications that the prophet's action was one of basic testimony to the gospel and the apostolic teaching, carried on within the community and contributing thereby to the growth of the community, there is no detailed account of the Christian prophet's role. One feature that is relevant to our study of ministry and priesthood is the link of prophetic ministry to the early celebration of Eucharist: the *Didache* gives explicit reference to this, and the New Testament texts give some implicit supporting evidence. Since the prophetic role is essentially that of bearing witness to the word of God revealed in Jesus' death and resurrection, and since the Eucharistic gather-

ing is seen as an action of proclaiming the death of the Lord until he comes, the prophet (if one is present in the community) seems a logical person to exercise liturgical leadership, roughly equivalent to what we would call the Eucharistic celebrant.

Teacher

There does not seem to have been the same overlap between prophet and teacher as between apostle and prophet, but there is some overlap between apostle and teacher, at least to the extent that apostles are described as teaching—so much so that the *didache ton apostolon* became very early a conventional designation for the instruction provided the early communities. There is, however, in at least some of the early communities, a ministry of teaching that is distinguishable from the role of apostle or prophet, a ministry that is carried on by individuals who were considered neither apostles nor prophets.[44] The very thing that would separate such teachers from the apostles was the fact that their function was one of explaining the teaching of the apostles, who were the original witnesses to the mystery of Christ Jesus.

Apostles would most probably have continued some teaching after the initial kerygma-conversion-baptism stage. After this first introduction of converts into the community, there ensued a continuing process of instruction; the very first stage of this would almost necessarily have fallen to the apostle who had evangelized the converts. Before long, however, other teachers could take over as the community became capable of developing its own life and the apostle moved on to further evangelization. Yet, it was the teaching of the original apostles that remained normative for this later instruction.

Presbyter

The term "*presbyteros*" does not as such denominate a specific ministry, though the one so designated could exercise one or other ministry; rather, it refers to a general situation of responsibility and service.[45] Within this broad "care for the community," what seems to have been most fundamental was the role of guidance or counsel, which at times could involve elements of judgment. Without denying the likelihood of presbyters exerting individual initiative in caring for needs that arose, the New Testament evidence indicates that presbyteral activity tended to be corporate. From the beginning, the presbyterate existed as a collegial group.

Though in the early decades the presbyterate was characteristic of the Palestinian communities and their offshoots, by very early second century the Pauline communities have the presbyterate as something well-established —Acts, 1 Clement, and the Pastorals make this clear. Any connection of *presbyteroi* with Eucharistic celebration in the first century can find no New Testament confirmation, unless one attempts a tenuous argumentation from the general situation of the early communities. There is greater foundation for believing that the presbyters were concerned for and at times actively involved in the catechesis of the community.

Episkopos

In informal fashion the presbyters performed some governance, perhaps more in making policy than in execution; so it is not surprising that the term "*episkopos*" (supervisor) was somewhat interchangeable with "*presbyteros*" in New Testament times.[46] In itself, however, "*episkopos*" is a term with more functional denotation. Basically it is a secular word (with no previous usage for a religious community function) which very early in Christianity is used to designate a supervisory role exercised by an individual or group. When this role is exercised by an individual as leader of a community it seems always to be in conjunction with the other presbyters. There is no clear evidence to justify Jerome's contention that in the infant church the *episkopos* was a chairman or executive officer chosen by the presbyterate to achieve unity and effectiveness. On the other hand, there is no suggestion that the presbyters come into existence as helpers or extension of the *episkopos*; instead, the presbyterate seems in many churches to have antedated the emergence of the single governing *episkopos*.

By the time of the Pastorals there is definite evidence that there was a common though not universal pattern of a single *episkopos*, charged specially with governance of teaching and worship and the community life of the group. As we will see, one cannot safely say that prior to the end of the second century this pattern is found in all the churches. And even the Pastorals, which reflect a structure of church order along much the same lines as that described in the letters of Ignatius, do not indicate a special ritual function for *episkopos* or *presbyteros*.

Deacon

One thing that helps confirm the contention that presbyters were not seen in the early church as assistants of the *episkopos* is the evidence that the deacons were just such aids to the head of the community.[47] In saying this, we do not wish to ignore the difficulty of discovering the origins and nature of the diaconate in the early church. Part of this difficulty stems from the fact that the word "*diakonia*" (and therefore to some extent "*diakonos*") is used generically to describe the entire range of early Christian ministry. Another element of the difficulty attaches to the use of "*diakonein*" for the seven chosen by the Twelve to attend to the needs of the Jerusalem community. The appointment of these seven has often been viewed as the beginnings of the diaconate, but it is far from clear that the function exercised by these men stands in continuity with that carried on by the men to whom Paul refers in his letter to the Philippians, or that described in the Ignatian letters. Instead, the deacons referred to in Acts, e.g., Stephen or Philip, exercised a great deal of autonomous apostolic endeavor and often engaged in activity that is not even remotely related to the internal service of the Jerusalem church. On the other hand, the deacons spoken of by Paul and those referred to in 1 Timothy 3:8–13 do seem to be serving the internal community needs of a local church, and to be doing so under the direction of the *episkopos*.

Slim as the evidence is, it does seem safe to say that those designated *"diakonoi"* had a special role in providing for the material well-being of the communities. On the other hand, there is nothing to suggest that the *diakonoi* functioned in early Christian liturgy as assistants to the celebrant—a role that is attributed to them by second-century Christian writing.

NOTES

1. On the meaning and varieties of cult, see J. Wach, *Sociology of Religion* (Chicago, 1944), pp. 25–26; L. Bouyer, *Rite and Man* (Notre Dame, 1963).

2. After a period of scholarly overemphasis on the influence of Hellenistic and Gnostic ideas and practices, there now seems to be increasing tendency to admit the uniqueness of Christian thought and institutions. See H. Rahner, *Greek Myth and Christian Mystery* (New York, 1968); W. van Unnik, "The Idea of the Gnostics Concerning the Church," *The Birth of the Church*, ed. J. Giblet (New York, 1968), pp. 225–41.

3. Gnostic impact resulted in a Christian Gnosticism which proved to be increasingly heterodox and which was eventually excommunicated as incompatible with the apostolic tradition. Judaism's influence, on the contrary, while explicitly resisted as a danger in first-century Christianity, subtly but importantly affects mainstream Christianity. See K. Baus, *Handbook of Church History* (New York, 1965), vol. 1, pp. 181–90.

4. See J. Jungmann, *The Early Liturgy* (Notre Dame, 1958), pp. 29–38.

5. See G. Schrenk, "Hiereus," *Theological Dictionary of the New Testament* (hereafter referred to as *TDNT*), vol. 3, pp. 263–65; J. Behm, "Thuo," *ibid.*, pp. 184–86.

6. Eph. 5:2; Rev. 7:14; 5:9.

7. Heb. 7:26–28. See A. Gelin, "The Priesthood of Christ in the Epistle to the Hebrews," *The Sacrament of Holy Orders* (Collegeville, Minn., 1962), pp. 30–43. Gelin's final remark (p. 43) bears mention: "The question of our own priesthood does not arise in Hebrews, nor does the eucharist. It can only be with the greatest caution that any conclusions can be drawn about priestly spirituality from this epistle." See also F. Durrwell, *The Resurrection* (New York, 1960), pp. 136–50.

8. On Jesus' relation to the Jewish priesthood, see R. Brown, *St. John* (Garden City, N.Y., 1966), vol. 1, pp. ixxi–ixxiii.

9. See R. Laurentin, *Structure et théologie de Luc I–II* (Paris, 1957), pp. 43–45, 146.

10. See H. Conzelmann, *The Theology of St. Luke* (New York, 1961), pp. 73–94.

11. On the Old Testament meaning of sacrifice, see R. de Vaux, *Ancient Israel* (New York, 1961), pp. 447–56.

12. Exod. 19.

13. Exod. 24. See W. Eichrodt, *Theology of the Old Testament* (Philadelphia, 1961), vol. 1, pp. 36–69; H. Renckens, *The Religion of Israel* (New York, 1966), pp. 179–87.

14. See de Vaux, pp. 451–53.

15. See *ibid.*, p. 416.

16. On the nature of Old Testament priesthood and its historical evolution, see *ibid.*, pp. 345–405. It might be relevant to our attempt to understand New Testament "offices" to reflect that charismatic prophets were also a set-apart, dedicated group in Old Testament history, but that the principle of their sacralization was different. In the case of the priests it seems that it was the contact with the altar which set them apart from the profane; in the case of the prophets it was their possession of and by the word of God that sanctified them.

17. See H. Kraus, *Worship in Israel* (Richmond, Va., 1966), pp. 61–66; de Vaux, pp. 495–502.

18. See Eichrodt, pp. 133–68.

19. See de Vaux, pp. 451–53; J. Pedersen, *Israel* (London, 1963–64).

20. Eph. 5:22 stresses the notion that Jesus' offering is a pleasing oblation to his Father, performed on mankind's behalf; however, in v. 25 of the same chapter the offering of Christ is placed in the context of a self-giving to the church.

21. Col. 1:9–23; 2 Cor. 5:17–21. Obviously, the very mentioning of this topic and the interpretation of New Testament texts in relation to it touch upon the question of New Testament eschatology, which is so keenly debated today and so closely intertwined with discussions of Christian secularity. See R. Richards, *Secularization Theology* (New York, 1967).

22. To some extent this revolution was anticipated by Old Testament prophetic thought, especially in the eschatological (as opposed to apocalyptic) viewpoint that characterized the ninth- to sixth-century prophets. See G. von Rad, *Old Testament Theology* (New York, 1965), vol. 2, pp. 112–19.

23. See W. Pannenberg, *Jesus—God and Man* (Philadelphia, 1968), pp. 378–97.

24. On the cultic dimension of *"agape"* see C. Spicq, *Agape* (Paris, 1959), vol. 2, pp. 194, 250–51.

25. This stands very close, of course, to the notion of Eucharist as prophetic proclamation and to the view that early Christianity saw the Eucharistic prayer as a benediction of God for his great deeds. See J.-P. Audet, "Esquisse historique du genre littéraire de la 'bénédiction' juive et de l'"eucharistie' chrétienne," *Revue biblique* 65 (1958), pp. 371–99.

26. See B. Neunheuser, *Baptism and Confirmation* (New York, 1964), pp. 16–22.

27. *Ibid.*, pp. 6–10; also, C. Davis, *Sacraments of Initiation* (New York, 1964), pp. 39–41; J. Delorme, "The Practice of Baptism in Judaism at the Beginning of the Christian Era," *Baptism in the New Testament* (Baltimore, 1964), pp. 25–60.

28. For a thorough study of Paul's teaching on baptism, see R. Schnackenburg, *Baptism in the Thought of St. Paul* (New York, 1964).

29. See Neunheuser, pp. 11–15.

30. See Schnackenburg, pp. 18–82.

31. See A. Richardson, *Introduction to the Theology of the New Testament* (New York, 1958), pp. 337–41.

32. For a fuller treatment of these elements, see B. Cooke, *Christian Sacraments and Christian Personality* (New York, 1965), pp. 15–24.

33. See E. Schweizer, *Church Order in the New Testament* (London, 1961), pp. 186–87.

34. See Audet, "Esquisse historique. . . ."

35. See Brown, pp. 272–94.

36. *Didache* 10.

37. See R. Schnackenburg, *The Church in the New Testament* (New York, 1965), pp. 40–45; E. Kilmartin, *The Eucharist in the Primitive Church* (Englewood Cliffs, N.J., 1965), pp. 141–53.

38. On relation of primitive Eucharist with Jewish liturgical meals, see J. Jeremias, *The Eucharistic Words of Jesus* (New York, 1966), pp. 15–88; J. Delorme, *The Eucharist in the New Testament* (Baltimore, 1964), pp. 21–67.

39. See Schnackenburg, *Church in the N.T.*, pp. 42–43; on specifically Christian meaning of *"anamnesis,"* see Cooke, pp. 134–36.

40. See H. Bietenhard, "Onoma," *TDNT*, vol. 5, pp. 270–80.

41. Since more detailed references have already been given on specific points, only a few selected works will be cited relative to the description of early Christian ministries. These references do not necessarily agree with one another or with the position taken in our presentation, but among them they represent most of the current opinions and summarize most of the modern discussion of the matter.

42. On *"apostolos,"* see K. Rengstorf, *TDNT*, vol. 1, pp. 420–47; H. Küng, *The Church* (New York, 1967), pp. 344–54; H. von Campenhausen, *Ecclesiastical Authority and*

Spiritual Power in the Church of the First Three Centuries (Palo Alto, Calif., 1969), pp. 12–29; Schnackenburg, *Church in the N.T.*, pp. 26–33; Schweizer, pp. 194–204.

43. On *"prophetes,"* see G. Friedrich, *TDNT*, vol. 6, pp. 848–61; von Campenhausen, pp. 60–62; Küng, pp. 184–86, 396–97; Schnackenburg, pp. 39–40; Schweizer, p. 197.

44. On *"didaskalos,"* see K. Rengstorf, *TDNT*, vol. 2, pp. 152–60; Küng, pp. 396–97; Schweizer, pp. 197–98; von Campenhausen, pp. 60–62; Schnackenburg, pp. 37–38, 99–102.

45. On *"presbyteros,"* see G. Bornkamm, *TDNT*, vol. 6, pp. 662–80; Küng, 404–7; Schweizer, pp. 216–18; von Campenhausen, pp. 76–123.

46. On *"episkopos,"* see H. Beyer, *TDNT*, vol. 2, pp. 615–22; Küng, pp. 399–400, 407–12; von Campenhausen, pp. 76–123; Schweizer, pp. 198–202, 216–19.

47. On *"diakonos,"* see H. Beyer, *TDNT*, vol. 2, pp. 89–93; Schweizer, pp. 198–202; Küng, p. 413.

CHAPTER 28

The Cult in the Ante-Nicene Period

As we move into the subapostolic period, there is still the striking absence of cultic language to refer to worship actions or leadership personnel. Even the final (and more "Catholic") portions of the New Testament literature, though they tend to reflect the emergence of a monarchical episcopate, do not reflect any tendency to look upon the leadership of the Christian communities as hieratic. By the end of the second century, however, there are clear evidences that *"hiereus"* is being applied in the Greek-speaking churches and *"sacerdos"* in the Latin-speaking churches. These terms are applied to Christ himself, to Christian *episkopoi* and *presbyteroi*, to the Christian people, and, of course, used frequently in referring back to Old Testament priesthood. Thus, the second century seems to have witnessed a startling shift from the New Testament mentality and in the direction of cult categories reminiscent of Old Testament thought, an evolution that is accelerated in the third century (finding its clearest expression in the *Didascalia*).

One finds very early use of *"hiereus"* (more often of *"archiereus"*) in reference to Christ.[1] We might expect this in the area of the early church to which the Epistle to the Hebrews was directed; but we find it also in the letter of Clement of Rome (61:3) and in Justin.[2] Somewhat surprisingly, because the general tone of his letters is quite liturgical, Ignatius of Antioch does not refer to Christ as high priest; but from the same part of the church, in the hymn placed on the lips of Polycarp in the account of his martyrdom, Christ is called the "eternal and heavenly

high priest."[3] Again, the early testimony of the *Didache* reflects no application of *"hiereus"* to Christ; even in its liturgical prayers (where we might expect *"hiereus"*) the term applied to Christ is "Servant."[4] In addition to Justin, whose use of the term is quite deliberate and conscious, the second century contains some incidental application of the term to Christ by Irenaeus and around the turn of the century by Clement of Alexandria.[5]

Early in the third century, a clearly conscious use of the term is found in Tertullian's *Adversus Judaeos*, chapter 6; but this is a situation much like the one faced in Hebrews.[6] In the *Apostolic Tradition*, also very early third-century, the liturgical prayers for the ceremony of ordination do not contain an explicit denomination of Christ as *"archiereus,"* but they say it by way of implication in speaking of the "high-priestly Spirit" and of Christ pouring out this Spirit on his disciples.[7] In mid-third century Origen's *De oratione* presents Christ, the high priest, as the model of Christian prayer.[8] Towards the end of the century, Cyprian speaks of Christ as the principal priest, links this with Christian celebration of the Eucharist, and presents Christ as the model of Christian priests.[9] But perhaps the most important evidence of the pre-Nicene period is that contained in the *Didascalia*, probably late third-century.[10] Here the idea of priesthood is central, its application to the episcopacy explicit and extended; its framework of reference is not noticeably that of Christ's priesthood. Christ is scarcely mentioned as high priest; instead, the antecedent of Christian priesthood from which the argumentation is drawn is the priesthood of the Old Testament.[11] This raises the question: What was it that underlay increased emphasis on the cultic aspects of Christian episcopacy and presbyterate, reflection on the priesthood of Christ or reintroduction of Old Testament categories?[12]

We have already mentioned the emphasis in the *Didascalia* on the priesthood of the *episkopos*; it is his priesthood that underlies all his other dignities and responsibilities. At about the same time in the West, Cyprian's references to the bishops are of such a nature that they seem to reflect a taken-for-granted view that the bishops are *sacerdotes*: it is the priests of the church who hold it together as cement;[13] Rome is the origin of the unity of the priesthood.[14] Quite clearly, by late third century *hiereus/sacerdos* is a well-established denomination of the episcopacy.

Earlier in the century the usage is already firm: the *Apostolic Tradition*, reflecting as it does a basic liturgical pattern from at least as early as the beginning of the third century, places the high-priestly role of the *episkopos* among the basic elements mentioned in the consecrating prayer for the *episkopos*.[15] So, too, a bit later, Origen gives clear testimony to the Alexandrian application of *"hiereus"* to the episcopacy.[16] Tertullian, also, gives us textual evidence that *"sacerdos"* and *"pontifex"* were used in African circles as referring to the bishops.[17]

When we move back into the second century, the evidence for use of the term *"hiereus"* for the *episkopoi* seems to be quite completely missing. Ignatius and Irenaeus who both speak clearly about the function of the bishop, and include in that function a role of leadership in Christian initiation and Eucharist, do not use *"hiereus"* of the bishop or parallel his role to that of the Old Testament high priest.[18] Justin applies *"hiereus"* both to Christ and to the Christian community, but not to the *episkopos*.[19] Nor do we find any application of the term to *episkopoi* (or for that matter to *presbyteroi*) in Hermas, the Apologetes, Clement of Rome, or any other second-century writer.[20]

One must be careful not to draw conclusions too hastily from this absence of hieratic terminology in the second century. First of all, it is dangerous to draw a strong negative conclusion from the limited second-century texts we have. Secondly, the liturgical texts in Hippolytus may reflect Roman (and perhaps much broader) usage and thinking from as early as mid-second century. Yet, in the light of what seems a determined effort on the part of the New Testament writers to avoid application of *"hiereus"* to the ministry of the Christian community, the second century seems to have retained this same reluctance for quite some time.

Use of *"hiereus"* to designate the presbyterate or its function is almost totally lacking, not just in the second century but in the entire ante-Nicene period. And this despite clear evidence that presbyters functioned along with the bishop (or as his substitute) in Eucharistic and other liturgical actions.[21]

The sole exception to this absence of evidence (but it is an exception of major importance) is the statement in the *Apostolic Tradition* where (in explaining why only the bishop imposes hands in diaconal ordination) it states that the deacon *"non in sacerdotio ordinatur, sed in ministerio episcopi. . . ."*[22] There are indications, too, both in the *Didascalia* and in Cyprian, that the presbyters share in the *sacerdotium* with the bishop, but the term "priest" is not explicitly applied to them.

Among the rare uses of *"hiereus"* in the second century, one finds several applications of the word to the Christian people as a whole.[23] No doubt the texts from 1 Peter and Revelation played an influential part in making explicit this view. However, in Justin there seems to be a somewhat independent process of personal reasoning connected with his use of the term. Because they have been called by God, Christians are a high-priestly race; and they exercise this by their offering of the one acceptable sacrifice.[24]

While the semantic study of *hiereus/sacerdos* is central to our examination, another term is of considerable influence because of its close link with the cult of the church:

namely, *"mysterion/sacramentum."* Fortunately, there have been a number of important and thorough studies of this term (or terms, for they do not totally coincide), so we will not have to undertake a repetition of that investigation here, but can simply draw on it as we treat of various topics.[25]

Liturgical Presidency

Apart from theological understandings they may (or may not) have had of priesthood and worship, the early Christian communities quickly developed a number of flexibly ritualized actions which were identifiably similar from one community to another. Most important of these were the Eucharist, baptismal initiation, the "laying on of hands" for ministerial ordination, and, as it came into existence a bit later, the ceremonies of the exomologesis. Since by sometime in the second century there was universal recognition that presidency over such ritual acts was part of the function attached to those called "priests," it is necessary to examine more carefully the exercise of such liturgical leadership.

From Didache to Hippolytus

Not that other evidence is without value (such as some of the indirect references in Hermas),[26] nor that further evolution does not occur in the third century, but it does seem that the essential development can be clarified by examining the *Didache*, Ignatius, Justin, and Hippolytus. In the *Didache*, presiding over the "breaking of the bread" seems to be the prerogative of the apostles and prophets, and in their absence (which was probably the more common situation) the prerogative of the presbyters and *episkopoi* chosen by the community.[27] In Ignatius of Antioch the leadership (even the control) of the ritual actions of Eucharist and baptism is firmly in the hands of the bishop, though others join him in Eucharistic celebration and some may even act as celebrants by his authorization.[28] That the pattern of monarchical episcopal direction of sacramental ritual is clearly indicated in Ignatius' letters is not the question. The question is the extent to which such a pattern prevailed at this time (apparently, to most of the churches to whom he addressed letters; the big exception being Rome), and the reasons for this quick emergence of tripartite ministry.

Appeal to the testimony of Justin is controlled, of course, by the disputed passage where he speaks of *ho proestos*, the "president" of the Eucharistic assembly.[29] While no completely convincing explanation of the usage will probably ever be given, the arguments used by Jalland and by Barnard seem to point quite strongly to an identity of the *proestos* with the *episkopos*.[30] If so, the episcopal role claimed in the Ignatian letters is described in greater detail by Justin. It is he who explains the meaning and implications of the day's readings; it is he who prays the Eucharistic prayer over the gifts which are thereby changed into the body of Christ.

In Hippolytus the picture is quite clear. The two detailed descriptions of liturgical ritual (the ordination rite and the initiation ceremony) give us, through the prayers for episcopal and presbyteral ordination, an invaluable insight into the understanding of those two offices and, through the description of the rite of initiation, a view of the episcopal celebrant in action.[31] There is no question about the presidency at both ceremonies. We can argue from them to the ordinary celebrations of the Eucharist: the regular celebrant is the bishop who is accompanied by the presbyterate and assisted by deacons. Allowing for the need, as numbers of Christians swelled, to have outlying Eucharist celebration under the delegated leadership of presbyters, the normative liturgy had the bishop as celebrant. Having said this, we must be careful not to read too monarchic a view of episcopacy into the situation. There are two possible ways of explaining theologically the situation described in Hippolytus and in other third-century documents; one can say that the bishop is celebrant and assisted by the presbyterate, or one can say that the presbyterate is celebrant under the presidency of its chosen bishop. The *Apostolic Tradition* does not demand either explanation.

Episcopal Presidency

In general, the textual evidence of the second and third century points with increasing clarity to four situations in which the principal liturgical role belongs to the bishop: baptismal initiation, Eucharist, ministerial ordination, exomologesis. In the initiation ceremony, there is a diversity of roles (at least from the time reflected in Hippolytus): the deacon (or deaconess) performs the prebaptismal anointings; the baptizing is done by the presbyter; but it is the bishop who presides over the entire ceremony, administers the chrismation, and is the chief celebrant at the initiation Eucharist.[32] Even prior to the initiation itself, it was the bishop who was responsible for the admission, training, and testing of the catechumens.

It seems legitimate to put together the evidence from Ignatius, Justin, and Hippolytus, and to say that the regular Sunday celebration of the *Eucharist* was essentially the same as the Eucharistic portion of the initiation and ordination ceremonies detailed in the *Apostolic Tradition*. This would make the bishop the chief celebrant, the regular homilist, and the one charged with principal responsibility for the manner in which the liturgy was performed. Such would seem to be the continuing situation as reflected in Tertullian, Cyprian, Origen, and the *Didascalia*.[33]

For the ordination ceremony the *Apostolic Tradition* stands as an isolated witness during the ante-Nicene period. However, all the other (somewhat fragmentary) textual evidence indicates the necessary involvement of the bishop in the ordination. What is not clear is the involvement of the presbyterate, especially in presbyteral ordination, and the manner in which that involvement was viewed.

When we come to the penitential discipline of the second and third centuries, we find traces of the exomologesis in second-century texts and much clearer evidence of its existence in third-century writing. Tertullian, just around the turn of the century, provides the sharpest picture prior to Cyprian; his writings reflect a discipline of penance and reconciliation that is already quite well established.[34] In Tertullian's treatment, despite his polemics against a "laxist" approach to forgiveness of sin by some bishops (whose identity is disputed), it is taken for granted that the bishop plays the chief role both for the assigning of appropriate penance and for the reconciliation of the penitent to the community.[35]

Prior to Tertullian the evidence, e.g., in the Second Clementine or in Hermas, is too uncertain to draw any conclusions, though in Hermas the presbyterate seems still active in judgment about such matters.[36] Testimony contemporaneous with that of Tertullian is provided by Hippolytus' *Philosophoumena* which in its attack on Callistus witnesses to the principal role exercised by the bishop at Rome in the forgiveness of sin.[37] In the controversy over the reconciliation of apostates, in which Cyprian found himself embroiled at Carthage, the assumption is that the traditional way of reconciling sinners was through the exomologesis over which the bishop presided; the problem that Cyprian faced was that of a challenge to this discipline, the claim that "confessors of the faith" had power of reconciliation comparable to that of the episcopacy.[38]

Presbyteral Presidency

Since the *episkopos* was the recognized chief celebrant for initiation, Eucharist, ordination, and exomologesis, it might seem that the presbyteral role in liturgical activity was definitely secondary and derivative. This was not exactly the situation. While the presbyterate seems definitely to be overshadowed by the bishop in the situation described in the *Didascalia*, the remainder of the second- and third-century evidence, even that provided by Cyprian, points to a somewhat autonomous function of the presbyterate at the Eucharist, a situation of collegial presbyteral celebration under the presidency of the bishop.[39] While the bishop was chief celebrant, concelebration was much more than a formality, more than an element of added solemnity.

As we mentioned earlier, there is some hint in Hermas that the presbyterate (which, in general, seems to have been fairly influential at Rome during the early stages of its history) had a role in the penitential discipline, but this is too vague to give us any evidence.[40] Where the presbyters do function, however, and in what seems to be a task reserved to them, is the anointing of the sick.[41] Tertullian does seem to give evidence for the role of presbyters in the penitential discipline, but it is not clear whether the *presbyteroi* in question might not be *episcopal presbyteroi*.[42]

What seems to be an assumption from the earliest stages of evidence we possess is that the presbyter is the proper agent to be selected by the *episkopos*, if this latter is unable personally to carry out some function proper to himself, such as, for example, the need to multiply celebrations of the Eucharist as the churches grew in size. Connected with this is the second assumption: as a notion of *sacerdotium* gradually emerges (it is already formally mentioned in Hippolytus) it seems always assumed that presbyters are included in this term.

Accompanying Notion of Eucharist

By the end of the third century, both East and West possess a fully developed notion of Christian cultic priesthood, shared in differing levels of dignity (i.e., orders) by bishops and presbyters. The cult act in which they most importantly function is, of course, the Eucharist. Hence, the actual understanding of priesthood that evolves in this period is inseparably linked with the evolution of thought about the nature of the Eucharistic action. As the Eucharist becomes more and more cultic, the function of the liturgical leadership is also seen increasingly as cultic.[43] This development is critically important for the view one has of Christianity, a development that becomes more accentuated in the immediate post-Constantinian period and that is further fortified by the anti-Arian reaction.[44]

Cult as Primary Role of Episkopoi

If one compares the description of early Christian community life and ministry as one finds it in Acts with the picture presented by the *Didascalia* or the writings of Cyprian, he is struck by the manner in which a more formal cultic image has come to the fore. That this is not just the product of the third century is proved by the extent to which the *Apostolic Tradition* already manifests this same trend; the Eucharistic celebration is fairly fixed into an approved form of worship, though undoubtedly a considerable amount of flexibility remained.[45]

As this happened, the *episkopoi* and *presbyteroi* became increasingly cult personnel, in their activity and in the view of the people. Whereas in the earlier stages of the Christian community the term "*episkopos*" did describe much better than "*hiereus*" the function of this ministry, i.e., one of pastorally supervising the life of the community, now the cultic aspects of his role begin to take precedence and it becomes appropriate to use the word "*hiereus/sacerdos*" as a simple designation for the person who is also *episkopos*. When Cyprian writes giving the reasons why the bishops should remain with their people despite the dangers of the persecution, the reasons have to do almost exclusively with liturgical activity.[46] In reality this is nothing more than the evolving establishment of certain recognized worship officials, already observable in inchoative form in the *Didache*, much more clearly in Ignatius, and unmistakably taken for granted in the *Apostolic Tradition*.[47]

Influence of Old Testament Thought

Perhaps one of the most potent forces in this cultifying of Christianity was the influence of the Old Testament. Deeply grounded though it is in the traditions and historical reality of the Old Testament dispensation, the Christianity of the New Testament writings is also a profound reaction against certain aspects of the Judaism known to the early Christians.[48] Above all, there was a conscious struggle against the Judaizing tendency to reintroduce the restrictions of Jewish law, and a deliberate break with the official Jewish ritual and priesthood.[49]

This is not precisely the place to study the

nature of this break with Judaism, nor the influence of other movements of the day, particularly Essenism, in stimulating this break.[50] A number of excellent studies in this regard already exists, presenting in technical detail the complicated dynamics of this relationship.[51] What does seem important from the point of view of Christian theology is that one take seriously the radical newness of the gospel. And so, in the discussion of the relation between the two covenants, it is necessary to insist that Christianity transcends Old Testament religion and that it can never be forced into Old Testament categories of thought or Old Testament institutional patterns.

Yet, there is considerable evidence to suggest that very early in the historical evolution of Christianity the radical nature of this transformation of Old Testament forms was forgotten and Old Testament categories and attitudes began to creep back in as interpretative of the gospel.[52] Nor was this done as it had been done by the New Testament community. Its mentality drew upon a profound typology grounded in the historical evolution of the salvific process, truly an evolution despite the incredible qualitative leap of the saving revelation in Jesus.[53] After centuries of serious theological probing into this relation between the two dispensations, we still find it extremely difficult to keep a clear vision of the uniqueness of Christianity *and* its deep intrinsic bond with Israel. Discussion today on the relation between Old and New Testaments is as current and polemic as it was in the patristic period, during the High Middle Ages, or at the time of the Reformation.[54] Little wonder, then, that Christians of the second and third century unconsciously began to drift back into an Old Testament way of viewing things, even the redemptive work of Christ. After all, it is hard enough to grasp Old Testament faith and the gospel is yet more challenging, with its message of "new life" and its faith in "the Word made flesh."[55]

In Ignatius of Antioch we still feel the freshness of the gospel thought. The community life Ignatius describes is paralleled

with that of Christ and his disciples, but not to that of Old Testament times. The same seems to be true of Justin, who sees Christians, and especially their act of spiritual worship, as fulfillment of Old Testament prophecy but by way of qualitative difference; this is the thrust of his argumentation in the *Dialogue with Trypho*.[56] On the other hand, as early as the Letter of Clement of Rome the Old Testament pattern of hierarchy is being invoked as explanation for some kind of hierarchical setup in Christianity.[57]

Whether or not it was due to the Latin attraction for law and established institutions, Tertullian is much influenced by Old Testament forms and thought.[58] He even utilizes Old Testament laws as guides for Christian behavior; for example, in his *De exhortatione castitatis* he refers to an undiscoverable text in Leviticus to justify the ban on remarriage for presbyters (an interesting conjunction of ideas: Christian presbyters are "priests," and Christian priests are to be governed by Old Testament law on priests).[59]

However, it is not just in the West that one observes this impact of Old Testament religion. The *Didascalia* is very importantly influenced by Jewish thinking, though it is hard to say whether the influence is directly from Old Testament writings or through sectarian interpretation.[60] For one thing, there is a strong possibility that the religious viewpoint of the Essenes had important influence on the Christianity depicted in the *Didascalia*. Benoit, discussing the possible contribution of Qumran to primitive Christianity, makes the point that it is more likely that at a somewhat later date the Essene heirs of Qumran influenced the portion of the church connected with the *Didascalia*.[61]

This impact of Old Testament patterns of thought and practice on Christian views of episcopal and presbyteral ministry will become increasingly noticeable over the succeeding centuries. It will affect the notion of sacrifice, the hierocratic theories of episcopal and papal authority, the understanding of the efficacy attaching to priestly action in sacraments, and it will be one of the major factors in that overconcentration on the cultic which tended to obliterate somewhat the noncultic aspects of the Christian ministry.[62]

Cult Actions as "Saving People"

One of the points of view regarding the pastoral office, later formulated as *cura animarum*, is already important but not yet theoretically explained. For this reason, it might be well to seek the understanding, if there was one, of the relation between cultic actions and salvation. This is reasonably easy to attain, at least in general terms, for baptismal initiation and for the exomologesis. In both instances, the person involved is seen to be taken from a situation of alienation from God and brought into reconciliation.[63] There does not seem to be much questioning about the causal efficacy of the action of the bishop (or presbyter) taken in isolation from the whole context of the sacramental action; but the minister of the sacrament was looked upon as playing a leading role (and a particularly necessary one) in the saving action.[64]

It is more difficult to make such statements about the celebration of the Eucharist. While it is seen as the celebration of the mystery of salvation in Christ, the Eucharist does not seem to have been viewed as itself saving the participating community; rather, the assembled faithful are expressing their gratitude for the salvation that came to them in baptism.[65] Yet, one must not overlook the element of *epiklesis* which looks primarily to the unification of the community but also touches upon the transformation of the individual.[66] On the whole, however, at this period one does not find the idea of Eucharistic action as source of saving grace or the idea of the celebrant as dispenser of Eucharistic graces. Rather, it would seem that the minister of Eucharist is viewed much more (as is the Eucharist itself) in terms of unifying the community in faith and charity.[67]

The Priesthood

While "ministry" is essentially a functional reality, and various types of ministry are distinguished by the different functions performed, "priesthood" resists such classification. It is more a state of being, a level of existence, an intrinsic qualification. However, there is danger of imposing even these notions on Christian priesthood, for they may prove to be nonappropriate categories. There is no doubt, though, that the notion of "priesthood" has always had overtones of dedication, of being set apart, whether the term was used of the whole Christian people or of some more restricted group.

Clearly the action, most commonly referred to in the early Christian centuries as *cheirotenia*, "imposition of hands," was some sort of special designation; it singled out the ordained for particular function but also some special dignity within the community.[68] Evidence for the existence of some such act of designating *episkopoi* and *presbyteroi* is as old as the pastoral Epistles, but there is no indication of the nature of this ceremony prior to the *Apostolic Tradition*.[69] There we have a rich source of insight, for the basic action is described and the accompanying prayers contain a precious witness to the meaning of the ceremony.[70]

Combining the evidence from this ordination ceremonial, which seems to have been typical of what took place from mid-second century through the ante-Nicene period, with other fragments of information,[71] we can apparently make several conclusions. The imposition of hands for episcopacy was strictly the action of the episcopacy, one or preferably more bishops. In presbyteral ordination, the imposition of hands involved the whole presbyterate but the bishop's imposition of the hand seems quite clearly to have had special significance.[72] In both instances, there was the idea of acceptance into a collegial reality, into the episcopacy or into the presbyterate.[73] In both, the imposition of the hands is associated with the giving of the Spirit.[74] In both ordinations the action is finalized in the collegial celebration of the Eucharist, which seems quite definitely to accentuate the cultic orientation of the role or function which results from the ordination. There is one interesting question that occurs with respect to presbyteral ordination. It arises from a remark in the *Apostolic Tradition* that no ordination to presbyterate is required for a person who has already witnessed to the faith in persecution.[75] This would seem to indicate that the kind of elder status (presumably with proved virtue, prudence, fidelity, etc.) recognized by the presbyteral ordination would already have been sufficiently indicated by the individual's heroic behavior in the face of persecution. If so, this gives us an important element of understanding: Ordination was seen as recognition of action of the Spirit already present in the ordinand, rather than as simple human choice which the Spirit would ratify. Ordination would not, then, be expected to infuse the qualifications desired in bishop or presbyter.

In any event, it seems that bishops and presbyters, in a way that was not shared by the deacons, formed a sacral group within the church. They had functions reserved to them, at least from fairly early in the second century, but they also had a position of dignity and prestige that had to do with special association with the divine. This was allied with the authority increasingly possessed by the bishop, but it was something other than that. Actually, it seems to have been seen more as sanctity than as authority. This probably ties in with the example expected of priests, which we will study a bit later.

During this period, however, there seems to be no indication that bishops or presbyters were considered to be in a different state of life.[76] This is especially true of presbyters, for it is not clear that this was even a full-time profession as episcopacy and diaconate may have been.[77] The idea that Christian life was basically one, that the ideals of the gospel applied to all in the community, kept any group (for the moment) from appropriating Christian holiness to itself. Yet, there is some kind of special holiness attached to ordination which in the next couple centuries will be poorly distinguished from the special holiness sought and often claimed by monasticism.

Some distinction between clergy and laity is in evidence very early. Clement of Rome explicitly indicates such a distinction, and advocates that each work in his proper order in the church.[78] Ignatius testifies to the same distinction between those connected with the tripartite ministry, i.e., the clergy, and the rank and file.[79] Justin, who himself was a layman, mentions the clergy/lay distinction as it functioned in the Eucharistic celebration.[80] However, in practically all the texts that mention such a clergy/laity distinction (and they are quite plentiful) one has the sense that despite the recognition of special functions and dignity attaching to the clergy the two groups still function within the more basic unity of the local church. Even with Cyprian one still has this feeling.[81] The exception is the *Didascalia*: there the bishop possesses a kind of regal-priestly eminence that lifts him (and by implication those closely associated with him) to a distinct level above his people;[82] they are more his charges and subjects than his fellow Christians.

Probably one of the great equalizers during this period was the fairly frequent occurrence of martyrdom. Though a large proportion of those singled out for persecution by the civil power were the leaders of the churches, there were also many of the laity who courageously faced torture and death. Martyrdom formed, as it were, its own hierarchy; it was the highest Christian ideal, the most potent witness to the gospel, and witness to the gospel was the very heart of the apostolic ministry itself. Thus, with confessors of the faith in a community commanding their own kind of respect (which clergy-confessors also had), the clergy could not that simply be viewed as "the better Christians."

Though one gets the impression that the episcopacy becomes very early a full-time occupation, and that the presbyterate gradually takes on this character, particularly as increasing numbers of presbyters are used in outlying situations as delegates of the bishop, there is no clear textual verification prior to Cyprian.[83] Cyprian seems to be reflecting a situation of fairly long standing when, objecting to a presbyter, Geminius Faustinus, being designated trustee for an estate, he says: ". . . Singuli divino sacerdotio honorati et in clerico ministerio constituti non nisi altari et sacrificiis deservire et precibus adque orationibus vacare debeant."[84]

Clerical Celibacy

Already in this period prior to Nicaea one finds traces of celibacy attached to priesthood.[85] There are more frequent references to and discussions of remarriage on the part of bishops and presbyters. For, despite the exegetical validity of the interpretation recently given by Audet[86] of the passage in 1 Timothy that advocates that the presbyter be a man of one wife, it was not read that way in the second and third centuries (or thereafter); it was heard as a prohibition of remarriage for a bishop or presbyter whose wife had died, or a prohibition of ordination for a man who had married a second time.[87]

Yet, we also find texts extolling celibacy, attributing to it an angelic kind of superiority,[88] a purity from earthly contamination,[89] that makes it specially appropriate for those functioning at the altar or professionally dedicated to contemplation and prayer.[90]

The exact roots of Christian thinking on celibacy are difficult to determine; many diverse influences seem to enter the picture. First of all, and probably most important, there was the exhortation of Paul and the impact of a few other New Testament texts (such as "There are some who are eunuchs for the kingdom of heaven" which had such drastic influence on Origen).[91] Secondly, there seem to have been from the earliest days some dedicated virgins who were pledged to celibate life. This immediate reaction makes one ask about the parallel instances in Roman or Greek religious groups of that time, and even more so about celibate practices in Jewish sects like the Essenes.[92] Thirdly, the preference of such men as Athenagoras for celibacy is strongly tinged with a depreciation of the bodily and material which is much more Neo-Platonic than Christian.[93] Tertullian is an interesting case in point, for he goes from the beautiful eulogy of Christian marriage in his

Catholic *Ad uxorem* to the *De exhortatione castitatis* of his Montanist phase, which treats remarriage as legalized debauchery.[94] It is notable, too, that (on the authority of Prisca, the Montanist prophetess) he links celibacy with ministry on the basis that one must be pure to deal properly with holy things.[95] Fourth, there seems to have been major influence from Old Testament thinking about priesthood. Even though the Levitical legislation did not prescribe a celibate clergy, it did place marital restrictions on the priests and even more on the high priest, thus indicating a certain relationship of sexuality with the sacred.[96] Fifth, in the developing theory of asceticism and contemplation, which will flow from Origen in particular into emerging monasticism,[97] sexual abstinence was considered well-nigh necessary for contemplation. Sexuality is symbolic of all that is imprisoning about man's bodiliness; moreover, it involves passion which tends to destroy the impassibility and self-possession needed for contemplative insight.[98] One cannot help but wonder how much of the source of this view is New Testament revelation and how much is Stoicism.[99] Moreover, the idea of sanctity was very closely bound up with that of "integrity," "untainted." Somehow the sexual act violated the bodily and spiritual integrity of the virgin, spoiling her previous unspotted condition.[100] The use of "her" seems appropriate, because the ideal of virginity (celibacy) seems to have been worked out essentially in terms of feminine imagery; this works out quite well, of course, when ascetic literature discusses the *anima christiana*.[101] Sixth, one must take a careful look at the socio-economic situation of the clergy as they became more numerous and the clerical ministry became a full-time profession. It is possible that economic pressures, and the trend for auxiliary clergy to live with the bishop (which one sees clearly a bit later with Augustine), both suggested celibacy for the clergy; if a man wished to marry he would, in many situations, have to find some other profession where he could earn enough to support a family.[102]

Priestly Power and Authority

In general, there was not much speculation about the metaphysics of Christianity during this period. What theological-philosophical speculation there was tended to deal with the problem of God and Christology, though inevitably there were overtones (in the discussions of the divine Logos and his revelation to men) that affected understanding of what went on in such sacraments as baptism and the Eucharist. We find, then, some tantalizing suggestions about the nature of priestly activity, but nothing developed or formalized. The closest thing to this comes with the first stage of the dispute on reordination.[103]

The principal effect of ordination seems to have been that of situating a man in a given order, be it episcopacy, presbyterate, or diaconate.[104] This gave him the right and responsibility to perform certain functions for the sake of the community such as preaching, offering the Eucharist, reconciling sinners in the exomologesis, and healing.[105] Presumably he also obtained thereby the ability to do such things effectively, i.e., he was given a certain power which was associated with a special possession of the Spirit. While the only detailed text on the subject that we possess from the ante-Nicene period is the ordination prayer from the *Apostolic Tradition*, a number of other brief remarks—in Tertullian, Origen, Cyprian, Irenaeus, and the *Didascalia*—agree with the view contained in Hippolytus and give us a consistent view.[106]

It is too early to speak of the "sacramental character" of the sacrament of orders. This formulation comes only with Augustine's solution to the reordination controversy.[107] But that controversy begins already in the third century not explicitly about ordination, but in the context of baptism, about the re-administration of unrepeatable sacraments. When the explicit controversy about reordination appears it is clear testimony to the underlying assumption that valid ordinations are a lifelong thing.[108] And obviously the doctrine of a sacramental character coming with ordination presumes that a lifelong reality is established in this sacrament.

It is not that clear, however, whether the imposition of hands already signified in the second and third centuries that kind of permanent designation. If the text of the *Apostolic Tradition* does point in the direction of a permanent office, for there seems never any question of this happening to a man more than once, it is not clear whether the power to celebrate Eucharist, to baptize, and to reconcile penitents is seen to be given in unqualified fashion to those ordained to the presbyterate or whether such powers were thought to come to them *toties-quoties* with specific delegation by the bishop.[109]

What does seem clear from the ante-Nicene documentation is that ordination affirmed a real distinction between the *sacerdotium* to which bishops and presbyters pertained and the universal priesthood of all members of the church.[110] Special ministerial functions were clearly recognized and these were to be performed by those designated in the ordination ceremony. Yet, "ministry" and "priesthood" do not coincide as notions, and "*sacerdotium*" seems to denominate a dignity rather than precisely a function, though cultic activity seems clearly implied in the term. One interesting feature (for which a satisfactory explanation, apart from practical need, is not apparent) of the view towards the efficacy of the ordination ceremony was that it could be annulled if the neighboring bishops did not approve.[111]

Clearly, from the time of the *Didache* the *episkopoi* and *diakonoi* were looked upon as providing for the needs of the community, as ministers in this sense.[112] True, the group referred to as "*diakonoi*" were charged in a particular fashion with the service of the community—their very designation indicates this. However, in doing so they were always looked upon as the strong right arm of the *episkopos*, as performing this *diakonia* as his assistants and under his direction; therefore the responsibility of *diakonia* which was theirs was also (and preeminently) that of the bishop.[113]

Thus, as leaders of the community, the bishops and presbyters, in somewhat differing ways in different situations of the ante-Nicene church, were ministers to the people. But what seems to have characterized them sacerdotally, and therefore distinguished them from the deacons, was their ministration to "the things of God."[114] This was more than their responsibility to help provide cultic ceremonial for the community. The deacons and other lower orders shared that responsibility. Rather, it involved the idea that they were used by God in the contact situation of the cult. Neither the notion of mediator nor that of instrument nor that of sacrament was formally present yet in this period; but one can find attitudes towards the activity of bishops (and presbyters) in baptism and Eucharist out of which such theological understandings could grow.[115]

In an earlier context, discussing the episcopal ministry of the word, we observed the strong emphasis on the example of the bishop; he was meant to exemplify in his own behavior the Christian way of life that he taught.[116] Certainly, this functioned to some extent during the celebration of the Christian liturgy —baptismal, Eucharistic, or penitential. For one thing, in the homiletic elements of these actions the effective preacher would have to be able to appeal at least implicitly to his own dedication to the Christian ideals he advocated. But beyond that there lies the wide range of symbolic representation, the celebrant exemplifying Christ, or God the Father, or the first apostles, and of this representation being merely pedagogical or extending beyond that to sacramental efficacy. One cannot, of course, raise such questions at this point in the church's life and expect any clear or systematic response; but in the light of many texts one cannot totally refrain from such questioning. Already in Ignatius this sacramental function of the *episkopos* is mentioned, and we find it suggested in Clement of Rome, Irenaeus, Origen, Cyprian, the *Apostolic Tradition*, and the *Didascalia*.[117]

It is not until the time of Cyprian and the rebaptizing controversy that arises that there is explicit discussion of the connection between sanctity (or possession of the Spirit) and sacerdotal efficacy.[118] The controversy between Cyprian and the bishops of Rome indicates the unsatisfactory state of awareness regarding the elements in the problem. What later came to be distinguished as character and grace (or in medieval theology as "*res et sacramentum*" and "*res*") were still lumped together under the vague notion of the action of the Spirit. The Spirit communicated in ordination was the same Spirit given in baptism, and it was hard to see how one could operate effectively as ordained minister if by his sinfulness or schism he had lost the Spirit.[119] Thus, sanctity (at least basic alliance with Christ and possession of his Spirit) seemed necessary for sacerdotal effectiveness.[120]

NOTES

1. For a basic description of the historical usage of "priest" in reference to Christ, see E. Scheller, *Das Priestertum Christi* (Paderborn, 1934).

2. *1 Clem.* 61. 3; Justin *Trypho* 42, 116.

3. *Martyrium Polycarpi* 14; however, this testimony is slightly later (A.D. 156) than the Ignatian epistles.

4. *Didache* 10. 1–4.

5. *Adv. Haer.* 3. 11. 8; *Strom.* 5. 6. However, the almost total absence of reference to Christ as priest in both writers is noteworthy. This is perhaps more significant in Irenaeus because of the centrality of his doctrine of "recapitulation" which lays stress on the mediatorial role of Christ and because of his rather developed theology of the Christian sacrifice.

6. However, there is a clear application of "*sacerdos*" to Christ in *Adv. Marcionem* 3. 7 and 4. 25.

7. *Apostolic Tradition* 3.

8. *De oratione* 15. 4. See also *In Leviticum*, Hom. 2. 3; and Hom. 6.

9. *Epist.* 63. 14.

10. On the dating and provenance of the *Didascalia*, see R. Connolly, *Didascalia Apostolorum* (Oxford, 1929), pp. ixxxvii–xci.

11. Esp. in chaps. 8 and 9.

12. Paralleling of Christian *presbyteroi* and *episkopoi* to the Old Testament priesthood is as early as *1 Clem.* 40, but as D. Power points out (*Ministers of Christ and His Church* [London, 1969], p. 39), the purpose of this Clementine passage is not to clarify the nature of Christian ministry by comparing it with Old Testament priesthood but simply to indicate the divine appointment of Christian ministers.

13. *Epist.* 66. 8.

14. *Ibid.*, 59. 14.

15. *Apostolic Tradition* 3.

16. *Hom. Is.* 4. 2; *Hom. Num.* 10. 1.

17. *De pudicitia* 1.

18. See Y. Congar, *Lay People in the Church* (Westminster, Md., 1956), pp. 123–27; on the absence of *hiereus* in Ignatius, see J. Colson, *Ministre de Jésus-Christ* (Paris, 1966), pp. 329–41.

19. *Trypho* 116.

20. With the possible exception of *1 Clem.* 40, which we discussed above (n. 12). "We have to wait until the beginning of the third century before it is accepted usage to speak of the hierarchy as priests . . ." (Power, p. 38).

21. This is already indicated in Ignatius of Antioch and clearly stated in Hippolytus, Cyprian, and the *Didascalia*.

22. *Apostolic Tradition* 9.

23. See Congar, pp. 123–30. On the early Christian connection of this priesthood of the people with baptism, see J. Lecuyer, *Le sacerdoce dans le mystère du Christ* (Paris, 1957), pp. 199–223.

24. *Trypho* 117.

25. See particularly the classic work of J. de Ghellinck and his collaborators, *Pour l'histoire du mot "sacramentum"* (Louvain, 1924). More specialized studies are K. Prumm, "'Mysterion' von Paulus vis Origenes," *Zeitschrift für katholische Theologie* 61 (1937), pp. 391–425; H. Marsh, "The Use of *mysterion* in the Writings of Clement of Alexandria with Special Reference to His Sacramental Doctrine," *Journal of Theological Studies* 37 (1936), pp. 64–80; A. Kolping, *Sacramentum Tertullianum* (Regensburg, 1948); and C. Kneller, "Sacramentum unitatis," *Zeitschrift für katholische Theologie* 40 (1916), pp. 676–703 (which deals with Cyprian's notion of *sacramentum*).

26. See *Vis.* 2. 4; *Simil.* 25–27.

27. *Didache* 10, 15.

28. *Smyrn.* 8. 1, 2.

29. *Apology 1* 62, 67.

30. See T. Jallard, "Justin Martyr and the President of the Eucharist," *Studia Patristica* 5 (1962), pp. 83–85; L. Barnard, *Justin Martyr: His Life and Thought* (Cambridge, 1967), p. 133.

31. *Apostolic Tradition* 3–10, 22–23.

32. *Ibid.*, 22–23.

33. Tertullian *De exhort. cast.* 11; Cyprian *Epist.* 63; Origen *De oratione* 28. 9; *Didascalia*, chaps. 8–9.

34. See B. Poschmann, *Penance and the Anointing of the Sick* (New York, 1964), pp. 39–49.

35. *Ibid.*, pp. 44–49.

36. *Vis.* 2. 4.

37. *Philos.* 9. 12.

38. See Poschmann, pp. 53–58. It is clear (e.g., *Epist.* 18. 1) that Cyprian held that power to forgive sins could be delegated to presbyters and even to deacons; but he complains in other letters (*Epist.* 15–17) that the presbyters have taken matters into their own hands.

39. See Power, pp. 39–52.

40. See H. von Campenhausen, *Ecclesiastical Authority and Spiritual Power in the Church of the First Three Centuries* (Palo Alto, Calif., 1969), pp. 141–42.

41. However, Pope Innocent I, early in the fifth century in his letter to Decentius, asserts that the claim of presbyters to exclusive ministry of anointing is unfounded and that even laity can so anoint. See Poschmann, pp. 239–41.

42. *De poenit.* 9.

43. The contrast is quite marked if one compares, for example, the relevant texts of Justin (*Apology 1* 62, 67) with the view of Cyprian in his *Epist.* 63.

44. On the changes in liturgical mentality during the fourth and fifth centuries, and the impact of non-Christian and heterodox influences, see J. Jungmann, *The Early Liturgy* (Notre Dame, 1958), pp. 109–98.

45. The picture of an orderly and "official" arrangement of cultic ministry is suggested as early as *1 Clem.* 40–44, which raises again the question of the influence exercised by Old Testament categories through Jewish Christianity.

46. *Epist.* 61; see also *Epist.* 67, which in describing the attributes to be sought in a bishop concentrates on the priestly function of sacrifice.

47. What remains unclear is the basis for the very early link of cultic leadership with the function of *episkopein*.

48. For a thorough study of the various elements in the attitude of early Christianity to Judaism, see J. Daniélou, *The Theology of Jewish Christianity* (London, 1964).

49. One immediately thinks of the Pauline position in Romans or Galatians, but synoptic themes such as Jesus as new lawgiver and new law, or Jesus' relation to the Temple, or Jesus' attitude towards the Sabbath, indicate that the anti-Judaizing was much broader than Paul.

50. One of the more intriguing aspects of this question is the link that may have existed between primitive Christianity and the Qumran community; see J. Daniélou, *Les manuscrits de la mer Morte et les origines du Christianisme* (Paris, 1956).

51. See, e.g., H.-J. Schoeps, *Urgemeinde, Judenchristentum, Gnosis* (Tübingen, 1956) and *Jewish Christianity* (Philadelphia, 1969), or L. Goppelt, *Jesus, Paul, and Judaism* (London, 1964), or D. Daube, *The New Testament and Rabbinic Judaism* (London, 1956).

52. There are, of course, two possible ways (at least) of interpreting this reappearance of Old Testament categories. One can see it as an obscuring of the new insights that are most characteristic of the earliest Christian decades, or one can see it as a more mature synthesis in which second- and third-century Christianity, having secured its own unique character, could enrich itself from the Israelitic heritage. While admitting all the enrichment to be gained by positive absorption of Old Testament thought, it seems that the evidence points to a process in Christian history by which many religious realities (law, sin, worship, etc.) came again to be thought of in largely pre-Christian (and specifically Old Testament) fashion.

53. Much of this mentality is linked with New Testament use of midrash; see R. Block, *Dictionnaire de la Bible, Supplement,* vol. 5, cols. 1263–81.

54. Historical events in the past half-century, especially the holocaust experience of European Jews under Nazism and the establishment of the state of Israel, have certainly provided the principal impetus for a new phase of Jewish-Christian studies (and, hopefully, of Jewish-Christian relations). But a number of developments in scholarly research have also opened up new avenues of insight: the discovery of Qumran documents (which suggested relationships between primitive Christianity

and first-century Jewish sectarianism), the findings of Nag Hammadi (with the light they threw on the link of Gnosticism to both Judaism and Jewish Christianity), and the very recent reappraisal of apocalyptic thought.

55. Two remarks seem necessary. First, in talking about a drift back to Old Testament thought we must remain conscious of the influence that late Judaism and early Jewish Christianity exerted on the way in which the Old Testament was understood by later Christian centuries. Secondly, while most of the discussion regarding the relation between Jewish and Christian thought tends to center on Christological evolution, it might be that an equally important question is the evolution (or nonevolution) of pneumatology. A number of elements in early Christian history seem to be linked with this: the decline of prophecy, the lessening interest in ecclesiology, the ethicizing of "the law of Christ," and the emergence of hierocracy.

56. Esp. chap. 41.

57. While we must be careful not to overread this passage (see above n. 12), it does illustrate the tendency, at least in some quarters of early Christianity, to look back to the Old Testament dispensation for precedents to guide Christian decisions and activity.

58. This is reflected particularly in his *Adversus Judaeos*. Although he argues that the Jewish refusal to accept the revelation in Jesus has meant the repeal of Old Testament law as such, he argues (as had Justin) for a spiritual interpretation of Old Testament texts; this process involves a christologizing of Old Testament references, but it also involves fitting Christian beliefs to these Old Testament references.

59. *De exhort. cast.* 7. See also the passage in *Adv. Marc.* 4. 23. In explaining the text "Let the dead bury the dead . . . ," he sees this as referring back to the law of Leviticus which concerns the sacerdotal office and forbids priests to be present at funerals even of their parents.

60. The fact that it is anti-Judaizing does not militate against strong Jewish influence; some (such as J. Quasten, *Patrology* [Westminster, Md., 1950], vol. 2, p. 147) lean to the view that the author was himself of Jewish descent, but even if this was not the case he seems to have been very familiar with Jewish thought. See von Campenhausen, pp. 239–41.

61. P. Benoit, "Qumran et le N.T.," *New Testament Studies* 7 (1961), pp. 276–96.

62. Our study can only suggest the research (which deserves to be made) into the historical evolution in liturgical understandings of Old Testament texts; this research would then form an integral part of the history of scriptural exegesis and complement the work done in this field by Spicq, De Lubac, Smalley, and others.

63. See B. Neunheuser, *Baptism and Confirmation* (New York, 1964), pp. 104–6; Poschmann, pp. 58–80.

64. Poschmann, pp. 58–80.

65. See Justin *Apology 1* 62.

66. See the formula of *epiklesis* in *Apostolic Tradition* 4.

67. See Cyprian *Epist.* 63. 13. However, in Irenaeus, though the notion of community achieved through Eucharist is prominent (*Adv. Haer.* 4. 18. 5), there is also the explicit notion that the new life eternal is nourished by the Eucharistic bread and wine (5. 2. 3).

68. See J. Coppens, *New Catholic Encyclopedia* (New York, 1967), vol. 7, p. 420.

69. See Acts 6:1–6; 1 Tim. 4:14; 5:22; 2 Tim. 1:6.

70. *Apostolic Tradition* 3–4, 8.

71. The letters of Cyprian are valuable in this respect.

72. In *Apostolic Tradition* 8 it is the bishop's imposition of the hand on the presbyteral ordinand that is mentioned first, and it is the bishop alone who pronounces the accompanying prayer.

73. See Cyprian *Epist.* 38–40.

74. *Apostolic Tradition* 3–4, 8. What is not clear is the extent to which the imposition of hands and accompanying prayer were viewed as a petition to God to grant the Spirit or as a collegial sharing of the Spirit; both elements seem to be present.

75. *Ibid.*, 10: "If a confessor has been in chains in prison for the Name, hands are not laid on him for the diaconate or the presbyterate; for he has the dignity of the presbyterate by his confession."

76. By the third century, there was a noticeable development away from primitive Christianity's more familial approach to ministry (for which see J.-P. Audet, *Structures of Christian Priesthood* [London, 1967]), but not yet the notion of clerical existence as a basic life-pattern different from and paralleling that of married Christians.

77. However, the letters of Cyprian seem to indicate that by his day, at least in the African church, the presbyters (as well as the bishops and deacons) are to receive their support from the alms of the community (*Epist.* 39. 5) and are therefore not to be involved in secular business (*Epist.* 1).

78. *1 Clem.* 40–42.

79. *Eph.* 4.

80. *Apology 1* 67.

81. Though his letters to his own church are addressed to the clergy, it is clearly with the idea that they will then communicate with the people. Much of the content of these letters has to do with the conduct of affairs in the entire community.

82. See von Campenhausen, pp. 240–44.

83. See G. d'Ercole, "The Presbyteral Colleges in the Early Church," *Historical Investigations*, vol. 17 of *Concilium* (New York, 1966), pp. 25–31.

84. *Epist.* 1. 1.

85. See P. Delhaye, *New Catholic Encyclopedia*, vol. 3, pp. 369–71; E. Vacandard, *Dictionnaire théologie catholique*, vol. 2, cols. 2068–78.

86. Audet, pp. 92–99.

87. Hippolytus *Philosophumena* 9. 12 (if his charge is correct that Callistus had not observed this more rigorous interpretation, it would witness to a division of view on the point). By the beginning of the fourth century, synods are forbidding even first marriages for clerics and Elvira (306) prohibits the continuance of married life for bishops, presbyters, and deacons. On the historical influences operative in Elvira's decisions, see S. Laeuchli, *Power and Sexuality* (Philadelphia, 1972).

88. Novatian *De bono pudicitiae* 7.

89. Athenagoras *Embassy* 33; Methodius *Banquet* 11. 2. 1–7.

90. Tertullian *De exhort. cast.* 7.

91. For present-day exegesis of this text, see Q. Quesnell, "Made Themselves Eunuchs for the Kingdom of Heaven," *Catholic Biblical Quarterly* 30 (1968), pp. 335–58.

92. See J. Daniélou and H. Marrou, *The Christian Centuries* (London, 1964), vol. 1, pp. 121–24.

93. Clement of Alexandria presents a special case. Against the Gnostic depreciation of marriage Clement gives what is probably the most exalted defense of Christian marriage in early patristic literature (*Paed.* 1. 4; *Strom.* 3. 10 and 7. 12). At the same time, throughout his treatment of Christian marriage in *Strom.* 3, he insists that it must rise above sexual desire and be only for the purpose of procreation. On this ambiguous attitude of Clement towards marriage and virginity, see H. Chadwick, *Alexandrian Christianity* (Philadelphia, 1954), pp. 33–39; and J. Quasten, pp. 34–35.

94. See Quasten, p. 304.

95. *De exhort. cast.* 10.

96. Lev. 21. This does not imply a negative Old Testament judgment on the compatibility of sexual relations and liturgical ministry; rather, what seems to be involved is an extension of the legislation regarding the physical integrity of the priestly personnel. Since the priest's wife becomes one flesh with him, some of the same "wholeness" demanded of him is also required of her.

97. On the influence of Origen on monasticism, see K. Baus, *Handbook of Church History* (New York, 1965—), vol. 1, pp. 236, 288–98. Another influence on the origins of monasticism that demands careful evaluation is that of Jewish Christianity; see Daniélou, *Jewish Christianity*, pp. 352–53.

98. Clement *Strom.* 3. 5; Origen *De orat.* 1–2.

99. Or, perhaps, how much is rooted in the Essene views that so deeply affected Jewish Christianity and what derived from it. See the discussion of holiness in Daniélou, *Jewish Christianity*, pp. 357–75.

100. See, e.g., the refrain of Methodius' *Banquet*: "I keep myself pure . . ." "I come in undefiled robes . . ." (11. 2).

101. Another element that needs further clarification is the extent to which celibacy on the part of some (and then later of all) clergy came in response to the existence of dedicated women celibates. Since they were in charge of the widows and virgins, the clergy often related specially to them. Apparently, this was not without its problems. For one thing, there was the curious practice of cohabitation by celibate "brother-sister" couples, something that more than one bishop and synod inveighed against. But more basically there is the question: How influential in instilling the atmosphere of clerical celibacy was the establishing of a special "clerical circle," in which the marriage of the clergy would offer a certain barrier to the clergy's dedication to care for the female celibates?

102. This clearly is a factor in later centuries, but the evidence for it in the early centuries still needs researching.

103. Actually, the question of reiteration of sacraments like baptism or ordination centers during the period we are studying on the matter of rebaptism; but the basic theological stances (represented by Cyprian and Stephen) will later control more explicit discussion of invalid ordinations. Fundamentally, the issue involves something that has never been satisfactorily explained: How can an ordained minister who, by his own repudiation of divine grace (i.e., his own grave sin) or schism from the recognized Christian community, is in a sense outside the community, act as the agent of grace and unity for that community? Historically, this came to be discussed in terms of the sacramental character, and we will later attempt to evaluate theological explanations of this notion.

104. On the transfer of the idea of "order" from secular to Christian usage, see P. Gy, "Notes on the Early Terminology of Christian Priesthood," *The Sacrament of Holy Orders* (Collegeville, Minn., 1962), pp. 98–115.

105. It would be good to insist again that the earlier understanding of presbyterate might not have been primarily functional (at least in terms of certain specific functions) and that it may be anachronistic to speak of tripartite ministry before the third century.

106. Actually, the explicit references to power relate to the power of the keys, as, for example, in *Apostolic Tradition* 3. 5, or Tertullian *De pudicitia* 21.

107. See L. Saltet, *Les reordinations* (Paris, 1907), pp. 387–88; also, B. Leeming, *Principles of Sacramental Theology*, 2d ed. (London, 1960), pp. 143–83.

108. Thus, there is never any question of reordaining if the first ordination was valid; the presupposition, if one does argue for reordination, is that the first ordination was not valid and that one is really ordaining for the first time.

109. Cyprian's letters, however, seem to indicate some abiding sacramental power given to presbyters by their ordination. At times he blames some presbyters for taking matters into their own hands, but he does not suggest that what they did had no validity.

110. So, in the *Apostolic Tradition*, even the deacon is not ordained to the *sacerdotium*, despite his recognized function as liturgical assistant.

111. See P. Van Beneden, "Het sacramenteel karakter van de ambstverlening," *Tijdschrift voor Theologie* 8 (1969), pp. 140–54. Basing his study on documents prior to the Edict of Milan, Van Beneden shows that the conferring of orders affirmed a real distinction between the ministerial priesthood and the universal priesthood, but that ordination was subject to annulment because of disapproval from neighboring bishops.

112. *Didache* 15.

113. The *Didascalia* is particularly emphatic on this close co-working of bishop and deacon (chaps. 9 and 11).

114. It is the presbyteral (and episcopal) ordination to such liturgical activity to which Cyprian appeals in *Epist.* 1: those who have been advanced into "sacerdotal ordination in the church" should not be involved in secular affairs and should "not withdraw from the altar and the sacrifices."

115. See R. Braun, *"Deus Christianorum": Recherches sur le vocabulaire doctrinal de Tertullian* (Paris, 1962), pp. 512–14, on the almost total absence of *mesites* in the apologists and apostolic fathers. One notion that is explicitly present is that of "acting for Christ"—e.g., Cyprian *Epist.* 63. 14, speaking of the celebrant's Eucharistic role says: "utique ille sacerdos vice Christi vere fungitur." And "mediator" does occur in *Didascalia* 8, but probably more in the sense of mediating teaching.

116. See above, pp. 264–66.

117. Ignatius *Magn.* 6. 1; *1 Clem.* 42–43; Irenaeus *Adv. Haer.* 4. 18. 5—4. 19. 1; Origen *Comm. Rom.* 5. 8; *Hom. Isa.* 4. 2; Cyprian *Epist.* 39; *Apostolic Tradition* 3. 3–5; *Didascalia*, chap. 5.

118. See Leeming, pp. 498–511.

119. Cyprian *Epist.* 70.

120. Interestingly (and of considerable importance for theological reflection on the nature of ministry), they did not draw the implication that possession of the Spirit, particularly by one of eminent sanctity, placed that person in a ministerial position. Even Origen, who inclined somewhat this way in his view of the role of spiritual Christians, bears witness to the enduring conviction that specialized ministry in the church flows from some kind of ministerial charism that is distinct from grace, a ministerial charism that is either recognized or granted in ordination.

CHAPTER 29

Cult and Sacrament in

the Patristic Period

By the time of Nicaea, whatever reluctance there had been in Christian circles to utilize the term *"hiereus/sacerdos"* has disappeared. It has become a standard category by which to describe Christ and the upper levels of the clergy, the bishop, and (rarely) the presbyter. During the eight centuries that stretch from Nicaea to Gregory VII a considerable evolution in usage takes place, one which reflects the changing structures of the church and the accompanying changes in ecclesiology.

Prior to this period (as far back as Hebrews) the priesthood of Jesus was explicitly acknowledged, but reference to it is relatively rare in the second century and gradually becomes more frequent in the third century.[1] From the fourth century onward, it is frequently mentioned and consciously used as a principle for understanding the *sacerdotium* of the church, since there is ultimately just the one priesthood of Christ.[2] The pattern of the following centuries does not change as to whether or not Christ is seen as high priest; it changes regarding the elements of that priesthood that are emphasized.

To treat in formal detail the theological history of Christian attribution of priesthood to Christ would be a volume in itself; since a number of studies already exist, we can simply summarize briefly the historical evolution they suggest, and then move on to the development of the idea of Christian ministerial priesthood.[3]

There is consistent reference to Christ as high priest, with both the Epistle to the Hebrews and the figure of Melchizedek in the background; but there is little developed explanation of this priesthood.[4] Rather, the fact that Christ is priest is an assumption that one finds operative as early as Justin and that runs through all the various patristic traditions: Clement, Origen and Cyril in Alexandria, Epiphanius, Theodore of Mopsuestia, Gregory of Nyssa, Ambrose, Leo I, and Ambrosiaster—and through Gregory I and Isidore into the Middle Ages. An accompanying assumption is that as high priest Christ is the mediator between God and men; but here divergence can be noticed as differing soteriologies dictate the functional understanding of Christ's high priesthood. Irenaeus' view is controlled by his notion of "recapitulation," and the Alexandrians tend to emphasize the divine and eternal aspects of Christ's mediation. Beginning with Tertullian the Latin fathers tend to lay relatively greater stress on the moral facet of this mediation. Antiocheans such as Chrysostom and Theodoret emphasize somewhat more the human side of Christ's mediation but concentrate on this humanness as it is glorified in the Resurrection. Yet, the differences are not sharp, and when one comes to Augustine one finds a synthesis of these various elements.[5]

Much the same is true of the belief that Jesus is victim as well as priest, that his priestly action is one of offering himself (his blood) as a redeeming sacrifice. There is widespread acceptance of this notion in all segments of patristic thought and it continues into medieval thought; but one finds in the Latin fathers a greater stress on the human suffering of Christ and on the compensatory aspect of his death on the cross, in contrast to the Greek emphasis on the consummation of Christ's sacrifice in his glorification.[6]

When one inquires about the relation between Christ's priestly sacrifice and the church's action of Eucharistic sacrifice, the patristic evidence is more difficult to interpret. References to this link are present, though explicit reference is comparatively infrequent. However, it is impossible to decide how much implicit Eucharistic reference is (or is not) contained in the statements that Christ is both priest and victim, and how much Eucharistic theology is contained in the varying views on Christ's sacrifice we mentioned above. One thing, though, is quite striking. In most of the texts explicitly linking the Eucharist and Christ's sacrifice there is question of Christ's glorification and of his continuing intercession for mankind. This is true even of Gregory I who in other discussion of Christ's mediation stresses the human virtue involved in Jesus' suffering and death.[7]

The pattern that seems to characterize the use of *"hiereus/sacerdos"* is the following: from Nicaea on through the fifth century there is constant and fairly exclusive use of *"sacerdos"* to denominate the bishop,[8] and strong emphasis on the bishop's function and authority in liturgical matters.[9] Presbyters are definitely in a subordinate role of cultic activity.[10] This is, of course, the period of great bishops, *the* fathers of the church. With the sixth to eighth centuries *"sacerdotium"* comes to signify an element in Christian society, a corporate function or corporate person in law and political theory;[11] the presbyter in most places takes on greater stature as ordinary cultic minister (though a higher cultic role is always reserved for the bishop);[12] administrative tasks assume greater importance in the view of the bishop's task;[13] monasticism is beginning to assume a greater leadership in spiritual formation of the laity and in the discipline of penance.[14] In the ninth to eleventh centuries, *"sacerdotium"* becomes even more markedly the term designating the clerical structure of the church as counterpoised with the *regnum*, and increasingly focused on the papacy.[15] On the other hand,

"sacerdos" (although commonly used of bishops) is already coming to the point where it is a proper designation for presbyters,[16] which indicates the fact that they were being increasingly identified in terms of their providing sacramental liturgy for the people or at least providing it![17]

Whereas the word *"ordo"* was used in conjunction with such terms as *"presbyterorum"* to denominate the collegial reality of the presbyterate or diaconate or episcopate (the abstract *"presbyteratus"* does not seem to have been used much by itself), it does not seem to have been used this way with *"sacerdotium."*[18] Even during the centuries when *"sacerdos"* was commonly used only for bishops, the *ordo episcopalis* is not called the *ordo sacerdotalis*—priesthood is not exactly an order.[19] *"Sacerdotium"* as used by Basil and Chrysostom and Ambrose and Cyril of Alexandria is the *cultic function* exercised principally by bishops but shared also with presbyters; it is the corporate provision for the worship of God through union with Christ's own priestly sacrifice.[20] The word is rarely used as a collective term for the *episkopoi* and presbyters of the church (or of a particular church); it is never used to name the basic priesthood possessed by the Christian people (even though in this latter case the adjectival form, *"sacerdotalis/hieratikos,"* is used).[21]

During this entire period, and the attitude continues unbroken for many centuries, there is a strong sense of the collegiality of the episcopacy, which probably extended to embrace in some fashion the presbyters, though there is much less evidence of this.[22] Bishops are at pains to keep in contact with fellow bishops; communion in faith and liturgy is highly prized. It was protocol for a visiting bishop to be asked to celebrate the Eucharist along with the local bishop as a sign of their communion, and synodal meetings become a common way of safeguarding faith and discipline.[23]

A gradual shift in the application of *"sacerdotium"* takes place from the late fifth century on. The word now denominates more the corporate reality of the clergy (with more direct reference to the higher clergy) and indirectly the function they exercise in the church. It is paralleled with *"imperium"* in the disputes over the relation of church and state that agitated the church during the sixth to eighth centuries and that marked the beginning of the cleavage between Latin and Greek Christianity. Just as *"imperium,"* an essentially functional term, was concretely embodied in the *basileus,* so also *"sacerdotium"* shifted in its denomination to the episcopacy (and increasingly the bishop of Rome) which exercised this function.[24]

However, the term as applied to the episcopacy had definite overtones that reached beyond a function to perform; it indicated that these men constituted a specially sacral element in human society. One can see this reflected in the manner in which the *basileus* was considered to pertain somehow to the *sacerdotium* (though there was never question of his functioning, e.g., as Eucharistic celebrant) because he was a sacred person.[25] Somehow, because of their ordination, those who belong to the *sacerdotium* are specially consecrated, stand closer to the realm of mystery and the divine, can approach the awesome precincts of the altar, have special appeal powers with God.[26] From one point of view the *sacerdotium* stands in dignity above any other group of men, even above temporal rulers.[27]

Moving into the period after Gregory the Great, *"sacerdotium"* still applies to a corporate reality (essentially the bishops), but several alterations seem to occur: (1) The focus of the corporate reality of the *sacerdotium* concentrates increasingly on the papacy (in the early stages, this is found principally in the view of Rome itself, but this is gradually imposed on the rest of the West by the end of the eleventh century);[28] it is the pope who is the source of the *unitas sacerdotalis* (to use Cyprian's term but not his exact meaning);[29] the struggle between *sacerdotium* and *regnum* becomes increasingly the struggle of Rome with secular rulers.[30] (2) Whereas in the period of the great councils and for some time thereafter the aura of sacrality connoted

by *"sacerdotium"* seems essentially connected with the Eucharistic mystery, in the early Middle Ages the dignity of the *sacerdotium* is attached rather to the power of the keys.[31] This would seem to reflect the shift in the whole context of Christian thinking, perhaps more strongly in the West but by no means exclusively there, a shift from a mystery-incorporation into Christ notion of sanctity to a possession of virtue notion of sanctity. Thus, the *sacerdotium* was an exemplar, a sign, not so much of *mystery-sacral* as of *moral-sacral.* And the effect of the *sacerdotium* upon the rest of the community was not so much in terms of Christianization as it was in terms of freeing from evil. (3) *"Sacerdotium"* in its functional import no longer embraces the whole of the episcopal office, even as that pertains to sacramental action; instead, the distinction between orders and jurisdiction begins to be used and reflects the presence of a concept regarding the ordained ministers of the church which is hard to reconcile with the New Testament writings: the notion that they possess a kind of authority different from that Christ gained in becoming "Lord" through his death and resurrection.[32] (4) Without contradicting what we said in (2), one finds increasing mention of the supreme sacerdotal power being that over the Body of Christ in the Eucharist. Since it touches Christ himself and not just the men and women who are the earthly members of his Body (which is what the "power of the keys" does), nothing can be of greater dignity.[33] Yet, this very explanation indicates the shift taking place in the understanding of the Eucharist action. It is now one of changing the bread and wine into Christ, and this is the precise concentration of priestly power in the action.[34] And so the disputes begin (in the ninth century with Ratramnus and Radbertus, more acrimoniously in the eleventh with Lanfranc and Berengarius), disputes as to whether the bread really becomes Christ;[35] if so, how this can be explained; the Eucharistic mode of presence becomes "the *real* presence"; and (to avoid any implication that Eucharistic presence might not be *real*) the term "mystical body of Christ" ceases to be applied to the Eucharist and now shifts to the church.[36] In such a shift of understanding about the action performed, the agent (i.e., the bishop or presbyter) is viewed differently. He becomes less the sign of mystery, less the mediator of God's saving action. He becomes more the worker of wonders (in some popular understanding, almost the worker of magic), the agent of transubstantiation (although that term has not yet emerged).

Although some distinction between laity and clergy appears very early, certainly by the beginning of the second century (in Clement of Rome and Ignatius),[37] this distinction becomes very rapidly accentuated with the Constantinian recognition of Christianity and increasingly solidified after that.[38] Yet, one must qualify this somewhat. As rural Christianity began to grow and become a commonplace style of Christian life and even of ecclesiastical structure, and as rural parish priests became more autonomous sociologically and attitudinally, these presbyters seem to have identified quite broadly with their parishioners, to have become an accepted part of the feudal society (even a somewhat subordinate part of feudal structures), and so the division between clergy and laity in this situation was not as great.[39] This, of course, caused numerous problems such as neglect of celibacy, control of church properties by non-ecclesiastical personnel, some bad examples from poorly educated and rude-mannered clergy.[40] So there was a constant episcopal and particularly papal struggle to alter this situation, a struggle that centers in the ninth to eleventh centuries in the lay investiture controversy.[41]

On the more theological level, the growing cleavage of laity and clergy was tied in with the Augustinian (Neo-Platonic) view of a strictly ordered, hierarchical world.[42] This view seemed to relate beautifully (as in another context did the Christian doctrine of the Trinity) to the various orders of ministry that one finds reflected in the *Apostolic Tradition*.[43] Christian community life was to be hierarchically ordered, just as the universe (of which it was the salvific element) was hier-

archically ordered. Quite early in the patristic period, the theologically refined Christian cosmology that gave philosophical rationality to the sociological reality of clerical-lay distinction began to emerge. To some extent, it was already on its way in the Alexandrian thinkers of the third and early fourth centuries, but it is further developed as their influence touches and fructifies in Augustine in the West and in the Cappadocian and Antiochean theologians in the East.[44] The two classics that epitomize this way of thought (though they do not completely converge in their view) are Augustine's *De civitate Dei* and Pseudo-Denis' *Hierarchia ekklesiastike*; the influence they exert on succeeding centuries is immeasurable.

What this rationalizing of the ecclesiastical structure of ministerial orders does is elevate to the status of an intrinsically necessary and essential reality a structural evolution that was, at least to some extent, the result of human decision and specific social needs. The pattern of ecclesiastical, and more specifically clerical, institutions which in actual historical reality changed drastically during its three centuries of ante-Nicene evolution is now looked upon as *de jure divino*.[45] This puts the divine stamp of approval on that clericalization of the church's faith, theology, liturgy, and spirituality which is quite clearly present by Nicaea, in the ascendancy during the period of the great councils, and thoroughly established by the time of Gregory I in the West and Justinian in the East.

This understanding of the clerical superiority in the church touched not only the claim by bishops (and in varying degrees by lower clergy) to possess superior powers of salvific action in Eucharist, penitential reconciliation, etc., but also the basic reality of being Christian, of being redeemed by Christ.[46] The clergy were the "better Christians"; they were called to a higher life and a different level of sanctity was expected of (and conferred upon) them than of ordinary Christians —and this higher way was interpreted throughout this period in terms of the asceticism which had its theological roots in the

Alexandrian fathers and which found its formulation in monasticism.[47]

Central to this asceticism, which was increasingly seen as highly appropriate to, even demanded of, the clergy in proportion to the elevation of their order, was sexual abstention.[48] Human sexuality was, after all, the very symbol of all that was opposed to truly spiritual existence, to tranquil contemplation, to mortification, and to despising of the world and its pleasures.[49] It was, of course, basic to monastic life that monks be celibate; but bishops and presbyters, who after all dealt with the heavenly realities in sacramental action, should not embrace an ordinary and earthly way of life.[50]

It is important to note, however, that there was considerably less than universal advocacy of clerical celibacy in the period of the great Fathers. Such could hardly be expected from someone like Gregory of Nazianzus, whose funeral eulogy of his father gives such a touching picture of the sanctity of a married bishop (i.e., Gregory's father).[51] Some writers in a later time, embarrassed by this ideal instance of married episcopacy, tried to point out that Gregory's younger brother (the youngest of the family) was born before his father became bishop, the implication being that he didn't live a normal married life as a bishop, but the facts do not substantiate this.[52]

What is not so expected is the view of Basil, the father of Eastern monasticism, who insisted on celibacy for monks but allowed bishops, presbyters, and deacons to keep their wives.[53] It is interesting to note that it was another monk-become-bishop (Paphnutius) who at the Council of Nicaea gave an impassioned plea against imposing celibacy on presbyters and kept the council from making any such law.[54] It is noteworthy, too, that as late as the Council of Seleucia (486) there was strong negative reaction to the introduction of clerical celibacy.[55]

Clerical celibacy did, however, have strong supporters, particularly in the West. Ambrose in his *De officiis* presents an unequivocal case for celibacy, based on principles of Old Testament law and theology![56] Augustine is the great source of the attitude in the Western church; not only his positive insistence on celibacy as appropriate for those belonging to the higher orders (bishop, presbyter, and deacon)[57] but also his basic negativity towards human sexuality passed into Leo I, Isidore of Seville, Gregory I, into monasticism, and so into the attitudes of Latin Christianity.[58] But it is not fair to lay all the blame at Augustine's door. To some extent, he but formulated currents of antisexual attitude that were widespread in the Mediterranean world of his day. However, in the actuality of historical influences it would be difficult to overestimate his impact in this regard.[59]

The history of the gradual imposition of clerical celibacy on the Latin church is a stormy one.[60] Really, there is not a situation that could justifiably be called universal clerical celibacy (i.e., celibacy of bishops, presbyters, and deacons) prior to the reform movement directed by Gregory VII in the eleventh century. Even this latter met with considerable (and bitter) opposition, and was eventually carried through only by utilization of raw social power and political pressure.[61] A satisfactory history of clerical celibacy in the Latin church remains to be written, not surprisingly, since it would have to include (or draw from) a good history of ascetical and contemplative theory, draw from careful sociological analysis of the various situations (city and rural) in which the clergy lived and worked century by century, and be part of a thoroughgoing study of sacramental practice and theory.[62]

In the absence of such a complete history, we can discern major stages in that history.[63] We are also able to indicate with considerable assurance some of the theological, political (ecclesiastical and civil), social, economic, and human dynamics that entered into that history.[64]

Several observations can be drawn from the revolution of the discipline of clerical celibacy in the patristic and very early medieval period: (1) It was a critical symbol of the otherworldliness of the clergy, of their independence of the affairs of ordinary life.[65] (2) It was the key issue in the whole matter of clerical morality and good example.[66] This was, of course, tied in with the shift in Christian thinking about morality which one observes around the fourth century. It is quite significant to observe in the preaching of the fourth century the manner in which charity as a dominant theme (which it had been for the first three centuries) gives way to emphasis on chastity.[67] Particularly in the Gregorian reform of the eleventh century, celibacy (and simony) is the element *standi aut cadendi* in evaluation of a bishop or presbyter.[68] (3) Celibacy was (as the practical problems of church property in the Merovingian and Carolingian periods made clear) most desirable from the point of view of keeping bishops and presbyters free from secular domination. In the feudal context, dependence upon a manor lord for the financial stability of one's family could be a serious drawback to freedom of apostolic activity.[69] (4) At every step of the way, the extension of clerical celibacy and its establishment finally as universal discipline was a matter of legislation and enforcement by means of threat and coercion, rather than by way of convincing through intrinsic argumentation or inspiration. This is not to say that such intrinsic reasons for celibacy did or did not exist, or that the ideal of celibacy should have convinced patristic and medieval clergy; it is simply to observe that the institutionalization of clerical celibacy came through law and sanction, and was effectively imposed only when church authority became absolutely monarchic (and effectively so) under Gregory VII and a succession of powerful medieval popes.[70] (5) In the theological justification (apart from the canonical justification) given during these centuries for clerical celibacy, three elements were constant and basic: argumentation from the classic texts ("eunuchs for the kingdom of heaven," "the married man must be solicitous for his wife . . . ," etc.) in the proof-text method, application of the ascetic ideal developed in monasticism, and appeal to Old Testament texts about priesthood (chiefly from Leviticus).[71] There seem to have been no

reasons drawn precisely from the characteristic nature of Christian worship or sacraments, unless one were to see as characteristic of Christianity the presumption that marriage prevents the total dedication expected in its priesthood.

The distinction of the clergy from the laity was greatly abetted, sociologically and psychologically, by the treatment given the clergy by the civil power. As part of his support of the church, Constantine granted to the clergy (at least those directly and professionally concerned with worship) exemption from civil and military service, from subjection to civil courts, and from taxation.[72] This grant, which was honored for the most part by Constantine's successors, passed in substance into the Theodosian and Justinian codes,[73] which in turn had their effect in passing on this clerical exemption to the feudal legislation of the Merovingian and Carolingian periods.[74]

Quite effectively, a clerical society, paralleling civil society, came into being and became more widespread, autonomous, and influential. It had its own courts and slowly developed its own body of law and custom, its own administrative structures (such as diocesan chanceries), and its own officials.[75] During the period prior to the twelfth century much of this was still in a loosely organized and uncoordinated state (the twelfth to fourteenth centuries saw the full structured development of this church machinery), but it is quite clear in its general outlines.[76]

At the time of Nicaea, the celebration of the Eucharist was quite universally a community affair, the assembly of the faithful of a given church under the liturgical leadership of the bishop and the presbyterate.[77] During the fourth and fifth centuries the Eucharist was apparently celebrated more frequently than each Sunday, but there is no trace of bishops or presbyters celebrating Eucharist more or less for and by themselves.[78]

Some traces of private masses can be found already in the sixth century and this gradually becomes more pronounced.[79] It is abetted by the ordination of more monk-priests, especially after Gregory I, and by the introduction of votive masses in abundance during the Carolingian period.[80] From the ninth century there is great emphasis on frequency of the Mass, and side altars are being placed in churches.[81]

Clearly, the introduction and gradual dominance of private masses changed the entire atmosphere of the Eucharistic action. From the point of view of the celebrant's role it is obvious that he could not act as a sacrament for the assembled people, for there were no assembled people except representatively in the acolyte, which preserved the external form of the Mass, but hardly respects its true operation as a sacrament effective of community. What it overemphasized was the notion that it was the priest who "did the Mass"; others, if they were even there, were "attending Mass." Moreover, the evangelical element in such situations was practically nonexistent except for the priest himself. Thus, the causality of the Eucharist was seen as operating in some almost magical fashion, somehow bringing grace at a distance to those for whom the Mass was being offered, or at least being the occasion for such grace being granted them. All of this was connected, of course, with the practice of stipends and the establishment of Mass-saying benefices.[82]

Private masses were not, though, the whole story. Particularly on Sunday and feast days, the Eucharist was celebrated for the rural or city congregation of the faithful. But what happened was that the liturgy for even these community liturgies was more and more influenced by the private Mass forms; and by a strange quirk, solemnity and simplicity disappeared concomitantly.[83]

With the evolution in function we have just indicated, there were still some basic notions that extended throughout the period we are studying, though they evolved in the actual understanding of theologians and ordinary faithful during these eight centuries. It is the pattern of this period that a large body of important formulation of faith was accomplished at the very beginning (in the period of the great councils), and then by and large repeated though not with unchanged meaning during the next six centuries.

It is explicitly clear throughout the patristic period that ministry of sacraments is seen as a primary, if not *the* primary, role of the bishop and presbyter.[84] And in the sacramental acts of baptism, ordination, and Eucharist we very early find the expressed insight that the minister of the sacrament acts as the instrument of Christ.[85] Augustine formulated the notion more extensively than most others, but he is not the only one, not even the first one, to say that in baptism or the Eucharist "it is Christ who baptizes, Christ who offers the sacrifice."[86] Chrysostom for one has a very clear teaching on the ministerial role of the bishop or presbyter: "For it is not only the priest who touches the head, but also the right hand of Christ, and this is shown by the very words of the one baptizing. He does not say 'I baptize so-and-so': but 'So-and-so is baptized,' showing that he is only the minister of grace and merely offers his hand because he has been ordained to this end by the Spirit."[87] Indeed, this notion of the ministerial role of the priest stands at the heart of Chrysostom's rather fully developed sacramental theology. He speaks explicitly of Christ's action as high priest in the Eucharist and in ordination; Christ continues to offer his sacrifice.[88]

Practically the same thing can be found in the baptismal catechesis of Theodore of Mopseustia[89] and in Ambrose: ". . . Sermo Christi hoc conficit sacramentum [i.e., the Eucharist]."[90] Through Leo I, Gregory I, Isidore of Seville, and Damascene the doctrine passes into medieval thought.[91] It forms a constant element in the background of the dispute over the necessity of sanctity in the minister of sacrament, though the very hesitation exhibited on this point shows a certain obscuring of the awareness of Christ's *active* presence in sacraments.[92]

The period we are studying opened with what might have given great impulse to the sense of the church's unity: the first general council. Nicaea triggered instead a century and a quarter of bitter doctrinal dispute which in one way or another continued for centuries.[93] Yet, the amazing thing was the endurance throughout the patristic period of the idea that there was but one church of

Christ, and this was symbolized by the fact that there was but one Eucharistic sacrifice.[94]

This meant that no celebration of the Eucharist was ever without the connotation that this same Eucharist was being offered throughout the Christian world—"From the rising of the sun to the going down thereof. . . ." The sign-action placed by the priest was not left to his own arbitrary invention; the sign he placed was the church's sign and in placing it he acted as the church's minister. The very fact that he was able to place it was due to his ordination by the church to do precisely this.[95] The Eucharistic celebrant was acting, then, not in a private capacity but as an official in that cultic society which was the church.

Throughout these eight hundred years there does not seem to be any increase or lessening in this conviction of acting for the church. What changed was the subtle but important pastoral orientation. In the earlier stages the priest was acting for the benefit of the present and worshiping community, placing the sign of the church so that they might become more deeply identified with and embodied in that church, giving them by virtue of the fact that he was providing the sign of the church a sense of identity with the "great church" and with the one mystery of Christ on which the life of the church depended.[96] In later stages, there is less of this emphasis and more stress on obtaining the benefits of the sacrifice of Christ for those present (if there were any present), but also for others, living or dead, for whom the Mass was being offered.[97]

Since the primary agent in the sacraments was Christ and since the ordained minister in his action was placing the sign expressive of the church's intention, it might be asked whether the priest's own intention or faith or sanctity made any difference in the action. Actually, this question was raised incessantly in the church's history, and is not yet in the late twentieth century satisfactorily answered.

In general, the doctrinal tradition of the church espoused the essential independence of sacramental action from the sanctity of the minister; at least this is true from the time of Augustine onward.[98] Having made the distinction between grace and character, which provided a solution for the rebaptism controversy, Augustine gave future theologians a basis for justifying what seems to be an enduring Christian instinct: that God would not condition the essential saving power of sacraments on the spiritual state of the ordained minister.[99]

By and large, then, the theologians prior to the twelfth century conceded essential reality and efficacy to a sacrament, even though celebrated by an unworthy minister.[100] They were not quite so certain if the minister in question was in schism, but they tended to recognize effectiveness even here.[101] As the controversy on celibacy and simony waxed strong in the ninth to eleventh centuries, there was considerable questioning about the power of simoniac (and to a lesser extent uncelibate) clergy to perform true sacramental actions.[102] But even so ardent a reformer as Peter Damian held that the efficacy of sacraments was not dependent on the minister's own possession of grace.[103] Gregory VII withdrew people from their pastoral care by and financial support of simoniac or married ministers, but he never declared the ministrations of such clergy lacking in saving efficacy.[104]

However, there was a fairly strong and enduring current of thought that questioned the very reality of sacraments celebrated by unworthy ministers. This will come to a head in Wyclif, but he was far from being an innovator in this regard. In the period we are now studying one can name Pseudo-Dionysius,[105] whose cosmology would logically lead to this position, and Humbert of Silva Candida,[106] whose teaching clashed with that of Peter Damian in the eleventh century. The controversy between Humbert and Damian witnessed to the continuing tension between the Cyprianic and Augustinian views on the question.[107] Significantly, in the twelfth century both Gratian and Peter Lombard testify to the prevailing theological uncertainty.[108]

One fact that ordinarily is not taken into consideration in this dispute, but one which may reflect important Christian insight, was the discipline of selecting candidates for ordination in monastic communities.[109] J. Leclercq (among others) has demonstrated quite clearly that a man was selected for ordination because of his recognized eminence in holiness.[110] It was not exactly a reward, something merited, but rather a recognition of the appropriateness of a man endowed with sanctity dealing with sacred realities.[111] There seems also to have been somewhat of the notion that the grace and dignity of priesthood would be a culminating element in the man's own sanctity, and that involvement with the Eucharist as celebrant would sanctify him more than participating in Eucharist as a lay person.[112] If nothing else, one can notice in such a view a surprising concentration on the celebrant; it is almost as if the private Mass he says is for his own sake.

At no time during the period from Nicaea to the twelfth century is there question of one acquiring the episcopate, presbyterate, or diaconate by any means other than ordination. Some minor complication arose in the feudal period when, for practical (particularly economic) reasons the theory was espoused that a man could upon his *election* (e.g., to bishop) legitimately begin to administer the church's affairs even prior to his *ordination*. However, even here there was never the suggestion that he could assume any sacramental functions prior to his own ordination. It is a bit anachronistic to ask whether ordination was considered to be a sacrament since the clear definition and numbering of sacraments comes only with the twelfth century, but it certainly was looked upon as a special and solemn liturgical action, always inseparably bound up with celebration of the Eucharist, employing as its central symbolic action the episcopal imposition of hands, and being effective of some kind of sanctification in the man being ordained.[113]

All the evidence throughout this period— patristic texts, synodal canons, ordination liturgy—points to the role of the bishop as essential, and probably self-sufficient, to the effectiveness of the ordination. Though it was common practice, and prescribed by a number of synods, that a bishop be ordained by the other bishops of the metropolitan area, or at least by three of them,[114] it does not seem that this was held absolutely necessary for effective ordination.[115] Again, though the participation of the local presbyterium in the imposition of hands in presbyteral ordination (which was already attested to by the *Apostolic Tradition*)[116] continues as unbroken tradition and liturgical direction throughout these centuries,[117] there is no evidence that it was considered as absolutely essential and certainly no evidence that it could in an emergency replace the episcopal imposition of hands.[118]

There is, however, little or no evidence as to whether the ordaining bishops were seen to be acting primarily as representatives of the episcopal *collegium* (extending back to the apostles) or as representatives of Christ. That is, it is not clear whether the imagery is primarily a vertical or horizontal one. With the increasing ascendancy of the papacy, the imagery becomes increasingly vertical. But to the end of our period it does not seem that the idea is ever abroad that consecrating bishops are acting as delegates of the pope.

In the earlier centuries of our period, until perhaps the time of Gregory I, the stress in the ordination ceremony seems to lie on the acceptance into a ministerial group, the episcopacy or the presbyterate.[119] With deacons it seems to have been rather an appointment to service of the bishop.[120] This was an established rank, or dignity, to which one was admitted, with the concomitant responsibilities and functions.[121] Naturally, being in the position of Eucharistic celebrant involved the power to so act, but the stress was not exactly on being given the powers to transubstantiate.

More and more the tendency grew to view ordination as the action whereby one is endowed with the power of the keys which is a social power and authority, and with the sacramental character, which is looked upon as a more intrinsic qualitative reality.[122] This latter endows one with the power of effectively transforming the elements in Eucharist by the words of consecration.[123] It also confers, at least on those entrusted with the pastoral charge of souls, the ability to forgive sin.[124] This latter power was never quite that clearly defined or understood. The attempt to clarify it as authoritative judgment, discernment through insight, or declarative proclamation carries on into the twelfth and thirteenth centuries and straight on into the Reformation disputes.[125]

It is difficult to ascertain any distinct teaching during this period on the matter of a sacramental character attached to episcopal, presbyteral, or diaconal ordination.[126] That something is actually effected in the person and ministerial capabilities of the ordinand is never doubted, but the exact nature of this change is not clearly determined.[127]

Throughout this period the notion that the ordained ministers were to be exemplary Christians, to teach by their example as well as by their words, persists as an explicit and dominant theme in explanations of the episcopal or presbyteral office, in synodal canons regarding the clergy, and in the criteria or instructions for selecting and training candidates for the clergy.[128] Though it is not formalized into a doctrine about the episcopacy and presbyterate being a *Sacrament of Orders*,[129] there is the understanding that somehow they are a sign of the presence of Christ's redemption, of the unity of the church, of the sanctifying power of the Spirit.[130] They (and, by an ill-defined association, the monks) are specially identified with the note of the church which is sanctity.[131]

For the most part it is moral example that is stressed, particularly as the martyrdom ideal gives way to the ascetic ideal, as it does early in the fourth century.[132] This is not just an ethical ideal, à la Stoicism (though Stoicism does exert an important influence);[133] essentially it is a question of exemplifying the way of Christ, the pattern of life presented by the New Testament writings.[134] One of the interesting features of the evolution that takes place in these centuries is the way in which the centrality of Christ as example, though never denied and actually mentioned repeatedly, gives way gradually to emphasis on the example of saints. Concomitantly, the intercession of these saints becomes more important in Christian prayer of petition.[135]

Not only is the bishop (and secondarily the presbyter) to be a source of development of sanctity by exhortation and example, he is also, in the Augustinian and Dionysian worldview, somehow an ontological source of the holiness that flows down to the laity, even to the monks.[136] Such a teaching raises many questions. It is tragically obvious that not all the higher clergy possess that holiness which would be appropriate to their office. So, the question: Do such clergy really possess the powers associated with that office? The question about the efficacy of sacramental actions performed by unworthy ministers becomes a classic canonical and theological point of discussion throughout the entire Middle Ages.[137]

There seems to be a shift in emphasis (not a total movement from one to the other, since they somewhat interpenetrate) from the bishop symbolizing the apostolic tradition to his symbolizing moral excellence. In the writings of Athanasius, Augustine, Chrysostom, Gregory of Nazianzus, and Leo I, there is still a strong reference to the episcopacy's relation to the apostolic tradition and its symbolizing of the presence of that tradition in the church.[138] This does, of course, imply moral example, for, as Clement of Rome had already indicated,[139] the apostles had first made clear how Christianity was to be lived; but the *historical signification* is retained.

From about Gregory I's time, however, a greater emphasis on the good example of the episcopacy is observable. This seems connected with the shift in the ministry of the word from instruction about the mystery to moral exhortation and admonition.[140] Bishops should provide example as part of the *cura animarum*. There is by this time the view that ordinary Christians should keep the commandments whereas the evangelical counsels pertained to those who had given up all to follow Christ.[141]

But if the symbolic link of episcopacy with the apostolic college diminished,[142] the liturgy of the sacraments, particularly the Eucharist, tended to keep alive another symbolism: that of the celebrant signifying the active presence of Christ. As we indicated earlier, a developed theology of bishops and presbyters acting ministerially for Christ in the sacraments was already in evidence in the late fourth century. The existence of such a theological teaching, seen most clearly in Chrysostom and Augustine, would seem to reflect the faith and understanding of Christians as they participated in the sacraments.

No doubt, there was considerable obscuring of this insight as the laity became more and more isolated from activity, or even physical proximity to the activity, in the Eucharist,[143]

and as the celebrant became more and more a dispenser of sacraments whose action was not meant to be particularly meaningful as long as it was causally effective.[144] Yet the retention of the patristic texts, both in canonical collections and in emergent theological discussion, that speak of Christ's acting in sacraments would seem to say that not all sense of the priest standing in for Christ was lost.[145] One thing, though, may be of major importance in this regard: it is the unquestioned shift from the celebrant as the sign of Christ's presence to the consecrated elements as that sign, which indicates the other basic shift in Eucharistic understanding, from mystery action to real presence.[146] By the twelfth century we begin to see quite clearly the view that the Eucharistic celebrant makes Christ present not by being there himself as a Sacrament but by transforming the bread and wine.[147]

NOTES

1. Origen, for example, not only speaks of Christ as priest, but attaches to this the notion of mediation (*In Levit.*, Hom. 2. 3) and of priestly sanctification of men by the shedding of his blood (*In Levit.*, Hom. 10).

2. Considerable work has been done on the patristic and early medieval teaching about the general priesthood of the faithful. See J. Lecuyer, "Essai sur le sacerdoce des fidèles chez les Pères," *Maison-Dieu* 27 (1951), pp. 7–50, and *Le sacerdoce dans le mystère du Christ*, pp. 199–223; P. Dabin, *Le sacerdoce royal des fidèles dans la tradition ancienne et moderne* (Paris, 1950); and the listing of patristic references in Y. Congar, *L'ecclésiologie du Haut Moyen Age* (Paris, 1968), p. 109, n. 216, and in S. Grabowski, *The Church: An Introduction to the Theology of St. Augustine* (St. Louis, 1957), pp. 96–97. Another basic historical study which, like Dabin's book, extends beyond the early periods is C. Eastwood's *The Royal Priesthood of the Faithful* (Minneapolis, 1963). Y. Congar's treatment of the topic in *Lay People in the Church* (Westminster, Md., 1956), pp. 112–221, remains a classic and provides ample reference to patristic and medieval texts.

   All these treatments tend to stress (and rightly so) the continuing tradition of the people being priestly, the tradition that the people are members of the one High Priest, the tradition of applying to the entire community the *regale sacerdotium* of 1 Peter 2:9. There was, however, an early and growing tradition of applying priesthood more exclusively to the episcopacy and presbyterate. In a passage which speaks a great deal about the common priesthood of the people, Leo I (*Sermo 4, P.L. 54. 149*) refers to "istam specialem nostri ministerii servitutem" and says that the people are "sacerdotalis officii consortes." Prosper of Aquataine, himself a layman, mentions the general priesthood: "Totus populus Christianus sacerdotalis est . . ."; but then adds: "verum plenius hoc ipsi rectores plebis accipiunt, qui speciatim summi pontificis et mediatoris personam gerunt" (*In Ps. 131, P.L. 51. 381*). Gregory I, discussing the sacrificial action of the ordained priest, says that it is "non solum . . .

utilis, sed etiam singularis" and then goes on to say that the ordained "honore ordinis superat" (*De cura past.* 1. 3).

The tendency of the clergy to appropriate to itself the priesthood of Christ is reflected also in the growing application to the episcopacy and presbyterate of 1 Peter 2:5–9; e.g., Isidore *De eccles. officiis* 2. 4; Rabanus Maurus *De cleric. instit.* 1. 3.

Another trend (which merits more careful study) is that towards a more individual rather than corporate interpretation of the common priesthood, i.e., towards seeing each Christian as possessing priesthood rather than seeing priesthood as something held corporate by Christians. For example, Peter Damian's remark (*Sermo* 45) "Constat ergo quemlibet Christianum esse per gratiam Christi sacerdotem" indicates that this mentality has crystallized by the eleventh century.

3. There is an obvious need for such a volume to complement the study attempted in this present book; this need is indicated briefly in the theological reflection at the end of Part One, where the point was made that all theological insight into the nature of Christian ministry and priesthood is controlled by the view one takes of soteriology, i.e., of Christ's own priestly act of salvation. There do exist a few historical studies, e.g., E. Scheller, *Das Priestertum Christi* (Paderborn, 1934), which is a very helpful assemblage of texts, or the work done by J. Lecuyer. But these need to be reworked and supplemented by new research because of the important new developments in Christological reflection (represented, for example, by the essays of K. Rahner, P. Schoonenberg, or E. Schillebeeckx). Inevitably, as we treat of the historical understanding of Christian ministry there will be frequent need to refer to the understanding of Christ's own priesthood, but no attempt will be made to give a separate systematizing of this latter.

4. On patristic reference to Melchizedek as a figure of Christ's priesthood, see the bibliography given by J. Lecuyer, *Le sacerdoce dans le mystère du Christ*, p. 89, n. 1; also J. Pintard, *Le sacerdoce selon Saint Augustin* (Paris, 1959), pp. 54–57.

5. Justin *Trypho* 42; Origen *In Levit.*, Hom. 6; Cyril Alex. *In Joan.* 11. 6–8; Epiphanius *Adv. Haer.* 2. 1; Theodore Mopsuestia *Hom.* 15. 19 (see R. Tonneau and R. Devreesse, *Les homelies catéchétiques de Théodore de Mopsueste* [Vatican City, 1949], p. 495); Gregory of Nyssa *De perfectione* (Jaeger ed., vol. 8, p. 175); Ambrose *Precatio prima* 1; Leo I *Sermo* 5. 1–2; Ambrosiaster *De Melchisadech* (*P.L.* 35. 2330).

6. Cyril Alex. *In Joan.* 2. 8: "He [i.e., Christ] indeed is victim and priest, he is mediator, he is the spotless sacrifice, he is the true lamb who takes away the sins of the world." See also, Origen *In Levit.*, Hom. 10; Ambrose *De fide ad Gratianum* 3. 11. 87; Greg. Nyssa *In Christi Resur.*, Or. 1; Augustine *Sermo* 374. 3; Leo I *Sermo* 64. 3 (where he speaks of the "altar of the cross") and *Sermo* 25. 5; Maximus *Sermo* 30; Fulgentius *De myst. mediat.* 1. 11; Isidore *Etymol.* 7. 2; Alcuin *In Hebr.* 5. 4. On the Eastern emphasis on the heavenly consummation of Jesus' sacrifice, see Lecuyer, *Le sacerdoce*, pp. 141–52; however, though the stress on the glorified stage of Christ's sacrifice is more noticeable in the East, the notion is present in the Latin fathers: e.g., Ambrose *Precatio prima* 4 ("Divinum et coeleste sacrificium . . . ubi tu es sacerdos et sacrificium mirabile et ineffabile constitutus"); Cassiodorus *In Ps.* 109; Leo I *Sermo* 5. 3.

7. Gregory I *Moral.* 22. 17. 42: ". . . Nisi pro nobis interpellatio Mediatoris intercederet, ab aure Dei procul dubio nostrarum precum voces silerent." See also Justin *Trypho* 116–17; Hilary *De trin.* 8. 15; Leo I *Sermo* 5; Ephraem *Sermo de sacerdotio*; Cyril Alex. *In Joan.* 11. 8.

8. See P. Gy, "Notes on the Early Terminology of Priesthood," *The Sacrament of Holy Orders* (Collegeville, Minn., 1962), pp. 109–12.

9. This is clearly reflected in the liturgical legislation of synods and councils during these centuries.

10. Yet they are considered to share in the *sacerdotium* and to exercise this in the liturgical celebration; see Gy, pp. 109–10.

11. This is crystallized in the East in the Justinian Code, and the same view is reflected in the papal discussions (e.g., by Gelasius) of the relation between *imperium* and

sacerdotium; see F. Dvornik, *Early Christian and Byzantine Political Philosophy* (Dumbarton Oaks, 1966), vol. 2, pp. 804–9.

12. See Gy, pp. 106–9.

13. See Isidore *De eccles. officiis* 2. 5, in which (as does his contemporary Gregory I) he refers to the bishop as *rector* and describes his task of ruling the church; however, this is closely intertwined with his role as teacher.

14. See B. Poschmann, *Penance and the Anointing of the Sick* (New York, 1964), pp. 123–38.

15. See Gy, pp. 105–6.

16. *Ibid.*

17. Another element enters the picture as the early medieval period evolves. Whereas in the earlier patristic period the notion of "*sacerdos*" was specified by Eucharistic cult, the early medieval use of the term implies increasingly the possession and use of "the keys" (see Congar, *Ecclésiologie*, pp. 138–51), though one continues to find texts pointing to the eminence of the Eucharistic power of priests.

18. See B. Botte, "Collegiate Character of the Presbyterate and Episcopate," *Sacrament of Holy Orders*, pp. 75–92.

19. It is considerably later that (in theological discussion but never in the liturgical formularies) episcopacy is viewed as part of the order of priesthood along with the presbyterate, but there is never complete acceptance of the position that episcopacy is not a distinct order.

20. See Congar, *Lay People*, pp. 120–58; J. Daniélou, "The Priestly Ministry in the Greek Fathers," *Sacrament of Holy Orders*, pp. 116–26.

21. See Leo I *Sermo* 4. 1. For a study of patristic use of "*regale sacerdotium*," see Dabin, *Le sacerdoce royal*.

22. See Botte, "Collegiate Character. . . ."

23. Another element that is prominent is the special episcopal obligation of hospitality (see Isidore *De eccl. officiis* 2. 5. 13), which is not confined to fellow bishops but has particular applicability to them.

24. See W. Ullmann, *Growth of Papal Government in the Middle Ages* (London, 1955), pp. 18–41; Dvornik, pp. 804–9.

25. On the manner in which the emperor was viewed as sacred and priestly, see Congar, *Ecclésiologie*, pp. 344–57; he makes an important distinction between the role of the *basileus* in the Byzantine situation and the priestly claims of Charlemagne in the West.

26. Rabanus Maurus, for example, in describing the celebrant's role in the Eucharist: "Missa autem est legatio inter Deum et homines, cujus legationis officio fungitur sacerdos, cum populi vota per preces et supplicationes ad Deum offert" (*De cleric. instit.* 1. 33).

27. This view found its sharpest expression in the Dionysian tradition, where the clergy (according to their respective orders) stand in greater ontological proximity to the divine sacredness. Thus, though there may not have been formal theological expression of the point, the ordained ministers of the church were looked upon as a sacrament, i.e., a symbolic presence of the divine redeeming power.

28. See Congar, *Ecclésiologie*, pp. 195–246.

29. Nicholas I goes even further in his claim: "Universitas credentium ab hac sancta Romana ecclesia, quae caput est omnium ecclesiarum, doctrinam exquirit, integritatem fidei deposcit" (*Epist.* 86).

30. See D. Knowles, *The Christian Centuries* (London, 1969), vol. 2, pp. 27–79.

31. This raises a key question. To what extent was the notion of "sacred" attached to the possession of special power, and to what extent therefore was it natural for the notion of "priest" to attach exclusively to those who held such powers (of penitential absolution or of Eucharistic consecration), thus overshadowing the traditional understanding of the priesthood of the entire church?

32. One of the important restrictions in the meaning of *"sacerdotium"* as applied to the episcopal (and presbyteral) function was a concentration on the cultic which involved a precision from ministry of the word. Such a precision is not possible, of course, if one realizes the inescapably evangelical nature of the Eucharistic (and other scaramental) symbolism, but this realization seems to have been increasingly lost.

33. ". . . Et, quod maximum est in Christiana religione . . . proprio ore corpus et sanguinem Domini conficere" (Gregory VII *Epist.* 21). It is interesting to note the shift from the glorification of priestly power that one finds in Chrysostom (*On the Priesthood* 3. 5) and Theodore of Mopsuestia (*Hom.* 15; Tonneau-Devreesse, pp. 495–96) where it is a question of offering the sacrifice of Christ, to the Latin medieval glorification of the priestly power to transform the bread and wine.

34. On the link of this development with the loss of appreciation of the Eucharist as *sacramental* action in which the people can participate, see J. Jungmann, *Mass of the Roman Rite* (New York, 1951), vol. 1, pp. 83–85.

35. See J. Fahey, *The Eucharistic Teaching of Ratramnus of Corbie* (Mundelein, Ill., 1951); C. Sheedy, *The Eucharistic Controversy of the Eleventh Century* (Washington, D.C., 1947).

36. On the shift in meaning of *"corpus mysticum,"* see H. de Lubac, *Corpus mysticum*, 2d ed. (Paris, 1949).

37. *1 Clem.* 42–44; *Eph.* 4.

38. As mentioned in an earlier chapter, the legal exemptions granted by Constantine contributed greatly to altering the sociological situation of the ordained ministry; they became public personages.

39. See A. Dumas, in A. Fliche and V. Martin, *Histoire de l'Eglise depuis les origines jusqu'à nos jours* (Paris, 1935—), vol. 7, pp. 265–90; J. Jungmann, *Handbook of Church History* (New York, 1965—), vol. 3, pp. 307–12.

40. See Knowles, pp. 165–71; Dumas, pp. 465–82.

41. On the various elements in this controversy, see Fliche-Martin, vols. 7 and 8.

42. See Grabowski, pp. 96–99; R. Markus, *Saeculum: History and Society in the Theology of St. Augustine* (Cambridge, 1970); H.-X. Arquillière, "Observations sur l'augustinisme politique," *Mélanges Augustiniens* (Paris, 1931), pp. 209–26.

43. However, the traditional theological explanation of the various orders in the clergy remains the parallel to the several orders of Old Testament priesthood; so, for example, Isidore in his *De eccles. officiis* and Rabanus Maurus in his *De cleric. instit.*

44. See R. Arnou, *Dictionnaire de théologie catholique*, vol. 12, cols. 2287–322; see also, J. Pépin, *Théologie cosmique et théologie chrétienne* (Paris, 1964).

45. See R. Roques, *L'univers dionysien* (Paris, 1954), pp. 176–78.

46. By the fourth century, the ordinary discipline of the exomologesis is no longer applied to clerics; see Poschmann, pp. 110–16.

47. See the first two volumes of L. Bouyer, J. Leclercq, F. Vandenbroucke, *History of Christian Spirituality* (London, 1963, 1968).

48. On the historical origins of the discipline of clerical celibacy, see E. Schillebeeckx, *Celibacy* (New York, 1968), pp. 26–72; and the essays of J. Noonan ("Celibacy in the Fathers of the Church," pp. 138–51) and P. Bilaniuk ("Celibacy in the Eastern Tradition," pp. 32–52) in *Celibacy: The Necessary Option*, ed. G. Frein (New York, 1968).

49. See Schillebeeckx, pp. 51–62.

50. On the link between the emerging notion of the cultic priest and the stress on clerical celibacy, see Schillebeeckx, pp. 57–60; and J. Blenkinsopp, *Celibacy, Ministry, Church* (New York, 1968), pp. 147–58.

51. See *Funeral Orations by Saint Gregory Nazienzen and Saint Ambrose*, vol. 22 of *Fathers of the Church* (New York, 1953), pp. 119–56.

52. See J. Cummings, *New Catholic Enyclopedia* (New York, 1967), vol. 6, p. 791.

53. See *Epist.* 199. 27.

54. See Bilaniuk, pp. 39–41.

55. On the early conciliar legislation regarding celibacy, see C. Hefele and H. Leclercq, *Histoire des Conciles* (Paris, 1909), vol. 2, pp. 1321–48.

56. *De officiis* 1. 50.

57. See *De coniug. adult* 2. 21.

58. Thus Leo I, explaining how Christ was innocently born, says ". . . Sine carnali concupiscentiae pollutione conceptus" (*Sermo* 25. 5). The heart of Augustine's influence must not, however, be sought in an isolated depreciation of sexuality. Actually, along with the patristic tradition as a whole he avoided the excessive opinions of Encratism and Manicheism and defended the essential goodness of marriage. Rather, the root of the problem lies in Augustine's explanation of original sin and concupiscence (see E. TeSelle, *Augustine the Theologian* [New York, 1970], pp. 314–19; E. Portalie, *Guide to the Thought of St. Augustine* [Chicago, 1960], pp. 204–11) in which even marital sexual activity is seen as tainted by the results of original sin.

59. See C. Baumgartner, *Le péché originel* (Paris, 1969), pp. 90–105; also, R. Bultot, *Pierre Damien* (Louvain, 1963), pp. 100–111 (where he studies the antecedents of Peter's negative view of sexuality).

60. See Schillebeeckx, pp. 26–50.

61. See A. Fliche in Fliche-Martin, vol. 8, pp. 70–106. On the widespread rejection of celibacy in the early medieval period, see Dumas, pp. 476–82.

62. One of the important distinctions that would need to be honored is that between celibacy as a spiritual ideal and celibacy as an element of clerical discipline, the first being an integral part of the historical evolution of Christian spirituality and the second an aspect of the development of ecclesiastical institutions. An interesting and instructive study of the complex interplay of forces behind adoption of clerical celibacy is provided by S. Laeuchli in his book on the Synod of Elvira, *Power and Sexuality* (Philadelphia, 1972). For a historical review of the attitude and influence of the papacy in the matter of celibacy, see G. Denzler, *Das Papstum und der Amtszolibat* (Stuttgart, 1973).

63. For a brief schematization of that history, see the article "Zolibat" by K. Morsdorff in *Lexikon für Theologie und Kirche*, 2d ed. (Freiburg, 1965).

64. Because the history of clerical celibacy is so much a matter of positive ecclesiastical legislation, a continuing historical witness to the *social phenomenon* of celibacy is provided by legal documents. There is not a parallel body of evidence regarding the historical evolution of *understanding* about clerical celibacy. Considering the official emphasis placed on celibacy, there is surprisingly little theological reflection about it.

65. Even in the East, where clerical celibacy was not imposed, the Justinian Code (*C.I.* 1. 3. 41) urges a celibate episcopacy: ". . . It is proper for such persons to be chosen and to be ordained bishops who have neither children nor grandchildren, since it cannot be that he, when occupied with life's cares (which children particularly provide for parents), should have his entire interest and good intention about the divine liturgy and ecclesiastical affairs."

66. This is reflected in the letters of such bishops as Cyprian or Augustine that deal with problem clerics and in the synodal legislation regarding "*mulieres subintroductae.*"

67. See W. Lecky, *History of European Morals from Augustus to Charlemagne*, 3d ed. (London, 1929), vol. 2.

68. See canon 3 of the First Lateran Council (in 1059) which was then reiterated and enforced through the Roman council of 1074 and Gregory VII's subsequent efforts; see also Fliche, pp. 70–74.

69. An allied factor was the serious danger of alienation of church property through clerical marriages, inheritances, etc. See E. Amann in Fliche-Martin, vol. 7, pp. 85–86; see also D. Herlihy, "Land, Family, and Women in Continental Europe, 700–1200," *Traditio* 18 (1962), pp. 97–98.

70. See Schillebeeckx, pp. 44–45. A key step in the legal enforcement of clerical celibacy

was the legislation (which came only with the Second Lateran Council in 1139) that made the marriage of subdeacons, deacons, and priests invalid.

71. *Ibid.*, pp. 51–62.

72. See J. Gaudemet, *L'Eglise dans l'Empire Romain* (Paris, 1958), pp. 176–79.

73. See G. Reilly, *Imperium and Sacerdotium According to St. Basil the Great* (Washington, D.C., 1945), pp. 86–98.

74. However, the more immediate and important bases for autonomy of the clerical establishment were the practical administrative needs and decisions of the Merovingian and Carolingian rulers. No little influence was exerted also by the "Donation of Constantine"; see G. Burr, *Cambridge Medieval History*, 2d ed. (Cambridge, 1966), vol. 2, pp. 584–89, and W. Ullmann, *New Catholic Encyclopedia*, vol. 4, pp. 1000–1001.

75. See F. Kempf, *Handbook of Church History*, vol. 3, pp. 258–99.

76. Particularly in the restoration of papal structures in the late tenth and eleventh centuries; see Dumas in Fliche-Martin, pp. 153–74.

77. See Jungmann, *Mass*, pp. 28–60.

78. Although it was fairly common to have smaller Eucharistic liturgies in homes or oratories; see *ibid.*, pp. 212–15.

79. See *ibid.*, p. 216.

80. *Ibid.*, pp. 216–21.

81. *Ibid.*, pp. 221–23.

82. See P. Boyle, *New Catholic Encyclopedia*, vol. 13, p. 715.

83. See Jungmann, *Mass*, pp. 195–233. In the High Middle Ages and thereafter in the Baroque period a newer and quite complicated form of solemnity comes to mark the more public celebrations of the Eucharist, particularly in episcopal masses.

84. Insistence on ministry of sacrament accompanies the increasing attention on the sacerdotal nature of episcopacy and presbyterate; however, the ministry of the word continues to be seen as an indispensable function of the bishop and presbyter. Leo I, for example, who clearly links priesthood with the offering of sacrifice (*Sermo* 4. 1) sees the role of the celebrant in the action of Eucharist as evangelical (*Sermo* 5. 6).

85. See Lecuyer, *Le sacerdoce*, pp. 288–99.

86. See Ambrose *De sacr.* 4. 14.

87. *Second baptismal instruction* 26.

88. *In Matt.*, Hom. 50. 5; *In Acta Apost.*, Hom. 14. 3; *In Epist. ad Hebr.*, Hom. 17.

89. *Hom.* 15, 19–21 (Tonneau-Devreesse), pp. 495–97.

90. *De sacr.* 4. 14.

91. See Congar, *L'ecclésiologie*, p. 109.

92. An important but subtle change in viewpoint occurs as the understanding of *"sacramentum"* shifts (see J. de Ghellinck, *Pour l'histoire du mot "sacramentum"* [Louvain, 1924]): As the view moves from mystery action to cause of grace, the ministry of the priest is viewed less as sacrament and more as instrument. Inevitably this has an influence on the theology of: the intention of the minister, the underlying intention of the church, the extent to which the efficacy of the sacramental act is dependent upon the minister's understanding and intent, the status of the minister as conscious or as impersonal agent. Concomitantly, as the mystery of the Eucharist came to be seen in the West in terms of changing the elements into Christ, the celebrant of Eucharist is seen more as the wonder-worker (of transubstantiation) than as the leader of a celebrating community.

93. See H. Marrou, *The Christian Centuries* (London, 1964), vol. 1, pp. 249–67, 335–75.

94. From at least as early as Victor I, communion in the Eucharist is seen as a sign of the unity of the church, and denial of such communion as excommunication. The constant presupposition, of course, for the oneness of the Eucharistic sacrifice is that it is the sacrifice of Christ himself.

95. Ambrosiaster *De Melchisedech* (*P.L.* 35. 2325–26). Apart from texts which speak of the powers given with ordination, there is little explicit witness to the sacramental celebrant being minister of the church; it is the kind of understanding that would logically have been taken for granted, for the celebrant was obviously functioning in a public action.

96. See M.-B. de Soos, *Le mystère liturgique d'après saint Léon le Grand* (Münster, 1968), pp. 100–103.

97. See Jungmann, *Mass*, pp. 215–33.

98. See B. Leeming, *Principles of Sacramental Theology*, 2d ed. (London, 1960), pp. 497–540.

99. *Ibid.*, pp. 516–18.

100. *Ibid.*, pp. 518–19.

101. However, this question shades off into the complicated matter of invalid ordinations, reordination, etc., on which no satisfactory history exists, although L. Saltet's *Les réordinations* (Paris, 1907) is still a valuable source. An important element that enters the problem during the period we are studying is the link between official approval and validity, a link whose legitimacy is still unclear; see Leeming, pp. 265–73, also F. van Beeck, "Towards an Ecumenical Understanding of the Sacraments," *Journal of Ecumenical Studies* 3 (1966), pp. 57–112.

102. See Leeming, pp. 534–35; Saltet, pp. 389–93.

103. *Liber gratissimus* (opus 6), 10 (*P.L.* 145. 112–13).

104. See Fliche, pp. 70–75.

105. See Roques, pp. 282–83.

106. See Leeming, p. 534; Kempf, pp. 354–55.

107. See Kempf, pp. 469–70.

108. See Leeming, pp. 535–38.

109. Our treatment will consider only Western monasticism, since the practice of presbyteral ordination did not become similarly prominent in the East.

110. J. Leclercq, "On Monastic Priesthood According to the Ancient Medieval Tradition," *Studia Monastica* 3 (1960), pp. 137–55.

111. *Ibid.*, pp. 144–45.

112. *Ibid.*, pp. 154–55.

113. Though the imposition of hands retained a central role in the liturgical action, there was not universal recognition that it constituted the essential action of the ordination; see Leeming, pp. 419–21.

114. See Botte, pp. 86–88.

115. *Ibid.*, p. 88. It seems quite clear that in situations of new evangelization, e.g., by Patrick or Boniface, some of the early episcopal consecrations would have been done by only one consecrator.

116. *Apostolic Tradition* 8. 1.

117. Though there is no direct evidence, it is highly probable that the imposition of hands by the attendant presbyters lessened in meaning and importance as the episcopal imposition of hands tended to be overshadowed by the anointing of hands, the vesting of the ordinand, and the *porrectio instrumentorum*. See D. Power, *Ministers of Christ and His Church* (London, 1969), pp. 53–88.

118. There is a constant body of evidence to indicate that presbyters were ordained by bishops without any attendant presbyters, particularly in missionary situations. For a discussion of the intrinsic question regarding the possibility of presbyters ordaining presbyters, see A. Piepkorn, "A Lutheran View of the Validity of Lutheran Orders," *Eucharist and Ministry*, vol. 4 of *Lutherans and Catholics in Dialogue* (New York, 1970), pp. 209–26.

119. See Botte, pp. 68–89.

120. Although there is also constant reference to the deacon's office of liturgical ministra-

tion (parallel to the Levites of the Old Testament); see Isidore *De eccl. officiis* 8. 1; Rabanus Maurus *De cler. instit.* 1. 7.

121. There were two aspects to the idea of rank: the notion of "situation in a certain societal status," which was most likely the earliest denotation of *"ordo"* as applied to the ordained ministers (see Botte, and Gy, pp. 98–105), and the notion of "situation at a certain ontological level in the cosmos," which one associates, for example, with the thinking of Pseudo-Dionysius (see Roques, pp. 281–83)—and the understanding of the powers and responsibilities proper to the ordained drew from both these aspects without clear distinction. This lack of clear differentiation between physical and societal power (sometimes denominated, though perhaps not too accurately, "physical" and "moral" power) continues to plague theological discussion up to our own day.

122. For a fuller treament of the power of the keys and its relation both to the sacramental character and to the power of Eucharistic confection, see above, pp. 436–37. On the origins and development of the notion of a sacramental character as conferred in ordination, see Leeming, pp. 129–273; and for a somewhat different explanation, see H. von Campenhausen, *Tradition and Life in the Church* (Philadelphia, 1968), pp. 222–30.

123. It is instructive to compare the view of Ambrose (e.g., *De sacr.* 4. 4) and Augustine (*In Joan.* 80. 3; *Sermo* 227; *De bapt.* 6. 25. 47), in which the presence of God's own word of power is emphasized in the explanation of Eucharistic transformation, with the later viewpoint of the celebrant "confecting the Eucharist" (see Peter Lombard *Sent.* 4. 11. 1). There is an evolution from the "sacramental" to the "instrumental" regarding the role of the minister, though these terms are not used to describe the two viewpoints.

124. Though he does not use the term "sacramental character," Chrysostom already has a developed notion of the abiding power conferred in ordination, but he sees it as the power of freeing from sin through baptism and the penitential discipline. See *On the Priesthood* 3. 5.

125. This evolution will be treated in subsequent chapters of this part.

126. There is a fairly extensive development during the fourth to sixth centuries of the notion of "character" as related to baptism, but little application of this to ordination. After the sixth century there is no development of a theology of the character until the major theological work of the twelfth and thirteenth centuries. "The doctrine of the sacramental character was almost forgotten from the seventh to the twelfth centuries" (P. Hanley, *New Catholic Encyclopedia*, vol. 12, p. 787).

127. This is, of course, only another side of the question as to what the minister of sacraments does: Does he cause grace and forgiveness of sin, or does he proclaim that God has effected such justification, or is his action the condition sine qua non of the divine justifying action? From the thirteenth century onward there is a consistent teaching that the sacramental character is an intrinsic and permanent causative power possessed by the ordained, but as late as Peter Lombard one feels that the word "character" as applied to the endowment granted the minister in ordination has the more general implications of our ordinary nontheological reference to a person's character. See Lombard *Sent.* 4, d. 6, c. 1.

128. In addition to the obvious expectation of spiritual leadership from those in positions of official leadership, there is a deeper current of thought (going back at least as far as Origen) that sees personal sanctity itself as a saving force within the life of the church and therefore as something that should be possessed by those who are ministers of salvation. See K. Delahaye, *Ecclesia Mater* (Paris, 1964), pp. 244–45.

129. Actually, the development of a formalized theology of the sacrament of orders, when it does occur from the twelfth century onward, concentrates on the ordination ceremony as the sacrament and pays little or no attention to the ordained ministers themselves as being the sacrament of orders.

130. See C. Couturier, *"Sacramentum et Mysterium* dans l'oeuvre de saint Augustin," *Etudes augustiniennes,* ed. H. Rondet (Paris, 1953), pp. 163–274, who argues that

Augustine's understanding of *"dispensator verbi et sacramenti"* (as applied to or-dained ministers) involved this broader sacramental context. "Cette expression [i.e., *dispensator verbi et sacramenti*], fréquente sous sa plume, se restreint parfois pour désigner le mystère de la prédication et l'administration des sacrements. Dans nom-bre de cas, elle nous paraît avoir une portée beaucoup plus générale." (P. 267, n. 22) See also Congar, *Ecclésiologie*, pp. 106–9; Lecuyer, *Le sacerdoce*, pp. 288–99; and O. Perler, "L'evêque, representant du Christ selon les documents des premiers siècles," *L'episcopat et l'Eglise universelle*, ed. Congar-Dupuy (Paris, 1962), pp. 31–66.

131. Though the formal explanation of "notes of the church" comes much later (with the polemical theology of the sixteenth century) the appeal to sanctity as a distinguish-ing and justifying characteristic of the church goes back as far as Justin's *Apologies*, and there is a continuing tradition that holiness should mark the life of the Christian community and particularly the life of "professional Christians."

132. On this process, see the latter half (pp. 190ff.) of L. Bouyer's *The Spirituality of the New Testament and the Fathers*, vol. 1 of *History of Christian Spirituality*.

133. Throughout the history of Christian asceticism Stoicism exercises a strong influence; the exact extent and character of this influence remains to be studied. M. Spanneut, *Le stoicisme des pères* (Paris, 1957), provides a thorough examination of the second century; nothing comparable has been done for later periods, although there are tantalizing insights in such books as H. Busson's *La religion des classiques* (Paris, 1948) and J. Fontaine's *Isidore of Seville* (Paris, 1959).

134. See Bouyer, pp. 523–27.

135. Various influences can be designated as contributing to this distancing of Christ—an excessive reaction to Arianism's denial of the divinity of Christ (J. Jungmann details some of this in his *Pastoral Liturgy* [New York, 1962], pp. 2–63), the Neo-Platonic world-view (particularly as expressed by Pseudo-Dionysius) with its layers of "inter-mediaries," the increase of moralizing in preaching and religious instruction. What-ever the causes, this evolution provided a subtle but important support to the status of the clergy, for they were the official mediators through whom the ordinary faithful were to deal with Christ.

136. See W. Völker, *Kontemplation und Ekstase bei Pseudo-Dionysius Areopagita* (Wies-baden, 1958), pp. 78–83.

137. See Leeming, pp. 535–41.

138. As Congar indicates (*Ecclésiologie*, p. 128) the notion of apostolicity continues in the early Middle Ages to stress the faith of the apostles. The critical shift in the under-standing of apostolic succession from possession of the *authentic apostolic teaching* to possession of the *jurisdiction proper to the apostolic office* shifts also the reason for episcopal good example: from the authenticity of behavior expected of the prophet to the edifying behavior expected of a public official.

139. *1 Clem.* 42–44.

140. On this evolution towards moralistic preaching, see above, pp. 257–59.

141. While the reservation of the evangelical counsels to monasticism is a gradual process, not yet achieved at the time of Gregory I (see J. Leclercq, *The Spirituality of the Middle Ages* [New York, 1968], pp. 3–67), there is a notable difference between the instructions given by Gregory (in part three of his *De cura pastorali*) for preaching to the laity and the Christmas sermon (*Sermo* 20) of Leo I which still proposes to all the ideal of heroic Christianity (see Bouyer, pp. 529–30).

142. This is not to say that there was any less claim to apostolic succession; indeed, such claim was constant, but it turned more in the direction of justifying the authority and power of the episcopate by reference to the apostolic office. See Congar, *Ecclésiolo-gie*, pp. 138–51.

143. See Jungmann, *Mass*, pp. 81–86.

144. So, e.g., Rabanus Maurus: "Iste autem ordo [i.e., ordained clerics] praeponitur in Ecclesia, quia jure in sanctis deservit, et sacramenta populis dispensat" (*De cler. instit.* 1. 2); "Sacerdos quidem nomen habet compositum ex Graeco et Latino, quasi sacrum

dans. Dispensat ergo mysteria coelestia, fidelibus baptismum tradit, corpus et sanguinem Christi distribuit. . . ." (*Ibid.* 1. 5.)

145. However, other notions often overshadow this *vicarius Christi* or *in persona Christi* role of the sacramental celebrant. In the ninth century, for example, a typical view was that the celebrant was a legate either of God or of the Christian people or both; see R. Reynolds, "A Florilegium on the Ecclesiastical Grades in CLM 19414: Testimony to Ninth-Century Clerical Instruction," *Harvard Theological Review*, vol. 63 (1970), p. 242.

146. This is unmistakable in the controversy between Lanfranc and Berengarius over the "real presence": the presupposition of the dispute (and of official attempts to resolve it) was that the question of real presence centered on the consecration of the bread and wine.

147. So, too, there seems little trace left of the idea that the community of Christians assembled for the Eucharist acts sacramentally to make the "mystery act of Christ" present; see Congar, *Ecclésiologie*, pp. 104–14.

CHAPTER 30

Sacramental Ministry in

the Middle Ages

Even though there was a general tendency of Christian liturgy as is typical of cult forms to be stable and relatively unchanging, the period from the twelfth to fourteenth centuries is one of notable unification and crystallization of liturgical forms, so much so that, until the very recent alterations in Roman Catholic liturgy, the sacramental ritual for the Roman church remained almost completely unchanged from the thirteenth to the twentieth century.[1] This says something, of course, about the basic understanding of worship and sacrament that prevailed during these centuries, and therefore about the understanding of priestly ministry in sacrament.

One of the most important influences in creating this situation of permanence and the accompanying view of sacraments and their ministry was the preeminence of canon law in the Middle Ages. Though appeal to legal precedent became increasingly important during the ninth to the eleventh centuries, the golden age of formal development of canon law was in the twelfth and thirteenth centuries. All that is required to see the prominence of legislation about sacraments is to glance at the table of contents of Gratian's *Decretum* and see the large portion of the work devoted to *"de sacramentis."*

True, in Gratian and in other canonists who treated of sacraments, the portion of their work devoted to this topic was generally in a vein different from that of their treatment of other topics; in the earlier stages before systematic theologians moved into the field, stimulated by the fourth book of Peter Lombard's *Sentences,* the canonical treatment was almost more theological in tone and method.[2] However, once one introduces the legal mentality into the explanation of sacraments and of sacramental ministry, the very positing of questions and selection of material worth discussing is governed in large part by this mentality.

With regard to the matter of sacramental ministry, the canonical influence draws attention to the official role of the minister and the question of his jurisdiction.[3] True, the distinction between orders and jurisdiction carries over from the preceding period and becomes even more important, but this tends to draw attention to jurisdiction rather than to orders and to give the impression that there is some kind of sacramental *potestas jurisdictionis* that is other than *potestas ordinis.*[4]

Again, this is the period of intense and thorough ecclesiastical organization culminating in the pontificates of Innocent III and IV.[5] Even the tempestuous situation of the fourteenth century, the Great Western Schism, and the attacks of rising national monarchies could not wipe out the structures developed during the two preceding centuries. Amazingly enough, some of them endured through Reformation and the eighteenth- and nineteenth-century revolutions into the twentieth century, though they no longer jibed with the sociological or intellectual development of modern Europe.

Such careful and detailed organization was bound to have a considerable effect on sacramental liturgy and its ministry. It would seem that a fair amount of the rubrical mentality which reigned supreme for many centuries was nurtured during this period.[6] And a study of Biel's *Canonis misse expositio* (from the fourteenth century) reveals the manner in which the least detail of liturgical action is given meaning.[7] In such a situation, the minister of the Eucharist (and *mutatis mutandis* of the other sacraments) becomes the performer of a ritualized action in which almost total emphasis is laid on conformity to determined pattern. Exactness of action rather than insight into what is taking place has the primacy. Clearly, to describe the medieval attitude towards Eucharistic ministry in this way is excessively harsh, for they were aware of the importance in the celebrant of faith and sincere personal identity with the sacrificial action, at least to the extent of questioning the effect this might have on the effectiveness of the Eucharist.[8] But to quite an extent the performance of the Eucharistic action by the ordinary bishop or presbyter was done with attention and care and little understanding.[9] The very bitterness and irrationality of the reaction when questions were first raised about the manner of Eucharistic real presence reflects the fact that theologians of that period did not possess an understanding of the Eucharistic action that was capable of satisfying a sincere Christian search for insight.[10]

Even though prepared for by the Irish penitential discipline which began to affect the Continent as early as the sixth century, the shift in the approach to forgiveness of sin which took place in the twelfth century was rapid and revolutionary. By the end of the century there is scarcely a trace of the classic discipline of the exomologesis. Instead, the emphasis has shifted determinatively to confession of sins and priestly absolution.[11] Internal contrition is seen as necessary, as is performance of some penance as satisfaction, but a theory of the sufficiency of attrition (plus, of course, priestly absolution) and the rapid growth of indulgences are beginning to detract from both contrition and penance.[12]

Actually, this caused an important shift in the external activity of the priests charged with the care of souls since a much greater portion of their time and effort was taken up with hearing confessions, especially when regularity in confession became a matter of law.[13] In their own self-image, too, the power of forgiving sins, the practice of passing some judgment on the culpability of their fellow Christians, was bound to have a major effect. More than ever, the notion of the pastoral office as one of ridding people from their sins became predominant. One preached in order to exhort people to leave their sins, to repent, and to approach the sacrament of reconciliation.[14] One celebrated the Eucharist so that the sin-effacing power of Christ's death might touch men.[15] And one exercised the power of the keys in order to free men from their sins and open up to them the gates of the kingdom.[16]

Ordination of monks to the priesthood had already influenced the understanding of the priestly function, for in many ways a large portion of these could hardly be considered pastors—for practical purposes they were "Mass-saying priests."[17] So, too, the formation of canons into regular communities, by Norbert in the twelfth century, introduced a monastic ideal into the very life and activity of nonmonastic priests.[18] However, the sociological reality of canons grouped around a cathedral church was already an approximation to monastic community life, and had historical precedents from as far back as Eusebius of Vercelli.[19] But the major new force was the foundation of the communities of friars regular, particularly the Dominicans and Franciscans. Intrinsically, it was the Dominicans rather than the Franciscans who should have affected the notion and exercise of the sacerdotal office. The Dominicans from the beginning were largely ordained presbyters, whereas the Franciscans were not meant to be clerics.[20] The idea of nonclerics going about teaching was much too innovative, however, and almost immediately the Franciscans were forced into the clerical mold, the result being a lasting rent in the soul of the Franciscan movement.[21]

The immense success of these new forms of dedicated priestly life and activity had deep effects on the idea of priestly ministry. For one thing, it introduced (or reintroduced) the missionary ideal into the already formulated patterns of ministry and so infused renewed dynamism into the *cura animarum*.[22] Moreover, even though it could not accomplish such a radical reversal with complete success, the advent of these friars regular marked a first break with the notion that dedicated life required flight from the world. Instead, there was a clearly pastoral orientation.[23] Actually, monasticism had been often forced out of seclusion and driven back to the care of Christians. Much of the evangelization of northern Europe was due to monks, but this was accidental, even inimical, to the basic genius of monasticism.[24] Now there were religious communities founded for the very purpose of working with people. However, the extent to which they still kept much of the monastic way of life and spirituality indicates how thoroughly the monastic ideal had penetrated into the theology of the pastoral function.

Then, too, the relative freedom of these friars from episcopal control, though the two orders became a rich source of candidates for the episcopacy, meant a source of power and support for the papacy in its efforts to Romanize the church.[25] It also meant the existence in the church of a powerful force for reforming the episcopacy and secular clergy, if this was needed. Nevertheless, it increased the tendency to a split within the presbyterium, a split that existed to some extent with the monastic institutions of previous centuries rivaling the diocesan clergy, but which was greatly increased as the mendicant orders became quite quickly powerful, rich, and prestigious. The opposition to admitting religious to the faculty of the University of Paris in the thirteenth century was but one manifestation of the tension, even hostility, which often existed between the two groups.[26]

Finally, the establishment of these mendicant orders, and the extent to which they soon developed a large group of eminent theologians, was most influential in emphasizing the theologian's role in the church's life, in coalescing the theologian's function with the presbyteral (and episcopal) office, and in giving the theologian autonomy and freedom vis-à-vis episcopal authority.[27]

Given the almost explosive growth of theology during the High Middle Ages, it would not be surprising to find a considerable theological clarification of Christian ministry and priesthood. Rather, the surprise is to find how relatively little attention was given it. When one puts together the various elements touching on Christian ministry which are scattered in various tracts—preaching and teaching in the treatise on faith, the power of the keys in the study of Penance, Eucharistic ministry in the question of transubstantiation—a respectable body of thought about ministry can be assembled; but one finds no lengthy systematic treatment of priesthood (and/or ministry) comparable to that given the Trinity, or grace, or Christian virtue.

One can find a number of lengthy systematic works *de sacramentis*,[28] though some of the early ones, like that of Hugh of St. Victor, take *sacramenta* in a very broad sense, practically equivalent to mysteries of faith.[29] But even in those which did explain what we ordinarily think of as "the sacraments," in the earlier stages one sometimes finds explanation of baptism, penance, and Eucharist, but no study of Orders. Petrus Cantor, writing towards the end of the twelfth century has no treatment of Orders.[30] Peter of Poitiers somewhat earlier gives us what may be the explanation for this absence. Explaining why he says nothing about Orders, though he does consider it a sacrament, he remarks, ". . . *Nil hic dicendum, eo quod decretistis disputatio de his potius quam theologis deservit.*"[31] His reference to the Decretists reminds us of the ample discussion contained in Gratian's *Decretum*, a mine of patristic and canonical tradition on the topic which was the source not only of the canonists' discussion of priesthood but also of Peter Lombard's (which in turn was the springboard for much of the thirteenth and fourteenth centuries' treatment of the topic).[32] From Lombard onward, theologians increasingly discuss various elements pertaining to ministry and priesthood and canonists continue their own commentary on *Decretum* and decretals.[33] Thus, a strong canonical flavor is introduced into the church's formalized thinking about ministry, even more so than about the other sacraments.

Patristic thought had already used Old Testament categories and the parallel of Old Testament priestly institutions as means of explaining more fully Christian priesthood. That thought, distilled in the florilegia and the canonical collections, was joined with the tendency of canonical thinking to go back to the Levitical legislation.[34] The result was a considerable impact of Old Testament thinking upon the development of Christian theology of worship, sacramental sanctification, and priestly ministry.[35]

The distinctive nature of Christ's priestly act of redemption was consistently mentioned, but generally the basis of the distinction was the difference between *type* and *fulfillment*. The distinction of Old Testament and Christian priesthood seen by a given theologian depended upon his view of the relation of the two covenants.[36] Moreover, the ethico-religious ideal of Leviticus with all its overtones of separation from the profane, separation from ordinary people, and man's need of professional mediators to get to God became a common source for reflection upon the sanctity expected of the New Testament priests and Levites.[37] It is interesting to see how often Leviticus is quoted as law in the campaign to enforce clerical celibacy.[38]

There is a good possibility, too, that constant reference to Old Testament ideas of priesthood was a major influence in bringing about the concentration on cultic ministration which is reflected in the common statement that the primary purpose of Christian ministry is cult.[39] What is interesting is that such statements are uncorrelated with the discussion in another tract about the power of the keys.[40]

It is not entirely accurate to single out the Dionysian influence, because much the same notion of a hierarchical universe was contained in the persistent and dominant Augustinian current of theology. However, in the Middle Ages the influence of Pseudo-Denis was greatly augmented; he was a frequent object of commentaries and because of his supposed apostolic authority a favorite among the *auctores* appealed to by theologians in their treatises.[41] It is interesting to notice how Denis was cited with quite a bit of discrimination, particularly when he disagreed with other commonly accepted traditions. For example, practically all the theologians who discussed the number of ministerial orders opted for seven distinct orders, despite the fact that nine would have fitted the neat arrangement of the Dionysian hierarchy.[42]

Within the intrinsic process of theology, an influence that was more critical than the others just discussed was the understanding of the priesthood of Christ.[43] All Christian thought has maintained that Christ is the one high priest in the Christian dispensation and that anything else that is named priesthood can be justifiably called that because it stands in some special relation to his unique priesthood. However, different historical periods and different Christian thinkers have understood the meaning of that statement quite diversely.

In the impressive systematizing of understanding about the mystery of God's revelation in Jesus Christ which is medieval theology, the explanation of Christ's priesthood was consciously used as a basis for explaining the priesthood possessed by the Christian people and, in some special way, by its ordained ministers.[44] Because it is one of those elements of faith that is close to the very core of the Christian mystery, for Christ's priesthood is *in concreto* indistinguishable from the finality of the incarnation, the priesthood of Christ was explained according to the particular genius of the divergent theological schools.[45]

A wide divergence of views marks twelfth-century reflection on the priesthood of Christ. Significantly, Anselm of Canterbury, whose influence was so determinative in turning the theology of redemption toward the notion of satisfaction, says nothing about the priesthood of Christ. Bernard of Clairvaux, on the contrary, is one of a long line of theologians who see Christ, the one true and supreme priest, acting in and through the visible minister of the sacraments.[46] There seems to be in Bernard's view an implicit assumption of some instrumental function on the part of the ordained minister. Christ works invisibly through the ordained priest's visible activity, but this is never spelled out theologically. Much the same is true of Abelard, who mentions almost in passing that Christ is the invisible high priest who can supply healing care to men even if the ministrations of a visible priest are unavailable.[47] Yet, this idea of the high priest healing the spiritual ailments of men must be read in terms of Abelard's view that Christ's passion redeems men by arousing in them that love by which they are freed from sin and brought to the liberty of the sons of God.[48]

In Peter Lombard's *Sentences* there is a lengthy discussion of Christ's role as mediator in his redeeming action;[49] but no explicit relation of this to priesthood is made until almost the end of his treatment when one succinct remark refers to Christ as priest, victim, and the price of reconciliation, but scarcely ties this in with the foregoing discussion of Christ's mediatorial function.[50]

One might expect Hugh of St. Victor to apply to Christ's continuing high-priestly role some of his rich insights into the sacramental dimension of Christian life, yet there seems to be practically none of this. Hugh does speak of Christ himself (at the Supper and on Calvary) acting as high priest and of ordained ministers (presbyters and bishops) acting as priest in the Eucharist and in Penance; but he treats the latter as a continuation (memorial) in historical sequence (i.e., ordained ministers in the church now do by commemoration what Christ *did*) rather than as a simultaneous action of Christ through the church's ministers.[51]

On the surface, Alexander of Hales (in the early thirteenth century) seems to bring together the notions of Christ's mediation and priesthood, but really there is more of a juxtaposition of the two since mediation pertains

to Christ's uniting of divinity and humanity, whereas his priesthood is a matter of his suffering on the cross and of his giving sacraments. Quite tellingly, in his explanation of Christ's redemptive work, Alexander begins with a citation from Augustine that speaks of Christ's priesthood, but then moves on without further advertence to the notion of priesthood to Anselm and the way in which Christ provided satisfaction for men's sin.[52]

Albertus Magnus lays the groundwork for an understanding of Christ's sacerdotal function in terms of Aristotelian categories of causation, refers explicitly to Christ's role as priest and victim, and makes passing reference to the grace of Orders as one that assimilates the ordinand to Christ as priest, but he never brings all this together into an integrated view of Christ's priestly and redeeming action. An indication of this is given by his discussion of the effectiveness of Christ's passion. He deals with the passion by using the categories of merit, redemption, and mediation, but no mention is made of the passion as an expression of Christ's priesthood.[53]

What Albertus Magnus suggested, Thomas Aquinas developed in systematic fashion. Dealing with mediation as the heart of priesthood, grounding this unique mediation of Christ in the Incarnation but insisting that the action of mediating is essentially Jesus' worship, his obedient acceptance of suffering and death, Aquinas can then give a consistent explanation of Christ's priestly action of offering himself as expiation, atonement, and source of mankind's justification.[54] Though it is in very compressed form, the treatment of Christ's priesthood in the *Summa theologica* is in effect a sketch for a sacerdotal interpretation of the entire Christ-mystery.

Unlike Aquinas, Bonaventure has no systematizing of theology about Christ's priesthood. He does, of course, repeat the traditional doctrine about Christ's high-priestly action of offering himself; however, apart from one or two tantalizing but incidental remarks, he does not introduce the notion of priesthood into the rather extensive discussion of Christ as mediator and redeemer.[55] Like

Bonaventure and the Franciscan tradition in general, Duns Scotus is markedly Christocentric in his theology; yet the strongly juridico-moral character of his soteriology leads him, when he discusses Christ's passion and death, to stress merit and satisfaction rather than priesthood. Indeed, Scotus distances Christ's priesthood from the church (and specifically from the Eucharist) much more than does Bonaventure.[56]

With Ockham, there is no attention paid to Christ's priesthood. In his treatment of the Eucharist, for example, the discussion deals entirely with such philosophical questions as the relation of substance and quantity in transubstantiation. More radically, however, the occasionalism of Ockham's explanation of the effectiveness of Jesus' passion (Ockham sees the passion as a condition sine qua non for God's granting of grace) undermines any attempt to put intrinsic power into Christ's exercise of priesthood.[57] Influential as Ockham's extrinsicism was to be, his lack of advertence to Christ's priesthood did not characterize all late medieval theologians, even those in the nominalistic school. Gabriel Biel, to take one prominent example, discusses Christ's exercise of priesthood in some detail —how he exercised it at the Supper by changing the elements into his own body and blood, how he (the one true high priest) offered himself on the altar of the cross, how he is mystically immolated in the daily celebration of Eucharist, how he acts still in Eucharist through the instrumentality of the ministers who are his vicars.[58]

Though the reason is not clear, by the time that systematized discussion of the sacraments evolves in the twelfth century the action of ordination is considered to be the sacrament of orders.[59] Perhaps this was due to the trend towards excessive categorizing: laying down a definition of sacrament, and then seeing how various instances of sacramental reality fit this definition, and not adverting to the fact that "sacrament" might be an *analogous* notion. And since other sacraments— baptism, confirmation, Eucharist—were obviously ritual actions, one looked for the ritual

action connected with Christian priesthood, namely, the ordination ceremony, as the sacrament. To some extent, the medieval explanations of the *res et sacramentum* resulting from this action (the sacramental character) could have retained the idea of the ecclesiastical orders themselves as sacrament, but the explanation of this *res et sacramentum* was situated too much in the realm of intrinsic change in the individual ordinand and so overlooked the collegial aspects of the effect.[60]

Whatever may have been the exact dynamics that explain the situation, the medieval treatises of the sacrament of orders (and thereafter, up to the present) were explanations of ordination.[61] This leaves practically untouched the theological explanation of the corporate causality of the episcopacy and presbyterate as a social force in a religious community. Most of this was left to canonists, in the context of legal power and jurisdiction.[62]

There seems to be no questioning of the necessary function of the bishop in the action of episcopal or presbyteral ordination.[63] Both the canonical traditions and the ordinals take this for granted, and the only questions have to do with jurisdictional disputes, e.g., the traditional rights of metropolitans to consecrate their suffragan bishops.

Though not much attention is paid to the point, the ordaining bishop is looked upon as the instrument of God (Christ) who is the principal cause of the ordinational sanctification.[64] This is merely an application of the general theory of sacramental effectiveness. In various authors the understanding of such instrumentality is controlled by their diverse metaphysics. The precise understanding of the episcopal action is also differentiated by the divergent opinions as to what is the essential action of the ordination, in the case of presbyteral ordination, whether it is the imposition of hands or the giving of the instruments or the anointing of the hands or the sum total of all these.[65]

To some extent, the earlier liturgy's clear emphasis on the giving of the Spirit, signified by the imposition of hands, was obscured by the liturgical complication of additional rites (e.g., the *traditio instrumentorum*) and the emphasis given them. This very emphasis indicated the extent to which the ceremony came to be seen as a conferring of various powers rather than the gift of the Spirit. Since the Middle Ages inherited from the preceding period the position that the power attached to the *sacerdotium* was the power of the keys, the ordination is seen as the conferring of the keys.[66] However, the picture is not entirely clear: the keys seem to pertain most clearly to the power of forgiving sins in the sacrament of reconciliation; but there seems to be some need to distinguish between the internal and external form, i.e., between sacramental absolution and lifting of excommunication, the former belonging to all those who have pastoral care, the latter reserved to the bishops.[67] More of a problem than this is the fact that the highest power belonging to priests is that involved in Eucharistic consecration, which does not seem to be precisely power of the keys.[68]

To this latter problem, two solutions were offered: the one, pursued by Bonaventure, consisted in seeing the Eucharistic power as implied in the keys (seeing the keys as the power of reconciliation);[69] the other, followed by Aquinas, was to ground the power of Eucharistic confection and the power of penitential absolution in the sacramental character.[70]

If one puts the discussion of ordination into a theological context governed, as was that of most medieval theologians, by a theory of ontological modifications, the sacrament was commonly considered to have two effects: the *res et sacramentum* which was the sacramental character of Orders, and the *res* which was grace.

Like all the sacraments, ordination was seen by the medieval theologians as a cause of grace, of sanctification provided for the ordinand to enable him to fit his new "level" in the ecclesiastical hierarchy and to perform worthily his function of ministry.[71] Interestingly, there is practically no discussion of what one would ordinarily think of as sancti-fying grace, but a fair amount of discussion about the gift of the discretion needed for penitential ministry.[72] In the twelfth-century treatises on the sacrament of penance, the two keys are seen as power of discretion and power of absolution.[73] And some sources, as the early twelfth-century *Liber de Sacramentis*, do not hesitate to attribute to the ordination an increase (or first gift) of discretion.[74]

While the thirteenth century sees the doctrine of a sacramental character caused by ordination as a theological commonplace, there is obviously quite a range of understanding character in this instance. One can, for example, contrast Alexander of Hales' view with that of Thomas Aquinas. For the former, there is a character but it is not equated with the *potestas*;[75] for Aquinas the character itself is the power of priestly action.[76] For most theologians of the Middle Ages, the doctrine of a character conferred in ordination is used as the key to explaining the efficacy of sacramental actions performed by an unworthy minister.[77] And obviously it is the root for the lasting effect of ordination and the nonrepetition of ordination.[78]

One of the persistent questions that one encounters in the theological discussions of this period is that of the distinction (or nondistinction) of episcopacy as an order. Contrary to the opinion of earlier periods and to the patristic overshadowing of presbyterate by episcopacy, the medieval theologians see the essence and loftiest powers of priesthood being conferred in presbyteral ordination.[79] The bishop is what a presbyter is, only a little more so—he can ordain, and his power of the keys extends to the realm of excommunication.[80] So, for the most part they do not see episcopacy as a distinct order.[81]

In a sense, this is a logical conclusion from the emphasis placed on the Eucharist as the changing of bread into Christ and on the priestly power of transubstantiating. Not that pastoral concerns have vanished, but priesthood as a cultic reality has gradually gained center stage in preference to apostolic proclamation of the gospel.[82] Relationship of bishops to the apostles had become by now a polemical argument for jurisdiction, rather than a sacramental making present of the apostolic tradition.[83]

As part of the attempt to distinguish what was proper to all priests as priests from what pertained only to the episcopacy, there developed in clear and constantly used form the distinction between *potestas ordinis* and *potestas jurisdictionis*.[84] This was not a distinction that was new to the Middle Ages[85] but it is theologically formulated and employed during the twelfth and thirteenth centuries,[86] becomes a basic principle of understanding during the fourteenth- and fifteenth-century disputes on relative power of pope and council,[87] and is important in the polemics about the relative and interlocking jurisdiction of pope and king.[88]

For centuries the ordained ministers of the church had been seen as the ministers of sacrament; the phrase *minister verbi et sacramenti* was already a patristic commonplace and is constantly repeated in the following centuries. However, there is a gradual increase of emphasis on the cultic aspect of this ministerial task, specifically on the Eucharistic celebration. To give but one illustration of this shift in emphasis: in its twenty-seventh canon, the Fourth Lateran Council speaks of the formation of clergy (which would, of course, reflect its view of what clergy should do): "Since spiritual guidance [*regimen animarum*] is the art of arts, we strictly command that bishops, either personally or through others who are well-fitted to the task, seriously instruct and train those who are to be advanced to the priesthood. Specifically, they should instruct them about liturgical celebrations and the Church's sacraments, so that they can perform them correctly."[89]

Presbyters are recognized ministers for baptism, penance, and anointing, bishops for confirmation and ordination.[90] This is already the pattern long before the twelfth century, but it is interesting to notice how this gradual increase of the autonomous ministry of presbyters differs from the patristic age (and earlier) when bishops were considered the ordinary ministers of baptism (at least in

a presidential position), Eucharist, penance, and marriage.[91] One really wonders if in the domain of sacramental activity the idea of the episcopal college had not in large part given way to the idea of the presbyteral college (controlled by the upper level priests).[92] Certainly there was the idea of a sacerdotal college, the *sacerdotium*, with priests *primi ordinis* (i.e., bishops) and *secundi ordinis* (presbyters).[93]

But it was for Eucharistic ministry that priests were primarily ordained, according to the constant teaching of the medieval theologians and canonists. "Consecrare enim est principalis actus, ad quem sunt actus omnium ordinum. . . ."[94] In this supreme action of priesthood, the confection of the Eucharist, there was no distinction between bishops and presbyters; this is the principle from which most medieval thinkers draw the conclusion that episcopacy is not a distinct order.[95]

Exact understanding of this priestly act of Eucharistic consecration depends, of course, on the various theories of Eucharistic transformation which, in turn, were dependent upon the diverse philosophical positions on such matters as causality.[96] In general, however, the celebrant of the Eucharist was seen to be in an instrumental role. The action of transubstantiating quite clearly goes beyond any human power, so God must be the principal agent in changing the bread and wine into Christ's body and blood. Moreover, the high priest who offers himself in each celebration of Eucharist is Christ; the human celebrant of Eucharist gives himself, as it were, to Christ as an instrument, though, of course a human agent, functioning with knowledge and intention.[97]

The action and words of Eucharistic consecration are essentially those of Christ; they are also the worship sign of the church as it joins itself to the offering of its Head. The celebrant of Eucharist acts representatively for both Christ and the church.[98] For this reason, the action of the Eucharist enjoys a basic freedom in its reality and effectiveness from the capabilities or sanctity of the celebrant. In a sense the fruitfulness of any given celebration of Eucharist is unlimited, since it makes Christ himself present and draws from the efficacy of his death on the cross.[99]

Actually, very little attention is paid theologically to the action of the priest in Eucharist. It seems taken for granted that his action consists essentially in the consecration of the elements, and that it is in one sense or another instrumental or ministerial.[100] The concentration of theological questioning and discussion falls on the change that takes place in the elements, on explanations of the real presence, on the sacramentality of the Eucharist (seen now not so much under the aspect of sacrificial mystery as under that of the providing the Eucharistic Body of Christ for adoration and reception in communion).[101]

Theologically, the development of the doctrine of the sacramental character conferred in ordination seemingly eliminated the question of Eucharist depending on the minister's sanctity, but the question still persists in some fashion throughout all medieval discussion of the Eucharist.[102] Interestingly, though nothing approaching an adequate explanation is ever provided, there is an enduring conviction that somehow a Mass celebrated by a holy priest is better than one celebrated by one in grave sin. With Wyclif this will extend to the point of denying essential priestly power to those in grave sin, but he seems definitely to have been an innovator in pressing the point that far.[103] In a sense, though, the prohibitions of Gregory VII and some of his successors which forbade Christians to attend Eucharist celebrated by a priest of known sinful life helped prepare the way for Wyclif, for such legislation definitely conveyed the impression that such sinful celebrations were of no value.[104]

As in the preceding centuries, it is taken for granted that the clergy, especially the higher clergy, should set an example for the rest of the Christian people. Unfortunately, the most common literary witness to this expectation comes in the frequent attacks upon clerical rapacity, grossness, and immorality. The level of Christian behavior among a great many diocesan priests and even among many

friars after the great revitalization they had provided in the late twelfth and early thirteenth centuries, left much to be desired.[105]

From a theological point of view, however, the important fact is that exemplary behavior was expected of priests and bishops. By this time, though, "example" is seen almost exclusively in terms of good ethical behavior, particularly in sexual matters. Fortunately, a good amount of the basic traditions of Christian evangelical life was preserved by successive waves of religious movements (some of them eventuating in institutionalized forms of religious community life, such as the Dominicans and Franciscans, some resulting in less formalized and less acceptable forms, such as the Beguardi and Beguini)[106] and are exemplified in some of the great saints of the period. Authentic mysticism developed and flowered in this period—Cistercian (Bernardine) mystics, Franciscans such as Bonaventure and Francis himself, the intellectualized mysticism of Aquinas and Suso and Rysbroeck and Gerson[107]—but the world of mystics was often so far removed from the ordinary world of clerics, even of bishops and popes, that little of it rubbed off on the ordinary priest or bishop. One can see this in the relative failure of the recurrent movements for clerical reform, which often emerged from the better educated and more genuinely prayerful circles of the clergy itself.[108]

Inheriting the victory of Gregory VII, the church of the twelfth to fourteenth centuries saw a relatively universal application of the regulation of clerical celibacy. Not that there was total observance of the discipline, but the legislation that made marriage of higher clergy not only illicit but invalid gave added impetus to the imposition of the regulation.[109] And even more so than in the preceding period, observance of celibacy was considered the touchstone to clerical morality. Establishment of the mendicant orders gave a strong support to the notion of a celibate clergy, but by the fourteenth century the nonobservance of celibacy by many of the friars and monks apparently became fairly widespread, though the form it took was not that of marriage.[110] In general, with marriage ruled out by legislation, many of the clergy drifted into a situation of concubinage that practically constituted common-law marriage.[111]

What one misses is anything that resembles a careful theological grounding for the discipline of celibacy. The elements of such a theology that are found in sermons, hortatory treatises, and complaints for the need of clerical reform are merely a repetition of argumentation that is centuries-old.[112]

What one does notice is the firm connection between celibacy and the separateness of the clergy. As official medieval thought sees it, there are two ways of Christian life, married and celibate, with the second obviously the superior.[113] Marriage reduces men to an ordinary fashion of life, and the higher clergy are not supposed to exist and function at that ordinary level.[114]

In the fully organized medieval civilization that flowered in the period we are studying, the clergy were a world within a world.[115] Even though there was extensive overlap and interpenetration of secular and ecclesiastical social and political structures, and the unitive notion of the church as *congregatio omnium fidelium* was a strong psychological force, there was a great gulf between the life of the common people and the life of higher clergy. In this regard, as in earlier centuries, one must distinguish between a fairly large group of poorly educated private priests and country pastors who in many ways identified with the common people, and who often ignored celibacy, and the group of priests who were better trained and worked in closer cooperation with the official structures.[116]

NOTES

1. See J. Jungmann, *Mass of the Roman Rite* (New York, 1951), vol. 1, pp. 103–27. The later Middle Ages (fourteenth and fifteenth centuries) saw a greater diversity, in many regions a proliferation, of different Mass books, and a number of serious abuses in alteration of the liturgy; this was resolved in the Roman Catholic church by the reform of Pius V (in 1570) which imposed the Roman *Missale*.

2. In the twelfth century, the line was not yet too sharply drawn between canon law and systematic theology. A number of prominent thinkers wrote extensively in both fields, and this had a decided influence on the systematizing of theology, particularly in the matter of sacraments. See A. Forest, in A. Fliche and V. Martin, *Histoire de l'Eglise depuis les origines jusqu'à nos jours* (Paris, 1935—), vol. 13, pp. 180–81; J. de Ghellinck, *Le mouvement théologique au XIIe siècle* (Bruxelles, 1948), pp. 499–510.

3. In the *Summas* of the thirteenth century, such jurisdictional questions tend to dominate the discussion about the minister of sacrament; even in Thomas Aquinas (who, in general, tends to be much more ontological in his approach) one can notice this tendency—see *Summa theol.* 3, qq. 67, 72, 82.

4. The critical instance is, as we saw in the previous part, the sacrament of penance, where by the thirteenth century the exercise of the *potestas ordinis* is itself tied in with possession of jurisdiction.

5. See G. Le Bras in Fliche-Martin, vol. 12, pp. 303–48.

6. On the rubrical regulation of liturgy in the thirteenth century, see S. Van Dijk and J. Walker, *The Origins of the Modern Roman Liturgy* (London, 1960).

7. This detailed allegorical explanation of the Eucharist was not new to Biel; it had dominated medieval understanding of the Eucharist since the influential writings of Amalar of Metz in the ninth century. See Jungmann, pp. 107–23.

8. E.g., Thomas Aquinas *Summa theol.* 3, q. 64, aa. 5–6; qq. 82, aa. 5–7.

9. This does not mean that one is justified in seeing this period as dominated by super-

stition and magic; in refutation of such negative judgments, see F. Clark, *Eucharistic Sacrifice and the Reformation,* 2d ed. (London, 1960).

10. See F. Kempf, *Handbook of Church History* (New York, 1965—), vol. 3, pp. 467–69.

11. See B. Poschmann, *Penance and the Anointing of the Sick* (New York, 1964), pp. 153–54.

12. On the *contritio/attritio* dispute during this period, see *ibid.,* pp. 156–93.

13. With Lateran IV (canon 21) in 1215.

14. See G. Owst, *Preaching in Medieval England* (Cambridge, 1926).

15. This was a basic influence in the historical development of private masses and the increase in the frequence of Eucharistic celebrations in the Middle Ages; see Jungmann, pp. 216–24.

16. Although (as we saw in the previous part) a large segment of theological opinion restricted the effectiveness of the penitential use of the keys to the penalty connected with sin, since forgiveness of sin was seen by these theologians to be an exclusively divine action.

17. See J. Leclercq, "On Monastic Priesthood According to the Ancient Medieval Tradition," *Studia Monastica,* vol. 3 (1960), pp. 137–55.

18. See D. Knowles, *The Christian Centuries* (London, 1969), vol. 2, p. 189.

19. See H. Marrou, *ibid.,* vol. 1, p. 278.

20. See W. Hinnebusch, *History of the Dominican Order* (New York, 1966), pp. 39–55; J. Moorman, *History of the Franciscan Order* (Oxford, 1968), pp. 10–31.

21. Moorman, pp. 91–122; D. Knowles, *Religious Orders in England* (Cambridge, 1956), vol. 1, pp. 114–26.

22. See Knowles, pp. 338–42.

23. See Hinnebusch, pp. 119–28.

24. Such a judgment about the intrinsic nature of monasticism is open to criticism, for a widespread discussion about monasticism is presently taking place in the churches; for a brief treatment of this (within the context of classic Benedictine monasticism), see D. Knowles, *Christian Monasticism* (New York, 1969), pp. 224–44.

25. See H. Wolter, *Handbook of Church History,* vol. 4, pp. 172–83.

26. See Knowles, *Christian Centuries,* vol. 4, pp. 348–50.

27. As is clear from these three historical effects, religious order involvement in theology had an ambiguous impact upon the freedom and autonomy of theologians. In taking theological activity out of the realm of episcopal delegation it helped establish the intrinsic autonomy of the theological function, but by emphasizing the limitation of theological activity to clerics it intensified the sociological link of theology to the clerical establishment, thereby bringing it under the umbrella of authoritative teaching, with all the tensions and disputes that that has caused for the past millennium.

28. For a brief listing of the early treatises on the sacraments, see B. Leeming, *Principles of Sacramental Theology,* 2d ed. (London, 1960), pp. xli–xliii.

29. See Hugh of St. Victor, *On the Sacraments of the Christian Faith,* trans. R. Deferrari (Cambridge, Mass., 1951); though entitled *De sacramentis* (and therefore suggesting to modern ears a rather limited scope), the work is a small *"summa"* of Christian theology that became (along with Lombard's *Sentences*) the forerunner of the great thirteenth-century *summas.*

30. See his *Summa de sacramentis;* also Forest, pp. 184–85.

31. *Libri V Sententiarum,* bk. 5, chap. 14.

32. On Gratian's influence on Peter Lombard's sacramental theories, see G. Le Bras, "Pierre Lombard, Prince du droit canon," *Miscellanea Lombardiana* (Novara, 1957), pp. 245–52. "Ce que l'on peut avancer sans exagération, c'est que le Decret fournit à Pierre Lombard un point de départ pour beaucoup de ses doctrines sur les sacréments" (p. 248). On the dogmatic richness of Gratian's treatment of sacraments, see J. de Ghellinck, *Dictionnaire de théologie catholique,* vol. 6, cols. 1740–41.

33. On a continuing interaction of canonical and theological thought into the thirteenth century, see de Ghellinck, *Mouvement Théologique*, pp. 499–510.

34. On the influence of the Old Testament on medieval theology, see M.-D. Chenu, *Nature, Man, and Society in the Twelfth Century* (Chicago, 1968), pp. 146–61.

35. *Ibid.*, p. 156: "The picture of the bishop as pastor is inspired more by the Old Testament than by the New. . . ."

36. Thus, Guido de Orchellis, in his *Tractatus de sacramentis*, ed. Van den Eynde (St. Bonaventure, N.Y., 1953), chap. 8, p. 179: ". . . Virtus sacerdotii Veteris Testamenti consistebat in significando, virtus autem Novi consistit in efficiendo."

37. This is quite logical, if one accepts what had become a theological commonplace by the twelfth century (see, e.g., Hugh of St. Victor *De sacramentis* 2. 3. 11), namely, that the Christian institution of priesthood actually had its origins in the Aaronic priesthood.

38. Usually, though, a passage like Lev. 8:33–35 is used as a basis for an *a fortiori* argument: if the Old Testament priesthood required such sexual abstinence, then certainly New Testament priesthood because of its greater dignity musι require clerical celibacy.

39. See Thomas Aquinas *Summa theol.* 3, q. 63, a. 3; Peter Lombard *Sent.* 4. 15. 9. However, there develops quite early the distinction between "priesthood" being directed to cultic celebration (specifically to Eucharistic confection) while "ministry" is directed to administration of sacraments. So, Hugh of St. Victor: ". . . Just as in the priesthood there is consecration, so in the ministry there is dispensing of the sacrament" (*De sacramentis* 2. 3. 10).

40. The general view of the relation between the two powers of consecration and absolution is that the penitential power enables the priestly minister to prepare people (the body of Christ) to participate in the Eucharistic body of Christ. So, e.g., Bonaventure *In Sent.* 4, d. 19, a. 2, q. 1.

41. See M.-D. Chenu, *Toward Understanding Saint Thomas* (Chicago, 1964), pp. 226–30.

42. The exception is Guido de Orchellis, *Tractatus de sacramentis*, chap. 8, who in true Dionysian fashion parallels the nine choirs of angels with nine "Holy Orders." He does this by making bishopric and archbishopric distinct orders.

43. On medieval theological understandings of the priesthood of Christ, see E. Scheller, *Das Priestertum Christi* (Paderborn, 1934), pp. 151–282.

44. The principle underlying this process was the one enunciated by Thomas Aquinas *Summa theol.* 3, q. 22, a. 4: "Christus est fons totius sacerdotii."

45. For a description of the theological positions of the various theologians and schools of theology in the High Middle Ages, see A. Forest, F. Van Steenberghen, and M. de Gandillac, *Le mouvement doctrinal du XIe au XIVe siècle*, vol. 13 of Fliche-Martin, *Histoire de l'Eglise*.

46. See Y. Congar, "L'ecclésiologie de S. Bernard," *Saint Bernard: Théologien*, ed. J. Leclercq (Rome, 1953), pp. 178–79.

47. *Epitome theologiae christianae*, chap. 36.

48. *In Epist. ad Rom.*, bk. 2 (*Petri Abaelardi Opera*, ed. V. Cousin [Paris, 1859], vol. 2, p. 207).

49. *Sent.* 3, d. 19, cc. 1–4.

50. *Ibid.*, d. 20, c. 5. Scheller, p. 160, sees Lombard as marking no advance in the theology of Christ's priesthood: "Die eigentliche Fruhscholastik ist also wenig ertragreich für die Geschichte vom Priestertum Christi. Petrus Lombardus enneurt nur den augustinischen Mittlerbegriff, wahrend Petrus von Poitiers ihn mit dem Priesterbegriff verbindet und damit, soweit sich bisher sagen lasst, den Anstoss fur eine neue Entwicklung gibt."

51. *De sacramentis* 2. 3. 10–12.

52. See *In Sent.* 3, dd. 1, 19, 20.

53. *De sacramentis*, tract. 1, q. 6; tract. 5, pars 3, q. 1; *De incarnatione*, tract. 6, q. 2, aa. 1–3.

54. *Summa theol.* 3, q. 22 (which deals in detail with Christ's priesthood); and q. 48 (a succinct theology of Christian redemption, which integrates Christ's passion and death *as sacrifice* with the other facets of soteriology). For a more detailed analysis, see Scheller, pp. 273–81.

55. See H. Berresheim, *Christus als Haupt der Kirche nach dem heiligen Bonaventura* (Bonn, 1939), pp. 242–44. One of the few places that suggests the link in Bonaventure's thought between Christ's priestly and redemptive functions is *In Sent.* 3, dist. 19, dub. 4: "Christus in offerendo sanguinem suum Deo, redemit nos a servitute diaboli, peccati et supplicii."

56. Whereas Bonaventure would see Christ as priest somehow present to the Eucharistic celebrant, Scotus denies that Christ is offering the Eucharistic sacrifice: "Christus etsi hic offeratur ut contentus in sacrificio, non tamen hic immediate offert sacrificium" (*Quodlib.*, q. 20, 22).

57. See E. Iserloh, *Gnade und Eucharistie in der philosophischen Theologie des Wilhelm von Ockham* (Wiesbaden, 1956), esp. pp. 272–78.

58. *Canonis Misse Expositio*, lect. 4. On the general trend of late medieval theology to neglect a theology of Christ's sacrificial act, see Iserloh, pp. 273–76.

59. See, e.g., Peter Lombard *Sent.* 4, dist. 24, 13.

60. However, if one compares the passage of Lombard cited in the previous note with the parallel treatment in the *Summa theologica* of Aquinas (*Suppl.*, q. 35), there is a clear historical progression towards understanding this *res et sacramentum* in terms of a "power to cause."

61. As recent and competent a book on sacraments as Leeming's *Principles of Sacramental Theology* still equates the sacrament of orders with ordination; the apostolic constitution of Pius XII in 1947, *Sacramentum ordinis* (*Acta Apost. Sed.* 40, 1948, pp. 5–7), did the same.

62. On the medieval canonists' development of legal explanation regarding presbyteral, episcopal, and papal responsibilities and rights in the church, see G. Le Bras, C. Lefebvre, J. Rambaud, *L'âge classique*, vol. 7 of *Histoire du droit et des institutions de l'Eglise en Occident* (Paris, 1965).

63. There were, of course, some instances where the papacy granted to abbots the power to ordain presbyters (see Leeming, pp. 241, 524); but the more elementary question about the community's capacity to ordain presbyters or bishops did not, apparently, surface during the Middle Ages. On this question, see the essays by A. Piepkorn and H. McSorley in *Eucharist and Ministry*, vol. 4 of *Lutherans and Catholics in Dialogue* (New York, 1970).

64. However, some qualification of this statement should be made. This merely instrumental role of the ordaining prelate did quite clearly apply to the giving of *potestas ordinis* and to the giving of grace to the ordinand; regarding the grant of *potestas jurisdictionis* there was much more inclination to see the bishop as sharing or delegating what was properly his by virtue of his office.

65. On the divergent medieval opinions regarding the essential sacramental sign of ordination, see A. Michel, *Dictionnaire de théologie catholique*, vol. 11, cols. 1322–30.

66. Peter Lombard *Sent.* 4, d. 19, c. 1; Bonaventure *In Sent.* 4, d. 19, a. 2, q. 1; Thomas Aquinas *Summa theol.*, *Suppl.*, q. 17, a. 2, ad 1.

67. This distinction is already explicit in the early Middle Ages and continues throughout the centuries we are now studying; see Y. Congar, *L'ecclésiologie du Haut Moyen Age* (Paris, 1968), pp. 138–63.

68. Albertus Magnus, ". . . Consecrare enim est principalis actus, ad quem sunt actus omnium ordinum . . ." (*De sacr.*, tract. 8, q. 2); Bonaventure (speaking of the powers given in ordination): ". . . Una principalis et prima, quae est ipse ordo ut potestas conficiendi . . ." (*In 4 Sent.*, d. 18, p. 1, a. 3, q. 2).

69. "Ad hoc autem ut possit esse mediator perfectus et competens inter Deum et hominem, oportet quod posse habeat offerendi dona et sacrificia pro peccatis, in quibus Deus placetur; ad hoc quod possit esse reconciliator, oportet quod possit reducere ad

corpus Christi mysticum, cujus caput est ipse Christus verus, et, ut recta sit et ordinata potestas, oportet quod habeat posse conficiendi sanctissimum corpus Christi. Hoc autem pertinet ad solos sacerdotes . . ." (*In 4 Sent.*, d. 19, a. 2, q. 1).

70. ". . . Ideo character et potestas conficiendi et potestas clavium est unum et idem per essentiam sed differt ratione" (*ibid.*, d. 18, q. 1. a. 1, qa. 3).

71. Duns Scotus, "Ordinatio est institutio alicuius in gradu Ecclesiae eminente . . . ex institutione divina efficaciter signans gratiam praeeminentem qua ordinatus digne aliquod ministerium exequatur" (*Ox.* 4, d. 24, q. unica, n. 8).

72. Alexander of Hales, for example, sees even the grace (i.e., the *res tantum*) of ordination as a power: "Similiter in Ordine: impositio manus vel collatio libri sive tonsura est signum tantum; character autem interior signum et signatum; gratia potestatis tantum signatum est; quia in quolibet Ordine confertur aliqua potestas" (*Quaest. disp.*, q. 57, d. 1, n. 12). At the root of the widespread medieval discussion of "the key of discretion," Congar (*Ecclésiologie*, p. 147) situates the distinction made by Bede between *clavis scientiae* and *clavis potestatis.*

73. "Claves istae non sunt corporales, sed spirituales, scilicet discernendi scientia et potentia judicandi . . ." (Peter Lombard *Sent.* 4, d. 18, c. 2). Problems arise early regarding the relation of these two keys, especially the problem about the effectiveness of an act of binding (particularly of excommunication) that is performed by a bishop (or presbyter) who lacks discernment; see Abelard's *Ethica*, chap. 26.

74. "Sciendum est pro certo quod si digne accedunt ad ordines discretio augetur, et si nulla fuit prius discretio tunc fit aliqua" (cited by P. Anciaux, *La théologie du sacrément de pénitence au XIIe siècle* [Louvain, 1949], p. 327).

75. *Quaest. disp.*, q. 57, d. 1.

76. *Summa theol.* 3, q. 63.

77. *Ibid.*, q. 82, aa. 5–8. Though weakened by Gregory VII's prohibition of attendance at sacraments celebrated by unworthy ministers, and openly challenged by Wyclif, the doctrine of the validity of sacramental actions performed by priests in grave sin remained the common opinion throughout the Middle Ages and was reiterated by the Council of Constance in its condemnation of Wyclif and Hus (see Denzinger-Schonmetzer, *Enchiridion Symbolorum* [Freiburg, 1965], no. 1262).

78. See Thomas Aquinas *Summa theol.* 3, q. 63, a. 5. On the permanence of the *potestas ordinis* (whether one equates it or not with the character), see Gerson, *De potest. eccles.*, consideratio secunda (Jean Gerson, *Oeuvres complètes*, ed. P. Glorieux [Tournai, 1965], vol. 6, p. 213). See also Le Bras in Fliche-Martin, vol. 12, pp. 214–15.

79. Hugh of St. Victor *De sacramentis* 2. 3. 11; Peter Lombard *Sent.* 4, d. 24, c. 11; Thomas Aquinas *In Sent.* 4, d. 23, q. 1, a. 3, qa. 3; G. Biel, *Canonis Misse expositio*, lect. 4.

80. Hugh of St. Victor *De sacramentis* 2. 3. 12; Peter Lombard *Sent.* 4, d. 24, c. 16; Thomas Aquinas *Summa theol.* 3, q. 82, a. 1, ad 4, and *Suppl.*, q. 40, a. 5.

81. Thus Albertus Magnus *De sacramentis*, tract. 8, q. 3, ad 4; Thomas Aquinas *Summa theol., Suppl.*, q. 40, 5; Bonaventure *Brevil.* 6. 12. 12–13; Hugh of St. Victor *De sacramentis* 2. 3. 11. However, Guido de Orchellis (*De sacramentis*, c. 8) maintains that episcopacy is a distinct order; and Duns Scotus (*In 4 Sent.*, d. 24, q. unica) also seems to favor the distinctness of episcopacy as an order. See J. Lecuyer, "La grâce de la consécration épiscopale," *Revue des sciences philosophique et théologique*, vol. 36 (1952), pp. 389–417; and "Aux origines de la théologie thomiste de l'Episcopat," *Gregorianum* 35 (1954), pp. 56–89.

82. This is reflected in medieval canon law, in which the bishop (and more so the pope) is seen as a sacred monarch, possessing the fullness of the keys and the fullness of the *potestas ordinis.* See Le Bras in Fliche-Martin, vol. 12, pp. 365–76.

83. Dominant as symbolism was in medieval understanding of the church (e.g., Hugh of St. Victor's *De sacramentis*), the emphasis was on cosmic ahistorical symbolism rather than on historical symbolism. This is reflected in the fascination with the allegorical meaning of the Bible. It may also have been reflected in the popes' assuming the

title of "vicar of Christ" rather than the earlier papal predilection for "vicar of Peter."

84. Obviously, application of this distinction was complicated by the intertwining of ecclesiastical and civil authority. It was further complicated by the increasing autonomy of the laity in secular pursuits (where they were outside the realm of the *potestas ordinis* and where they felt ever less need to acknowledge any clerical *potestas jurisdictionis*) and by the rapid expansion of the mendicant orders; see J. Leclercq, *Jean de Paris et l'ecclésiologie du XIIIe siècle* (Paris, 1942), pp. 119–120.

85. See above, p. 88.

86. E.g., Thomas Aquinas *Summa theol., Suppl.*, q. 8, aa. 5, 7.

87. See Gerson's *De potestate ecclesiastica* (*Oeuvres complètes*, vol. 6, pp. 212–27) where this distinction is the basis for the division of material, and in which he situates the *potestas jurisdictionis in foro exteriori* in a general council (p. 217).

88. Two stages in this dispute should be distinguished. In the earlier stage, the context is the one *populus christianus* in which two authorities (two swords) interact and in which there is question about pope and emperor being two parallel possessors of jurisdiction (spiritual and temporal). In the second stage (from the fifteenth century onward), with rising nationalism making the Holy Roman Empire more of an empty symbol, the pope is in the matter of *potestas jurisdictionis secularis* a sovereign among peers. In the first stage the discussion of papal *potestas* is more juridico-theological, in the second stage more politico-philosophical. See A. Black, *Monarchy and Community* (Cambridge, 1970), pp. 53–84.

89. Lateran IV, canon 27 (*Mansi* 22. 1015).

90. Peter Lombard *Sent.* 4, d. 24, c. 11.

91. Without passing any judgment on this historical development, it does represent a considerable removal of the episcopacy from contact with the faithful, and a considerable evolution in episcopal self-identity from the sacramental to the jurisdictional.

92. To illustrate: as far as people's experience of sacraments was concerned, the presbyter-celebrant was the primary analogate; if they experienced a bishop as celebrant of penance or anointing or baptism or even the Eucharist, they saw him as an exceptional minister of the action that was proper to their parish priest.

93. See Leclercq, *Jean de Paris*, p. 123.

94. Albertus Magnus *De sacramentis*, tract. 8, q. 2, ad 18.

95. ". . . Ordinatur omnis ordo ad Eucharistiae sacramentum. Unde cum episcopus non habeat potestatem superiorem sacerdote quantum ad hoc, episcopatus non erit ordo" (Thomas Aquinas *Summa theol., Suppl.*, q. 40, a. 5).

96. On the variety of opinion in this matter, see Leeming, pp. 283–339.

97. Hugh of St. Victor *De sacramentis* 2. 3. 12 and 2. 6. 6; Peter Lombard *Sent.* 4, d. 13, c. 1; Thomas Aquinas *Summa theol.* 3, q. 82. Already in the eleventh century, Peter Damian gives a fairly lengthy description of the Eucharistic celebrant's *ministerial* role (*Liber qui dicitur gratissimus*, cc. 2–3).

98. Perhaps because of Augustine's texts that speak of the effective word of sacrament as being the word of Christ, there was much more stress on the Eucharistic celebrant as representing Christ than as representing the church. The notion of the Mass as a legation in which the celebrant carries the petitions of the people to God, a notion that was prominent in the ninth and tenth centuries (e.g., Rabanus Maurus *De cleric. institutione*, bk. 1, c. 33), practically disappears, though it resurfaces in the sixteenth century. One can notice the clear emphasis on the priest as *acting upon* the bread and wine by transubstantiating them, and the people by administering sacraments to them, rather than as *representing* the people before God: "Sacerdos . . . est sacrum dans sacerdos a sanctificando vocatus est: consecrat enim et sanctificat" (Peter Lombard *Sent.* 4, d. 24, c. 11). And Gratian entitles the section of his *Decretum* which deals with the ministry of sacrament *"De consecratione."* The continuity of this mentality throughout the Middle Ages can be seen in Biel's *Canonis Misse Ex-*

positio (lect. 4): "Apellantur et sacerdotes quia sacra ministrantes seu dantes. Solis enim sacerdotibus ratione officii inest sacrorum sacramentorum ministrandi potestas. Vel sacerdotes quasi sacra dicentes, quia verbum dei predicare habent, horas dicere, missas celebrare. Vel sacerdotes quasi sacra conficientes, conficiunt nanque sacratissimum christi corpus."

99. All the medieval treatments of the Eucharist ask the question about the fruitfulness of the Eucharist when celebrated by an unworthy minister, and quite universally maintain an essential effectiveness to the action, independent of the celebrant's state of soul. This begins to shift somewhat with Wyclif and the resurgence (in fourteenth and fifteenth centuries) of Donatism; see H. Oberman, *Harvest of Medieval Theology* (Cambridge, Mass., 1963), pp. 220–22.

   One of the important elements that develops in the theology of sacramental ministry is that of "applying the merits of Christ (or of the church)." The notion that this is what the Eucharistic celebrant (or the celebrant of other sacraments) does, ties in with an increasing stress on a moralistic interpretation of sacraments and an increasing intrusion of jurisdiction into the realm of the *potestas ordinis*. See Bonaventure *Brev.* 6. 10. 7.

100. However, an important distinction develops in the explanation of the Eucharistic celebrant's role—between his consecration of the elements (which is seen as his cultic or priestly role) and his administering Communion (which is seen as his ministerial role). Hugh of St. Victor (*De sacramentis* 2. 3. 10) already enunciates the principle ". . . just as in the priesthood there is consecration, so in the ministry there is dispensation of the sacrament"—though he sees the one action as proper to presbyter and the other to deacon. In Thomas Aquinas (*Summa theol.* 3, q. 82, a. 3) there is a close relation of consecrating and administering the Eucharist, but it is quite clear that the distinction is a common one with which he has to deal and that it is related to the practical question of the deacon's role in the Eucharistic action. However, in Bonaventure the distinction is greater and carries over into a distinction between performing the act of worship and administering the sacraments that will heal sinners. (*Brevil.* 6. 12. 9–16.)

   One of the clearest medieval summations of the ordained priest's (including presbyters and bishops) role and powers is that given by John of Paris in chap. 12 of his *De potestate regia et papali*: "Potestas consecrationis que interdum dicitur character vel potestas ordinis . . . potestas administrationis sacramentorum et precipue sacramenti penitentie . . . potestas sive auctoritas apostolatus sive predicationis . . . potestas iudiciaria scilicet correctionis in foro exteriori . . . potestas disponendi ministros ecclesie et determinandi iurisdictionem [a power reserved to the pope] . . . potestas accipiendi necessaria ad congruentem vite sustentationem." Interestingly, there is no specific mention of sacrifice in this passage (actually, "*sacerdotium*" is defined in other terms: ". . . Sacerdotium non est aliud nisi potestas spiritualis ministris ecclesiae collata ad dispensandum fidelibus sacramenta gratiam continentia qua ordinamur in vitam aeternam"), but in chap. 19 it is clear that the offering of sacrifice is the proper and specifying action of priesthood.

101. Even in Thomas Aquinas' treatment in the *Summa theologica* (3, qq. 73–83) there is a striking absence of any explanation of the Eucharistic action—how it is the sacrifice of Christ and of the church, how it operates sacramentally, how it is a "mystery-action," how it is supreme worship, etc.

102. See Leeming, pp. 497–541; Anciaux, pp. 116–17; J. Leclercq, *Saint Pierre Damien* (Rome, 1960), pp. 231–34; Berresheim, p. 266; Oberman, pp. 220–21; J. Gerson, *De potest. eccles.*, consid. prima.

103. On the roots and development of Wyclif's views, see E. Delaruelle in Fliche-Martin, vol. 14, pp. 943–59.

104. On Gregory VII's decree (in connection with the Roman council of 1074) and its relative failure to accomplish Gregory's purposes, see A. Fliche in Fliche-Martin, vol. 8, pp. 70–75.

105. See E. Iserloh, *Handbook of Church History*, vol. 4, pp. 580–85; also Delaruelle, pp. 883–941, 1031–100, who indicates the elements of increasing spiritual decline but

describes also the important movements of reform that arose during the late Middle Ages.

106. Of particular interest and importance were the confraternities, which were prominent throughout the Middle Ages and even more so towards the end of that period; see Delaruelle, pp. 666–93.

107. See J.-M. Dechanet and F. Vandenbroucke, *Dictionnaire de spiritualité*, vol. 2, cols. 1948–2013.

108. One of the most far-reaching and perhaps the most important of the late medieval reform movements was the so-called *devotio moderna* (see R. Garcia-Villoslada, *New Catholic Encyclopedia*, vol. 4, pp. 831–32; Delaruelle, pp. 911–41). Among those associated with this broad current of Christian revival none was more prominent and influential than Gerson, who in many ways exemplifies the best in late medieval clerical culture and the sincere attempts by clerics themselves to halt and reverse the decadence of the church's life in the fourteenth and fifteenth centuries. See Delaruelle, pp. 837–60.

109. See E. Vacandard, *Dictionnaire de théologie catholique*, vol. 2, cols. 2085–87; P. Delhaye, *New Catholic Encyclopedia*, vol. 3, pp. 372–73.

110. There is fairly frequent mention of this abuse in fourteenth- and fifteenth-century writings; however, the nature and motivation of such writing needs to be carefully assessed. If there was criticism of the friars and their way of life, there was also a great deal of popular support for them. See Moorman, pp. 346–49. The Black Death apparently paved the way for much of the decadence which did set in, and official documentation of the mendicant orders along with their reform decrees point to the presence of serious scandals; see Delaruelle, pp. 1067–68, 1085–87.

111. This is reflected, for example, in the reform decrees of the various synods convoked by Nicholas of Cusa when (in 1451 and 1452) he journeyed about much of Europe as papal legate. Clerical concubinage shows up regularly in these reform regulations, which would seem to indicate its prevalence. See Iserloh, *Handbook*, pp. 588–90.

112. Among the dominant elements in this argumentation (apart from all the practical aspects of seeing that ecclesiastical property was not alienated, that church ministers did not come too much under secular control, etc.) were the notions that sexual relations somehow "soiled" one, somehow diminished one's bodily and personal integrity; that sexuality was an entangling force that drew one away from the realm of the spirit and therefore from contemplation; that sexuality was too closely allied with the profane and therefore inappropriate in one as deeply involved in the cult and the sacred as an ordained priest was; that the ordained priest who offered sacrifice should himself live a life of sacrifice which was somehow epitomized in the sacrifice of celibate life. All of these had been expressly developed during the patristic period; see H. Crouzel, "Le célibat et la continence dans l'Eglise primitive: Leurs motivations," *Sacerdoce et célibat*, ed. J. Coppens (Louvain, 1971), pp. 333–71. See also in the same volume the essay of A. Stickler, "L'évolution de la discipline du célibat dans l'Eglise en Occident de la fin de l'âge patristique au Concile de Trente" (pp. 373–442).

113. On the extent to which "married or "celibate" became the discriminating mark between laity and clergy, see Congar, "L'ecclésiologie de S. Bernard," p. 166.

114. There are a number of fascinating interrelationships between the view of celibacy as a superior way of life and other viewpoints that downgrade the ordinary and the secular: the suspicion that many in religious circles felt towards secular pursuits of knowledge as not being pious enough, the idea that one had to push beyond the literal meaning of Scripture so that one could find the religious meaning in the allegorical sense, the view that genuine involvement with human life and its concerns was a barrier to contact with God in prayer.

115. See the development of this view in H. Daniel-Rops, *Cathedral and Crusade* (New York, 1963), pp. 220–58.

116. See C. Brooke, *Medieval Church and Society* (London, 1971), pp. 69–99.

CHAPTER 31

Challenge and Response

Apart from the second and third centuries, which witnessed the evolution of Christian ministry from its primitive Christian community function into a pattern of institutionalized existence, no period of history is more critical to a study of Christian ministry and priesthood than is the sixteenth century. This century of the Reformation was the time when there emerged explicitly and unavoidably questions that had long agitated theologians and Christian pastors, questions of doctrine and questions of practice. More dramatically, this century saw the explosion of Christian cultic life into a fragmented pattern, into greatly diversified forms of worship. Accompanying this, there arose a wide variety of theological views regarding the nature and necessity of Christian ministry. So determinative were the theological and pastoral positions taken by Reformers and Roman Catholicism during that period that they have provided the pattern of faith and life for the various churches up to the present time.

Basic Background Positions

If historical study of the Protestant Reformation has proved anything it is that the Reformation was to a great extent an outgrowth of religious unrest that had long been present and a coalescence of theological opinions that had existed for at least two centuries. For that reason, it is good to reiterate three theological views of the cult role of the ordained minister, views that represent the three principal schools of theology at the beginning of the sixteenth century and which

therefore typify the theological positions that the reformers, Protestant and Catholic alike, either reacted against or accepted. These are the positions of Thomas Aquinas, Duns Scotus, and Gabriel Biel.

Thomas Aquinas

Of the various medieval explanations of ministry and priesthood, particularly as related to cult, the one that was destined to have the widest apparent influence was that of Thomas Aquinas. This is particularly true if one considers only the more obvious elements of Aquinas' explanation, without probing to the metaphysical presuppositions that give deeper and more precise meaning to his theological insights into Christian ministry.[1] Much of later Catholic theology on priesthood consists in repetition or comment upon Aquinas' explanation; the formulations of Trent on this point, while not tied to any particular school position, are open to the Thomistic interpretation given by many post-Tridentine theologians.

Assuming (as does all Christian theology of priesthood) that the only per se priesthood in the Christian dispensation is that of Christ himself, who is the unique and eternal high priest, Thomas Aquinas sees the entire Christian people as having a basic share in this priesthood; they are a priestly people.[2] At the same time, there is another mode of sharing in this priesthood of Christ, a mode that comes with the sacrament of ordination and that is active in its orientation as opposed to the somewhat passive (or receptive) nature of the common priesthood that follows upon baptism; this priesthood of the ordained is the power of *giving* rather than simply *receiving* sacraments.[3]

Since the key manifestation of Christ's own priesthood comes in the supreme cultic act of his death and resurrection,[4] the principal function of the ordained Christian priest is the celebration of the Eucharist;[5] it is here that Christ's own priestly worship is made effectively present in the midst of the worshiping community.[6] The basic power involved in the *potestas ordinis* that comes with presbyteral ordination is that of confecting the Eucharist, of transforming the bread and wine into the sacramental body and blood of Christ.[7] Subordinate to this, which is the supreme exercise of ministerial office and the supreme moment of the church's existence, are the other powers of the ordained; these are the powers of preparing the Christian people for the Eucharist by providing penitential absolution, preaching the gospel, and governing the community so that harmony is maintained.[8]

Presbyterate and episcopacy together form the reality of Christian ministerial priesthood to which diaconate (and to a much lesser degree the other "orders") is joined.[9] Though episcopacy is not a distinct order, it is the fullness of the *ordo sacerdotalis* and has reserved to itself certain powers, particularly that of ordination.[10] Ontologically, ordained priesthood is constituted by the sacramental character of orders, caused in the person by his ordination and lasting irremovably to the end of life.[11] Distinct from both grace and faith, the character is a modification of the spiritual aspect of man (more specifically of his intellectual power) which assimilates him to Christ as priest and enables him to perform effectively the rites of sacramental worship.[12]

In the performance of the Christian ritual the ordained minister, bishop or presbyter, acts as the instrument of Christ, who is the principal agent of the sacraments. But the Christian minister acts as a *human* instrument, i.e., precisely as *minister Christi*, channeling and specifying by his own understanding and intent the divine causative intentionality.[13] Thus, the Eucharistic celebrant does not primarily give expression to his own intent and understanding but to the communal faith and intent of the church, and beyond that to the redeeming intent of the Head of the church.[14]

Duns Scotus

While some subtle differences can be noticed, e.g., in the discussion as to whether episcopate is a distinct order, Scotus inclines more than does Aquinas towards accepting episcopate as a distinct order,[15] the basic positions of Aquinas and Scotus on the cultic reality of Christian ministry seem very close. However, this is true if one is looking at the positive theological elements of their teaching; on the level of metaphysical interpretation of this positive doctrinal data there is, of course, the deep difference that comes from their diverse views of sacramental causality.[16]

With Aquinas (and for that matter with the entirety of medieval theology) Scotus sees the essential power of the ordained priest to be that of effecting the transubstantiation of the bread and wine and thus confecting the Eucharist.[17] He does not see this as the basic power of the keys (as Bonaventure does), but he seems to hold that the power of the keys follows by way of congruity from this power of transubstantiation.[18] Like Aquinas, Scotus links this Eucharistic power to the sacramental character conferred in ordination,[19] but in accord with his basic philosophical categories he locates the reality of the character in a title to divine concurrence rather than in an intrinsic modification of man's intellectual power.[20]

When we turn from Scotus' discussion of the sacrament of orders to his explanation of the Eucharistic sacrifice and of the ordained priest's role in this sacrificial action, we discover a basic and (in the light of sixteenth-century theological disputes about the Mass) very significant opposition to the view of Thomas Aquinas. He does not develop the point at length, but it seems quite clear that Aquinas understands the action of the Mass as one in which Christ himself is present and active, working through the celebrant as his minister; the celebrant acts essentially *in persona Christi*—he is the *minister of Christ*.[21] Scotus on the contrary sees the celebrant acting rather *in persona ecclesiae*; Christ himself is not immediately present and actively offering the sacrifice, but it is the will and intent of the church that is effective of the sacrificial offering and the celebrant is the instrument (minister) of this intention of the church.[22] Thus, the way is open to considering the Mass as the church's own sacrificial action, related to and drawing upon Christ's own act of sacrifice but not identified with it.

Gabriel Biel

Though a devoted follower of Ockham and a prominent representative of the theological *via moderna* which along with Thomism and Scotism provided the three dominant schools at the beginning of the sixteenth century, Biel is quite close to Scotus in his notions of priesthood and ministry.[23] Discussing the various meanings of *"sacerdos"* in his explanation of the canon of the Mass, Biel lists three functions: "They are called priests because they administer or give sacred things; for only priests have by reason of their office the power of administering the sacred sacraments. Or they are priests in so far as they say sacred things; because they preach the word of God, recite the divine office, and celebrate Mass. Or they are priests in so far as they confect sacred things, for they confect the most holy body of Christ."[24]

Several things might be noted about this statement. Not only does Biel distinguish the function of ministering to the word from that of Eucharistic ministration or that of Eucharistic transubstantiation, but he distinguishes the latter two from one another. This is not new to Biel. Scotus had already done so, and others like Bonaventure before him. What is interesting in Biel is that pastoral administration of the Eucharist is not a function of *ministry* (which can therefore be shared with the deacons, since they are ministers, though not priests), whereas confection of the Eucharist is seen as a cultic or strictly *priestly* act; both are viewed as properly *priestly*. Among the priestly functions mentioned in this passage, that which is unquestionably preeminent is confection of the Eucharist.[25] However, in his explanation of the manner in which the Eucharistic celebrant participates in the effecting of transubstantiating,[26] Biel follows faithfully the Scotus-Ockham concentration on the divine *will*: God has so determined things that when the Eucharistic celebrant performs the proper external acts with the proper intent, etc., the creative power of God will bring about the change of bread into the body of Christ.[27] Though his causal explanation of the celebrant's role may differ radically from some theologians, particularly those in the Thomistic school, Biel's insistence on the preeminence of priestly dignity because of the power to bring about the Eucharistic change is a late medieval commonplace. The superiority of the Christian priesthood over that of Old Testament Israel consists precisely in this that the former is taken from among men "in order to prepare, consecrate, offer, consume and dispense that purest food of the soul."[28]

One of the most interesting and important aspects of Biel's teaching about the efficacy (and reality) of the Eucharistic action is his emphasis on the faith and intention of the church. Perhaps it was because of his strong conviction about the power of the church's faith and intention that he opts in favor of the reality and effectiveness of sacraments performed by an unworthy minister, a long-standing question that was hotly debated in Biel's day because of a rising current of Donatism.[29] Linked with this view (as well as with his view on Eucharistic causality) is Biel's relatively greater emphasis on the Eucharistic celebrant as *minister ecclesiae* rather than as *minister Christi*, another similarity to Scotus.[30]

The Cultic Aspect of Ministry

Because of the obvious overlap in the understanding of cultic ministry and the

understanding of the nature of cult, a theological investigation of Reformation thought
about the cultic aspect of Christian ministry
must incorporate study of the various Reformation views on worship. Concretely, theological discussion in the sixteenth century
about the nature of Christian cultic ministry
is but a part of the basic Reformation dispute
about the nature of the Eucharist as sacrifice.

Lutheranism

Without detracting from the distinctive
contribution of Martin Luther or from the
unparalleled influence of his own activity and
teaching, a consideration of Lutheran origins
(particularly a consideration of the genesis of
Lutheran understanding of worship) must
reach beyond him to include the developments that resulted in the documents contained in the *Book of Concord*. It is this
entire sixteenth-century evolution of thought
that provides the foundation for the seventeenth-century construction of Lutheran theological orthodoxy.

Brunotte in his lengthy study of Luther's
understanding of Christian ministry concludes that Luther's thought remains constant
from "The Babylonian Captivity" (1520) to
"On the Councils and Churches" (1539),[31]
but it seems hard to avoid the impression that
there was an evolution (at the very least an
evolution in emphasis) from the very strong
reaction against traditional Roman stress on
sacramentalism that one finds in early writings (e.g., in the *Babylonian Captivity*) to a
more positive acceptance in later writings of
sacraments and their importance. This shift
touches Luther's explanation both of the nature of Christian worship and of the nature of
cultic ministry. To some extent this evolution
was tied to Luther's involvement after 1524 in
the disputes about Christ's presence in the
Eucharist.[32] It would be a misreading of
Luther to accentuate the polarities involved
by saying that he rejects ordained sacramental
ministry in his earliest works, or by suggesting
that he gradually comes to agree with Roman
Catholic teaching as represented by Trent's
decree on Holy Orders. However, the *De in-*

stituendis ministris ecclesiae (in 1523) already
seems to offer more possibility of positive relation to Catholic theology, particularly in the
way it develops the key distinction between
priesthood and ministry, than does the *De
captivitate babylonica*.[33]

Perhaps Luther's position can be clarified
by relating it to a distinction that had been
developing in medieval theology since the
thirteenth century: the distinction between
offering sacrifice and administering sacraments. This distinction applied to the function of the Eucharistic celebrant takes different forms in different theologians (as, for
example, in Scotus and Biel), but it seems in
general to correspond to a distinction between
cultic and pastoral functions of the celebrant.
When the celebrant is seen as offering the
Eucharist in worship of God, he is "priestly"
in his role; when he is seen as providing for
the people the sacred food of the Eucharist or
performing the action of the Mass so that the
merits of Christ's passion and death can be
applied to people's salvation, he is "ministerial" in his activity. When we come to the
Protestant Reformers, it seems that they (each
in his own way) utilize this distinction and
reject the cult role and distinctive priestliness
of the ordained while retaining a special and
official ministerial function regarding sacraments. Luther fits into this picture, not in
the sense that he opposes emphasis on the
Lord's Supper as worship but in the sense that
he sees the priesthood that is exercised in this
action as being that of the entire people.

Central, of course, to Luther's view of
Christian ministry and priesthood is his teaching about the basic priesthood possessed by all
believers. Intertwined with this is his treatment of the two critical distinctions: that
between clergy and laity, and that between
ministry and priesthood.[34] In itself, the
teaching of the common priesthood possessed
by Christians because of their baptismal faith
and share in the priesthood of Christ was not
new. Based on texts such as 1 Peter 2:5, traditional theology had always taught the existence of this fundamental priestly identity of
the Christian people. The doctrine is fre-

quently mentioned during the patristic period, carries on into the Middle Ages as a theological commonplace, and continues through the period of the Reformation into modern theology, both Catholic and Protestant.[35] However, the operative understanding of this fundamental Christian priesthood had been obscured for many centuries by the claim of the bishops and presbyters that they were the *sacerdotium*, and long before the sixteenth century the word "priest" had become a proper denomination for the presbyters in the church. Moreover, in the life of the church, most critically in the celebration of Eucharistic liturgy, the laity had been deprived of practically all active roles and so could scarcely think of themselves as either priestly or ministerial. Luther's great contribution was to draw attention again to this basic reality of Christianity and to utilize it as a principle for theological analysis and for practical structuring of Christian community.

Grounded in this insight into the priesthood of believers, Luther's denial of an essential difference between clergy and laity is unmistakable, appears immediately in his reformation thought, and persists throughout his writings.[36] Luther does not deny the need for a designated ministerial group in the church, nor does he understand the priesthood of each believer in an individualistic sense.[37] However, he denies to any group within the church a special claim to priestly powers or priestly prerogatives; all Christians are basically equal in their Christian dignity, spiritual capabilities, and evangelical responsibilities. While some may be designated to perform more officially the tasks of preaching the word and administering sacraments, these are only doing what each Christian has the power to do. One of the things that makes it easier for Luther to insist on the radical possession of priestly power and responsibility by each Christian is his emphasis on the evangelical rather than cultic nature of this priesthood.[38]

We have already treated the essentially evangelical understanding of the office in Luther and in Lutheranism after him, but it is good to advert here to the emphasis on the ministry of sacrament as itself being an element in the ministry of the word.[39] The focus comes, of course, in Luther's understanding of the Eucharist. One must be careful not to distort Luther's rejection of what he considered erroneous Roman views on the Mass as sacrifice, nor to overlook his important stress on the prophetic (or proclamation) aspect of the Eucharistic action. Luther's theology of the Eucharist is not, nor could it under the circumstances be expected to be, an adequate development of his seminal insights; but it does not itself allow for the unfortunate cleavage between word and sacrament which is found in so much later Reformation and post-Reformation theology.

It is difficult to say which came first in the evolution of Luther's thought, the denial of distinction between clergy and laity or the assertion of distinction between priesthood and ministry. Ultimately the denial and the assertion are inseparable, but the distinction between priesthood and ministry is much harder to clarify and to maintain. One can, of course, reserve the term "ministry" for the official function by which a designated few provide in public and permanent fashion for the preaching of the word and the performance of sacrament. This is the common way in which Luther himself (and his commentators) distinguish ministry from priesthood.[40] The problem comes, though, when one tries to compare the nature of ministry to the nature of priesthood. At this point, the two seem to coincide in Luther's theology: all believers, by virtue of their common priesthood, are meant to minister evangelically; the designated minister is performing on behalf of the priestly community the tasks that rest basically on the community as a whole. It seems that one must conclude that Luther, though he had the insight to distinguish between the priesthood possessed by the entire people and the ministry belonging to the ordained, was never able satisfactorily to distinguish and relate these two realities.[41]

In conformity with his insistence that two elements are required for the existence of a true Christian community, genuine preaching of the word and authentic celebration of sacrament, Luther sees the principal function of the ordained minister to lie in pastoral preaching of the gospel, to which is linked the administration of sacraments. The fact that someone is chosen, ultimately by God but more proximately by the community,[42] to minister in this regard does not mean that he possesses such ministerial authority more intrinsically than any other member of the community; rather, it means that he is commissioned by the community to function in this regard as its representative and by its comission.[43]

For Luther, the officially recognized minister has the role and function he possesses because of community choice and delegation, but his ordination does not add any new spiritual quality to him. Whatever he has by way of enabling power he possesses in virtue of the priesthood that he shares with his fellow believers.[44] That is why, in case of need, any baptized Christian can perform the actions ordinarily considered the proper task of the official ministers.

Confessional and Orthodox Lutheranism

Moving from Luther's own views to the understandings reflected in documents gathered in the *Book of Concord*, one notices not a change from Luther's teaching but a somewhat different stress on some of the elements with which Luther dealt.[45] Whether it is due to Melanchthon's influence or not, the confessions stress even more than Luther the fundamental and all-embracing ministry of the *word*, pay relatively little attention to the priesthood of all believers, and insist on the divine institution of the office of ministry, emphases which one finds in Melanchthon.[46] Accepting the medieval distinction between orders and jurisdiction, the confessions consider both the preaching and administration of sacraments (which are the *potestas ordinis*) and the reconciliation and excommunication of sinners (the *potestas jurisdictionis*) as belonging to the ordained ministry *de jure divino*. Moreover, the divine authentication of the ministry extends to the tasks of judging doctrine, leading the community, and providing for community discipline.[47] While the ministry is considered basically as a function, the confessions do treat it also as an order in the church,[48] without denying Luther's rejection of a basic clergy-laity dichotomy. One of the aspects of the confessions' treatment that highlights the official and public nature of the ordained ministry is the clearly anti-Donatist position regarding the activity of unworthy ministers. While obviously the presence of such in the church is regrettable, the unworthiness of the minister does not deprive preaching or administration of sacraments of their efficacy.[49]

With the doctrinal position of Lutheranism clearly established by the 1580 recognition of the *Book of Concord* as official confession, the next logical step of development was an analysis of the principles involved in these confessional statements and a systematic realignment into a theological synthesis. This was accomplished by Lutheran orthodoxy in the seventeenth century.[50] Considering only this movement's explanation of worship and cultic ministry, it seems at first sight that this development of Lutheran scholasticism was quite faithful to Luther's own views.[51] There is clear emphasis on the primacy of the ministry of the word, on the worship liturgy as evangelical, and on faith as the key activity of the Christian in the Eucharistic action.

Facing the question "Is not participation in the Lord's Supper a 'good work' that wins reconciliation with God?" Lutheran orthodoxy worked out a more detailed exposition of the passive role of the believer vis-à-vis the word of God.[52] Such a position highlights the activity of God in the liturgical act and concomitantly the instrumental role of the officiating minister. "God not only instituted the sacraments, but He also dispenses them; not indeed directly (if we except the first Supper, which was administered by Christ Himself), but by ministers of the church. For since the minister dispensing the sacraments does not act in his own name, but in the name of God, and does not dispense some gift of his own, but that of another; therefore God Himself is rightly declared to be the principal dispenser of the sacraments."[53] However, the ordained minister acts not only in the name of God but also as the minister of the worshiping congregation, expressing its sacrificial offering of self to God.[54] While any baptized Christian could, if necessary, take over this ministerial role, the established ecclesiastical office of minister exists by divine right.[55]

Lutheran orthodoxy's divergence from Luther's own view of worship and sacramental ministry appears in terms of a legal-moralistic approach to the *obligation* of participating in the Lord's Supper. Not unlike early patristic reintroduction of Old Testament law in relation to Christian worship, Lutheran orthodoxy sees the celebration of Christian liturgy as fulfillment of the third command of the Decalogue.[56] This tends to shift the attitude from Luther's response of faith to the word to an act of obedience in conformity to law, a development that is quite un-Lutheran. And it is in this context that the *public* aspect of official worship is stressed in opposition to Pietism's emphasis on inner worship, for it is this established liturgy, under the leadership of ordained ministers, that fulfills the command to "keep holy the Sabbath."[57] It does not require much reflection to see lurking in this position the danger of clericalism in worship.

Bucer

Martin Bucer's views on ministry and priesthood did not find expression (as did those of Luther and Calvin) in a lasting institutionalization, yet his thought exerted important influence on other Reformers. His *De vera animarum cura* and *De regno Christi* are among the most significant treatments of ministry in the literature of the Reformation.[58] Even more so than Luther, Bucer represents a strong element of continuity with the Christian situation which preceded the Reformation, though his views on Christian worship gradually came to diverge much more than Luther's from the pre-Reformation understanding of the Eucharist. His empathy with late medieval Christian thought and practice is reflected in his irenic views and important involvement in attempts to avert a final split between Reformation and Rome;[59] it was reflected also in his insistence on church discipline as one of the three "notes" of the church. Closely identified as he was with the reform developments in Strasbourg where so much of the early thrust towards change dealt with revitalization of the liturgy, Bucer quite expectedly emphasized correct understanding of the Eucharist and authentic community involvement in this action. Yet, his emphasis in ministry is typical of the Reformation: the pastor is basically a minister of the word; through him Christ exhorts, forgives, and consoles his people.[60]

In line with his stress on the Christian community, Bucer emphasizes the priesthood of all believers; at the same time, he sees the offices of bishop, presbyter, and deacon as of divine origin[61] and their effectiveness as rooted in the Spirit's action through them.[62] Despite his early strong reaction against Roman views of church office and ministry, and his stress on mutual service of all Christians in the community, Bucer drew increasing attention to the pastoral office.[63] This office of pastor (in which bishops are included) involves the task of preaching and supervision of doctrine, and also supervision of the parishioners. In these tasks the pastors are assisted by elders who are meant to be models of Christian behavior and to share in the disciplinary government of the community.[64] The tasks in which these elders assisted the pastor were: *doctrina, exhortatio, monitio, correctio, increpatio, castigatio, precum usus, et tota officii pastoralis administratio*—a listing which clearly reflects emphasis on the ministry of the word and on discipline.[65] On the other hand, the leadership role in liturgy seems to be reserved to the pastor.

Obviously, Bucer's understanding of the nature of Eucharist controlled his understanding of the nature of sacramental ministry. Thus, his rapidly changing views on the Eucharist must have been reflected in his view of the ministerial role, but there is no clear indication of this in his writings.[66] Perhaps the most enduring and controlling elements in Bucer's theology of ministry were the salvific presence of the Spirit in the action of the ministry, and the function of the ministry in helping achieve truly Christian community.

Calvin

Grasping the view of Calvin on sacramental ministry and situating it in the spectrum of Reformation thought is difficult, precisely because Calvin's understanding of the Eucharist is hard to describe. Much of his thought on sacrament and sacramental ministry is contained in the Eucharistic controversies with Luther and Zwingli and more radically (if somewhat less voluminously) with Roman Catholicism. It probably is in his opposition to what he considered the abuses and errors of pre-Reformation teaching and practice that Calvin's most important convictions about the nature of priesthood, worship, and ministry are apparent.[67] He clearly rejects an excessive realism regarding the presence of Christ in Eucharist and a concentration on the elements of bread and wine, though he does not reject a real presence of Christ in the Christian celebration of the Lord's Supper.[68] He rejects the Roman theology of Eucharist as sacrificial action, though he does not deny that in a correct sense the Eucharistic action can be called a sacrifice.[69] He does follow the basic Reformation tendency of opting for administration of sacrament rather than cultic offering of sacrifice as the proper role of the Eucharistic celebrant; but it would be a mistake to underestimate the importance of cultic worship (understood, of course, in his own fashion) in Calvin's view of Christian faith and life.[70]

Like Luther, Calvin sees the church as truly existent wherever there is authentic preaching of the gospel and genuine celebration of sacrament, and like Luther he places the dynamism and efficacy of sacrament within the operation of the word.[71] However, the understanding of word and sacrament in Calvin's theology is quite distinct from that found in Luther and his followers.[72] For one thing, there is greater emphasis on what might be called the spiritual character of Christian worship. The word "spiritual" here can be applied both to Calvin's stress on the psychological element of human faith response to the Eucharist as "word of promise" and to his stress on the action of the Spirit in Eucharist.[73] While Luther rejected any crass understanding of the bodily presence of Christ in the Eucharist, and rejected also the doctrine of transubstantiation, he still kept a static and spatially realistic view of the real presence. Calvin, on the contrary, espoused a more dynamic view without denying a bodily presence of Christ which makes it possible for the believer to enter into communion with Christ.[74] Sacraments, and the Lord's Supper in particular, are professions of faith and acts of worship, but they can be this on man's part only because they are more radically God's actions of promise, i.e., they are proclamation of the gospel.[75]

Calvin's outlook on worship and sacramental act has a number of implications for Christian ministry. First, the institution of official ministry does not grow out of the priesthood of all believers nor depend upon it; rather, the ordained ministry comes from God. It is an order instituted by God and it functions effectively because the Spirit works in and through it.[76] It is meant to be a service to the universal priesthood of the people. A man entrusted with the ministry must be duly selected by the community (or by leadership within the community), but such human designation should be essentially a recognition of the gifts already bestowed by the Spirit.[77] Somewhat paradoxically, this insistence on the divine origin of ministry (which gives it an authority to which the community owes obedience) coexists in Calvin's thought with a rejection of any lay-clergy distinction. Part of the solution to this paradox lies in Calvin's reestablishment (according to a New Testament pattern, and as he saw it practiced in Basel and Strasbourg) of elders and deacons, ministers who can be identified simply neither as clergy nor as laity, and who effectively undertake much of the government of the community.[78]

The authority which attaches to official ministry comes not from any special personal dignity of the minister nor even from the office he holds[79] but from the power of the Word and the Spirit which works in the ministry. For Calvin, the pastoral ministry is essentially the proclamation of the gospel through word and sacrament; the pastor is servant of the word.[80] This concentration on the ministry of the word is reflected in Calvin's emphasis on teaching. Not only is the pastor essentially a transmitter of the word of God but another distinct office, teacher, exists exclusively for the explanation of the word.[81] It is reflected also in Calvin's understanding of the sacraments themselves as evangelical,[82] though his view is not as purely homiletic as is that of Zwingli.[83]

In the sacramental acts, as in his other preaching, the ordained pastor is the ambassador of Christ himself in bringing reconciliation to the Christian community.[84] He acts as a principle of unity for the community, and in helping achieve this objective he is servant both of the Lord and of the community.[85] More correctly, the word which he proclaims in his sacramental role is the source of unity among the people; the role of the minister is to be servant of the sacramental sign which he places as the ambassador of Christ.[86] It is the word they proclaim, not the ministers themselves, which possesses authority; if their ministry is effective, this is due to the power of the Spirit which accompanies the word and works through their ministry. Thus, Calvin's view of the action of ministers in the sacraments, particularly in the Lord's Supper, is truly sacramental.[87] One of the intriguing questions about Calvin's view of ministry is why, in the light of his emphasis on the evangelical nature of sacrament, he does not describe this ministerial function as prophetic; instead, he links the role of *teacher* with the ministry of prophecy.[88]

Finally, there is the question of the relation

(if any) which Calvin sees between the ordained ministry and a ministerial priesthood. On the explicit level, Calvin does not apply the word "priest" to any of the ministerial functions, even the pastoral role of Eucharistic minister; the term is reserved for the unique priesthood of Christ and secondarily for the universal priesthood of the people. On the implicit level, Calvin does see the pastor as the ambassador of Christ's priestly work of reconciliation, therefore reductively a priest in his ministry.[89] But clearly this is a much different notion of "priest" than that of a cultic offerer of sacrifice.

Zwingli

In even more pronounced fashion, Zwingli emphasizes the preaching element in the ministerial role practically to the exclusion of what one would ordinarily think of as cultic. The worship assembly, having developed into a key didactic occasion, tends to lose its character as presence of the numinous or even as acknowledgment of the divine in favor of the congregation's religious education. This is connected, of course, with Zwingli's suspicion of sacraments as at least potentially idolatrous and more fundamentally with his almost Nestorian approach to Christology.[90] Since nothing bodily is capable of mediating the spiritual influence of God upon the faith of the assembled Christians, there can be no question of the external actions of the worship ceremony (or of the actions of the ordained minister) acting in a sacramental fashion.[91]

This is more than an underlying implication of Zwingli's teaching. In the successive actions of the Zurich city council regarding public worship, actions that were inspired and guided by Zwingli's reforming agitation, one can see clearly a progressive decultifying of the liturgy.[92] Moreover, Zwingli's establishment in 1525 of a training program in prophecy (i.e., careful education in Scripture with the practical aim of preparing trained preachers) gives clear evidence of the strictly evangelical function he planned for the ordained ministry.[93] For Zwingli, the pastor seems to have only two identities: minister of the word and leader of the community.

Anglicanism

Insight into the Anglican understanding of priesthood and ministry is complicated by the pluralism of theological opinion and the oscillation of official policy within the Church of England, by the fact that the Church of England's origin is to be explained to quite an extent by political pragmatism rather than by theological interest, and by the manner in which the struggles within the Church of England between episcopalianism and presbyterianism were interlocked with the conflict between monarchical and representative forms of civil government.[94] Moreover, the geographical and political situation of Britain made it impractical to resolve doctrinal conflicts by the continental strategy of *cujus regio, ejus religio*, and so the government (civil and ecclesiastical) of England, in order to preserve national unity, moved more towards tolerant acceptance of divergent religious views than it did towards theological unanimity.[95]

Granted the political origins of the English Reformation and Henry VIII's less than enthusiastic attitude towards Protestant theology, there was from the beginning an influential and determined Protestant-minded party within the leadership of the English church-state complex. Until his fall from power, Thomas Cromwell was the aggressive political angel of this Protestantizing thrust, but the principal ecclesiastical and theological agent in this movement was Thomas Cranmer. Thus, though he was by no means an isolated figure,[96] Cranmer's key role gives his theological views a particular significance not just for his own age but for the subsequent history of Anglicanism.[97]

Perhaps it is impossible to ascertain with certainty Cranmer's view (or views) on the nature of the Lord's Supper; but whether it was the same as Zwingli's,[98] or closer to Calvin's,[99] or coincident with Bullinger's developed Zwinglianism,[100] it is clear that the Eucharistic celebrant is not considered a cultic personage, a priest who is officiating at a sacrificial action.[101] Instead, the ordained minister is simply the one who administers to the faithful the Holy Communion; his principal and all-embracing function is (as in the Reformed tradition) clearly that of the ministry of the word.[102]

While the decidedly Protestant view of ministry held by Cranmer and associates such as Latimer and Ridley was not universally accepted in the sixteenth century (even apart from the reign of Mary Tudor), for on the one side the Puritans agitated for a more radically Reformed doctrine of the church and its ministry and on the other side the Catholic party insisted on a more priestly understanding of the clerical (and especially episcopal) office, the English church under Henry and Edward and Elizabeth definitely moved towards an evangelical and away from a cultic view of ministry. This is manifested not only in statements like those of the influential Bishop Jewel (early in Elizabeth's reign) which stressed the primacy of Scripture and the pre-eminence of the ministry of the word but in the somewhat paradoxical fact that there was conflict between Elizabeth and the bishops she had supported because she wished more attention given to liturgical ministry and they were instead fostering an emphasis on preaching.[103] At the same time, there was a basic liturgical emphasis in Anglicanism that preserved, despite a theological drift towards Calvinism, a more sacramental view of ministry.[104]

During the reign of Elizabeth, the English Reformation finds its systematic theological explanation in the *Ecclesiastical Polity* of Richard Hooker; but on the matter of sacramental (and especially Eucharistic) ministry, Hooker takes a practical (even pietist) line of solution rather than a truly theological approach to the questions that had agitated the sixteenth-century English church.[105] However, he gives much more of a genuine instrumentality to the Eucharist as source of grace than does Cranmer.[106] Though he favors "presbyter" rather than "priest" as a title for the ordained,[107] and clearly rejects the notion that the Eucharistic celebrant is offering sacrifice,[108] he speaks of "the principal work of the ministry . . . which consists in doing the services of God's house, and in applying unto men the sovereign medicines of grace."[109] And then, in most un-Protestant language, he goes on to speak of the ordained minister's power over both the mystical and natural body of Christ and to say that this power is not inappropriately "termed a kind of mark or character and acknowledged to be indelible."[110] It seems quite consonant with Hooker's statements to say that his emphasis in ministry is strongly sacramental, but pastoral rather than cultic (i.e., stressing the gift of grace through administration of sacrament).

Following upon Hooker's sacramental emphasis, the Caroline Divines gave to Anglican faith and the liturgy of the *Book of Common Prayer* an understanding that can truly be called both Catholic and reformed. Without drawing back from the Reformation stress on the key importance of the ministry of the word, Andrewes and Laud and Jeremy Taylor reversed the tendencies towards Zwinglian understanding of the Eucharist and its ministry. Applying to the Eucharist the implications of his understanding of the Incarnation, Andrewes sees the union of reality and symbol in sacrament as analogous to the union of divine and human in Christ. The Eucharist is memorial, hence the unsurpassed evangelical importance of this action. But it is a true sacrificial act of memorial in which Christ is offered. It is an important reflection of the Eucharistic discussion of the Reformation and post-Reformation period that Andrewes distinguishes the Eucharist as *sacrifice* and *sacrament* in the best scholastic tradition, and that he links the sacrificial aspect of the Eucharist exclusively to the historical death of Jesus.[111] In his controversy with Bellarmine, Andrewes states clearly that the point of difference between them is not whether the Eucharist is a sacrifice but whether the understanding of Eucharistic sacrifice is tied to the notion of transubstantiation (which Andrewes rejects). This in turn leads to the difference in emphasis between private masses

and adoration of the host (which, says Andrewes, Bellarmine is defending) or reception of Christ in communion.[112] Thus, though he does not speak explicitly of the Eucharistic minister's role, Andrewes seems to indicate that the minister functions in official fashion in an act of memorial and sacrifice but with emphasis on his administration of the sacrament to the people.

William Laud is important not so much as the theorist among Caroline prelates but rather as the one who tried to give practical implementation to the theology of such men as Andrewes and Taylor. Perhaps his greatest contribution was the negative one of his own tragic failure: the lesson that liturgical reform cannot be achieved by legal imposition. However, though his own efforts to revitalize Eucharistic celebration collapsed with the Puritan ascendancy in mid-seventeenth century, the ideas contained in them found some continuity in the ecclesiastical provisions of the Restoration and in the Catholic wing of later Anglicanism. Laud was intent upon reviving the memorial aspect of the Eucharistic liturgy, and he saw this as linked with the notion of Eucharist as sacrifice. For him, the sacrificial reality of the Eucharist is threefold: there is the commemorative sacrifice of Christ's death (represented in the bread broken and the wine poured out), the offering made by the officiating priest alone; there is the communal sacrifice of praise and thanksgiving that is made by priest and people together; and there is the personal self-oblation of each individual.[113] Laud's emphasis on the sacrificial nature of the Eucharist was reflected in his efforts to restore the altar to its position in the churches, a practical measure that inevitably provided a somewhat different image of the officiating minister.

Of the Caroline divines, Jeremy Taylor provides the lengthiest and most detailed explanation of Eucharist and sacramental ministry. Much of his theology is polemic, though quite gentle in tone, and concentrated on the classic disputes about real presence, and transubstantiation. In these writings his thought is noticeably consonant with pre-

Reformation scholasticism and even with post-Tridentine Roman Catholic theology, except on the question of transubstantiation.[114] When his opponent is not Roman Catholicism but British presbyterianism, his treatment of the ministerial offices and functions of episcopacy and presbyterate is undeniably Catholic. He speaks of ordination (diaconal, presbyteral, and episcopal) as involving "the impress of a distinct character; that is, the person is qualified with a new capacity to do certain offices, which, before his ordination, he had no power to do."[115] One of these powers is that of Eucharistic consecration, which Taylor recognizes as common to presbyter and bishop.[116] But it is in his more devotional writings that Taylor's clearest and most positive understandings of sacramental ministry are enunciated: the ministry of Eucharist is both evangelical and sacramental, "the Lord's Supper is an appointed enunciation and declaration of Christ's death, and it is a sacramental participation of it";[117] Christ himself continues his priestly activity in heaven, and this heavenly liturgy is imaged forth in the Eucharistic action of the ordained priest who is Christ's minister;[118] and the Eucharist is a truly sacrificial offering which Christ makes of himself through the ministry of the Eucharistic celebrant.[119]

The impact of the Caroline theologians is hard to assess because of the divergent reactions within the English church to their views. Yet, it seems that in the establishment of Anglican tradition they performed a function not unlike that of seventeenth-century orthodoxy within the Lutheran communion.[120]

The Radical Reformation

The difficulty of discovering consistent currents of thought (or even discernible lines of evolution) about ministry in the Radical Reformation would tempt one to avoid the topic. Yet, discussion of the Reformation's approach to the question of priesthood and ministry would be truncated without some brief mention of the Radical Reformers. In some ways, these various fringe movements represent a more thoroughgoing expression of the Reformation's deepest searchings and aspirations than does the Magisterial Reformation, and so they help us see the important underlying issues. For one thing, the Radical Reformers asserted in sharper fashion the primacy of the individual Christian, the normative role of his faith and inspiration by the Spirit, and his radical independence from ecclesiastical structures in establishing rapport with the divine. Thus, though they developed little formalized theology about the ordained ministry (or about the reasons for abandoning it), and in some instances were inconsistent in their attitudes towards it, the radical reform communities present an important challenge to reappraise one's understandings of priesthood and ministry.[121]

The basically pneumatic and therefore charismatic character of these radical reform groups found expression in their worship. For the most part it moved away from what ordinarily would be thought of as liturgical or cultic and consisted rather in a prayer meeting devoted to explanation of and response to the Scripture. For the most part, such worship followed the basic Reformation accent on the preaching of the scriptural word; but in some instances (as in the Quaker meeting) there was a strong emphasis on the charismatic direction of prayer and community decision.

In such communities, the need for ordained ministers is less obvious: the call to community leadership lies more in the direction of prophetic charism than of ecclesiastical function or office, and emphasis on the universal priesthood (or some equivalent manner of expressing basic equality within the community) eliminates the role of ordained cultic professionals. At the same time, the continuing orderly existence of a community demands sociologically the gradual emergence of a governing group; this is found in each of the free churches, though it takes varied forms. In none of them, however, does such a leadership group have the character of a priestly ministry directed towards cult. To some extent, this is linked with the radical secularization of worship that takes place in these communities, i.e., application of the notion of worship to the entirety of life rather than to certain formally ritual activities; it is this that may constitute the Radical Reformation's deepest challenge to traditional theology of ministry.

Reformation Views of Ordination

For centuries prior to the Reformation, discussion of Holy Orders as a sacrament had quite exclusively dealt with the action of ordination rather than with the sacramental role of the ordained within the community. So, it is no surprise to find that ordination (its nature and necessity, its sacramentality, its effect) is a central issue in Reformation and post-Reformation controversy about ministry. What may be a surprise is to find that it is not possible to say simply that the Reformers reject ordination as a sacrament.

There is, of course, the classic Reformation tendency to limit the application of "sacrament" to baptism and the Lord's Supper, since only those two seem clearly instituted by Christ himself. But practically all the Reformers are willing to extend the term (with certain qualifications) to other rites. To some extent, the controversy over the number of sacraments is a matter of semantics, but it is complicated by the fact that the sixteenth century inherited an excessively univocal use of "sacrament" and a misleading set of theological questions about the nature of sacramental causality. All this finds special reference to the ritual of ordination, where it had long been realized that the giving of grace to the ordinand was secondary to his receiving spiritual power to serve the altar and the community.

Among the Reformers there is unanimity in seeing God himself as the source of designation for ministry, and the ceremony of ordination (whatever form it takes) as essentially a recognition of this divine calling.[122] Thus, whether one wishes to attribute any particular efficacy to the ordination ritual or not, the making of a minister of the gospel is looked

upon as basically the action of God and to this extent, at least, the ordination is sacramental of the divine choice.[123]

From Luther and Zwingli onward, the Reformation recognizes the need for public designation in some observable ceremony of men and women to perform ministerial functions in the church. However, the Lutheran tradition in particular insists that in case of need any Christian can perform any ministry by virtue of his baptismal priesthood. Such designation cannot, of course, be an arbitrary or sheerly pragmatic judgment by the community or by its leadership; two elements must be certified in a prospective minister: his vocation by God and his capability to perform the ministry in question.[124] The precise qualifications that are ratified by the community (or for practicality's sake more often ratified by the already existent ministerial group) vary according to the ministry in question, whether it is the "pastor" envisaged by Luther, or the "doctor" in Calvin's Geneva, or the "pastor" of Zwingli's Zurich. Differing mechanisms of selection, formation, screening, approbation, and appointment develop within the different Reformation communities, but some such mechanism is found quite universally, even to some extent in the Radical Reformation communities.

But though ordination in some sense is commonly accepted, there is a notable absence of the idea that such ordination places the individual on a special sacred level of Christian existence.[125] Yet, even this statement, which could be supported by innumerable texts in which the Reformers attack the pretensions to superiority on the part of the Roman clerics, has to be carefully delimited. Even the Reformers who stress the universal priesthood and basic equality of all Christians stress also the special good example expected from the ordained. Almost inevitably, the ordained ministers soon come to be looked upon as official Christians. Despite express and emphatic verbal rejection of a clergy/laity dichotomy, such a dichotomy continues into and throughout Protestantism's history. Ordination gave the minister a special social eminence, which (particularly in established church situations) often involved some political and economic and social prestige. Ordination also laid on the minister a heavier responsibility for society as a whole and he was expected to preach and exemplify moral respectability and the civic virtues. However, what had been the central image of the ordained presbyter, that of a sacrificing cult priest, is replaced in Protestantism by the image of the public functionary in religious matters.

One of the theological positions that is most widely held among Protestants of the sixteenth and seventeenth centuries is the denial that ordination causes any sacramental character in the minister. For Luther, ordination confers upon a man the function or office of ministry, but no new power is required to carry out this office, for the necessary power is possessed by each believing Christian.[126] For Calvin, ordination places a man in the position of being an instrument of God, but the efficacy of his ministerial activity depends not upon some new power inherent in him but upon the accompanying work of the Spirit.[127] Zwingli is quite explicit in his rejection of any *character indelibilis* by which the ordained would have special spiritual powers or status.[128] Yet, as one reads the various Reformers and discovers their strongly functional view of ministry, one cannot but wonder whether they would have rejected a view of sacramental character that was more dynamic and ecclesial and not so tied to hierarchical rank and to transubstantiation.

The Council of Trent

Though faced with serious and radical questioning of its traditional understandings of priesthood and ministry, the Roman Catholic church at the Council of Trent did little more than insist on certain theological explanations and ecclesiastical viewpoints that had been in existence for several centuries. Despite this fact, namely, its lack of creativity in facing the issues raised by the Reformation,[129] the council did provide in its doc-

trinal decree on Holy Orders an influential synthesis of one portion of Catholic understanding as it existed at the time of the Protestant Reformation. Trent's doctrinal formulation is historically important, of course, because it was the springboard for Catholic theology on this question until the mid-twentieth century. However, it is not just in the decree on the sacrament of orders that Trent's position on ministry is to be sought. The doctrinal decrees on sacraments in general and on the sacrifice of the Mass and the disciplinary decree on clerical reform are an integral part of the council's view on the nature and function of Christian ministry. The reform decrees in particular reflect that notion of priesthood and ministry which controlled the council's understanding of the ideal ordained minister, i.e., the goal towards which the reform measures are directed.

There are few things that one can say about the theological situation of the early sixteenth century without risk of argument. One thing, however, that seems quite clear is that Roman Catholic theology was ill-prepared for the challenge of the Reformation. It was particularly unprepared to deal with, or even to recognize clearly, the fundamental issues raised concerning ministry, priesthood, worship—issues that were central to the more commonly recognized questions of justification, ecclesiastical authority, or criteria for faith. To some extent, this unpreparedness is difficult to explain. The explicit questions raised by the Reformers and the solutions they proposed were not all that innovative; they had been proposed more than once before, quite explicitly and in rather harsh form by Wyclif (to give but one example). But for a variety of reasons, Catholic theology and ecclesiastical thought in general had been slow to recognize the deeper implications of these questions and the religious need to confront them straightforwardly. The Reformers understood that religious need without seeing adequately the theological issues involved.

For all practical purposes there is no advance in sixteenth-century Roman Catholic theology of priesthood and ministry beyond the scholasticism of the High Middle Ages. Driedo, Eck, Tapper, Gropper, Pighius, and others were competent theologians, and their treatment of priesthood and ministry is solid, respectable, and traditional. Their confrontations with theologians from the Reformation make it clear that they were skilled as theological debaters, but that very involvement in polemical discussion worked against their grasping the deeper issues and underlying suppositions of Reformation thought, and it also worked against the development of an imaginative and constructive approach to understanding Christianity and its ministry. Though it is always difficult to justify such judgments, it does seem (at least in the questions touching ministry) that the evolution of Roman Catholic theology as a counterattack against the teachings of the Reformers diverted attention from some of the better theological reflection and directed it to less important or even specious questions. Positions were taken in the heat of controversy which theologians on both sides would probably not have otherwise taken, positions which sometimes stand in open contradiction to statements made in other more pacific circumstances. An important case in point is the dispute over the priesthood of all believers. Two issues are at stake, and very often confused. There is the question about the distinction, if any, between the priesthood possessed by all Christians and that possessed by the ordained; and there is the question about the nature of Christian priesthood, whether it is priestly in a cultic sense or whether "priestly" should be translated as "prophetic." Or, to put it another way, there was the question of distinction between ordained and nonordained Christians, and the question as to whether Christianity was evangelical or sacramental. In many instances, including the Council of Trent, the tendency is to safeguard the preeminence of the ordained clergy by attributing genuine sacramental activity to them alone.[130]

Eck, for instance, in his dispute with Oeclampadius in 1526, seems to push into the background the active role of Christ as agent of the Eucharist, and to insist instead on the ordained minister as the one who offers sacrifice *"sicut minister Christianae ecclesiae."*[131] Apparently, this position persists into his later thought, for it is repeated almost verbatim in his Enchiridion in 1530.[132] At the same time, he is quite clearly not thinking of the entire community (i.e., the Body of Christ) actually entering into Christ's own offering of himself to the Father. This is evidenced by the way in which he reduces the common priesthood of the Christian people to priesthood in a purely spiritual and applied sense, sharply distinguished from the sacramental priesthood of the ordained.[133]

It was not as if Eck was unacquainted with the idea that Christ, working through the instrumentality of the priestly community which is his Body, constantly exercised his priesthood in the Eucharistic sacrifice. This view (which seems more profound, better calculated to confront the real issues being raised by Luther and his allies, and in less danger of separating the church's Eucharistic sacrifice from Christ's own sacrifice) was clearly proposed by Eck's contemporary, Schatzgeyer, whom Eck himself cites.[134] Much the same position was espoused by Bishop Michael Helding: ordination gives a man the power to function *in persona Christi* and so to offer Christ's own sacrifice, but when he does so in Eucharist he functions also as servant of the entire church, for the Eucharistic celebration is the action of the entire assembled community. Christ's own priesthood thus finds expression in the entire church, though with special sacramentality in the ordained minister of Eucharist.[135] Helding was thus able to admit with Luther the basic importance of the universal priesthood, but able also to preserve not just an evangelical priesthood of witnessing to the gospel but a genuine sacramental role of the laity in the sacrificial act of Christian worship.

A much less conciliatory attitude towards Luther's teaching on the priesthood of all believers was taken by Bishop John Fisher.[136] Ordination, which is of divine origin, gives the ordained a special measure of grace and places them in clear distinction to the laity: they are the rulers, the laity are the ruled; they are the tillers of the Lord's field, the laity are that field.[137] Christ himself was anointed by the Spirit in order to evangelize; only the ordained pastors of the church share in this anointing.[138] One can speak of a priesthood of all Christians, but one must immediately add that there is a distinctive priesthood and ministry which belongs only to the ordained; obviously, not all in the church are meant to be pastors, but the distinctive role and responsibility of the pastors would be meaningless if all Christians were priests in the same sense.[139] Fisher's objective seems quite clearly that of proving a substantive distinction between ordained priests (presbyters and bishops) and the Christian people.

The Sacrament of Orders

From a theological point of view, the Council of Trent's discussion of ordained ministry is disappointing; but it was the intent of the council fathers to set limits between acceptable Catholic teaching and unacceptable views (presumably those of the Reformers), though after some dispute the council agreed not to condemn any Reformers by name,[140] and not to give any extended theological treatment.[141] Even granting this delimited purpose, the council exhibited little interest in the basic theological issues. The groundwork for discussion of sacraments in general had been laid by collecting a list of questionable views on sacraments, to quite an extent from Luther's *Babylonian Captivity*, and formulating theological response to them. Yet, in the ensuing debates about the basic principles of Catholic doctrine on sacraments there is no real probing into the issues raised by the Reformers nor indeed into the issues raised by the council's own theologians. Instead, there is unmistakable intent on the part of the council to avoid theological questions.[142] One can appreciate this when there was a question of avoiding the centuries-old school debate as to whether sacraments involved physical or moral causality. But it is more difficult to see how the council could prescind

from deeper study of the relation between faith and sacrament.

If the council's discussion of the basic principles of sacramental doctrine avoided theological issues, the lengthy debate about the sacrament of orders (from September to December of 1562) seems scarcely aware of the Reformation challenge to traditional understanding of Christian ministry.[143] There is some time devoted to examination and reassertion of ordination as one of the seven sacraments; but the great bulk of the discussion focuses on episcopal prerogatives, and represents a continuation of the controversies that had been going on for centuries regarding the extent of episcopal superiority over ordained presbyters and the dependence or independence of bishops vis-à-vis the papacy in the matter of jurisdiction. The classic distinction between *potestas ordinis* and *potestas jurisdictionis* is the unchallenged foundation for this lengthy debate, and invariably the controversy centers on the source and limits of episcopal *jurisdiction*. Beneath the surface of this discussion lay not the questions raised by Reformation theology but rather the power struggle between papacy and episcopacy, a struggle that threatened to disrupt the council until a compromise formulation was accepted by both sides.[144]

In its own way, though, it is significant that the bulk of Trent's decree on the sacrament of orders[145] raised little question among the council participants and that debate centered on canon seven.[146] This would seem to indicate that it found positive resonance in the beliefs of the council fathers, and could therefore be legitimately used (as it was) by later Roman Catholic theologians as a principle of theological reflection. Perhaps the most important element in the decree, at least from a theological perspective, is its very beginning: the fact that the opening clause "Sacrificium et sacerdotium ita Dei ordinatione coniuncta sunt . . ." takes for granted that ordained ministry is to be considered under the notion of "priesthood" and that this priesthood-ministry is primarily characterized by its orientation to sacrifice. The power that is given to the ordained priest (be he bishop or presbyter) is that of "consecrating, offering, and administering" the body and blood of Christ and, linked with this, the power of forgiving and retaining sins.[147] Nothing is said about the ministry of the word except in the jurisdictional framework of canon seven, where it says that only those who have been ordained and commissioned by recognized church authorities are legitimate ministers of word and sacraments.

There is no further clarification of this sacrificial role of the ordained minister, neither in the decree on Orders nor in the decree on the sacrifice of the Mass, and one is left with the task of drawing out the assumptions implicit in both documents.[148] The ordained priest truly offers the body and blood of Christ, in commemoration and representation of Christ's once-for-all sacrifice on the cross. This action of the Mass is truly a propitiatory sacrifice, for Christ himself is the offered and the offerer through the ministry of the ordained priest. Even when he celebrates Eucharist privately, i.e., with no other Christians sharing in the action, the ordained priest performs an act that is effective of salvation, since he is acting as a public minister of the church.

What he does in Eucharist the ordained minister does by virtue of the power given him in ordination, power that comes from the sacramental character which is permanently impressed upon him and which remains a source of effective sacramental action even when the ordained lapses from grace. Only the ordained possess this priestly character which distinguishes them intrinsically from the laity; therefore any notion of a common priesthood of the faithful which denies the essentially hierarchical structure of the church is to be rejected. And as a result, only those who have been duly ordained by proper ecclesiastical authority can legitimately function as ministers of sacrament.[149]

Post-Tridentine Catholic Theology

Perhaps it is misleading to designate the Catholic theological activity of the late sixteenth and early seventeenth centuries as particularly "post-Tridentine"; in effect, almost all Roman Catholic theology up to about 1950 has been truly Tridentine. Yet, a brief look at the patterns of theological discussion about ministry and priesthood during the decades immediately following the council can be valuable. One finds already present the basic methods, the essential content, and the common arguments that characterize the theological discussion of the consequent four centuries.[150]

Thomas Stapleton

One of the most prominent and influential Catholic controversialists of the immediate post-Tridentine period was Thomas Stapleton, who left his native England in 1563 and spent the remainder of his life in exile in the Low Countries, devoting himself to teaching and to voluminous theological writings.[151] Central to Stapleton's theological contribution was his massive work on justification, the issue which he judged most basic to the controversies between Catholics and Protestants. It is a tribute to his theological acumen that he viewed this essentially soteriological question as the root of the differing Catholic/Protestant positions on ministry.[152] Though his accusation that the Reformers, having once espoused their position of justification by faith alone, had to establish new churches in which they could take refuge with such heterodox theology, is patently naive and unfair,[153] still the link between the Reformation views on justification and the new ecclesiastical polities that emerged was real and intrinsic, indeed, more profound than Stapleton admitted.

However, Stapleton in his attack upon Reformation theology and practice of ministry does not seem to concentrate much on the inner nature of ministry; rather, his battleground is the question of ministerial authority. Commenting on the Reformation churches' use of the ceremony of imposition of hands (and without, apparently, making any distinction in the various usages this practice had in different Reformation communities), Stapleton focuses on the illegitimacy of such actions because of the lack of true episcopal succession.[154] What is at the root of the

Protestant opposition to the Roman Catholic church is not the Reformers' choice *for* the Scriptures but their attitude *against* the teaching authority of Rome.[155] And because the Reformers have rejected the authority of the "true church of Christ" neither their teaching nor their other ministerial acts can bear true witness to Christ.[156]

Stapleton's polemic against the Reformers stresses much more the illegitimacy of their teaching, since they have not been properly sent by Christ through succession from the apostles; but he extends this to sacramental acts as well. In sacraments the ordained minister acts as God's instrument; the efficacy of the sacrament is not the result of the minister's own human power but results instead from the power of the Spirit working through him. So, there can be no saving power in the sacramental acts (or the preaching) of those who cannot have the Spirit because they are not legitimately commissioned by true successors of the apostles.[157] Not surprisingly, Stapleton sees the ministerial *potestas ordinis* and *potestas jurisdictionis* as very closely linked; they are two aspects of a single office.[158] And though in his lengthy disputes with Anglican theologians about legitimate authority he stressed the basically spiritual nature of genuine ecclesiastical jurisdiction,[159] Stapleton does seem to see even the *potestas ordinis* in an essentially jurisdictional context. An ordained minister's activity is effective if and because he is authorized.[160]

Robert Bellarmine

Though his role in helping to shape post-Tridentine theology is both praised and criticized, Robert Bellarmine was unquestionably one of the most influential Roman Catholic theologians in the latter part of the sixteenth century. His impact was especially important in the emergence of the modern theological treatise *"De ecclesia"* and therefore of the post-Tridentine understanding of priesthood and ministry.[161] At the beginning of his short explanation of the sacrament of orders (in the twelfth of his *Controversies*), Bellarmine mentions that this treatise should be comple-

mented by what he has said in other places about ecclesiastical power, sacraments in general, the nature and functions of various church offices, and priesthood. Still, this treatise on Orders does give a succinct expression of his views on priesthood and ordained ministry.[162]

Following the common understanding of his day (as of several centuries previous), Bellarmine identifies the sacrament of orders with the ordination ceremony, and spends a good portion of his explanation in establishing (through "proofs" from Scripture, tradition, and reason) that ordination is truly a sacrament. Incidentally, it is interesting to note that he sees the imposition of hands (not the *traditio instrumentorum*) as the essential sacramental gesture.[163] Basically, the ministry to which ordination is directed is sacramental; the power that is given the ordinand is the *potestas conficiendi et ministrandi sacramenta*.[164] In line with the thought of Thomas Aquinas (whom, in general, he follows quite closely) he identifies this *potestas ordinis* with the sacramental character; however, unlike Aquinas (who views the character as an intrinsic modification, a power to act), Bellarmine views the character as a covenanted assurance of (or title to) God's concurring activity in sacramental actions.[165]

In discussing the relationship of bishops and presbyters and the question of whether episcopacy is a distinct order, Bellarmine appeals to the principle that the sacrament of orders is finalized by the Eucharist, and says that the highest power of ordained priests (presbyters and bishops) is that of Eucharistic consecration.[166] Another insight into his view of episcopate and presbyterate as more or less of the same thing comes with his statement that episcopate, if it were conferred upon one who had not previously been an ordained presbyter, would contain presbyterate within itself.[167] Episcopate and presbyterate together form one ordained priesthood, but episcopate is more eminent than presbyterate and its source.

Conscious of the fact that denial of a sacramental character in the ordained is a cardinal tenet of Protestantism,[168] Bellarmine insists that ordination confers a spiritual power which permanently distinguishes the ordained from the laity, and the character is the sign of this power. Ministry is, therefore, more than a simple function that can be given one day and taken away the next.[169] However, this does not mean that Bellarmine denigrates the functional importance of the ordained minister but just the opposite. In his sacramental ministry the ordained priest is to function *humanly*; he is not meant to place unthinkingly a sacramental sign that works with some kind of impersonal force *ex opere operato*. Nor is his role as agent of Christ and of the church one of performing rigidly an external rite. Instead, he is to carry out the commission of his ordination with awareness and discretion. This is how Bellarmine seems to read the traditional insistence upon the need in sacraments of the minister's intention.[170]

Francis Suarez

When reading Bellarmine one gets the feeling that he is on the verge of developing what in twentieth-century theology has been called the ecclesial dimension of sacraments, though his treatment of elements such as the sacramental character is still situated against the background of medieval scholasticism and its underlying philosophical anthropology. In the writings of Francis Suarez, a contemporary of Bellarmine's but representing the intellectual world of Spanish theology rather than the movements of thought in Louvain and Rome (to which Bellarmine had been exposed), one notices a somewhat different spirit. There is unquestionably a strong influence of the political model of thought. Suarez moves very much in the mentality of law and jurisdiction, but the structures of reality (including human society and the church in particular) are ontologically monarchical, all truth and life and grace come down from above in a chain of causes.

One can talk about this hierarchical structure of reality in a purely philosophical fashion, or one can take the more complete religious perspective and see it all in terms of Christ's priesthood, for it is as the *mediator* of all created reality (and more specifically of all grace) that Christ is the high priest. It is quite illuminating to watch Suarez' procedure in his commentary on Thomas Aquinas' treatment of Christ's priesthood in the *Summa theologica*.[171] In the commentary directly on the text, Suarez follows Aquinas in placing almost exclusive emphasis on the notion of offering sacrifice and in stressing the identity between the sacrifice of the cross and Christ's sacrificial offering in the Eucharist.[172] This continues into the first part of the *disputatio* which immediately follows, but Suarez then shifts attention to the *monarchical* power of High Priesthood and ends with the statement that royal dignity and power belong to the very notion of priesthood, at least as this is found in the High Priesthood of Christ himself and of his vicar on earth (the pope).[173]

Suarez sees only the pope as entering fully into this priestly possession of monarchical spiritual authority, but this perspective definitely controls his notion of how other ordained ministers function. The ordained minister of the new law offers sacrifice as the minister of Christ, through his power, and in terms of applying to those who need it the merits of Christ's propitiatory sacrifice.[174] This he is able to do because of the consecration he received in ordination, a consecration that consists in the impression of the sacramental character.[175] The primary function of the ordained is to worship God by offering sacrifice in the name of the whole people, and while this is definitely a representative role it seems to have clear overtones of surrogate.[176] Secondly, the ordained minister has the role of preparing the faithful for, and leading them to, the worship of God and the salvation of their souls. He is to do this by teaching, by governing, and by judging. This last-named function while belonging intrinsically to priesthood should be exercised only by the one possessing fullness of authority, i.e., the pope.[177]

In the action of Eucharistic sacrifice, Christ himself is the principal agent; the ordained minister acts *in persona Christi*.[178] Because he possesses the power to consecrate (the *potestas ordinis*) which flows from the sacramental character he received in ordination,[179] and because the act of Eucharistic sacrifice consists in consecrating the bread and wine,[180] only the duly ordained minister is able to offer the sacrifice. Christ himself concurs in the ordained minister's sacrificing action not only in the causal context of being a special instrumental cause (an *instrumentum coniunctum*) of the divine action which effects the transubstantiation through the instrumentality of the ordained minister (who is an *instrumentum separatum*) but in the sense that Christ himself continues in heaven to worship his Father and to intercede for men.[181] If one understands it correctly, it is true to say that the entire church is priestly and that the entire community offers sacrifice. This means that the ordained celebrant is acting officially and publicly in the name of the entire church (therefore in the name of each member of the church) and it is presumed that each Christian joins his own intention to that of the celebrant who represents him. A lay person can increase his participation in the sacrificing action by intensifying his own interior consent to the act, or even by some external cooperation (such as giving a stipend for the Mass), but this does not mean that he becomes an immediate principle of the sacrificing action. This is reserved to the ordained minister.[182]

Pierre de Bérulle

While not representing a clearly different theological position on priesthood and ministry, the so-called French school of spirituality that is grounded in the thought of Cardinal Pierre de Bérulle did develop a distinctive emphasis in its understanding of priesthood and of the pastoral ministry. Bérulle himself was the moving spirit in the establishment of the French Oratory, whose purpose was to foster the sanctity of the diocesan clergy and to do so precisely by communicating an exalted notion of the priestly office.[183] Vincent de Paul and Jean-Jacques Olier, two of the leading disciples of Bérulle, founded communities of priests (the Lazarists and the Sulpicians) that have been in the forefront of seminary education for the past three centuries. Hence, the widespread influence and historical importance of this approach to understanding priesthood and ministry.[184]

In Bérulle's view the role of the ordained minister has two objectives: to worship God and to produce Christ in the souls of men.[185] Thus, cult and spiritual direction play a dominant part in priestly ministry, but Bérulle's (and the French school's) understanding of these two functions is controlled by his basic world-view, a view that focuses on the Incarnation and specifically on the priestly aspect of God-becoming-man, but a view that is also grounded in the Pseudo-Dionysian vision of a world and a church ordered in strict hierarchical fashion.[186] All creation exists to manifest and to pay witness to the grandeur of God; in this process Christ is *the* mediator, he is the unique adorer of the Father, he is the great Sacrament of religion.[187] Thus, all the mysteries of Jesus' life are the object of meditation and interior imitation. This finds a paramount expression in the celebrations of the liturgical cycle.[188] However, Jesus' own mission as unique mediator and adorer of the Father came to focus in his redeeming sacrifice;[189] the self-immolation of Jesus continues on in the Eucharistic act in which he empties himself for the sake of his Father and for men.[190]

Bérulle's understanding of sacrifice is central to his notion of Christian spirituality, and therefore to his notion of ordained ministry, since it is the ordained who are to live out in superior fashion the Christian ideal of life.[191] Christ's own adoration of his Father, especially in his act of sacrifice, consists in his utter self-emptying. This is the essence of his priestly function of worship. So, also, are ordained priests in the church to do: they are to be living sacrifices, they are to empty themselves utterly of self so that Christ can completely take over in them. This state of soul is to be specially realized in the ordained as he stands at the altar to celebrate the most sacred of sacrificial actions. In a sense, he is to lose his own identity in this action so that Christ and the entire church (both the church now and the church in glory) can work through him in offering Christ's sacrifice to the Father.[192] Eucharist and life are, then, to be one unbroken process of sacrifice, of self-denial in a most radical sense; when one is completely empty of self, Christ can take over and by the power of his Spirit rule the whole course of one's activity.

This ideal of sacrifice is to find more perfect expression in the ordained, for it is their particular function to be the ministers of the Eucharistic sacrifice; but it is the basic law of perfection for all Christians. For this reason, the object of the ordained minister's care of souls is to form Christ in the hearts of men.[193] This he does by proclaiming the gospel to them,[194] by spiritual direction, but most of all by his own life of prayer. The care of souls is (as Gregory the Great said) "ars artium"; but it is the art of humbly letting God work through one's ministry. And the science connected with this art is no ordinary kind of human knowing, but that enlightenment which comes in prayer.[195] In this way, the French school develops a refined synthesis of cult and pastoral ministry, one which places the contemplative life of the ordained minister at the very heart of his ministerial activity.[196]

Characteristics of Post-Tridentine Theology

The century and a half that followed the Council of Trent was marked by theological production of massive proportions, and despite the normative impact of the council's decrees there was still great complexity and divergence of opinion within Roman Catholic theology. Nevertheless, one can point to certain basic approaches of post-Tridentine theology to the question of ministry and priesthood, approaches that continue to control Catholic theology until mid-twentieth century. By the end of the seventeenth century, Europe is already passing out of the post-medieval, post-Renaissance period of the *ancien régime* and is coming increasingly under the influence of the Enlightenment. Radical as were the implications for Christian faith of this development in European intellectual life, Roman Catholic theology tended to be relatively untouched by it except insofar as it reacted negatively against it.

During the immediate post-Reformation period, the enemy for Catholic theologians was not yet modern rationalism but rather the various theologies of the Reformation churches. Understandably, in these decades of religious conflict (even bitter religious war) much of the theology is quite polemic in purpose and in tone. This can serve to sharpen the issues, which in some cases happened; but what happened in most cases was that polemical discourse concentrated on disproving the theological position of the adversary rather than on constructive reflection about the intrinsic issues. Positive theology was clearly coming into its own (both in Catholic and Protestant theology). Quite a number of eminent positive theologians (for example, Estius, Thomassinus, Morin, Maldonatus), contributed importantly to scholarly research in this field. An increasing number of systematic theologians incorporated masses of positive theological data into their work (so, for example, Cano, Bellarmine, Gonet). Not all the use of scholarly work in Scripture, patristics, and history was unprejudiced, for the proof-text method of arguing against false theological or confessional positions often wrenched texts out of context and gave them dubious interpretations. At the same time, a most impressive contribution to the task of gathering and collating textual and historical data was made by theologians of this period.[197]

Prior to the sixteenth century there was already a definite split of theological opinion into several schools (Thomist, Scotist, etc.), and in the post-Tridentine centuries this differentiation of theological views is even more marked.[198] However, the theological discussion of priesthood and ministry is quite homogeneous and is largely a process of using texts from Thomas Aquinas to expand on the statements of Trent. In a way, this was quite logical. Trent had purposely avoided attaching its decrees on the sacrament of orders and allied topics to any theological school, but it had depended quite noticeably on the Council of Florence, especially on its *Decretum pro Armenis*; the section of this Decretum that deals with Orders is very close to and clearly based upon Aquinas' *Opusculum de fidei articulis et septem sacramentis*.[199] Yet, it meant that there was relatively little penetration into or criticism of the views of Thomas Aquinas on the topic; rather, there was a repetition of the structure and doctrinal elements of his treatment. Such dependence on Aquinas' statements is a recurring element in the discussion at Trent about Orders. This was particularly and importantly true of his explanation of ministerial priestly power and function in terms of the sacramental character. Whatever new elements came into the picture came not so much from formal theological discussion of the topic but from theories of spirituality, particularly from the French school and from the notion of Christ's priesthood implicit in the *Spiritual Exercises* of Ignatius Loyola.

Unquestionably, the shock of the Protestant Reformation drove Catholic theology to clarify and deepen its understandings of many issues, but all too often there was the understandable but unprofitable tendency to seek justification for perpetuating practices and viewpoints of the past, rather than subjecting them to critical evaluation. Thus, for example, the presentations of Christian ministerial priesthood that appeared in the ascetical writings (intended particularly for seminarians, priests, and clerical religious) of the French school or of the Carthusian Anthony de Molina or of Barthelemy Holzhauer all emphasized the need for holiness in the ordained, the values of reciting the breviary and celebrating Mass, and the lofty dignity of the clerical state. Or, again, the emphasis on ecclesiastical jurisdiction that had grown up over the centuries is continued and further developed in the structured ecclesiologies of such men as Bellarmine or Suarez. An important

extension of this mentality appears (as it does in a key seventeenth-century treatise on priesthood, F. Hallier's *De sacris electionibus et ordinationibus, ex antiquo et novo Ecclesiae usu*) in the increasing attention given to the moral and canonical aspects of the sacrament of orders. But perhaps more deleterious than this desire to defend what the Reformation attacked were the false presuppositions and acceptance by theologians both Catholic and Protestant of false questions as the basis for dispute.[200] In the matter of ministry and priesthood two crucial areas of false problematic were the sacrificial character of the Eucharist and the nature of sacramental causation. Neither Protestant nor Catholic theologians questioned the simple identification of Christ's sacrifice with his death on Calvary, and the resultant identification of sacrifice with some form of giving up or immolation. So the Protestant solution to the problem of relating Christ's sacrifice to the Christian celebration of Eucharist lay in denying the sacrificial character of the Eucharist, and Catholic theologians devoted their efforts to devising various theories of mystic immolation or unbloody sacrifice.

Obviously, all such views controlled the idea one had of the minister's role in Christian worship. In Roman Catholic circles, the attempts to explain how the Eucharistic celebrant was at the moment of consecrating the bread and wine an instrument of symbolic immolation pushed into the background any study of the evangelical, prophetic, or personally charismatic elements of his function. Linked with this were the philosophical presuppositions about the nature and effectiveness of sacraments. Instead of picking up some of the more profound probings of twelfth- and thirteenth-century theologians into the functioning of symbols, later medieval thought settled into an attempt to explain sacramental causation as either physical causality (i.e., classifying sacraments and therefore sacramental ministers under the rubric of instrumental cause) or moral causality (bringing in legalistic notions, theories of extrinsic denomination). Continuation of such lines of thought into the Reformation period and thereafter cut off the convergence of genuine emphasis on faith's role in sacraments and genuine understanding of sacramental symbolism. The result was a false opposition between evangelical and sacramental approaches to Eucharist and its ministry.

Great as were the theological contributions of the sixteenth and seventeenth centuries, and it would be a mistake to minimize them, they left unresolved the basic question about the nature of Christ's own priestly ministry, and therefore the resultant questions about ordained ministry within the church.

NOTES

1. At the root of Aquinas' views on Christian priesthood lies his theological explanation of the Incarnation. The differing interpretation within the Thomistic school of Aquinas' theology of the Incarnation (e.g., the divergent explanations of Cajetan and Capreolus), to say nothing of the rejection of Aquinas' approach by a broad spectrum of theological opinion (Scotist, nominalist, Augustinian), should indicate the need for caution in presenting a given explanation of priesthood and ministry as "Thomist."

2. *Summa theol.* 3, q. 63, aa. 3–6.

3. *Ibid.,* a. 6.

4. *Ibid.,* q. 48, a. 3; q. 49, a. 4.

5. *Summa theol., Suppl.,* q. 37, a. 2; q. 40, a. 4.

6. See E. Schillebeeckx, *Christ, the Sacrament of the Encounter with God* (New York, 1963), pp. 54–63. Schillebeeckx' treatment is an excellent example of the manner in which the theological insights of Aquinas are open to contemporary theological developments, in this case, the present-day emphasis on the Eucharist as action. However, attention should be drawn to the absence in Thomas Aquinas' own systematic theology of any explanation of Eucharist as ritual action; instead, his treatment of Eucharist follows the traditional medieval emphasis on real presence and he views the sacerdotal *potestas ordinis* as focusing on the act of transubstantiating. Thus, his theological exposition of priesthood and of Eucharist is a good example of the lack of theology of cultic action which the Reformation period inherited.

7. *Summa theol., Suppl.,* q. 36, a. 2, ad 1; q. 37, a. 5; q. 40, a. 4.

8. ". . . Sacerdos habet duos actus: unum principalem, scilicet consecrare corpus Christi; alterum secundarium, scilicet preparare populum Dei ad susceptionem hujus sacramenti . . ." *(ibid.,* q. 40, a. 4; see also, q. 37, a. 2).

9. *Contra Gent.* 4, chap. 75.

10. *Summa theol., Suppl.,* q. 40, a. 5.

11. *Ibid.;* see also q. 34, aa. 2–4; and *Summa theol.* 3, q. 63, a. 5.

12. *Summa theol.* 3, q. 63, aa. 2–3.

13. *Ibid.*

14. *Ibid.,* q. 64, a. 8.

15. See *Rep.* 4, dist. 24, n. 7; *Ox.* 4, dist. 24, q. 1, n. 4.

16. See *Ox.* 4, dist. 1, q. 5, 4–17 (where Scotus explicitly challenged Aquinas' explanation); also *ibid.,* dist. 14, q. 4, n. 11; dist. 19, n. 23.

17. *Ibid.,* dist. 13, q. 1, n. 40; q. 2, nn. 3–4.

18. *Ibid.,* dist. 19, q. 1, n. 11. As a matter of fact, it probably would be more accurate to say that both the power of Eucharistic consecration and that of the keys follow (and in that sequence) from the exalted ecclesial position to which one is raised in ordination. Scotus sees ordination—which, incidentally, is for him the sacrament of orders—as essentially an establishment of a person in a superior grade in the church: "Ordinatio est institutio alicuius in gradu Ecclesiae eminente, cui convenit

aliquod ministerium circa Eucharistiam exhibendum . . ." (*ibid.*, dist. 24, q. unica, n. 8).

19. *Ibid.*

20. *Ibid.*, dist. 6, q. 10, nn. 7–8.

21. *Summa theol.* 3, q. 82, aa. 1, 3.

22. *Quod.*, q. 19, n. 22.

23. This raises, of course, the difficult question of the relation between Duns Scotus and Ockham and between both of them and the so-called nominalist school. Some notion of this complicated problem and some idea of present research into the problem can be found in H. Oberman's *Harvest of Medieval Theology* (Cambridge, Mass., 1963), esp. in the introduction; see also C. Feckes, *Die Rechtfertigungslehre des Gabriel Biel* (Münster, 1925), pp. 139ff.

24. "Appellantur et sacerdotes, quia sacra ministrantes seu dantes. Solis enim sacerdotibus ratione officii inest sacrorum sacramentorum ministrandi potestas. Vel sacerdotes quasi sacra dicentes, quia verbum dei predicare habent, horas dicere, missas celebrare. Vel sacerdotes quasi sacra conficientes, conficiunt nanque sacratissimum christi corpus." (Gabrielis Biel, *Canonis Misse Expositio*, ed. H. Oberman and W. Courtenay [Wiesbaden, 1963], vol. 1, lect. 4, D [p. 33].)

25. Earlier in this same lectio 4 (p. 31) Biel says: "Hec operatio consecrandi omnium nobilissima est ecclesie militanti concessarum, propter quam merito sacerdotium venit extollendum."

26. *Ibid.*, pp. 37–38.

27. "Hec autem virtus [i.e. the power by which transubstantiation is effected] est virtus creatoris, ipsa videlicet dei voluntas. Determinavit enim deus se ad efficiendum predicta omnia, cum sacerdos intentione debita profert verba super materiam debitam ad hunc effectum a se domino instituta." (*Ibid.*, p. 38.)

28. *Ibid.*, p. 35.

29. See Oberman, pp. 22–222.

30. In the section of his work on the Mass where he discusses the role of the celebrant's intention and its relation to the faith and intention of the church, Biel explicitly draws upon Scotus and Alexander of Hales (lect. 6, C, p. 46).

31. W. Brunotte, *Das geistliche Amt bei Luther* (Berlin, 1959), pp. 114–15, 199–200.

32. The remarks about this shift in Luther's thought as it touched the Lord's Supper made by P. Althaus (in his *The Theology of Martin Luther* [Philadelphia, 1966], pp. 318–22) deserve careful reflection. He suggests that in his earliest writings Luther stressed the nature of the Eucharist as a principle and expression of community, and therefore understood the "priesthood of all believers" in this context, but that this element of Luther's theology remained undeveloped after his attention was diverted to the polemics about the real presence.

33. Even though their discussion deals explicitly with the evolution (or nonevolution) of Luther's thought on the relation between ordained ministry and the priesthood of all believers, the differing opinions expressed in the articles of B. Gerrish ("Luther on Priesthood and Ministry," *Church History* 34 [1965], pp. 404–22), L. Green ("Change in Luther's Doctrine of the Ministry," *Lutheran Quarterly* 18 [1966], pp. 173–83), and R. Fischer ("Another Look at Luther's Doctrine of the Ministry," *Lutheran Quarterly* 18 [1966], pp. 260–71) indicate the delicacy with which one must approach the question of development in Luther's thought. If this is true of the relation between two clearly expressed elements, the priesthood of all believers and the ordained ministry, it is much more true of a shift in tonality from anticultic to cultic—which is what we suggest.

34. Because of its fundamental position in Lutheran doctrine, the priesthood of all believers has been the object of innumerable studies; a selective bibliography is given by G. Hoyer on pp. 194–95 of his article "Christianhood, Priesthood, and Brotherhood," *Accents in Luther's Theology*, ed. H. Kadai (St. Louis, 1967), pp. 148–98. To this might be added the works of Brunotte and Althaus previously cited.

35. For a gathering of relevant textual evidence, see P. Dabin, *Le sacerdoce royal des fidèles dans la tradition ancienne et moderne* (Paris, 1950).

36. At the end of his analysis of Luther's letter *To the Christian Nobility of the German Nation* (written in 1520), Brunotte summarizes: "Grundsätzlich hebt Luther die Scheidung von 'Klerus' and 'Laien' auf. Jeder Christ hat 'gleiche Gewalt,' d. h. er ist vor Gott gleich wie der andere und hat grundsäzlich die gleiche geistliche Würde ..." (p. 46).

37. See the articles cited above of Gerrish and Fischer, both of which oppose the notion that Luther's doctrine of the priesthood of believers is individualistic, i.e., that each Christian is a priest for himself and needs no mediation between himself and God. However, even when one admits that "one is a priest for others" (Gerrish, pp. 410–11) the question remains whether Luther thought of Christian priesthood as a truly communal and corporate reality or whether his view of the priesthood of all believers fits into the increased emphasis on individualism that marked the late medieval and Reformation periods. Fischer in his notion that "the church is a priesthood" (p. 270) and Althaus in his treatment of Luther's idea of communion (pp. 294–322) open up a possibility of interpreting Luther's "priesthood of believers" in a truly corporate sense.

38. See Gerrish, p. 412.

39. On the evangelical understanding of sacraments in Luther, see J. Pelikan, "The Theology of the Means of Grace," *Accents in Luther's Theology*, pp. 124–47.

40. See Gerrish, pp. 413–20; Althaus, pp. 323–32.

41. As far as solving the exegetical question of Luther's own understanding, Fischer's approach (pp. 270–71) seems as acceptable as any. It is neatly summarized in the sentence he quotes from Schlink's *Theology of the Lutheran Confessions:* " 'Ministerial,' then, means that in the congregation the preacher of the Gospel serves the priestly commission which God has given the whole congregation."

42. On the derivation of the ministerial office, see Althaus, pp. 323–32.

43. See Brunotte, pp. 84–86.

44. *Ibid.*, p. 88. As Gerrish points out (pp. 412–13), Luther's treatment of the distinction between the ordained ministers and the community as a whole turns around the distinction between possession of power and use of power: all believers in the community possess the powers, but (at least ordinarily) the exercise of these powers is reserved to the ordained.

45. *The Book of Concord*, trans. and ed. T. Tappert (Philadelphia, 1959). A helpful summary of the Lutheran confessions on ministry is given by J. Reumann, "Ordained Minister and Layman in Lutheranism," vol. 4 of *Lutherans and Catholics in Dialogue* (Washington–New York, 1970), pp. 233–42. More detailed studies are provided by A. Piepkorn's study in the same volume, "The Sacred Ministry and Holy Ordination in the Symbolical Books of the Lutheran Church," pp. 101–19, and by the article of G. Lindbeck, "The Lutheran Doctrine of the Ministry: Catholic and Reformed," *Theological Studies* 30 (1969), pp. 588–612.

46. ". . . Though [because?] he was a layman, Melanchthon seems to have stressed the dignity of the ministerial office more than Luther did and was more emphatic about its divine institution, omitting connections with the universal priesthood." J. Reumann, p. 233; for a fuller treatment of Melanchthon's views, see H. Lieberg, *Amt und Ordination bei Luther und Melanchthon* (Göttingen, 1962).

47. See Lindbeck, p. 596; Piepkorn, pp. 102–5. Though the ministry is *de jure divino*, no particular structuring of this ministry is divinely ordained; the question of church polity is basically an *adiaphoron*.

48. Piepkorn, p. 105.

49. See Lindbeck, p. 595.

50. On the methodology and basic orientations of this theological development, see R. Preus, *The Theology of Post-Reformation Lutheranism* (St. Louis, 1970).

51. Unfortunately we must bypass the difficult but important question of Lutheran ortho-

doxy's relationship to Pietism and to the rationalism that comes to the fore in the eighteenth century, a matter upon which Lutheran scholars are in considerable disagreement. See *ibid.*, pp. 15–44.

52. See F. Kalb, *Theology of Worship in Seventeenth-Century Lutheranism* (St. Louis, 1965), pp. 28–36.

53. J. Gerhard *Loci theologici* 4. 148 (quoted by Kalb, p. 28).

54. See Kalb, p. 31.

55. "The ecclesiastical ministry is a sacred and public office, divinely instituted and entrusted to certain suitable men through a legitimate call, so that, equipped with a peculiar power, they may teach the Word of God, administer the sacraments, and preserve church discipline to the glory of God and to promote the salvation of men." (D. Hollaz, *Examen theologicum acroamaticum* [quoted by Kalb, p. 29].)

56. See Kalb, pp. 61–64.

57. *Ibid.*, pp. 166–71.

58. On the influence of Bucer, see D. Steinmetz, *Reformers in the Wings*, (Philadelphia, 1971), p. 121; F. Littell, "New Light on Bucer's Significance," *Reformation Studies*, ed. F. Littell (Richmond, 1962), pp. 145–67.

59. See J. Dolan, *History of the Reformation* (New York, 1965), pp. 311–14.

60. See J. Courvoisier, *La notion d'Eglise chez Bucer* (Paris, 1933), pp. 98–101; also W. Stephens, *The Holy Spirit in the Theology of Martin Bucer* (Cambridge, 1970), pp. 173–85.

61. See J. van de Poll, *Martin Bucer's Liturgical Ideas* (Groningen, 1954), pp. 68–69.

62. See Stephens, pp. 257–59.

63. See van de Poll, pp. 67–68.

64. His interest in and development of the role of elders, though to some extent influenced by contact with Oecolampadius, is an indication of the way in which Bucer went to the New Testament writings for his models of the community and its ministries. For somewhat divergent views of Bucer's thought about the elders (particularly about their identity as clergy or laity), see *ibid.*, p. 32; and Courvoisier, pp. 101–3.

65. See van de Poll, p. 70.

66. Probably, the final position arrived at by Bucer is stated in chaps. 6–9 of his *De regno Christi* (written towards the end of his life for Edward VI of England). For an English translation, see pp. 232–37 in W. Pauck, *Melanchthon and Bucer*, vol. 19 of *Library of Christian Classics* (Philadelphia, 1969); a brief exposition of this passage is given by Courvoiser, pp. 125–30. On the evolution of Bucer's Eucharistic theology, see K. McDonnell, *John Calvin, the Church, and the Eucharist* (Princeton, 1967), pp. 75–85.

67. See the excellent expansion of this point in McDonnell, pp. 105–55. On Calvin's notion of ministry, see A. Ganoczy, *Calvin: Théologien de l'Eglise et du ministère* (Paris, 1944), esp. pp. 223–402; R. N. Caswell, "Calvin's View of Ecclesiastical Discipline," *John Calvin*, vol. 1 of *Courtenay Studies in Reformation Theology* (London, 1966), pp. 210–26; J. Ainslie, *The Doctrine of Ministerial Order in the Reformed Churches of the 16th and 17th Centuries* (Edinburgh, 1940); J. McNeill, "The Doctrine of the Ministry in Reformed Theology," *Church History* 12 (1943), pp. 77–97. The last two references are particularly helpful in relating Calvin's own views to subsequent Reformed theology.

68. McDonnell, pp. 223–31; also F. Wendel, *Calvin: The Origins and Development of His Religious Thought* (Fontana ed., London, 1965), pp. 329–55.

69. See McDonnell, pp. 280–88.

70. For this reason the judgment of H. von Campenhausen seems a bit excessive: ". . . The Reformation won back spiritual freedom from the consecrated order of the sacerdotal office, by reverting to the conception of the *ministerium*, as viewed solely in relation to its evangelical task and to the order this entails." (*Tradition and Life in the Church* [Philadelphia, 1968], p. 136.)

71. ". . . The sacraments have effectiveness among us in proportion as we are helped by their ministry sometimes to foster, confirm, and increase the true knowledge of Christ in ourselves; at other times, to possess him more fully and enjoy his riches. But that happens when we receive in true faith what is offered there." (*Instit.* 4. 1. 16 [trans. F. Battles, Library of Christian Classics edition of Calvin's *Institutes*, vol. 2, p. 1291].)

72. See Wendel, pp. 329–32. Calvin's position was closer to that of Melanchthon, particularly in its stress on the evangelical aspect of sacrament and on the action of the Spirit; see McDonnell, pp. 95–104.

73. See McDonnell, pp. 239–41.

74. See Wendel, pp. 350–55; also L. Schummer, *Le ministère pastoral dans l'Institution Chrétienne de Calvin* (Wiesbaden, 1965), pp. 59–61.

75. "It seems to me that a simple and proper definition [of sacrament] would be to say that it is an outward sign by which the Lord seals on our consciences the promises of his good will toward us in order to sustain the weakness of our faith; and we in turn attest our piety toward him in the presence of the Lord and of his angels and before men." (*Instit.* 4. 14. 1.) See J. Boisset, *Sagesse et sainteté dans la pensée de Jean Calvin* (Paris, 1959), pp. 117–18.

76. See B. Milner, *Calvin's Doctrine of the Church* (Leiden, 1970), pp. 134–39.

77. See Wendel, pp. 302–5.

78. See *ibid.*, pp. 301–9. It is particularly difficult in Calvin, even allowing for progression in his views, to discover the exact application of the term "elder"; at times it seems to apply to a group distinct from the other three ministries (pastor, teacher, deacon), at other times it quite clearly includes pastors and perhaps teachers. See W. Niesel, *The Theology of Calvin* (Philadelphia, 1956), pp. 200–202.

79. Calvin treats the ministries in the church as functions rather than offices; a person may exercise more than one function. See W. Dankbaar, "L'office des docteurs chez Calvin," *Regards contemporains sur Calvin* (Paris, 1965), pp. 123–24.

80. *Instit.* 4. 3. 1–8; see Boisset, p. 113.

81. See Dankbaar, pp. 123–26.

82. ". . . The sacraments have the same office as the Word of God: to offer and set forth Christ to us, and in him the treasures of heavenly grace. . . . They do not bestow any grace of themselves, but announce and tell us, and (as they are guarantees and tokens) ratify among us those things given us by divine bounty." (*Instit.* 4. 17. 17.)

83. See Schummer, pp. 59–62; Wendel, pp. 329–55.

84. See Schummer, pp. 49–51.

85. See Milner, pp. 135–37.

86. See Schummer, p. 60.

87. "We say that this is a sacramental view of the ministry but what actually appears here is the scheme which we have discovered everywhere in Calvin's theology, viz., that when the efficacious work of the Spirit is correlated with the *ordinatio Dei* in the ministry of a given man, there occurs the restoration of order, the salvation of the church" (Milner, p. 138). Here we seem quite clearly in contact with a basic soteriological insight in Calvin, which controls his understanding of ministry.

88. *Instit.* 4. 3. 5.

89. This is the conclusion drawn by Schummer, pp. 93–95. "Il y a, chez Calvin, un sacerdoce d'ambassade par délégation. Si un tel mot rebute—qu'important les mots!—on peut essayer d'en trouver un autre, mais sans supprimer tout ce que le premier contient. J'estime pourtant que si l'on parle sans rougir et frémir du sacerdoce universel, on peut de même parler du sacerdoce du pasteur." (P. 95)

90. See McDonnell, pp. 85–95; Dolan, pp. 203–310.

91. See McDonnell, pp. 89–93; Y. Brilioth, *Eucharistic Faith and Practice* (London, 1930), pp. 153–64.

92. See Thompson, *Reformers in Profile*, ed. B. Gerrish (Philadelphia, 1967), pp. 121–30.

93. *Ibid.*, p. 130.

94. Another element is the retardation of pastoral reform in the English reformation. In many ways, the kind of break with established patterns and movement towards more evangelical forms of pastoral effort which one associates with the great continental reformers did not find adequate expression until the Wesleyan revival of the eighteenth century.

95. Obviously, one must be careful not to exaggerate the extent or the nature of this tolerance. The movement towards genuine religious tolerance was very slow (in England, as in other countries), and the repression of opposing views and practices by the Church of England in the Restoration (at the close of the seventeenth century) makes it quite clear how minimal and pragmatic freedom of religion still was at that time. On the sixteenth-century evolution of religious toleration, between Roman Catholics and Reformation churches and within the Reformation itself, see the two volumes of J. Lecler's *Toleration and the Reformation* (London, 1960).

96. One could find essentially the same tendencies in Ridley, Latimer, Hooper, or Coverdale. For a lengthier discussion of the influence in England of the continental Reformation, the formation of a Protestant party within English churchmen and theologians, and the influence of this on the formation of Church of England credal and liturgical forms, see F. Clark, *Eucharistic Sacrifice and the Reformation* (Oxford, 1967), pp. 116–205.

97. See C. Richardson, *Zwingli and Cranmer on the Eucharist* (Evanston, 1949), p. 1. He points to the contribution of Cranmer to the *Book of Common Prayer*, but remarks (quite justly) that the Church of England's understanding of its liturgy is not tied to Cranmer's view. "Cranmer's opinions did not, of course, triumph in the English Church, and the 39 Articles represent, in Eucharistic doctrine, a rejection of some of his views. The liturgy he has bequeathed the Anglican Communion cannot, therefore, be read by Anglicans in the same sense in which he composed it. What the Church intends, and not what Cranmer intended, is the construction to be put upon it."

98. See *ibid.* Richardson concludes that there is a slight difference between Cranmer and Zwingli, for Cranmer grants a certain effective instrumentality to the Lord's Supper (pp. 48–49).

99. So Brilioth, pp. 200–201; H. Davies in the first volume of his monumental *Worship and Theology in England* (Princeton, 1970) situates Cranmer somewhere between Zwingli and Calvin (pp. 118–20).

100. Clark, pp. 159–75, at the end of his review of various interpretations of Cranmer's position, seems to incline towards identifying Cranmer's and Bullinger's views: "In general, this view [i.e., Bullinger's] of the memorial aspect of the Eucharist can be recognized in the writings of Cranmer and his associates" (p. 174).

101. On the thoroughgoing Protestantism of Cranmer's attack on the Mass as sacrifice, see *ibid.*, pp. 127–58.

102. On the Anglican stress on and development of preaching, see Davies, vol. 1, pp. 227–54; for a more general (i.e., not concentrating on Cranmer) picture of the Protestant understanding of ministry in the sixteenth-century English church, see C. and K. George, *The Protestant Mind of the English Reformation* (Princeton, 1961), pp. 320–41.

103. See Davies, pp. 14–15.

104. H. Davies' conclusions in this regard are worth pondering: ". . . There was a different order of priorities in the Christian life for Anglicans and Puritans. Anglicans give the primacy to sacraments, and Puritans to sermons, as channels of the knowledge and the grace of God. . . . This differing evaluation of sacraments and sermons led to functional differences between the Anglican priest and the Puritan minister. . . . For the Anglican the sacramental was the primary mode of Christ's presence, but for the Puritan, the primary mode of Christ's presence was kerygmatic." (Pp. 64–65) See also J. New, *Anglican and Puritan* (Stanford, Calif., 1964), pp. 68–76.

105. Davies, pp. 122–23.

106. *Eccles. Polity* 5. 67. 12.

107. *Ibid.*, 5. 78. 3–4.

108. *Ibid.*, 5. 78. 2.

109. *Ibid.*, 5. 76. 10.

110. *Ibid.*, 5. 77. 2.

111. "Will ye mark one thing more, that *epulemur* doth here refer to *immolatus*? To Christ, not every way considered, but as when he was offered. Christ's body that now is. True; but not Christ's body as now it is, but as then it was, when it was offered, rent, and slain, and sacrificed for us. Not, as now He is, glorified, for so He is not, so He cannot be immolatus for He is immortal and impassible. But as then He was when He suffered death, that is, passible and mortal. . . . And we are in this action not only carried up to Christ (*Sursum corda*), but we are also carried back to Christ as He was at the very instant, and in the very act of His offering." (*Sermon 7 on the Resurrection* [1612], *Works of Andrewes* [Oxford, 1841—Parker ed.], vol. 2, p. 301.)

112. See *Responsio ad Apologiam Card. Bellarmini* 184–85 (*Works of Andrewes*, vol. 8, pp. 250–51).

113. See Brilioth, pp. 208–9.

114. See particularly his *Real Presence and Spiritual of Christ in the Blessed Sacrament, Proved Against the Doctrine of Transubstantiation*, vol. 9 of *Collected Works*, 3d ed. (London, 1839), pp. 421–512.

115. *Of the Sacred Order and Offices of Episcopacy* 31. 3 (*Collected Works*, vol. 7, p. 122).

116. *Ibid.*

117. *The Worthy Communicant* 4. 3 (*Collected Works*, vol. 15, p. 435).

118. "Christ, in heaven, perpetually offers and represents that sacrifice to his heavenly Father, and, in virtue of that, obtains all good things for his Church. Now what Christ does in heaven, he hath commanded us to do on earth; that is, to represent his death, to commemorate this sacrifice, by humble prayer and thankful record; and, by faithful manifestation and joyful eucharist, to lay it before the eyes of our heavenly Father, so ministering in his priesthood, and doing according to his commandment and his example; the Church being the image of heaven; the priest, the minister of Christ; the holy table being a copy of the celestial altar; and the eternal sacrifice of the Lamb slain from the beginning of the world being always the same; . . . as Christ, in virtue of his sacrifice on the cross, intercedes for us with his Father, so does the minister of Christ's priesthood here." (*Ibid.*, 4. 4 [*Collected Works*, vol. 15, pp. 437–38].)

119. "As Christ is a priest in heaven forever and yet does not sacrifice himself afresh nor yet without a Sacrifice could He be a priest, but by a daily ministration and intercession represents His Sacrifice to God and offers Himself as sacrificed, so He does upon earth by the ministry of His servants." *The Great Exemplar* 3. 15 (*Collected Works*, vol. 3, p. 297).

120. Concluding her study of the Anglican church during the years 1559–1662, F. Higham remarks: ". . . Something had emerged worthy of man's devotion, a faith and worship and practice in well-being that have given to the Anglican branch of Christendom its own spiritual insights and the validity of a living Church" (*Catholic and Reformed* [London, 1962], p. 337).

121. See G. Williams, *The Radical Reformation* (Philadelphia, 1962), pp. xxix–xxx, for a brief summation of radical reform views on ministry.

122. There are, however, somewhat divergent views as to how the divine call is related to the call coming from the community. On the Lutheran position, see E. Schlink, *Theology of the Lutheran Confessions* (Philadelphia, 1960), pp. 241–47; and Piepkorn, pp. 112–16. On Calvin, see Schummer, pp. 14–27, and Niesel, pp. 203–5.

123. *The Apology for the Augsburg Confessions* (13. 9–13) says that the term "sacrament" can be applied to the laying on of hands in ordination, if the ministry in question is correctly understood: *Instit.* 4. 19. 28.

124. Naturally, the second of these qualifications can be viewed as a sign of the first. As

the Magisterial Reformation becomes more institutionalized and orthodox the emphasis on education, pastoral training, etc., becomes increasingly the criteria for ordination, whereas in the Radical Reformation there is more stress on the charismatic call to ministry.

125. One must make exception here (as in much of our discussion of Reformation theology of ordination) for the "Catholic" wing in Anglican theology.

126. See J. Heubach, *Die Ordination zum Amt der Kirche* (Berlin, 1956), pp. 66–73; Brunotte, pp. 199–201.

127. See Milner, pp. 134–44.

128. See F. Schmidt-Clausing, *Zwingli als Liturgiker* (Berlin, 1965), pp. 72–73.

129. As we suggested earlier, the truly critical issues underlying dispute about the nature of priesthood and ministry, issues that were Christological and soteriological, had not surfaced sufficiently by the sixteenth century to be enunciated clearly by either Protestant or Catholic theologians. Perhaps the deepest probings came in the arguments about justification, whereas the arguments about the Eucharist (which more obviously and immediately touched upon priesthood) were relatively superficial and polemical. However, as we hope to indicate, some of the most balanced and promising theological understandings about Christian ministry were gradually pushed into the background under the pressure of polemics.

130. However, it is important to recall, and we will mention a few instances as illustration, that there were exceptions to this tendency both in the sixteenth century and to lesser extent in later centuries.

131. See E. Iserloh, *Die Eucharistie in der Darstellung des Johannes Eck* (Münster, 1950), pp. 156–63.

132. "Christus semel oblationem perfecit in ara crucis . . . sacerdos in persona ecclesiae praesentat Deo patri memoriam huius oblationis" (*Ench.* H 8v [cited by Iserloh, p. 161]).

133. See Iserloh, pp. 229–33.

134. See *ibid.*, pp. 157–58; for some key texts of Schatzgeyer, see Clark, pp. 266, 530–31.

135. See E. Feifel, *Grundzüge einer Theologie des Gottesdienstes* (Freiburg, 1960), pp. 226–31.

136. See esp. his *Sacri sacerdotii defensio contra Lutherum* (1525), ed. H. Schmeink (Münster, 1925), vol. 9 in *Corpus Catholicorum*.

137. *Ibid.*, 2. 27–28.

138. *Ibid.*, 2. 29.

139. *Ibid.*, 3. 3–4; 3. 18–20.

140. See H. Jedin, *A History of the Council of Trent* (New York, 1961), vol. 2, pp. 380–81.

141. *Ibid.*, pp. 386–92.

142. *Ibid.*, pp. 380–91. While one cannot say that it was typical, the remark of Audet, the Carmelite general, at the end of discussion on the sacramental character, met with no dissent: "There is general consent in the Catholic Church that the sacramental character is a spiritual sign indelibly imprinted upon the soul; in my opinion, those who delight in the discussion of controverted questions should be silenced" (*Concilium Tridentinum* 5, p. 969).

143. See *Concilium Tridentinum* 9, pp. 5–243.

144. See L. Willaert, *La restauration catholique*, vol. 18 of A. Fliche and V. Martin, *Histoire de l'Eglise depuis les origines jusqu'à nos jours* (Paris, 1935—), pp. 336–40.

145. Promulgated in session 7 (23), July 15, 1563. See *Concilium Tridentinum* 9, pp. 620–22.

146. It was canon seven that dealt with episcopal prerogatives and which in its final form represents a political compromise and an avoidance of the much-disputed phrase *de jure divino*. "Si quis dixerit, episcopos non esse presbyteris superiores; vel non habere potestatem confirmandi et ordinandi, vel eam, quam habent, illis esse cum presbyteris communem; vel ordines ab ipsis collatos sine populi vel potestatis saecu-

laris consensu aut vocatione irritos esse; aut eos, qui nec ab ecclesiastica et canonica potestate rite ordinati nec missi sunt, sed aliunde veniunt, legitimos esse verbi et sacramentorum ministros: anathema sit." (*Ibid.*, p. 622.)

147. The council had earlier discussed these two powers: that of penitential absolution in its decree on the sacrament of penance (*Concilium Tridentinum*, vol. 7, pp. 343–59), and that of Eucharistic celebration in its decree on the sacrifice of the Mass, (*Concilium Tridentinum* 8, pp. 959–64).

148. For an analysis of the dogmatic content of the decree on Orders, see A. Michel, *Dictionnaire de théologie catholique*, vol. 11, cols. 1354–63; also A. Duval, *The Sacrament of Holy Orders* (Collegeville, Minn., 1962), pp. 219–45. On Trent's decree on the Mass, see Clark, *passim*.

149. In his "The Roman Catholic Doctrine of the Competent Minister of the Eucharist in Ecumenical Perspective" (vol. 4 of *Lutherans and Catholics in Dialogue* [Washing-New York, 1970], pp. 120–37), H. McSorley raises the question of whether Trent's limitation of legitimate ministry of word and sacrament to the duly ordained is intended to deny the reality of sacramental actions performed by the nonordained. The question is germane, of course, to the recent ecumenical study of validity in sacramental actions.

150. In many ways, the seventeenth century (beginning actually in the latter half of the sixteenth century) sees a development of Roman Catholic neoscholasticism comparable to that in Lutheran orthodoxy and Caroline theology in England. To give a detailed analysis of this rich theological writing, even on the limited topic of Christian ministry, would require several volumes; this can be seen from Willaert's excellent introduction (cited in n. 143 above). We will examine only a few theologians, hopefully typical and influential, and three major aspects of the post-Tridentine theological treatment of ministry.

151. See M. O'Connell, *Thomas Stapleton and the Counter Reformation* (New Haven, 1964).

152. *Ibid.*, pp. 110–25.

153. *Ibid.*, pp. 125–29.

154. *Ibid.*, pp. 128–32.

155. "Thus the question today is not about the Word of God or the Scripture, nor has this question even separated Catholics from heretics. Rather, the question is, from whom ought we to receive the Scripture, and through whom ought we to understand it." (Cited in *ibid.*, p. 134.)

156. See M. Seybold, *Glaube und Rechtfertigung bei Thomas Stapleton* (Paderborn, 1967), pp. 324–25.

157. *Ibid.*, pp. 325–27, esp. the lengthy texts of Stapleton in the footnotes.

158. *Ibid.*, p. 324.

159. See O'Connell, pp. 184–210.

160. Earlier, pp. 292–93, we drew attention to the way in which this stress on jurisdiction colored both Trent's decree on reform of preaching and Suarez' explanation of the ministry of the word; Stapleton's stress on jurisdiction was not, then, proper to himself, but reflected a developing emphasis within Roman Catholic thought.

161. Speaking of Bellarmine, X.-M. Le Bachelet (*Dictionnaire de théologie catholique*, vol. 2, col. 1365) says: "Ce théologien est vraiment à la fin du XVIe siècle, l'initiateur du traité moderne du sacrement de l'ordre. . . ." On Bellarmine's theological method and his role in post-Tridentine theology, see E. Ryan, *The Historical Scholarship of Saint Bellarmine* (New York, 1936); X.-M. Le Bachelet, *Bellarmin avant son cardinalat* (Paris, 1911); and J. de la Servière, *La théologie de Bellarmin* (Paris, 1909), pp. 495–96, discuss Bellarmine's theology of priesthood.

162. *De sacramento ordinis, Opera omnia*, ed. J. Fevre (Paris, 1873), pp. 21–35.

163. *Ibid.*, chap. 2, p. 22.

164. *Ibid.*, chap. 4, p. 26.

165. "Nam licet character non agat reipsa, sed sit solum signum pacti Dei cum homine de concursu divino in actionibus illis sacramentalibus, tamen hoc signum reale est, et ideo sicut ubi est spiritualis potestas, colligimus realem esse in anima characterem . . ." (*ibid.*, chap. 5, p. 27). Clearly, the difference of opinion between Bellarmine and Aquinas lies in their differing philosophical views of instrumental causality, though they concur in the view that God uses the ordained minister instrumentally in the sacramental actions.

166. *Ibid.*

167. *Ibid.*, p. 28.

168. "Haeretici hujus temporis characterem praecipue negant" (*ibid.*, chap. 9, p. 34).

169. *Ibid.*

170. See B. Leeming, *Principles of Sacramental Theology* (London, 1960), p. 484.

171. *Summa theol.* 3, q. 22.

172. *In Summa theol.* 3, q. 22 (*Opera omnia* [Vives ed., Paris, 1860], vol. 18, pp. 411–48).

173. *Disputatio* 47. 1. 2: ". . . Christum Dominum simul cum summo sacerdotio habuisse regnum spirituale, vel potius de ratione talis sacerdotii fuisse regiam hanc dignitatem et potestatem . . ." (p. 461). *Ibid.*, 2. 4.: ". . . Non solum potuit Christus per hanc potestatem leges condere, sed etiam potuit Vicario suo hanc potestatem impartiri, quam illi communicavit . . ." (p. 464).

174. *Ibid.*, 46. 3. 2 (p. 452).

175. *Ibid.*

176. *Ibid.*, 47, introd. (p. 460).

177. *Ibid.*

178. *In Summa theol.* 3, q. 83, a. 1; *Disput.* 77. 1. 1–6 (*Opera omnia*, vol. 21, pp. 689–92).

179. *Disput.* 77. 2. 5 (p. 694).

180. *Ibid.*, 2. 3–5 (pp. 693–95).

181. *Ibid.*, 1. 6 (p. 692).

182. *Ibid.*, 3. 3 (pp. 697–98).

183. "L'Oratoire a une mission essentiellement doctrinale: il doit restaurer et glorifier l'idée même du sacerdoce catholique" (H. Bremond, *Histoire littéraire du sentiment religieux en France* [Paris, 1925], vol. 3, p. 159).

184. In the early seventeenth century, France became the center of post-Tridentine Catholic reform, and Bremond (p. 156) sees Bérulle's foundation of the Oratory as "le point culminant de la Contre-réforme française." On the French school and its role in sacerdotal reform in seventeenth-century France, see P. Pourrat, *Le sacerdoce, doctrine de l'Ecole française* (Paris, 1931); L. Broutin, *La réforme pastorale en France au XVIIe siècle* (Paris, 1956); L. Cognet, *Les origines de la spiritualité française au XVIIe siècle* (Paris, 1949); J. Le Brun, *Dictionnaire de spiritualité*, vol. 5, cols. 933–36.

185. *Oeuvres complètes du Cardinal Bérulle* (Montsoult, 1644), p. 622.

186. On Bérulle's thought, see A. Molien, *Le Cardinal de Bérulle* (Paris, 1947), and his earlier article in the *Dictionnaire de spiritualité*, vol. 1, cols. 1539–81; J. Dagens, *Bérulle et les origines de la restauration catholique* (Paris, 1952); J. Orcibal, *Le Cardinal de Bérulle: Evolution d'une spiritualité* (Paris, 1965).

187. *Oeuvres complètes*, p. 933: "Le P. de Bérulle est plus original quand il fait du Christ un moyen, un principe d'adoration; pour lui, le Christ est l'adorateur par excellence de son Père, le parfait religieux, le Dieu-Homme qui, en raison de l'union des deux natures en une personne unique, peut offrir à Dieu une adoration infinie. La religion, qui s'adresse à Dieu comme term ultime, a ainsi un Dieu comme moyen. Cela est vrai de toute le vie du Christ, *heri, hodie, in saecula*; particulièrement dans l'Eucharistie." (A. Molien, *Dictionnaire de théologie catholique*, vol. 1, col. 1554; see also Bremond, pp. 62–64.)

188. *Oeuvres complètes*, pp. 940–41, 952. The spiritual revival connected with the French school (though by no means exclusively with them) in the early seventeenth century

had important impact on the liturgy. For one thing, its strong theological orientation acted to correct and deepen popular understandings of the sacramental acts. Unfortunately, much of the promise of this nascent liturgical revival was lost in the controversy over Jansenism. See L. Bouyer, *Life and Liturgy* (New York, 1956), pp. 49–51.

189. See Bremond, pp. 365–67.

190. *Ibid.*, pp. 491–93.

191. Following the Pseudo-Dionysian view, Bérulle sees an essential division between laity and ordained clergy, with the latter called to a level of holiness beyond even that proper to members of religious orders. See *ibid.*, pp. 168–71.

192. See *ibid.*, pp. 405–7. As Bremond points out, the formal emphasis on sacrifice is developed most fully in the French school of Bérulle's disciple (and second superior-general of the French Oratory), Charles de Condren, but it is already central in Bérulle's own thought.

193. *Oeuvres complètes*, pp. 622–24.

194. The notion of "sacrifice" dominates the French school's view of the ministry of the word: the preacher (or teacher) is to be certain that his auditor hears God's word and not his (i.e., the preacher's) word; he is to so empty himself that God can use him completely as an instrument of the word.

195. *Oeuvres complètes*, pp. 623–25.

196. There is a fascinating similarity and yet difference between the viewpoint of Bérulle and that of Ignatius Loyola *"in actione contemplativa."* The similarity is to quite an extent explainable by the influence of the *Spiritual Exercises* upon Bérulle in his early years. Bremond discusses this relationship a number of times, but since Bremond's treatment (in 1925) there has been considerable study of Loyola's insights on this point, so that the *theological* relationship of the two positions needs re-examination.

197. On the evolution of positive theology in this period, see L. Willaert, *La restauration catholique* (Paris, 1960), pp. 230–58. His judgment on the precise contribution made by these scholars is quite justified: ". . . Les historiens de l'Eglise à cette époque ont accumulé un immense trésor de matériaux; ils ont conçu le manière scientifique de les critiquer, ils les ont utilisés dans des constructions 'analistiques' ou partielles. Mais il ne s'est pas trouvé parmi eux de génie capable d'expliquer, dans une vision de synthèse désinteressée, le déroulement de la vie des siècles."

198. *Ibid.*, pp. 264–84.

199. See Michel, cols. 1315–16, for an analysis of this connection.

200. The anti-Protestant orientation of theology led to the increased falsification of some issues as, for example, the relation between Scripture and tradition. E. Feifel (in his *Grundzüge einer Theologie des Gottesdienstes*, p. 26, n. 160) makes an interesting suggestion about the manner in which Protestant stress on justification and particularly on the justice of God led to an overbalanced emphasis in Catholic theology on the sin-offering aspect of the Eucharist.

CHAPTER 32

Post-Reformation Sacramental Ministry

One of the developments that has marked the evolution of Christianity in the twentieth century has been widespread liturgical revival. From several points of view, this development was a bit surprising, particularly as it touched not only communities like the Anglican and Roman Catholic which had traditionally given more attention to sacraments but communities like the Reformed and Methodists whose orientation was more characteristically evangelical.[1] In the seventeenth and eighteenth centuries there was little indication that liturgical revitalization might lie in the future. Lutheranism, which had manifested elements of liturgical creativity in the sixteenth century, witnessed a serious decline of meaningful worship in the next two centuries. In the churches of the Reformed tradition, the ascendancy of the Zwinglian understanding of Eucharist logically led away from the modified sacramentalism of Calvin's own position, and so worship services of this wing of Protestantism became occasions for hearing a sermon, with some accompanying prayers and songs. Anglicanism, except for the abortive attempts of Laud at liturgical reestablishment, drifted into a moralistic rationalism and liturgical torpor. Roman Catholicism, having achieved an important unification and clarification of liturgy as a result of Trent, settled into a period of frozen sacramental performance and of emphasis on various devotional practices.

Then, slowly, in the course of the nineteenth century a liturgical awakening began; but throughout the century it remained, in those cases where it became identifiable, a liturgical movement within one or other church. It was not until well into the twentieth century that it became more apparent that what seemed to be an enthusiasm of a given group within a church might be something basic to the life of the entire church. Even up to World War II, however, there was considerable suspicion of attempts to revive and emphasize liturgy. With some justification, the liturgical movement was identified in many minds with restoration of archaic ceremonies and vestments, or with Gregorian chant, or with rubrical formalism. In Protestant communities the popular level of understanding rejected any infiltration of sacramentalism as opposed in principle to the Reformation. However, the current of liturgical revival was strong enough to force theologians in the various churches to reassess their theology of worship, sacrament, and ministry; this proved to be one of the major stimuli of the mid-twentieth-century theological explosion.

The Protestant Traditions

The leading reformers of the sixteenth century shared a common repudiation of crass popular misunderstanding of Eucharist (as did Roman Catholic theologians of the period), but they tended to retain a special role for and special reverence towards the celebration of the Lord's Supper; this was, of course, more noticeable in the Lutheran developments and less the case where the influence of Zwingli was strong. During the seventeenth and eighteenth centuries this residue of sacramental cult was often submerged under the growing dominance of the sermon, but not totally lost. So, the resurgence of emphasis upon the cult aspects of the Lord's Supper, with its accompanying shift in the role of the ordained minister, has been quite legitimately seen as a development of confessional traditions that were present from the Reformation onwards, traditions which themselves are grounded in the most authentic currents of pre-Reformation faith.[2]

Among the Protestant churches, both in Europe and in America, the clearest acceptance of a cult role for the ordained minister has come in Lutheranism. While it did not embrace all Lutheran thought and practice in mid-nineteenth-century Germany, the return to sacramentalism that was fostered by Lohe, Delitzsch, and Thomasius slowly gained ground (incidentally, finding much of its support in American Lutheranism) and had a lasting effect in moving Lutheranism away from the Calvinist influence that had earlier infiltrated its theology.[3] This led to a scholarly investigation, both of classic sixteenth-century Lutheran thought and of primitive Christian sources, attempting to clarify the nature of ministerial office and/or charism and particularly the distinctiveness of ministerial ordination and function vis-à-vis the universal priesthood of believers.[4] The century or more of serious discussion, even controversy, about these questions has not resolved all the issues, but it has drawn attention back to the spiritual character of the ordained ministry. It has made quite clear that this ministry is basically one of word and sacrament, and with typical Lutheran stress on "the word" it has insisted on the evangelical activity of the ministry, even in sacrament.[5] At the same time, in reasserting the divine institution of the ordained ministry, not just in terms of its original institution but in terms of the vocation of a candidate to the pastoral function, modern Lutheran thought has subtly stressed the image of the pastor when he preaches or officiates at the Lord's Supper as the instrument of God's saving action, an instrument who functions not individually but rather within the context of the universal priesthood and of the church as the body of Christ.[6]

Not surprisingly, the churches of the Reformed tradition have been slower to move towards a liturgical revival. The notion that sacramental forms were foreign to genuine Protestant worship was slow to die, even when nineteenth- and twentieth-century scholarship began to show that such denigration of liturgy was not shared by such men as Calvin and Knox. Yet, the existence of the liturgy of Taizé, or the liturgies adopted in situations of church union (such as that for the United Church of Canada, when it was formed in 1925), or the profound sacramental theology developed by such Reformed theologians as von Allmen or Leenhardt or Thurian are signs that the movement towards recovery of Christian sacraments has touched in unmistakable fashion the modern disciples of Calvin.[7]

Precisely because of the greater freedom that had been exercised by the minister in Reformed worship services, even in the celebration of the Lord's Supper, it is more difficult to discover how the understanding of the minister's cultic role changed (if at all) during the past two centuries. However, the increasing tendency to bring some unity into ministerial practice by urging use of official directories is itself significant. It points up the community role of the minister and emphasizes the form of the worship service as a sign of the faith of the entire church. To the extent that one can use such directories as a guide (and along with them the theological writings out of which they have grown or which attempt to explain them),[8] it seems quite clear that the ordained minister sees himself to be leading the congregation in an act of worship, though it also seems quite clear that the heart of this worship is the sermon. At the same time, there is a recognition that the external action of the Lord's Supper has a certain autonomous effectiveness independent of the minister who performs it, though Reformed theologians are rightly wary of drifting towards a faulty *ex opere operato* view.[9] What has remained unclear, and, of course, it has been the controlling problem in the disputes over the minister's role, is the manner in which ministers in the Calvinist tradition understand Christ to be present in the action of the Lord's Supper and therefore understand their own activity to relate to Christ's act of salvation.[10]

One of the most intriguing instances of liturgical traditions being preserved in an evangelically oriented community occurred in Methodism. John Wesley's own rooting in the liturgical traditions of the Church of England, his use of the Anglican books of ritual as the source for his own *The Sunday Service,* and the role of this latter document as the foundation for all Methodist worship forms in North America have given Methodism a strong link with the sacramental views of Anglicanism and Roman Catholicism.[11] Yet, there has been no loss of the evangelical emphasis which is characteristic of Methodist ministry.

John Wesley himself accepted a threefold ordained ministry, though he preferred the title "supervisor" to "bishop"; but his understanding of the ministry stressed function rather than office. Thus, he rejected apostolic succession as the only validation of ministerial orders and held that effective work in "turning men to righteousness" gave proof of a genuine ministry.[12] At the same time, he maintained that ministerial ordination (which, however, could come from a presbyter as well as a supervisor, since they were not distinct orders) was required for one to administer sacraments. A layman could appropriately be permitted to preach but he could not function as minister of sacraments.[13] And although he denied that ordination was a sacrament (he held that it did empower the ordinand for ministry but did not give grace) and rejected the Eucharist as a *propitiatory* sacrifice, his statements in this vein are a repetition of the standard Reformation objections to what they saw as Roman teaching. There is solid reason for thinking that he considered the ministry he exercised as priestly and the

worship act of the Lord's Supper as a sacrifice.[14]

One of the most interesting, and perhaps theologically most significant, elements of liturgy and of ministerial function that Wesley bequeathed to Methodism was the solemn renewal of covenant.[15] It is not clear whether, in Wesley's own usage, the covenant ceremony was integrated with the Communion service; Wesley himself made no theoretical explanation of the link.[16] However, in later Methodist theology there is a positive utilization of covenant-renewal as a principle for understanding the Lord's Supper.[17] This would seem to promise that Methodist theology could mediate between churches with strongly sacramental (Eucharistic) ecclesiologies and churches with strong emphasis on covenant in their ecclesiology.

Anglican Understandings of Cultic Ministry

The Stuart Restoration might have meant the return to power of the Church of England, but it did nothing to bring closer relations to the dissenting churches; indeed, the notion of some form of working union of the two groups quite completely evaporated. However, this split did not mean that the Catholic wing in Anglicanism came into control and that the Protestant emphasis no longer found a strong voice within the Church of England. Actually, just the opposite happened in the eighteenth century and well into the nineteenth. With the general trend towards rationalism and moralizing, with the increasing emphasis on preaching within this context, with the Latitudinarian theology gaining prominence, there was general neglect of traditional liturgy and little theological effort to make that liturgy more intelligible.[18] Actually, the creative liturgical thrust in the eighteenth century came rather from the Unitarians and the Methodists, the first more philosophical, the second more evangelical.[19]

Different as the two movements are in many respects, the evangelicalism of the eighteenth century both in Methodism and in Anglicanism prepared for the Oxford movement of the early nineteenth century.[20] Despite the strong practical impact it would have on the ministerial activity of the Church of England, the Tractarian movement was essentially a scholarly effort to regain a theology of the church that was compatible with genuine Christian tradition.[21] Naturally, this involved a study of the Catholic tradition throughout the centuries prior to the Reformation; but this was mediated through the thought of the Caroline Divines, who were the more direct religious ancestors of the Tractarian theologians. Working consciously to redirect the Church of England away from the Protestant understandings of grace, salvation, and sacraments, which in their opinion had drawn the Anglican communion away from a true understanding of the church and its ministry, the Tractarians stressed the objective aspect of the sacraments as part of an incarnational understanding of Christianity.[22] While themselves stressing the ministry of preaching, they saw their ministerial identity as priestly, they saw this priesthood as being derived from a sacramental ordination, and they saw the reality of such priestly ordination as grounded in apostolic succession of the episcopacy. This priestly role found its primary expression in the celebration of the Eucharist, an action they understood in terms both of real presence and of sacrifice.[23]

The foundations for a Catholic understanding of Anglican ministry were quite adequately laid by the Oxford Tractarians, and two important essays on the topic appeared towards the end of the century: C. Gore's *The Church and the Ministry* (1882, revised in 1889 as *The Ministry of the Christian Church*) and R. Moberly's *Ministerial Priesthood* (in 1897).[24] Grounding his understanding of Christian priesthood in the identity of the church as the body of Christ, Moberly sees this priesthood as a share in the priesthood of Christ himself, and ministerial priesthood as a reality that operates within the broader priesthood of the entire community.[25] It finds its highest expression in leadership of the Eucharistic action, but it is also

intended to manifest itself in preeminent priestliness of spirit as the ordained minister provides pastorally for his people.[26]

Neither in the nineteenth century nor in the twentieth has this Anglo-Catholic theology of ordained ministry gone unchallenged in the Church of England. One of the more recent indications of this diversity of Anglican understandings of ministry and priesthood came with the publication in 1946 of *The Apostolic Ministry*, an impressive collection of essays by Anglo-Catholic scholars.[27] Still more recently, some heated controversy has grown out of conversations on reunion between Methodists and the Church of England.[28] Yet, there are indications that the liturgical movement in the Anglican church became increasingly in the first half of the twentieth century a broadly based and theologically grounded reality.[29]

Roman Catholic Understanding of Priestly Ministry

Clearly subject to the same rationalizing and secularizing forces that deeply influenced other Christian churches in the eighteenth to twentieth centuries, the Roman Catholic church had been (at least until well after World War I) strikingly unchanging in her theory and practice of sacramental ministry. To a large extent this was the result of Trent, which had formulated a doctrinal statement on the Mass and on the sacrament of orders, initiated an important unification of Eucharistic ritual (actually executed by Pius V shortly after the council), and rather effectively placed Roman Catholic liturgy in a deep freeze.[30] There was a rich Baroque embellishment of the liturgical ceremony and of church buildings, but this did little else than hide still further the genuine nature of the Eucharist as a community action.[31] In the eighteenth century there were voices raised for a purification and simplification of the liturgy, voices demanding that somehow the faithful who had been reduced to almost total silence and inaction be given a share in the Eucharistic action. Some elimination of obvious Baroque excesses was achieved, but for the most part the cries for true liturgical reform were as little effective as had been the attempts made by the Bérullian circle in the seventeenth century.[32]

But if the Council of Trent and the subsequent laws and official actions that implemented it were at the root of the static condition of sacramental liturgy, the theological developments of those centuries served to support and justify the practice and to make creative change that much more difficult, since such change, when it was attempted, tended to be suspect as heterodox. At the heart of this conservative theology was the explanation of Eucharistic ministry, an explanation that treated the ordained minister's role in sacrament as a self-contained reality, that reacted excessively against Reformation discussion of the universal priesthood of Christians, and that cast even the ordained minister's action in a context of objective validity that was grounded in jurisdiction and conformity to rubrical law.[33] Thus, while the course of modern theological discussion of sacramental ministry does not give us a full insight into the development of Roman Catholic thought on that ministry, it can serve as an accurate indication of that development.

Eighteenth-Century Theology

Since Thomas Aquinas' explanation of Christian priesthood had been so influential in shaping the doctrinal formulations of Florence and Trent, the more competent commentators on Aquinas in any century give a reliable presentation of the classic and officially acceptable theology. In the eighteenth century, no theologian in this tradition of Thomistic commentary was more prominent than Billuart nor a greater influence on subsequent Thomistic thought. The Belgian Dominican, in his treatment of the sacrament of orders,[34] follows the standard teaching that a double power is given in ordination: the power touching the real body of Christ in the Eucharistic consecration and the power touching the mystical body of Christ. Thus, though the essence of priesthood as such deals

with sacrifice, the priesthood of the new law instituted by Christ is directed both to sacrifice and to judgment—the Christian priest is sacrificer and judge.[35] The highest power that can be given to man is that over the body of Christ in Eucharistic consecration; it far surpasses the power over the mystical body of Christ.[36] Thus, though a bishop has the fullness of this latter power, the episcopacy is not clearly a distinct order but rather the fullness of the *sacerdotium*. However, Billuart maintains that bishops are, by divine institution, superior to presbyters both in power of orders and power of *jurisdictionis*.[37]

His notion of the bishop's role is very governmental. Bishops were instituted by Christ to rule the church, to define dogmas of faith and religion, to correct. At the same time, his overall view of the priestly-episcopal role does seem to be slightly less authority-conscious than that espoused by Gonet, Billuart's seventeenth-century Thomistic predecessor. In his *Clypeus Theologiae Thomisticae* (which was still being reprinted and exercising considerable influence in the nineteenth century) Gonet also speaks of the sublime privilege of ordained priesthood, but he expresses it in terms of power: he has power over souls, because he can remit or retain sin; he has power over the church, for he illumines and perfects and deifies it; he has power over the real body of Christ, because his word of command makes the incarnate Word present on the altar.[38]

When he discusses more directly the role played by the ordained celebrant in the Eucharistic action, Billuart distinguishes two elements of Eucharistic ministration: consecration and distribution. Only the ordained are able to consecrate, and only they licitly dispense the consecrated elements, though anyone can effectively distribute the elements once they have been consecrated.[39] It is clearly the ordained celebrant who alone effects the sacrifice of the Mass, since the essence of that sacrificial act consists in the consecration.[40] Billuart gives no particular clarification of the relation between the priest celebrant and Christ, whereas Gonet had taught that the priest offering the sacrifice of the Mass is the vicar of Christ, since Christ himself no longer immediately offers this sacrifice.[41]

Not all the theological discussion of ministry and priesthood in the eighteenth century was as scholastic in language and form, but the viewpoint was basically the same as that held by Billuart and Gonet. In the series of conferences he gave to his clergy in the early part of the century (from about 1723 onward), Massillon, the bishop of Clermont, stresses the indispensable mediatorial role of the priest, uses this to exhort his hearers to truly pastoral concern, and laments the extent of priestly negligence. With a bit of rhetorical exaggeration he attributes the evils of the age to the negligence and infidelity of priests.[42]

It is the priest who stands before God on behalf of his people; he is the one who presents their needs and petitions, for his greater dignity (as priest) gives him closer access to the throne of mercy. His prayer, above all the recitation of the divine office, is not just his personal prayer; it is public prayer and has special efficacy for that reason. And if he is the link from the people to God, he is also the channel by which grace comes down from God to men. Consequently, the prayer life of the priest and his personal intimacy with God are basic to his function; for how can he obtain from God what the people need if he himself is not close to God in prayer?[43] Clearly, Massillon reflects the French school of spirituality with its emphasis on the priest's own prayer as an act of ministry.

But the priest is also meant to reconcile men to God, particularly by offering the propitiatory sacrifice of the Mass. As he stands at the altar he exercises a public ministry on behalf of his people; he presents to the Father the saving blood of his Son; he immolates the living victim. In this exalted role, it is sacrilege for him to function with sinful hands; an unworthy priest desecrates the altar and the sacred mysteries he performs.[44] Clearly, Massillon's exhortations are grounded in a strongly cultic, mystery understanding of the Eucharistic action. In this action, the precise role of the priest is not delineated, beyond the view that he represents the people, prays officially on their behalf, and is the "co-worker with God in the salvation of souls; for he applies to men the blood of Jesus Christ by the channels of the sacraments. . . ."[45] Significantly, Massillon continues his description of the priest as co-worker with God by turning to the ministry of word: "He announces to the people the word of life and reconciliation; he nourishes them with the bread of teaching and of truth." Thus, without explicitly making the point, he indicates the intrinsic link between the ministry of word and sacrament. Actually, in his view the key element to this double ministry lies in the personal behavior of the priest, in his own holiness and in the example he gives his people. It is this latter which preaches louder than words: "For most people, the Gospel is preached by the lives of the priests they see; what counts is not that which we proclaim in the pulpit, rather it is that which they observe in our behavior."[46] If the priest is to deal salvifically with his people, he must, as did Moses, first go up on the mountain and deal with God; then he can come armed with truth and holiness. To some extent, Massillon's treatment of the ministry of preaching breaks out of the context of supernatural causality and deals with the more obvious level of the psychological effect caused by a sincere and competent speaker. But basically he remains in the same theology of redemption which controls his view of sacramental ministry: salvation is brought about by grace which is won by the prayer of the church and particularly by the Mass, which then flows down to men through sacramental channels—in which up-and-down flow of grace the ordained priest plays a unique and controlling function.

Massillon's devotional theology of the priestly office seems to have been typical of the century; one finds much the same viewpoint (though in less hortatory style) in the *De officiis sacerdotalibus et pastoralibus* of J. Soettler, which appeared in the eighteenth century but was reprinted in 1825 at the urging of Pope Leo XII, so that it might provide guidance and edification for priests.[47] This little treatise stresses the sanctity and life-style of the priest. Its order of material is revealing: first it deals with what a priest should observe regarding himself (his conduct, prayer, etc.); then, what he should do about the temporal goods entrusted to his administration; then, what he should do for his parishioners. Under the first part the function of celebrating Eucharist is treated, and it is put into the context of the priest's own personal praise of God in prayer. He is urged to celebrate Mass devoutly and frequently, for if he neglects to say Mass without good reason "he deprives the Trinity of praise and glory, the angels of joy, sinners forgiveness, the just the support of grace, solace to those in purgatory, the Church the spiritual benefit of Christ, and himself the medicine and help against daily sins and infirmities."[48] Somewhat later, Soettler mentions the things that the pastor should do for his people; the last of these is to provide religious services and administer the sacraments.[49] Only two short paragraphs deal with the Eucharist, and these are concerned almost totally with the question of the frequency of Communion. It would seem that there is no notion of forming the faith of the people by the action of the Eucharist; the celebration of the Eucharist was still very much the priest's own thing, even though he did it to win grace for the church.

By and large, Roman Catholic theology took little account of the intellectual developments connected with the Enlightenment, and so the theological treatment of the ministerial office continued in its traditional course without much reference to the eighteenth-century rationalism that so deeply affected many of the other Christian churches. An exception to this was the late eighteenth-century theologian and bishop (of Regensburg), Johann Michael Sailer, whose pioneering work in the development of a *Pastoraltheologie* had widespread influence in the German-speaking sections of the church. Sailer was very concerned with the practical effects of ministry,

with the psychological transformation of insight and attitude which hopefully could be accomplished by competent preaching and instruction; but he was insistent that the "conversion" he saw as the goal of ministry was a truly religious reality, a deepening or regaining of genuine faith, which could in no way be reduced to the changes of understanding achieved by secular ethical teaching.[50] What he criticized in this latter kind of Enlightenment preaching was its loss of the notion of mystery; salvation was reduced to moral good, and philosophy replaced faith. True Christian preaching is meant to be the proclamation of God's saving activity, not just ethical instruction and exhortation;[51] for this reason, he urged a careful formation of seminarians in Scripture studies.[52]

With this general perspective in his pastoral theology, Sailer logically resisted the attempts of rationalistic thought to reduce the celebration of Eucharist to an exercise of morality, though he saw the Eucharist as the foremost and continuing situation of true Christian conversion.[53] Preaching was important, but the essential action of the ordained minister is to stand at the altar and "along with Christ, whose offering he renews, to offer himself and the community to the eternal Father."[54] The Mass is the supreme instruction about the mystery of salvation, because it is the real effecting of that mystery: Christ is acting and the Christian community is working with him in its own salvation. The entire community is meant to join its own sacrificial attitude to that of the celebrant who prays, and offers, and gives thanks in the name of the community.[55] Thus, Sailer gives full scope for the evangelical aspect of the Eucharistic action; he sees that the depth of the Eucharistic ministry of the word lies in the real presence of the mystery that is effected through the sacramental ministration of the ordained priest.

The Nineteenth Century

Though the influence of Sailer was lasting and his thought found resonance in many who regretted the barrenness of Eucharistic liturgy, the treatment of ministerial priesthood in treatises of systematic theology remained largely unchanged in the nineteenth century. As for several centuries, the questions relative to sacramental ministry that drew most attention were the type of causality involved in sacraments, the essence of the Mass (theories of sacrifice, mystic immolation, etc.), and transubstantiation.[56] And a representative treatise on the sacrament of orders, like that of G. Perrone which was included in Migne's *Cursus Completus*, is an orderly but uncreative repetition of standard post-Tridentine theology. He stresses the basic link of priesthood with sacrifice, argues for the *reality* of the celebrant's Eucharistic offering of Christ, and sees this sacrificing action, accomplished essentially in the consecration of the elements, as the proper and defining action of the Christian minister.[57]

Early in the century, Möhler began to lay the foundations for what would be the twentieth-century revolution in ecclesiology, but the effect of his thought was only slowly felt in the formal theology of Christian ministry. Möhler's contribution lay basically in his organic and pneumatic understanding of the Christian community, so different in emphasis from the classic post-Tridentine defense of the institutional elements in the church.[58] He stressed the union of the inner and outer aspects of the church and of its ministerial offices: the Spirit who works from within to unify the church, and the hierarchy (around the papacy) which is the external sign and instrument of the Spirit. True power to form community does belong to the hierarchy, and in extended fashion to the presbyters, but it is always power from above, the power of the Spirit.[59]

Möhler's emphasis on the community, and especially on its mystery identity as the body of Christ, influences his view of the Eucharistic action and of the ordained minister's role in this act. He does not admit any notion of a priesthood of the faithful which is not grounded in acceptance of episcopacy and papacy, but he does take this broader priesthood of the community seriously. In the Eucharistic act the entire people offers Christ to the Father, though the power of consecration is proper to the ordained celebrant, and the celebrant has a special role in the offering of the sacrifice. However, the ordained minister acts not in isolation but united with the community; thus, the Eucharist expresses and deepens their unity with one another.[60]

In general, in his treatment of the Eucharistic action Möhler broadens out the notion of sacrifice at the same time that he insists on the unity exhibited: unity of the assembled Christians among themselves, more specifically the unity of celebrant and people, unity of a given celebrating community with the entire body of Christ, unity of the Christian people with Christ, unity of Christ's sacrificial act with the sacrificing act of the church. The Eucharist is essentially an act of community. And unlike the main stream of medieval and post-medieval theology (Catholic and Protestant), Möhler extends the sacrificing act of Christ himself to more than Calvary, thus preparing the way for mid-twentieth-century developments in Eucharistic theology.[61]

More representative of nineteenth-century theology of ministry was J. Franzelin, whose career as professor of dogmatic theology in Rome at the time of Vatican I and for more than a decade thereafter and whose elevation to the cardinalate gave him a somewhat unique position of influence. He was by no means a conservative thinker and urged a much greater openness of Catholic thought to modern intellectual currents. For this very reason, the traditionalism of his theological explanation of ministry indicates how stabilized and unmoving that area of ecclesiology (and, as a matter of fact, the whole of ecclesiology) had grown.

Franzelin's most extended and profound analysis of the ordained ministry occurs in his discussion of the sacramental character, where he examines the cooperative relationship between the ordained minister and Christ in the sacramental actions.[62] His point-by-point exposition of the nature of the sacramental character follows the treatment of Thomas Aquinas[63] and adds nothing substantial to it. The character is a supernatural quality that grounds a special relationship to Christ and to the acts of Christian cult; it is an ontological consecration that conforms one to Christ (member to head, citizen to king through baptism; minister to high priest through ordination); it is a spiritual sign of power and office in the area of the church's cult, a participation in Christ's priesthood; it is teleologically directed to sanctification.[64]

When Franzelin comes to explain the kind of causality exercised by the minister in the sacramental actions, it becomes apparent that he denies to the minister any intrinsic effectiveness. Instead, he has by virtue of the sacramental character the official power to act as Christ's legate or vicar, and as such to place the external sacramental sign which by divine institution can effect grace and salvation. The ordained minister acts in the name and person of Christ, but the *dignitas supernaturalis* which calls into being the effect of the sacrament is attached not to the minister but to the external action (the *sacrum signum*) itself.[65] What Franzelin seems to hold is the view that the external sign has by itself, in considerable independence of the minister (who apparently is not considered part of the sign, since it is something he places), a supernatural efficacy that was attached to it by Christ's own direct act of institution some two thousand years ago.[66] In such an understanding of sacraments, which pushes the *ex opere operato* principle to the edge of its acceptability, there is little room for an evangelical interpretation of sacrament and not much need for personal involvement on the part of either people or minister.

While they might prefer an explanation of ministerial activity in sacrament that leaned towards physical causality rather than towards the moral causality that Franzelin espoused, most of the theological manuals in the latter part of the nineteenth century and into the early decades of the twentieth century con-

tained an explanation of ministerial priesthood much like that presented by Franzelin; the reediting and wide usage of his own books is an indication of this.[67]

In the early decades of the twentieth century there was in Roman Catholicism a dialectical interaction between more creative currents of Eucharistic theology and the growing movement for liturgical reform: the newer theological insights suggesting what the practical conduct of liturgy should be, and the growing experience of better liturgy revealing the insufficiency of existent Eucharistic theory. Progressive theology was suspect, partially because of the pervading worry especially in official circles about modernism, partially because it obviously led to the practical conclusion that basic reform of the Eucharistic celebration was needed. Two great pioneers, De la Taille and Casel, prepared for the reorientation of sacramental theology that came around mid-century: the first by reintroducing the importance of the meal element in the Eucharist and by pushing theological discussion out of the sterile post-Tridentine debates about unbloody immolation of Christ in the Eucharistic sacrifice; the second by drawing attention to the mystery dimension of the Eucharistic celebration.[68] Both men drew widespread criticism from more conservative quarters. The theories of both men (at least in their explicit elements) have been bypassed in the theological developments of the 1950s and 60s, but it is difficult to see how post–World War II evolution of Roman Catholic thought about the Eucharist and its ministry could have happened as it did without the contribution of these two men. Neither man produced (except in fragments) a new theological explanation of the sacramental role of the ordained minister, but they made the emergence of such an explanation inevitable because of the radical reorientation they gave to the understanding of Christ's own priesthood.

NOTES

1. On Roman Catholic liturgical developments, see O. Rousseau, *The Progress of the Liturgy* (Westminster, Md., 1951); and L. Bouyer, *Life and Liturgy* (London, 1956). For Lutheranism, see L. Reed, *The Lutheran Liturgy* (Philadelphia, 1947), chaps. 7–10; for Anglicanism, H. Davies, *Worship and Theology in England* (Princeton, 1970), vols. 3–5; for the Calvinist tradition, K. Phifer, *A Protestant Case for Liturgical Renewal* (Philadelphia, 1965), pp. 66–136, and J. Melton, *Presbyterian Worship in America* (Richmond, 1967); for Methodism, J. Bowmar, *The Lord's Supper in Methodism* (London, 1961).

2. Speaking of the *tendance sacramentaliste* in the nineteenth century, E. Léonard, *Histoire générale du Protestantisme* (Paris, 1964), vol. 3, says: "Elle a été si forte, qu'on a vu une tentative ou un risque de catholicisation du protestantisme. . . . Mais il apparaîtra, sans doute, que ces tentatives restent 'protestantes' et sont davantage dues à une interprétation particulière des principes de la Réforme, qu'à une volonté de les méconnaître ou de les enfreindre." (P. 306)

3. See *ibid.*, pp. 306–11; Reed, pp. 140–55, 228–45. The essay by J. Reumann, "Ordained Minister and Layman in Lutheranism," in vol. 4 of *Lutherans and Catholics in Dialogue* (Washington–New York, 1970), pp. 227–82, gives special emphasis to the American developments.

4. See Reumann, "Ordained Minister and Layman"; G. Hasenhüttl, *Charisma, Ordnungsprinzip der Kirche* (Freiburg, 1969).

5. See E. Schlink, *Theology of the Lutheran Confessions* (Philadelphia, 1960), pp. 241–51.

6. See J. Heubach, *Die Ordination zum Amt der Kirche* (Berlin, 1956), pp. 66–73.

7. On the evolution and nature of this litugical renewal in the Reformed tradition, see J. Barkley, *The Worship of the Reformed Church* (Richmond, 1967); and Phifer, *Protestant Case for Liturgical Renewal*.

8. E.g., D. Macleod, *Presbyterian Worship: Its Meaning and Method* (Richmond, 1965).

9. See *ibid.*, pp. 61–65.

10. One can cite the Eucharistic theology of Leenhardt (in his *Ceci est mon corps* [Neuchatel, 1955]; reprinted in English translation in *Essays on the Lord's Supper* by O. Cullmann and F. Leenhardt [Richmond, 1958]) or of Thurian (*The Eucharistic Memorial* [London, 1969]) as important modern Calvinist treatments of this point, but their views could not yet be considered typical.

11. On the origin and revisions of the Methodist forms of worship, see the essays in *Companion to the Book of Worship*, ed. W. Dunkle and J. Quillian (Nashville, Tenn., 1970).

12. See A. Lawson, *John Wesley and the Christian Ministry* (London, 1963), pp. 71–83.

13. *Ibid.*, pp. 83–87.

14. *Ibid.*, pp. 93–96.

15. See D. Tripp, *The Renewal of the Covenant in the Methodist Tradition* (London, 1969). Wesley's *Sunday Service*, which he prepared for the American Methodists, did not contain the covenant renewal service, but it is included in the 1944 *Book of Worship*.

16. Tripp, pp. 30–32.

17. *Ibid.*, pp. 108–23.

18. See Davies, vol. 3, pp. 19–37, 52–75; G. Cragg, *The Church and the Age of Reason*, rev. ed. (London, 1970), pp. 65–80.

19. See Davies, pp. 76–93, 143–209.

20. See E. Fairweather, *The Oxford Movement* (Oxford, 1964), pp. 10–11.

21. On the nature and evolution of the Oxford movement, see the volume of E. Fairweather cited above; also Davies, vol. 3, pp. 243–82; A. Vidler, *The Church in an Age of Revolution* (London, 1961), pp. 45–55. In my treatment of the Tractarian movement, I have been much helped by an unpublished study of a confrere, the Rev. Robert Wittaker.

22. See Fairweather, pp. 8–11.

23. See the essays by Pusey, Keble, and Wilberforce in Fairweather, pp. 281–383. Though large segments of the Anglican church disagreed (and still disagree) with the Catholic Eucharistic theology espoused by these men, "the Oxford Movement has contributed largely to a spectacular transformation of Anglican eucharistic worship" (Fairweather, p. 12).

24. On the sequence of events in the Church of England preceding and following the appearance of Moberly's book, see A. Hanson's introduction to the 1969 reprinting of *Ministerial Priesthood*.

25. "The priesthood of Christ we found in His offering of Himself as a perfect sacrifice, an offering which is not more an outward enactment than an inward perfecting of holiness and of love; an offering whose outward enactment is but the perfect utterance of a perfect inwardness; an offering which, whilst, so to say, containing Calvary in itself, is consummated eternally by His eternal self-presentation before the presence and on the throne of God. The sacrificial priesthood of the Church is really her identification with the priesthood and sacrifice of Christ. . . . The priesthood of the ministry follows as corollary from the priesthood of the Church. What the one is, the other is. If the priesthood of the Church consists *ceremonially* in her capacity of self-identification, through Eucharistic worship, with the eternal presentation of Christ's atoning sacrifice, and *spiritually* in her identification of inner life with the spirit of sacrifice which is the spirit of love uttering itself in devoted ministry to others, so it is by necessary consequence with the priesthood of the ministry. For the priesthood of the ministry is nothing distinct in kind from the priesthood of the Church. . . . They [i.e., ordained ministers] are Priests because they are personally consecrated to be the representatives and active organs of the priesthood of the Church." (*Ministerial Priesthood*, pp. 254–59.)

26. *Ibid.*, pp. 259–62.

27. For a short description of this reaction, see J. R. Nelson, *The Realm of Redemption*, 7th ed. (London, 1964), pp. 155–56. His discussion of ministry, pp. 142–59, is a succinct but balanced appraisal of twentieth-century views (he does not treat the Roman Catholic position).

28. See R. Beckwith, *Priesthood and Sacraments* (Appleford, Eng., 1964), pp. 15–41.

29. "Above all, there has been growing a clearer and more cogent conviction of the Divine origin and empowering of the Church as manifested in the Eucharist. However strong the forces of secularism and materialism, there is great encouragement in the thought that the Church has never lost sight of her calling to adore God and to serve mankind. And it is precisely this calling which has been renewed in the Church of England through more than half a century's concentration on worship." (Davies, vol. 5, p. 346.)

30. See J. Jungmann, *Mass of the Roman Rite* (New York, 1951), vol. 1, pp. 132–45.

31. *Ibid.*, pp. 148–52.

32. *Ibid.*, pp. 151–59.

33. If this judgment appears too harsh, it might be well to reflect on the way in which the teaching of Pius XII's "*Mediator Dei*"—a document that is certainly not revolutionary when compared with Vatican II's *Constitution on the Liturgy*—was considered such a drastic breakthrough when it was issued in 1947.

34. His treatise on Orders is in vol. 7 of *Summa Sancte Thomae*, original edition in 1769.

35. *Ibid.*, diss. 2, a. 1 (p. 328).

36. *Ibid.*, diss. 4, a. 2 (p. 364).

37. *Ibid.*, diss. 4, a. 1 (p. 359).

38. *Tract. 7 (De angelis)*, disp. 2, digressio brevis, vol. 3 of *Clypeus Theol. Thom.* (Paris, 1876), p. 42: "Praeterea natura humana insigni gaudet privilegio, quo caret angelica, dignitate scilicet sacerdotii; quae ex triplici capite summopere commendatur: Primo, quod imperium in animas exerceat, et potestatem ligandi atque solvendi habeat, ut dicitur Matt. 16. Secundo, quod mystici Christi corpori, videlicet Ecclesiae, dominetur: hanc enim expiat Sacerdos, illustrat, perficit, ac deificat, ut docet Dionysius in libro de Eccles Hierarch. . . . Tertio, Sacerdos ipsi etiam vera [*sic*] Christi corpori

imperat: quia ipsum . . . Sacro ore conficit, et ad ejus verbum, praesens altari sistitur ipsum Dei Verbum, per quod omnia facta sunt."

39. *Summa Sancte Thomae*, vol. 6, diss. 7, a. 1 (p. 523). Gonet makes a comparable distinction (vol. 5, tract. 5 [*De Eucharistia*], disp. 10, aa. 1–2 [pp. 458–61]); and though he sees the administration of Communion as part of the priest's mediatorial role (a. 2, p. 460), he still introduces the notion of jurisdiction: "Non omnes Sacerdotes possunt hoc Sacramentum licite ministrare, sed solum illi qui habent potestatem jurisdictionis. . . . Ratio vero est quia etsi administratio Eucharistiae non sit actus judicialis, sicut est Poenitentiae administratio, est tamen proprius pastoris actus, et quidem magis quam actus publico docendi populum, cum sit actus pascendi gregem Christi spirituali pabulo carnis Domini." (P. 461)

40. Vol. 6, diss. 8, a. 2 (p. 537): "Essentia sacrificii Missae non consistit in oblatione sive praecedente sive consequente consecrationem, neque in elevatione hostiae, neque in fractione et mixtione specierum, neque in distributione. . . . Sumptio non est de essentia sacrificii. . . . Essentia sacrificii Missae adaequate consistit in consecratione corporis et sanguinis, cum ordine ad sumptionem tamquam ad partem integrantem. Sacerdotium per se primo consistit in potestate consecrandi: ergo sacrificium in ipsa consecratione; sacerdotium enim essentialiter est propter sacrificium."

41. Gonet *Clypeus* Tract. de Eucharistia, vol. 5, disp. 11, a. 3 (p. 471).

42. *Oeuvres de Massillon* (Paris, 1835), vol. 2, p. 229.

43. *Ibid.*, pp. 228–29.

44. *Ibid.*, pp. 229–30.

45. *Ibid.*, p. 251.

46. *Ibid.*, p. 232.

47. See J. Migne, *Theologiae Cursus Completus* (Paris, 1841), vol. 25, cols. 107–227.

48. *Ibid.*, chap. 1, 8 (col. 117).

49. The other things he should do for his parishioners are (1) be kind and charitable, (2) give good example, (3) pray for them, and (4) preach and instruct.

50. See H. Müller, *Die ganze Bekehrung* (Salzburg, 1956), pp. 186–87.

51. *Ibid.*, pp. 187–89.

52. *Ibid.*, p. 190.

53. *Ibid.*, pp. 192–94.

54. *Ibid.*, p. 194.

55. *Ibid.*, pp. 194–95.

56. See E. Hocedez, *Histoire de la théologie au XIXe siècle* (Paris, 1952), vol. 3, pp. 272–306.

57. Migne, cols. 18–20.

58. See P. Riga, "The Ecclesiology of Johann Adam Möhler," *Theological Studies* 22 (1961), pp. 563–87.

59. See *Symbolik*, ed. J. Geiselmann (Cologne, 1958), vol. 1, pp. 448–56.

60. See J. Geiselmann, *Die theologische Anthropologie Johann Adam Möhlers* (Freiburg, 1955), pp. 48–52.

61. See *Symbolik*, pp. 352–76.

62. *De sacramentis in genere*, 5th ed. (Rome, 1910), pp. 165–94.

63. Franzelin cites *Summa theol.* 3, q. 63 as his source.

64. *De sacramentis in genere*, p. 166.

65. *Ibid.*, p. 193.

66. He supports the postion (p. 181) that Christ directly instituted the sacramental signs.

67. A good summation of this classical position (along with presentation of more recent theological developments) is given by J. Brinktrine, *Die Lehre von den heiligen Sakramenten der katholischen Kirche* (Paderborn, 1962), vol. 2, pp. 159–202.

68. M. de la Taille, *Mysterium Fidei* (Paris, 1921); and O. Casel, *Das christliche Opfermysterium*, ed. V. Warnach (Graz, 1968).

CHAPTER
33

Theological Reflections on Sacramental Ministry

In an earlier part we argued that differences of soteriology are the root of divergent opinions about Christian ministry; nowhere is this clearer than in the discussion of sacramental ministry. Differing confessional views and differing theological explanations are controlled by the manner in which Christ's own priestly function is understood. For that reason, analysis of Christ's priesthood is an inevitable first step in any attempt to reflect upon the cultic (priestly) role of the ordained ministry.

Whether one works from the New Testament theology of Jesus as the realization of the prophetic witness to God, from the Gospel evidence that Jesus' teaching was a constant public acknowledgment of his Father, from the less obvious but basic biblical theology of Jesus as the new Temple, or from the Johannine theology of Jesus as incarnated Son and Word, one arrives at the conclusion that Jesus' whole being and activity was understood by primitive Christianity to be an act of worship. More than that, it constituted a radical transformation of the very notion of worship because it said "son" in relationship to God in an absolutely unprecedented and unparalleled fashion. Jesus' own human experience, even though it included participation in Jewish cult as a most precious element, was the paradigm of that secularization of worship which marks the early decades of Christianity. Lest there be any misunderstanding, it might be well to mention proleptically that what is really involved is not a movement from the sacred to the secular but a profound sacralization of what might be considered the realm of the secular.

But of course that which fulfills the meaning of Jesus' life and ministry is the unique event of his Passover, the event that stretches from the Cenacle to Pentecost, the event in which (as all Christian faith has seen) he becomes definitively Messiah and Lord and High Priest. For centuries, Christian devotion and theology particularly in the West have centered on Jesus' death on Calvary as the element in this complex redeeming act which is most properly and fully priestly. Such a separation of Christ's suffering and death from what precedes and follows it is artificial and misleading, and though Calvary is not the supreme moment of priestly sacrifice, we might start our reflection with the commonly accepted belief that Christ's death on the cross was an act of sacrifice, i.e., a preeminently priestly act, and see what that implies.

Worship is an acknowledgment of God; Jesus' acceptance of his suffering and death was essentially such an acknowledgment. It was not an abstract acceptance of a divine existent, not just faith in some beneficent divinity, but a realistic and highly personal trust in the fidelity of this God who is his Father. Dying in itself was obviously not the redemptive force on Calvary; the redeeming agency was the human consciousness and loving decision of Jesus. His awareness of the fact that his witness to truth and his love for people (i.e., doing his Father's will) had somehow led with a certain inevitability to Calvary, and to his decision to trust that his Father's Spirit of truth and love would conquer death and bring new life to himself and to all his fellow humans. Calvary was, then, a moment of supreme witness to the God who is revealed in Jesus, a trusting benediction of that God as faithful (even though this was expressed in hope); it was a total coincidence of worship and prophetic proclamation.

But Calvary has always been seen as that particular form of worship which we call "sacrifice"; it was a sacrificial action that fulfilled in transcendent fashion all the sacrificial liturgies of Old Testament Israel and that made any further sacrifice unnecessary. Like Old Testament holocaust, Calvary was a total giving over to God; it was a conversion from previous existing to a new way of being. This illustrated the hidden meaning that had been contained in the transformation of Israel's sacrificial gifts by the fire. It was conversion, too, in the deeply personal sense; for, like Abraham, Jesus was asked to leave the land he knew and venture into the unknown. It was an emptying, a loss, the ultimate risk. It was death. Even if one stresses the positive side of that moment, Calvary was still on Jesus' part a giving over of himself to be utterly transformed by his Father's Spirit, something that threatens destruction of one's individuality unless one trusts the life-giving and freedom-respecting character of love.

Calvary is not, however, an event in itself; it is a moment in and inseparable from the integrated event that is Jesus' Passover. The intrinsic meaning of Jesus' death as his personally experienced action and the manifestation of that meaning were provided by the Supper. It was the act of Jesus in the Cenacle, explicitly linking his Passover with the Old Testament exodus and with the centuries-long and evolving liturgical commemoration of that exodus. It initiated the new covenant in a sacred meal that is unmistakably related to the covenant-renewing peace offerings of Israelitic liturgy, that placed the shedding of his blood in a sacrificial context. Jesus' decisive placing of himself in the role of victim, which is the internal and essential element of his sacrificial offering, is one unbroken act that extends from the Supper into his death.

It is this internal act that finds symbolic expression in the Supper. Without the Supper, Christian faith would not have known how to interpret the enigma of Calvary, for without the Supper Calvary would have been in itself a meaningless tragedy.

It is most important, then, to realize that the meaning of what Jesus did and said at the Supper was sacrificial, but that the sacrificial meaning was that of *giving* himself to his friends, so that they might live, rather than that of *giving up* his life as the price of our salvation. In order to transform the entire context of human life and life-giving, Jesus combined the two basic symbols of giving life, food and the human body, and poured into them the new meaning of his own gift-of-self-as-source-of-life. The most basic structures of meaning in human experience were thereby Christianized, and the Christian sacramental system was instituted. Obviously, the Supper cannot possess such profound symbolic power by itself, for like Calvary it is existentially and symbolically inseparable from the entire Passover event. However, it is the moment in that event which is uniquely interpretative of the entirety, and so its symbolic forms continue to be used as proclamation of the Christian Passover throughout the church's history.

The Last Supper was not just a promise of Passover, not just a commitment (however solemn and irrevocable) to give oneself in death and resurrection. It is already the beginning of such self-giving, and so in the most profound fashion gives promise of continuation and fulfillment. It is already the once-for-all act of sacrifice in progress. This makes clear that the essence of Jesus' sacrifice does not consist in dying, nor even in accepting death, but in giving himself to others as a life principle. To be a sacrifice means for Jesus to be irrevocably set aside for this purpose of vivifying his brethren.

Jesus' choice at the Supper, for himself and others, was the choice of life—the new life for which he hoped, and in expectation of which he was willing to pass through death. Thus, risen life entered into the conscious dimension of both Cenacle and Calvary as a finalizing force. New human existing of a kind that would make possible his self-gift to men was precisely what Jesus chose; he chose to enter into this new and uncharted manner of life so that he might be personally for all other men. Paul, in Ephesians, is not speaking, then, in metaphor when he describes Jesus' death and resurrection as a marital giving of self.

Without in any way demeaning the intrinsic value of Jesus' human activity in his Passover, or in any way denying the essential role Jesus played (and plays) in human redemption, it is important to remember that the redeeming sacrifice of Christ is most basically the action of God. Divine love initiated the entire process of Word-becoming-flesh which comes to fulfillment in the Christian Passover, and so there can be no question of Jesus' sacrifice being appeasement or even of being reconciliation with some God who is not himself doing the reconciling. In giving himself to men as their life principle, Jesus is doing the will of his Father, he is fulfilling the mission on which he was sent; his self-offering to men is his self-offering to his Father. And in the resurrection moment of the Passover the sacrifice (the "making sacred") is accomplished by the divine action. Jesus is definitively established in a state of human existing that permits him to be life-giving for all men. He is the totally sacralized, existentially constituted victim by the divine Spirit of vitalizing love which is the source of his new and unending life and which springs forth from him (the new Temple) to enliven all who accept this life.

So, the resurrection of Jesus is the full moment of sacrifice. Even as man Jesus' participation in this sacrificial situation is more profound and meaningful than it was at the Supper or on Calvary, because he now accepts with full understanding the victim role of being for others, and is now fully endowed to achieve it. One can, of course, speak of this situation as one in which "Christ still prays for us to the Father," in which "he still offers sacrifice"; but it is good to remain aware that in actuality Jesus is continuously being sent (now with full possession of the Spirit) from

the Father to share risen life and sonship. In thus giving life and sonship by giving himself, the risen Christ sacramentalizes the Father's own life-giving love and so bears witness to the Father. Christ's transforming gift of self to others is his worship service of his Father; the heavenly nuptials of the Lamb, the risen Christ's marital self-giving to men and women, constitute the heavenly liturgy.

Jesus' priestly act of sacrifice, precisely because it is constituted by his dynamic relationship to others, is formative of community. This is by no means an incidental by-product: the entire mystery of creation and divine revelation that culminates in God revealing himself in Jesus is a matter of communicating and thereby bringing community into being. Divine-human community is the goal that finalizes the Incarnation itself, the mission of Jesus, and therefore his priesthood. Because the human sharing in this communion with God consists in loving acceptance of sonship, i.e., grateful personal acknowledgment that Christ's Father is indeed *our* Father, the human community that springs from faith in the resurrection is a worship community. The risen Christ still acts as high priest, leading his church to ever more authentic and profound benediction of his Father and celebration of the *magnalia Dei*.

This liturgical profession of faith is critical in the process of salvation that the risen Christ carries on in men's lives. Since salvation means the heightened vitalization of men and women, it is a life process that develops by the exercise of that new life, and no one else (including God) can do this living and internal growing for them. The living in question is, of course, the activity of believing and hoping and loving. Since this activity must be carried on (at least partially) in community, corporate profession of faith (i.e., liturgical celebration) is a basic element in the process of Christian salvation. How salvation occurs in the lives of those who are not involved in formal Christian faith and liturgy is another question, which is not our present topic but which can find some reasonable explanation along analogous lines.

It is obvious that if one explains the saving action of Jesus in his death and resurrection as we have just done, notions that are closely connected with priesthood and ministry appear in a somewhat different light. Grace, if one is speaking about the sanctification of a Christian, is that transformation of human persons as persons which results from the loving presence of God. Under the impact of the divine self-gift (i.e., God's graciousness), the human's structures of consciousness and affectivity are quite radically reorientated. Since the concrete context for all such divine self-giving is God's self-revelation in Christ, the grace-transformation of a person is "Christianization"—the polarization of one's personal existing by the presence (accepted in faith) of the risen Christ, who himself is sacramental of the presence of his Father.

What this implies, as one reflects on it, is the change of a person's awareness of himself and of all other reality, a change brought about by the insights proper to faith and revelation, a change that touches the deepest constitutive elements of a person's psychic structure and which can therefore be called a basic ontological transformation. Simply put, the presence of the risen Christ to a believer transforms the most fundamental meaning of that person; it is a basic "transignification" and could also be called a "transubstantiation." This is not something totally hidden and mysterious, though obviously we are not explicitly conscious of all the complexities of our psychic functions. The mystery and the "supernaturality" and the gratuity of a Christian's transformation consist precisely in the totally inexplicable fact that "God so loved the world that he has sent his only-begotten son, so that those who believe may not perish but may have unending life." The mystery lies in what theologians have called uncreated grace.

Such a profoundly personal reorientation certainly deserves to be called "conversion." Even in the case of a Christian who is deeply committed in faith to Christ, there is a continuing movement away from inadequate response to divine love and towards a more adequate response. And since sin is the alienation from God (as well as from other humans and from one's self) that results from the refusal to love, the transformation of a person by divine presence is identical with freeing a person from sin. For that reason, a sinner's contrition should not be looked upon as a prelude to forgiveness of sin and reconciliation with God; it is already a response to divine love, a positive reorientation that replaces the lack of that orientation, which lack is what the sin was. Liberation from sin can be viewed as the reintegration of a person's affective power, a reintegration that can be more fully accomplished because of the loving presence of God. The reason this is so is that the source of psychic integration is a person's own acts of loving, and the divine offer of friendship opens up a new level of loving response—man's capacity to love is transformed.

This transformation of a person by the presence of Christ constitutes a "consecration" of the most ultimate sort. If one works from the etymological meaning of the term, then there could be no fuller associating a person with sacred things than the personal relatedness of a Christian with the risen Christ and his Father, a relatedness which the Johannine tradition describes as a mutual indwelling. The ultimate dimension of this relatedness comes in the fact that the Christian shares one common Spirit with Christ and his Father. This Spirit, the principle of Christ's own human consecration and therefore of all Christian consecration, is the supreme "blessing" that Christ confers on his disciples. Christ's gift of his Spirit is the gift of "eternal life," for this Spirit is the source of that new life which Jesus has in resurrection; Christ's Eucharistic gift of his own life involves a continuous Pentecost. Moreover, if the term "applying the merits of Christ" has any meaning, it can only refer to this life-giving blessing of the Spirit, for it is precisely the full possession of life and the Spirit of life that Jesus gained by passing through death into resurrection.

When one comes to the important term

"mediation," there is question of the agency by which God's transforming self-gift is made present to men. The risen Christ is admittedly the unique mediator, but in understanding his mediation it seems important to deal with the following distinction: One can think of mediation as *transient* activity or as *immanent* activity. In other words, one can think of mediation in terms of some agent causing an effect from outside, or one can think of it in terms of one part of a living thing acting upon another part, but doing so because it is an organic expression of the life that is common to both parts. Significantly, both the Pauline notion of the church as body and the Johannine description of the church as vine place us in the context of immanent activity, though, obviously, there is no intent of denying either the continuing human individuality of the risen Christ or his preeminence as head. This distinction seems even more applicable to whatever mediation belongs to persons or institutions or processes in the church. Are we to think of some mediator (e.g., the episcopal college) as standing between Christ and the rest of the church and instrumentally passing on grace? Or is it more correct to think of Christ and his Spirit being present most immediately to the Christian community, and that the community then mediates life and mission in specialized (organic) fashion to individuals or groups so that they can then nurture the community's life or carry out its mission?

In any event, if grace (consecration, Christianization, and sanctification) is effected by the divine presence, "mediation" can mean nothing other than making such presence possible. And because presence is what it is, something that takes place in terms of consciousness and personal communication, the mediating of God's presence to men must in the last analysis coincide with sacramentality: Christ as sacrament makes his Father present; the church as sacrament makes Christ present, and it does so most formally in those symbolic activities that have traditionally been called the sacraments.

To return, then, to the notion of priest-

hood: When we speak of the priesthood of Christ himself, we are referring to that basic directedness of his human existing and activity towards the establishment of a worship community. Another way of expressing this is to say that the mission of the son-become-man is to establish the kingdom of his Father, for the kingdom of God is coextensive with the acknowledgment and acceptance (explicit or implicit) of God. Still another way of pointing to the same reality is to say that the glory of God is the finality of the Incarnation, "glory" referring both to the action of formally glorifying God and to the realization of human potential in this act of glorification, i.e., man thus perfected in the act of contemplating and loving God is "the glory of God." But however one wishes to categorize this priestly orientation of the being and action of the man Jesus, it is clear that it is accomplished essentially by his being the sacrament of his Father's self-gift to men and the sacrament of men's acceptance and reciprocal self-gift. Being the embodied Word of the Father, Jesus realizes uniquely the oracular aspect of priesthood; being a victim committed by resurrection to self-giving as the life source of all other humans, Jesus realizes uniquely the sacrificial aspect of priesthood.

Since Jesus, the risen Lord, communicates to his Body, the church, his own life and his own Spirit, the church's very existence is finalized by Jesus' own priestly mission. Thus, the entire Christian community is priestly. Its priesthood is not some office or function entrusted to it, nor some quality that attaches to it because it was founded by Christ's priestly sacrifice on Calvary; its priesthood is the fundamental dynamism and purposefulness of its being. Concretely, the Christian community exists "priestly" because it exists "sacramentally." Being the Body of the risen Christ, the Christian community, in everything it is and does, *bears witness* to the presence of Christ; its loving and faith-filled concern for bettering human life makes present Christ's own salvific concern; it is *oracular*. But the church is the Body-Sacrament of Christ in freedom and faith. Men and women are Christians if they give themselves in belief and love to Christ and with him to all other humans; as Christians they are a living sacrifice in which Christ's own sacrificial self-gift is made present to mankind.

Because it is thus priestly to the depths of its being, everything about the church—all its activities, all its institutions, all its ministries, all its members—are marked with a priestly character; but no one aspect or agency of the church can claim to be the priesthood. At the same time, since the corporate life of the church (rooted as it is in the Spirit) is extremely rich and capable of manifold expression, this life manifests itself organically (charismatically) through diverse ministries that safeguard and nurture the diverse aspects of the community's being. One of the things that needs to be safeguarded and nurtured is the formal expression of Christian sacramentality that takes place in the community's liturgical celebrations. The need for a ministry of liturgical leadership, whose purpose is to unify a group of assembled Christians into a true *koinonia* of Christian worship, flows from the very priestliness of the church. All the ministries of the church are priestly, for the church is priestly, but the ministry of liturgical leadership bears a special relationship to the community's sacramentality and priesthood, for it exists in order to bring that priesthood to its fullest sacramental expression. It flows from the more basic priesthood of the community, functions for the sake of that community priesthood, and in a sense is a specialized or intensified expression of that common priesthood.

To say all this is not yet to say that there must be some institutionalized group of ministers who are set aside to perform this function. It is simply to say that this ministry-to-sacrament function is required by the nature of the church. History indicates, however, that very early in the church's life there emerged the institution of permanent, "professional" orders of liturgical ministers, and that very early these ministers were designated and empowered by a ritual of ordination. Historically, it is a bit unclear when and in

what manner this ordination rite came into use, or exactly how it was understood in early Christianity.

In more recent centuries, there has been debate among the Christian confessions as to whether ordination is a genuine sacrament. There is no question but that this liturgical ceremony was considered sacramental in a full sense for many centuries prior to the Reformation when the question arose in more acerbated form, so much so that the term "sacrament of orders" came to be applied to it rather than to the ordained ministers who are "the orders" within the community. Theological study of the sacrament of orders pretty well confined itself to reflection on the ordination ceremony. To some extent the Reformation and post-Reformation controversy on the question has been a *lis verborum*, depending upon the limitation or breadth of meaning that one wished to give to the term "sacrament." Much of the controversy flowed from the divergent understandings of Christian ministry that marked the sixteenth century, particularly the extent to which ministry, and therefore ordination to ministry, was tied to the function of offering sacrifice. And another important element in the difference of views was the notion of sacraments "giving grace."

Today, however, it seems that there is broad acceptance, confessional and theological, of some special Christian sacramentality in the ritual by which the various churches designate ministers to lead their worship services. There is general agreement that the designation and empowering (however one may wish to understand these two notions) are not purely human, that somehow the call from God and the empowering by the Spirit enter into the picture. There is much less agreement, even within confessional traditions, as to whether the ordination ceremony is the community's recognition of the charism given by the Spirit, or whether the gift of the Spirit in the ordination ratifies the community's choice of an individual to perform a function, or whether the community (or a group within the community, the episcopal college) actually confers the charism on the ordinand.

Perhaps one can avoid some (if not all) of the traditional conflict of opinion by transposing the question to another context. If ministries emerge organically from the church's inner life as specialized agencies to nurture that life, and if the ministry of liturgical leadership emerges from the life of the church *as sacrament* so that the church can become more profoundly sacramental, then the process of that emergence (i.e., the historical sequence of ordinations) must surely be sacramental. Moroever, if the ministerial charism in question is one that belongs corporately to what we might call tentatively the "sacerdotal *collegium*" and an individual ordinand shares in this charism by initiation into the *collegium*, there can be an ordinational gift of the Spirit which is quite clearly other than the vocation that attracted him to this ministry, and other than the gifts of grace that mark him as a suitable candidate for ministerial ordination. That these latter two can constitute a designation by the Spirit, a designation that should be honored by the community as it discerns those to be ordained is quite clear; but an individual cannot share in the properly collegial charism except by becoming a member of the *collegium*.

But is the ordination of liturgical ministers such a collegial initiation? Both history and theological reflection suggest an affirmative answer. For many centuries (before geographical dispersal, private masses, and a growing individualism corroded the sense of corporate Christian worship) the common pattern of Eucharistic leadership was concelebration. Again, in the ordination of bishops there was, if at all possible, an imposition of hands by a number of the bishops of the region. In the ordination of presbyters there was an imposition of hands by all the presbyters present at the ceremony. In several Christian traditions, this liturgical practice has continued unbroken up to the present time, despite a long period of time when the sense of collegiality was quite dim. Thirdly, if one tries to recapture the understanding

that the early Christian centuries had of ordination, it seems to have been that of a man being incorporated into an "order" (an "official level") of the community and beginning to share the responsibilities and powers proper to that order. For quite some time there was little notion that ordination gave the ordinand a new physical power to cause such sacramental effects as Eucharistic changing of bread and wine. Actually, when presbyteral ordination came to be viewed as the conferring of such causal power (the sacramental character of orders, the *potestas ordinis*), this diminished the sense of collegial sacerdotal activity.

The role of liturgical leadership includes a sacramentalizing of the unity between a given Eucharistic celebration and the Eucharist of the entire church. Thus, this particular ministry appears to be a collegial ministry that is meant to be exercised corporately. An individual cannot function as liturgical celebrant without some membership in the *collegium*. This does not rule out a temporary association with the *collegium*, or an ad hoc delegation to be celebrant on a single occasion, nor even the emergency measure of a community that is deprived of ordinary means of obtaining liturgical leaders selecting someone to function in this role. In these instances, also, the liturgical celebrant would be acting collegially.

If we are to consider the ritual of ordination as admission to a ministerial *collegium*, we face the problem of identifying the *collegium* in question. Historical evidence on the point is both important and confusing. It suggests at least three collegial realities (the episcopacy, the presbyterate, the ministerial priesthood), but it is not at all clear how these are to be distinguished from, related to, or identified with, one another. What adds to the confusion is the historical evolution of meaning attached to such terms as "*sacerdotium*" or "*presbyterus*," and the historical decline of appreciation for the collegiality of Christian ministry. It does seem, however, that we can prescind from any historical use of words to denominate a given group of men, and approach the problem in terms of the functions to which episcopal and presbyteral ordination point. Then, perhaps, we can discover to which group or groups a given function belongs.

Certainly, there is some question of a collegial witness to the apostolic experience and faith; there is also a collegial function of officiating at liturgical celebrations, providing sacral contact between the community and God, and praying officially for the community. There is a third, less specific, function of governing the orderly conduct of a community, including the orderly conduct of its liturgical activity. And there is a fourth, even less specific, role (for it is not really a particular function) of exerting leadership in a way appropriate to a believing and Eucharistically worshiping community. The third and fourth of these groups are inadequately distinct from one another. Those exercising the function of governing would inevitably be part of the leadership group, but not vice versa. And in the practical order it might make good sense in a given situation to assign the function of liturgical officiating to those who are governing or to the community's leadership; but there does not seem to be any necessitating intrinsic reason for such an assignment. Again, there seems to be no compelling theological reason for identifying the function of special apostolic witness with the function of governing, though such convergence occurred very early in the emergence of the historical episcopate. On the contrary, there does seem to be an intrinsic connection between the function of liturgical leadership (part of which is to sacramentalize the apostolicity of the community) and the function of special apostolic witness.

It seems that a certain amount of ambiguity arose because the two functions of governing and bearing special witness were confused in the episcopal function, and the notion of oligarchy rather than collegiality characterized the understanding of episcopal government. Things were further confused when preeminence in liturgical leadership, which was intrinsically linked to the episcopal college's witness function, was incorrectly thought to be a result of its governing function. Theoretically, it seems that the *collegium* of special witness to the apostolic tradition could cease all governing apart from the normative proclamation of their witness, and an entirely different group could provide for the necessary practical management of the community's life, but that no such separation could occur between the "witnessing college" and the "liturgical leadership college," since the proper function of the former is instrinsic to the functioning of the latter. Christian liturgy requires apostolic witness, and only in that liturgy can the witness finds its fullest expression. At the same time, the witness college is not coextensive with the liturgical leadership college; the witness college functions within the liturgical leadership college to make the function of the latter possible, just as the liturgical leadership college functions within the community as a whole so that the community can celebrate its priesthood sacramentally.

Ordination, then, is the initiation into the *collegium* of liturgical leaders. Episcopal consecration (or whatever term one wishes to apply to the designation of higher clergy) is a second-step initiation into the witness college. By receiving a new member into its midst, each *collegium* shares with him the charism and function it possesses in common, and the initiate undertakes the corporate responsibilities and contributes to the corporate activity of the group. Since the witness college possesses a certain eminence within the liturgical leadership college, it is intrinsically appropriate (though apparently not necessary) that a member of the witness college act as the special agent of initiation; however, it is most basically the entire liturgical leadership college that receives a new member.

The Sacramental Character of Orders

Explaining ordination in this fashion implies no denial of the classic teaching that ordination confers a special power of orders, a sacramental character. Rather, it opens up the way for giving such teaching a more deeply ecclesial interpretation and for explaining what is essentially a societal (relational) reality in societal terms, rather than trying to fit it into an anthropology of intrinsic powers of action. The very word "ordination" suggests a "being directed toward," a new relatedness to a function that is to be performed within a community and to a community goal that is to be achieved. Although one obviously has to employ certain bodily or psychological powers to fulfill this function, none of these gives the relatedness to community function. Such relatedness derives from one's membership and/or special role in the community.

In Christ himself, it is his mission (which is identical with the finality of the Incarnation and with the eschatological impulse of the prophetic Spirit) that sets the context for his human existing and provides its special priestly character. His human endowments and the activities that flow from them are directed to fulfillment of that mission. Concretely, that mission is the establishment of the divine-human community which is the kingdom of God; everything Jesus is and does is marked by his ordination to the achievement of that goal. His priesthood is clearly a societal reality; it is a directedness to establishing the ultimate society.

When he communicates his mission to his followers, which he does by sharing with them his own destiny and his own Spirit, Christ automatically gives his priestly character to their human existing and to their life as sons of his Father. The church, Christ's Body that is animated by his Spirit, cannot have a finality other than that proper to the risen Christ himself; the church exists with the same priestly orientation, the same character as does Christ. This is the priesthood that is corporately possessed by the Christian community, and in which each Christian shares by his baptismal entry into the community. This priesthood that is common to all the faithful is a directedness towards nurturing human community, and precisely at the level of faith.

Since a community in faith can only exist and develop through the sharing of faith, which implies necessarily the external profession of faith, the Christian community's priestly character directs it to formal worship, to public acknowledgment of the Father. Each Christian, by virtue of belonging to this community, participates in this responsibility and is obviously therefore empowered to profess his faith sacramentally in Christian liturgy. The priestly character in which one shares by baptism does not point to one specific function in Christian life. Rather, it is a fundamental, all-embracing specification of one's human existing; it conditions one's entire life of faith and grace by placing it in the context of priestly purpose. This is not an individual modification that comes to each person with baptism; it is the Christian community that is priestly/sacramental in its whole being.

One can link "sacramental" with "priestly" in this matter, because the priestly mission of Christ himself is accomplished in his existing sacramentally. His Father's love is the ultimate source of that human community towards which Jesus' priesthood is directed, and this love is made salvifically present to men in Christ as the sacrament of his Father. So, too, the church is fundamentally sacramental. The professed faith of Christians (particularly in Eucharist) makes present Christ in his Passover mystery, i.e., the very power of life and unity that will eventually accomplish the kingdom of God. As in Christ, priesthood is something more basic than any particular action or power of action, so in the church the common priesthood is more basic than any power to act, even the power to celebrate Eucharist, because it is the community's very way of existing as the sacrament of Christ.

It is different when one speaks of a sacramental character resulting from ministerial ordination. Here, it is a matter of a specific directedness to some function that enables the community to express its priestly character. If the ordination in question is that of liturgical ministers (for "ordination" could apply to the public designation of other ministers as well), the ordinand is directed towards the function of liturgical leadership. And he is so directed by sharing in the corporate function of the liturgical leadership *collegium* into which his ordination introduces him. Because of the very manner in which it serves the common priesthood of the community, the special mission or charism (i.e., sacramental character, power of orders) of liturgical ministry belongs to this *collegium* which functions as a sacrament within a sacrament, in order that the community can give formally sacramental expression to its priestly existence. Those who belong to this special ministerial group are not more priestly than other Christians, but they are called to give special sacramental expression to Christ's priestly action of Passover so that the entire community can celebrate more authentically and fully its priestly character. Probably the best way of gaining some insight into the special power or character possessed by this ministerial *collegium* is to examine the specific role exercised by the ordained liturgical leader.

As we approach the focal question of the precise role of the ordained minister in the action of sacraments, certain theological presuppositions must be kept in mind. First of all, the sacraments are actions of the entire community and not just of the officiating celebrant; they are actions of the local assembled community that is actually performing the ritual act, and they are also actions of the "great church," i.e., the entire church, which is linked with and involved in the local community's profession of faith. In the celebration of the sacramental act, some individuals or groups have special functions so that the community can "do the sacrament"; but *the* basic action of the sacrament is the community's "sacrificial" profession of its faith. Incidentally, it is good to remember that the ordained celebrant shares with the community as it makes this corporate profession, i.e., he acts in a special role but he also acts as a member of the community.

Secondly, the basic structure of all the sacramental rituals is that of evangelization and response: there is a proclamation of the Passover of Christ and the community's "yes" to this proclamation. How this happens in each of the sacramental contexts is quite different,

for "sacrament" can be applied only analogously to the various human experiences that are Christianized in sacrament by applying to them the transforming meaning of Christ's death and resurrection.

Thirdly, the actions of sacramental ritual are actions of the risen Christ himself, actions that he performs in and through the Christian community which is his Body. It is the faith of this community which provides the matrix for Christ's saving presence; his gift of himself as word and life is received in the community's consciousness of its faith. In this sense, the assembled Christians act as the instrument of Christ, enabling him to speak to them and through them to others his saving word of self-gift.

Fourthly, the sacramental actions are the ritual moment in a much broader sacramental process: the entire corporate living of the community, involving the whole life experience of its individual members, is sacramental because the church as Body of Christ is a sacrament of his presence. The entirety of Christian living is a continuous act of worship; the sacramental rituals are specially formalized expressions of that worship.

What, then, is the particular function of the ordained minister who acts as liturgical leader? For one thing, his function is clearly prophetic (or to put "prophetic" into a precisely Christian context, his function is evangelical): he is to proclaim to the assembled community the word of Christ's death and resurrection. All preaching of the gospel involves more than just the psychological effectiveness of human language. All authentic preaching of the gospel is sacramental, but the Eucharistic proclamation (which, of course, includes the entire liturgical action as a "word") possesses a unique symbolic depth. Briefly put, it not only proclaims the Passover mystery, it *is* that Passover mystery. In Eucharist, there is total convergence of prophecy and priesthood; both of these realities take on a new meaning by being identified with Christian celebration of Passover.

Like all prophetic proclamation, the Eucharistic action gives meaning to the present by interpreting it in terms of the past and future activity of God; it places man's life experience within the context of human history interpreted eschatologically. If such a giving-of-meaning is really to happen in a particular Eucharistic celebration, someone must make clear to the assembled Christians that this is what is happening—this is the role of the celebrant. In all the elements of explanation, particularly in the homily, that clarify for the community the meaning of what they are doing in Eucharist, the celebrant is more than a teacher; he is exercising a properly prophetic function. This prophetic activity is intensified in the Eucharistic prayer, which is the great prayer of blessing God because of his great deeds. This is the supreme act of prophetic witness in which the celebrant, because he is symbolizing both the witness of Christ and the witness of the church, unites in himself (as a symbol) all authentic worship of God.

Certainly, it is not the celebrant by himself who acts prophetically in Eucharist; even the Eucharistic prayer, though the celebrant alone enunciates it, is the corporate prayer (and proclamation) of the entire group. But it is the liturgical leader who by placing the symbol, i.e., his words and his other actions, gives the form to the community's prophetic act. Animated by the Spirit of prophecy, a community of Christians gathers to bear witness to God; but to do so, it must utter an appropriate word. This the celebrant does for the community (or better: enables the community to do) by utilizing essentially that symbol-word which was employed by Jesus at the Supper and which has been the heart of all Christian Eucharist.

Basically, the function of the celebrant is not to perform an action (whether one views it as prophetic, worship, or sacrifice) that the assembled community observes, nor to perform an action representatively for the community and in its place. By his liturgical leadership he is to help bring into being a deepened community of faith and worship in the very act of Eucharist so that the assembled community can more authentically and pro-

foundly celebrate the Eucharistic mystery. Since the community, if its action is to be a response in faith to God's word, must appreciate the action as a word of God in Christ that is here and now spoken to it, the special prophetic role of the celebrant is to convey such an insight. He does this by the didactic elements of his activity, but even more importantly by the "word" which he himself is during the Eucharistic act. The celebrant is specially sacramental.

Before probing a bit further the meaning of "sacramental" as applied to the Eucharistic minister, it would be good to recall that the more ancient meaning of a "sacrament of orders" applies to the group of ordained ministers rather than to the ordination ceremony. The collegial group of publicly designated liturgical leaders is the sacrament of orders. So, even though in the last few paragraphs we have been speaking of the liturgical celebrant as an individual (and for the sake of simplicity will continue to do so), it is important to keep in mind that the ministry of Eucharistic leadership is essentially collegial, and that any exercise of this ministry by an individual is always in its deeper reality a sharing in the corporate ministry of the liturgical leadership *collegium*. Fortunately, it is much easier for us to appreciate this since the reinstitution of the ancient Christian practice of ministerial concelebration of Eucharist.

Theological reflection seems to indicate that no characterization of the liturgical celebrant's function is more basic or more precise than to say that he acts sacramentally, that he is a "sacrament within a sacrament." He forms a community of faith by sacramentalizing that community. In him, as he gives expression to the community's faith, that faith finds a unified statement; as he witnesses externally to his own faith, that witness acts to unify and confirm the faith of his brethren. As he sacramentalizes the corporate faith of the liturgical leadership *collegium*, that faith works to deepen the faith of the assembled Christians. But the faith of that *collegium* (which is the corporate minister of all Eucharist) is itself a sacrament of the faith of the great church (i.e., of all the various local communities), and the unity of the collegial faith acts sacramentally in Eucharist to unify the faith and worship of the entire church.

However, the unity of the Christian people is not just a unity that applies geographically at any given time (e.g., Christians today throughout the world are one community); it is a unity that extends through history, so that Christians at any point of time can identify with Christians at any other time despite all the changes that history brings. This aspect of Christian unity is critically important when one is dealing with the Christian sacraments, for the most essential dimension of their symbolism is historical: they *must* bear the significance of that happening which is the life and death and resurrection of Jesus Christ. Thus, the sacramentality of any celebration of Eucharist must include a recognizable link of the community's faith with the faith of all previous Christians, all the way back to the faith experience of the Twelve; Eucharist must always express the apostolic tradition. And while it is true that the entire community celebrating Eucharist bears this mark of apostolicity, and the liturgical employment of New Testament literature is a special witness to apostolic tradition, the collegial leadership of Eucharist, as it sacramentalizes the witness of the Twelve, has a specific role in linking the faith of Christians today with the faith of previous generations of Christians.

If the various kinds of sacramentalizing we have described are to take place, the Eucharistic minister must be publicly recognizable as symbolizing the assembled community and the liturgical leadership *collegium*; this is what ordination provides. However, there is another aspect of the minister's sacramental function, and historically this has been stressed in the interpretation of ordination's effectiveness: the liturgical celebrant acts as the sacrament of Christ. The special representative function of the liturgical leader in relationship to Christ has been variously described: he is the vicar of Christ, he is the legate of Christ, he is the minister of Christ, he

acts *in persona Christi*, he is the instrument of Christ. And each of these descriptions has found multiple interpretation, dependent upon the basic soteriological understanding of the risen Christ's relationship to the church. However, it seems safe to say that no interpretation allows for a more immediate involvement of Christ himself in the action of Eucharist than to see the minister's function as *sacramental* in the strict sense.

Sacrament is that which makes present by its very symbolizing; the Christian Eucharist is an unparalleled instance of such "making present." Fundamentally, and most importantly, it is the Christian community's faith that provides the location of Christ's presence. Presence in the strictest sense is a matter of a person *being for* someone else in friendship, which can only happen if that other person is consciously aware and accepting of this loving self-communication. Christian faith is such a conscious acceptance of Christ's self-gift, and consequently Christ is personally present wherever there are Christians who believe in him. So, when a group of Christians gathers for Eucharist, the risen Christ is present because of their faith. It is inaccurate to suppose that he becomes present only with the consecration of the bread and wine. However, because presence is the kind of reality it is, it is intensified in proportion as the consciousness and acceptance and reciprocal self-giving deepen. The level of presence is commensurate with the level of friendship.

So, by being a specialized expression or sacrament of Christ's self-giving to a Eucharistic community, the liturgical celebrant can lead to an intensification of Christ's presence to that group of men and women, and through them to others as well. Concretely, the celebrant makes Christ more intensely present to the community by communicating Christ to them—in the total liturgical action of the Eucharist which includes the "embodiment" of Christ in the liturgical use of Scripture, the "embodiment" of Christ in the ritual transformation of the bread and wine, in the distribution of the consecrated species in Communion. Obviously, all this is an action of

Christ's own self-giving, but it takes place precisely in and through the celebrant's symbolic activity, i.e., through the celebrant's action as a sacrament. Though it has been historically misleading to isolate it from the rest of the Eucharistic action and to make it, almost by itself, the focal instant of worship and sacrifice and sanctification, the Eucharistic changing of the bread and wine is a key aspect of the liturgical minister's special function. Bread and wine as transformed in Eucharistic celebration are clearly the means for Christ's gift of self to the assembled Christians. It is the liturgical leader who "Christianizes" (i.e., attaches a Christ-meaning to, or transignifies) these elements of food and drink, a Christianization that takes on full depth because Christ is sacramentally present in this action and uses the visibility of the bread and wine as a principle of communicating his gift of self.

Because he is thus giving himself in the Eucharistic action, Christ is still offering sacrifice. The fullness of Jesus' priestly act of sacrifice comes in his resurrection, which places him irrevocably in the sacred victim state of being for his brethren as source of new life; but he can actually *be for others* only if he can be present to them. By his liturgical use of the bread and wine, the celebrant of Eucharist becomes the sacrament through and in whom the risen Christ is able to be more explicitly present to the assembled community; Christ is thus able to give himself in presence to these Christians. Concomitantly, these assembled Christians are enabled to respond to Christ's word of self-gift by committing themselves to *be for others*, for Christ and for their fellow humans, thus offering the sacrifice of themselves in union with Christ's own sacrifice. The liturgical celebrant does not offer the sacrifice himself (except insofar as he shares in the community's act of sacrifice), but it is he who makes possible the reciprocal self-giving of Christ and the community, i.e., their unified sacrifice. The celebrant does lead the Eucharistic assembly as it gives voice to its sacrificial decision, but it is the entire community that corporately professes this decision, and thereby offers sacrifice.

The liturgical celebrant's sacramental activity, his word, is simultaneously Christ's word to the community, the community's word of response to Christ, and the conjoined word of both Christ and the community to the Father; for this reason, the Eucharistic leader's role is one of mediation in this sense of sacramental unification. He does not stand between Christ and the community; rather, it is in his word that Christ and the community meet and commune. Too much of the historical discussion about the Eucharistic celebrant's function was controlled (at least implicitly) by the image of the risen Christ being "up in heaven" and being represented in the earthly liturgy by his legate; in such a view the celebrant stands in the place of Christ. However, such an approach worked against the understanding of Eucharist as a mystery of Christ's presence; the celebrant tended to be more a sign of Christ's absence. Instead of being seen as the sacrament of Christ's presence, the liturgical celebrant came to be viewed more and more as the wonder-worker who effected the unique miracle of transubstantiation; practically all notion of sacramentality became attached to the consecrated elements. Moreover, theological study of the Eucharist artificially and inaccurately separated discussion of the Eucharist as sacrament from discussion of the Eucharist as sacrifice, and separated the role of the celebrant in offering sacrifice from his role in administering the sacrament. This almost completely obscured the fact that the celebrant's role (in everything he did, including the distribution of Communion) was one of sacramentalizing Christ's sacrificial self-giving. As theologians lost sight of the very specific kind of mediation that was exercised by the Eucharistic celebrant (or for that matter, by the Eucharistic community and by Christ himself), "priesthood" and "mediation" came to be seen as totally coincident: to be priest was to be mediator, to be mediator was to be priest. Thus, since any form of ministry involves some element of mediation, all the ministerial functions in the church came to be absorbed into the priestly ministry.

Today, with the regaining of an insight

into Christ's presence to men, particularly to those men and women who are members of his Body, the church, we can work towards a more accurate understanding of mediation as applied to Christ himself, to the church, to various ministries in the church, and specifically to the celebrant's role in Eucharistic liturgy. If we might borrow a helpful distinction from scholastic philosophy, the Eucharistic leader's action is more of a medium *in which* Christ gives himself to the community (and vice versa) than a medium *through which* this happens; thus it seems much more helpful to speak of the celebrant as a sacrament than as an instrument. One can speak of the sacramental celebrant as the instrument God uses to give grace to people, but when one examines more closely the meaning of his giving of grace, it is clear that what is involved is a process of Christianizing and that the liturgical celebrant helps effect such Christianizing by being the sacrament of Christ's self-giving. It would seem, then, that the most precise and distinguishing description we can give of the liturgical celebrant's function is in terms of its special sacramentality. It is *one* of the kinds of mediation that operate in the church's life; it is the one in which the liturgical leaders minister to the community's formally sacramental expression of its priesthood. It is a specially priestly ministry, for it is a ministry to the church's priesthood.

Before concluding our treatment of the ministry of liturgical leadership, a word needs to be said about the ecclesiastical discipline of clerical celibacy. Further reflection and experience by the Christian community may well indicate that celibacy is not intrinsic to the meaning or to the exercise of this sacramental ministry. But for many centuries a large portion of the church has seen celibacy as very closely, if not inseparably, linked with priestly ministry, and this widespread view is a piece of experiential data that the theologian cannot ignore in a conscientious attempt to clarify the nature of Christian ministry and priesthood.

Reasons for the discipline of imposed clerical celibacy can be roughly grouped into three classes: practical, theological, and ascetical—though the last two somewhat overlap. Our treatment will concentrate on these last two types of reasons, since both theological and ecclesiastical justification for the official policy have insisted that the grounds for clerical celibacy are ultimately ascetical and theological—a brief mention of the practical reasons that have been given historically for celibacy will suffice. Some of these practical reasons seem obvious: If sacramental ministry is to be a full-time profession, it should be less expensive for the community to employ a celibate than a married man with a family. Again, a man without family responsibilities could be moved more easily from one position to another, from one place to another; he could be asked to submit to living conditions that a married man would hesitate to inflict on his family and he could be more totally at people's disposal in his pastoral work. Moreover, an unmarried man can (in exercising the prophetic aspects of his ministry) witness to unpopular elements of the gospel without having to worry about the social impact on his family. Then, too, a celibate minister is more likely to identify with the clerical establishment, more likely to be amenable to administrative control, more willing to submerge himself in a team effort. Other practical reasons might be added, but precisely because these are in the order of practical judgment, they must be evaluated by the experience of history (which does not fully support all of these reasons) and by the circumstances of a given situation.

Turning to the theological grounds for clerical celibacy, which is our particular concern here, it seems that the reasons given for celibacy center around its special symbolic impact. Sometimes appeal is made to the fact that clerical celibacy can symbolize the celibate situation of Christ himself; since Christ himself was unmarried, those who most closely link themselves with his priestly ministry should imitate him in his celibacy. Much more basic, however, in the classical argumentation is the view that sexual intercourse is fundamentally inappropriate to the realm of the sacred. Without going into the whole question of the origin and the extent of the negative attitude towards sexuality that crept into Christianity at an early date, it is clear that not long after the first Christian century the opinion grew that sexual activity should be excluded from the life of those who exercised liturgical leadership (concomitantly there was increased application of the term priest to such liturgical leaders). There seems no way of avoiding the conclusion that in its earliest stages the move towards clerical celibacy was motivated by a view that sexual intercourse was, if not evil, at least much less good. Married men who were ordained were not required to free themselves from any of the practical burdens of family life; they remained with their families, but they were not to have marital relations. Those who were ordained for liturgical celebration were *consecrated*, and somehow sexual acts violated this consecration. Though they might have shunned such a direct statement, the Christian theologians during the time when celibacy was emerging as a pattern of clerical life looked upon sexual intercourse as a defiling activity. A basic belief in the sacredness of the married state was preserved, but one gets the impression from patristic literature that marriage itself would be better if it did not involve sex.

Because the Eucharistic minister was involved in offering the sacrifice of Christ, he himself should symbolize Christ's sacrificial victimhood; the ordained minister should be a living sacrifice. Celibacy was the key symbol of such sacrificial existence. Obviously, in such an understanding of "sacrifice" the emphasis is placed on giving up, and celibacy is presupposed to be a more difficult decision than marriage. After all, sexual activity in marriage is a concession granted by God so that the human race can continue, and truly Christian exercise of marital relations will be only for the purpose of procreation. If one wished to go the whole way, to be truly an unblemished sacrifice, this involved celibacy. One who bore the title "priest" should be such an undefiled sacrificial victim.

Again, the very notion of "sacred" (or of "consecrated") involved a removal from the profane, a distancing from the world and its entanglements. All Christians were to be otherworldly, to be pilgrims without any permanent roots in this world, to be free from involvement with mundane affairs; so much the more should specially consecrated priests be separated from ordinary life. And what is more symbolic than sex of men and women's involvement in this world and all its many absorbing activities and responsibilities? Sexual intercourse is intrinsically a commitment to mankind's continuing existence on this planet. Thus, the celibacy of ordained ministers was meant to symbolize their noninvolvement in human affairs; historically it has done this, both for good and for ill.

Slightly different is the eschatological symbolism of celibacy, something that is much appealed to in today's discussion of celibacy. Because humans are presumably destined to live a-sexually (like the angels) in the next life, those who live a celibate existence are already living, as it were, in the next life; and so they are a sign to the whole church and to others also of the life to come. Unless there were the hope of this future reward, the sacrifice of foregoing married life would be meaningless; so the ordained celibate gives witness to his faith in this eschatological fulfillment.

Closely connected with such theological views were the ascetical views that stressed freedom from sex as basic to Christian perfection. Not accidentally, such views came into prominence at the time when the ascetic was replacing the martyr as Christian ideal, at the time when chastity was replacing charity as the preeminent Christian virtue, and at the time when monasticism (whose origins show some signs of Essene influence) was giving a social formulation to the ideal of freedom from this world in order to gain the next world.

In this ascetic theory, man had to condition himself (with God's grace, of course) by stringent self-discipline so that he would be free and undistracted when he turned to contemplation. Progress in contemplation was what really marked a Christian's progress in sanctity and familiarity with God, but there had to be an accompanying ascetic endeavor that gradually freed a man from any enslaving link to the terrestrial. Since it involved not just the personal responsibilities of caring for a wife and children but also the deeply distracting and disturbing forces of human passion, sexual activity was such an enslaving link and was incompatible with an ascetic-contemplative striving for union with God.

Now, ordained ministers were not monks, but they were thought to possess a higher position in the church than even the monks; hence, a higher level of perfection should be expected of them—obviously implying celibacy. Besides, for a liturgical minister to perform his function with understanding and symbolic depth, he needed contemplation as a basic element in his life; and this contemplation dictated celibacy as a prerequisite. Then, too, because his sanctity was to bear witness to Christ's own sacrificial holiness, the ordained minister had even more reason than the monk to live a celibate existence.

All this did not mean that the ordained minister was to be an unloving person. Just the contrary: the fact that he had not focused his human love on his own wife and children meant that the celibate was freer to love all the members of the community; in this way he reflected the universality of Christ's own celibate love. More basically, and this is probably the most profound and most authentic element in Christian celibacy, the celibate gave all his deepest personal affection and devotion to Christ himself in exclusive fashion; his love for Christ was such that it left no place for rivals. With Christ he was lovingly concerned for all men and women; but Christ was the one love of his life.

Such (at least in essential lines) has been the theological and ascetical argumentation in support of clerical celibacy. None of it is, of course, particularly supportive of a discipline that imposes celibacy by law and enforces it by harsh penalty. Progress in true Christian sanctity is a movement towards increased freedom, and the symbolic value of personal witness depends upon the freedom of the witness. Celibacy is authentically Chris-

tian only if it is the expression of love; but love of its nature cannot be legislated. But even apart from this element of imposition, there is much to make one question the arguments for linking celibacy with the ordained ministry. Incidentally, this is quite a different question from that of the relevance of committed celibacy (the "vow of chastity") to the communal life of dedicated religious groups, or the value of choosing a celibate way of life for any one of several good reasons —including the performance of certain ministerial functions.

For one thing, the historical picture of clerical celibacy is a very mixed one. Unquestionably, the context of celibate life has been a profoundly inspiring and Christianizing force in the lives of many ordained ministers; the celibacy of the clergy (even with its imposed character) has been a genuine witness to the ministerial dedication of many of the ordained. On the other hand, the centuries-long battle to enforce celibacy and the severity of the measures used to make it a universally accepted pattern in the Roman Catholic community make one wonder about the intrinsic persuasiveness of the arguments used to defend it. Even more tellingly, one finds it difficult not to be disturbed by the widespread damage done to people for centuries, by the severity (even cruelty) and administrative arrogance of the procedures used to force acceptance of the discipline, by the almost total lack (on the part of the masculine church authorities in question) of any compassion or even sense of justice towards the women affected by the discipline. Perhaps all this evil that has been attached to retention of imposed celibacy can be justified as the price that had to be paid to preserve the cherished jewel of celibacy; but it does seem difficult to see it as a reflection of the Christian gospel that says nothing about clerical celibacy and a great deal about justice and compassion. Finally, one must ask what it is that clerical celibacy has actually symbolized. Certainly a large part of that symbolism has had to do with clerical superiority and separation from the rest of the community. Celibacy has been *the* distinguishing mark of the clergy, *the* sign of the clergy/lay dichotomy in the church, and in a subtle but real way *the* sign of masculine domination in the church.

Theologically, the case for celibacy as *the* way of life for ordained liturgical ministers, even as the better way, seems to be based on weak foundations: on an inadequate theology of Christian sacrifice, on an inadequate understanding of Christian sanctity, on an inadequate appreciation of the basic sacramentality of human sexuality and of the manner in which it has been Christianized by Jesus' death and resurrection. No doubt such a statement will be rather hotly contested, but it is time for the debate about clerical celibacy to deal openly and thoroughly with such fundamental theological questions.

If discussion of Christian sacrifice is governed by what Jesus actually did in his Passover and not by categorized understandings of sacrifice drawn from other sources, it does seem that we can argue that Jesus' act of sacrifice is his giving of himself to men as the source of their life. In the New Testament literature this self-giving by Christ is seen as a marital gift to his bride, the Christian community; the sexual intercourse by which a Christian husband and wife become one flesh is seen to become more profoundly significant because of Christ's Passover. Moreover, this Paschal involvement of Christ in the lives of men and women is only the realization, in full intensity and intimacy, of the finality of the Incarnation, i.e., of Jesus' priesthood. The Incarnation is a mystery of God seeking familiarity, even radical identification, with human beings; the Word-made-flesh in no way held himself aloof from the ordinary concerns and activities of men and women.

Christian marriage is, then, a *sacrificial* reality; a man and a woman exist for one another in a dedicated fidelity that makes present Christ's own fidelity to mankind. All their actions of giving themselves to one another, including their sexual self-gift, are a communication of life in love. Their love for one another is an act of *sanctifying*, for all

sanctification is the impact of God's love made present in the sacrament of human love. Their act of sexual intercourse is an act of *consecrating* one another; it is a gift of the total life each possesses (including the Spirit) so that together they can live (i.e., believe and hope and love and experience) more fully than they could do separately. Because the Christian faith and love of each is enriched by the faith and love of the other, a Christian couple is enabled to give a richer witness and to be a more effective sacrament of Christ, i.e., to fulfill the communal priesthood of the church.

When one reflects on the transformation of human love and sexuality effected by Christ in his death and resurrection, it is indeed strange to hear the statement that celibacy is more eschatological in its significance. The very act of a human loving another person is a promise of yet fuller love in the future (and, of course, a pattern of promise and fulfillment is the basic structure of Israelitic and Christian eschatology); and the more solemn the commitment of love, the more prominent is the element of eschatology. That would make marital intercourse profoundly eschatological, which of course it is as a Christian sacrament. The eschatological dimension of human love is sacramental of the eschatological hope men have because of God's love; even in the observable psychological order, the love that human beings have for one another can make the reality of God's love credible. Again, the very link of love with the giving of life which is manifested in the generation of children points to the future. Along this line, it might be instructive to reflect on the command of celibacy laid on the prophet Jeremiah: he was told by God not to marry, so that this might be a sign that the inhabitants of Jerusalem did not have that hopeful a future.

One could develop at much greater length the theology of Christian marriage as part of a theology of the church's priesthood, but these few suggestions may enable us to suggest some of the priestly spirituality appropriate to married Christians, and therefore the appropriateness of married liturgical ministers. All development in Christian holiness is basically a growth in mature human love, a growth that occurs within the context of faith, i.e., the acceptance of God's loving self-gift in the risen Christ. A married couple are committed to confronting head-on the demanding task of learning how to love. Moreover, it is the nature of genuine love to be expansive. Learning to love one person more deeply enables one to love others more authentically; while there is a uniqueness to certain love relationships, these (if they are mature and healthy) do not establish walls. Indeed, a profound love relationship to someone, particularly if it carries the mutual commitment of fidelity that Christian marriage does, is an influence that works to free one from the anxieties and confusions that limit so many people's affective and sexual life. This power of love to liberate is central to the entire process of salvation. The experience of Christian married love is a revelation of the manner in which the assumption of great responsibility is part of the process of gaining mature freedom. Celibacy, too, can be meaningful if it involves such responsibility for loving people; but to the extent that it signifies an escape from such responsibility, it is countersymbolic of Christianity. Many an ordained celibate would have been better able to deal with his own sexuality and the sexuality of his fellow Christians, and better able to open himself to others in human warmth and loving concern (i.e., in love that could sacramentalize Christ's own love), if he had been married.

Marital spirituality is not peripheral to Christian spirituality, for it is a living out of the sacramental significance that is central not only to Christian marriage but to the Eucharist, and particularly to the Eucharistic symbolisms of bread and body. Christian sacraments are the transformation (Christianization) of the meaning of men and women's most basic human experiences—birth, death, and decision. Therefore they depend upon this substratum of experience for their very existence. The experience of sexual intercourse and parenthood form such a substra-

tum not just for Christian marriage but for the Eucharist, and in some fashion for all the other sacraments. To give but one example of this: Christian marriage gives to the two persons involved the experience of human bodiliness vitalized by a new level of life that has come with love; this can provide an insight into the mystery of the new bodiliness that comes with Christ's gift of risen life, which, incidentally, is important to any appreciation of Christian eschatology.

Obviously, for Christian marriage to have for the two persons concerned the significance we have been describing, faith and insight are required. This implies that contemplation is as intrinsic to Christian marriage as it is to any other situation of Christian life (monasticism, for example). Nor is marriage a barrier to genuine prayer, as has all too often been supposed. This supposition was based on the theory that one had to retire from the world, get away from distractions, in order to pray. Though there is an element of truth in this theory, it often overlooked the basic pattern of all genuine Christian prayer, which is to be a response to the word of God. Most basically, the word of God comes to each person in and through his particular life experience. Scripture, sacrament, church teaching—all function as elements in the word of God, clarifying the meaning of one's life. But it is the experience itself that speaks most clearly and with greatest impact.

Thus, a Christian's prayer is a careful listening to and reverence for the meaning of his life, and then an appropriate response of loving gratitude to God. Christian marriage is a life experience in which the wonder of human love sacramentalizes God's creative life-giving love; it is in a strict sense a continuing revelation, to be accepted in faith and responded to in prayer. It is, therefore, strange to think that one would have to be free from this situation in order to pray. Actually, in the theories of asceticism that saw sexual intercourse as a hindrance to contemplation, there was suspicion of human passion as something that obscured clear insight and unbalanced one's motivations and values. With all due respect for the amount of confusion connected with sexuality in human life (confusion that is injected *into* sexuality by fears and insecurities and arrogance and other evils), passion contributes importantly to man's religious insights and motivations. To give again but one element as example: the force of the passion attached to sexual love can give one an intuition into the manner in which love for his fellow humans led Jesus to the excess of confronting death.

There is no solid theological basis, then, for excluding married Christians from genuine contemplation and the pursuit of Christian holiness. Fortunately, the recovery in the church today of a sense of the layman's belonging to the church in the full sense has been accompanied by a realization that it was wrong for any group to appropriate to itself the evangelical counsels, as if the rest of the church was not to follow the idealism of the gospel. If all this is true, then the prayer and spirituality and pastoral effectiveness of an ordained minister can be enhanced by marriage.

Of course, this implies a considerable amount of idealism regarding the actual situation of a Christian marriage. Not all marriages of Christians possess the kind of understanding and love and Christian sacramentality we have described, and not all marriages of ordained ministers would. However, this is a challenge to be faced rather than a convincing argument against a married ministry. As a matter of fact, it might suggest several imaginative approaches to Christian ministry. For one thing, it might be appropriate in some (perhaps many) cases to ordain a couple as a couple for joint ministry. Since it might be specially important for both man and woman to face together the decisions and the difficulties and the challenges that a ministry would entail, would not the ministerial vocation be really a shared charism, and could not the ordaining to a function be a shared designation by the community?

Even if such a practice as the one we just suggested were to prove valuable in many cases, it would certainly not be universal.

And this leads us to what seems the most sensible practical conclusion on the matter of celibacy. By their respective life-styles, both celibate ministers and married ministers signify complementary aspects of Christian ministry; the full richness of the community's ministry requires both, just as the full richness requires both men and women ministers. Whether a man or a woman decides to combine marriage or celibacy with a ministerial function should be a matter of that person's judgment regarding the manner in which he or she will most deeply believe and hope and love and sacramentalize the saving presence of the risen Christ. For this is what Christianity and its ministry and priesthood is all about: the Christian community exists sacramentally to make the risen Christ redemptively present to mankind, by doing this the community shares in Christ's own priestly mission, and the specialized ministries within the community (and specifically the ministry of liturgical leadership) exist to enable the community to function in this priestly sacramental fashion.

Closely linked in its symbolic implications with the question of clerical celibacy is the matter of recognizing women's right to full participation in the church's ministries. Ordinarily, this question is posed in terms of the "ordination of women"; actually, several interwoven questions are involved. The factual question (should women be admitted to full sharing in ministry?) is somewhat difficult to treat theologically. From a theological point of view it is really a nonquestion. There is no apparent reason why the ability and right of women to function in this manner should even be questioned. Negation of this right to women in most Christian churches has been rooted in sociological, legal, and cultural presuppositions rather than in theological principles. The present task of theologians is to indicate the injustice and religious irrelevance of such cultural arguments against women in the ministry. The positive arguments for women's sharing in ministry are, really, the arguments for any Christian participating in ministry.

However, the question is not quite that

simple; its complexity is related to several of the items we have discussed earlier in this book. First of all, in the concrete situation of present-day ecclesiastical structures, official admission to ordained ministry involves entry into a professional caste, the clergy. Earlier portions of this book have already questioned the value of perpetuating in the church the anomalous division of Christians into clergy and laity; and it would seem to intensify this anomaly if women were to seek identification as clergy at the very moment when any such identification is being seen as undesirable. Moreover, there is a radical inappropriateness in women becoming clergy, because the very reality of clergy has historically been an important element in the masculine domination proper to a patriarchal culture. In seeking to become clergy, women would be seeking identification with "the male establishment" at one of the key points where it claims superiority over women. Perhaps *strategy* dictates some feminine participation in the clerical caste in order to hasten its disappearance; if so—and the wisdom of such a decision is dubious—this would be a very short-term arrangement and not desirable as a continuing solution.

This is not to suggest that nothing be done about asserting women's rights in this regard; rather, it is to suggest that a more genuine solution may come in a different way. As we have several times noted—and there is growing awareness of the situation—a plurality of distinct ministries in the church is not only desirable, it is already in existence, though not yet fully recognized. In many of these ministries, e.g., teaching, women are engaged in large numbers. They are functioning with considerable autonomy in many instances, and to a considerable degree they are designated, or at least recognized with approval, by some community. That is to say, these women do effectively minister, and they do so with "ordination," whether that takes the form of a special religious ceremony or not. Very significantly, then, these women are functioning in Christian ministry without being clergy.

But the question then comes: Can such a situation be extended so that women come to exercise all the various ministerial functions? Obviously, this question focuses on the episcopate and the presbyterate. Looking at it theologically, this seems to concern three functions: governing, witnessing as a member of the episcopal (and presbyteral) *collegium*, and ministering as liturgical celebrant. Putting aside arguments drawn from tradition in the sense of ecclesiastical legislation and customary practice, women (with the charisms one would expect from anyone exercising these roles) are perfectly capable of doing what is intrinsically proper to these three ministries.

Granted that there is no intrinsic barrier to admitting women to all the various ministerial functions of the church, should we move this direction? Will it, after all, make any significant difference, contribute anything to the church's internal development or to its apostolic effectiveness? The most immediate and obvious response is that basic justice demands that women be no longer denied their full rights within the church; in moving this direction we will honor the radical egalitarianism that is meant to characterize the Christian community. Only experience will indicate the multifaceted advantage of women's participation in the entire range of Christian ministries, but theological reflection suggests some of the benefits that will follow from such a course of action.

First, with both men and women functioning in full sacramental fashion, we will have a fuller and more balanced reflection of the church's faith, and therefore an integral expression of the Christian community's sacramental existence. Because the church's fundamental role in human history is to be the sacrament of the redeeming presence of the risen Lord, the recognition of women's rights to full ministerial activity, by increasing the extent to which the church can express sacramentally the saving action that Christ is carrying on through and in it, will permit the church to realize its historical destiny more adequately. And by opening up the possibilities of men and women interacting creatively at every level of the church's existence, the ordaining of women to full sacramental ministry will help humanity realize its revealing role as the image of God.

The dialectical relationship of men and women—distinctness and complementarity, challenge that requires no aggressive response, reciprocal need in order to achieve fulfillment, mutual enrichment through interaction of difference—images forth the divine. This relationship, which is but one particularly symbolic aspect of the more basic and richer dialectic of all personal relationships, is an intrinsic element in all Christian sacraments, especially in the Eucharist. And this dialectic is bound to have much fuller play as both men and women minister actively in sacramental liturgy.

Second, the activity of women in the three roles we mentioned (governing, collegial witness, liturgical celebration) will probably be a major factor in separating the intrinsic symbolisms of Christian ministry from the countersymbolisms of "professional clergy." Loss of this clerical significance will permit these ministerial functions to achieve their purpose much more effectively. These ministries are meant to bring about the unification of Christians (and others also) into a genuine personal community, something that has been partially blocked by the "separation from the laity" symbolism attached to "clergy." Extending full ministry to women will not automatically break down this wall of division between "professional" and "ordinary" Christians, for women could probably be as clerical as men, but it would offer an unprecedented opportunity to make the church one community.

Third, it is almost certain that the exercise by women of full ministry in the church will force a clearer understanding of the authority that is appropriate to the Christian community. Much of the misinterpretation of that authority that has occurred historically has come about because of a mistaken application of the model of "dominative political authority," a model that is inextricably bound up with the masculine assertion of superiority in a patriarchal culture. With women involved in sacramental leadership and in governing, we will most likely come to reflect on the distinctive authority proper to the church, the authority of Christ's own truth and love.

No doubt, we will become aware of many other gains that will follow from the recognition of women's right to participate fully in the church's life. Perhaps the most fundamental and far-reaching effect will be the enrichment of the church's faith life as that is expressed in liturgical worship, because for the first time the life experience and faith-consciousness of half of the community will have full play in the "speaking" of the sacramental symbols, and such experience and consciousness are the stuff of which sacraments and a sacramental community are made.

Selected Bibliography

Ministry to Sacrament

Quite a number of the works cited in earlier bibliographies are relevant to this section. The following studies deal more exclusively with the sacramental and "priestly" aspects of ministry.

GENERAL STUDIES:

Congar, Y. *Lay People in the Church*. London, 1957.
Lash, N. and Rhymer, J., eds. *The Christian Priesthood*. London, 1970.
Lecuyer, J. *Le sacerdoce dans la mystère du Christ*. Paris, 1957.
Power, D. *Ministers of Christ and His Church*. London, 1969.

EARLY CHRISTIANITY:

Blenkinsopp, J. *Celibacy, Ministry, Church*. New York, 1968.
Brown, R. *Priest and Bishop*. New York, 1970.
Jungmann, J. *The Early Liturgy*. Notre Dame, 1958.

PATRISTIC AND MEDIEVAL CHRISTIANITY:

Brooke, C. *Medieval Church and Society*. London, 1971.
Hinnebusch, W. *History of the Dominican Order*. Vols. 1 and 2. New York, 1966, 1973.
Moorman, J. *History of the Franciscan Order*. Oxford, 1968.
Pintard, J. *La sacerdoce selon Augustin*. Paris, 1960.

POST-MEDIEVAL CHRISTIANITY:

Ainslie, J. *The Doctrine of Ministerial Order in the Reformed Churches of the Sixteenth and Seventeenth Centuries*. Edinburgh, 1940.
Clark, F. *Eucharistic Sacrifice and the Reformation*. 2d ed. London, 1960.
Fischer, R. "Another Look at Luther's Doctrine of the Ministry." *Lutheran Quarterly* 18 (1966), pp. 260–71.
Gerrish, B. "Luther on Priesthood and Ministry." *Church History* 34 (1965), pp. 404–22.
Green, L. "Change in Luther's Doctrine of the Ministry." *Lutheran Quarterly* 18 (1966), pp. 173–83.
Kalb, F. *Theology of Worship in Seventeenth-Century Lutheranism*. St. Louis, 1965.
Lutherans and Catholics in Dialogue, vol. 4 (*Eucharist and Ministry*), Washington, D.C., 1970.
Lindbeck, G. "The Lutheran Doctrine of the Ministry: Catholic and Reformed." *Theological Studies* 30 (1969), pp. 588–612.
McDonnell, K. *John Calvin, the Church, and the Eucharist*. Princeton, 1967.
Van de Pol, J. *Martin Bucer's Liturgical Ideas*. Croningen, 1954.
Rahner, K., ed. *The Identity of the Priest*. Vol. 43 of *Concilium*. New York, 1969.

Indexes

Index of Names

661

INDEX OF NAMES

Index of Subjects

Albigensianism, 124, 280, 470–71
Anglicanism, 144–45, 149, 498, 600–602, 626–27
  sacramental/evangelical view of ministry, 149
Anointing of sick, 213, 400, 541
Anticlericalism, 135, 138, 147, 163, 373, 499–500
Apostle, 206, 213–14, 332–34, 531–32
Apostles (the Twelve)
  as disciples, 223
  functions, 223–25, 241, 407–8, 531–32
Apostleship, 531
Apostolic succession, 65, 237–40, 420, 438–39, 513, 608
Arminianism, 151
Ars praedicandi, 279
Auctoritas, 93, 255, 278, 447, 577
Authority
  attached to Bible, 164, 236–37
  attached to office, 68, 208, 236–37, 255, 258, 352, 417–18, 515–20, 608
  derived from knowledge, 242–45, 411, 415, 419, 500–501, 513–14
  derived from love, 411, 515
  derived from ordination, 199, 418–19, 431, 516–17
  derived from patron saint, 433–34, 439
  derived from sanctity, 356–57, 419, 489
  and disestablishment of the church, 485, 503
  episcopal, 88–89, 364–65, 415–17, 420–22, 428–29, 437–38, 449, 469, 482, 486, 505–7, 516, 518–20, 628
  of lower clergy, 506
  nature of church authority, 411, 421, 432–33, 481–83, 489, 501–3, 516–20
  papal, 438–42, 446–50, 464, 470–72, 504–5
  presbyteral, 421, 428
  questioning of absolute, 162–64, 465–67
  relation to charism, 408, 414–18, 490, 514–15
  societal, 431, 497–99
  teaching, 15, 226, 242–45, 255, 280, 293, 352, 415–16, 470–73, 487, 500–503, 608
Asceticism
  Christian, character of, 265
  as Christian ideal, 235, 245, 265

Baptism
  bishop's role, 239, 241, 261–64, 356, 417–18, 540
  cult action of, 528–29, 543
  developing doctrine of, 260–64
  dimming of "mystery" understanding, 263–64
  faith and, 264, 529

  initiation into Christian "myth," 228–29, 262–63
  original sin and, 264
  transmission of mystery, 263
Baptismal churches, 362–63
Basileia, 86, 444, 447–48
Basileus, 83–84, 428, 447–48, 556
Benefice system, 285–86, 387 (n. 2)
Bible
  basis of preaching, 259, 278–79, 288
  interpretation of, 259, 490
  link with liturgy, 322–23
  medieval exegesis of, 123–24, 279
  role in teaching, 241, 254, 257–59, 312
  typology, 263
  as word of God, 329–31
Bishop, functions of, 78, 80–81, 83–84, 170–71, 199, 338–39, 444, 506
  baptismal role, 239, 241, 261–64, 356, 417–18, 540
  civil judge, 76, 354, 431
  doctrinal judge, 243, 256–57, 277, 354, 434–35, 490
  Eucharistic celebrant, 64–65, 86, 90–91, 96–97, 247, 539–41, 581–82
  healer, 81, 94, 256–57, 351, 356
  initiator into mystery, 228, 241, 263
  judge (ecclesiastical), 62–63, 364, 431, 434–36, 442–43
  minister of ordination, 71, 418–19
  model and example, 264–66, 563
  principle of unity, 62, 354–55, 415, 631
  primacy of preaching, 95, 239, 255, 258–59, 288
  sacerdos, 79, 90, 538, 541, 554–55, 628
  teacher, 63, 78, 227, 240–43, 254–61, 434–35
  theologian, 78–79, 243–44, 254–55, 276–77, 471
  witness to tradition, 237–40, 244, 258, 262–63, 330, 337–38, 415–16
Bishops
  consecration of, 418–19, 430–31, 516, 540, 562
  relation between deacons and, 348, 353–54, 358 (n. 6), 421
  relation between presbyters and, 11, 19, 77, 80, 89–90, 200, 255, 363–65, 415–16, 421–22, 486, 506, 608
  selection of, 175, 418–19, 429–30, 505, 516
Brethren of the Common Life, 295

Calvinism
  ministerial role in, 144, 150–51, 377, 488–90, 625–26
  soteriology of, 291–92
Cambridge Platonists, 162